SEVENTH EDITION

ADJUSTMENT AND GROWTH

THE CHALLENGES OF LIFE

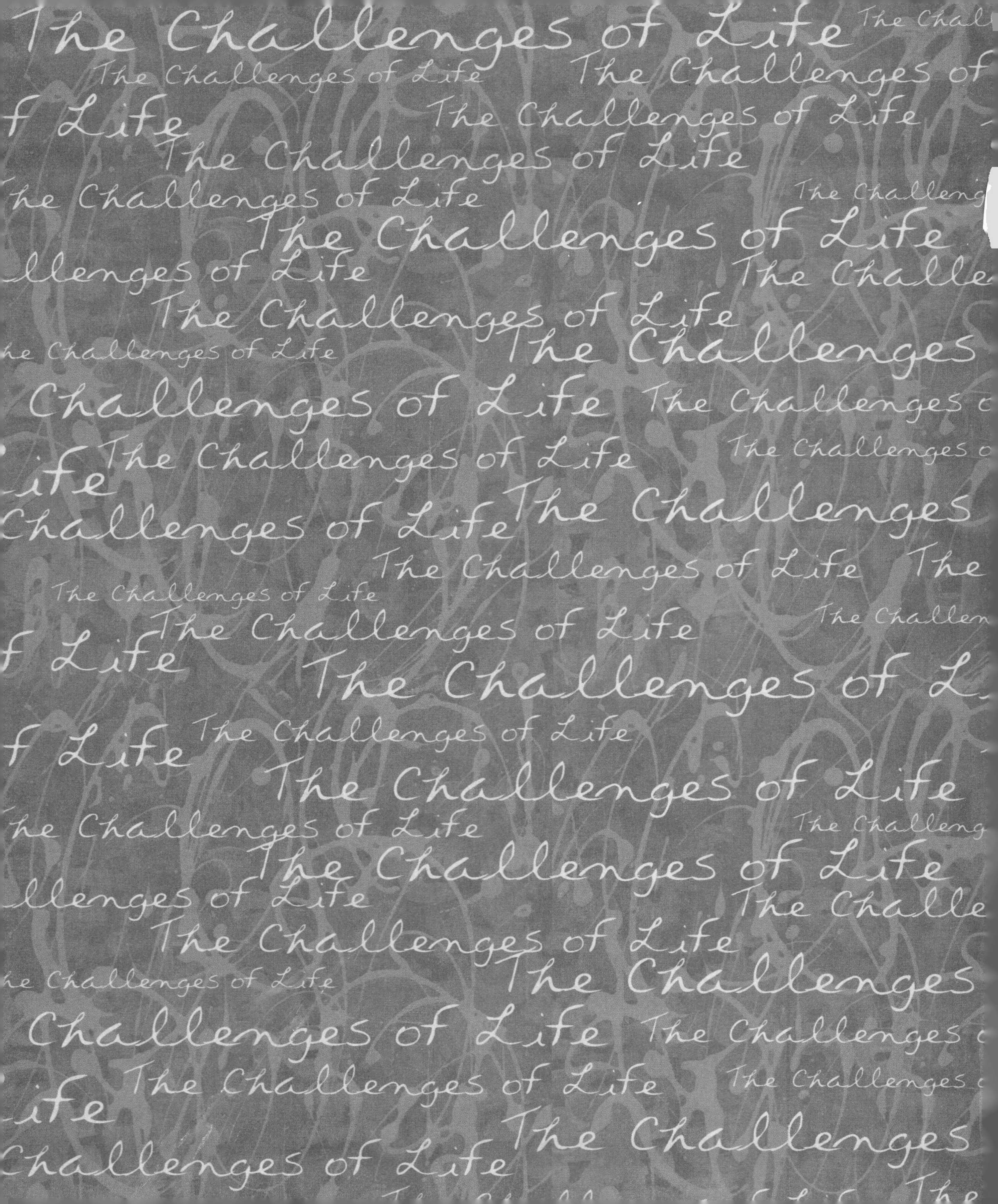
The Challenges of Life

SEVENTH EDITION

ADJUSTMENT AND GROWTH

THE CHALLENGES OF LIFE

SPENCER A. RATHUS
MONTCLAIR STATE UNIVERSITY

JEFFREY S. NEVID
HOFSTRA UNIVERSITY

HARCOURT COLLEGE PUBLISHERS

FORT WORTH PHILADELPHIA SAN DIEGO NEW YORK ORLANDO AUSTIN SAN ANTONIO
TORONTO MONTREAL LONDON SYDNEY TOKYO

Publisher Earl McPeek
Executive Editor Carol Wada
Market Strategist Kathleen Sharp
Project Editor Angela Williams Urquhart
Art Director Carol Kincaid
Production Manager Andrea A. Johnson

Cover credit: 1998 Scott Spiker / Alaska Stock.

ISBN: 0-15-508043-1

Library of Congress Catalog Card Number: 98-88489

Copyrights and acknowledgments appear on page 667, which constitutes a continuation of the copyright page.

Address for Domestic Orders
Harcourt College Publishers, 6277 Sea Harbor Drive, Orlando, FL 32887-6777
800-782-4479

Address for International Orders
International Customer Service
Harcourt, Inc., 6277 Sea Harbor Drive, Orlando, FL 32887-6777
407-345-3800
(fax) 407-345-4060
(e-mail) hbintl@harcourt.com

Address for Editorial Correspondence
Harcourt College Publishers, 301 Commerce Street, Suite 3700, Fort Worth, TX 76102

Web Site Address
http://www.harcourtcollege.com

Printed in the United States of America

0 1 2 3 4 5 6 7 8 9 032 10 9 8 7 6 5 4

Harcourt College Publishers

BRIEF CONTENTS

CONTENTS

CONTENTS

PREFACE

When we wrote the first edition of *Adjustment and Growth,* we were aware of a comment from the literary past:

> *Books should be tried by a judge and jury as though they were crimes.*
>
> —Samuel Butler (1835–1902)

Of course, Samuel Butler had to live his life without the benefits of reading *Adjustment and Growth.* If he had lived to the turn of the new millennium, he would have seen that at least one book can all at once offer valuable suggestions for living, captivate students, and accurately portray the rigorous academic discipline of psychology.

This book has also been tried through six successful editions. And since its first edition, its core goals have not changed: to show how psychology provides the basis for meeting many of the challenges of contemporary life, to offer students concrete advice that is based on psychological knowledge, and to do it all in a way that stimulates and engages students. *Adjustment and Growth* is part of the solution.

The seventh edition of *Adjustment and Growth* was written explicitly for the instructor who requires a textbook that:

- Communicates the true scientific nature of psychology through coverage of research methods and classic studies in psychology
- Applies psychological theory and research to help readers solve problems and reach their unique potentials
- Reflects the importance of human diversity in students' lives
- Motivates students through the abundant use of humor, personal anecdotes, and "Truth or Fiction?" items
- Presents abstract, complex concepts in energetic, accessible prose

Psychological theory and research now encompass aspects of our daily lives that range from doing well in college to adjustment in the workplace, from weight control to safe(r) sex in the age of AIDS, from figuring out what to say in social encounters to the quests for values and personal identity. With these issues and others, we report the pertinent psychological theory and research. We then show readers how to apply this information to their own lives.

■ WHAT'S NEW IN THIS EDITION

There are two major changes in the seventh edition of *Adjustment and Growth.* One is the inclusion of "Adjustment in the New Millennium" features, which help bring the psychology of adjustment into the twenty-first century. Second is the inclusion of a new chapter on "Substance Abuse and Adjustment."

A New Feature: "Adjustment in the New Millennium"

Our new "Adjustment in the New Millennium" features help students prepare for life in the new millennium by exploring the interfaces between technological advances, cultural changes, psychology, and our individual styles of life. Here is a sampling of some of the current topics discussed in "Adjustment in the New Millennium":

- If There Were 100 "You's," Just How Unique Would You Be?
- Are Pills for Self-Improvement in the Offing?
- Can Psychologists Use Attribution Theory to Enhance International "Adjustment"?
- Psychology and Health in the New Millennium
- Will We Be Competing With Virtual Babes and Hunks in the New Millennium?
- Will We See Gender Differences in Fitness Evaporate in the New Millennium?
- Will We Find Ways to Make Nicotine (Gasp!) Good for You?
- Will Your Problems Be Diagnosed by Computer?
- Looking Ahead to "Designer Drugs"
- Reaching New Heights With Virtual Reality
- Who Are the Ideal Men for the New Millennium?
- http://www.planetout.com
- Sex Becomes "Interactive"
- Will We Finally Have "Love Potions" in the New Millennium?
- Enter the "Brave New World" of Viagra?
- Two Views of Parenting in the New Millennium
- Will We Discover a Real Fountain of Youth?
- Careers—What's Hot, What's Not
- Sperm and Egg "Donations" for Overnight Delivery?

A New Chapter: "Substance Abuse and Adjustment"

The seventh edition has expanded, full-chapter coverage of substance abuse. As noted in that chapter,

> The world is a supermarket of . . . drugs. The United States is flooded with hundreds of drugs that distort perceptions and change mood—drugs that take you up, let you down, and move you across town. Some people use drugs because their friends do, or because their parents tell them not to. Others get started with doctors' prescriptions, coffee, or their first aspirin tablet.
>
> Some are seeking pleasure; others, relief from pain; still others, inner truth.

Chapter 8 is intended to help students evaluate such substances and to help them find ways of coping without resorting to them. Our coverage of these substances contains no phony horror stories; in most cases, the problems connected with substance abuse are all too real. The chapter's "Self-Assessment" features offer students insight into why they drink and why they smoke (if, of course, they do at all). The "Adjustment and Modern Life" feature contains concrete suggestions on "How to Use Self-Control Strategies to Quit and Cut Down on Smoking." Chapter 8 also includes a section titled "Getting There Without Drugs: Don't Just Say No, *Do* Something Else."

GENERAL COVERAGE

The seventh edition of *Adjustment and Growth* covers the following topics, as summarized here.

Chapter 1 ("What Is Adjustment?") defines psychology and relates psychology to adjustment and growth. It explores controversies in psychology and adjustment and addresses the nature of human diversity. It explains research methods in psychology.

Chapter 2 ("Personality and Behavior: Understanding People") explores the major approaches to understanding personality and behavior. The nature of the healthy personality is discussed.

Chapter 3 ("Social Perception: How We See Others and Ourselves") applies the social psychology of person perception to students' daily lives. It covers schemas, primacy and recency effects, body language, prejudice, the self, and attribution theory.

Chapter 4 ("Social Influence: Being Influenced By—and Influencing—Others") explores the contributions of the psychology of social influence to our understanding of how people influence each other's behavior. Topics range from sales resistance to mob behavior.

Chapter 5 ("Stress: Sources and Moderators") covers the sources of stress, ranging from life changes and daily hassles to pain and environmental stressors. It covers moderators of the impact of stress, from psychological hardiness to self-efficacy expectancies, humor, predictability, and social support.

Chapter 6 ("Psychological Factors and Health") provides up-to-date coverage of the mind-body connection, including topics such as the immune system and the biological effects of stress. Here we discuss stress-related disorders including headaches, menstrual problems, coronary heart disease, and—yes—cancer.

Chapter 7 ("Issues in Personal Health: Nutrition, Fitness, and Sleep") covers obesity, anorexia nervosa and bulimia nervosa, the benefits of exercise, and insomnia.

Chapter 8 ("Substance Abuse and Adjustment") emphasizes two dangerous but legal drugs—alcohol and cigarettes. Students are given up-to-date information, no phony horror stories. They can assess why they drink and smoke, and there are ample suggestions for coping without resorting to drugs.

Chapter 9 ("Psychological Disorders") provides rigorous coverage of adjustment disorders, anxiety disorders, dissociative disorders, somatoform disorders, mood disorders, schizophrenia, and personality disorders. Vivid case studies illustrate the disorders.

Chapter 10 ("Therapies: Ways of Helping") covers contemporary methods of psychotherapy and biological therapies. Methods of therapy receive rigorous evaluation. Case studies illuminate the methods of therapy.

Chapter 11 ("Methods of Coping: Ways of Helping Ourselves") is the text's major do-it-yourself chapter. Concrete, well illustrated advice is offered on controlling stressful cognitions, alleviating the Type A behavior pattern, enhancing psychological hardiness, and managing the emotions of fear and anger. (Whew!)

Chapter 12 ("Gender Roles and Gender Differences") covers gender roles and stereotypes, sexism, and gender differences and their origins.

Chapter 13 ("Interpersonal Attraction: Of Friendship, Love, and Loneliness") covers interpersonal attraction, friendship, love, and loneliness—as advertised.

Chapter 14 ("Relationships and Communication: Getting From Here to There") introduces students to the ABC(DE)'s of relationships, marriage, and alternative styles of life.

Chapter 15 ("Sexual Behavior") covers timely topics in the biology of sex, sexual orientation, rape, sexual dysfunctions, the most up-to-date information on AIDS and other sexually transmitted diseases, and contraception.

Chapter 16 ("Adult Development: Going Through Changes") covers the physical, cognitive, and personality developments of the stages and transitions of adulthood.

Chapter 17 ("The Challenge of the Workplace") covers reasons for working (it's more than money!), vocational development, job satisfaction and adjustment in the workplace, and women in the workplace.

Chapter 18 ("Having and Rearing Children") begins with a discussion of whether or not to have children. Then we survey issues concerning conception, pregnancy, childbirth, and childrearing. We offer advice on coping with infertility, detecting fetal abnormalities, and rearing competent children.

PEDAGOGICAL AIDS AND FEATURES

Most students who take the psychology of adjustment course are first- and second-year students. Many of them have not had an introductory course in psychology. For others, the psychology of adjustment *is* the introductory course in psychology. We include a number of pedagogical aids and features to foster learning and to underscore the relevance of psychology to everyday life.

Chapter Outlines

Each chapter opens with a chapter outline that provides students with "advance organizers"—that is, expectations about what is to come. One of the themes of the text is that predictability helps us manage events. We hope that students will use the outlines to construct cognitive categories and read the chapters to flesh out the categories with specific knowledge.

"Truth or Fiction?" and "Truth or Fiction Revisited" Items

A "Truth or Fiction?" box appears at the beginning of each chapter. This feature is intended to stimulate students to delve into the subject matter by challenging folklore and common sense (which is just as often really "common *non*sense").

Many students consider themselves psychologists. Psychology involves the study of human behavior, and even by the age at which students first attend college, they have observed people for many years. The "Truth or Fiction?" items prod them to reflect upon the accuracy of their observations and to reconsider conclusions they may have drawn about human nature.

Over the years, we have heard repeatedly that the "Truth or Fiction?" items are the text's most salient pedagogical feature—one that helps give it its unique stamp. Students and even instructors find themselves reading the chapters in order to learn just what the authors have to say about these items. Sometimes they even agree with the answers.

"Truth or Fiction Revisited" inserts are found throughout the chapters, where the subjects of the "Truth or Fiction?" items are discussed in the text. The inserts provide students with feedback as to whether their assumptions about psychology and adjustment were accurate.

Running Glossary

Key terms are defined in the margins, on the pages where they occur in the text. Research shows that many students do not make use of a glossary at the back of a book. Moreover, ready access to glossary items permits students to maintain their concentration on the flow of material in the chapter. Students need not flip back and forth between different sections of the book to decode the vocabulary.

Key terms are boldfaced the first time they appear in the chapter, to signal students that definitions are available.

"Adjustment in a World of Diversity"

The profession of psychology is committed to the dignity of the individual, and we cannot understand individuals without reference to the richness of human diversity. People differ not only as individuals, but also in terms of their culture, gender, age, sexual orientation, and other factors. As psychology students, we cannot hope to understand the behavior and mental processes of people without reference to their diversity. "Adjustment in a World of Diversity" features explore and celebrate the rich variety of adjustment issues found throughout the world. The United States alone is a nation of hundreds of different ethnic and religious groups. This diversity extends to the "global village" of nearly 200 nations and to those nations' own distinctive subcultures.

Studying perspectives other than our own helps us to understand the role of a culture's beliefs, values, and attitudes on adjustment. It helps us to understand why other people behave in ways that are so different, and why adjustment may have different meanings for them.

Here is a sampling of the text's "Adjustment in a World of Diversity" titles:

- On Increasing Diversity in American Higher Education
- Including Women and Members of Diverse Ethnic Groups in Research
- A Sex Survey That Addresses Sociocultural Factors
- African American Women—Happier With Themselves
- "But You're Not in Hong Kong": Asian Americans Fight a Stereotype Through Assertiveness Training
- Stress and Ethnic Pride Among African Americans
- Health and Socioeconomic Status: The Rich Get Richer and the Poor Get . . . Sicker?
- Eating Disorders: Why the Gender Gap?
- Fitness Is for Everyone: Exercise and the Physically Disabled
- Alcoholism, Gender, and Ethnicity
- Psychological Disorders Among Native Americans—Loss of a Special Relationship With Nature?
- The Case of Women and Depression
- Should We Match Clients and Therapists According to Ethnicity?
- Machismo/Marianismo Stereotypes and Hispanic Culture
- School Days, School Days—Dear Old Sexist School Days?
- "Your Daddy's Rich and Your Ma Is Good Lookin'": Gender Differences in the Importance of Physical Attractiveness
- "Let's Make a Deal": On Gender and Lonely Hearts Ads
- Snug in Their Beds for Christmas Eve—In Japan, December 24th Has Become the Hottest Night of the Year
- The Ritual Destruction of Female Sexuality
- Is There a *Man*opause?

- Why Does Mommy Work?
- Some Notes on Prenatal Care: A Tale of Three Neighborhoods

"Self-Assessment"

"Self-Assessment" features are intended to stimulate student interest by involving them more deeply in the subject matter, and also to help students evaluate where they stand in relation to the issues raised in the text. For example, when we explain the concept of self-efficacy expectancies, we provide a "Self-Assessment" questionnaire that enables students to learn how self-efficacious they perceive themselves to be. When we raise the topic of life changes as a source of stress, we provide students with a questionnaire that permits them to assess the stress caused by changes in their own lives.

Each chapter of the text contains at least one "Self-Assessment," including the following:

- Dare You Say What You Think? The Social-Desirability Scale
- Will You Be a Hit or a Miss? The Expectancy for Success Scale
- Do You Strive to Be All That You Can Be?
- How Content Are You With Your Physical Self?
- Values Clarification—What Is Important to You?
- Are You One of Your Favorite People?
- Do You Speak Your Mind or Do You Wimp Out? The Rathus Assertiveness Schedule
- Have You Been Going Through Changes? The Social Readjustment Rating Scale
- Are You Type A or Type B?
- Who's in Charge Here? The Locus-of-Control Scale
- How Optimistic Is Your Outlook? The Life Orientation Test
- The Eating Smart Quiz
- Check Your Physical Activity and Heart Disease IQ
- Why Do You Drink?
- Why Do You Smoke?
- Do Your Own Thoughts Put You Down in the Dumps?
- Are You Making Yourself Miserable? The Irrational-Beliefs Questionnaire
- Do You Choke Up During Tests? The Suinn Test Anxiety Behavior Scale (STABS)
- Are You Blue? The Self-Rating Depression Scale
- What Turns You On? The Pleasant Events Schedule
- Are You a "Chesty" Male or a "Fluffy" Female? The ANDRO Scale
- Has Cupid Shot His Arrow Into Your Heart? Sternberg's Triangular Love Scale
- Do You Endorse a Traditional or a Liberal Marital Role?
- Do You Subscribe to Cultural Myths That Create a Climate That Supports Rape?
- The AIDS Awareness Inventory
- How Long Will You Live? The Life-Expectancy Scale

- What Are Your Attitudes Toward Aging?
- How Concerned Are You About Death?
- How Do You Feel About Your Work? The Job Satisfaction Index
- What's Your Vocational Type? Attend the Job Fair and Find Out!
- Should You Have a Child?

"Adjustment and Modern Life"

"Adjustment and Modern Life" features are found at the conclusion of each chapter. These features apply psychological knowledge to help students cope with the challenges in their own lives. Many of them include step-by-step instructions. They are the book's major how-to or do-it-yourself sections. The "Adjustment and Modern Life" features of the seventh edition discuss the following topics:

- Becoming a Successful Student
- Understanding Yourself: Will the One True Theory of Human Nature Please Stand Up?
- Taking Charge of Fears
- Getting in Touch With the Untouchable Through Biofeedback Training
- Controlling Bad Habits Through Aversive Conditioning
- Managing First Impressions
- Using Body Language to Foster Adjustment and Enhance Social Relationships
- Coping With Prejudice and Discrimination
- Enhancing Self-Esteem
- How to Become an Assertive Person (How to Win Respect and Influence People)
- Using the Balance Sheet to Make Decisions
- Choosing a Physician
- How to Take It Off and Keep It Off — Weight, That Is
- How to Use Self-Control Strategies to Quit and Cut Down on Smoking
- Suicide
- Psychotherapy and Human Diversity
- Relaxing (Chilling, That Is)
- Coping With Test Anxiety
- Alleviating Depression (Getting Out of the Dumps)
- Costs of Gender-Role Stereotyping
- Coping With Loneliness
- Making It Work: Ways of Coping With Conflict in a Relationship
- Preventing Rape (Shout "Fire!" not "Rape!")
- Preventing STDs in the Age of AIDS
- Dying With Dignity
- Finding a Career That Fits
- Dealing With Day Care
- Coping With Child Abuse

"What Do You Say Now?"

The interactive "What Do You Say Now?" features place students in challenging social situations, ask them to write down what they would say, and then present authors' suggestions for managing the situations. Students thus have the opportunity to compare their own ideas with ours. These situations are real and happen often enough. We believe that these exercises will help students respond to them, and to similar situations, effectively. Here are some examples:

- Responding to Lowballing
- Encouraging a Friend to Seek Help
- Resisting an Invitation to Eat
- Handling a Sexist Remark
- How to Wow the Job Interviewer
- Selecting an Obstetrician

Chapter Summaries

Chapter summaries are numbered and presented in an interactive question-and-answer format so as to be consistent with the SQ3R study method outlined in Chapter 1. These summaries help students actively review the subject matter by posing questions and suggesting responses.

THE ANCILLARIES

The seventh edition of *Adjustment and Growth: The Challenges of Life* is accompanied by an array of ancillaries that are intended to optimize learning and teaching. In the seventh edition, the ancillaries are combined into two texts, as shown in the descriptions below:

Self-Scoring Study Guide/Student Activities Manual

Each chapter of this ancillary includes an outline; learning objectives; key terms with an exercise for reviewing those terms; tear-out activities and questionnaires; a chronological chapter review with fill-in-the-blank, true/false, and matching exercises; and a sample test including multiple-choice, true/false, and essay items. The chapter review sections have been expanded from the previous edition with additional questions and activities that reflect the revision of the main text. In the seventh edition, the *Study Guide* has been combined with the *Student Activities Manual.*

Instructor's Manual/Test Bank

The *Instructor's Manual* furnishes instructors with many helpful tools for each chapter, including an outline, an overview, teaching objectives, lecture and discussion ideas based on concepts covered in the main text, and activities for distribution to students. The *Test Bank* consists of an average of 100 multiple-choice questions, 30 to 40 true/false questions, and 10 to 20 essay questions for each chapter. The questions are designed to test students' factual, conceptual, and applied knowledge of the material presented in the main text.

Computerized Test Bank

The *Computerized Test Bank* is available in CD-ROM or 3.5" disk format for Windows and Macintosh computers. The computerized version also includes the student activities from the *Instructor's Manual* for each chapter that instructors can edit and print out.

Harcourt Brace Teaching Modules

With this edition, there are 15 teaching modules from the video series *Discovering Psychology* to supplement classroom lectures in adjustment and growth. Interviews with famous researchers and footage of actual experiments make this a valuable teaching aid. The *Instructor's Manual* gives suggestions on using these videos in class and provides questions for relating the videos to the text material. Contact your local Harcourt Brace sales representative for more information on these and other videos.

ACKNOWLEDGMENTS

At times writing can seem a solitary task. However, many of our professional colleagues participated in the growth and development of *Adjustment and Growth*. They painstakingly read manuscripts, and they suggested many insightful adjustments. We take this opportunity to express our sincere gratitude to those instructors who contributed to the development of the seventh edition:

Bernardo Carducci
Shyness Research Institute
Indiana University Southeast

Robert Higgins
Oakland Community College

Dorothy (Dot) McDonald
Sandhills Community College

Robert Osman
Onondaga Community College

Scott Potter
Marion Technical College

Richard W. Rogers
Daytona Beach Community College

Robert Schultz
Fulton-Montgomery Community College

We also take this opportunity to express our sincere gratitude to those who have reviewed previous editions:

Harold D. (Doug) Andrews
Miami-Dade Community College
Wolfson Campus

Bob Arndt
Delta College

Bela Baker
University of Wisconsin—Green Bay

Helene Bakewell
Stephen F. Austin University

Jacinth Baubitz
Northwood Institute

Nancy Bowers
Pikes Peak Community College

Edward N. Brady
Belleville Area College

Kyle Ann Campos
Des Moines Area Community College

Desmond Cartwright
University of Colorado

David Chance
Central State College

Steven Coccia
Orange County Community College

Norma Crews
DeKalb Community College

Jean De Vany
Auburn University

Richard Dienstbier
University of Nebraska

Steve Donahue
Grand Canyon College

William Dugmore
Central Washington University

Thomas Eckle
Modesto Junior College

Richard M. Ehlenz
Rochester Community College

Ron Evans
Washburn University

Jennie Fauchier
Metro Technical Community College

Eugene Fichter
Northern Virginia Community College

Ronnie Fisher
Miami-Dade Community College

Sharon Fisher
El Paso Community College

Lynn Godat
Portland Community College

Peter Gram
Pensacola Community College

Lawrence Grebstein
University of Rhode Island

Myree Hayes
East Carolina University

Barbara J. Hermann
Gainesville College

Glady Hiner
Rose State College

Joseph Horvat
Weber State College

Richard Hudiburg
University of North Alabama

Gordon M. Kimbrell
University of South Carolina

Guadelupe King
Milwaukee Area Technical College

Clint Layne
Western Kentucky University

Gary Lesniak
Portland Community College

Arnold LeUnes
Texas A & M University

Phyllis McGraw
Portland State University

Joseph McNair
Miami-Dade Community College North Campus

Louis A. Martone
Miami-Dade Community College

Frederick Medway
University of South Carolina

Roland Miller
Sam Houston State University

Norma Mittenthal
Hillsborough Community College

Patrick Murphy
Spokane Community College

Tony Obradovich
DeVry Institute of Technology

Ginger T. Osborne
Rancho Santiago College

Arne Parma
Massachusetts Bay Community College

Carola Pedreschi
Miami-Dade Community College

Kathy Petrowsky
Southwestern Oklahoma State University

Robert Petty
University of Santa Clara

A. R. Peyrnan
Mississippi State University

Gary Piggrem
DeVry Institute of Technology

Chris Potter
Harrisburg Area Community College

Jay Pozner
Jackson Community College

Rosemary Price
Rancho Santiago College

James B. Riley
Southeastern Massachusetts University

Suzanne Rucker
Miami-Dade Community College

Robert W. Schaeffer
Auburn University

Paul Schwartz
Mt. Saint Mary College

Richard W. Seefeldt
University of Wisconsin—River Falls

Patricia W. Smith
Del Gado Community College

Claudia Sowa
University of Virginia

Arthur Swanson
University of Missouri—Columbia

Marilyn Thomas
Prince George Community College

Robert Thomlinson
University of Wisconsin—Eau Claire

Brenda K. Vance
Seminole Junior College

Catherine Wambach
University of Minnesota

Deborah Weber
University of Akron

David Weight
Brigham Young University

Robert Wrenn
University of Arizona

I am also grateful, as always, to the fine group of publishing professionals at Harcourt Brace who helped translate my book dreams into the finished product you are holding in your hands. First is Carol Wada, Executive Editor, whose faith in this book almost literally breathed new life into it. Christine Abshire, Developmental Editor, helped me formulate the improvements you will find over the sixth edition. Angela Urquhart, Senior Project Editor, and Andrea

Johnson, Production Manager, handled the myriad details that go into making a bound book. Carol Kincaid, Art Director, is to be credited for the book's stunning new design—a design that brings us into the new millennium in many, many ways. Finally, let me express my gratitude to the company's upper management team, including Earl McPeek, Chris Klein, and Ted Buchholz. You have been there for me for many years; I have shared confidences with you, and I consider you to be close friends.

Spencer A. Rathus
Montclair State University
Upper Montclair, New Jersey

To the memory of Gustave and Sophie Rathus.
—S. A. R.

To Judy, Michael, and Daniella who fill my life with love.
—J. S. N.

Chapter 1

What Is Adjustment?

Truth or Fiction?

T F

- ☐ ☐ You can't buy happiness.
- ☐ ☐ Women were not permitted to attend college in the United States until 1833.
- ☐ ☐ Americans in their forties have had more sex partners than Americans in their twenties.
- ☐ ☐ You are less likely to get a divorce if you live together with your future spouse before getting married.
- ☐ ☐ Pretest cramming is more effective than distributed learning.
- ☐ ☐ You shouldn't reward yourself simply for meeting daily study goals.

OUTLINE

BETH, 22, A FOURTH-YEAR CHEMISTRY MAJOR, HAS been accepted to medical school in Boston. She wants to do cancer research, but this goal means another 7 or 8 years at the grindstone. Kevin, her fiancé, has landed a solid engineering position in "Silicon Valley," California. He wants Beth to come with him, take a year to start a family, and then go to medical school in California. But Beth hasn't applied to medical school in California, and there's no sure bet that she would be accepted there. If she surrenders her educational opportunity now, another one might not come along. Should she demand that Kevin accompany her to Boston, even though he hasn't been offered work there? Would he go? What if he gives up his golden opportunity and their relationship falters because of resentment? Also, if she has children, she doesn't want to hand them over to a stranger all day, every day, so she can go to school. And how long can she safely put off childbearing? She's "a kid" now, but the biological clock is ticking and she won't be finishing her graduate training—assuming she goes to medical school—until she's 30. And what if having children even then threatens to prevent her from getting established in her career? Beth has just been accepted to medical school—shouldn't she be happy?

John, 21, is a business student who is all business. Every day he reads the *Wall Street Journal* and the business pages of the *New York Times*. He is dedicated to his books and invests most of his energy in trying to construct a solid academic record so that he will get his career off on the right foot. He represents the first generation in his African American family to attend college, and he is determined to do college right. But sometimes he wonders why he bothers; he thinks of himself as one of those people who "just can't take tests." He begins to shake 2 days before a test. His thoughts become jumbled when the papers are distributed. He finds himself wondering whether his professors will attribute poor grades to his ethnicity. By the time the papers are on his desk, his hand is shaking so badly that he can hardly write his name. His grades suffer.

Maria, 19, is a first-year college student. She has seen the TV talk shows and has gone to the R-rated films. She has read the books and the magazine articles about the new sexual openness, but her traditional Mexican American upbringing has given her a strong sense of what is right and wrong for her. Yes, she is acculturated in that her English is fluent and in that she has excelled in her education. Yet despite the social and sexual pressures she finds in the dominant culture, she would prefer to wait for Mr. Right. At the very least, she is not going to allow social pressure to prevent her from carefully sorting out her values and her feelings. The young man she has been seeing, Mark, has been patient—from his point of view. But lately he's been pressuring Maria, too. He has told Maria they have more than a fly-by-night relationship and that other women are more willing to "express their sexual needs" with him. Maria's girlfriends say they understand her feelings. Yet they tell her that they fear that Mark will eventually turn elsewhere. Quite frankly, Maria is concerned about more than virginity; she also thinks about diseases such as herpes and AIDS. After all, Mark is 22 years old and she doesn't know every place he's been. True, they can take precautions, but what is completely safe? In any event, Maria does not want to be pressured.

Lisa, 20, a hard-working college junior, is popular with faculty, dutiful with relatives. She works out regularly and is proud of her figure. But Lisa also has a secret. When she is sipping her coffee in the morning, she hopes that she won't go off the deep end again, but most of the time she does. She usually starts by eating a doughnut slowly; then she eats another, picking up speed; then she voraciously downs the remaining four in the box. Then she eats two or three bagels with cream cheese. If there is any leftover pizza from the evening before, that goes down, too. She feels disgusted with herself, but she hunts through her apartment for food. Down go the potato chips, down go the cookies. Fifteen minutes later she feels as though she will burst and cannot take in anymore. Half nauseated, she finds her way to the bathroom and makes herself throw up the contents of her binge eating. Tomorrow, she tells herself, will be different. But deep inside she suspects that she will buy more doughnuts and more cookies, and that tomorrow might be much the same. She has read about something called bulimia nervosa. Does she have it? Does she need professional help?

David, 32, is not sleeping well. He wakes before dawn and cannot get back to sleep. His appetite is off, his energy level is low, he has started smoking again. He has a couple of drinks at lunch and muses that it's lucky that any more alcohol makes him sick to his stomach—otherwise, he'd probably be drinking too much, too. Then he thinks, "So what difference would it make?" Sometimes he is sexually frustrated; at other times he wonders whether he has any sex drive left. Although he's awake, each day it's getting harder to drag himself out of bed in the morning. This week he missed one day of work and was late twice. His supervisor has suggested in a nonthreatening way that he "do something about it." David knows that her next warning will not be unthreatening. It's been going downhill since Sue walked out. Suicide has even crossed David's mind. He wonder's whether he's going crazy.

Beth, John, Maria, Lisa, David—each of them is experiencing a challenge to adjustment and growth.

Beth is experiencing role conflict. She wants to attend medical school but also wants to maintain the relationship with Kevin and start a family. Although she might become a physician, she would probably retain the primary responsibility for childrearing. Even women who have become officers of their companies most often remain the ones who do the laundry and dress the kids. Kevin is not a chauvinist, however; he accompanies Beth to Boston and looks for work there.

John's problem is test anxiety, plain but not-so-simple. Years of anxiety and fluctuating grades have led to a vicious cycle: He becomes so anxious that he often finds himself paying more attention to his bodily sensations and his troubled thoughts than to the test items themselves. His distraction then leads to poor grades and heightens his anxiety. His concerns have prevented him from performing up to his full potential. Fortunately, there is a notice on a bulletin board that his college counseling center is running a program to help students with test anxiety. He follows techniques like those outlined in Chapter 11 and his grades pick up.

Maria is in conflict—with Mark and with herself. She decides not to be pressured into a sexual relationship, and it happens that Mark turns elsewhere.

It hurts, but Maria is confident that other men who are more sensitive to her values will understand and appreciate her.

Lisa does have **bulimia nervosa**, an eating disorder discussed in Chapter 7. Bulimia has reached epidemic proportions on college campuses. The causes of bulimia are complex and not fully understood, but bulimia seems to be related to the slender feminine ideal that prevails in the United States.

David is depressed. Depression is normal following a loss, such as the end of a relationship, but David's feelings have lingered. His friends tell him that he should get out and do things, but David is so down that he hasn't the motivation. After much prompting David consults a psychologist who, ironically, also pushes him to get out and do things—pleasant events of the sort described in Chapter 11. The psychologist also shows David that part of his problem is that sees himself as a failure who cannot make meaningful changes.

Beth, John, Maria, Lisa, and David all need to make adjustments to the challenges in their lives. The challenges of life touch us all at one time or another. That is what this book is about: adjusting to challenges as we get on with the business of living—growing, learning, building relationships, making sense of our value systems, establishing careers, making ends meet, and striving to feel good about ourselves. This book portrays our quest for self-development and brings psychological knowledge to bear on problems that may block self-development. Some of these problems, such as anxiety, depression, or obesity, are personal. Some involve intimate relationships and sexuality. Some involve the larger social context—the workplace, prejudice and discrimination, community disasters, pollution, and urban life.

Most challenges offer us the opportunity to grow. Most of the time we solve the problems we encounter by ourselves. But when personal solutions are not at hand, we can often turn to modern psychology for help. In this book you will learn how you can apply psychological knowledge to your own life. You will also learn about the professional helpers and when and how to seek their intervention. This knowledge is important because life in the new millennium has in many ways become more challenging than ever.

In this chapter we first define the science of psychology and see that it is well suited to gathering information about, and suggesting applications for, our own adjustment and growth. We explore the richness of human diversity—the facets of ourselves that can make us unique yet can instill in us a sense of cultural pride. Then we examine the scientific procedures that psychologists use in gathering knowledge. Finally, we explore what psychologists have learned about making study habits more effective.

PSYCHOLOGY AND ADJUSTMENT

The science of **psychology** is ideally suited to helping people meet the challenges of contemporary life. Psychology is a scientific approach to the study of behavior and mental processes. Psychologists traditionally attempt to understand or explain behavior in terms of the workings of the nervous system, the interaction of genetic and environmental influences ("nature" and "nurture"), the ways in which we sense and mentally represent the world, the roles of learning and motivation, and the nature of personality and social interaction.

Psychology also has an applied side that helps foster personal adjustment. Clinical, counseling, and health psychologists—to name but a few—assess individuals' personal strengths and weaknesses through psychological tests and structured interviews, and they help individuals cope with problems and optimize their personal development through psychotherapy and behavior therapy.

Adjustment, or coping, is behavior that permits us to meet the demands of the environment. Sometimes the demands are physical. When we are cold, we

BULIMIA NERVOSA • An eating disorder characterized by cycles of binge eating and a dramatic method for purging, such as vomiting.

PSYCHOLOGY • The science that studies observable behavior and mental processes.

ADJUSTMENT • Processes by which people respond to environmental pressures and cope with stress.

Getting Started. Sometimes the demands of adjustment are psychological, as in assuming the academic and social demands of college life.

can adjust by dressing warmly, turning up the thermostat, or exercising. Holding down a job to keep the bill collector from our doors, drinking to quench our thirst, meeting the daily needs of our children—these, too, are forms of adjustment.

Sometimes the demands of adjustment are more psychological, as in leaving home for the first time, a major exam, a job interview, the death of a loved one. We may adjust to demands such as these by making new friends, adding up the pluses and minuses of studying versus going to the movies, rehearsing what we'll say in a job interview, or being with supportive relatives.

We can also make inferior adjustments. We can pretend that problems do not exist, we can avoid thinking about the exam, or we can believe that we'll get that job because we're basically deserving. We can medicate ourselves, dull our anxieties and fears with alcohol or other drugs. We can deceive ourselves that we hurt others for the noblest of reasons—that we have the best of intentions when we're simply reluctant to look within ourselves. We can tell ourselves that our problems are so awful that there's no point to trying to cope with them.

The strongest, most effective forms of adjustment involve seeing pressures and problems for what they are. Then we can make decisions and plans that will allow us to change them, or, in those cases where they cannot be changed, perhaps we can work to change self-defeating response patterns so that they trouble us less.

CONTROVERSIES IN PSYCHOLOGY AND ADJUSTMENT

There are a number of controversies in the psychology of adjustment that reflect debates in the broader field of psychology. They are important because they address our concepts of human nature.

Adjustment Versus Personal Growth

One controversy concerns the meaning of the word *adjustment.* Literally speaking, to adjust is to change so as better to conform to, or meet, the demands of one's environment. Adjustment is essentially reactive. The ball is perpetually in the environment's court. We can only wait to see what forces the environment will unleash on us.

However, a premise of this book is that people are not merely reactors to their environments. People are also actors. Things not only happen to us. We also make things happen. Not only does the environment affect us. We also affect the environment. Now and then, we create novel environments to suit our needs.

We must extend the concept of adjustment to accommodate the active aspects of human nature—self-initiated growth and development. Not only do we react to stress. We also act to become.

When we achieve greatness, or when our lives seem filled with meaning, it is not because we have adjusted. It is because we have acted in order to become. It is because of personal growth.

ADJUSTMENT in the NEW MILLENNIUM

Where Are We Headed?

How many people's lives have straddled two millennia? New years bring new hope, and we make resolutions to improve our lives. What, then, of the new millennium? The thought of entering the new millennium stirs yet greater hope and still more resolve to enhance our lives and those of our children.

The rapid pace of the development of new technologies seems to offer many opportunities to promote adjustment and growth. The "Adjustment in the New Millennium" features in the text explore the connections between technological advances, the science of psychology, and our styles of life. In some cases we explore the future of psychological knowledge and applications.

The first of these features contains a wish list—a partial list of developments that are being ushered in with the refreshing breezes of the new millennium. Some of them are here already. Others seem around the corner. Still others seem to be more elusive. All of them are being researched or developed as you read these pages:

- Enhancement of knowledge about the links between biological processes and psychological processes so that we can better understand psychological processes and promote human adjustment and growth. For example, increased knowledge of the various functions of serotonin, a chemical messenger in the brain, is likely to lead to improved treatments for depression and obesity.
- Applications of the Human Genome Project to the psychology of adjustment. The human genome consists of all our genes—the basic units of heredity. The government-funded Human Genome Project is expected to be completed early in the new millennium and aims to identify all the genes that make up the human being—that is, the *human genome.* In so doing, researchers will be able to determine whether people have genes that contribute to physical adjustment problems such as cancer and to psychological adjustment problems such as bipolar mood disorder and schizophrenia. We may also learn how to change these genes to enhance adjustment and growth.
- Application of research in developmental psychology, social psychology, and consumer psychology

Nature Versus Nurture: Is Biology Destiny?

Psychologists are concerned about the degree to which our traits and behavior patterns reflect our nature, or genetic factors, and our nurture, or environmental influences. Physical traits such as height, race, and eye color are biologically transmitted from generation to generation by **genes.** Genes are segments of deoxyribonucleic acid (DNA), the stuff of which our **chromosomes** are composed. Genes give rise to our biological structures and physical traits.

It has been clear that genes play roles in the development of physical disorders such as heart disease and cancer. Now it appears that genetic factors are also involved in personality and behavior. For example, genes have an influence on traits such as intelligence, sociability, emotional stability, shyness, aggressiveness, social dominance and leadership, effectiveness as a parent or a therapist, even on interest in arts and crafts (Lykken and others, 1992). Genetic influences are involved in psychological disorders such as anxiety disorders, mood disorders, and schizophrenia (DiLalla and others, 1996). There are also roles for heredity in obesity and vulnerability to addiction to substances such as alcohol and nicotine (Azar, 1995; Newlin & Thomson, 1990; Pomerleau and others, 1993).

GENE • The basic unit of heredity, consisting of a segment of deoxyribonucleic acid (DNA).

CHROMOSOME • A strand of DNA that consists of genes. People normally have 23 pairs of chromosomes.

(for example, advertising methods) to prevent substance abuse—including smoking cigarettes—among young people.

- Development of effective methods of preventing violence against women and children.
- Development of effective methods of educating all groups in the United States about HIV infection and AIDS and of encouraging them to take preventive measures.
- Development of effective methods for teaching the public to think critically so that it will be more resistant to appeals to authority, to celebrity endorsements, and to other tyrants of the mind.
- Determination of which methods of therapy work best for various psychological disorders as they appear in different populations (e.g., the same methods of intervention might not work as well with Asian Americans as they do with Americans of European origin).
- Development of systems for bringing psychological services to populations with little access to health care, including members of some ethnic minority groups and homeless people.
- Increasing the sensitivity of psychologists and other health professionals to the needs of women, people from diverse ethnic groups, disabled people, and gay males and lesbians.
- Increased utilization of computers in the diagnosis and treatment of psychological problems.
- Determination of the most effective ways to encourage people to help maintain the environment—for example, encouraging recycling and the use of mass transportation or of vehicles that emit fewer (or no) pollutants.
- Development of better methods to determine the kinds of careers individuals are suited for.
- Extension of the human life span through improvements in sanitation and diet, possible use of hormone supplements, increasing the number of times human cells can divide, and—perhaps—genetic engineering.

These are just a couple of handfuls of the developments we can expect in the new millennium. What kinds of adjustment problems do you imagine people will encounter in the new millennium? How do you think we will be able to cope with them? ■

Truth or Fiction Revisited

It is apparently true that you can't buy happiness. Heredity seems to be a more important determinant of happiness than money and other social factors. (But let's face it: At the very least, having money means that one needn't worry about money.)

Studies of pairs of twins carried out by psychologist David Lykken (1996) suggest that people even inherit a tendency toward a certain level of happiness. Despite the ups and downs of experience, people tend to drift back to their usual levels of cheerfulness or grumpiness. Factors such as availability of money, level of education, and marital status may be less influential than heredity when it comes to human happiness.

Although genetic factors play a role in psychological adjustment and effective behavior, they do not in themselves give rise to specific behavior patterns. They interact with environmental factors and with self-determination to affect behavior (Azar, 1997a). Although people may have a genetic predisposition toward becoming dependent on various substances, including alcohol, cocaine, and nicotine, peer pressures and other psychological factors may be just as important as genes in determining whether or not people become addicted to them.

Genetic factors can be powerful influences; for example, our genetic codes do not permit us to fly or breathe underwater. But in many cases, human adjustment ability can modify the impact of genes. For example, we can build airplanes and submarines (or scuba gear). Biology is not always destiny. The degree to which you marshal your inherited resources to adjust and develop your potential is largely up to you.

The Clinical Approach Versus the Healthy-Personality Approach

Most psychology-of-adjustment textbooks are written according to one of two major approaches—a clinical approach or a healthy-personality approach. The clinical approach primarily focuses on ways in which psychology can help people correct personal problems and cope with stress. The healthy-personality approach primarily focuses on healthful patterns of personal growth and development, including social and vocational development. Books with a clinical approach are frequently written from psychodynamic and behaviorist perspectives, whereas books with a healthy-personality approach are more likely to be written from phenomenological perspectives.

The book you are holding in your hands was written with awareness of both approaches to the psychology of adjustment. There is ample discussion of stress and disorder and ways of coping. But there is equal emphasis on optimizing our potentials through preventive and self-actualizing behavior. We aim to be comprehensive and balanced in our approach, to provide ample theory, research, and applications for coping and for optimal development.

HUMAN DIVERSITY AND ADJUSTMENT

Psychologists focus mainly on individual people and are committed to the dignity of the individual. Yet we cannot understand individuals without an awareness of the richness of human diversity (Basic Behavioral Science Task Force, 1996b). People diverge, or differ, from one another in many ways. Human diversity gives rise to numerous kinds of adjustment problems and to various resources for adjustment.

Ethnic Diversity

The nation and the world at large contain more kinds of people and more ways of doing and viewing things than most of us might imagine. One kind of

HUMAN DIVERSITY.
Psychologists focus mainly on individual people and are committed to the dignity of the individual. Yet we cannot understand individuals without an awareness of the richness of human diversity.

diversity involves people's **ethnic groups.** Ethnic groups are subgroups within the general population who have a common cultural heritage, as distinguished by factors such as their customs, race, language, and common history.

One reason for studying ethnic diversity is that the experiences of various ethnic groups in the United States highlight the impact of social, political, and economic factors on human behavior and development (Basic Behavioral Science Task Force, 1996b; Phinney, 1996). Another reason is the dramatically changing ethnic makeup of the United States. Figures 1.1 and 1.2 highlight the changes under way due to patterns of reproduction and immigration. The U.S. Bureau of the Census (1998) projects that the nation's non-Hispanic White population will increase from 196 million in 1999 to 208 million by the year 2050, an increase of 12 million people (Figure 1.1). But because the populations of other ethnic groups in the United States are projected

ETHNIC GROUP • A group of people who can be distinguished by characteristics such as their cultural heritage, common history, race, and language. Not all ethnic groups differ according to all these features. For example, French Catholics and Protestants can be said to belong to different ethnic groups, but both groups are predominantly White, speak French, and share much of their cultural heritage and history.

to increase relatively more rapidly, the *percentage* of non-Hispanic white Americans in the total population will *decrease* from 72 percent in 1999 to 53 percent in 2050 (see Figure 1.2). The fastest growing ethnic groups consist of Asians and Pacific Islanders (to whom we refer as Asian Americans) and of Hispanic Americans. In 1999 there were 10 million Asian Americans in the United States, and they are expected to increase to 32 million by 2050 (Figure 1.1), rising from 4 percent to 8 percent of the total U.S. population (Figure 1.2). Hispanic Americans (who may be White, Black, or Native American) are projected to increase from 31 million to 97 million people, or from about 11 percent to nearly 25 percent of the population. As shown in Figures 1.1 and 1.2, the numbers of African Americans and Native Americans are growing more slowly than those of Hispanic and Asian Americans, but still more rapidly than those of non-Hispanic White Americans. The African American population is expected to grow from 33 million people (12 percent of the current population) in 1999 to nearly 54 million people (13.6 percent) by the year 2050. The cultural heritages of ethnic minority groups are thus likely to have increasing impacts on the cultural life of the United States.

Studying human diversity also enables students to appreciate the cultural heritages and historical problems of various ethnic groups (Murray, 1995). Too often throughout our history, the traditions, languages, and achievements of ethnic minority groups have been judged by majority standards or denigrated (Jones, 1991; Sue, 1991). For example, Ebonics (the English dialect spoken by many African Americans) has been considered inferior to standard English, although it is as complex. Bilingualism has also been erroneously considered to be inferior to being reared to speak English only.

FIGURE 1.1
PROJECTED GROWTH OF ETHNIC GROUPS IN THE UNITED STATES, 1999–2050
Although non-Hispanic White Americans are more numerous than the other ethnic groups within the United States that are shown in this figure, their growth rate is projected to be lower.

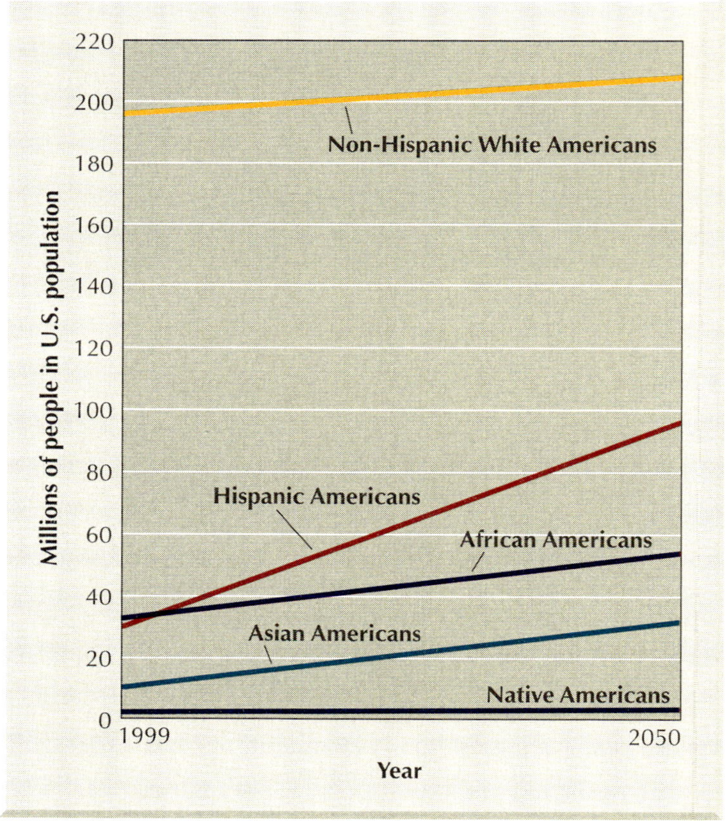

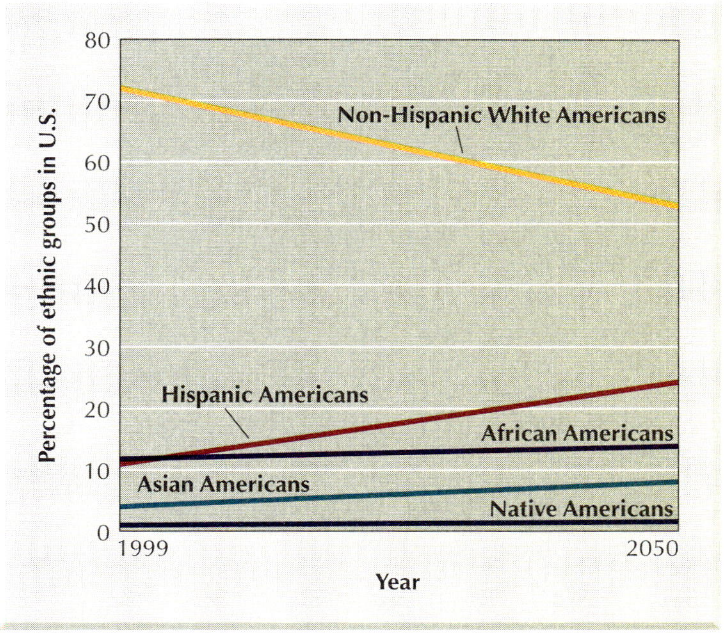

FIGURE 1.2
CHANGES IN THE ETHNIC MAKEUP OF THE UNITED STATES, ACCORDING TO THE NUMBERS OF EACH ETHNIC GROUP AS A PERCENTAGE OF THE OVERALL POPULATION, 1999–2050

Although the numbers of non-Hispanic White Americans will increase between 1999 and 2050, trends in reproduction and immigration suggest that non-Hispanic White Americans will make up a much smaller percentage of the overall U.S. population by the year 2050.

Another reason for studying diversity concerns psychological intervention and consultation. Psychologists are called upon to help people of all ethnic groups solve personal problems, for example. How can psychologists hope to understand the aspirations and problems of individuals from an ethnic group without understanding the history and cultural heritage of that group (Nevid and others, 1997)? How can psychologists understand African Americans or Hispanic Americans, for example, without sensitivity to the histories of prejudice to which members of these ethnic groups have been exposed? Moreover, should psychologists from the White majority attempt to practice psychotherapy with people from ethnic minority groups? If so, what kinds of special education or training might they need in order to do so? What is meant by "culturally sensitive" forms of psychotherapy? We address these issues in Chapter 10.

Throughout the text we consider many issues that address ethnic minority groups and psychology. Just a handful include the following:

- Prejudice
- Alcohol and substance abuse among adolescents from various ethnic minority groups
- The influence of ethnic stereotypes on our perceptions and memories
- Ethnic differences in vulnerability to various physical problems and disorders, ranging from obesity to hypertension and cancer
- Ethnic differences in the utilization of health care for physical and psychological problems
- The prevalence of suicide among members of different ethnic minority groups
- Considerations in the practice of psychotherapy with clients from different ethnic groups
- Machismo/Marianismo stereotypes and Hispanic culture

Adjustment in a World of DIVERSITY

On Increasing Diversity in American Higher Education[1]

The increasing diversity of American higher education has been created not only by demographic changes in American society, but, just as importantly, by the rising awareness in the United States of various group identities and cultures. At one time, most American colleges and universities were relatively homogeneous, even those that were not were able to persuade their students to leave their ethnicity and other cultural "baggage" at the campus gate. Today, that would no longer be realistic, even if it were desirable.

Students now enter college with their group identity intact, and they expect the institution to respond accordingly. Although that is a fairly new situation, it is rooted in events of the 1960s and 1970s, when Black students began demanding Black studies. Since then, people have come to identify themselves not only according to race, gender, or ethnic identity, but also by class, sexual orientation, disability, and age.

This new reality suggests a need for students to learn about groups that were formerly ignored in the curriculum, not only so that they may more fully appreciate the rich variety of cultures that make up our national community, but so that they will better understand the complex ways in which cultural identity and personal identity interact. Today's multicultural world also requires critical inquiry into culture, not mere naive acceptance or celebration of it. And since the critical study and mastery of one's own culture is the best preparation for critical encounters with the cultures of others, the curriculum should not only teach students about those who are different, but help them discover themselves culturally as well.

Perhaps the most far-reaching result of the intercultural discourse beginning on today's campuses will be the introduction of *all* participants to unfamiliar cultures. That, of course, can put the received cultural traditions at some risk, one that some of their guardians may be unwilling to take. Closely held cultures, like closely held companies, control access jealously. If conducted in an open spirit, however, critical inquiry can open borders, introduce outside influences, and ultimately create new cultural values.

Gender

Another way in which people differ concerns their **gender**—that is, the state of being male or being female. A person's gender is not simply a matter of her or his anatomy. Gender involves a complex web of cultural expectations and social roles that affect people's self-concepts and hopes and dreams as well as their behavior. How can sciences such as psychology and medicine hope to understand the particular viewpoints, qualities, and problems of women if most research is conducted with men, by men, and for the benefit of men (Matthews and others, 1997)?

GENDER • The state of being female or being male. (In this book, the word *sex* refers to sexual behavior and is also used in phrases such as *sex hormones*.)

[1] This "Adjustment in a World of Diversity" feature is extracted from Edgar F. Beckham (1993), "Campus Diversity: Facing New Realities," *The Ford Foundation Report, 23*(4), 8–9.

Just as there have been historic prejudices against members of ethnic minority groups, so, too, have there been prejudices against women. Even much of the scientific research into gender roles and gender differences assumes that male behavior represents the norm (Ader & Johnson, 1994; Matlin, 1996; Walsh, 1993). The careers of women have been traditionally channeled into domestic chores, regardless of their wishes as individuals. Not until relatively modern times were Western women generally considered suitable for education. (Women are still considered unsuited to education in many parts of the world!) Women have attended college in the United States only since 1833, when Oberlin opened its doors to women. Today, however, more than half (54 percent) of U.S. postsecondary students are women. As noted in Figure 1.3, African Americans and Native Americans contribute relatively higher percentages of women. Other gains by women are suggested by the numbers of women who received doctoral degrees in various areas in the 1970s, 1980s, and 1990s (see Table 1.1).

Truth or Fiction Revisited

It is true that women were not permitted to attend college in the United States until 1833; 1833 is the year that Oberlin began to accept women as students.

Others Kinds of Diversity

Human diversity also touches upon differences in age, physical ability, and sexual orientation. Older people, disabled people, and gay males and lesbians have all suffered from discrimination. The dominant culture has from time to time been loath to consider and profit from the particular sensitivities and perspectives afforded by individuals from each of these groups. For example, physical disabilities can affect people's lifestyles and adjustment by creating communication barriers with able-bodied people, complicating transportation, making many buildings inaccessible, and requiring costly devices such as wheelchairs (APA Task Force, 1998).

Our focus on human diversity throughout the text will help us to better understand and fully appreciate the true extent of human behavior and mental processes. This broader view of psychology—and the world—is enriching for its own sake and heightens the accuracy and scope of our presentation.

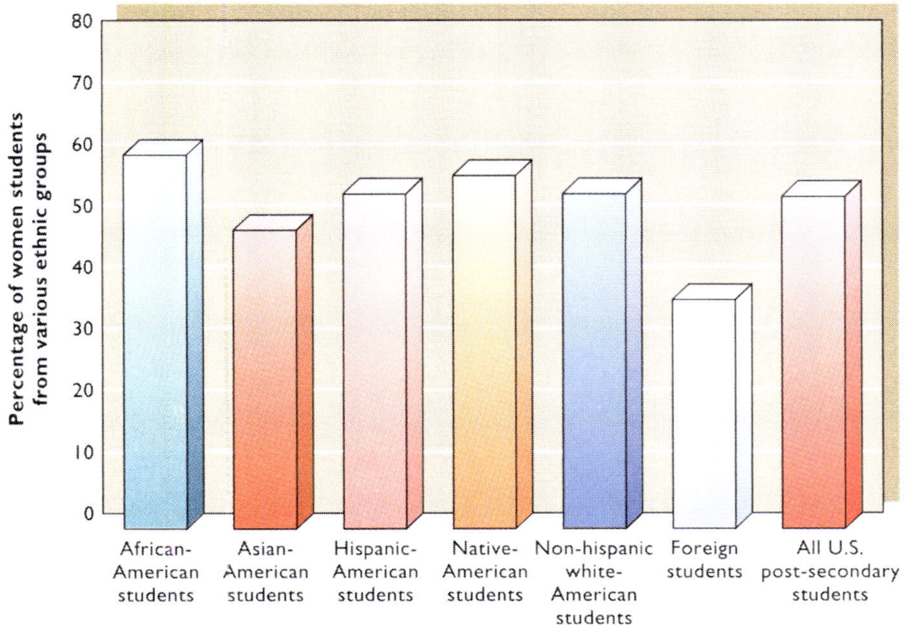

FIGURE 1.3

THE PERCENTAGES OF WOMEN POSTSECONDARY STUDENTS IN THE UNITED STATES, ACCORDING TO ETHNIC GROUP

Note that the percentages of African American and Native American women among postsecondary students are relatively high, whereas the percentages of Asian American and foreign women are relatively low. Why do you think this is so?
Source: *The Chronicle of Higher Education,* March 18, 1992, p. A35.

TABLE 1.1 PERCENTAGE OF DOCTORAL DEGREES AWARDED TO WOMEN IN VARIOUS MAJOR FIELDS AND PROFESSIONS

Major Field (degree awarded)	*Percentage of Women*		
	1971	**1981**	**1991**
Biology (Ph.D.)	14.5	25.5	38.7
Dentistry (D.D.S. or D.M.D.)	1.1	14.0	32.1
Education (Ph.D.)	21.9	47.2	58.1
Engineering (Ph.D.)	0.4	3.9	8.7
Humanities (Ph.D.)	24.2	41.3	46.5
Law (J.D.)	7.1	32.0	42.9
Mathematics (Ph.D.)	7.8	15.4	18.7
Medicine (M.D.)	9.1	25.0	35.9
Physical Sciences	5.9	11.8	18.3
Psychology (Ph.D.)	24.7	43.9	61.2
Sociology and Anthropology (Ph.D.)	19.7	40.0	49.5
Veterinary Medicine (D.V.M.)	7.8	36.4	57.2

Source: From Pion, G. M., and others (1996), The shifting gender composition of psychology: Trends and implications for the discipline, *American Psychologist, 51*, 509–528.

HOW PSYCHOLOGISTS STUDY ADJUSTMENT

Are women better than men at spelling? Are city dwellers less friendly toward strangers than small town residents? Do laws against discrimination reduce prejudice? Does alcohol cause aggression? Is exercise good for your heart? What are the effects of day care and divorce on children?

Many of us have expressed *opinions* on questions such as these at one time or another, and psychological and medical theories also suggest a number of possible answers. But psychology is a science, and scientific statements about behavior must be supported by *evidence*. Strong arguments, reference to authority figures, celebrity endorsements, even tightly knit theories are not considered adequate as scientific evidence. Scientific evidence is obtained by means of the *scientific method*.

The Scientific Method

The **scientific method** is an organized way of expanding and refining knowledge. It consists of a group of principles that generally guide scientists' research endeavors.

SCIENTIFIC METHOD • A method for obtaining scientific evidence in which a hypothesis is formed and tested.

Psychologists usually begin by *formulating a research question*. Some research questions arise from daily experience. Daily experience in using day care centers may motivate us to conduct research into whether day care influences children's development of social skills or the bonds of attachment between children and their mothers. Some research questions arise from psychological theory, as we see in later chapters. Widespread beliefs such as "Opposites attract" and "Beauty is in the eye of the beholder" may also give rise to research questions. That is, *do* opposites attract? *Is* beauty in the eye of the beholder?

A research question may be studied in its question format, or it may be reworded into a **hypothesis.** A hypothesis is a specific statement about behavior or mental processes that is tested through research. One hypothesis about day care might be that preschoolers placed in day care will acquire greater social skills in relating to peers than preschoolers who are cared for in the home. A hypothesis about TV violence might be that elementary school children who watch more violent TV shows tend to behave more aggressively toward their peers.

Psychologists next examine the research question or *test the hypothesis* through carefully controlled methods such as naturalistic or laboratory observation and the experiment. For example, we could introduce day-care and non-day-care children to a new child in a college child research center and observe how each group fares with the new acquaintance.

To undertake research we must provide **operational definitions** for the variables under study. Concerning the effects of TV violence, we could have parents help us tally which TV shows their children watch and rate the shows for violent content. Each child could receive a composite "exposure-to-TV-violence score." We could also operationally define aggression in terms of teacher reports on how aggressively the children act toward their peers. Then we could determine whether more-aggressive children also watch more violence on television.

How might we test the hypothesis that the verbal expression of feelings of anger decreases feelings of depression? Researchers would have to decide, for example, whether they should use feelings of anger that people already have or use a standardized set of angry statements that address common areas of parent-child conflict. Would their **subjects** include people in therapy or, say, students taking a psychology of adjustment course? What would be the operational definition of feelings of depression? Self-ratings of depression according to a numerical scale? Scores on psychological tests of depression? Reports of depressive behavior by informants such as spouses? Psychologists frequently use a combination of definitions to increase their chances of tapping into targeted behavior patterns and mental processes.

Psychologists draw conclusions about their research questions or the accuracy of their hypotheses on the basis of their research observations or findings. When their observations do not bear out their hypotheses, they may modify the theories from which the hypotheses were derived.

In our research on day care, we would probably find that day-care children show somewhat greater social skills than children cared for in the home. We would probably also find that more-aggressive children spend more time watching TV violence.

As psychologists draw conclusions from research evidence, they try not to confuse connections between the findings with cause and effect. Although more-aggressive children apparently spend more time watching TV violence, it may be erroneous to conclude from this kind of evidence that TV violence *causes* aggressive behavior. Perhaps there is a **selection factor** at work, for example, such that more-aggressive children are more likely than less-aggressive children to tune into violent TV programs.

To better understand the potential effects of the selection factor, consider a study on the relationship between exercise and health. If we were to compare a group of people who exercised regularly with a group who did not, we might find that the exercisers were physically healthier than the couch potatoes. Could we conclude from this research approach that exercise is a causal factor in good health? Perhaps not. The selection factor—the fact that one group

HYPOTHESIS • An assumption about behavior that is tested through research.

OPERATIONAL DEFINITION • A definition of a variable in terms of the methods used to create or measure that variable.

SUBJECT • A participant in a scientific study.

SELECTION FACTOR • A source of bias that may occur in research findings when subjects are allowed to determine for themselves whether or not they will receive a treatment condition in a scientific study. Do you think, for example, that there are problems in studying the effects of a diet or of smoking cigarettes when we allow study participants to choose whether or not they will try the diet or smoke cigarettes? Why or why not?

chose to exercise and the other did not—could also suggest that healthy people are more apt to choose to exercise.[2] Later we shall consider the kinds of research studies that do permit us to draw conclusions about cause and effect.

Psychologists similarly attempt to avoid oversimplifying or overgeneralizing their results. The effects of day care are apparently complex, for example. Although children in day care usually exhibit better social skills than children who are not, there is also a tendency for them to be somewhat more aggressive. If we conducted our research into the benefits of expressing feelings of anger with clients in therapy, do you think that we would be justified in generalizing the results to the population at large? If we conducted that research with psychology students, could we extend or generalize the results to people who sought psychotherapy to relieve feelings of depression? Why or why not?

Some psychologists include publication of research reports in professional journals as a crucial part of the scientific method. Psychologists and other scientists are obligated to provide enough details of their work that other scientists will be able to repeat or **replicate** it. Psychologists may attempt to replicate a study in detail to corroborate the findings, especially when the findings are significant for people's welfare. Sometimes psychologists replicate research methods with different kinds of subjects to determine, for example, whether findings with women can be generalized to men, whether findings with non-Hispanic white Americans can be generalized to ethnic minority groups, or whether findings with people who have sought psychotherapy can be generalized to people at large.

Let us now consider the research methods used by psychologists: methods of sampling, methods of observation, the use of correlation, and the queen of the empirical approach—the experiment.

Samples and Populations: Representing Human Diversity

Consider a piece of "history" that never happened: The Republican candidate Alf Landon defeated the incumbent president, Franklin D. Roosevelt, in 1936. Or at least Landon did so in a poll conducted by a popular magazine of the day, the *Literary Digest.* In the actual election, however, Roosevelt routed Landon in a landslide of 11 million votes. How, then, could the *Digest* predict a Landon victory? How was so great a discrepancy possible?

The *Digest,* you see, had phoned the voters it surveyed. Today, telephone sampling is a widely practiced and reasonably legitimate technique. But the *Digest* poll was taken during the Great Depression, when Americans who had telephones were much wealthier than those who did not. Americans at higher income levels are also more likely to vote Republican. No surprise, then, that the overwhelming majority of those sampled said that they would vote for Landon.

The principle involved here is that samples must accurately *represent* the population they are intended to reflect if we are to be able to **generalize** from research samples to populations.

In surveys such as that conducted by the *Literary Digest,* and in other research methods, the individuals, or subjects, who are studied are referred to as a **sample.** A sample is a segment of a **population.** Psychologists and other scien-

REPLICATE • Repeat, reproduce, copy. What are some reasons that psychologists replicate the research conducted by other psychologists?

GENERALIZE • To extend from the particular to the general; to apply observations based on a sample to a population.

SAMPLE • Part of a population selected for research.

POPULATION • A complete group of organisms or events.

---

[2] I am not trying to suggest that exercise does *not* make a contribution to health. I am merely pointing out that research that compares people who have chosen to exercise with people who have not is not a valid way to study the issue.

tists need to ensure that the subjects they observe *represent* their target population, such as Americans, and not subgroups such as southern California yuppies or non-Hispanic White members of the middle class.

One way to achieve a representative sample is by means of **random sampling.** In a random sample, each member of a population has an equal chance of being selected to participate. Researchers can also use a **stratified sample,** which is drawn so that identified subgroups in the population are represented proportionately in the sample. For instance, 12 percent of the American population is African American. A stratified sample would thus be 12 percent African American. As a practical matter, a large, randomly selected sample will show reasonably accurate stratification. A random sample of 1,500 people will represent the general American population reasonably well. A haphazardly drawn sample of 1 million, however, might not.

Large-scale magazine surveys of sexual behavior such as those run by *Redbook* (Tavris & Sadd, 1977) and *Cosmopolitan* (Wolfe, 1981) have asked readers to fill out and return questionnaires. Although many thousands of readers completed the questionnaires and sent them in, did they represent the general American population? Probably not. These studies and similar ones may have been influenced by **volunteer bias.** The concept behind volunteer bias is that people who offer to participate in research studies differ systematically from people who do not. In the case of research into sexual behavior, volunteers may represent subgroups of the population—or of readers of the magazines in question—who are willing to disclose intimate information (Rathus and others, 1997). Volunteers may also be more interested in research than nonvolunteers, as well as having more spare time. How might such volunteers differ from the population at large? How might such differences slant or bias the research outcomes?

Adjustment in a World of DIVERSITY

Including Women and Members of Diverse Ethnic Groups in Research

There is a historic bias in favor of conducting research with men (Matthews and others, 1997). Inadequate resources have been devoted to conducting health-related research with women (Matthews and others, 1997). For example, most of the large-sample research on the relationships between lifestyle and health has been conducted with men. There is a crucial deficiency of research into women's health (including disease prevention), women and depression, and women and chemical dependence.

More research with women is also needed in other areas. One of these is the effects of violence on women. One fifth to one third of U.S. women will be physically assaulted—slapped, beaten, choked, or attacked with a weapon—by a partner with whom they share an intimate relationship (Browne, 1993). As many as one woman in four has been raped (Koss, 1993). Many psychologists believe that the epidemic of violence against women will only come to an end when people in the United States confront and change the social and cultural traditions and institutions that give rise to violence (Goodman and others, 1993). (Some of these traditions are discussed in Chapter 15.)

Another area in which more research is needed is the impact of work on women's lives. For example, how does working outside the home affect the division of labor within the home? Numerous studies have found that women

RANDOM SAMPLE • A sample drawn such that every member of a population has an equal chance of being selected.
STRATIFIED SAMPLE • A sample drawn such that known subgroups within a population are represented in proportion to their numbers in the population.
VOLUNTEER BIAS • A source of bias or error in research that reflects the prospect that people who offer to participate in research studies differ systematically from people who do not.

IS ADEQUATE RESEARCH BEING CONDUCTED ON THE ADJUSTMENT OF WOMEN? Women's groups and health professionals argue that there is a historic bias in favor of conducting research with men. For example, most of the large-sample research into lifestyle and health has been conducted with male subjects. There is a crucial deficiency of research with women subjects on topics such as the promotion of women's health, the effects of violence on women, and the impact of work on women's lives.

are more likely than men to put in a "double shift." Women, that is, tend to put in a full day of work along with an equally long "shift" of shopping, mopping, and otherwise caring for their families (Chitayat, 1993; Keita, 1993). Even so, research shows that women who work outside the home have lower cholesterol levels and fewer illnesses than full-time homemakers (Weidner and others, 1997).

It is now fairly widely accepted that findings of research with men cannot be generalized to women (Ader & Johnson, 1994). However, psychology may now be in danger of overgeneralizing findings of research with White, privileged women to *all* women (Yoder & Kahn, 1993). When women of color and of lower socioeconomic status are not included in research studies, or when their responses are not sorted out from those of non-Hispanic White women, issues of interest to them tend to get lost.

Research samples have also tended to underrepresent minority ethnic groups in the population. For example, personality tests completed by non-Hispanic White Americans and by African Americans may need to be interpreted in diverse ways if accurate conclusions are to be drawn (Nevid and others, 1997). The well known Kinsey studies on sexual behavior (Kinsey and others, 1948, 1953) did not adequately represent African Americans, poor people, older people, and numerous other groups. The results of the National Health and Social Life Survey (NHSLS), reported later in the chapter, *do* reflect the behavior of diverse groups.

Methods of Observation: The Better to See You With

Many people consider themselves experts on behavior and mental processes on the basis of their life experiences. How many times have grandparents, for example, told us what they have seen in their lives and what it means about human nature?

We see much indeed during our lifetimes. Our personal observations tend to be fleeting and uncontrolled, however. We sift through experience for the minutiae that interest us. We often ignore the obvious because it does not fit our preexisting ideas (or "schemes") of the ways that things ought to be.

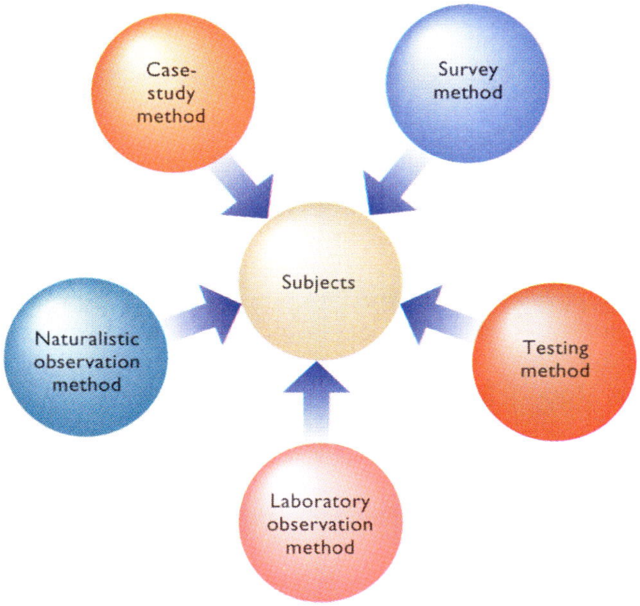

FIGURE 1.4
METHODS OF OBSERVATION IN PSYCHOLOGY

Scientists, however, have devised more controlled ways of observing others. Let us consider the case-study, survey, testing, naturalistic-observation, and laboratory-observation methods (see Figure 1.4).

THE CASE-STUDY METHOD We begin with the case-study method because our own informal ideas about human nature tend to be based on **case studies,** or information we collect about individuals and small groups. But most of us gather our information haphazardly. Often, we see what we want to see. Unscientific accounts of people's behavior are referred to as *anecdotes.* Psychologists attempt to gather information about individuals more carefully.

Sigmund Freud developed his theory of personality largely on the basis of case studies. Freud studied his patients in great depth, seeking factors that seemed to contribute to notable patterns of behavior. He followed some patients for many years, meeting with them several times a week.

Of course, there are bound to be gaps in memory when people are questioned. People may also distort their pasts because of social desirability and other factors. Interviewers may also have certain expectations and subtly encourage their subjects to fill in gaps in ways that are consistent with their theoretical perspectives (Bandura, 1986).

Case studies are often used to investigate rare occurrences, as in the case of "Eve." "Eve" (in real life, Chris Sizemore) was an example of a multiple personality (see Chapter 8). "Eve White," as we shall see, was a mousy, well intentioned woman who had two other "personalities" living inside her. One was "Eve Black," a promiscuous personality who now and then emerged to take control of her behavior.

THE SURVEY METHOD Psychologists conduct **surveys** to learn about behavior and mental processes that cannot be observed in the natural setting or studied experimentally. Psychologists making surveys may employ questionnaires and interviews or examine public records. By distributing questionnaires and analyzing answers with a computer, psychologists can survey many thousands of people at a time.

CASE STUDY • A carefully drawn biography that may be obtained through interviews, questionnaires, and psychological tests.

SURVEY • A scientific method in which large samples of people are questioned.

Adjustment in a World of DIVERSITY

A Sex Survey That Addresses Sociocultural Factors

Is it possible for scientists to describe the sex lives of people in the United States? There are many difficulties in gathering data, such as the refusal of many individuals to participate in research. Moreover, we must specify *which* people we are talking about. Are we talking, for example, about the behavior of women or men, younger people or older people, White Americans or African Americans?

The National Health and Social Life Survey (NHSLS) sample included 3,432 people (Laumann and others, 1994). Of this number, 3,159 were English-speaking adults aged 18 to 59. The other 273 respondents were obtained by purposefully oversampling African American and Hispanic American households in order to obtain more information about these ethnic groups. While the sample probably represents the overall U.S. population aged 18 to 59 quite well, it may include too few Asian Americans, Native Americans, and Jews to offer much information about these groups.

The NHSLS research team identified sets of households in various locales—addresses, not names. They sent a letter to each household describing the purpose and methods of the study. An interviewer visited each household one week later. The people targeted were assured that the purposes of the study were important and that their identities would be kept confidential. Incentives of up to $100 were offered to obtain a high completion rate of close to 80 percent.

The NHSLS considered the sociocultural factors of gender, age, level of education, religion, and race/ethnicity in the numbers of sex partners people have (Laumann and others, 1994; see Table 1.2). Males in the survey report having higher numbers of sex partners than females do. For example, 1 male in 3 (33 percent) reports having 11 or more sex partners since the age of 18. This compares with fewer than 1 woman in 10 (9 percent). On the other hand, most people in the United States appear to limit their numbers of sex partners to a handful or fewer.

Truth or Fiction Revisited

It is true that Americans in their forties have had more sex partners than Americans in their twenties. Perhaps they have had more opportunity to have sexual relationships.

Note that the number of sex partners appears to rise with age into the forties. Why? As people gain in years, have they had more opportunity to accumulate life experiences, including sexual experiences? But reports of the numbers of partners fall off among people in their fifties. People in this age group entered adulthood when sexual attitudes were more conservative.

Level of education is also connected with sexual behavior. Generally speaking, it would appear that education is a liberating influence. People with some college, or who have completed college, are likely to report having more sex partners than those who attended only grade school or high school. But if education has a liberating influence on sexuality, conservative religious experience appears to be a restraining factor. Liberal Protestants (for example, Methodists, Lutherans, Presbyterians, Episcopalians, and United Churches of Christ) and people who say they have no religion report higher numbers of sex partners than Catholics and conservative Protestants (for example, Baptists, Pentecostals, Churches of Christ, and Assemblies of God).

Ethnicity is also connected with sexual behavior. The research findings in Table 1.2 suggest that White (non-Hispanic) Americans and African Americans have the highest numbers of sex partners. Hispanic Americans are mostly Catholic. Perhaps Catholicism provides a restraint on sexual behavior. Asian Americans would appear to be the most sexually restrained ethnic group.

TABLE 1.2 NUMBER OF SEX PARTNERS SINCE AGE 18 AS FOUND IN THE NHSLS* STUDY

SOCIOCULTURAL FACTORS	*NUMBER OF SEX PARTNERS (%)*					
	0	1	2–4	5–10	11–20	21+
GENDER						
Male	3	20	21	23	16	17
Female	3	32	36	20	6	3
AGE						
18–24	8	32	34	15	8	3
25–29	2	25	31	22	10	9
30–34	3	21	29	25	11	10
35–39	2	19	30	25	14	11
40–44	1	22	28	24	14	12
45–49	2	26	24	25	10	14
50–54	2	34	28	18	9	9
55–59	1	40	28	15	8	7
EDUCATION						
Less than high school	4	27	36	19	9	6
High school graduate	3	30	29	20	10	7
Some college	2	24	29	23	12	9
College graduate	2	24	26	24	11	13
Advanced degree	4	25	26	23	10	13
RELIGION						
None	3	16	29	20	16	16
Liberal, moderate Protestant	2	23	31	23	12	8
Conservative Protestant	3	30	30	20	10	7
Catholic	4	27	29	23	8	9
RACE/ETHNICITY						
White (non-Hispanic)	3	26	29	22	11	9
African American	2	18	34	24	11	11
Hispanic American	3	36	27	17	8	9
Asian American†	6	46	25	14	6	3
Native American†	5	28	35	23	5	5

* National Health and Social Life Survey, conducted by a research team centered at the University of Chicago.
† These sample sizes are quite small.
Source: Adapted from *The Social Organization of Sexuality: Sexual Practices in the United States* (Table 5.1C, p. 179), by E. O. Laumann, J. H. Gagnon, R. T. Michael, & S. Michaels, 1994, Chicago: University of Chicago Press.

SELF-ASSESSMENT

DARE YOU SAY WHAT YOU THINK? THE SOCIAL-DESIRABILITY SCALE

Do you say what you think, or do you tend to misrepresent your beliefs to earn the approval of others? Do you answer questions honestly, or do you say what you think other people want to hear?

Telling others what we think they want to hear is making the socially desirable response. Falling prey to social desirability may cause us to distort our beliefs and experiences in interviews or on psychological tests. The bias toward responding in socially desirable directions is also a source of error in the case study, survey, and testing methods. You can complete the Social-Desirability Scale devised by Crowne and Marlowe to gain insight into whether you have a tendency to produce socially desirable responses.

Directions: Read each item and decide whether it is true (T) or false (F) for you. Try to work rapidly and answer each question by circling the T or the F. Then turn to the scoring key in the Appendix to interpret your answers. ■

T	F	1.	Before voting I thoroughly investigate the qualifications of all the candidates.
T	F	2.	I never hesitate to go out of my way to help someone in trouble.
T	F	3.	It is sometimes hard for me to go on with my work if I am not encouraged.
T	F	4.	I have never intensely disliked anyone.
T	F	5.	On occasions I have had doubts about my ability to succeed in life.
T	F	6.	I sometimes feel resentful when I don't get my way.
T	F	7.	I am always careful about my manner of dress.
T	F	8.	My table manners at home are as good as when I eat out in a restaurant.
T	F	9.	If I could get into a movie without paying and be sure I was not seen, I would probably do it.
T	F	10.	On a few occasions, I have given up something because I thought too little of my ability.
T	F	11.	I like to gossip at times.
T	F	12.	There have been times when I felt like rebelling against people in authority even though I knew they were right.
T	F	13.	No matter who I'm talking to, I'm always a good listener.

However, the sample sizes of Asian Americans and Native Americans are relatively small.

THE TESTING METHOD Psychologists also use psychological tests—such as intelligence, aptitude, and personality tests—to measure various traits and characteristics among a population. There is a wide range of psychological tests, and they measure traits ranging from verbal ability and achievement to anxiety, depression, the need for social dominance, musical aptitude, and vocational interests.

T	F	14.	I can remember "playing sick" to get out of something.
T	F	15.	There have been occasions when I have taken advantage of someone.
T	F	16.	I'm always willing to admit it when I make a mistake.
T	F	17.	I always try to practice what I preach.
T	F	18.	I don't find it particularly difficult to get along with loudmouthed, obnoxious people.
T	F	19.	I sometimes try to get even rather than forgive and forget.
T	F	20.	When I don't know something I don't mind at all admitting it.
T	F	21.	I am always courteous, even to people who are disagreeable.
T	F	22.	At times I have really insisted on having things my own way.
T	F	23.	There have been occasions when I felt like smashing things.
T	F	24.	I would never think of letting someone else be punished for my wrong-doings.
T	F	25.	I never resent being asked to return a favor.
T	F	26.	I have never been irked when people expressed ideas very different from my own.
T	F	27.	I never make a long trip without checking the safety of my car.
T	F	28.	There have been times when I was quite jealous of the good fortune of others.
T	F	29.	I have almost never felt the urge to tell someone off.
T	F	30.	I am sometimes irritated by people who ask favors of me.
T	F	31.	I have never felt that I was punished without cause.
T	F	32.	I sometimes think when people have a misfortune they only got what they deserved.
T	F	33.	I have never deliberately said something that hurt someone's feelings.

Source: D. P. Crowne and D. A. Marlowe, A new scale of social desirability independent of pathology, *Journal of Consulting Psychology 24* (1960): 351. Copyright 1960 by the American Psychological Association. Reprinted by permission.

Psychological test results, like the results of surveys, can be distorted by respondents who answer in a socially desirable direction or attempt to exaggerate problems. For these reasons, some commonly used psychological tests have items built into them called **validity scales.** Validity scales are sensitive to misrepresentations and alert the psychologist when test results may be deceptive.

The Naturalistic-Observation Method You use **naturalistic observation** every day of your life. That is, you observe people in their natural habitats.

So do scientists. The next time you opt for a fast-food burger lunch, look around. Pick out slender people and overweight people and observe whether

Validity scale • Groups of test items that suggest whether or not the test results are valid (measure what they are supposed to measure).

Naturalistic observation • A scientific method in which organisms are observed in their natural environments.

they eat their burgers and fries differently. Do the overweight eat more rapidly? Chew less frequently? Leave less food on their plates? This is just the type of research psychologists have recently used to study the eating habits of normal-weight and overweight people.

In naturalistic observation, psychologists and other scientists observe behavior in the field, or "where it happens." They try to avoid interfering with the behaviors they are observing by using **unobtrusive** measures. The naturalistic-observation method provides descriptive information, but it is not the best method for determining the causes of behavior.

THE LABORATORY-OBSERVATION METHOD Psychologists at times place lower animals and people into controlled laboratory environments where they can be readily observed and where the effects of specific conditions can be discerned. With people, the **laboratory** takes many forms.

Figure 4.2 (see p. 112), for example, diagrams a laboratory setup at Yale University, where human subjects (the "Teacher" in the diagram) were urged to deliver electric shock to other people (so-called "Learners") as a way of signaling them that they had made errors on a learning task. You will see that this study was inspired by the atrocities committed by apparently typical German citizens during World War II, and its true purpose was to determine how easy it would be to induce normal people to hurt others. In studies on sensation and perception, human subjects may be placed in dark or quiet rooms in order to learn how bright or loud a stimulus must be before it can be detected.

The Correlational Method: Seeing What Goes Up and What Comes Down

Are people with higher intelligence more likely to do well in school? Are people with a stronger need for achievement likely to climb higher up the corporate ladder? What is the relationship between stress and health?

Correlation follows observation. By using the **correlational method,** psychologists investigate whether one observed behavior or measured trait is related to, or correlated with, another. Consider the variables of intelligence and academic performance. The variables of intelligence and academic performance are assigned numbers such as intelligence test scores and academic averages. Then the numbers or scores are mathematically related and expressed as a **correlation coefficient.** A correlation coefficient is a number that varies between $+1.00$ and -1.00.

DO CIGARETTES CAUSE CANCER?
Correlational evidence with humans and experiments with animals strongly suggest that they do. Why haven't experiments on the effects of smoking been carried out with humans?

Numerous studies report **positive correlations** between intelligence and achievement. Generally speaking, the higher people score on intelligence tests, the better their academic performance is likely to be. The scores attained on intelligence tests are positively correlated (about $+0.60$ to $+0.70$) with overall academic achievement (see Figure 1.5).

There is a **negative correlation** between stress and health. As the amount of stress affecting us increases, the functioning of our immune systems decreases (see Chapter 6). Under high levels of stress, many people show poorer health.

Correlational research may suggest but does not show cause and effect. For instance, it may seem logical to assume that high intelligence makes it possible for children to profit from education. Research has also shown, however, that education contributes to higher scores on intelligence tests. Children placed in richly stimulating Head Start programs at an early age do better later on intelligence tests than age-mates who did not have this experience. The relationship between intelligence and academic performance may not be as simple as you might have thought. What of the link between stress and health? Does stress impair health, or is it possible that people in poorer health encounter higher levels of stress?

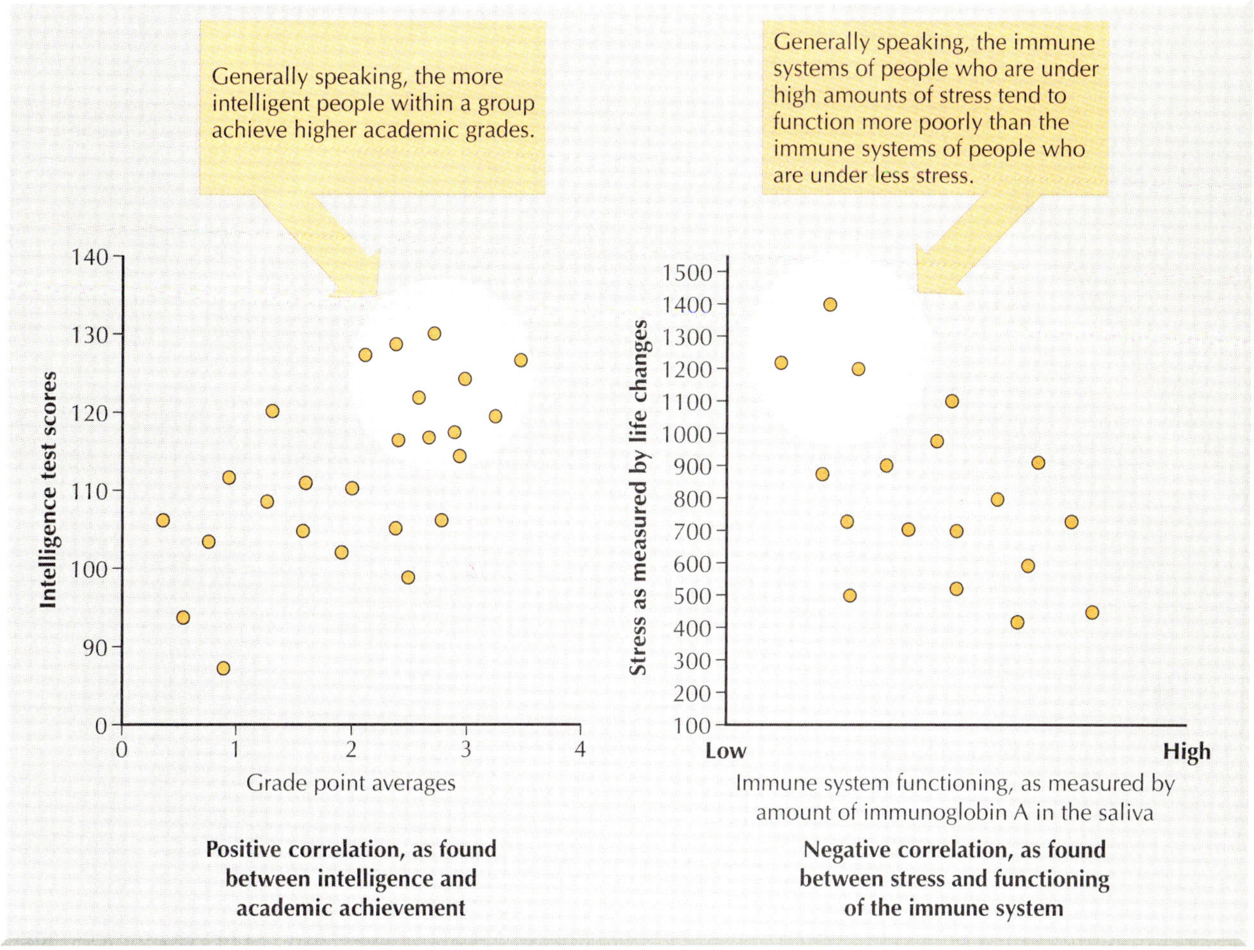

FIGURE 1.5

POSITIVE AND NEGATIVE CORRELATIONS

When there is a positive correlation between variables, as there is between intelligence and achievement, one tends to increase as the other increases. By and large, the higher people score on intelligence tests, the better their academic performance is likely to be, as in the diagram on the left. (Each dot is located to represent an individual's intelligence test score and grade point average.) Similarly, there is a positive correlation between engaging in exercise and physical health, as we will see in Chapter 7. On the other hand, there is a negative correlation between stress and health. As the amount of stress we experience increases, the functioning of our immune systems tends to decrease. Correlational research may suggest but does not demonstrate cause and effect.

Thus, correlational research does not allow us to pin "cause" and "effect" labels on variables. Nevertheless, correlational research can point the way to profitable experimental research. That is, if there were no correlation between intelligence and achievement, there would be little purpose in running experiments to determine causal relationships. If there were no relationship between the need for achievement and success, it would be pointless to ask whether the need for achievement contributes to success.

Consider the results of research on cohabitation. A kind of folklore has developed concerning the advantages of premarital cohabitation, or of trial marriage with one's future spouse. Many people believe that a trial period allows them to test their feelings and find out whether they can adjust to another's quirks before they make a permanent commitment. It is thus ironic that studies of divorce rates show that 38 percent of those who had cohabited were divorced

UNOBTRUSIVE • Not interfering.

LABORATORY • A place in which theories, techniques, and methods are tested and demonstrated.

CORRELATIONAL METHOD • A scientific method that studies the relationships between variables.

CORRELATION COEFFICIENT • A number between +1.00 and −1.00 that expresses the strength and direction (positive or negative) of the relationship between two variables.

POSITIVE CORRELATION • A relationship between variables in which one variable increases as the other also increases.

NEGATIVE CORRELATION • A relationship between two variables in which one variable increases as the other decreases.

Truth or Fiction Revisited

It is not true that you are less likely to get a divorce if you live together with your future spouse before getting married. Although a Swedish study showed that cohabitors are *more* likely to get divorces, the evidence is correlational. Therefore, the causal relationships remain speculative.

within 10 years after the wedding, as compared with 27 percent of those who tied the knot before setting up joint housekeeping (Barringer, 1989).

Do not jump to the conclusion that living together before marriage causes, or even heightens the risk of, divorce. We cite this research because it highlights the fact that correlational research does not demonstrate cause and effect. Both variables—the high divorce rate and the choice to live together before marriage—might reflect another factor: liberalism. Liberal attitudes, that is, could contribute to cohabitation and divorce. Similarly, people do not grow taller *because* they weigh more. People do not become depressed, usually, because they lose weight.

The Experimental Method: Trying Things Out

Most psychologists agree that the preferred method for determining cause and effect—for answering questions such as whether physical activity lowers the incidence of heart disease, smoking causes cancer, alcohol causes aggression, or psychotherapy relieves feelings of anxiety—is the **experiment.** In an experiment, a group of participants, or subjects, receives a **treatment**—for example, 8 weeks of fast walking around a track, smoking the equivalent of a pack a day, a half-ounce of alcohol, or 3 months of therapy. Then the subjects are observed carefully to determine whether the treatment makes a difference in their behavior.

EXPERIMENTAL AND CONTROL SUBJECTS Ideal experiments randomly assign subjects to experimental and control groups. **Experimental subjects** receive some amount of the experimental treatment—alcohol in the above example. **Control subjects** do not. Every effort is made to hold all other conditions constant for both groups. In this way the experimenters can be reasonably sure that it was the experimental treatment, and not uncontrolled factors such as room temperature or time of day, that influenced the outcome.

RANDOM ASSIGNMENT In an experiment, subjects are assigned to experimental treatments at random. If we allow subjects to determine for themselves whether they would like to drink the alcohol or not, we could not determine the effects of alcohol. For example, subjects who chose to drink might also be more aggressive to begin with than the nondrinkers. Certainly their expectations about the effects of alcohol would differ from those of the nondrinkers; otherwise they, too, would choose not to drink.

CONTROLLING FOR SUBJECTS' EXPECTATIONS The effects of treatments usually stem from the treatments and our expectations about the treatments. In well designed experiments, researchers thus try to control for the effects of subjects' expectations about the treatments. In doing so, they often create conditions in which subjects are **blind** as to whether or not they have received the treatment. For instance, people could behave aggressively after drinking alcohol because they *believe* that alcohol causes aggression, not because of the alcohol itself. Thus, if subjects do not *know* whether they have drunk alcohol, we can control for this expectation.

Control subjects are very often given a "sugar pill," or **placebo** treatment, to control for the effects of expectations. For example, in a study on the effects of Therapy A on mood, it would be inadequate to randomly assign a single treatment group to Therapy A and the control group to a no-treatment waiting list. The Therapy A group might show improvement because group membership leads them to expect improvement. For this reason it would be wise to randomly fill a placebo-treatment group, one in which subjects also expect to improve. In such studies, the placebo-treatment groups frequently have general discussions of problems or general education about problems instead of specific therapies. Sometimes it's difficult to find a "placebo" that doesn't do some good!

EXPERIMENT • A scientific method that seeks to discover cause-and-effect relationships by introducing independent variables and observing their effects on dependent variables.

TREATMENT • In experiments, a condition received by participants so that its effects may be observed.

EXPERIMENTAL SUBJECTS • Subjects receiving a treatment in an experiment.

CONTROL SUBJECTS • Experimental participants who do not receive the experimental treatment but for whom all other conditions are comparable to those of experimental subjects.

BLIND • In experimental terminology, unaware of whether one has received a treatment.

PLACEBO • A bogus treatment that has the appearance of being genuine.

adjustment and modern life

The "Adjustment and Modern Life" features in this book are found at the end of each chapter and apply psychology to the challenges that are likely to occur in your own life.

BECOMING A SUCCESSFUL STUDENT

Your first author had little idea of what to expect when he first went off to college. New faces, a new locale, responsibility for doing his own laundry, new courses—it added up to an overwhelming assortment of changes. Perhaps the most stunning change of all was his new-found freedom. It was completely up to him to plan ahead to get his coursework completed but somehow to manage to leave time for socializing and his addiction to the game of bridge.

Another big surprise was that it was not enough for him just to enroll in a course and plant himself in a seat. To see what we mean, visualize a simple experiment. Imagine that you put some water into a bathtub and then sit in the tub. Wait a few moments, then look around. Unless strange things are happening, you'll notice that the water is still there, even though you may have displaced it a bit. You are not a sponge, and you will not simply soak up the water. You have to take active measures to get it inside—perhaps a straw and patience would help.

Taking an Active Approach to Learning—We Don't Really "Soak Up" Knowledge

The problems of soaking up knowledge from this and other textbooks are not entirely dissimilar. You won't accomplish much by sitting on it, except, perhaps, looking an inch taller. But psychological theory and research have taught us that an active approach to learning results in better grades than a passive approach. It is more efficient to look ahead and seek the answers to specific questions than to just flip through the pages "like a good student." It is also helpful not to try to do it all in one sitting, as in cramming before tests—especially when a few bathtubsful of academic material are floating around you.

> ***Truth or Fiction Revisited***
>
> It is not true that pretest cramming is more effective than distributed learning. Distributed, or spaced, learning is more effective than massed learning (cramming).

PLAN AHEAD Begin your active approach to studying by assessing the amount of material you must master during the term and considering your rate of learning. How long does it take you to learn the material in a chapter or in a book? How many hours do you spend studying each day? How much material is there? Does it add up right? Will you make it? It may be that you will not be able to determine the answers until you have gotten into your textbooks for a week or two. But once you have, be honest with yourself about the mathematics of how you are doing. Be willing to revise initial estimates.

Once you have determined the amount of study time you will need for each course, try to space it out fairly evenly. For most of us, spaced or distributed learning is more efficient than massed learning or cramming. So outline a study schedule that will provide nearly equal time periods each weekday. But leave weekends relatively open so that you can have some time for yourself and your friends and some extra hours to digest topics or assignments that are not going down so smoothly.

The following suggestions are derived from Rathus and Fichner-Rathus (1994):

1. Determine where and when the next test will be and what material will be covered.
2. Ask your instructor what will be most important for you to know, and check with students who have already taken the course to determine the sources of test questions—chapters in the text, lecture notes, student study guides, old exams, and so on.
3. Determine the number of chapters to be read between now and the test.
4. Plan to read a specific number of chapters each week and try to "psych out" your instructor by generating possible test questions from the chapters.
5. In generating possible test questions, keep in mind that good questions often start with phrases such as:

   Give several examples of . . .

   Which of the following is an example of . . .

   Describe the functions of . . .

   What is most important about . . .

   List the major . . .

   Compare and contrast . . .

   Describe the structure of . . .

   Explain how psychologists have determined that . . .

   Why do psychologists advise clients to . . .

   Identify the parts of . . .
6. Plan specific study periods each week during which you will generate questions from lecture notes, old exams, the student study guide, and so on.
7. Plan for weekly study periods during which you will compose and take practice tests.
8. Take the practice quizzes in the student study guide. Many instructors reinforce use of the study guide by occasionally taking some exam questions directly from them.
9. Keep a diary or log in which you record your progress, including when, where, and how long you study and how well you perform on practice tests.

STUDY A VARIETY OF SUBJECTS EACH DAY Also remember that variety is the spice of life—that is, we are more responsive to novel stimulation. Don't

study the psychology of adjustment all day Monday, physics all day Tuesday, and literature all day Wednesday. Study each for a little while each day so that you won't feel bored or dulled by too lengthy an immersion in one subject.[3]

ACCEPT YOUR CONCENTRATION SPAN If you can't push yourself at first into studying enough each day, start at a more comfortable level and build toward the amount of study time you'll need by adding a few minutes every day. See what your concentration span is like for your subjects—how long you can continue to focus on coursework without your attention slipping away and, perhaps, lapsing into daydreaming. Plan to take brief study breaks before you reach your limit. Get up and stretch. Get a sip of water.

COPE WITH DISTRACTIONS Find a study place that is comfortable and free from distractions. To better understand how distractions work, consider the case of Schuyler:

> All through high school, Schuyler withdrew to her bedroom to study—the one room where she had complete privacy—and studied in her bed. She assumed that it would be easy to do the same thing in college. But in college she has two roommates, and they very often want to chat while Schuyler is hitting the books. Or if they're not talking together, one of them may be on the phone. Or if no one's on the phone, someone is likely to come knocking at the door. Schuyler has put a sign up on the door that says "No knocking between 7:00 and 10:00 P.M.—This means you!" Nevertheless, someone's always coming by and saying, "Oh, but I wanted to see if Nicky or Pam was in. I didn't mean to disturb you."
>
> Pam, it happens, likes to study with the stereo on—soft, but on, nevertheless. Nicky eats in bed—incessantly. While Schuyler is trying to concentrate on the books, she's assailed by the chomping of potato chips or pretzels.
>
> Finally, Schuyler gets disgusted and gets up to go for a brief walk to clear her head. She passes the lounge and is intrigued by glimpses of a new hit series. A friend calls her over to pass the time. Before she knows it, it's 8:30 and she hasn't really begun to get to work. (Adapted from Rathus & Fichner-Rathus, 1994.)

Avoid Schuyler's pitfalls by letting your spot for studying—your room, a study lounge, a place in the library—come to mean studying to you. Do nothing but study there—no leafing through magazines, no socializing, no snacking. But after you have met a goal, such as finishing half of your studying, you may want to reward yourself with a break and do something like people watching in a busier section of the library.

USE SELF-REWARD Reward yourself for meeting daily study goals. Don't be a martyr and postpone all pleasures until the end of the term.

Truth or Fiction Revisited

It is not true that you should resist rewarding yourself for meeting daily study goals. Sure, you should! Why not?

[3] Here, of course, we are referring to those other subjects. Obviously, you could study this book for several hours every day without ever becoming bored.

When you meet your daily study goals, you may want to select one or two of the activities from the Pleasant Events Schedule (pp. 354–355) to reward yourself the following day or on the weekend.

Survey, Question, Read, Recite, and Review

Don't question some of your instructors' assignments. Question all of them. By so doing, you can follow the active SQ3R study technique originated by educational psychologist Francis Robinson (1970). In SQ3R, that is, you phrase questions about your assignments as you go along and then seek to answer them. SQ3R has helped students raise their grades at several colleges (Adams et al., 1982; Anderson, 1985; Benecke & Harris, 1972). There are five steps to SQ3R: surveying, questioning, reading, reciting, and reviewing.

SURVEY Skipping through the pages of a "whodunit" to identify the killer is a sure-fire way to destroy the impact of a mystery novel, but it can help you learn textbook material. In fact, many textbooks are written with devices that stimulate you to survey the material before reading it. This book has chapter outlines, "Truth or Fiction?" sections, major and minor section heads throughout each chapter, and chapter summaries. If drama and suspense are your goals, begin the chapters with the "Truth or Fiction?" sections and then read them page by page. But if learning the facts comes first, it may be more effective (sigh) first to examine the chapter outlines, skim the minor heads not covered in the outlines, and read the summaries—before you get to the meat of the chapters. Familiarity with the skeletons or advance organizers of the chapters will provide you with frameworks for learning the meat of the chapters as you ingest them page by page.

QUESTION Phrase questions for each head in the chapter and write them down in a notebook. Some questions can also be based on material within sections. For courses in which the textbooks do not have helpful major and minor heads, get into the material page by page and do the best you can at phrasing questions as you go along. You will develop questioning skills with practice, and your questions will help you perceive the underlying structure of each chapter, even when the authors do not use heads. Most of the following questions recast major and minor heads in Chapter 6. Notice that they are indented according to the outlined chapter structure, providing an immediate sense of how the material is organized:

A. What is health psychology?

A. What is the immune system?

    B. What are the functions of the immune system?

    B. What are the effects of stress on the immune system?

A. What are the relationships between stress and physical disorders?

    B. How are headaches related to stress?

- C. What are muscle-tension headaches?
- C. What are migraine headaches?
- C. How do psychologists help people cope with headaches?

B. What are cardiovascular disorders? What kinds of cardiovascular disorders are there?

- C. What are the risk factors for cardiovascular disorders?
- C. How can we modify our behavior to reduce the risk of cardiovascular disorders?

The questions you would have phrased from these heads might have been different, but they might have been as useful as these, or more useful. As you study, you will learn what works best for you.

READ AND WRITE Once you have phrased questions, read the subject matter with the purpose of answering them. This sense of purpose will help you focus on the essential points of the material. As you answer each question, write down a few key words in your notebook that will telegraph that answer to you when you recite and review later on. Many students find it helpful to keep two columns in their notebooks: questions in the column to the left, and key words (to the answer) in the column to the right.

If the material you are reading happens to be fine literature, you may wish to read it once just to appreciate its poetic features. But when you reread it, use SQ3R in order to tease out the essential information it contains.

RECITE Once you have read a section and jotted down the key words to the answer, recite each answer aloud if possible. (Your ability to do so may depend on where you are, who's around, and your level of concern over how you think they'll react to you.) Reciting answers aloud helps us remember them and provides a check on the accuracy of the key words.

REVIEW Review the material according to a reasonably regular schedule, such as once weekly. Cover the answer column and read the questions as though they were a quiz. Recite your answers and then check them against the key response words. Reread the subject matter when you forget an answer. Forgetting too many answers may mean that you haven't phrased the questions efficiently for your own use or that you haven't reviewed the material frequently enough. By taking a more active approach to studying, you may find that you are earning higher grades and gaining more pleasure from the learning process. ■

SUMMARY

1. **What are the challenges of life?** Challenges are changes, events, and problems that require adjustment and provide us with the opportunity to grow. Some challenges, such as anxiety, depression, or obesity, are personal. Other challenges involve intimate relationships and sexuality. Still others involve the larger social context—the workplace, prejudice and discrimination, natural and technological disasters, pollution, and urban life.
2. **What is psychology?** Psychology is a scientific approach to the study of behavior and mental processes.
3. **What is adjustment?** Adjustment is behavior that permits us to meet the challenges of life.
4. **What is the difference between adjustment and personal growth?** Adjustment is reactive—meeting the challenges of life. Personal growth is conscious, active self-development.
5. **Is biology destiny?** Not necessarily. Genes (nature) may determine the ranges for the expression of traits, but our chosen behavior patterns can minimize genetic risk factors and maximize genetic potential.
6. **What is the difference between the clinical and healthy-personality approaches to the psychology of adjustment?** The clinical approach focuses on ways in which problems can be corrected, whereas the healthy-personality approach focuses on optimizing our development along personal, social, physical, and vocational lines.
7. **Why is it important to study human diversity?** Awareness of the richness of human diversity enhances our understanding of the individual and enables students to appreciate the cultural heritages and historical problems of various ethnic groups. Knowledge of diversity helps psychologists understand the aspirations and problems of individuals from various groups so that they can successfully intervene to help group members.
8. **What is an "ethnic group"?** An ethnic group may share factors such as cultural heritage, common history, race, and language. Minority ethnic groups have frequently experienced prejudice and discrimination by members of the dominant culture.
9. **What is meant by gender?** Gender is the state of being female or being male.
10. **What prejudices have been experienced by women?** There have been historic prejudices against women. Much of the scientific research into gender roles and gender differences assumes that male behavior represents the norm. The careers of women have been traditionally channeled into domestic chores, regardless of women's wishes as individuals.
11. **What is the scientific method?** This method is a systematic approach to gathering scientific evidence. It involves formulating a research question, developing a hypothesis, testing the hypothesis, and drawing conclusions.
12. **What is the relationship between a sample and a population?** The subjects who are studied are referred to as a sample. A sample is a segment of a population. Samples must accurately represent the population they are intended to reflect. Women's groups and health professionals argue that there is a historic bias in favor of conducting research with men. Research samples have also tended to underrepresent minority ethnic groups in the population.
13. **How do researchers ensure that their samples represent the targeted populations?** Two ways are the use of random and stratified samples. In a random sample, each member of a population has an equal chance of being selected to participate. In a stratified sample, identified subgroups in the population are represented proportionately.
14. **What are the methods of observation used by psychologists?** These include the case-study, survey, testing, naturalistic-observation, and laboratory-observation methods. Case studies consist of information about the lives of individuals or small groups. The survey method employs interviews, questionnaires, or public records to provide information about behavior that cannot be observed directly. Psychological tests are used to measure various traits and characteristics among a population. The naturalistic-observation method observes behavior carefully and unobtrusively where it happens—in the "field." The laboratory-observation method observes behavior in a controlled environment created by the psychologist.

15. **What is correlational research?** Correlational research reveals relationships between variables, but it does not determine cause and effect. In a positive correlation, variables increase simultaneously. In a negative correlation, one variable increases while the other decreases.

16. **What is the experimental method?** Experiments are used to seek cause and effect—that is, the effects of independent variables on dependent variables. Experimental subjects are given a treatment, whereas control subjects are not. Blinds may be used to control for the effects of expectations.

CHAPTER 2

Personality and Behavior: Understanding People

TRUTH OR FICTION?

✔ T F

- ☐ ☐ According to psychodynamic theory, the human mind is like a vast submerged iceberg, only the tip of which rises above the surface into awareness.
- ☐ ☐ Biting one's fingernails or smoking cigarettes as an adult is a sign of conflict during very early childhood.
- ☐ ☐ It is normal for boys to be hostile toward their fathers.
- ☐ ☐ According to behaviorists, we may believe that we have freedom of choice, but our preferences and choices are forced on us by the environment.
- ☐ ☐ We are more motivated to tackle difficult tasks if we believe that we shall succeed at them.
- ☐ ☐ We all have unique ways of looking at ourselves and at the world outside.
- ☐ ☐ Psychologists helped a young boy overcome his fear of rabbits by having him eat cookies while a rabbit was brought nearer and nearer to him.
- ☐ ☐ You can learn to raise your heart rate or to lower your blood pressure by being hooked up to a machine that "bleeps" when you make the desired response.
- ☐ ☐ One of the treatments designed to help people to stop smoking cigarettes is . . . smoking cigarettes.

OUTLINE

There is a Hindu tale about three blind men who encounter an elephant. Each touches a different part of the elephant, but each is stubborn and claims that he alone has grasped the true nature of the beast. One grabs the elephant by the leg and describes the animal as firm, strong, and upright, like a pillar. The blind man who touched the ear of the elephant objects. From his perspective, the animal is broad and rough, like a rug. The third man has become familiar with the trunk. He is astounded at the gross inaccuracy of the others. Clearly the elephant is long and narrow, he declares, like a hollow pipe.

Each of this trio came to know the elephant from a different perspective. Each was blind to the beliefs of his fellows and to the real nature of the beast—not just because of his physical limitations, but also because his initial encounter led him to think of the elephant in a certain way.

In much the same way, different ways of encountering people also lead scientists to view people from different perspectives. Theories as to why people think what they think, feel what they feel, and do what they do may thus differ as widely as the blind men's concepts of the elephant.

In this chapter we explore four key approaches to understanding people: psychodynamic, trait, learning, and phenomenological. We shall see what each has to say about human nature, and what each suggests about our abilities to cope with the challenges of life and to develop as individuals.

PSYCHODYNAMIC THEORY

There are several **psychodynamic** theories of personality, but they all have some things in common. Each teaches that people encounter a dynamic struggle as drives like sex, aggression, and the need for superiority come into conflict with laws, social rules, and moral codes. The laws and social rules become internalized. We make them parts of ourselves. After doing so, the dynamic struggle becomes a clashing of opposing *inner* forces. Our behaviors, thoughts, and emotions represent the outcome of these clashes.

Each psychodynamic theory owes its origin to Sigmund Freud.

Sigmund Freud's Theory of Psychosexual Development

Sigmund Freud (1856–1939) was a mass of contradictions. He has been lauded as the greatest thinker of the twentieth century, and criticized as overrated, even as a "false and faithless prophet." He preached liberal views on sexuality but was himself a model of sexual restraint. He invented a popular form of psychotherapy but experienced lifelong psychologically related problems such as migraine headaches, bowel problems, fainting under stress, hatred of the

Psychodynamic • Descriptive of Freud's view that various forces move through the personality and determine behavior.

telephone, and an addiction to cigars. He smoked 20 cigars a day and could not or would not break the habit even after he developed cancer of the jaw.

Freud was trained as a physician. Early in his practice, he was astounded that some people apparently experienced loss of feeling in a hand or paralysis of the legs in the absence of any medical disorder. These strange symptoms often disappeared once patients had recalled and discussed distressful events and feelings of guilt or anxiety that seemed to be associated with the symptoms. For a long time these events and feelings were hidden beneath the surface of awareness. Even so, they could influence patients' behavior.

From this sort of clinical evidence, Freud concluded that the human mind is like an iceberg (Figure 2.1). Only the tip of an iceberg rises above the surface of the water, while the greater mass darkens the deep. Freud suggested that people, similarly, were aware of but a few of the ideas and the impulses that dwelled within their minds. The greater mass of the mind—our deepest images, thoughts, fears, and urges—remained beneath the surface of awareness, where little light illumined them. He labeled the region that poked through into the light of awareness the *conscious* part of the mind. He called the regions that lay below the surface the *preconscious* and the *unconscious*.

The **preconscious** contains elements of experience that are presently out of awareness, but can be made conscious by focusing on them. The **unconscious** is shrouded in mystery. It contains biological instincts such as sex and aggression. Some unconscious urges cannot be experienced consciously because mental images and words cannot portray them in their full color and fury. Other unconscious urges may be kept below the surface by **repression.** Repression is the automatic ejection of anxiety-evoking ideas from awareness. Repression protects us from recognizing impulses we would consider immoral.

The unconscious is the largest part of the mind. Here the dynamic struggle between biological drives and social rules is most fierce. As drives seek expression, and values exert counterpressures, conflict can give rise to psychological disorders and behavioral outbursts. Because we cannot view the unconscious mind directly, Freud developed a method of mental detective work called **psychoanalysis.** In psychoanalysis, people are prompted to talk about anything that pops into their mind while they remain comfortable and relaxed. People may

Truth or Fiction Revisited

It is true that according to psychodynamic theory, the human mind is like a vast submerged iceberg, only the tip of which rises above the surface into awareness. This statement is consistent with Freud's postulation of an unconscious psychic structure (the id) and a partly unconscious psychic structure (the ego). However, empirical evidence does not confirm the existence of these structures.

PRECONSCIOUS • In psychodynamic theory, something not in awareness but capable of being brought into awareness by focusing of attention.

UNCONSCIOUS • In psychodynamic theory, something not available to awareness by simple focusing of attention.

REPRESSION • In psychodynamic theory, a defense mechanism that protects the person from anxiety by ejecting anxiety-evoking ideas and impulses from awareness.

PSYCHOANALYSIS • In this usage, Freud's method of exploring human personality.

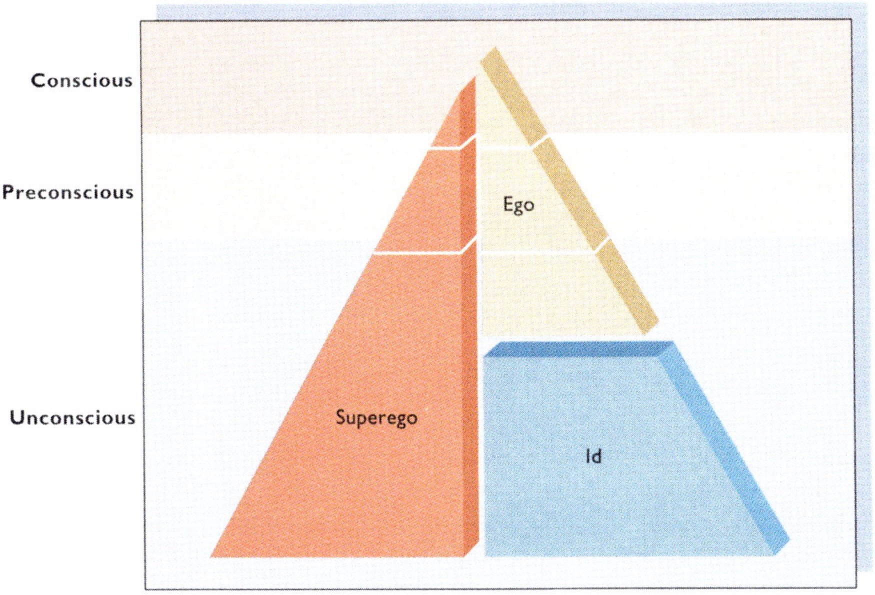

FIGURE 2.1

THE HUMAN ICEBERG, ACCORDING TO FREUD.

According to psychoanalytic theory, only the tip of human personality rises above the surface of the mind into conscious awareness. Material in the preconscious can become conscious if we direct our attention to it, but unconscious material tends to remain shrouded in mystery.

gain self-insight by pursuing some of the thoughts that arise. But they are also motivated to avoid threatening subjects. The same repression that has ejected unacceptable thoughts from awareness prompts *resistance,* or the desire to avoid thinking about or discussing them. Repression and resistance can make psychoanalysis a tedious process that lasts for years, or even decades.

THE STRUCTURE OF PERSONALITY When is a structure not a structure? When it is a mental or **psychic structure.** Freud labeled the clashing forces of personality psychic structures. They could not be seen or measured directly, but their presence was suggested by observable behavior such as expressed thoughts and emotions. Freud hypothesized the existence of three psychic structures: the *id, ego,* and *superego.*

The **id** is present at birth. It represents physiological drives and is fully unconscious. Freud described the id as "a chaos, a cauldron of seething excitations" (Freud, 1964, p. 73). The conscious mind might find it inconsistent to love and hate the same person at the same time, but Freud believed that conflicting emotions can dwell side by side in the id. In the id, we can experience hatred for our mothers for failing to immediately gratify all our needs, even at the same time that we love them. The id demands instant gratification without consideration of law, social custom, or the needs of others.

The **ego** begins to develop during the first year of life, largely because not all of a child's demands for gratification can be met immediately. The ego "stands for reason and good sense" (Freud, 1964, p. 76), for rational ways of coping with frustration. It curbs the appetites of the id and makes plans that are in keeping with social convention, so that a person can find gratification yet avoid the disapproval of others. The id lets you know that you are hungry. The ego creates the idea of walking to the refrigerator, heating up some tacos, and pouring a glass of milk. The ego weighs the practical and possible, as well as what is urged. Within Freudian theory, the ego provides the conscious sense of self.

Although most of the ego is conscious, some of its business is carried out unconsciously. For instance, the ego also acts as a watchdog or censor that screens the impulses of the id. When the ego senses that socially unacceptable impulses are rising into awareness, it may use psychological defenses to prevent them from surfacing. Repression is one such defense, or **defense mechanism.** (Defense mechanisms are discussed in Chapter 10.)

The **superego** develops throughout middle childhood, usually incorporating the moral standards and values of parents and significant members of the community through **identification.** The superego can hold forth shining examples of an ideal self and also acts like the conscience, an internal moral guardian. Throughout life, the superego monitors the intentions of the ego and hands out judgments of right and wrong. It floods the ego with feelings of guilt and shame when the verdict is in the negative.

The ego hasn't an easy time of it. It stands between id and superego, braving the arrows of each. It strives to satisfy the demands of the id and the moral sense of the superego. The id may urge, "You are sexually aroused!" But the superego may warn, "You're not married." The poor ego is caught in the middle.

PSYCHIC STRUCTURE • In psychodynamic theory, a hypothesized mental structure that helps explain different aspects of behavior.

ID • The psychic structure, present at birth, that represents physiological drives and is fully unconscious. (A Latin word meaning "it.")

EGO • The second psychic structure to develop, characterized by self-awareness, planning, and the delay of gratification. (A Latin word meaning "I.")

DEFENSE MECHANISM • In psychodynamic theory, an unconscious function of the ego that protects it from anxiety-evoking material by preventing accurate recognition of this material.

SUPEREGO • The third psychic structure, which functions as a moral guardian and sets forth high standards for behavior.

IDENTIFICATION • In psychodynamic theory, the unconscious assumption of another person's behavior—usually the parent of the same gender.

STAGES OF PSYCHOSEXUAL DEVELOPMENT Freud stirred controversy within the scientific establishment of his day by arguing that sexual impulses, and their gratification, are central factors in children's development. Freud believed that children's basic ways of relating to the world, such as sucking their mothers' breasts and moving their bowels, involve sexual feelings.

Freud believed that there is a major instinct to preserve and perpetuate life—*Eros.* Eros contains a certain amount of energy, which Freud labeled

THE ORAL STAGE?
According to Freud, the first year of life is the oral stage of psychosexual development. What, according to Freud, are the effects of insufficient or excessive gratification during the oral stage? Does research evidence support his views?

libido. This energy is psychological in nature and involves sexual impulses, so Freud considered it *psychosexual.* Libidinal energy is expressed through sexual feelings in different parts of the body, or *erogenous zones,* as the child develops. To Freud, human development involves the transfer of libidinal energy from one zone to another. He hypothesized five stages of **psychosexual development:** oral, anal, phallic, latency, and genital.

During the first year of life, a child experiences much of its world through the mouth. If it fits, into the mouth it goes. This is the *oral stage.* Freud argued that oral activities such as sucking and biting bring the child sexual gratification as well as nourishment.

Freud believed that children would encounter conflicts during each stage of psychosexual development. During the oral stage, conflict centers around the nature and extent of oral gratification. Early weaning can lead to frustration. Excessive gratification, on the other hand, can lead an infant to expect it will automatically be handed everything in life. Inadequate or excessive gratification in any stage can lead to **fixation** in that stage, and the development of characteristic traits. Oral traits include dependency, gullibility, and optimism or pessimism.

Freud theorized that adults with an *oral fixation* can experience exaggerated desires for "oral activities," such as smoking, overeating, alcohol abuse, and nail biting. Like the infant whose very survival depends on the mercy of an adult, adults with oral fixations may be disposed toward clinging, dependent interpersonal relationships. Freud saw people as being at the mercy of events that occur long before they can weigh alternatives and make decisions.

During the *anal stage,* sexual gratification is attained through contraction and relaxation of the muscles that control elimination of waste products. Elimination, which was controlled reflexively during most of the first year of life, comes under voluntary muscular control, even if such control at first is not reliable. The anal stage is said to begin in the second year of life.

During the anal stage, children learn to delay the gratification of eliminating as soon as they feel the urge. The general issue of self-control may create parent-child conflict. Anal fixations may stem from this conflict and lead to two sets of anal traits. So-called *anal retentive* traits involve excessive self-control. They include perfectionism, a strong need for order, and exaggerated neatness and cleanliness. *Anal expulsive* traits, in contrast, "let it all hang out." They include carelessness, messiness, even sadism.

Truth or Fiction Revisited

It is not true that biting one's fingernails or smoking cigarettes as an adult is a sign of conflict during very early childhood. Although the statement is consistent with the psychodynamic view that adult problems can reflect fixations during early stages of psychosexual development, there is no evidence that biting fingernails or smoking is a sign of childhood conflict.

LIBIDO • (1) In psychoanalytic theory, the energy of Eros; the sexual instinct. (2) Generally, sexual interest or drive.

PSYCHOSEXUAL DEVELOPMENT • In psychodynamic theory, the process by which libidinal energy is expressed through different erogenous zones during different stages of development.

FIXATION • In psychodynamic theory, arrested development. Attachment to objects of a certain stage when one's development should have advanced so that one is attached to objects of a more advanced stage.

Truth or Fiction Revisited

There is no evidence that it is normal for boys to be hostile toward their fathers. This is another statement that is consistent with Freud's theoretical views—in this case, his views concerning the Oedipus complex.

Children enter the *phallic stage* during the third year of life. During this stage the major erogenous zone is the phallic region (the clitoris in girls). Parent-child conflict is likely to develop over masturbation, which parents may treat with punishment and threats. During the phallic stage children may develop strong sexual attachments to the parent of the opposite gender and begin to view the parents of the same gender as a rival in love. Boys may want to marry Mommy, and girls may want to marry Daddy. Freud labeled this conflict in boys the **Oedipus complex,** after the legendary Greek king who unwittingly killed his father and married his mother.

Feelings of lust and jealousy are difficult for children to handle. Home life would be tense indeed if they were aware of them. So these feelings remain unconscious, although their influence is felt through fantasies about marriage and hostility toward the parent of the same gender.

Oedipal feelings are thought to be resolved by about the age of 5 or 6. Children then repress their hostilities toward and identify with the parent of the same gender. Identification leads to playing the social and gender roles of the parent of the same gender, and internalizing that parent's values. Sexual feelings toward the parent of the opposite gender are repressed for several years. When they emerge during adolescence, they are *displaced,* or transferred, onto socially appropriate members of the opposite gender.

Freud believed that by 5 or 6 children would have been in conflict with their parents over sexual feelings for several years. The pressures of Oedipal feelings would motivate them to repress all sexual urges. In so doing, they would enter the *latency stage,* a period of life during which sexual feelings remain unconscious.

Freud wrote that we enter the final stage of psychosexual development, or *genital stage,* at puberty. Adolescent boys reexperience sexual urges toward their mothers, and adolescent girls toward their fathers. But the incest taboo motivates repression of these impulses, and they are displaced onto other adults or adolescents of the opposite gender. Yet boys may gravitate toward girls "just like the girl that married dear old Dad." Girls may be attracted to men who resemble their fathers.

People in the genital stage prefer, by definition, to find sexual gratification through intercourse with a member of the opposite gender. In Freud's view, oral or anal stimulation, masturbation, and homosexual activity all represent *pregenital* fixations and immature forms of sexual conduct. They are not in keeping with the life instinct, Eros.

Other Psychodynamic Views

A number of personality theorists are intellectual descendants of Sigmund Freud. Their theories, like Freud's, include roles for unconscious motivation, for motivational conflict, and for defensive responses to anxiety that involve repression and cognitive distortion of reality. In other respects, they differ markedly.

The Swiss psychiatrist Carl Jung (1875–1961) was a member of Freud's inner circle who developed his own psychodynamic theory. Jung downplayed the role of the sexual instinct. He saw sex as one of several important instincts. Jung also believed in the **Self,** a unifying force of personality that gives direction and purpose to human behavior. According to Jung, heredity dictates that the self will persistently strive to achieve wholeness or fullness. Jung believed that an understanding of human behavior must incorporate self-awareness and self-direction as well as knowledge of unconscious impulses.

Alfred Adler (1870–1937), another follower of Freud, also believed that Freud had placed too much emphasis on sex in determining human behavior. Adler believed that an **inferiority complex** also plays a important role. In some

OEDIPUS COMPLEX • A conflict of the phallic stage in which the boy wishes to possess his mother sexually and perceives his father as a rival in love.

SELF • According to Jung, a unifying force of personality that provides people with direction and purpose.

INFERIORITY COMPLEX • Feelings of inferiority hypothesized by Adler to serve as a central motivating force in the personality.

people, feelings of inferiority may be based on physical problems and the need to compensate for them. But Adler believed that all of us encounter some feelings of inferiority because of our small size as children, and that these feelings give rise to a **drive for superiority.** Adler, like Jung, believed that self-awareness plays a major role in the formation of personality. Adler spoke of a *creative self,* a self-aware aspect of personality that strives to overcome obstacles and develop the individual's potential.

Karen Horney (1885–1952) was ostracized by the New York Psychoanalytic Institute because she took issue with the way in which psychoanalytic theory portrayed women. Early in the twentieth century, psychodynamic theory taught that a woman's place was in the home. Women who sought to compete with men in the business world were assumed to be suffering from unconscious penis envy. Psychodynamic theory taught that little girls feel inferior to boys when they learn that boys have a penis and they do not. Horney argued that this view perpetuated the treatment of women as second-class citizens. Yet Horney agreed with Freud that childhood experiences play a major role in personality development. Like many other neoanalysts, however, she believed that sexual and aggressive impulses take a back seat to social relationships.

Erik Erikson (1902–1994) also believed that Freud had placed undue emphasis on sexual instincts and asserted that social relationships are more crucial determinants of personality. To Erikson, the general climate of the mother-infant relationship is more important than the details of the feeding process or the sexual feelings that might be stirred by contact with the mother. Erikson also argued that to a large degree we are the conscious architects of our own personalities—a view that grants more powers to the "ego" than Freud had allowed. Within Erikson's theory, we make real choices; within Freud's theory, we may think that we are making choices when we are only rationalizing the compromises forced upon us by intrapsychic warfare.

Erikson, like Freud, devised a developmental theory of personality. But whereas Freud proposed stages of psycho*sexual* development, Erikson proposed stages of psycho*social* development. Rather than label a stage after an erogenous zone, Erikson labeled stages after the traits that might be developed during that stage (Table 2.1). Each stage is named according to the possible outcomes, which are polar opposites. For example, the first stage of **psychosocial development** is named the stage of *trust versus mistrust* because of the two possible major outcomes:

1. A warm, loving relationship with the mother (and others) during infancy might lead to a sense of basic trust in people and the world.
2. A cold, nongratifying relationship might lead to a pervasive sense of mistrust.

Erikson believed that most of us would develop some combination of trust and mistrust—hopefully more trust than mistrust. A basic sense of mistrust could impair the development of relationships for a lifetime.

ERIKSON'S VIEWS ON ADOLESCENT AND ADULT DEVELOPMENT Erikson extended Freud's five developmental stages to eight to include the evolving concerns of adulthood.

For Erikson, the goal of adolescence is the attainment of **ego identity,** not genital sexuality. Adolescents who attain ego identity develop a firm sense of who they are and what they stand for. One aspect of ego identity is learning how to "connect the roles and skills cultivated [during the elementary school years] with the occupational prototypes of the day" (Erikson, 1963, p. 261)—that is, with jobs. Ego identity also extends to sexual, political, and religious beliefs and commitments. According to Erikson, adolescents who do not

DRIVE FOR SUPERIORITY • Adler's term for the desire to compensate for feelings of inferiority.

PSYCHOSOCIAL DEVELOPMENT • Erikson's theory of personality and development, which emphasizes social relationships and eight stages of growth.

EGO IDENTITY • One's sense of who one is and what one stands for.

TABLE 2.1 ERIK ERIKSON'S STAGES OF DEVELOPMENT

TIME PERIOD	*LIFE CRISIS*	*THE DEVELOPMENTAL TASK*
Infancy (0–1)	Trust vs. mistrust	Coming to trust the mother and the environment—to associate surroundings with feelings of inner goodness
Early childhood (2–3)	Autonomy vs. shame and doubt	Developing the wish to make choices and the self-control to exercise choice
Preschool years (4–5)	Initiative vs. guilt	Adding planning and "attacking" to choice; becoming active and on the move
Grammar school years (6–12)	Industry vs. inferiority	Becoming eagerly absorbed in skills, tasks, and productivity; mastering the fundamentals of technology
Adolescence	Identity vs. role diffusion	Connecting skills and social roles to formation of career objectives
Young adulthood	Intimacy vs. isolation	Committing the self to another; engaging in sexual love
Middle adulthood	Generativity vs. stagnation	Needing to be needed; guiding and encouraging the younger generation; being creative
Late adulthood	Integrity vs. despair	Accepting the timing and placing of one's own life cycle; achieving wisdom and dignity

Source: E. H. Erikson (1963), *Childhood and society,* New York: Norton, 247–269.

develop a firm sense of identity are especially subject to peer influences and short-sighted hedonism. We explore Erikson's stages of adult development in Chapter 16.

The Healthy Personality

Psychodynamic theories were developed by working with troubled individuals, and so the theoretical emphasis has been on the development of psychological disorders, not a healthy personality. Nevertheless, the thinking of the major theorists can be combined to form a picture of psychological health.

THE ABILITIES TO LOVE AND TO WORK Freud is noted to have equated psychological health with the abilities *lieben und arbeiten*—that is, "to love and to work." Healthy people can care deeply for others. They can engage in sexual love within an intimate relationship and lead a productive work life. To accomplish these ends, sexual impulses must be allowed expression in a relationship with an adult of the opposite gender, and other impulses must be channeled into socially productive directions.

EGO STRENGTH The ego of the healthy individual has the strength to control the instincts of the id and to withstand the condemnation of the superego. The presence of acceptable outlets for the expression of some primitive impulses decreases the pressures within the id, and, at the same time, lessens the burdens of the ego in repressing the remaining impulses. Being reared by reasonably tolerant parents might prevent the superego from becoming overly harsh and condemnatory.

A CREATIVE SELF Jung and Adler both spoke of a self (or Self)—a unifying force that provides direction to behavior and helps develop a person's potential. The notion of a guiding self provides bridges between psychodynamic theories, social-cognitive theory (which speaks of self-regulatory processcs), and phenomenological theories (which also speak of a self and the fulfillment of potential).

COMPENSATION FOR FEELINGS OF INFERIORITY None of us can be "good at everything." According to Adler, we attempt to compensate for feelings of inferiority by excelling in one or more of the arenas of human interaction. So choosing productive arenas in which to contend—finding out what we are good at and developing our talents—constitutes healthful behavior from Adler's perspective.

ERIKSON'S POSITIVE OUTCOMES A positive outcome within each of Erik Erikson's psychosocial stages also contributes to the healthy personality. It is healthful to develop a basic sense of trust during infancy, to develop a sense of industry during the grammar school years, to develop a sense of who we are and what we stand for during adolescence, to develop intimate relationships during young adulthood, to be productive during middle adulthood, and so on.

TRAIT THEORY

> *In most of us by the age of thirty, the character has set like plaster, and will never soften again.*
>
> WILLIAM JAMES

The notion of traits is very familiar. If I asked you to describe yourself, you would probably do so in terms of traits such as bright, sophisticated, and witty. (That is you, is it not?) We also describe other people in terms of traits.

Traits are reasonably stable elements of personality that are inferred from behavior. If you describe a friend as "shy," it may be because you have observed social anxiety or withdrawal in that person's encounters with others. Traits are assumed to account for consistent behavior in diverse situations. You probably expect your "shy" friend to be retiring in most social confrontations—"all across the board," as the saying goes. The concept of traits is also found in other approaches to personality. Recall that Freud linked the development of certain traits to children's experiences in each stage of psychosexual development.

The trait approach dates back to the Greek physician Hippocrates (ca. 460–377 B.C.) and could be even older (Maher & Maher, 1994). It has generally been assumed that traits are embedded in people's bodies, but *how?* Hippocrates believed that traits were embedded in bodily fluids, which gave rise to certain types of personalities. In his view, an individual's personality depended on the balance of four basic fluids, or "humors," in the body. Yellow bile was associated with a choleric (quick-tempered) disposition; blood with a sanguine (warm, cheerful) one; phlegm with a phlegmatic (sluggish, calm, cool) disposition; and black bile with a melancholic (gloomy, pensive) temperament. Disease was believed to reflect an imbalance among the humors. Methods such as bloodletting and vomiting were recommended to restore the balance (Maher & Maher, 1994). Although Hippocrates' theory was pure speculation, the terms *choleric, sanguine,* and so on are still used in descriptions of personality.

More enduring trait theories assume that traits are heritable and are embedded in the nervous system. They rely on the mathematical technique of factor analysis in attempting to determine basic human traits.

More than 50 years ago, Gordon Allport and a colleague (Allport & Odbert, 1936) catalogued some 18,000 human traits from a search through word lists like dictionaries. Some were physical traits such as *short, black,* and *brunette.* Others were behavioral traits such as *shy* and *emotional.* Still others were moral traits such as *honest.* This exhaustive list has served as the basis for personality research by many other psychologists. Other psychologists have used factor analysis to reduce this universe of traits to smaller lists of traits that show common features.

British psychologist Hans J. Eysenck (Eysenck & Eysenck, 1985) has focused much of his research on the relationships between two important traits: **introversion-extraversion** and emotional stability-instability. (Emotional *in*stability is also known as **neuroticism**). Carl Jung was first to distinguish between introverts and extraverts. Eysenck added the dimension of emotional stability-instability to introversion-extraversion. He has catalogued various personality traits according to where they are situated along these dimensions or factors (see Figure 2.2). For instance, an anxious person would be high in both introversion and neuroticism—that is, preoccupied with his or her own thoughts and emotionally unstable.

INTROVERSION • A trait characterized by intense imagination and the tendency to inhibit impulses.
EXTRAVERSION • A trait characterized by tendencies to be socially outgoing and to express feelings and impulses freely.
NEUROTICISM • Eysenck's term for emotional instability, as expressed, for example, by anxiety and restlessness.

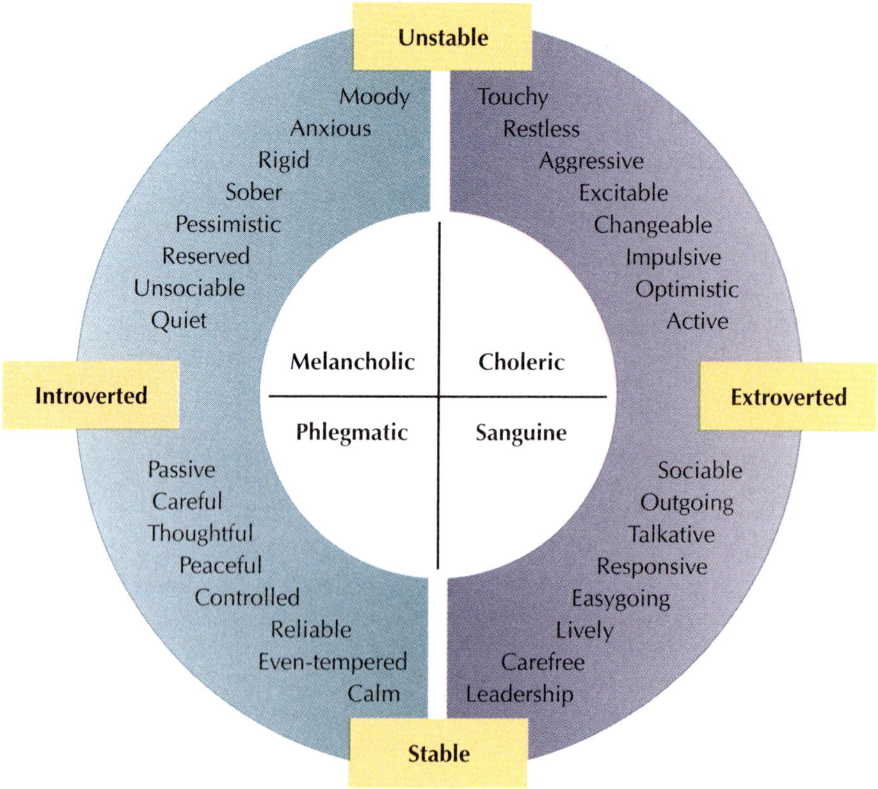

FIGURE 2.2
EYSENCK'S PERSONALITY DIMENSIONS AND HIPPOCRATES' PERSONALITY TYPES.
Various personality traits shown in the outer ring fall within the two major dimensions of personality suggested by Hans Eysenck. The inner circle shows how Hippocrates' four major personality types — choleric, sanguine, phlegmatic, and melancholic — fit within Eysenck's dimensions.

TABLE 2.2 THE FIVE-FACTOR MODEL

FACTOR	NAME	TRAITS
I	Extraversion	Contrasts talkativeness, assertiveness, and activity with silence, passivity, and reserve
II	Agreeableness	Contrasts kindness, trust, and warmth with hostility, selfishness, and distrust
III	Conscientiousness	Contrasts organization, thoroughness, and reliability with carelessness, negligence, and unreliability
IV	Neuroticism	Contrasts traits such as nervousness, moodiness, and sensitivity to negative stimuli with coping ability
V	Openness to experience	Contrasts imagination, curiosity, and creativity with shallowness and lack of perceptiveness

Eysenck notes that his scheme is reminiscent of that suggested by Hippocrates. According to Eysenck's dimensions, the choleric type would be extraverted and unstable; the sanguine type, extraverted and stable; the phlegmatic type, introverted and stable; and the melancholic type, introverted and unstable.

More recent research suggests that there may be five basic personality factors (McCrae, 1996). These include the two found by Eysenck—extraversion and neuroticism—along with conscientiousness, agreeableness, and openness to new experience (see Table 2.2). Cross-cultural research has found that these five factors appear to define the personality structure of American, German, Portuguese, Hebrew, Chinese, Korean, and Japanese people (McCrae & Costa, 1997).

The Healthy Personality

Trait theory is mainly descriptive, and it is generally assumed that heredity has a great deal to do with the development of personality traits. From this perspective, people with healthy personalities may be seen as having come out on the positive side of the "luck of the (genetic) draw." Genetic factors provide a broad range for the expression of traits, but people have some ability to shape themselves into what they would like to become.

Adjustment, from the trait perspective, partly means seeking jobs and social activities that are compatible with one's genetically-based traits. For example, a short individual is not likely to fare well in athletic contests that require great height. In terms of psychological traits, it seems reasonable to seek a fit between one's traits and the requirements of various jobs. For example, a creative, tactile, and visually stimulated individual may fare better as an artist than as an accountant.

CHANGING THE UNCHANGEABLE: IS BIOLOGY DESTINY? What can be done by people with a number of counterproductive traits, such as shyness and tenseness? Such traits tend to be enduring and are at least partly biologically based. Is it healthful to be self-accepting and say, "That's me—that's my personality," and then settle for what one's "traits" will allow? Or is it more healthful to try to change self-defeating behavior patterns, such as social withdrawal and tenseness?

Rather than thinking in terms of changing embedded traits, it may be more productive to think about changing, or modifying, *behaviors.* Rather than attempting to change an abstract trait such as social withdrawal, one can work on modifying socially withdrawn *behavior.* Rather than eliminating *tenseness* per se, one can modify the body responses and thoughts that people connect with tenseness. If people acquire consistent new behavior patterns, aren't they, in effect, changing their traits, whether or not the traits are biologically based? Even when a trait seems to be "deeply imbedded," it may sometimes only mean that we need to work relatively harder to change our behavior.

This is a perfect time to consider learning theories, particularly behaviorism. Behaviorism suggests that if we practice hard enough (if we work at it), new adaptive behavior patterns can become habits. Once adaptive behavior patterns become habitual, perhaps they may as well be considered traits.

LEARNING THEORIES

Psychodynamic theories look at personality and behavior in terms of the outcomes of internal conflict. Trait theory largely sees personality as inherited. Learning theories focus on the great capacity of human beings to learn about their environments—to mentally represent the world outside and to learn to manipulate it to bring about desired consequences. In this section we consider two approaches to understanding learning: behaviorism and social-cognitive theory.

Behaviorism

At Johns Hopkins University in 1924, psychologist John B. Watson announced the battle cry of the **behaviorist** movement:

> Give me a dozen healthy infants, well-formed, and my own specified world to bring them up in and I'll guarantee to take any one at random and train him to become any type of specialist I might suggest—doctor, lawyer, merchant-chief and, yes, even beggar-man and thief, regardless of his talents, penchants, tendencies, abilities, vocations, and the race of his ancestors. (p. 82)

Watson thus proclaimed that situational variables, or environmental influences—not internal variables like intrapsychic forces, traits, and conscious choice—shape our preferences and behavior. Watson argued that if psychology were to be accepted as a science, unseen, undetectable mental structures must be rejected in favor of measurable behaviors.

Behaviorism largely discounts concepts of personal freedom, choice, and self-direction. We tend to assume that our wants originate within us. But behaviorists suggest that environmental influences, such as parental approval and social custom, shape us into *wanting* certain things and *not wanting* others. Even our thinking that we have free will is determined by the environment.

Let us consider two basic types of learning that have been studied by behaviorists: classical and operant conditioning.

Truth or Fiction Revisited

It is true that behaviorists believe that our preferences and choices are forced on us by the environment (even if we believe that we have freedom of choice). This statement reflects the behaviorist view that behavior, including preferences, is situationally determined. (Other theorists have other points of view.)

BEHAVIORIST • A person who explains and predicts behavior in terms of the stimuli acting on organisms and organisms' responses.

CLASSICAL CONDITIONING • A simple form of learning in which one stimulus comes to bring forth the response usually brought forth by a second stimulus as a result of being paired repeatedly with the second stimulus.

CLASSICAL CONDITIONING **Classical conditioning** was discovered by accident. The Russian physiologist Ivan Pavlov (1849–1936) was studying the biological pathways of dogs' salivation glands, but the animals botched his results

FIGURE 2.3
PAVLOV'S DEMONSTRATION OF CONDITIONED REFLEXES IN LABORATORY DOGS.
From behind the one-way mirror, a laboratory assistant rings a bell and then drops meat powder on the dog's tongue. After several repetitions, the dog salivates to the bell alone. Saliva is collected by means of a tube. The amount of saliva is a measure of the strength of the dog's learned responses.

by what, at first, looked like random salivation. Upon investigation, Pavlov noticed that the dogs were actually salivating in response to his assistants' entering the lab or the inadvertent clanking of metal on metal. So Pavlov initiated a series of experiments to demonstrate that the dogs salivated in response to **stimuli** that had been *associated* with being fed.

If you place meat on a dog's tongue, it will salivate. Salivation in response to food is a reflex—a simple form of unlearned behavior. We, too, have many reflexes, such as the knee jerk in response to a tap below the knee and the eye blink in response to a puff of air.

A change in the environment, such as placing meat on a dog's tongue or tapping below the knee, is called a *stimulus.* A reflex is one kind of response to a stimulus. Reflexes are unlearned, but they can also be associated with, or *conditioned* to, different stimuli.

Pavlov (1927) strapped a dog into a harness (see Figure 2.3). He placed meat powder on the dog's tongue, and the dog salivated. He repeated the process several times, with one difference. Each time he preceded the meat with the ringing of a bell. After several pairings of bell and meat, Pavlov rang the bell but did not present the meat. What did the dog do? It salivated anyway. The dog had learned to salivate in response to the bell because the bell had been repeatedly paired with the meat.

In this experiment, meat is an **unconditioned stimulus** (abbreviated US or UCS), and salivation in response to meat is an **unconditioned response** (abbreviated UR or UCR). "Unconditioned" means unlearned. At first the bell is a meaningless, or neutral, stimulus. But by being paired repeatedly with the US (meat), the bell becomes a learned or **conditioned stimulus** (CS), and it becomes capable of evoking, or eliciting, the salivation response. Salivation to the bell is a learned or **conditioned response** (CR).

Conditioning of Fears Can you identify classical conditioning in your own life? Perhaps you automatically cringe or grimace in the waiting room when you hear the dentist's drill. The sound of the drill may have become a conditioned stimulus (CS) for conditioned responses (CRs) of muscle tension and fear. John Watson and his future wife Rosalie Rayner (1920) demonstrated how fears could be conditioned. They presented an 11-month-old lad, "Little Albert," with a laboratory rat and then clanged steel bars behind his head. At first the boy reached out to play with the animal. After several pairings of animal and clanging, however, the boy cried when he saw the rat and attempted to avoid it.

STIMULUS • An environmental condition that elicits a response. (Plural: *stimuli.*)
UNCONDITIONED STIMULUS • A stimulus that elicits a response from an organism without learning.
UNCONDITIONED RESPONSE • An unlearned response. A response to an unconditioned stimulus.
CONDITIONED STIMULUS • A previously neutral stimulus that elicits a conditioned response because it has been paired repeatedly with a stimulus that already brought forth that response.
CONDITIONED RESPONSE • A response to a conditioned stimulus.

Adjustment often requires responding appropriately to conditioned stimuli—stimuli that have taken on the meaning of other events. After all, if we did not learn to fear touching a hot stove after one or two pairings of seeing the reddened burner and experiencing pain, we would suffer many needless burns. If we did not develop an aversion to food that nauseates us, we might become poisoned.

But adjustment can also require coping with excessive or irrational conditioned fears. If the sound, or the thought, of the drill is enough to keep you away from the dentist's office, you may wish to consider one of the fear-reduction techniques we discuss below and in Chapters 9 and 10.

Extinction and Spontaneous Recovery Conditioned responses (CRs) may become "extinguished" when conditioned stimuli (CSs) are presented repeatedly but no longer paired with unconditioned stimuli (USs). Pavlov found that **extinction** of the salivation response (CR) would occur if he presented the bell (CS) repeatedly but no longer followed it with the meat (US). Extinction, too, is adaptive. After all, if your dentist becomes more skillful or uses an effective painkiller, why should the sound of the drill continue to make you cringe? If you acquire effective social skills, why should you continue to experience anxiety at the thought of meeting new people or asking someone out on a date?

However, extinguished responses may return simply as a function of the passage of time; that is, they may show **spontaneous recovery.** After Pavlov extinguished his dogs' salivation in response to a bell, a few days later they would again salivate if they heard a bell. You might cringe again in the office of the (recently painless) dentist if a year has passed between checkups. If you haven't dated for several months, you might experience anxiety at the thought of asking someone out. Is spontaneous recovery adaptive? It seems so; as time passes, situations may change again.

In classical conditioning we learn to connect stimuli, so that a simple, usually passive response evoked by one is then evoked by the other. In the case of Little Albert, clanging noises were associated with a rat, so that the rat came to elicit the fear response brought forth by the noise. Let us now turn our attention to operant conditioning, in which we learn to engage in certain behavior patterns because of their effects. After classical conditioning took place, Albert's avoidance of rats would be an example of voluntary, or operant, behavior that has desired effects—in this case, allowing the boy to avoid a dreaded object and, by so doing, to avert discomforting sensations of fear. Similarly, the sight of a hypodermic syringe might elicit an involuntary fear response because a person once had a painful injection. But subsequent avoidance of injections is voluntary, operant behavior. It has the effect of reducing fear. In other cases we engage in operant behavior to attain rewards, not to avert unpleasant outcomes.

OPERANT CONDITIONING In **operant conditioning,** an organism learns to engage in certain behavior because of the effects of that behavior. Behavior that operates upon, or manipulates, the environment in order to attain desired consequences is referred to as operant behavior.

Operant conditioning can occur mechanically with lower organisms. B. F. Skinner (1938) showed that hungry pigeons will learn to peck buttons when pecking is followed by food pellets dropping into their cages. It may take the pigeons a while to happen upon the first response (button-pecking) that is followed by food, but after the pecking-food association has occurred a few times, pecking becomes fast and furious until the birds have eaten their fill. Similarly,

EXTINCTION • In classical conditioning, repeated presentation of the conditioned stimulus in the absence of the unconditioned stimulus, leading to suspension of the conditioned response.

SPONTANEOUS RECOVERY • In classical conditioning, the eliciting of an extinguished conditioned response by a conditioned stimulus after some time has elapsed.

OPERANT CONDITIONING • A simple form of learning in which the frequency of behavior is increased by means of reinforcement or rewards.

hungry rats will learn to press levers to attain food, or for a burst of electrical stimulation in the so-called pleasure center of the brain.

In operant conditioning, organisms are said to acquire responses or skills that lead to **reinforcement.** A reinforcement is a change in the environment (that is, a stimulus) that increases the frequency of the behavior that precedes it. A **reward,** by contrast, is defined as a *pleasant* stimulus that increases the frequency of behavior. Skinner preferred the concept of reinforcement to that of reward because it is fully defined in terms of observable behaviors and environmental contingencies. The definition of reinforcement does not rely on "mentalistic" assumptions about what another person or lower organism finds pleasant or unpleasant. However, some psychologists use the terms *reinforcement* and *reward* interchangeably.

Types of Reinforcers Psychologists speak of various kinds of reinforcers, and it is useful to be able to distinguish among them.

Positive reinforcers increase the frequency of behavior when they are applied. Money, food, opportunity to mate, and social approval are common examples of positive reinforcers. **Negative reinforcers** increase the frequency of behavior when they are removed. Pain, anxiety, and social disapproval usually function as negative reinforcers. That is, we will usually learn to do things that lead to the removal or reduction of pain, anxiety, or the disapproval of other people.

Adjustment requires learning responses or skills that enable us to attain positive reinforcers and to avoid negative reinforcers. In the examples given, adjustment means acquiring skills that allow us to attain money, food, and social approval, and to avoid pain, anxiety, and social disapproval. *When we do not have the capacity, the opportunity, or the freedom to learn these skills, our ability to adjust is impaired.*

We can also distinguish between primary and secondary, or conditioned, reinforcers. **Primary reinforcers** have their values because of the biological makeup of the organism. We seek primary reinforcers such as food, liquid, affectionate physical contact with other people, sexual excitement and release, and freedom from pain because of our biological makeup. Conditioned reinforcers, or **secondary reinforcers,** acquire their value through association with established reinforcers. We may learn to seek money because money can be exchanged for primary reinforcers such as food and heat (or air conditioning). Or we may learn to seek social approval—another secondary reinforcer—because approval may lead to affectionate embraces or the meeting of various physical needs.

Punishment **Punishments** are painful, or aversive, events that suppress or decrease the frequency of the behavior they follow. *Recall that* negative reinforcers *are defined in terms of increasing the frequency of behavior, although the increase occurs when the negative reinforcer is removed.*

Punishment can rapidly suppress undesirable behavior. For this reason it may be warranted in emergencies, such as when a child tries to run out into the street. But many theorists suggest that punishment is usually undesirable, especially in rearing children. For example, punishment does not in and of itself suggest an alternate, acceptable form of behavior. Punishment also tends to suppress undesirable behavior only under circumstances in which delivery is guaranteed. It does not take children long to learn that they can "get away with murder" with one parent, or one teacher, but not with another. Moreover, punishment may be imitated as a way of solving problems or of coping with stress. Children learn by observing other people. Even if they do not immediately

Reinforcement • A stimulus that increases the frequency of behavior.
Reward • A pleasant stimulus that increases the frequency of behavior.
Positive reinforcer • A reinforcer that increases the frequency of behavior when it is presented (e.g., food and approval).
Negative reinforcer • A reinforcer that (e.g., pain, anxiety, and social disapproval).
Primary reinforcer • An unlearned reinforcer, such as food, water, warmth, or pain.
Secondary reinforcer • A stimulus that gains reinforcement value as a result of association with established reinforcers. Money and social approval are secondary reinforcers.
Punishment • An unpleasant stimulus that suppresses behavior.

imitate behavior, they may do so as adults when they are under stress, with their own children as targets.

It is considered preferable to focus on rewarding children and adults for desirable behavior rather than to punish them for misbehavior. Ironically, some children can gain the reward of adult attention only by misbehaving. In such cases, punishment may function as a positive reinforcer—that is, children may learn to misbehave in order to gain the attention (expressed through punishment) of the people they care about.

Operant conditioning is not just a laboratory procedure. It is used every day in the real world. Consider the **socialization** of children. Parents and peers inspire children to acquire behavior patterns that are appropriate to their gender through rewards and punishments. Parents usually praise children for sharing and punish them for being too aggressive. Peers take part in socialization by playing with children who are generous and nonaggressive and, often, by avoiding those who are not.

Social-Cognitive Theory

Social-cognitive theory[1] is a contemporary view of learning developed by Albert Bandura (1986, 1991) and other psychologists (e.g., Mischel & Shoda, 1995). It focuses on the importance of learning by observation and on the cognitive processes that underlie individual differences. Social-cognitive theorists see people as influencing their environment just as their environment influences them. Bandura terms this mutual pattern of influence **reciprocal determinism.** Social-cognitive theorists agree with behaviorists and other empirical psychologists that discussions of human nature should be tied to observable experiences and behaviors. They assert, however, that variables within people—which they call **person variables**—must also be considered if we are to understand them.

One goal of psychological theories is the prediction of behavior. We cannot predict behavior from **situational variables** alone. Whether a person will behave in a certain way also depends on the person's expectancies about the outcomes of that behavior and the emotions we feel as a result of those expectancies.

To social-cognitive theorists, people are not simply at the mercy of the environment. Instead, they are self-aware and purposefully engage in learning. They seek to learn about their environment and to alter it in order to make reinforcers available.

OBSERVATIONAL LEARNING

Observational learning (also termed **modeling** or *cognitive learning*) refers to acquiring knowledge by observing others. For operant conditioning to occur, (1) an organism must engage in a response, and (2) that response must be reinforced. But observational learning occurs even when the learner does not perform the observed behavior. Therefore, direct reinforcement is not required either. Observing others extends to reading about them or seeing what they do and what happens to them in books, television, radio, and film.

Our expectations stem from our observations of what happens to ourselves and other people. For example, teachers are more likely to call on males and are more accepting of "calling out" in class by males than by females (Sadker & Sadker, 1994). As a result, many males expect to be rewarded for calling out.

SOCIALIZATION • The process of fostering socially acceptable behavior by means of rewards and punishments.

SOCIAL-COGNITIVE THEORY • A cognitively oriented theory in which observational learning, values, and expectations play major roles in determining behavior. Formerly termed *social-learning theory.*

RECIPROCAL DETERMINISM • Bandura's term for the social-cognitive view that people influence their environment just as their environment influences them.

PERSON VARIABLES • Factors within the person, such as expectancies and competencies, that influence behavior.

SITUATIONAL VARIABLES • In social-cognitive theory, determinants of behavior that lie outside the person.

MODELING • In social-cognitive theory, an organism that exhibits behaviors that others will imitate, or acquire, through observational learning.

[1] The name of this theory is in flux. It was formerly referred to as social learning theory. Today it is also sometimes referred to as *cognitive social theory* (Miller and others, 1996).

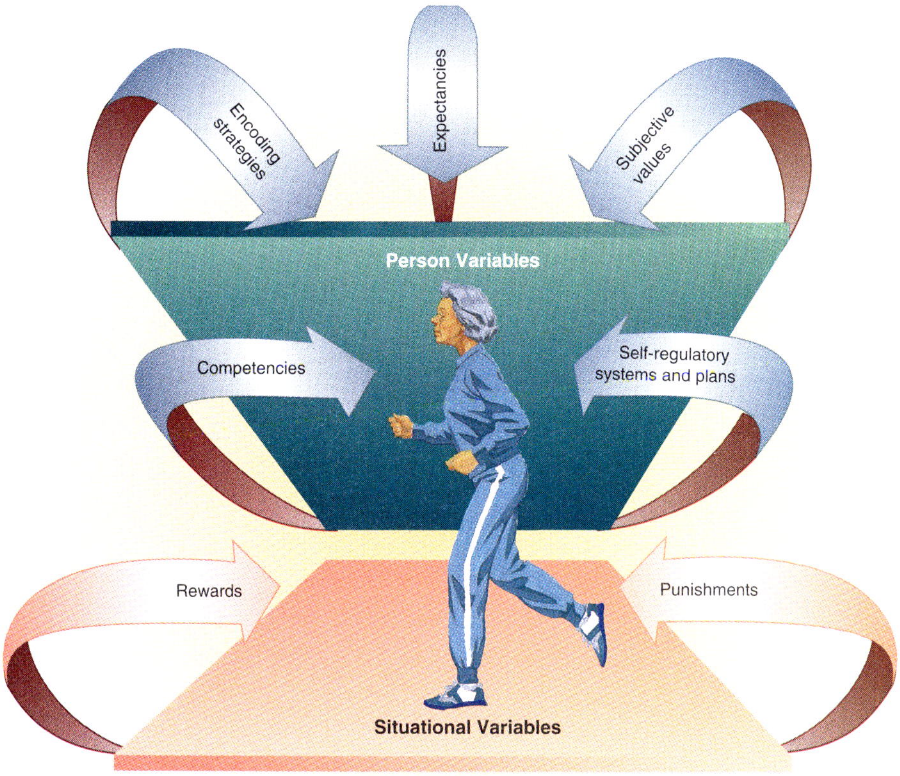

FIGURE 2.4
PERSON AND SITUATIONAL VARIABLES IN SOCIAL-COGNITIVE THEORY.
According to social-cognitive theory, person and situational variables interact to influence behavior.

Females, however, may learn that they will be reprimanded for behaving in what some might term an "unladylike" manner.

Social-cognitive theorists believe that behavior reflects person variables and situational variables. Person variables include competencies, encoding strategies, expectancies, emotions, and self-regulatory systems and plans (Mischel & Shoda, 1995; see Figure 2.4).

COMPETENCIES: WHAT CAN YOU DO? *Competencies* include knowledge of rules that guide conduct, concepts about ourselves and other people, and skills. Our ability to use information to make plans depends on our competencies. Knowledge of the physical world and of cultural codes of conduct are important competencies. So are academic skills such as reading and writing, athletic skills such as swimming and tossing a football, social skills such as knowing how to ask someone out on a date, and many others.

Individual differences in competencies reflect genetic variation, learning opportunities, and other environmental factors. People do not perform well at given tasks unless they have the competencies needed to do so.

ENCODING STRATEGIES: HOW DO YOU SEE IT? Different people **encode** (symbolize or represent) the same stimuli in different ways. Their encoding strategies are an important factor in their behavior. One person might encode a tennis game as a chance to bat the ball back and forth and have some fun. Another person might encode the game as a demand to perfect his or her serve. One person might encode a date that doesn't work out as a sign of her or his

ENCODE • Interpret; transform.

WILL YOU BE A HIT OR A MISS? THE EXPECTANCY FOR SUCCESS SCALE

Life is filled with opportunities and obstacles. What happens when you are faced with a difficult challenge? Do you rise to meet it, or do you back off?

Social-cognitive theorists note the importance of our expectancies in influencing our behavior. Of particular importance, according to Albert Bandura, are our self-efficacy expectations. When we believe that we are capable of accomplishing difficult things through our own efforts, we marshal our resources and apply ourselves. When we believe that our efforts will pay off, we are more likely to persist.

The following scale, created by Hale and Fibel (1978), can provide you with insight as to whether you believe that your own efforts are likely to meet with success. You can compare your own expectancies for success with those of other undergraduates taking psychology courses by taking the questionnaire and then turning to the scoring key in the Appendix. ■

Directions: Indicate the degree to which each item applies to you by circling the appropriate number, according to this key:

1 = highly improbable
2 = improbable
3 = equally improbable and probable; not sure
4 = probable
5 = highly probable

In the Future I Expect That I Will:

1.	Find that people don't seem to understand what I'm trying to say.	1	2	3	4	5
2.	Be discouraged about my ability to gain the respect of others.	1	2	3	4	5
3.	Be a good parent.	1	2	3	4	5
4.	Be unable to accomplish my goals.	1	2	3	4	5
5.	Have a stressful marital relationship.	1	2	3	4	5
6.	Deal poorly with emergency situations.	1	2	3	4	5
7.	Find my efforts to change situations I don't like are ineffective.	1	2	3	4	5
8.	Not be very good at learning new skills.	1	2	3	4	5
9.	Carry through my responsibilities successfully.	1	2	3	4	5
10.	Discover that the good in life outweighs the bad.	1	2	3	4	5
11.	Handle unexpected problems successfully.	1	2	3	4	5
12.	Get the promotions I deserve.	1	2	3	4	5
13.	Succeed in the projects I undertake.	1	2	3	4	5
14.	Not make any significant contributions to society.	1	2	3	4	5
15.	Discover that my life is not getting much better.	1	2	3	4	5
16.	Be listened to when I speak.	1	2	3	4	5
17.	Discover that my plans don't work out too well.	1	2	3	4	5
18.	Find that no matter how hard I try, things just don't turn out the way I would like.	1	2	3	4	5
19.	Handle myself well in whatever situation I'm in.	1	2	3	4	5
20.	Be able to solve my own problems.	1	2	3	4	5
21.	Succeed at most things I try.	1	2	3	4	5
22.	Be successful in my endeavors in the long run.	1	2	3	4	5
23.	Be very successful working out my personal life.	1	2	3	4	5
24.	Experience many failures in my life.	1	2	3	4	5
25.	Make a good first impression on people I meet for the first time.	1	2	3	4	5
26.	Attain the career goals I have set for myself.	1	2	3	4	5
27.	Have difficulty dealing with my superiors.	1	2	3	4	5
28.	Have problems working with others.	1	2	3	4	5
29.	Be a good judge of what it takes to get ahead.	1	2	3	4	5
30.	Achieve recognition in my profession.	1	2	3	4	5

Source: Reprinted with permission from Hale and Fibel, 1978, p. 931.

social incompetence. Another person might encode the date as reflecting the fact that people are not always "made for each other."

Some people make themselves miserable by encoding events in self-defeating ways (see Chapter 15). A linebacker may encode an average day on the field as a failure because he didn't make any sacks. Cognitive therapists foster adjustment by challenging people to view life in more optimistic ways.

EXPECTANCIES: WHAT WILL HAPPEN? There are various kinds of expectancies. Some are predictions about what will follow various stimuli or signs. For example, some people predict other people's behavior on the basis of signs such as "tight lips" or "shifty eyes" (Ross & Nisbett, 1991). Other expectancies involve what will happen if we engage in certain behaviors. **Self-efficacy expectations** are beliefs that we can accomplish certain things, such as speaking before a group or doing a backflip into a swimming pool or solving math problems (Pajares & Miller, 1994).

Competencies influence expectancies. Expectancies, in turn, influence motivation to perform. People with positive self-efficacy expectations are more likely to try difficult tasks than people who do not believe that they can master those tasks. One way that psychotherapy helps people is by changing their self-efficacy expectations from "I can't" to "I can" (Bandura, 1986). As a result, people are motivated to try new things.

HOW DO COMPETENCIES CONTRIBUTE TO PERFORMANCE?
There are great individual differences in our competencies, based on genetic variation, nourishment, differences in learning opportunities, and other environmental factors. What factors contribute to this young woman's performance on the balance beam?

Truth or Fiction Revisited

It is true that we are more likely to persist at difficult tasks when we believe we shall succeed. Positive self-efficacy expectations motivate us to persevere.

EMOTIONS: HOW DOES IT FEEL? Because of our different learning histories, similar situations can arouse different feelings in us—anxiety, depression, fear, hopelessness, and anger. What frightens one person may entice another. What bores one person may excite another. From the social-cognitive perspective, in contrast to the behaviorist perspective, we are not controlled by stimuli. Instead, stimuli arouse feelings in us, and feelings influence our behavior. Hearing Chopin may make one person weep and another person switch to a rock 'n' roll station.

SELF-REGULATORY SYSTEMS AND PLANS: HOW CAN YOU ACHIEVE IT? We tend to regulate our own behavior, even in the absence of observers and external constraints. We set our own goals and standards. We make plans to achieve them. We congratulate or criticize ourselves, depending on whether or not we achieve them (Bandura, 1991).

Self-regulation helps us influence our environments. We can select the situations to which we expose ourselves and the arenas in which we will compete. Depending on our expectancies, we may choose to enter the academic or athletic worlds. We may choose marriage or the single life. And when we cannot readily select our environment, we can to some degree select our responses within an environment—even an aversive one. For example, if we are undergoing an uncomfortable medical procedure, we may try to reduce the stress by focusing on something else—an inner fantasy or something in the environment such as the cracks in the tiles on the ceiling. This is one of the techniques used in prepared or "natural" childbirth.

The Healthy Personality

Behaviorists do not usually speak in terms of a healthy personality, since a personality cannot be observed or measured directly. They prefer to speak in terms of adaptive or productive behaviors.

Ideally, we should learn to anticipate positive events with pleasure and potentially harmful events with fear. In this way we shall be motivated to

SELF-EFFICACY EXPECTATIONS • Beliefs to the effect that one can handle a task.

approach desirable stimuli and to avoid noxious stimuli. Fears should be sufficient to warn of real danger, but not so extreme that they inhibit necessary exploration of the self and the environment.

Similarly, "healthy" people have acquired skills (operants) that enable them to meet their needs and avert punishments.

Social-cognitive theorists view the healthy personality in terms of opportunities for observational learning and in terms of person variables.

RICH OPPORTUNITIES FOR OBSERVATIONAL LEARNING Because most human learning occurs by observation, it is desirable for us to be exposed to a diversity of models. In this way we can form complex, comprehensive views of the social and physical world.

LEARNING OF COMPETENCIES Getting along and getting ahead require competencies—knowledge and skills. Competencies are acquired by combinations of observational learning and operant conditioning. We require accurate, efficient models and the opportunities to practice and improve skills.

ACCURATE ENCODING OF EVENTS We need to encode events accurately and productively. One failure should not be magnified as a sign of total incompetence. A social provocation may be better encoded as a problem to be solved than as an injury that must be avenged.

ACCURATE EXPECTATIONS AND POSITIVE SELF-EFFICACY EXPECTATIONS Accurate expectancies enhance the probability that our efforts will pay off. Positive self-efficacy expectations increase our motivation to take on challenges and our persistence in meeting them.

EMOTIONS It is useful for our emotional reactions to reflect our needs. Then we shall pursue the things we need, and we shall not squander our efforts by running after things that we do not need.

EFFICIENT SELF-REGULATORY SYSTEMS Methodical, efficient self-regulatory systems facilitate our performances. For example, thoughts such as "One step at a time" and "Don't get bent out of shape" help us to cope with difficulties and pace ourselves.

Now let us turn our attention to phenomenological theories, which, like social-cognitive theory, emphasize cognitive processes and conscious experience.

PHENOMENOLOGICAL THEORY

We discuss two **phenomenological** approaches to personality: the theories of Abraham Maslow and Carl Rogers. They have a number of things in common: Each proposes that the personal, or subjective, experiencing of events is the most important aspect of human nature and that we, as unique individuals, are our own best experts on ourselves.

Abraham Maslow and the Challenge of Self-Actualization

PHENOMENOLOGICAL • Having to do with subjective experience.

Maslow's views owe much to the European school of philosophy called *existentialism,* which holds that we are free to choose and so adaptable that human

SELF-ASSESSMENT

DO YOU STRIVE TO BE ALL THAT YOU CAN BE?

Are you a self-actualizer? Do you strive to be all that you can be? Maslow attributed the following eight characteristics to the self-actualizing individual. How many of them are characteristic of you? Why not check them and undertake some honest self-evaluation? ■

YES	NO		
____	____	1.	*Do you fully experience life in the present—the here and now?* (Self- actualizers do not focus excessively on the lost past or wish their lives away as they stride toward distant goals.)
____	____	2.	*Do you make growth choices rather than fear choices?* (Self-actualizers take reasonable risks to develop their unique potentials. They do not bask in the dull life of the status quo. They do not "settle.")
____	____	3.	*Do you seek to acquire self-knowledge?* (Self-actualizers look inward; they search for values, talents, and meaningfulness. The questionnaires in this book offer a decent jumping-off point for getting to know yourself. It might also be enlightening to take an "interest inventory"—a test frequently used to help make career decisions—at your college testing and counseling center.)
____	____	4.	*Do you strive toward honesty in interpersonal relationships?* (Self-actualizers strip away the social facades and games that stand in the way of self-disclosure and the formation of intimate relationships.)
____	____	5.	*Do you behave self-assertively and express your own ideas and feelings, even at the risk of occasional social disapproval?* (Self-actualizers do not bottle up their feelings for the sake of avoiding social disapproval.)
____	____	6.	*Do you strive toward new goals? Do you strive to be the best that you can be in a chosen life role?* (Self-actualizers do not live by the memory of past accomplishments. Nor do they present second-rate efforts.)
____	____	7.	*Do you seek meaningful and rewarding life activities?* Do you experience moments of actualization that phenomenological psychologists refer to as peak experiences? (Peak experiences are brief moments of rapture filled with personal meaning. Examples might include completing a work of art, falling in love, redesigning a machine tool, suddenly solving a complex problem in math or physics, or having a baby. Again, we differ as individuals, and one person's peak experience might bore another person silly.)
____	____	8.	*Do you remain open to new experiences?* (Self-actualizers do not hold themselves back for fear that novel experiences might shake their views of the world, or of right and wrong. Self-actualizers are willing to revise their expectations, values, and opinions.)

nature is whatever we believe it to be. Existentialists asserted that the main task of life is to come to grips with the experiences of being mortal and free to choose. It is up to us to make our lives meaningful by exercising free will and seeking goals and values that lead to individual fulfillment.

Maslow believed that we each have needs for **self-actualization**—to become whatever we are capable of being. He also believed that each of us is unique. Thus, no two people can follow quite the same path to self-actualization. Expressing our unique potentials and finding fulfillment requires setting out on our own—taking risks. Otherwise, our lives may degenerate into the drab and the routine.

SELF-ACTUALIZATION • In humanistic theory, an innate tendency to strive to realize one's potential. Self-initiated striving to become all one is capable of being.

Truth or Fiction Revisited

It is true that we all have unique ways of looking at ourselves and at the world outside. Since all of us, with the exception of identical twins, are geneticallty unique, and not even twins have exactly the same experiences, it is probably true that we all have unique points of view. The statement is also consistent with phnenomenological theories of personality.

The "Self-Assessment" feature "Do You Strive to Be All That You Can Be?" will provide you with insight as to whether or not you are a self-actualizer.

THE HIERARCHY OF NEEDS: WHAT DO YOU DO WHEN YOU'RE NO LONGER HUNGRY? Maslow believed that there was an order, or **hierarchy of needs,** that range from basic biological needs, such as hunger and thirst, to self-actualization (see Figure 2.5).

Freud saw all motivation as stemming from the id, and he argued that our ideas that we have conscious and noble intentions were defensive and self-deceiving. By contrast, Maslow saw all levels of needs as equally valid and real. Maslow believed that once we had met our lower-level needs, we would strive to fulfill higher-order needs for personal growth. We would not snooze away the hours until lower-order needs stirred us once more to act. In fact, some of us—as in the stereotype of the struggling artist—will sacrifice basic comforts to devote ourselves to higher-level needs.

Maslow's hierarchy of needs includes:

1. *Biological needs.* Water, food, elimination, warmth, rest, avoidance of pain, sexual release, and so forth.
2. *Safety needs.* Protection from the physical and social environment by means of clothing, housing, and security from crime and financial hardship.
3. *Love and belongingness needs.* Love and acceptance through intimate relationships, social groups, and friends. Maslow believed that in a well fed and well housed society, a principal source of maladjustment lay in the frustration of needs at this level.

HIERARCHY OF NEEDS • Maslow's progression from basic, physiological needs to social needs to aesthetic and cognitive needs.

FIGURE 2.5

MASLOW'S HIERARCHY OF NEEDS.

Maslow believed that we progress toward higher psychological needs once our basic survival needs have been met. Where do you fit into this picture?

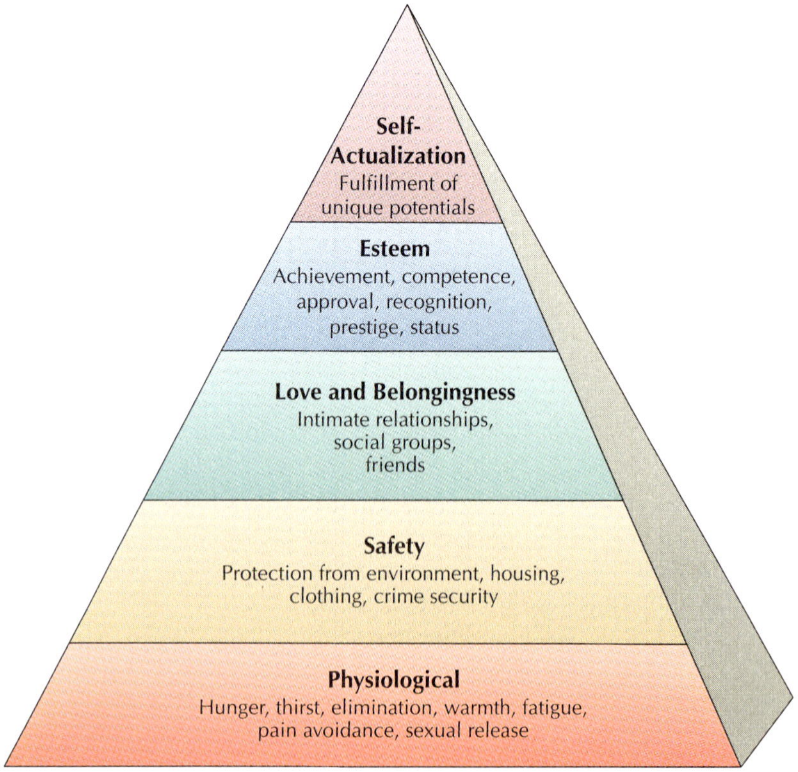

4. *Esteem needs.* Achievement, competence, approval, recognition, prestige, status.
5. *Self-actualization.* Personal growth, the development of our unique potentials. At the highest level are also found needs for cognitive understanding (as found in novelty, understanding, exploration, and knowledge) and aesthetic experience (as found in order, music, poetry, and art).

How far have your personal growth and development proceeded up through the hierarchy of needs? At what levels have you adequately met your needs? What levels are you attacking now?

UNIQUE.
According to humanistic psychologists like Carl Rogers, each of us views the world from a unique frame of reference. What matters to one person may mean little to another.

Carl Rogers's Self Theory

> My *experience in therapy and in groups makes it impossible for me to deny the reality and significance of human choice. To me it is not an illusion that man is to some degree the architect of himself.*
>
> CARL ROGERS (1974, p. 119)

According to Rogers, people tend to shape themselves through freedom of choice and action.

Rogers's views are labeled "self theory" because of his focus on the relationships between the self and other aspects of life. Your self is your center of experience. It is your ongoing sense of who and what you are, your sense of how and why you react to the environment, and how you choose to act upon the environment. Your choices are made on the basis of your values, and your values are also parts of your self.

To Rogers the sense of self is inborn, or innate. The self provides the experience of being human in the world. It is the guiding principle behind personality structure and behavior.

Rogers stated that we all have unique ways of looking at ourselves and the world, or unique **frames of reference.** It may be that we each use a different set of dimensions in defining ourselves, and that we judge ourselves according to different sets of values. To one person achievement-failure may be the most important dimension. To another person the most important dimension may be decency-indecency. A third person may not even think in terms of decency.

SELF-ESTEEM AND POSITIVE REGARD Rogers assumes that we all develop a need for self-regard or self-esteem as we develop and become self-aware. Self-esteem at first reflects the esteem others hold us in. Parents help children develop self-esteem when they show them **unconditional positive regard.** But when parents show children **conditional positive regard,** they may learn to disown the thoughts, feelings, and behaviors that parents have rejected. Conditional positive regard may lead children to develop **conditions of worth,** to think that they are worthwhile only if they behave in certain ways.

Rogers, like Maslow, saw each of us as having a unique potential. Therefore, children who develop conditions of worth must wind up somewhat dissatisfied with themselves. We cannot fully abide by the wishes of others and remain true to ourselves. This does not mean that the expression of the self inevitably leads to conflict. Rogers was optimistic about human nature. He believed that we hurt others only when we are frustrated in our efforts to develop our potentials. But

FRAME OF REFERENCE • One's unique patterning of perceptions and attitudes, according to which one evaluates events.

UNCONDITIONAL POSITIVE REGARD • Acceptance of others as having intrinsic merit regardless of their behavior of the moment. Consistent expression of esteem for the value of another person.

CONDITIONAL POSITIVE REGARD • Judgment of another person's value on the basis of the acceptability of that person's behaviors.

CONDITIONS OF WORTH • Standards by which the value of a person is judged.

ADJUSTMENT in the NEW MILLENNIUM

If There Were 100 "You's," Just How Unique Would You Be?

Most Americans believe in the uniqueness, value, and dignity of the individual. Yet how valuable would your individual existence be if a copy of you could be developed on demand? What adjustment problems would be posed if a dozen or more of you could be brought to life?

Some fear that our increasing control of genetics will make possible scenarios like that portrayed by Aldous Huxley in his still-powerful 1939 novel *Brave New World.* Through a science fiction method called "Bokanovsky's Process," egg cells from parents who were ideally suited to certain types of labor were made to "bud." From these buds, up to 96 people with identical genetic makeups were developed—easily meeting the labor needs of society.

In the novel, the director of a "hatchery" leads a group of students on a tour. One student is foolish enough to question the advantage of Bokanovsky's Process:

> "My good boy!" The Director wheeled sharply round on him. "Can't you see? Can't you see?" He raised a hand; his expression was solemn. "Bokanovsky's Process is one of the major instruments of social stability!"
>
> Major instruments of social stability (wrote the student).
>
> Standard men and women; in uniform batches. The whole of a small factory staffed with the products of a single Bokanovskied egg.
>
> "Ninety-six identical twins working 96 identical machines!" The voice was almost tremulous with enthusiasm. "You really know where you are. For the first time in history." He quoted the planetary motto. "Community, Identity, Stability." Grand words. "If we could Bokanovskify indefinitely the whole problem would be solved."

Bokanovsky's Process was science fiction when Huxley wrote *Brave New World.* Today, however, cloning technology has made the creation of genetically identical people possible. Techniques similar to that described by Huxley have been developed for making identical cattle. For example, an ovum (egg cell) would be fertilized with sperm in the laboratory (in vitro). The fertilized ovum would begin to divide. The dividing mass of cells would be separated into clusters so that each cluster develops into a separate organism. The embryos would then be implanted in one or more "mothers" to develop to maturity. Or else some embryos would be

when parents and others are loving and tolerant of our differentness, we, too, shall be loving—even if our preferences, abilities, and values differ.

But children in some families learn that it is bad to have ideas of their own, especially about sexual, political, or religious matters. When they perceive their parents' disapproval, they may come to see themselves as rebels and label their feelings as selfish, wrong, or evil. If they wish to retain self-esteem, they may have to deny their genuine feelings, or disown parts of themselves. According to Rogers, anxiety often stems from partial perception of feelings and ideas that we are trying to deny.

According to Rogers, the path to self-actualization requires getting in touch with our genuine feelings, accepting them as ours, and acting upon them. This is frozen to be implanted if the natural parents (or adoptive parents) desired a genetically identical offspring.

In an approach that has been used successfully with sheep, a DNA-containing cell nucleus would be surgically extracted from an egg cell donated by a woman. The nutrients that will nourish the development of the egg would be retained. A DNA-containing cell from another person (male or female, child or adult) would be fused with the egg cell. An electric charge might jump-start cell division, and the embryo would be implanted in a woman's uterus. There it would develop into a person with the genetic traits determined by the nucleus.

These technologies have been used successfully with cattle and sheep (Kolata, 1997), but they would raise many ethical concerns if they were applied to people. One involves human dignity—the core concern for psychologists. One reason that we consider people to be dignified and valuable is their uniqueness. Imagine a world, however, in which every child and adult had one or more frozen identical twins in embryo form:

- If a child died by accident, would the parents develop a frozen embryo to replace the lost child? *Would* this method "replace" the lost child?
- Would some frozen embryos be developed to term to provide donor organs for people who were ill?
- Would society desire that a dozen twins be developed to maturity when a Toni Morrison, a Wolfgang Amadeus Mozart, a Mary Cassatt, or an Albert Einstein was discovered?
- Would society, on the other hand, attempt to lower the incidence of certain genetic disorders or antisocial behavior by *preventing* the twins of less fortunate individuals from being developed to maturity?
- Would parents "invest" frozen embryos that were the twins of their children in embryo banks? As their children developed, would they take photographs and administer psychological tests? Could it happen that the twins of the brightest, most attractive children would be sold to the highest bidder?
- What would happen in societies that valued brawny soldiers? In societies that valued dull workers of the sort envisioned by Huxley? In societies that valued boys more than girls or girls more than boys?

Some ethicists argue that parents' embryos are their own and that it is not society's place to prevent parents from cloning them. Others argue that cloning would devalue the individual and change society in ways that we cannot foresee. Today, nearly three out of five people in the United States say that cloning is a bad thing (Berke, 1997). Only one in four or five say it is a good thing. As we head into the new millennium, the development of many technologies is outpacing ethical considerations. As citizens, it is our duty to keep abreast of technical innovations and to ensure that their applications are beneficial.

the goal of Rogers's method of psychotherapy, **person-centered therapy** (see Chapter 10). Person-centered therapists help clients cope with the anxiety they experience when they focus on disowned parts of the self.

Rogers also believes that we have *self-ideals,* or mental images of what we are capable of becoming. We are motivated to reduce the discrepancy between our self-concepts and our self-ideals. But as we undertake the process of actualizing ourselves, our self-ideals may gradually grow more complex. Our goals may become higher or change in quality. The self-ideal is something like a carrot dangling from a stick strapped to a burro's head. The burro strives to reach the carrot, as though it were a step or two away, without recognizing that its own progress also causes the carrot to advance. Our own forward movement

PERSON-CENTERED THERAPY • Rogers's form of therapy, which provides a warm, therapeutic atmosphere to encourage client self-exploration.

creates more distant goals. It may be that we are happiest when our goals seem attainable, almost within our grasp, and we are striving with confidence to achieve them. We may never be completely satisfied with what we attain, but, according to Rogers, the process of striving to meet meaningful goals, the good struggle, yields happiness.

The Healthy Personality

Phenomenological theorists have written volumes about the healthy personality. In fact, their focus has been on the functioning of the psychologically healthy individual. According to phenomenological theorists, persons with a healthy personality possess a number of advantageous traits.

EXPERIENCE LIFE HERE AND NOW They do not dwell excessively on the past or wish their days away as they strive toward future happiness.

BE OPEN TO NEW EXPERIENCE They do not turn away from ideas and ways of life that might challenge their own perceptions of the world and values.

EXPRESS FEELINGS AND IDEAS They assert themselves in interpersonal relationships and are honest about their feelings.

TRUST INTUITIVE FEELINGS They believe in their own inner goodness and are not afraid of their urges and impulses.

ENGAGE IN MEANINGFUL ACTIVITIES They strive to live up to their self-ideals, to enact fulfilling roles. As a result, they may have peak experiences.

BE CAPABLE OF MAKING MAJOR LIFE CHANGES They can find more convenient ways to interpret experiences, strive toward new goals, and act with freedom.

BE ONE'S OWN PERSON They have developed their own values and their own ways of construing events. As a consequence they take risks and can anticipate and control events.

THIS HISPANIC AMERICAN WOMAN IS HIGHLY ACCULTURATED TO LIFE IN THE UNITED STATES.
Some immigrants are completely assimilated by the dominant culture and abandon the language and customs of their country of origin. Others retain the language and customs of their country of origin and never become comfortable with those of their new country. Still others become bicultural. They become fluent in both languages and blend the customs and values of both cultures.

THE SOCIOCULTURAL PERSPECTIVE

In multicultural societies such as those of the United States and Canada, personality cannot be understood without reference to the **sociocultural perspective.** Moreover, as we head into the new millennium, trends in immigration are making the population an even richer mix. Different cultural groups within these countries have different attitudes, beliefs, norms, self-definitions, and values (Basic Behavioral Science Task Force, 1996c; Triandis, 1996).

Consider Hannah—a Korean American teenager. She strives to become a great violinist, yet she talks back to her parents and insists on choosing her own friends, clothing, and so on. She is strongly influenced by her peers and

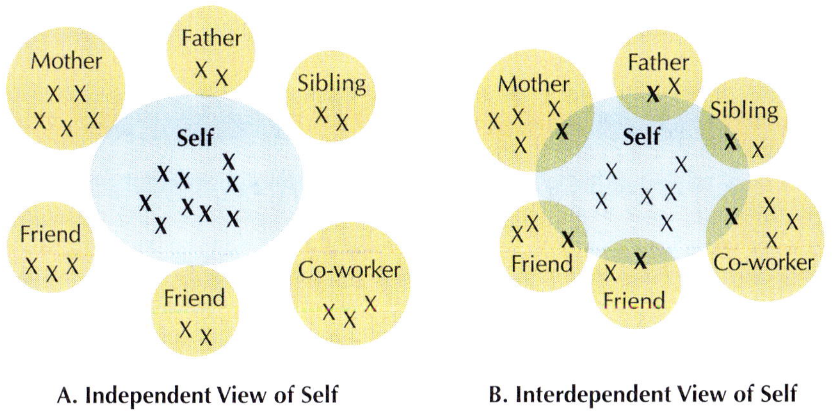

FIGURE 2.6
THE SELF IN RELATION TO OTHERS FROM THE INDIVIDUALIST AND COLLECTIVIST PERSPECTIVES.
To an individualist, the self is separate from other people (Part A). To a collectivist, the self is complete only in terms of relationships to other people (Part B).
Source: Based on Markus & Kitayama (1991).

completely at home wearing blue jeans and eating french fries. She is also a daughter in an Asian American immigrant group that views education as the key to success in American culture (Gibson & Ogbu, 1991; Ogbu, 1993). Belonging to this ethnic group had certainly contributed to her ambition. But being a Korean American had not prevented her from becoming an outspoken American teenager, when children back in Korea—especially girls—generally followed the wishes of their parents. Her outspoken behavior strikes her traditional mother as brazen and inappropriate (Lopez & Hernandez, 1986).

Let us consider some of the connections between culture and adjustment.

Individualism Versus Collectivism

Hannah saw herself as an individual and an artist to a greater extent than as a family member and a Korean girl. Cross-cultural research reveals that people in the United States and many northern European nations tend to be individualistic. **Individualists** tend to define themselves in terms of their personal identities and to give priority to their personal goals (Triandis, 1995). When asked to complete the statement "I am . . . ," they are likely to respond in terms of their personality traits ("I am outgoing," "I am artistic") or their occupations ("I am a nurse," "I am a systems analyst") (Triandis, 1990). In contrast, many people from cultures in Africa, Asia, and Central and South America tend to be collectivistic (Basic Behavioral Science Task Force, 1996c). **Collectivists** tend to define themselves in terms of the groups to which they belong and to give priority to the group's goals (Triandis, 1995). They feel complete in terms of their relationships with others (Markus & Kitayama, 1991; see Figure 2.6). They are more likely than individualists to conform to group norms and judgments (Bond & Smith, 1996; Okazaki, 1997). When asked to complete the statement "I am . . . ," they are more likely to respond in terms of their families, gender, or nation ("I am a father," "I am a Buddhist," "I am a Japanese") (Triandis, 1990, 1994).

The seeds of individualism and collectivism are found in the culture in which a person grows up. The capitalist system fosters individualism to some degree. It assumes that individuals are entitled to amass personal fortunes and that the process of doing so creates jobs and wealth for large numbers of people. The individualist perspective is found in the self-reliant heroes and antiheroes of Western literature and mass media—from Homer's Odysseus to Clint Eastwood's gritty cowboys and Walt Disney's Pocahontas. The traditional writings of the East have exalted people who resisted personal temptations in order to do their duty and promote the welfare of the group.

SOCIOCULTURAL PERSPECTIVE • The view that focuses on the roles of ethnicity, gender, culture, and socioeconomic status in personality, behavior, and adjustment.
INDIVIDUALIST • A person who defines herself or himself in terms of personal traits and gives priority to her or his own goals.
COLLECTIVIST • A person who defines herself or himself in terms of relationships to other people and groups and gives priority to group goals.

Sociocultural Factors and the Self

Sociocultural factors affect the self-concept and self-esteem. Carl Rogers noted that our self-concepts tend to reflect how other people see us. Thus, members of the dominant culture in the United States are likely to have a positive sense of self. They share in the expectations of personal achievement and respect that are accorded to those who ascend to power. Similarly, members of ethnic groups that have been subjected to discrimination and poverty often have poorer self-concepts and lower self-esteem than members of the dominant culture (Greene, 1993, 1994; Lewis-Fernández & Kleinman, 1994).

Acculturation and Self-Esteem

Should Hindu women who emigrate to the United States surrender the sari in favor of California casuals? Should Russian immigrants try to teach their children English at home? Should African American children be acquainted with the music and art of African peoples or those of Europe? How do these activities, which are examples of **acculturation,** affect the psychological well-being of immigrants and their families?

Self-esteem is connected with patterns of acculturation among immigrants. Those patterns take various forms. Some immigrants are completely assimilated by the dominant culture. They lose the language and customs of their country of origin and become like the dominant culture in the new host country. Others maintain separation. They retain the language and customs of their country of origin and never become comfortable with those of the new country. Still others become bicultural. They remain fluent in the language of their country of origin while learning that of their new country. Bicultural people blend the customs and values of both cultures.

Research evidence suggests that people who identify with the bicultural pattern have the highest self-esteem (Phinney and others, 1992). For example, Mexican Americans who are more proficient in English are less likely to be anxious and depressed than less proficient Mexican Americans (Salgado de Snyder and others, 1990). The ability to adapt to the ways of the new society, combined with a supportive cultural tradition and a sense of ethnic identity, apparently helps people adjust.

The Healthy Personality

FUNCTION WITHIN AN INDIVIDUALISTIC OR COLLECTIVISTIC SOCIETY

In Western nations, adjustment may mean having an individualist perspective—for example, experiencing and trying to actualize personal ambitions, being self-assertive, and so on. In other parts of the world, adjustment may mean viewing oneself and society from a collectivist point of view. Yet some of us, like Hannah, need to function within different societies out in the academic or business worlds and at home. It would probably be healthiest for many young people like Hannah not to take her parents' restrictions personally and to attempt to regulate her behavior according to where she is and whom she is with.

COPING WITH DISCRIMINATION Most of us belong to groups that have experienced—or are currently experiencing—discrimination. People experience discrimination on the basis of their ethnic background, their gender, their sexual orientation, their age, and so on. People with healthy personalities try not to

ACCULTURATION • The process of adaptation in which immigrants and native groups identify with a new, dominant culture by learning about that culture and making changes in their behavior and attitudes.

allow discrimination to affect their self-esteem. If you have experienced discrimination, it is not you as an individual who is at fault. The problem lies within those who judge you on the basis of your sociocultural background rather than your individual traits and abilities. You will find advice for coping with prejudice and discrimination in Chapter 3.

Becoming Acculturated Research suggests that it may be healthiest for people in a new country to retain the values, language, and other trappings of their ethnic background while they also gain the ability to navigate successfully within their host country. If you have the opportunity, become (or remain) bilingual. Nurture all parts of you, including interests within your own sociocultural background as well as within the dominant culture.

Each of the major approaches to understanding personality and behavior has a number of strengths to recommend it, and a number of drawbacks, or at least question marks. Each theory views the "elephant" from a different perspective, but each sheds light on aspects of human nature.

Adjustment in a World of DIVERSITY

One Nation Under Gods[2]

Although the United States fosters the freedom to practice or not to practice a religion, it is one of the more religious nations in the world. Religion is one of the shapers of human beliefs, attitudes, and behavior. People's religions reflect and contribute to human nature. Religions not only provide a sense of people's place in the universe and moral codes of conduct, but they also provide traditions that help people adjust to life cycle events such as birth, marriage, and death. In Chapter 1 we explored diversity in the United States in terms of ethnicity and gender. In this chapter we consider religious diversity.

There has never been a nation so religiously diverse as the United States. With new immigrants, the country becomes ever more diverse each year. Not only does the United States continue to house the various Judeo-Christian faiths that populated the original colonies, but there are now 700 to 800 other denominations. Half of these are imported varieties of standard world religions, mostly from Asia. Then there is the chaotic and creative mix of U.S.-born religions.

While adding creeds new to the United States, recent immigration has also increased the varieties of Christianity. Hispanic Americans have brought a fervent sensibility into U.S. Catholicism. They challenge a church hierarchy that remains dominated to some degree by the descendants of Irish immigrants, who, because of dwindling numbers, are trying to recruit Hispanic priests. Spanish-speaking peoples are also being recruited by Pentecostal and Baptist missionaries. Koreans, meanwhile, have brought an evangelistic zeal back to Protestantism.

---

[2] Most of the information for this feature is derived from Richard N. Ostling (Fall 1993), One nation under Gods: Not without conflict, an unprecedented variety of faiths blooms across the land, *Time, 142* (21), 62–63.

THE NATION'S CONSENSUS FAITH Although Christianity still accounts for 9 Americans in 10, talk of a "Christian nation" is increasingly inaccurate. Instead, the country's consensus faith is a biblical monotheism, which includes Judaism and a major new player, Islam. Islam is expanding rapidly both through immigration and conversion of African Americans. The Interfaith Conference of Metropolitan Washington includes Muslims alongside Catholics, Protestants, Jews, Mormons, and Sikhs. Hindus may soon follow, as may Buddhists and Baha'is.

Despite some doctrinal hostility, America remains by and large tolerant. In places like Beirut, Belfast, Bombay, and Bosnia, interreligious conflicts are being fought out in the streets. In the United States, the same conflicts are usually argued out in courtrooms, zoning boards, and school boards. Consider some recent events in the state of Georgia, where Protestantism once reigned supreme. A number of Baptists recently joined non-Christians to prevent the state from erecting a statue of Jesus along a highway. A prison inmate is suing to keep the dreadlocks that are mandated by his Rastafarian faith. Atlanta Muslims have won from their employer the right to attend Friday worship, and Muslim women are planning to petition to be able to obtain a driver's license without removing their veils for license photos. A family of agnostic Native Americans persuaded the federal courts to prohibit prayers before high school football games.

HERE, TOO, AMERICANIZATION Although newly emerging religions may encounter conflict with society at large, in subtle ways they are Americanizing their operations. For example, many Asians now incorporate their temples and organize their boards just as churches and synagogues do. As a result, lay leaders may bear more authority than spiritual leaders do. U.S. holidays such as the Fourth of July and New Year's may be meaningless in traditional religious terms but are adopted for significant gatherings. Although Sunday has no religious significance for Hindus as it does for Christians, Sunday is nevertheless the most crowded day for worship at the Hindu Temple in New York City.

ISLAMIC GUIDELINES The temptation to Americanize is often resisted when it encroaches on basic religious tenets, however. For example, the guidelines for public school administrators published by the Islamic Society of North America entreats schools to honor the needs of Muslim students. The guidelines request that boys and girls be seated separately, that Islamic students be exempted from drama and music classes, that they be permitted to attend afternoon prayers, and that they be allowed to wear gym clothing that is consistent with Islamic traditions of modesty.

Whether they are Hispanic American Catholics, traditionally minded Korean Protestants, Hindus, or Muslims, the faithful in the United States also tend to be exposed to influences like Madonna, Beavis and Butthead, and R-rated movies. Personality formation in this nation clearly reflects diverse influences.

adjustment and modern life

Students are often frustrated after reading about different psychological theories of human nature. Which theory, they want to know, is the real one? The true theory? The fact of the matter is that human nature is so rich, so complex, that no single theory has been able to capture it completely. If you think about it, that fact should make you happy, even a bit smug. Don't be frustrated by it.

In this "Adjustment and Modern Life" section, we first consider what each theory has to offer. Then we consider some of the concrete contributions made by behavioral concepts of classical and operant conditioning.

UNDERSTANDING YOURSELF: WILL THE ONE TRUE THEORY OF HUMAN NATURE PLEASE STAND UP?

Despite their diversity, each theory touches on meaningful aspects of human nature. Rather than worry about which is the one true theory, why not consider how each might contribute to your self-understanding? Let us put together a list of some of the basic ideas set forth by these theories. Each item on the list might not apply equally to everyone, but such a list might reflect something of what you see in yourself and in other people. Let's try it out:

1. Early childhood experiences can have lasting influences on us.
2. Our cognitive processes can be distorted so that we may see what we want to see and hear what we want to hear.
3. Some of your traits, such as your intelligence, outgoingness, emotional stability, social dominance, and your interest in arts and crafts may be in part genetically determined.
4. It is useful to consider seeking jobs and social activities that are compatible with your psychological traits. (Rather than focusing on your limitations, why not take steps to learn about your individual talents, strengths, and interests so that you can develop yourself to the fullest as a unique individual?)
5. We are influenced by our circumstances as well as by inner preferences, talents, and emotional conflicts.
6. Experience can lead us to anticipate events with pleasure or fear.
7. We generally seek rewards and avoid punishments.
8. We model much of our behavior after that of people we observe, especially those we admire.
9. We are more likely to persevere in difficult tasks when we believe that our efforts will pay off.
10. Our conceptions of who we are and what we can do have an impact on our behavior.

11. Each of us has something unique to offer, although it may not always seem very important to other people.
12. We are, to some degree, the architects of our own personalities and of the abilities we choose to develop.
13. When we close ourselves off to new experiences, we are less likely to find things that are of value to us and to develop as individuals.
14. We strive to become like our mental images of what we are capable of being.
15. Our behavior and personalities are affected by our sociocultural backgrounds.

What is your mental image of what you are capable of being? Are you comfortable with that image? If not, what will you do about it?

TAKING CHARGE OF FEARS

Each theory has given rise to ways in which psychologists have helped people meet the challenges of contemporary life. Psychodynamic theory, for example, spawned psychoanalysis, a method of psychotherapy that aims to help clients uncover unconscious childhood conflicts and find ways of coping with them to attain a reasonable amount of gratification as adults. Psychoanalysis and other methods of therapy will be fully described and evaluated in Chapter 10.

Trait theorists have helped develop psychological tests to measure traits. These tests have been used to help diagnose psychological disorders (see Chapter 9) and to help point clients toward careers that fit their interests and abilities.

Behaviorists have devised methods of therapy that might not have been derived from other theoretical perspectives. Consider the fear-reduction methods of flooding, systematic desensitization, and counterconditioning.

Flooding

Flooding is based on extinction. In this method, a person is exposed to a fear-evoking but harmless stimulus until fear is extinguished. Watson and Rayner did not extinguish Little Albert's fear of the laboratory rat, but they might have been able to reduce or eliminate his fear by placing him in contact with the rat until fear became fully extinguished. Technically speaking, the CS (in this case, the rat) would be presented repeatedly in the absence of the US (clanging of the steel bars) until the CR (fear) became extinguished.

Systematic Desensitization

Flooding is usually effective, but it is unpleasant. When you are afraid of rats, sharing a room with one is not a holiday. For this reason, behavior therapists often prefer a second method, systematic desensitization. In this method, people are gradually exposed to fear-evoking stimuli under circumstances in which they remain relaxed. Systematic desensitization is described more fully in Chapters 10 and 11. Systematic desensitization, like flooding, is highly effective. It takes longer to work but is less unpleasant.

Counterconditioning

Some psychologists explain systematic desensitization as extinguishing fear gradually, in progressive amounts. Others explain it in terms of counterconditioning; by remaining relaxed in the presence of fear-evoking stimuli, we associate, or condition, feelings of relaxation to these stimuli. Feelings of relaxation then *counteract* our fear responses—hence the term, *counter*conditioning.

In counterconditioning, one pairs a pleasant stimulus with a fear-evoking object in order to counteract the fear response. Consider a historic application of this principle. Eating sweets is a pleasant activity for most of us (sigh), and psychologists discovered early in the twentieth century that a rabbit could be gradually introduced into a room where a boy, Peter, who feared rabbits was eating cookies (Jones, 1924). The pleasure from the cookies counteracted fear and apparently generalized to, or "rubbed off on," the rabbit, so that the animal could be brought closer gradually without causing discomfort. Eventually Peter played with it.

Truth or Fiction Revisited

It is true that a psychologist helped a young boy overcome his fear of rabbits by having him eat cookies while a rabbit was brought nearer and nearer to him. This is how University of California psychologist Mary Cover Jones counterconditioned "Peter's" fear of rabbits.

GETTING IN TOUCH WITH THE UNTOUCHABLE THROUGH BIOFEEDBACK TRAINING

Biofeedback training (BFT) is based on principles of operant conditioning. It has been an important innovation in the treatment of health-related problems and has allowed people to gain control over automatic functions like blood pressure and heart rate.

In a landmark series of experiments on BFT, Neal E. Miller (1969) placed electrodes in the "pleasure centers" of rats' brains. Electrical stimulation of these centers is reinforcing. The heart rates of the rats were monitored. One group of rats received electrical stimulation (reinforcement) when their heart rates increased. Another group received stimulation when their heart rates decreased. After a single 90-minute training session, the rats had altered their heart rates by as much as 20 percent in the targeted direction. Somehow laboratory rats had learned to manipulate their heart rate—an autonomic function—because of reinforcement. Human beings can also gain control over autonomic functions such as heart rate and blood pressure through BFT. Moreover, they can improve control over voluntary health-related functions, such as muscle tension in various parts of the body.

When people receive BFT, reinforcement takes the form of information, not electrical stimulation of the brain. The targeted biological function is monitored, by instruments such as the electroencephalograph (EEG) for brain waves, the electromyograph (EMG) for muscle tension, and the blood pressure cuff.

A "bleep" on an electronic console can change in pitch or frequency to signal a bodily change in the desired direction. Brain waves referred to as alpha waves tend to be emitted when we are relaxed. By pasting or taping electrodes to our scalps, and providing us with feedback about the brain waves we are emitting, we can learn to emit alpha waves more frequently—and, as a result, to feel more relaxed. The "bleep" can be sounded more frequently whenever alpha waves are emitted, and the biofeedback instructor can simply instruct

Truth or Fiction Revisited

It is true that you can learn to raise your heart rate or to lower your blood pressure by being hooked up to a machine that "bleeps" when you make the desired response. The method is called *biofeedback training.*

clients to "make the bleep go faster." Muscle tension in the forehead or the arm can be monitored by the EMG, and people can learn to lower tension by means of "bleeps" and instructions. But lessened muscle tension is usually signaled by a slower rate of bleeping. Lowered muscle tension also induces feelings of relaxation.

CONTROLLING BAD HABITS THROUGH AVERSIVE CONDITIONING

Aversive conditioning is another method based on operant conditioning. It has been used to help people control harmful habits, such as smoking or excessive drinking. In this method, painful or aversive stimuli are paired with drug abuse or abuse-related stimuli to render the substance less appealing. In the case of excessive drinking, tastes of alcoholic beverages are frequently connected with drug-induced nausea and vomiting or with electric shock. As a result, alcohol may come to evoke an aversive conditioned response, like fear or nausea, that inhibits drinking. Avoidance of alcohol is negatively reinforced by relief from fear or nausea.

One large-scale study of aversive conditioning in the treatment of alcoholism found that 63 percent of 685 people treated stayed abstinent for 1 year afterward. Nearly one third remained abstinent for at least 3 years (Wiens & Menustik, 1983). However, do the effects of aversive conditioning last? Aversively conditioned responses are apparently readily extinguished because exposure to alcohol in real-life settings is not paired with aversive stimuli.

Truth or Fiction Revisited

It is true that a treatment designed to help people to stop smoking cigarettes involves smoking cigarettes. However, the cigarettes are smoked excessively, as in the technique called *rapid smoking*.

Aversive conditioning for smoking aims to make smoke aversive through some kind of overexposure. In rapid smoking, smokers inhale frequently, about once every 6 seconds, until they begin to feel nauseated. Nausea acts as an unconditioned stimulus that becomes connected with stimuli like the taste and aroma of cigarette smoke and the feel of the cigarette between the fingers. After repeated pairings, cigarette smoke becomes aversive and smokers are motivated to avert nausea by quitting. All in all, however, the long-term results of aversive conditioning in maintaining abstinence have been only poorly to modestly successful. Taylor and colleagues (1991) report an average quit rate across studies of rapid smoking at 1-year follow-ups of 25 percent. Interest in rapid smoking appears to have waned because of questions about the safety of inhaling so much nicotine and carbon monoxide so quickly, and because of the availability of nicotine-replacement methods such as gum and skin patches. ■

Summary

1. **What are the major features of the psychodynamic view of human nature?** Freud's psychodynamic view of human nature suggests that our behavior is determined by the outcome of internal and largely unconscious conflict. Conflict is inevitable as the primitive instincts of sex and aggression come up against social pressures to follow laws, rules, and moral codes.
2. **What are the three psychic structures and how do they function?** The unconscious id represents psychological drives. The ego is the sense of self, or "I," and seeks realistic ways of gratifying the id. The superego acts like a conscience, handing out judgments of right and wrong.
3. **What are the stages of psychosexual development?** People undergo psychosexual development as psychosexual energy, or libido is transferred from one erogenous zone to another. There are five stages of psychosexual development: the oral, anal, phallic, latency, and genital stages.
4. **What is the Oedipus complex?** The Oedipus complex is a conflict of the phallic stage. In this conflict, children long to possess the parent of the opposite gender and resent the parent of the same gender. Under normal circumstances, these complexes eventually become resolved by identifying with the parent of the same gender.
5. **How do neoanalysts' views differ from Freud's?** Most neoanalysts downplay the importance of the sexual instinct. Jung believed in the Self, a unifying force in the personality that provides us with direction and purpose. Adler believed that people are basically motivated by an inferiority complex, and that this complex gives rise to a compensating drive for superiority. Horney was more optimistic than Freud about children's ability to overcome early emotional hardships. Erikson highlights the importance of early social relationships rather than the gratification of childhood sexual impulses and extended Freud's five developmental stages to eight.
6. **What is the focus of trait theory?** Trait theory catalogues human traits and assumes that they are largely inherited. Eysenck theorized that there are two key personality dimensions: introversion-extraversion and emotional stability. More recent research adds another three basic traits: conscientiousness, agreeableness, and openness to new experience.
7. **What are the views of the behaviorists?** John B. Watson, the father of modern behaviorism, rejected notions of mind and personality altogether. Watson and B. F. Skinner discarded notions of personal freedom, and argued that environmental contingencies can shape people into wanting to do the things that the physical environment and society require of them. Behaviorists explain behavior in terms of conditioning.
8. **What are the views of social-cognitive theory?** Social-cognitive theory focuses on the importance of person variables in individual differences: competencies, encoding strategies, expectancies, emotions, and self-regulatory systems and plans.
9. **What do phenomenological theories have in common?** Phenomenological theories each propose that the personal, or subjective, experiencing of events is the most important aspect of human nature. They also propose that we each have unique ways of perceiving the world.
10. **What are the major ideas of Abraham Maslow's phenomenological theory?** Maslow believed that we are motivated by self-actualization—the urge to become everything we are capable of being. He stated that people traveled up through a hierarchy of needs, with biological needs at the bottom and self-actualization at the top.
11. **What are the major ideas of Carl Rogers's self theory?** According to Rogers, the self is an innate, organized, and consistent way in which a person perceives his or her "I" to relate to others and the world. The self attempts to develop its unique potential when the person receives unconditional positive regard.
12. **What is sociocultural theory?** Sociocultural theory focuses on the roles of ethnicity, gender, culture, and socioeconomic status in personality formation, behavior, and mental processes. Sociocultural theorists are interested in issues such as individualism versus collectivism and the effects of discrimination and acculturation on the sense of self.

The Challenges of Life

Chapter 3

Social Perception: How We See Others and Ourselves

Truth or Fiction?

T	F	
☐	☐	First impressions last.
☐	☐	Waitresses who touch their patrons while making change receive higher tips.
☐	☐	A rose by any other name, contrary to William Shakespeare, could smell just plain awful.
☐	☐	Children with strict parents have higher self-esteem than children with permissive parents.
☐	☐	We can build our self-esteem by becoming good at something.
☐	☐	We hold other people responsible for their misdeeds, but we tend to see ourselves as victims of circumstances.
☐	☐	We tend to attribute our successes to our abilities and hard work, but we attribute our failures to external factors such as lack of time or obstacles placed in our paths by others.
☐	☐	Children who have been victims of discrimination are less likely to practice discrimination themselves.
☐	☐	Contact between members of different racial groups can reduce feelings of prejudice.
☐	☐	One way of combating prejudice is to seek compliance with the law.
☐	☐	The self-esteem of an average student may exceed that of a scholar.

OUTLINE

You say you've had it tough getting from place to place? You complain that you've waited in lines at airports, or you've been stuck in freeway traffic? These are ordeals, to be sure, but according to Greek mythology, some ancient travelers had a harder time of it. They met up with a highwayman named Procrustes (pronounced "pro-CRUSS-tease").

Procrustes had a quirk. Not only was he interested in travelers' pocketbooks, but also in their height. He had a concept—a **schema**—of how tall people should be. When people did not fit his schema, they were in for it. You see, Procrustes also had a very famous bed—a "Procrustean bed." He made his victims lie in the bed. When they were too short for it, he stretched them to make them fit. When they were too long for it, he is said to have practiced surgery on their legs. Many unfortunate passersby failed to survive.

ON SOCIAL PERCEPTION AND SCHEMAS: PROCESSING SOCIAL INFORMATION

The myth of Procrustes may sound absurd, but it reflects a quirky truth about us as well. We all carry cognitive Procrustean beds around with us—our unique ways of perceiving the world. And we try to make things and people fit. Many of us carry around the Procrustean beds of gender-role stereotypes—an example of a **role schema**—and we try to fit men and women into them. For example, when the career woman oversteps the bounds of the male chauvinist's role schema, he metaphorically chops off her legs.

We carry many other kinds of schemas around with us, and they influence our adjustment and personal development. Some are **person schemas**, as formed, for example, by first impressions. Our first impressions of others often form schemas, or kinds of cognitive anchors, that color our future observations. Other schemas concern our ways of "reading" body language. We infer personality traits from behavior. Other schemas concern groups of people; they involve prejudices concerning racial and ethnic groups. We shall examine the origins of prejudice and make a number of suggestions as to what you can do about prejudice when it affects you.

We shall also see that we carry inward-directed schemas, or **self-schemas,** in the form of self-concepts and self-ideals. Self-schemas affect our feelings about ourselves and influence our behavior. Finally, we shall see that we carry schemas that influence the ways in which we interpret the successes and shortcomings of other people and ourselves. These particular schemas are called "attributions," and they have a major impact on our relationships with others.

Schema • A set of beliefs and feelings about something. Examples include stereotypes, prejudices, and generalizations.

Role schema • A schema about how people in certain roles (e.g., boss, wife, teacher) are expected to behave.

Person schema • A schema about how a particular individual is expected to behave.

Self-schema • The set of beliefs, feelings, and generalizations we have about ourselves.

As we progress, a theme will emerge: We do not perceive other people and ourselves directly. Instead, we process information about others and ourselves through our schemas. We perceive the social and the personal worlds as through a glass—and sometimes darkly. And when other people do not quite fit our schemas, we have a way of perceptually stretching them or of chopping off their legs. Ironically, we do not spare ourselves this cognitive pruning.

PERCEPTION OF OTHERS

Let us begin by seeing how first impressions prompt the development of schemas that resist change. Then we shall discuss our schemas concerning body language and prejudice.

Primacy and Recency Effects: The Importance of First Impressions

Why do you wear your best outfit to an interview for an attractive job? Why do defense attorneys dress their clients immaculately before they go before the jury? Because first impressions are important.

When one of us was a teenager, a young man was accepted or rejected by his date's parents the first time they met. If he was considerate and made small talk, her parents would allow them to stay out past curfew, even to attend "submarine races" at the beach. If he was boorish or uncommunicative, he was a cad forever. Her parents would object to him, no matter how hard he worked to gain their favor later on.

First impressions often make or break us. This is the **primacy effect.** We tend to infer traits, or to form person schemas, from behavior. If we act considerately at first, we are labeled considerate. The trait of considerateness is used to explain and predict our future behavior. If, after being labeled considerate, one keeps a date out past curfew, this behavior is likely to be seen as an exception to a rule—as justified by circumstances or external factors. But if at first one is seen as inconsiderate, several months of considerate behavior may be perceived as a cynical effort to "make up for it" or to camouflage one's "real personality."

Truth or Fiction Revisited

It is true that first impressions last. First impressions are not engraved in stone, however. New information, or advice to focus on all the evidence, can modify them.

In a classic experiment on the primacy effect, psychologist Abraham Luchins (1957) had subjects read different stories about "Jim." The stories consisted of one or two paragraphs. One-paragraph stories portrayed Jim as friendly or unfriendly. These paragraphs were also used in the two-paragraph stories, but presented to different subjects in opposite order. Of subjects reading only the "friendly" paragraph, 95 percent rated Jim as friendly. Of those who read just the "unfriendly" paragraph, 3 percent rated him as friendly. Seventy-eight percent of those who read two-paragraph stories in the "friendly-unfriendly" order labeled Jim as friendly. But when they read the paragraphs in the reverse order, only 18 percent rated Jim as friendly.

How can we encourage people to pay more attention to more recent impressions? Luchins accomplished this by allowing time to elapse between presenting the paragraphs. In this way, fading memories allowed more recent information to take precedence. We call the phenomenon in which the most recent impressions govern the formation of the person schema the **recency effect.** Luchins found a second way to counter first impressions: He simply counseled subjects to avoid snap judgments and to weigh all the evidence.

PRIMACY EFFECT • The tendency to evaluate others in terms of first impressions.

RECENCY EFFECT • The tendency to evaluate others in terms of the most recent impression.

BODY LANGUAGE. We infer much about people's thoughts and feelings from their body language. What does the body language of this couple suggest about their feelings toward one another?

Body Language

Body language provides important information about other people's thoughts and feelings. They contribute heavily to our person schemas.

ON BEING "UPTIGHT" AND "HANGING LOOSE" The ways that people carry themselves provide cues as to how they feel and are likely to behave. When people are "uptight," their bodies are often rigid and straight-backed. Relaxed people often literally "hang loose." Various combinations of eye contact, posture, and distance between people provide cues as to their moods and their feelings toward their companions.

When people face us and lean toward us, we may assume that they like us or are interested in us. If we are privy to a conversation between a couple and observe that the woman is leaning toward the man but that he is sitting back and toying with his hair, we may rightly infer that he is not having any of what she is selling (DePaulo and others, 1978).

Truth or Fiction Revisited

It is true that waitresses who touch their patrons while making change receive higher tips. Touching often induces positive behavior.

TOUCHING Touching also communicates. Women are more likely than men to touch other people when they are interacting with them (Stier & Hall, 1984). In one touching experiment, Kleinke (1977) showed that appeals for help can be more effective when the distressed person engages in physical contact with people being asked for aid. A woman received more dimes for phone calls when she touched the arm of the person she was asking for money. Similarly, waitresses who touch customers' arms are likely to receive higher tips.

In these experiments, touching was noncontroversial. It was usually gentle, brief, and done in familiar settings. However, when touching suggests greater intimacy than is desired, it can be seen as negative. A study in a nursing home found that responses to being touched depended on factors such as the status of the staff member, the type of touch, and the part of the body that was touched (Hollinger & Buschmann, 1993). Touching was considered positive when it was appropriate to the situation and did not appear to be condescending. It was seen as negative when it was controlling, unnecessary, or overly intimate. Put it this way: If you do it wrong, people may be touchy about your touching them.

GAZING AND STARING: THE EYES HAVE IT We usually feel that we can learn much from eye contact. When other people "look us squarely in the eye," we may assume that they are being assertive or open with us. Avoidance of eye contact may suggest deception or depression. Gazing is interpreted as a sign of liking or friendliness (Kleinke, 1986). In one penetrating study, men and women were asked to gaze into each other's eyes for two minutes (Kellerman and others, 1989). After doing so, they reported having passionate feelings toward one another. (Watch out!)

Gazes are different, of course, from persistent "hard" stares. Hard stares are interpreted as provocations or signs of anger (Ellsworth & Langer, 1976). When the first author was in high school, adolescent males engaged in "staring contests" to assert their dominance. The adolescent who looked away first "lost."

In a series of field experiments, Phoebe Ellsworth and her colleagues (1972) subjected drivers stopped at red lights to hard stares from riders of motor scooters. Recipients of the stares crossed the intersection more rapidly than other drivers did when the light changed. Greenbaum and Rosenfeld (1978) found that recipients of hard stares from a man seated near an intersection also drove off more rapidly after the light turned green (see Figure 3.1).

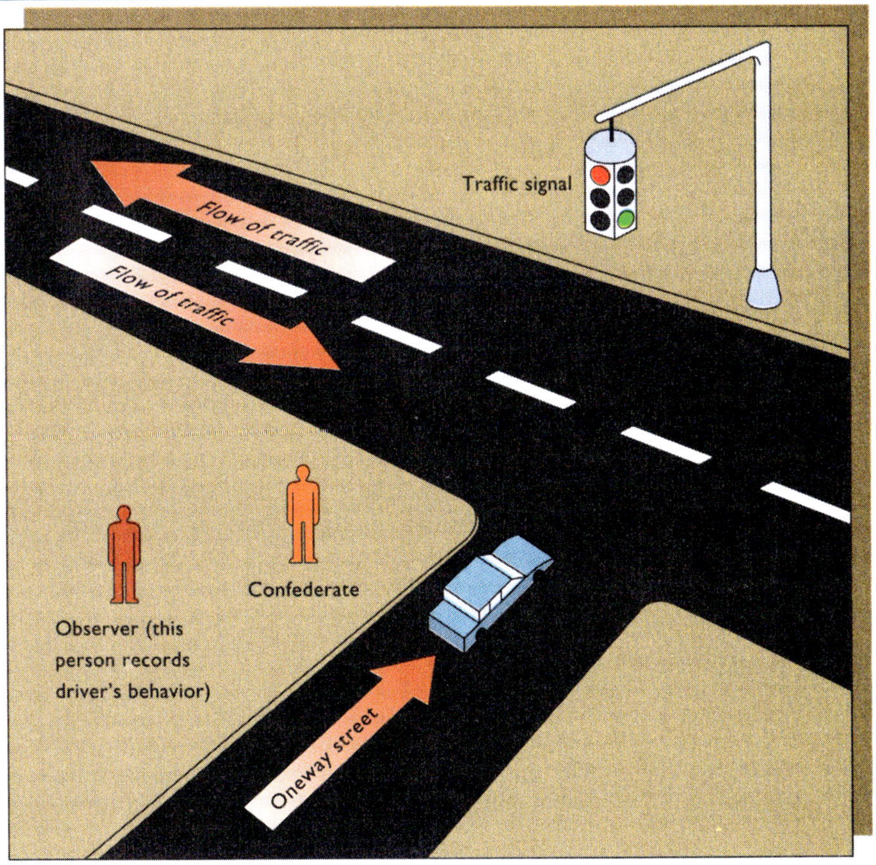

FIGURE 3.1
DIAGRAM OF AN EXPERIMENT IN HARD STARING AND AVOIDANCE.
In the Greenbaum and Rosenfeld study, the confederate of the experimenter stared at some drivers and not at others. Recipients of the stares drove across the intersection more rapidly once the light turned green. Why?

Prejudice

> *Too often we consider race as something only Blacks have, sex orientation as something only gays have, gender as something only women have. If we don't fall into any of these categories, then we don't have to worry.*
>
> HENRY LOUIS GATES, JR., CHAIR, HARVARD UNIVERSITY'S AFRICAN AMERICAN STUDIES DEPARTMENT

> *I imagine one of the reasons people cling to their hates so stubbornly is because they sense, once hate is gone, they will be forced to deal with pain.*
>
> JAMES BALDWIN

People have condemned billions of other people. Without ever meeting them. Without ever learning their names.

Prejudice is an attitude toward a group that leads people to evaluate members of that group negatively. As a person schema, prejudice is linked to expectations that the target group will behave badly, in the workplace, say, or by engaging in criminal activity. On an emotional, or **affective**, level, prejudice is associated with negative feelings such as dislike or hatred. Behaviorally, prejudice is associated with avoidance behavior, aggression, and discrimination.

SEXISM, RACISM, AND AGEISM Women are often expected to produce inferior work. This form of prejudice is called sexism. In **racism**, one race or ethnic group holds negative person schemas of, or attitudes toward, the other. For example, many white Americans are more likely than African Americans to assume that African Americans are guilty of crimes of violence. African Americans, by contrast, are more likely to attribute guilt for such crimes to white Americans (Ugwuegbu, 1979).

In recent years, we have become more sensitive to **ageism.** "Ageists" assume that the elderly are less capable of performing on the job, that they will hold old-fashioned moral and political views, and that they are easily irritated, or "crotchety." Many ageists assume that senior citizens cannot (or should not) engage in sexual activity (Rathus and others, 1997). None of these schemas necessarily conforms to the facts. Yet senior citizens may also acquire the schemas and disqualify themselves from productive work or sex.

DISCRIMINATION **Discrimination** is one form of negative behavior that results from prejudice. Many groups have been discriminated against from time to time in the United States. They include, but are not limited to, African Americans, Asian Americans, Hispanic Americans, Irish Americans, Jewish Americans, Native Americans, gay males and lesbians, the aged, and women (Takaki, 1993). Discrimination takes many forms, including denial of access to jobs, housing, even the voting booth. Many people have forgotten that African Americans gained the right to vote decades before it was obtained by women.

STEREOTYPES Are women emotional? Are Jews shrewd? Are African Americans flashy? Are Asians inscrutable? If you believe such ideas, you are falling for stereotyped person schemas—prejudices about a group that can lead us to process information about members of these groups in a biased fashion. Table 3.1 shows common stereotypes about cultural and ethnic groups. Do you believe any of these stereotypes? What is the evidence for your beliefs?

PREJUDICE • The belief that a person or group, on the basis of assumed racial, ethnic, sexual, or other features, will possess negative characteristics or perform inadequately.

AFFECTIVE • Emotional.

RACISM • The preconception that a person, on the basis of race, will perform inadequately or have negative characteristics.

AGEISM • The preconception that a person, on the basis of age, will perform inadequately or have negative characteristics.

DISCRIMINATION • The denial of privileges to a person or group on the basis of prejudice.

Stereotyping.
How well is this child doing? Research shows that our expectations concerning a child's performance on a test are linked to our awareness of that child's socioeconomic background.

TABLE 3.1 SOME STEREOTYPES OF ETHNIC GROUPS WITHIN THE UNITED STATES

African Americans Physically powerful and well coordinated Unclean Unintelligent and superstitious Musically talented Excellent as lovers Lazy Emotional and aggressive Flashy (gaudy clothes and big cars)	**Irish Americans** Sexually repressed Heavy drinkers Overly religious Political and nationalistic Outgoing, witty, and literary Hot-tempered ("fighting Irish")	**Jewish Americans** Cheap, shrewd in business Clannish Control banks, Wall Street, and the media Wealthy and showy Big-nosed Pushy Smothering mother
Chinese Americans Deceitful Inscrutable Wise Cruel Polite, quiet, and deferential Possessing strong family ties Law-abiding	**Italian Americans** Overly interested in food Ignorant, suspicious of education Clannish Great singers Great shoemakers and barbers Hot-tempered and violent Connected to the Mafia Talk with their hands Cowardly in battle	**Polish Americans** Unintelligent and uneducated Overly religious Dirty Racist, bigoted Boorish, uncultured
Hispanic Americans Macho Unwilling to learn English Disinterested in education Not concerned about being on welfare Warm, expressive Lazy Hot-tempered and violent	**Japanese Americans** Ambitious, hardworking, and competitive Intelligent, well educated Obedient, servile women Sneaky Poor lovers Possessing strong family ties Great imitators, not originators Law-abiding	**White Anglo-Saxon Protestants (WASPs)** Hardworking, ambitious, thrifty Honorable Wealthy, powerful Insensitive, emotionally cold Polite, well mannered, genteel Snobbish Guilt-ridden do-gooders

Stereotypes are fixed, conventional ideas about groups of people and can give rise to prejudice and discrimination. Do you believe the stereotypes listed in this table? What is the evidence for your beliefs?
Sources: W. Kornblum, (1997), *Sociology in a changing world,* 4th ed., Fort Worth: Harcourt Brace College Publishers; R. Takaki, (1993), *A different mirror: A history of multicultural America,* Boston: Little, Brown & Company.

SOURCES OF PREJUDICE The sources of prejudice are many and varied. Let us consider some contributors.

1. *Assumptions of Dissimilarity.* We are apt to like people who share our attitudes. In forming impressions of others, we are influenced by attitudinal similarity and dissimilarity (Duckitt, 1992). People of different religions and races often have different backgrounds, however, giving rise to dissimilar attitudes. Even when people of different races share important values, they may assume that they do not.
2. *Social Conflict.* There is also a lengthy history of social and economic conflict between people of different races and religions. For example, Southern Whites and African Americans have competed for jobs, giving rise to negative attitudes, even lynchings (Hepworth & West, 1988).
3. *Social Learning.* Children acquire some attitudes from others, especially parents. Children tend to imitate their parents, and parents reinforce their children for doing so (Duckitt, 1992). In this way, prejudices can be transmitted from generation to generation.
4. *Information Processing.* One cognitive view is that prejudices act as cognitive filters through which we perceive the social world. Prejudice is a way of processing social information. It is easier to attend to, and remember, instances of behavior that are consistent with our prejudices than it is to reconstruct our mental categories (Bodenhausen, 1988; Devine, 1989; Dovidio and others, 1986; Fiske, 1989). If you believe that Jews are stingy, it is easier to recall a Jew's negotiation of a price than a Jew's charitable donation. If you believe that Californians are "airheads," it may be easier to recall TV images of surfing than of scientific conferences at Caltech and Berkeley.
5. *Social Categorization.* A second cognitive perspective focuses on people's tendencies to divide the social world into "us" and "them." People usually view those who belong to their own groups—the "ingroup"—more favorably than those who do not—the "outgroup" (Duckitt, 1992; Linville and others, 1989; Schaller & Maas, 1989). Moreover, there is a tendency for us to assume that outgroup members are more alike, or homogeneous, in their attitudes and behavior than members of our own groups (Judd & Park, 1988; Wilder, 1986). Our isolation from outgroup members makes it easier to maintain our stereotypes.
6. *Victimization by Prejudice.* Ironically, people who have been victims of prejudice sometimes attempt to gain a sense of pride by asserting superiority over other socioeconomic or ethnic groups (Van Brunt, 1994). For example, *some* Irish immigrants who had been subjected to prejudice and discrimination by British Americans then discriminated against Polish and Italian Americans. *Some* Polish and Italian Americans then discriminated against African Americans. *Some* African Americans then discriminated against recent waves of Hispanic Americans and Asian Americans. In many cases, of course, experiencing discrimination leads people to *combat* prejudice and discrimination.

SELF-PERCEPTION

Some of our most important person schemas are directed inward. These schemas are called *self-schemas.* Our self-schemas influence our behavior and the ways that we feel about ourselves.

In this section we define what is meant by the self and explore the parts of the self: the physical, social, and personal selves. We see that aspects of our personal selves include our names, values, self-concepts, even our self-efficacy expectations. All can contribute to, and reflect, our adjustment and personal growth.

The Self as a Guiding Principle of Personality

Many psychologists have written about the **self.** The psychodynamic theorists Carl Jung and Alfred Adler both spoke of a self (or Self) that serves as a guiding principle of personality. Erik Erikson and Carl Rogers spoke of ways in which we are, to some degree, the conscious architects of ourselves. Your self is your ongoing sense of who and what you are, your sense of how and why you react to the environment, and, more important, how you choose to act on your environment. To Rogers, the sense of self is inborn—a "given." It is an essential part of the experience of being human in the world, and the guiding principle behind personality structure and behavior.

Let us consider some parts of the self.

The Parts of the Self

In this section we discuss the physical self, the social self, and the personal self.

THE PHYSICAL SELF The physical person you carry around with you plays an enormously influential role in your self-concept. You may tower above others or always have to look up to them—literally. Because of your physical appearance, others may smile and seek your gaze, or they may pretend that you do not exist. Your health and conditioning may be such that you assume that you will be up to athletic challenges or that the sporting life is not for you. *The New Our Bodies, Ourselves* (Boston Women's Health Book Collective, 1993) emphasizes repeatedly how having female features and sex organs is intertwined with women's self-identities. Men's features and organs are no less central to their self-concepts.

SELF • The totality of our impressions, thoughts, and feelings, such that we have a conscious, continuous sense of being in the world.

THE PHYSICAL SELF.
The physical person we carry around with us has an enormous influence on our self-concepts. Because of our physical appearance, others may smile at us and seek our gaze. Or, they may shudder or act as though we do not exist. The social approval or disapproval we receive can foster very different patterns of self-esteem.

How Content Are You With Your Physical Self?

Imagine a future society in which cosmetic surgery and other methods allowed you to have your entire body sculpted to your exact specifications. You might leaf through a "Whole Human Catalogue" and select your preferred dimensions of face and form. Then your physical self would spring forth custom-made.

But could satisfaction be guaranteed? Would nonclassic forms such as Barbra Streisand's nose or Clark Gable's ears be tolerated in this mix-and-match society? Would there be one perfect body and one perfect face, or would some people select less than "ideal" features to lend their physical selves an air of individuality? And when everyone is beautiful, does the allure of beauty fade away?

How satisfied are you with your physical features? Complete the following questionnaire, and then check the Appendix to compare your satisfaction with your physical self to that expressed by *Psychology Today* readers. ■

Directions: For each of the following, check the column that indicates your degree of satisfaction or dissatisfaction.

Body Part	**Quite or Extremely Dissatisfied**	**Somewhat Dissatisfied**	**Somewhat Satisfied**	**Quite or Extremely Satisfied**
My overall body appearance				
FACE				
overall facial attractiveness				
hair				
eyes				
ears				
nose				
mouth				
teeth				
voice				
chin				
complexion				
EXTREMITIES				
shoulders				
arms				
hands				
feet				
MID-TORSO				
size of abdomen				
buttocks (seat)				
hips (upper thighs)				
legs and ankles				
HEIGHT, WEIGHT, AND TONE				
height				
weight				
general muscle tone or development				

Source: Berscheid, Walster, and Bohrnstedt, 1973.

Whereas some aspects of the physical self, such as hair length and weight, change as we grow, gender and race are permanent features of our physical identities. For most of us, adjustment to traits such as height, gender, and race is connected with our self-acceptance and self-esteem (Steinem, 1992). Other physical traits, such as weight, athletic condition, and hairstyle, can be modified. Our determination, behavior, and choices can be more influential than heredity in shaping these latter aspects of the self.

Adjustment in a World of DIVERSITY

African American Women—Happier With Themselves

Large numbers of Americans, particularly American women, are dissatisfied with their physical selves (Williams, 1992). Many, if not most, women would prefer to be thinner. Jennifer Brenner (1992), a psychology professor at Brandeis University, notes that women models, who tend to represent the female ideal, are 9 percent taller and 16 percent slimmer than the average woman.

Despite the persistence of racial prejudices, a survey by the American Association of University Women (1991) found that African American girls are likely to be happier with the way they are than White girls. Sixty-five percent of African American elementary schoolgirls said they were happy with the way they were, as compared to 55 percent of White girls. By high school age, however, 58 percent of African American girls remained happy with the way they were, as compared with only 22 percent of White girls. Why the great discrepancy? It appears that the parents of African American girls teach them that there is nothing wrong with them if they do not match the American ideal; the world treats them negatively because of prejudice (Williams, 1992). The White girls are more likely to look inward and blame themselves for not attaining the unreachable American ideal.

In later chapters we shall see that dieting has become a way of life for the majority of American women. American women are also likely to be unhappy with their breast size, however. Whereas they perceive themselves as generally too heavy, they are likely to think of their bust size as too small. Through 1991, about 120,000 U.S. women a year had breast-implant surgery for purely cosmetic reasons—including Cher and Mariel Hemingway (Williams, 1992).

The Social Self The social self refers to the social masks we wear, the social roles we play—suitor, student, worker, husband, wife, mother, father, citizen, leader, follower. Roles and masks are adaptive responses to the social world. In a job interview you might choose to project enthusiasm, self-confidence, and commitment to hard work but not to express self-doubts or serious reservations about the company. You may have prepared a number of such roles for different life situations.

Are social roles and masks deceptions and lies? Usually not. Our roles and masks often reflect different features within us. The job hunter has strengths and weaknesses but logically aims to project the strengths. You may perceive yourself to be something of a rebel, but it would be understandable if you were respectful when stopped by a highway patrol officer. This is not dishonesty; it is an effort to meet the requirements of the situation. If you did not understand what respect is, or did not have the social skills to act respectfully, you would not be able to enact a respectful role—even when required to do so.

ADJUSTMENT in the NEW MILLENNIUM

Are Pills for Self-Improvement in the Offing?

Biological therapies for psychological disorders may date to prehistoric times. They hark back at least to ancient times, when the Greeks and Romans used mineral water (containing lithium) to treat people with bipolar disorder. Only in recent years, however, have we gained insights into how biological approaches to therapy affect the biochemical processes of the human body. This knowledge raises the possibility that biological treatments may soon be used to take us a step beyond freedom from disorder. They may be used to improve people's personalities—their selves.

One current drug that some have seen as self-enhancing is the antidepressant drug Prozac (Newman, 1994). In *Listening to Prozac,* psychiatrist Peter D. Kramer (1993) writes that Prozac not only lifted depression in a number of his patients, but also caused a transformation in personality. Kramer claimed that Prozac could give introverted people the social skills of the salesperson. Prozac could free the inhibited person to be impetuous. Kramer argues that Prozac not only leads to predictable improvements such as reduced sluggishness (that is, reversal of the depressive symptom of psychomotor retardation) and enhanced ability to concentrate, but he believes that Prozac also improves memory functioning, enhances social poise, increases resilience to setbacks, allows people to slough off insults, and heightens mental agility and thoughtfulness.

Kramer's critics, such as Daniel X. Freedman (1993), former editor of the journal *Archives of General Psychiatry,* argue that Prozac's effects are much more limited. Freedman allows that Kramer's *Listening to Prozac* demonstrates how drugs and psychotherapy can together provide helpful treatment for depression and other psychological problems. Yet Freedman argues that the number of users of Prozac "who experience startling personality changes is rather small. Indeed, it will be news to the millions of [people] who take it for depres-

When our entire lives are played behind masks, however, it may be difficult to discover our inner selves. Partners tend to be reasonably genuine with one another in a mature intimate relationship. They drop the masks that protect and separate them. Without an expression of genuine feelings, life can be the perpetual exchange of one cardboard mask for another.

THE PERSONAL SELF In Mark Twain's *The Prince and the Pauper,* a young prince is sabotaged by enemies of the throne. He seeks to salvage the kingdom by exchanging places with Tom Canty, a pauper who happens to look just like him. It is a learning experience for both of them. The pauper is taught social graces and learns how the powerful are flattered and praised. The prince learns what it means to stand or fall on the basis of his own behavior, not his royalty.

Toward the end of the tale, there is a dispute. Which is the prince and which is Tom Canty? The lads are identical in appearance and behavior, even highly similar in experience. Does it matter? Both, perhaps, can lead the realm as well. But court officials seek the one whose personal self—whose *inner identity*—is that of the prince. The tale ends happily. The prince retakes the throne and Tom earns the permanent protection of the court.

sion [and other psychological problems] that this drug can cause dramatic changes in temperament" (p. 6).

Regardless of the effects—or limitations—of Prozac, many biological therapies, including drugs with psychological effects, are in the research pipeline (Newman, 1994). One or more of them may foster remarkable changes in personality. If that is so, what questions are raised for society to ponder?

The value of psychological and biological approaches to alleviating psychological disorders would appear to be unquestioned. But who will decide what is an ideal self? Who will decide on the directions into which we take the normal into the supernormal?

If drugs that can eliminate shyness are available, will outgoing mothers use them on timid children? Will people who are naturally reserved, and who might prefer to remain diffident, feel pressured to use drugs that abolish reservations so that they can compete in a millennium of "drug-engineered personalities" (Freedman, 1993, p. 6)? In ousting shyness, do we also eradicate introversion and introspection? Do we risk having a society of smiling, outgoing risk-takers?

If chemicals are available to make us well adjusted, do we risk forgoing the fruits of people with "tortured" personalities such as Vincent Van Gogh, Sylvia Plath, and Edgar Allan Poe? Would the person with antisocial personality disorder obtain a chemical conscience? Would Shakespeare's *Hamlet,* which is about the internal conflicts of literature's "melancholy Dane," be reinterpreted as a reminder of the perils of remaining pill-free?

If politicians—or the style—were to dictate that gender differences created the dangers of prejudice and discrimination, would gender differences in cognition and personality be chemically or surgically erased? On the other hand, if political powers—or, again, the style—were to revert to a fierce traditionalism, would all men be chemically hyped into macho males and all women chemically laced into supernurturant, ultrafeminine modes?

If the new millennium brings ways of transforming the self in specified directions, we will face many ethical and practical issues concerning what it means to be human. Will psychologists argue that "perfecting" the individual actually destroys the dignity of the individual? If so, why?

Your personal self is visible to you and you alone. It is the day-to-day experience of being you, a changing display of sights, thoughts, and feelings to which you hold the only ticket of admission.

There are many aspects of our personal selves, or self-schemas. We now discuss some of them, including our names, values, and self-concepts.

Aspects of the Self-Schema: Names, Values, and Self-Concept

Names: Labels for the Self

ALICE: *Must a name mean something?*
HUMPTY-DUMPTY: *Of course it must. . . . My name means the shape I am. . . . With a name like yours, you might be any shape, almost.*

Lewis Carroll, *Through the Looking Glass*

What's in a name? Quite a bit, perhaps. The voyages of the starship *Enterprise* are more dynamic with Captain Kirk and Mr. Spock at the helm than they would be with Captain Milquetoast and Mr. Anderson. Marilyn Monroe was sexier than Norma Jean Baker. Doc Gooden hurls a mean fastball; Dwight Gooden sounds like an assistant in a chemistry lab. Reggie Jackson hit more home runs than Reginald. Richard Starkey might well be a factory worker in Liverpool, but Ringo Starr is, well, a star.

Names even have an influence on perceptions of physical attractiveness. In one experiment, photographs of women who had been rated equal in attractiveness were assigned various names at random (Garwood and others, 1980). They were then rated by a new group of subjects with the assigned names in view. Women given names such as Jennifer, Kathy, and Christine were rated as significantly more attractive than women assigned names such as Gertrude, Ethel, and Harriet. There are two messages in this: First, names do not really serve as an index to beauty. But second, if your name is a constant source of dismay, there might be little harm in using a more appealing nickname.[1]

Truth or Fiction Revisited

Regardless of William Shakespeare's view, it is true that a rose by any other name, contrary to William Shakespeare, could smell just plain awful. Names have an influence on our perceptions.

Our names and nicknames can also reflect our attitudes toward ourselves. Although we may have one legal given name, the variations or nicknames we select says something about our self-schemas. For example, are you a Bob, Bobby, or Robert? An Elizabeth, Betty, or Liz? Shakespeare wrote that a rose by any other name would smell as sweet, but perhaps a rose by the name of skunkweed would impress us as smelling just plain awful.

According to Berne (1976b), the names our parents give us, and the ways in which they refer to us, often reflect their expectations about what we are to become:

> Charles and Frederick were kings and emperors. A boy who is steadfastly called Charles or Frederick by his mother, and insists that his associates call him that, lives a different life style from one who is commonly called Chuck or Fred, while Charlie and Freddie are likely to be horses of still another color. (p. 162)

Berne offers another example, the names of two famous neurologists—H. Head and W. R. Brain.

Unusual names may create childhood problems, but seem linked to success in adulthood. In an American study, men with names such as David, John, Michael, and Robert were rated more positively than men with names such as Ian, Dale, and Raymond (Marcus, 1976). People with common names may tend to be more popular, but college professors and upper-level army brass frequently have unusual names: *Omar* Bradley, *Dwight* Eisenhower. Unique, even odd, names are common enough in *Who's Who.* In a survey of 11,000 North Carolina high school students, boys and girls with unusual first names earned more than their fair share of academic achievements (Zweigenhaft, 1977). In another study, no personality differences were found between men with common or unusual names (Zweigenhaft and others, 1980). However, women with unusual names scored more optimally than their counterparts with common names on the California Psychological Inventory.

The Zweigenhaft group (1980) found no differences in personality between students with common names and students with names that were ambiguous with regard to gender (e.g., Ronnie and Leslie) or misleading (e.g., boys named Marion or Robin) names. But another study found that college women with masculine names (such as Dean or Randy)—who *used* them—were less anxious, more culturally sophisticated, and had greater leadership potential than women with masculine names who chose to use feminine nicknames (Ellington

[1] Yes, we are being inconsistent. Remember Ralph Waldo Emerson's remark, "A foolish consistency is the hobgoblin of little minds."

and others, 1980). The women who used their masculine names showed no signs of maladjustment. A woman who uses a given masculine name may be asserting that she is not about to live up to the stereotype of taking a backseat to men.

VALUES Our values involve the importance we place on objects and things. If we're hot, we may value air conditioning more than pizza. We may value love more than money, or money more than love. How many of us are in conflict because our values do not mesh fully with those of our friends, spouses, or employers?

Our values give rise to our personal goals and tend to place limits on the means we shall use to reach them. The medical corpsman's values caused him to renounce violence and adopt the goal of seeking to aid the wounded. His psychological problems developed when he was compelled to engage in behavior that was inconsistent with his values.

We all have unique sets of values, but we probably get along best with people whose values resemble our own. Values are often derived from parents and other childhood influences. But we may also derive values and **ethics,** our standards of conduct or behavior, through logic and reasoning. According to psychologist Lawrence Kohlberg (1981), the highest level of moral functioning requires us to use ethical principles to define our own moral standards and then to live in accord with them.

Clarifying our values is a crucial aspect of self-development. If we do not have personal values, our behavior seems meaningless, purposeless. During some periods of life, especially during adolescence, our values may be in flux. For most of us, this is an unsettling experience, or crisis in self-identity, and we are motivated to make our beliefs consistent and meaningful. But until we do, we may be subject to the whims and opinions of others—concerned about risking social disapproval because we have not yet established stable standards for self-approval.

THE SELF-CONCEPT Your **self-concept** is your impression or concept of yourself. It includes your own listing of the personal traits (fairness, competence, sociability, and so on) you deem important, and your evaluation of how you rate according to these traits.

You can sketch out your own self-concept as follows. First, think of your personal traits as existing along bipolar dimensions of the kind shown in Figure 3.2 (p. 88). Use the dimensions in Figure 3.2 so that you and your classmates will have a common reference point.

Now, you can sketch your own self-concept by placing a checkmark in one of the seven spaces for each dimension. Use the number code of 1 through 7 as your guide, as in the following example for the trait of fairness:

1 = extremely fair
2 = rather fair
3 = somewhat fair
4 = equally fair and unfair; or not sure
5 = somewhat unfair
6 = rather unfair
7 = extremely unfair

The self-concept is multifaceted. In addition to your self-evaluation it includes your sense of personal worth (or self-esteem), your sense of who and what you would like to be (your ideal self), and your sense of your competence

ETHICS • Standards for behavior. A system of beliefs from which one derives standards for behavior.
SELF-CONCEPT • One's perception of oneself, including one's traits and an evaluation of these traits. The self-concept includes one's self-esteem and one's ideal self.

SELF-ASSESSMENT

VALUES CLARIFICATION — WHAT IS IMPORTANT TO YOU?

Freedom, recognition, beauty, eternal salvation, a world without war—which is most important to you? Are people who put pleasure first likely to behave differently from people who rank salvation, wisdom, or personal achievement number 1?

Milton Rokeach devised a survey of values that allows us to rank our life goals according to their relative importance to us. How will you rank yours? ■

Directions: Eighteen values are listed below in alphabetical order. Select the value that is most important to you and write a 1 next to it in Column I. Then select your next most important value and place a 2 next to it in the same column. Proceed until you have ranked all 18 values. By turning to the key in the Appendix, you can compare your rankings to those of a national sample of American adults.

Now would you like to participate in a brief experiment? If so, imagine how someone very close to you, perhaps an old, trusted friend or relative, would rank the 18 values. Place his or her rankings in Column II. Then think of someone with whom you have had a number of arguments, someone whose way of life seems at odds with your own. Try to put yourself in his or her place, and rank the values as he or she would in Column III. Now compare your own ranking to the rankings of your friend and your adversary. Are your own values ranked more similarly to those in Column II or in Column III? Do you and your good friend or close relative have rather similar values? Is it possible that you and the person represented in Column III do not get along, in part, because your values differ?

As a class exercise, compare your rankings to those of classmates, or to the class average rankings. Do class members share similar values? Do they fall into groups with characteristic values? Does the behavior of different class members reflect differences in values?

Value	**I**	**II**	**III**
A COMFORTABLE LIFE a prosperous life	______	______	______
AN EXCITING LIFE a stimulating, active life	______	______	______
A SENSE OF ACCOMPLISHMENT lasting contribution	______	______	______
A WORLD AT PEACE free of war and conflict	______	______	______

to meet your goals (your self-efficacy expectations). Self-esteem depends on many factors, including social approval, competence, and the discrepancy between the way you see yourself and what you think you ought to be.

SELF-ESTEEM

Oh, that God the gift would give us
To see ourselves as others see us.

ROBERT BURNS

Actually, we do largely see ourselves as others see us. That is, **self-esteem** appears to begin with parental love and approval. Children who are cherished by

SELF-ESTEEM • Self-approval. One's self-respect or favorable opinion of oneself.

Value	I	II	III
A WORLD OF BEAUTY beauty of nature and the arts	______	______	______
EQUALITY brotherhood, equal opportunity for all	______	______	______
FAMILY SECURITY taking care of loved ones	______	______	______
FREEDOM independence, free choice	______	______	______
HAPPINESS contentedness	______	______	______
INNER HARMONY freedom from inner conflict	______	______	______
MATURE LOVE sexual and spiritual intimacy	______	______	______
NATIONAL SECURITY protection from attack	______	______	______
PLEASURE an enjoyable, leisurely life	______	______	______
SALVATION saved, eternal life	______	______	______
SELF-RESPECT self-esteem	______	______	______
SOCIAL RECOGNITION respect, admiration	______	______	______
TRUE FRIENDSHIP close companionship	______	______	______
WISDOM a mature understanding of life	______	______	______

their parents usually come to see themselves as being worthy of love. They are likely to learn to love and accept themselves.

Coopersmith (1967) studied self-esteem patterns among fifth- and sixth-grade boys and found that boys with high self-esteem more often came from homes with strict but not harsh or cruel parents. Such parents were highly involved in their sons' activities. Parents of boys low in self-esteem were generally more permissive, but tended to be harsh when they did administer discipline.

The parents of boys with higher self-esteem were more demanding but also highly involved in their lives. Involvement communicates worthiness. Encouraging children to develop competence not only contributes to their self-esteem but is an expression of love and caring. Resultant competencies in intellectual

Truth or Fiction Revisited

It is true that children with strict parents have higher self-esteem than children with permissive parents. Children whose parents demand more accomplish more, and accomplishment is linked to self-esteem.

tasks (Flippo & Lewinsohn, 1971) or in physical activities, such as swimming (Koocher, 1971), heighten self-esteem.

Once established, self-esteem seems to endure. Coopersmith (1967) found high similarities between his subjects' self-esteem at 3-year intervals. We may all fail at our endeavors now and then, but if our self-esteem is initially high, perhaps we shall retain belief in our ability to master adversity. But low self-esteem may become a self-fulfilling prophecy: People with low self-esteem may carve out little to boast of in life.

Our self-concepts may be described according to our perceptions of our positions along dimensions like those shown in Figure 3.2. Our self-esteem tends to depend on our approval of our self-positioning. It is related to the discrepancy between our self-placement along these dimensions and the placement our values suggest we ought to have. That is, self-esteem is based on the discrepancy between our self-descriptions and our ideal selves.

IDEAL SELF • One's perception of what one ought to be and do. Also called the self-ideal.

THE IDEAL SELF Our concepts of what we ought to be are called our **ideal selves,** or self-ideals. How about you? What "oughts" and "shoulds" are you carrying around about your ideal self? You can gain some insight into the nature of your ideal self through the following exercise. Look again at Figure 3.2. Use a pencil of a different color or make another kind of mark, perhaps an *x* instead of a checkmark. This time around, mark the spaces that indicate where you think you *ought* to be, not where you think you are. Try not to be influenced by the first set of marks.

FIGURE 3.2
RATING SCALES FOR MEASUREMENT OF THE SELF-CONCEPT.

Fair	1	2	3	4	5	6	7	Unfair
Independent	1	2	3	4	5	6	7	Dependent
Religious	1	2	3	4	5	6	7	Irreligious
Unselfish	1	2	3	4	5	6	7	Selfish
Self-confident	1	2	3	4	5	6	7	Lacking confidence
Competent	1	2	3	4	5	6	7	Incompetent
Important	1	2	3	4	5	6	7	Unimportant
Attractive	1	2	3	4	5	6	7	Unattractive
Educated	1	2	3	4	5	6	7	Uneducated
Sociable	1	2	3	4	5	6	7	Unsociable
Kind	1	2	3	4	5	6	7	Cruel
Wise	1	2	3	4	5	6	7	Foolish
Graceful	1	2	3	4	5	6	7	Awkward
Intelligent	1	2	3	4	5	6	7	Unintelligent
Artistic	1	2	3	4	5	6	7	Inartistic
Tall	1	2	3	4	5	6	7	Short
Obese	1	2	3	4	5	6	7	Skinny

Now look at Table 3.2, which is a summary of the list of traits in Figure 3.2. Select a few traits (perhaps four or five) that make you feel good about yourself and place a plus sign (+) in the blank space in front of them. Then select an equal number of traits about which you feel somewhat disappointed, and place a minus sign (−) in front of each. What, you have only one "bad" trait? Then select only one good trait as well.[2]

Now return to Figure 3.2 and make some comparisons. Compare your self-concept with your ideal self. Observe that the mark that describes your ideal self is usually placed closer to the end of the dimension that *you* value more positively. (For example, some people wish that they were taller, but others would prefer that they were shorter.)

Now let us note the discrepancies, or differences, between your self-description and your ideal self for the dimensions to which you assigned pluses and minuses. For instance, let's say that you are 5′9″ tall but would like to be a star center in basketball. The discrepancy between your self-description (S) and your ideal self (I) might be illustrated like this:

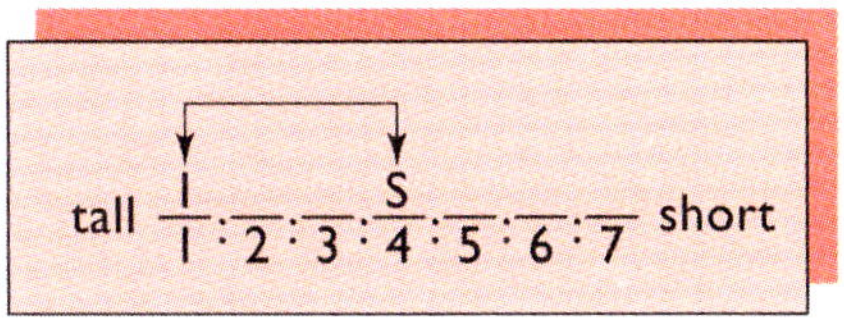

Mathematically, the discrepancy between your self-description and your ideal self on the tallness dimension is $4 - 1 = 3$. Or, more generally,

$$\text{Discrepancy} = \text{Ideal Self} - \text{Self-Description}$$

Now figure out the discrepancies for each trait that pleased you and displeased you, as listed in Table 3.2. For instance, if you placed plus signs in front of fairness, kindness, and sociability, add the discrepancies for these three dimensions. If you placed minus signs before the dimensions of competence, education, and wisdom, also add these three numbers together. Now compare the total discrepancy scores for the positive and negative clusters of traits. We would be pleased

TABLE 3.2 SUMMARY LIST OF TRAITS SHOWN IN FIGURE 3.1

_____	fair–unfair
_____	independent–dependent
_____	religious–irreligious
_____	unselfish–selfish
_____	self-confident–lacking confidence
_____	competent–incompetent
_____	important–unimportant
_____	attractive–unattractive
_____	educated–uneducated
_____	sociable–unsociable
_____	kind–cruel
_____	wise–foolish
_____	graceful–awkward
_____	intelligent–unintelligent
_____	artistic–inartistic
_____	tall–short
_____	obese–skinny

[2] Of course, it is somewhat difficult for your authors to empathize with people who have bad traits. After all, we have not been able to find any of our own.

Self-Assessment

Are You One of Your Favorite People?

Self-acceptance and self-esteem are vital to our feelings about ourselves and to our social relationships. Self-acceptance may originate in the way other people act and react to us. However, our self-acceptance then influences the ways in which we interact with others. High self-acceptance frees us to be ourselves and interact spontaneously; low self-acceptance renders us irresolute and touchy. ■

Directions: Following are a series of statements that are suggestive of your self-acceptance. Read each one and indicate how true or false it is for you according to the code given below. Then check the scoring key in the Appendix.

1 = Completely true
2 = Mostly true
3 = Half true, half false
4 = Mostly false
5 = Completely false

____ 1. I'd like it if I could find someone who would tell me how to solve my personal problems.

____ 2. I don't question my worth as a person, even if I think others do.

____ 3. When people say nice things about me, I find it difficult to believe they really mean it. I think maybe they're kidding me or just aren't being sincere.

____ 4. If there is any criticism or anyone says anything about me, I just can't take it.

____ 5. I don't say much at social affairs because I'm afraid that people will criticize me or laugh if I say the wrong thing.

____ 6. I realize that I'm not living very effectively, but I just don't believe I've got it in me to use my energies in better ways.

____ 7. I look on most of the feelings and impulses I have toward people as being quite natural and acceptable.

____ 8. Something inside me just won't let me be satisfied with any job I've done—if it turns out well, I get a very smug feeling that this is beneath me, I shouldn't be satisfied with this, this isn't a fair test.

____ 9. I feel different from other people. I'd like to have the feeling of security that comes from knowing I'm not too different from others.

____ 10. I'm afraid for people that I like to find out what I'm really like, for fear they'd be disappointed in me.

____ 11. I am frequently bothered by feelings of inferiority.

Truth or Fiction Revisited

It is true that the self-esteem of an average student may exceed that of a scholar. The average student may not value scholarship and may be very pleased with his or her other attributes and accomplishments; the scholar, meanwhile, may be perfectionistic and fault his or her scholarly achievements.

to take bets that the total for the traits that disappoint you is *larger* than the total for the traits that please you.

Why are we so confident? Simply because the *reason* that certain traits please you is that there is little or no discrepancy between your ideal self and where you perceive yourself to be on them. These are the traits that are likely to contribute to your self-esteem. (Whenever you feel a bit low, why not sit back for a moment and think of how you sparkle along these dimensions!) In general, the closer your self-description is in keeping with your ideal self, the higher your self-esteem will be. The farther away you are, the bleaker your self-description will look to you.

____ 12. Because of other people, I haven't been able to achieve as much as I should have.
____ 13. I am quite shy and self-conscious in social situations.
____ 14. In order to get along and be liked, I tend to be what people expect me to be rather than anything else.
____ 15. I seem to have a real inner strength in handling things. I'm on a pretty solid foundation and it makes me pretty sure of myself.
____ 16. I feel self-conscious when I'm with people who have a superior position to mine in business or at school.
____ 17. I think I'm neurotic or something.
____ 18. Very often, I don't try to be friendly with people because I think they won't like me.
____ 19. I feel that I'm a person of worth, on an equal plane with others.
____ 20. I can't avoid feeling guilty about the way I feel toward certain people in my life.
____ 21. I'm not afraid of meeting new people. I feel that I'm a worthwhile person and there's no reason why they should dislike me.
____ 22. I sort of only half believe in myself.
____ 23. I'm very sensitive. People say things and I have a tendency to think they're criticizing me or insulting me in some way and later when I think of it, they may not have meant anything like that at all.
____ 24. I think I have certain abilities and other people say so too. I wonder if I'm not giving them an importance way beyond what they deserve.
____ 25. I feel confident that I can do something about the problems that may arise in the future.
____ 26. I guess I put on a show to impress people. I know I'm not the person I pretend to be.
____ 27. I do not worry or condemn myself if other people pass judgment against me.
____ 28. I don't feel very normal, but I want to feel normal.
____ 29. When I'm in a group, I usually don't say much for fear of saying the wrong thing.
____ 30. I have a tendency to sidestep my problems.
____ 31. Even when people do think well of me, I feel sort of guilty because I know I must be fooling them—that if I were really to be myself, they wouldn't think well of me.
____ 32. I feel that I'm on the same level as other people and that helps to establish good relations with them.
____ 33. I feel that people are apt to react differently to me than they would normally react to other people.
____ 34. I live too much by other people's standards.
____ 35. When I have to address a group, I get self-conscious and have difficulty saying things well.
____ 36. If I didn't always have such hard luck, I'd accomplish much more than I have.

ATTRIBUTION THEORY

At the age of 3, the first author's daughter Allyn believed that a friend's son was a boy because he *wanted* to be a boy. Because she was 3 at the time, this error in her **attribution** for the boy's gender is charming and understandable. But we as adults tend to make somewhat similar attribution errors. No, we do not usually believe that people's preferences have much to do with their gender, but as we shall see, we may tend to exaggerate the role of conscious choice in other aspects of their behavior.

Attribution • A belief concerning why people behave in a certain way.

ADJUSTMENT *in the* NEW MILLENNIUM

Can Psychologists Use Attribution Theory to Enhance International "Adjustment"?

One of the most pressing adjustment problems concerns conflict and warfare. It would be nice to think that technological advances would somehow minimize human brutality. However, the fact is that technological innovations have been repeatedly used by warlords and governments as more efficient ways of maiming and killing.

Fortunately, psychologists have not given in to the view that we are helpless to prevent people from harming others (Kelman, 1997). Many psychologists are focusing on "zealous nationalism and what motivates some groups to start war [while others] are able to live in peace" (Meade, 1994, p. 15). Let us consider how psychologists might use what they know about attributional processes to heighten the chances of peace.

CAN ATTRIBUTION THEORY BE USED TO MEDIATE INTERNATIONAL CONFLICTS? Biases in the attribution process interfere with people's ability to understand other nations' motives for their behavior. As a result, they may unfairly blame citizens of those nations, and conflict may result.

Psychologists conduct individual and group therapy. Can they also mediate international conflicts? Research on attribution process suggests the following possibilities:

Helping Nations Avoid Jumping to the Conclusion That Other Nations Are Always to Blame for Their Behavior. Nations, like people, tend to attribute too much of other nations' behavior to dispositional factors. That is, they make the fundamental attribution error. The fact is that nations are influenced by situational variables as well as by dispositional variables. These include financial hardship, short-sighted leaders, conflict among ethnic groups, unwise alliances, the promise of reward, and the threat of punishment.

When one nation is offended by another nation's behavior, leaders might try to imagine the internal and external pressures that are influencing the other nation and its leaders. Empathy might foster understanding and encourage more suitable behavior.

Helping Nations Avoid Jumping to the Conclusion That They Are Never to Blame for Their Own Behavior. Psychologists have also learned that nations, like people, tend to be highly aware of the situa-

An assumption as to why people do things is called an attribution for behavior. Our inference of the motives and traits of others through the observation of their behavior is called the **attribution process.** We now focus on attribution theory, or the processes by which people draw conclusions about the factors that influence one another's behavior. Attribution theory is important to adjustment because our attributions lead us to perceive other people, and ourselves, either as purposeful actors or as victims of circumstances.

ATTRIBUTION PROCESS • The process by which people draw inferences about the motives and traits of others.

DISPOSITIONAL ATTRIBUTION • An assumption that a person's behavior is determined by internal causes, such as personal attitudes or goals.

Dispositional and Situational Attributions

Social psychologists describe two types of attributions—dispositional attributions and situational attributions. In making **dispositional attributions,** we ascribe a person's behavior to internal factors, such as personality traits and free tional forces that are influencing their behavior. They may focus on situational factors to the point that they ignore dispositional factors—for example, the rolc of their leaders' decisions. A nation may see itself as leaning toward war because of a shortage of natural resources and pressure from an ally. However, its leaders make decisions on the basis of numerous factors in addition to these. Recognizing the importance of decision making can help place the blame for bad decisions where it belongs—on specific leaders rather than entire nations.

Do you ever say to yourself, "How can I be expected to relax and be a nice guy when I'm going to this pressure cooker of a college?" or "How can I let such an insult go unpunished?" Situational and dispositional variables affect nations' behavior as well as our own. When nations focus on the situational variables, they may lose sight of their own causal role in aggressive behavior.

Helping a Nation Recognize That Other Nations May Tend to Blame It for Things That Are Not Its Fault. Partly because of its wealth, partly because of its history, and partly because it is a big target, the United States is frequently blamed for problems that are not of its making. Other people may attribute too much of our nation's behavior to dispositional factors. When in conflict, it is useful for a nation to explain the forces that it perceives to be acting upon it. In this way it can give other nations the information that will help them empathize with its situation.

Helping a Nation Recognize That Other Nations Often See Themselves as Forced to Act as They Do. We tend to see ourselves as victims of circumstances, compelled by situations. Consider the United States' involvement in Vietnam in the 1960s and 1970s. The nation perceived itself as coming to the aid of its South Vietnamese allies, who valued democracy and sought U.S. protection against invaders from the north. But many North Vietnamese perceived themselves as attempting to unify their country and resist the influence of a superpower from the other side of the world.

It is helpful to try to see things through the eyes of one's adversary. Other people can feel that they are forced to behave as they do, just as we can. Then we can begin to focus on the forces that compel us all—not just on our own sense of injury.

Can psychologists help make the new millennium an age of peace? Can they enhance "international adjustment" where national leaders, philosophers, kings and queens, and great historic figures have failed? Perhaps they can. Perhaps not. But there are two compelling reasons why psychologists will try to help. One is that psychology brings a unique perspective to the problems of nations as well as those of individuals. Another is that even if psychologists fail, the greater crime would be not to try to help.

will. In making **situational attributions,** we attribute a person's actions to external factors such as social influence or socialization.

The Fundamental Attribution Error

We frequently attribute too much of other people's behavior to internal, dispositional factors. This bias in the attribution process is what social psychologists refer to as the **fundamental attribution error.** Apparently, when we observe the behavior of others, we focus excessively on their actions and too little on the contexts within which their actions take place. But we do tend to be more aware of the networks of forces acting on ourselves.

One reason for the fundamental attribution error is that we tend to infer traits from behavior. When we overhear a woman screaming at her husband in a

SITUATIONAL ATTRIBUTION • An assumption that a person's behavior is determined by external circumstances, such as the social pressure found in a situation.

FUNDAMENTAL ATTRIBUTION ERROR • The tendency to assume that others act on the basis of choice or will, even when there is evidence suggestive of the importance of their situations.

supermarket, we tend to assume that she is impulsive and boisterous. We are usually not aware of the many things that her husband might have done to infuriate her.

The fundamental attribution error is linked to another bias in the attribution process: the actor-observer effect.

The Actor-Observer Effect

Truth or Fiction Revisited

It is true that we hold other people responsible for their misdeeds, but we tend to see ourselves as victims of circumstances. This bias in the attribution process is referred to as the actor-observer effect.

When we or others engage in behavior that we do not like, we tend to see the others as willful, but to perceive ourselves as victims of circumstances. The tendency to attribute the behavior of others to internal, dispositional factors, and our own behavior to external, situational influences is called the **actor-observer effect.**

Let us consider an example of the actor-observer effect that may hit home. Surely you have dated someone whom your parents thought should be placed in an institution. When parents and children argue about the children's choice of friends or dates, the parents infer traits from behavior and tend to perceive their children as stubborn, difficult, and independent. But the children also infer traits from behavior and may perceive their parents as bossy and controlling. Parents and children alike attribute the other's behavior to internal causes. That is, they make dispositional attributions about the behavior of others.

But how do the parents and children perceive themselves? The parents probably see themselves as forced into combat by their children's foolishness. If they become insistent, it is in response to their children's stubbornness. The children probably see themselves as responding to peer pressures, and, perhaps, to sexual urges that may come from within but do not seem "of their own making." The parents and the children both tend to see their own behavior as motivated by external factors. That is, they make situational attributions for their own behavior.

The Self-Serving Bias

Truth or Fiction Revisited

It is true that we tend to attribute our successes to our abilities and hard work, but we attribute our failures to external factors such as lack of time or obstacles placed in our paths by others. This perceptual bias is referred to as the self-serving bias.

ACTOR-OBSERVER EFFECT • The tendency to attribute our own behavior to external, situational factors but to attribute the behavior of others to internal, dispositional factors such as choice or will.

SELF-SERVING BIAS • The tendency to view one's successes as stemming from internal factors and one's failures as stemming from external factors.

There is also a **self-serving bias** in the attribution process. We are more likely to attribute our successes to internal, dispositional factors, but our failures to external, situational influences (Baumgardner and others, 1986; O'Malley & Becker, 1984). When we have done well on a test or impressed a date, we are more likely to attribute these outcomes to our intelligence and charm. But when we fail, we are more likely to attribute these outcomes to bad luck, an unfairly difficult test, or our date's bad mood.

There are exceptions to the self-serving bias, however. Depressed people are more likely than other people to attribute their failures to internal factors, even when dispositional attributions are not justified (see Chapter 9).

Another interesting attribution bias is a gender difference in attributions for friendly behavior. Men are more likely than women to interpret a woman's friendliness toward men as flirting (Abbey, 1987). Perhaps gender roles apparently still lead men to expect that decent women are passive.

adjustment and modern life

This chapter has to do with social perception: the ways in which we see other people and ourselves. We noted that we all carry certain expectations—our cognitive Procrustean beds—around with us. Our expectations shape the ways in which we perceive the world and ourselves. When expectations are inaccurate, or irrational, they can harm social relationships and make us—and the people we care about—unhappy.

Let us consider a number of ways in which the topics we discussed in the chapter can help shape, or reshape, social perceptions to foster social adjustment and create greater happiness.

MANAGING FIRST IMPRESSIONS

The first impressions you make on others, and the first impressions others make on you, are quite important to your interpersonal relationships. There are a number of ways in which you can manage first impressions to enhance your relationships:

1. First, be aware of the first impressions you make on others. When you meet people for the first time, remember that they are forming person schemas about you. Once formed, these schemas resist change.
2. When you apply for a job, your "first impression" may reach your prospective employer before you walk through the door. It is your vita or résumé. Make it neat and present some of your more important accomplishments at the beginning.
3. Why not plan and rehearse your first few remarks for a date or a job interview? Imagine the situation and, in the case of a job interview, things you are likely to be asked. If you have some relatively smooth statements prepared, along with a nice smile, you are more likely to be considered as socially competent, and competence is respected.
4. Smile. You're more attractive when you smile.
5. Be well dressed for job interviews, college interviews, first dates, or other important meetings. Even be well dressed when you go to the doctor's office with a physical complaint! The appropriate dress to make an impression on a first date might differ from what you would wear to a job interview. In each case, ask yourself, "What type of dress is expected for this occasion? How can I make a positive first impression?"
6. When you answer essay questions, attend to your penmanship. It is the first thing your instructor notices when looking at your paper. Present relevant knowledge in the first sentence or paragraph of the answer, or restate the question by writing something like, "In this essay I shall show how . . . "
7. In class, seek eye contact with your instructors. Look interested. That way, if you do poorly on a couple of quizzes, your instructor may

conceptualize you as a basically good student who made a couple of errors rather than a poor student who is revealing his/her shortcomings. (Don't tell your instructor that this paragraph is in the book. Maybe he/she won't notice.)

8. The first time you talk to your instructor outside of class, be reasonable and sound interested in his/her subject.
9. When you pass someone in a race, put on a burst of speed. That way the other guy may think that trying to catch you will be futile.
10. Ask yourself if you are being fair to other people in your life. If your date's parents are a bit cold toward you the evening of your first date, maybe it's because they don't know you and are concerned about their son/daughter's welfare. If you show them that you are treating their son/daughter decently, they may come around. Don't assume that they're basically prunefaces.
11. Before you eliminate people from your life on the basis of first impressions, ask yourself, "Is the first impression the 'real person' or just one instance of that person's behavior?" Give other people a second chance, and you may find that they have something to offer. After all, would you want to be held accountable for everything you've ever said and done? Haven't you changed for the better as time has gone on? Haven't you become more sophisticated and knowledgeable? (You're reading this book, aren't you?) People are not always at their best. Don't carve person schemas in stone on the basis of one social exchange.

USING BODY LANGUAGE TO FOSTER ADJUSTMENT AND ENHANCE SOCIAL RELATIONSHIPS

There are several ways in which you can use information about body language to foster adjustment and social relationships:

1. Be aware of what other people are telling you with their body language. If they are looking away as you are telling them something, perhaps you are "turning them off." If they are leaning toward you, nodding, and meeting your gaze, they are probably agreeing with you. Make mental notes of their reactions to get a fix on their attitudes and feelings about you.
2. Pay attention to your own body language as a way of helping to make the desired impressions on other people. Are you maintaining eye contact and nodding "yes" when you want to say "no"? If so, you can't be very happy with yourself. Would you like to be encouraging but wear a perpetual frown? If so, you may be pushing other people away without intending to.
3. Pay attention to your own body language as a way of learning about yourself—as a way of getting "in touch" with your own feelings. If you are agreeing to something, but you are leaning away from the other person and your back is rigid, perhaps you would like to rethink your assent. Or perhaps you are staring when you think you might be gazing. Could it

be that you are more upset by something than you had imagined? Gestalt therapists encourage their clients to pay very close attention to what their bodies are "telling them" about their genuine feelings.

COPING WITH PREJUDICE AND DISCRIMINATION

Prejudice has existed throughout history and we doubt that "miracle cures" are at hand to eradicate it fully. However, as we shall see, a number of measures have met with success. In many cases, it is easier to deal with discrimination, the behavioral manifestation of prejudice. For example, laws now prohibit denial of access to jobs, housing, and other social necessities on the basis of race, religion, handicaps, and related factors.

Let us consider a number of things that can be done.

Role Reversal: An Immunization Technique?

A classic experiment by Weiner and Wright (1973) tested the implications of Jane Elliot's informal demonstration with blue- and brown-eyed children. White third-graders were assigned at random to "Green" or "Orange" groups and identified with armbands. First, the "Green" people were labeled inferior and denied social privileges. After a few days, the pattern was reversed. Children in a second class did not receive the "Green-Orange treatment" and served as a control group.

Following this treatment, children from both classes were asked whether they wanted to go on a picnic with African American children from another school. Ninety-six percent of the "Green-Orange" group expressed desire to go on the picnic, as compared with 62 percent of the controls. The experience of prejudice and discrimination apparently led the "Green-Orange" children to think that it is wrong to discriminate on the basis of color. Perhaps being discriminated against made the children more mindful of the sensitivities and feelings of members of outgroups. Unless we are encouraged to actively consider our attitudes toward others, we may automatically rely upon previously conceived ideas, and these ideas are very often prejudiced (Langer and others, 1985).

Truth or Fiction Revisited

It is true that children who have been victims of discrimination are less likely to practice discrimination themselves. Role reversal apparently heightens their awareness of the unfairness of, and pain induced by, discrimination.

Intergroup Contact

A stereotype is a fixed, conventional schema about a *group* of people. Intergroup contact can break down stereotypes. Contact reveals that groups consist of individuals who are not so homogeneous. They have different abilities, interests, personalities, and attitudes.

Intergroup contact best reduces prejudice when the individuals work toward common goals rather than compete (Clore and others, 1978; Kennedy & Stephan, 1977; Wilder & Thompson, 1980). Competition stirs feelings of antipathy. Second, the individuals should come from similar socioeconomic backgrounds so that they have a number of things in common. Third, contacts should

Truth or Fiction Revisited

It is true that contact between members of different racial groups can reduce feelings of prejudice. This is especially so when contact involves working toward common goals.

INTERGROUP CONTACT. Intergroup contact can reduce feelings of prejudice when people work together toward common goals.

be informal. Highly structured contacts distance participants from one another. Finally, prolonged contact is more effective than brief contact (Skrypnek & Snyder, 1982).

Seeking Compliance With the Law

Truth or Fiction Revisited

It is true that one way of combating prejudice is to seek compliance with the law. Laws prohibit discrimination in hiring and housing.

On a personal level, it is appropriate to demand legal support if we have been discriminated against on the basis of race, religion, or other ethnic factors. It may be that "We can't legislate morality," but people can be compelled to modify illegal behavior.

Self-Examination

I'm starting with the man in the mirror,
I'm asking him to change his ways,
And no message could have been any clearer,
If you want to make the world a better place,
Take a look at yourself and make that change.

"THE MAN IN THE MIRROR," A MICHAEL JACKSON SONG

Very often we say or do things that remind us that we have prejudices. Recently a Catholic acquaintance said "that damned Jew" when someone disappointed

him. He was asked if he had ever been disappointed by a Catholic, and, of course, the answer was yes. He was then asked, "Did you call him 'that damned Catholic'?" No, he hadn't. The thought had not occurred to him. Individuals of all groups have done, or might do, things that disappoint or disturb us. In such cases we need not deny the harm, but we should remember to attribute the behavior to them as *individuals,* not as *group representatives.*

ENHANCING SELF-ESTEEM

> *No one can make you feel inferior without your consent.*
>
> ELEANOR ROOSEVELT

In this chapter we reviewed theory and research concerning the self-schema. Now let us focus on ways in which you can raise your own self-esteem.

Improve Yourself

This is not an absurd suggestion of the sort that one of our (less well liked!) literature professors made when he told a student, "Get a new brain." Here we are talking about undertaking strategies that can lead to improvement in specific areas of life.

You can begin, for example, by thinking about reducing some of the discrepancies between your self-description and your ideal self. Consider again the traits in Figure 3.2. Are you miserable because of overdependence on another person? Perhaps you can enhance your social skills or your vocational skills in an effort to become more independent. Are you too heavy? Perhaps you can follow some of the suggestions in Chapter 7 for losing weight.

Truth or Fiction Revisited

It is true that we can build our self-esteem by becoming good at something. Competence boosts self-esteem.

Challenge the Realism of Your Ideal Self

Our "oughts" and "shoulds" can create such perfectionistic standards that we are constantly falling short and experiencing frustration. One way of adjusting to perfectionistic self-demands is to challenge them and, when appropriate, to revise them. It may be harmful to abolish worthy and realistic goals, even if we do have trouble measuring up now and then. However, some of our goals or values may not stand up under our close scrutiny, and it is always healthful to be willing to consider them objectively.

Substitute Realistic, Attainable Goals for Unattainable Goals

It may be that we shall never be as artistic, as tall, or as graceful as we would like to be. We can work to enhance our drawing skills, but if it becomes clear that we shall not become Michelangelos, perhaps we can just enjoy our scribbles for what they are and also look to other fields for satisfaction. We cannot make ourselves taller (once we have included our elevator shoes or heels, that is), but we can take off 5 pounds and we can cut our time for running the mile by a few seconds. We can also learn to whip up a great fettuccine Alfredo.

Build Self-Efficacy Expectations

Our self-efficacy expectations are a major factor in our willingness to take on the challenges of life and persist in meeting them. Our self-efficacy expectations define the degree to which we believe that our efforts will bring about a positive outcome. We can build self-efficacy expectations by selecting tasks that are consistent with our interests and abilities and then working at them. Many tests have been devised to help us focus in on our interests and abilities. They are often available at your college testing and counseling center. But we can also build self-efficacy expectations by working at athletics and on hobbies.

Remember, realistic self-assessment, realistic goals, and a reasonable schedule for improvement are the keys to building self-efficacy expectations. The chances are that you will not be able to run a 4-minute mile, but after a few months of reasonably taxing workouts under the advice of a skilled trainer, you might be able to put a few 7-minute miles back to back. You might even enjoy them!

SUMMARY

1. **How do schemas influence our perception of ourselves and others?** Schemas are expectations that influence our perceptions of other people (person schemas), social roles (role schemas), and ourselves (self-schemas). Schemas bias us to see things in certain ways.
2. **Do first impressions matter?** Very much so. According to the primacy effect, we tend to interpret people's behavior in terms of our first impressions of them. However, we may also focus on our most recent impressions of people (the so-called recency effect), especially when we are advised to weigh all the evidence in impression formation.
3. **How shall we read other people's body language?** People who are anxious are usually rigid in posture, whereas people who are relaxed usually "hang loose." When people lean toward one another they are usually interested in each other. Gazing is a sign of interest, and sometimes of love; hard staring is an aversive challenge.
4. **What is prejudice?** Prejudice is an attitude toward a group that leads us to evaluate group members negatively. Prejudice is associated with negative feelings and with discriminatory behavior.
5. **Where does prejudice come from?** Possible sources of prejudice include attitudinal differences (real or assumed) between groups, social conflict, authoritarianism, and social learning. Prejudices in the form of stereotypes also make it easier to process information about unknown individuals.
6. **What is the self?** The self is a guiding principle of personality. The self is an organized, consistent way of perceiving our "I" and our perceptions of the ways in which we relate to the world.
7. **What are the parts of the self?** The self has physical, social, and personal aspects. Our social selves are the masks and social roles we don to meet the requirements of our situations. Our personal selves are our private inner identities.
8. **What is the relationship between our names and our self-identities?** Names are linked to expectations by parents and society at large. People with common names are usually rated more favorably, but people with unusual names often accomplish more. People of higher status often sign their names larger and less legibly.
9. **What do our values imply about us?** Our values indicate the importance we place on objects and behavior. Values give rise to goals and set limits on behavior. We are more subject to social influences when we do not have personal values or when our values are in flux.
10. **What is the self-concept?** Our self-concept is our self-description in terms of bipolar traits, or dimensions.
11. **What is self-esteem?** Our self-esteem is our sense of self-worth. Our self-esteem rests on our self-approval of our placement along the dimensions we use to describe ourselves. The smaller the discrepancy between our self-concepts and our ideal selves, the higher our self-esteem.
12. **What is the attribution process?** The attribution process refers to our inferences of the motives and traits of others through observing their behavior.
13. **What kinds of attributions are there?** There are dispositional and situational attributions. In dispositional attributions, we attribute people's behavior to internal factors, such as personality traits and choice. In situational attributions, we attribute people's behavior to their circumstances, or external forces.
14. **What is the fundamental attribution error?** This error is the tendency to attribute too much of other people's behavior to dispositional factors.
15. **What is the actor-observer effect?** According to this effect, we tend to attribute the negative behavior of others to internal, dispositional factors, but we tend to attribute our own shortcomings to our situations.
16. **What is the self-serving bias?** This bias is the tendency to attribute our successes to dispositional factors, such as talent and hard work, but our failures to our situations.

The Challenges of Life

CHAPTER 4

Social Influence: Being Influenced By — and Influencing — Others

TRUTH OR FICTION?

T	F	
☐	☐	Admitting your product's weak points in an ad is the death knell for sales.
☐	☐	Most of us are swayed by ads that offer useful information, not by emotional appeals or celebrity endorsements.
☐	☐	People who worry about what other people think of them are likely to be low in sales resistance.
☐	☐	Most people would refuse to deliver painful electric shock to an innocent party, even under powerful social pressure.
☐	☐	Many people are late to social gatherings because they are conforming to a social norm.
☐	☐	Nearly 40 people stood by and did nothing while a woman was being stabbed to death.

OUTLINE

Most of us would be reluctant to wear blue jeans to a funeral, to walk naked on city streets, or, for that matter, to wear clothes at a nudist colony. Other people and groups can exert enormous pressure on us to behave according to their wishes or according to group norms. **Social influence** is the area of social psychology that studies the ways in which people alter the thoughts, feelings, and behavior of other people.

In this chapter we elaborate on some of the situational factors that affect our behavior—in particular, the influences of other people. In doing so, we explore some rather fascinating topics, such as the power of TV commercials to persuade us to buy and the possibility that most if not all of us can be pressured to do things that are repugnant to us.

But this chapter offers more than a warning. We suggest a way in which you can prevent yourself from being pressured by other people: the adoption of assertive behavior. Assertive behavior allows you to express your genuine feelings and to say no to unreasonable requests. Assertive behavior not only helps you resist the demands of others, it also helps you to express positive feelings of appreciation, liking, and love.

■ PERSUASION

To get some quick insight into the topic of persuasion, let's go back to the year 1741. In that year Jonathan Edwards, a Puritan minister, delivered a famous sermon, "Sinners in the Hands of an Angry God," to his Connecticut congregation. As you can see from the following excerpt, he wanted his audience to shape up:

> The God that holds you over the pit of hell, much as one holds a spider or some loathsome insect over the fire, abhors you and is dreadfully provoked. He looks upon you as worthy of nothing else but to be cast into the fire. . . . You are ten thousand times so abominable in his eyes as the most hateful venomous serpent is in ours. . . . Oh, sinner! Consider the fateful danger you are in. . . . You hang by a slender thread, with the flames of divine wrath flashing about it, and ready every moment to singe it and burn it asunder.

We're sure you get the message, so we'll cut the sermon short. It's getting a bit warm around here. Through his highly charged appeals, Edwards was hoping to return his congregation to the orthodoxy of the generation that had settled Massachusetts. If logic would not persuade them to rededicate themselves, perhaps the **emotional appeal**—*fear,* that is—would do the job.

There are two routes to persuading others to change their attitudes and behavior (Petty and others, 1994). With the central route, change results from weighing the arguments and evidence (Eagly & Chaiken, 1992). The peripheral

Social influence • The area of social psychology that studies the ways in which people influence the thoughts, feelings, and behavior of other people.

Emotional appeal • A type of persuasive communication that influences behavior on the basis of feelings that are aroused instead of on the basis of rational analysis of the issues.

route associates things or proposed behavioral changes with positive or negative "cues." These cues include rewards (such as physically attractive actors and models) and punishments (such as parental disapproval), positive and negative emotional reactions (such as the fear generated by Jonathan Edwards's harangue), and factors such as the trustworthiness of the communicator.

Advertisements—one form of persuasive communication—also take central and peripheral routes. Some advertisements focus on the quality of the product (central route). Others connect the product with appealing images (peripheral route). Ads for Total cereal, which emphasize its nutritional benefits, provide information about the quality of the product. So do the "Pepsi challenge" taste-test ads, which claim that Pepsi-Cola tastes better than Coca-Cola. The Marlboro cigarette ads, by contrast, focused on the masculine, rugged image of the "Marlboro man" and offered no information about the product itself.

In this section we examine one central factor in persuasion—the nature of the message itself—and three peripheral factors: (1) the person delivering the message, (2) the context in which the message is delivered, and (3) the audience. We also consider two methods of persuasion used frequently by people seeking charitable contributions and by salespeople: the foot-in-the-door technique and lowballing.

The Persuasive Message: Say What? Say How? Say How Often?

How do we respond when TV commercials are repeated until we have memorized every dimple on the actors' faces? Research suggests that familiarity breeds content, not contempt (Baron & Byrne, 1997):

- Political candidates who become familiar through frequent TV ads attain more votes.
- People respond more favorably to abstract art, to classical music, and to photographs of Black people and of college students on the basis of repetitive viewing. Love for classical art and music may begin through exposure in the nursery—not the college appreciation course.
- The more complex the stimuli, the more likely it is that frequent exposure will have favorable effects. The hundredth repetition of a Bach concerto may be less tiresome than the hundredth repetition of a pop tune.

Two-sided arguments, in which the communicator recounts the arguments of the opposition in order to refute them, can be effective when the audience is at first uncertain about its position (Hass & Linder, 1972). Theologians and politicians sometimes expose followers to the arguments of the opposition. By refuting these arguments, they give their followers a sort of psychological immunity to them. Swinyard found that two-sided product claims, in which advertisers admit their product's weak points as well as highlight its strengths, have the greatest credibility (in Bridgwater, 1982).

Truth or Fiction Revisited

It is not true that admitting your product's weak points in an ad is the death knell for sales. Admitting a product's weak points lends the communicator credibility.

It would be nice to think that people are too sophisticated to be persuaded by an emotional appeal. However, women warned of the dire risks of failing to be screened for breast cancer are more likely to obtain mammograms than women who are informed of the benefits of mammography (Banks and others, 1995). Fear appeals are also more effective at persuading college students to use condoms to prevent transmission of the AIDS virus (Struckman-Johnson and others, 1994). Suntanning has been shown to increase the likelihood of skin cancer. Interestingly, however, warnings against suntanning were shown to be more effective among a group of Wake Forest University students when they were based on risks to students' *appearance* (premature aging, wrinkling, and scarring of the skin) rather than on the risk to their health (Jones & Leary, 1994). That is, students who read essays about the sun's cosmetic effects were

Truth or Fiction Revisited

It is not true that most of us are swayed by ads that offer useful information. Emotional appeals and endorsements work quite well, especially when we are not experts on the products being advertised.

more likely to say they would protect themselves from the sun than were students who read essays about the sun and cancer. Generally speaking, fear appeals are most effective when they are strong, when the audience believes the dire outcomes, and when the audience believes that it can change (Eagly & Chaiken, 1993).

Audiences also tend to believe arguments that appear to run counter to the personal interests of the communicator (Wood & Eagly, 1981). People may pay more attention to a whaling-fleet owner's claim that whales are becoming extinct than to a conservationist's. If the president of Chrysler or General Motors were to state that Toyotas and Hondas are superior, you can bet that we would prick up our ears.

The Persuasive Communicator: Whom Do You Trust?

Would you buy a used car from a person convicted of larceny? Would you attend weight-control classes run by a 350-pound leader? Would you leaf through fashion magazines featuring clumsy models? Probably not. Research shows that convincing communicators show expertise (Hennigan and others, 1982a), trustworthiness, attractiveness, or similarity to their audiences (Mackie and others, 1990; Wilder, 1990). Because of the adoration of their fans, sports superstars such as Michael Jordan of the Chicago Bulls have also solidified their places as endorsers of products (Goldman, 1993). Basketball fans may consider Jordan to be an MVP, or Most Valuable Player. To Madison Avenue, however, Jordan is an MVE, or Most Valuable Endorser (Goldman, 1993).

Health professionals enjoy high status in our society and are considered experts. It is not coincidental that toothpaste ads boast that their products have the approval of the American Dental Association.

We are reared not to judge books by their covers, but we are more likely to find attractive people persuasive. Corporations do not gamble millions on unappealing actors to hawk their products. Some advertisers seek out the perfect combination of attractiveness and plain, simple folksiness with which the audience can identify. Ivory Soap commercials sport "real folks" with comely features who are so freshly scrubbed that you might think you can smell Ivory Soap emanating from the TV set.

TV news anchorpersons also enjoy high prestige. One study (Mullen and others, 1987) found that before the 1984 presidential election, Peter Jennings of ABC News had shown significantly more favorable facial expressions when reporting on Ronald Reagan than when reporting on Walter Mondale. Tom Brokaw of NBC and Dan Rather of CBS had not shown measurable favoritism. The researchers also found that viewers of ABC News voted for Reagan in greater proportions than viewers of NBC or CBS News. It is tempting to conclude that viewers were subtly persuaded by Jennings to vote for Reagan. However, Sweeney and Gruber (1984) have shown that viewers do not simply absorb like a sponge whatever the tube feeds them. Instead, they show **selective avoidance** and **selective exposure.** They tend to switch channels when they are faced with news coverage that seems to run counter to their own attitudes, and they seek communicators whose attitudes coincide with their own. So Jennings might have had an influence on his audience's attitudes toward Reagan, but Reaganites might also have preferred Jennings to Brokaw and Rather.

SELECTIVE AVOIDANCE • Diverting one's attention from information that is inconsistent with one's attitudes.

SELECTIVE EXPOSURE • Deliberately seeking and attending to information that is consistent with one's attitudes.

The Context of the Message: "Get 'Em in a Good Mood"

You are too clever and insightful to allow someone to persuade you by buttering you up, but perhaps someone you know would be influenced by a sip of

Would You Buy These Shoes?

Advertisers use a combination of central and peripheral cues to hawk their wares. What factors contribute to the persuasiveness of messages? To the persuasiveness of communicators? Why is Michael Jordan considered an MVE ("most valuable endorser")?

wine, a bite of cheese, and a sincere compliment. Seduction attempts usually come at the tail end of a date—after the Szechuan tidbits, the nouveau Fresno film, the party, and the wine that was sold at its time. An assault at the outset of a date would be viewed as . . . well, an assault. Atmospheric elements like good food and pleasant music boost acceptance of persuasive messages. When we are in a good mood, we are apparently less likely to carefully evaluate the situation (Petty and others, 1991; Schwarz and others, 1991).

It is also counterproductive to call your dates fools when they disagree with you—even if you believe their views are foolish if they do not coincide with yours. Agreement and praise are more effective at encouraging others to accept your views. Appear sincere, or else your compliments will look manipulative. It seems unfair to divulge this information.

The Persuaded Audience: Are You a Person Who Can't Say No?

Why do some people have sales resistance, whereas others enrich the lives of every door-to-door salesperson? For one thing, people with high self-esteem might be more likely to resist social pressure than people with low self-esteem (Santee & Maslach, 1982). Santee and Maslach (1982) suggest that people

Do You Speak Your Mind or Do You Wimp Out?

The Rathus Assertiveness Schedule

What about you? Do you enrich the pockets of every telemarketer, or do you say no? Do you stick up for your rights, or do you allow others to walk all over you? Do you say what you feel or what you think other people want you to say? Do you initiate relationships with attractive people, or do you shy away from them?

One way to gain insight into how assertive you are is to take the Rathus Assertiveness Schedule. Once you have finished, turn to the Appendix to find out how to calculate your score. A table in the Appendix will allow you to compare your assertiveness to that of a sample of 1,400 students drawn from 35 college campuses across the United States.

If you believe that you are not assertive enough, why not take the quick course in self-assertion offered at the end of the chapter? You need not go through life imitating a doormat. ■

Directions: Indicate how well each item describes you by using this code:

3 = very much like me	−1 = slightly unlike me
2 = rather like me	−2 = rather unlike me
1 = slightly like me	−3 = very much unlike me

____ 1. Most people seem to be more aggressive and assertive than I am.*
____ 2. I have hesitated to make or accept dates because of shyness.*
____ 3. When the food served at a restaurant is not done to my satisfaction, I complain about it to the waiter or waitress.
____ 4. I am careful to avoid hurting other people's feelings, even when I feel that I have been injured.*
____ 5. If a salesperson has gone to considerable trouble to show me merchandise that is not quite suitable, I have a difficult time saying no.*
____ 6. When I am asked to do something, I insist upon knowing why.
____ 7. There are times when I look for a good, vigorous argument.
____ 8. I strive to get ahead as well as most people in my position.
____ 9. To be honest, people often take advantage of me.*
____ 10. I enjoy starting conversations with new acquaintances and strangers.
____ 11. I often don't know what to say to people who are sexually attractive to me.*
____ 12. I will hesitate to make phone calls to business establishments and institutions.*
____ 13. I would rather apply for a job or for admission to a college by writing letters than by going through with personal interviews.*
____ 14. I find it embarrassing to return merchandise.*
____ 15. If a close and respected relative were annoying me, I would smother my feelings rather than express my annoyance.*
____ 16. I have avoided asking questions for fear of sounding stupid.*
____ 17. During an argument I am sometimes afraid that I will get so upset that I will shake all over.*
____ 18. If a famed and respected lecturer makes a comment which I think is incorrect, I will have the audience hear my point of view as well.
____ 19. I avoid arguing over prices with clerks and salespeople.*
____ 20. When I have done something important or worthwhile, I manage to let others know about it.
____ 21. I am open and frank about my feelings.
____ 22. If someone has been spreading false and bad stories about me, I see him or her as soon as possible and have a talk about it.
____ 23. I often have a hard time saying no.*
____ 24. I tend to bottle up my emotions rather than make a scene.*
____ 25. I complain about poor service in a restaurant and elsewhere.
____ 26. When I am given a compliment, I sometimes just don't know what to say.*
____ 27. If a couple near me in a theater or at a lecture were conversing rather loudly, I would ask them to be quiet or to take their conversation elsewhere.
____ 28. Anyone attempting to push ahead of me in a line is in for a good battle.
____ 29. I am quick to express an opinion.
____ 30. There are times when I just can't say anything.*

Source: Reprinted from Rathus, 1973, pp. 398–406.

high in social anxiety are more readily persuaded than people with low social anxiety.

A study by Schwartz and Gottman (1976) reveals the cognitive nature of the "social anxiety" that can make it hard for some of us to say no to requests. Schwartz and Gottman found that people who comply with unreasonable requests are more likely to report thinking such things as "I was worried about what the other person would think of me if I refused," "It is better to help others than to be self-centered," or "The other person might be hurt or insulted if I refused." People who did not comply reported thoughts like "It doesn't matter what the other person thinks of me," "I am perfectly free to say no," or "This request is an unreasonable one" (p. 916).

Familiarity with the areas that a communicator is discussing also tends to decrease persuadability (Wood, 1982). If we know a great deal about cars, we are less open to the unrealistic claims of salespersons.

Truth or Fiction Revisited

It is true that people who worry about what other people think of them are likely to be low in sales resistance. Such people may be overly concerned about what the disappointed salesperson will be thinking.

The Foot-in-the-Door Technique

You might think that giving money to door-to-door solicitors for charity will get you off the hook. That is, they'll take the cash and leave you alone for a while. Actually, the opposite is true: The next time the organization mounts a campaign, they are more likely to call on generous you. In fact, they may even recruit you to go door to door! Giving an inch apparently encourages others to try to take a yard. They have gotten their "foot in the door."

In order to gain insight into the **foot-in-the-door technique,** consider a classic experiment by Freedman and Fraser (1966). In this study, groups of women received phone calls from a consumer group who asked whether they would allow a six-man crew to drop by their homes to inventory every product they used. It could take several hours to complete the chore. Only 22 percent of one group acceded to this rather troublesome request. But 53 percent of another group of women agreed to a visit from this wrecking crew. Why was the second group more compliant? The more compliant group had been phoned a few days earlier and had agreed to answer a few questions about the soap products they used. They had been primed for the second request. The caller had gotten his "foot in the door." Perhaps people who have acceded to a small request become more likely to accede to a larger one, because they come to view themselves as the type of people who help others (Snyder & Cunningham, 1975).

Regardless of how the foot-in-the-door technique works, if you want to say no, it may be easier to say no (and stick to your guns) the first time a request is made, and not later. And organizations have learned that they can compile lists of persons they can rely on.

Lowballing

Have you ever had a salesperson promise you a low price for merchandise, committed yourself to buy at that price, and then had the salesperson tell you that he or she had been in error, or that the manager had not agreed to the price? Have you then canceled the order or stuck to your commitment?

You might have been a victim of **lowballing,** a sales method also referred to as "throwing the low ball." In lowballing, you are persuaded to make a commitment on favorable terms; the persuader then claims that he or she must revise the terms. Perhaps the car you agreed to buy for $9,400 did not have the automatic transmission and air conditioning you both assumed it had. Perhaps the yen or the mark has just gone up against the dollar, and the price of the car has to be raised proportionately.

FOOT-IN-THE-DOOR TECHNIQUE • A method for inducing compliance in which a small request is followed by a larger request.

LOWBALLING • A method in which extremely attractive terms are offered to induce a person to make a commitment. Once the commitment is made, the terms are revised.

WHAT DO *YOU* SAY NOW?

RESPONDING TO LOWBALLING

Imagine that you're shopping for a new stereo set. You know just what you want and you see it advertised by a discount store at the excellent price of $350. You rush to the store and find a salesperson.

"Uh-oh," says the salesperson, shaking his head. "These sets have been going fast. I'll have to check on whether it's in stock. Give me a couple of minutes." Then he disappears into the back.

Fifteen minutes pass, and you're getting fidgety. But then the salesperson returns looking more upbeat. You are optimistic.

"I looked everywhere," he says, "and we're all out of the speakers." You have a sinking feeling. "But I checked with my manager," he continues, "and he says we can give you the same amplifier and CD player with more powerful speakers for $425. That's a bargain when you consider the sound you'll be getting."

You're no sucker, so you ask, "Won't you be getting them in stock again?"

"Sure," says the salesperson, "but not at $350. The dollar's been going down against the yen, and Japanese electronics are going up every day. Look, we don't want you to be unhappy. Believe me, at $425, the set with bigger speakers is a very good deal."

You want the set, but you don't need bigger speakers. And the price in the paper was $350 with the speakers you wanted.

What do you say now? Consider a number of possible responses, and write them here. Then check the sample answers that follow.

1. ______________________________
____

2. ______________________________
____

3. ______________________________
____

So, what did you say?

You have probably been a victim of lowballing. In this kind of lowballing, the customer is lured into the store by a good price on unavailable merchandise and then offered substitute goods at a higher price. Sad to say, this is not a rare sales practice. What kinds of things might you have said? There is no single right answer, but here are some possibilities:

1. "I think you had better let me talk to that manager myself. Please show me the way." (If the salesperson hems and haws, or if he says he'll "bring the manager out to you" in a few minutes, it might be that he had not spoken to the manager but was following a preplanned tactic.)
2. "It's illegal to advertise merchandise that's unavailable. Why don't you recheck with the manager and go through the storeroom again?" (If the salesperson—or the manager—is concerned about your veiled threat of a legal suit, he might be able to come up with the advertised merchandise.)
3. "Thank you for looking. I'll find the set I want at a decent price elsewhere." (This lets the salesperson know you're not going to be suckered, and perhaps you will find that set elsewhere—at a good price.)
4. Or you could simply walk out. ■

Lowballing is an aggravating technique, and there are few protections against it. One possibility is to ask the salesperson whether he or she has the authority to make the deal, and then to have him or her write out the terms and sign the offer. Unfortunately, the salesperson might later confess to misunderstanding what you meant by his or her having the "authority" to make the deal. Perhaps the best way to combat lowballing is to be willing to take your business elsewhere when the salesperson tries to back out of an arrangement.

OBEDIENCE TO AUTHORITY

Richard Nixon resigned the presidency of the United States in August 1974. For 2 years the business of the nation had almost ground to a halt while Congress investigated the 1972 burglary of a Democratic party campaign office in the Watergate office and apartment complex. It turned out that Nixon supporters had authorized the break-in. Nixon himself might have been involved in the cover-up of this connection later on. For 2 years Nixon and his aides had been investigated by the press and by Congress. Now it was over. Some of the bad guys were thrown in jail. Nixon was exiled to the beaches of southern California. The nation returned to work. The new president, Gerald Ford, declared "Our national nightmare is over."

But was it over? Have we come to grips with the implications of the Watergate affair?

According to psychologist Stanley Milgram (*APA Monitor,* January 1978), the Watergate cover-up, like the Nazi slaughter of the Jews, was made possible through the compliance of people who were more concerned about the approval of their supervisors than about their own morality. Otherwise they would have refused to abet these crimes. The broad questions are: (1) How pressing is the need to obey authority figures at all costs? (2) What can we do to ensure that we follow the dictates of our own consciences and not the immoral commands of authority figures?

The Milgram Studies: Shocking Stuff at Yale

Stanley Milgram also wondered how many of us would resist authority figures who made immoral requests. To find out, he ran a series of experiments at Yale University. In an early phase of his work, Milgram (1963) placed ads in New Haven, Connecticut, newspapers for subjects for studies on learning and memory. He enlisted 40 men ranging in age from 20 to 50—teachers, engineers, laborers, salespeople, men who had not completed elementary school, men with graduate degrees. The sample was a cross section of the population of New Haven.

Let us suppose you had answered the ad. You would have shown up at the university for a fee of $4.50, for the sake of science, and for your own curiosity. You might have been impressed. After all, Yale was a venerable institution that dominated the city. You would not have been less impressed by the elegant labs where you would have met a distinguished behavioral scientist dressed in a white laboratory coat and another newspaper recruit—like you. The scientist would have explained that the purpose of the experiment was to study the *effects of punishment on learning.* The experiment would require a "teacher" and a "learner." By chance you would be appointed the teacher, and the other recruit the learner.

You, the scientist, and the learner would enter a laboratory room with a rather threatening chair with dangling straps. The scientist would secure the learner's cooperation and strap him in. The learner would express some concern, but this was, after all, for the sake of science. And this was Yale University, was it not? What could happen to a person at Yale?

You would follow the scientist to an adjacent room from which you would do your "teaching." This teaching promised to be effective. You would punish the "learner's" errors by pressing levers marked from 15 to 450 volts on a fearsome-looking console (Figure 4.1). Labels described 28 of the 30 levers as running the gamut from "Slight Shock" to "Danger: Severe Shock." The last two

FIGURE 4.1
THE "AGGRESSION MACHINE."
In the Milgram studies on obedience to authority, pressing levers on the "aggression machine" was the operational definition of aggression.

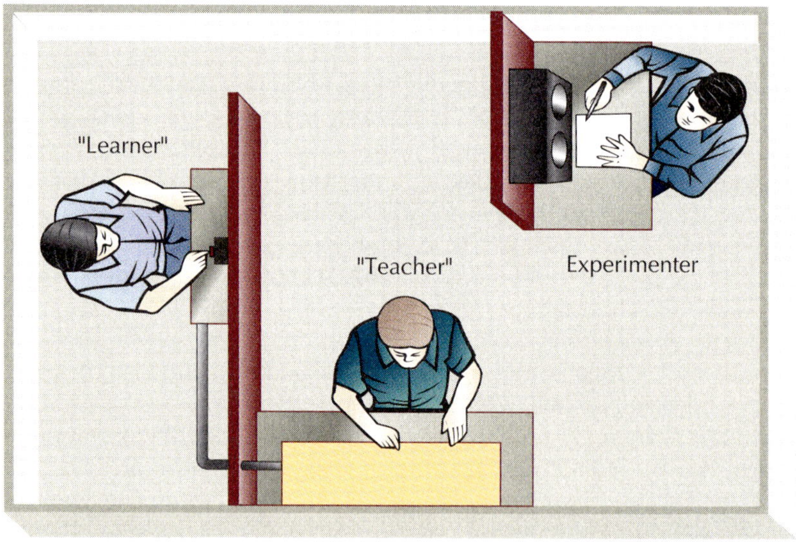

FIGURE 4.2
THE EXPERIMENTAL SETUP IN THE MILGRAM STUDIES.
When the "learner" makes an error, the experimenter prods the "teacher" to deliver a painful electric shock.

levers resembled a film unfit for anyone under age 17: They were rated simply "XXX." Just in case you had no idea what electric shock felt like, the scientist gave you a sample 45-volt shock. It stung. You pitied the fellow who might receive more.

Your learner was expected to learn word pairs. Pairs of words would be read from a list. After hearing the list once, the learner would have to produce the word that was paired with the stimulus word. He would do so by pressing a switch that would signify his choice from a list of four alternatives. The switch would light one of four panels in your room (see Figure 4.2). If it was the correct panel, you would proceed to the next stimulus word. If not, you would

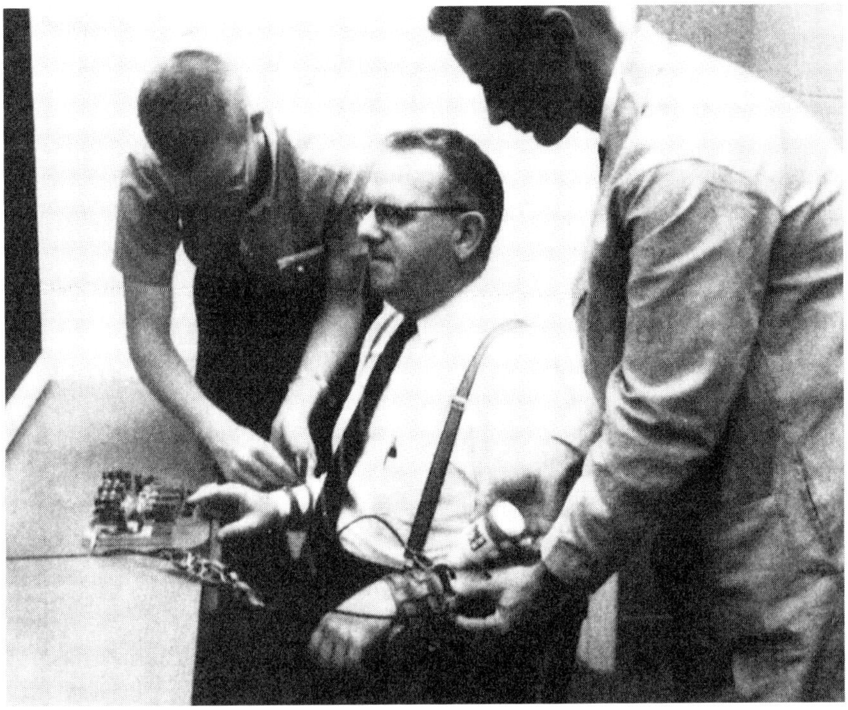

FIGURE 4.3
A "LEARNER" IN THE MILGRAM STUDIES ON OBEDIENCE TO AUTHORITY.
This "learner" could be in for quite a shock.

deliver an electric shock. With each error, you would increase the voltage of the shock.

You would probably have some misgivings. Electrodes had been strapped to the learner's wrists (see Figure 4.3), and the scientist had applied electrode paste to "avoid blisters and burns." You were also told that the shocks would cause "no permanent tissue damage," although they might be extremely painful. Still, the learner was going along, and, after all, this was Yale.

The learner answered some items correctly and then made some errors. With mild concern you pressed the levers up through 45 volts. You had tolerated that much yourself. Then a few more mistakes were made. You pressed the 60-volt lever, then 75. The learner made another mistake. You paused and looked at the scientist. He was reassuring: "Although the shocks may be painful, there is no permanent tissue damage, so please go on." Further errors were made, and quickly you were up to a shock of 300 volts. But now the learner was pounding on the other side of the wall! Your chest tightened, and you began to perspire. Damn science and the $4.50! you thought. You hesitated, and the scientist said, "The experiment requires that you continue." After the delivery of the next stimulus word, there was no answer at all. What were you to do? "Wait for five to ten seconds," the scientist instructed, "and then treat no answer as a wrong answer." But after the next shock, there was again that pounding on the wall! Now your heart was racing, and you were convinced that you were causing extreme pain and discomfort. Was it possible that no lasting damage was being done? Was the experiment that important, after all? What to do? You hesitated again. The scientist said, "It is absolutely essential that you continue." His voice was very convincing. "You have no other choice," he said, "you *must* go on." You could barely think straight, and for some unaccountable reason you felt laughter rising in your throat. Your finger shook above the lever. What were you to do?

On Truth at Yale

Milgram (1963, 1974) found out what most people would do. Of the 40 men in this phase of his research, only 5 refused to go beyond the 300-volt level, at which the learner first pounded the wall. Nine more "teachers" defied the scientist within the 300-volt range. But 65 percent of the participants complied with the scientist throughout the series, believing that they were delivering 450-volt, XXX-rated shocks.

Were these newspaper recruits simply unfeeling? Not at all. Milgram was impressed by their signs of stress. They trembled, they stuttered, they bit their lips. They groaned, they sweated, they dug their fingernails into their flesh. There were fits of laughter, though laughter was inappropriate. One salesperson's laughter was so convulsive that he could not continue with the experiment.

Milgram wondered if college students, heralded for independent thinking, would show more defiance. But a replication of the study with Yale undergraduates yielded similar results. What about women, who were supposedly less aggressive than men? Women, too, shocked the "learners"—and all of this in a nation that values independence and the free will of the individual. Our "national nightmare" may not be over at all.

On Deception at Yale

You are probably skeptical enough to wonder whether the "teachers" in the Milgram study actually shocked the "learners" when they pressed the levers on the console. They didn't. The only real shock in this experiment was the 45-volt sample given to the teachers. Its purpose was to lend credibility to the procedure.

The learners in the experiment were actually confederates of the experimenter. They had not answered the newspaper ads, but were in on the truth from the start. "Teachers" were the only real subjects. They were led to believe that they were chosen at random for the teacher role, but the choosing was rigged so that newspaper recruits would always become teachers.

The Big Question: Why?

We have shown that most people obey the commands of others, even when pressed to immoral tasks. But we have not answered the most pressing question: *Why?* Why did Nazis "just follow orders" and commit atrocities? Why did "teachers" obey orders from the experimenter? We do not have all the answers, but we can offer a number of hypotheses:

1. *Socialization.* Despite the expressed American ideal of independence, we are socialized to obey authority figures such as parents and teachers from early childhood on. Obedience to immoral demands may be the ugly sibling of socially desirable respect for authority figures (Blass, 1991).
2. *Lack of Social Comparison.* In Milgram's experimental settings, experimenters showed command of the situation, whereas "teachers" (subjects) were on the experimenter's ground. Being on their own, teachers did not have the opportunity to compare their ideas and feelings with those of people in the same situation. They were thus less likely to have a clear impression of what to do.
3. *Perception of Legitimate Authority.* The phase of Milgram's research described here took place within the hallowed halls of Yale University. Subjects there might be overpowered by the reputation and authority of the

setting. An experimenter at Yale might appear very much the legitimate authority figure—as might a government official or a high-ranking officer in the military. Further research showed that the university setting contributed to compliance but was not fully responsible for it. The percentage of subjects complying with the experimenter's demands dropped from 65 percent to 48 percent when Milgram (1974) replicated the study in a dingy storefront in a nearby town. In the less prestigious setting, slightly fewer than half of the subjects were willing to administer the highest levels of shock.

At first glance this finding might seem encouraging. But the main point of the Milgram studies is precisely that most of us remain willing to engage in morally reprehensible acts at the behest of a legitimate-appearing authority figure. Hitler and his henchmen were very much the legitimate authority figures in Nazi Germany. Nixon was the authority figure in the White House of the early 1970s. "Science" and Yale University legitimized the authority of the experimenters in the Milgram studies. The problem of acquiescence to authority figures remains.

4. *The Foot-in-the-Door Technique.* The foot-in-the-door technique might also have contributed to the obedience of the teachers (Gilbert, 1981). That is, after teachers had begun the process of delivering graduated shocks to learners, perhaps they found it progressively more difficult to extricate themselves from the project. Soldiers, similarly, are first taught to obey unquestioningly in innocuous matters such as dress and drill. By the time they are ordered to risk their lives and storm that hill, they have been saluting smartly and following commands for quite some time.

5. *Inaccessibility of Values.* People are more likely to behave in ways that are consistent with their values and other attitudes when their attitudes are readily accessible, or when they easily "come to mind" (Fazio, 1986; Fazio and others, 1986). But we become subject to confused and conflicting thoughts and motives as our levels of anxiety shoot up. As teachers in the Milgram experiments became more and more aroused, their values might have become less accessible. As a consequence, it might have become progressively more difficult for them to behave in ways that were consistent with their moral values.

6. *Buffers.* Social psychologist Daryl Bem (1993) also notes that several buffers decreased the immediate impact of the teachers' violence. Learners (confederates of the experimenter), for example, were in another room. When learners were in the same room with teachers—that is, when subjects had full view of their victims—the compliance rate dropped from 65 to 40 percent. Moreover, when the subject was given the task of holding the learner's hand on the shock plate, the compliance rate dropped to 30 percent. Similarly, many bomber pilots during World War II said that they could not have carried out their missions if they had seen the faces of their victims. In modern warfare, opposing soldiers tend to be separated by great distances. It is one thing to press a button to launch a missile, or to aim a piece of artillery at a distant troop carrier or a distant ridge. It is another thing to hold the weapon to the throat of the victim.

There are thus many reasons for obedience. Regardless of the exact nature of the forces that acted upon the subjects in the Milgram studies, his research has alerted us to a real and present danger—the tendency of most people to obey authority figures, even when the figures' demands contradict their own values. It has happened before. Unhappily, unless we remain alert, it may happen again. Who are the authority figures in your life? How do you think you

Truth or Fiction Revisited

It is not true that most people would refuse to deliver painful electric shock to an innocent party when they are under powerful social pressure. Most people, sad to say, would shock an innocent party, as shown by the Milgram studies on obedience.

would have behaved if you had been a "teacher" in the Milgram studies? Are you sure?

GROUP BEHAVIOR

To be human is to belong to groups. Families, classes, religious groups, political parties, circles of friends, bowling teams, sailing clubs, conversation groups, therapy groups—to how many groups do you belong? How do groups influence the behavior of individuals?

In this section we have a look at two important aspects of group behavior: mob behavior and the bystander effect.

Mob Behavior and Deindividuation

Gustave Le Bon (1960), the French social thinker, branded mobs and crowds irrational, like a "beast with many heads." Mob actions such as race riots and lynchings sometimes seem to operate on a psychology of their own. Do mobs elicit the beast in us? How is it that mild-mannered people will commit mayhem as members of a mob? In seeking an answer, let us examine a lynching and the baiting type of crowd that often seems to attend threatened suicides.

THE LYNCHING OF ARTHUR STEVENS In *Social Learning and Imitation,* Neal Miller and John Dollard (1941) vividly described a southern lynching. Arthur Stevens, a Black man, was accused of murdering his lover, a White woman, when she wanted to break up with him. Stevens was arrested and confessed to the crime. The sheriff feared violence and moved Stevens to a town 200 miles distant during the night. But his location was uncovered. The next day a mob of a hundred persons stormed the jail and returned Stevens to the scene of the crime.

Outrage spread from person to person like a plague bacillus. Laborers, professionals, women, adolescents, and law enforcement officers alike were infected. Stevens was tortured and killed. His corpse was dragged through the streets. Then the mob went on a rampage in town, chasing and assaulting other Black people. The riot ended only when troops were sent in to restore law and order.

DEINDIVIDUATION When we act as individuals, fear of consequences and self-evaluation tend to prevent antisocial behavior. But as members of a mob,

MOB BEHAVIOR?
Do groups of people sometimes act like a "beast with many heads"? Have you ever been swept up by a mob? What can you do to maintain your individuality?

we may experience **deindividuation,** a state of reduced self-awareness and lowered concern for social evaluation (Baron & Byrne, 1997; Diener, 1980). Many factors lead to deindividuation, including anonymity, **diffusion of responsibility,** arousal due to noise and crowding, and focusing of individual attention on the group process. Individuals also tend to adopt the emerging norms and attitudes of the group. Under these circumstances, crowd members behave more aggressively than they would as individuals.

Police know that mob actions are best averted early, by dispersing the small groups that may gather into a crowd. On an individual level, perhaps we can resist deindividuation by instructing ourselves to stop and think whenever we begin to feel highly aroused as group members. If we dissociate ourselves from such groups when they are in the formative process, we shall be more likely to retain critical self-evaluation and avoid behavior that we shall later regret.

Conformity

Earlier we noted that most of us would be reluctant to wear blue jeans to a funeral or to walk naked on city streets. Such behavior would fly in the face of social norms, and other people would show us disapproval for it. We are said to **conform** when we change our behavior in order to adhere to social norms. **Social norms** are widely accepted expectations concerning social behavior. Explicit social norms require us to whisper in libraries and to slow down when driving past a school. One unspoken or implicit social norm is to be fashionably late for social gatherings.

Truth or Fiction Revisited

It is true that many people are late to social gatherings because they are conforming to a social norm. Being "fashionably late" is an example of an implicit (unspoken) social norm.

A couple of unspoken social norms operate in elevators. One norm is to face the front (Zuckerman and others, 1983). The other is to mind one's own business, especially when the elevator is crowded. The first author likes to test the second elevator norm now and then by making friendly comments to strangers. The strangers usually smile perfunctorily and say as little as possible.

The tendency to conform to social norms is often a good thing. Many norms have evolved because they favor comfort and survival. In the tight confines of the elevator, people seem to hold on to dignity in the face of others pressing against them and literally breathing down their necks by pretending that the other people are not there. The pretense works as long as everyone plays the same game. Given the discomfort of being crowded in with strangers, the distance provided by minding one's own business seems adaptive. But group norms can also promote maladaptive behavior, as in pressuring businesspeople to wear coats and ties in summer in buildings cooled only, say, to 78 degrees Fahrenheit. At that high temperature the only motive for conforming to a dress code may be to show that we have been adequately socialized and are not threats to social rules.

Let us examine some of the factors that promote conformity.

Factors That Influence Conformity Several personal and situational factors prompt conformity to social norms. Personal factors include low self-esteem, high self-consciousness, social shyness (Santee & Maslach, 1982), familiarity with the task, and the desires to be liked by other members of the group and to be right (Insko, 1985). Situational factors include group size and social support.

Familiarity with the task at hand promotes self-reliance (Eagly, 1978). In one experiment, for example, Sistrunk and McDavid (1971) found that women were more likely to conform to group pressure on tasks involving identification of tools (such as wrenches) that were more familiar to men. But men were more

Deindividuation • The process by which group members may discontinue self-evaluation and adopt group norms and attitudes.

Diffusion of responsibility • The sharing of responsibility for behavior by the members of a group.

Conform • To changes one's attitudes or behaviors to adhere to social norms.

Social norms • Explicit and implicit rules that reflect social expectations and influence the ways people behave in social situations.

likely to conform on tasks involving identification of cooking utensils, with which women, in our society, are usually more familiar.

Situational factors include the number of people who hold the majority opinion and the presence of at least one other who shares the discrepant opinion. Probability of conformity, even to incorrect group judgments, increases rapidly as a group grows to five members. Then it increases at a slower rate up to eight members (Gerard and others, 1968; Wilder, 1977), at which point maximum probability of conformity is reached.

But finding just one other person who supports your minority opinion is apparently enough to encourage you to stick to your guns (Morris and others, 1977).

Helping Behavior and the Bystander Effect: Some Watch While Others Die

We are all part of vast social networks—schools, industries, religious groups, communities, and society at large. Although we may have individual pursuits, in some ways our adjustment and personal development are intertwined. To some degree we depend on one another. What one person produces, another consumes. Goods are available in stores because other people have transported them, sometimes halfway around the world. A medical discovery in Boston saves a life in Taiwan. An assembly-line foul-up in Detroit places an accident victim in a hospital in Florida.

Truth or Fiction Revisited

It is true that nearly 40 people stood by and did nothing while a woman was being stabbed to death. Kitty Genovese was the victim, and her tragic end sparked much research into the so-called bystander effect.

Because of such mutual dependency, one might think that we would come to the aid of others in trouble—especially when their lives are threatened. And sometimes we do, even at risk to ourselves. But now and then we let others down, as in the murder of 28-year-old Kitty Genovese in New York City in 1964. Murder was not unheard-of in the "Big Apple," but Kitty had screamed for help as her killer had repeatedly stabbed her (Rosenthal, 1994). Nearly 40 neighbors had heard the commotion. Many watched. Nobody helped. Why? Are we a callous bunch who would rather watch than help others who are in trouble? According to Stanley Milgram, the Genovese case "touched on a fundamental issue of the human condition. If we need help, will those around us stand around and let us be destroyed or will they come to our aid?" (in Dowd, 1984).

Social psychologists refer to helping behavior as **altruism.** Let us consider some of the factors that determine whether we will come to the aid of others who are in trouble.

THE HELPER: WHO HELPS? Many factors affect helping behavior:

1. Empathic observers are more likely to help. Most psychologists focus on the roles of a helper's mood and personality traits. By and large, we are more likely to help others when we are in a good mood (Baron & Byrne, 1997; George, 1991). Perhaps good moods impart a sense of personal power (Cunningham and others, 1990). People who are empathic are also more likely to help people in need (Darley, 1993). Empathic people feel the distress of others, feel concern for them, and can imagine what it must be like to be in need. Women are more likely than men to be empathic, and thus more likely to help people in need (Trobst and others, 1994).
2. Bystanders may not help unless they believe that an emergency exists (Baron & Byrne, 1997). Perhaps some people who heard Kitty Genovese's calls for help were not certain as to what was happening. (But remember that others admitted they did not want to get involved.)

ALTRUISM • Unselfish concern for the welfare of others.

3. Observers must assume the responsibility to act (Baron & Byrne, 1997). It may seem logical that a group of people would be more likely to have come to the aid of Kitty Genovese than a lone person. After all, a group could more effectively have overpowered her attacker. Yet research by Darley and Latané (1968) suggests that a lone person may have been more likely to try to help her.

   In their classic experiment, male subjects were performing meaningless tasks in cubicles when they heard a (convincing) recording of a person apparently having an epileptic seizure. When the men thought that four other persons were immediately available, only 31 percent tried to help the victim. When they thought that no one else was available, however, 85 percent of them tried to help. As in other areas of group behavior, it seems that *diffusion of responsibility* inhibits helping behavior in groups or crowds. When we are in a group, we are often willing to let George (or Georgette) do it. When George isn't around, we are more willing to help others ourselves. (Perhaps some who heard Kitty Genovese thought, "Why should I get involved? Other people can hear her too.")
4. Observers must know what to do (Baron & Byrne, 1997). We hear of cases in which people impulsively jump into the water to save a drowning child and then drown themselves. Most of the time, however, people do not try to help unless they know what to do. For example, nurses are more likely than people without medical training to try to help accident victims (Cramer and others, 1988). Observers who are not sure that they can take charge of the situation may stay on the sidelines for fear of making a social blunder and being ridiculed. Or they may fear getting hurt themselves. (Perhaps some who heard Kitty Genovese thought, "If I try to intervene, I may get killed or make an idiot of myself.")
5. Observers are more likely to help people they know (Rutkowski and others, 1983). Aren't we also more likely to give to charity when asked directly by a co-worker or supervisor in the socially exposed situation of the office as compared with a letter received in the privacy of our own homes?

   Some theorists (e.g., Guisinger & Blatt, 1994) suggest that altruism is a natural aspect of human nature. Self-sacrifice sometimes helps close relatives or others who are similar to us to survive. Ironically, self-sacrifice is selfish from a genetic or sociobiological point of view. It helps us perpetuate a genetic code similar to our own. This view suggests that we are more likely to be altruistic with our relatives than with strangers, however. The Kitty Genoveses of the world may remain out of luck unless they are surrounded by kinfolk or friends.
6. Observers are more likely to help people who are similar to themselves (Baron & Byrne, 1997). Similarity also seems to promote helping behavior. Poorly dressed people are more likely to succeed in requests for a dime with poorly dressed strangers. Well dressed people are more likely to get money from well dressed strangers.

What will you do the next time you pass by someone who is obviously in need of aid? Will you help, or will you stand by?

adjustment and modern life

There is no simple, single answer to the adjustment problems that are brought about by social influence. Running off to an island on the other side of the world would be a poor, if not impossible, solution for most of us. Other people provide us with exciting and needed stimulation, and so averting social influence by avoiding social contact is a punitive prospect for most of us. But there are a number of things we can do about social influence, and one of them is to become more self-assertive.

Assertive behavior involves many things—the expression of your genuine feelings, standing up for your legitimate rights, and refusing unreasonable requests. It means withstanding undue social influences, disobeying *arbitrary* authority figures, and refusing to conform to *arbitrary* group standards. Since many of our feelings are positive, such as love and admiration, assertive behavior also means expressing them.

Assertive people also use the power of social influence to achieve desired ends. That is, they influence others to join them in worthwhile social and political activities. They may become involved in political campaigns, consumer groups, conservationist organizations, and other groups to advance their causes.

Alternatives to assertive behavior include submissive, or *unassertive*, behavior and *aggressive* behavior. When we are submissive, our self-esteem plummets. Unexpressed feelings sometimes smolder as resentments and then catch fire as socially inappropriate outbursts. Aggressive behavior includes physical and verbal attacks, threats, and insults. Sometimes we get our way through aggression, but we also earn the condemnation of others. And, unless we are unfeeling, we condemn ourselves for bullying others.

Becoming More Assertive. Sometimes what you do is what you are. You can become more assertive by greeting people cheerfully, making eye contact, and talking about your feelings.

HOW TO BECOME AN ASSERTIVE PERSON (HOW TO WIN RESPECT AND INFLUENCE PEOPLE)

Perhaps you can't become completely assertive overnight. But you can decide *now* that you have been unassertive long enough and make a plan for change. There may be times when you want to quit and revert to your unassertive ways. Expressing your genuine beliefs may lead to some immediate social disapproval. Others may have a stake in your remaining a doormat, and the people we wind up confronting are sometimes those who are closest to us: parents, spouses, supervisors, and friends.

You can use the following four methods to become more assertive: (1) self-monitoring, (2) challenging irrational beliefs, (3) modeling, and (4) behavior rehearsal.

Self-Monitoring: Following Yourself Around the Block

Self-monitoring of social interactions can help you pinpoint problem areas and increase your motivation to behave more assertively. Keep a diary for a week or so. Jot down brief descriptions of any encounters that lead to negative feelings such as anxiety, depression, or anger. For each encounter, record the following:

The situation

What you felt and said or did

How others responded to your behavior

How you felt about the behavior afterward

Here are some examples of self-monitoring. They involve an office worker (Jane), a teacher (Michael), and medical student (Leslie), all in their 20s:

Jane: Monday, April 6

9:00 A.M. I passed Artie in the hall. I ignored him. He didn't say anything. I felt disgusted with myself.

NOON Pat and Kathy asked me to join them for lunch. I felt shaky inside and lied that I still had work to do. They said all right, but I think they were fed up with me. I felt miserable, very tight in my stomach.

7:30 P.M. Kathy called me and asked me to go clothes shopping with her. I was feeling down and I said I was busy. She said she was sorry. I don't believe she was sorry—I think she knows I was lying. I hate myself. I feel awful.

Jane's record reveals a pattern of fear of incompetence in social relationships and resultant avoidance of other people. Her avoidance may once have helped her to reduce the immediate impact of her social anxieties, but it has led to feelings of loneliness and depression. Now, because of Jane's immediate self-disgust, her defensive avoidance behavior doesn't even seem to help her in the short run.

Michael: Wednesday, December 17

8:30 A.M. The kids were noisy in homeroom. I got very angry and screamed my head off at them. They quieted down, but sneaked looks at each other as if I were crazy. My face felt red and hot, and my stomach was in a knot. I wondered what I was doing.

4:00 P.M. I was driving home from school. Some guy cut me off. I followed him closely for two blocks, leaning on my horn but praying he wouldn't stop and get out of his car. He didn't. I felt shaky as hell and thought someday I'm going to get myself killed. I had to pull over and wait for the shakes to pass before I could go on driving.

8:00 P.M. I was writing lesson plans for tomorrow. Mom came into the room and started crying—Dad was out drinking again. I yelled it was her problem. If she didn't want him to drink, she could confront him with it, not me,

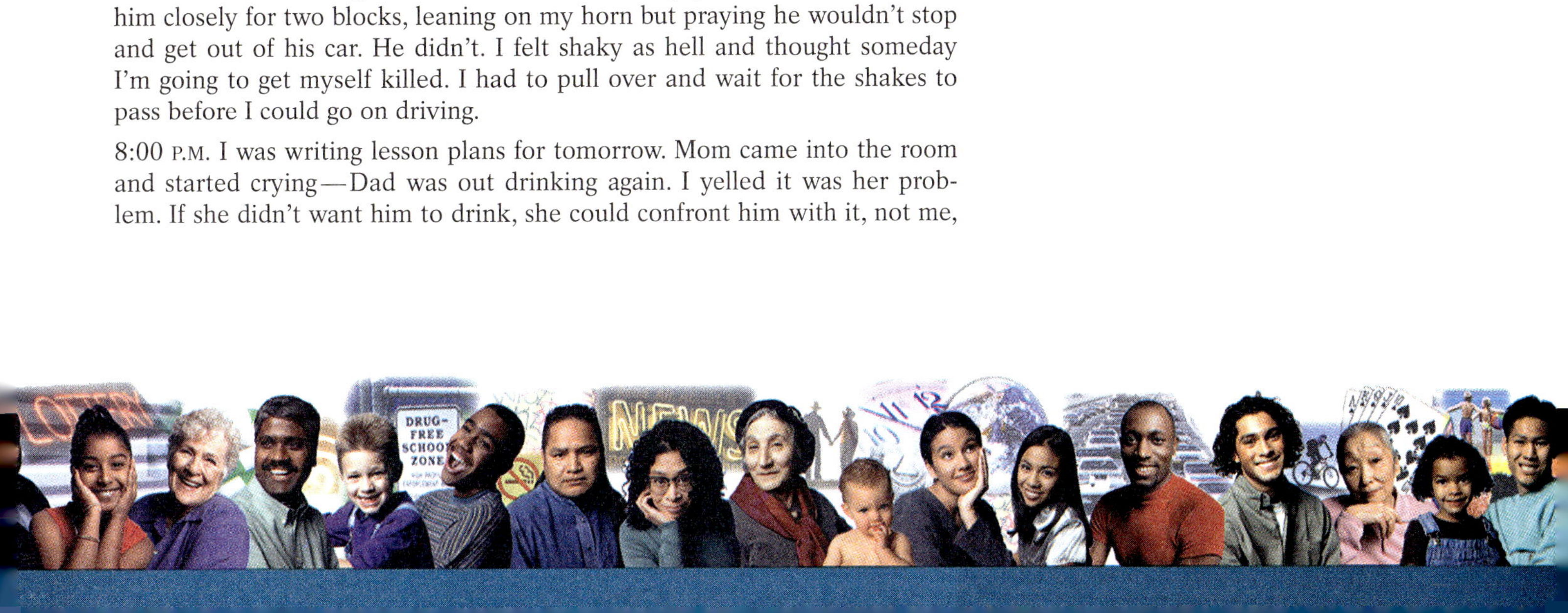

> or divorce him. She cried harder and ran out. I felt pain in my chest. I felt drained and hopeless.

Michael's record showed that he was aggressive, not assertive. The record pinpoints the types of events and responses that had led to higher blood pressure and many painful bodily sensations. The record also helped him realize that he was living with many ongoing frustrations instead of making decisions—as to where he would live, for example—and behaving assertively.

Leslie was a third-year medical student whose husband was a professor of art and archaeology:

Leslie: Tuesday, October 5

> 10:00 A.M. I was discussing specialization interests with classmates. I mentioned my interest in surgery. Paul smirked and said, "Shouldn't you go into something like pediatrics or family practice?" I said nothing, playing the game of ignoring him, but I felt sick and weak inside. I was wondering if I would survive a residency in surgery if my supervisors also thought that I should enter a less pressured or more "feminine" branch of medicine.

Leslie: Thursday, October 7

> 7:30 P.M. I had studying to do, but was washing the dinner dishes, as per usual. Tom was reading the paper. I wanted to scream that there was no reason I should be doing the dishes just because I was the woman. I'd worked harder that day than Tom, my career was just as important as his, and I had studying to do that evening. But I said nothing. I felt anxiety or anger—I don't know which. My face was hot and flushed. My heart rate was rapid. I was sweating.

Even though Leslie was competing successfully in medical school, men apparently did not view her accomplishments as being as important as their own. It may never have occurred to Tom that he could help her with the dishes, or that they could rotate responsibility for household tasks. Leslie resolved that she must learn to speak out—to prevent male students from taunting her and to enlist Tom's cooperation around the house.

Confronting Irrational Beliefs: Do Your Own Beliefs Lead to Unassertive or Aggressive Behavior?

While you are monitoring your behavior, try to observe irrational beliefs that may lead to unassertive or to aggressive behavior. These beliefs may be fleeting and so ingrained that you no longer pay any attention to them. But by ignoring them, you deny yourself the opportunity to evaluate them, and to change them if they are irrational.

Jane feared social incompetence. Several irrational beliefs heightened her concerns. She believed, for example, that she must be perfectly competent in her social interactions or else avoid them. She believed that it would be awful if she floundered at a social effort and another person showed disapproval of her, even for an instant. She also believed that she was "naturally shy"—that heredity and her early environment must somehow have forged a fundamental shy-

ness that she was powerless to change. She also told herself that she could gain greater happiness in life through inaction and "settling" for other-than-social pleasures like reading and television—that she could achieve a contentment even if she never confronted her avoidance behavior. When shown Albert Ellis's list of 10 basic irrational beliefs (see p. 303), even Jane had to admit that she had unknowingly adopted nearly all of them.

Many of Michael's frustrations stemmed from a belief that life had singled him out for unfair treatment. How *dare* people abuse him? The *world* should change. With the world so unfair and unjust, why should he have to search out his *own* sources of frustration and cope with them? For many reasons: For example, Michael was attributing his own miseries to external pressures and hoping that if he ignored them they would go away. With an alcoholic father and a weak mother, he told himself, how could *he* be expected to behave appropriately?

Women and Assertive Behavior: Problems Caused by Early Socialization Messages Leslie failed to express her feelings because she harbored subtle beliefs to the effect that women should not be "pushy" and cause resentments when they compete in areas traditionally reserved for men. She kidded herself that she could understand and accept the fact that Tom had simply been reared in a home atmosphere in which women carried out the day-to-day household chores. She kidded herself that it was easier for her to remain silent on the issue instead of making a fuss and expecting Tom to modify lifelong attitudes.

Women like Leslie have typically received early socialization messages that underlie many of their adult irrational beliefs. Among these messages are the following: "I need to rely on someone stronger than myself—a man," "Men should handle large amounts of money and make the big decisions," "It is awful to hurt the feelings of others," "A woman does not raise her voice," and "I should place the needs of my husband and children before my own." In the area of sexual behavior, women have frequently received these early socialization messages: that they need to be guided by men to achieve satisfaction, that only men should initiate sexual activity, that sexually assertive women are sluttish or castrating, and that women must use artificial means such as makeup and scented sprays to make themselves attractive. Beliefs such as these endorse the stereotypical feminine gender role and traits like dependence, passivity, and nurturance (at all costs). In short, they deny women *choice*.

Changing Irrational Beliefs Do any of Jane's, Michael's, or Leslie's irrational beliefs also apply to you? Do they prevent you from behaving assertively? From making the effort to get out and meet people? From expressing your genuine feelings? From demanding your legitimate rights? Do they sometimes prompt aggressive rather than assertive behavior?

If so, you may decide to challenge your irrational beliefs. Ask yourself if they strike you as logical or simply as habit. Do they help you behave assertively, or do they give you excuses for being submissive or aggressive? What will happen if you try something new? What if your new behavior has a few rough edges at first? Will the roof cave in if someone disapproves of

you? Will the Ice Age be upon us if you try to speak up and flub it once or twice? Will the gods descend from Mount Olympus and strike you with lightning if you question an authority figure who makes an unreasonable request?

Modeling: Creating the New—Well, Almost New—You

Much of our behavior is modeled after that of people we respect and admire, people who have seemed capable of coping with situations that posed some difficulty for us. Here and there we adopt a characteristic, a gesture, a phrase, a tone of voice, a leer, a sneer.

Therapists who help clients become more assertive use extensive modeling. They may provide examples of specific things to say. When we are interacting with other people, our degrees of eye contact, our postures, and our distances from them also communicate strong messages (Schwarz and others, 1983). Direct eye contact, for example, suggests assertiveness and honesty. So therapists help clients shape nonverbal behaviors as well—whether to lean toward the other person, how to hold one's hands, how far away to stand, and so on. Then the client tries it. The therapist provides feedback, telling the client how well he or she did.

Behavior Rehearsal: Practice Makes Much Better

At first it is a good idea to try out new assertive behaviors in nonthreatening situations, such as before your mirror or with trusted friends. This is behavior rehearsal. It will accustom you to the sounds of assertive talk as they are born in your own throat.

Therapists have clients rehearse assertive responses in individual or group sessions. They may use role-playing, in which they act the part of a social antagonist or encourage you or other group members to take the roles of important people in your life. They alert you to posture, tone of voice, and the need to maintain eye contact.

Joan was a recently divorced secretary in her twenties. She returned home to live with her parents, and 6 months later her father died. Joan offered support as her mother, in her fifties, underwent several months of mourning. But Joan eventually realized that her mother had become excessively dependent on her. She no longer drove or went anywhere alone. Joan felt she must persuade her mother to regain some independence—for both their sakes.

Joan explained her problem in an assertiveness training group. The therapist and group members suggested things that Joan could say. A group member then role-played her mother while Joan rehearsed responses to her mother's requests. Her goal was to urge independent behavior in such a way that her mother would eventually see that Joan was interested in her welfare. Joan showed that she understood her mother's feelings by using the technique of *fogging,* or by paraphrasing them. But she clung to her basic position through the *broken-record technique,* as in this sample dialogue:

MOTHER ROLE: Dear, would you take me over to the market?
JOAN: Sorry, Mom, it's been a long day. Why don't you drive yourself?

MOTHER ROLE: You know I haven't been able to get behind the wheel of that car since Dad passed away.

JOAN: I know it's been hard for you to get going again (fogging), but it's been a long day (broken record) and you've got to get started doing these things again sometime.

MOTHER ROLE: You know that if I could do this for myself, I would.

JOAN: I know that you believe that (fogging), but I'm not doing you a favor by driving you around all the time. You've got to get started sometime (broken record).

MOTHER ROLE: I don't think you understand how I feel. *(Cries.)*

JOAN: You can say that, but I think I really do understand how awful you feel (fogging). But I'm thinking of your own welfare more than my own, and I'm not doing you a favor when I drive you everywhere (broken record).

MOTHER ROLE: But we need a few things.

JOAN: I'm not doing you any favor by continuing to drive you everywhere (broken record).

MOTHER ROLE: Does that mean you've decided not to help?

JOAN: It means that I'm not helping you by continuing to drive you everywhere. I'm thinking of your welfare as well as my own, and you have to start driving again sometime (broken record).

Joan's task was difficult, but she persisted. She and her mother reached a workable compromise in which Joan at first accompanied her mother while her mother drove. But after an agreed-upon amount of time, her mother began to drive by herself.

We can use modeling on our own by carefully observing friends; business acquaintances; characters on television, in films, and in books—and noting how effective they are in their social behavior. If their gestures and words seem effective and believable in certain situations, we may try them out. Ask yourself whether the verbal and nonverbal communications of others would fit you if you trimmed them just a bit here and there. Sew bits and pieces of the behavior patterns of others together; then try them on for size. After a while you may find that they need a bit more altering. But if you wear them for a while once they have been shaped to fit you, you may come to feel as if you have worn them all your life.

Adjustment in a World of DIVERSITY

"But You're Not in Hong Kong": Asian Americans Fight a Stereotype Through Assertiveness Training

The United States is an individualistic society, and Japan is a collectivistic society. Therefore, in many cases the Japanese corporate culture encourages consensus building, whereas individualism and face-to-face confrontation are common American approaches to arriving at corporate decisions. In the United

States, many groups of Asian Americans, including Japanese Americans and Chinese Americans, also tend to be stereotyped as passive, soft-spoken, and unassertive—and consequently as poor managers and poor decision makers (Louie, 1993). A young Chinese American executive at a California high-tech firm complains that his efforts to build consensus are often criticized with statements such as, "Why can't you come out and make a decision?" (cited in Louie, 1993).

In many Asian cultures, direct eye contact, expansive movements, and impassioned speech during a discussion are often considered threatening (Louie, 1993). Asians and many Asian Americans are thus socialized into less confrontational patterns of body language. Either way, many Asian Americans are stereotyped. Politeness is often misinterpreted as wimpiness. Yet because forceful behaviors run counter to the stereotype, many Asian Americans who are simply being dynamic and decisive in typical American fashion are branded as aggressive—just as dynamic, decisive women are often besmirched as masculine or bitchy.

ENTER ASSERTIVENESS TRAINING? Assertiveness training, which was at the height of its popularity during the Me Decade of the 1970s, is making a comeback among Asian Americans (Louie, 1993). Participants in assertiveness training workshops are taught both nonverbal and verbal assertive behaviors. Nonverbal assertiveness includes direct eye contact, sitting upright, and leaning toward the person one is addressing. Verbal exercises focus on expressing one's feelings, using the word *I* rather than being self-deprecating, making reasonable requests, saying no, and emphatic repetition of one's positions.

Training also focuses on the clashes between Asian and American cultures. Participants talk through their feelings about the place of Asian values such as desire for harmony, respect for authority, loyalty toward one's group or corporation, perseverance at difficult tasks without making complaints, and control of emotions in the American workplace.

A participant in one such workshop complained that none of this would be necessary if she had remained in Hong Kong. "But you're not in Hong Kong," replied the workshop leader (cited in Louie, 1993). "So what are you going to do about that?" ■

SUMMARY

1. **What "routes" are involved in persuasion?** People can be persuaded to change attitudes by central and peripheral routes. The central route involves change by consideration or arguments and evidence. The peripheral route involves associating the objects of attitudes with positive or negative cues, such as attractive communicators.
2. **How does the nature of the message influence whether or not it will be persuasive?** Repeating messages also makes them more persuasive. Messages that are too discrepant with audience views, however, may fail to persuade.
3. **What peripheral factors influence whether or not a message will be persuasive?** We tend to be persuaded by communicators who appear to have expertise, trustworthiness, and attractiveness. Emotional appeals are more effective with most people than are logical presentations. We are more likely to be persuaded by people who compliment and agree with us. Food and music also create an atmosphere in which we are more compliant.
4. **Are some people more readily persuaded than others?** Yes. People who feel inadequate, or who believe that it is awful to earn the disapproval of others, show less sales resistance.
5. **What is the foot-in-the-door technique?** This is a method for inducing compliance with requests in which another person makes a small request to which you are likely to accede. Having gotten his or her "foot in the door," he or she follows with a larger request.
6. **What is lowballing?** This is a persuasive, or sales, technique in which you are induced to make a commitment (such as to buy a product) by being offered extremely favorable terms. Then the persuader, or salesperson, alters the terms in hopes that you will retain your commitment.
7. **What happened during the Milgram studies on obedience, and what factors are thought to account for the behavior of the subjects?** In the Milgram studies, most subjects, in obeying an authority figure, administered to an innocent person what they believed to be an electric shock. Factors that heighten the tendency to obey other people include socialization, lack of social comparison, perception of a legitimate authority figure, the foot-in-the-door technique, inaccessibility of values, and buffers between the actor and the victim.
8. **How does our behavior as members of the crowd differ from our behavior as individuals? Why?** As members of crowds, many people engage in behavior they would find unacceptable if they were acting alone, to some degree because of high arousal and anonymity. In doing so, they set aside their own values and adopt the norms of the group. The adoption of group norms is called deindividuation, and once people have become deindividuated, their responsibility for their own behavior becomes diffused.
9. **Why do we sometimes help people in trouble and at other times stand by and do nothing?** When we are members of groups or crowds, we may ignore people in trouble because of diffusion of responsibility. We are more likely to help others when we think we are the only ones available to help, when we understand the situation, when we believe that our efforts will succeed, and when we feel responsible for helping.
10. **What is assertive behavior?** Assertive behavior helps us withstand social influence. It is assertive to express our genuine feelings and stand up for our legitimate rights. It is aggressive, not assertive, to insult, threaten, or attack verbally or physically.
11. **How can we become more assertive?** We can become more assertive through techniques such as self-monitoring, challenging irrational beliefs that prevent us from speaking up, modeling, and behavior rehearsal. In doing so, we should attend to nonverbal communications such as eye contact, posture and gestures, and distance from others, as well as to the things we say.

CHAPTER 5

Stress: Sources and Moderators

TRUTH OR FICTION?

✔ T F

- ☐ ☐ The more change the merrier—variety's the spice of life.
- ☐ ☐ Our own bodies produce chemicals that are similar in function to the narcotic morphine.
- ☐ ☐ Video games help child cancer patients cope with the side effects of chemotherapy.
- ☐ ☐ Commuting on the freeway elevates our blood pressure.
- ☐ ☐ Many people create their own sources of stress.
- ☐ ☐ Children in noisy classrooms do not learn to read as well as children in quiet classrooms.
- ☐ ☐ Auto fumes may lower your children's IQs.
- ☐ ☐ Hot temperatures make us hot under the collar—that is, they prompt aggression.
- ☐ ☐ Crowding a third roommate into a dorm room built for two usually makes somebody unhappy.
- ☐ ☐ The belief that we can handle stress is linked to lower levels of adrenaline in the bloodstream.
- ☐ ☐ Some people are psychologically hardier than others.
- ☐ ☐ A sense of humor helps buffer the effects of stress.
- ☐ ☐ Single men live longer.

OUTLINE

PERHAPS TOO MUCH OF A GOOD THING CAN MAKE you ill. You might think that marrying Mr. or Ms. Right, finding a prestigious job, and moving to a better neighborhood all in the same year would propel you into a state of bliss. It might. But the impact of all these events, one on top of the other, could also lead to headaches, high blood pressure, and asthma. As pleasant as the events may be, they all involve major life changes, and change is a source of *stress.*

STRESS

In the science of physics, stress is a pressure or force exerted on a body. Tons of rock pressing against the earth, one car smashing into another, a rubber band stretching—all are physical stressors. Psychological forces, or stresses, also "press," "push," or "pull." We may feel "crushed" by the "weight" of a big decision, "smashed" by misfortune, or "stretched" to the limit.

In psychology, **stress** is the demand made on an organism to adapt, cope, or adjust. Some stress is necessary to keep us alert and occupied (Selye, 1980). But stress that is too intense or prolonged can overtax our adjustive capacity, dampen our moods, impair our ability to experience pleasure, and harm the body (Berenbaum & Connelly, 1993; Cohen and others, 1993; Repetti, 1993). Stress is the number one reason that college students seek help at college counseling centers (Gallagher, 1996; Murray, 1996). See Table 5.1 for further reasons they seek help.

SOURCES OF STRESS

Change is one source of stress. Other sources include daily hassles, pain and discomfort, frustration, conflict, Type A behavior, the need for power, and environmental factors like natural disasters, noise, and crowding.

Daily Hassles

STRESS • An event that exerts physical or psychological force or pressure on a person. The demand made on an organism to adjust.

DAILY HASSLES • Lazarus's term for routine sources of annoyance or aggravation that have a negative impact on health.

UPLIFTS • Lazarus's term for regularly occurring enjoyable experiences.

The "last" straw will break the camel's back—so goes the saying. Similarly, stresses can pile atop each other until we can no longer cope. Some stresses take the form of **daily hassles** (Lazarus, 1984a); others are life changes. Lazarus and his colleagues (1985) analyzed a scale that measures daily hassles and their opposites—**uplifts**—and found that examples of hassles could be grouped as follows (see also Figure 5.1):

TABLE 5.1 STUDENTS' REASONS FOR SEEKING COUNSELING

Reason	*Percent Reporting Reason*
Stress, anxiety, nervousness	51
Romantic relationships	47
Low self-esteem, self-confidence	42
Depression	41
Family relationships	37
Academic problems, grades	29
Transition to the career world	25
Loneliness	25
Financial problems	24

Source: From Baum, M. C. & Rardin, D. K. (1993). Counseling center clients: Have they really changed. Reprinted by permission of Student Counseling Services, Illinois State University.

1. *Household hassles:* preparing meals, shopping, and home maintenance
2. *Health hassles:* physical illness, concern about medical treatment, and the side effects of medication
3. *Time-pressure hassles:* having too many things to do, too many responsibilities, and not enough time
4. *Inner-concern hassles:* being lonely and fear of confrontation
5. *Environmental hassles:* crime, neighborhood deterioration, and traffic noise
6. *Financial-responsibility hassles:* concern about owing money, such as mortgage payments and loan installments
7. *Work hassles:* job dissatisfaction, not liking one's work duties, and problems with co-workers
8. *Future-security hassles:* concerns about job security, taxes, property investments, stock market swings, and retirement

These hassles are linked to psychological features like nervousness, worrying, inability to get going, feelings of sadness, feelings of aloneness, and so on.

Life Changes: "Going Through Changes"

Researchers have also focused on the impact of life changes. Life changes differ from daily hassles in two ways: (1) Many life changes are positive and desirable, whereas hassles are defined as negative. (2) Hassles tend to occur on a daily basis, whereas life changes are relatively more isolated, such as changes in financial state or living conditions.

It is understandable that hassles and life changes—especially negative life changes—will have psychological effects such as causing worry and dampening our moods. But hassles and life changes (even positive ones) may also lead to physical illness.

LIFE CHANGES.

Life changes are more episodic than daily hassles. Moreover, life changes can be positive (like marriage) or negative (like the death of a loved one), whereas all hassles are negative. What is the relationship between life changes and illness? Is the relationship causal?

FIGURE 5.1

DAILY HASSLES.

Daily hassles are recurring sources of aggravation. Which of the hassles shown here are regular parts of your life?

Richard Lazarus and his colleagues (e.g., Kanner and others, 1981) assess exposure to hassles by having subjects indicate which of 117 hassles they have encountered and how intense they were, according to a 3-point scale. Holmes and Rahe (1967) constructed a scale to measure the impact of life changes. They assigned marriage an arbitrary weight of 50 "life-change units" and then asked samples of people to assign units to other life changes, using marriage as the baseline. Most events were rated less stressful than marriage, but a few—such as the death of a spouse (100 units) and divorce (73 units)—were considered more stressful. Positive life changes such as outstanding personal achievement (28 units) and going on vacation (13 units) also made the list (see Figure 5.2).

HASSLES, LIFE CHANGES, AND ILLNESS Hassles and life changes—especially negative life changes—affect us psychologically. They can cause us to worry and can affect our moods. But stressors such as hassles and life changes also predict health problems such as heart disease and cancer and even athletic injuries (Smith and others, 1990; Stewart and others, 1994). Holmes and Rahe found that people who "earned" 300 or more life-change units within a year, according to their scale, were at greater risk for health problems. Eight of 10 developed health problems, compared with only 1 of 3 people whose totals of life-change units for the year were below 150.

Moreover, people who remain married to the same person live longer than people who experience marital breakups and remarry (Tucker and others, 1996). Apparently the life changes of divorce and remarriage—or the instability associated with them—can be harmful to health.

Truth or Fiction Revisited

Actually, the adage "the more change the merrier" is not necessarily true. Variety may be "the spice of life" but changes are sources of stress that require adjustment. Some changes are necessary to keep us alert and occupied, but high numbers of life changes within a short time frame have been connected with illness. Changes, even changes for the better, are sources of stress that require adjustment.

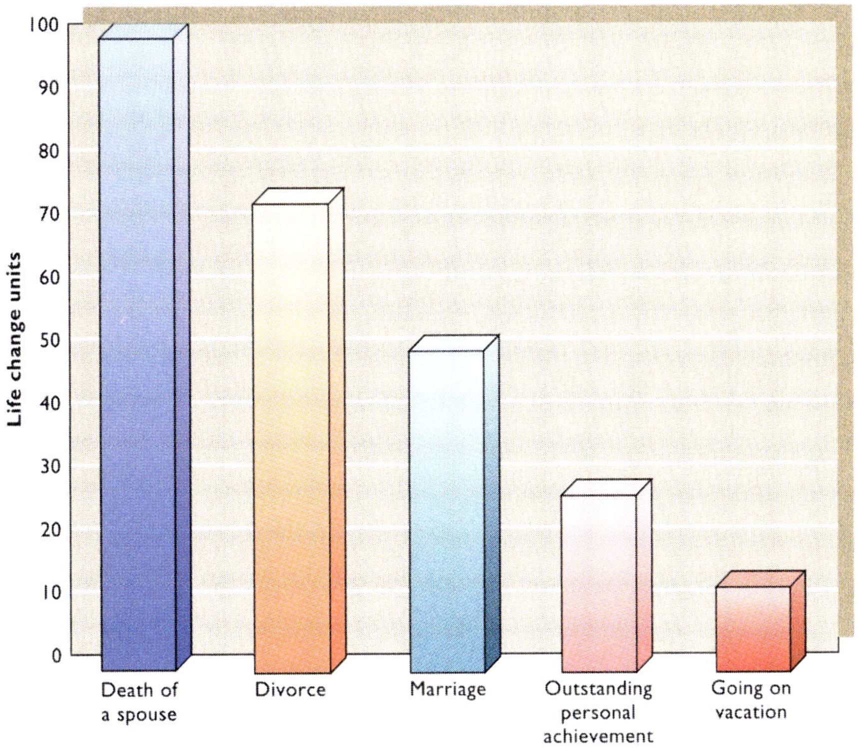

FIGURE 5.2
LIFE CHANGES AND STRESS.
According to Holmes and Rahe, both positive and negative life changes can be stressful. Some life changes and the numbers of "life-change units" assigned to them are shown here.

HAVE YOU BEEN GOING THROUGH CHANGES? THE SOCIAL READJUSTMENT RATING SCALE

Life changes are a source of stress. How many life changes have you gone through in the past year? In order to compare the amount of change-related stress you have encountered with that of other college students, complete this questionnaire. ■

Directions: Indicate how many times ("frequency") you have experienced the following events during the past 12 months. Then multiply the frequency (do not enter a number larger than 5) by the number of life-change units ("value") associated with each event. Write the product in the column to the right ("total"). Then add up all the points and check the key in the Appendix.

Event	Value	Frequency	Total
1. Death of a spouse, lover, or child	94		
2. Death of a parent or sibling	88		
3. Beginning formal higher education	84		
4. Death of a close friend	83		
5. Miscarriage or stillbirth of pregnancy of self, spouse, or lover	83		
6. Jail sentence	82		
7. Divorce or marital separation	82		
8. Unwanted pregnancy of self, spouse, or lover	80		
9. Abortion of unwanted pregnancy of self, spouse, or lover	80		
10. Detention in jail or other institution	79		
11. Change in dating activity	79		
12. Death of a close relative	79		
13. Change in marital situation other than divorce or separation	78		
14. Separation from significant other whom you like very much	77		
15. Change in health status or behavior of spouse or lover	77		
16. Academic failure	77		
17. Major violation of the law and subsequent arrest	76		
18. Marrying or living with lover against parents' wishes	75		
19. Change in love relationship or important friendship	74		
20. Change in health status or behavior of a parent or sibling	73		
21. Change in feelings of loneliness, insecurity, anxiety, boredom	73		
22. Change in marital status of parents	73		
23. Acquiring a visible deformity	72		
24. Change in ability to communicate with a significant other whom you like very much	71		
25. Hospitalization of a parent or sibling	70		
26. Reconciliation of marital or love relationship	68		
27. Release from jail or other institution	68		
28. Graduation from college	68		
29. Major personal injury or illness	68		
30. Wanted pregnancy of self, spouse, or lover	67		
31. Change in number or type of arguments with spouse or lover	67		
32. Marrying or living with lover with parents' approval	66		
33. Gaining a new family member through birth or adoption	65		
34. Preparing for an important exam or writing a major paper	65		
35. Major financial difficulties	65		
36. Change in the health status or behavior of a close relative or close friend	65		
37. Change in academic status	64		
38. Change in amount and nature of interpersonal conflicts	63		
39. Change in relationship with members of your immediate family	62		
40. Change in own personality	62		
41. Hospitalization of yourself or a close relative	61		
42. Change in course of study, major field, vocational goals, or work status	60		
43. Change in own financial status	59		
44. Change in status of divorced or widowed parent	59		
45. Change in number or type of arguments between parents	59		

Event		Value	Frequency	Total
46.	Change in acceptance by peers, identification with peers, or social pressure by peers	58	____	____
47.	Change in general outlook on life	57	____	____
48.	Beginning or ceasing service in the armed forces	57	____	____
49.	Change in attitudes toward friends	56	____	____
50.	Change in living arrangements, conditions, or environment	55	____	____
51.	Change in frequency or nature of sexual experiences	55	____	____
52.	Change in parents' financial status	55	____	____
53.	Change in amount or nature of pressure from parents	55	____	____
54.	Change in degree of interest in college or attitudes toward education	55	____	____
55.	Change in the number of personal or social relationships you've formed or dissolved	55	____	____
56.	Change in relationship with siblings	54	____	____
57.	Change in mobility or reliability of transportation	54	____	____
58.	Academic success	54	____	____
59.	Change to a new college or university	54	____	____
60.	Change in feelings of self-reliance, independence, or amount of self-discipline	53	____	____
61.	Change in number or type of arguments with roommate	52	____	____
62.	Spouse or lover beginning or ceasing work outside the home	52	____	____
63.	Change in frequency of use or amounts used of drugs other than alcohol, tobacco, or marijuana	51	____	____
64.	Change in sexual morality, beliefs, or attitudes	50	____	____
65.	Change in responsibility at work	50	____	____
66.	Change in amount or nature of social activities	50	____	____
67.	Change in dependencies on parents	50	____	____
68.	Change from academic work to practical fieldwork experience or internship	50	____	____
69.	Change in amount of material possessions and concomitant responsibilities	50	____	____
70.	Change in routine at college or work	49	____	____
71.	Change in amount of leisure time	49	____	____
72.	Change in amount of in-law trouble	49	____	____
73.	Outstanding personal achievement	49	____	____
74.	Change in family structure other than parental divorce or separation	48	____	____
75.	Change in attitude toward drugs	48	____	____
76.	Change in amount and nature of competition with same sex	48	____	____
77.	Improvement of own health	47	____	____
78.	Change in responsibilities at home	47	____	____
79.	Change in study habits	46	____	____
80.	Change in number or type of arguments or close conflicts with close relatives	46	____	____
81.	Change in sleeping habits	46	____	____
82.	Change in frequency of use or amounts of alcohol	45	____	____
83.	Change in social status	45	____	____
84.	Change in frequency of use or amounts used of tobacco	45	____	____
85.	Change in awareness of activities in external world	45	____	____
86.	Change in religious affiliation	44	____	____
87.	Change in type of gratifying activities	43	____	____
88.	Change in amount or nature of physical activities	43	____	____
89.	Change in address or residence	43	____	____
90.	Change in amount or nature of recreational activities	43	____	____
91.	Change in frequency of use or amounts used of marijuana	43	____	____
92.	Change in social demands or responsibilities due to your age	43	____	____
93.	Court appearance for legal violation	40	____	____
94.	Change in weight or eating habits	39	____	____
95.	Change in religious activities	37	____	____
96.	Change in political views or affiliations	34	____	____
97.	Change in driving pattern or conditions	33	____	____
98.	Minor violation of the law	31	____	____
99.	Vacation or travel	30	____	____
100.	Change in number of family get-togethers	30	____	____

Source: Peggy Blake, Robert Fry, & Michael Pesjack, *Self-assessment and behavior change manual* (New York: Random House, 1984), pp. 43–47. Reprinted by permission of Random House, Inc.

Criticisms of the Research Links Between Hassles, Life Changes, and Illness

Although the links between daily hassles, life changes, and illness seem to have been supported by a good deal of research, there are some limitations.

CORRELATIONAL EVIDENCE The links that have been uncovered between hassles, life changes, and illness are correlational rather than experimental. It may seem logical that the hassles and life changes caused the disorders, but these variables were not manipulated experimentally. Other explanations of the data are possible. One is that people who are predisposed toward medical or psychological problems encounter more hassles and amass more life-change units. For example, undiagnosed medical disorders may contribute to sexual problems, arguments with spouses or in-laws, changes in living conditions and personal habits, and changes in sleeping habits. People may also make certain changes in their lives that lead to physical and psychological disorders (Simons and others, 1993).

POSITIVE VERSUS NEGATIVE LIFE CHANGES Other aspects of the research on the relationship between life changes and illness have also been challenged. For instance, positive life changes may be less disturbing than hassles and negative life changes, even though the number of life-change units assigned to them is high (Lefcourt and others, 1981).

THE NEED FOR NOVEL STIMULATION In a similar vein, keep in mind the saying that "variety is the spice of life." People seem motivated to seek change, or novel stimulation. Stress researcher Hans Selye (1980) also noted that a certain amount of stress was necessary, even healthful. He referred to healthful stress as **eustress** (pronounced "yoo-stress," and derived from the Greek *eu*, meaning "good" or "well"). Stress is apparently sometimes in the eye of the beholder. That is, one person's stress might be another person's eustress, because each encodes experiences in a different way.

PERSONALITY DIFFERENCES People with different kinds of personalities respond to life stresses in different ways (Vaillant, 1994). For example, people who are easygoing or psychologically hardy are less likely to become ill under the impact of stress.

A ROLE FOR COGNITIVE APPRAISAL The stress of an event reflects the meaning of the event to the individual (Whitehead, 1994). Pregnancy, for example, can be a positive or negative life change, depending on whether one wants and is prepared to have a child. We cognitively appraise hassles, traumatic experiences, and life changes (Creamer and others, 1992; Kiecolt-Glaser, 1993). In responding to them, we take into account their perceived danger, our values and goals, our beliefs in our coping ability, our social support, and so on. The same event is perceived as less taxing by people who have greater coping ability and social support.

Pain and Discomfort

Pain and discomfort impair performance and coping ability. Athletes report that pain interferes with their abilities to run, swim, and so forth, even when the source of the pain does not directly weaken them.

EUSTRESS • Healthful stress. (Derived from the Greek *eu*, meaning "good" or "well.")

PROSTAGLANDINS • Substances derived from fatty acids; they are involved in body responses such as inflammation and menstrual cramping.

ANALGESIC • Not feeling pain, although fully conscious.

ENDORPHINS • Neurotransmitters that are composed of chains of amino acids and are functionally similar to morphine.

What Pain Is Pain is a signal that something is wrong in the body. Pain is adaptive in the sense that it motivates us to do something about it. But for some of us, chronic pain—pain that lingers once injuries or illnesses have otherwise cleared up—saps our vitality and the pleasures of everyday life.

As shown in Figure 5.3, pain originates at the point of contact, as with a stubbed toe. At the site of injury, a number of chemicals are released, including **prostaglandins.** Prostaglandins facilitate transmission of the pain message to the brain and heighten circulation to the injured area, causing the redness and swelling we refer to as inflammation. Inflammation attracts infection-fighting blood cells to the area to protect against invading bacteria. **Analgesic** drugs such as ibuprofen (brand names Motrin, Advil, Medipren, Nuprin) and aspirin work by inhibiting the production of prostaglandins and thus decreasing fever, inflammation, and pain.

Endorphins In response to pain, the brain triggers the release of **endorphins,** a kind of chemical that is involved in transmitting messages within the body. The word *endorphin* is the contraction of *endogenous morphine. Endogenous* means "developing from within." Endorphins are similar to the narcotic morphine in their functions, and we produce them in our own bodies. They occur naturally in the brain and the bloodstream. Endorphins act by "locking into" receptors in the nervous system for chemicals that transmit pain messages to the brain. Once the endorphin "key" is in the "lock," pain-causing chemicals are prevented from transmitting their messages.

Truth or Fiction Revisited

It is true that our bodies produce chemicals that are similar in function to the narcotic morphine. The chemicals are called *endorphins*—the contraction of *endogenous morphine.*

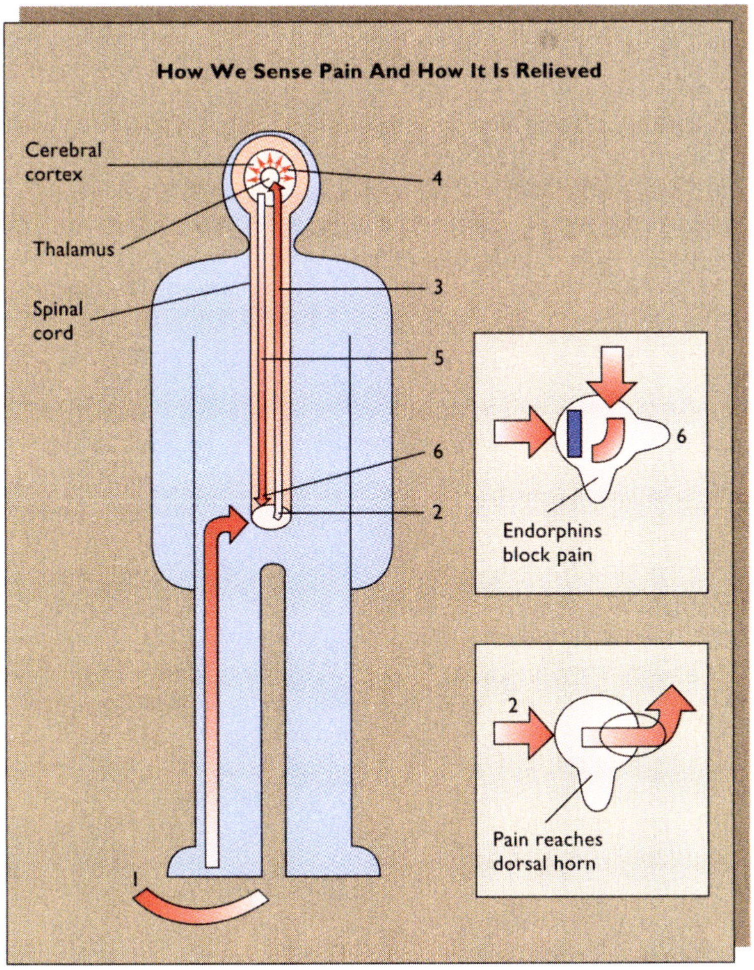

Figure 5.3
Perception of, and Response to, Pain.
Pain originates at the point of contact. Transmission of the pain message to the brain is initiated by release of prostaglandins and other substances. The body responds by releasing endorphins, which block part of the pain message.

THE RICHTER EXPERIMENT In a classic experiment, psychiatrist Curt Richter (1957) dramatized the effects of pain on behavior. First, Richter obtained baseline data by recording the amount of time rats could swim to stay afloat in a tub of water. In water at room temperature, most rats could keep their noses above the surface for about 80 hours. But when Richter blew noxious streams of air into the animal's faces, or kept the water uncomfortably hot or cold, the rats could remain afloat for only 20 to 40 hours.

When rats were traumatized immediately before their dunking by having their whiskers noisily cropped off, some managed to remain afloat for only a few minutes. Yet the clipping itself had not weakened them. Rats that were allowed several minutes to recover from the clipping before being launched swam for the usual 80 hours. Because of results such as these, psychologists recommend that we space aggravating tasks or chores so that discomfort does not build to the point where it compounds stress and impairs our performance.

PAIN MANAGEMENT Psychologists have been of major help in the management of pain. Pain management has traditionally been a medical issue, with the main type of treatment being chemical, as in the use of analgesic drugs. But drugs are not always effective (Flor & Birbaumer, 1993). Moreover, patients can develop tolerance for many analgesic drugs, such as morphine or Demerol. Increased doses thus become required to achieve the same effects. Because of limitations and problems such as these, health psychologists have increasingly focused their efforts on psychological methods for managing pain (Ross & Berger, 1996).

Accurate Information One psychological method for pain management is the provision of accurate and thorough information (Jacox and others, 1994; Ross & Berger, 1996). Most people try not to think about their symptoms (and their implications!) during the early phases of an illness. However, when it comes to administering painful or discomforting treatments, as with chemotherapy for cancer, knowledge of the details of the treatment, including how long it will last and how much pain will be entailed, often helps patients cope—particularly patients who prefer to receive high levels of information in an effort to maintain control over their situations (Burish and others, 1991). Accurate information even helps small children cope with painful procedures (Jay and others, 1983).

Truth or Fiction Revisited

It is true that video games help children who are cancer patients cope with the side effects of chemotherapy. The games distract them from unpleasant body sensations.

Distraction and Fantasy Ignoring pain and diverting one's attention enhance the ability to cope with pain (Jensen & Karoly, 1991; Keefe and others, 1992). Though it is helpful for patients to have accurate and detailed explanations of painful procedures, psychologists also study ways of minimizing discomfort once the procedures are under way. A number of methods involve the use of distraction or fantasy. For example, patients can distract themselves from pain by focusing on environmental details, as by counting ceiling tiles or the hairs on the back of a finger or by describing the clothing of medical personnel or passersby. Studies with children ranging in age from 9 into their teens have found that playing video games diminishes the pain and discomfort of the side effects of chemotherapy (Kolko & Rickard-Figueroa, 1985; Redd and others, 1987). Other distraction methods that help children deal with pain include combing one's hair and blowing on a noisemaker (Adler, 1990).

Hypnosis In 1842 London physician W. S. Ward amputated a man's leg after using a rather strange anesthetic: hypnosis. According to reports, the man experienced no discomfort. Several years later, operations at Ward's infirmary were being performed under hypnosis routinely. Today hypnosis is often used to reduce chronic pain (Flor and others, 1992; Patterson & Ptacek, 1997) and as an anesthetic in dentistry, childbirth, and even some forms of surgery.

In using hypnosis to manage pain, the hypnotist usually instructs the person that he or she feels nothing or that the pain is distant and slight. Hypnosis can also aid in the use of distraction and fantasy. For example, the hypnotist can instruct the person to imagine that he or she is relaxing on a warm, exotic shore.

Relaxation Training and Biofeedback **Relaxation training** refers to a number of psychological techniques that relax muscles and lower sympathetic activity. Some relaxation methods focus on relaxing muscle groups (see Chapter 11). Some involve breathing exercises. Some focus on guided imagery, including suggestions that limbs are becoming warmer and heavier. However, none of them claims to induce a trance, and their benefits are explained by theories that link behavior to human physiology. Biofeedback that helps people relax muscles at the site of the pain has been shown to be more effective than most medications at reducing chronic pain in the lower back and jaw (Flor & Birbaumer, 1993).

Coping With Irrational Beliefs Irrational beliefs can heighten pain (Ukestad & Wittrock, 1996). For example, telling oneself that the pain is unbearable and that it will never cease increases discomfort (Keefe and others, 1992). Some people seem to feel obligated to focus on things that distress them. They may be unwilling to allow themselves to be distracted from pain and discomfort. Thus, cognitive methods aimed at changing irrational beliefs hold some promise (Jensen and others, 1994).

Social Support Supportive social networks also seem to help us cope with discomfort. Having friends visit the patient and encourage a return to health is thus as consistent with psychological findings as it is with tradition and folklore (Rook & Dooley, 1985).

Frustration

You may wish to play the line for the varsity football team, but you may weigh only 120 pounds or you may be a woman. You may have been denied a job or educational opportunity because of your ethnic background or favoritism. We all encounter *frustration*—the thwarting of a motive to attain a goal (see Figure 5.4, Part A). Frustration is another source of stress.

RELAXATION TRAINING • Methods for inducing relaxation that focus on relaxing imagery, systematic relaxation of muscle groups, and so on.

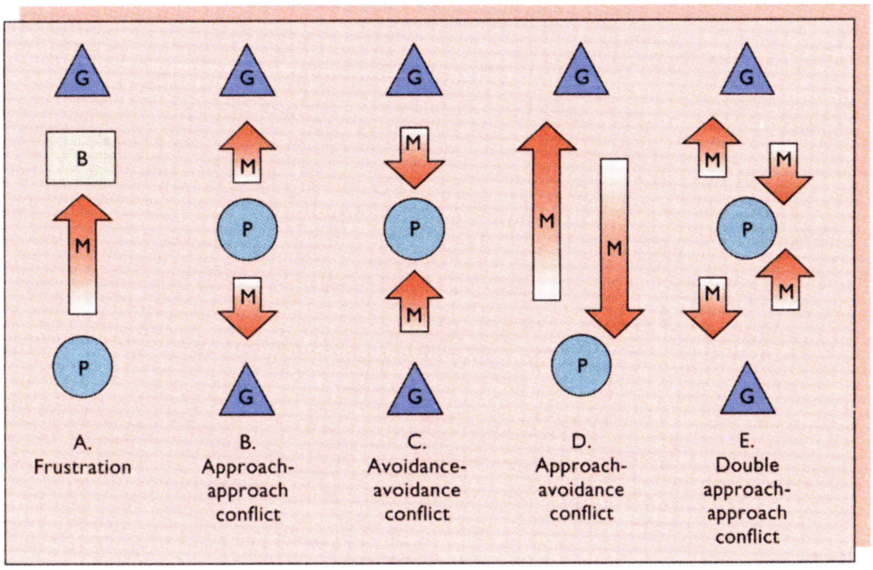

FIGURE 5.4

MODELS FOR FRUSTRATION AND CONFLICT.

Part A is a model for frustration in which a person (P) has a motive (M) to reach a goal (G), but is thwarted by a barrier (B). Part B shows an approach-approach conflict, in which the person cannot simultaneously approach two positive goals. Part C shows an avoidance-avoidance conflict in which avoiding one negative goal requires approaching another. Part D shows an approach-avoidance conflict in which the same goal has positive and negative features. Part E shows a multiple — in this case, double — approach-avoidance conflict in which more than one goal has positive and negative features.

Many sources of frustration are obvious. Adolescents are used to being too young to wear makeup, drive, go out, engage in sexual activity, spend money, drink, or work. Age is the barrier that requires them to delay gratification. We may frustrate ourselves as adults if our goals are set too high or if our self-demands are irrational. If we try to earn other people's approval at all costs, or insist on performing perfectly in all of our undertakings, we doom ourselves to failure and frustration.

Truth or Fiction Revisited

It is true that commuting on the freeway elevates our blood pressure. Especially when traffic is heavy!

THE FRUSTRATIONS OF COMMUTING One of the common frustrations of contemporary life is commuting. Distance, time, and driving conditions are some of the barriers that lie between us and our work or schooling. How many of us fight the freeways or crowd ourselves into train cars or buses for an hour or more *before* the workday begins? For most people, the stresses of commuting are mild but persistent (Stokols & Novaco, 1981). Still, lengthy commutes on crowded highways are linked to increases in heart rate, blood pressure, chest pain, and other signs of stress. Noise, humidity, and air pollution all contribute to the frustration involved in driving to work.

If you commute by car, try to pick times and roads that provide lower volumes of traffic. It may be worth your while to take a longer, more scenic route that has less stop-and-go traffic.

EMOTIONAL BARRIERS Anxiety and fear may serve as emotional barriers that prevent us from acting effectively to meet our goals. A high school senior who wishes to attend an out-of-state college may be frustrated by the fear of leaving home. A young adult may not ask an attractive person out on a date because of fear of rejection. A woman may be frustrated in her desire to move up the corporate ladder, fearing that co-workers, friends, and family may view her assertiveness as compromising her femininity.

TOLERANCE FOR FRUSTRATION Getting ahead is often a gradual process that demands that we must be able to live with some frustration and delay gratification. Yet our **tolerance for frustration** may fluctuate. Stress heaped upon stress can lower our tolerance, just as Richter's rats, stressed from their close shaves, sank quickly to the bottom of the tub. We may laugh off a flat tire on a good day. But if it is raining, or if we have just waited for an hour in a gas line, the flat may seem like the last straw. People who have encountered frustration but learned that it is possible to surmount barriers or find substitute goals are more tolerant of frustration than those who have never experienced it or those who have experienced excesses of frustration.

Conflict

I *am*
At war 'twixt will and will not.

SHAKESPEARE, *MEASURE FOR MEASURE*

Have you ever felt "damned if you did and damned if you didn't"? Have you regretted that you couldn't do two things or be in two places at the same time? Have you ever wanted to go to a film but had to study for a test? This is **conflict**—being torn in two or more directions by opposing motives. Conflict is frustrating and stressful. Conflict may also be looked at as a type of frustration in which the barrier to achieving a goal is an opposing impulse or motive. Psychologists often break conflicts down into four types.

TOLERANCE FOR FRUSTRATION • Ability to delay gratification, to maintain self-control when a motive is thwarted.

CONFLICT • A condition characterized by opposing motives, in which gratification of one motive prevents gratification of the other.

Approach-Approach Conflict An **approach-approach conflict** (Figure 5.4, Part B) is the least stressful form of conflict. Here each of two goals is positive and within reach. You may not be able to decide between pizza or tacos, Tom or Dick, or a trip to Nassau or Hawaii. Conflicts are usually resolved by making decisions. People in conflict may vacillate until they make decisions, and afterward there may be some regrets, especially if their choices fall short of expectations.

Avoidance-Avoidance Conflict An **avoidance-avoidance conflict** (Figure 5.4, Part C) is more stressful, because you are motivated to avoid each of two negative goals. However, avoiding one requires approaching the other. You may be fearful of visiting the dentist yet also fear that your teeth will decay if you do not. You may not want to contribute to the Association for the Advancement of Lost Causes yet fear that your friends will consider you cheap or uncommitted if you do not. Each goal is negative in an avoidance-avoidance conflict. When an avoidance-avoidance conflict is highly stressful and no resolution is in sight, some people withdraw from the conflict by focusing their attention on other matters or by suspending behavior altogether. For example, some highly conflicted people refuse to get out of bed in the morning to start the day.

Approach-Avoidance Conflict The same goal can produce both approach and avoidance motives, as in the **approach-avoidance conflict** (Figure 5.4, Part D). People and things have their pluses and minuses, their good points and their bad points. Cream cheese pie may be delicious, but oh, the calories! Why are so many attractive goals immoral, illegal, or fattening?

Multiple Approach-Avoidance Conflict The most complex form of conflict is the **multiple approach-avoidance conflict,** in which each of several alternative courses of action has its promising and distressing aspects. Consider the example in which there are two goals, as in Figure 5.4, Part E. This sort of conflict might arise on the evening of an examination, when you are faced with the choice of studying or, say, going to a film. Each alternative has its positive and negative aspects: "Studying's a drag, but I won't have to worry about flunking. I'd love to see the movie, but I'd just be worrying about how I'll do tomorrow."

Similarly, should you take a job or go on for advanced training when you complete your college program? This is another double approach-avoidance conflict. If you opt for the job, money will soon be jingling in your pockets, but later you might wonder if you have the education to reach your potential. By furthering your education you may have to delay the independence and gratification that are afforded by earning a living, but you may find a more fulfilling position later on.

This chapter's "Adjustment and Modern Life" feature (pp. 156–158) will help you make decisions that can reduce some of the conflicts in your life.

Type A Behavior

Some of us behave as though we were dedicated to the continuous creation of our own stress through the **Type A behavior** pattern. Type A people are highly driven, competitive, impatient, and aggressive (Thoresen & Powell, 1992). They feel rushed and under pressure and keep one eye glued firmly to the clock. They are not only prompt for appointments, but are frequently early. They eat, walk, and talk rapidly, and they become restless when they see others working slowly.

Approach-approach conflict • Conflict involving two positive but mutually exclusive goals.

Avoidance-avoidance conflict • Conflict involving two negative goals, with avoidance of one requiring approach of the other.

Approach-avoidance conflict • Conflict involving a goal with positive and negative features.

Multiple approach-avoidance conflict • Conflict involving two or more goals, each of which has positive and negative aspects.

Type A behavior • Stress-producing behavior, characterized by aggressiveness, perfectionism, unwillingness to relinquish control, and a sense of time urgency.

ARE YOU TYPE A OR TYPE B?

Are you Type A or Type B? Type A's are ambitious, hard driving, and chronically discontent with their current achievements. Type B's, by contrast, are more relaxed, more involved with the quality of life, and—according to cardiologists Meyer Friedman and Ray Rosenman—less prone to heart attacks. The following checklist will help give you insight into whether you are closer in your behavior patterns to the Type A or the Type B individual. ■

Directions: place a checkmark under the *Yes* if the behavior pattern is typical of you, and under the *No* if it is not. Try to work rapidly and leave no item blank. Then turn to the scoring key in the Appendix.

Yes	No		Do You . . .
____	____	1.	Strongly accent key words in your everyday speech?
____	____	2.	Eat and walk quickly?
____	____	3.	Believe that children should be taught to be competitive?
____	____	4.	Feel restless when watching a slow worker?
____	____	5.	Hurry other people to get on with what they're trying to say?
____	____	6.	Find it highly aggravating to be stuck in traffic or waiting for a seat at a restaurant?
____	____	7.	Continue to think about your own problems and business even when listening to someone else?
____	____	8.	Try to eat and shave, or drive and jot down notes at the same time?
____	____	9.	Catch up on your work on vacations?
____	____	10.	Bring conversations around to topics of concern to you?
____	____	11.	Feel guilty when you spend time just relaxing?
____	____	12.	Find that you're so wrapped up in your work that you no longer notice office decorations or the scenery?
____	____	13.	Find yourself concerned with getting more *things* rather than developing your creativity and social concerns?
____	____	14.	Try to schedule more and more activities into less time?
____	____	15.	Always appear for appointments on time?
____	____	16.	Clench or pound your fists, or use other gestures, to emphasize your views?
____	____	17.	Credit your accomplishments to your ability to work rapidly?
____	____	18.	Feel that things must be done *now* and quickly?
____	____	19.	Constantly try to find more efficient ways to get things done?
____	____	20.	Insist on winning at games rather than just having fun?
____	____	21.	Interrupt others often?
____	____	22.	Feel irritated when others are late?
____	____	23.	Leave the table immediately after eating?
____	____	24.	Feel rushed?
____	____	25.	Feel dissatisfied with your current level of performance?

TYPE A BEHAVIOR.
The Type A behavior pattern is characterized by a sense of time urgency, competitiveness, and hostility.

They attempt to dominate group discussions. They are reluctant to delegate authority in the workplace and thus tend to increase their own workloads. Type A people accentuate the negative. They are merciless in their self-criticism when they fall short (Moser & Dyck, 1989). They seek out negative information about themselves in order to better themselves (Cooney & Zeichner, 1985).

Type A people find it difficult just to go out on the tennis court and bat the ball back and forth. They watch their form, perfect their strokes, and demand regular self-improvement. The irrational belief that they must be perfectly competent in everything they undertake seems to be their motto.

Type B people, by contrast, relax more readily and focus more on the quality of life. They are less ambitious and less impatient, and they pace themselves. Type A's perceive time as passing more rapidly than do Type B's, and they work more quickly. Type A's earn higher grades and more money than Type B's of equal intelligence (Glass, 1977). Type A's also seek greater challenges than Type B's (Ortega & Pipal, 1984).

Truth or Fiction Revisited

It is true that many people create their own sources of stress. Some do so through perfectionism, and others do so by means of Type A behavior.

Environmental Stressors

The impact of environmental stressors has been one of the key spurs of the development of the psychology of adjustment. Among these stressors are natural disasters, technological disasters, noise, air pollution, extremes of temperature, and crowding.

NATURAL DISASTERS: OF FIRE AND ICE

Some say the world will end in fire,
Some say in ice.

ROBERT FROST

In 1989 an earthquake heaved the Bay Area of northern California. Dozens of automobile passengers were killed in the collapse of an Oakland freeway. In 1992 Hurricane Andrew ripped the coasts of Florida and Louisiana, leaving hundreds of thousands homeless. In 1993, the Mississippi and other central U.S. rivers overleapt their banks and flooded surrounding communities. In 1994, another earthquake shook southern California, collapsing apartment buildings and killing more than 40 people. In 1998 Montreal was struck by an ice storm that killed at least 15 people and left the city without power for days. Earthquakes, hurricanes, blizzards, tornadoes, wind storms, ice storms, monsoons, floods, mudslides, avalanches, and volcanic eruptions—these are a sampling of the natural disasters to which we are prey. In some cases we are warned of natural disasters. We may know that we live in an area that is prone to earthquakes or flooding. In the case of Hurricane Andrew, meteorologists followed the track of the storm as it approached the shore. In others cases we are stunned by the suddenness of natural disasters and left numb. Even when we expect a storm, its gray menace and massiveness may stun us.

Natural disasters are hazardous in themselves and also cause life changes to pile atop one another by disrupting community life. Services that had been taken for granted, such as electricity and water, may be lost. Businesses and homes may be destroyed, so that people must rebuild or relocate. Natural disasters reveal the thinness of the veneer of technology on which civilization depends. It is understandable that many survivors report stress-related problems such as anxiety and depression for months after the fact. Perhaps it is also understandable that the suicide rate rises after natural disasters like hurricanes, floods, and earthquakes (Krug and others, 1998). Étienne Krug and his colleagues (1998) at the Centers for Disease Control and Prevention in Atlanta speculate that well intentioned government disaster loans contribute to the suicide rate by placing victims under the stress of repaying the loans.

Adjustment in a World of DIVERSITY

One Quake, Two Worlds[1]

The following story came out of the 1994 Los Angeles earthquake, which killed more than 40 people and left thousands homeless. It says something about social support and coping in a time of stress. It says much more.

There's always a positive media spin for tragedy. In Los Angeles, it is that a city wracked by racial and class divisions has come together after the earthquake. On TV and in the papers we are told how African Americans, Latinos (Hispanic Americans), Asians, Middle Easterners, and Anglos (non-Hispanic White Americans) have laid down their arms—literal and rhetorical—to pitch in and help their neighbors. But the truth is that even in disaster, the fault lines that divide L.A. are there for all to see.

Take the way the city's two largest ethnic groups responded. The quake thrust Anglo suburbia into an unaccustomed dramatic role: When the shaking stopped, neighbors spilled into the streets, offering each other gallons of water, flashlights, words of reassurance. Normally, the brick walls between their homes are so high that neighbors rarely speak, much less borrow sugar. Now, with all those bricks in dusty piles on the sidewalks, people greet each other like long-lost relatives.

---

[1] Reprinted with permission from Rubén Martínez (1994, January 20), One quake, two worlds, *New York Times*, p. A21.

A world away in the Latino immigrant barrios, such solidarity is the survival mechanism of daily life. The firetrap apartment buildings have the thinnest of walls. Trained for disaster by war and poverty in their native countries, residents see tragedy as inevitable as a heart attack, a car accident, or a stray bullet. After the quake, there was more resignation in the barrios than chaos or hysteria. Once again tragedy had struck, and once again it had to be overcome.

And so we see culturally divided images on the tube: Suburbanites rush to the city-run emergency shelters while Latinos build impromptu tent cities in whatever open space they can find. The TV crews are particularly fascinated with the people camping out in the parks. (Most are from Mexico and Central America and are well-acquainted with nature's violent whims.) The immigrants fashion tents with blankets and scrap wood, and the extended families—grandparents and parents and aunts and uncles and children—start cookouts at dusk.

These are the same immigrants that many California politicians insist have come here to strike it rich on welfare. And yet here they are, looking far more self-sufficient than their suburban counterparts. They know from experience that emergency aid always goes to the rich neighbors before (maybe) trickling down to the poor. In post-quake L.A., it's the suburbanites—the longtime enemies of big government—who cry first and loudest for services.

On the morning of the quake, in the pancaked parking lot of the Northridge Fashion Mall, Salvador Peña, an immigrant from El Salvador, was trapped beneath tons of concrete. He was saved because the street sweeper he was driving around the lot at 4:30 A.M. protected him from falling debris like a steel womb. Live on TV, firefighters worked for hours before freeing him. Throughout the ordeal, rescuers assured us, the man was in good spirits, although few could be sure what he was saying since only one spoke Spanish.

Yes, this rescue assured us, good will can guide us through tragedy. Still, although many commentators missed it, the drama had greater meaning. It asked us to pause and consider a Salvadoran man, perhaps an undocumented immigrant, working in the darkness while suburbia slept, making sure the parking lot would be spotless for middle class mallgoers the next day.

An army of hundreds of thousands of Salvador Peñas toils from dusk to dawn in L.A., cleaning office buildings, preparing meals for the white collars. They do so because without work there is no future, and without a future there is no hope.

The old L.A., the suburbanites who are quickly becoming the minority, have something to learn from this new L.A. The suburbanites, if they look hard enough, would see hope: the solace and solidarity of extended families, the innocent ambition to succeed that was once synonymous with America. For the moment, however, it appears that the only walls that have fallen in L.A. are the ones that separate one suburban dwelling from another.

TECHNOLOGY: WHEN HIGH-TECH FAILS We owe our dominance over the natural environment to technological progress. Yet technology can also fail or backfire and cause disaster. The 1984 leakage of poisonous gas at Bhopal, India; the 1983 collapse of a bridge along the Connecticut Turnpike; the 1979 nuclear accident at Three Mile Island; the 1976 collapse of the dam at Buffalo Creek; the 1977 Beverly Hills Supper Club fire (Green and others, 1983); airplane accidents, blackouts, and the leakage of toxic chemicals—these are a sampling of the technological disasters that befall us. When they do, we feel as though we have lost control of things and suffer stress (Davidson and others, 1982).

After the dam burst at Buffalo Creek, thousands of tons of water coursed onto Saunders, West Virginia. The flood lasted only 15 minutes, but 125 people were killed and over 5,000 were left homeless. Reactions to the flood included anxiety, numbness, depression, anger, and sleep disturbances. Many survivors felt guilty that they had been spared when family members and friends had been taken by the waters.

For many days after the leakage of radioactive gases and liquids at the Three Mile Island nuclear plant in Pennsylvania, it was feared that there might be a nuclear explosion, a meltdown, or massive releases of radiation. Evacuation was advised, contributing to fears. The psychological and physical effects of stress lingered for nearly 2 years after the accident (Baum and others, 1983; Schaeffer & Baum, 1982).

In technological disasters, as opposed to natural disasters, there is someone to blame (Baum, 1988). As a consequence, there may be legal suits. Suits tend to linger for years. They provide an enduring source of stress to the victims and to those identified as responsible.

NOISE: OF ROCK 'N' ROLL AND LOW-FLYING AIRCRAFT How do you react when a fingernail is scraped along a blackboard or an airplane roars overhead? Noise can be aversive, especially loud noise (Staples, 1996).

The **decibel** (dB) is the unit that is used to express the loudness of noises (see Figure 5.5). The hearing threshold is defined as zero dB. The noise level in your school library is probably about 30 to 40 dB. Noise on a freeway is about 70 dB; 140 dB is painfully loud, and 150 dB can rupture your eardrums. After 8 hours of exposure to 110 to 120 dB, your hearing may be damaged (rock groups play at this level). High noise levels are stressful and can lead to illnesses such as hypertension, neurological and intestinal disorders, and ulcers (Cohen and others, 1986; Staples, 1996).

High noise levels also impair daily functioning. They can lead to forgetfulness, perceptual errors, even dropping things. Children who are exposed to louder traffic noise on the lower floors of apartment buildings or to loud noise from low-flying airplanes at school may experience stress, hearing loss, and impairments in learning and memory (Cohen and others, 1986). Time to adjust and subsequent noise abatement do not seem to reverse their cognitive and perceptual deficits.

Truth or Fiction Revisited

It is true that children in noisy classrooms do not learn to read as well as children in quiet classrooms. Research carried out near the Los Angeles International Airport bears out this statement.

DECIBEL • A unit expressing the loudness of a sound.

FIGURE 5.5

DECIBEL RATINGS OF SOME FAMILIAR SOUNDS.

Loud noise is an environmental stressor that can raise the blood pressure, foster aggressive behavior, and interfere with learning and performance.

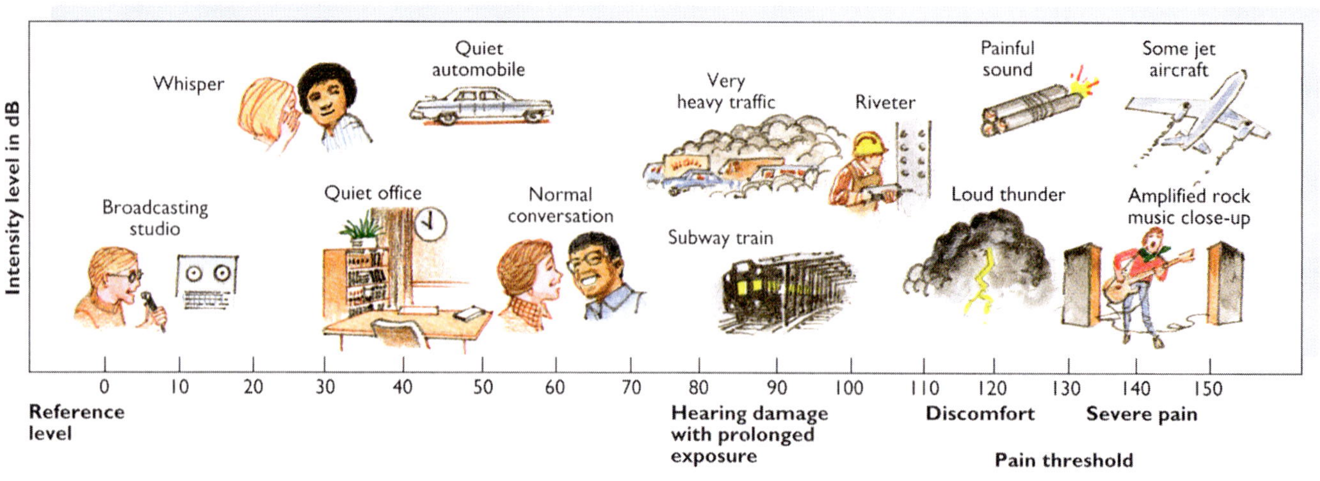

Couples may enjoy high noise levels at nightclubs, but grating noises of 80 dB seem to decrease feelings of attraction. They cause people to stand farther apart. Loud noise also reduces helping behavior. People are less likely to help pick up a dropped package when the background noise of a construction crew is at 92 dB than when it's at 72 dB (Staples, 1996). They're even less willing to make change for a quarter.

If you and your date have had a fight and are then exposed to a tire blowout, look out. Angry people are more likely to behave aggressively when exposed to a sudden noise of 95 dB than when exposed to one of 55 dB (Donnerstein & Wilson, 1976).

AIR POLLUTION: FUSSING AND FUMING Auto emissions, industrial smog, cigarette smoke, smoke from fireplaces and burning leaves—these are some of the air pollutants that affect us. Carbon monoxide, the most common air pollutant, combines with the substance in the blood that carries oxygen, thus preventing organs such as the brain and heart from receiving adequate oxygen. Prolonged exposure to high levels of carbon monoxide can impair learning and contribute to headaches, memory disturbances, fatigue, even epilepsy. High concentrations of carbon monoxide may thus contribute to highway accidents. The lead in auto fumes may impair children's intellectual functioning in the same way that chewing lead paint does.

Truth or Fiction Revisited

It is true that auto fumes may lower your children's IQs. Auto exhaust contains chemicals that can impair learning, memory, and other cognitive functions that are related to overall intellectual functioning.

Carbon monoxide, a colorless, odorless gas found in cigarette smoke and auto fumes, decreases the oxygen-carrying capacity of the blood. Carbon monoxide impairs learning ability and perception of the passage of time. It may also contribute to highway accidents. Residents of Los Angeles, New York, and other cities are accustomed to warnings to stay indoors or remain inactive in order to reduce air consumption when atmospheric inversions allow smog to accumulate. In December 1952, high amounts of smog collected in London, causing nearly 4,000 deaths (Schenker, 1993). High levels of air pollution have also been connected with higher mortality rates in U.S. cities (Dockery and others, 1993).

People tend to become psychologically accustomed to air pollution. For example, newcomers to polluted regions like southern California are more concerned about the air quality than long-term residents (Evans and others, 1982). Acceptance of pollution backfires when illness results.

Unpleasant-smelling pollutants, like other forms of aversive stimulation, decrease feelings of attraction and heighten aggression (Baron & Byrne, 1997). When there is a stink, some people are more likely to . . . well, make a stink.

EXTREMES OF TEMPERATURE A hot car engine makes great demands on the circulatory system. The water can overheat, and the radiator can pop its cap. Excesses of heat also make demands on our own circulatory systems and can cause dehydration, heat exhaustion, heatstroke, even a heart attack. When it is too cold, the body tries to generate and retain heat. The metabolism increases and we shiver. Blood vessels in the skin constrict, decreasing blood supply to the periphery of the body, where its warmth can be lost more easily.

Hot and cold temperatures are both aversive events that increase arousal. In other words, they get your attention (Bell, 1981). Minor shifts in temperature may facilitate learning and behavior, increase feelings of attraction, and have generally positive effects, but extreme changes in temperature tax our ability to adjust; our performance and activity levels tend to deteriorate.

Heat apparently makes some people hot under the collar, because high temperatures are connected with aggression. In Houston, murders and rapes are most likely to occur when the temperature is in the nineties Fahrenheit

(Anderson, 1989). In Raleigh, North Carolina, the incidence of rape and aggravated assault escalates with the average monthly temperature (Cohn, 1990; Simpson & Perry, 1990). The frequency of car honking at traffic lights in Phoenix increases with the temperature (Kenrick & MacFarlane, 1986).

Truth or Fiction Revisited

It is true that heat prompts aggression (makes us "hot under the collar"). Cooling off apparently helps us to . . . cool off.

Some psychologists (e.g., Anderson & DeNeve, 1992) suggest that the probability of aggressive behavior continues to increase as the temperature soars. If so, one must wonder whether global warming will heat up people's tempers as well as the climate (Anderson & Bushman, 1998). Other psychologists (e.g., Bell, 1992) argue that once temperatures become extremely aversive, people tend to avoid aggressive behavior so that they will not be doubly struck by hot temper and hot temperature. The evidence does not absolutely support either view, so the issue remains, well, heated.

CROWDING: LIFE IN RAT CITY AND BEYOND Sometimes you do everything you can for rats. You give them all they can eat, sex partners, a comfortable temperature, and protection from predators such as owls and pussycats. And how do they reward you. By acting like, well, rats.

In classic research, John Calhoun (1962) allowed rats to reproduce with no constraints but for space (see Figure 5.6). At first, all was bliss in rat city. Males scurried about, gathered females into harems, and defended territories. They did not covet their neighbors' wives. They rarely fought. Females, unliberated, built nests and nursed their young. They resisted the occasional advance of the passing male.

But unchecked population growth proved to be the snake in rat paradise. Beyond a critical population, the mortality rate rose. Family structure broke down. Packs of delinquent males assaulted inadequately defended females. Other males shunned all social contact. Some females avoided sexual advances and huddled with the fearsome males. There were instances of cannibalism. Upon dissection, many rats showed biological changes characteristic of stress.

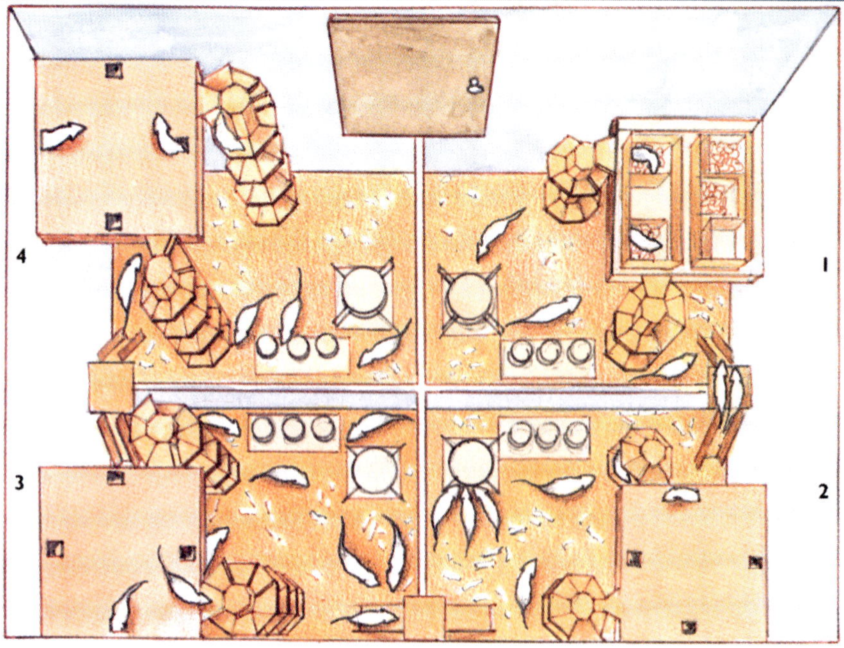

FIGURE 5.6
THE "RAT UNIVERSE."
In Calhoun's "rat universe," unlimited food supply and ready access between compartments (with the exception of compartments 1 and 4, between which access was not direct) caused compartments 2 and 3 to become a "behavioral sink." The "sink" was characterized by overpopulation, breakdown of the social order, and a higher-than-normal mortality rate. Do some cities function as behavioral sinks?

High density can be a source of stress in people, too. People who live in crowded institutional settings, such as prisons, hospitals, and college dormitories, may share some of the problems encountered by Calhoun's rats. Crowded prison inmates, for example, show higher blood pressure, more psychiatric illness, and a higher mortality rate than uncrowded prisoners (D'Atri, 1975; Paulus and others, 1975).

You may have been shoehorned with other roommates into a dorm room intended only for two. Students in high-density living situations sometimes adjust by withdrawing from optional social interactions (Baum & Valins, 1977; Paulus, 1979). Crowded students are more likely to complain about roommates and label them uncooperative (Baron and others, 1976).

There is also a "tripling" effect. When three students live together, a coalition frequently forms between two of them so that the third feels isolated. The isolate reports the crowding to be more aversive than the pair who have formed the coalition (Aiello and others, 1981; Reddy and others, 1981). Findings such as these suggest that with humans it is not crowding per se that is so aversive. Instead, it is the sense that one does not have control over the situation. We shall learn more about the importance of a sense of control in coping with stress in the next section, when we discuss psychological hardiness.

Truth or Fiction Revisited

It is true that crowding a third roommate into a dorm room built for two can make somebody unhappy. According to the "tripling effect," two roommates frequently form an alliance against the third.

MODERATORS OF THE IMPACT OF STRESS

There is no one-to-one relationship between the amount of stress we experience and outcomes such as physical disorders or psychological distress. Physical factors account for some of the variability in our responses. For example, some people apparently inherit predispositions toward certain physical and psychological disorders. But psychological factors also play a role. Psychological factors can influence, or *moderate,* the impact of sources of stress.

In this section we discuss a number of moderators of stress: self-efficacy expectations, psychological hardiness, a sense of humor, predictability, and social support (Figure 5.7).

FIGURE 5.7
PSYCHOLOGICAL MODERATORS OF STRESS.
There is no one-to-one connection between the intensity of a stressor and its impact on us. Factors such as those shown here can moderate, or buffer, the effects of stress.

Self-Efficacy Expectancies

Truth or Fiction Revisited

It is true that the belief that we can handle stress is linked to lower levels of adrenaline in the bloodstream. As a result, we are likely to feel less nervous.

Cognitive social theorists (e.g., Bandura, 1989, 1991) argue that our **self-efficacy expectations** have important influences on our abilities to withstand stress. For example, when we are faced with fear-inducing objects, high self-efficacy expectations are accompanied by *low* levels of the hormone **adrenaline** in the bloodstream (Bandura and others, 1985). Adrenaline arouses the body (see Chapter 6). As a result, we may experience shakiness, "butterflies in the stomach," and feelings of nervousness. So people with higher self-efficacy expectations have biological as well as psychological reasons for remaining calmer.

Further evidence of the importance of self-efficacy expectations to psychological well-being is suggested by research that shows that normal people have higher levels of perceived self-efficacy than do people who visit psychiatrists (Rosenbaum & Hadari, 1985).

People with high self-efficacy expectations complete tasks more successfully than people of comparable ability but lower self-efficacy expectations. Subjects with high self-efficacy expectations show lower emotional arousal as they work, allowing them to maintain more of a task orientation. A combination of high self-efficacy expectations *and a detailed plan* helps overweight college students lose weight (Schifter & Ajzen, 1985). People with higher self-efficacy expectations are less likely to relapse after they have lost weight or quit smoking (Condiotte & Lichtenstein, 1981; Marlatt & Gordon, 1980). They are more likely to seriously consider nontraditional and challenging career options (Betz & Hackett, 1981). They are also more likely to profit from psychotherapy for problems such as depression (Steinmetz and others, 1983).

When intelligence and aptitudes are held constant, it appears that people with higher self-efficacy expectations regulate problem-solving behavior more effectively and bounce back more readily from failure. In these ways it seems that life's challenges may be less stressful for them.

The connection between self-efficacy expectations and performance is a two-way street. People with high self-efficacy are more effective in athletic competition (Weinberg and others, 1980). Feltz (1982) also found that improved performance (in women who were back-diving) heightens self-efficacy expectations. If you think you can, perhaps you can.

Psychological Hardiness

Truth or Fiction Revisited

It is true that some people are psychologically hardier than others. They are more capable of resisting the harmful effects of stress. Psychological hardiness is characterized by commitment, challenge, and control.

Psychological hardiness also apparently helps people resist stress. The research on psychological hardiness is largely indebted to the pioneering work of Suzanne Kobasa and her colleagues (Kobasa, 1990; Kobasa and others, 1994). They studied business executives who resisted illness despite heavy loads of stress. In one phase of her research, Kobasa administered a battery of psychological tests to hardy and nonhardy executives. The hardy executives differed from the nonhardy in three notable ways (Kobasa and others, 1982, pp. 169–170):

1. Hardy individuals were high in *commitment*. They tended to involve themselves in, rather than feel alienated from, whatever they were doing or experiencing.
2. Hardy individuals were high in *challenge*. They saw change rather than stability as the norm. They considered change a stimulating incentive to personal growth, not a threat to security.
3. Hardy individuals were high in perceived *control* over their lives. They felt that they were instrumental in reaping personal rewards and

SELF-EFFICACY EXPECTATIONS • Beliefs to the effect that one can handle a task or manage a stressor.

ADRENALINE • A hormone manufactured by the adrenal glands, which lie above the kidneys. Adrenaline arouses the body to cope with stress in many ways, for example, by increasing the heart and respiration rates.

PSYCHOLOGICAL HARDINESS • A cluster of traits that buffer stress and are characterized by commitment, challenge, and control.

avoiding punishments. Psychologically hardy people tend to show what Rotter (1990) terms an internal **locus of control.**

According to Kobasa, hardy people are more resistant to stress because they see themselves as *choosing* their stress-producing situations. They interpret, or encode, the stress impacting upon them as making life more interesting, not as compounding pressure. Their activation of control allows them to regulate the amount of stress they encounter (Maddi & Kobasa, 1984). Of the three aspects of psychological hardiness that help people resist stress, Hull and his colleagues (1987) argue that commitment and control make the most difference.

Kobasa and Pucetti (1983) suggest that psychological hardiness helps individuals resist stress by providing buffers between themselves and stressful life events. Buffering allows people the opportunity to draw upon social supports (Ganellen & Blaney, 1984) and to use successful coping mechanisms, such as controlling what they will be doing from day to day. And Type A individuals who show psychological hardiness are more resistant to illness, including coronary heart disease, than Type A individuals who do not (Booth-Kewley & Friedman, 1987; Kobasa and others, 1983).

CONTROL AS AN ADJUSTMENT STRATEGY FOR COPING WITH CROWDING Examples from everyday life suggest that a sense of control—a sense of making choices—fosters adjustment. Consider the role of control in our responses to crowding. When we are at a concert, a nightclub, or a sports event, we may experience greater crowding than we do in those frustrating registration lines. But we may be having a wonderful time. Why? Because we have *chosen* to be at the concert and are focusing on our good time (unless a tall or noisy person sits in front of us). We feel that we are in control.

How, then, can we handle registration lines? First, we must challenge the irrational idea that we have no choice about being there. Haven't we decided to be there because the pluses of waiting outweigh the negatives? By waiting, for example, aren't we less likely to get closed out of desired courses? We can also plan ahead and bring a novel or wait with a friend and chat.

Sense of Humor: "Doeth a Merry Heart Good Like a Medicine?"

The idea that humor lightens the burdens of the day and helps us cope with stress has been with us for millennia (Lefcourt & Martin, 1986). Consider the biblical maxim, "A merry heart doeth good like a medicine" (Proverbs 17:22).

Writer and editor Norman Cousins (1979) once recovered from a lengthy bout with a painful illness. He reported that 10 minutes of belly laughter had a powerful anesthetic effect, allowing him to sleep for at least 2 hours without analgesic medication. Laughter also appeared to reduce his inflammation, a finding that has led some writers to speculate that laughter might stimulate the output of endorphins. But the benefits of humor might also be explained in terms of the sudden cognitive shifts they entail and the emotional changes that accompany them (Dixon, 1980).

Until recently, the benefits of humor were speculative and anecdotal. But an important psychological study of the moderating effects of humor on stress was run by Martin and Lefcourt (1983). They administered a negative-life-events checklist and a measure of mood disturbance to college students. The mood-disturbance measure also yielded a stress score. In addition, each student was given a self-report scale concerning his or her sense of humor, and also a behavioral assessment of his or her ability to produce humor under stressful conditions. Overall, high accumulations of negative life events predicted high levels of stress. However, students who produced humor in difficult situations were

Truth or Fiction Revisited

It is true that a sense of humor helps buffer the effects of stress. Research by Martin and Lefcourt supports the biblical maxim that "A merry heart doeth good like a medicine."

LOCUS OF CONTROL • The place (locus) to which an individual attributes control over the receiving of reinforcers—either inside or outside the self.

SELF-ASSESSMENT

WHO'S IN CHARGE HERE? THE LOCUS-OF-CONTROL SCALE

Psychologically hardy people tend to have an internal locus of control. They believe that they are in control of their own lives. Persons with an external locus of control, by contrast, tend to see their fates as being out of their hands.

Are you more of an "internal" or more of an "external"? To learn more about your perception of your locus of control, complete the Locus-of-Control Scale developed by Nowicki and Strickland (1973). ■

Directions: Place a checkmark in either the *Yes* or the *No* column for each question. When you have finished, turn to the answer key in the Appendix.

		Yes	No
1.	Do you believe that most problems will solve themselves if you just don't fool with them?	___	___
2.	Do you believe that you can stop yourself from catching a cold?	___	___
3.	Are some people just born lucky?	___	___
4.	Most of the time, do you feel that getting good grades meant a great deal to you?	___	___
5.	Are you often blamed for things that just aren't your fault?	___	___
6.	Do you believe that if somebody studies hard enough he or she can pass any subject?	___	___
7.	Do you feel that most of the time it doesn't pay to try hard because things never turn out right anyway?	___	___
8.	Do you feel that if things start out well in the morning, it's going to be a good day no matter what you do?	___	___
9.	Do you feel that most of the time parents listen to what their children have to say?	___	___
10.	Do you believe that wishing can make good things happen?	___	___
11.	When you get punished, does it usually seem it's for no good reason at all?	___	___
12.	Most of the time, do you find it hard to change a friend's opinion?	___	___
13.	Do you think cheering helps a team win more than luck does?	___	___
14.	Did you feel that it was nearly impossible to change your parents' minds about anything?	___	___
15.	Do you believe that parents should allow children to make most of their own decisions?	___	___
16.	Do you feel that when you do something wrong there's very little you can do to make it right?	___	___
17.	Do you believe that most people are just born good at sports?	___	___

		Yes	No
18.	Are most other people your age stronger than you are?	____	____
19.	Do you feel that one of the best ways to handle most problems is just not to think about them?	____	____
20.	Do you feel that you have a lot of choice in deciding who your friends are?	____	____
21.	If you find a four-leaf clover, do you believe that it might bring you good luck?	____	____
22.	Did you often feel that whether or not you did your homework had much to do with what kind of grades you got?	____	____
23.	Do you feel that when a person your age is angry with you, there's little you can do to stop him or her?	____	____
24.	Have you ever had a good-luck charm?	____	____
25.	Do you believe that whether or not people like you depends on how you act?	____	____
26.	Did your parents usually help you if you asked them to?	____	____
27.	Have you ever felt that when people were angry with you, it was usually for no reason at all?	____	____
28.	Most of the time, do you feel that you can change what might happen tomorrow by what you did today?	____	____
29.	Do you believe that when bad things are going to happen they are just going to happen no matter what you try to do to stop them?	____	____
30.	Do you think that people can get their own way if they just keep trying?	____	____
31.	Most of the time, do you find it useless to try to get your own way at home?	____	____
32.	Do you feel that when good things happen, they happen because of hard work?	____	____
33.	Do you feel that when somebody your age wants to be your enemy there's little you can do to change matters?	____	____
34.	Do you feel that it's easy to get friends to do what you want them to do?	____	____
35.	Do you usually feel that you have little to say about what you get to eat at home?	____	____
36.	Do you feel that when someone doesn't like you, there's little you can do about it?	____	____
37.	Did you usually feel it was almost useless to try in school, because most other children were just plain smarter than you were?	____	____
38.	Are you the kind of person who believes that planning ahead makes things turn out better?	____	____
39.	Most of the time, do you feel that you have little to say about what your family decides to do?	____	____
40.	Do you think it's better to be smart than to be lucky?	____	____

less affected by negative life events than other students. Humor, that is, apparently played its assumed historic stress-buffering role.

Predictability

Ability to predict the onset of a stressor also apparently moderates its impact. Predictability lets us brace ourselves for the inevitable and, in many cases, permits us to plan ways of coping. Most people who are aware of medical procedures and what they will feel cope with pain more effectively than people who do not (e.g., Shipley and others, 1978; Staub and others, 1971). Crowding is also less aversive when we are forewarned as to how we may react (Baum and others, 1981).

On the other hand, there is a relationship between personality factors, such as the desire to exercise control over one's situation, and the usefulness of information about stressors (Lazarus & Folkman, 1984). Predictability is apparently of greater benefit to "internals"—that is, to people who desire exercise of control over their situations—than to "externals." People who want information about medical procedures and what they will experience cope better with pain when they undergo those procedures (Ludwick-Rosenthal & Neufeld, 1993).

Social Support

Social support, like psychological hardiness, seems to buffer the effects of stress (Cohen & Wills, 1985; Pagel & Becker, 1987). Although social support is a situational variable, it should be noted that we can choose to seek support. In fact, children who thrive despite environmental hardships show an uncanny knack for seeking out the support of adults (Farber & Egeland, 1987). Social support, in turn, helps the child behave more resiliently.

Forms of social support include the following:

1. *Emotional concern.* Emotional concern means listening to people's problems and expressing sympathy, caring, understanding, and reassurance.
2. *Instrumental aid.* Instrumental aid refers to material supports and services that make adaptive behavior possible. For example, after a disaster, the government may arrange for low-interest loans to help survivors rebuild. Foodstuffs, medicines, and temporary living quarters are further examples.
3. *Information.* This form of support refers to cognitive guidance (advice) that will enhance people's abilities to cope. The seeking of information as to how to cope is a prominent motivation for undertaking psychotherapy.
4. *Appraisal.* Appraisal is feedback from others as to how one is doing. This kind of support involves helping people interpret, or make sense of, what has happened to them.
5. *Socializing.* Beneficial effects are derived from socializing itself, even if socialization is not aimed at helping solve problems. Examples include simple conversation, recreation, even shopping with company.

Research shows that social support moderates the impact of stress in situations ranging from problems at work to technological disasters. Consider the nuclear accident at the Three Mile Island nuclear plant in Pennsylvania. Nearby residents who had solid networks of social support—relatives and friends with whom they could share the experience—reported less stress than those who did not (Fleming and others, 1982).

Psychologists know that it is useful for people who encounter stress to get together and talk about their ideas and feelings so that they can support one another. Return to the effects of crowding. When compared with men who are crowded in with other men, women find being crowded in with women less aversive. An experiment by Karlin suggests that the effects of the stress of crowding are moderated for women because women feel freer to share their feelings about it (Karlin and others, 1976). Men who conform to the tough, independent masculine stereotype tend to keep a "stiff upper lip." Women are thus more likely to form supportive social networks.

People who receive social support may even live longer, as was found in studies of Alameda County, California (Berkman & Syme, 1979; Berkman & Breslow, 1983), and Tecumseh, Michigan (House and others, 1982). In the Tecumseh study, 2,754 adults were followed from 1967 through 1979. Over this 12-year period, the mortality rate was significantly lower for men who were married, who regularly attended meetings of voluntary associations, and who engaged in frequent social leisure activities.

Truth or Fiction Revisited

It is not true that single men live longer. According to a long-term study carried out in Tecumseh, Michigan, married men outlive their unmarried peers. Perhaps it is because they receive more social support. It is also possible that more stable men (men likelier to be reasonably prudent in their behaviors) are also more likely to choose to get married.

Adjustment in a World of DIVERSITY

Stress and Ethnic Pride Among African Americans

African Americans are at greater risk than non-Hispanic White Americans of incurring stress-related health problems such as obesity, hypertension, coronary heart disease, diabetes, and certain cancers. Researchers suspect that the stressors faced by African Americans— such as racism, poverty, violence, and overcrowding—play a role in explaining their heightened health risks (Anderson, 1991).

Yet stress appears to have a different impact on individual African Americans. Many factors appear to mediate the effects of stress among African Americans, just as they do among other ethnic groups in the United States. These include social support from family and friends, belief in one's ability to manage stress (one's self-efficacy expectations), coping skills, and one's feelings about one's ethnic identity. Ironically, African Americans who may be in the greatest need of social support, such as single parents and the elderly, are frequently the most reluctant to seek support from family members (Anderson, 1991).

As among other ethnic groups, self-esteem is connected with ethnic identity among African Americans. Pride in one's racial identity and cultural heritage apparently helps African Americans—and other ethnic minorities—withstand the stresses imposed by prejudice. Although more research is needed to clarify the connections between self-esteem, racial identity, and ability to manage or tolerate stress, the evidence suggests that African Americans who become alienated from their cultural backgrounds develop more negative self-images. They are also at greater risk of developing physical and psychological disorders, academic underachievement, and marital conflicts (Anderson, 1991).

adjustment and modern life

Modern life is filled with conflict—motives that aim in opposite directions. When one motive is much stronger than the other—as when you feel starved and are only slightly concerned about your weight—it will probably not be too stressful to act in accord with the powerful motive and, in this case, eat. But when each conflicting motive is powerful, you may encounter high levels of stress and confusion about the proper course of action. At such times you are faced with the need to make a decision. Yet making decisions can also be stressful, especially when there is no clear correct choice. Let us see how psychologists have helped people use the balance sheet to make decisions.

USING THE BALANCE SHEET TO MAKE DECISIONS

Making decisions involves choosing among goals or courses of action to reach goals. In order to make rational decisions, we weigh the pluses and minuses of each possible course of action. We need to clarify the subjective values of our goals, our abilities to surmount the obstacles in our paths, and the costs of surmounting them. Frequently, we need to gather information about the goals and about our abilities to attain them.

There is nothing new in the concept of weighing pluses and minuses, but Janis and Mann (1977) have found that use of a balance sheet can help us make sure that we have considered the information available to us. Sheri Oz (1994, 1995) suggests that it is crucial to attend to the costs of deciding one way or another.

The balance sheet also helps highlight gaps in information. The balance sheet has been shown to help high school students select a college and to help adults decide whether or not to go on diets and attend exercise classes. Balance sheet users show fewer regrets about the road not taken and are more likely to stick to their decisions.

To use the balance sheet, jot down the following information for each choice (see Table 5.2):

1. Projected tangible gains and losses for oneself
2. Projected tangible gains and losses for others
3. Projected self-approval or self-disapproval
4. Projected approval or disapproval of others

Consider a case from our files. Meg was a 34-year-old woman whose husband, Bob, beat her. She had married Bob at 27, and for 2 years life had run smoothly. But she had been bruised and battered, fearful of her life, for the

TABLE 5.2 Meg's Balance Sheet for the Alternative of Getting a Divorce From Bob

	Positive Anticipations	***Negative Anticipations***
Tangible gains and losses for me	1. Fear of being beaten or killed will be eliminated.	1. Loneliness 2. Fear of starting a new social life 3. Fear of not having children owing to age 4. Financial struggle 5. Fear of personal emotional instability
Tangible gains and losses for others	1. Mother will be relieved.	1. Bob might harm himself or others (he has threatened to commit suicide if I leave him).
Social approval or social disapproval		1. I might consider myself a failure because I could not help Bob or save our marriage.
Social approval or social disapproval		1. People who believe that marriage is sacred and must be maintained at any cost will blame me for "quitting." 2. Some men may consider me an easy mark.

When making a decision, weighing up the pluses and minuses for the various alternatives can lead to more productive choices and fewer regrets. Meg's balance sheet for the alternative of getting a divorce from an abusive husband showed her psychologist that her list of positive anticipations was incomplete.

past 5. She sought psychotherapy to cope with Bob, her fears, her resentments, and her disappointments. The therapist asked if Bob would come for treatment too, but Bob refused. Finally, unable to stop Bob from abusing her, Meg considered divorce. But divorce was also an ugly prospect, and she vacillated.

Table 5.2 shows the balance sheet, as filled out by Meg, for the alternative of divorce. Meg's balance sheet supplied Meg and her therapist with an agenda of concerns to work out. It also showed that Meg's anticipations were wanting. Would she really have no positive thoughts about herself if she got a divorce from Bob? Would no one other than her mother applaud the decision? Did she have an irrational need to avoid the disapproval of others? Meg's list of negative anticipations pointed to the need to develop financial independence by acquir-

ing job skills. Her fears about undertaking a new social life also seemed overblown. Yes, making new acquaintances might not be easy, but it was not impossible. And what of Meg's feelings about herself? Wouldn't she be pleased that she had done what she thought was necessary, even if divorce also entailed problems?

Meg concluded that many negative anticipations were exaggerated. Many fears could be collapsed into an umbrella of fear of change. Fear of change had also led her to underestimate her need for self-respect. Meg did get a divorce, and at first she was depressed, lonely, and fearful. But after a year, she was working and dating regularly. She was not blissful but had regained a sense of forward motion. She took pride in being independent and no longer dwelled in fear. It is fortunate that this story has a relatively happy ending. Otherwise, we would have had to look for another.

Are you now putting off making any decisions in your own life? Could using the balance sheet be of any help?

In this chapter we have explored the nature of stress and factors that moderate the impact of stress. In the next chapter we explore the effects of stress on the body and examine a number of stress-related illnesses. In Chapter 9 we examine the ways in which stress apparently contributes to a number of psychological disorders, and in Chapters 10 and 11 we discuss ways of coping with stress.

SUMMARY

1. **What is stress?** Stress is the demand made on an organism to adjust. Whereas some stress is desirable ("eustress") to keep us alert and occupied, too much stress can tax our adjustive capacities and contribute to physical illness.
2. **What are some sources of stress?** Sources of stress include daily hassles; life changes; pain; frustration; conflict; Type A behavior; and environmental stressors such as disasters, noise, and crowding.
3. **What is the difference between daily hassles and life changes?** Daily hassles are regularly encountered sources of aggravation or annoyance. Life changes occur on an intermittent basis and may be positive (such as a major achievement or a vacation) as well as negative.
4. **How do daily hassles and life changes affect us?** Hassles and life changes require adjustment, although negative life changes are more taxing than positive life changes. People who earn more than 300 life-change units within a year, according to the Holmes and Rahe scale, are at high risk for medical and psychological disorders.
5. **What are the limitations of the data on daily hassles, life changes, and illness?** The data on these relationships are correlational rather than experimental. It is possible that people about to develop illnesses encounter more hassles or lead lifestyles with more life changes. Also, the degree of stress imposed by an event is linked to one's appraisal of that event.
6. **What are pain and discomfort, and how do they affect us?** Pain originates at a source of body injury and is transmitted to the brain. Pain and discomfort impair our ability to perform, especially when severe demands are made on the heels of a traumatic experience.
7. **What are some psychological methods of pain management?** These include provision of accurate information about the source, intensity, and duration of the pain; distraction and fantasy; hypnosis; relaxation training; coping with irrational beliefs; and social support.
8. **What is frustration?** Frustration results from having unattainable goals or from barriers to reaching our goals.
9. **What kinds of conflict are there?** Conflict results from opposing motives. We often vacillate when we are in conflict. Approach-approach conflicts are least stressful. Multiple approach-avoidance conflicts are most complex. Making decisions is often the way out of conflict. We can use the balance sheet to help list and weigh the pluses and minuses for the alternatives available to us.
10. **What is Type A behavior, and how does it affect us?** Type A behavior is characterized by aggressiveness, a sense of time urgency, and competitiveness. Type A people are more aggressive and more reluctant to relinquish control or power than are Type B's. Type A people also respond to challenge with higher blood pressure than Type B's. Evidence as to whether Type A's are at greater risk for heart attacks is mixed.
11. **What are some environmental stressors?** Environmental stressors include natural disasters, technological disasters, high noise levels, air pollution, extremes of temperature, and crowding.
12. **How do self-efficacy expectations moderate the impact of stress?** Self-efficacy expectations encourage us to persist in difficult tasks and to endure pain and discomfort.
13. **What is psychological hardiness, and how does it help us cope with stress?** Psychological hardiness is characterized by commitment, challenge, and control. Persons with an internal locus of control ("internals") endure stress more successfully than people with an external locus of control ("externals"). Internals seek information about their situations, which increases the chances of coping.
14. **Does humor help us cope with stress?** Yes. The ability to produce humor under stress apparently buffers the impact of stress.
15. **Are there times when we seek stress, or is stress always aversive?** Yes, we may seek stress from time to time. When we are in a goal-directed mode of functioning, we tend to be serious-minded and to try to decrease the stress impinging on us by lowering our levels of arousal. However, when we are in a playful mode (e.g., involved in a tennis match), we may seek to increase the amount of arousal we experience.
16. **How does predictability moderate the impact of stress?** Predictability buffers stress by allowing us to brace ourselves and to plan ways of coping.
17. **How does social support moderate the impact of stress?** Social support buffers the impact of stress in five ways: expression of emotional concern, instrumental aid, provision of information, appraisal, and socialization activities.

The Challenges of Life
The Challenges of Life
The Challenges of Life
The Challenges of Life
The Challenges of Life
Challenges of Life
The Challenges of Life
Challenges of Life

CHAPTER 6

Psychological Factors and Health

TRUTH OR FICTION?

T F

- ☐ ☐ Optimistic people recover more rapidly than pessimistic people from coronary artery bypass surgery.
- ☐ ☐ Fear can give you indigestion.
- ☐ ☐ At any given moment, myriads of microscopic warriors within our bodies are carrying out search-and-destroy missions against foreign agents.
- ☐ ☐ Poor Americans eat less than more affluent Americans do.
- ☐ ☐ Most headaches are caused by muscle tension.
- ☐ ☐ Most women are severely impaired by premenstrual syndrome.
- ☐ ☐ Your diet can influence the likelihood that you will contract cancer.
- ☐ ☐ Stress can influence the course of cancer.

OUTLINE

Some of us are our own best friends. We mind what we eat, we exercise regularly, and we monitor the sources of stress in our lives so that we can regulate their impact.

But some of us are our own worst enemies. Some of us share contaminated needles or engage in reckless sexual behavior despite knowledge that AIDS can be transmitted in these ways. Many of us eat foods high in cholesterol and fats despite knowledge that we heighten the risks of coronary heart disease and cancer. And, of course, many of us continue to smoke even though we know full well that we are *not* invulnerable.

In this chapter we consider some findings in the field of health psychology. In the following chapter we explore the effects of nutrition, fitness, and sleep on personal health, and we look at ways of maximizing their benefits.

HEALTH PSYCHOLOGY

Health psychology has recently emerged as a prominent field of psychology. Health psychologists study the relationships between psychological factors (behavior, emotions, stress, beliefs, and attitudes) and the prevention and treatment of physical illness (Taylor, 1990). Health psychologists investigate the ways in which stress affects the body—especially the immune system. Stress apparently helps pave the way for physical disorders ranging from headaches to cornonary heart disease. Health psychologists have examined the ways in which our behavior patterns—such as smoking, drinking, and exercise—contribute to or can help us prevent and cope with physical disorders. They have also explored the psychology of being sick—factors that induce us to seek medical advice, ways in which we conceptualize illness, and how we "play" the sick role. They have also identified factors that foster compliance with medical advice.

BIOLOGICAL, EMOTIONAL, AND COGNITIVE EFFECTS OF STRESS

In this section we review a number of biological, emotional, and cognitive effects of stress. We see how stress can set the stage for, or exacerbate, physical illness.

Effects of Stress on the Body

Health psychology • The field of psychology that studies the relationships between psychological factors (e.g., attitudes, beliefs, situational influences, and overt behavior patterns) and the prevention and treatment of physical illness.

How does too much of a good thing or anxiety or frustration or conflict make us ill? We do not yet have all the answers, but those we have suggest that the

How Optimistic Is Your Outlook? The Life Orientation Test

Over the years, laypeople and professionals have speculated on the relationships between psychological factors such as attitudes and emotions, on the one hand, and health on the other. Later we shall see that some relationships have been discovered concerning the will to resist, anger, and the course of cancer. Here, as an example of the connections between attitudes and health, let us consider the roles of optimism and pessimism.

According to Scheier and Carver, optimism is what cognitive social theorists refer to as a generalized outcome expectancy. It is generalized because it addresses many areas of life, from vocational and family life to ability to cope with physical problems. In one study, Scheier and Carver (1985) administered their Life Orientation Test (LOT)—a measure of optimism—to college undergraduates. They also had the students track their physical symptoms over a 4-week period. Students who scored higher on optimism reported fewer symptoms like dizziness, fatigue, muscle soreness, and blurred vision. (Subjects' symptom levels at the beginning of the study were mathematically taken into account so that it could not be argued that the results simply show that healthier people are more optimistic.) The researchers suggest that optimistic people are less bothered by physical symptoms because they tend to assume that they will be able to cope with them—or in spite of them.

Optimism has been related to many aspects of health (Peterson & Bossio, 1991), such as postpartum depression and recovery from coronary artery bypass surgery (CABP). For example, Carver and Gaines (1987) found that optimistic women were less likely than pessimistic women to be depressed following the birth of their children. Scheier and his colleagues (1989) showed that cardiac patients who are optimistic recover relatively more rapidly from CABP. They take fewer days after surgery to get up and walk around their rooms, show a more favorable physical recovery, have fewer postoperative complications at a 6-week follow-up, and are more likely to have returned to their preoperative routines (including work and physical exercise) by 6 months after surgery.

Do you see the cup as half full or half empty? Are you generally optimistic or pessimistic? Do you expect good things to happen, or do you find the cloud around the silver lining? The Life Orientation Test may provide you with insight into your general outlook on life. ■

Truth or Fiction Revisited

It is true that optimistic people recover more rapidly than pessimistic people from coronary artery bypass surgery. Our attitudes are apparently connected with aspects of our physical well-being.

Directions: Indicate whether or not each of the items represents your feelings by writing a number in the black space according to the following code. Then turn to the scoring key in the Appendix.

4 = strongly agree
3 = agree
2 = neutral
1 = *dis*agree
0 = strongly *dis*agree

____ 1. In uncertain times, I usually expect the best.
____ 2. It's easy for me to relax.
____ 3. If something can go wrong for me, it will.
____ 4. I always look on the bright side of things.
____ 5. I'm always optimistic about my future.
____ 6. I enjoy my friends a lot.
____ 7. It's important for me to keep busy.
____ 8. I hardly ever expect things to go my way.
____ 9. Things never work out the way I want them to.
____ 10. I don't get upset too easily.
____ 11. I'm a believer in the idea that "every cloud has a silver lining."
____ 12. I rarely count on good things happening to me.

Source: Michael F. Scheier & Charles S. Carver (1985), Optimism, coping, and health: Assessment and implications of generalized outcome expectancies, *Health Psychology*, 4, 219–247.

ADJUSTMENT in the NEW MILLENNIUM

Psychology and Health in the New Millennium

During the 1980s, coronary-prone behavior received the lion's share of attention from researchers in health psychology. Although some observers questioned this emphasis, it now seems that it was extremely valuable. For example, the focus on coronary-prone behavior led to vastly increased understanding of the roles of stressors, cognitive appraisal, and personality factors (especially hostility) in CHD.

In the 1990s, AIDS became the focus of research in health psychology, and again some researchers wondered whether too much attention was being paid to this illness. Margaret A. Chesney (1993) argues that this focus is appropriate because AIDS has such a devastating effect on the lives of so many people. Moreover, the AIDS epidemic has pointed health psychology toward five trends that are likely to become even more prominent in the twenty-first century:

- *Early identification of people at risk for disease.* The experience of the AIDS epidemic is showing that health psychology needs to encourage early identification of people who are at risk for health problems. Risk for many disorders, such as cancer, is defined largely in terms of family history and patterns of consumption such as poor diet, smoking, and drinking alcohol. In the case of AIDS, however, risk is defined more in terms of behavior and mental processes—factors that place people at risk of being infected with the AIDS virus (HIV). Sociocultural considerations are also connected with risk. In the United States, for example, non-Hispanic white men are most likely to be infected with HIV through engaging in sex with male partners. African American men are equally likely to be infected through sex with other men and by injecting ("shooting up") drugs (Centers for Disease Control and Prevention, 1997). Throughout the world, however, sex between men and women is the most common way in which the virus is transmitted (Weniger & Brown, 1996).

body, under stress, is like a clock with an alarm system that does not shut off until its energy is dangerously depleted.

GENERAL ADAPTATION SYNDROME The body's response to different stressors shows some similarities, whether the stressor is a bacterial invasion, perceived danger, a major life change, inner conflict, or a wound. Selye (1976) has labeled this response the **general adaptation syndrome** (GAS). The GAS consists of three stages: an alarm reaction, a resistance stage, and an exhaustion stage.

GENERAL ADAPTATION SYNDROME • Selye's term for a hypothesized three-stage response to stress. Abbreviated *GAS*.

ALARM REACTION • The first stage of the GAS, which is "triggered" by the impact of a stressor and characterized by sympathetic activity.

FIGHT-OR-FLIGHT REACTION • Cannon's term for an innate adaptive response to the perception of danger.

THE ALARM REACTION The **alarm reaction** is triggered by perception of a stressor. It mobilizes or arouses the body in preparation for defense. Cannon (1929) had earlier termed this alarm system the **fight-or-flight reaction.** The alarm reaction involves body changes that are initiated by the brain and regulated by the endocrine system and the sympathetic division of the autonomic nervous system. Let us consider the roles of these two body systems.

- *Rising expectations for programs that encourage people to change high-risk behavior.* Health psychology needs to learn more about the planning and execution of programs that foster healthful behavioral changes. For example, most people in the United States have become generally aware of the threat and modes of transmission of HIV. Yet knowledge of danger alone apparently does not lead to necessary changes in sexual practices and drug use (Klepinger and others, 1993; Rotheram-Borus and others, 1991). (Nor does knowledge of danger alone stop people from smoking or drinking to excess.)
- *Growing numbers of people who are coping with chronic diseases.* Health psychologists are developing more effective ways to help people cope with chronic diseases. Today more than 31 million Americans are age 65 or older. That number will increase to about 60 million by 2020. Almost four out of five people age 65 or older have at least one chronic condition such as heart disease, hypertension, arthritis, or declining cognitive functioning (Chesney, 1993). In addition to younger people who are at risk for serious illnesses like AIDS, the increasing numbers of older people will profit from better coping strategies that are being devised and tested today.
- *A shift toward inclusion of community and public health perspectives.* Psychology promotes the dignity of the individual, and health psychology has traditionally focused on the health of the individual. However, the AIDS epidemic has spurred health psychologists to also consider community and public health perspectives. Health psychologists, for example, are working with community psychologists to explore more effective ways of changing norms and values in the community at large. They are studying barriers to behavioral change among groups that are likely to engage in high-risk behavior.
- *The need to address health problems on a global scale.* There is increasing awareness that health psychology must address health problems on a global scale. Since chronic illnesses such as cancer and heart disease know no boundaries, it appears that the international perspective is here to stay. ■

THE ROLE OF THE ENDOCRINE SYSTEM The **endocrine system** consists of ductless glands such as those shown in Figure 6.1. Glands such as tear glands send their secretions (in this case, tears) to their destinations (the eyes) by ducts (tear ducts). Ductless glands pour their secretions, known as **hormones,** directly into the bloodstream. Although hormones are poured into the bloodstream and circulate throughout the body, they only act on receptors in certain locations. Some hormones released by the hypothalamus influence only the pituitary gland. Some hormones released by the pituitary gland influence the adrenal cortex, while others influence the testes and ovaries, or other parts of the body.

The hypothalamus, a tiny structure in the brain, is essential to the alarm reaction. The hypothalamus secretes corticotrophin-releasing hormone (CRH), which stimulates the pituitary gland to secrete adrenocorticotrophic hormone (ACTH). ACTH, in turn, acts upon the outer part of the adrenal glands (the adrenal cortex), causing the glands to release a number of hormones referred to as **corticosteroids.** Corticosteroids help the body respond to stress by fighting inflammation and allergic reactions (such as difficulty breathing). Cortisol is an

ENDOCRINE SYSTEM • The body's system of ductless glands that secrete hormones and release them directly into the bloodstream.

HORMONES • Substances that are secreted by endocrine glands and that regulate various body functions. (From the Greek *horman,* meaning "to stimulate" or "to excite.")

CORTICOSTEROIDS • Hormones produced by the adrenal cortex that increase resistance to stress in ways such as fighting inflammation and causing the liver to release stores of sugar. Also called *cortical steroids.*

ARE THEIR ALARM SYSTEMS GOING OFF AS THEY TAKE OUT A LOAN?

The alarm reaction of the general adaptation syndrome can be triggered by daily hassles and life changes — such as taking out a large loan — as well as by physical threats. When the stressor persists, diseases of adaptation may develop.

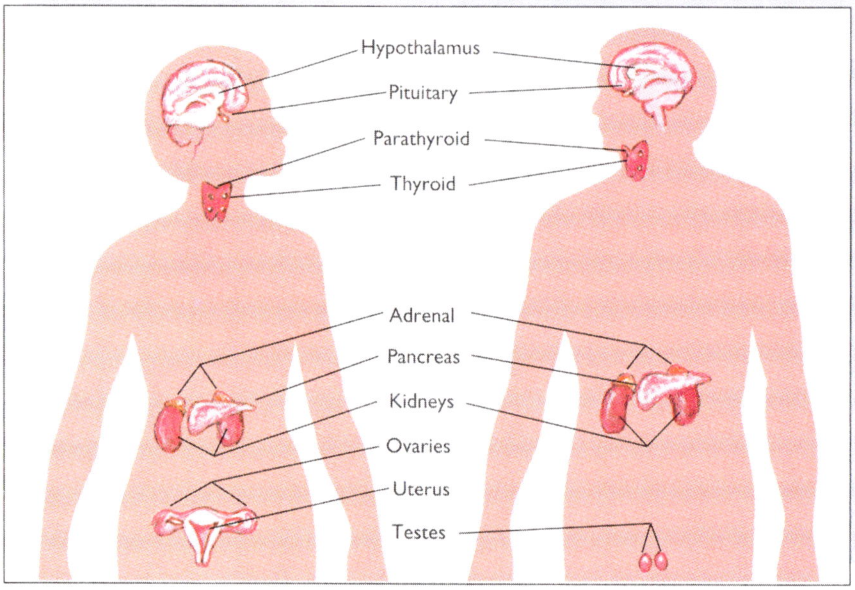

FIGURE 6.1

LOCATION OF SOME GLANDS OF THE ENDOCRINE SYSTEM.

When we are under stress, the hypothalamus signals the pituitary gland to secrete a hormone that causes the adrenal cortex to release steroids such as cortisol. The adrenal medulla secretes adrenaline and noradrenaline, which heighten the functioning of the sympathetic division of the autonomic nervous system. Note the position of the adrenal glands atop the kidneys.

important corticosteroid. Steroids also cause the liver to release stored glucose (sugar), making energy available. The names of these hormones are a "mouthful," but note the logic to them: the *cortico-* in each one refers to the adrenal *cortex*, indicating that they act, in a domino effect, to cause the adrenal cortex to secrete steroids. Moreover, *cortex* is the Latin word for "bark," or outer covering.

The adrenal medulla (or inner part [*medulla* means "marrow"] of the adrenal glands) secretes two hormones that play a major role in the alarm reaction. These are adrenaline (also known as epinephrine) and noradrenaline (also known as norepinephrine). *Ad-renal* is Latin for "near the kidneys," and *epinephros* has the same meaning in Greek. Figure 6.1 shows that the adrenal glands are located on top of the kidneys. Adrenaline is manufactured exclusively by the adrenal glands, but noradrenaline is also produced at other sites in the body. Adrenaline acts on the sympathetic branch of the autonomic nervous system (see the discussion following) to arouse the body to cope with threats and stress. Noradrenaline raises the blood pressure and helps transmit messages in the nervous system.

Since cortisol and adrenaline are secreted in response to stress, the amounts of these substances in the body serve as an objective measure of stress. Psychologists frequently use the amount of cortisol in the saliva and the amount of adrenaline in the urine as biological measures of stress.

Since adrenaline acts on the autonomic nervous system, let us now consider the role of that system in the alarm reaction.

THE ROLE OF THE AUTONOMIC NERVOUS SYSTEM *Autonomic* means "automatic." The **autonomic nervous system,** or ANS, regulates the glands and involuntary activities such as heartbeat, digestion, and dilation of the pupils of the eyes.

The ANS has two branches or divisions, the **sympathetic** division and the **parasympathetic** division (see Figure 6.2). These branches of the ANS have largely opposing effects; when they work at the same time, their effects can average out to some degree. Many organs and glands are stimulated by both branches. In general, the sympathetic division is stimulated by adrenaline and is

AUTONOMIC NERVOUS SYSTEM • The part of the nervous system that regulates glands and involuntary activities such as heartbeat, respiration, digestion, and dilation of the pupils of the eyes. Abbreviated *ANS*.

SYMPATHETIC • The division of the ANS that is most active during activities and emotional responses—such as anxiety and fear—that spend the body's reserves of energy.

PARASYMPATHETIC • The division of the ANS that is most active during processes that restore the body's reserves of energy, such as digestion.

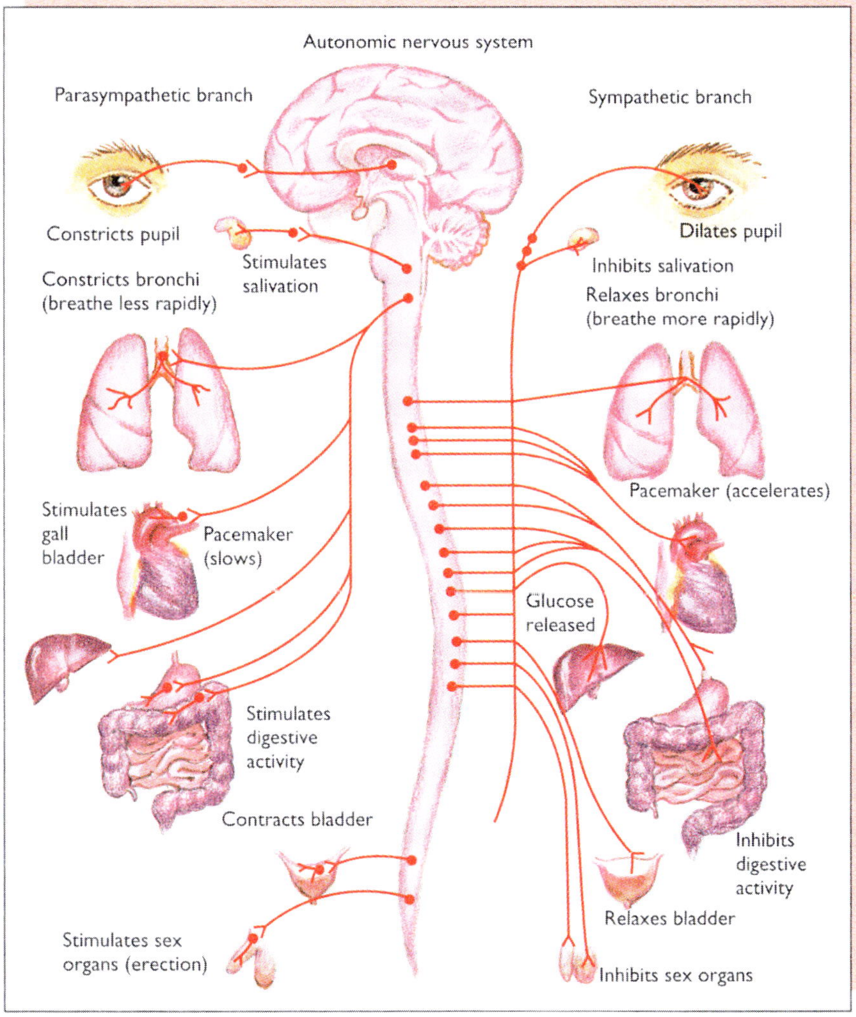

FIGURE 6.2
ACTIVITIES OF THE BRANCHES OF THE AUTONOMIC NERVOUS SYSTEM.
The parasympathetic branch or division of the autonomic nervous system (ANS) is generally dominant during activities that replenish the body's stores of energy, such as digesting and relaxing. The sympathetic branch or division of the ANS is most active during activities that spend energy, such as fighting or fleeing from an enemy, and when we feel emotions such as fear and anxiety. For this reason, most of the organs shown are stimulated to heightened activity by the sympathetic division of the ANS. Digestive processes are an exception; they are inhibited by sympathetic activity.

TABLE 6.1 COMPONENTS OF THE ALARM REACTION

Corticosteroids are secreted	Muscles tense
Adrenaline is secreted	Blood shifts from internal organs to the skeletal musculature
Noradrenaline is secreted	Digestion is inhibited
Respiration rate increases	Sugar is released from the liver
Heart rate increases	Blood coagulability increases
Blood pressure increases	

The alarm reaction is triggered by various types of stressors. It is defined by release of corticosteroids and adrenaline and by activity of the sympathetic branch of the autonomic nervous system. It prepares the body to fight or flee from a source of danger.

most active when the body is spending energy from stored reserves, such as when you chafe at the bit in stop-and-go traffic or when you find out that your mortgage or rent payment is going to be increased. Adrenaline increases the heart and respiration rates, the blood sugar level, and so on.

Truth or Fiction Revisited

It is true that fear can give you indigestion. Fear is characterized by sympathetic arousal, and sympathetic arousal inhibits digestive processes.

The parasympathetic division is most active during processes that replenish reserves of energy, as during eating. For instance, when we are anxious, the sympathetic division of the ANS accelerates the heart rate. When we relax, the parasympathetic division decelerates the heart rate. The parasympathetic division stimulates digestion, but the sympathetic branch inhibits digestion. Since the sympathetic division predominates when we feel anxiety or fear, fear or anxiety can give you indigestion.

The sympathetic division of the ANS provides more energy for muscular activity, which can be used to fight or flee from a source of danger, and decreases the body's vulnerability to wounds. These and other changes are outlined in Table 6.1. The fight-or-flight reaction is inherited from a long-ago time when many stressors were life-threatening. It was triggered by a predator at the edge of a thicket or by a sudden rustling in the undergrowth. Once the threat is removed, the body returns to a lower state of arousal.

Our ancestors lived in situations in which the alarm reaction would not be activated for long. They fought or ran quickly or, to put it bluntly, they died. Sensitive alarm reactions contributed to survival.

Highly sensitive alarm reactions may no longer be an advantage. Our ancestors did not spend years in the academic grind or carry 30-year mortgages. Contemporary pressures may activate our alarm systems for hours, days, or months at a time. For this reason, highly sensitive systems may now be a handicap. Pardine and Napoli (1983) administered a life-events questionnaire to college undergraduates. Students who reported high levels of recent stress showed higher levels of heart rate and blood pressure in response to an experimentally induced stressor than students who reported low levels of stress. Apparently, students with more sensitive alarm reactions recover less rapidly from stressors and find their lives more stressful. We cannot change our heredity—sensitive alarm systems will tend to remain sensitive to some degree. (In Chapter 11 we explore methods for lowering our levels of arousal—for turning the alarm system down.)

RESISTANCE STAGE • The second stage of the GAS, characterized by prolonged sympathetic activity in an effort to restore lost energy and repair damage. Also called the *adaptation stage.*

THE RESISTANCE STAGE If the alarm reaction mobilizes the body and the stressor is not removed, we enter the adaptation stage, or **resistance stage,** of the GAS. Levels of endocrine and sympathetic activity are not as high as in the alarm reaction but are still greater than normal. In this stage, the body attempts to restore energy and repair damage.

The Exhaustion Stage If the stressor is still not adequately dealt with, we may enter the final or **exhaustion stage** of the GAS. Our individual capacities for resisting stress vary, but all of us eventually become exhausted when stress persists. Our muscles become fatigued, and we deplete our bodies of resources required for combating stress. With exhaustion, the parasympathetic division of the ANS may become predominant. As a result, our heartbeats and respiration rates slow down. Many of the body responses that had characterized sympathetic activity are reversed. It might sound as if we would profit from the respite, but remember that we are still under stress—and, perhaps, still confronting a real threat. Continued stress in the exhaustion stage may lead to what Selye terms "diseases of adaptation"—from allergies and hives to coronary heart disease—and, ultimately, to death.

Later in the chapter we explore a number of these stress-related illnesses.

Emotional Effects of Stress

Emotions color our lives. We are green with envy, red with anger, blue with sorrow. The poets paint a thoughtful mood as a brown study. Positive emotions such as love and desire can fill our days with pleasure, but negative emotions, such as those induced by stress, can fill us with dread and make each day an intolerable chore. Let us consider three important emotional responses to stress: anxiety, anger, and depression.

Anxiety Anxiety tends to occur in response to *threats* of stressors such as physical danger, losses, and failure. Anxiety is a stressor in its own right as well as an emotional response to stress.

Psychologists frequently distinguish between trait anxiety and state anxiety. **Trait anxiety** is a personality variable. People with trait anxiety have persistent feelings of dread and foreboding—cognitions that something terrible is about to happen. They are chronically worried and concerned. **State anxiety** is a temporary condition of arousal that is triggered by a specific situation, such as a final exam, a big date, a job interview, or a visit to the dentist.

On a biological level, anxiety of either type involves predominantly sympathetic arousal (rapid heartbeat and breathing, sweating, muscle tension, and so on).

Anger Anger usually occurs in response to stressors such as frustration and social provocation. Hostility differs from anger in that it is an enduring trait. Biologically, anger can arouse both sympathetic and parasympathetic arousal. Anger usually involves cognitions to the effect that the world has no right to be the way it is (in the case of frustration) or that another person has no right to treat us in a certain way (in the case of a social provocation).

Depression Depression usually occurs in response to stressors such as the loss of a friend, lover, or relative; to failure; to inactivity or lack of stimulation; and to prolonged stress. Why does depression sometimes stem from inactivity and lack of stimulation? People have needs for stimulation, and some stress, which Selye referred to as "eustress," is desirable and healthful.

Why does depression stem from prolonged exposure to stress? On a biological level, depression is characterized by parasympathetic dominance, and parasympathetic activity is characteristic of the exhaustion stage of the GAS.

Exhaustion stage • The third stage of the GAS, characterized by weakened resistance and possible deterioration.
Trait anxiety • Anxiety as a personality variable, or persistent trait.
State anxiety • A temporary condition of anxiety that may be attributed to a situation.

EMOTIONS AND BEHAVIOR Emotions motivate certain kinds of behavior. Negative emotions such as anxiety, anger, and depression can motivate us to behave in maladaptive ways. For example, anxiety tends to motivate escapist behavior; anger, aggressive behavior; and depression, withdrawal.

It is helpful for us to perceive negative emotional responses as signs that something is wrong, to learn what we can about the sources of stress, and then to plan behavior that will enable us to remove or buffer stressors. But when our emotions "run too high," they can disrupt our cognitive processes and interfere with adaptive behavior.

Cognitive Effects of Stress

There are continuous interactions between the physiological, emotional, and cognitive aspects of human nature. Emotions include physiological and cognitive "components." High levels of bodily arousal in response to stress heighten our emotional responses and influence our cognitions.

EFFECTS OF HIGH AROUSAL ON BEHAVIOR It appears that we are motivated to seek *optimal* levels of arousal at which we feel best and function most efficiently. By and large, our levels of arousal are determined by the levels of activity of the sympathetic and parasympathetic divisions of the ANS. Most of us seek a balance between the two divisions—preferring to avoid the extremes characterized by, say, anxiety (sympathetic dominance) and depression and inactivity (parasympathetic dominance).

EVOCATION OF DOMINANT COGNITIONS AND OVERT BEHAVIOR PATTERNS Strong physiological and emotional responses to stress, which are characterized by high levels of arousal, can impair cognitive activity and problem-solving ability. One source of impairment is the evocation of our dominant cognitions and behavior patterns by high levels of arousal. So, even if we have been working to find adaptive ways of responding to threats and social provocations, we may revert to fleeing or fighting under high arousal.

WHAT DO WE FOCUS ON WHEN THE ADRENALINE IS PUMPING? High arousal also impairs cognitive functioning by distracting us from the tasks at hand. We may focus on our body responses—and, as a result, cognitions to the effect that perhaps we need to escape or are doomed to failure—rather than on the problems to be solved.

In later chapters we see that adaptive coping methods include ways of lowering arousal and maintaining a task orientation.

THE IMMUNE SYSTEM

Given the complexities of our bodies and the fast pace of scientific change, it is common for us to think of ourselves as highly dependent on trained professionals, such as physicians, to cope with illness. But we actually do a great deal for ourselves by means of our **immune system.**

Functions of the Immune System

IMMUNE SYSTEM • The system of the body that recognizes and destroys foreign agents (antigens) that invade the body.

PATHOGENS • Microscopic organisms (e.g., bacteria or viruses) that can cause disease.

One way in which we combat physical disorders is by producing white blood cells that routinely engulf and kill **pathogens** such as bacteria, fungi, and

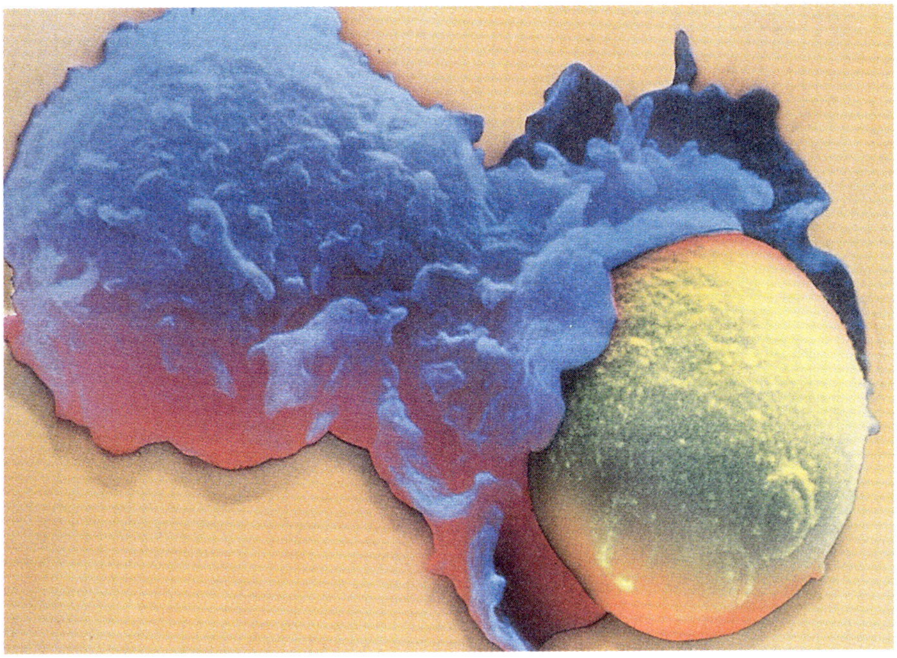

MICROSCOPIC WARFARE.
Beneath the level of awareness, our immune systems are engaged in a constant struggle against invaders. Here, a white blood cell engulfs and destroys an invading pathogen.

viruses; worn out body cells; even cells that have become cancerous. White blood cells are termed **leukocytes** (pronounced "LOO-coh-sites"). Leukocytes carry on microscopic warfare. They engage in search-and-destroy missions in which they "recognize" and eliminate foreign agents and unhealthy cells.

Leukocytes recognize foreign agents to enhance the effectiveness of future combat. The surfaces of the foreign agents are termed **antigens** because the body reacts to their presence by developing specialized proteins, or **antibodies,** that attach to the foreign bodies, inactivating them and marking them for destruction. The second function of the immune system is to "remember" how to battle these antigens by maintaining antibodies in the bloodstream. **Vaccination** is the introduction of a weakened form of an antigen (usually a bacterium or a virus) into the body to stimulate the production of antibodies. Antibodies can confer immunity for many years, in some cases for a lifetime. Smallpox has been eradicated by means of vaccination, and scientists are searching for a vaccine against the AIDS virus.

Inflammation is a third function of the immune system. When injury occurs, blood vessels in the area first contract (stemming bleeding) but then dilate. Dilation increases the flow of blood to the damaged area, causing the redness and warmth that characterize inflammation. The increased blood supply also brings in large numbers of white blood cells to combat invading microscopic life forms, such as bacteria, that might use the local damage as a port of entry into the body.

Truth or Fiction Revisited

It is true that myriads of microscopic warriors within our bodies are carrying out search-and-destroy missions against foreign agents at any given moment. These warriors are white blood cells.

Effects of Stress on the Immune System

Psychologists, biologists, and medical researchers have combined their efforts in a field of study that addresses the relationships between psychological factors, the nervous system, the endocrine system, the immune system, and disease: **psychoneuroimmunology** (Maier and others, 1994). One of the major concerns of psychoneuroimmunology is the effect of stress on the immune system.

One of the reasons that stress eventually exhausts us is that it stimulates us to produce steroids. Steroids suppress the functioning of the immune system. Suppression has negligible effects when steroids are secreted intermittently, but

LEUKOCYTES • White blood cells. (Derived from the Greek words *leukos,* meaning "white," and *kytos,* literally meaning "a hollow," but used to refer to cells.)

ANTIGENS • Substances that stimulate the body to mount an immune-system response to them. (The contraction for *anti*body *gen*erators.)

ANTIBODIES • Substances that are formed by white blood cells and that recognize and destroy antigens.

VACCINATION • Purposeful infection with a small amount of an antigen so that in the future the immune system will recognize and efficiently destroy the antigen.

INFLAMMATION • Increased blood flow to an injured area of the body, resulting in redness, warmth, and an increased supply of white blood cells.

PSYCHONEUROIMMUNOLOGY • The field that studies the relationships between psychological factors (e.g., attitudes and overt behavior patterns) and the functioning of the immune system.

persistent secretion impairs the functioning of the immune system by decreasing inflammation and interfering with the formation of antibodies. As a consequence, susceptibility to various illnesses, including the common cold (Cohen and others, 1991), increases.

RESEARCH CONCERNING STRESS–IMMUNE-SYSTEM RELATIONSHIPS Research supports the hypothesized links between stress and the immune system (Coe, 1993; Kiecolt-Glaser, 1993). Research also demonstrates the moderating effects of psychological factors such as control and social support.

An experiment conducted by Laudenslager and associates (1983) studied the activity of the immune system in laboratory rats. The rats were exposed to electric shocks—but one group of rats could learn to terminate the shock. The rats that could *not* exert control over the stressor showed immune-system deficits, but the rats that could end the shock showed no drop-off in their immune-system functioning.

One study focused on dental students (Jemmott and others, 1983). Students showed lower immune-system functioning, as shown by lower levels of antibodies in the saliva, during stressful school periods than immediately following vacations. Students with many friends showed relatively less suppression of the immune system. Social support apparently buffered school stresses.

Another study with students found that the stress of examinations depressed immune-system response to the Epstein-Barr virus, which causes fatigue and other physical problems (Glaser and others, 1991). Moreover, students who were lonely showed greater suppression of the immune system than students who had more social support. In a study of elderly people it was found that relaxation training, which decreases sympathetic activity, and training in coping skills *improve* immune-system functioning (Glaser and others, 1991). We shall detail training in relaxation and coping skills in Chapters 10 and 11.

Psychologist Barbara Andersen and her colleagues (1998) found that anxiety following breast cancer surgery was connected with a lower white blood cell count. White blood cells, of course, are the warriors of the immune system. Andersen is still attempting to determine whether the functioning of the immune system affects the long-term outcome of breast cancer.

FACTORS IN PHYSICAL HEALTH AND ILLNESS

The only way to keep your health is to eat what you don't want, drink what you don't like, and do what you'd rather not.

MARK TWAIN

Diseases ranging from heart problems to cancer are best understood in the context of many variables or factors. Biological factors such as family history of disease, pathogens, inoculations, injuries, age, and gender may strike us as the most obvious causes (or moderators) of disease. As you can see in Figure 6.3, however, many other factors also play key roles in health and illness. Many diseases have psychological aspects to them or are influenced by psychological factors, such as our attitudes and patterns of behavior (Ader, 1993; Angell, 1993; Farley, 1993). Many are affected by stressors. Our sociocultural backgrounds can affect which health problems we will develop, how we will react to them, and the eventual outcome.

This broad view of illness not only provides insight into the causes of illness, but also suggests avenues of prevention and treatment.

Biological Factor
Family history of illness
Exposure to infectious organisms (e.g., bacteria and viruses)
Functioning of the immune system
Inoculations
Medication history
Congenital disabilities, birth complications
Physiological conditions (e.g., hypertension, serum cholesterol level)
Reactivity of the cardiovascular system to stress (e.g., "hot reactor")
Pain and discomfort
Age
Gender
Ethnicity (e.g., genetic vulnerability to Tay-Sachs disease or sickle-cell anemia)

Sociocultural Factor
Socioeconomic status
Family circumstances (social class, family size, family conflict, family disorganization)
Access to health care (e.g., adequacy of available health care, availability of health insurance, availability of transportation to health care facilities)
Prejudice and discrimination
Health-related cultural and religious beliefs and practices
Health promotion in the workplace or community
Health-related legislation

Environmental Factor
Vehicular safety
Architectural features (e.g., crowding, injury-resistant design, nontoxic construction materials, aesthetic design, air quality, noise insulation)
Aesthetics of residential, workplace, and communal architecture and landscape architecture
Water quality
Solid waste treatment and sanitation
Pollution
Radiation
Global warming
Ozone depletion
Natural disasters (earthquakes, blizzards, floods, hurricanes, drought, extremes of temperature, tornadoes)

Personality
Seeking (or avoiding) information about health risks and stressors
Self-efficacy expectations
Psychological hardiness
Psychological conflict (approach-approach, avoidance-avoidance, approach-avoidance)
Optimism or pessimism
Attributional style (how one explains one's failures and health problems to oneself)
Health locus of control (belief that one is or is not in charge of one's own health)
Introversion/extroversion
Coronary-prone (Type A) personality
Tendencies to express or hold in feelings of anger and frustration
Depression/anxiety
Hostility/suspiciousness

Behavior
Diet (intake of calories, fats, fiber, vitamins, etc.)
Consumption of alcohol
Cigarette smoking
Level of physical activity
Sleep patterns
Safety practices (e.g., using seat belts; careful driving; practice of sexual abstinence, monogamy, or "safer sex"; adequate prenatal care)
Having (or not having) regular medical and dental checkups
Compliance with medical and dental advice
Interpersonal/social skills

Stressors
Daily hassles (e.g., preparing meals, illness, time pressure, loneliness, crime, financial insecurity, problems with co-workers, day care)
Major life changes such as divorce, death of a spouse, taking out a mortgage, losing a job
Frustration
Pain and discomfort
Availability and use of social support vs. peer rejection or isolation
Climate in the workplace (e.g., job overload, sexual harassment)

FIGURE 6.3
FACTORS IN HEALTH AND ILLNESS.
Various factors figure in a person's state of health or illness. Which of the factors in this figure are you capable of controlling? Which are beyond your control?

Human Diversity and Health: A Land of Many Nations

Today we know more about the connections between behavior and health than ever before. The United States also has the resources to provide the most advanced health care in the world. But not all Americans take advantage of contemporary knowledge. Nor do all profit equally from the health care system. Health psychologists note, therefore, that from the perspective of health and health care we are many nations and not just one. Many factors influence whether people engage in good health practices or let themselves go. Many factors affect whether they act to prevent illness or succumb to it. These factors include ethnicity, gender, level of education, and socioeconomic status.

ETHNICITY AND HEALTH The life expectancy of African Americans is 7 years shorter than that of White Americans (Kilborn, 1998). The time of "healthy life"—that is, life without serious infirmity—is 8 years shorter (Kilborn, 1998). It is unclear whether this difference is connected with ethnicity per se or with factors such as income and level of education (Kilborn, 1998).

Because of lower socioeconomic status, African Americans have less access to health care than White Americans do (Flack and others, 1995; Penn and others, 1995). They are also more likely to live in unhealthful neighborhoods, eat high-fat diets, and smoke (Pappas and others, 1993).

African Americans also experience different treatment by medical practitioners. Even when they have the same medical conditions as White people, African Americans are less likely to receive treatments such as coronary artery bypass surgery, hip and knee replacements, kidney transplants, mammography, and flu shots (Geiger, 1996). Why? Various explanations have been offered, including cultural differences, patient preferences, and lack of information about health care. Another possible explanation, of course, is racism (Geiger, 1996).

Disproportionate numbers of deaths from AIDS occur within ethnic minority groups in the United States, predominantly among African Americans and

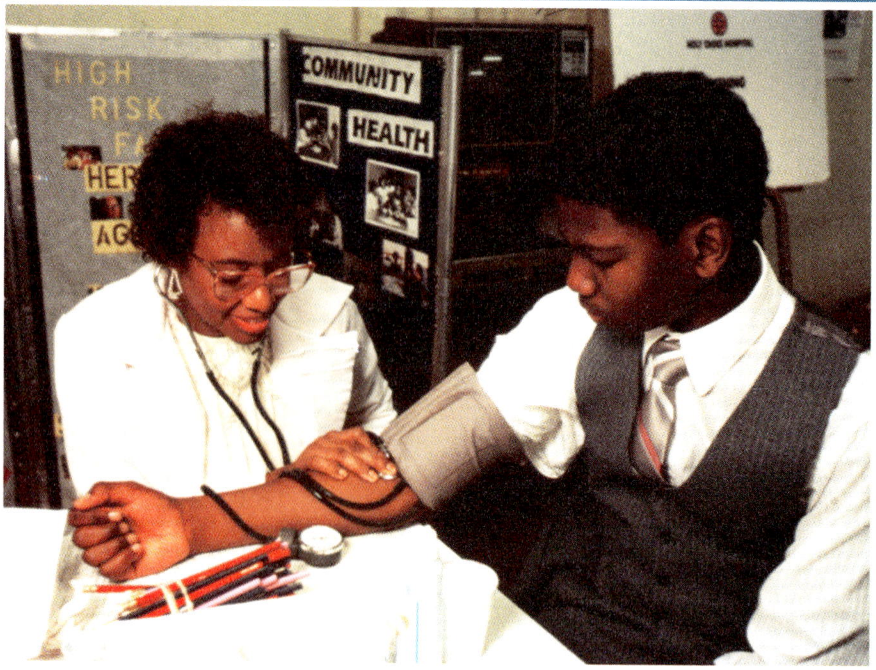

ETHNICITY AND HYPERTENSION. African Americans are more likely than non-Hispanic White Americans to suffer from hypertension. Research suggests that a genetic vulnerability to hypertension interacts with environmental factors such as stress, smoking, and diet to produce the problem.

Hispanic Americans (Centers for Disease Control and Prevention, 1997). Only 12 percent of the U.S. population is African American, but African American men account for 31 percent of people with AIDS. African American women account for 55 percent of women with AIDS. Only 9 percent of the population is Hispanic American, but Hispanic American men account for 17 percent of the men with AIDS. Hispanic American women account for 20 percent of women with AIDS.

African Americans are five to seven times more likely than European Americans to have hypertension (Leary, 1991). However, African Americans are also more likely to suffer from hypertension than Black Africans are. Many health professionals thus infer that environmental factors found among many African Americans—such as stress, diet, and smoking—contribute to high blood pressure in people who are genetically vulnerable to it (Betancourt & López, 1993; Leary, 1991).

African Americans are more likely than White Americans to have heart attacks and to die from them (Becker and others, 1993). Early diagnosis and treatment might help decrease the racial gap (Ayanian, 1993). African Americans with heart disease are less likely than White Americans to obtain procedures such as bypass surgery, even when it appears that they would benefit equally from the procedure (Peterson and others, 1997).

African Americans are also more likely than White Americans to contract most forms of cancer (Kilborn, 1998). Possibly because of genetic factors, the incidence of lung cancer is significantly higher among African Americans than among White Americans (Blakeslee, 1994; "Smoke Rises," 1993). Once they contract cancer, African Americans are more likely than White Americans to die from it. The results for African Americans are connected with their lower socioeconomic status and relative lack of access to health care (Meyerowitz and others, 1998). African Americans are also more likely than White Americans to have tuberculosis, asthma, diabetes, and strokes, and to die from these diseases as well (Kilborn, 1998).

Also consider some cultural differences in health. Death rates from cancer are higher in such nations as the Netherlands, Denmark, England, Canada, and—yes—the United States, where average rates of daily fat intake are high (Cohen, 1987). Death rates from cancer are much lower in such nations such as Thailand, the Philippines, and Japan, where average daily fat intake is much lower. Don't assume that the difference is racial just because Thailand, the Philippines, and Japan are Asian nations! The diets of Japanese Americans are similar in fat content to those of other Americans—and so are their rates of death from cancer.

There are health care "overusers" and "underusers" among cultural groups. For example, Hispanic Americans visit physicians less often than African Americans and non-Hispanic White Americans do because of lack of health insurance, difficulty speaking English, misgivings about medical technology, and—for illegal aliens—fear of deportation (Ziv & Lo, 1995).

GENDER AND HEALTH Also consider a few gender differences. Men are more likely than women to have coronary heart disease before women enter menopause (Keil and others, 1993), as women are apparently protected from it by high levels of estrogen until that time (Davidson, 1995). After menopause, women are dramatically more likely to incur heart disease (although this can be counteracted by estrogen replacement therapy).

The gender of the physician can also make a difference. According to a study of more than 90,000 women, women whose internists or family practitioners are women are more likely to have screening for cancer (mammograms and Pap smears) than women whose internists or family practitioners are men (Lurie and others, 1993). It is unclear from this study, however, whether female physicians are more likely than their male counterparts to encourage women to seek preventive care, or whether women who choose female physicians are also more likely to seek preventive care. Other research shows that female physicians are more likely than male physicians to conduct breast examinations properly (J. A. Hall and others, 1990).

Men's life expectancy is 7 years shorter, on the average, than women's. A survey of 1,500 physicians suggests that this difference is due, at least in part, to women's greater willingness to seek health care ("Doctors tie male mentality," 1995). Men often let symptoms go until a problem that could have been prevented or readily treated becomes serious or life threatening.

Adjustment in a World of DIVERSITY

Health and Socioeconomic Status: The Rich Get Richer and the Poor Get . . . Sicker?

Socioeconomic status (SES) and health are intimately connected. Generally speaking, people with higher SES enjoy better health and lead longer lives (Leary, 1995). The question is *why*.

Consider three possibilities (Adler and others, 1994). One is that there is no causal connection between health and SES. Perhaps both SES and health reflect genetic factors. For example, "good genes" might lead both to good health and to high social standing. Second, poor health might lead to socioeconomic "drift" (that is, loss of social standing). Third, SES might affect biological functions that, in turn, influence health.

How might SES influence health? SES is defined in part in terms of education. That is, people who attain low levels of education are also likely to have low SES. Less well educated people are more likely to smoke (Winkleby and others, 1991), and smoking has been linked to many physical illnesses. People with lower SES are also less likely to exercise and more likely to be obese—both of which, again, are linked to poor health outcomes (Ford and others, 1991).

Truth or Fiction Revisited

It is not true that poor people in the United States eat less than more affluent people. Obesity is actually most prevalent among the lowest socioeconomic groups. (This is not to deny the fact that some poor people in the United States cannot afford food.)

Anorexia and bulimia nervosa are uncommon among poor people, but obesity is most prevalent among the poor. The incidence of obesity is also greater in cultures that associate obesity with happiness and health—as is true of some Haitian and Puerto Rican groups. People living in poor urban neighborhoods are more likely to be obese because junk food is heavily promoted in those neighborhoods and many residents tend to eat as a way of coping with stress (Johnson and others, 1995).

Let us also not forget that poorer people also have less access to health care (Leary, 1995). The problem is compounded by the fact that people with low SES are less likely to be educated about the benefits of regular health checkups and early medical intervention when symptoms arise.

Headaches

Headaches are among the most common stress-related physical ailments. The single most frequent kind of headache is the muscle-tension headache. A survey of more than 13,000 people in Baltimore County found that nearly half had occasional muscle-tension headaches (Schwartz and others, 1998). Two in five had them at least once a month. Women were about 15 percent more likely than men to have muscle-tension headaches, and more educated people were more likely to have them than less educated people. The connection with education is not understood, but it may reflect the kinds of work done by more educated people, such as looking at computer screens for several hours a day. Some researchers suggest that more educated people experience more stress, with the graduate student perhaps experiencing the most stress.

Why are muscle-tension headaches connected with stress? We are likely to contract muscles in the shoulders, neck, forehead, and scalp during the first two stages of the GAS. Recurring stress can lead to persistent muscle contraction and consequent chronic muscle-tension headaches. Psychological factors, such as the tendency to catastrophize negative events—that is, blow them out of proportion—can bring on a tension headache (Ukestad & Wittrock, 1996). Tension headaches usually come on gradually. They involve dull, steady pain on both sides of the head and feelings of tightness or pressure.

Truth or Fiction Revisited

It is true that most headaches are caused by muscle tension. Muscle tension can also increase the pain of headaches that stem from other causes.

MIGRAINE HEADACHES Most other headaches, including the severe migraine headache, are vascular in nature. They stem from changes in the blood supply to the head. **Migraine headaches** have preheadache phases, during which the arteries that supply the head with blood are constricted, decreasing blood flow; and headache phases, during which the arteries are dilated, increasing the flow of blood. Migraine attacks are frequently accompanied by sensitivity to light; nausea, vomiting and loss of appetite; sensory and motor disturbances, such as loss of balance; and mood changes. The "common migraine" headache is identified by sudden onset and throbbing on one side of the head. In the "classic migraine," sensory and motor disturbances precede the pain.

The origins of migraine headaches are not clearly understood. It is believed, however, that they can be induced by barometric pressure; pollen; specific drugs; the chemical monosodium glutamate (MSG), which is often used to enhance the flavor of food; chocolates; aged cheeses; beer, champagne, and red wines; and the hormonal changes of the period prior to and during menstruation (Brody, 1992).

Type A behavior may also be an important contributor to migraine headaches. In one study, 53 percent of 30 migraine sufferers showed the Type A behavior pattern, as compared with 23 percent of 30 muscle-tension headache sufferers (Rappaport and others, 1988).

Regardless of the source of a headache, we can unwittingly propel ourselves into a vicious cycle: Headache pain is a stressor that can lead us to increase, rather than relax, muscle tension in the neck, shoulders, scalp, and face.

TREATMENT Aspirin, ibuprofen, and acetaminophen frequently decrease pain, including headache pain, by inhibiting the production of the prostaglandins that help initiate transmission of pain messages to the brain. Behavioral methods can also help. Progressive relaxation (described in Chapter 11) focuses on decreasing muscle tension and has been shown to be highly effective in relieving muscle-tension headaches (Blanchard, 1992; Blanchard and others, 1990a, 1991). Biofeedback training that alters the flow of blood to the head has been used effectively to treat migraine headaches (Blanchard, 1992; Blanchard and others, 1990b). People who are sensitive to MSG or red wine can ask that MSG be left out of their dishes and can switch to a white wine.

Why, under stress, do some of us develop headaches, others develop coronary heart disease, and still others suffer no bodily problems? In the following discussions we see that there may be an interaction between stress and

MIGRAINE HEADACHES • Throbbing headaches caused by changes in the supply of blood to the head.

predisposing biological and psychological differences between individuals (Nevid and others, 1998).

Menstrual Problems

Menstruation is a perfectly natural biological process. Nevertheless, most women experience some discomfort prior to or during menstruation. Table 6.2 contains a list of commonly reported symptoms of menstrual problems. Let us focus on the problems of dysmenorrhea, amenorrhea, and premenstrual syndrome (PMS).

DYSMENORRHEA Pain or discomfort during menstruation is called dysmenorrhea, and is the most common type of menstrual problem. Most women at some time have at least mild menstrual pain or discomfort. Pelvic cramps are the most common source of discomfort. Cramps may be accompanied by headache, backache, nausea, or bloated feelings. Dysmenorrhea is usually caused by hormonal changes but can also be caused by health problems such as endometriosis, pelvic inflammatory disease (PID), and ovarian cysts. Painful menstruation was reported by nearly 75 percent of the participants in a sample of college women (Wildman & White, 1986). The symptoms varied not only from person to person but also according to whether or not the women had been pregnant. Women who had been pregnant reported a lower incidence of menstrual pain but a higher incidence of premenstrual symptoms and menstrual discomfort.

Menstrual cramps appear to be caused by uterine spasms that are triggered by heavy secretion of hormones called prostaglandins. Prostaglandins cause muscle fibers in the uterine wall to contract, as during labor. Women with more intense menstrual discomfort may produce more prostaglandins. Prostaglandin-inhibiting drugs such as ibuprofen, indomethacin, and aspirin are thus often of help. (Ask your doctor or go to your college or university health center.) Pelvic pressure and bloating may be traced to pelvic edema (Greek for "swelling")—the congestion of fluid in the pelvic region. Fluid retention can lead to a gain of

TABLE 6.2 SYMPTOMS OF MENSTRUAL PROBLEMS

PHYSICAL SYMPTOMS	*PSYCHOLOGICAL SYMPTOMS*
Swelling of the breasts	Depressed mood, sudden tearfulness
Tenderness in the breasts	Loss of interest in usual social or recreational activities
Bloating	Anxiety, tension (feeling "on edge" or "keyed up")
Weight gain	Anger
Food cravings	Irritability
Abdominal discomfort	Changes in body image
Cramping	Concern over skipping routine activities, school, or work
Lack of energy	A sense of loss of control
Sleep disturbance, fatigue	A sense of loss of ability to cope
Migraine headache	
Pains in muscles and joints	
Aggravation of chronic disorders such as asthma and allergies	

several pounds, sensations of heaviness, and *mastalgia*—a swelling of the breasts that sometimes causes premenstrual discomfort. Menstrual migraine headaches arise from changes in the blood flow in the brain. These headaches are typically limited to one side of the head and are often accompanied by visual difficulties.

AMENORRHEA Amenorrhea is the absence of menstruation and is a primary sign of infertility. Amenorrhea has various causes, including abnormalities in the structures of the reproductive system, hormonal problems, growths such as cysts and tumors, and stress. Amenorrhea is normal during pregnancy and following menopause. Amenorrhea is also a symptom of anorexia nervosa—an eating disorder characterized by an intense fear of putting on weight and a refusal to eat enough to maintain a normal body weight. Anorexia results in extreme—sometimes life threatening—weight loss. Hormonal changes that accompany loss of body fat are believed responsible for the cessation of menstruation. Amenorrhea may also occur in women who exercise strenuously, such as competitive long-distance runners.

PREMENSTRUAL SYNDROME (PMS) **Premenstrual syndrome** (PMS) refers to the biological and psychological symptoms that may affect women during the 4- to 6-day interval that precedes menstruation (see Table 6.3). For many women, premenstrual symptoms persist during menstruation. Nearly three women in four experience symptoms at this time (Brody, 1996a). Most cases involve mild to moderate discomfort. Only about 2.5 percent of women report symptoms severe enough to markedly impair their social, academic, or occupational functioning (Mortola, 1998).

The causes of PMS are not fully understood. It was once believed that psychological factors such as negative attitudes toward menstruation played a crucial role. Now the prevailing view is that attitudes toward menstruation—for example, seeing the menstrual flow as an unclean thing—can worsen menstrual problems, but that PMS primarily has a biological basis. Today's researchers are searching out relationships between menstrual problems, including PMS, and chemical imbalances in the body. There are probably no differences in levels of estrogen or progesterone between women with severe PMS and those with mild symptoms or none (Mortola, 1998; Rubinow & Schmidt, 1995). Research in which these hormone levels were controlled suggests that it is not the levels of hormones that contribute to PMS, but unusual sensitivity to them (Schmidt and

Truth or Fiction Revisited

It is not true that most women are severely impaired by premenstrual syndrome. Premenstrual and menstrual symptoms are mild to moderate in most women.

PREMENSTRUAL SYNDROME • A cluster of physical and psychological symptoms that afflict some women prior to menstruation. Abbreviated *PMS*.

TABLE 6.3 SYMPTOMS OF PMS*

Depression	Insomnia or too much sleeping
Anxiety	Feelings of being out of control or overwhelmed
Mood swings	Physical problems such as headaches, joint or muscle pain, weight gain or feeling bloated (both from fluid retention), tenderness in the breasts
Anger and irritability	
Loss of interest in usual activities	
Difficulty concentrating	
Lack of energy	
Overeating or cravings for certain foods	

* Most women experience only a few of these symptoms, if they experience any at all.
Source: Jane E. Brody (1996, August 28), PMS need not be the worry it was just decades ago, *New York Times*, p. C9.

others, 1998). PMS also appears to be linked with imbalances in neurotransmitters such as serotonin (Mortola, 1998; Steiner and others, 1995). (Neurotransmitters are the chemical messengers in the nervous system.) Serotonin imbalances are also linked to changes in appetite. Women with PMS show greater increases of appetite during the luteal phase than other women do. Another neurotransmitter, gamma-aminobutyric acid (GABA) also appears to be involved in PMS, because medicines that affect the levels of GABA help many women with PMS (Mortola, 1998). Premenstrual syndrome may well be caused by a complex interaction between ovarian hormones and neurotransmitters (Mortola, 1998).

Only a generation ago, PMS was seen as something a woman must put up with but it is no longer viewed that way. Today there are many treatment options. These include exercise, dietary control (for example, eating several small meals a day rather than two or three large meals; limiting salt and sugar; taking vitamin supplements), hormone treatments (usually progesterone), and medications that affect concentrations of GABA or serotonin in the nervous system (Mortola, 1998).

HOW TO HANDLE MENSTRUAL DISCOMFORT Most women experience some degree of menstrual discomfort. Women with persistent menstrual distress may profit from the suggestions listed below. Why not adopt the techniques that sound right for you? You can use all of them, if you wish.

1. First of all, don't blame yourself! Again, this is where *psychological* as opposed to *medical* advice comes in handy. Menstrual problems were once erroneously attributed to women's "hysterical" nature. This is nonsense. Menstrual problems appear, in large part, to reflect chemical fluctuations in the brain during the menstrual cycle. Even though researchers have not yet fully identified all the causal elements and patterns, there is no evidence that women who have menstrual problems are "hysterical."
2. Keep track of your menstrual symptoms to help you (and your doctor) identify patterns.

MANAGING MENSTRUAL DISCOMFORT. Most women have some menstrual discomfort, but there is much that you can do about it. For example, you can check into whether your attitudes toward menstruation are compounding your discomfort. You can watch your diet and, like the women in this photo, try exercise. Many drugs are also of help. Check with your doctor.

3. Develop strategies for dealing with days during which you experience the greatest distress—strategies that will help enhance your pleasure and minimize the stress affecting you on those days. Psychologists have found that it is useful to engage in activities that distract people from pain. Why not try things that will distract you from your menstrual discomfort? Go see a movie or get into that novel you've been meaning to read.
4. Ask yourself whether you harbor any self-defeating attitudes toward menstruation that might be compounding distress. Do close relatives or friends see menstruation as an illness, a time of "pollution," a "dirty thing"? Have you adopted any of these attitudes—if not verbally, then in ways that affect your behavior, as by restricting your social activities during your period?
5. See a doctor about your concerns, especially if you have severe symptoms. Severe menstrual symptoms are often caused by health problems such as endometriosis and pelvic inflammatory disease (PID). Check it out.
6. Develop nutritious eating habits—and continue them throughout the entire cycle (that means *always*). Consider limiting intake of alcohol, caffeine, fats, salt, and sweets, especially during the days preceding menstruation.
7. If you feel bloated, eat smaller meals (or nutritious snacks) throughout the day, rather than a couple of highly filling meals.
8. Some women find that vigorous exercise—jogging, swimming, bicycling, fast walking, dancing, skating, even jumping rope—helps relieve premenstrual and menstrual discomfort. Try it out. But don't engage in exercise *only* prior to and during your period! You'll be placing more stress on yourself. Make exercise a part of your lifestyle.
9. Check with your doctor about vitamin and mineral supplements (such as calcium and magnesium). Vitamin B_6 appears to have helped some women.
10. Ibuprofen (brand names: Medipren, Advil, Motrin, and so on) and other medicines available over the counter may be helpful for cramping. Prescription drugs such as antianxiety drugs (e.g., alprazolam) and antidepressant drugs (serotonin-reuptake inhibitors) may also be of help (Mortola, 1998). Ask your doctor for a recommendation. *Note that in these cases, you are not taking the antianxiety drug to treat anxiety or the antidepressant to treat depression. You are taking the drugs to treat imbalances in neurotransmitters that can also give rise to anxiety and depression.*
11. Remind yourself that menstrual problems are time limited. Don't worry about getting through life or a career. Just get through the next couple of days.

Coronary Heart Disease

Coronary heart disease (CHD) is the leading cause of death in the United States, most often from heart attacks (National Center for Health Statistics, 1996). Consider the risk factors for CHD:

1. *Family History.* People with a family history of CHD are more likely to develop the disease themselves (Marenberg and others, 1994).

2. *Physiological Conditions.* Obesity, high **serum cholesterol** levels (Keil and others, 1993; Rossouw and others, 1990; Stampfer and others, 1991), and **hypertension** are risk factors for CHD.

   About one American in five has hypertension, or abnormally high blood pressure (Leary, 1991). When high blood pressure has no identifiable cause, it is referred to as essential hypertension. This condition appears to have a genetic component (Caulfield and others, 1994). However, blood pressure also rises when we inhibit the expression of strong feelings or are angry or on guard against threats (Jorgensen and others, 1996; Suls and others, 1995). When we are under stress, we may believe that we can feel our blood pressure "pounding through the roof," but this notion is usually false. Most people cannot recognize hypertension. Therefore it is important to have blood pressure checked regularly.
3. *Patterns of Consumption.* Patterns include heavy drinking, smoking, overeating, and eating food that is high in cholesterol, like saturated fats (Castelli, 1994; Jeffery, 1991).
4. *Type A Behavior.* Most studies suggest that there is at least a modest relationship between Type A behavior and CHD (Thoresen & Powell, 1992). It also seems that alleviating Type A behavior patterns may reduce the risk of *recurrent* heart attacks (Friedman & Ulmer, 1984).
5. *Hostility and Holding in Feelings of Anger* (Miller and others, 1996; Powch & Houston, 1996). Hostility appears to raise the blood pressure, especially in men (Guyll & Contrada, 1998).
6. *Stress.* Mental stress of the sort created by tests of memory and cognition can raise the blood pressure by blocking blood vessels (Kamarck and others, 1997). A particularly troublesome form of stress is job strain. Overtime work, assembly line labor, and exposure to conflicting demands can all contribute to CHD. High-strain work, which makes heavy demands on workers but gives them little personal control, puts workers at the highest risk (Kamarck and others, 1998; Krantz and others, 1988). As shown in Figure 6.4, the work of waiters and waitresses may best fit this description. Sudden stressors are also dangerous. For example, after the 1994 Los Angeles earthquake there was an increased incidence of death from heart attacks in people with heart disease (Leor and others, 1996).
7. *Chronic Fatigue.*
8. *Chronic Emotional Strain.*
9. *A Physically Inactive Lifestyle* (Dubbert, 1992; Lakka and others, 1994).

REDUCING CHD THROUGH BEHAVIOR MODIFICATION Once CHD has been diagnosed, a number of medical treatments, including surgery and medication, are available. However, people who have not had CHD (as well as those who have) can profit from behavior modification techniques designed to reduce the risk factors. These methods include the following:

1. *Stopping Smoking.* (See Chapter 8.)
2. *Weight Control.* (See Chapter 7.)
3. *Reducing Hypertension.* There is medication for reducing hypertension, but behavioral changes such as the following often do the trick: relaxation training (Agras and others, 1983), meditation (Benson and others, 1973), aerobic exercise (Danforth and others, 1990), eating more fruits and vegetable and less fat (Appel and others, 1997), and eating less salt.

SERUM CHOLESTEROL • A fatty substance (cholesterol) in the blood (serum) that has been linked to heart disease.
HYPERTENSION • High blood pressure.

FIGURE 6.4
THE JOB-STRAIN MODEL.
This model highlights the psychological demands made by various occupations and the amount of personal (decision) control they allow. Occupations characterized by both high demand and low decision control place workers at greatest risk for cardiovascular disorders.

4. *Lowering Low-Density Lipoprotein (Harmful) Serum Cholesterol.* Major methods involve exercise, medication, and cutting down on foods that are high in cholesterol and saturated fats (Castelli, 1994; Shepherd and others, 1995).
5. *Modifying Type A Behavior.* See the section on coping with the Type A behavior pattern in Chapter 11, pp. 326–329.
6. *Exercise.* Sustained physical activity protects people from CHD (Castelli, 1994; Curfman, 1993b). If you haven't exercised for a while, check with your physician about getting started. Also check out the advice in Chapter 7's section on fitness, pp. 201–214.

We conclude this discussion with good news. Many risk factors for coronary heart disease, such as smoking and diet, have been known for 25 years or more. Many Americans have responded to this knowledge by changing their lifestyles, and the incidence of coronary heart disease has declined. There is one particular message for readers of this book: *better educated* individuals are more likely to modify health-impairing behavior patterns and reap the benefits of change (Kilborn, 1998; Pappas and others, 1993).

Cancer

Cancer is the number one killer of women in the United States, and it is the number two killer of men (Andersen, 1996). Cancer is characterized by the development of abnormal, or mutant, cells that may take root anywhere in the body: in the blood, bones, digestive tract, lungs, and genital organs. If their spread is not controlled early, the cancerous cells may *metastasize*—that is, spread by establishing colonies elsewhere in the body. It appears that our bodies develop cancerous cells frequently. However, these are normally destroyed by the immune system. People whose immune system is damaged by physical or psychological factors are more likely to develop tumors (Azar, 1996b, 1996c).

Truth or Fiction Revisited

It is true that your diet can influence the likelihood that you will contract cancer. Vitamin deficiencies and fats, for example, heighten the risk.

RISK FACTORS As with many other disorders, people can inherit a disposition toward cancer (Croyle and others, 1997; Lerman and others, 1997; Vernon and others, 1997). Carcinogenic genes may remove the brakes from cell division, allowing cells to multiply wildly. Or genes may allow mutations to accumulate unchecked. However, many behavior patterns markedly heighten the risk for cancer. These include smoking, drinking alcohol (especially in women), eating animal fats, and sunbathing (which may cause skin cancer due to exposure to ultraviolet light). Agents in cigarette smoke, such as benzopyrene, may damage a gene that would otherwise block the development of many tumors, including lung cancer ("Damaged gene," 1996). Prolonged psychological conditions such as depression or stress may also heighten the risk of cancer (Azar, 1996b). The nearby "Self-Assessment" feature will help you assess whether or not your dietary habits increase or decrease the risk of cancer.

STRESS AND CANCER In recent years, researchers have begun to uncover links between stress and cancer (Andersen, 1998; Azar, 1996b). One study of children with cancer revealed that a significant percentage had encountered severe life changes within a year of the diagnosis, often involving the death of a loved one or the loss of a close relationship (Jacobs & Charles, 1980).

As in many other areas of psychology, experimental research has been conducted with animals that could not be conducted with humans. In one type of study, animals are injected with cancerous cells or with viruses that cause cancer and then exposed to a variety of conditions, so that we can determine whether or not these conditions influence the likelihood that the animals' immune systems will be able to fend off the antigens. Experiments with rodents suggest that once cancer has affected the individual, stress can influence its course. In one study, rats were implanted with numbers of cancer cells that were small enough so that their immune systems would have a chance to resist them (Visintainer and others, 1982). Some of the rats were then exposed to inescapable shocks, whereas others were exposed to escapable shocks or to no shock. The rats exposed to the most stressful condition—inescapable shock—were half as likely as other rats to reject the cancer, and two times as likely to die from it.

In an experiment with mice, Riley (1981) studied the effects of a cancer-causing virus that can be transmitted by nursing. The virus usually produces breast cancer in 80 percent of female offspring by the time they have reached 400 days of age. Riley placed one group of female offspring at risk for cancer in a stressful environment of loud noises and noxious odors. Another group was placed in a less stressful environment. By the age of 400 days, 92 percent of the mice who developed under stressful conditions had contracted breast cancer, as compared to 7 percent of the controls. Moreover, the high-stress mice showed increases in cortisol and depressed immune-system functioning. However, the "bottom line" in this experiment is of major interest: By the time another 200 days had elapsed, the low-stress mice had nearly caught up to their high-stress peers in the incidence of cancer. Stress appears to have hastened the inevitable for many of these mice, but the ultimate outcomes for the high-risk rodents were not overwhelmingly influenced by stress.

Stress may thus influence the timing of the onset of diseases such as cancer. Genetic predispositions and the presence of powerful antigens will in many or most cases eventually do their damage, however. An extreme expression of this position was published in *The New England Journal of Medicine:* "The inherent biology of [cancer] alone determines the prognosis, overriding the potentially mitigating influence of psychosocial factors" (Cassileth and others, 1985, p. 1555). Even if this pessimistic view is largely accurate, we can still do four things:

1. We can control our exposure to behavioral risk factors for cancer. Consider diet. Your authors have tried to decrease their intake of fats and to eat more fiber and vitamins in order to decrease the risk of cancers of the digestive tract. One of us stopped eating food with nitrate preservatives, such as frankfurters. Nitrates form nitrosamines—a powerful **carcinogen.** The other learned that ascorbic acid (vitamin C) prevents formation of nitrosamines. So he pops vitamin C pills whenever he eats hot dogs, even though evidence as to the usefulness of vitamin C is fairly weak. Our wives think of us as fanatics and down their occasional hot dogs with abandon.

   Our wives upped their milk intake after learning that calcium might serve to protect against **osteoporosis** later in life and against certain kinds of cancers of the digestive tract.

   One of us became a carrot and sweet-potato "freak" after learning that vitamin A and beta carotene were linked to a lower-than-average incidence of cancer. Moderate amounts of these vitamins may afford some protection against head and neck, stomach, and lung cancers (Hinds and others, 1984; Hong and others, 1990; Stehr and others, 1985).
2. We can have regular screenings for cancer to catch it early.
3. We can regulate the amount of stress impacting upon us. Health psychologists have also found that the stressful feelings of depression and helplessness that often accompany the diagnosis of cancer can hinder recovery among humans (Andersen, 1998), perhaps by depressing the responsiveness of the immune system. For example, a 10-year follow-up of breast cancer patients found a significantly higher survival rate for patients who met their diagnosis with anger and a "fighting spirit" rather than helplessness or stoic acceptance (Pettingale and others, 1985). This brings us to our fourth recommendation:
4. If we are struck by cancer, we can fight the illness vigorously. Health psychologists are also investigating the role of chronic stress in inflammatory diseases, such as arthritis; premenstrual distress; digestive diseases, such as colitis; even metabolic diseases, such as diabetes and hypoglycemia. The relationships between behavior patterns, attitudes, and illness are complex and under intense study. With some stress-related illnesses, it may be that stress determines whether or not the person will contract the disease at all. In others, it may be that an optimal environment merely delays the inevitable, or that a stressful environment merely hastens the onset of the inevitable. Then, too, in different illnesses stress may have different effects on the patient's ability to recover.

Truth or Fiction Revisited

It is true that stress can influence the course of cancer. Stress seems to hasten the progress of the disease, although it may be that in most cases the ultimate outcome would be the same regardless of level of stress.

Carcinogen • An agent that gives rise to cancerous changes.

Osteoporosis • A condition caused by calcium deficiency and characterized by brittleness of the bones.

The Eating Smart Quiz

The American Cancer Society provides guidelines for dietary habits that may help prevent cancer of the mouth, larynx, throat, esophagus, stomach, bladder, colon, rectum, lungs, breast, prostate, and uterus:

- Watch your weight; avoid obesity.
- Decrease your total intake of fats.
- Eat more of foods that are high in fiber.
- Eat foods that are rich in vitamins A and C on a daily basis.
- Eat cruciferous (cabbage-family) vegetables.
- Decrease intake of salt-cured, smoked, and nitrite-cured foods.
- If you drink, keep alcohol consumption moderate.

The society's Eating Smart Quiz can help you assess whether your own dietary habits are consistent with the society guidelines. ■

Directions: Read each group of three items, and select the number (0, 1, or 2) that best describes your own eating habits. Write that number in the blank space in the Points column. Then add up the points and write that number in the Total Score space at the end of the quiz. Finally, interpret your score according to the key in the Appendix.

		Points
Oils and Fats		
butter, margarine, shortening, mayonnaise, sour cream, lard, oil, salad dressing		
I always add these foods in cooking and/or at the table.	0	
I occasionally add these to foods in cooking and/or at the table.	1	
I rarely add these to foods in cooking and/or at the table.	2	___
I eat fried foods 3 or more times a week.	0	
I eat fried foods 1–2 times a week.	1	
I rarely eat fried foods.	2	___
Dairy Products		
I drink whole milk.	0	
I drink skim or low-fat milk.	1	
I seldom eat frozen desserts or ice cream.	2	___
I eat ice cream almost every day.	0	
Instead of ice cream, I eat ice milk, low-fat frozen yogurt, and sherbet.	1	
I drink only fruit juices, seldom eat frozen dairy dessert.	2	___
I eat mostly high-fat cheese (jack, cheddar, colby, Swiss, cream).	0	
I eat both low- and high-fat cheeses.	1	
I eat mostly low-fat cheeses (cottage, skim milk mozzarella).	2	___
Snacks		
potato/corn chips, nuts, buttered popcorn, candy bars		
I eat these every day.	0	
I eat some occasionally.	1	
I seldom or never eat these snacks.	2	___
Baked Goods		
pies, cakes, cookies, sweet rolls, doughnuts		
I eat them 5 or more times a week.	0	
I eat them 2–4 times a week.	1	
I seldom eat baked goods or eat only low-fat baked goods.	2	___
Poultry and Fish*		
I rarely eat these foods.	0	
I eat them 1–2 times a week.	1	
I eat them 3 or more times a week.	2	___
Low-Fat Meats*		
extra lean hamburger, round steak, pork loin roast, tenderloin, chuck roast		
I rarely eat these foods.	0	

	Points	
I eat these foods occasionally.	1	
I eat these foods often.	2	___
High-Fat Meats*		
luncheon meats, bacon, hot dogs, sausage, steak, regular and lean ground beef		
I eat these every day.	0	
I eat these foods occasionally.	1	
I rarely eat these foods.	2	___
Cured and Smoked Meats, and Fish*		
luncheon meats, hot dogs, bacon, ham, and other smoked or pickled meats and fish		
I eat these foods 4 or more times a week.	0	
I eat some 1–3 times a week.	1	
I seldom eat these foods.	2	___
Legumes		
dried beans and peas: kidney, navy, lima, pinto, garbanzo, split-pea, lentil		
I eat legumes less than once a week.	0	
I eat these foods 1–2 times a week.	1	
I eat them 3 or more times a week.	2	___
Whole Grains and Cereals		
whole grain breads, brown rice, pasta, whole grain cereals		
I seldom eat such foods.	0	
I eat them 2–3 times a day.	1	
I eat them 4 or more times daily.	2	___
Vitamin C–Rich Fruits and Vegetables		
citrus fruits and juices, green peppers, strawberries, tomatoes		
I seldom eat them.	0	
I eat them 3–5 times a week.	1	
I eat them 1–2 times a day.	2	___
Dark Green and Deep Yellow Fruits and Vegetables†		
broccoli, greens, carrots, peaches		
I seldom eat them.	0	
I eat them 3–5 times a week.	1	
I eat them daily.	2	___
Vegetables of the Cabbage Family		
broccoli, cabbage, brussels sprouts, cauliflower		
I seldom eat them.	0	
I eat them 1–2 times a week.	1	
I eat them 3–4 times a week.	2	___
Alcohol		
I drink more than 2 oz. daily.	0	
I drink alcohol every week but not daily.	1	
I occasionally or never drink alcohol.	2	___
Personal Weight		
I'm more than 20 pounds over my ideal weight.	0	
I'm 10–20 pounds over my ideal weight.	1	
I am within 10 pounds of my ideal weight.	2	___
	Total Score	___

*If you do not eat meat, fish, or poultry, give yourself a 2 for each meat category.
†Dark green and yellow fruits and vegetables contain beta carotene, which your body can turn into vitamin A, which helps protect you against certain types of cancer-causing substances.
Reprinted with permission from American Cancer Society, *Eating smart* (1987).

ENCOURAGING A FRIEND TO SEEK HELP

You have a friend who has been complaining of chest pains for a few days but who has not gone to have them evaluated by a physician. There may be nothing seriously wrong, but you are becoming concerned. What do you say now?

Write some possible responses in the following spaces. Then look at the authors' suggestions.

1. ____

2. ____

3. ____

Your friend might be avoiding medical evaluation for fear of the possible consequences of whatever illness he or she might have. Note the following suggestions:

1. Your friend might have told you what he or she suspects the symptoms might mean, but if not you can say something like, "You've been having these pains now for at least a week. Do you have any idea what they might be from?" This is a relatively nonthreatening way of drawing your friend out to find out how he or she conceptualizes the symptoms. You can get an impression of whether he or she is minimizing them, as many of us do, or assuming "the worst"—that is, something like a life-threatening cardiovascular disorder.
2. If your friend has been minimizing symptoms and says, "Oh, they're nothing," you can follow up with something like, "Yes, they might mean nothing at all, but they could mean something. I care about you, and it would make me very happy if you would get looked at." You can add an offer to go with your friend to the doctor; correcting minimization and social support are of help.
3. If your friend has been catastrophizing the symptoms and is afraid to seek medical advice, you can say something like, "I understand your concern. I'm no doctor, but I understand that lots of the time chest pains mean something like indigestion. Why don't you get looked at? It's probably something you can take care of, and at least it'll put your mind at ease." Again, you can follow up by offering to go along with your friend. ■

adjustment and modern life

The United States has the world's most sophisticated medical technology, as evidenced, for example, by the development of new treatments for the underdeveloped lungs of premature and low-birth-weight babies ("Infant deaths drop," 1993). Yet many people fail to make use of that technology. Where do we begin? One answer lies in choosing a physician.

CHOOSING A PHYSICIAN

One aspect of health is choosing competent health care professionals. The single most important of these is your personal physician, because he or she will hold the major responsibility for your medical care. Yet many people spend more time picking out a TV set or stereo system than selecting a physician. They may assume (erroneously) that all physicians are equally competent. Or they may not think that they know enough to make an informed choice. Yet you need not be a medical expert to make an informed decision about who will be your primary health care provider. Here are some suggestions:

1. *Get recommendations.* Ask around. Seek recommendations from friends and family members, especially from people whose opinions you trust. Try asking other medical professionals whom they would use or to whom they would refer a sick relative. Another suggestion: Call your local medical center or medical school and ask for the unit or department in the area of specialty that you are inquiring about, such as pediatrics, internal medicine, or obstetrics and gynecology. Ask to speak to the head nurse on the unit. Explain that you are seeking a primary care physician and would like a recommendation for two or three doctors in your area.
2. *Set up an appointment.* Before making a choice, take a "test drive." Make an appointment for a routine physical examination or to ask about a relatively minor medical problem. See whether the physician makes the grade on the following factors:

   Empathy. Empathic physicians are warm and supportive. They express understanding and concern. They have what used to be called a "good bedside manner." Ask yourself whether the physician seems genuinely interested in you as a person, or as just another case. See whether the physician takes time to get to know you or seems abrupt.

   Availability. Ask about office hours, coverage for emergencies, weekend and evening availability, and back-up coverage during vacations.

   Ability to communicate in language you can understand. Steer clear of a doctor who speaks only in "doctorese." Choose someone who provides precise answers in a way that you can understand.

Credentials. Ask the doctor about his or her professional background. Pose questions such as the following: From what medical school did you graduate? Where did you complete your residency training, and in what area or areas? In which specialty areas are you board-certified?

Almost two thirds of the nearly 700,000 physicians in the United States are board-certified. Board certification is the minimum standard that doctors must meet to obtain hospital privileges and be accepted in managed care plans. Also ask with which hospitals the doctor is affiliated. More prestigious hospitals tend to weed out doctors with questionable records.

You can check your doctor's credentials by using the American Medical Association's *Directory of Physicians in the U.S.* The book contains information about each doctor's medical and residency training, hospital affiliations, teaching positions, and board certification. Many public libraries have copies of the directory. You can also find out whether your doctor is board-certified by calling the American Board of Medical Specialties at 800-776-CERT. Don't be misled by the term "board-eligible." This means that the doctor has completed the required training in a specialty but has not yet taken the exam to become certified, or perhaps has taken the test and flunked it.

3. *Listen to yourself.* When you have interviewed the doctor, ask yourself how you really feel about him or her. If you have the feeling that there is something missing, maybe there is. If you are concerned that you didn't quite connect, maybe you'll find a better fit with someone else. Give it a little time and effort. After all, your health is at stake.

In this chapter we have examined relationships between psychological factors and health. In the following chapter we focus on health-enhancing behaviors that involve nutrition, fitness, and sleep. ■

SUMMARY

1. **What is health psychology?** Health psychology studies the relationships between psychological factors (e.g., behavior, emotions, stress, beliefs, and attitudes) and the prevention and treatment of physical illness.
2. **What is the general adaptation syndrome (GAS)?** Selye suggested that the general adaptation syndrome is triggered by perception of a stressor and consists of three stages: alarm, resistance, and exhaustion.
3. **What is the role of the endocrine system in the body's response to stress?** In response to stress, the hypothalamus and pituitary glands secrete hormones which stimulate the adrenal cortex to release cortisol and other corticosteroids. Corticosteroids help the body resist stress by fighting inflammations and allergic reactions. Adrenaline and noradrenaline are also secreted by the adrenal medulla, and adrenaline arouses the body by activating the sympathetic division of the autonomic nervous system.
4. **What is the role of the autonomic nervous system in the body's response to stress?** The sympathetic division of the ANS is highly active during the alarm and resistance stages of the GAS and is characterized by rapid heartbeat and respiration rate, release of stores of sugar, muscle tension, and other responses that spend the body's stores of energy. The parasympathetic division of the ANS predominates during the exhaustion stage of the GAS and is characterized by responses, such as digestive processes, that help restore the body's reserves of energy.
5. **What are some of our emotional responses to stress?** Emotional responses to stress include anxiety, anger, and depression. Anxiety involves sympathetic ANS activity. Anger is a response to frustration and social provocations. Depression involves predominantly parasympathetic ANS activity and is a response to a loss, to failure, or to prolonged stress.
6. **What are some of our cognitive responses to stress?** Stress can distract us from focusing on the tasks at hand.
7. **What are the functions of the immune system?** The first function of the immune system is to engulf and kill pathogens, worn out body cells, and cancerous cells. The second function of the immune system is to "remember" pathogens to facilitate future combat against them. The third function is inflammation, which increases the numbers of white blood cells brought to a damaged area.
8. **What are the effects of stress on the immune system?** By stimulating the release of corticosteroids, stress depresses the functioning of the immune system (e.g., steroids counter inflammation).
9. **What kinds of headaches are there, and how are they related to stress?** The most common kinds of headaches are muscle-tension headaches and migraine headaches. Stress causes and compounds headache pain by stimulating muscle tension.
10. **What is PMS?** Premenstrual syndrome is a combination of psychological (e.g., mood changes) and physical symptoms (e.g., bloating, cramping) that afflicts many women for a few days prior to menstruation. In most cases, the symptoms are mild to moderate.
11. **What are the risk factors for cardiovascular disorders?** There are seven major risk factors for cardiovascular disorders: family history, physiological conditions such as hypertension and high levels of serum cholesterol, behavior patterns such as smoking and eating fatty foods, Type A behavior, work overload, chronic fatigue and emotional strain, and physical inactivity.
12. **What behavioral measures contribute to the prevention and treatment of cardiovascular disorders?** Stopping smoking, controlling one's weight, reducing hypertension, lowering serum cholesterol, and modifying Type A behavior can all help in prevention and treatment of these disorders.
13. **What are the risk factors for cancer?** Risk factors for cancer include family history, smoking, drinking alcohol, eating animal fats, sunbathing, and stress.
14. **What behavioral measures contribute to the prevention and treatment of cancer?** Controlling our exposure to behavioral risk factors for cancer, going for regular medical checkups, regulating the amount of stress impacting upon us, and vigorously fighting cancer if we are afflicted can all help in preventing and/or treating this serious disease.

USA

CHAPTER 7

Issues in Personal Health: Nutrition, Fitness, and Sleep

TRUTH OR FICTION?

✓ T F

- ☐ ☐ Most of us should eat more protein and less fat.
- ☐ ☐ One adult American in three is obese.
- ☐ ☐ Americans overeat by enough to feed the nation of Germany.
- ☐ ☐ Dieting has become the normal way of eating for women in the United States.
- ☐ ☐ Some college women control their weight by going on cycles of binge eating followed by self-induced vomiting.
- ☐ ☐ Exercise can alleviate feelings of depression.
- ☐ ☐ We act out our forbidden fantasies in our dreams.
- ☐ ☐ Trying to get to sleep may keep you up at night.
- ☐ ☐ A 220-pound person burns more calories running around the track than a 125-pound person does.

OUTLINE

. . . mens sana in corpore sano.
(A sound mind in a sound body.)

JUVENAL, A.D. 60–CA. 130

MARK TWAIN QUIPPED THAT IT WAS EASY TO GIVE up smoking—he had done it a thousand times. Your authors have both quit smoking cigarettes to reduce the chances of coronary heart disease and the threat of cancers of the lungs, pancreas, bladder, larynx, and esophagus. We gave it up a dozen times—between us.

In recent years knowledge of the benefits of exercise and the hazards of various substances has been amassed. Health food stores have opened in every shopping mall. The fitness craze is upon us. Large numbers of us have taken to exercise and modified our diets in an effort to enhance our physical well-being and attractiveness. Some of us have even kept to our regimens.

In this chapter we examine a number of issues in personal health, including nutrition, fitness, and sleep. In the next chapter we discuss substance abuse and adjustment. We begin our discussion with nutritional patterns, and we see that there are ways in which we can do ourselves much more good than harm.

NUTRITION

A cucumber should be well-sliced, dressed with pepper and vinegar, and then thrown out.

SAMUEL JOHNSON

One should eat to live, not live to eat.

MOLIÈRE, *L'AVARE*

In general mankind, since the improvement of cookery, eats twice as much as nature requires.

BENJAMIN FRANKLIN

Never eat more than you can lift.

MISS PIGGY

Since much knowledge about nutrition has accumulated in recent years, you might think that young people would pay more attention than older people to what they eat. But according to a *New York Times* poll, you would be wrong (Burros, 1988). Of the 1,870 respondents, those aged 30 and older reported better eating habits than those aged 18 to 29. As Table 7.1 shows, women paid more attention to their diets than did men.

Why do young people pay less attention to their diets? Nutritionist Bonnie Liebman notes that "Instead of teaching good nutrition in schools, we subject our kids to television commercials that push fast foods, soft drinks, candy bars, and sugary cereals. And then we wonder why kids don't ask for fruits and

TABLE 7.1 PERCENTAGE OF RESPONDENTS TO THE *NEW YORK TIMES* POLL WHO PAY ATTENTION TO THESE DIETARY COMPONENTS AT EVERY MEAL

	GENDER		*AGE*	
DIETARY COMPONENT	**MEN**	**WOMEN**	**18–29**	**30 AND ABOVE**
Cholesterol	19	31	13	30
Salt	43	60	39	57
Fats	31	46	26	44
Additives and preservatives	20	25	16	25
Sugar and sweets	34	42	30	42
Calories	16	36	21	29
Fiber	12	21	10	19
Caffeine	21	30	20	28

Source: The *New York Times*, January 6, 1988, p. C6.

vegetables" (quoted in Burros, 1988, pp. C1, C6). Consumer researcher Fabian Linden adds that "Youth has a magic feeling that they are invulnerable. They don't pay attention to the medical wisdom we have accumulated" (in Burros, 1988, p. C6).

NUTRITION.
Do you pay attention to what you eat, or do you fancy yourself to be invulnerable to the ills associated with poor diets? Americans tend to eat too much protein and fat and too little carbohydrates.

Nutrients

Foods provide **nutrients.** Nutrients furnish energy and the building blocks of muscle, bone, and other tissues. Essential nutrients include protein, carbohydrates, fats, vitamins, and minerals.

NUTRIENTS • Essential food elements that the body cannot produce on its own.

PROTEINS Proteins are amino acids that build muscles, blood, bones, fingernails, and hair. Proteins also serve as enzymes, hormones, and antibodies. We must obtain several proteins from food. We manufacture others for ourselves. The most popular sources of protein are meat, poultry, eggs, fish, and dairy products like milk and cheese. Legumes (beans, lentils, and peas) and grains are also fine sources of protein. Americans tend to eat more protein than they need. Meat, fish, and dairy products provide all of the proteins that we cannot manufacture for ourselves. Legumes and grains provide some, but not all of them. Vegetarians thus need to eat complementary protein sources—legumes and grains that, in combination, provide essential proteins.

CARBOHYDRATES Carbohydrates consist of carbon, hydrogen, and oxygen. They provide the body with energy. Sugars are simple carbohydrates that offer little more than a spurt of energy. Starches are complex carbohydrates that provide vitamins, minerals, and a steadier flow of energy. Americans typically do not eat enough starches. Starches should account for 50 to 60 percent of the diet. Foods rich in carbohydrates include cereals; citrus fruits; crucifers, such as broccoli, cabbage, and cauliflower; green, leafy vegetables; legumes; pasta (also high in protein, low in fats); root vegetables such as potatoes and yams; and yellow fruits and vegetables, such as carrots and squash. Many starches are also rich in fiber, which aids the digestion and may protect us from some cancers, such as cancer of the colon.

Truth or Fiction Revisited

It is not true that most of us should eat more protein and less fat. The statement is too all-inclusive: It is true enough that Americans should eat less fat, but most Americans eat more protein than they need. (Look, we're entitled to one tricky Truth-or-Fiction item.)

FATS Fats provide stamina, insulate us from extremes of temperature, nourish the skin, and store vitamins A, D, E, and K. However, most Americans, especially fast-food addicts, eat more fat than they need. A tablespoon of vegetable oil a day is plenty. Olive oil is a relatively healthful unsaturated fat that is excellent for salads. Saturated fats, which come from animal sources, greatly increase levels of cholesterol. All in all, no more than 10 percent of our calorie intake should be from saturated fats.

VITAMINS AND MINERALS Vitamins are essential organic compounds that need to be eaten regularly. Vitamin A is found in orange produce, such as carrots and sweet potatoes, and deep green vegetables. It is also abundant in liver, but organ meats such as liver are extremely high in cholesterol; find more healthful sources. Vitamins A and D are found in fortified dairy products. B vitamins are abundant in legumes, vegetables, nuts, and whole-grain products. Fruits and vegetables are rich in vitamin C. Vitamins like A, C, and E are antioxidants; that is, they deactivate substances in some foods (called *free radicals*) that might otherwise contribute to the development of cancer.

We also need minerals such as calcium (for conducting nerve impulses and bones and teeth), iron, potassium, and sodium. Readers are advised to consult with physicians, pharmacists, and dieticians about their daily requirements of vitamins and minerals. Overdoses can be harmful. Don't assume that more is better and mindlessly pop megavitamin pills. Table 7.2 lists some foods that are high in fats or cholesterol and some more healthful foods.

TABLE 7.2 FOODS HIGH IN FATS AND CHOLESTEROL AND MORE HEALTHFUL FOODS

FOODS HIGH IN CHOLESTEROL AND SATURATED FATS

Bacon and sausage	Crab	French fries	Palm oil
Beef	Cream (half & half)	Fried foods	Pie
Butter, lard	Croissants	Ice cream (ice milk)	Potato chips
Cake	Egg yolks	Lobster	Salad dressing (most)
Cheese	Frankfurters and luncheon meats	Organ meats (liver, etc.)	Shrimp
Chocolate			Whole milk
Coconut			

MORE HEALTHFUL FOODS

Beans	Fruits	Popcorn (without the butter)
Bagels	Lean meats (broiled, in moderation)	Taco sauce (hot or mild; read the contents)
Breads	Legumes	Tomato sauces (meatless)
Cereals (most; read the contents)	Low-fat ice cream	Turkey (without skin—watch the dressing and the gravy)
Chicken (white meat; skinless; broiled, baked, or barbecued)	Nonfat milk and dairy products	Vegetables
Egg whites	Nonfat yogurt	Whole-grain products
Fish (baked, broiled)	Pasta	
	Peas	

Nutrition and Health

Relationships between nutritional patterns and health have grown clearer in recent years. For example, many cases of cancer can be linked to diet. Food preservatives, a high intake of animal fat, and vitamin deficiencies pose particular risks. High levels of cholesterol heighten the risks of cardiovascular disorders. On the other hand, vitamins, calcium, and fruits and vegetables appear to reduce the risk of cancer.

One basic component of the diet is calories. The intake of excessive calories can lead to what might well be our number one nutrition-related problem—obesity.

Obesity

We need food to survive, but food means more than survival to many of us. Food is a symbol of family togetherness and caring. We associate food with the nurturance of the parent-child relationship, with visits home during the holidays. Friends and relatives offer food when we enter their homes. Saying no may be interpreted as a personal rejection. Bacon and eggs, coffee with cream and sugar, meat and mashed potatoes—all seem part of sharing American values and agricultural abundance. But many of us are paying the price of abundance:

- The prevalence of obesity in the United States has increased by 25 percent in the past decade (Brownell, 1997).
- One American adult in three is now obese (Fox, 1998; Meyer, 1997).
- Nearly half of African American women are obese, possibly because they have lower metabolic rates than White women do (Brody, 1997).
- Americans eat more than a total of 800 billion calories of food each day (200 billion calories more than they need to maintain their weights). The extra calories could feed a nation of 80 million people.
- Compared with other women, overweight women are less likely to get married, have lower incomes, and complete fewer years of school (Gortmaker and others, 1993).
- Within a few years, most dieters regain most of the weight they have lost, even when they have used diet pills "successfully" (Kassirer & Angell, 1998; Rosenbaum and others, 1997).
- About 300,000 Americans die each year because of excess weight (Brownell, 1997).

Truth or Fiction Revisited

It is true that one adult American in three is obese.

Truth or Fiction Revisited

Yes, Americans do overeat by an amount great enough to feed the entire nation of Germany. The excess calories would feed another 80 million people!

This nation idealizes slender heroes and heroines. For many of us who measure more-than-up to TV and film idols, food may have replaced sex as the central source of guilt. The obese also encounter more than their fair share of illnesses, including cardiovascular diseases, diabetes, gout, and even certain types of cancer (Brownell & Wadden, 1992; Kassirer & Angell, 1998).

Why do so many of us overeat? Research suggests that psychological and biological factors both play a role in obesity.

HEREDITY Obesity runs in families. It was once assumed that obese parents encouraged their children to be overweight by having fattening foods in the house and setting poor examples. However, a study of Scandinavian adoptees by Stunkard and his colleagues (1990) found that children bear a closer resemblance in weight to their biological parents than their adoptive parents. Research with mice suggests that a so-called *ob* gene may fail to signal the brain when one has eaten enough to satisfy one's nutritional needs (Angier, 1994; Lindpaintner, 1995). However, we shall see that environmental factors also play a role in obesity.

FAT CELLS The efforts of obese people to maintain a slender profile might be sabotaged by microscopic units of life within their own bodies: **fat cells.** No, fat cells are not overweight cells. They are adipose tissue, or cells that store fat. Hunger might be related to the amount of fat stored in these cells. As time passes after a meal, the blood-sugar level drops. Fat is then drawn from these cells to provide further nourishment. At some point, referred to as the **set point,** fat cells signal the hypothalamus of the deficiency with hormones (e.g., leptin), triggering the hunger drive (Fox, 1998).

People with more adipose tissue than others feel food-deprived earlier, even though they may be equal in weight. This might be because more signals are being sent to the brain. Obese people, and *formerly* obese people, tend to have more adipose tissue than people of normal weight. Thus, many people who have lost weight complain that they are always hungry when they try to maintain normal weight levels.

Fatty tissue also metabolizes food more slowly than muscle. For this reason, a person with a high fat-to-muscle ratio will metabolize food more slowly than a person of the same weight with a lower fat-to-muscle ratio. In other words, two people identical in weight will metabolize food at different rates, according to their bodies' distribution of muscle and fat. Obese people are therefore doubly handicapped in their efforts to lose weight—not only by their extra weight but by the fact that much of their body is composed of adipose tissue.

In a sense, the normal distribution of fat cells could be considered sexist. The average man is 40 percent muscle and 15 percent fat, whereas the average woman is 23 percent muscle and 25 percent fat. Therefore, if a man and woman with typical distributions of muscle and fat are of the same weight, the woman—who has more fat cells—will have to eat less to maintain that weight.

Truth or Fiction Revisited

It is true that dieting has become the normal way of eating for women in the United States. Surveys show that the majority of women are on diets at one time or another. Dieting, therefore, is normal from a statistical perspective.

DIETING AND METABOLISM People on diets and those who have lost substantial amounts of weight burn fewer calories. That is, their metabolic rates slow down (Leibel and others, 1995; Schwartz & Seeley, 1997).

Other factors, such as emotional state, also play a role in obesity. Negative emotional states such as depression and anxiety can interfere with efforts to diet (Nevid and others, 1997).

But now, some good news for readers who would like to shed a few pounds. Psychological research has led to a number of helpful suggestions for dieting, such as those found in the chapter's "Adjustment and Modern Life" feature.

Eating Disorders

Did you know that today the eating habits of the "average" American woman are characterized by dieting? Efforts to restrict the intake of food have become the norm (Kassirer & Angell, 1998)! However, the eating disorders that we discuss here are characterized by gross disturbances in patterns of eating. They include *anorexia nervosa* and *bulimia nervosa.*

ANOREXIA NERVOSA **Anorexia nervosa** is a life-threatening disorder characterized by refusal to maintain a healthful body weight, intense fear of being overweight, a distorted body image, and, in females, **amenorrhea.** Anorexic persons usually weigh less than 85 percent of their expected body weight.

FAT CELLS • Cells that contain fat; adipose tissue.
SET POINT • A theoretical setting in the hypothalamus that governs when we feel satiated.
ANOREXIA NERVOSA • An eating disorder characterized by maintenance of an abnormally low body weight, intense fear of weight gain, a distorted body image, and, in females, amenorrhea.
AMENORRHEA • Absence of menstruation.

By and large, anorexia afflicts girls and young women. Anorexia nervosa and bulimia nervosa are epidemic among adolescent girls and young women in middle schools, high school, and college (Kassirer & Angell, 1998). Anorexic females greatly outnumber anorexic males. Onset is most often during the teenage years.

Anorexic girls may be full height but weigh 60 pounds or less. They may drop 25 percent or more of their body weight in a year. Severe weight loss triggers amenorrhea. The girl's general health declines, and she may experience slowed heart rate, low blood pressure, constipation, dehydration, and a host of other problems. The mortality rate for girls with anorexia nervosa or bulimia nervosa is as high as 20 percent (Kassirer & Angell, 1998). The singer Karen Carpenter died in her thirties from a heart attack that may have been caused by her long battle with anorexia.

In the typical pattern, girls notice some weight gain after menarche and decide that it must come off. However, dieting and often exercise continue at a fever pitch—long after the girls reach normal body weights and even after family members and others have told them that they are losing too much weight. Anorexic girls almost always adamantly deny that they are wasting away. They may point to their fierce exercise regimens as proof. Their body images are distorted. Whereas others perceive them as "skin and bones," they frequently sit before the mirror and see themselves as getting where they want to be. Or they focus on nonexistent "remaining" pockets of fat.

Although the thought of eating can be odious to anorexic girls, now and then they may feel quite hungry. Many anorexics become obsessed with food and are constantly "around it." They may engross themselves in cookbooks, take on the family shopping chores, and prepare elaborate dinners for others.

ON A BINGE.
Bulimia nervosa is defined as recurrent cycles of binge eating and the taking of dramatic measures, such as self-induced vomiting, to purge the food. Why do you think that many more women than men suffer from the eating disorders of anorexia nervosa and bulimia nervosa?

BULIMIA NERVOSA Consider the case of Nicole:

> Nicole awakens in her cold dark room and already wishes it was time to go back to bed. She dreads the thought of going through this day, which will be like so many others in her recent past. She asks herself the question every morning, "Will I be able to make it through the day without being totally obsessed by thoughts of food, or will I blow it again and spend the day bingeing?" She tells herself that today she will begin a new life, today she will start to live like a normal human being. However, she is not at all convinced that the choice is hers. (Boskind-White & White, 1983, p. 29)

This day, it turns out, Nicole begins by eating eggs and toast. Then she binges on cookies; doughnuts; bagels smothered with butter, cream cheese, and jelly; granola; candy bars; and bowls of cereal and milk—all within 45 minutes. Then she cannot take in any more food and turns her attention to purging what she has eaten. She goes to the bathroom, ties back her hair, turns on the shower to mask any noise she will make, drinks a glass of water, and makes herself vomit. Afterward she vows, "Starting tomorrow, I'm going to change." But she knows that tomorrow it will probably be the same story.

Nicole has **bulimia nervosa.** Bulimia nervosa is defined as recurrent cycles of binge eating, especially of foods rich in carbohydrates,[1] and the taking of dramatic measures to purge the food, once consumed. These measures include self-induced vomiting, fasting or strict dieting, use of laxatives, and vigorous

Truth or Fiction Revisited

It is true that some college women control their weight by going on cycles of binge eating followed by self-induced vomiting. Many do, in fact. Cycles of binge eating and purging define the disorder of bulimia.

BULIMIA NERVOSA • An eating disorder characterized by recurrent episodes of binge eating followed by purging, and persistent overconcern with body shape and weight.

[1] Examples include candy, cookies, and cakes. Meats contain protein and fat, so they are of relatively less interest to bulimic bingers.

exercise. As with anorexia, there is overconcern about body shape and weight. The problem usually begins in adolescence or early adulthood, and afflicts women more so than men.

Adjustment in a World of DIVERSITY

Eating Disorders: Why the Gender Gap?

The typical person with anorexia or bulimia is a young White female of higher socioeconomic status. Yet anorexia is becoming more prevalent among males, other ethnic groups, and older people (DeAngelis, 1997a; Gilbert, 1996b).

Women with eating disorders vastly outnumber men with these disorders. Theorists account for the gender gap in different ways. Because anorexia is connected with amenorrhea, some psychodynamic theorists suggest that anorexia represents an effort by the girl to revert to a prepubescent stage. Anorexia allows the girl to avoid growing up, separating from her family, and taking on adult responsibilities. Because of the loss of fatty deposits, her breasts and hips flatten. In her fantasies, perhaps, a woman with anorexia remains a child, sexually undifferentiated.

Cognitive-behavioral approaches suggest that weight loss has strong reinforcement value because it provides feelings of personal perfectibility (Vitousek & Manke, 1994). Yet perfection is an impossible goal for most people. Fashion models, who represent the female ideal, are 9 percent taller and 16 percent slimmer than the average woman (Williams, 1992). Sixteen percent! For most women, that is at least 16 pounds!

Consider the sociocultural aspects of eating disorders: As the cultural ideal leans more toward slimmer bodies, women with average or heavier-than-average figures come under more pressure to control their weight. Agras and Kirkley (1986) documented interest in losing weight by counting the numbers of diet articles printed in three women's magazines—*Ladies' Home Journal, Good Housekeeping,* and *Harper's Bazaar*—since 1900. Diet articles were absent until the 1930s. During the 1930s and 1940s, only about one such article appeared in every 10 issues. During the 1950s and 1960s, the number of diet articles jumped to about one in every other issue. During the 1980s, however, the number mushroomed to about 1.3 articles per issue. This means that in recent years there has been an average of *more than one* diet article per issue!

Many men with eating disorders are involved in sports or occupations that require them to remain within certain weight ranges, such as dancing, wrestling, and modeling (Gilbert, 1996b). (Women ballet dancers are also at special risk of developing eating disorders [Dunning, 1997].) Men are more likely than women to control their weight through intense exercise. Men, like women, are under social pressure to conform to an ideal body image—one that builds their upper bodies and trims their abdomens (DeAngelis, 1997a).

THEORETICAL VIEWS Many psychologists link eating disorders to the cultural idealization of the (very) slender female and a consequent irrational fear of gaining weight. This cultural ideal may contribute to distortion of the body image. Women college students generally see themselves as significantly heavier than the figure that is most attractive to males and as heavier, still, than the ideal (Fallon & Rozin, 1985). College men actually prefer women to be heavier than women expect—about halfway between the girth of the average woman and what the woman thinks is most attractive.

Other psychological hypotheses concerning the origins of anorexia nervosa and bulimia nervosa have been advanced. For example, as discussed in the accompanying "Adjustment in a World of Diversity" feature, the frequent link between anorexia and **menarche** (pronounced "men-ARE-key") has led psychoanalysts to suggest that anorexia may represent an effort to remain **prepubescent.** Some psychoanalysts thus hypothesize that anorexic women are conflicted about their sexuality, especially the possibility of pregnancy.

Other theorists note that self-starvation may be intended to punish parents. Perhaps adolescents use refusal to eat as a weapon when family relationships become disturbed.

FITNESS: RUN FOR YOUR LIFE?

Fitness is not just a matter of strength or of whether you can run the mile in 8 minutes or less. Fitness is the ability to engage in moderate to vigorous levels of physical activity without undue fatigue. If you cannot walk from the parking lot to the classroom or the office, or climb the stairs without shortness of breath or fatigue, consider yourself unfit. The good news is that you may not be destined to remain unfit. The great majority of readers can improve their fitness by making exercise a regular part of their lifestyles.

In this section we discuss types of exercise, the physiological effects of exercise, the health benefits (and hazards) of exercise, the psychological effects of exercise, and, for you couch potatoes out there, some hints on getting started.

Types of Exercise

There are many kinds of exercise. Let us distinguish between aerobic exercise and anaerobic exercise. **Aerobic exercise** is any kind of exercise that requires a sustained increase in the consumption of oxygen. Aerobic exercise promotes cardiovascular fitness. Examples of aerobic exercise include running and jogging, running in place, walking (at more than a leisurely pace), aerobic dancing, jumping rope, swimming, bicycle riding, basketball, racquetball, and cross-country skiing (see Table 7.3).

MENARCHE • The beginning of menstruation.
PREPUBESCENT • Descriptive of people during the years just prior to puberty.
AEROBIC EXERCISE • Exercise that requires sustained increase in oxygen consumption, such as jogging, swimming, or riding a bicycle.

AN AEROBICS CLASS.
Aerobic exercise requires a sustained increase in the consumption of oxygen and promotes cardiovascular fitness. Examples of aerobic exercise include running, walking (at more than a leisurely pace), dancing, jumping rope, swimming, cycling, basketball, racquetball, and cross-country skiing.

TABLE 7.3 TYPES OF PHYSICAL ACTIVITIES

INDOOR ACTIVITIES

ACTIVITY	PROS	CONS	TIPS
Working out with exercise equipment (e.g., ski machine, treadmill, stationary bike, step aerobics, weight training, rowing machine, stair climber, etc.) 	Weight training can strengthen muscles and build bones; aerobics equipment like treadmills, stair climbers, skiers, and rowers can give you a good aerobics workout to build cardiovascular endurance, take off pounds, and strengthen and tone selected muscle groups (e.g., the rowing machine is great for the biceps, quads, glutes, upper back, abs, and legs). Most types of equipment these days have electronic gauges that give you feedback on intensity, calories expended, and time spent exercising.	Equipment can be expensive if you purchase it for home use, especially motorized treadmills. Club memberships too tend to be expensive and may not guarantee access to the equipment when you want to use it, especially during peak hours. Many people are initially attracted to exercise equipment (some in the misguided belief that the equipment will do the work for them), but quickly lose interest as they find the routines too demanding or monotonous. May result in injuries if you push yourself too hard too fast.	Don't overdo it. Build up intensity and duration slowly. Allow your body to adjust to the increased demand. Alternate between machines to increase variety and combat boredom. Also, combat boredom and help the time pass more quickly by watching TV, reading (if possible), or listening to music on your personal stereo while you exercise. Most important: Get checked out first by a health professional.
Working out with an exercise video 	Great for aerobics training without the expense and effort of going to an exercise studio or health club; only a one-time expense for the video.	May get bored with same routine; may lose motivation if someone isn't there exhorting you on.	Start with an exercise program at a local club or studio to learn proper technique and style. Ask the instructor for recommended videos that fit your needs and style. Have several exercise videos available and alternate among them to prevent boredom. Invite a friend over and exercise together.
Swimming laps 	Improves cardiovascular endurance; great for shedding pounds and toning muscles; as a low-impact activity, poses little risk of injury; relaxing and soothing to the mind as well.	Pools may be crowded or inconvenient. Use of pools may require expensive membership fees.	Start slowly and build up gradually. Don't push yourself to extremes. Increase the number of laps and lap speed gradually. Find a pool with swim hours that fit your particular schedule.
Aerobics classes 	Good way to build up cardiovascular endurance and drop excess pounds. If you're the type of person who needs a push every now and then, having an instructor exhorting you on may help you to get the most out of yourself. Instructors also help you with technique and can tailor the routine to your ability and level of endurance.	Can be expensive. Classes may not be offered at convenient times or locations. Some people may be intimidated or self-conscious about exercising in front of others. Depending on the instructors, some classes may be too demanding. The repetitive routines may become boring or mind numbing.	Choose an instructor who is right for you, someone who takes the time to get to know your personal capabilities and needs. Start with a beginner's class and gradually work your way up to more challenging classes. Go with a friend. It's more likely that you'll stick with it if you feel that someone else is depending on you.

TABLE 7.3 TYPES OF PHYSICAL ACTIVITIES (CONTINUED)

OUTDOOR ACTIVITIES

ACTIVITY	PROS	CONS	TIPS
Competitive sports (baseball, basketball, handball, racquetball, tennis, golf, etc.) 	Sports that require more continuous exertion, such as basketball and tennis, can improve cardiovascular fitness. Even sports requiring less frequent bursts of physical activity, like baseball or softball, can burn calories and help you meet your goal of 30 minutes daily of moderate physical activity. Golfing can be a good workout, but only if you leave the golf cart in the clubhouse and carry your own golf bag.	Competition can bring out the best in people, but also the worst. It may also diminish self-esteem if you connect your self-worth with winning and you wind up on the losing end. Team sports may be difficult to coordinate with people's busy schedules. Accessibility to playing courts or ball fields may be limited. Games may be rained out due to the weather.	Choose a sport you enjoy and for which you have a modicum of skill. Play for enjoyment, not to trounce your opponent. Remember, it is only a game.
Brisk walking 	Depending on the pace, it can be a source of cardiovascular endurance (at 5+ mph) or general fitness (3–4 mph); requires no special equipment other than good walking shoes; can enjoy the scenery, which may be especially appealing on long nature walks.	Not too much on the downside, which is perhaps why walking is America's most popular fitness activity. Yet there are potential disadvantages. Walking may be unpleasant or difficult in inclement weather. It may become boring if you walk the same route every time. Injuries can occur if you fail to warm up correctly, use improper shoes, take a misstep because of an uneven surface, or push your body too hard too fast.	Wear a comfortable, well fitting athletic shoe that is specially designed for walking. Remember to start any workout, including brisk walking, with some warm-up exercises, including stretching. This will help cut down on the chances of injuries such as sprains and strains. Afterward, cool down by walking at a slower pace for about 5 to 7 minutes and then finish off with some stretching. Start with a slower pace and for a limited period of time, say about 10 or 15 minutes. Then gradually increase your speed to about 3 to 4 miles an hour for about a 30-minute period.
Running 	Excellent aerobic exercise for cardiovascular fitness and weight reduction. Requires minimal equipment, though good running shoes are a must.	Injuries to feet and ankles are common due to high impact of running, especially on hard surfaces. Excessive running can overtax body resources, impairing immunological functioning.	Get doctor's approval before beginning any vigorous exercise routine. Stretching exercises are a must when warming up and cooling down. Run in pairs or groups for safety, especially at night. Like other exercises, take it slow at first and build up speed and endurance gradually. Seek medical attention for any persistent pain or soreness.
Cycling 	Can set the pace for moderate or vigorous activity; improves cardiovascular fitness at speeds of 15 mph; less impact on feet and ankles than running, reducing the risk of injury; love that passing scenery!	Potential risk of injuries from falls; requires purchase of quality bicycle ($125+) and accessories including (a must) a Snell-certified helmet; may be dangerous on slippery surfaces and city streets; not suitable for inclement weather.	Never bicycle without a safety helmet; like other demanding exercises, work up pace and distance gradually and consult your doctor first; alternate between level and hilly terrain; have your bicycle checked regularly for malfunctions; avoid cycling on congested city streets.

Continued

TABLE 7.3 TYPES OF PHYSICAL ACTIVITIES (CONTINUED)

OUTDOOR ACTIVITIES (continued)

ACTIVITY	PROS	CONS	TIPS
Roller-blading 	With the fitness boom of the 1990s, the numbers of in-line skaters are surpassing those of cyclists in some city parks. Depending on the pace, can be a source of moderate or vigorous exercise with less impact on feet than running or fast walking.	High risk of injuries to wrists, knees, and ankles from falls; especially dangerous if weaving around other in-line skaters or cyclists; expense of initial outlay for in-line skates and safety accessories.	Learn proper technique before setting out and check first with your doctor concerning any physical restrictions; use proper safety equipment, which includes safety helmet, wrist and knee pads, and a quality pair of in-line skates that provide good ankle support; avoid highly congested areas and never skate in vehicular traffic.
Cross-country skiing 	Excellent aerobic exercise, which spares the feet of the pounding associated with running. Enjoy the beauty of nature in all its winter wonder. Less expensive than downhill skiing and may be free in public areas or parks.	Limited to winter and available only in colder climates; requires purchase of skis, boots, and ski clothing; risk of injury to lower extremities from falls or severe twists of the ankles or knees; risk of cold-weather injuries.	Get doctor's approval before beginning any vigorous exercise routine. Learn proper technique from an expert before setting out; dress warmly in removable layers; waterproof outer clothing a must. Work up gradually.

Anaerobic exercises, by contrast, involve short bursts of muscle activity. Examples include weight training, calisthenics (which allow rest periods between exercises), and sports such as baseball, in which there are sporadic bursts of strenuous activity.

Cardiovascular benefits are obtained from aerobic exercise, although anaerobic exercises can strengthen muscles and improve flexibility. Table 7.3 highlights the pros and cons of various kinds of exercise.

Effects of Exercise

The major physiological effect of aerobic exercise is *fitness.* Fitness is a complex concept that includes muscle strength; muscle endurance; suppleness or flexibility; cardiorespiratory, or aerobic, fitness; and, through building muscle and reducing fat, an increase in the muscle-to-fat ratio.

Muscle strength is promoted by contracting muscles and then returning gradually to the starting position. Weight training and calisthenics such as push-ups and chin-ups facilitate muscle development by offering resistance. Flexibility is enhanced by slow, sustained stretching exercises. Flexibility is desirable in its own right and also because it helps prevent injuries from other types of exercises. This is why many people stretch before running. Stretching exercises can be incorporated into the warm-up and cool-down phases of an aerobic exercise program.

Cardiovascular fitness, or condition, means that the body can use greater amounts of oxygen during vigorous activity and pump more blood with each heartbeat. Since the conditioned athlete pumps more blood with each beat, he or she usually has a slower pulse rate—fewer heartbeats per minute. But during aerobic exercise, the person may double or triple his or her resting heart rate for minutes at a time.

ANAEROBIC EXERCISE • Exercise that does not require sustained increase in oxygen consumption, such as weight lifting.

Exercise raises the metabolic rate and burns more calories. To lose weight, one should exercise regularly. Exercise promotes weight loss in ways other than burning calories. The body often compensates for lessened food intake by slowing the metabolic rate, but regular aerobic exercise elevates the metabolic rate of dieters throughout the day (Wadden and others, 1997). Failure to reach the set point in the brain may trigger persistent feelings of hunger, but sustained exercise may lower the set point in the hypothalamus so that dieters who exercise feel less hungry. However, the connection between exercise and the set point remains somewhat speculative.

EXERCISE AND HEALTH Not only does sustained activity foster cardiovascular fitness. It also appears to reduce the risks of cardiovascular disorders, as measured by incidence of heart attacks and mortality rates (Curfman, 1993b). Paffenbarger and his colleagues (1986, 1993) have been tracking 17,000 Harvard University alumni through university records and questionnaires. Among the alumni, the incidence of heart attacks declines as the physical activity level rises to burning about 2,000 calories a week—the exercise equivalent of jogging some 20 miles a week (see Figure 7.1). Inactive alumni run the highest risks of heart attacks. Alumni who burn at least 2,000 calories a week live 2 years longer, on the average, than their less active counterparts.

Long daily walks also appear to cut the mortality rate. Amy Hakim of the University of Virginia School of Medicine and her colleagues (1998) reviewed 12 years of data on 707 retired men from the Honolulu Heart Program and found that 43.1 percent of the men who walked less than a mile per day died during that period, as compared with 27.7 percent of those who walked from 1 to 2 miles a day and 21.5 percent of those who walked at least 2 miles daily (see Figure 7.2). Additional findings: 6.6 percent of the men who walked less than a mile a day died from coronary heart disease or strokes, as compared with only 2.1 percent of those who walked upward of 2 miles (see Figure 7.3). Moreover, 13.4 percent of them men who walked less than a mile died from

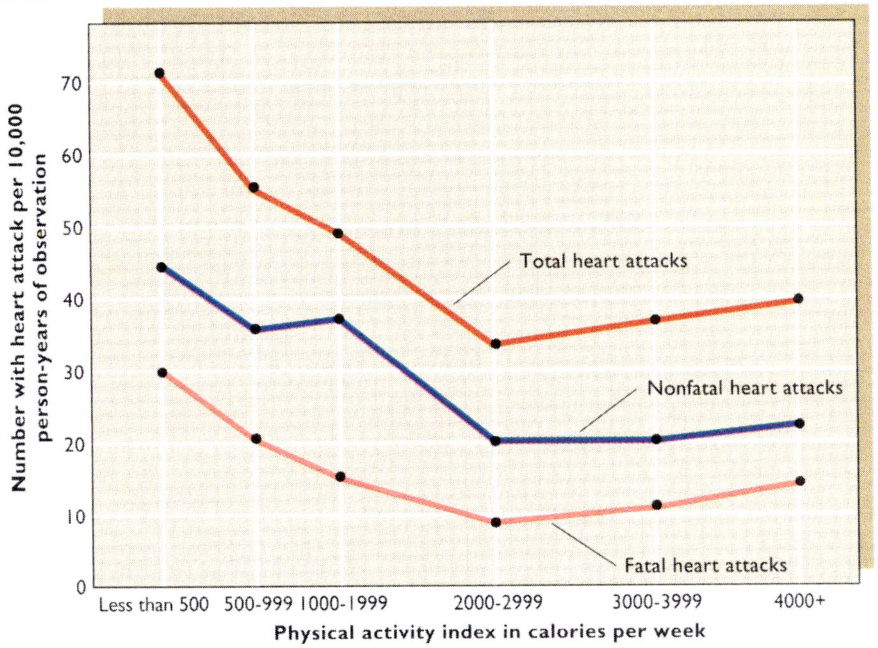

FIGURE 7.1
THE RELATIONSHIP BETWEEN EXERCISE AND HEART ATTACKS.
A longitudinal study of Harvard University alumni found that the probability of having a heart attack declines as the number of calories expended in exercise increases up to about 2,000 calories per week. We can expend about 2,000 calories a week by jogging 3 miles a day or walking for about an hour a day.

ADJUSTMENT *in the* NEW MILLENNIUM

Will We Be Competing With Virtual Babes and Hunks in the New Millennium?

At the turn of the millennium, many American women find themselves competing against the ideal of the tall, slender, "buffed up" woman (Williams, 1992). That image of the ideal has sent millions of women, young and older, to their mirrors, searching out that extra ounce of fat. It has given rise to an epidemic of eating disorders, as women take drastic measures to lose weight.

Men, too, have been feeling the pressure to slim down—and buff up. Many dancers, wrestlers, and male models have also developed eating disorders (DeAngelis, 1997a; Gilbert 1996b).

It is difficult enough for women and men to compete against the flesh-and-blood supermodels they see in the media. But what of the *virtual* models that will be assaulting us from every medium imaginable—and some that may be not so imaginable? Consider Lara Croft, the 29-year-old epitome of female perfection. She's tall (5′9″), slim (110 pounds), and well-muscled. Unreal, you say. Well, you won't find her sitting in your class. It's not that she's opposed to education; it's that she's *unreal* in more ways than one. Lara's not a flesh-and-blood "babe"—she's what her devotees call a "cyberbabe," and you'll find her on video games and in ads. Ads, ads, and more ads.

Her name is Lara Croft, and she seems to be everywhere (Barboza, 1998).

Her image is popping up in magazines, on television and computer screens, even on pinup posters like the one in the January 1998 issue of *PC Games* magazine, which shows her reclining in a bikini, a handgun resting suggestively on her hip.

And she's not even real. Lara is a digitized female image from one of the hottest-selling video games of 1998, Tomb Raider 2, which is published by Eidos Interactive, based in London.

But that has not stopped Lara—whose tanned, voluptuous cyberframe is the equivalent of 34-24-34—from becoming a popular female icon. She is a far cry from Betty Boop, and she is no Barbie doll. She is more like a female Indiana Jones, but pumped up, vertically and horizontally.

Her fans say she is gritty, sexy, sassy, smart and, well, virtually real. And that's exactly what her British creators were hoping for.

"It's really a strange phenomenon because people talk about her as if she's a real person," said Cindy Church, a spokeswoman for Eidos. "A lot of people who play video games fantasize about her."

Unsure of just how to portray the silicon icon, Church went on, "She's not overly sexual," then paused. "OK, she is physically sexual, but she has a personality behind her."

Because of those attributes, Eidos executives are being flooded with gifts and presents for the silicon princess. There are flowers, Christmas gifts, even vows from young boys and men. "People all over the world have sent in their pictures," said Tricia Gray at the Eidos office in San Francisco. "She's had dozens of marriage proposals and all these cheesy letters."

Indeed, in Britain, only the bubbly Spice Girls are said to be more popular. And in the United States, her Indiana Jones–like video exploits are being sold in large quantities to game players who are well into their thirties.

LARA CROFT, THE "STAR" OF THE TOMB RAIDER VIDEO GAMES.
In the new millennium, will we be competing with "cyberbabes" and "cyberhunks," as well as with people made of flesh and blood?

Lara's first game, Tomb Raider, was released in November 1996 and sold about 3.5 million copies worldwide. Tomb Raider 2, which came out in November of 1997, has sold several million, according to Eidos.

As a result, just about every game and computer magazine wants to reprint Lara's sexy image. There are even entire World Wide Web sites devoted to her and sites created by individuals who even take the liberty of posing the digital Lara in the nude.

"The most obvious reason Lara Croft is so popular is that 99.5 percent of the gaming population is young men," says Steve Klett, editor of *PC Games* magazine, which has Lara gracing its cover this month. "And it doesn't hurt that she's so outrageously proportioned."

Indeed, the craze surrounding Lara (there is also an online newspaper dedicated to chronicling her life) might be yet another sign that technological advances in human imagery are creating lifelike portraits that further blur the line between reality and fantasy.

Devoted fans, who see a three-dimensional image and hear a real British voice projecting out of their computer speakers, have dubbed Lara a "cyberbabe" and the "silicon chick."

And to bolster such realism, Lara has her own biography and a rebellious past. Born into an aristocratic family in Wimbledon, England, Lara Croft—whose given age is 29—grew up in a world of private tutors, boarding schools, and a Swiss finishing school.

But on a skiing trip to the Himalayas, her plane crashed. Lara, who was the sole survivor, soon realized that she could not stand the "suffocating atmosphere of the upper-class British society" and preferred a new adventurous life. Thus she began searching for ancient artifacts and fighting villains and a zoo of animals, like tigers and wolves.

But her creators say that Lara's future is not about slaying dragons but winning eyeballs. "The digital Lara is going to sign a modeling contract with a big agency," Church boasts. "She'll become a supermodel, like Naomi Campbell and Linda Evangelista."

Even her creators think she's real. ■

Source: Written with the aid of David Barboza (1998, January 19), "Video World Is Smitten by a Gun-Toting, Tomb-Raiding Sex Symbol," *New York Times*, p. D3.

FIGURE 7.2

CUMULATIVE MORTALITY ACCORDING TO YEAR OF FOLLOW-UP AND DISTANCE WALKED PER DAY AMONG PARTICIPANTS IN THE HONOLULU HEART PROGRAM

After 12 years of follow-ups, retired men who walked more than 2 miles a day had lower mortality rates than men who walked shorter distances.
Source: Hakim and others, 1998.

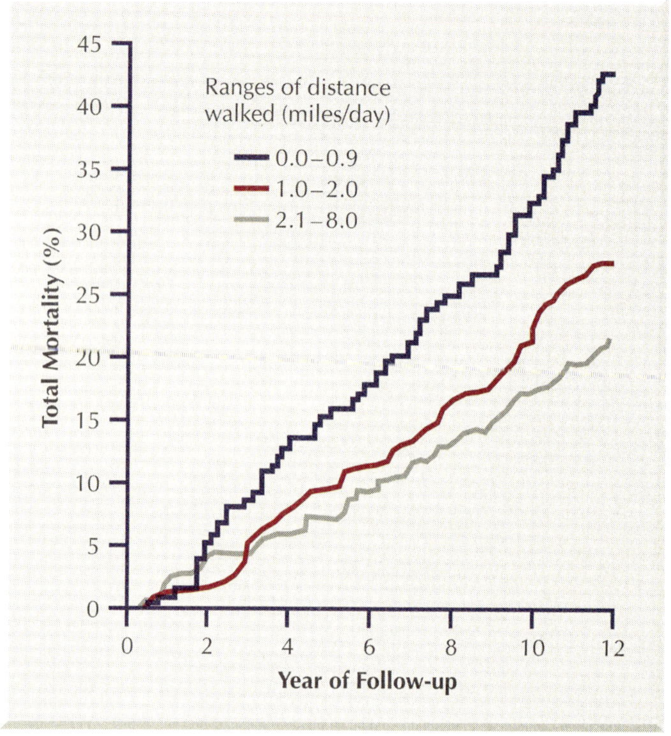

FIGURE 7.3

CAUSES OF DEATH AND DISTANCE WALKED IN MILES PER DAY AMONG PARTICIPANTS IN THE HONOLULU HEART PROGRAM

Men who walked more than 2 miles a day had a lower mortality rate than men who walked between 1 and 2 miles a day and men who walked less than a mile a day. Men who took long walks were less likely to die from cancer and heart disease.
Source: Hakim and others, 1998.

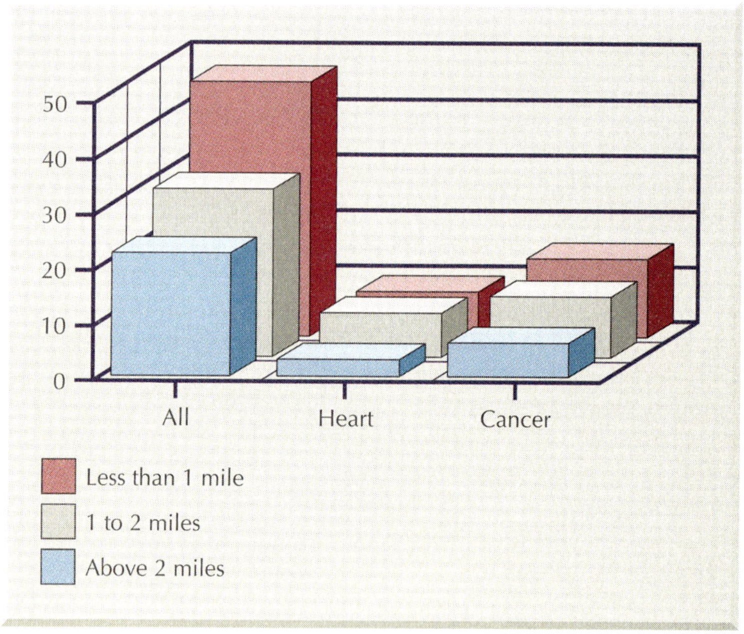

cancer, as compared with 5.3 percent of men who walked more than 2 miles a day. Since the study was not experimental, one can ask whether those who walked less died sooner because they were hobbled by health problems that made them less able or willing to walk. Hakim and her colleagues recognized this problem and got around it partly by using data only on nonsmokers who were physically able to walk a few miles.

SELF-ASSESSMENT

CHECK YOUR PHYSICAL ACTIVITY AND HEART DISEASE IQ

Test how much you know about how physical activity affects your heart. Mark each question true or false. See how you did by checking the Appendix. ■

T	F	1.	Regular physical activity can reduce your chances of getting heart disease.
T	F	2.	Most people get enough physical activity from their normal daily routine.
T	F	3.	You don't have to train like a marathon runner to become more physically fit.
T	F	4.	Exercise programs do not require a lot of time to be very effective.
T	F	5.	People who need to lose some weight are the only ones who will benefit from regular physical activity.
T	F	6.	All exercises give you the same benefits.
T	F	7.	The older you are, the less active you need to be.
T	F	8.	It doesn't take a lot of money or expensive equipment to become physically fit.
T	F	9.	Many risks and injuries can occur with exercise.
T	F	10.	You should always consult a doctor before starting a physical activity program.
T	F	11.	People who have had a heart attack should not start any physical activity program.
T	F	12.	To help stay physically active, include a variety of activities.

Source: NHLBI (1995, May), *Obesity education initiative.* National Heart, Lung, and Blood Institute: NIH Publication No. 95-3795.

PSYCHOLOGICAL EFFECTS OF EXERCISE: "RUNNING THERAPY"? Psychologists are also interested in the effects of exercise on psychological variables such as depression. Articles have been appearing on exercise as "therapy"—for example, "running therapy" (Greist, 1984).

Depression is characterized by inactivity and feelings of helplessness. Aerobic exercise is, in a sense, the opposite of inactivity. Success at it might also help alleviate feelings of helplessness. In a notable experiment, McCann and Holmes (1984) assigned mildly depressed college women at random to aerobic exercise, a progressive-relaxation placebo, and a no-treatment control group. The relaxation group showed some improvement, but aerobic exercise made dramatic inroads on students' depression.

ADJUSTMENT *in the* NEW MILLENNIUM

Will We See Gender Differences in Fitness Evaporate in the New Millennium?

Not so long ago, women who were interested in athletics were not taken seriously or were perceived as unfeminine. If they did take up a sport, like tennis, they were expected to approach it in a "ladylike" way, which meant they weren't expected to compete too hard, let alone to grunt when serving the ball, like many male players do. Today, though women athletes are accorded greater respect than in the past, they still have to fight for parity with their male counterparts. With the exception of figure skating and perhaps professional tennis, the rule still holds that male athletes are awarded more lucrative contracts and endorsements and receive the lion's share of television exposure.

The belief that competitive sports are male preserves, especially sports that demand muscle strength and physical endurance, reflects an underlying premise that women are not strong enough or fit enough to compete. But is it so?

ARE MEN NATURALLY STRONGER? In muscle strength, especially upper-body strength, the average man does have an advantage over the average woman (Wells, 1991; Wilmore, 1991). This is not surprising when you consider that the average man is 35 pounds heavier, has more muscle mass, less body fat, and is 5 inches taller than the average woman. Men also have broader shoulders, slimmer hips, and slightly longer legs proportionally to their height. Prior to puberty (beginning around age 12 or 13), boys and girls are well matched in physical strength and ability. Girls can run just as fast, lift as much, and otherwise match boys in physical strength. Differences begin to emerge, however, as children pass through puberty.

Hormonal influences play a large role in accounting for growth differences between males and females during puberty. At the onset of puberty, males experience a steep rise in testosterone production, the so-called male sex hormone ("so-called" because females also have testosterone, although in far lesser amounts). This leads to a number of changes in males, not the least of which is a growth spurt lasting about 2 years longer than in females. The result is greater height, denser bones, and larger muscles.

Females also undergo many changes during puberty. These are caused by a surge in estrogen and other female hormones. One effect of these hormones is to increase body fat—which is why women taking birth control pills or estrogen supplements often experience a weight gain. Some of this fat directly prepares the body for reproduction (for instance, fat around internal organs and in the breasts). A greater amount of fat becomes stored in the buttocks, hips, and thighs, giving women a more rounded shape.

Even if women manage to reduce the amount of stored fat to levels comparable to males—and it's harder to do this, since estrogen slows the metabolism of stored fat— they are left with a minimum of 10 percent more fat than men. This means that a woman's body has proportionately less muscle than it did before puberty and proportionately less muscle mass than a man's. The female's pelvis also broadens during puberty in preparation for childbearing; this, along with shorter thigh bones, results in a greater inward sloping of the upper leg (causing knock-knees in some women).

Given the fact that the average man has greater muscle mass, greater body weight, and a lower percentage of body fat, is it fair to compare men and women directly in terms of muscle strength? In professional boxing, we hardly would expect a 155-pound middleweight to go head-to-head with a 215-pound heavyweight? On the football field, we're not likely to see any 150-pound defensive linemen. If we just compare men and women of the same age, the average woman has about half the upper-body strength and about three quarters the lower-body strength of the average man. However, if we take into account body weight and composition, men and women are actually quite similar in lower-body strength, though men still retain an advantage in upper-body strength. Consider, too, that with weight training, women can develop upper-body strength that is similar to that of men of the same weight and body composition whose muscles are similarly trained. Yes, there may be some male body builders who have not (not yet at least) met their match in women competitors. But when we look more broadly at the general population, differences in strength relate more to the use to which we put our muscles than to our gender.

ARE MEN NATURALLY MORE FIT? Fitness is the ability of the body to withstand stress and sustain physically demanding work. One measure of fitness is cardiorespiratory fitness—the ability of the body to pump oxygen-rich blood to the muscles in order to sustain vigorous physical activity. Here men do have an advantage. The typical male heart beats at a slower rate because it can pump out a greater amount of blood per beat (Wells, 1991; Wilmore, 1991). Men also have a higher concentration of hemoglobin-rich (oxygen-carrying) red blood cells in their bloodstream. The smaller heart volumes and lower levels of hemoglobin in women mean that the female heart must beat faster to provide the same amount of blood and oxygen. At rest, the female heart beats about 7 to 10 beats per minute faster than males of comparable age and fitness levels. At a given level of exercise, the female heart is working harder. So female joggers, for instance, work their hearts harder to run a 10-minute mile than do their male counterparts. These cardiovascular differences account for the fact that cardiorespiratory endurance, measured by maximum oxygen uptake relative to body weight, is 28 percent higher in men than women.

Once again, however, to accurately assess the differences in cardiorespiratory endurance between males and females, we need to compare males and females with both similar-sized hearts (and bodies) and who also carry around the same body fat. When this is done—by adding weight to males to simulate extra body fat—it turns out that body fat does account for about one third of the differences between men and women in cardiorespiratory endurance. Nonetheless, even when body fat is taken into account, males still have greater cardiorespiratory endurance (about 16 percent more than comparable females). This 16 percent advantage appears to be due to the fact that males are born with higher hemoglobin levels. Hemoglobin is the part of blood that carries oxygen, so males can use oxygen more efficiently than females.

END OF THE STORY? Across the board, women athletes are narrowing the gender gap in sports achievement. The reason is their rigorous training schedules. Elite female athletes of today have body fat levels between 10 percent and 15 percent—the same as or lower than male athletes—and cardiorespiratory fitness greater than that of most men. Elite female runners have been steadily closing the gap between their marathon times and those of male athletes (Whipp & Ward, 1992). In 1971, for instance, the women's marathon record was 38 minutes slower than the men's record. In 1981 this difference was 21.5 minutes. In the 1990s, a mere 15 minutes separated the fastest male and female marathon runners. This rapid rate of improvement indicates that women athletes are on their way to catching up to their male counterparts.

But what of the great majority of us who aren't elite athletes? The fact is that differences in fitness, like differences in muscle strength, are largely a function of training. Sedentary people of either gender are less fit when it comes to cardiorespiratory fitness, muscle strength, and ability to endure hard physical activity like running or swimming laps than are those who regularly train. When it comes to muscle strength and fitness, the issue is not so much which gender you are, but how well conditioned you are. ■

Truth or Fiction Revisited

It is true that exercise can alleviate feelings of depression. Research has shown that exercise has positive effects on the moods of many people.

Other experiments also suggest that aerobic exercise alleviates feelings of depression, at least among mildly and moderately depressed individuals (Buffone, 1984). Buffone (1980) found that 8 weeks of treatment combining cognitive-behavioral methods and running helped clinically depressed patients. Greist (1984) assigned depressed subjects at random to aerobic exercise, relaxation training, or group therapy. All treatments helped, but the exercise and relaxation groups outpaced the verbal therapy patients at a 3-month follow-up.

Still other research suggests that sustained exercise alleviates anxiety (Long, 1984) and boosts self-esteem (Sonstroem, 1984). However, Sonstroem points out that in all these studies it might not be the exercise itself that is responsible for the psychological benefits. The apparent benefits of exercise might also be attributed to the following:

1. Feelings of physical well-being
2. Improved physical health
3. Achievement of (exercise) goals
4. An enhanced sense of control over one's body
5. The social support of fellow exercisers
6. Even the attention of the researchers

Of course, benefits 1 through 5 still provide very good reasons for exercising.

Starting an Exercise Program

How about you? Are you considering climbing aboard the exercise bandwagon? If so, consider the following suggestions:

1. Unless you have engaged in sustained and vigorous exercise recently, seek the advice of a medical expert. If you smoke, have a family history of cardiovascular disorders, are overweight, or are over 40, get a stress test.
2. Consider joining a beginner's aerobics class. Group leaders are not usually experts in physiology, but at least they know the steps. You'll also be among other beginners and derive the benefits of social support.
3. Get the proper equipment to facilitate performance and help avert injury.
4. Read up on the activity you are considering.
5. Try to select activities that you can sustain for a lifetime. Don't worry about building yourself up rapidly. Enjoy yourself and your strength and endurance will progress on their own. If you do not enjoy what you're doing, you're not likely to stick to it.
6. Keep a diary or log and note your progress. If running, note the paths or streets you follow, the distance you run, the weather conditions, and any remarkable details that come to mind. Check your notes now and then to remind yourself of enjoyable paths and experiences.
7. If you feel severe pain, don't try to "exercise through it." Soreness is to be expected for beginners (and some old-timers now and then). In that sense, soreness, at least when intermittent, is normal. But sharp pain is abnormal and a sign that something is wrong.
8. Have fun!

Adjustment in a World of DIVERSITY

Fitness Is for Everyone: Exercise and the Physically Disabled

Janet Reed's videotape workout is similar in many ways to other exercise videos. For example, Reed's workout does not require special expertise or equipment. Viewers are encouraged to consult with their health professionals before participating. And like other exercise tapes, Reed's has warm-up stretches, activities that foster relaxation and range of motion, and exercises that enhance flexibility, strength, balance, and coordination.

But Reed's workout differs in a very important way: It is aimed at participants who are temporary or permanent users of wheelchairs.

Reed was thrown from a horse and suffered spinal cord injuries that paralyzed her from the waist down. She had difficulty accepting these new limitations for many years. One year, however, a friend asked her to dance during a fund-raiser, and her outlook began to change. The friend manipulated her wheelchair while she moved her upper body in tune with the music. It was the most fun she had since her accident and eventually led to the idea that she could help other physically disabled people profit from physical activity. She put together her "Wheelchair Workout" with the assistance of a physical therapist and found that creating the program helped her again to take charge of her life. Working out regularly "strengthens the body, relaxes the mind and toughens the spirit," she says. "It can prove to you that you have what it takes to do what is necessary" (cited in Brody, 1990c).

When people are consigned to wheelchairs or to generally sedentary lives, their cardiovascular functioning suffers, their muscles atrophy, and their joints stiffen. People in wheelchairs can also encounter pressure sores. Exercise, of course does not cure paralysis. However, it helps people with spinal cord injuries to improve their upper-body strength and flexibility, their cardiovascular condition, the functioning of other body systems—such as the nervous and urogenital systems—their overall outlooks on life, and their self-esteem. Exercise may actually be more crucial to the well-being of the physically disabled than it is for other people.

The benefits of exercise for physically disabled people are well known. Physical activities, including tournaments, were organized as therapy for wounded war veterans after World War II. Wheelchair athletic organizations today encourage physically disabled people to participate in archery, basketball, bowling, Ping-Pong, racquetball, softball, swimming, track and field events, even weight lifting. The Special Olympics aims to foster independence and a sense of achievement among people with mental disabilities such as mental retardation. It provides training and competition in 22 sports to some 750,000 participants, many of whom are also physically disabled. A ranking system—a sort of literal "handicap" ranking—gives everyone a more or less equal chance to win.

Even group marathon "wheelchairing" is available to physically disabled people. At the Boston Marathon, wheelchair participants leave the starting gate a half hour ahead of runners. The runners do not catch up to them until they hit the area of "Heartbreak Hill" on Commonwealth Avenue in Newton, some 20 miles into the race. During one race, a burly-shouldered wheelchair contestant hit a rock on Heartbreak Hill and flew from his chair, landing on the road. Lead runners and members of the crowd spontaneously sprang to help him, but he waved them off. He made himself erect and walked on his hands to obtain tools from a kit on the back of his damaged wheelchair. Within minutes he had made appropriate minor repairs, replaced the tools, fairly flung himself back into his seat, and rejoined the race.

Rehabilitation specialists suggest isometric exercises to enhance muscle strength in wheelchair users, such as pressing the palms together and making a fist. Isotonic exercises can help increase range of motion and stamina. One example is wheelchair sit-ups. This is accomplished by locking the chair wheels, grasping the arms of the chair, and straightening the elbows, which lifts the person off of the seat. After letting themselves down, the exercise is repeated several times.

Swimming is an ideal exercise for physically disabled people. Swimming is a low-impact activity that fosters flexibility, strength, and cardiovascular conditioning. The water helps support the body and swimming provides opportunities for social interaction (unless you stick to your own pool in your own backyard).

At Philadelphia's Moss Rehabilitation Hospital, people in wheelchairs receive upper-body versions of martial arts training so that they can better protect themselves from molesters as well as enhance their strength and coordination. They learn to jolt or fend off assailants with their fists, fingers, and arms.

In addition to the more standard fare, the Handicapped Sports Program at Denver's Children's Hospital has programs in golf, horseback riding, river rafting, and skiing. One 15-year-old boy without a left leg and with a small right leg learned to ski with a brace on his one leg, one ski, and special ski "poles" with ski tips. In addition to enhancing his coordination and strength, skiing got him onto the slopes where he made friends and gained self-confidence.

Although exercise confers many benefits on disabled people, there are also some special hazards. For example, wheelchair-using athletes may overuse their upper bodies so that they incur more than their fair share of injuries to muscles and joints in their hands, arms, shoulders, and necks. Wheelchair-using athletes are also apparently more susceptible to dangerous changes in body temperature—hyperthermia and hypothermia. Forcing fluids helps avert hyperthermia. Getting out of sweaty clothes at the end of a session and getting wrapped in a blanket can help prevent hypothermia. Like other athletes, physically disabled people are encouraged to consult with health professionals before undertaking exercise regimens.

SLEEP

Sleep has always been a fascinating topic. We spend about one third of our adult lives sleeping. Most animals relax their muscles and collapse when they sleep, but birds and horses sleep upright. Their antigravity muscles are at work all night long. Most of us complain when we have not gotten several hours of sleep, but some people sleep for an hour or less a day and appear to lead otherwise normal lives.

Why do we sleep? Why do some of us have trouble getting to sleep, and what can we do about it?

Functions of Sleep

One outdated theory of sleep suggested that sleep allowed the brain to rest and recuperate from the stresses of "being on" all day. But research with the electroencephalograph (EEG), an instrument that measures the electrical activity of the brain, has shown that brain cells are active all night long. So the power isn't switched off at night.

But what of sleep and the rest of the body? Sleep helps rejuvenate a tired body. What will happen to you if you miss sleep for one night? For several nights?

Tina Adler (1993c) compares people who are highly sleep deprived with people who have been drinking heavily. Their abilities to concentrate and perform normal tasks may be seriously impaired, but they may be the last ones to recognize their limitations. Research shows that sleep deprivation mainly affects attention (Adler, 1993c). There are related psychological problems, however, including impaired memory formation, which in part may reflect lessened motivation to focus on details.

Sleep researcher Wilse Webb (1993) notes that most students can pull successful "all-nighters." That is, they can cram for a test through the night and then perform reasonably well on the test the following day. His rationale is that students will generally be highly motivated to pay attention to the details of the test. When we are sleep deprived for several nights, aspects of psychological functioning such as attention, learning, and memory deteriorate notably. Webb (1993) also notes that many people sleep late or nap on their days off. Perhaps they suffer from mild sleep deprivation during the week and catch up on the weekend.

The amount of sleep we need seems to be in part genetically determined, like our heights (Webb, 1993). People also tend to need more sleep during periods of change and stress such as a change of jobs, an increase in workload, or an episode of depression. Perhaps sleep helps us recover from the stresses of life.

Dreams

Just what is the "stuff"[2] of dreams? What are they "made on"? Like memories and fantasies, dreams involve imagery in the absence of external stimulation. Some dreams seem very real. You may have had an "anxiety dream" the night before a test. Perhaps you dreamed that you had taken the test and it was all over. (Ah, the disappointment when you woke up and realized that such was not the case!)

Dreams are most vivid during the period designated as REM sleep. That is when they are most likely to have vivid imagery. Images are vaguer and more fleeting during NREM sleep. You may dream every time you are in REM sleep. Therefore, if you sleep for 8 hours and undergo five sleep cycles, you may have five dreams. Upon waking, you may think that time seemed to expand or contract during your dream, so that during 10 or 15 minutes of actual time, the content of your dream ranged over days or weeks. But dreams actually tend to take place in real time. Therefore 15 minutes of events fills about 15 minutes of dreaming. Your dream theater is quite flexible. You can dream in black and white or in full color.

THE STUFF OF DREAMS: THEORIES OF THE CONTENT OF DREAMS You may recall dreams involving fantastic adventures, but most dreams involve memories of the activities and problems of the day (Wade, 1998a). If we are preoccupied with illness or death, sexual or aggressive urges, or moral dilemmas, we are likely to dream about them. The characters in our dreams are more likely to be friends and neighbors than spies, monsters, and princes.

---

[2] The phrase "such stuff as dreams are made on" comes from Shakespeare's *The Tempest*.

TABLE 7.4 DREAM SYMBOLS IN PSYCHODYNAMIC THEORY

SYMBOLS FOR THE MALE GENITAL ORGANS				
Airplanes	Fish	Neckties	Tools	Weapons
Bullets	Hands	Poles	Trains	
Feet	Hoses	Snakes	Trees	
Fire	Knives	Sticks	Umbrellas	
SYMBOLS FOR THE FEMALE GENITAL ORGANS				
Bottles	Caves	Doors	Ovens	Ships
Boxes	Chests	Hats	Pockets	Tunnels
Cases	Closets	Jars	Pots	
SYMBOLS FOR SEXUAL INTERCOURSE				
Climbing a ladder		Entering a room		
Climbing a staircase		Flying in an airplane		
Crossing a bridge		Riding a horse		
Driving an automobile		Riding a roller coaster		
Riding an elevator		Walking into a tunnel or down a hall		
SYMBOLS FOR THE BREASTS				
Apples	Peaches			

Note: Freud theorized that the content of dreams symbolizes urges, wishes, and objects of fantasy that we would censor if we were awake.

"A dream is a wish your heart makes," goes the song from the Disney film *Cinderella.* Freud theorized that dreams reflect unconscious wishes and urges. He argued that through dreams we can express impulses that we would censor during the day. Moreover, he said that the content of dreams is symbolic of unconscious fantasized objects such as genital organs (see Table 7.4). (Nevertheless, Freud admitted, "Sometimes a cigar is just a cigar.") A key part of Freud's method of psychoanalysis involved interpretation of his clients' dreams. Freud also believed that dreams "protect sleep" by providing imagery that helps keep disturbing, repressed thoughts out of awareness.

Truth or Fiction Revisited

It is not true that we act out our forbidden fantasies in our dreams. Most dreams are humdrum.

The theory that dreams protect sleep has been challenged by the observation that disturbing events tend to be followed by disturbing dreams on the same theme—not by protective imagery (Reiser, 1992). Our behavior in dreams is also generally consistent with our waking behavior. Most dreams, then, are unlikely candidates for the expression of repressed urges (even disguised). A person who leads a moral life tends to dream moral dreams.

There are a number of biological views of the meanings of dreams. According to the **activation-synthesis model,** acetylcholine and the pons stimulate responses that lead to dreaming (Hobson, 1992). One is *activation* of the reticular activating system (RAS), which arouses us, but not to waking. During the waking state, firing of these cells in the reticular formation is linked to movement, particularly the semiautomatic movements involved in walking, running, and other physical acts. During REM sleep, however, neurotransmitters generally inhibit activity so that we don't thrash about as we dream (Blakeslee, 1992). In this way, we save ourselves (and our bed partners) some wear and tear. The eye muscles are stimulated and thus show the rapid eye movement associated with dreaming. The RAS also stimulates neural activity in the parts of the cortex involved in memory. The cortex then *synthesizes,* or puts together, these sources of stimulation to some degree to yield the "stuff" of dreams. Yet

ACTIVATION-SYNTHESIS MODEL • The view that dreams reflect biological activation of cognitive activity and the synthesis of this activity into a pattern.

research with the PET scan shows that the frontal lobes of the brain, which make sense of experience, are pretty much shut down during sleep (Braun & Balkin, 1998; Hobson, 1998). Dreams are therefore more likely to be emotionally gripping than coherent in plot.

Another view of dreams is that with the brain cut off from the world outside, memories are replayed and consolidated during sleep (Wade, 1998a). Another possibility is that REM activity is a way of testing whether the individual has benefited from the restorative functions of sleep (Braun & Balkin, 1998). When restoration is adequate, the brain awakens. According to this view, dreams are purposeless by-products of the testing.

NIGHTMARES Have you ever dreamed that something heavy was on your chest and watching as you breathed? Or that you were trying to run from a terrible threat but couldn't gain your footing or coordinate your leg muscles?

In the Middle Ages, such nightmares were thought to be the work of demons. By and large, they were seen as a form of retribution. That is, they were sent to make you pay for your sins. They might sit on your chest and observe you fiendishly. (How else would a fiend observe, if not "fiendishly"?) If you were given to sexual fantasies or behavior, they might have sexual intercourse with you.

Nightmares, like most pleasant dreams, are generally products of REM sleep. College students keeping dream logs report an average of two nightmares a month (Wood & Bootzin, 1990). Traumatic events can spawn nightmares, as reported by survivors of the San Francisco earthquake of 1989 (Wood and others, 1992) and the Los Angeles earthquake of 1994 (Kolbert, 1994). People who suffer frequent nightmares are more likely than other people to also suffer from anxieties, depression, and other kinds of psychological discomfort (Berquier & Ashton, 1992).

Insomnia: "You Know I Can't Sleep at Night"

About one third of American adults are affected by insomnia in any given year (Gillin, 1991). Women complain of insomnia more often than men do (Kupfer & Reynolds, 1997).

INSOMNIA.
"You know I can't sleep at night" goes the song from the 1960s by the Mamas and the Papas. Why are women more likely than men to have insomnia? What can people do about insomnia?

As a group, people with insomnia show greater restlessness and muscle tension than other people do (Lacks & Morin, 1992). People with insomnia also have greater "cognitive arousal"; that is, they are more likely to worry and have "racing thoughts" at bedtime (White & Nicassio, 1990). Insomnia comes and goes with many people, increasing during periods of anxiety and tension (Gillin, 1991).

Truth or Fiction Revisited

It is true that trying to get to sleep may keep you up at night. Trying to get to sleep may create tension, which keeps you awake.

Insomniacs tend to compound their sleep problems through their efforts to force themselves somehow to get to sleep (Lacks & Morin, 1992). Their concern heightens sympathetic nervous system activity and muscle tension. The fact is that you cannot force yourself to get to sleep. You can only set the stage for sleep by lying down and relaxing when you are tired. If you focus on sleep too closely, it might elude you. Yet millions of us go to bed each night dreading the prospect of insomnia.

Following are a number of suggestions for getting to sleep and sleeping through the night.

GETTING TO SLEEP AND STAYING ASLEEP Our most common method for fighting insomnia is popping sleeping pills (Murtagh & Greenwood, 1995). Pill popping is often effective—for a while. Sleeping preparations work by reducing arousal, and lowered arousal can induce sleep. At first, focusing on changes in arousal may also distract you from efforts to get to sleep. Expectations of success may also help.

But problems are associated with sleeping pills. First, you attribute your success to the pill and not yourself. You are thus at risk for becoming dependent on the pills. Second, you develop tolerance for sleeping pills and must increase the dose if they are to continue to work. Third, high doses of these chemicals can be dangerous, especially if mixed with alcohol.

Let us now consider psychological strategies for coping with insomnia. They include using relaxation to reduce tension, challenging irrational beliefs that otherwise heighten tension, using techniques that distract from the task of somehow *getting* to sleep, and stimulus control.

Relax! Releasing muscle tension has been shown to reduce the amount of time needed to fall asleep and the incidence of waking up during the night. It increases the number of hours slept and leaves us feeling more rested in the morning (Murtagh & Greenwood, 1995). Biofeedback training (BFT) for insomnia usually focuses on reducing muscle tension in the forehead or in the arms. BFT has also been used to teach people to produce the kinds of brain waves that are associated with relaxation and sleep.

Challenge Irrational Beliefs You need not be an expert on insomnia to realize that thinking that the following day will be ruined unless you get to sleep *right now* will increase, rather than decrease, body arousal at bedtime. Still, we often catastrophize the problems that will befall us if we do not sleep. Table 7.5 lists some irrational beliefs that are reported by many insomniacs, and suggests some rational alternatives.

Don't Ruminate in Bed Don't plan or worry about tomorrow while in bed (Kupfer & Reynolds, 1997). When you lie down for sleep, you may organize your thoughts for the day for a few minutes, but then allow yourself to relax or engage in fantasy. If an important idea comes to you, jot it down on a handy pad so that you won't lose it. If thoughts persist, however, get up and follow them elsewhere. Let your bed be a place for relaxation and sleep—not your second office. A bed—even a waterbed—is not a think tank.

TABLE 7.5 SOME IRRATIONAL BELIEFS ABOUT SLEEP AND RATIONAL ALTERNATIVES

IRRATIONAL BELIEF	*RATIONAL ALTERNATIVE*
"If I don't get to sleep, I'll feel wrecked tomorrow."	"Not necessarily. If I'm tired, I can go to bed early tomorrow night."
"It's unhealthy for me not to get more sleep."	"Not necessarily. Some people get only a few hours of sleep each night and lead apparently normal lives. I may not need 8 hours at all."
"I'll wreck my schedule for the whole week if I don't get to sleep very soon."	"Not at all. I don't need a schedule for the week. I'll just get up in time to do what I have to do in the morning. I can catch up by going to bed early tomorrow night, if I'm tired."
"If I don't get to sleep, I won't be able to concentrate on that big test/conference in the morning."	"Possibly, but my fears may also be exaggerated. I may just as well relax, or get up and do something enjoyable. There's no point to just lying here and worrying."

Note: Irrational thoughts increase our tensions at bedtime, contributing to insomnia. Rational alternatives tend to lower our tensions by granting us a proper perspective.

Establish a Regular Routine Sleeping late can encourage insomnia. Set your alarm for the same time each morning and get up, regardless of how many hours you have slept (Lacks & Morin, 1992). By rising at a regular time, you'll encourage yourself to go to sleep at a regular time as well.

Using Fantasy: Taking Nightly Mind Trips Mind trips have advantages over real trips. They're less expensive and you conserve energy. In bed at night, mind trips may also distract you from what you may see as your nightly burden—confronting insomnia and forcing yourself to somehow get to sleep. You may be able to ease yourself to sleep by focusing on pleasant images, such as lying on a sun-drenched beach and listening to waves lapping on the shore or walking through a summer meadow high among the hills.

Above all, accept the idea that it really doesn't matter if you don't get to sleep early *this night*. You will survive. (You really will, you know.) In fact, you'll do just fine.

adjustment and modern life

One third of Americans are obese and half are on a diet at any point in time. There is thus little doubt that weight control is central to adjustment in the United States. Here, we consider self-control strategies for weight control.

HOW TO TAKE IT OFF AND KEEP IT OFF—WEIGHT, THAT IS

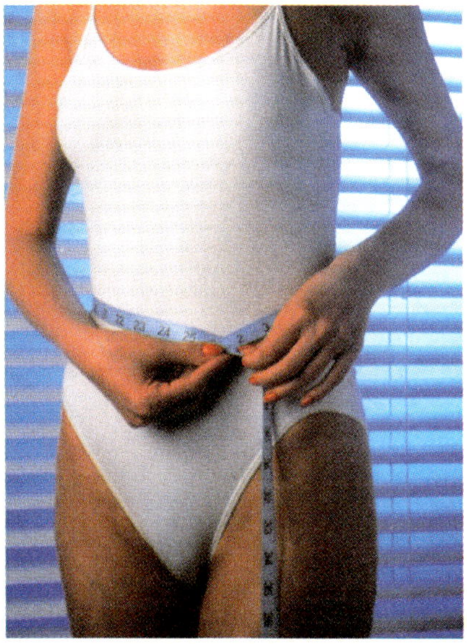

How Does She Measure Up?
Successful dieters do not rely on dangerous fads. Instead, they make changes in lifestyle that involve setting reasonable goals, improving nutritional knowledge, controlling calorie intake, and exercise.

Research shows that successful weight control does not require drastic and dangerous fad diets, such as fasting, eliminating carbohydrates, or downing gobs of grapefruit or rice. Successful diets involve changes in lifestyle that allow you to reduce and then to maintain a more healthful weight. The methods include setting reasonable goals, improving nutritional knowledge, decreasing calorie intake, exercise, modifying behavior, and tracking your progress.

Setting Reasonable Goals

Select a reasonable goal for your post-diet weight. You can use standard height/weight tables, but your ideal weight also depends on how much muscle you have (muscle weighs more than fat). Your physician may be able to make a judgment about how much fat you have by using (painless) skinfold calipers.

Gradual weight loss is usually more effective than crash dieting. Don't expect to lose 10 pounds a week through some fad diet. All you'll probably lose is water weight, if you lose that, and you may jeopardize your health into the bargain. Assume that you'll lose 1 to 2 pounds per week, and focus on the long-term outlook.

Improving Nutritional Knowledge

Eating fewer **calories** is the central method for decreasing weight, so we need some nutritional knowledge. Knowledge will prevent us from depriving ourselves of essential food elements and can suggest strategies for losing tonnage without feeling overly deprived. Taking in fewer calories doesn't only mean eating smaller portions. It means switching to some lower-calorie foods—relying more on fresh, unsweetened fruits and vegetables (apples rather than apple pie); lean meats; fish and poultry; and skim milk and cheese. It means cutting down on—or eliminating—butter, margarine, oils, and sugar.

Calories • Food energy; scientifically, units expressing the ability to raise temperature or give off body heat.

The foods that help us control our weight also tend to be high in vitamins and fiber and low in fats. So they also lower our risk of cardiovascular disorders, cancer, and other illnesses.

TABLE 7.6 CALORIES EXPENDED IN 1 HOUR ACCORDING TO ACTIVITY AND BODY WEIGHT

	BODY WEIGHT (in pounds)				
ACTIVITY	***100***	***125***	***150***	***175***	***200***
Sleeping	40	50	60	70	80
Sitting quietly	60	75	90	105	120
Standing quietly	70	88	105	123	140
Eating	80	100	120	140	160
Driving, housework	95	119	143	166	190
Desk work	100	125	150	175	200
Walking slowly	133	167	200	233	267
Walking rapidly	200	250	300	350	400
Swimming	320	400	480	560	640
Running	400	500	600	700	800

One pound of body weight roughly equals 3,500 calories. As a rule of thumb, if you eat 3,500 more calories than your body requires in order to maintain its proper weight, you will gain a pound or so.[3] If you eat 3,500 fewer calories than you burn, you will lose a pound or so. How many calories do you burn in a day? As you can see from Table 7.6, your calorie expenditure is a function of your activity level and, yes, of your weight. Gender and age figure in somewhat, but not as much.

The guidelines in Table 7.6 will help you arrive at an estimate. Let's follow Paul, a rather sedentary office worker, through his day. He weighs 150 pounds. First, he records 8 hours of sleep a night. As we see in Table 7.7, that's 8 times 60, or 480 calories. He spends about 6 hours a day at the desk, for another 900 calories. He eats for about an hour (120 calories) and drives for an hour (143 calories). He admits to himself that he spends about 5 hours a day in quiet sitting, watching television and reading (525 calories). He has begun an exercise program of walking rapidly for an hour a day—that's 300 calories. Another couple of hours of desk work at home—working on his stamp collection and other hobbies (300 calories)—accounts for the remainder of the day. In this typical weekday, Paul burns up about 2,768 calories.

If you weigh less than Paul, your calorie expenditure will probably be less than his, unless you are more active.

The information in Table 7.7 can help you estimate the number of calories you burn each day. To lose weight you need to take in fewer calories, burn more, or do both.

Truth or Fiction Revisited

It is true that a 220-pound person burns more calories running around the track than a 125-pound person does. The heavier person is doing more work. (Do *not* interpret this fact to mean that one should gain weight to lose weight, however!)

[3] Actually, you may gain a bit less because the body makes some effort to compensate for excess calories by using more of them to digest excess food. But you will gain weight.

TABLE 7.7 APPROXIMATE NUMBER OF CALORIES BURNED BY PAUL* ON A TYPICAL WEEKDAY

ACTIVITY	*HOURS/DAY*		*CALORIES/ HOUR*		*SUBTOTAL*
Sleeping	8	×	60	=	480
Desk work	6	×	150	=	900
Eating	1	×	120	=	120
Driving	1	×	143	=	143
Sitting quietly	5	×	105	=	525
Walking rapidly	1	×	300	=	300
Hobbies	2	×	150	=	300
TOTALS	**24**				**2,768**

*Based on a body weight of 150 pounds.

Decreasing Calorie Intake

To lower calorie intake, consult a calorie book and a physician. The book will suggest what to eat and what to avoid and enable you to track your calorie intake. The physician will tell you how extensively you may restrict your calorie intake.

Establish specific weight-loss plans, including daily calorie intake goals. If the daily goal sounds forbidding—such as eating 500 calories a day fewer than you do now—you can gradually approach it. For example, reduce daily intake, say, by 100 calories for a few days or a week, then 200 calories, and so on.

Behavior modification programs employ self-monitoring or tracking. In weight control it is usually better to track calorie intake than weight. Temporary fluctuations, such as water retention, can make tracking of weight a frustrating experience.

Before cutting down, determine your calorie-intake baseline. Record the calories you consume throughout the day *and* the sorts of encounters that make it difficult to exercise self-control.[4] Keep a notebook and jot down the following:

What you have eaten

Estimated number of calories (use the calorie book)

Time of day, location, your activity, and your reactions to eating

Your record may suggest foods that you need to cut down on or eliminate; places you should avoid; and times of day, such as midafternoon or late

[4] If it is difficult to continue to overeat while engaging in tracking of calories, feel free to cut down and thereby sacrifice the integrity of the record somewhat.

evening, when you are particularly vulnerable to snacking. Planning small, low-calorie snacks (or distracting activities) for these times will prevent you from feeling deprived and inhaling two shelves of the refrigerator.

Once you have established your baseline, maintain a daily record of calories consumed throughout the weight-loss program. Weigh yourself as often as you wish, but use calories, not weight, as your guiding principle.

Exercise

Why exercise? For many reasons. First of all, exercise burns calories. Dieting plus exercise is more effective than dieting alone for shedding pounds and keeping them off. When we restrict our intake of calories, our metabolic rate compensates by slowing down (Wadden and others, 1997). Exercise burns calories and builds muscle tissue, which metabolizes more calories than fatty tissue does.

Behavior Modification

The self-monitoring of calorie intake is a behavior modification method. Let us expand your use of behavior modification by adding a number of self-control strategies (described in Chapter 9). Pick ones that sound right for you. If they work, continue with them. If not, discard them and try others.

Restricting the Stimulus Field

- Eat in the dining area only.
- Break the habit of eating while watching television or studying.

Avoiding Powerful Triggers for Eating

- Avoid trouble spots identified in your baseline record. Shop at the mall with the Alfalfa Sprout Restaurant, not the Gushy Gloppy Shoppe.
- Use smaller plates. Remove or throw out leftover foods quickly.
- Don't starve yourself—deprivation may lead to binge eating.
- Don't read that appetizing restaurant menu. Order according to prearranged plan.
- Pay attention to your own plate only—not the sumptuous dish at the next table.
- Shop from a list. Walk briskly through the market, preferably after dinner, when you're no longer hungry. Don't browse. The colorful, appetizing packages may stimulate you to make unwise purchases.
- Keep out of the kitchen. Study, watch television, write letters elsewhere.

Response Prevention

- Keep fattening foods out of the house.
- Prepare only enough food to remain within the restrictions of your diet.

What Do You Say Now?

RESISTING AN INVITATION TO EAT

Part of the challenge of following a self-control program for losing weight is maintaining control in a social environment. It's relatively easy to rid your own house of fattening foods, but what do you do when you're with the relatives over the holidays, or at a party, and your host brings out the Boston cream pie, "made especially for you"?

"Look at what I've got!" your host exclaims. "Your favorite. I baked it just for you, and I know you're going to love it."

What do you say now? Write down the responses that come to mind in the spaces below, and then note some of the following suggestions.

1. ______________________________

2. ______________________________

3. ______________________________

What a dilemma! It's not easy to disappoint a close relative or friend, yet you have been doing such an excellent job of maintaining control. It is helpful if you have anticipated situations such as this—they're bound to arise—and prepared responses for them, such as the following:

1. "That looks great, Uncle Harry! I really appreciate your going to all this trouble for me, but I've been on a diet for 3 months now, and it's important to me. So I'll have to be content with that marvelous turkey you served!"
2. "That looks wonderful, but I've been feeling so much better since I've cut back on desserts. I'll feel good while I'm eating it, but then I'll feel terrible for days, so I have to pass.
3. "I'd love a piece, but I'm determined to fit into my bikini this July."
4. If Uncle Harry says, "Don't be silly, this is Thanksgiving—come on, now," you can say something like, "Yes, and I want to have something to be thankful about, like staying on my diet!" (If it's Christmas, you can say, "Yes, and I'd like to have something to be merry about," etc.)
5. If Uncle Harry says, "Oh, just have a mouthful. I made it especially for you," you can say something like, "I really appreciate it, but it will be torture for me to just have one mouthful, especially of your delicious pie. Have mercy!"
6. If Uncle Harry says, "Don't be silly, you're already skinny as a rail," you can say something like, "Thanks for the compliment, but I've still got a way to go." By the way, if many people are telling you that you're skinny and should stop dieting, perhaps it wouldn't hurt to get an impartial medical opinion on the subject.

Note, too, that it's possible to make occasional exceptions when you are dieting—so long as you continue to conceptualize yourself as being on a diet and do not catastrophize the exception. If you believe that the possibility of making exceptions will be of help to you, include it as part of your original dieting plan—make a note of it. But if your experiences lead you to believe that it would do you more harm than good to make exceptions and eat the pie, or a few mouthfuls, stick to your guns.

And if you still eat the pie, notice that the world hasn't caved in on you. Try not to catastrophize; return to your diet right after you brush the taste of the pie out of your mouth—which it would be advisable to do quickly. ■

Using Competing Responses

- Stuff your mouth with celery, not ice cream or candy.
- Eat premade, low-calorie snacks instead of losing control and inhaling a jar of peanuts.
- Try jogging for half an hour instead of eating an unplanned snack.
- Reach for your mate, to coin a phrase—not for your plate.

Chain Breaking—Making Emily Post Happy

- Always make a place setting before eating, even a snack.
- Take small bites. Chew slowly and thoroughly.
- Put down your utensils between bites.
- Take a 5-minute break during the meal to allow your blood sugar level to rise and signal that you're no longer famished. Ask yourself if you need to finish *every* bite when you return.

Building Desired Habits by Successive Approximations

- Increase your daily calorie deficit by 100 calories each week so that you won't feel deprived by a sudden plunge.
- Schedule frequent, low-calorie snacks as dieting gets under way. Gradually space them farther apart and eliminate one or two.
- Build your daily exercise routine by just a few minutes each week.
- Eliminate fattening foods from your diet one by one.

Making Rewards Contingent on Desired Behavior

- Do not eat dinner unless you have exercised during the day.
- Do not go to see that great new film unless you have met your weekly calorie-intake goal. Each time you meet your weekly calorie-intake goal, put cash in the bank toward a vacation or new camera.

Response Cost

- Keep a dollar bill in a stamped envelope addressed to your least favorite cause. If the cheesecake wins, mail it at once.
- Dock yourself a dollar toward the camera every time the cheesecake wins.

Covert Reinforcement and Covert Sensitization

- Imagine reaching for something fattening—Stop! and congratulate yourself for doing so. Imagine your pride; imagine friends patting you on the back.
- Imagine how wonderful you're going to look in that brief swimsuit on the beach next summer. Mentally rehearse your next visit to relatives who usually try to stuff you with your favorite foods. Imagine how you will po-

litely but firmly refuse seconds. Think of how proud of yourself you'll be.

- Tempted by a fattening dish? Imagine that it's rotten, that you would be nauseated by it and have a sick taste in your mouth for the rest of the day.
- Tempted to binge? Strip before the mirror and handle a fatty area of your body. Ask yourself if you *really* want to make it larger or would prefer to exercise self-control?
- When tempted, think of the extra work your heart must do for every pound of extra weight. Imagine your arteries clogging with dreaded substances (not far off base).
- Keep 6 to 10 business-size cards in your wallet. On half of them print proreducing statements such as "I'll be able to fit in that new swimsuit if I'm careful," "I can get rid of this awful roll of fat," and "I'll be sexually appealing." Print anti-overeating statements on the others, such as "Think of the way you look in a mirror," "Think of how sick you feel after you binge on cake," and so on. Shuffle the cards and read them each time you're about to leave home or engage in another frequent activity. Keep them fresh by rotating them with alternate messages. The benefits of losing and the perils of gaining will tend to remain in your mind.

Tracking Your Progress

Keep a record of how you are doing. Day-to-day weight measures can be misleading, but in the intermediate term (say, monthly scale readings) and in the long run (say, 6-month readings), your weight should be dropping.

An alternative is to track the body circumferences measurements that are of concern to you every 3 or 4 weeks. Measure your waist, thighs, hips, or anything else of interest to you. ■

SUMMARY

1. **What are the essential food elements?** People need to eat proteins, carbohydrates, fats, vitamins, and minerals. Americans tend to eat too much protein and fats. Complex carbohydrates (starches) are superior to simple carbohydrates (sugars) as sources of nutrients.
2. **How do nutritional patterns influence our health?** Cholesterol, fats, and obesity heighten the risk of cardiovascular disorders. Salt raises the blood pressure. Fats and preservatives heighten the risk of cancer. Diets high in fiber, vitamins, fruits and vegetables, and fish are apparently healthful.
2. **What factors contribute to obesity?** Risk factors for obesity include family history, overeating, and a low level of activity. Obese people have more fat cells than normal-weight people.
4. **What is anorexia nervosa?** Anorexia nervosa is an eating disorder characterized by dramatic weight loss and intense fear of being overweight. Anorexic females also show amenorrhea; that is, they stop menstruating. Anorexic women have a distorted body image in which they view themselves as overweight when others perceive them as dangerously thin.
5. **What is bulimia nervosa?** In bulimia nervosa, the individual also fears becoming overweight, but goes on eating binges, especially of carbohydrates. Binge eating is followed by severe weight-loss methods such as fasting or self-induced vomiting.
6. **How do activity patterns influence our health?** Physical inactivity is a risk factor for cardiovascular disorders. Exercise has the benefits of promoting muscle strength, muscle endurance, flexibility, cardiorespiratory fitness, and a higher muscle-to-fat ratio. Exercise also appears to alleviate depression and anxiety and to boost self-esteem.
7. **How do sleeping patterns influence our health?** Sleep appears to serve a general restorative function, although the mechanisms are unclear. Sleep deprivation over a few days does not appear particularly harmful, although there are some cognitive lapses and drowsiness during the day.
8. **Why are psychologists opposed to using sleeping pills to get to sleep?** We develop a tolerance for sleeping pills so that we need progressively larger doses. Moreover, we attribute getting to sleep to the pills, not our self-efficacy.
9. **What are some psychological methods of coping with insomnia?** Psychological methods include lowering arousal, challenging irrational beliefs (such as the thought that something awful will happen if you don't get enough sleep tonight), using fantasy to distract yourself from the "task" of getting to sleep, and using stimulus control so that your bed comes to mean "sleep" to you.
10. **What are some psychological methods of weight control?** Psychologists focus on setting reasonable goals, improving nutritional knowledge (e.g., substituting healthful food for fattening, harmful foods), decreasing calorie intake, exercise in order to raise the metabolic rate, behavior modification to help us avoid temptations and eat less, and tracking progress.

CHAPTER 8

Substance Abuse and Adjustment

TRUTH OR FICTION?

✓ T F

- ☐ ☐ People can inherit a tendency to become dependent on certain drugs.
- ☐ ☐ Alcohol goes to women's heads more quickly than to men's.
- ☐ ☐ Nicotine enhances memory functioning.
- ☐ ☐ The number of people who die from smoking-related causes is greater than the total number lost to motor vehicle accidents, abuse of alcohol and all other drugs, suicide, homicide, and AIDS combined.
- ☐ ☐ Coca-Cola once "added life" by using cocaine.
- ☐ ☐ Marijuana facilitates social interaction.
- ☐ ☐ Heroin was once used as a cure for addiction to morphine.
- ☐ ☐ It is helpful to tell relatives and friends of plans to quit smoking.

OUTLINE

THE WORLD IS A SUPERMARKET OF **PSYCHOACTIVE** substances, or drugs. The United States is flooded with hundreds of drugs that distort perceptions and change mood—drugs that take you up, let you down, and move you across town. Some people use drugs because their friends do, or because their parents tell them not to. Others get started with doctors' prescriptions, coffee, or their first aspirin tablet. Some are seeking pleasure; others, relief from pain; still others, inner truth.

Given laws, moral pronouncements, medical warnings, and an occasional horror story, drug use has declined somewhat in recent years (Johnston and others, 1996). But overall, drugs—especially alcohol, cigarettes, and marijuana—remain an integral part of American life (see Table 8.1).

SUBSTANCE ABUSE, DEPENDENCE, INTOXICATION, AND WITHDRAWAL

Where does drug use end and abuse begin? The American Psychiatric Association (1994) defines **substance abuse** as repeated use of a substance despite the fact that it is causing or compounding social, occupational, psychological, or physical problems. If you are missing school or work because you are drunk or "sleeping it off," you are abusing alcohol. The amount you drink is not as crucial as the fact that your pattern of use disrupts your life.

Substance dependence is more severe than abuse. Dependence has both behavioral and biological aspects (American Psychiatric Association, 1994). Behaviorally, dependence is often characterized by loss of control over one's use of the substance. Dependent people may organize their lives around getting and using a substance. Biological or physiological dependence is typified by tolerance, withdrawal symptoms, or both.[1] **Tolerance** is the body's habituation to a substance, so that with regular usage, higher doses are required to achieve similar effects. There are characteristic withdrawal symptoms, or an **abstinence syndrome,** when the level of usage suddenly drops off. The abstinence syndrome for alcohol includes anxiety, tremors, restlessness, weakness, rapid pulse, and high blood pressure.

When doing without a drug, people who are *psychologically* dependent show signs of anxiety (shakiness, rapid pulse, and sweating are three) that overlap abstinence syndromes. Because of these signs, they may believe that they are physiologically dependent on a drug when they are psychologically dependent. Still, symptoms of abstinence from certain drugs are unmistakably physio-

Psychoactive • Having psychological effects.

Substance abuse • Continued use of a substance despite knowledge that it is dangerous or that it is linked to social, occupational, psychological, or physical problems.

Substance dependence • Dependence on a substance, shown by signs such as persistent use despite efforts to cut down, marked tolerance, and withdrawal symptoms.

Tolerance • The body's habituation to a drug, so that with regular use, increasingly higher doses of the drug are needed to achieve similar effects.

Abstinence syndrome • A characteristic cluster of symptoms that results from sudden decrease in the level of use of an addictive drug.

---

[1] The lay term *addiction* is usually used to mean physiological dependence, but here, too, there may be inconsistency. After all, some people speak of being "addicted" to work or to love.

TABLE 8.1 TRENDS IN DRUG USE AMONG COLLEGE STUDENTS DURING LIFETIME AND DURING LAST 30 DAYS (IN PERCENTS)

DRUG	*USED*	*1980*	*1982*	*1984*	*1986*	*1988*	*1990*	*1992*	*1994*
Marijuana	Ever?	65.0	60.5	59.0	57.9	51.3	49.1	44.1	42.2
	Last 30 days?	34.0	26.8	23.0	22.3	16.3	14.0	14.6	15.1
Inhalants	Ever?	10.2	10.6	10.4	11.0	12.6	13.9	14.2	12.0
	Last 30 days?	1.5	0.8	0.7	1.1	1.3	1.0	1.1	0.6
Hallucinogens (includes LSD)	Ever?	15.0	15.0	12.9	11.2	10.2	11.2	12.0	10.0
	Last 30 days?	2.7	2.6	1.8	2.2	1.7	1.4	2.3	2.1
Cocaine (includes crack)	Ever?	22.0	22.4	21.7	23.3	15.8	11.4	7.9	5.0
	Last 30 days?	6.9	7.9	7.6	7.0	4.2	1.2	1.0	0.6
MDMA	Ever?	NA	NA	NA	NA	NA	3.9	2.9	2.1
	Last 30 days?	NA	NA	NA	NA	NA	0.6	0.4	0.2
Heroin	Ever?	0.9	0.5	0.5	0.4	0.3	0.3	0.5	0.1
	Last 30 days?	0.3	0.0	0.0	0.0	0.1	0.0	0.0	0.0
Stimulants (other than cocaine)	Ever?	NA	30.1	27.8	22.3	17.7	13.2	10.5	9.2
	Last 30 days?	NA	9.9	5.5	3.7	1.8	1.4	1.1	1.5
Barbiturates	Ever?	8.1	8.2	6.4	5.4	3.6	3.8	3.8	3.2
	Last 30 days?	0.9	1.0	0.7	0.6	0.5	0.2	0.7	0.4
Alcohol	Ever?	94.3	95.2	94.2	94.9	94.9	93.1	91.8	88.1
	Last 30 days?	81.8	82.8	79.1	79.7	77.0	74.5	71.4	67.5
Cigarettes	Ever?	NA	NA	NA	NA	NA	NA	NA	NA
	Last 30 days?	25.8	24.4	21.5	22.4	22.6	21.5	23.5	23.5

Source: From Johnston, L. D., O'Malley, P. M., & Bachman, J. G. (1996). *National Survey Results on Drug Use From the Monitoring the Future Study, 1975–1994. Volume II. College Students and Young Adults.* U.S. Department of Health and Human Services, Public Health Service, National Institutes of Health: National Institute on Drug Abuse, tables 23 (p. 160) and 25 (p. 162).

logical. One is **delirium tremens** (known as "the DTs"), encountered by some chronic alcoholics when they suddenly lower intake. The DTs are characterized by heavy sweating, restlessness, general **disorientation,** and terrifying **hallucinations**—often of creepy, crawling animals.

Causal Factors in Substance Abuse and Dependence

Substance abuse and dependence usually begin with experimental use (Kessler, 1995; Petraitis and others, 1995). Why do people experiment with drugs? Reasons include curiosity, conformity to peer pressure, parental use, rebelliousness, and escape from boredom or pressure (Chassin and others, 1996; Curran and others, 1997). Another reason is self-handicapping. By using alcohol or another drug when faced with a problem, we can blame failure on the alcohol, not on ourselves. Alcohol and other drugs are used as excuses for behaviors such as aggression, sexual forwardness, and forgetfulness.

Consider some psychological and biological theories of substance abuse.

PSYCHOLOGICAL VIEWS Psychodynamic explanations of substance abuse propose that drugs help people control or express unconscious needs and impulses. Alcoholism, for example, may reflect the need to remain dependent on an overprotective mother.

DELIRIUM TREMENS • A condition characterized by sweating, restlessness, disorientation, and hallucinations.

DISORIENTATION • Gross confusion. Loss of sense of time, place, and the identity of people.

HALLUCINATIONS • Perceptions in the absence of sensation that are confused with reality.

Social-cognitive theorists suggest that people commonly try tranquilizing agents such as Valium and alcohol on the basis of a recommendation or observation of others. Cognitive psychologists note that expectancies about the effects of a substance are powerful predictors of its use (Schafer & Brown, 1991; Sher and others, 1996). Use may be reinforced by the drug's positive effects on mood and its reduction of unpleasant sensations such as anxiety, fear, and tension. For people who are physiologically dependent, avoidance of withdrawal symptoms is also reinforcing. Carrying a supply of the substance is reinforcing because one need not worry about doing without it. Some people, for example, will not leave home without taking along some Valium.

Parents who use drugs may increase their children's knowledge of drugs. They also, in effect, show their children when to use them—for example, when they are seeking to reduce tension or to "lubricate" social interactions (Stacy and others, 1991).

Truth or Fiction Revisited

It is true that people can inherit a tendency to become dependent on certain drugs. But this does not mean that other people are immune from becoming dependent on them.

BIOLOGICAL VIEWS Certain people may have a genetic predisposition toward physiological dependence on various substances, including alcohol, cocaine, and nicotine (Azar, 1995; Haney and others, 1994; Pomerleau and others, 1993). For example, the biological children of alcoholics who are reared by adoptive parents seem more likely to develop alcohol-related problems than the natural children of the adoptive parents. An inherited tendency toward alcoholism may involve greater sensitivity to alcohol (that is, greater enjoyment of it) and greater tolerance of it (Finn and others, 1997; Newlin & Thomson, 1990). College students with alcoholic parents exhibit better muscular control and visual-motor coordination when they drink than do college students whose parents are not alcoholics. They also feel less intoxicated when they drink (Pihl and others, 1990).

Let us now consider the effects of a number of drugs, beginning with alcohol.

ALCOHOL

One friend had been struck by Leslie's piercing green eyes. Another recounted how Leslie had loved to dance barefoot at parties. Leslie spent a semester in Italy, and another friend recalled how they had been stranded one night in Rome. They had needed a bus ride but were without a transit pass. Leslie had impetuously jumped aboard a bus and quipped that they could hop out the back door if someone objected. A roommate remembered Leslie studying curled up on the couch in wool socks and a heavy sweater. She described how Leslie ate handfuls of chocolate chips straight from the bag and picked the marshmallows out of Lucky Charms cereal. She even remembered the time that Leslie baked a tuna casserole without removing the Saran Wrap. Leslie had been an art major and her professors described her work as promising (Winerip, 1998). Her overall GPA at the University of Virginia had been 3.67 and she had been in the middle of preparing her senior essay on a Polish-born sculptor. But she did not finish the essay or graduate. Instead, Leslie died from falling down a flight of stairs after binge drinking alcohol. While deaths from heroin or cocaine overdoses may get more publicity, hundreds of college students die from alcohol-related causes (overdoses, accidents, and the like) each year. As many as 10 or so University of Virginia students alone wind up in a hospital emergency room each weekend due to alcohol-related causes.

Why alcohol?

Perhaps because no drug has meant so much to so many as alcohol. Alcohol is our dinnertime relaxant, our bedtime sedative, our cocktail-party social facilitator. We celebrate holy days, applaud our accomplishments, and express joyous wishes with alcohol. The young assert their maturity with alcohol (nearly nine in ten college students have used it, and two of three have done so within the past

DOES ALCOHOL GO TO WOMEN'S HEADS MORE QUICKLY THAN MEN'S?

Research suggests that women may be more sensitive to the psychoactive effects of alcohol than men are. Why? Similarly, there are apparently genetic and ethnic differences in sensitivity to the effects of alcohol.

month [Johnston and others, 1996]). The elderly use alcohol to stimulate circulation in peripheral areas of the body. Alcohol kills germs on surface wounds.

Alcohol is the tranquilizer you can buy without prescription. It is the relief from anxiety you can swallow in public without criticism or stigma. A man who pops a Valium tablet may look weak. A man who chug-a-lugs a bottle of beer may be perceived as "macho."

No drug has been so abused as alcohol. Ten to 20 million Americans are **alcoholics.** By contrast, 200,000 use heroin regularly, and 300,000 to 500,000 abuse sedatives.

Alcohol remains the BDOC (Big Drug on Campus). In 1996, more than two out of three college students reported using alcohol at least once in the past month (Johnston and others, 1996). Perhaps two out of five were binge drinkers.

Consider a survey of 1,100 undergraduates at the University of Virginia (Grossman, 1991). Results showed that 43 percent of the respondents were "heavy drinkers"—meaning that they had imbibed at least five alcoholic beverages in a row on one occasion within the 2 weeks preceding the survey. This pattern of drinking is also termed *binge drinking* (Winerip, 1998). *More than half* of the binge drinkers reported that under the influence of alcohol, they had engaged in sexual relations with someone they would not otherwise have become involved with. All in all, between one in four and one in five students in the total sample had engaged in sexual relations they considered to be unwise when they were under the influence of alcohol!

ALCOHOLIC • A person whose drinking persistently impairs his or her personal, social, or physical well-being.

Adjustment in a World of DIVERSITY

Alcoholism, Gender, and Ethnicity

Men are much more likely than women to become alcoholics. A cultural explanation is that tighter social constraints are usually placed on women. A biological explanation is that alcohol hits women harder. If, for example, you have the impression that alcohol "goes to women's heads" more quickly than to men's, you are probably correct. Women seem to be more affected by alcohol because they metabolize very little of it in the stomach. Thus, alcohol reaches women's bloodstreams and brains relatively intact. (Women have less of an enzyme that metabolizes alcohol in the stomach than men do [Lieber, 1990].) Women mainly metabolize alcohol in the liver. For women, reports one health professional, "drinking alcohol has the same effect as injecting it intravenously" (Lieber, 1990). Strong stuff, indeed.

Despite their greater responsiveness to small quantities of alcohol, women who drink heavily are apparently as likely as men to become alcoholics.

Some ethnic factors are connected with alcohol abuse. Native Americans and Irish Americans have the highest rates of alcoholism in the United States (Lex, 1987; Moncher and others, 1990). Jews have relatively low rates of alcoholism, and a cultural explanation is usually offered. Jews tend to expose children to alcohol (wine) early in life, within a strong family or religious context. Wine is offered in small quantities, with consequent low blood-alcohol levels. Alcohol is thus not connected with rebellion, aggression, or failure in Jewish culture.

There are also biological explanations for low levels of drinking among some ethnic groups such as Asians. Asians are more likely than White people to show a "flushing response" to alcohol, as evidenced by rapid heart rate, dizziness, and headaches (Ellickson and others, 1992). Sensitivity to alcohol may inhibit immoderate drinking among Asians as among women.

Truth or Fiction Revisited

It is true that alcohol goes to women's heads more quickly than to men's. Women are less likely to metabolize alcohol before it affects psychological functioning.

SELF-ASSESSMENT

WHY DO YOU DRINK?

Do you drink? If so, why? To enhance your pleasure? To cope with your problems? To help you in your social encounters? Because you will feel withdrawal symptoms if you don't? Half of all Americans use alcohol, and as many as 1 user in 10 is an alcoholic. The expectation that alcohol helps reduce tension encourages many college students to drink. ■

Directions: To gain insight into your reasons for using alcohol, respond to the following items by checking off *T* if an item is true or mostly true for you, or *F* if an item is false or mostly false for you. Then turn to the answer key in the Appendix.

✔ T	F		
☐	☐	1.	I find it painful to go without alcohol for any period of time.
☐	☐	2.	It's easier for me to relate to other people when I have been drinking.
☐	☐	3.	I drink so that I will look more mature and sophisticated.
☐	☐	4.	My future prospects seem brighter when I have been drinking.
☐	☐	5.	I enjoy the taste of beer, wine, or hard liquor.
☐	☐	6.	I don't feel disturbed or uncomfortable in any way if I go for a long time without having a drink.
☐	☐	7.	When I drink, I feel calmer and less edgy about things.
☐	☐	8.	I drink in order to fit in better with the crowd.
☐	☐	9.	When I am drinking, I worry less about things.
☐	☐	10.	I have a drink when I'm together with my family.
☐	☐	11.	Drinking is a part of my religious ceremonies.
☐	☐	12.	I'll have a drink to help deaden the pain of a toothache or some other physical problem.
☐	☐	13.	I feel that I can do almost anything when I'm drinking.
☐	☐	14.	You really can't blame people for the things they do when they have been drinking.
☐	☐	15.	I'll have a drink before a big exam or a big date so that I feel less concerned about how things will go.
☐	☐	16.	I like to drink for the taste of it.
☐	☐	17.	There have been times when I've found a drink in my hand even though I can't remember placing it there.
☐	☐	18.	I tend to drink when I feel down or when I want to take my mind off my troubles.
☐	☐	19.	I find that I do better both socially and sexually after I've had a drink or two.
☐	☐	20.	I have to admit that drinking sometimes makes me do reckless and asinine things.

✔ T	F		
☐	☐	21.	I have missed classes or work because of having a few too many.
☐	☐	22.	I feel that I am more generous and sympathetic when I have been drinking.
☐	☐	23.	One of the reasons I drink is that I like the look of a drinker.
☐	☐	24.	I like to have a drink or two on festive occasions and special days.
☐	☐	25.	My friends and I are likely to go drinking when one of us has done something well, like "aced out" a tough exam or made some great plays on the team.
☐	☐	26.	I'll have a drink or two when some predicament is gnawing away at me.
☐	☐	27.	Drinking gives me pleasure.
☐	☐	28.	Frankly, one of the lures of drinking is getting high.
☐	☐	29.	Sometimes I'm surprised to find that I've poured a drink when another one is still unfinished.
☐	☐	30.	I find that I'm better at getting other people to do what I want them to do when I've been drinking.
☐	☐	31.	Having a drink keeps my mind off my problems at home, at school, or at work.
☐	☐	32.	I get a real gnawing hunger for a drink when I haven't had one for a while.
☐	☐	33.	One or two drinks relax me.
☐	☐	34.	Things tend to look better when I've been drinking.
☐	☐	35.	I find that my mood is much improved when I've had a drink or two.
☐	☐	36.	I can usually see things more clearly when I've had a drink or two.
☐	☐	37.	One or two drinks heightens the pleasure of food and sex.
☐	☐	38.	When I run out of alcohol, I buy more right away.
☐	☐	39.	I think that I would have done better on some things if it hadn't been for the alcohol.
☐	☐	40.	When I'm out of alcohol, things are practically unbearable until I can obtain some more.
☐	☐	41.	I drink at fraternity or sorority parties.
☐	☐	42.	When I think about the future and what I'm going to do, I often go and have a drink.
☐	☐	43.	I like to go out for a drink when I've gotten a good grade.
☐	☐	44.	I usually have a drink or two with dinner.
☐	☐	45.	There have been times when it's been rough to get through a class or through practice because I wanted a drink.

Alcohol and Health

As a food, alcohol is fattening. Yet chronic drinkers may be malnourished. Though high in calories, alcohol does not contain nutrients such as vitamins and proteins. Moreover, alcohol can interfere with the body's absorption of vitamins, particularly thiamine, a B vitamin. Chronic drinking can thus lead to a number of disorders, such as **cirrhosis of the liver,** which has been linked to protein deficiency, and to **Wernicke-Korsakoff syndrome,** which has been linked to vitamin B deficiency (Nevid and others, 1998). Chronic drinking has also been linked to coronary heart disease and high blood pressure (Nevid and others, 1998). Drinking by a pregnant woman may harm the embryo.

CIGARETTES (NICOTINE)

> *Smoking: a "custome lothesome to the Eye, hatefull to the Nose, harmefull to the Braine, dangerous to the Lungs."*
>
> KING JAMES I, 1604

Truth or Fiction Revisited

It is true that nicotine enhances memory functioning. (No, this is not an adequate reason to take up smoking.)

Nicotine is the stimulant in cigarettes. Nicotine stimulates discharge of the hormone adrenaline and the release of many neurotransmitters, including dopamine and acetylcholine. Adrenaline creates a burst of autonomic activity that accelerates the heart rate and pours sugar into the blood. Acetylcholine is vital in memory formation, and nicotine appears to enhance memory and attention (Leary, 1997); improve performance on simple, repetitive tasks (Kinnunen and others, 1996; O'Brien, 1996); and enhance the mood. If you think about it, a stimulant is the opposite of a depressant, and some people apparently use nicotine (smoke) in order to battle feelings of depression (Lerman and others, 1998). Even though nicotine is a stimulant, it also appears to relax people and reduce feelings of stress (O'Brien, 1996).

Some people smoke in order to control their weight (Califano, 1995; Meyers and others, 1997). Nicotine depresses the appetite and raises the metabolic rate (Audrain and others, 1995; Hultquist and others, 1995). People also tend to eat more when they stop smoking (Klesges and others, 1997). This tendency leads some quitters to return to smoking.

Nicotine is the agent that creates physiological dependence on cigarettes (Kessler, 1995). Nicotine may be as addictive—or more addictive—than heroin or cocaine (MacKenzie and others, 1994). Regular smokers adjust their smoking to maintain fairly even levels of nicotine in their bloodstream (Drobes & Tiffany, 1997; Shiffman and others, 1997). Symptoms of withdrawal from nicotine include nervousness, drowsiness, loss of energy, headaches, irregular bowel movements, lightheadedness, insomnia, dizziness, cramps, palpitations, tremors, and sweating. Since many of these symptoms resemble those of anxiety, it was once thought that smoking might be a habit rather than an addiction.

The Perils of Smoking

It's no secret. Cigarette packs sold in the United States carry messages such as "Warning: The Surgeon General Has Determined That Cigarette Smoking Is Dangerous to Your Health." Cigarette advertising has been banned on radio and television. Nearly 420,000 Americans die from smoking-related illnesses each year (Rosenblatt, 1994). This is the equivalent of two jumbo jets colliding in midair each day with all passengers lost. It is higher than the number of people who die from motor vehicle accidents, alcohol and drug abuse, suicide, homicide, and AIDS *combined* (Rosenblatt, 1994).

CIRRHOSIS OF THE LIVER • A disease caused by protein deficiency in which connective fibers replace active liver cells, impeding circulation of the blood. Alcohol does not contain protein; therefore, persons who drink excessively may be prone to this disease.

WERNICKE-KORSAKOFF SYNDROME • A brain dysfunction that is characterized by confusion and disorientation, memory loss for recent events, and visual problems.

The percentage of American adults who smoke declined overall from 42.2 percent in 1966 to about 25 percent in the 1990s, but there have been increases among women, African Americans, and eighth- to twelfth-graders (Feder, 1997; Gold and others, 1996). The incidence of smoking is connected with gender, age, ethnicity, level of education, and socioeconomic status (see Table 8.2). Better-educated people are less likely to smoke. They are also more likely to quit smoking (Rose and others, 1996).

Every cigarette smoked steals about 7 minutes of a person's life. The carbon monoxide in cigarette smoke impairs the blood's ability to carry oxygen, causing shortness of breath (Gold and others, 1996). It is apparently the hydrocarbons ("tars") in cigarette smoke that lead to lung cancer (Stout, 1996). Heavy smokers are about 10 times as likely as nonsmokers to die of lung cancer (Nevid and others, 1998). Cigarette smoking is also linked to death from heart disease, chronic lung and respiratory diseases, and other health problems. Women who smoke show reduced bone density, significantly increasing the risk of fracture of the hip and back (Brody, 1996b; Hopper & Seeman, 1994). Pregnant women who smoke risk miscarriage, premature birth, and birth defects.

Passive smoking is also connected with respiratory illnesses, asthma, and other health problems and accounts for more than 50,000 deaths per year (Nevid and others, 1998). Prolonged exposure to household tobacco smoke during childhood is a risk factor for lung cancer (Janerich and others, 1990). Because of the noxious effects of secondhand smoke, smoking has been banished from many public places such as airplanes, restaurants, and elevators.

Why, then, do people smoke? For many reasons—such as the desire to look sophisticated (though these days smokers may be more likely to be judged foolish than sophisticated), to have something to do with their hands, and—of course—to take in nicotine.

In the chapter's "Adjustment and Modern Life" feature, we describe a number of strategies for cutting down and quitting smoking.

TABLE 8.2 HUMAN DIVERSITY AND SMOKING, UNITED STATES

FACTOR	*GROUP*	*PERCENTAGE IN GROUP WHO SMOKE*
GENDER	Women	23.5
	Men	28.1
AGE	18–24	22.9
	25–44	30.4
	45–64	26.9
	65–74	16.5
	75 and older	8.4
ETHNIC GROUP	African American	29.2
	Asian American/Pacific Islander	16.0
	Hispanic American	20.2
	Native American	31.4
	Non-Hispanic White American	25.5
LEVEL OF EDUCATION	Fewer than 12 years	32.0
	12	30.0
	13–15	23.4
	16 and above	13.6
SOCIOECONOMIC STATUS (SES)	Below poverty level	33.3
	At poverty level or above	24.7

Source: Office of Smoking and Health, Centers for Disease Control (1993).

Truth or Fiction Revisited

It is true that the number of people who die from smoking-related causes is greater than the total number lost to motor vehicle accidents, abuse of alcohol and all other drugs, suicide, homicide, and AIDS.

CIGARETTES: SMOKING GUNS?

The perils of cigarette smoking are widely known today. Cigarette smoking is the chief preventable cause of death in the United States. The numbers of Americans who die from smoking are comparable to two jumbo jets crashing *every day*. If flying were that unsafe, would the government ground all flights? Would the public continue to book airline reservations?

PASSIVE SMOKING • Inhaling smoke from other people's tobacco products; also called *secondhand smoking*.

SELF-ASSESSMENT

WHY DO YOU SMOKE?

These are some statements made by people to describe what they get out of smoking cigarettes. If you smoke, indicate how often you feel the way described in the statement by circling the appropriate number. ■

Important: Answer every question.

1 = never
2 = seldom
3 = occasionally
4 = frequently
5 = always

A.	I smoke cigarettes in order to keep myself from slowing down.	1 2 3 4 5
B.	Handling a cigarette is part of the enjoyment of smoking it.	1 2 3 4 5
C.	Smoking cigarettes is pleasant and relaxing.	1 2 3 4 5
D.	I light up a cigarette when I feel angry about something.	1 2 3 4 5
E.	When I have run out of cigarettes I find it almost unbearable until I get them.	1 2 3 4 5
F.	I smoke cigarettes automatically without even being aware of it.	1 2 3 4 5
G.	I smoke cigarettes to stimulate me, to perk myself up.	1 2 3 4 5
H.	Part of the enjoyment of smoking a cigarette comes from the steps I take to light up.	1 2 3 4 5
I.	I find cigarettes pleasurable.	1 2 3 4 5
J.	When I feel uncomfortable or upset about something, I light up a cigarette.	1 2 3 4 5
K.	I am very much aware of the fact when I am not smoking a cigarette.	1 2 3 4 5
L.	I light up a cigarette without realizing I still have one burning in the ashtray.	1 2 3 4 5
M.	I smoke cigarettes to give me a lift.	1 2 3 4 5
N.	When I smoke a cigarette, part of the enjoyment is watching the smoke as I exhale it.	1 2 3 4 5
O.	I want a cigarette most when I am comfortable and relaxed.	1 2 3 4 5
P.	When I feel blue or want to take my mind off cares and worries, I smoke cigarettes.	1 2 3 4 5
Q.	I get a real gnawing hunger for a cigarette when I haven't smoked for a while.	1 2 3 4 5
R.	I've found a cigarette in my mouth and didn't remember putting it there.	1 2 3 4 5

Source: U.S. Department of Health and Human Services, Public Health Service, National Institutes of Health. *Why Do You Smoke?* (NIH publication No. 87-1822), Bethesda, MD: National Cancer Institute, 1987.

ADJUSTMENT *in the* NEW MILLENNIUM

Will We Find Ways to Make Nicotine (Gasp!) Good for You?

In his movie *Sleeper,* Woody Allen woke up in the new millennium and was informed that research had revealed that cigarettes were actually good for you.

No, cigarettes are *not* good for you. Smoking causes many kinds of cancer and is involved in heart disease and many other health problems, even dental problems (Nevid and others, 1998). Chewing tobacco also causes cancer and other health problems. Nor is there any question that nicotine is addictive. (It is.)

However, nicotine has some positive qualities that are under study and may lead to the development of useful medications in the new millennium. Nicotine turns out to hold potential for the treatment of health problems ranging from Alzheimer's and Parkinson's diseases to schizophrenia (Grady, 1997; Leary, 1997). Nicotine binds to receptors (called *nicotinic cholinergic receptors*) on many kinds of cells, particularly in the brain. There it stimulates the release of neurotransmitters, including dopamine and acetylcholine. Deficiencies of these neurotransmitters are implicated in Parkinson's and Alzheimer's diseases. It has been observed that smokers are less likely to develop these diseases (Leary, 1997). Nicotine may also block the formation of the plaque deposits in the nervous system that characterize Alzheimer's disease (Zagorski, 1997).

It has also been observed that people with schizophrenia smoke heavily (Grady, 1997). People with schizophrenia have difficulty filtering out distractions such as irrelevant sounds, thus impairing their concentration and thought processes. One possible result is hearing voices—sounds that are not really there. This may be connected with a defective structure in the brain whose functioning is aided by nicotine. Thus, when people with schizophrenia smoke, they may be seeking relief from interference in their thought processes (Grady, 1997).

Nobody is suggesting that people take up smoking to alleviate these health problems. The risks of smoking outweigh any potential benefits. However, researchers are developing nicotine-like compounds that are intended to target the symptoms of Parkinson's and Alzheimer's diseases without the problems connected with nicotine (Leary, 1997). ■

COCAINE

Do you recall the commercials claiming that "Coke adds life"? Given its caffeine and sugar content, Coca-Cola should provide quite a lift. But Coca-Cola hasn't been "the real thing" since 1906. At that time the manufacturers discontinued use of the coca leaves from which the soft drink derived its name. Coca leaves contain **cocaine,** a powerful stimulant that produces a state of euphoria (or high), reduces hunger, deadens pain, and bolsters self-confidence.

One of the prominent advocates of cocaine, at least initially, was Sigmund Freud. Freud found that cocaine enabled people to work longer without sleep or food. Freud also found that cocaine helped relieve pain and had desirable psychoactive effects:

Truth or Fiction Revisited

It is true that Coca-Cola once "added life" by using cocaine. However, the Coca-Cola company discontinued using cocaine as soon as the drug became controversial.

COCAINE • A powerful stimulant that provides feelings of euphoria and bolsters self-confidence.

SNORTING COCAINE. Cocaine is a powerful stimulant that boosts self-confidence and may enhance performance in the short run. Health professionals have become concerned about cocaine's constriction of blood vessels and its acceleration of the heart rate. Many well known people have died from cocaine overdoses.

> The psychic effect of cocaine consists of exhilaration and lasting euphoria, which does not differ in any way from the normal euphoria of a healthy person.... One senses an increase of self-control and feels more vigorous and more capable of work.... Long lasting intensive mental or physical work can be performed without fatigue; it is as though the need for food and sleep, which otherwise makes itself felt peremptorily at certain times of the day, were completely banished. (Freud, "On Coca," 1884)

However, Freud quit using cocaine when he discovered that it was habit forming. Cocaine does cause physiological dependence (Brown & Massaro, 1996).

In addition to enhancing performance, cocaine heightens vigilance and bolsters confidence—properties that have made it popular among professional athletes like Lawrence Taylor, formerly of the New York Giants, and Dexter Manley, formerly of the Washington Redskins. Cocaine's popularity with college students seems to have peaked during the 1980s (Johnston and others, 1996). The majority of high school students now believe that use of cocaine is harmful (Johnston and others, 1996). It thus seems that the health warnings about cocaine may have gotten through to students. The percentage who had used crack within the past 30 days was less than 1 percent during the past few years. Questions remain about the prevalence of cocaine use among minority youth, high school dropouts, and young people who do not attend college, however (Rhodes & Jason, 1990).

Cocaine is brewed from coca leaves as a "tea," breathed in ("snorted") in powder form, and injected ("shot up") in liquid form. Repeated snorting constricts blood vessels in the nose, drying the skin and, at times, exposing cartilage and perforating the nasal septum. These problems require cosmetic surgery.

The potent derivatives *crack* and *bazooka* are inexpensive because they are unrefined. Crack "rocks"—so-called because they look like small white pebbles—are available in small, ready-to-smoke amounts that are priced at about \$10 to \$15 a dose and considered to be the most habit-forming street drug available (Weiss & Mirin, 1987). Crack produces a prompt and potent rush that wears off in a few minutes. The rush from snorting is milder and takes a while to develop, but it tends to linger longer than the rush of crack.

Cocaine constricts blood vessels in the brain, which can lead to problems in learning and memory and can also lead to strokes (Kaufman and others, 1998). Moreover, many of the effects of cocaine are cumulative. For example, prior use of cocaine increases the constriction of blood vessels the next time cocaine is used (Kaufman and others, 1998). This has been referred to as a *kindling effect.* Health problems connected with the use of cocaine are summarized in Table 8.3.

MARIJUANA

MARIJUANA • A hallucinogenic substance made up of the dried vegetable matter of the *Cannabis sativa* plant.

PSYCHEDELIC • Causing hallucinations and delusions or heightening perceptions.

HALLUCINOGENIC • Giving rise to hallucinations.

HASHISH • A drug that is stronger than, and similar to, marijuana in its effects and derived from the resin of the cannabis sativa plant.

Marijuana is produced from the *cannabis sativa* plant, which grows wild in many parts of the world. Marijuana helps some people relax and can elevate the mood. It also sometimes produces mild hallucinations. It is thus a **psychedelic** or a mild **hallucinogenic** drug. Its major psychoactive substance is delta-9-tetrahydrocannabinol, which, fortunately, can be abbreviated THC. THC is found in the branches and leaves of cannabis, but it is highly concentrated in the sticky resin of the female plant. The more potent **hashish** ("hash") is derived from this resin.

Marijuana use burgeoned during the Swinging Sixties and through the 1970s, but it dropped off after 1980. In 1981, one college student in three re-

TABLE 8.3 HEALTH RISKS OF COCAINE USE

PHYSICAL EFFECTS AND RISKS	
Increased heart rate	Accelerated heart rate may give rise to heart irregularities that can be fatal, such as ventricular tachycardia (extremely rapid contractions) or ventricular fibrillation (irregular, weakened contractions).
Increased blood pressure	Rapid or large changes in blood pressure may place too much stress on a weak-walled blood vessel in the brain, which can cause it to burst, producing cerebral hemorrhage or stroke.
Increased body temperature	Can be dangerous to some individuals.
Possible grand-mal seizures (epileptic convulsions)	Some grand-mal seizures are fatal, particularly when they occur in rapid succession or while driving a car.
Respiratory effects	Overdoses can produce gasping or shallow, irregular breathing that can lead to respiratory arrest.
Dangerous effects in special populations	Various special populations are at greater risk from cocaine use or overdose. People with coronary heart disease have died because their heart muscles were taxed beyond the capacity of their arteries to supply oxygen.
MEDICAL COMPLICATIONS OF COCAINE USE	
Nasal problems	When cocaine is administered intranasally (snorted), it constricts the blood vessels serving the nose, decreasing the supply of oxygen to these tissues, leading to irritation and inflammation of the mucous membranes, ulcers in the nostrils, frequent nosebleeds, and chronic sneezing and nasal congestion. Chronic use may lead to tissue death of the nasal septum, the part of the nose that separates the nostrils, requiring plastic surgery.
Malnutrition	Cocaine suppresses the appetite, so weight loss, malnutrition, and vitamin deficiencies may accompany regular use.
Seizures	Grand-mal seizures, typical of epileptics, may occur due to irregularities in the electrical activity of the brain. Repeated use may lower the seizure threshold, described as a type of kindling effect.
Sexual problems	Despite the popular belief that cocaine is an aphrodisiac, frequent use can lead to sexual dysfunctions, such as impotence and failure to ejaculate among males and decreased sexual interest in both genders. Although some people report initial increased sexual pleasure with cocaine use, they may become dependent on cocaine for sexual arousal or lose the ability to enjoy sex for extended periods following long-term use.
Other effects	Cocaine use may increase the risk of miscarriage among pregnant women. The sharing of infected needles is associated with transmission of hepatitis, endocarditis (infection of the heart valve), and AIDS. Repeated injections often lead to skin infections as bacteria are introduced into the deeper levels of the skin.

ported using marijuana in the last month, as compared with about one in six or seven in more recent years (Johnston and others, 1996).

Marijuana smokers report different sensations at different levels of intoxication. Early intoxication is frequently characterized by restlessness, which gives way to calmness. Fair to strong intoxication is linked to reports of heightened perceptions and increases in self-insight, creative thinking, and empathy. Strongly intoxicated users perceive time as passing more slowly and are more aware of their bodily sensations, such as their heartbeats. Smokers also report that strong intoxication heightens sexual sensations and that a song might seem to last an hour rather than a few minutes. Strong intoxication may also cause disorientation, nausea, and vomiting. Needless to say, smokers with such experiences smoke infrequently, or just once. Some people report that marijuana helps them socialize at parties. But the friendliness characteristic of early stages of intoxication may give way to self-absorption and social withdrawal as the smoker becomes higher (Fabian & Fishkin, 1981).

Truth or Fiction Revisited

It is not true that marijuana facilitates social interaction. The statement is too broad to be true. Marijuana may aid socializing by relaxing users during the early stages of intoxication. Heavy intoxication is connected with social withdrawal, however.

In the nineteenth century, marijuana was used almost as aspirin is used today for headaches and minor aches and pains. It could be bought without prescription in any drugstore. Today marijuana use and possession are illegal in most states, but medical applications are being explored. For example, marijuana has been used to treat health problems, including glaucoma and the nausea experienced by cancer patients undergoing chemotherapy ("More research needed," 1997). Marijuana may even offer some relief from asthma. However, in most cases other drugs are available for these purposes.

But there are causes for concern, as noted in 1982 by the Institute of Medicine of the National Academy of Sciences. For example, marijuana impairs motor coordination and perceptual functions used in driving and the operation of other machines. It impairs short-term memory and slows learning. Although it causes positive mood changes in many people, there are disturbing instances of anxiety, confusion, even occasional psychotic reactions. Marijuana boosts the heart rate to 140 to 150 beats per minute and, in some people, raises blood pressure, posing a threat to people with cardiovascular disorders.

OPIOIDS

Opioids are a group of **narcotics.** Some opioids are derived from the opium poppy, from which they obtain their name. Others are similar in chemical structure but synthesized. The ancient Sumerians gave the opium poppy its name: It means "plant of joy." Opioids include morphine, heroin, codeine, Demerol, and similar drugs whose major medical application is **analgesia,** or pain relief (Rosenthal, 1993a).

Morphine was introduced at about the time of the Civil War in the United States and the Franco-Prussian War in Europe. It was used liberally to deaden pain from wounds. Physiological dependence on morphine became known as the "soldier's disease." There was little stigma attached to dependence until morphine became a restricted substance.

Truth or Fiction Revisited

It is true that heroin was once used as a cure for addiction to morphine. Today, methadone is used to help addicts avert withdrawal symptoms from heroin.

Heroin was so named because it made people feel "heroic" and was hailed as the "hero" that would cure physiological dependence on morphine.

Heroin is a powerful narcotic that can provide a euphoric rush. Users of heroin claim that it is so pleasurable it can eradicate any thought of food or sex. Soon after its initial appearance, heroin was used to treat so many problems that it became known as G.O.M. ("God's own medicine").

Heroin is illegal. Because the penalties for possession or sale are high, it is also expensive. For this reason, many physiologically dependent people support their habits through dealing (selling heroin), prostitution, or selling stolen goods. But the chemical effects of heroin do not directly stimulate criminal or aggressive behavior. On the other hand, people who use heroin regularly may be more likely than nonusers to engage in *other* risky criminal behaviors as well.

The word seems to have gotten out that HIV (the AIDS virus) can be transmitting by sharing needles to inject ("shoot up") heroin and other drugs. More and more heroin users are thus "snorting" heroin (breathing it in through the nose in powder form) rather than injecting it in liquid form (Smolowe, 1993).

Although regular users develop tolerance for heroin, high doses can cause drowsiness, stupor, altered time perception, and impaired judgment.

Methadone is a synthetic opioid. Methadone has been used to treat physiological dependence on heroin in the same way that heroin was once used to treat physiological dependence on morphine. Methadone is slower acting than heroin and does not provide the thrilling rush. Most people treated with it simply swap dependence on one drug for dependence on another. Because they are

OPIOIDS • A group of narcotics derived from the opium poppy, or similar in chemical structure, that provide a euphoric rush and depress the nervous system.

NARCOTICS • Drugs used to relieve pain and induce sleep. The term is usually reserved for opioids.

ANALGESIA • A state of not feeling pain, although fully conscious.

MORPHINE • An opioid introduced at about the time of the U.S. Civil War.

HEROIN • An opioid. Heroin, ironically, was used as a cure for morphine addiction when first introduced.

METHADONE • An artificial narcotic that is slower acting than, and does not provide the "rush" of, heroin. Methadone use allows heroin addicts to abstain from heroin without experiencing an abstinence syndrome.

unwilling to undergo withdrawal symptoms or to contemplate a lifestyle devoid of drugs, they must be maintained on methadone indefinitely.

Withdrawal Symptoms

Opioids can have distressing abstinence syndromes, especially when used in high doses. Such syndromes may begin with flulike symptoms and progress through tremors, cramps, chills alternating with sweating, rapid pulse, high blood pressure, insomnia, vomiting, and diarrhea. However, these syndromes are somewhat variable from person to person. Many soldiers who used heroin regularly in Vietnam are reported to have suspended usage with relatively little trouble when they returned to the United States. Moreover, many pain patients who use small to moderate doses of narcotics for pain relief neither experience a euphoric rush nor become psychologically dependent on them (Taub, 1993). If they no longer need the drugs but have become physiologically dependent, they can frequently gradually decrease their dosage with few if any side effects (Rosenthal, 1993a).

SEDATIVES: BARBITURATES AND METHAQUALONE

Barbiturates such as amobarbital, phenobarbital, pentobarbital, and secobarbital are sedatives that are used to treat anxiety and tension, pain, epilepsy, high blood pressure, and insomnia. Barbiturates lead rapidly to dependence. **Methaqualone,** sold under the brand names Quaalude and Sopor, is a sedative similar in effect to barbiturates.

Psychologists generally oppose using barbiturates and methaqualone for anxiety, tension, and insomnia, since they lead rapidly to dependence and do nothing to teach the individual how to alter disturbing patterns of behavior. Physicians, too, have grown concerned about barbiturates.

Barbiturates and methaqualone are popular as street drugs, because they are relaxing and produce a mild euphoric state. High doses of barbiturates cause drowsiness, motor impairment, slurred speech, irritability, and poor judgment. A dependent person who undergoes withdrawal abruptly may experience severe convulsions and die. High doses of methaqualone may cause internal bleeding, coma, and death. Because of synergistic effects, it is dangerous to mix alcohol and other depressants at bedtime—or at any time.

AMPHETAMINES

Stimulants known as amphetamines were first used by soldiers during World War II to help them remain alert through the night. Truck drivers have used them to drive through the night. But amphetamines have become more widely known through students who have used them for all-night cram sessions and through dieters who use them because they reduce hunger.

Amphetamines and a related stimulant, Ritalin (methylphenidate), increase self-control in hyperactive children, increase their attention span, decrease fidgeting, and lead to academic gains (Whalen & Henler, 1991; Wolraich and others, 1990). The paradoxical calming effect of stimulants on hyperactive children may be explained by assuming that a cause of hyperactivity is immaturity of the areas of the brain that govern thought and self-control. Amphetamines may stimulate these areas of the brain to exercise control over more

BARBITURATE • An addictive depressant used to relieve anxiety or induce sleep.

METHAQUALONE • An addictive depressant. Often referred to as "ludes."

ADJUSTMENT in the NEW MILLENNIUM

Use and Abuse of Drugs: More Research Needed

Drugs remain very much a part of U.S. society. Children and teenagers continue to become involved with drugs that impair their ability to learn at school and that are connected with reckless behavior (Cooper and others, 1994). There are also questions about the proper therapeutic use of drugs that are illicit under most circumstances. Such drugs include opioids, marijuana, and stimulants.

Let us consider a few key research questions about drugs—their use and abuse—that may be answered in the new millennium. The twentieth century saw the chemical description of psychoactive drugs and the beginnings of knowledge about how these drugs act on the nervous system. Perhaps the twenty-first century will see developments in the following areas.

SUBSTANCE ABUSE IN TEENAGERS More research is needed into effective means of fighting substance abuse by children. Curiosity, peer pressure, parental use, rebelliousness, and the desire to escape from boredom or pressure are among the reasons children become involved with drugs. Inner-city youth are especially likely to become involved because of peer usage and the effort to escape a painful existence. Many means of fighting substance abuse have been tried with teenagers, including residential treatment centers, but their effectiveness has been shown to be modest at best (Nevid and others, 1997).

Efforts being made with younger children seem to hold somewhat more promise. For example, community psychologists are now experimenting with ways of tutoring youths to boost their self-esteem and success experiences in the schools (deGroot, 1994a, 1994b). In addition to boosting IQ scores, early childhood intervention programs also appear to decrease the likelihood of delinquent behavior, including substance abuse (Schweinhart & Weikart, 1993; Zigler and others, 1992). Perhaps these early approaches will succeed in helping children break away from poverty, a sense of lack of a future, and drug abuse.

Another positive note is that many teenagers now recognize that drugs such as crack cocaine are harmful (Johnston and others, 1996). In the 1970s and 1980s, teenagers were relatively more likely to attribute reports of drugs' harmfulness to horror stories concocted to scare them away from drugs. Perhaps the new millennium will also see more application of knowledge about the complex web of sociocultural factors that act on youths from various ethnic groups.

TREATMENT OF ALCOHOLISM More research is needed into effective ways of treating alcoholism. Alcoholics Anonymous (AA) is the most widely used program to treat alcoholism, yet research suggests that other approaches work as well for most people (Ouimette and others, 1997; "Tailoring treatments," 1997). The National Institute on Alcohol Abuse and Alcoholism funded an 8-year study in which more than 1,700 problem drinkers were randomly assigned to AA's 12-step program, cognitive-behavioral therapy, or motivational-

primitive centers in the brain. A combination of stimulants and cognitive-behavior therapy may treat hyperactivity most effectively (Whalen & Henler, 1991).

Called speed, uppers, bennies (for Benzedrine), and dexies (for Dexedrine), these drugs are often used for the euphoric "rush" they can produce, especially in high doses. Regular users may stay awake and "high" for days on end. Such highs must come to an end. People who have been on prolonged highs sometimes "crash," or fall into a deep sleep or depression.

enhancement therapy. The cognitive-behavioral treatment taught problem drinkers how to cope with temptations and how to refuse offers of drinks. Motivational enhancement was designed to enhance drinkers' desires to help themselves. The treatments worked equally well for most people with some exceptions. For example, people with psychological problems fared somewhat better with cognitive-behavioral therapy.

Research is also under way on the use of medicines in treating problem drinking. Disulfiram, for example, cannot be mixed with alcohol. People who take disulfiram experience symptoms such as nausea and vomiting if they drink (Schuckit, 1996). Many problem drinkers have lower than normal levels of serotonin. Medicines that boost serotonin levels therefore may be helpful for problem drinkers (Azar, 1997b).

Therapeutic Applications of Illicit Drugs More research is needed into the therapeutic application of various illicit drugs. For example, many pain patients who use small to moderate doses of opioids for pain relief neither experience a euphoric rush nor become psychologically dependent on them (Lang & Patt, 1994; Taub, 1993). If pain patients no longer need the drugs but have become physiologically dependent, they can usually quit by gradually decreasing their dosage and suffer few, if any, side effects (Rosenthal, 1993a).

On the other hand, serious questions have been raised about using marijuana to decrease the nausea and vomiting often experienced by people with cancer who are taking chemotherapy. Supporters of marijuana argue that marijuana should be made widely available for medical purposes (Grinspoon & Bakalar, 1994). But detractors contend that carefully controlled studies on marijuana's medical benefits have not been conducted and that other drugs for nausea are available (Kolata, 1994a).

The therapeutic usages of opioids, marijuana, and other substances need further investigation. If drugs like opioids and marijuana are to be used therapeutically, researchers need to demonstrate that they provide necessary benefits that are unavailable from more socially acceptable substances.

Treatment of Children With Attention-Deficit/Hyperactivity Disorder (ADHD) More research is needed into the treatment of children with ADHD. The two major treatment methods have been stimulant medication (Ritalin) and cognitive behavior therapy. Some researchers have argued for the benefits of cognitive behavior therapy alone, whereas others argue for a combination of Ritalin and cognitive-behavior therapy (Whalen & Henler, 1991). Although some research evidence suggests that Ritalin alone is as effective as a combination of Ritalin and cognitive-behavior therapy (Pelham and others, 1993), Ritalin has side effects that are a cause of concern. Its use is connected with restlessness and loss of appetite. It may also suppress growth and give rise to tics and cardiovascular changes. These side effects are usually reversible with "drug holidays" or dosage decreases (Whalen & Henler, 1991). However, it would be highly desirable to develop effective drugs that have fewer side effects or to refine cognitive-behavioral techniques so that drug therapy is not necessary.

As we gather new knowledge of the nervous system and the actions of drugs, perhaps we will develop more effective therapeutic drugs and find more effective ways of helping people discontinue harmful use of drugs. ■

People can become psychologically dependent on amphetamines, especially when they are used to cope with depression. Tolerance develops rapidly, but opinion is mixed as to whether they lead to physiological dependence. High doses may cause restlessness, insomnia, loss of appetite, and irritability. In the so-called amphetamine psychosis, there are hallucinations and delusions that mimic the symptoms of paranoid schizophrenia.

LSD, PCP, AND OTHER HALLUCINOGENICS

LSD is the abbreviation for lysergic diethylamide acid, a synthetic hallucinogenic drug. Users of "acid" claim that it expands consciousness and opens new worlds. Sometimes people believe they achieved great insights while using LSD, but when it wears off they usually cannot apply or recall them.

As a powerful hallucinogenic, LSD produces somewhat unpredictable and colorful hallucinations or "trips." Some regular users have only "good trips." Others have one bad trip and swear off. Regular users who have had no bad trips argue that people with bad trips were psychologically unstable prior to using LSD.

Other hallucinogenic drugs include mescaline (derived from the peyote cactus) and phencyclidine (PCP). PCP is a dangerous tranquilizer that is intended for use with animals. About 1 percent of high school seniors reported PCP use within the past 30 days (Berke, 1990).

Regular use of hallucinogenics may lead to tolerance and psychological dependence. They are not known to lead to physiological dependence. High doses can induce frightening hallucinations, impaired coordination, poor judgment, mood changes, and paranoid delusions.

GETTING THERE WITHOUT DRUGS: DON'T JUST SAY NO, DO SOMETHING ELSE

All of us feel depressed, tense, or just plain bored from time to time. (Really.) Many of us are intrigued by the possibility of exploring the still dark reaches of our inner selves. Many feel inadequate to face the challenges of college life now and then. Some of us see our futures as bleak and unrewarding. A vast wilderness or desert seems to lie before us.

So we all have feelings like these now and then. Then what? Do we turn to drugs to provide the magical answers, or do we seek healthful alternatives—alternatives without drugs? If you are wavering on whether or not to get involved with drugs, here are some drug-free alternatives to consider:

If You Are . . .

- Feeling tense or anxious, try practicing self-relaxation or meditation, or exercise, or listen to relaxing music.
- Feeling bored, find a new activity or interest. Get involved in athletics. Take up a hobby. Become involved in a political campaign or social cause.
- Feeling angry, write down your feelings or channel your anger into constructive pursuits.
- Feeling worthless, hopeless, or depressed, or putting yourself down, seek assistance from a friend or loved one. Focus on your abilities and accomplishments, not on your deficits. If that doesn't help, visit the college counseling center or health center. You may be suffering from a treatable case of depression.
- Wanting to probe the inner depths of your consciousness, try meditation or yoga. Or seek the counsel of a counselor, minister, priest, or rabbi.
- Pressured to using drugs by friends, learn how to say no politely but firmly. If you need help saying no, read a self-help book on self-assertion or go to the college counseling center for advice. (A real friend will not

LSD • Lysergic diethylamide acid. A hallucinogenic drug.

push you into doing anything that makes you feel uncomfortable, including using drugs.)

- Seeking to heighten your sensations, try dancing, jogging, parachuting, bungee-jumping, snowboarding, roller-blading, or mountain climbing. There are many ways to get your adrenaline flowing without relying on chemical stimulants.
- Feeling stressed out to the point where you can't take it anymore, sit down to figure out the pressures acting upon you. List your priorities. What must be done *right now?* What can wait? If this approach fails, see your academic adviser or visit the college counseling center or health center. If you can afford the time, you may choose to take a day or two off. Sometimes the key is to establish more reasonable expectations of yourself. No drug will help you do that.
- Wanting to discover new insights on the human condition, take classes or workshops on philosophy and theology. Attend lectures by prominent thinkers. Read great works of literature. Ponder great works of art. Attend the symphony. Visit a museum. Let your mind connect with the great minds of the past and present.
- Searching for deeper personal meaning in life, become more involved in spiritual activity in your church, synagogue, or mosque. Do volunteer work in hospitals or charitable organizations. Get involved in a cause you believe in. Or seek personal counseling to get in touch with your inner self.

adjustment and modern life

Although the perils of smoking have been well publicized, one American in four still smokes cigarettes. There is thus little doubt that cutting down on, or quitting, smoking is central to adjustment in the United States. Here, we consider self-control strategies for freeing oneself from cigarettes.

HOW TO USE SELF-CONTROL STRATEGIES TO QUIT AND CUT DOWN ON SMOKING

Although quitting smoking is a difficult task, some 45 percent of American smokers have managed to do so (Shiffman, 1993a).

Some smokers find it more effective to quit all at once (to go "cold turkey"). Others find cutting down gradually to be more effective. Either approach can work (Cinciripini and others, 1995; Gunther and others, 1992).

SUGGESTIONS FOR QUITTING COLD TURKEY

Psychologists have compiled suggestions such as the following for helping people to quit smoking:

Truth or Fiction Revisited

It is true that in quitting smoking, it is helpful to tell relatives and friends of plans to quit. Making a public commitment to stop smoking heightens one's motivation.

1. Tell your family and friends that you're quitting—make a public commitment.
2. Think of specific things to tell yourself when you feel the urge to smoke: how you'll be stronger, free of fear of cancer, ready for the marathon, and so on.
3. Tell yourself that the first few days are the hardest—after that, withdrawal symptoms weaken dramatically.
4. Remind yourself that you're "superior" to nonquitters.
5. Start when you wake up, at which time you've already gone 8 hours without nicotine.
6. Go on a smoke-ending vacation to get away from places and situations in which you're used to smoking.
7. Throw out ashtrays and don't allow smokers to visit you at home for a while.
8. Don't carry matches or light other people's cigarettes.
9. Sit in nonsmokers' sections of restaurants and trains.
10. Fill your days with novel activities—things that won't remind you of smoking.

11. Use sugar-free mints or gum as substitutes for cigarettes. (Don't light them.)
12. Interpret withdrawal symptoms as a sign that you're winning and getting healthier. After all, you wouldn't have withdrawal symptoms if you were smoking.
13. Buy yourself presents with all that cash you're socking away.
14. Ask your physician or pharmacist about nicotine replacement therapy in the form of nicotine gum or a skin patch. The use of nicotine replacements helps to avert withdrawal symptoms when dependent smokers discontinue cigarettes. Nicotine gums and skin patches help some people (Cepeda-Bcnito, 1993; Martin and others, 1997; O'Brien, 1996). Once the smoking habit is interrupted, many ex-smokers can wean themselves from the patches or gum. This technique is referred to as *nicotine fading.* But other people find it difficult to wean themselves from nicotine replacement methods. Nicotine gum also appears to help many people avoid gaining weight after they quit smoking (Doherty and others, 1996). A combination of cognitive-behavior therapy and nicotine patches looks promising: People experience less discomfort from withdrawal than they do from cognitive-behavior therapy alone (Cinciripini and others, 1996).

The addictive agent in cigarette smoke is nicotine. Smokers tend to smoke enough to maintain fairly even levels of nicotine in the bloodstream. Since the carcinogenic agents in cigarette smoke are the hydrocarbons ("tars"), not the nicotine, it is possible to switch from cigarettes to a less harmful source of nicotine and, at the same time, to avert withdrawal symptoms from nicotine.

Experiments with nicotine replacement show that it can help people quit smoking, even though users report cravings for cigarettes now and then. There are apparently satisfactions in inhaling that are not imparted by the nicotine substitutes. A combination of nicotine replacement and psychotherapy is apparently more effective than either one alone (Cepeda-Benito, 1993).

There is also a high relapse rate for people who quit smoking. Be on guard: We are most likely to relapse—that is, return to drugs such as alcohol and nicotine—when we feel highly anxious, angry, or depressed (Cooney and others, 1997; Kinnunen and others, 1996). If you are tempted, you can reduce the risk of relapse by using almost any of the strategies described here, such as reminding yourself of reasons for quitting, having a mint, or going for a walk.

SUGGESTIONS FOR CUTTING DOWN GRADUALLY

Psychologists have compiled suggestions such as the following for people who would rather try to cut down than quit altogether:

1. Count your cigarettes to establish your smoking baseline.
2. Set concrete goals for controlled smoking. For example, plan to cut down baseline consumption by at least 50 percent.
3. Gradually restrict the settings in which you allow yourself to smoke.
4. Get involved in activities where smoking isn't allowed or practical.

5. Switch to a brand you don't like.
6. Hold your cigarettes with your nondominant hand only.
7. Keep only enough cigarettes to meet the (reduced) daily goal. Never buy more than a pack at a time.
8. Use sugar-free candies or gum as a substitute for a few cigarettes each day.
9. Jog instead of having a cigarette. Or walk, swim, or make love.
10. Pause before lighting up. Put the cigarette in an ashtray between puffs. Ask yourself before each puff if you really want more. If not, throw the cigarette away.
11. Put the cigarette out before you reach the end. (No more eating the filter.)
12. Gradually lengthen the amount of time between cigarettes.
13. Imagine living a prolonged, noncoughing life. Ah, freedom!
14. As you smoke, picture blackened lungs, coughing fits, the possibilities of cancer and other lung diseases.

Using strategies such as these, many individuals have gradually cut down their cigarette consumption and eventually quit. ■

Summary

1. **What is the difference between substance abuse and substance dependence?** Substance abuse is use despite the fact that abuse is causing social, occupational, or other problems. Dependence is characterized by inability to control use, tolerance, and withdrawal symptoms.
2. **What are the effects of alcohol?** Alcohol is a depressant that can induce feelings of euphoria, lead to cirrhosis of the liver, Wernicke-Korsakoff syndrome, cardiovascular disorders, and cancer.
3. **What are the effects of smoking cigarettes?** Smoking heightens the risks of cancer, cardiovascular disorders, lung and respiratory disorders, miscarriage, and—in the offspring of pregnant smokers—premature birth, low birth weight, respiratory ailments, and birth defects.
4. **What are the effects of cocaine?** As a psychoactive substance, cocaine provides feelings of euphoria and bolsters self-confidence. Overdoses can lead to restlessness, insomnia, psychotic reactions, and cardiorespiratory collapse.
5. **What are the effects of marijuana?** Marijuana is a mild hallucinogenic drug that produces heightened and distorted perceptions and feelings of relaxation.
6. **What are the effects of opioids?** The opioids morphine and heroin are depressants that reduce pain, but they are also bought on the street because of the euphoric rush they provide. Opioids lead to physiological dependence.
7. **What are the effects of sedatives?** The sedative barbiturates are depressants used to treat epilepsy, high blood pressure, anxiety, and insomnia. They lead rapidly to physiological dependence.
8. **What are the effects of amphetamines?** Amphetamines are stimulants that produce feelings of euphoria when taken in high doses. High doses may also cause restlessness, insomnia, psychotic symptoms, and a crash upon withdrawal. Amphetamines and a related stimulant, Ritalin, are commonly used to treat hyperactive children.
9. **What are the effects of LSD and other hallucinogenics?** Hallucinogenic substances produce hallucinations. Hallucinogenics are not known to cause physiological dependence.

The Challenges of Life

CHAPTER 9

Psychological Disorders

TRUTH OR FICTION?

✔ T F

- ☐ ☐ If the breakup of a recent romance has led you to have trouble concentrating on your schoolwork, you may have a diagnosable psychological disorder.
- ☐ ☐ Native Hawaiians lead a carefree existence.
- ☐ ☐ Some people are suddenly flooded with feelings of panic, even when there is no external threat.
- ☐ ☐ Some people have irresistible urges to wash their hands—over and over again.
- ☐ ☐ Stressful experiences can lead to recurrent nightmares.
- ☐ ☐ Some people have not one, but two or more distinct personalities dwelling within them.
- ☐ ☐ People have lost the use of their legs or eyes under stress, even though there was nothing medically wrong with them.
- ☐ ☐ It is abnormal to feel depressed.
- ☐ ☐ Some people ride an emotional roller coaster, with cycles of elation and depression.
- ☐ ☐ In some mental disorders, people see and hear things that are not actually there.
- ☐ ☐ Some people persistently injure others and violate their rights without feeling guilty.
- ☐ ☐ African Americans are more likely than White Americans to commit suicide.
- ☐ ☐ People who threaten suicide are only seeking attention.

OUTLINE

THE OHIO STATE CAMPUS EXISTED IN A STATE OF terror one long fall semester. Four college women were abducted, forced to cash checks or obtain money with their instant-cash cards, and then raped. A mysterious phone call led to the arrest of a 23-year-old drifter, William, who had been dismissed from the Navy.

William was not the boy next door.

Several psychologists and psychiatrists who interviewed William concluded that 10 personalities resided within him, eight male and two female (Scott, 1994). His personality had been "fractured" by an abusive childhood. The personalities showed distinct facial expressions, vocal patterns, and memories. They even performed differently on personality and intelligence tests.

Arthur, the most rational personality, spoke with a British accent. Danny and Christopher were normal, quiet adolescents. Christene was a 3-year-old girl. It was Tommy, a 16-year-old, who had enlisted in the Navy. Allen was 18 and smoked. Adelena, a 19-year-old lesbian personality, had committed the rapes. Who had made the mysterious phone call? Probably David, aged 9, an anxious child personality.

The defense claimed that William was suffering from **dissociative identity disorder.** That is, his sense of identity—of who he was—had dissociated or split apart. In dissociative identity disorder, which was once termed *multiple personality disorder,* several distinct personalities dwell within an individual. In William's case, some personalities were aware of the others; some believed that they were the sole occupants. Billy, the core personality, had learned to sleep as a child to avoid the abuse of his father. A psychiatrist asserted that Billy had also been "asleep," in a "psychological coma," during the abductions. Therefore Billy should be found innocent by reason of insanity.

Billy was found not guilty. He was committed to an institution for the mentally ill and released 6 years later.

In 1982, John Hinckley, was also found not guilty of the assassination attempt on President Reagan by reason of insanity. Expert witnesses testified that he was suffering from **schizophrenia.** Hinckley, too, was committed to an institution for the mentally ill.

Dissociative identity disorder and schizophrenia are two types of psychological disorders, or abnormal behavior patterns. In this chapter we first define *psychological disorder.* Then we discuss classification of psychological disorders and various kinds of psychological disorders, including *adjustment disorders, anxiety disorders, dissociative disorders, somatoform disorders, mood disorders, schizophrenia,* and *personality disorders.*

Dissociative identity disorder • A disorder in which a person appears to have two or more distinct identities or personalities, which may alternate in controlling the person.

Schizophrenia • A psychotic disorder characterized by loss of control of thought processes and inappropriate emotional responses.

WHAT ARE PSYCHOLOGICAL DISORDERS?

There is quite a range of psychological disorders. Some are characterized by anxiety or depression, but many of us are anxious or depressed now and then, without having psychological disorders. It is normal to be anxious before a big date or on the eve of a midterm examination. It is appropriate to be depressed if a friend is upset with you or if you have done poorly on a test or in a job.

Anxiety and depression are abnormal, or signs of psychological disorders, when they are not appropriate for our situations. It is normal to be depressed because of a poor performance on a test, but not when everything is going well. It is normal to be anxious before a job interview, but not when one is looking out a fourth-story window or about to receive a harmless vaccination. The magnitude of the problem may also suggest a psychological disorder. Again, anxiety is to be expected before a job interview, but feeling that your heart is pounding so severely that it might leap out of your chest—and then avoiding the interview—are not. Nor is sweating so profusely that you drench your clothing.

Most psychologists agree that we show a psychological disorder when our behavior meets some combination of the following criteria:

1. *Our behavior is unusual.*
2. *Our behavior is socially unacceptable.* Each society has standards or norms for acceptable behavior in a given context. In our society, walking naked is normal in a locker room, but abnormal on a crowded boulevard.
3. *Our perception or interpretation of reality is faulty.* In our culture it is all right to say that you talk to God through prayer, but if you say that God talks back, you may be committed to a mental institution. "Hearing voices" and "seeing things" are considered **hallucinations.** Similarly, **ideas of persecution**, such as believing that the Mafia or the CIA are out to get you—all are considered signs of disorder. (Unless they *are* out to get you, of course.)
4. *We are in severe personal distress.*
5. *Our behavior is self-defeating.* Behavior that leads to misery rather than happiness and fulfillment may be considered disordered. Chronic drinking and avoidance of other people are examples of self-defeating behavior.
6. *Our behavior is dangerous.* People who threaten or attempt suicide may be considered abnormal, as may people who threaten or attack others.

CLASSIFYING PSYCHOLOGICAL DISORDERS

Toss some people, apes, seaweed, fish, and sponges into a room—preferably a well-ventilated room. Stir slightly. What do you have? It depends on how you classify this hodgepodge.

Classify them as plants versus animals and you lump the people, chimpanzees, fish, and, yes, sponges together. Classify them as stuff that carries on its business on land versus underwater, and we throw in our lots with just the chimps. How about those that swim versus those that don't? Then the chimps, the fish, and some of us are pigeonholed together.

HALLUCINATION • A perception in the absence of sensory stimulation that is confused with reality.

IDEAS OF PERSECUTION • Erroneous beliefs that one is being victimized or persecuted.

Classification is at the heart of science (Barlow, 1991). Without labeling and ordering psychological disorders, investigators would not be able to communicate with each other, and progress would be at a standstill. Although psychologists are working on their own system of classification of psychological disorders (Mjoseth, 1998), today the most widely used system is the *Diagnostic and Statistical Manual* (DSM) of the American Psychiatric Association. The DSM was developed to provide a uniform way of classifying psychological disorders, and it has undergone several revisions.

The current edition of the DSM—the DSM-IV—employs a multiaxial, or multidimensional, system of assessment. It provides a broad range of information about an individual's functioning, not just a diagnosis. The axes are shown in Table 9.1.

People may receive Axis I or Axis II diagnoses, or a combination of the two. Axis III, general medical conditions, lists physical disorders or problems

TABLE 9.1 THE MULTIAXIAL CLASSIFICATION SYSTEM OF THE DSM-IV

AXIS	TYPE OF INFORMATION	DESCRIPTION
Axis I	Clinical syndromes (a wide range of diagnostic classes, such as substance-related disorders, anxiety disorders, mood disorders, schizophrenia, somatoform disorders, and dissociative disorders)	Patterns of abnormal behavior that impair functioning and are stressful to the individual
Axis II	Personality disorders	Deeply ingrained, maladaptive ways of perceiving others and behaviors that are stressful to the individual or those who relate to the individual; notable personality traits can be listed here, even when no personality disorder per se is diagnosed
Axis III	General medical conditions	Chronic and acute illnesses, injuries, allergies, and so on, that affect functioning and treatment, such as cardiovascular disorders, athletic injuries, and allergies to medication
Axis IV	Psychosocial and environmental problems	Stressors that occurred during the past year that may have contributed to the development of a new mental disorder or the recurrence of a prior disorder or that may have exacerbated an existing disorder, such as divorce occurring during a depressive episode; stressors can be marital, parental, occupational, financial, legal, developmental, physical, and so on
Axis V	Global assessment of functioning	Overall judgment of current functioning and the highest level of functioning in the past year according to psychological, social, and occupational criteria

TABLE 9.2 PSYCHOSOCIAL AND ENVIRONMENTAL PROBLEMS

PROBLEM CATEGORIES	*EXAMPLES*
Problems with primary support groups	Death of family members; health problems of family mem bers; marital disruption in the form of separation, divorce, or estrangement; physical or sexual abuse in the family; birth of a sibling
Problems related to the social environment	Death or loss of a friend; living alone or in social isolation; problems in adjusting to a new culture (acculturation problems); discrimination; problems in adjusting to the transitions of the life cycle, such as retirement
Educational problems	Academic problems; illiteracy; problems with classmates or teachers; impoverished or inadequate school environment
Occupational problems	Work-related problems, including problems with supervisors and co-workers, heavy workload, unemployment, adjusting to a new job, job dissatisfaction, sexual harassment, discrimination
Housing problems	Homelessness or inadequate housing; problems with landlords or neighbors; an unsafe neighborhood
Economic problems	Financial hardships or poverty; inadequate public support
Problems with access to health care	Lack of health insurance; inadequate health care services; problems with transportation to health care facilities
Problems related to the legal or criminal justice systems	Victimization by crime; involvement in a lawsuit or trial; arrest, imprisonment
Other psychosocial or environmental problems	Natural or technological disaster; war; lack of social services

Source: Adapted from DSM-IV (American Psychiatric Association, 1994).

that may affect people's functioning or response to psychotherapy or drug treatment. Axis IV, psychosocial and environmental problems, includes difficulties that may affect the diagnosis, treatment, or outcome of a psychological disorder (see Table 9.2). Axis V, the global assessment of functioning, allows the clinician to rate the client's current level of functioning and highest level of functioning prior to the onset of the psychological disorder. The purpose is to help set goals as to what kinds of behavioral and mental functioning are to be restored.

The DSM-IV groups disorders on the basis of observable features or symptoms. However, early editions of the DSM, which was first published in 1952, grouped many disorders on the basis of assumptions about their causes. Because Freud's psychodynamic theory was widely accepted at the time, one major diagnostic category contained so-called neuroses.[1] From the psychodynamic perspective, all neuroses—no matter how differently people with various neuroses might behave—were caused by unconscious neurotic conflict. Each neurosis was thought to reflect a way of coping with the unconscious fear that

[1] The neuroses included what are today referred to as anxiety disorders, dissociative disorders, somatoform disorders, mild depression, and some other disorders, such as sleepwalking.

ADJUSTMENT *in the* NEW MILLENNIUM

Will Your Problems Be Diagnosed by Computer?

Imagine yourself seated in a comfortable chair in a room with a computer as we enter the new millennium. The computer has powerful voice-recognition software and asks for your name. Not wanting to offend, you pronounce your name carefully. The computer says "Thank you" and prints your name on the screen. "Did I get it right?" the computer asks self-effacingly. "Yes," you respond. In the same way, you provide your address, telephone number, and PIN (personal identification number). The computer then says, "I'm now going to ask you some questions so that I can learn more about you. Whatever you tell me will be shared only with a psychologist who is bound by professional ethics to keep it confidential. May I begin?" Without thinking, you nod your head yes. "Do I take that for a yes?" the computer asks. You realize that you hadn't spoken aloud and that the computer's body language-recognition software picked up your head nod and is seeking confirmation. "Yes," you say again. "Let's get on with it."

This scenario presupposes that you have decided to seek help for some personal problems. The helping professional asked if you would have a dialogue with her computer as a way of learning more about your problems. Living in a world of computers, you assumed that the interaction would be worthwhile. So here you are.

Sound far-fetched? Actually, primitive computers have been interviewing clients for more than 20 years. One current system is named CASPER, which stands for Computerized Assessment System for Psychotherapy Evaluation and Research. A CASPER interview covers a wide range of topics, such as age, income, family relations, social activities, sexual behavior, life satisfaction, and health problems. Questions and response options, such as the following, are shown on the screen:

> "About how many days in the past month did you have difficulty falling asleep, staying asleep, or waking too early (include sleep disturbed by bad dreams)?"

primitive impulses might break loose. As a result, sleepwalking was included as a neurosis (psychoanalysts assumed that sleepwalking reduced this unconscious fear by permitting the partial expression of impulses during the night). Now that the focus is on observable behaviors, sleepwalking is classified as a sleep disorder, not as a neurosis. We mention all this because the words *neurosis* and *neurotic* are still frequently used. Without some explanation, it might seem strange that they have been largely abandoned by professionals.

Some professionals, such as psychiatrist Thomas Szasz, believe that the categories described in the DSM are really "problems in living" rather than "disorders." At least, they are not disorders in the sense that high blood pressure, cancer, and the flu are disorders. Szasz argues that labeling people with problems in living as being "sick" degrades them and encourages them to evade their personal and social responsibilities. Since sick people are encouraged to obey doctors' orders, Szasz (1984) also contends that labeling people as "sick" accords too much power to health professionals. Instead, he believes, troubled people need to be encouraged to take greater responsibility for solving their own problems.

"During the past month, how have you been getting along with your spouse/partner? (1) Very satisfactory; (2) Mostly satisfactory; (3) Sometimes satisfactory, sometimes unsatisfactory; (4) Mostly unsatisfactory; (5) Very unsatisfactory." (Farrell and others, 1987, p. 692)

The client presses a numeric keypad to respond. CASPER is a branching program that follows up on problems suggested by responses to earlier questions. If the client reports difficulty sleeping, CASPER delves into whether sleep has become a key problem—"something causing you great personal distress or interfering with your daily functioning" (Farrell and others, 1987, p. 693). If the client responds yes, the computer will investigate still more deeply. The program allows clients to add or drop complaints. That is, clients can change their minds.

Most clients respond favorably to a CASPER interview (Bloom, 1992; Farrell and others, 1987). It also appears that clients are willing to report a greater number of problems to CASPER than to a live clinician. Perhaps the computer helps identify problems that the client would be unwilling to report otherwise. Or perhaps the computer seems more willing to take the time needed to record complaints. Computer diagnostic programs offer some advantages over traditional human interviewers (Farrell and others, 1987):

1. Computers can be programmed to ask specific sets of questions in a definite order. Clinicians sometimes omit important questions or allow the interview to veer off course into less critical issues.
2. Clients may be less disconcerted about reporting personal matters to a computer because computers do not respond emotionally or judgmentally.
3. Use of the computer for diagnosis frees clinicians to spend more time providing direct clinical services.

As such programs become capable of handling vastly increased amounts of information, they are also likely to become more accurate at diagnosis and more capable of identifying unusual problems. They may also connect the client's complaints to similar cases in the literature, indicating what treatment has been most effective in the past. On the other hand, computerized interviews may not be for everyone. Research shows that younger, better-educated people who are experienced with computers react more favorably to computerized assessment (Spinhoven and others, 1993). ■

■ ADJUSTMENT DISORDERS

Although adjustment to stress can be painful and difficult, **adjustment disorders** are among the mildest psychological disorders. Adjustment disorders are maladaptive reactions to identified stressors. They are typified by academic, occupational, or social problems that exceed those normally caused by the stressor. The maladaptive response can be resolved if the person learns to cope with it or if the stressor is removed.

If a love relationship ends and you cannot keep your mind on your coursework, you may fit the bill for an adjustment disorder. The diagnosis sounds more official than "not being able to get one's homework done," but it alludes to similar kinds of problems. If Uncle Paul has been feeling down and pessimistic since his divorce from Aunt Debbie, he too may be diagnosed as having an adjustment disorder. If, since the breakup, Cousin Billy has been cutting classes and spraying obscene words on the school walls, he may also have an adjustment disorder.

ADJUSTMENT DISORDER • A maladaptive reaction to one or more identified stressors that occurs shortly following exposure to the stressor(s) and causes signs of distress beyond that which would be normally expected or impairs functioning.

Considering an adjustment disorder to be a psychological or mental disorder highlights the problem of attempting to define where normal behavior leaves off and abnormal behavior begins. When something important goes wrong, it is normal to feel bad about it. If we experience a business crisis, if we are victimized by violent crime, if there is an earthquake or a flood, anxiety and depression are understandable reactions. Under such circumstances, it might be abnormal *not* to react maladaptively—at least temporarily.

Truth or Fiction Revisited

It is true that if the breakup of a recent romance has led you to have trouble concentrating on your schoolwork, you may have a diagnosable psychological disorder. The diagnosis would most likely be adjustment disorder.

A student who leaves home for the first time to attend college is encountering an identified stressor. Temporary feelings of loneliness and mild depression because of separation from one's family and friends or anxiety about successful completion of academic assignments and making new friends may be normal adjustments to such a stressor. But when a person's emotional complaints exceed the expected level, or when her or his ability to function is impaired, the diagnosis of adjustment disorder may be warranted. For example, if the student avoids social interactions at college or has difficulty getting out of bed or attending classes, the adjustment reaction may be excessive and warrant the diagnosis. But there are no precise boundaries between an expected reaction and an adjustment disorder.

In the following case study, the identified stressor is learning that one is infected with HIV, the virus that causes AIDS. Learning that one is infected with HIV normally generates strong feelings of anxiety and depression (Kelly & Murphy, 1992), but the diagnosis of adjustment disorder was made because of Bill's impairment in occupational functioning:

> Bill is a 35-year-old journalist who tested positive for HIV, but he was presently in good health, except for some bothersome allergies that produced a sore throat and other physical symptoms. He worries that his symptoms might represent the first signs of AIDS and has been bothered by frequent and intrusive thoughts about dying and recurrent fantasies of becoming seriously ill and dependent on others. His anxiety has become so severe that he finds it difficult to concentrate at work and is worried that exposure to job-related stress may weaken his body's immune system, leaving him more vulnerable to the disease. He is considering quitting his job and retiring to a country home, where he could lead a simpler life. His anxiety was heightened in the past week when he heard that two acquaintances were diagnosed as having AIDS. He now avoids reading anything about AIDS in the newspaper or attending social situations in which AIDS may be discussed. Bill has never contacted a mental health professional before and has always regarded himself, until now, as a happy person who was fulfilled in his work and personal relationships. (Adapted from Nevid and others, 1997)

Adjustment in a World of DIVERSITY

Psychological Disorders Among Native Americans—Loss of a Special Relationship With Nature?

When you envision hula dancing, luaus, and wide tropical beaches, you may assume that Native Hawaiians are a carefree people. Research shows, however, that Native Hawaiians also suffer a disproportionate share of physical diseases and mental health problems. The death rate for Native Hawaiians is 34 percent higher than that of the general U.S. population, largely because of an

How Many Native Hawaiians Are Described by This Photo?
The stereotype of Hawaiians includes hula dancing, luaus, and wide tropical beaches. Native Hawaiians are not a carefree people, however. They suffer a disproportionate share of physical diseases and mental health problems. Native Hawaiians are one Native American group. Native Americans are, on the whole, among the most impoverished ethnic groups in the country. Psychological disorders among Native Americans may reflect the loss of land and a way of life that resulted from colonization by European cultures.

increased rate of serious diseases including cancer and heart disease (Mokuau, 1990). Other groups in Hawaii also outlive Native Hawaiians by 5 to 10 years (Hammond, 1988). Compared to other Hawaiians, Native Hawaiians have higher rates of psychological disorders, higher suicide rates, higher rates of substance abuse, and higher rates of antisocial behavior (Mokuau, 1990). Depression and associated feelings of despair and a sense of hopelessness and self-doubt are also common among the Native Hawaiian population.

Native Hawaiians are one Native American group. Native Americans include American Indians and Alaskan Natives. According to the 1990 censuses, nearly 2 million people describe themselves as either American Indian or Alaskan Native (Aleut Eskimo, or Indian). Native American populations are found in virtually every state but are largely concentrated in states west of the Mississippi River. On the whole, the Native American population is among the most impoverished ethnic groups in the country. Like other groups who are socially and economically disadvantaged, Native Americans suffer from a disproportionate incidence of psychological problems, such as alcoholism, depression, drug abuse, and delinquency (USDHHS, 1991). One in four Native American teenagers has attempted suicide—a rate that is four times higher than that of other U.S. teenagers (Resnick and others, 1992). Among Zuni adolescents of New Mexico, the rate of completed suicides is more than twice the national rate (Howard-Pitney and others, 1992).

Psychological disorders among Native Americans and Native Hawaiians may reflect the loss of land and a way of life that resulted from colonization by European cultures. Native peoples often attribute psychological problems, especially depression and alcoholism, to the collapse of their traditional culture (Timpson and others, 1988). Here some researchers describe how a Native Canadian elder in northwestern Ontario explained depression in his people:

> Before the White Man came into our world we had our own way of worshiping the Creator. We had our own church and rituals. When hunting was good, people would gather together to give gratitude. This gave us close contact with the Creator. There were many different rituals depending on the tribe. People would dance in the hills and play drums to give recognition to the Great Spirit. It was like talking to the Creator and living daily with its spirit. Now people have lost this. They can't use these methods and have lost conscious contact with this high power. . . . The more distant we are from the Creator the more complex things are because we have no sense of direction. We don't recognize where life is from. (Timpson and others, 1988, p. 6)

Truth or Fiction Revisited

It is not true that Native Hawaiians lead a carefree existence. They have the highest death rates of any U.S. ethnic group and show greater-than-average incidences of suicide, drug abuse, and antisocial behavior in relation to other Hawaiians. Another reason for studying the relationships between ethnicity and abnormal behavior is to debunk erroneous stereotypes.

ANXIETY DISORDERS

Anxiety is characterized by subjective and physical features (Zinbarg & Barlow, 1996). Subjective features include worrying, fear of the worst things happening, fear of losing control, nervousness, and inability to relax. Physical features reflect arousal of the sympathetic branch of the autonomic nervous system. They include trembling, sweating, a pounding or racing heart, elevated blood pressure (a flushed face), and faintness. Anxiety is an appropriate response to a real threat. It can be abnormal, however, when it is excessive or when it "comes out of the blue"—that is, when events do not seem to warrant it.

Types of Anxiety Disorders

The anxiety disorders include phobic, panic disorder, generalized anxiety, obsessive-compulsive, and stress disorders.

PHOBIAS Phobias are often broken down into *specific phobias, social phobias,* and *agoraphobia.* Specific phobias are excessive, irrational fears of specific objects or situations. Social phobias are persistent fears of scrutiny by others and of doing something that will be humiliating or embarrassing. Stage fright and speech anxiety are common social phobias. Phobias can seriously intrude on one's life. A person may know that a phobia is irrational, yet experience acute anxiety and avoid the phobic object or situation.

One specific phobia is fear of elevators. Some people will not enter elevators despite the hardships they incur as a result (such as walking up six flights of steps). Yes, the cable *could* break. The ventilation *could* fail. One *could* be stuck in midair waiting for repairs. These problems are uncommon, however, and it does not make sense for most people to walk up and down several flights of stairs to elude them. Similarly, some people with a specific phobia for hypodermic needles will not have injections, even to treat profound illness. Injections can be painful, but most people with a phobia for needles would gladly suffer an even more painful pinch if it would help them fight illness. Other specific phobias include claustrophobia (fear of tight or enclosed places), acrophobia (fear of heights), and fear of mice, snakes, and other creepy-crawlies. Fears of animals and imaginary creatures are common among children.

Agoraphobia is among the most widespread phobias affecting adults. Agoraphobia is derived from Greek words meaning "fear of the marketplace," or fear of being out in open, busy areas. Persons with agoraphobia fear being in places from which it might be difficult to escape or in which help might not be available if they get upset. In practice, people who receive this diagnosis often refuse to venture out of their homes, especially by themselves. They find it difficult to hold a job or to maintain an ordinary social life.

PANIC DISORDER

> My *heart would start pounding so hard I was sure I was having a heart attack. I used to go to the emergency room. Sometimes I felt dizzy, like I was going to pass out. I was sure I was about to die.*
>
> KIM WEINER (1992)

PANIC DISORDER • The recurrent experiencing of attacks of extreme anxiety in the absence of external stimuli that usually elicit anxiety.

Panic disorder is an abrupt attack of acute anxiety that is not triggered by a specific object or situation. People with panic disorder have strong physical symptoms, such as shortness of breath, heavy sweating, tremors, and pounding of the heart. Like Kim Weiner (1992), they are particularly aware of cardiac sensations (Schmidt and others, 1997). It is not unusual for them to think they are having a heart attack (Clark and others, 1997). Many fear suffocation (McNally & Eke, 1996). People with the disorder may also experience choking sensations, nausea, numbness or tingling, flushes or chills, and fear of going crazy or losing control. Panic attacks may last minutes or hours. Afterward, the person usually feels drained.

Many people panic now and then. The diagnosis of panic disorder is reserved for those who undergo a series of attacks or live in fear of attacks.

Panic attacks seem to come from nowhere. Thus, some people who have had them stay home for fear of having an attack in public. They are diagnosed as having panic disorder with agoraphobia.

Truth or Fiction Revisited

It is true that some people are suddenly flooded with feelings of panic, even when there is no external threat. Such people are said to have panic disorder.

GENERALIZED ANXIETY DISORDER The central feature of **generalized anxiety disorder** is persistent anxiety of at least 6 months' duration. As in the panic disorder, the anxiety cannot be attributed to a phobic object, situation, or activity. It seems free-floating. Signs may include motor tension (shakiness, inability to relax, furrowed brow, fidgeting, etc.); autonomic overarousal (sweating, dry mouth, racing heart, light-headedness, frequent urinating, diarrhea, etc.); feelings of dread and foreboding; and distractibility, insomnia, and irritability.

OBSESSIVE-COMPULSIVE DISORDER **Obsessions** seem to be irrational and beyond control. Obsessions are so intrusive that they interfere with daily life. They may include doubts as to whether one has locked the doors and shut the windows; impulses, such as the wish to strangle one's spouse; and images, such as one mother's recurrent fantasy that her children had been run over by traffic on the way home from school. Consider the case of Bonnie:

> Bonnie was a 29-year-old who complained of being obsessed by fantasies that her 8- and 11-year-old children were run over on their way home from school. It was April and the fantasies had begun in September, gradually occupying more time during the day.
>
> "I'm usually all right for most of the morning," she explained. "But after lunch the pictures come back to me. There's nothing I can do about it. The pictures are in my head. I see them walking home and crossing the street, and I know what's going to happen and I think 'Why can't I do something to stop it?' but I can't. They're walking into the street and a car is coming along speeding, or a truck, and then it happens again, and they're lying there, and it's a horrible mess." She broke into tears. "And I can't function. I can't do anything. I can't get it out of my head.
>
> "Then sometimes it bothers me at night and [my husband] says 'What's wrong?' He says I'm shaking and white as a ghost and 'What's wrong?' I can't tell him what's going on because he'll think I'm crazy. And then I'm in and out of [the children's] bedrooms, checking that they're all right, tucking them in, kissing them, making sure I can see that they're breathing. And sometimes I wake [the 11-year-old] up with my kissing and he says 'Mommy' and I start crying as soon as I get out of the room." (Nevid and others, 1997)

In other cases, a 16-year-old boy found "numbers in my head" whenever he was about to study or take a test. A housewife became obsessed with the notion that she had contaminated her hands with Sani-Flush and that the contamination was spreading to everything she touched.

Compulsions are frequent and forceful, interfering with daily life. The woman who felt contaminated by Sani-Flush engaged in elaborate hand-

GENERALIZED ANXIETY DISORDER • Feelings of dread and foreboding and sympathetic arousal of at least 6 months' duration.

OBSESSION • A recurring thought or image that seems beyond control.

COMPULSION • An apparently irresistible urge to repeat an act or engage in ritualistic behavior, such as lengthy, elaborate washing after using the bathroom.

A TRAUMATIC EXPERIENCE FROM THE VIETNAM WAR. Physical threats and other traumatic experiences can lead to posttraumatic stress disorder (PTSD). PTSD is characterized by intrusive memories of the experience, recurrent dreams about it, and the sudden feeling that it is, in fact, recurring (as in "flashbacks").

Truth or Fiction Revisited

It is true that some people have irresistible urges to wash their hands—over and over again. These people are said to have a compulsion.

washing rituals. She spent 3 to 4 hours daily at the sink and complained, "My hands look like lobster claws."

POSTTRAUMATIC STRESS DISORDER Fires, stabbings, shootings, suicides, medical emergencies, accidents, bombs, and hazardous material explosions—these are just some of the traumatic experiences firefighters confront on a fairly regular basis. Because of such experiences, one study found that the prevalence of **posttraumatic stress disorder** (PTSD) among firefighters is 16.5 percent. This rate is 1 percent higher than the rate among Vietnam veterans and far above that for the general population, which is 1 percent to 3 percent (DeAngelis, 1995a).

PTSD is characterized by a rapid heart rate and feelings of anxiety and helplessness that are caused by a traumatic experience. Such experiences may include a threat or assault, destruction of one's community, or witnessing a death. PTSD may occur months or years after the event. It frequently occurs among combat veterans, people whose homes and communities have been swept away by natural disasters or who have been subjected to toxic hazards, and survivors of childhood sexual abuse (Baum & Fleming, 1993; Rodriguez and others, 1997). A study of victims of Hurricane Andrew, which devastated South Florida in 1992, found that one man in four and about one woman in three (36 percent) had developed PTSD (Ironson, 1993). A national study of more than 4,000 women found that about one woman in four who had been victimized by crime experienced PTSD (Resnick and others, 1993; see Figure 9.1).

Truth or Fiction Revisited

It is true that stressful experiences can lead to recurrent nightmares. Recurrent nightmares are one of the features of posttraumatic stress disorder.

The traumatic event is revisited in the form of intrusive memories, recurrent dreams, and flashbacks—the sudden feeling that the event is recurring. People with PTSD typically try to avoid thoughts and activities connected to the traumatic event. They may also have sleep problems, irritable outbursts, difficulty concentrating, extreme vigilance, and an intensified "startle" response.

The case of Margaret illustrates many of the features of PTSD:

> Margaret was a 54-year-old woman who lived with her husband Travis in a small village in the hills to the east of the Hudson River. Two winters earlier, in the middle of the night, a fuel truck had skidded down one of the icy inclines that led into the village center. Two blocks away, Margaret was shaken from her bed by the explosion ("I thought the world was coming to an end. My husband said the Russians must've dropped the

POSTTRAUMATIC STRESS DISORDER • A disorder which follows a psychologically distressing event that is outside the range of normal human experience and that is characterized by signs such as intense fear, avoidance of stimuli associated with the event, and reliving of the event. Abbreviated *PTSD*.

H-bomb.") when the truck slammed into the general store. The store and the apartments above were immediately engulfed in flames. The fire spread to the church next door. Margaret's first and most enduring visual impression was of shards of red and black that rose into the air in an eerie ballet. On their way down, they bathed the centuries-old tombstones in the church graveyard in hellish light. A dozen people died, mostly those who had lived above and in back of the general store. The old caretaker of the church and the truck driver were lost as well.

Margaret shared the village's loss, took in the temporarily homeless, and did her share of what had to be done. Months later, after the general store had been leveled to a memorial park and the church was on the way toward being restored, Margaret started to feel that life was becoming strange, that the world outside was becoming a little unreal. She began to withdraw from her friends and scenes of the night of the fire would fill her mind. At night she now and then dreamt the scene. Her physician prescribed a sleeping pill which she discontinued because "I couldn't wake up out of the dream." Her physician turned to Valium, a minor tranquilizer, to help her get through the day. The pills helped for a while, but "I quit them because I needed more and more of the things and you can't take drugs forever, can you?"

Over the next year and a half, Margaret tried her best not to think about the disaster, but the intrusive recollections and the dreams came and went, apparently on their own. By the time Margaret [sought help], her sleep had been seriously distressed for nearly two months and the recollections were as vivid as ever. (Nevid and others, 1994)

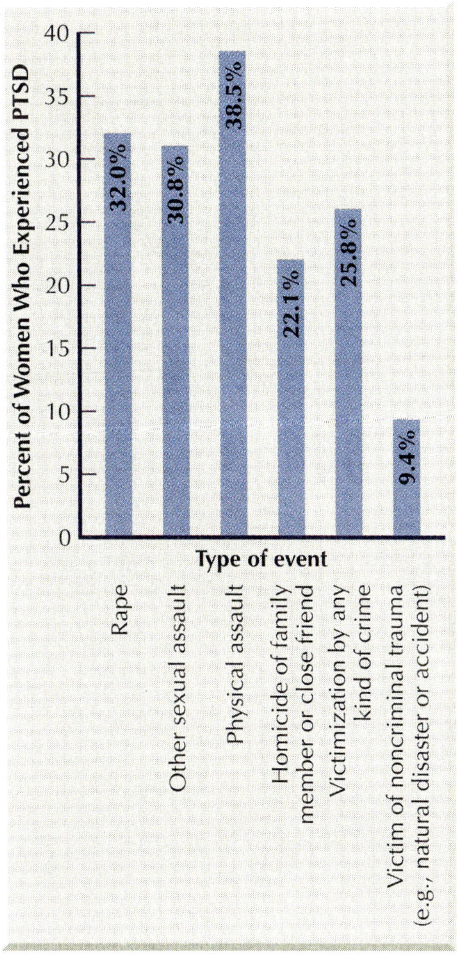

FIGURE 9.1

POSTTRAUMATIC STRESS DISORDER AMONG FEMALE VICTIMS OF CRIME AND AMONG OTHER WOMEN

According to Resnick and her colleagues (1993), about one woman in four (25.8 percent) who was victimized by crime could be diagnosed with PTSD at some point following the crime. By contrast, fewer than one woman in ten (9.4 percent) who was not victimized by crime experienced PTSD.

ACUTE STRESS DISORDER **Acute stress disorder,** like PTSD, is characterized by feelings of anxiety and helplessness that are caused by a traumatic event. However, PTSD can occur 6 months or more after the traumatic event and tends to persist. Acute stress disorder occurs within a month of the event and lasts from 2 days to 4 weeks. Women who have been raped, for example, experience acute distress that tends to peak in severity about 3 weeks after the assault (Davidson & Foa, 1991; Rothbaum and others, 1992).

ACUTE STRESS DISORDER • A disorder which, like PTSD, follows a psychologically distressing event and is characterized by fear, avoidance of stimuli associated with the event, and reliving of the event. The features of acute stress disorder, however, appear earlier than those of PTSD and do not persist as long.

Theoretical Views

According to the psychodynamic perspective, phobias symbolize conflicts originating in childhood. Psychodynamic theory explains generalized anxiety as persistent difficulty in repressing primitive impulses. Obsessions are explained as leakage of unconscious impulses, and compulsions are seen as acts that allow people to keep such impulses partly repressed.

Some learning theorists consider phobias to be conditioned fears that were acquired in early childhood. Therefore, their origins are beyond memory. Avoidance of feared stimuli is reinforced by the reduction of anxiety.

Social-cognitive theorists note that observational learning plays a role in the acquisition of fears (Basic Behavioral Science Task Force, 1996b). If parents squirm, grimace, and shudder at the sight of mice, blood, or dirt on the kitchen floor, children might assume that these stimuli are awful and imitate their parents' behavior. Cognitive theorists suggest that anxiety is maintained by thinking that one is in a terrible situation and helpless to change it. People with anxiety disorders may be cognitively biased toward paying more attention to threats than other people do (Foa and others, 1996; Mineka, 1991). Psychoanalysts and learning theorists generally agree that compulsive behavior reduces anxiety.

Cognitive theorists note that people's appraisals of the magnitude of threats help determine whether they are traumatic and can lead to PTSD (Creamer and others, 1992). People with panic attacks tend to misinterpret bodily cues and to view them as threats (Meichenbaum, 1993). Obsessions and compulsions may serve to divert attention from more frightening issues, such as "What am I going to do with my life?" When anxieties are acquired at a young age, we may later interpret them as enduring traits and label ourselves as "people who fear ________" (you fill it in). We then live up to the labels. We also entertain thoughts that heighten and perpetuate anxiety such as "I've got to get out of here," or "My heart is going to leap out of my chest." Such ideas intensify physical signs of anxiety, disrupt planning, make stimuli seem worse than they really are, motivate avoidance, and decrease self-efficacy expectations. The belief that we will not be able to handle a threat heightens anxiety. The belief that we are in control reduces anxiety (Bandura and others, 1985).

Biological factors play a role in anxiety disorders. Genetic factors are implicated in most psychological disorders, including anxiety disorders (Carey & DiLalla, 1994). For one thing, anxiety disorders tend to run in families (Michels & Marzuk, 1993b). Studies of twins also find a higher agreement rate for anxiety disorders among identical twins than among fraternal twins (Torgersen, 1983). Studies of adoptees who are anxious similarly show that the biological parent places the child at risk for anxiety and related traits (Pedersen and others, 1988).

Susan Mineka (1991) suggests that humans (and nonhuman primates) are genetically predisposed to respond with fear to stimuli that may have once posed a threat to their ancestors. Evolutionary forces would have favored the survival of individuals who were predisposed toward acquiring fears of large animals, spiders, snakes, heights, entrapment, sharp objects, and strangers.

Perhaps a predisposition toward anxiety—in the form of a highly reactive autonomic nervous system—can be inherited. What might make a nervous system "highly reactive"? In the case of panic disorder, faulty regulation of levels of serotonin and norepinephrine may be involved. In other anxiety disorders, receptor sites in the brain may not be sensitive enough to *gamma-aminobutyric acid* (GABA), a neurotransmitter that may help calm anxiety reactions. The *benzodiazepines,* a class of drugs that reduce anxiety, may work by increasing the sensitivity of receptor sites to GABA. However, it is unlikely that GABA levels fully explain anxiety disorders (Michels & Marzuk, 1993a).

In many cases anxiety disorders may reflect the interaction of biological and psychological factors. In panic disorder, biological imbalances may initially trigger attacks. However, subsequent fear of attacks—and of the bodily cues that signal their onset—may heighten discomfort and give one the idea there is nothing one can do about them (McNally, 1990; Meichenbaum, 1993). Feelings of helplessness increase fear. People with panic disorder therefore can be helped by psychological methods that provide ways of reducing physical discomfort—including regular breathing—and show them that there are, after all, things they can do to cope with attacks (Klosko and others, 1990).

DISSOCIATIVE DISORDERS

A dissociative disorder is characterized by a disturbance in the normal functions of identity, memory, or consciousness that allow us to feel whole.

Types of Dissociative Disorders

DISSOCIATIVE DISORDERS • Disorders in which there are sudden, temporary changes in consciousness or self-identity.

There are four major **dissociative disorders:** *dissociative amnesia, dissociative fugue, dissociative identity disorder,* and *depersonalization.*

DISSOCIATIVE AMNESIA In **dissociative amnesia,** there is sudden inability to recall important personal information. Memory loss cannot be attributed to organic problems, such as a blow to the head or alcoholic intoxication. Thus it is a psychological dissociative disorder, and not an organic disorder. Usually, the person cannot recall events for a number of hours after a stressful incident, as in warfare or as in the case of the uninjured survivor of an accident. In generalized amnesia, people forget their entire lives. Amnesia may last for hours or years. Termination of amnesia is also sudden.

DISSOCIATIVE FUGUE In **dissociative fugue** (pronounced "FYOOG"), the person shows loss of memory for the past, travels suddenly from his or her home or place of work, and assumes a new identity. Either the person does not think about the past, or reports a past filled with bogus memories that are not recognized as false. Following recovery, the events that occurred during the fugue are not recalled.

DISSOCIATIVE IDENTITY DISORDER Dissociative identity disorder (formerly *multiple personality disorder*) is the name given William's disorder, as described in the beginning of the chapter. In this disorder, two or more "personalities," each with distinct traits and memories, "occupy" the same person, with or without awareness of the others. Different personalities may even have different eyeglass prescriptions.

In the celebrated case that became the subject of the film *The Three Faces of Eve,* a timid housewife named Eve White harbored two other personalities: Eve Black, a sexually aggressive, antisocial personality, and Jane, an emerging personality who was able to accept the existence of her primitive impulses, yet show socially appropriate behavior. Finally, the three faces merged into one: Jane. Ironically, Jane (Chris Sizemore, in real life) reportedly split into 22 personalities later on. Another publicized case is that of Sybil, a woman with 16 personalities, played by Sally Field in a film based on Sybil's experience.

DEPERSONALIZATION DISORDER **Depersonalization disorder** is the persistent feeling that one is not real. Persons with the disorder may feel detached from their own bodies, as if they are observing their thought processes from the outside. Or they may feel that they are functioning on automatic pilot, or as if in a dream.

The following case describes feelings of depersonalization, although they were not persistent enough to be diagnosed as depersonalization disorder:

> We went to Orlando with the children after school let out. I had also been driving myself hard, and it was time to let go. We spent three days "doing" Disney World, and it got to the point where we were all wearing shirts with mice and ducks on them and singing Disney songs like "Yo ho, yo ho, a pirate's life for me." On the third day I began to feel unreal and ill at ease while we were watching these middle-American Ivory-soap teenagers singing and dancing in front of Cinderella's Castle. The day was finally cooling down, but I broke into a sweat. I became shaky and dizzy and sat down on the cement next to the 4-year-old's stroller without giving [my wife] an explanation. There were strollers and kids and [adults'] legs all around me, and for some strange reason I became fixated on the pieces of popcorn strewn on the ground. All of a sudden it was like the people around me were all silly mechanical creatures, like the dolls in the It's a Small World [exhibit] or the animals on the Jungle Cruise. Things sort of seemed to slow down, the way they do when you've smoked marijuana, and there was this invisible wall of cotton between me and everyone else.

Truth or Fiction Revisited

It is apparently true that some people have two or more distinct personalities dwelling within them. Such people are said to have dissociative identity disorder. In this disorder, different identities may have different eyeglass prescriptions and perform differently on intelligence tests.

DISSOCIATIVE AMNESIA • A dissociative disorder marked by loss of memory or self-identity. Skills and general knowledge are usually retained. Previously termed *psychogenic amnesia.*

DISSOCIATIVE FUGUE • A dissociative disorder in which one experiences amnesia, then flees to a new location and establishes a new lifestyle. Previously termed *psychogenic fugue.*

DEPERSONALIZATION DISORDER • Persistent or recurrent feelings that one is not real or is detached from one's own experiences or body.

> Then the concert was over and my wife was like "What's the matter?" and did I want to stay for the Electrical Parade and the fireworks or was I sick? Now I was beginning to wonder if I was going crazy and I said I was sick, that my wife would have to take me by the hand and drive us back to the motel. Somehow we got back to the monorail and turned in the strollers. I waited in the herd [of people] at the station like a dead person, my eyes glazed over, looking out over kids with Mickey Mouse ears and Mickey Mouse balloons. The mechanical voice on the monorail almost did me in and I got really shaky.
>
> I refused to go back to the Magic Kingdom. I went with the family to Sea World, and on another day I dropped [my wife] and the kids off at the Magic Kingdom and picked them up that night. My wife thought I was goldbricking or something, and we had a helluva fight about it, but we had a life to get back to and my sanity had to come first. (The authors' files)

Theoretical Views

According to psychodynamic theory, dissociative disorders involve massive use of repression to prevent recognition of unacceptable impulses. In psychogenic amnesia and fugue, the person forgets a profoundly disturbing event or impulse. In multiple personality, people express unacceptable impulses through alternate personalities. In depersonalization, the person stands outside—removed from the turmoil within.

Cognitive social theorists generally regard dissociative disorders as conditions in which people learn *not to think* about disturbing acts or impulses in order to avoid feelings of guilt and shame. This is an example of negative reinforcement: *Not thinking about these matters* is reinforced by *removal* of the aversive stimuli of guilt and shame.

Cognitive social theory also suggests that many people come to role-play people with multiple personality through observational learning. This is not exactly the same thing as faking a disorder, because people can "forget to tell themselves" that they have assumed a role. Reinforcers are made available by role-playing individuals with multiple personality: drawing attention to oneself and escaping responsibility for unacceptable behavior are two (Spanos and others, 1985; Thigpen & Cleckley, 1984). Although role-playing is not the same as faking, many psychologists are suspicious that people in individual cases claim to have dissociative identity disorder as a way of evading responsibility for unacceptable behavior (McMinn & Wade, 1995).

One cognitive perspective explains dissociative disorders in terms of deployment of attention. Perhaps all of us are capable of dividing our awareness so that we become unaware, at least temporarily, of events that we usually focus more attention on. Perhaps the marvel is *not* that attention can be divided, but that human consciousness normally integrates experience into a meaningful whole.

SOMATOFORM DISORDERS

SOMATOFORM DISORDERS • Disorders in which people complain of physical (somatic) problems, although no physical abnormality can be found.

In **somatoform disorders,** people show or complain of physical problems, such as paralysis, pain, or the persistent belief that they have a serious disease, yet no evidence of a physical abnormality can be found.

Types of Somatoform Disorders

In this section we shall discuss two somatoform disorders: *conversion disorder* and *hypochondriasis*.

CONVERSION DISORDER **Conversion disorder** is characterized by a major change in or loss of physical functioning, although there are no medical findings to support the loss of functioning. The problems are not intentionally produced; that is, the person is not faking.

If you lost the ability to see at night, or if your legs became paralyzed, you would show understandable concern. But some victims of conversion disorder show indifference to their problem, a remarkable feature referred to as **la belle indifférence**. Conversion disorder is so named because it appears to transform a source of stress into a physical problem. Instances are rare and short in duration, but their existence led the young Sigmund Freud to believe that subconscious processes were at work in people.

During World War II a number of bomber pilots developed night blindness. They could not carry out their nighttime missions, although no damage to the optic nerves was found. In Freud's classic case study of "Anna O.," a woman with a large family became paralyzed in the legs, again with no medical findings.

Conversion disorder, like dissociative disorders, seems to serve a purpose. The "blindness" of the pilots may have afforded them temporary relief from stressful missions or allowed them to avoid the guilt of bombing civilian populations. The paralysis of a woman who prematurely commits herself to a large family and a life at home may prevent her from doing housework or from engaging in sexual intercourse and becoming pregnant again. She accomplishes certain ends without having to recognize them or make decisions.

Truth or Fiction Revisited

It is true that people have lost the use of their legs or eyes under stress, even though there was nothing medically wrong with them. Such people are said to have conversion disorder, in which stress is converted into loss or disturbance of a bodily function.

HYPOCHONDRIASIS Persons with **hypochondriasis** hold the persistent belief that they are suffering from serious disease, although no medical evidence can be found for it. Sufferers often become preoccupied with minor physical sensations and maintain an unrealistic belief that something is wrong despite medical reassurance. *Hypochondriacs* may go from doctor to doctor, seeking the one who will find the cause of the sensations. Fear may impair work or home life.

MOOD DISORDERS

The mood disorders are characterized by disturbance in expressed emotions and generally involve depression or elation. If you have failed an important test, if you have lost a business investment, or if your closest friend becomes ill, it is understandable and fitting for you to be sad about it. It would be odd, in fact, if you were *not* affected by adversity.

Truth or Fiction Revisited

It is not true that feelings of depression are abnormal. The statement is too broad to be true. Depression is an appropriate response to a loss or failure. But depression can be abnormal when it is excessive or inappropriate to one's situation.

Types of Mood Disorders

In this section we discuss two mood disorders: *major depression* and *bipolar disorder*.

MAJOR DEPRESSION Depression is the common cold of psychological problems—the most common psychological problem we face (Murstein & Fontaine, 1993). People with "run-of-the-mill" depression may feel sad, blue, or "down in the dumps." They may complain of lack of energy, loss of self-esteem, difficulty

CONVERSION DISORDER • A disorder in which anxiety or unconscious conflicts are "converted" into physical problems that often have the effect of helping the person cope with anxiety or conflict.

LA BELLE INDIFFÉRENCE • A French term descriptive of the lack of concern sometimes shown by people with conversion disorders.

HYPOCHONDRIASIS • Persistent belief that one has a medical disorder despite lack of medical findings.

in concentrating, loss of interest in other people and usually enjoyable activities, pessimism, crying, and thoughts of suicide.

People with **major depression** may share most or all of these feelings, but they tend to be more severe. In addition, people with major depression may show poor appetite and significant weight loss, agitation or severe **psychomotor retardation,** and an inability to concentrate and make decisions. They may also complain of "not caring" anymore, and they may have recurrent thoughts of death or make suicide attempts.

Persons with major depression may also show faulty perception of reality or psychotic features such as delusions of unworthiness, guilt for imagined great wrongdoing, even ideas that one is rotting away from disease. There may also be hallucinations, as of the Devil administering just punishment or of strange sensations in the body.

Truth or Fiction Revisited

It is true that some people ride an emotional roller coaster, with cycles of elation and depression. They are said to have bipolar mood disorder.

BIPOLAR DISORDER **Bipolar disorder** is characterized by mood swings from elation to depression. These cycles seem unrelated to external events. In the elated or **manic** phase, people may show excessive excitement or silliness, carrying jokes too far. They may show poor judgment, sometimes destroying property, and may be argumentative. Roommates may avoid them, finding them abrasive. Manic people often speak rapidly ("pressured speech") and jump from topic to topic, showing **rapid flight of ideas.** It is hard to "get a word in edgewise." They may show extreme generosity by making unusually large contributions to charity or giving away expensive possessions. They may not be able to sit still or to sleep restfully.

Depression is the other side of the coin. Bipolar depressed people often sleep more than usual and are lethargic. People with major (or *unipolar*) depression are more likely to show insomnia and agitation. Bipolar depressed individuals show social withdrawal and irritability.

Some persons with bipolar disorder attempt suicide "on the way down" from the elated phase of the disorder. They report that they will do almost anything to escape the depths of depression that they realize lie ahead.

Theoretical Views

Depression is an appropriate reaction to losses and unpleasant events. Problems such as marital discord, physical discomfort, incompetence, and failure or pressure at work all contribute to feelings of depression. We tend to be more depressed by things we bring upon ourselves, such as academic problems, financial problems, unwanted pregnancy, conflict with the law, arguments, and fights (Simons and others, 1993). Many people recover from depression less readily than others, however. People who remain depressed have lower self-esteem (Andrews & Brown, 1993), are less likely to be able to solve social problems (Marx and others, 1992), and have less social support.

MAJOR DEPRESSION • A depressive disorder in which the person may show loss of appetite, psychomotor abnormalities, and impaired reality testing.
PSYCHOMOTOR RETARDATION • Slowness in motor activity and thought.
BIPOLAR DISORDER • A disorder in which the mood alternates between poles of elation and depression.
MANIC • Elated, showing excessive excitement.
RAPID FLIGHT OF IDEAS • Rapid speech and topic changes, characteristic of manic behavior.

Adjustment in a World of DIVERSITY

The Case of Women and Depression

Women are about two times more likely to be diagnosed with depression than men (Culbertson, 1997; Leutwyler, 1997). Some therapists, like many laypeople, assume that biological gender differences largely explain why women are more likely to become depressed. How often do we hear degrading remarks such as "It must be that time of the month" when a woman expresses feelings of anger or irritation?

Hormonal changes during the menstrual cycle and childbirth may contribute to depression in women (McGrath and others, 1990). However, a panel convened by the American Psychological Association attributed most of the difference to the greater stresses placed on women (McGrath and others, 1990). Women are more likely to experience physical and sexual abuse, poverty, single parenthood, and sexism. Women are also more likely than men to help other people who are under stress. Supporting other people heaps additional burdens on the caregiver (Shumaker & Hill, 1991). One panel member, Bonnie Strickland, expressed surprise that even more women are not depressed, given that they are often treated as second-class citizens.

Belle (1990) argues that social inequality creates many of the problems that lead people to seek therapy. This is particularly true among members of oppressed groups, such as women (Brown, 1992). Women—especially single mothers—have lower socioeconomic status than men, and depression and other psychological disorders are more common among poor people (Hobfoll and others, 1995). Even capable, hard-working women are likely to become depressed when they see how society limits their opportunities (Rothbart & Ahadi, 1994).

A part of "therapy" for women, then, is to modify the overwhelming demands that are placed on women today (Comas-Diaz, 1994). The pain may lie in the individual, but the cause often lies in society.

PSYCHODYNAMIC VIEWS Psychoanalysts suggest various explanations for depression. In one, depressed people are overly concerned about hurting others' feelings or losing their approval. As a result, they hold in rather than express feelings of anger. Anger becomes turned inward and is experienced as misery and self-hatred.

LEARNING VIEWS Many people with depressive disorders have an external locus of control. That is, they do not believe that they can control events so as to achieve desired outcomes (Weisz and others, 1993).

Research has also found links between depression and **learned helplessness.** In classic research, Seligman taught dogs that they were helpless to escape an electric shock by preventing them from leaving a cage in which they received repeated shock. Later a barrier to a safe compartment was removed, allowing the animals a way out. But when they were shocked again, the dogs made no effort to escape. Apparently they had learned that they were helpless. Seligman's dogs were also, in a sense, reinforced for doing nothing. That is, the shock *eventually* stopped when the dogs were showing helpless behavior—inactivity and withdrawal. "Reinforcement" may have increased the likelihood of repeating their "successful behavior"—that is, doing nothing—in a similar situation. This helpless behavior resembles that of depressed people.

COGNITIVE FACTORS The concept of learned helplessness bridges learning and cognitive approaches in that it is an attitude, a general expectation. Other cognitive factors also contribute to depression. For example, perfectionists set themselves up for depression through irrational self-demands. They are likely to fall short of their (unrealistic) expectations and, as a result, to feel depressed (Blatt and others, 1995; Hewitt and others, 1996).

The case of Christie illustrates a number of cognitive factors in depression:

> Christie was a 33-year-old real estate sales agent who suffered from frequent episodes of depression. Whenever a deal fell through, she would

LEARNED HELPLESSNESS • Seligman's model for the acquisition of depressive behavior, based on findings that organisms in aversive situations learn to show inactivity when their operants are not reinforced.

WHY DID HE MISS THAT TACKLE? This football player is compounding his feelings of depression by attributing his shortcomings on the field to factors that he cannot change. For example, he tells himself that he missed the tackle because of general stupidity and lack of athletic ability. He ignores the facts that his coaching was also poor and that his teammates failed to come to his support.

> blame herself, "If only I had worked harder . . . negotiated better . . . talked more persuasively . . . the deal would have been set." After several successive disappointments, each one followed by self-recriminations, she felt like quitting altogether. Her thinking became increasingly dominated by negative thoughts, which further depressed her mood and lowered her self-esteem: "I'm a loser. . . . I'll never succeed. . . . It's all my fault. . . . I'm no good and I'm never going to succeed at anything."
>
> Christie's thinking included cognitive errors such as the following: (1) *personalization* (believing herself to be the sole cause of negative events); (2) *labeling and mislabeling* (thinking of herself as a "nothing"); (3) *overgeneralization* (predicting a dismal future on the basis of a present disappointment); and (4) *mental filter* (judging her entire personality on the basis of her disappointments). In therapy, Christie was helped to think more realistically about events and not to jump to conclusions that she was automatically at fault whenever a deal fell through, or to judge her whole personality on the basis of disappointments or perceived flaws within herself. In place of this self-defeating style of thinking, she began to think more realistically when disappointments occurred, as in telling herself, "Okay, I'm disappointed. I'm frustrated. I feel lousy. So what? It doesn't mean I'll never succeed. Let me discover what went wrong and try to correct it the next time. I have to look ahead, not dwell on disappointments in the past." (Nevid and others, 1997)

People who ruminate about feelings of depression are more likely to prolong them (Just & Alloy, 1997). Women are more likely than men to ruminate about feelings of depression (Nolen-Hoeksema and others, 1993). Men seem more likely to try to fight off negative feelings by distracting themselves. Men are also more likely to distract themselves by turning to alcohol (Nolen-Hoeksema, 1991). They thus expose themselves and their families to further problems.

Seligman (1996) suggests that when things go wrong we may think of the causes of failure as either *internal* or *external, stable* or *unstable, global* or *specific.* These various **attributional styles** can be illustrated using the example of having a date that does not work out. An internal attribution involves self-blame, as in "I really loused it up." An external attribution places the blame elsewhere (as in "Some couples just don't take to each other" or "She was the wrong sign for me"). A stable attribution ("It's my personality") suggests a problem that cannot be changed. An unstable attribution ("It was because I had a head cold") suggests a temporary condition. A global attribution of failure ("I have no idea what to do when I'm with other people") suggests that the problem is quite large. A specific attribution ("I have problems making small talk at the beginning of a relationship") chops the problem down to a manageable size.

Research has shown that people who are depressed are more likely to attribute the causes of their failures to internal, stable, and global factors—factors that they are relatively powerless to change (Kinderman & Bentall, 1997; Simons and others, 1995). Such attributions can give rise to feelings of hopelessness.

The "Self-Assessment" feature may afford you insight into some of your own cognitions that may contribute to feelings of depression.

BIOLOGICAL FACTORS Researchers are also searching for biological factors in mood disorders. Depression, for example, is often associated with the trait of *neuroticism*, which is heritable (Clark and others, 1994). Anxiety is also connected with neuroticism, and mood and anxiety disorders are frequently found in the same person (Clark and others, 1994).

ATTRIBUTIONAL STYLE • One's tendency to attribute one's behavior to internal or external factors, stable or unstable factors, and so on.

SELF-ASSESSMENT

Do Your Own Thoughts Put You Down in the Dumps?

Cognitive theorists note that we can depress ourselves through negative thoughts. The following list contains negative thoughts that are linked to depression. ■

Directions: Using the code given below, indicate how frequently you have the following thoughts. There is no scoring key for this inventory. Try, however, to consider whether your negative thoughts are accurate and appropriate to your situation.

1. Never
2. Seldom
3. Often
4. Very often

____ 1. It seems such an effort to do anything.
____ 2. I feel pessimistic about the future.
____ 3. I have too many bad things in my life.
____ 4. I have very little to look forward to.
____ 5. I'm drained of energy, worn out.
____ 6. I'm not as successful as other people.
____ 7. Everything seems futile and pointless.
____ 8. I just want to curl up and go to sleep.
____ 9. There are things about me that I don't like.
____ 10. It's too much effort even to move.
____ 11. I'm absolutely exhausted.
____ 12. The future seems just one string of problems.
____ 13. My thoughts keep drifting way.
____ 14. I get no satisfaction from the things I do.
____ 15. I've made so many mistakes in the past.
____ 16. I've got to really concentrate just to keep my eyes open.
____ 17. Everything I do turns out badly.
____ 18. My whole body has slowed down.
____ 19. I regret some of the things I've done.
____ 20. I can't make the effort to liven up myself.
____ 21. I feel depressed with the way things are going.
____ 22. I haven't any real friends anymore.
____ 23. I do have a number of problems.
____ 24. There's no one I can feel really close to.
____ 25. I wish I were someone else.
____ 26. I'm annoyed at myself for being bad at making decisions.
____ 27. I don't make a good impression on other people.
____ 28. The future looks hopeless.
____ 29. I don't get the same satisfaction out of things these days.
____ 30. I wish something would happen to make me feel better.

Source: Reprinted with permission of The Free Press, a division of Macmillan, Inc., from *The Psychological Treatment of Depression: A Guide to the Theory and Practice of Cognitive-Behavior Therapy* by J. Mark G. Williams. Copyright (1984) by J. Mark G. Williams.

Genetic factors appear to be involved in bipolar disorder. Mood swings tend to run in families (Rose, 1995; Wachtel, 1994). There is also a higher concordance rate for bipolar disorder among identical twins than among fraternal twins (Goodwin & Jamison, 1990).

Other researchers focus on the actions of the **neurotransmitters** serotonin and noradrenaline (Cooper and others, 1991; Michels & Marzuk, 1993b). A deficiency in serotonin may create a general disposition toward mood disorders. Serotonin deficiency *combined with* noradrenaline deficiency may be linked with depression. People with severe depression often respond to antidepressant drugs that heighten the action of noradrenaline and serotonin. Moreover, the metal lithium, which is a major chemical treatment for bipolar disorder, seems to flatten out manic-depressive cycles by moderating levels of noradrenaline.

Relationships between mood disorders and biological factors are complex and under intense study. Even if people are biologically predisposed toward depression, self-efficacy expectations and attitudes—particularly attitudes about whether one can change things for the better—may also play a role.

Although the precise causes of depression remain unknown, we know all too well that for some people suicide is one of the possible outcomes of depression. We discuss suicide in the "Adjustment and Modern Life" feature at the end of this chapter.

SCHIZOPHRENIA

> Joyce was 19. Her husband Ron brought her into the emergency room because she had slit her wrists. When she was interviewed, her attention wandered. She seemed distracted by things in the air, or something she might be hearing. It was as if she had an invisible earphone.
>
> She explained that she had cut her wrists because the "hellsmen" had told her to. Then she seemed frightened. Later she said that the hellsmen had warned her not to reveal their existence. She had been afraid that they would punish her for talking about them.
>
> Ron and Joyce had been married for about a year. At first they had been together in a small apartment in town. But Joyce did not want to be near other people and had convinced him to rent a bungalow in the country. There she would make fantastic drawings of goblins and monsters during the days. Now and then she would become agitated and act as if invisible things were giving her instructions.
>
> "I'm bad," Joyce would mutter. "I'm bad." She would begin to jumble her words. Ron would then try to convince her to go to the hospital, but she would refuse. Then the wrist-cutting would begin. Ron thought he had made the cottage safe by removing knives and blades. But Joyce would always find something.
>
> Then Joyce would be brought to the hospital, have stitches put in, be kept under observation for a while, and medicated. She would explain that she cut herself because the hellsmen had told her that she was bad and must die. After a few days she would deny hearing the hellsmen, and she would insist on leaving the hospital.
>
> Ron would take her home. The pattern continued.

When the emergency room staff examined Joyce's wrists and heard that she believed she had been following the orders of "hellsmen," they suspected that she could be diagnosed with schizophrenia. Schizophrenia touches every aspect of a person's life. It is characterized by disturbances in thought and language,

NEUROTRANSMITTERS • Chemical substances that are involved in the transmission of messages in the nervous system.

perception and attention, motor activity, and mood, and by withdrawal and absorption in daydreams or fantasy.

Schizophrenia has been referred to as the worst disorder affecting human beings (Carpenter & Buchanan, 1994). It afflicts nearly 1 percent of the population worldwide. Its onset occurs relatively early in life, and its adverse effects tend to endure. It has been estimated that one third to one half of the homeless people in the United States have schizophrenia (Bachrach, 1992).

People with schizophrenia have problems in memory, attention, and communication (Docherty and others, 1996). Their thinking becomes unraveled. Unless we are allowing our thoughts to wander, our thinking is normally tightly knit. We start at a certain point, and thoughts that come to mind (the associations) tend to be logically connected. But people with schizophrenia often think illogically. Their speech may be jumbled. They may combine parts of words into new words or make meaningless rhymes. They may jump from topic to topic, conveying little useful information. They usually do not recognize that their thoughts and behavior are abnormal.

Many people with schizophrenia have **delusions**—for example, delusions of grandeur, persecution, or reference. In the case of delusions of grandeur, a person may believe that he is a famous historical figure, such as Jesus, or a person on a special mission. He may have grand, illogical plans for saving the world. Delusions tend to be unshakable even in the face of evidence that they are not true. People with delusions of persecution may believe that they are sought by the Mafia, CIA, FBI, or some other group. A woman with delusions of reference said that news stories contained coded information about her. A man with such delusions complained that neighbors had "bugged" his walls with "radios." Other people with schizophrenia have had delusions that they have committed unpardonable sins, that they were rotting away from disease, or that they or the world did not exist.

The perceptions of people with schizophrenia often include hallucinations—imagery in the absence of external stimulation that the person cannot distinguish from reality. In Shakespeare's *Macbeth*, for example, after killing King Duncan, Macbeth apparently experiences a hallucination:

> Is this a dagger which I see before me,
> The handle toward my hand? Come, let me clutch thee:
> I have thee not, and yet I see thee still.
> Art thou not, fatal vision, sensible
> To feeling as to sight? or art thou but
> A dagger of the mind, a false creation,
> Proceeding from the heat-oppressed brain?

Joyce apparently hallucinated the voices of "hellsmen." Other people who experience hallucinations may see colors or even obscene words spelled out in midair. Auditory hallucinations are the most common type.

In individuals with schizophrenia, motor activity may become wild or become so slow that the person is said to be in a *stupor*. There may be strange gestures and facial expressions. The person's emotional responses may be flat or blunted, or inappropriate—as in giggling upon hearing bad news. People with schizophrenia have problems understanding other people's feelings (Penn and others, 1997), tend to withdraw from social contacts, and become wrapped up in their own thoughts and fantasies.

Truth or Fiction Revisited

It is true that people with some psychological disorders see or hear things that are not really there. Schizophrenia is an example of such a disorder.

Types of Schizophrenia

There are three major types of schizophrenia: paranoid, disorganized, and catatonic.

DELUSIONS • False, persistent beliefs that are unsubstantiated by sensory or objective evidence.

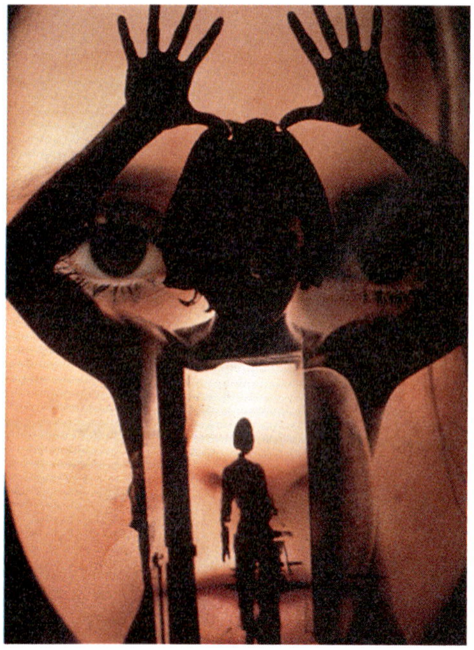

PARANOID SCHIZOPHRENIA. Paranoid schizophrenics hold systematized delusions, often involving ideas that they are being persecuted or are on a special mission. Although they cannot be argued out of their delusions, their cognitive functioning is relatively intact compared to that of disorganized and catatonic schizophrenics.

PARANOID TYPE People with **paranoid schizophrenia** have systematized delusions and, frequently, related auditory hallucinations. They usually have delusions of grandeur and persecution, but they may also have delusions of jealousy, in which they believe that a spouse or lover has been unfaithful. They may show agitation, confusion, and fear, and they may experience vivid hallucinations that are consistent with their delusions. People with paranoid schizophrenia often construct complex or systematized delusions involving themes of wrongdoing or persecution.

DISORGANIZED TYPE People with **disorganized schizophrenia** show incoherence, loosening of associations, disorganized behavior, disorganized delusions, fragmentary delusions or hallucinations, and flat or highly inappropriate emotional responses. Extreme social impairment is common. People with this type of schizophrenia may also exhibit silliness and giddiness of mood, giggling, and nonsensical speech. They may neglect their appearance and personal hygiene and lose control of their bladder and bowels.

CATATONIC TYPE People with **catatonic schizophrenia** show striking impairment in motor activity. It is characterized by a slowing of activity into a stupor that may suddenly change into an agitated phase. Catatonic individuals may maintain unusual, even difficult postures for hours, even as their limbs grow swollen or stiff. A striking feature of this condition is **waxy flexibility,** in which the person maintains positions into which he or she has been manipulated by others. Catatonic individuals may also show **mutism,** but afterward they usually report that they heard what others were saying at the time.

Theoretical Views

Psychologists have investigated various factors that may contribute to schizophrenia. They include psychological and biological factors.

PSYCHODYNAMIC VIEWS According to the psychodynamic perspective, schizophrenia occurs because the ego is overwhelmed by sexual or aggressive impulses from the id. The impulses threaten the ego and cause intense inner conflict. Under this threat, the person regresses to an early phase of the oral stage in which the infant has not yet learned that it and the world are separate. Fantasies become confused with reality, giving rise to hallucinations and delusions. Yet critics point out that schizophrenic behavior is not the same as infantile behavior.

LEARNING VIEWS Learning theorists explain schizophrenia in terms of conditioning and observational learning. From this perspective, people engage in schizophrenic behavior when it is more likely to be reinforced than normal behavior. This may occur when a person is reared in a socially unrewarding or punitive situation. Inner fantasies then become more reinforcing than social realities.

Patients in a psychiatric hospital may learn what is expected by observing others. Hospital staff may reinforce schizophrenic behavior by paying more attention to patients who behave bizarrely. This view is consistent with folklore that the child who disrupts the class attracts more attention from the teacher than the "good" child.

Critics note that many people are reared in socially punitive settings but apparently are immune to the extinction of socially appropriate behavior. Others

PARANOID SCHIZOPHRENIA • A type of schizophrenia characterized primarily by delusions—commonly of persecution—and by vivid hallucinations.

DISORGANIZED SCHIZOPHRENIA • The type of schizophrenia characterized by disorganized delusions and vivid hallucinations.

CATATONIC SCHIZOPHRENIA • The type of schizophrenia characterized by striking impairment in motor activity.

WAXY FLEXIBILITY • A sign of catatonic schizophrenia in which persons maintain postures into which they are placed.

MUTISM • Refusal to talk.

develop schizophrenic behavior without having had opportunities to observe other people with schizophrenia.

SOCIOCULTURAL VIEWS Many investigators have considered whether and how social and cultural factors such as poverty, discrimination, and overcrowding contribute to schizophrenia—especially among people who are genetically vulnerable to the disorder. A classic study in New Haven, Connecticut, showed that the rate of schizophrenia was twice as high in the lowest socioeconomic class as in the next-higher class on the socioeconomic ladder (Hollingshead & Redlich, 1958). Some sociocultural theorists therefore suggest that treatment of schizophrenia requires reforming society so as to alleviate poverty and other social ills, rather than trying to change people whose behavior is deviant.

Critics of this view suggest that low socioeconomic status may be a result, rather than a cause, of schizophrenia. People with schizophrenia may drift toward low social status because they lack the social skills and cognitive abilities to function at higher social class levels. Thus, they may wind up in poor neighborhoods in disproportionately high numbers.

Evidence for the hypothesis that people with schizophrenia drift downward to lower socioeconomic status is mixed (Nevid and others, 1997). Many people with schizophrenia do drift downward occupationally in comparison with their fathers' occupations. Many others, however, were reared in families in which the father came from the lowest socioeconomic class. Because the stresses of poverty may play a role in the development of schizophrenia, many researchers are interested in the possible interactions between psychosocial stressors and biological factors (Carpenter & Buchanan, 1994).

BIOLOGICAL RISK FACTORS Research suggests that there are three biological risk factors for schizophrenia: heredity, complications during pregnancy and birth, and birth during winter (Carpenter & Buchanan, 1994; Goleman, 1996a).

Schizophrenia, like many other psychological disorders, runs in families (Grove and others, 1991). People with schizophrenia constitute about 1 percent of the population. However, children with one parent who has been diagnosed as schizophrenic have about a 10 percent chance of being diagnosed as schizophrenic themselves. Children with two such parents have about a 35 percent to 40 percent chance of being so diagnosed (Gottesman, 1991; Straube & Oades, 1992). Studies of twins also find about a 40 percent to 50 percent concordance rate for the diagnosis among pairs of identical (MZ) twins, whose genetic codes are the same, compared with about a 10 percent rate among pairs of fraternal (DZ) twins (Gottesman, 1991; Straube & Oades, 1992). Moreover, adoptee studies find that the biological parent typically places the child at greater risk for schizophrenia than the adoptive parent—even though the child has been reared by the adoptive parent (Carpenter & Buchanan, 1994; Gottesman, 1991). Sharing genes with relatives who have schizophrenia apparently places a person at risk of developing the disorder

There seems to be strong evidence for a genetic role in schizophrenia. However, heredity cannot be the sole factor. If it were, we would expect a 100 percent concordance rate between identical twins, as opposed to the 40 percent to 50 percent rate found by researchers (Carpenter & Buchanan, 1994). It also turns out that many people with schizophrenia underwent complications during pregnancy and birth (Goleman, 1996a). For example, the mothers of many people with schizophrenia had influenza during the sixth or seventh month of pregnancy (Barr and others, 1990). Maternal starvation has also been implicated (Susser & Lin, 1992). Individuals with schizophrenia are also somewhat more likely to have been born during winter than would be predicted by chance

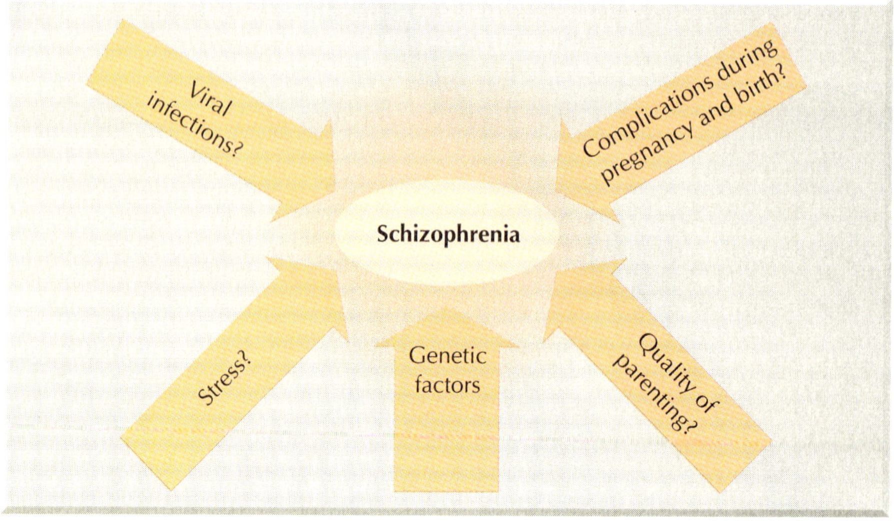

FIGURE 9.2
A MULTIFACTORIAL MODEL OF SCHIZOPHRENIA
According to the multifactorial model of schizophrenia, people with a genetic vulnerability to the disorder experience increased risk for schizophrenia when they encounter problems such as viral infections, birth complications, stress, and poor parenting. People without the genetic vulnerability would not develop schizophrenia despite such problems.

(Carpenter & Buchanan, 1994). Considered together, these three biological risk factors suggest that schizophrenia involves atypical development of the central nervous system. Problems in the nervous system may involve neurotransmitters as well as the development of brain structures, and research on these problems has led to the dopamine theory of schizophrenia.

THE DOPAMINE THEORY OF SCHIZOPHRENIA Much research has been conducted on the chemistry of schizophrenia. Numerous chemical substances have been suspected of playing a role. Much recent research has focused on the neurotransmitter dopamine (Carpenter & Buchanan, 1994). According to the dopamine theory of schizophrenia, people with schizophrenia *use* more dopamine than other people do, although they may not *produce* more of it. Why? They may have more dopamine receptors in the brain than other people, or their dopamine receptors may be hyperactive (Davis and others, 1991). Postmortem studies of the brains of people with schizophrenia have yielded evidence that is consistent with both possibilities.

Many researchers agree that dopamine plays a role in schizophrenia but argue that other neurotransmitters are also involved (Maas and others, 1993; van Kammen and others, 1990). Supportive evidence is found in the fact that drugs that act on dopamine alone are not always effective in the treatment of schizophrenia (Carpenter & Buchanan, 1994).

Because so many psychological and biological factors have been implicated in schizophrenia, most investigators today favor a *multifactorial* model. According to this model, genetic factors create a predisposition toward schizophrenia (see Figure 9.2). Genetic vulnerability to the disorder interacts with other factors, such as complications during pregnancy and birth, stress, and quality of parenting, to cause the disorder to develop (Michels & Marzuk, 1993a; Venables, 1996).

PERSONALITY DISORDERS

PERSONALITY DISORDERS • Enduring patterns of maladaptive behavior that are a source of distress to the individual or others.

Personality disorders are characterized by enduring patterns of inflexible and maladaptive behavior. They impair personal or social functioning and are a source of distress to the individual or to others.

Types of Personality Disorders

There are a number of personality disorders, including the *paranoid, schizotypal, schizoid,* and *antisocial personality disorders.* The defining trait of the **paranoid personality disorder** is the tendency to interpret other people's behavior as deliberately threatening or demeaning. Although persons with the disorder do not show grossly disorganized thinking, they are mistrustful of others, and their social relationships suffer. They may be suspicious of co-workers and supervisors, but they can generally hold onto jobs.

Schizotypal personality disorder is characterized by pervasive oddities in thought, perception, and behavior, such as fantasy and suspiciousness, feelings of being unreal, or odd usage of words. The bizarre psychotic behaviors that characterize schizophrenia are absent, so this disorder is schizo*typal* instead of schizophrenic. Because of their oddities, persons with the disorder are often maladjusted on the job.

Schizoid personality disorder is defined by indifference to social relationships and flat emotional response. Schizoid personalities are loners who do not develop warm, tender feelings for others. They have few friends and rarely marry. Some schizoid personalities do very well on the job, so long as continuous social interaction is not required. Hallucinations and delusions are absent.

Persons with **antisocial personality disorders** persistently violate the rights of others, show indifference to commitments, and encounter conflict with the law (see Table 9.3). In order for the diagnosis to be used, the person must be at least 18 years old. Whereas women are more likely than men to be anxious and depressed, men are more likely to show antisocial personality disorder (Russo, 1990). Cleckley (1964) notes that persons with antisocial personalities often show a superficial charm and are at least average in intelligence. Perhaps their most striking feature, given their antisocial behavior, is their lack of guilt and low level of anxiety.

People with antisocial personalities seem largely undeterred by punishment. Though they have usually received punishment from parents and others for their misdeeds, they continue their impulsive, irresponsible styles of life.

Truth or Fiction Revisited

It is true that some people persistently injure others and violate their rights without feeling guilty. Persons with antisocial personalities feel little or no guilt over their misdeeds.

TABLE 9.3 CHARACTERISTICS OF PEOPLE DIAGNOSED WITH ANTISOCIAL PERSONALITY DISORDER

KEY CHARACTERISTICS	***OTHER COMMON CHARACTERISTICS***
History of delinquency and truancy	Lack of loyalty or of formation of enduring relationships
Persistent violation of the rights of others	Failure to maintain good job performance over the years
Impulsiveness	Failure to develop or adhere to a life plan
Poor self-control	Sexual promiscuity
Lack of remorse for misdeeds	Substance abuse
Lack of empathy	Inability to tolerate boredom
Deceitfulness and manipulativeness	Low tolerance for frustration
Irresponsibility	Irritability
Glibness; superficial charm	
Exaggerated sense of self-worth	

Sources: Harris and others, 1994; White and others, 1994; Widiger and others, 1996.

PARANOID PERSONALITY DISORDER • A disorder characterized by persistent suspicion, but not the disorganization of paranoid schizophrenia.

SCHIZOTYPAL PERSONALITY DISORDER • A disorder characterized by oddities of thought and behavior, but not bizarre psychotic behaviors.

SCHIZOID PERSONALITY DISORDER • A disorder characterized by social withdrawal.

ANTISOCIAL PERSONALITY DISORDER • The diagnosis given a person who is in frequent conflict with society, yet who is undeterred by punishment and experiences little or no guilt and anxiety.

Theoretical Views

Many of the theoretical accounts of personality disorders derive from the psychodynamic model. Traditional Freudian theory focuses on Oedipal problems as the foundation for many psychological disorders, including personality disorders. Faulty resolution of the Oedipus complex might lead to antisocial personality disorder since the moral conscience, or superego, is believed to depend on proper resolution of the Oedipus complex. Learning theorists suggest that childhood experiences can contribute to maladaptive ways of relating to others (personality disorders) in adulthood. Empirically speaking, various factors appear to contribute to antisocial behavior, including an antisocial father, parental lack of love and rejection during childhood, and inconsistent discipline.

Genetic factors may be involved in antisocial personality disorder because antisocial personalities tend to run in families. Adoptee studies, for example, reveal higher incidences of antisocial behavior among the biological than the adoptive relatives of persons with the disorder (Maher & Maher, 1994). There is also evidence that genetic influences are moderate at best, however, and that the family environment is a crucial contributor to antisocial behavior (Carey, 1992).

If there are genetic factors in antisocial personality disorder, they may influence the individual's characteristic level of arousal of the nervous system. Consider that antisocial personalities are unlikely to show guilt for their misdeeds or to be deterred by punishment. Low levels of guilt and anxiety may reflect lower-than-normal levels of arousal, which, in turn, may have a partial genetic basis (Lykken, 1957, 1982). Experiments show, for example, that antisocial subjects do not learn as rapidly as others equal in intelligence when the payoff is avoidance of impending electric shock. But when the levels of arousal of the antisocial subjects are increased by injections of adrenaline, they learn to avoid punishment as rapidly as others (Chesno & Kilmann, 1975; Schachter & Latané, 1964).

A lower-than-normal level of arousal would not ensure the development of an antisocial personality. Perhaps a person must also be reared under conditions that do not foster the self-concept of a law-abiding citizen. Punishment for deviant behavior would then be unlikely to induce feelings of guilt and shame. The individual might well be undeterred by punishment.

Although the causes of many psychological disorders remain in dispute, a number of therapies have been devised to manage them. Those methods are the focus of Chapter 10.

adjustment and modern life

In the United States today there are great opportunities and great challenges. Millions are pleased with their financial accomplishments. Millions are generally happy with their families and their social lives. Yet millions of others feel that their lives are failures and that they cannot cope with the stresses they face. In the United States of the 1990s, about 30,000 people each year commit suicide (Michels & Marzuk, 1993a).

SUICIDE

Consider some facts about suicide:

- Suicide is more common among college students than among nonstudents. About 10,000 college students attempt suicide each year.
- Suicide is the second leading cause of death among college students.
- Teenage suicides loom large in the media spotlight, but older people are actually much more likely to commit suicide (McIntosh and others, 1995; Richman, 1993; see Figure 9.3). The suicide rate among older people is nearly twice the national rate.
- Nearly 200,000 people attempt suicide each year in the United States.
- Three times as many women as men attempt suicide, but about four times as many men succeed (see Figure 9.3; Rich and others, 1988; CDC, 1985a).
- Men prefer to use guns or to hang themselves, but women prefer to use sleeping pills. Males, that is, tend to choose quicker-acting and more lethal means. A study of 204 San Diego County suicides that took place in the early 1980s found that males who committed suicide were more likely to use guns (60 percent of the males versus 28 percent of the females) (Rich and others, 1988). Females who committed suicide more often used drugs or poisons (44 percent of the females versus 11 percent of the males).
- Although African Americans are more likely than White Americans to live in poverty and suffer from discrimination, the suicide rate is about twice as high among White Americans (see Figure 9.3).
- Suicide is especially common among physicians, lawyers, and psychologists, although it is found among all occupational groups and at all age levels.

Why do people take their lives? Most suicides are linked to feelings of depression and hopelessness (Beck and others, 1990; Lewinsohn and others, 1994a, 1994b). Additional factors connected with suicide include anxiety, panic attacks, lack of pleasure, alcohol abuse, problems concentrating, and insomnia (Sommers-Flanagan & Sommers-Flanagan, 1995). People who attempt suicide are usually trying to end extreme psychological anguish (Shneidman, 1985).

Truth or Fiction Revisited

It is not true that African Americans are more likely than White Americans to commit suicide. White Americans are actually more likely than African Americans to commit suicide, despite African Americans' greater social and socioeconomic burdens.

FIGURE 9.3
SUICIDE RATES ACCORDING TO GENDER AND RACE

Men are more likely than women to commit suicide. Women, however, make more suicide attempts. How can we account for this discrepancy? Non-Hispanic White Americans are also more likely to commit suicide than African Americans.

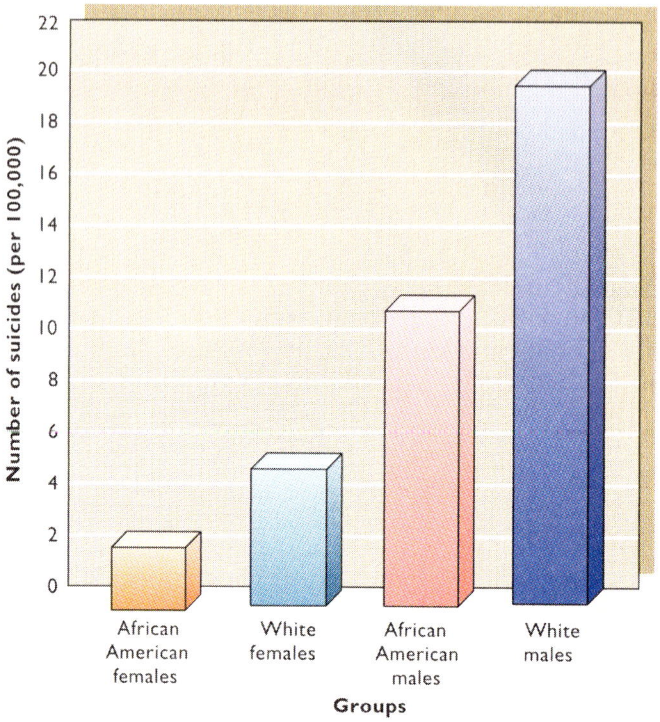

Suicide attempts are more frequent following stressful life events, especially events that involve loss of social support such as loss or death of a spouse, relative, or close friend. People who consider suicide in response to stress have also been found less capable of solving their problems than those who do not consider suicide (Rotheram-Borus and others, 1990; Schotte and others, 1990).

Now let us consider a number of myths about suicide—and the realities.

Myths About Suicide

Truth or Fiction Revisited

It is not true that people who threaten suicide are only seeking attention. Most people who commit suicide have informed others of their intentions.

Some believe that people who threaten suicide are only seeking attention. The serious just "do it." Actually, most people who commit suicide provide some clues to their intentions. About one third of them leave suicide notes (Black, 1993).

Some believe that those who fail at suicide attempts are only seeking attention. But the majority of people who take their lives have made prior attempts (Nevid and others, 1997). Contrary to myth, discussion of suicide with a depressed person does not prompt suicide. In fact, extracting a promise that the person will not commit suicide before calling or visiting a mental health worker seems to have prevented suicides.

Some believe that only "insane" people (meaning people who are out of touch with reality) would take their own lives. However, Shneidman points out that suicidal thinking is not necessarily a sign of psychosis, neurosis, or personality disorder. Instead, contemplation of suicide reflects a narrowing of the range of options that people think they have (Rotheram-Borus and others, 1990; Schotte and others, 1990). Finally, most people with suicidal thoughts, contrary to myth, do *not* act on them. Suicidal thinking is not uncommon when we are under stress. ■

HOW TO HELP PREVENT SUICIDE

You are having a heart-to-heart talk with one of your best friends on campus, Jamie. Things haven't been going well, you know. Jamie's grandmother died a month ago, and they were very close. Jamie's coursework has been suffering, and things have also been going downhill with the person Jamie has been seeing regularly. But you are not prepared when Jamie looks you straight in the eye and says, "I've been thinking about this for days, and I've decided that the only way out is to kill myself."

What do you say now? Write down three possible responses, and then check below for our suggestions.

1. ______________________________
   ____
2. ______________________________
   ____
3. ______________________________
   ____

If someone tells you that he or she is considering suicide, you may feel frightened and flustered, or you may feel that an enormous burden has been placed on you. It has. In such cases, your objective should be to encourage the person to consult a professional mental health worker, or you should consult a worker yourself as soon as possible. But if the person refuses to talk to anyone else and you feel that you can't break free for a consultation, there are a number of things you can do:

1. Draw the person out. Shneidman suggests asking questions like "What's going on?" "Where do you hurt?" "What would you like to see happen?" (1985, p. 11). Questions like these may encourage people to express frustrated needs and provide some relief. They also give you time to assess the danger and think.
2. Be empathetic. Show that you understand how upset the person is. Do *not* say, "Don't be silly."
3. Suggest that measures other than suicide may solve the problem, even if they are not evident at the time. Shneidman (1985) suggests that suicidal people can typically see only two solutions to their problems—either death or a magical answer. Therapists thus try to "widen the mental blinders" of suicidal people.
4. Ask how the person intends to commit suicide. People with concrete plans and a weapon are at greater risk. Ask if you may hold on to the weapon for a while. Sometimes the person says yes.
5. Suggest that the person go *with you* to obtain professional help *now*. The emergency room of a general hospital, the campus counseling center or infirmary, the campus or local police will do. Some campuses have hot lines. Some cities have suicide prevention centers with hot lines that can be called anonymously.
6. Extract a promise that the person will not commit suicide before seeing you again. Arrange a concrete time and place to meet. Get professional help as soon as you are apart.
7. Do *not* tell people threatening suicide that they're silly or crazy. Do *not* insist that people threatening suicide contact specific people, like parents or a spouse. Conflict with these people may have led to the suicidal thinking. Above all, remember that your primary objective is to consult a helping professional. Don't go it alone any longer than you must. ■

SUMMARY

1. **What are psychological disorders?** Behavior is likely to be labeled disordered when it is unusual, socially unacceptable, involves faulty perception of reality, or is personally distressful, dangerous, or self-defeating.
2. **How are psychological disorders classified?** The most commonly used system for classifying psychological disorders is the *Diagnostic and Statistical Manual* (DSM) of the American Psychiatric Association. The current edition of the DSM—the DSM-IV—has a multiaxial system with five axes: axes that assess clinical syndromes, personality disorders, general medical conditions, psychosocial and environmental problems, and global assessment of functioning.
3. **What are adjustment disorders?** Adjustment disorders are maladaptive reactions to one or more identified stressors that occur shortly following exposure to the stressor(s) and cause signs of distress beyond that which would be normally expected or impair functioning. Adjustment disorders are usually resolved when the stressor is removed or the person learns to cope with it.
4. **What are anxiety disorders?** Anxiety disorders are characterized by motor tension, feelings of dread, and autonomic overarousal. Anxiety disorders include irrational, excessive fears, or phobias; panic disorder, which is characterized by sudden attacks in which people typically fear that they may be losing control or going crazy; generalized, or free-floating, anxiety; obsessive-compulsive disorders, in which people are troubled by intrusive thoughts or impulses to repeat some activity; and the stress disorders (posttraumatic stress disorder and acute stress disorder), in which stressful events are followed by persistent fears and intrusive thoughts about them.
5. **What are dissociative disorders?** Dissociative disorders are characterized by a sudden temporary change in consciousness or self-identity. They include dissociative amnesia, or "motivated forgetting" of personal information; dissociative fugue, which involves forgetting plus fleeing and adopting a new identity; dissociative identity disorder, in which a person behaves as if distinct personalities occupied the body; and depersonalization, which is characterized by feelings that one is not real or that one is standing outside one's body and observing one's thought processes.
6. **What are somatoform disorders?** In somatoform disorders, people show or complain of physical problems, although no evidence of a medical abnormality can be found. The somatoform disorders include conversion disorder and hypochondriasis. In a conversion disorder, there is loss of a body function with no organic basis. Hypochondriacs insist that they are suffering from illnesses, although there are no medical findings.
7. **What are mood disorders?** Mood disorders are characterized by disturbance in expressed emotions. Major depression is characterized by persistent feelings of sadness, loss of interest, feelings of worthlessness or guilt, inability to concentrate, and physical features that may include disturbances in the regulation of eating and sleeping. Feelings of unworthiness and guilt may be so excessive that they are considered delusional. In bipolar disorder there are mood swings from elation to depression and back. Manic people also tend to show pressured speech and rapid flight of ideas.
8. **What is schizophrenia?** Schizophrenia is characterized by disturbances in thought and language, such as loosening of associations and delusions; disturbances in perception and attention, as found in hallucinations; disturbances in motor activity, as shown by a stupor or by excited behavior; disturbances in mood, as in flat or inappropriate emotional responses; and by withdrawal.

9. **What are the subtypes of schizophrenia?** There are three major types of schizophrenia: paranoid, disorganized, and catatonic. Paranoid schizophrenia is characterized by paranoid delusions. Disorganized schizophrenia is characterized by disorganized delusions and vivid, abundant hallucinations. Catatonic schizophrenia is characterized by impaired motor activity.

10. **What are personality disorders?** Personality disorders are inflexible, maladaptive behavior patterns that impair personal or social functioning and are a source of distress to the individual or others. Persons with antisocial personality disorders persistently violate the rights of others and encounter conflict with the law. They show little or no guilt or shame over their misdeeds and are largely undeterred by punishment.

CHAPTER 10

Therapies: Ways of Helping

TRUTH OR FICTION?

✓ T F

- ☐ ☐ Some psychotherapists interpret clients' dreams.
- ☐ ☐ If psychotherapy is to be of help, you must stick with it for several years.
- ☐ ☐ Some psychotherapists encourage their clients to take the lead in the therapy session.
- ☐ ☐ Some psychotherapists tell their clients precisely what to do.
- ☐ ☐ Lying around in your reclining chair and fantasizing can be an effective way of confronting your fears.
- ☐ ☐ You may be able to gain control over bad habits merely by keeping a record of where and when you practice them.
- ☐ ☐ Some psychotherapists purposefully argue with clients.
- ☐ ☐ Individual therapy is preferable to group therapy.
- ☐ ☐ Drugs are never a solution to psychological problems.
- ☐ ☐ The originator of a surgical technique intended to reduce violence learned that it was not always successful when one of his patients shot him.

OUTLINE

Jasmine, a 19-year-old college sophomore, has been crying almost without letup for several days. She feels that her life is falling apart. Her college aspirations are in a shambles. She has brought shame upon her family. Thoughts of suicide have crossed her mind. She can barely drag herself out of bed in the morning. She is avoiding her friends. She can pinpoint some sources of stress in her life: a couple of poor grades, an argument with a boyfriend, friction with roommates. Still, her misery seemed to descend on her out of nowhere.

Jasmine is depressed—so depressed that her family and friends have finally prevailed upon her to seek professional help. Had she broken her leg, her treatment by a qualified professional would have followed a fairly standard course. Yet, treatment of psychological problems and disorders like depression may be approached from very different perspectives. Depending on whom Jasmine sees, she may be treated by any of the following methods:

- Lying on a couch talking about anything that pops into her awareness and exploring the hidden meanings of a recurrent dream.
- Sitting face-to-face with a gentle, accepting therapist who places the major responsibility for what happens in therapy on Jasmine's shoulders.
- Listening to a frank, straightforward therapist assert that her problems stem from self-defeating attitudes and perfectionistic beliefs.
- Taking antidepressant medication.
- Participating in some combination of these approaches.

These methods, though different, all represent methods of therapy. In this chapter we explore various methods of psychotherapy and biological therapy.

WHAT IS THERAPY?

Psychotherapy may be defined as a systematic interaction between a therapist and a client that brings psychological principles to bear on influencing the client's thoughts, feelings, or behavior in order to help the client overcome psychological disorders, adjust to problems in living, or develop as an individual.

Quite a mouthful? True. But note the essentials:

1. Psychotherapy is a *systematic interaction* between a client and a therapist. The client's needs and goals and the therapist's theoretical point of view determine how the therapist and client relate to one another.
2. Psychotherapy brings *psychological principles* to bear on the client's problems or goals. Psychotherapy is based on the psychologies of personality, learning, motivation, and emotion. Psychotherapy is not based on, say, religious or biological principles, although it can be compatible with both.

PSYCHOTHERAPY • A systematic interaction between a therapist and a client that brings psychological principles to bear on influencing the client's thoughts, feelings, or behavior in order to help that client overcome psychological disorders or adjust to problems in living.

3. Psychotherapy influences clients' *thoughts, feelings, and behaviors.* Psychotherapy can address any or all of these.
4. Psychotherapy helps the client *overcome psychological disorders, adjust to problems in living, or develop as an individual.*

Now let us consider the main methods of therapy available today.

PSYCHOANALYSIS

Psychoanalysis is based on the thinking of Sigmund Freud. Freudians see our problems as largely reflecting early childhood experiences and internal conflicts. When primitive urges threaten to break through from the id, or when the superego floods us with excessive guilt, they give rise to defenses and distress. Psychoanalysis bulwarks the ego against the torrents of energy loosed by the id and the superego. With impulses and feelings of guilt placed under greater control, clients are emotionally freed to develop adaptive behavior.

Not all psychoanalysts view internal conflict in terms of unconscious forces, however. In this section we first outline Freud's methods, frequently referred to as "traditional" psychoanalysis. Then we examine more modern psychoanalytic approaches and find that their concepts of conflict and their methods differ from those of Freud.

Traditional Psychoanalysis: Where Id Was, There Shall Ego Be

Canst thou not minister to a mind diseas'd,
Pluck out from the memory a rooted sorrow,
Raze out the written troubles of the brain,
And with some sweet oblivious antidote
Cleanse the stuff'd bosom of that perilous stuff
Which weighs upon the heart?

SHAKESPEARE, *MACBETH*

In this passage, Macbeth asks a physician to minister to Lady Macbeth after she has gone mad. In the play, her madness is caused partly by events—namely, her role in murders designed to seat her husband on the throne of Scotland. There are also hints of mysterious, deeply rooted problems, such as conflicts about infertility.

If Lady Macbeth's physician had been a traditional psychoanalyst, he might have asked her to lie on a couch in a slightly darkened room. He would have sat behind her and encouraged her to talk about anything that came to mind, no matter how trivial, no matter how personal. To avoid interfering with her self-exploration, he might have said little or nothing for session after session. That would have been par for the course. A traditional psychoanalysis can extend for months or even years.

Psychoanalysis is the clinical method devised by Freud for plucking "from the memory a rooted sorrow," for razing "out the written troubles of the brain." It aims to provide *insight* into the conflicts that are presumed to lie at the roots of a person's problems. Insight means many things, including knowledge of the experiences that lead to conflicts and maladaptive behavior, recognition of unconscious feelings and conflicts, and conscious evaluation of one's thoughts, feelings, and behavior.

Psychoanalysis also aims to help the client express feelings and urges that have been repressed. By so doing, Freud believed that the client spilled forth the psychic energy that had been repressed by conflicts and guilt. He called this

PSYCHOANALYSIS • Freud's method of psychotherapy.

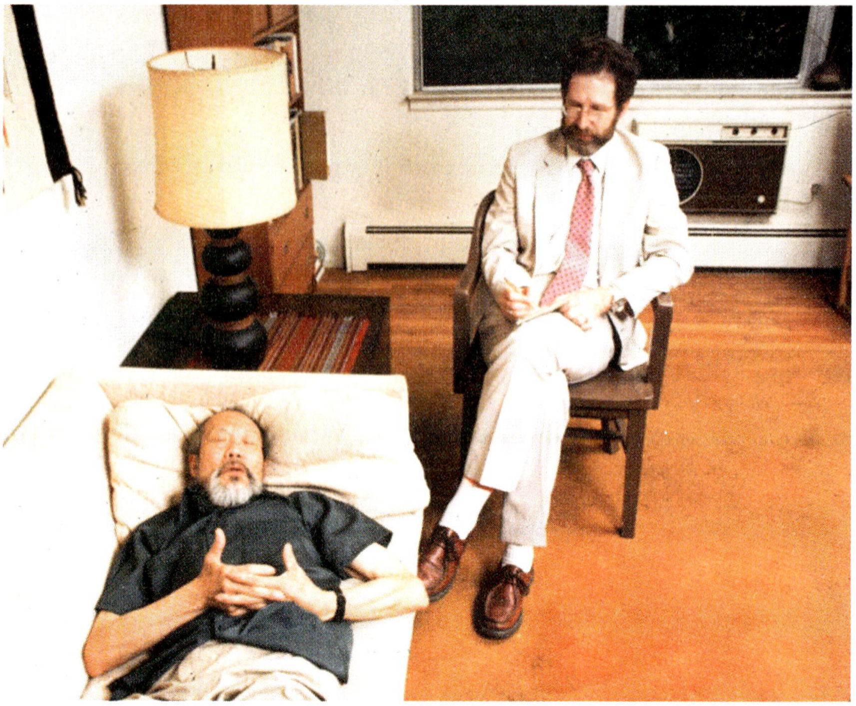

TRADITIONAL PSYCHOANALYSIS. In traditional psychoanalysis, the analyst sits in a chair by the head of a couch while a client free-associates. The cardinal rule of free association is that no thought is to be censored.

spilling forth **catharsis.** Catharsis would provide relief by alleviating some of the forces assaulting the ego.

Freud was also fond of saying, "Where id was, there shall ego be." In part, he meant that psychoanalysis could shed light on the inner workings of the mind. He also sought to replace impulsive and defensive behavior with coping behavior. In this way, for example, a man with a phobia for knives might discover that he had been repressing the urge to harm someone who had taken advantage of him. He might also find ways to confront the person verbally.

FREE ASSOCIATION Early in his career as a therapist, Freud found that hypnosis allowed his clients to focus on repressed conflicts and talk about them. The relaxed "trance state" provided by hypnosis seemed to allow clients to "break through" to topics of which they would otherwise be unaware. Freud also found, however, that many clients denied the accuracy of this material once they were out of the trance. Other clients found them to be premature and painful. Freud therefore turned to **free association,** a more gradual method of breaking through the walls of defense that block a client's insight into unconscious processes.

In free association, the client is made comfortable—for example, lying on a couch—and is asked to talk about any topic that comes to mind. No thought is to be censored—that is the basic rule. Psychoanalysts ask their clients to wander "freely" from topic to topic, but they do not believe that the process occurring *within* the client is fully free. Repressed impulses clamor for release.

The ego persists in trying to repress unacceptable impulses and threatening conflicts. As a result, clients might show *resistance* to recalling and discussing threatening ideas. A client about to entertain such thoughts might claim that "my mind is blank." The client might accuse the analyst of being demanding or inconsiderate. He or she might "forget" the next appointment when threatening material is about to surface.

CATHARSIS • In psychoanalysis, expression of previously repressed feelings and impulses to allow the psychic energy associated with them to spill forth.

FREE ASSOCIATION • In psychoanalysis, the uncensored uttering of all thoughts that come to mind.

The therapist observes the dynamic struggle between the compulsion to utter certain thoughts and the client's resistance to uttering them. Through discreet remarks, the analyst subtly tips the balance in favor of utterance. A gradual process of self-discovery and self-insight ensues. Now and then the analyst offers an *interpretation* of an utterance, showing how it suggests resistance or deep-seated feelings and conflicts.

Dream Analysis

Sometimes a cigar is just a cigar.

SIGMUND FREUD, ON DREAM ANALYSIS

Freud often asked clients to jot down their dreams upon waking so that they could be discussed in therapy. Freud considered dreams the "royal road to the unconscious." He believed that the content of dreams is determined by unconscious processes as well as by the events of the day. Unconscious impulses tend to be expressed in dreams as a form of **wish fulfillment.**

Truth or Fiction Revisited

It is true that some psychotherapists interpret clients' dreams. Psychoanalysis is a case in point.

But unacceptable sexual and aggressive impulses are likely to be displaced onto objects and situations that reflect the client's era and culture. These objects become symbols of the unconscious wishes. For example, long, narrow dream objects might be **phallic symbols,** but whether the symbol takes the form of a spear, rifle, stick shift, or spacecraft partially reflects the dreamer's cultural background.

In psychodynamic theory, the perceived content of a dream is referred to as its shown or *manifest content.* Its presumed hidden or symbolic content is its *latent content.* Suppose a man dreams that he is flying. Flying is the manifest content of the dream. Freud usually interpreted flying as being symbolic of erection, so issues concerning sexual potency might make up the latent content of such a dream.

Modern Psychodynamic Approaches

Some psychoanalysts adhere faithfully to Freud's techniques. In recent years, however, briefer, less intense forms of psychodynamic therapy have been devised. They make treatment available to clients who do not have the time or money for long-term therapy. Many of these therapists also believe that prolonged therapy is not needed or justifiable in terms of the ratio of cost to benefits.

Truth or Fiction Revisited

It is not true that psychotherapy must continue for many months or years to be effective. There are many effective brief forms of psychotherapy.

Some modern psychodynamic therapies continue to focus on revealing unconscious material and breaking through psychological defenses. Nevertheless, they differ from traditional psychoanalysis in several ways. One is that the client and therapist usually sit face-to-face (the client does not lie on a couch). The therapist is usually directive. That is, modern therapists often suggest helpful behavior instead of focusing on insight alone. Finally, there is usually more focus on the ego as the "executive" of personality, and less emphasis on the id. For this reason, many modern psychodynamic therapists are considered **ego analysts.**

Many of Freud's followers, the "second generation" of psychoanalysts—from Jung and Adler to Horney and Erikson—believed that Freud had placed too much emphasis on sexual and aggressive impulses and underestimated the role of the ego. For example, Freud aimed to establish conditions under which clients could spill forth psychic energy and eventually shore up the egos. Erikson, in contrast, spoke to clients directly about their values and concerns, encouraging them to develop desired traits and behavior patterns. Even Freud's daughter, the psychoanalyst Anna Freud (1895–1982), was more concerned with the ego than with unconscious forces and conflicts.

WISH FULFILLMENT • A primitive method used by the id to attempt to gratify basic instincts.

PHALLIC SYMBOL • A sign that represents the penis.

EGO ANALYST • A psychodynamically oriented therapist who focuses on the conscious, coping behavior of the ego instead of the hypothesized unconscious functioning of the id.

Today there are many approaches to psychoanalysis. Let us now consider phenomenological approaches to therapy.

PHENOMENOLOGICAL THERAPIES

Psychodynamic therapies focus on internal conflicts and unconscious processes. Phenomenological therapies, in contrast, focus on clients' subjective, conscious experiences. Psychodynamic therapies tend to focus on the past, and particularly on early childhood experiences. Phenomenological therapies usually focus on what clients are experiencing today—here and now.

Having noted these differences, we must point out that they are differences in *emphasis*. The happenings of the past have a way of influencing the thoughts, feelings, and behavior of the present. Carl Rogers, the originator of client-centered therapy, recognized that childhood experiences gave rise to conditions of worth that troubled his clients in the here and now. Rogers and Fritz Perls, the originator of Gestalt therapy, recognized that early incorporation of other people's values can lead clients to "disown" parts of their own personalities in the here and now.

Let us now consider client-centered therapy and Gestalt therapy to elaborate some of these ideas.

Client-Centered Therapy: Removing Roadblocks to Self-Actualization

Client-centered therapy was originated by Carl Rogers (1951), who believed that we have natural tendencies toward health, growth, and fulfillment. Given this view, Rogers wrote that psychological disorders stem largely from roadblocks placed in the path of our own self-actualization. Because others show us selective approval when we are young, we learn to disown the disapproved parts of ourselves. We don masks and facades to earn social approval. As a result we might experience stress and discomfort and the feeling that we—or the world—are not real.

Client-centered therapy aims to provide insight into parts of us that we have disowned, so that we can feel whole. It stresses the importance of a warm, therapeutic atmosphere that encourages client self-exploration and self-expression. Therapist acceptance of the client is thought to lead to client self-acceptance and self-esteem. Self-acceptance frees the client to make choices that foster development of his or her unique potential.

Client-centered therapy is nondirective. The client takes the lead, listing and exploring problems. The therapist reflects or paraphrases expressed feelings and ideas, helping the client get in touch with deeper feelings and to follow the strongest leads in the quest for self-insight.

An effective client-centered therapist has several qualities:

- **Unconditional positive regard:** Respect for clients as human beings with unique values and goals.
- **Empathic understanding:** Recognition of the client's experiences and feelings. Therapists view the world through the client's *frame of reference* by setting aside their own values and listening closely.
- **Genuineness:** Openness and honesty in responding to the client. Client-centered therapists must be able to tolerate differentness, because they believe that every client is different in important ways.

Client-centered therapy is practiced widely in college and university counseling centers, not just to help students experiencing, say, anxieties or depres-

Truth or Fiction Revisited

It is true that some psychotherapists encourage their clients to take the lead in the therapy session. Client-centered therapists provide an example.

CLIENT-CENTERED THERAPY • Carl Rogers's method of psychotherapy, which emphasizes the creation of a warm, therapeutic atmosphere that frees clients to explore and express themselves.

UNCONDITIONAL POSITIVE REGARD • Acceptance of the value of another person, although not necessarily acceptance of all of that person's behaviors.

EMPATHIC UNDERSTANDING • Ability to perceive a client's feelings from the client's frame of reference. A quality of the effective person-centered therapist.

GENUINENESS • Open expression of the therapist's own feelings.

sion but also to help them make decisions. Many college students have not yet made career choices or wonder whether they should become involved with particular people or in sexual activity. Client-centered therapists do not tell clients what to do. Instead, they help clients arrive at their own decisions.

Gestalt Therapy: Getting It Together

Gestalt therapy was originated by Fritz Perls (1893–1970). Like client-centered therapy, it aims to help people integrate conflicting parts of their personalities. Perls used the term *Gestalt* to signify his interest in providing the conflicting parts of the personality an integrated form or shape. He aimed to have his clients become aware of inner conflict, accept the reality of conflict rather than deny or repress it, and make productive choices despite misgivings and fear.

Although Perls's ideas about conflicting personality elements owe much to psychoanalysis, his form of therapy focuses on the here and now. In Gestalt therapy, clients undergo exercises to heighten awareness of current feelings and behavior, not to explore the past. Perls, like Rogers, believed that people are free to make choices and to direct their personal growth. Unlike client-centered therapy, however, Gestalt therapy is directive. The therapist leads the client through planned experiences.

Truth or Fiction Revisited

It is true that some psychotherapists tell their clients precisely what to do. Gestalt therapists provide an example.

One Gestalt technique that increases awareness of internal conflict is the *dialogue.* Clients undertake verbal confrontations between opposing wishes and ideas. An example of these clashing personality elements is "top dog" and "underdog." One's top dog may conservatively suggest, "Don't take chances. Stick with what you have or you may lose it all." One's frustrated underdog may then rise up and assert, "You never try anything. How will you ever get out of this rut if you don't take on new challenges?" Heightened awareness of the elements of conflict can clear the path toward resolution, perhaps through compromise.

Body language also provides insight into conflicting feelings. Clients may be instructed to attend to the ways in which they furrow their eyebrows and tense their facial muscles when they express ideas that they think they support. In this way they often find that their body language asserts feelings that they have been denying.

In order to increase clients' understanding of opposing points of view, Gestalt therapists may encourage them to argue in favor of ideas opposed to their own. They may also have clients role-play people who are important to them in order to get more in touch with their points of view.

Whereas psychodynamic theory views dreams as the "royal road to the unconscious," Perls saw the stuff of dreams as disowned parts of the personality. He would often ask clients to role-play the elements in their dreams to get in touch with these parts.

BEHAVIOR THERAPY: ADJUSTMENT IS WHAT YOU DO

Behavior therapy—also called *behavior modification*—applies principles of learning to directly promote behavioral changes (Wolpe & Plaud, 1997). Behavior therapists rely heavily on principles of conditioning and observational learning. They help clients discontinue self-defeating behavior patterns such as overeating, smoking, and phobic avoidance of harmless stimuli. They help clients acquire adaptive behavior patterns such as the social skills required to start social relationships or say no to insistent salespeople.

Gestalt therapy • Fritz Perls's form of psychotherapy, which attempts to integrate conflicting parts of the personality through directive methods designed to help clients perceive their whole selves.

Behavior therapy • Systematic application of the principles of learning to the direct modification of problem behavior.

Behavior therapists may help clients gain "insight" into maladaptive behavior in the sense of fostering awareness of the circumstances in which it occurs. They do not foster insight in the psychoanalytic sense of unearthing the childhood origins of problems and the symbolic meanings of maladaptive behavior. Behavior therapists, like other therapists, may also build warm, therapeutic relationships with clients, but they see the efficacy of behavior therapy as deriving from specific, learning-based procedures (Wolpe, 1990). They insist that their methods be established by experimentation and that therapeutic outcomes be assessed in terms of observable, measurable behavior. Let us look at some behavior therapy techniques.

Fear-Reduction Methods

Behavior therapists use many methods for reducing fears, including flooding (see Chapter 2), systematic desensitization, and modeling.

SYSTEMATIC DESENSITIZATION Adam has a phobia for receiving injections. His behavior therapist treats him as he reclines in a comfortable padded chair. In a state of deep muscle relaxation, Adam observes slides projected on a screen. A slide of a nurse holding a needle has just been shown three times, 30 seconds at a time. Each time Adam has shown no anxiety. So now a slightly more discomforting slide is shown: one of the nurse aiming the needle toward someone's bare arm. After 15 seconds, our armchair adventurer notices twinges of discomfort and raises a finger as a signal (speaking might disturb his relaxation). The projector operator turns off the light, and Adam spends 2 minutes imagining his "safe scene"—lying on a beach beneath the tropical sun. Then the slide is shown again. This time Adam views it for 30 seconds before feeling anxiety.

Adam is undergoing **systematic desensitization,** a method for reducing phobic responses originated by psychiatrist Joseph Wolpe (1990). Systematic desensitization is a gradual process in which the client learns to handle increasingly disturbing stimuli while anxiety to each one is being counterconditioned. About 10 to 20 stimuli are arranged in a sequence, or *hierarchy,* according to their capacity to elicit anxiety. In imagination or by being shown photos, the client travels gradually up through this hierarchy, approaching the target behavior. In Adam's case, the target behavior was the ability to receive an injection without undue anxiety.

SYSTEMATIC DESENSITIZATION • Wolpe's method for reducing fears by associating a hierarchy of images of fear-evoking stimuli with deep muscle relaxation.

OVERCOMING FEAR OF FLYING. This woman has undergone group systematic desensitization in order to overcome her fear of flying. For several sessions, she engaged in tasks such as viewing pictures of airplanes and imagining herself in one. Now in the final stages of her program, she actually flies in an airplane with the support of group members and her therapist.

Wolpe developed systematic desensitization on the assumption that anxiety responses, like other behaviors, are learned or conditioned. He reasoned that they can be unlearned by means of **counterconditioning** or extinction. In counterconditioning, a response that is incompatible with anxiety is made to appear under conditions that usually elicit anxiety. Muscle relaxation is incompatible with anxiety. For this reason, Adam's therapist is teaching him to relax in the presence of (usually) anxiety-evoking slides of needles.

Remaining in the presence of phobic imagery, rather than running away from it, is also likely to enhance self-efficacy expectations (Galassi, 1988). Self-efficacy expectations are negatively correlated with levels of adrenaline in the bloodstream (Bandura and others, 1985). Raising clients' self-efficacy expectations thus may help lower their adrenaline levels and reduce their feelings of nervousness.

The case of David offers more insight into systematic desensitization:

> David, a 25-year-old art teacher, was scheduled to begin his first full-time teaching job in a month and a half. During the prior weeks he had begun to ruminate about his shaky student teaching the spring before. He was growing more and more fearful of going before his classes. He had even considered resigning before he began. He had developed shakiness, light-headedness, cold hands, loose bowels, and "spells" during which he forgot what he was going to do. A friend who had taken a few psychology courses told David that he was "really" afraid that if he became a competent teacher he would run out of excuses for continuing to live with his mother. Sad to say, neither this "insight" nor David's haphazard attempts to medicate himself with beer were useful.
>
> When David consulted a professional, it was suggested that systematic desensitization might help him overcome his fear of teaching within the few weeks remaining before the school year began. David received two weeks of intensive relaxation training. A fear-stimulus hierarchy was constructed along two dimensions: time left to go before teaching and the amount of threat in various teaching situations. He listed the items on index cards and sorted them until he was satisfied that they were in the proper order. In a couple of cases, an item from one dimension induced as much anxiety as an item from another, and their order was randomized. The list was as follows:
>
> 1. It is four weeks before classes begin
> 2. It is three weeks before classes begin
> 3. Talking after school with a student about the possibility of a career in art
> 4. It is two weeks before classes begin
> 6. It is ten days before classes begin
> 7. Supervising one student during class while other students work independently in the classroom
> 8. It is one week before classes begin
> 9. Supervising two students working on a project while other students work independently in the classroom
> 10. Supervising a group of three students working on a project while other students work independently in the classroom
> 11. It is five days before classes begin
> 12. Asking a class involved in independent projects if there are any questions

Truth or Fiction Revisited

It is true that lying in a reclining chair and fantasizing can be an effective way of confronting fears. This is what happens in the method of systematic desensitization.

COUNTERCONDITIONING • The repeated pairing of a stimulus that elicits a certain response (say, fear) with a stimulus that elicits an antagonistic response (say, relaxation instructions) in such a way that the first stimulus loses the capacity to elicit the problematic (fear) response.

13. It is two days before classes begin
14. Preparing a lesson plan for the first day of classes
15. It is the night before classes begin
16. Driving to work the first morning of classes
17. Greeting a new class, talking about the course, and fielding questions

So that he would not worry about how to greet his classes, David prepared concrete initial talks for his students. He rehearsed them until they seemed "natural." Parts of clinical sessions were spent in behavior rehearsal, during which David delivered pieces of lessons. Now and then the therapist role-played difficult students, asking confusing questions or making sarcastic remarks. David rehearsed responses to these students in the unthreatening therapeutic situation.

When David appeared before his classes, he experienced mild anxiety. He took a deep breath, told himself to relax, and exhaled. The effect was calming. By the time David introduced himself to his last class, he was enjoying his first day as a teacher. He had increased his perceived self-efficacy by learning that he could control his level of arousal and focus on his teaching rather than on his fear. (Rathus & Nevid, 1977, pp. 52–54)

MODELING **Modeling** relies on observational learning. In this method clients observe, and then imitate, people who approach and cope with the objects or situations that the clients fear. Bandura and his colleagues (1969) found that modeling worked as well as systematic desensitization—and more rapidly—in reducing fear of snakes. Like systematic desensitization, modeling is likely to increase self-efficacy expectations in coping with feared stimuli.

Aversive Conditioning

Aversive conditioning is one of the more controversial procedures in behavior therapy. In this method painful or aversive stimuli are paired with unwanted impulses, such as desire for a cigarette or desire to engage in antisocial behavior, in order to make the impulse less appealing. For example, to help people control alcohol intake, tastes of different alcoholic beverages can be paired with drug-induced nausea and vomiting or with electric shock.

Aversive conditioning has been used with problems as diverse as cigarette smoking, sexual abuse (Rice and others, 1991), and retarded children's self-injurious behavior. *Rapid smoking* is an aversive conditioning method designed to help smokers quit. In this method, the would-be quitter inhales every 6 seconds. In another method the hose of a hair dryer is hooked up to a chamber containing several lit cigarettes. Smoke is blown into the quitter's face as he or she also smokes a cigarette. A third method uses branching pipes so that the smoker draws in smoke from several cigarettes at the same time. In all of these methods overexposure causes once-desirable cigarette smoke to become aversive. The quitter becomes motivated to avoid, rather than seek, cigarettes. Many reports have shown a quit rate of 60 percent or higher at 6-month follow-ups. Yet interest in these methods for quitting smoking has waned because of side effects such as raising blood pressure and the availability of nicotine-replacement techniques.

In one study of aversive conditioning in the treatment of alcoholism, 63 percent of the 685 people treated remained abstinent for 1 year afterward, and about a third remained abstinent for at least 3 years (Wiens & Menustik, 1983). It may seem ironic that punitive aversive stimulation is sometimes used to stop children from punishing themselves, but people sometimes hurt themselves in

MODELING • A technique in which a client observes and imitates a person who approaches and copes with feared objects or situations.

AVERSIVE CONDITIONING • A technique in which undesired responses are inhibited by pairing repugnant or offensive stimuli with them.

order to obtain sympathy and attention. If self-injury leads to more pain than anticipated and no sympathy, it might be discontinued.

Operant Conditioning Methods

Behavior therapists have used operant conditioning principles to manage problems as widespread as lack of cooperation on hospital wards and high blood pressure.

The staff at one mental hospital was at a loss as to how to induce withdrawn schizophrenic patients to eat regularly. Ayllon and Haughton (1962) observed that the staff exacerbated the problem by coaxing patients into the dining room, even feeding them. Increased staff attention apparently reinforced the patients' lack of cooperation. The rules were changed. Patients who did not arrive at the dining hall within 30 minutes after serving were locked out. Staff could not interact with patients at mealtime. With uncooperative behavior no longer reinforced, patients quickly changed their eating habits. Patients were then required to pay one penny to enter the dining hall. Pennies were earned by showing socially appropriate behaviors, such as socializing with other patients. These target behaviors also increased in frequency.

TOKEN ECONOMY Many psychiatric wards and hospitals now use **token economies.** Tokens such as poker chips are used by patients to purchase TV-viewing time, extra visits to the canteen, or private rooms. Tokens are provided as reinforcements for productive activities such as making beds, brushing teeth, and socializing. Whereas token economies have not eliminated all signs of schizophrenia, they have enhanced patient activity and cooperation. Tokens have also been used successfully to modify the behavior of children with conduct disorders. For example, Schneider and Byrne (1987) gave children tokens for helpful behaviors such as volunteering, and removed tokens for behaviors such as arguing and inattention.

SUCCESSIVE APPROXIMATIONS We can use the operant conditioning method of **successive approximations** to build good habits. Let us use a (not uncommon!) example: You wish to study 3 hours an evening but can only maintain concentration for half an hour. Rather than attempting to increase study time all at once, you could do so gradually, say by 5 minutes an evening. After every hour or so of studying, reinforce yourself with something like 5 minutes of people watching in a busy section of the library.

SOCIAL-SKILLS TRAINING In **social-skills training,** behavior therapists decrease social anxiety and build social skills through operant conditioning procedures that employ self-monitoring, coaching, modeling, role-playing, behavior rehearsal, and feedback. Social-skills training has been used to help formerly hospitalized mental patients maintain jobs and apartments in the community. Assertiveness training, a kind of social-skills training described in Chapter 4, helps clients demand their rights and express their genuine feelings.

BIOFEEDBACK TRAINING Through **biofeedback training** (BFT), therapists have helped many clients become more aware of, and gain control over, their stress responses. In BFT, therapists attach devices to clients that measure bodily changes, such as heart rate. "Bleeps" or other electronic signals are used to indicate (and thereby reinforce) bodily changes in the desired direction. (Knowledge of results is a powerful reinforcer.) The electromyograph (EMG), for

TOKEN ECONOMY • A controlled environment in which people are reinforced for desired behaviors with tokens (such as poker chips) that may be exchanged for privileges.

SUCCESSIVE APPROXIMATIONS • In operant conditioning, a series of behaviors that gradually become more similar to a target behavior.

SOCIAL-SKILLS TRAINING • Operant conditioning methods that build social skills through techniques like self-monitoring, coaching, modeling, role-playing, behavior rehearsal, and feedback.

BIOFEEDBACK TRAINING • An operant conditioning procedure in which an organism is fed back continuous information about a bodily function and thereby gains control over that function. Abbreviated *BFT.*

example, monitors muscle tension. It has been used to augment control over muscle tension in the forehead and elsewhere, thereby alleviating anxiety and stress.

BFT also helps clients to voluntarily regulate functions, such as heart rate and blood pressure, that were previously thought to be beyond conscious control. Hypertensive clients have used a blood-pressure cuff and electronic signals to gain control over their blood pressure. The electroencephalograph (EEG) monitors brain waves and can be used to teach people how to produce alpha waves, which are associated with relaxation. People have even overcome insomnia by learning to produce brain waves associated with sleep.

Self-Control Techniques

Do mysterious forces sometimes seem to be at work in your life? Forces that delight in wreaking havoc on New Year's resolutions and other efforts to put an end to your bad habits? Just when you go on a diet, that juicy pizza stares at you from the TV set. Just when you resolve to balance your budget, that sweater goes on sale. Behavior therapists have developed a number of self-control techniques to help people cope with such temptations.

Truth or Fiction Revisited

It is true that you might be able to put an end to bad habits merely by keeping a record of where and when you engage in them. The record may help motivate you, make you more aware of the problems, and suggest strategies for behavior change.

FUNCTIONAL ANALYSIS OF BEHAVIOR Behavior therapists usually begin with a **functional analysis** of the problem behavior. In this way, they help determine the stimuli that trigger the behavior and the reinforcers that maintain it. You can use a diary to jot down each instance of a problem behavior. Note the time of day, location, your activity at the time (including your thoughts and feelings), and reactions (yours and others'). Functional analysis serves a number of purposes. It makes you more aware of the environmental context of your behavior and can increase your motivation to change.

Brian used functional analysis to master his nail biting. Table 10.1 shows a few items from his notebook. He discovered that boredom and humdrum activities seemed to serve as triggers for nail biting. He began to watch out for feelings of boredom as signs to practice self-control. He also made some changes in his life so that he would feel bored less often.

There are numerous self-control strategies aimed at the stimuli that trigger behavior, the behaviors themselves, and reinforcers. Table 10.2 looks at some of these strategies.

TABLE 10.1 EXCERPTS FROM BRIAN'S DIARY OF NAIL BITING FOR APRIL 14

INCIDENT	*TIME*	*LOCATION*	*ACTIVITY (thoughts, feelings)*	*REACTIONS*
1	7:45 A.M.	Freeway	Driving to work, bored, not thinking	Finger bleeds, pain
2	10:30 A.M.	Office	Writing report	Self-disgust
3	2:25 P.M.	Conference	Listening to dull financial report	Embarrassment
4	6:40 P.M.	Living room	Watching evening news	Self-disgust

A functional analysis of problem behavior, like nail biting, increases awareness of the environmental context in which it occurs, spurs motivation to change, and, in highly motivated people, may lead to significant behavioral change.

FUNCTIONAL ANALYSIS • A systematic study of behavior in which one identifies the stimuli that trigger it and the reinforcers that maintain it.

TABLE 10.2 Behavior Therapy Self-Control Strategies

TARGET OF STRATEGIES	STRATEGY	EXAMPLE
Strategies aimed at stimuli that trigger behavior	Restriction of the stimulus field	Gradually exclude the problem behavior from more environments. For example, at first make smoking off limits in the car, then in the office. Or practice the habit only outside the environment in which it normally occurs. Smoke, for example, only in a "stimulus-deprived" (boring) corner of the basement.
	Avoidance of powerful stimuli that trigger habits	Avoid obvious sources of temptation. People who go window-shopping often wind up buying more than windows. If eating at The Pizza Glutton tempts you to forget your diet, eat at home or at The Celery Stalk instead.
	Stimulus control	Place yourself in an environment in which desirable behavior is likely to occur. Maybe it's difficult to lift your mood directly at times, but you can place yourself in the audience of that uplifting concert or film. It might be difficult to force yourself to study, but how about rewarding yourself for spending time in the library?
Strategies aimed at behavior	Response prevention	Make unwanted behavior difficult or impossible. Impulse buying is curbed when you shred your credit cards, leave your checkbook home, and carry only a couple of dollars. You can't reach for the strawberry cream cheese pie in your refrigerator if you have left it at the supermarket (that is, have not bought it).
	Competing responses	Engage in behaviors that are incompatible with the bad habits. It is difficult to drink a glass of water and a fattening milk shake simultaneously. Grasping something firmly is a useful competing response for nail biting or scratching.
	Chain breaking	Interfere with unwanted habitual behavior by complicating the process of engaging in it. Put your cigarette in the ashtray between puffs, or put your fork down between mouthfuls of dessert. Each time, ask yourself if you really want more.
Strategies aimed at reinforcements	Reinforcement of desired behavior	Make pleasant activities such as going to films, walking on the beach, or reading a new novel contingent upon meeting reasonable, daily behavioral goals. Put a few dollars away toward that camera or vacation trip each day you remain within your calorie limit.
	Response cost	Heighten awareness of the long-term reasons for dieting or cutting down on smoking by punishing yourself for not meeting a daily goal or for practicing a bad habit. Make out a check to your most hated cause and mail it at once if you bite your nails or inhale that cheesecake.
	"Grandma's method"	Remember Grandma's method for inducing children to eat their vegetables? Simple: no veggies, no dessert. In this method, desired behaviors such as studying and brushing teeth can be increased by insisting that they be done before you carry out a favored or frequently occurring activity. For example, don't watch television unless you have studied first. Don't leave the apartment until you've brushed your teeth.
	Covert sensitization	Create imaginary horror stories about problem behavior. Psychologists have successfully reduced overeating and smoking by having clients imagine that they become acutely nauseated at the thought of fattening foods or that a cigarette is made from vomit. Some horror stories are not so "imaginary." Deliberately focusing on heart strain and diseased lungs every time you overeat or smoke, rather than ignoring these long-term consequences, might also promote self-control.
	Covert reinforcement	Create rewarding imagery for desired behavior. When you have achieved a behavioral goal, fantasize about how wonderful you are. Imagine friends and family patting you on the back.

COGNITIVE THERAPIES

There is nothing either good or bad,
But thinking makes it so.

SHAKESPEARE, *HAMLET*

A *thing is important if anyone* think *it Important.*

WILLIAM JAMES

Cognitive therapies focus on the beliefs, attitudes, and automatic types of thinking that create and compound people's problems. Cognitive therapists, like psychodynamic and phenomenological therapists, are interested in fostering self-insight, but they heighten insight into *current cognitions,* not the distant past. Cognitive therapists also aim to *change* maladaptive cognitions to reduce negative feelings, provide more accurate perceptions of the self and others, and orient the client toward solving problems.

Let us have a look at some of the major cognitive therapists and at some of their approaches and methods.

Cognitive Therapy: Correcting Cognitive Errors

Aaron Beck, the originator of a key approach to cognitive therapy, used cognitive and behavioral techniques on himself before he became a psychiatrist. One of the reasons he went into medicine was to confront his own fear of blood. He had had a series of operations as a child, and from then on the sight of blood had made him feel faint. During his first year of medical school, he forced himself to watch operations. In his second year, he became a surgical assistant. Soon the sight of blood became normal to him. Later he essentially argued himself out of an irrational fear of tunnels. He convinced himself that the tunnels did not cause the fear because the symptoms of faintness and shallow breathing would appear before he entered them.

As a psychiatrist, Beck, like Albert Ellis, first practiced psychoanalysis. However, he could not find scientific evidence for psychoanalytic beliefs. Psychoanalytic theory explained depression as anger turned inward, so that it is transformed into a need to suffer. Beck's own clinical experiences led him to believe that it is more likely that depressed people experience cognitive distortions such as the *cognitive triad.* That is, they expect the worst of themselves ("I'm no good"), the world at large ("This is an awful place"), and their future ("Nothing good will ever happen").

Beck's cognitive therapy is active. Beck encourages clients to become their own personal scientists and challenge beliefs that are not supported by evidence. He questions people in a way that encourages them to see the irrationality of their ways of thinking. For example, depressed people tend to minimize their accomplishments and to assume that the worst will happen. Both distortions heighten feelings of depression. Beck (1991, 1993) notes that cognitive distortions can be fleeting and automatic, difficult to detect. His therapy methods help clients pin down such distortions and challenge them.

Beck notes in particular the pervasive influence of four basic types of cognitive errors that contribute to clients' miseries:

COGNITIVE THERAPY • A form of therapy that focuses on how clients' cognitions (expectations, attitudes, beliefs, etc.) lead to distress and may be modified to relieve distress and promote adaptive behavior.

1. Clients may *selectively perceive* the world as a harmful place and ignore evidence to the contrary.

2. Clients may *overgeneralize* on the basis of a few examples. They may perceive themselves as worthless because they were laid off at work or as grossly unattractive because they were refused a request for a date.
3. Clients may *magnify*, or blow out of proportion, the significance of negative events. Clients may catastrophize flunking a test by assuming they will flunk out of college, or catastrophize losing a job by believing that they will never work again and that serious harm will befall their families.
4. Clients may engage in *absolutist thinking*, or looking at the world in black and white rather than in shades of gray. In doing so, a rejection on a date assumes the meaning of a lifetime of loneliness; a nagging illness takes on life-threatening proportions.

The concept of pinpointing and modifying errors may become more clear from a case in which a 53-year-old engineer was treated with cognitive therapy for severe depression. The engineer had left his job and become inactive. The first treatment goal was to foster physical activity—even things like raking leaves and preparing dinner—because activity is incompatible with depression. Then:

> [The engineer's] cognitive distortions were identified by comparing his assessment of each activity with that of his wife. Alternative ways of interpreting his experiences were then considered.
>
> In comparing his wife's résumé of his past experiences, he became aware that he had (1) undervalued his past by failing to mention many previous accomplishments, (2) regarded himself as far more responsible for his "failures" than she did, and (3) concluded that he was worthless since he had not succeeded in attaining certain goals in the past. When the two accounts were contrasted, he could discern many of his cognitive distortions. In subsequent sessions, his wife continued to serve as an "objectifier."
>
> In midtherapy, [he] compiled a list of new attitudes that he had acquired since initiating therapy. These included:
>
> (1) I am starting at a lower level of functioning at my job, but it will improve if I persist.
>
> (2) I know that once I get going in the morning, everything will run all right for the rest of the day.
>
> (3) I can't achieve everything at once.
>
> (4) I have my periods of ups and downs, but in the long run I feel better.
>
> (5) My expectations from my job and life should be scaled down to a realistic level.
>
> (6) Giving in to avoidance [e.g., staying away from work and social interactions] never helps and only leads to further avoidance.
>
> He was instructed to re-read this list daily for several weeks even though he already knew the content (Rush and others, 1975).

Rereading the list of productive attitudes is a variation on the cognitive therapy theme of having clients rehearse accurate and rational ideas so that they will replace cognitive distortions and irrational beliefs. The engineer became gradually less depressed in therapy and returned to work and an active social life. Along the way he learned to combat inappropriate self-blame, perfectionistic expectations, and overgeneralizations from failures.

Becoming aware of cognitive errors and modifying catastrophizing thoughts helps provide us with coping ability under stress.

WHAT DO *You* SAY NOW?

HOW TO RESPOND TO A SOCIAL PROVOCATION

Cognitive therapists sometimes help clients get in touch with their feelings and beliefs by having them "run movies," or place themselves in imaginary situations. For example, picture yourself in this situation: You are pushing a cart down an aisle in a supermarket, looking at the containers on the shelves. Maybe you're not paying attention to other people and you wander out into the middle of the aisle. Suddenly, someone pushes into you, so hard that it seems purposeful. He then says, "What the hell's the matter with you? Why don't you watch where you're going!"

What do you say now? Write down a number of responses you might make and then check the suggested responses below.

1. ______________________________
2. ______________________________
3. ______________________________

Cognitive therapists believe that your responses will reflect the way in which you interpret your antagonist's behavior. For example, would you perceive his behavior as a challenge to your "honor" or as a problem to be solved?

We suggest responses such as the following:

1. Say *nothing*. Perhaps it will be dropped if you let it pass. (This person might be angry at the world because of personal failures and shortcomings and might be spoiling for a fight. Or for some reason, he might really think that *you* bumped into *him* and that *you* are looking for trouble. How can you know what is motivating him or how dangerous he is?)
2. Say something like, "No harm intended." (It might not be necessary to actually apologize in order to avert a fight. This remark, or one like it, is almost neutral in terms of affixing blame, but might help diffuse your antagonist's feelings of outrage.)
3. If your antagonist will accept nothing short of an apology, you might strongly consider apologizing. (He might be carrying a weapon, or he might be so enraged that he is not thinking clearly about the consequences of trying to hurt you severely. You might be able to fight him off, but is it worth risking your life to find out? Why should your self-esteem suffer for making a wise decision? And why should *your antagonist* be in control of *your* behavior? If you allow him to press you into a fight, he is.)

Of course, our suggestions assume that you will be motivated not to get into a fight with a stranger over this silly business. If you do think that the bump is worth fighting about, we suggest that you closely examine your beliefs about it and ask yourself why. ■

Rational-Emotive Behavior Therapy: Ten Doorways to Distress

The deepest principle of Human Nature is the craving to be appreciated.

WILLIAM JAMES

RATIONAL-EMOTIVE BEHAVIOR THERAPY • Albert Ellis's method of cognitive therapy, which focuses on how irrational beliefs give rise to negative emotions and maladaptive behavior, and urges clients to challenge and correct these beliefs.

Not very modestly, Albert Ellis refers to himself as "the father of REBT **[rational-emotive behavior therapy]** and the grandfather of cognitive-behavioral therapy." Like Aaron Beck, Ellis first practiced psychoanalysis. However, he found Freud's methods to be slow and ineffective. He noted that people who were undergoing analysis often *felt* better, at least for a while, because of talking about their problems and getting attention from the therapist. But he did not believe that they *got* better. He also was not convinced that it was useful for the therapist to be so passive, so he became more active and began to offer direct advice.

Ellis (1977, 1993) points out that our beliefs *about* events, not only the events themselves, shape our responses to them. Consider a case in which one is fired from a job and is anxious and depressed about it. It might seem logical that losing the job is responsible for all the misery, but Ellis points out how beliefs about the loss compound misery.

Let us examine this situation according to Ellis's A-B-C approach: Losing the job is an *activating event* (A). The eventual outcome, or *consequence* (C), is misery. But between the activating event (A) and the consequences (C) lies a set of *beliefs* (B), such as the following: "This job was the most important thing in my life," "What a no-good failure I am," "My family will starve," "I'll never find a job as good," "There's nothing I can do about it." Beliefs such as these compound misery, foster helplessness, and divert us from planning and deciding what to do next. The belief "There's nothing I can do about it" fosters helplessness. The belief "What a no-good failure I am" internalizes the blame and is also an exaggeration that might be based on perfectionism. The belief "My family will starve" is also probably an exaggeration.

We can diagram the situation like this:

Activating events ⟶ Beliefs ⟶ Consequences

Anxieties about the future and depression over a loss are normal enough. However, the beliefs of the person who lost the job tend to **catastrophize** the extent of the loss and contribute to anxiety and depression. By heightening negative feelings and fostering helplessness, these beliefs also impair coping ability. They lower self-efficacy expectancies and divert people from attempting to solve their problems.

Ellis proposes that most of us harbor a number of the following 10 irrational beliefs. We lug them everywhere as our personal doorways to distress. They give rise to problems in themselves, and when other problems besiege us, they magnify their impact. How many of these beliefs do you harbor? Are you sure?

1. You must have sincere love and approval almost all the time from the people who are important to you.
2. You must prove yourself thoroughly competent, adequate, and achieving. Or you must at least have real competence or talent at something important.
3. Things must go the way you want them to go. Life proves awful, terrible, and horrible when you don't get your first choices in everything.
4. Other people must treat everyone fairly and justly. When people act unfairly or unethically, they are terrible and rotten.
5. When there is danger or fear in your world, you must be preoccupied with and upset by it.
6. People and things should turn out better than they do. It's awful and horrible when you don't find quick solutions to life's hassles.
7. Your emotional misery comes almost completely from external pressures that you have little or no ability to control. Unless these external pressures change, you must remain miserable.
8. It is easier to evade life's responsibilities and problems than to face them with self-discipline.
9. Your past influenced you immensely and must therefore continue to determine your feelings and behavior today.

CATASTROPHIZING • Exaggerating, making into a catastrophe; blowing out of proportion.

SELF-ASSESSMENT

ARE YOU MAKING YOURSELF MISERABLE? THE IRRATIONAL-BELIEFS QUESTIONNAIRE

Are you making yourself miserable? Are your attitudes and beliefs setting you up for distress? Do you expect that other people are obligated to put you first? Do you make such great demands of yourself that you must fall short? Do you think that you can be happier by sliding along than by applying yourself? Do you feel like dirt when other people disapprove of you? Albert Ellis points out that our own attitudes and beliefs can make us miserable just as surely as failing that test or not getting that job. ■

Directions: Following are a number of irrational beliefs that serve as examples of Ellis's 10 basic irrational beliefs. Place a checkmark to the left of each one that might apply to you. (If you're in doubt check it—nobody's going to fault you for having more checkmarks than the person sitting next to you and it'll give you something to think about!) Recognizing irrational beliefs is not the same as overcoming them, but it's a valuable first step. It will enhance your self-knowledge and give you some things to work on.

____ 1. Since your parents don't approve of your date, you must give him/her up.

____ 2 Since your date doesn't approve of your parents, you must give them up.

____ 3. It is awful if your teacher doesn't smile at you.

____ 4. It's awful when your boss passes you in the hall without saying anything.

____ 5. You're a horrible parent if your children are upset with you.

____ 6. How can you refuse to buy the vacuum cleaner when the salesperson will be disappointed?

____ 7. Unless you have time to jog 5 miles, there's no point in going out at all.

____ 8. You must get A's on all your quizzes and tests; a B+ now and then is a disaster.

____ 9. Your nose (mouth, eyes, chin, etc.) should be (prettier/more handsome) or else your face is a mess.

____ 10. Since you are 15 pounds overweight, you are totally out of control and must be sickened by yourself.

____ 11. Since you can't afford a Mercedes, how can you possibly enjoy your Mazda?

____ 12. Every sexual encounter should lead to a huge orgasm.

____ 13. You can't just go out on the courts and bat the ball back and forth a few times—you have to perfect your serves, returns, and volleys.

____ 14. You can't be happy with your life from day to day when people who are no more talented or hard-working make more money than you do.

____ 15. The cheerleader/quarterback won't go out with you, so why go out at all?

10. You can achieve happiness by inertia and inaction, or by just enjoying yourself from day to day.

Ellis points out that it is understandable that we would want the approval of others, but it is irrational to believe we cannot survive without it. It would be nice to be competent in everything we do, but it's unreasonable to demand it. Sure, it would be nice to serve and volley like a tennis pro, but most of us haven't the time or natural ability to perfect the game. Demanding self-perfection prevents us from going out on the courts on weekends and just batting the

____ 16. Your boss is awful because a co-worker got a promotion and you didn't.

____ 17. White people are awful because they'd usually rather associate with other White people.

____ 18. Black people are awful because they'd usually rather associate with other Black people.

____ 19. Since there is the possibility of nuclear war, you must spend all your time worrying about it—and, of course, there's no point to studying.

____ 20. How can you be expected to do your best on the job after you didn't get the raise?

____ 21. Given all your personal problems, how can your teachers expect you to study?

____ 22. Since the quizzes are hard, why should you study for them?

____ 23. How can your spouse expect you to be nice to him/her when you've had an awful day on the job?

____ 24. Your spouse (boyfriend, girlfriend, etc.) should know what's bugging you and should do something about it.

____ 25. It should be possible to get A's in your courses by quick cramming before tests.

____ 26. Since you have the ability, why should you have to work at it? (That is, your teacher/boss should appraise you on the basis of your talents, not on your performance.)

____ 27. You should be able to lose a lot of weight by dieting for just a few days.

____ 28. Other people should be nicer to you.

____ 29. How can you be expected to learn the subject matter when your instructor is a bore? (Note: This belief couldn't possibly apply to this course.)

____ 30. Your spouse (boyfriend, girlfriend, mother, father, etc.) is making you miserable, and unless your spouse changes, there's nothing you can do about it.

____ 31. Since you didn't get the promotion, how can you be happy?

____ 32. How can you be expected to relax unless college gets easier?

____ 33. Since college is difficult, there's a bigger payoff in dropping out than in applying yourself for all those years.

____ 34. You come from a poor background, so how can you ever be a success?

____ 35. Your father was rotten to you, so how can you ever trust a man?

____ 36. Your mother was rotten to you, so how can you ever trust a woman?

____ 37. You had a deprived childhood, so how can you ever be emotionally adjusted?

____ 38. You were abused as a child, so you are destined to abuse your own children.

____ 39. You come from "the street," so how can you be expected to clean up your act and stop cursing with every other word?

____ 40. It's more fulfilling just to have fun than to worry about college or a job.

____ 41. You can be happier dating a bunch of people than by investing yourself in meaningful relationships.

ball back and forth for fun. Belief 5 is a prescription for perpetual emotional upheaval. Beliefs 7 and 9 lead to feelings of helplessness and demoralization. Sure, Ellis might say, childhood experiences can explain the origins of irrational beliefs, but our own cognitive appraisal—here and now—causes us misery.

Rather than sitting back like the traditional psychoanalyst, Ellis urges clients to seek out their irrational beliefs, which can be fleeting and hard to pin down. He then disputes these beliefs. He shows clients how they lead to misery and challenges them to change their beliefs.

Truth or Fiction Revisited

It is true that some psychotherapists purposefully argue with clients. Cognitive therapists might do so in pointing out client beliefs that are irrational and self-defeating.

The case of Jane will afford insight into rational emotive behavior therapy:

> Jane, a 27-year-old woman, was socially inhibited and especially shy with attractive men. Therapy helped her identify some of the irrational beliefs that contributed to her inhibitions, such as "I must speak well to people I find attractive," and, "When I don't speak well and impress people as I should, I'm a stupid, inadequate person!" Therapy helped Jane distinguish between irrational beliefs and rational alternatives, such as, "If people do reject me for showing them how anxious I am, that will be most unfortunate, but I can stand it." Therapy encouraged Jane to dispute her irrational beliefs by asking herself, "*Why* must I speak well to people I find attractive?" and, "When I don't speak well and impress people, how does that make me a *stupid and inadequate person?*" Jane learned to answer herself rationally: "There is no reason I must speak well to people I find attractive, but it would be desirable if I do so, so I shall make an effort—but not kill myself—to do so," and, "When I speak poorly and fail to impress people, that only makes me a *person who* spoke unimpressively this time—not a *totally stupid or inadequate person.*"
>
> Jane also rehearsed rational thoughts several times a day. For example, "I would like to speak well, but I never *have to,*" and, "When people I favor reject me, it often reveals more about them and their tastes than about me." After 9 months of therapy, Jane was able to talk calmly to attractive men and was readying herself for a job as a teacher, a post she had avoided because of fear of facing a class. (Adapted from Ellis & Dryden, 1987, pp. 68–70)

Ellis also straddles behavioral and cognitive therapies. He originally dubbed his method of therapy *rational-emotive therapy,* because his focus was on the cognitive—irrational beliefs and how to change them. However, Ellis has also always promoted behavioral changes to cement cognitive changes and provide "a fuller experience of life" (Albert Ellis Institute, 1997, p. 2). In keeping with his broad philosophy, he recently changed the name of rational-emotive therapy to rational-emotive *behavior* therapy.

■ GROUP THERAPY

When a psychotherapist has several clients with similar problems—whether stress management, adjustment to divorce, lack of social skills, or anxiety—it may make sense to treat them in groups of 6 to 12 rather than conduct individual therapy. Group methods reflect the needs of the members and the theoretical orientation of the leader. In a psychoanalytic group, clients may interpret one another's dreams. In a client-centered group, they may provide an accepting atmosphere for self-exploration. Clients in a transactional analysis (TA) group may comment on each other's games. Behavior-therapy groups may undergo joint desensitization to anxiety-evoking stimuli or model and rehearse social skills.

There are several advantages to group therapy:

1. Group therapy is economical. It allows the therapist to work with several clients at once.
2. As compared with one-to-one therapy, group therapy provides a greater fund of information and life experiences for clients to draw upon. When a

group member explains how something worked out (or didn't work out) for him or her, it may have more impact than a theoretical discussion or a secondhand story from the leader.

3. Appropriate behavior receives group support. A spontaneous outpouring of approval from peers is a potent reinforcer for appropriate behavior.
4. When we run into troubles, it is easy to imagine that we are different from other people, and possibly inferior. Group members may reassuringly find that other people have had similar problems, similar self-doubts, similar failure experiences.
5. Group members who show improvement provide hope for others.
6. Many individuals seek therapy because of problems in relating to other people, and people who seek therapy for other reasons are also frequently socially inhibited. Members of therapy groups have the opportunity to rehearse social skills with one another in a relatively unthreatening atmosphere. In a group consisting of men and women of different ages, group members can role-play one another's employers, employees, spouses, parents, children, and friends. A 20-year-old can practice refusing unreasonable requests from a 47-year-old as a way of learning how to refuse such requests from a parent. Members can role-play asking one another out on dates, saying no (or yes) to sexual requests, and so on.

Truth or Fiction Revisited

It is not necessarily true that individual therapy is preferable to group therapy. The statement is too broad to be true. Groups give clients social support and the benefits of the experience of the other members.

Although there are advantages to group treatment, many clients prefer individual therapy, and they may have valid reasons. They may not wish to disclose their problems to a group. They may be inhibited in front of others, or they may desire individual attention. Because many clients who are willing to enter groups also share these concerns, the therapist must insist that group disclosures be kept confidential, establish a supportive atmosphere, and see that group members receive adequate attention.

GROUP THERAPY.
Group therapy has a number of advantages over individual therapy for many clients. It is economical, provides a fund of information and experience for clients to draw upon, elicits group support and reassurance, and provides the opportunity to relate to other people. On the other hand, some clients do require individual attention.

Many types of therapy can be conducted either individually or in groups. Encounter groups and family therapy can be conducted in group-format only.

Encounter Groups

Encounter groups are not appropriate for treating serious psychological problems. Rather, they are meant to promote personal growth by heightening awareness of one's own needs and feelings and those of others. This goal is sought through intense confrontations, or encounters, between strangers. Like ships in the night, group members come together out of the darkness, touch one another, then sink back into the shadows of one another's lives. But something is thought to be gained from the passing.

Encounter groups stress interactions between group members in the here and now. Discussion of the past may be outlawed. Interpretation is out. Expression of genuine feelings toward others is encouraged. When group members think that a person's social mask is phony, they may descend en masse to rip it off.

Professionals recognize that encounter groups can be damaging when they urge overly rapid disclosure of intimate matters, or when several members attack one member in unison. Responsible leaders do not tolerate these abuses and try to keep groups moving in growth-enhancing directions.

Family Therapy

In **family therapy,** one or more families constitute the group. Family therapy may be undertaken from various theoretical viewpoints. One is the "systems approach," in which the family system of interaction is studied and modified to enhance the growth of family members and of the family unit (Annunziata & Jacobson-Kram, 1995; Mikesell and others, 1995).

Family members with low self-esteem often cannot tolerate different attitudes and behaviors from other family members. Faulty family communications also create problems. It is not uncommon for the family to present an "identified patient"—that is, the family member who has *the* problem and is *causing* all the trouble. But family therapists usually assume that the identified patient is a scapegoat for other family problems. It is a sort of myth: Change the bad apple, or identified patient, and the barrel, or family, will be functional once more.

The family therapist teaches the family to communicate more effectively and encourages the growth and eventual autonomy, or independence, of each member. In doing so, the family therapist will also show the family how the identified patient has been used as a lightning rod for the problems of other family members.

There are many other types of groups: couples groups, marathon groups, sensitivity-training groups, and psychodrama groups, to name just a few.

DOES PSYCHOTHERAPY WORK?

Many of us know people who swear by their therapists, but the evidence is often shaky—for example, "I was a wreck before, but now . . . ," or "I feel so much better now." Anecdotes like these are encouraging, but we do not know what would have happened to these people had they not sought help. Many people feel better about their problems as time goes on, with or without therapy. Sometimes, happily, problems seem to go away by themselves. Sometimes people find solutions on their own. Then, too, we hear some stories about how

ENCOUNTER GROUP • A type of group that aims to foster self-awareness by focusing on how group members relate to each other in a setting that encourages open expression of feelings.

FAMILY THERAPY • A form of therapy in which the family unit is treated as the client.

therapy was useless and about people who hop fruitlessly from one therapist to another.

Problems in Conducting Research on Psychotherapy

Before we report on research dealing with the effectiveness of therapy, let us look at two key problems in conducting this kind of research. As noted by psychologist Hans Strupp, "The problem of evaluating outcomes from psychotherapy continues to bedevil the field" (1996, p. 1017).

PROBLEMS IN RUNNING EXPERIMENTS ON PSYCHOTHERAPY The ideal method for evaluating a treatment—such as a method of therapy—is the experiment (Shadish & Ragsdale, 1996). However, experiments on therapy methods are difficult to arrange and control. The outcomes can be difficult to define and measure.

Consider psychoanalysis. In well run experiments, people are assigned at random to experimental and control groups. A true experiment on psychoanalysis would require randomly assigning people seeking therapy to psychoanalysis and to a control group or other kinds of therapy for comparison (Luborsky and others, 1993). But a person may have to remain in traditional psychoanalysis for years to attain beneficial results. Could we create control treatments that last as long? Moreover, some people seek psychoanalysis per se, not psychotherapy in general. Would it be ethical to assign them at random to other treatments or to a no-treatment control group? Clearly not.

DOES THERAPY HELP BECAUSE OF THE METHOD OR BECAUSE OF "NONSPECIFIC FACTORS"? Sorting out the benefits of therapy per se from other aspects of the therapy situation is a staggering task. These other aspects are termed *nonspecific factors.* They refer to features that are found in most therapies, such as the client's relationship with the therapist. Most therapists, regardless of theoretical outlook, show warmth and empathy, encourage exploration, and instill hope (Blatt and others, 1996; Burns & Nolen-Hoeksema, 1992). The benefits of therapy thus could stem largely from these behaviors. If so, the method itself might have little more value than a "sugar pill" has in combating physical ailments.

Analyses of Therapy Effectiveness

Despite these evaluation problems, research on the effectiveness of therapy has been encouraging (Barlow, 1996; Shadish and others, 1997; VandenBos, 1996). This research has relied heavily on a technique termed **meta-analysis.** Meta-analysis combines and averages the results of individual studies. Generally speaking, the studies included in the analysis address similar issues in a similar way. Moreover, the analysts judge them to have been conducted in a valid manner.

In their classic early use of meta-analysis, Mary Lee Smith and Gene Glass (1977) analyzed the results of dozens of outcome studies of various types of therapies. They concluded that people who obtained psychodynamic therapy showed greater well-being, on the average, than 70 percent to 75 percent of those who did not obtain treatment. Similarly, nearly 75 percent of the clients who obtained client-centered therapy were better off than people who did not obtain treatment. Psychodynamic and client-centered therapies appear to be most effective with well educated, verbal, strongly motivated clients who report

META-ANALYSIS • A statistical averaging method that combines the results of a number of studies.

problems with anxiety, depression (of light to moderate proportions), and interpersonal relationships. Neither form of therapy appears to be effective with people with psychotic disorders such as major depression, bipolar disorder, and schizophrenia. Smith and Glass (1977) found that people who obtained Gestalt therapy showed greater well-being than about 60 percent of those who did not obtain treatment. The effectiveness of psychoanalysis and client-centered therapy thus was reasonably comparable. Gestalt therapy fell behind.

Smith and Glass (1977) did not include cognitive therapies in their meta-analysis because at the time of their study many cognitive approaches were relatively new. Because behavior therapists also incorporate many cognitive techniques, it can be difficult to sort out which aspects—cognitive or otherwise—of behavioral treatments are most effective. However, many meta-analyses of cognitive-behavioral therapy have been conducted since the early work of Smith and Glass. Their results are encouraging (Lipsey & Wilson, 1993).

A number of studies of cognitive therapy per se have also been conducted. For example, they show that modifying irrational beliefs of the type described by Albert Ellis helps people with problems such as anxiety and depression (Engels and others, 1993; Haaga & Davison, 1993). Modifying self-defeating beliefs of the sort outlined by Aaron Beck also frequently alleviates anxiety and depression (Robins & Hayes, 1993; Whisman and others, 1991). Cognitive therapy may be helpful with people with severe depression, who had been thought responsive only to biological therapies (Jacobson & Hollon, 1996; Simons and others, 1995). Cognitive therapy has also helped people with personality disorders (Beck & Freeman, 1990). It has helped many people with schizophrenia (who are also using drug therapy) modify their delusional beliefs (Chadwick & Lowe, 1990). Cognitive therapy has even helped people manage pain—an outcome not sought by most kinds of therapy (Gil and others, 1996).

Behavior therapy has provided people with strategies for alleviating anxiety, depression, social skills deficits, and problems in self-control (Lazarus, 1990). Behavior therapists have also innovated treatments for anxiety disorders and sexual disorders for which there previously were no effective treatments. Overall, Smith and Glass (1977) found behavior therapy techniques to be somewhat more effective than psychodynamic or humanistic-existential methods. About 80 percent of people who obtained behavior therapy treatments such as systematic desensitization and strategies for self-control showed greater well-being than people who did not obtain such treatments. The 80 percent figure compares favorably with percentages in the low to middle 70s for people who obtained psychodynamic and humanistic-existential therapies.

Many studies that directly compare treatment techniques find behavior therapy, psychodynamic, and humanistic-existential approaches to be about equal in overall effectiveness (Berman and others, 1985; Smith and others, 1980). Psychodynamic and humanistic-existential approaches seem to foster greater self-understanding. Behavior therapy (including cognitive-behavioral therapy) shows superior results in treatment of specific problems such as headaches (Blanchard, 1992) and anxiety disorders (Borkovec & Costello, 1993). Behavior therapy has also been effective in helping to coordinate the care of institutionalized patients, including people with schizophrenia and mental retardation (Spreat & Behar, 1994). However, there is little evidence that behavior therapy alone is effective in treating the quirks of thought exhibited in people with severe psychotic disorders (Wolpe, 1990).

Thus, it is not enough to ask which type of therapy is most effective. We must ask which type is most effective for a particular problem and a particular patient. What are its advantages? Its limitations? Clients may successfully use systematic desensitization to overcome stage fright, as measured by ability to speak to a group of people. If clients also want to know why they have stage fright, however, behavior therapy alone will not provide the answer.

Adjustment in a World of DIVERSITY

Should We Match Clients and Therapists According to Ethnicity?

Most psychotherapists in the United States are non-Hispanic White Americans whose primary language is English (Allison and others, 1994; Bernal & Castro, 1994). Many of them receive little education or training concerning working with people from minority groups (Mintz and others, 1995; Pope-Davis and others, 1995). Can such therapists be as effective as therapists drawn from clients' own ethnic groups?

According to the "cultural-responsiveness hypothesis," clients respond better to psychotherapy when the therapist shares their ethnic background, including their language (Sue and others, 1991). Yet the evidence is mixed on whether ethnic matching actually enhances the benefits of therapy (Sue, 1988). A large-scale study of the Los Angeles mental health system found partial support for the cultural-responsiveness hypothesis (Sue and others, 1991). Matching of therapists and clients was connected with lower rates of premature dropping out from therapy, as after only one session. It also led to greater length of treatment for all ethnic groups in the study (that is, African, Asian, Mexican, and non-Hispanic White Americans). Ethnic matching, however, was not linked to treatment outcome, except in the case of Mexican Americans. The benefits of ethnic matching were greatest for Mexican Americans and Asian Americans whose primary language was not English. Both groups remained in therapy longer and had better treatment outcomes.

Although matching therapists to clients on the basis of ethnicity has some benefits, ethnicity is not the sole determinant of therapeutic effectiveness. Therapist sensitivity and ability to establish rapport are also crucial factors in therapeutic effectiveness, whether one is treating clients of one's own ethnicity or from a different background (Sue, 1988).

BIOLOGICAL THERAPIES

In the 1950s Fats Domino popularized the song "My Blue Heaven." Fats was singing about the sky and happiness. Today "blue heavens" is the street name for the 10-milligram dose of one of the more widely prescribed drugs in the world: Valium. The antianxiety drug Valium became popular because it reduces feelings of anxiety and tension. The manufacturer once claimed that people could not become addicted to Valium nor readily kill themselves with overdoses. Today Valium looks more dangerous. Some regular users are reported to go into convulsions when they suspend usage. And now and then someone dies from mixing Valium with alcohol, or someone shows unusual sensitivity to the drug.

Psychiatrists and other physicians prescribe Valium and other drugs for various psychological disorders. In this section we discuss *drug therapy, electroconvulsive therapy,* and *psychosurgery,* three biological or medical approaches to treating psychological disorders.

Drug Therapy

The major forms of drug therapy include antianxiety drugs, antipsychotic drugs, antidepressants, and lithium.

AN ARSENAL OF CHEMICAL WEAPONS AGAINST PSYCHOLOGICAL DISORDERS. Many drugs are available for treatment of psychological problems and disorders such as anxiety, depression, schizophrenia, and bipolar disorder. Would you want to use a tranquilizer before taking a big test, going on a date, or having a job interview? Why or why not?

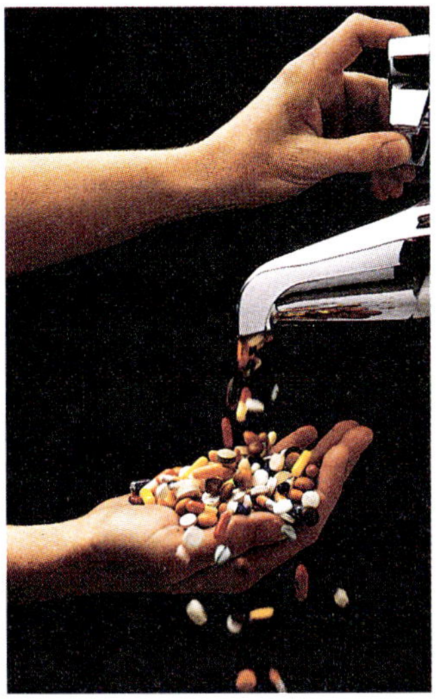

ADJUSTMENT *in the* NEW MILLENNIUM

Looking Ahead to "Designer Drugs"

The National Institute of Mental Health labeled the 1990s the "Decade of the Brain" (Goleman, 1996b) and encouraged researchers to push back the frontiers of knowledge about the brain. One of the expected payoffs will be a new generation of "designer drugs." The miracle drugs of the previous decade, such as Prozac for depression and Xanax for anxiety, may be little more than chemical dinosaurs in the new millennium.

Current research has shown that there are many different kinds of receptors for neurotransmitters. For example, there are at least 15 different kinds of receptors for serotonin, a neurotransmitter implicated in mood disorders, eating disorders, sexual response, and other aspects of behavior and mental activity (Goleman, 1996b). There are at least five kinds of receptors for dopamine, a neurotransmitter involved in schizophrenia.

One of the problems with the current generation of psychiatric drugs is that they affect all of the receptors for the neurotransmitter they target, rather than the one or two they ought to be targeting. Consider the case of depression and serotonin. Only one or a few of serotonin's receptors are likely to be involved in depression. Current antidepressant drugs therefore cause unwanted side effects, such as digestive and sexual problems.

Once we know exactly how each kind of receptor is involved in psychological disorders, we may be able to increase the potency of drug therapies and reduce side effects. The ultimate goal, of course, would be to prevent psychological disorders altogether. Dare we dream that we will reach this goal sometime in the new millennium? ■

ANTIANXIETY DRUGS Antianxiety drugs are also called *minor tranquilizers.* Valium is an antianxiety drug. Other antianxiety drugs include Librium, Serax, and Xanax. Antianxiety drugs are usually prescribed for people who complain of generalized anxiety or panic attacks, although many people also use them as sleeping pills. Valium and other antianxiety drugs depress the activity of the central nervous system. The nervous system, in turn, reduces the heart rate, respiration rate, and feelings of nervousness and tension.

Some people come to tolerate small dosages of these drugs very quickly. When tolerance occurs, dosages must be increased for the drug to remain effective.

Sedation (feelings of being tired or drowsy) is the most common side effect of antianxiety drugs. Problems that may be associated with withdrawal from them include *rebound anxiety.* That is, some patients who have been using these drugs regularly report that their anxiety returns in exacerbated form once they stop them. Antianxiety drugs can induce physical dependence, as evidenced by withdrawal symptoms such as tremulousness, sweating, insomnia, and rapid heartbeat.

ANTIPSYCHOTIC DRUGS People with schizophrenia are often given antipsychotic drugs (also called *major tranquilizers*). In most cases these drugs reduce agitation, delusions, and hallucinations (Kane, 1996). Many antipsychotic drugs, including phenothiazines (for example, Thorazine) and clozapine (Clozaril) are thought to act by blocking dopamine receptors in the brain (Kane, 1996).

ANTIDEPRESSANTS People with major depression often take so-called **antidepressant** drugs. These drugs are also helpful for some people with eating disorders, panic disorder, obsessive-compulsive disorder, and social phobia (Abramowitz, 1997; Lydiard and others, 1996; Thase & Kupfer, 1996). Problems in the regulation of noradrenaline and serotonin may be involved in eating and panic disorders as well as in depression. Antidepressants increase the concentration of noradrenaline or serotonin in the brain.

Typically, antidepressant drugs must build up to a therapeutic level over several weeks. Because overdoses of antidepressants can be lethal, some people enter a hospital during the buildup period to prevent suicide attempts. There are also side effects, such as a racing heart and weight gain (Sleek, 1996).

LITHIUM The ancient Greeks and Romans were among the first people to use the metal lithium as a psychoactive drug. They prescribed mineral water for people with bipolar disorder. They had no inkling as to why this treatment sometimes helped, but it might have been because mineral water contains lithium. A salt of the metal lithium (lithium carbonate), in tablet form, flattens out cycles of manic behavior and depression in most people. It is not known precisely how lithium works, although it is clear that it affects the functioning of the neurotransmitters dopamine, acetylcholine, serotonin, and norepinephrine (Price & Heninger, 1994).

It might be necessary for people with bipolar disorder to use lithium indefinitely, just as a person with diabetes must continue to use insulin to control the illness. Lithium also has been shown to have side effects such as hand tremors, memory impairment, and excessive thirst and urination (Price & Heninger, 1994). Memory impairment is reported as the main reason why people discontinue lithium.

Antipsychotic drugs, antidepressants, and lithium help many persons with severe psychiatric disorders. They enable thousands of formerly hospitalized patients to return to the community and lead productive lives.

Drug therapy seems desirable for severe disorders that do not respond to psychotherapy or behavior therapy alone. But psychological methods of therapy are preferable for problems such as anxiety, mild depression, and interpersonal conflict. No chemical can show a client how to change an idea or to solve an interpersonal problem.

Truth or Fiction Revisited

Actually, drugs may very well be the solution (or at least a partial solution) to some psychological problems. This was another truth-or-fiction item that was too broad to be true. Antipsychotic drugs, antidepressants, and lithium have been shown to be of help in many cases.

Electroconvulsive Therapy

Electroconvulsive therapy (ECT) was introduced by the Italian psychiatrist Ugo Cerletti in 1939 for use with people with psychological disorders. Cerletti had noted that some slaughterhouses used electric shock to render animals unconscious. The shocks also produced convulsions. Along with other European researchers of the period, Cerletti erroneously believed that convulsions were incompatible with schizophrenia and other major psychological disorders.

ECT was originally used for a variety of psychological disorders. Because of the advent of antipsychotic drugs, however, it is now used mainly for people with major depression who do not respond to antidepressants (Thase & Kupfer, 1996).

People typically obtain one ECT treatment three times a week for up to 10 sessions. Electrodes are attached to the temples and an electrical current strong enough to produce a convulsion is induced. The shock causes unconsciousness, so the patient does not recall it. Nevertheless, patients are given a sedative so that they are asleep during the treatment.

ANTIDEPRESSANT • Acting to relieve depression.
ELECTROCONVULSIVE THERAPY • Treatment of disorders by passing a seizure-inducing electric current through the head. Abbreviated *ECT.*

ECT is controversial for many reasons. First, many professionals are distressed by the thought of passing an electric shock through a patient's head and producing convulsions. Second, there are side effects, including memory problems (Coleman, 1990). Third, nobody knows *why* ECT works.

Psychosurgery

Truth or Fiction Revisited

It is true that the originator of a surgical technique intended to reduce violence learned that it was not always successful when one of his patients shot him. The surgeon's name was Moniz and he was the originator of the prefrontal lobotomy.

Psychosurgery is more controversial than ECT. The best-known modern technique, the *prefrontal lobotomy*, has been used with severely disturbed patients. In this method, a pick-like instrument is used to crudely sever the nerve pathways that link the prefrontal lobes of the brain to the thalamus. The prefrontal lobotomy was pioneered by the Portuguese neurologist Antonio Egas Moniz and was brought to the United States in the 1930s. Although the prefrontal lobotomy often reduces violence and agitation, it is not universally successful. One of Dr. Moniz's failures shot him, leaving a bullet lodged in his spine and causing paralysis in the legs.

The prefrontal lobotomy also has a host of side effects, including hyperactivity and distractibility, impaired learning ability, overeating, apathy and withdrawal, seizures, reduced creativity, and, now and then, death. Because of these side effects, and because of the advent of antipsychotic drugs, the prefrontal lobotomy has been largely discontinued.

In this chapter we explored the ways in which professionals help people with psychological disorders and adjustment problems. In the following chapter, we examine a number of the ways in which we can apply these techniques to help ourselves cope with the challenges of life.

PSYCHOSURGERY • Surgery intended to promote psychological changes or to relieve disordered behavior.

adjustment and modern life

PSYCHOTHERAPY AND HUMAN DIVERSITY

The United States is changing. The population is becoming an ever-richer ethnic mix (USBC, 1998). Yet most of the "prescriptions" for psychotherapy discussed in this chapter were originated by, and intended for use with, European Americans (Hall, 1997)—and especially for male heterosexuals. People from ethnic minority groups are less likely than European Americans to seek therapy (Penn and others, 1995). Reasons for their lower participation rate include:

- Unawareness that therapy would help
- Lack of information about the availability of professional services, or inability to pay for them (DeAngelis, 1995b)
- Distrust of professionals, particularly White professionals and (for women) male professionals (Basic Behavioral Science Task Force, 1996c)
- Language barriers (American Psychological Association, 1993)
- Reluctance to open up about personal matters to strangers—especially strangers who are not members of one's own ethnic group (LaFramboise, 1994)
- Cultural inclinations toward other approaches to problem solving, such as religious approaches and psychic healers (LaFramboise, 1994)
- Negative experiences with professionals and authority figures

Women and gay males and lesbians have also sometimes found therapy to be insensitive to their particular needs. Let us consider ways in which psychotherapy can be of more use to people from ethnic minority groups, women, and gay males and lesbians.

Psychotherapy and Ethnic Minority Groups

Clinicians need to be sensitive to the cultural heritage, language, and values of the people they see in therapy (American Psychological Association, 1993; Comas-Diaz, 1994). Let us consider some of the issues involved in conducting psychotherapy with African Americans, Asian Americans, Hispanic Americans, and Native Americans.

African Americans In addition to addressing the psychological problems of African American clients, therapists often need to help them cope with the effects of prejudice and discrimination. Beverly Greene (1993) notes that some African Americans develop low self-esteem because they internalize negative stereotypes.

African Americans often are reluctant to seek psychological help because of cultural assumptions that people should manage their own problems and because of mistrust of the therapy process. They tend to assume that people are supposed to solve their own problems. Signs of emotional weakness such as tension, anxiety and depression are stigmatized (Boyd-Franklin, 1995; Greene, 1993).

Many African Americans are also suspicious of their therapists—especially when the therapist is a non-Hispanic White American. They may withhold personal information because of the society's history of racial discrimination (Boyd-Franklin, 1995; Greene, 1993).

Asian Americans Asian Americans tend to stigmatize people with psychological disorders. As a result, they may deny problems and refuse to seek help for them (Sue, 1991). Asian Americans, especially recent immigrants, also may not understand or believe in Western approaches to psychotherapy. For example, Western psychotherapy typically encourages people to express their feelings openly. This mode of behavior may conflict with the Asian tradition of restrain in public. Many Asians prefer to receive concrete advice rather than Western-style encouragement to develop their own solutions.

Because of a cultural tendency to turn away from painful thoughts, many Asians experience and express psychological complaints as physical symptoms (Zane & Sue, 1991). Rather than thinking of themselves as being anxious, they may focus on physical features of anxiety such as a pounding heart and heavy sweating. Rather than thinking of themselves as depressed, they may focus on fatigue and low energy levels.

Hispanic Americans Many Hispanic Americans adhere to a patriarchal (male-dominated) family structure and strong kinship ties. Many Hispanic Americans also share the values described in the following passage:

> One's identity is in part determined by one's role in the family. The male, or *macho,* is the head of the family, the provider, the protector of the family honor, and the final decision maker. The woman's role *(marianismo)* is to care for the family and the children. Obviously, these roles are changing, with women entering the work force and achieving greater educational opportunities. Cultural values of *respeto* (respect), *confianza* (trust), *dignidad* (dignity), and *personalismo* (personalism) are highly esteemed and are important factors in working with many [Hispanic Americans]. (De La Cancela & Guzman, 1991, p. 60)

Therapists need to be aware of potential conflicts between the traditional Hispanic American value of interdependency in the family and the typical non-Hispanic White American belief in independence and self-reliance (De La Cancela & Guzman, 1991). Measures like the following may help bridge the gaps between psychotherapists and Hispanic American clients:

1. Interacting with clients in the language requested by them or, if this is not possible, referring them to professionals who can do so.
2. Using methods that are consistent with the client's values and levels of *acculturation,* as suggested by fluency in English and level of education.
3. Developing therapy methods that incorporate clients' cultural values. Malgady and his colleagues (1990), for example, use *cuento* therapy with

Puerto Ricans. *Cuento* therapy modifies Hispanic folktales, or *cuentos*, such that the characters serve as models for adaptive behavior.

Native Americans Many psychological disorders experienced by Native Americans involve the disruption of their traditional culture caused by European colonization (LaFramboise, 1994). Native Americans have also been denied full access to key institutions in Western culture (LaFramboise, 1994). Loss of cultural identity and social disorganization have set the stage for problems such as alcoholism, substance abuse, and depression. Theresa LaFramboise (1994) argues that if psychologists are to help Native Americans cope with psychological disorders, they must do so in a way that is sensitive to their culture, customs, and values. Efforts to prevent such disorders should focus on strengthening Native American cultural identity, pride, and cohesion. They should help Native Americans regain a sense of mastery over their world. When cultural and language differences create so great a gulf between Native Americans and the dominant culture, perhaps only trained Native Americans will be able to provide effective counseling.

Some therapists use ceremonies that reflect clients' cultural or religious traditions (Edwards, 1995). Purification and cleansing rites are therapeutic for many Native Americans (Lefley, 1990). Such rites are commonly sought by Native Americans who believe that their problems are caused by failure to placate malevolent spirits or perform required rituals (Lefley, 1990).

Feminist Psychotherapy

Feminist psychotherapy is not a particular method of therapy. It is an approach to therapy that is rooted in feminist political theory and philosophy. Feminism challenges the validity of stereotypical gender role stereotypes and the traditional of male dominance (Greene, 1993).

Feminist therapy developed as a response to male dominance of health professions and institutions. It suggested that the mental health establishment often worked to maintain inequality between men and women by trying to help women "adjust" to traditional gender roles when they wished to challenge these roles in their own lives. Feminist therapists note that many women experience depression and other psychological problems as a result of being treated as second-class citizens, and they argue that society rather than the individual woman must change if these psychological problems are to be alleviated.

Psychotherapy and Sexual Orientation The American Psychiatric Association (1994) does not consider a gay male or a lesbian sexual orientation to be a psychological disorder. The association did list homosexuality as a mental disorder until 1973, however, and there have been many efforts to "help" gay males and lesbians change their sexual orientation. For example, William Masters and Virginia Johnson (1979) adapted methods they had innovated for the treatment of sexual dysfunctions and reported that the majority of gays seen in therapy "reversed" their sexual orientations. However, most of these individuals were bisexuals and not exclusively gay. More than half were married, and they all were motivated to change their sexual behavior.

Many critics argue that it is unprofessional to try to help people change their sexual orientations (Sleek, 1997). They note that the great majority of gay males and lesbians are satisfied with their sexual orientations and only seek therapy because of conflicts that arise from social pressure and prejudice. They believe that the purpose of therapy for gay males and lesbians should be to help relieve conflicts caused by prejudice so that they will find life as gay people to be more gratifying.

In sum, psychotherapy is most effective when therapists attend to and respect people's sociocultural as well as individual differences. Although it is the individual who experiences psychological anguish, the fault often lies in the cultural setting and not the individual. ■

SUMMARY

1. **What is psychotherapy?** Psychotherapy is a systematic interaction between a therapist and client that brings psychological principles to bear in helping the client overcome psychological disorders or adjust to problems in living.
2. **What are the goals of psychoanalysis?** Goals are to provide self-insight, allow the spilling forth (catharsis) of psychic energy, and replace defensive behavior with coping behavior.
3. **What are the methods of psychoanalysis?** Methods include free association and dream analysis.
4. **How do modern psychodynamic approaches differ from traditional psychoanalysis?** Modern approaches are briefer and more directive, and the therapist and client usually sit face-to-face.
5. **What is client-centered therapy?** Client-centered therapy uses nondirective methods to help clients overcome obstacles to self-actualization. Therapists show unconditional positive regard, empathic understanding, and genuineness.
6. **What are some behavior therapy methods for reducing fears?** These include flooding, systematic desensitization, and modeling. Systematic desensitization counterconditions fears by gradually exposing clients to fear-evoking stimuli while they remain deeply relaxed.
7. **What is aversive conditioning?** This is a behavior therapy method for discouraging undesirable behavior by repeatedly pairing the goals (e.g., alcohol, cigarette smoke, deviant sex objects) with aversive stimuli so that the goals become aversive rather than tempting.
8. **What is operant conditioning?** This is a behavior therapy method that fosters adaptive behavior through principles of reinforcement. Examples include extinction of maladaptive behavior, successive approximations, social-skills training, and biofeedback training.
9. **What are self-control methods?** These are behavior therapy methods for adopting desirable behavior patterns and breaking bad habits. They focus on modifying the antecedents of behavior, the behavior itself, and reinforcers.
10. **What is cognitive therapy?** Cognitive therapies aim to provide clients insight into irrational beliefs (such as excessive needs for approval and perfectionism) and cognitive distortions, and to replace these cognitive errors with rational beliefs and accurate perceptions. Beck notes that clients may become depressed because of minimizing accomplishments, catastrophizing failures, and general pessimism.
11. **What are the advantages of group therapy?** Group therapy is more economical than individual therapy. Moreover, group members profit from one another's social support and experiences.
12. **Does psychotherapy work?** Apparently it does. People receiving most forms of psychotherapy fare better than people left untreated. Psychoanalytic and client-centered approaches are particularly helpful with highly verbal and motivated individuals. Cognitive and behavior therapies are probably most effective, and behavior therapy also helps in the management of retarded and severely disturbed populations.
13. **What are some issues concerning the practice of psychotherapy with clients from ethnic minority groups?** Various cultural and ethnic factors are related to therapeutic processes with African Americans, Asian Americans, Hispanic Americans, and Native Americans. For example, clinicians must avoid stereotypes and be sensitive to the values, languages, and cultural beliefs of members of minority groups.
14. **What are the uses of drug therapy?** Antipsychotic drugs often help schizophrenic individuals, apparently by blocking the action of dopamine. Antidepressants often help severely depressed people, apparently by raising the levels of noradrenaline and serotonin. Lithium often helps persons with bipolar disorder, apparently by moderating levels of noradrenaline.
15. **What is electroconvulsive therapy (ECT)?** ECT passes an electrical current through the temples, inducing a seizure and frequently relieving major depression.
16. **What is psychosurgery?** Psychosurgery is an extremely controversial method for alleviating severe agitation by severing nerve pathways in the brain.

CHAPTER 11

Methods of Coping: Ways of Helping Ourselves

TRUTH OR FICTION?

✔ T F

- ☐ ☐ The best way to change catastrophizing thoughts is to . . . change them.
- ☐ ☐ Modification of Type A behavior helps prevent recurrent heart attacks.
- ☐ ☐ Visiting museums and art galleries is one of the methods for treating Type A behavior.
- ☐ ☐ Telling someone you love them is another method for treating Type A behavior.
- ☐ ☐ When your spouse insists on getting a divorce, learning to ski can help you cope.
- ☐ ☐ We cannot be expected to stand still for it when someone insults us or threatens our honor.
- ☐ ☐ Meditation can help people with hypertension lower their blood pressure.
- ☐ ☐ If you ask people just to allow their muscles to relax, many will have no idea what to do.
- ☐ ☐ One way of coping with test anxiety is not to allow it to distract us from the test items.
- ☐ ☐ Psychologists have compiled scientifically derived lists of turn-ons that can elevate your mood without popping pills.

OUTLINE

JUST DO IT. THIS IS THE TEXT'S MAIN DO-IT-YOURself chapter. Consider it a self-help manual. In Chapter 10, we saw how psychologists and other health professionals use methods of therapy to help people in distress. In this chapter, we explore methods of stress management that enable us to help ourselves.

First, however, we offer an overview of the defensive and active coping methods that constitute **stress management.**

STRESS MANAGEMENT

What do you do when the pressures of work or school begin to get to you? What do you do when you feel that your instructor or your supervisor doesn't appreciate your performance? When your steady date finds someone else? When you're uptight before a test, or irritated because you're stuck in traffic?

Defensive Coping

Many techniques for coping with stress are defensive. **Defensive coping** reduces the immediate impact of the stressor, but at a cost. Costs include socially inappropriate behavior (as in alcoholism, aggression, or regression), avoidance of problems (as in withdrawal), or self-deception (as in rationalization or denial).

Defensive coping grants us time to marshal our resources but does not deal with the source of stress or enhance the effectiveness of our responses to stress. In the long run, defensive methods can be harmful if we do not use the chance they provide to find better ways of coping. In this section we consider the following methods of defensive coping: use of alcohol and other drugs, aggression, withdrawal, fantasy, and defense mechanisms.

ALCOHOL AND OTHER DRUGS Alcohol, tranquilizers, and some other depressants blunt feelings of tension, anxiety, and frustration. Alcohol can also subdue self-awareness. In this way, it reduces negative feelings that might stem from recognition that our behavior has fallen short of our standards.

People may also attribute inappropriate aggressive or sexual behavior to alcohol. Regular use of drugs to cope with stress constitutes psychological dependence. People may become dependent on drugs to blunt awareness of stress or distort perception of what has become, for them, an unpleasant reality.

AGGRESSION Violence is often used to cope with social provocations and, sometimes, as a response to frustration. In warfare and self-defense, aggression is usually valued. Most violence in society is frowned upon, however, and its benefits can be short-lived. Attacking a police officer who is writing a summons

STRESS MANAGEMENT • A generic term for a number of techniques that moderate the effects of stress by, for example, lowering arousal, increasing one's sense of control, and reconceptualizing one's situation.

DEFENSIVE COPING • Coping methods that reduce the immediate impact of the stressor, but at costs such as socially inappropriate behavior, avoidance of problems, or self-deception.

Withdrawal.
Sometimes it is healthy to withdraw from stress. Withdrawal can allow us to examine a situation and to marshal our resources. Prolonged withdrawal, however, can prevent us from reaping the social and other rewards of life.

will not earn a judge's approval. Aggressive behavior usually heightens interpersonal conflict by creating motives for retaliation.

Withdrawal When you are petrified, or feel helpless, or believe that any decision would be futile, you may wish to withdraw from the situation. Withdrawal can also be emotional, as in loss of interest, or physical, as in moving or changing one's lifestyle. Victims of rape frequently move to a new location in order to avoid painful memories and future threats. City dwellers tend to withdraw from social contacts with strangers to protect themselves from crime and the "stimulus overload" created by crowding.

Temporary withdrawal can be beneficial. It can provide the chance to find better methods of coping. Withdrawal may also be appropriate when there is no productive way to cope with stress. But withdrawal from social interaction and social responsibility is harmful to the social fabric and accounts for some of the more disturbing aspects of contemporary urban life.

Fantasy Fantasy is not for children only. Have you ever daydreamed about the future, testing career and marital choices through cognitive trial and error? Fantasy serves many functions and is useful so long as it does not become an indefinitely prolonged substitute for effective action.

Defense Mechanisms Sigmund Freud believed that **defense mechanisms** operate unconsciously to protect the ego from anxiety that might stem from recognition of unacceptable ideas and impulses. Some learning theorists (e.g., Dollard & Miller [1950]) view defense mechanisms as ways of responding to stress that become habitual because they reduce discomfort, anxiety, or frustration. As shown in Table 11.1, defense mechanisms are used by normal and abnormal people alike. They become problems when they are the sole means used to cope with stress.

Active Coping

Direct or **active coping** methods for managing stress aim to manipulate the environment (in socially acceptable ways) to remove stressors, or to change our response patterns to buffer their harmfulness. Active coping faces and

Defense mechanisms • In psychodynamic theory, unconscious functions of the ego that protect it from anxiety-evoking material by preventing accurate recognition of the material.

Active coping • Methods of manipulating the environment to remove stressors, or to change our response patterns to cushion their harmfulness.

TABLE 11.1 SOME DEFENSE MECHANISMS OF THE EGO, ACCORDING TO PSYCHODYNAMIC THEORY

DEFENSE MECHANISM	WHAT IT IS	THEORETICAL EXAMPLES OF DEFENSE MECHANISMS IN NORMAL BEHAVIOR	THEORETICAL EXAMPLES OF DEFENSE MECHANISMS IN PSYCHOLOGICAL DISORDERS
Repression	The ejection of anxiety-evoking ideas from awareness.	A student forgets that a difficult term paper is due. A client in psychoanalysis forgets an appointment when anxiety-evoking material is about to be brought up.	A person who has hurt people close to him cannot recall his identity or the facts concerning his personal life.
Regression	The return, under stress, to a form of behavior characteristic of an earlier stage of development.	An adolescent cries when forbidden to use the family car. An adult becomes highly dependent on his parents following the breakup of his marriage.	Under extreme stress a person regresses to the first months of life, where she is ruled by impulses and cannot distinguish between fantasy and reality.
Rationalization	The use of self-deceiving justifications for unacceptable behavior.	A student blames her cheating on her teacher for leaving the room during a test. A man explains his cheating on his income tax by saying "Everyone does it."	A man justifies raping a woman by claiming that she was dressing provocatively.
Displacement	The transfer of ideas and impulses from threatening or unsuitable objects to less threatening objects.	A worker picks a fight with her spouse after being criticized sharply by her supervisor.	A man who is frustrated at work kills his family.
Projection	The thrusting of one's own unacceptable impulses onto others so that others are assumed to harbor them.	A hostile person perceives the world as being a dangerous place. A sexually frustrated person interprets innocent gestures of others as sexual advances.	A hostile person develops delusions that others are attempting to destroy him.
Reaction formation	Assumption of behavior in opposition to one's genuine impulses in order to keep impulses repressed.	A person who is angry with a relative behaves in a "sickly sweet" manner toward that relative. A sadistic individual becomes a physician.	A conservative woman who cannot accept her sexual desires goes on a compulsive holy crusade to ban pornography.
Denial	Refusal to accept the true nature of a threat.	Belief that one will not contract cancer or heart disease although one smokes heavily. "It can't happen to me."	A person denies that his house is in danger from the rising flood waters of a nearby river and refuses to leave, despite imminent danger of being drowned.
Sublimation	The channeling of primitive impulses into positive, constructive efforts.	A person paints nudes for the sake of "beauty" and "art." A hostile person becomes a tennis star.	(Sublimation is not usually associated with abnormal behavior.)

recognizes stressors for what they are. Sometimes stressors cannot be eliminated or modified. Active coping then involves rational evaluation of our capacities to manage them and planning efficient ways to cushion their impact.

We explored a number of active coping methods in Chapter 5's sections on pain management and decision making. The methods we explore in this chapter begin with ways of controlling irrational and catastrophizing thoughts that compound, and sometimes create, stressors. Our biological responses to stress are characterized by arousal of the nervous system. In this chapter's

"Adjustment and Modern Life" feature, we thus examine two methods for relaxing or lowering arousal: meditation and progressive relaxation. Elsewhere in this chapter, we describe methods for coping with Type A behavior. We look at ways of increasing psychological hardiness, a moderator of the impact of stress. We consider ways of coping with the three basic emotional responses to stress—fears and phobias, anger, and, in the "Adjustment and Modern Life" section, depression.

CONTROLLING STRESSFUL COGNITIONS

Have you had any of these experiences?

1. You have difficulty with the first item on a test and become convinced that you will flunk?
2. You want to express your genuine feelings but think that you might upset another person by doing so?
3. You haven't been able to get to sleep for 15 minutes and assume that you will lie awake the whole night and feel "wrecked" in the morning?
4. You're not sure what decision to make, so you try to put your conflicts out of your mind by going out, playing cards, or watching TV?
5. You decide not to play tennis or go jogging because your form isn't perfect and you're in less-than-perfect condition?

If you have had such experiences, it may be because you harbor irrational beliefs identified by Albert Ellis (see pp. 303–304). These beliefs may make you overly concerned about the approval of others (experience 2) or perfectionistic (experience 5). They may lead you to think that you can relieve yourself of life's problems by pretending that they do not exist (experience 4), or that a minor setback must lead to greater problems (experiences 1 and 3).

How, then, do we change irrational or catastrophizing thoughts? The answer is deceivingly simple: We change these thoughts by changing them. However, change can require some work. Before we can change our thoughts we must first be, or become, aware of them.

Controlling Irrational and Catastrophizing Thoughts

Canadian psychologist Donald Meichenbaum suggests a three-step procedure for controlling irrational and catastrophizing thoughts that often attend feelings of pain, anxiety, frustration, conflict, or tension:

1. Develop awareness of them through careful self-examination. Study the examples at the beginning of this section and in Table 11.2 to see if they apply to you. (Also ponder whether any of Ellis's "ten doorways to distress" govern your behavior.) When you meet anxiety or frustration, scrutinize your thoughts. Do they point to a solution, or do they compound your problems?
2. Prepare thoughts that are **incompatible** with the irrational and catastrophizing thoughts. Practice saying them firmly to yourself. (If nobody is nearby, why not vocalize them?)
3. Reward yourself with a mental pat on the back for effective changes in beliefs and thought patterns.

Controlling catastrophizing thoughts reduces the impact of a stressor, whether it is pain, anxiety, or feelings of frustration. It gives you a chance to

INCOMPATIBLE • Not capable of occurring simultaneously.

TABLE 11.2 CONTROLLING IRRATIONAL, CATASTROPHIZING BELIEFS AND THOUGHTS

IRRATIONAL, CATASTROPHIZING THOUGHTS	*RATIONAL (COPING) THOUGHTS*
"Oh my God, I'm going to lose all control!"	"This is painful and upsetting, but I don't have to go to pieces."
"This will never end."	"This will come to an end, even if it's hard to see right now."
"It'll be awful if Mom gives me that look."	"It's more pleasant when Mom's happy with me, but I can live with it if she isn't."
"How can I go out there? I'll look like a fool."	"So you're not perfect; that doesn't mean that you're going to look stupid. And so what if someone thinks you look stupid? You can live with that, too. Just stop worrying and have some fun."
"My heart's going to leap out of my chest! How much can I stand?"	"Easy—hearts don't leap out of chests. Stop and think! Distract yourself. Breathe slowly, in and out."
"What can I do? There's nothing I can do!"	"Easy—stop and think. Just because you can't think of a solution right now doesn't mean there's nothing you can do. Take it a minute at a time. Breathe easy."

Do irrational beliefs and catastrophizing thoughts compound your stress? Psychologists suggest that we can cope with stress by becoming aware of self-defeating thoughts and replacing them with rational, calming thoughts.

Truth or Fiction Revisited

It is true that the best way to change catastrophizing thoughts is to . . . change them. Practicing rational alternatives is one method for doing so.

develop a plan for effective action. When effective action is not possible, controlling our thoughts increases our capacity to tolerate discomfort. So does relaxing, which we discuss in the chapter's "Adjustment and Modern Life" section.

COPING WITH THE TYPE A BEHAVIOR PATTERN

Truth or Fiction Revisited

According to the results of the Recurrent Coronary Prevention Project, it is true that the modification of Type A behavior helps prevent recurrent heart attacks.

Type A behavior is identified by characteristics such as a sense of time urgency and hostility. Cardiologist Meyer Friedman, one of the originators of the Type A concept, and Diane Ulmer reported in 1984 on some of the results of the San Francisco Recurrent Coronary Prevention Project (RCPP). The RCPP was designed to help Type A heart attack victims modify their behavior in an effort to avert future attacks. After 3 years, subjects who learned to reduce Type A behavior patterns had only one third as many recurrent heart heart attacks a control group.

Two of the RCPP guidelines addressed participants' sense of time urgency and their hostility.

Alleviating Your Sense of Time Urgency

Stop driving yourself—get out and walk! Too often we jump out of bed to an abrasive alarm, hop into a shower, fight commuter crowds, and arrive at class or work with no time to spare. Then we first become involved in our hectic day. For Type A people, the day begins urgently and never lets up.

The first step in coping with a sense of time urgency is confronting and replacing the beliefs that support it. Friedman and Ulmer (1984) note that Type A individuals tend to harbor the following beliefs:

1. "My sense of time urgency has helped me gain social and economic success" (p. 179). The idea that impatience and irritation contribute to success, according to Friedman and Ulmer, is absurd.
2. "I can't do anything about it" (p. 182). Of course, the belief that we cannot change ourselves is also one of Ellis's doorways to distress (see Chapter 10). Even in late adulthood, note Friedman and Ulmer, old habits can be discarded and new habits can be acquired.

Friedman and Ulmer (1984) also use many exercises to help combat thc sense of time urgency. Note these examples:

1. Engage in more social activities with family and friends.
2. Spend a few minutes each day recalling events from the distant past. Check old photos of family and friends.
3. Read books—literature, drama, politics, biographies, science, nature, science fiction. (Not books on business or on climbing the corporate ladder!)
4. Visit museums and art galleries for their aesthetic value—not for speculation on the price of paintings.
5. Go to the movies, ballet, and theater.
6. Write letters to family and friends.
7. Take a course in art, or begin violin or piano lessons.
8. Remind yourself daily that life is by nature unfinished and you do not need to have all your projects finished on a given date.
9. Ask a family member what he or she did that day, and actually *listen* to the answer.

Psychologist Richard Suinn (1982, 1995) also suggests:

10. Get a nice-sounding alarm clock!
11. Move about slowly when you awake. Stretch.
12. Drive more slowly. This saves energy, lives, and traffic citations. It's also less stressful than racing the clock.
13. Don't wolf lunch. Get out; make it an occasion.

Truth or Fiction Revisited

It is true that visiting museums and art galleries is one of the methods for treating Type A behavior. Such visits help alleviate the sense of time urgency.

Easing Out of the Type A Behavior Pattern.
Type A behavior is characterized by time urgency and hostility. Pursuing (relaxing!) leisure activities, visiting museums and art galleries, taking the time to write letters to friends, expressing feelings of love, caring for a pet, even offering a cheerful "Good morning!" can all help ease us out of the Type A behavior pattern.

14. Don't tumble words out. Speak more slowly. Interrupt less frequently.
15. Get up earlier to sit and relax, watch the morning news with a cup of tea, or meditate. This may mean going to bed earlier.
16. Leave home earlier and take a more scenic route to work or school. Avoid rush-hour jams.
17. Don't car-pool with last-minute rushers. Drive with a group that leaves earlier or use public transportation.
18. Have a snack or relax at school or work before the "day" begins.
19. Don't do two things at once. Avoid scheduling too many classes or appointments back-to-back.
20. Use breaks to read, exercise, or meditate. Limit intake of stimulants like caffeine. Try decaffeinated coffee (tasty when brewed, not instant).
21. Space chores. Why have the car and typewriter repaired, work, shop, and drive a friend to the airport all in one day?
22. If rushed, allow unessential work to go to the next day. Friedman and Ulmer add, "Make no attempt to get everything finished by 5:00 P.M. if you must pressure yourself to do so" (1984, p. 200).
23. Set aside some time for yourself: for music, a hot bath, exercise, relaxation. (If your life will not permit this, get a new life.)

Alleviating Your Hostility

Hostility, like time urgency, is supported by a number of irrational beliefs. Again, we need to begin by recognizing our irrational beliefs and replacing them. Beliefs that support hostility include:

1. "I need a certain amount of hostility to get ahead in the world" (Friedman & Ulmer, 1984, p. 222). Becoming readily irritated, aggravated, and angered does not contribute to getting ahead.
2. "I can't do anything about my hostility" (p. 222). Need we comment?
3. "Other people tend to be ignorant and inept" (p. 223). Yes, some of them are, but the world is what it is. As Ellis notes, we expose ourselves to aggravation by demanding that other people be what they are not.
4. "I don't believe I can ever feel at ease with doubt and uncertainty" (p. 225). There are ambiguities in life; certain things remain unpredictable. Becoming irritated and aggravated doesn't make things less uncertain.
5. "Giving and receiving love is a sign of weakness" (p. 228). This belief is rugged individualism carried to the extreme. It can isolate us from social support.

Friedman and Ulmer offer suggestions beyond replacing irrational beliefs:

Truth or Fiction Revisited

It is true that telling someone you love them is another method for treating Type A behavior. Doing so helps alleviate feelings of hostility.

1. Tell your spouse and children that you love them.
2. Make some new friends.
3. Let friends know that you stand ready to help them.
4. Get a pet. (Take care of it!)
5. Don't get into discussions on topics about which you know that you and the other party hold divergent and heated opinions.
6. When other people do things that fall short of your expectations, consider situational factors such as level of education or cultural background that may limit or govern their behavior. Don't assume that they "will" the behavior that upsets you.

7. Look for the beauty and joy in things.
8. Stop cursing so much.
9. Express appreciation for the help and encouragement of others.
10. Play to lose, at least some of the time. (Ouch?)
11. Say "Good morning" in a cheerful manner.
12. Look at your face in the mirror throughout the day. Search for signs of aggravation and ask yourself if you need to look like that.

ENHANCING PSYCHOLOGICAL HARDINESS

Psychological hardiness buffers the effects of stress and is characterized by "three C's"—commitment, challenge, and control (see Chapter 5). Psychologist Salvatore Maddi, who along with Susanne Kobasa originated the concept of psychological hardiness, maintains that hardiness can be enhanced by teaching people three coping strategies: situational reconstruction, focusing, and compensatory self-improvement. These methods heighten our sense of commitment and control and provide meaningful challenges.

Maddi piloted the methods with small groups of male and female Illinois Bell managers (Fischman, 1987). After treatment, participants showed significant gains on paper-and-pencil tests of hardiness constructed by Maddi. They reported greater job satisfaction, fewer headaches, and improved sleep patterns. Moreover, their blood pressure dropped from a pretreatment average of 130/92 to 120/87. These findings are promising, but there are some methodological flaws. For example, Maddi taught all the participants. Thus we cannot really say whether the benefits of the treatment can be attributed to hardiness training per se or to Maddi's personal skills.

Although questions remain about the evidence for the benefits of these techniques, let's have a look at them. They are consistent with other methods presented in this book and they may very well be of help to *you*.

Situational Reconstruction: "It's Not So Bad, But How Can You Make It Better?"

In **situational reconstruction,** you place stressful situations in perspective by reconsidering your assumptions. You also enhance your problem-solving skills. The case of Arthur illustrates the use of situational reconstruction:

> Arthur was upset by a mediocre appraisal of his work that gave him a salary increase but cost him a promotion. Maddi had Arthur imagine outcomes that would have been worse, such as not getting any raise or being fired, and outcomes that would have been better, such as upper-level management promoting him despite the evaluation. Since Arthur hadn't been fired and had been given a raise, he realized that his performance hadn't been all that bad, enhancing his sense of competence and self-esteem. Also, the promotion was not likely to come about unless upper-level management became aware of him and his work. Arthur realized that he could foster management's awareness of him by taking on more challenging assignments, and he initiated conferences with his much-surprised supervisor (took control of the situation) to explore ways of enhancing his value to Illinois Bell.

SITUATIONAL RECONSTRUCTION • In psychological-hardiness training, modifying the way in which one interprets one's situation so that one's senses of commitment, challenge, and control are enhanced.

COMPENSATORY SELF-IMPROVEMENT. Barbara's husband insisted on getting a divorce, and she saw herself as a failure. She could not win back her husband, but she could take up skiing. Her excellence in the sport eventually dulled some of the anguish of her personal loss and opened social opportunities.

Focusing: "What's Really Bothering You?"

Focusing offers insight to people who are unhappy or distressed but unable to locate the causes of their feelings. Maddi has such people focus on negative bodily sensations, such as tightness in the chest, and reflect on the circumstances in which they usually occur. The case of Roger illustrates focusing:

> Roger, another Illinois Bell executive, realized that tightness in the chest and churning in the stomach had originated in elementary school when he had not done his homework and was consequently afraid of failure. Now he had similar feelings when he feared that there would not be enough time to meet his work assignments. Roger's recognition of the origins of his problem challenged him to work on something specific—not just a nameless feeling. As a result, his sense of control was restored.

Compensatory Self-Improvement: "If Love Eludes You, Take Up Skiing?"

The idea behind compensatory self-improvement is this: If you're knocked out of one arena, and lose your sense of control, find a more suitable arena and build up your self-confidence and sense of control by excelling in it:

> Barbara, another Illinois Bell manager, was up against a roadblock in her personal life—her husband's insistence on getting a divorce. Nothing she could do would change his mind, so she saw herself as a failure and became depressed. Also, her failure to win back her husband seemed emblematic, to her, of general inability to control her life.
>
> After discussion back and forth, Maddi suggested to Barbara that she go out and learn how to ski. Skiing may seem irrelevant when one's marriage is in a shambles, but the sport was important in the area of the country where Barbara lived, and she had always seen herself as too timid and incompetent to learn.

FOCUSING • In psychological-hardiness training, attending to one's body responses in order to gain insight into the causes of negative feelings.

So Barbara signed up for skiing lessons. At first with her heart in her mouth, she gingerly descended the slopes. Gradually, as her skills increased, she began to look forward to her lessons and to assault the slopes. Not only did she enhance her skiing skills, she also made new acquaintances on the slopes and had something to share with them. She also felt that she was taking charge of her life once more, not just letting things happen to her.

Isn't that the trick to things?

Truth or Fiction Revisited

It is true that learning to ski can help you cope when your spouse insists on getting a divorce. Learning to ski is an example of compensatory self-improvement.

COPING WITH EMOTIONAL RESPONSES TO STRESS

Emotional responses to stress include fear, depression, and anger. In this section we explore cognitive-behavioral methods for coping with fear and anger. In the chapter's "Adjustment and Modern Life" feature, we consider ways of dealing with depression.

Coping With Fears and Phobias

Adjustment often requires that we approach and master the objects and situations that frighten us. Maintaining our health can require mastering fear of what the doctor may tell us. Getting ahead in school or in business can require speaking before groups, so some of us may need to cope with stage fright. Getting better grades may require mastering test anxiety.

Cognitive-behavioral methods for mastering fears reverse the common tendency to avoid feared objects. In an emergency, of course, we can simply "do what we have to" despite fear—for example, have a dreaded injection. We can control our body sensations by relaxing, by reminding ourselves that injections don't last forever, and, perhaps, by thinking about lying on a beach somewhere. If continued exposure to frightening objects, such as hypodermic needles, is necessary, flooding may actually extinguish much of the fear. But most psychologists suggest approaching feared objects and situations *under undistressing circumstances.* Lack of discomfort gives us the opportunity to reappraise dreaded objects.

Fear-reduction methods that you may be able to use on your own include gradual approach and systematic desensitization. One can reduce fears by gradually approaching, or confronting, the feared object or situation. Systematic desensitization combines Jacobson's method of progressive relaxation with gradual movement up an imagined or symbolized (as with photographic slides) fear-stimulus hierarchy. Relaxation apparently counterconditions anxiety. Gradual approach and systematic desensitization both allow people to reappraise the objects and situations that they fear.

GRADUAL APPROACH To use this method, define the feared object or situation as the target. Then list specific behaviors that make up a gradual approach of the target. A hierarchy of fear-evoking stimuli is called a **fear-stimulus hierarchy.** Strategies may include decreasing the distance between yourself and the target step-by-step; first approaching it with a friend, then approaching it alone; and gradually increasing the amount of time you remain in contact with the target. To be certain that the behaviors are listed in order of increasing difficulty, you can write down 10 to 20 steps on index cards. Then order and reorder the cards until you are satisfied that they are in a hierarchy. If there seems to be too great a jump between steps, one or two intermediary steps can be added.

FEAR-STIMULUS HIERARCHY • The arrangement of fear-evoking objects or situations in order, from least to most aversive. Used in fear-reduction methods such as gradual approach and systematic desensitization.

ADJUSTMENT *in the* NEW MILLENNIUM

Reaching New Heights With Virtual Reality

Chris Klock peered down a dizzying height. He was 40 floors above the ground in a tiny glass-walled atrium in the Atlanta Marriott Marquis. Or so it seemed. In weekly sessions lasting 45 minutes each, he was going higher and higher in the elevator, until his fear at each level faded, allowing him to move on. In addition to looking down into the hotel's cavernous atrium, the Georgia Institute of Technology junior was also looking out from small balconies at various heights and scrambling across a narrow bridge high above a rapid river. Or so it seemed.

The reality was quite different from the apparent reality, or virtual reality. The elevator, balconies, and bridge were all displays in a virtual reality setup designed to help people with acrophobia.

In "exposure therapy" for phobias, psychologists accompany people into feared situations. For example, they help them get on airplanes standing still in the airport or on to high balconies. Then they help them remain in the situation until the anxiety fades. People feel less anxious on subsequent exposures and can accept greater challenges, like actually flying or standing on a higher balcony. Through repetition in progressively more frightening situations, people eventually overcome their fears.

The virtual reality treatment used by Chris Klock was created by psychologist Barbara O. Rothbaum of Emory University and computer scientist Larry F. Hodges of Georgia Tech. The balcony scene was a cartoonlike rendering of the view from a balcony. Klock stood at a real railing in the lab room. He wore a virtual reality headset and stood by the rail. As he moved, it seemed that he was getting closer to or farther away from the edge of the balcony.

Although he knew it wasn't real, Klock felt as though he were on the edge of the ledge. "Even though it looks like animated reality," he said, "all the depth and movement cues are realistic, so it feels real."

Klock recalled his initial experience with fear of heights. He was 10 years old and was climbing the stairs to the top of the Statue of Liberty. Halfway up there was a view of the surrounding harbor. "It just terrified me," Klock reported. "I turned around and walked right down the steps."

Klock is one of 12 people with acrophobia who were successfully treated by Rothbaum (1995) with the virtual reality apparatus. Other researchers are trying virtual reality to treat other phobias like agoraphobia and speech anxiety. Virtual reality technology is expanding into other areas. There is even virtual reality group therapy. One "group" for men with erectile problems meets with simulated faces in an Internet chat room. (The men in the group meet several times a week by signing on simultaneously. They each have virtual reality goggles and gloves so that they seem to be in the same room.) One day, clients and their therapists may share virtual worlds peopled by significant figures in the clients' lives, such as their parents.

"I think virtual reality is a potentially great advance for psychotherapy, especially for treating phobias," notes psychologist David Barlow (1995), director of the Phobia and Anxiety Disorders Clinic at the State University of New York at Albany. "You can have people experience scary situations through the virtual reality goggles that can be very difficult to arrange for in real life." ■

Kathy's case illustrates such a gradual approach:

> Kathy experienced fear of driving, which made her dependent on family and friends for commuting to work, shopping, and recreation. Driving 30 miles back and forth to work was identified as the target. She constructed this fear-stimulus hierarchy:

1. Sitting behind the wheel of her car with an understanding friend
2. Sitting alone behind the wheel of her car
3. Driving around the block with her friend
4. Driving around the block alone
5. Driving a few miles back and forth with her friend
6. Driving a few miles back and forth alone
7. Driving the route to work and back on a nonworkday with her friend
8. Driving the route to work and back on a nonworkday alone
9. Driving the route to work and back on a workday with her friend
10. Driving the route to work and back on a workday alone

Kathy repeated each step until she experienced no discomfort. As the procedure progressed, Kathy became aware of how her cognitive appraisal of driving had created and compounded her fears. Later she saw how cognitive *reappraisal* aided her coping efforts. At first she catastrophized: "What a baby I am! Marian is being so understanding and here I am ruining her day with my stupidity."

After discussing her self-defeating thoughts with a professional, Kathy learned to forgive herself for imperfect performances. She recognized her growing self-efficacy and rewarded herself for progress. As time passed, she entertained thoughts like, "I don't like my fears, but I didn't get them on purpose and I'm working to overcome them. I am grateful to Marian, but I don't have to feel guilty about inconveniencing her. In the long run, this will make things easier for her, too. Now, this isn't so bad—you're sitting behind the wheel without going bananas, so give yourself a pat on the back for that and stop condemning yourself. You're gradually gaining control of the situation. You're taking charge and mastering it, bit by bit."

SYSTEMATIC DESENSITIZATION To use systematic desensitization, first develop facility with progressive relaxation, explained in the "Adjustment and Modern Life" feature later in the chapter. Learn to relax yourself in a few minutes through abbreviated instructions or by letting go only. Prepare a vividly imagined "safe scene," such as lying on the beach or walking in the woods, that you can focus on when you encounter anxiety. Use index cards to construct a fear-stimulus hierarchy. The first item should elicit only the slightest anxiety. If you cannot progress from one item to another, try placing one or two in between.

Relax in a recliner or on a couch. Imagine hierarchy items vividly, or project slides onto a screen. Control the projector yourself or have a friend help. Focus on each item until it produces some anxiety. Then imagine the safe scene until you regain complete relaxation. Focus on the item again. When you can focus on a hierarchy item without anxiety for 30 seconds three times in a row, move on to the next item. Once you have completed the hierarchy, approach the actual target, gradually if necessary. The case of David in Chapter 10 (pp. 295–296) may provide additional hints.

Coping With Anger

Anger is a common emotional response to negative feelings such as frustration (Berkowitz, 1990), and to social provocations such as insults or threats. Anger is adaptive when it motivates us to surmount obstacles in our paths or to defend ourselves against aggressors. But anger is troublesome when it leads to excessive arousal or self-defeating aggression. Prolonged arousal is stressful and may lead to diseases of adaptation such as high blood pressure. Insulting, threatening, or attacking other people can cause us to get fired, be expelled from school, get into legal trouble, and get hurt or hurt people we care about.

A RATIONAL-EMOTIVE ANALYSIS OF ANGER AND AGGRESSION Why do we respond aggressively when we are frustrated or provoked? Many of us are aware of deciding to act aggressively under such circumstances. In these cases, we can weigh the effects of our aggression to determine whether we should change our behavior. But some of us feel that we just "explode" when others insult or argue with us, and that there is little we can do about it.

Not so. Aggressive responses may occur automatically with lower animals that are subjected to aversive stimulation, but aggressive behavior in humans involves cognitive processes (Berkowitz, 1990). Yet thoughts can be so automatic and fleeting that we are not fully in touch with them. At an extreme, no injury may have been done us. Because of automatic thoughts, however, we may blow up when a parent asks if we had a nice time on a date or when a supervisor offers a helping hand.

Many automatic thoughts (see Table 11.3) are irrational and reflect ongoing sources of frustration, such as conflicts and fears. Conflicts over independence, sex, and personal competence may plague us incessantly, yet we may be barely aware of them. In such cases, we have to work to tune in to them.

In a rational-emotive analysis, a parent's inquiry about a date, or a supervisor's offer to help, serves as an *activating event*. Subtle, ongoing frustrations—say, frustrated wishes to be independent or to be recognized as competent on the job—lead to irrational *beliefs*. So we may interpret a parent's or supervisor's innocent expression of interest as an effort to control or undermine us. Such irrational beliefs, in turn, trigger the *consequences* of intense feelings of anger and, perhaps, aggressive behavior. If we are not fully aware of the *beliefs* in this chain, our aggression may seem a mystery to us. We may wonder why we become so upset or explode. Our behavior may seem unauthentic, and we may disown it. We wind up feeling alienated and disappointed in ourselves.

Table 11.3 provides a number of examples of how ongoing frustrations can set the stage for the irrational *beliefs* behind the *consequences* of anger and aggression.

Because anger often stems from frustration, an ideal method for coping with anger is to remove sources of frustration. This may require creating plans for surmounting barriers or finding substitute goals. But when we choose to, or must, live with our frustrations we can still get in touch with our irrational beliefs, challenge them, and replace them with rational alternatives.

As with anxiety-evoking and depressing beliefs, we can pinpoint enraging beliefs by closely attending to our fleeting thoughts when we feel ourselves becoming angry. Or we can get in touch with them by "running a movie" (see Chapter 10). Once we have noted our automatic thoughts, let us consider: Are we jumping to conclusions about the motives of others? Are we overreacting to our own feelings of frustration? If so, we can construct and rehearse rational alternatives to our irrational beliefs, as in Table 11.4.

The rational alternatives in Table 11.4 help you in several ways:

1. They help you focus on your fleeting cognitive responses to an activating event and to weigh them.
2. They help you control your level of arousal.
3. They help prevent you from jumping to conclusions about other people's intentions. Some people, of course, may have ulterior motives when they

TABLE 11.3 How Frustrations Set the Stage for Activating Events to Trigger Irrational Thoughts and Consequences of Anger and Aggression

POSSIBLE SOURCES OF FRUSTRATION	*ACTIVATING EVENT*	→	*IRRATIONAL THOUGHTS*	→	*POSSIBLE CONSEQUENCES*
Unresolved dependence-independence conflict. Need for privacy from parents.	Your mother asks, "Did you see a nice movie?"	→	"Why does she always ask me that?" "That's my business!"	→	"I don't want to talk about it!" You walk away angrily. You make a noncommittal grunt and then walk away.
Concern about your worth as a person. Concern about competent behavior (work, date, athletics, etc.) at destination.	You are caught in a traffic jam.	→	"Who the hell are they to hold me up?" "I'll never get there! It'll be a mess!"	→	You lean on the horn. You weave in and out of traffic. You curse at drivers who respond to the jam nonchalantly.
Frustration with gender-role expectations. Concern with your adequacy as a parent.	Your husband says, "The baby's crying pretty hard this time."	→	"Are you blaming me for it?" "So do something about it!"	→	"So what the hell do you want from me?" "Just leave me alone, will you?"
Concern with your adequacy as a student. Competition (social, academic, etc.) with a roommate.	Your roommate asks, "How's that paper of yours coming?"	→	"He's got nothing to do tonight, has he?" "Wouldn't he love it if I failed!"	→	"Why do you ask?" "I don't feel like talking about it, okay?" "Mind your own damn business!"
Concern with your adequacy on the job. Concern that your boss is acting like a parent—thwarting needs for independence and privacy.	Your boss asks, "So how did that conference turn out?"	→	"I can handle conferences by myself!" "Always checking up on me!" "Dammit, I'm an adult!"	→	You get flustered and feel your face reddening. You are so enraged that you can barely speak. You excuse yourself. When alone, you kick your desk.
Conflict over expression of sexual needs. Concerns about sexual adequacy.	Your fiancée asks, "Did you have a good time tonight?"	→	"She's always testing me!" "Didn't *she* have a good time?"	→	You feel your face redden. You scream, "Why do you always have to talk about it?"

make "innocent" remarks, but we learn who they are and can handle them differently. We need not assume that everyone has such motives.

4. They help you focus on what is happening *now,* rather than on misinterpreting events because of years of ongoing frustration.

Sometimes you may feel yourself becoming angered by what someone says or does, but not be able to grasp the fleeting beliefs that are intensifying your feelings. In such a situation you can say things to yourself like "Stop and think!" "Don't jump to conclusions," or "Wait a minute before you do anything." Here are some suggestions from Novaco (1977):

"I can work out a plan to handle this. Easy does it."
"As long as I keep my cool, I'm in control of the situation."

TABLE 11.4 IRRATIONAL THOUGHTS THAT INTENSIFY FEELINGS OF ANGER AND RATIONAL ALTERNATIVES TO THESE THOUGHTS

ACTIVATING EVENT	*IRRATIONAL THOUGHTS*	*RATIONAL ALTERNATIVES*
Your mother asks, "Did you see a nice movie?"	"Why does she always ask me that?"	"She probably just wants to know if I had a good time."
	"That's my business!"	"She's not really prying. She just wants to share my pleasure and make conversation."
You are caught in a traffic jam.	"Who the hell are they to hold me up?"	"They're not doing it on purpose. They're probably just about as frustrated by it as I am."
	"I'll never get there! It'll be a mess!"	"So I'm late. It's not my fault and there's nothing I can do about it. When I get there, I'll just have to take a few minutes to get things straightened out. Breathe slowly in and out. Take it easy. I'll do what I can—no more, no less."
Your husband says, "The baby's crying pretty hard this time."	"Are you blaming me for it?"	"Don't jump to conclusions. He just made a statement of fact."
	"So do something about it!"	"Stop and think. Why not ask Mr. Macho to handle it this time?"
Your roommate asks, "How's that paper of yours coming?"	"He's got nothing to do tonight, has he?"	"The paper is difficult, but that's not his fault."
	"Wouldn't he love it if I failed!"	"I shouldn't assume I can read his mind. Maybe it's a sincere question. And if it's not, why should I let him get me upset?"
Your boss asks, "So how did that conference turn out?"	"I can handle conferences by myself!"	"Take it easy! Relax. Of course I can handle them. So why should I get bent out of shape?"
	"Always checking up on me!"	"Maybe she's just interested, but checking up is a part of her job, after all is said and done."
	"Dammit, I'm an adult!"	"Of course I am. So why get upset?"
Your fiancée asks, "Did you have a good time tonight?"	"She's always testing me!"	"Stop and think! Maybe it's an innocent question—and if she is checking, maybe it's because she cares about my feelings."
	"Didn't *she* have a good time tonight?"	"Stop reaching and digging for reasons to be upset. She only asked if I had a good time. Deal with the question."

By replacing irrational, enraging thoughts with rational alternatives, we can avert uncalled-for feelings of anger and aggressive outbursts.

"You don't need to prove yourself. Don't make more out of this than you have to."
"There's no point in getting mad. Think of what you have to do."
"Muscles are getting tight. Relax and slow things down."
"My anger is a signal of what I need to do. Time for problem solving."
"He probably wants me to get angry, but I'm going to deal with it constructively."

Other strategies for coping with feelings of anger include relaxation training, assertive behavior, and self-reward for self-control.

Relaxation You can use a relaxation method to counteract the arousal that accompanies feelings of anger. If you have practiced progressive relaxation, try the following: When you feel angry take a deep breath, tell yourself to relax, and exhale. Allow the bodily sensations of relaxation to "flow in" and replace feelings of anger. If you are stuck in midtown traffic, take a breath, think "Relax," exhale, and then think about some pleasant activities or events. (But continue to pay some attention to other cars.)

Assertive Behavior Assertive behavior entails expressing genuine feelings and sticking up for one's rights. Assertive behavior does *not* include insulting, threatening, or attacking. However, it is assertive (not aggressive) to express strong disapproval of another person's behavior and to ask that person to change his or her behavior.

In Table 11.5, we review some of the situations noted earlier, but now we suggest assertive responses as a substitute for aggressive responses to activating events. In Table 11.6, we present new situations and compare potential assertive and aggressive responses.

Self-Reward When you have coped with frustrations or provocations without becoming enraged and aggressive, pat yourself on the back. Tell yourself you did a fine job. Think, "This time I didn't say or do anything I'll regret later," or "This time I caught myself, and I'm proud of the way I handled things." Novaco (1977) suggests some additional self-rewarding thoughts:

"I handled that one pretty well. That's doing a good job."
"I could have gotten more upset than it was worth."
"My pride can get me into trouble, but I'm doing better at this all the time."
"I actually got through that without getting angry."

Truth or Fiction Revisited

It is not true that we cannot be expected to stand still for it when someone insults us or threatens our honor. Of course we can! Why should we let someone else control our behavior, especially when we don't like what they are doing?

Table 11.5 Assertive Responses to Activating Events

Activating Event	*Assertive Responses*
You are caught in a traffic jam.	You admit to yourself, "This is damned annoying." But you also think, "But it is *not* a tragedy. *I* will control the situation rather than allow the situation to control me. *Relax.* Let those muscles in the shoulders go. When I arrive, I'll just take things step by step and make an honest effort. If things work out, fine. If they don't, getting bent out of shape about it won't make things better."
Your roommate asks, "How's that paper of yours coming?"	You say, "It's a pain! I absolutely hate it! I can't wait till it's over and done with. Don't tell me you have free time on your hands. I'd find that annoying."

TABLE 11.6 A COMPARISON OF AGGRESSIVE AND ASSERTIVE RESPONSES TO PROVOCATIVE ACTIVATING EVENTS

PROVOCATION (ACTIVATING EVENT)	*AGGRESSIVE RESPONSE*	*ASSERTIVE RESPONSE*
Your supervisor says, "I would have handled that differently."	"Well, that's the way I did it. If you don't like it, fire me."	"What is your concern?" If the supervisor becomes argumentative, say, "I believe that I handled it properly because . . ." If you think that you were wrong, admit it straightforwardly. (It is assertive to express genuine recognition of incorrect behavior.)
A co-worker says, "You are a fool."	"Drop dead."	"That's an ugly thing to say. It hurts my feelings, and if you have any hope of maintaining our relationship, you will apologize."
A provocateur says, "So what're yuh gonna do about it?"	You shove or strike the provocateur.	You say "Goodbye" and leave.
Your roommate has not cleaned the room.	"Dammit, you're a pig! Living with you is living in filth!"	"It's your turn to clean the room. You agreed to clean it, and I expect you to stick to it. Please do it before dinner." (Reminding someone of an agreement and requesting compliance is assertive.)

When we commit ourselves to monitoring and working on our negative feelings, we take direct charge of our emotional lives rather than condemning ourselves to passively riding out the winds of whatever emotion is driving us from moment to moment.

adjustment and modern life

Modern life is filled with stresses and strains. This chapter is about taking charge of our lives rather than riding out the winds of our situations and our emotional responses. Our "Adjustment and Modern Life" feature addresses cognitive-behavioral strategies for relaxing in the midst of a sea of stress, managing test anxiety, and lifting ourselves out of depression. You may not always succeed, but when faced with these situations you will now have something to do about them. And remember, if your emotional responses are strong, and are not managing well enough by yourself, talk to klyour professor, visit your college counseling center, or contact a private psychologists or other helping professional. Much of the time we can solve our problems on our own, but it is comforting to know that there are others who can, and would like to, help us.

MEDITATION.
Meditation is a way of reducing arousal that involves focusing on a relaxing, repetitive stimulus, such as a mantra. The concerns of the day are allowed to fade.

RELAXING (CHILLING, THAT IS)

Once you are aware that a stressor is acting on you, and have developed a plan to cope with it, it is no longer helpful to have blood pounding so fiercely through your arteries. Helping professionals have developed many methods for teaching people to relax or lower arousal that you may be able to use on your own. They include meditation and progressive relaxation.

Meditating

Meditation involves narrowing your consciousness so that the stresses of the outside world fade away. The yogis stare at a pattern on a vase or mandala. The ancient Egyptians gazed upon an oil-burning lamp—the origin of the fable of Aladdin's magic lamp. Islamic mystics of Turkey, referred to as "whirling dervishes," concentrate on their body movements and the rhythms of their breathing.

These methods of meditation share a common thread: Through passive observation, the normal person-environment relationship is altered. Problem solving, planning, worry, the concerns of the day are suspended (Clay, 1997). By focusing on peaceful, repetitive stimuli—and thereby narrowing consciousness—we can also lower our levels of arousal.

Meditation has been historically associated with magic. Some meditators may thus report that they have "merged" with the object of meditation (e.g., the vase or mantra) and then transcended it, leading to "oneness with the universe," rapture, or some great insight. Psychologists have no way of measuring oneness with the universe, so these claims are unscientific. But meditation can cause stress-buffering body changes, as we shall see.

Thousands of Americans regularly engage in **transcendental meditation,** or TM, a simplified form of meditation brought to the United States from India in the 1950s by the Maharishi Mahesh Yogi. TM is practiced by repeating **mantras,** which are relaxing words or sounds such as *ieng* and *om.*

MEDITATION • As a method for coping with stress, a systematic narrowing of attention that slows the metabolism and helps produce feelings of relaxation.
TRANSCENDENTAL MEDITATION • The simplified form of meditation brought to the United States by the Maharishi Mahesh Yogi. Abbreviated *TM.*
MANTRA • A word or sound that is repeated in TM.

Truth or Fiction Revisited

It is true that meditation can help people with hypertension lower their blood pressure. Research by Benson and others provides evidence for the statement.

Effects of Transcendental Meditation Herbert Benson (1975) of Harvard Medical School studied practitioners of TM ranging in age from 17 to 41—businesspeople, students, artists. His subjects included people who had practiced TM anywhere from a few weeks to 9 years. Benson found that TM produces what he labels a **relaxation response** in many people. This response is typified by a lower rate of metabolism, as measured by oxygen consumption. The blood pressure of people with hypertension decreases. In fact, people who meditate twice daily tend to show normalized blood pressure throughout the day (Benson and others, 1973). Meditators also produce more frequent and intense alpha waves—brain waves that are associated with relaxation.

Other researchers agree that meditation lowers arousal, but argue that the same effects can be achieved through other relaxing activities, even by resting quietly (Holmes, 1984). Holmes (1984) and his colleagues found no differences between experienced meditators and novice "resters" in heart rate, respiration rate, blood pressure, and sweat in the palms of the hands. Most critics of meditation do not argue that the method is useless, but rather that meditation may have no special benefits as compared with a respite from a stressful routine.

If you want to try out meditation for yourself, the following measures may be of help:

1. Begin by meditating once or twice daily for 10 to 20 minutes.
2. What you *don't* do is more important than what you do do: Adopt a passive, "what happens, happens" attitude.
3. Create a quiet, undisruptive environment. Don't face a light directly.
4. Don't eat for an hour beforehand. Avoid caffeine for at least two.
5. Assume a comfortable position. Change it as needed. It's okay to scratch or yawn.
6. For a concentrative device, you may focus on your breathing or seat yourself before a calming object such as a plant or burning incense. Benson suggests "perceiving" (rather than "mentally saying") the word *one* on every outbreath. This means thinking the word, but "less actively" than usual (good luck). You can also think or "perceive" the word *in* as you are inhaling and *out,* or *ah-h-h,* as you are exhaling. Carrington also suggests mantras such as *ah-nam, shi-rim,* and *ra-mah.*
7. If you are using a mantra, you can prepare for meditation by vocalizing it several times. Enjoy it. Then say it more and more softly. Close your eyes and think only the mantra. Allow the thinking to become "passive" so that you sort of "perceive," rather than actively think, the mantra. Again, adopt a passive, "what happens, happens" attitude. Continue to perceive the mantra. It may grow louder or softer, or disappear for a while and then return.
8. If disruptive thoughts come in as you are meditating, allow them to "pass through." Don't get wrapped up in trying to squelch them, or you may raise your level of arousal.
9. Above all, "take what you get." You cannot force the relaxing effects of meditation. You can only set the stage for it and allow it to happen.
10. Allow yourself to drift. (You won't go too far.) What happens, happens.

Relaxation response • Benson's term for a group of responses which can be brought about by meditation. They involve lowered activity of the sympathetic branch of the autonomic nervous system.

Using Progressive Relaxation

Edmund Jacobson (1938), the originator of **progressive relaxation,** noted that people tense their muscles when they are under stress, compounding their discomfort. He reasoned that if they could relax these contractions, they could lower their tension. Yet when he asked clients to relax their muscles, they often had no idea what to do.

He devised progressive relaxation to teach people how to relax these tensions. In this method, people purposefully tense a muscle group before relaxing it. This sequence helps them to develop awareness of their muscle tensions, to differentiate between tension and relaxation. The method is "progressive" because people move on, or progress, from one muscle group to another. Since its beginnings in the 1930s, progressive relaxation has undergone development by behavior therapists, including Wolpe and Lazarus (1966).

> ***Truth or Fiction Revisited***
>
> It is true that many people will have no idea what to do if you ask them just to allow their muscles to relax. This is one reason that Jacobson devised the method of progressive relaxation.

You can practice progressive relaxation by using the following instructions. Why not tape them or have a friend read them aloud?

First, create a conducive setting. Settle down on a reclining chair, a couch, or a bed with a pillow. Pick a time and place where you're not likely to be interrupted. Be sure that the room is warm and comfortable. Dim the lights. Loosen tight clothing.

Use the following instructions (Wolpe & Lazarus, 1966, pp. 177–180). Tighten each muscle group about two thirds as hard as you could if you were using maximum strength. If you feel that a muscle may go into spasm, you are tensing too hard. When you let go of your tensions, do so completely.

The instructions can be memorized (slight variations from the text will do no harm), taped, or read aloud by a friend. An advantage to having someone read them is that you can signal the person to speed up or slow down by lifting a finger or two.

After you have practiced alternate tensing and relaxing for a couple of weeks, you can switch to relaxing muscles only.

> **Relaxation of Arms (time: 4–5 minutes)** Settle back as comfortably as you can. Let yourself relax to the best of your ability. . . . Now, as you relax like that, clench your right fist, just clench your fist tighter and tighter, and study the tension as you do so. Keep it clenched and feel the tension in your right fist, hand, forearm . . . and now relax. Let the fingers of your right hand become loose, and observe the contrast in your feelings. . . . Now, let yourself go and try to become more relaxed all over. . . . Once more, clench your right fist really tight . . . hold it, and notice the tension again. . . . Now let go, relax; your fingers straighten out, and you notice the difference once more. . . . Now repeat that with your left fist. Clench your left fist while the rest of your body relaxes; clench that fist tighter and feel the tension . . . and now relax. Again enjoy the contrast. . . . Repeat that once more, clench the left fist, tight and tense. . . . Now do the opposite of tension—relax and feel the difference. Continue relaxing like that for a while. . . . Clench both fists tighter and together, both fists tense, forearms tense, study the sensations . . . and relax; straighten out your fingers and feel that relaxation. Continue relaxing your hands and forearms more and more. . . . Now bend your elbows and tense your biceps, tense them harder and study the tension feelings . . . all right, straighten out your

PROGRESSIVE RELAXATION • A method for lowering arousal in which the individual alternately tenses then relaxes muscle groups throughout the body.

arms, let them relax and feel that difference again. Let the relaxation develop. . . . Once more, tense your biceps; hold the tension and observe it carefully. . . . Straighten the arms and relax; relax to the best of your ability. . . . Each time, pay close attention to your feelings when you tense up and when you relax. Now straighten your arms, straighten them so that you feel most tension in the triceps muscles along the back of your arms; stretch your arms and feel that tension. . . . And now relax. Get your arms back into a comfortable position. Let the relaxation proceed on its own. The arms should feel comfortably heavy as you allow them to relax. . . . Straighten the arms once more so that you feel the tension in the triceps muscles; straighten them. Feel that tension . . . and relax. Now let's concentrate on pure relaxation in the arms without any tension. Get your arms comfortable and let them relax further and further. Continue relaxing your arms even further. Even when your arms seem fully relaxed, try to go that extra bit further; try to achieve deeper and deeper levels of relaxation.

Relaxation of Facial Area With Neck, Shoulders, and Upper Back (time: 4–5 minutes) Let all your muscles go loose and heavy. Just settle back quietly and comfortably. Wrinkle up your forehead now; wrinkle it tighter. . . . And now stop wrinkling your forehead, relax and smooth it out. Picture the entire forehead and scalp becoming smoother as the relaxation increases. . . . Now frown and crease your brows and study the tension. . . . Let go of the tension again. Smooth out the forehead once more. . . . Now close your eyes tighter and tighter . . . feel the tension . . . and relax your eyes. Keep your eyes closed, gently, comfortably, and notice the relaxation. . . . Now clench your jaws, bite your teeth together; study the tension throughout the jaws. . . . Relax your jaws now. Let your lips part slightly. . . . Appreciate the relaxation. . . . Now press your tongue hard against the roof of your mouth. Look for the tension. . . . All right, let your tongue return to a comfortable and relaxed position. . . . Now purse your lips, press your lips together tighter and tighter. . . . Relax the lips. Note the contrast between tension and relaxation. Feel the relaxation all over your face, all over your forehead and scalp, eyes, jaws, lips, tongue, and throat. The relaxation progresses further and further. . . . Now attend to your neck muscles. Press your head back as far as it can go and feel the tension in the neck; roll it to the right and feel the tension shift; now roll it to the left. Straighten your head and bring it forward, press your chin against your chest. Let your head return to a comfortable position, and study the relaxation. Let the relaxation develop. . . . Shrug your shoulders, right up. Hold the tension. . . . Drop your shoulders and feel the relaxation. Neck and shoulders relaxed. . . . Shrug your shoulders again and move them around. Bring your shoulders up and forward and back. Feel the tension in your shoulders and in your upper back. . . . Drop your shoulders once more and relax. Let the relaxation spread deep into the shoulders, right into your back muscles; relax your neck and throat, and your jaws and other facial areas as the pure relaxation takes over and grows deeper . . . deeper . . . ever deeper.

Relaxation of Chest, Stomach, and Lower Back (time: 4–5 minutes) Relax your entire body to the best of your ability. Feel that comfortable heaviness that accompanies relaxation. Breathe easily and freely in and

out. Notice how the relaxation increases as you exhale . . . as you breathe out just feel that relaxation. . . . Now breathe right in and fill your lungs; inhale deeply and hold your breath. Study the tension. . . . Now exhale, let the walls of your chest grow loose and push the air out automatically. Continue relaxing and breathe freely and gently. Feel the relaxation and enjoy it. . . . With the rest of your body as relaxed as possible, fill your lungs again. Breathe in deeply and hold it again. . . . That's fine, breathe out and appreciate the relief. Just breathe normally. Continue relaxing your chest and let the relaxation spread to your back, shoulders, neck and arms. Merely let go . . . and enjoy the relaxation. Now let's pay attention to your abdominal muscles, your stomach area. Tighten your stomach muscles, make your abdomen hard. Notice the tension. . . . And relax. Let the muscles loosen and notice the contrast. . . . Once more, press and tighten your stomach muscles. Hold the tension and study it. . . . And relax. Notice the general well-being that comes with relaxing your stomach. . . . Now draw your stomach in, pull the muscles right in and feel the tension this way. . . . Now relax again. Let your stomach out. Continue breathing normally and easily and feel the gentle massaging action all over your chest and stomach. . . . Now pull your stomach in again and hold the tension. . . . Now push out and tense like that; hold the tension . . . once more pull in and feel the tension . . . now relax your stomach fully. Let the tension dissolve as the relaxation grows deeper. Each time you breathe out, notice the rhythmic relaxation both in your lungs and in your stomach. Notice thereby how your chest and your stomach relax more and more. . . . Try and let go of contractions anywhere in your body. . . . Now direct your attention to your lower back. Arch up your back, make your lower back quite hollow, and feel the tension along your spine . . . and settle down comfortably again relaxing the lower back. . . . Just arch your back up and feel the tensions as you do so. Try to keep the rest of your body as relaxed as possible. Try to localize the tension throughout your lower back area. . . . Relax once more, relaxing further and further. Relax your lower back, relax your upper back, spread the relaxation to your stomach, chest, shoulders, arms and facial area. These parts relax further and further and further and ever deeper.

Relaxation of Hips, Thighs, and Calves Followed by Complete Body Relaxation (time: 4–5 minutes) Let go of all tensions and relax. . . . Now flex your buttocks and thighs. Flex your thighs by pressing down your heels. . . . Relax and note the difference. . . . Straighten your knees and flex your thigh muscles again. Hold the tension. . . . Relax your hips and thighs. Allow the relaxation to proceed on its own. . . . Press your feet and toes downward, away from your face, so that your calf muscles become tense. Study that tension. . . . Relax your feet and calves. . . . This time, bend your feet towards your face so that you feel tension along your shins. Bring your toes right up. . . . Relax again. Keep relaxing for a while. . . . Now let yourself relax further all over. Relax your feet, ankles, calves and shins, knees, thighs, buttocks and hips. Feel the heaviness of your lower body as you relax still further. . . . Now spread the relaxation to your stomach, waist, lower back. Let go more and more. Feel the relaxation all over. Let it proceed to your upper back, chest, shoulders and arms and right to the tips of your

fingers. Keep relaxing more and more deeply. Make sure that no tension has crept into your throat; relax your neck and your jaws and all your facial muscles. Keep relaxing your whole body like that for a while. Let yourself relax.

Now you can become twice as relaxed as you are merely by taking in a really deep breath and slowly exhaling. With your eyes closed so that you become less aware of objects and movements around you and thus prevent any surface tensions from developing, breathe in deeply and feel yourself becoming heavier. Take a long, deep breath and let it out very slowly. . . . Feel how heavy and relaxed you have become.

In a state of perfect relaxation you should feel unwilling to move a single muscle in your body. Think about the effort that would be required to raise your right arm. As you *think* about raising your right arm, see if you can notice any tensions that might have crept into your shoulder and your arm. . . . Now you decide not to lift the arm but to continue relaxing. Observe the relief and the disappearance of the tension. . . .

Just carry on relaxing like that. When you wish to get up, count backwards from four to one. You should then feel fine and refreshed, wide awake and calm.

Letting Go Only Once you have practiced progressive relaxation through alternate tensing and letting go, you may be able to relax fully by letting go alone. Focus on the muscle groups in your arms and allow them to relax. Keep letting go. Allow sensations of relaxation, warmth, and heaviness to develop. Repeat for your facial area, neck, shoulders and upper back; chest, stomach and lower back; hips, thighs, and calves.

You may find that you can skip over some areas. Relaxation from one area may "flow" into relaxation in another. Tailor the instructions to your needs.

You can probably achieve deep relaxation by letting go alone in about 5 minutes. Continue to relax and enjoy the sensations for another 10 to 20 minutes. Now and then you can search your body for pockets of residual tension and let them go, too. But you may want to return to the full-length instructions once in a while to maintain your relaxation skills.

Once you have learned how to relax, you can call on your skills as needed. You can relax bodily tensions when you want the alarm turned down. You can also relax once or twice daily to reduce high blood pressure throughout the working day (Agras and others, 1983), or to cut down on Type A behavior.

COPING WITH TEST ANXIETY

Are these complaints familiar? "I just know I'm going to flunk." "I study hard and memorize everything, but when I get in there my mind goes blank." "I don't know what's wrong with me—I just can't take tests." "The way I do on standardized tests, I'll never get into graduate school." When we study diligently, test anxiety seems a particularly cruel hurdle.

Truth or Fiction Revisited

It is true that one way of coping with test anxiety is not to allow it to distract us from the test items. This is because one way in which test anxiety impairs test performance is by distracting us from the tasks at hand.

WHY DO SOME OF US ENCOUNTER TEST ANXIETY? We are not born with test anxiety. Test-anxious students show high arousal, as shown, for example, by dryness in the mouth and rapid heart rate. They also have more negative

TABLE 11.7 PERCENT OF POSITIVE AND NEGATIVE THOUGHTS FOR UNIVERSITY STUDENTS WITH LOW OR HIGH TEST ANXIETY

	THOUGHT	*LOW TEST ANXIETY*	*HIGH TEST ANXIETY*
Positive Thoughts	Will do all right on test	71%	43%
	Mind is clear, can concentrate	49	26
	Feel in control of my reactions	46	23
Negative Thoughts	Wish I could get out or test was over	46	65
	Test is hard	45	64
	Not enough time to finish	23	49
	Work I put into studying won't be shown by my grade	16	44
	Stuck on a question and it's making it difficult to answer others	13	34
	Mind is blank or can't think straight	11	31
	Going to do poorly on test	11	28
	Think how awful it will be if I fail or do poorly	11	45

Students who are highly anxious about tests report fewer positive thoughts and more negative thoughts while taking tests than other students. Their negative thoughts are linked to signs of sympathetic arousal such as dryness in the mouth and rapid heart rate.
Source of data: Galassi, Frierson, & Sharer, 1981, pp. 56, 58.

thoughts and are more self-critical than people with low or moderate test anxiety, even when they are performing just as well (Galassi and others, 1981, 1984; Meichenbaum & Butler, 1980). Moreover, they allow self-criticisms and negative thoughts of the sort shown in Table 11.7 to *distract* them from the test (Bandura, 1977).

COGNITIVE RESTRUCTURING OF TEST ANXIETY Since test anxiety is often linked to catastrophic, irrational thoughts that distract test-takers, it is fitting to cope with test anxiety by challenging these thoughts and returning your attention to the test (Goldfried, 1988). College students on several campuses have reduced test anxiety and improved their test grades through such a method of cognitive restructuring.

Participants in one study of this method (Goldfried and others, 1978) selected 15 anxiety-evoking items from the Suinn Test Anxiety Behavior Scale (STABS). Three of the items were presented for four 1-minute trials during each of five treatment sessions. During these trials, subjects first pinpointed the irrational or catastrophizing thoughts that were evoked. Then they restructured their responses to them by constructing rational alternative thoughts.

One student's irrational thoughts included, "I'm going to fail this test, and then everyone's going to think I'm stupid." Restructuring of these catastrophizing

Do You Choke Up During Tests? The Suinn Test Anxiety Behavior Scale (STABS)

How about you? Do you look upon tests as an opportunity to demonstrate your knowledge and test-taking ability, or do you drive yourself bananas by being overly self-critical and expecting the worst? How does your level of test anxiety compare to that of others? To find out, take the Suinn Test Anxiety Behavior Scale (STABS) items listed below. Then compare your results to those of others by turning to the key in the Appendix. ■

Directions: The items in the questionnaire refer to experiences that may cause fear or apprehension. For each item, place a checkmark under the column that describes how much you are frightened by it nowadays. Work quickly but be sure to consider each item individually.

	Not at all	A little	A fair amount	Much	Very much
1. Rereading the answers I gave on the test before turning it in.	_____	_____	_____	_____	_____
2. Sitting down to study before a regularly scheduled class.	_____	_____	_____	_____	_____
3. Turning in my completed test paper.	_____	_____	_____	_____	_____
4. Hearing the announcement of a coming test.	_____	_____	_____	_____	_____
5. Having a test returned.	_____	_____	_____	_____	_____
6. Reading the first question on a final exam.	_____	_____	_____	_____	_____
7. Being in class waiting for my corrected test to be returned.	_____	_____	_____	_____	_____
8. Seeing a test question and not being sure of the answer.	_____	_____	_____	_____	_____

ideas might be as follows: "Chances are I probably won't fail. And even if I do, people probably won't think I'm stupid. And even if they do, that doesn't mean I *am* stupid" (Goldfried and others, 1978, p. 34).

You can use these four steps to restructure your own cognitions concerning test-taking:

1. Pinpoint irrational, catastrophizing thoughts.
2. Construct incompatible, rational alternatives.

	Not at all	A little	A fair amount	Much	Very much
9. Studying for a test the night before.	______	______	______	______	______
10. Waiting to enter the room where a test is to be given.	______	______	______	______	______
11. Waiting for a test to be handed out.	______	______	______	______	______
12. Waiting for the day my corrected test will be returned.	______	______	______	______	______
13. Discussing with the instructor an answer I believed to be right but which was marked wrong.	______	______	______	______	______
14. Seeing my standing on the exam relative to other people's standing.	______	______	______	______	______
15. Waiting to see my letter grade on the test.	______	______	______	______	______
16. Studying for a quiz.	______	______	______	______	______
17. Studying for a midterm.	______	______	______	______	______
18. Studying for a final.	______	______	______	______	______
19. Discussing my approaching test with friends a few weeks before the test is due.	______	______	______	______	______
20. After the test, listening to the answers my friends selected.	______	______	______	______	______

3. Practice thinking the rational alternatives.
4. Reward yourself for doing so.

You can pinpoint irrational thoughts by studying the STABS items in the accompanying "Self-Assessment" box. Jot down several items that cause you concern. Include other items that come to mind as you review the STABS. Sit back, relax, imagine yourself in each situation. After a while, jot down the irrational thoughts that have come to mind.

TABLE 11.8 RATIONAL ALTERNATIVES TO IRRATIONAL COGNITIONS CONCERNING TEST-TAKING

IRRATIONAL, CATASTROPHIZING THOUGHTS	*RATIONAL ALTERNATIVES*
"I'm the only one who's going so bananas over this thing."	"Nonsense, lots of people have test anxiety. Just don't let it take your mind off the test itself."
"I'm running out of time!"	"Time is passing, but just take it item by item and answer what you can. Getting bent out of shape won't help."
"This is impossible! Are all the items going to be this bad?"	"Just take it item by item. They're all different. Don't assume the worst."
"I just can't remember a thing!"	"Just slow down and remember what you can. Take a few moments and some things will come back to you. If not, go on to the next item."
"Everyone else is smarter than I am!"	"Probably not, but maybe they're not distracting themselves from the test by catastrophizing. Just do the best you can and take it easy. Breathe easy, in and out."
"I've got to get out of here! I can't take it anymore!"	"Even if I feel that I need to leave now and then, I don't have to act on it. Just focus on the test items, one by one."
"I just can't do well on tests."	"That's only true if you believe it's true. Back to the items, one by one."
"There are a million items left!"	"Quite a few, but not a million. Just take them one by one and answer as many as you can. Focus on each item as it comes, not on the number of items."
"Everyone else is leaving. They're all finished before me."	"Fast work is no guarantee of good work. Even if most of them do well, it doesn't have to mean that you *won't* do well. Take all the time you need. Back to the items, one by one."
"If I flunk, everything is ruined!"	"You won't be happy if you fail, but it won't be the end of the world either. Just take it item by item and don't let worrying distract you. Breathe easy, in and out."

In order to restructure your cognitions concerning test-taking, prepare rational alternatives to your irrational thoughts and rehearse them. Don't let catastrophizing distract you from the test items.

Examine each thought carefully. Is it rational and accurate, or is it irrational? Does it catastrophize? Construct incompatible rational alternatives for each thought that is irrational, as in Table 11.8.

Arrange practice tests that resemble actual tests. Time yourself. If the tests are GRE's or civil service exams, buy the practice tests and make testing conditions as realistic as possible.

Attend to your thoughts while you take the practice tests. Can you find additional irrational thoughts? If so, prepare additional rational alternatives.

Whenever an irrational thought comes to mind, think the rational alternative firmly. If you are alone, say it out loud. If no irrational thoughts pop into mind, mentally rehearse the ones that you usually think in such a situation. For each one, think the rational alternative firmly.

Reward yourself for thinking rational alternatives. Say to yourself, for example, "That's better, now I can return to the test," or, "See, I don't have to be at the mercy of irrational thoughts. I can decide what I'm going to say to myself." When the test is over, think something like, "Well, I did it. What's done is done, but I certainly got through that feeling much better, and I may have done better as well."

Additional hints: Practice progressive relaxation. If you feel uptight during a test, allow feelings of relaxation to drift in, especially into your shoulders and the back of your neck. Take a deep breath, tell yourself to relax, and let the breath out (Suinn, 1995). Also, try **overlearning** the material you're studying. Study it even after you feel you know it fully. Overlearning aids retention of material and increases your belief in your ability to recall it. Finally, when a test is over, *let it be over.* Check answers to help master important material, if you wish, but not just to check your score. Do something that's fun. (Go ahead. You've earned it.)

ALLEVIATING DEPRESSION (GETTING OUT OF THE DUMPS)

> *Be not afraid of life. Believe that life is worth living and your belief will help create the fact.*
>
> WILLIAM JAMES

In this section, we discuss methods for coping with the inactivity, feelings of sadness, and cognitive distortions that characterize depression. People who feel that their situations may fit the picture of a major depressive episode or bipolar disorder, as described in Chapter 9, are advised to talk over their problems with their instructors or a health professional. However, there are many strategies that we can use to cope with lingering feelings of depression that accompany losses, failures, or persistent pressures. These include using pleasant events, modifying depressing thoughts, exercise, and assertive behavior. But first you may wish to check into how depressed you are by taking the Self-Rating Depression Scale on page 350.

Using Pleasant Events to Lift Your Mood

Bill's romance had recently disintegrated, and he was now at a low ebb, weepy and withdrawn. Depression is an appropriate emotional response to a loss, but after weeks of moping, Bill's friends became concerned. After much argument, they finally prevailed on him to accompany them to a rock concert. It took Bill a while to break free from his own ruminations and begin to focus on the music and the electricity of the crowd, but then Bill found himself clapping, shouting,

OVERLEARNING • Continuing to study academic material that has already been learned adequately.

ARE YOU BLUE? THE SELF-RATING DEPRESSION SCALE

Depression has been referred to as the common cold of psychological problems. What about you? Are you blue? ■

Directions: Below are 20 statements about feelings each of us has at one time or another. Read each one and place a check in the space which best describes how you are feeling at this time. Interpret your answers by turning to the key in the Appendix.

	None OR a little of the timc	**Some of the time**	**Good part of the time**	**Most OR all of the time**
1. I feel downhearted, blue, and sad.	_______	_______	_______	_______
2. Morning is when I feel the best.	_______	_______	_______	_______
3. I have crying spells or feel like it.	_______	_______	_______	_______
4. I have trouble sleeping through the night.	_______	_______	_______	_______
5. I eat as much as I used to.	_______	_______	_______	_______
6. I enjoy looking at, talking to and being with attractive women/men.	_______	_______	_______	_______
7. I notice that I am losing weight.	_______	_______	_______	_______
8. I have trouble with constipation.	_______	_______	_______	_______
9. My heart beats faster than usual.	_______	_______	_______	_______
10. I get tired for no reason.	_______	_______	_______	_______
11. My mind is as clear as it used to be.	_______	_______	_______	_______
12. I find it easy to do the things I used to.	_______	_______	_______	_______
13. I am restless and can't keep still.	_______	_______	_______	_______
14. I feel hopeful about the future.	_______	_______	_______	_______
15. I am more irritable than usual.	_______	_______	_______	_______
16. I find it easy to make decisions.	_______	_______	_______	_______
17. I feel that I am useful and needed.	_______	_______	_______	_______
18. My life is pretty full.	_______	_______	_______	_______
19. I feel that others would be better off if I were dead.	_______	_______	_______	_______
20. I still enjoy the things I used to do.	_______	_______	_______	_______

and moshing with his friends. Depressive feelings did not return until the following morning. At that time Bill thought, "Well, what could I expect? I was really depressed *underneath it all.*"

Bill's thoughts were understandable, if irrational. He had a right to feel sad that his romance had ended. But after several weeks had passed, his belief that sadness was the only emotion he ought to feel was irrational. (He also seemed to believe that his feelings were subject to the whims of others, and that there was nothing he could do to elevate his mood so long as his love life was in a shambles.) For Bill, the rock concert was incompatible with depression. He could not listen to the heavy metal group, The Naked and the Dead, and remain miserable.[1] Although his friends were helpful, it is unfortunate that they, and not Bill, were responsible for placing him in the audience. Bill eventually profited from the experience, but he attributed his improvement to his friends' actions, and not to his own resources. Again, his own mood was attributed to, and dependent upon, the behavior of others.

In any event, there is a significant relationship between our moods and our activities. Pressures and failures can trigger feelings of depression. It seems that the opposite also holds true: Feelings of happiness and joy can be generated by pleasant events. Lewinsohn and Graf (1973) had subjects track their activities and feelings of depression for 30 days, using checklists they mailed to the researchers on a daily basis. A number of items that contributed to a positive mood are listed in Table 11.9. The researchers classify them into three groups: (1) activities that counteract depression by producing positive, or incompatible, emotional responses; (2) social interactions; and (3) ego-supportive activities or events. Ego-supportive activities help raise self-efficacy expectancies.

Truth or Fiction Revisited

It is true that psychologists have compiled scientifically derived lists of turn-ons that can elevate your mood without your popping pills. These are lists of pleasant events.

If you have been down in the dumps for a while, it may help you to engage in activities that are incompatible with depression. You can systematically use pleasant events to lift your mood—or enrich the quality of your daily life—through the following steps:

1. Check off items that appeal to you on the Pleasant Events Schedule.
2. Engage in at least three pleasant events each day.
3. Record your pleasant activities in a diary. Add other activities and events that struck you as pleasant, even if they were unplanned.
4. Toward the end of each day, rate your response to each activity using a scale like:

   +3 Wonderful
   +2 Very nice
   +1 Somewhat nice
   0 No particular response
   −1 Somewhat disappointing
   −2 Rather disappointing
   −3 The pits

5. After a week or so, check the activities and events in the diary that received positive ratings.
6. Make a point of repeating highly positive activities and continue to experiment with new ones.

[1] Your authors, however, would be able to accomplish this feat.

TABLE 11.9 ACTIVITIES LINKED TO POSITIVE FEELINGS IN THE LEWINSOHN AND GRAF STUDY

ACTIVITIES PRODUCING INCOMPATIBLE EMOTIONAL RESPONSES	Thinking about something good in the future Listening to music Being relaxed Wearing clean clothes Breathing clean air Sitting in the sun Watching wild animals Seeing beautiful scenery
SOCIAL INTERACTIONS	Being with happy people Having a frank and open conversation Having coffee, tea, a Coke with friends Watching people Being told I am loved Meeting someone new of the same sex Being with friends Smiling at people Expressing my love to someone Having a lively talk Kissing Having sexual relations Complimenting or praising someone
EGO-SUPPORTIVE ACTIVITIES OR EVENTS	Doing a project in my own way Planning trips or vacations Reading stories, novels, poems, or plays Planning or organizing something Doing a job well Learning to do something new

Lewinsohn and Graf (1973) found that many activities seem to contribute to positive feelings and raise self-efficacy expectancies. How frequently do you do things such as these for yourself?

Challenging Irrational, Depressing Thoughts

> *Public opinion is a weak tyrant compared with our own private opinion. What a man thinks of himself, that it is which determines . . . his fate.*
>
> HENRY DAVID THOREAU, *WALDEN*

Depressed people tend to have excessive needs for social approval and to be perfectionistic in their self-demands. They also tend to blame themselves for failures and problems, even when they are not at fault. They *internalize* blame and see their problems as *stable* and *global*—as all but impossible to change. Depressed people also make the cognitive errors of tending to *catastrophize* their problems and to *minimize* their accomplishments.

Consider Table 11.10. Column 1 illustrates a number of (often) irrational, depressing thoughts. How many of them have you had? Column 2 indicates the type of cognitive error being made (such as internalizing or catastrophizing), and column 3 shows examples of more rational, less depressing alternatives.

You can pinpoint irrational, depressing thoughts by focusing on what you are thinking when you feel low. Pay particular attention to the rapid, fleeting thoughts that can trigger mood changes. It helps to jot down the negative thoughts. Then challenge their accuracy. Do you characterize difficult situations as impossible and hopeless? Do you expect too much from yourself and minimize your achievements? Do you internalize more than your fair share of blame?

You can use Table 11.10 to classify your own cognitive errors and as a guide in constructing rational alternatives to your own depressing thoughts. Jot down rational alternatives next to each irrational thought. Review them from time to time. When you are alone, read the irrational thought aloud, then follow it by saying, firmly, "No, that's irrational!" Then read aloud the rational alternative twice, *emphatically*.

TABLE 11.10 IRRATIONAL, DEPRESSING THOUGHTS AND RATIONAL ALTERNATIVES

IRRATIONAL THOUGHT	*TYPE*	*RATIONAL ALTERNATIVE*
"There's nothing I can do."	Catastrophizing, minimizing, stabilizing	"I can't think of anything to do right now, but if I work at it, I may."
"I'm no good."	Internalizing, globalizing, stabilizing	"I did something I regret, but that doesn't make me evil or worthless as a person."
"This is absolutely awful."	Catastrophizing	"This is pretty bad, but it's not the end of the world."
"I just don't have the brains for college."	Stabilizing, globalizing	"I guess I really need to go back over the basics in that course."
"I just can't believe I did something so disgusting!"	Catastrophizing	"That was a bad experience. Well, I won't be likely to try that again soon."
"I can't imagine ever feeling right."	Stabilizing, catastrophizing	"This is painful, but if I try to work it through step by step, I'll probably eventually see my way out of it."
"It's all my fault."	Internalizing	"I'm not blameless, but I wasn't the only one involved. It may have been my idea, but he went into it with his eyes open."
"I can't do anything right."	Globalizing, stabilizing, catastrophizing, minimizing	"I sure screwed this up, but I've done a lot of things well, and I'll do other things well."
"I hurt everybody who gets close to me."	Internalizing, globalizing, stabilizing	"I'm not totally blameless, but I'm not responsible for the whole world. Others make their own decisions, and they have to live with the results, too."
"If people knew the real me, they would have it in for me."	Globalizing, minimizing (the positive in yourself)	"I'm not perfect, but nobody's perfect. I have positive as well as negative features, and I am entitled to self-interests."

Many of us create or compound feelings of depression because of cognitive errors such as those in this table. Have you had any of these irrational, depressing thoughts? Are you willing to challenge them?

SELF-ASSESSMENT

WHAT TURNS YOU ON? THE PLEASANT EVENTS SCHEDULE

Walking, loving, reading, collecting, redecorating—different people enjoy different things. Here is a list of 116 activities and events enjoyed by many. The first 114 are derived from research by MacPhillamy and Lewinsohn (1971). The last two are a contemporary update. ■

Directions: You can use the 116 items to get in touch with what turns you on by rating them according to the scale given below. Then you may want to enrich the quality of your daily life by making sure to fit one or more of them in.

2 = very pleasant
1 = pleasant
0 = not pleasant

____ 1. Being in the country
____ 2. Wearing expensive or formal clothes
____ 3. Making contributions to religious, charitable, or political groups
____ 4. Talking about sports
____ 5. Meeting someone new
____ 6. Going to a rock concert
____ 7. Playing baseball, softball, football, or basketball
____ 8. Planning trips or vacations
____ 9. Buying things for yourself
____ 10. Being at the beach
____ 11. Doing art work (painting, sculpture, drawing, moviemaking, etc.)
____ 12. Rock climbing or mountaineering
____ 13. Reading the Scriptures
____ 14. Playing golf
____ 15. Rearranging or redecorating your room or house
____ 16. Going naked
____ 17. Going to a sports event
____ 18. Going to the races
____ 19. Reading stories, novels, poems, plays, magazines, newspapers
____ 20. Going to a bar, tavern, club
____ 21. Going to lectures or talks
____ 22. Creating or arranging songs or music
____ 23. Boating
____ 24. Restoring antiques, refinishing furniture
____ 25. Watching television or listening to the radio
____ 26. Camping
____ 27. Working in politics
____ 28. Working on machines (cars, bikes, radios, television sets)
____ 29. Playing cards or board games
____ 30. Doing puzzles or math games
____ 31. Having lunch with friends or associates
____ 32. Playing tennis
____ 33. Driving long distances
____ 34. Woodworking, carpentry
____ 35. Writing stories, novels, poems, plays, articles
____ 36. Being with animals
____ 37. Riding in an airplane
____ 38. Exploring (hiking away from known routes, spelunking, etc.)
____ 39. Singing
____ 40. Going to a party
____ 41. Going to church functions
____ 42. Playing a musical instrument
____ 43. Snow skiing, ice skating
____ 44. Wearing informal clothes, "dressing down"
____ 45. Acting
____ 46. Being in the city, downtown
____ 47. Taking a long, hot bath
____ 48. Playing pool or billiards
____ 49. Bowling

____ 50. Watching wild animals
____ 51. Gardening, landscaping
____ 52. Wearing new clothes
____ 53. Dancing
____ 54. Sitting or lying in the sun
____ 55. Riding a motorcycle
____ 56. Just sitting and thinking
____ 57. Going to a fair, carnival, circus, zoo, amusement park
____ 58. Talking about philosophy or religion
____ 59. Gambling
____ 60. Listening to sounds of nature
____ 61. Dating, courting
____ 62. Having friends come to visit
____ 63. Going out to visit friends
____ 64. Giving gifts
____ 65. Getting massages or backrubs
____ 66. Photography
____ 67. Collecting stamps, coins, rocks, etc.
____ 68. Seeing beautiful scenery
____ 69. Eating good meals
____ 70. Improving your health (having teeth fixed, changing diet, having a checkup, etc.)
____ 71. Wrestling or boxing
____ 72. Fishing
____ 73. Going to a health club, sauna
____ 74. Horseback riding
____ 75. Protesting social, political, or environmental conditions
____ 76. Going to the movies
____ 77. Cooking meals
____ 78. Washing your hair
____ 79. Going to a restaurant
____ 80. Using cologne, perfume
____ 81. Getting up early in the morning
____ 82. Writing a diary
____ 83. Giving massages or backrubs
____ 84. Meditating or doing yoga
____ 85. Doing heavy outdoor work
____ 86. Snowmobiling, dune buggying
____ 87. Being in a body-awareness, encounter, or "rap" group
____ 88. Swimming
____ 89. Running, jogging
____ 90. Walking barefoot
____ 91. Playing frisbee or catch
____ 92. Doing housework or laundry, cleaning things
____ 93. Listening to music
____ 94. Knitting, crocheting
____ 95. Making love
____ 96. Petting, necking
____ 97. Going to a barber or beautician
____ 98. Being with someone you love
____ 99. Going to the library
____ 100. Shopping
____ 101. Preparing a new or special dish
____ 102. Watching people
____ 103. Bicycling
____ 104. Writing letters, cards, or notes
____ 105. Talking about politics or public affairs
____ 106. Watching attractive women or men
____ 107. Caring for houseplants
____ 108. Having coffee, tea, or Coke, etc., with friends
____ 109. Beachcombing
____ 110. Going to auctions, garage sales, etc.
____ 111. Water skiing, surfing, diving
____ 112. Traveling
____ 113. Attending the opera, ballet, or a play
____ 114. Looking at the stars or the moon
____ 115. Surfing the Internet
____ 116. Playing video games

Source of first 114 items: Adapted from D. J. MacPhillamy & P. M. Lewinsohn, *Pleasant Events Schedule, Form III-S,* University of Oregon, Mimeograph, 1971.

After you have thought or read aloud the rational alternative, think or say things like, "That makes more sense! That's a more accurate view of things! It feels better now that I have things in perspective."

Irrational thoughts do not just happen. Nor are you stuck with them. You can learn to exert control over your thoughts and, in this way, to exert a good deal of control over your feelings—whether the feelings are of anxiety, depression, or anger.

Exercise

Exercise, particularly aerobic exercise, not only fosters physical health. It can enhance our psychological well-being and help us cope with stress (Berger, 1993; Hays, 1995). Depression is characterized by inactivity and feelings of helplessness. Exercise is, in a sense, the opposite of inactivity. Success at exercise might also help alleviate feelings of helplessness. In one experiment, McCann and Holmes (1984) assigned mildly depressed college women at random to aerobic exercise, a progressive-relaxation placebo, and a no-treatment control group. The relaxation group showed some improvement, but aerobic exercise made dramatic inroads on students' depression. Other experiments also suggest that exercise alleviates feelings of depression, at least among mildly and moderately depressed individuals (Buffone, 1984; Greist, 1984; Norvell & Belles, 1993).

Assertive Behavior

Since we humans are social creatures, our social interactions are very important to us. Unassertive behavior patterns, as measured by the Rathus Assertiveness Schedule (see Chapter 4), are linked to feelings of depression (Gotlib, 1984). Learning to express our feelings and relate to others, on the other hand, has been shown to alleviate feelings of depression (Hersen and others, 1984). Assertive behavior permits more effective interactions with our families, friends, co-workers, and strangers. Thus we remove sources of frustration and expand our social support. Expressions of positive feelings—saying you love someone or simply saying "Good morning" brightly—help reduce feelings of hostility and pave the way for further social involvement. ■

SUMMARY

1. **What are some ways of coping with stress?** Psychologists usually speak of defensive and active methods. Defensive coping methods blunt the immediate impact of stressors, but there is usually a personal or social cost—as in socially inappropriate behavior, withdrawal, or self-deception. Direct or active coping methods manipulate the environment to reduce or remove sources of stress. They also involve changing our responses to unavoidable stressors so that their harmfulness is abated.
2. **What are Meichenbaum's methods of controlling irrational and catastrophizing thoughts?** Meichenbaum suggests pinpointing irrational thoughts, replacing them with rational thoughts, and rewarding ourselves for doing so.
3. **How does meditation help us lower arousal?** Meditation lowers arousal by reducing awareness of the surrounding world and the problems of the day.
4. **How does progressive relaxation help us lower arousal?** Progressive relaxation reverses the muscle tension associated with arousal and may also help through its suggestions of warm and heavy limbs.
5. **How can we alleviate the Type A behavior pattern?** Friedman and Ulmer suggest various methods for alleviating our sense of time urgency and hostility.
6. **How can we enhance our psychological hardiness?** Maddi and Kobasa suggest techniques that enhance our senses of commitment, challenge, and control over our situations. These include situational reconstruction, focusing, and compensatory self-improvement.
7. **How can we cope directly with fears and phobias?** We can use gradual approach and systematic desensitization. Each approach allows us to reappraise fear-evoking stimuli.
8. **How can we cope directly with anger?** We can begin by analyzing the ways in which social provocations can trigger irrational beliefs. Then we can challenge the beliefs, lower our arousal, and replace aggressive behavior with assertive behavior.

The Challenges of Life

Chapter 12

Gender Roles and Gender Differences

Truth or Fiction?

T F

- ☐ ☐ Men behave more aggressively than women.
- ☐ ☐ Five- and 6-year-olds tend to distort their memories so that they "remember" boys playing with trains and sawing wood—even when these activities were actually carried out by girls.
- ☐ ☐ Adolescent girls who show a number of masculine traits are more popular than girls who thoroughly adopt the traditional feminine gender role.
- ☐ ☐ An essay written by a woman is poorer in quality than an essay written by a man—even when it is the same essay.
- ☐ ☐ Teachers are more likely to accept calling out in class from boys than girls.
- ☐ ☐ Throughout most of human history, girls were considered unsuited to education.

OUTLINE

I like men to behave like men—strong and childish.

Françoise Sagan

We're halfway there. We've begun to raise our daughters more like sons—so now women are whole people. But fewer of us have the courage to raise our sons more like daughters. Yet until men raise children as much as women do—and are raised to raise children, whether or not they become fathers—they will have a far harder time developing in themselves those human qualities that are wrongly called "feminine," but are really those necessary to raise children: empathy, flexibility, patience, compassion, and the ability to let go.

Gloria Steinem[1]

"Why Can't a Woman Be More Like a Man?" You may remember this song from the musical *My Fair Lady.* In the song, Henry Higgins laments that women are emotional and fickle, whereas men are logical and dependable. The emotional woman is a **stereotype**—a fixed conventional idea about a group. The logical man is also a stereotype. Stereotypes shape our expectations so that we assume that unknown individuals who belong to the group share the stereotypes we attribute to the group.

We begin this chapter by exploring the masculine and feminine gender-role stereotypes. Then we examine research on gender differences in cognitive functioning and personality and explore how we develop "masculine" and "feminine" traits. Next, we examine the concept of psychological androgyny. *Physical* androgyny, or the possession of the sex organs of both genders, can pose towering adjustment problems and is usually corrected medically at an early age—when it can be. But *psychological androgyny* may be desirable because it places a wide range of traits and adjustment strategies at our disposal. In the chapter's "Adjustment and Modern Life" feature, we see that sharp stereotyping has been linked to sexism directed, in particular, against women. We explore sexism and the costs of traditional stereotyping to adjustment in several spheres—in education, in activities and career choices, and in interpersonal relationships.

GENDER POLARIZATION: GENDER ROLES AND STEREOTYPES

Henry Higgins's stereotypes reflect cultural beliefs. Cultural beliefs about men and women involve clusters of stereotypes called **gender roles.** Gender roles define the ways in which men and women are expected to behave.

Sandra Lipsitz Bem (1993) writes that three beliefs about women and men have prevailed throughout the history of Western culture:

1. Women and men have basically different psychological and sexual natures.
2. Men are the superior, dominant gender.
3. Gender differences and male superiority are "natural."

Stereotype • A fixed, conventional idea about a group.

Gender roles • Complex clusters of ways in which males and females are expected to behave.

[1] Commencement address, Smith College, May 1995.

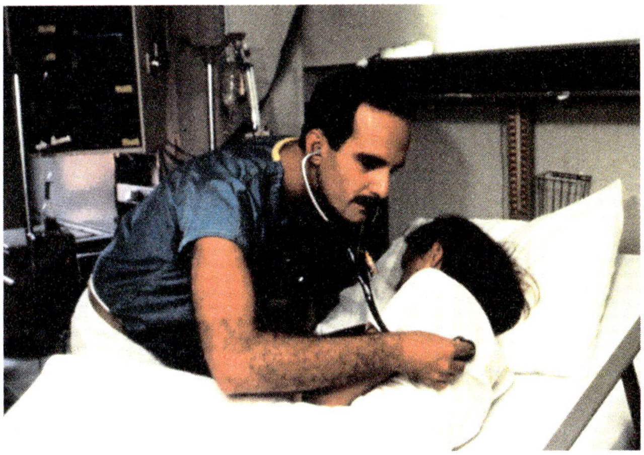

Bucking the Stereotype. Many contemporary women and men are bucking the stereotypes and pursuing careers in fields that previously were reserved for the other gender. Women now make up a sizable minority of the armed forces, although conflict continues over housing them with men and sending them into combat. Some men are now found in nursing.

These beliefs have tended to polarize our views of women and men. It is thought that gender differences in power and psychological traits are natural, but what does "natural" mean? Throughout most of history, people viewed naturalness in terms of religion, or God's scheme of things (S. L. Bem, 1993). For the past century or so, naturalness has been seen in biological, evolutionary terms—at least by most scientists. But these views ignore cultural influences.

What are perceived as the "natural" gender roles? In our society, people tend to see the feminine gender role as warm, emotional, dependent, gentle, helpful, mild, patient, submissive, and interested in the arts (S. L. Bem, 1993). The typical masculine gender role is perceived as independent, competitive, tough, protective, logical, and competent at business, math, and science. Women are typically expected to care for the kids and cook the meals. Cross-cultural studies confirm that these gender-role stereotypes are widespread (see Table 12.1). For example, in their survey of 30 countries, John Williams and Deborah Best (1994) found that men are more likely to be judged to be active, adventurous, aggressive, arrogant, and autocratic (and we have only gotten through the *a*'s). Women are more likely to be seen as fearful, fickle, foolish, frivolous, and fussy (and these are only a handful of *f*'s).

Gender polarization in the United States is linked to the traditional view of men as breadwinners and women as homemakers (Eagly & Steffen, 1984; Hoffman & Hurst, 1990). Despite the persistence of this stereotype in the United States, 6 of every 10 new jobs are held by women (National Institute of Occupational Safety and Health, 1990). Stereotypes also affect the opportunities open to men and women in Hispanic communities, as can be seen in the following discussion of *machismo* and *marianismo*.

Adjustment in a World of DIVERSITY

Machismo/Marianismo Stereotypes and Hispanic Culture[2]

The concept of **machismo** is a cultural stereotype that defines masculinity in terms of an idealized view of manliness. To be *macho* is to be strong, virile, and dominant. Each Hispanic culture puts its own particular cultural stamp on

[2] This guest feature was written by Rafael Art. Javier, Ph.D., associate clinical professor of psychology and director of the Center for Psychological Services and Clinical Studies at St. John's University in Jamaica, NY.

Machismo • The Hispanic American cultural stereotype that defines masculinity in terms of strength, virility, dominance, and emotional restraint.

the meaning of machismo, however. In the Spanish-speaking cultures of the Caribbean and Central America, the macho code encourages men to restrain their feelings and maintain an emotional distance. In my travels in Argentina and some other Latin American countries, however, I have observed that men who are sensitive and emotionally expressive are not perceived as compromising their macho code. More research is needed into differences in cultural conceptions of machismo and other gender roles among various Hispanic groups.

In counterpoint to the macho ideal among Hispanic peoples is the cultural idealization of femininity embodied in the concept of **marianismo.** The marianismo stereotype, which derives its name from the Virgin Mary, refers to the ideal of the virtuous woman as one who "suffers in silence," submerging her needs and desires to those of her husband and children. With the marianismo stereotype, the image of a woman's role as a martyr is raised to the level of a cultural ideal. According to this cultural stereotype, a woman is expected to demonstrate her love for her husband by waiting patiently at home and having dinner prepared for him at any time of day or night he happens to come home, to have his slippers ready for him, and so on. The feminine ideal is one of suffering in silence and being the provider of joy, even in the face of pain. Strongly influenced by the patriarchal Spanish tradition, the marianismo stereotype has historically been used to maintain women in a subordinate position in relation to men.

Acculturation—the merging of cultures that occurs when immigrant groups become assimilated into the mainstream culture—has challenged this traditional machismo/marianismo division of marital roles among Hispanic couples in the United States. I have seen in my own work in treating Hispanic American couples in therapy that marriages are under increasing strain from the conflict between traditional and modern expectations about marital roles. Hispanic American women have been entering the workforce in increasing numbers, usually in domestic or child care positions, but they are still expected to assume responsibility for tending their own children, keeping the house, and serving their husbands' needs when they return home. In many cases, a reversal of traditional roles occurs in which the wife works and supports the family, while the husband remains at home because he is unable to find or maintain employment.

It is often the Hispanic American husband who has the greater difficulty accepting a more flexible distribution of roles within the marriage and giving up a rigid set of expectations tied to traditional machismo/marianismo gender expectations. Although some couples manage to reshape their expectations and marital roles in the face of changing conditions, many relationships buckle under the strain and are terminated in divorce. While I do not expect either the machismo or marianismo stereotype to disappear entirely, I would not be surprised to find a greater flexibility in gender role expectations as a product of continued acculturation.

PSYCHOLOGICAL GENDER DIFFERENCES: VIVE LA DIFFÉRENCE OR VIVE LA SIMILARITÉ?

MARIANISMO • The Hispanic American cultural stereotype that defines the feminine ideal as subordinating her needs and desires to those of her husband and children and, when necessary, suffering in silence.

The French have an expression "Vive la différence," which means "Long live the difference" (between men and women). Yet modern life has challenged our concepts of what it means to be a woman or a man. The anatomical differences between women and men are obvious and are connected with the biological

TABLE 12.1 GENDER-ROLE STEREOTYPES AROUND THE WORLD

STEREOTYPES OF MALES		***STEREOTYPES OF FEMALES***	
Active	Opinionated	Affectionate	Nervous
Adventurous	Pleasure-seeking	Appreciative	Patient
Aggressive	Precise	Cautious	Pleasant
Arrogant	Quick	Changeable	Prudish
Autocratic	Rational	Charming	Self-pitying
Capable	Realistic	Complaining	Sensitive
Coarse	Reckless	Complicated	Sentimental
Conceited	Resourceful	Confused	Sexy
Confident	Rigid	Dependent	Shy
Courageous	Robust	Dreamy	Softhearted
Cruel	Sharp-witted	Emotional	Sophisticated
Determined	Show-off	Excitable	Submissive
Disorderly	Steady	Fault-finding	Suggestible
Enterprising	Stern	Fearful	Superstitious
Hardheaded	Stingy	Fickle	Talkative
Individualistic	Stolid	Foolish	Timid
Inventive	Tough	Forgiving	Touchy
Loud	Unscrupulous	Frivolous	Unambitious
Obnoxious		Fussy	Understanding
		Gentle	Unstable
		Imaginative	Warm
		Kind	Weak
		Mild	Worrying
		Modest	

Source of data: Williams & Best, 1994, p. 193, Table 1.
Psychologists John Williams and Deborah Best (1994) found that people in 30 nations around the world tended to agree on the nature of masculine and feminine gender-role stereotypes. Men are largely seen as more adventurous and hardheaded than women. Women are generally seen as more emotional and dependent.

aspects of reproduction. Biologists therefore have a relatively easy time of it describing and interpreting the gender differences they study. The task of psychology is more complex and is wrapped up with sociocultural and political issues (Eagly, 1995; Marecek, 1995). Psychological gender differences are not as obvious as biological gender differences. In fact, in many ways women and men are more similar than different.

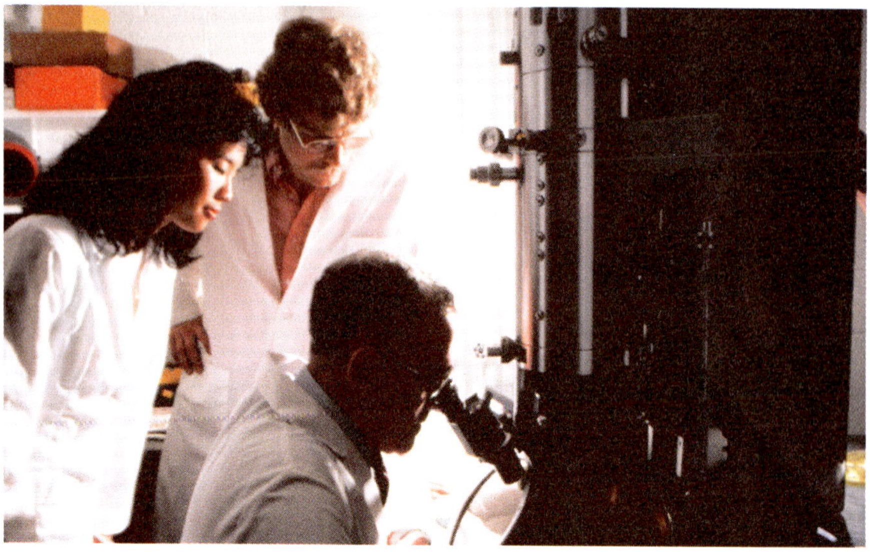

ARE THERE COGNITIVE DIFFERENCES BETWEEN MEN AND WOMEN?
Females appear to excel in language abilities, whereas males seem to excel in some math and spatial-relations skills. However, these differences are small and may reflect cultural stereotypes rather than genetic differences.

To put it another way: To reproduce, women and men have to be biologically different. Throughout history, it has also been assumed that women and men must be psychologically different in order to fulfill different roles in the family and society (S. L. Bem, 1993). But what are the psychological differences between women and men? Key studies on this question span three decades.

Cognitive Abilities

It was once believed that males were more intelligent than females because of their greater knowledge of world affairs and their skill in science and industry. We now know that greater male knowledge and skill did not reflect differences in intelligence. Rather, it reflected the systematic exclusion of females from world affairs, science, and industry. Assessments of intelligence do not show overall gender differences in cognitive abilities. However, reviews of the research suggest that girls are somewhat superior to boys in verbal abilities, such as verbal fluency, ability to generate words that are similar in meaning to other words, spelling, knowledge of foreign languages, and pronunciation (Halpern 1997). Males, on the other hand, seem to be somewhat superior in visual-spatial abilities. Differences in mathematical ability are more complex (Neisser and others, 1996).

Girls seem to acquire language somewhat faster than boys do (Hyde & Linn, 1988). Also, in the United States far more boys than girls have reading problems, ranging from reading below grade level to severe disabilities (Halpern, 1997; Neisser and others, 1996). On the other hand, at least the males headed for college seem to catch up in verbal skills.

Males apparently excel in visual-spatial abilities of the sort used in math, science, and even reading a map (Voyer and others, 1995). Tests of spatial ability assess skills such as mentally rotating figures in space (see Figure 12.1) and finding figures embedded within larger designs (see Figure 12.2).

In math, differences at all ages are small and seem to be narrowing (Hyde and others, 1990). Females excel in computational ability in elementary school, however. Males excel in mathematical problem solving in high school and college (Hyde and others, 1990). Boys outperform girls on the math part of the Scholastic Aptitude Test (Byrnes & Takahira, 1993). According to Byrnes and Takahira (1993), boys' superiority in math does not reflect gender per se.

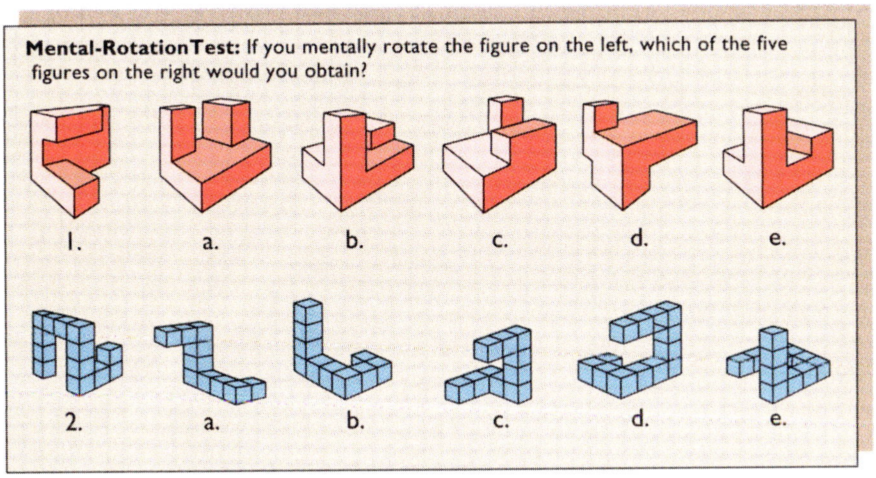

FIGURE 12.1
ROTATING FIGURES IN SPACE.
Males as a group usually outperform females on spatial-relations tasks. Females do as well as males, however, when they receive some training in the tasks.

Instead, boys do as well as they do because of greater experience in solving math problems.

In any event, psychologists note three factors that should caution us not to attach too much importance to apparent gender differences in cognition:

1. In most cases, the differences are small (Hyde & Plant, 1995). In addition, differences in verbal, mathematical, and spatial abilities are getting smaller (Hyde and others, 1990; Voyer and others, 1995).
2. These gender differences are *group* differences. There is greater variation in these skills between individuals *within* the groups than between males and females (Maccoby, 1990). That is, there may be a greater difference in, say, verbal skills between two women than between a woman and a man. Millions of females outdistance the "average" male in math and spatial abilities. Men have produced their Shakespeares. Women have produced their Madame Curies.
3. Some differences may largely reflect sociocultural influences. In our culture spatial and math abilities are stereotyped as masculine. Women who are given just a few hours of training in spatial skills—for example, rotating geometric figures or studying floor plans—perform at least as well men on tests of these skills (Baenninger & Elenteny, 1997; Lawton & Morrin, 1997).

FIGURE 12.2
ITEMS FROM AN EMBEDDED-FIGURES TEST.
This is another measure of spatial-relations ability.

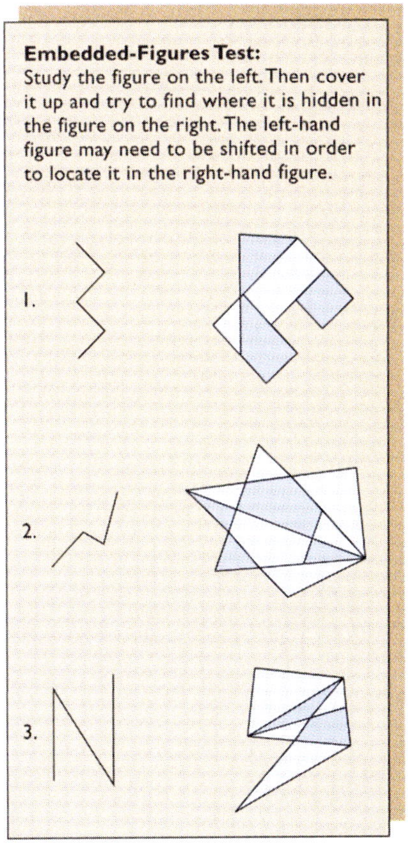

Social Behavior

There are many other psychological differences between males and females. For example, women exceed men in extraversion, anxiety, trust, and nurturance (Feingold, 1994). Men exceed women in assertiveness and tough-mindedness. In the arena of social behavior, women seem more likely than men to cooperate with other people and hold groups, such as families, together (Bjorklund & Kipp, 1996).

Despite the stereotype of women as gossips and chatterboxes, research in communication styles suggests that in many situations men spend more time talking than women do. Men are more likely to introduce new topics and to interrupt (Hall, 1984). Women, on the other hand, seem more willing to reveal their feelings and personal experiences (Dindia & Allen, 1992).

Women interact at closer distances than men do. They also seek to keep more space between themselves and strangers of the other gender than men do

(Rüstemli, 1986). Men are made more uncomfortable by strangers who sit across from them, whereas women are more likely to feel "invaded" by strangers who sit next to them. In libraries, men tend to pile books protectively in front of them. Women place books and coats in adjacent seats to discourage others from taking them.

There are also gender differences in social behavior (Archer, 1996). Let us consider differences in sex and relationships, and in aggression.

SEX AND RELATIONSHIPS Men are more interested than women in casual sex and in having more than one sex partner (Leitenberg & Henning, 1995). In our society there are constraints on unbridled sexual behavior, so most men are not promiscuous (Archer, 1996). Women are more likely to want to combine sex with a romantic relationship.

Truth or Fiction Revisited

It is true that men behave more aggressively than women do—at least in the great majority of cultures. The issue is whether this gender difference is inborn or reflects sociocultural factors.

AGGRESSION In most cultures, it is the males who march off to war and battle for glory (and sneaker ads in TV commercials). Psychological studies of aggression find that male children and adults behave more aggressively than females do (Archer, 1996).

In a classic review of 72 studies concerning gender differences in aggression, Ann Frodi and her colleagues (1977) found that females are more likely to act aggressively under some circumstances than others:

1. Females are more likely to feel anxious or guilty about aggression. Such feelings inhibit aggressive behavior.
2. Females behave as aggressively as males when they have the means to do so and believe that aggression is justified.
3. Females are more likely to empathize with the victim—to put themselves in the victim's place. Empathy encourages helping behavior, not aggression.
4. Gender differences in aggression decrease when the victim is anonymous. Anonymity may prevent females from empathizing with their victims.

There thus seem to be a number of gender differences. Now we consider the development of these differences.

ON BECOMING A MAN OR A WOMAN: THEORETICAL VIEWS

Like mother, like daughter; like father, like son—at least often, if not always. Why is it that little boys (often) grow up to behave according to the cultural stereotypes of what it means to be male? That little girls (often) grow up to behave like female stereotypes? Let us have a look at biological and psychological factors that appear to contribute to the development of gender differences.

Biological Influences

Biological views on gender differences tend to focus on the roles of sex hormones.

PRENATAL DEVELOPMENT Sex hormones are responsible for prenatal differentiation of sex organs. The sex organs of genetic females who are prenatally exposed to excess androgens may become masculinized. Prenatal sex hormones may also "masculinize" or "feminize" the brain by creating predispositions that are consistent with some gender-role stereotypes (Money, 1987). Language skills seem to be based more in the left hemisphere of the brain. The right hemisphere of the brain may be relatively more involved in spatial relations and aesthetic and emotional responses. Prenatal hormonal influences may cause the hemispheres to become relatively more specialized in males (Bryden, 1982). For example, men with damage to the left hemisphere are more likely than similarly injured women to show verbal deficits (McGlone, 1980). Men with damage to the right hemisphere are relatively more likely to show spatial-relations deficits. Gender differences in brain organization may partly explain why women excel in verbal skills that require some spatial organization, such as reading, spelling, and crisp articulation of speech. But men may be superior at more specialized spatial-relations tasks, such as interpreting road maps and visualizing objects in space.

Let us now consider psychological views of the development of gender differences.

Psychodynamic Theory

Sigmund Freud explained the acquisition of gender roles in terms of **identification.** In psychodynamic theory, identification is the process of incorporating within ourselves the behaviors and our perceptions of the thoughts and feelings of others. Freud believed that gender identity remains flexible until the resolution of the Oedipus and Electra complexes at about the age of 5 or 6. Appropriate gender-typing requires that boys identify with their fathers and surrender the wish to possess their mothers. Girls would have to surrender the wish to have a penis and identify with their mothers. But, as noted earlier, children display stereotypical gender-role behaviors long before the arrival of the hypothetical conflicts of the phallic stage.

Cognitive Social Theory

Cognitive social theorists (formerly termed *social learning theorists*) explain the acquisition of gender roles and gender differences in terms such as observational learning, identification,[3] and socialization.

Children learn much of what is considered masculine or feminine by observational learning, as suggested by an experiment conducted by David Perry and Kay Bussey (1979). In this study, children learned how behaviors are gender-typed by observing the *relative frequencies* with which men and women performed them. However, the adult role models expressed arbitrary preferences for one of each of 16 pairs of items—pairs such as oranges vs. apples, and toy cows vs. toy horses—as 8- and 9-year-old boys and girls observed. Then the children were asked to show their own preferences. Boys selected an average of 14 of 16 items that agreed with the "preferences" of the men. Girls selected an average of only 3 of 16 items that agreed with the choices of the men.

Cognitive social theorists view identification as a broad, continuous learning process in which children are influenced by rewards and punishments to imitate adults of the same gender—particularly the parent of the same gender. In identification as opposed to imitation, children not only imitate a certain behavior pattern, they also try to become broadly like the model.

[3] But the social learning concept of identification differs from the psychodynamic concept, as noted in this section.

IDENTIFICATION • In psychodynamic theory, the process of incorporating within the personality elements of others. In cognitive social theory, a broad, continuous process of learning by observation and imitation.

Socialization also plays a role. Parents and other adults—even other children—inform children as to how they are expected to behave. They reward children for behavior they consider gender-appropriate. They punish (or fail to reinforce) children for behavior they consider inappropriate. Girls, for example, are given dolls while they still sleep in cribs. They are encouraged to rehearse caretaking behaviors in preparation for traditional feminine adult roles.

COGNITIVE SOCIAL VIEWS ON GENDER DIFFERENCES IN AGGRESSIVE BEHAVIOR Concerning the greater aggressiveness of boys, Maccoby and Jacklin note that:

> Aggression in general is less acceptable for girls, and is more actively discouraged in them, by either direct punishment, withdrawal of affection, or simply cognitive training that "that isn't the way girls act." Girls then build up greater anxieties about aggression, and greater inhibitions against displaying it. (1974, p. 234)

Girls frequently learn to respond to social provocations by feeling anxious about the possibility of acting aggressively. Boys, however, are often encouraged to retaliate (Frodi and others, 1977). Parents usually squelch aggression in their daughters. Boys are likely to be permitted to express some aggression toward their parents. Many boys are encouraged to fight with peers, when necessary, in order to defend themselves and their property.

Experiments highlight the importance of cognitive social factors in female aggressiveness. Studies by Albert Bandura and his colleagues (1963) found that boys are more likely than girls to imitate film-mediated aggressive models, because the social milieu more often frowns upon aggressiveness in girls. Other investigators find that the development of aggressive behavior in females is influenced by situational variables, such as the nature of a provocation and the possibility that someone will disapprove of them (Richardson and others, 1979; Taylor & Epstein, 1967).

SOCIALIZATION • The fostering of "gender-appropriate" behavior patterns by providing children with information and using rewards and punishments.

In the Taylor and Epstein study, aggressive behavior was measured by the strength of the electric shock selected for delivery to another person. Subjects used the console in Figure 12.3 to take turns shocking other participants when

FIGURE 12.3
THE "AGGRESSION MACHINE."
Psychologists frequently use consoles like the one pictured here in studies on aggression. In the Taylor and Epstein study, the intensity of aggression was defined as the amount of shock selected by the subject.

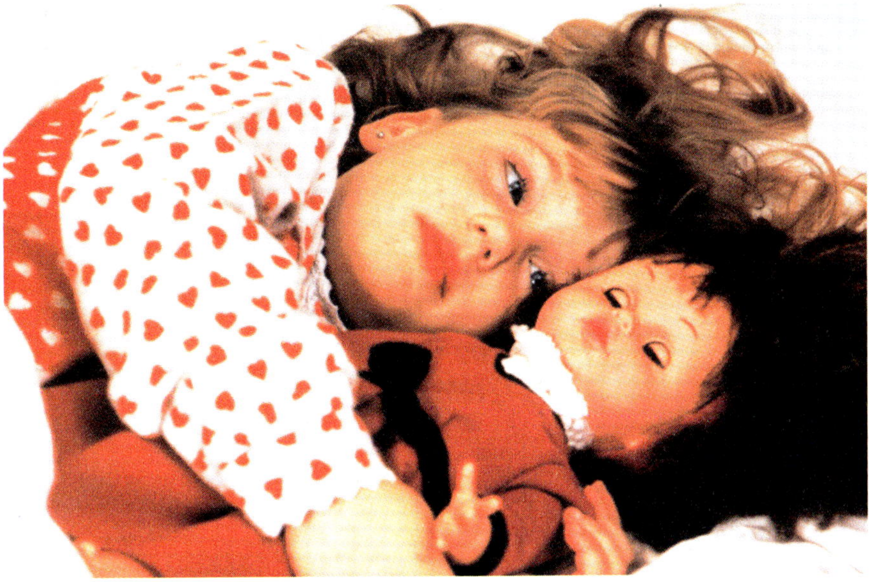

GENDER TYPING.
According to cognitive theories of gender typing, children are motivated to behave in ways they believe are consistent with their genders. Children actively seek information as to what behaviors are deemed appropriate for people of their gender.

they failed to respond to a stimulus fast enough. Subjects could select the strength of the shock. When men set low or moderate shock levels for women, the women generally chose somewhat lower shock levels for the men. In this way, they adhered to the feminine stereotype of nonaggressiveness. But when the men violated the **gender norm** of treating women favorably by setting high levels of shock for them, the women retaliated by setting shock levels that were equally high. Apparently the women decided that what was sauce for the gander was sauce for the goose. If men could violate gender norms and treat women aggressively, women could also violate gender norms and respond just as aggressively.

The development of aggressive behavior in girls is influenced by the responses of those who monitor their behavior and reward or punish them. In the Richardson study, college women competed with men to respond quickly to a stimulus. There were four blocks of trials, with six trials in each block. Subjects could not see their opponents. The loser of each trial received an electric shock whose intensity was set by the opponent. Women competed under one of three experimental conditions: "public," "private," or with a "supportive other." In the public condition, another woman observed her silently. In the private condition, there was no observer. In the supportive-other condition, another woman urged her to retaliate when her opponent selected high shock levels. As shown in Figure 12.4, women in the private and supportive-other conditions selected increasingly higher retaliatory shocks. Presumably, the women in the study assumed that an observer—though silent—would frown on aggressive behavior. This assumption probably reflects their own early socialization experiences. Women who were unobserved or urged on by a supportive-other apparently felt free to violate the gender norm of nonaggressiveness when their situations called for aggressive responses.

Cognitive social theory has helped outline the ways in which rewards, punishments, and modeling foster "gender-appropriate" behavior. Gender-schema theory suggests that we tend to assume gender-appropriate behavior patterns as a result of blending our self-concepts with society's expectations for us.

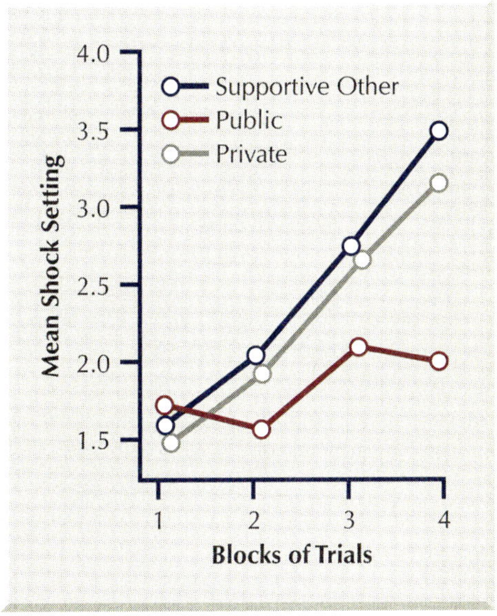

FIGURE 12.4
MEAN SHOCK SETTINGS SELECTED BY WOMEN IN RETALIATION AGAINST MALE OPPONENTS.
Women in the Richardson study chose higher shock levels for their opponents when they were alone or when another person (a supportive "other") urged them on.

GENDER NORM • An expectation about what sort of behavior is considered appropriate in social interactions between males and females.

Gender-Schema Theory: "If That's What I Am, What Do I Do?"

Gender-schema theory holds that children use gender as a way of organizing their perceptions of the world (Bem, 1981, 1985, 1993; Martin & Halverson, 1981). Gender has a good deal of prominence, even to young children. Children thus mentally group people of the same gender.

Consider the example of strength and weakness. Children learn that strength is linked to the male gender-role stereotype, and weakness to the female's. But they also learn that some traits, such as strong-weak, are more relevant to one gender than the other—in this case, for males. Bill will learn that the strength he displays in weight training or wrestling has an impact on the way others perceive him. But most girls do not find this trait so important, unless they are competing in sports such as gymnastics, tennis, or swimming. Even so, boys are expected to compete in these sports, and girls are not. Jane is likely to find that her gentleness and neatness are more important in the eyes of others than her strength.

Children thus learn to judge themselves according to the traits considered relevant to their genders. In so doing, their self-concepts become blended with the gender schema of their culture. The gender schema provides standards for comparison. Children whose self-concepts are consistent with society's gender schema are likely to have higher self-esteem.

From the viewpoint of gender-schema theory, gender identity would be sufficient to prompt "gender-appropriate" behavior. As soon as children understand the labels *boy* and *girl,* they have a basis for blending their self-concepts with the gender schema of their society. Children with gender identity will actively seek information concerning the gender schema. Their self-esteem will soon become wrapped up in the ways in which they measure up to the gender schema.

A number of studies support the view that children process information according to the gender schema (Cann & Newbern, 1984; List and others, 1983). Boys, for example, show better memory for "masculine" toys and objects, whereas girls show better memory for "feminine" objects and toys (Bradbard & Endsley, 1984).

In one study, Martin and Halverson (1983) showed 5- and 6-year-old children pictures of actors engaged in "gender-consistent" or "gender-inconsistent" activities. The gender-consistent pictures showed boys in activities such as playing with trains or sawing wood and girls in activities such as cooking and cleaning. Gender-inconsistent pictures showed actors of the opposite gender engaged in these gender-typed activities. A week later, the children were asked who had engaged in a pictured activity, a male or a female. Boys and girls both replied incorrectly significantly more often when the picture they had seen showed gender-inconsistent activity. The processing of information was distorted to conform to the gender schema.

Truth or Fiction Revisited

It is true that 5- and 6-year-olds tend to distort their memories so that they "remember" boys playing with trains and sawing wood—even when these activities were actually carried out by girls. Such patterns of processing information lend support to the gender-schema theory of gender-typing.

In sum, sex hormones may contribute to gender-typed behavior. Yet the effects of social learning may be strong enough to counteract most biological predispositions. Cognitive social theory helps outline the environmental factors that influence children to assume "gender-appropriate" behavior. Gender-schema theory highlights the ways in which children process information to blend their self-concepts with the gender schema of their culture.

ADJUSTMENT AND PSYCHOLOGICAL ANDROGYNY: THE MORE TRAITS THE MERRIER?

GENDER-SCHEMA THEORY • The view that one's knowledge of the gender schema in one's society (the distribution of behavior patterns that are considered appropriate for men and women) guides one's assumption of gender-typed preferences and behavior patterns.

Most of us think of masculinity and femininity as opposite poles of one continuum (Storms, 1980). We assume that the more masculine people are, the less feminine they are, and vice versa. So a man who shows "feminine" traits of nurturance, tenderness, and emotionality might be considered less masculine for it. Women who compete with men in the business world are not only seen as more masculine than other women, but also as less feminine.

ARE MASCULINITY AND FEMININITY OPPOSITES ON THE SAME CONTINUUM OR INDEPENDENT DIMENSIONS? But today many psychologists look upon masculinity and femininity as independent dimensions (Figure 12.5). That is, people who score high on measures of masculine traits need not score low on feminine traits. People who show skill in the business world can also be warm and loving. People who possess both stereotypically masculine and feminine traits are said to show **psychological androgyny.** People who are low in both stereotypical masculine and feminine traits are "undifferentiated" according to masculinity and femininity.

Undifferentiated women, for example, are viewed less positively than more feminine or more masculine women, even by their friends (Baucom & Danker-Brown, 1983). And undifferentiated women are less satisfied with their marriages (Baucom & Aiken, 1984). However, psychologically androgynous people, as we shall see, may be more resistant to stress.

CONTRIBUTIONS OF PSYCHOLOGICAL ANDROGYNY TO WELL-BEING, ADJUSTMENT, AND PERSONAL DEVELOPMENT There is a good deal of evidence that androgynous people are relatively well adjusted, apparently because they can summon both "masculine" and "feminine" traits to express their talents and desires and to meet the demands of their situations.

In terms of Erik Erikson's concepts of **ego identity** and intimacy, androgynous college students are more likely than feminine, masculine, and undifferentiated students to show a combination of "high identity" and "high intimacy" (Schiedel & Marcia, 1985). That is, they are more likely to show a firm sense of who they are and what they stand for (identity), and they have a greater capacity to form intimate, sharing relationships.

Psychologically androgynous people of both genders show "masculine" independence under group pressures to conform and "feminine" nurturance in interactions with a kitten or a baby (Bem, 1975; Bem and others, 1976). They feel

PSYCHOLOGICAL ANDROGYNY • Possession of stereotypical masculine and feminine traits.

EGO IDENTITY • One's sense of who one is and what one stands for.

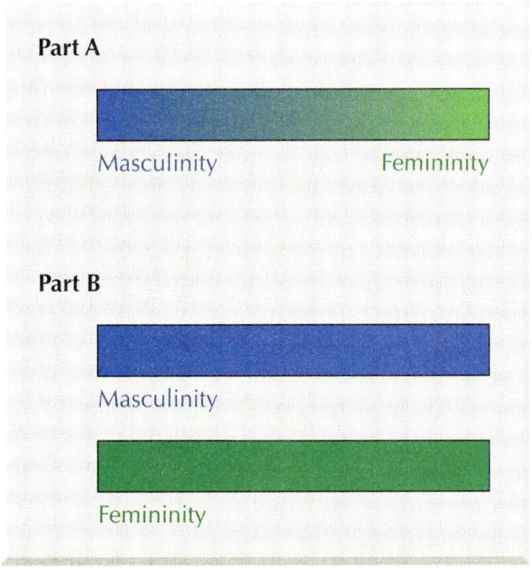

FIGURE 12.5
ARE MASCULINITY AND FEMININITY OPPOSITE POLES ON ONE DIMENSION, SEPARATE DIMENSIONS, OR ARBITRARY DISTINCTIONS?
Most people consider masculinity and femininity to be opposite poles of one continuum (Part A). Thus, the more masculine people are, the less feminine they are assumed to be, and vice versa. But many psychologists look upon masculinity and femininity as independent dimensions (Part B), so that the presence of traditional masculine traits need not prevent one from expressing stereotypical feminine behaviors, and vice versa. Many social critics, of course, challenge the basic distribution of behavior patterns into feminine and masculine. To them, the lists of so-called feminine and masculine traits are sexist and polarizing.

more comfortable performing a wider range of activities, including (the "masculine") nailing of boards and (the "feminine") winding of yarn (Bem & Lenney, 1976; Helmreich and others, 1979). In adolescence, they report greater interest in pursuing nontraditional occupational roles (Motowidlo, 1982). They show greater self-esteem (Flaherty & Dusek, 1980; Spence and others, 1975) and greater ability to bounce back from failure (Baucom & Danker-Brown, 1979). They are more likely to try to help others in need. Androgynous people are more willing to share the leadership in mixed-gender groups; masculine people attempt to dominate such groups and feminine people tend to be satisfied with taking a back seat (Porter and others, 1985). Androgynous women rate stressful life events as less undesirable than do feminine women (Shaw, 1982).

"Feminine" traits contribute to marital happiness, whether found in women *or men.* Antill (1983) found not only that husbands' happiness was positively related to their wives' femininity, but also that wives' happiness was positively related to their husbands' femininity. Wives of psychologically androgynous husbands are happier than women whose husbands adhere to a strict, stereotypical masculine gender role. Androgynous men are more tolerant of their wives' or lovers' faults and more likely to express loving feelings than are "macho" males (Coleman & Ganong, 1985). Women, like men, appreciate spouses who are sympathetic, warm, tender, and who love children.

Truth or Fiction Revisited

It is true that adolescent girls who show a number of masculine traits are more popular than girls who thoroughly adopt the traditional feminine gender role. Apparently the presence of some masculine-typed traits does not compromise their "femininity."

In adolescence, "masculinity" and androgyny are associated with popularity and higher self-esteem in *both* genders (Lamke, 1982). Given the prevalence of sexism, it is not surprising that young men fare better than their peers when they show masculine traits. It is of greater interest that young women also fare better when they exhibit masculine traits. Apparently these traits do not compromise their femininity in the eyes of others. The more traits would, indeed, appear the merrier. The ANDRO Scale on pages 374–375 will offer you insight into your own adherence to gender-role stereotypes.

A CHALLENGE TO ANDROGYNY: DOES MASCULINITY ACCOUNT FOR GREATER SELF-ESTEEM? These findings on adjustment have not gone unchallenged. Self-esteem is an important factor in our psychological well-being. Yet it may be that the benefits of psychological androgyny in terms of self-esteem do *not* derive from the combination of masculine and feminine traits, but rather from the presence of "masculine" traits, whether they are found in males or females (Whitley, 1983; Williams & D'Alessandro, 1994). That is, traits such as independence and assertiveness contribute to high self-esteem in both genders.

THE FEMINIST CHALLENGE TO ANDROGYNY Some feminists have criticized the view that psychological androgyny is a worthwhile goal—for a quite different reason. Feminists note that psychological androgyny is defined as the possession of both masculine and feminine personality traits. However, this very definition relies upon the presumed authenticity of masculine and feminine gender-role stereotypes. Feminists would prefer to see the stereotypes dissolved (Matlin, 1996).

In any event, Sandra Bem (1974) has found that about 50 percent of her samples of college students have adhered to their own gender-role stereotypes on her own test for measuring psychological androgyny—the Bem Sex Role Inventory. About 15 percent have been cross-typed (described by traits stereotypical of the opposite gender), and 35 percent have been androgynous. So many young people are challenging stereotypical gender roles and deciding that it is okay to show competence in the realm of objects and also express feelings of warmth and tenderness.

Since large numbers of college students are androgynous, and since college students will play a powerful role in shaping American society in the twenty-first century, it may be that gender stereotypes will become less rigid. Perhaps opportunities for self-expression will expand for both men and women. Dare we go so far as to hope that mothers who enter the workforce might even get a bit more help from their spouses?

Now that we've considered the scientific aspects of psychological androgyny, let's have a bit of a look at the lighter side. The following feature on diversity looks at what we could perhaps call the "gender intensity" of various names in the United States.

Adjustment in a World of DIVERSITY

Name That Baby! Thoughts on Macho, Wimpy, Feminine, "Feminissima," and Androgynous Names

Congratulations! You have decided to rear your children to be psychologically androgynous. When do you begin doing so, however? Perhaps as soon as you name your child.

Children's names express parental attitudes toward them, and, as the children develop, they may contribute to children's self-concepts. For example, in their fascinating name book, *Beyond Jennifer and Jason*, Linda Rosenkrantz and Pamela Satran (1988) note that the following names are rather "macho" and tend to encourage a little boy to act like "a bull on testosterone" (p. 160):

Angelo	Dominic	Rip
Bart	Ford	Rocco
Bubba	Jock	Thor
Clint	Mack	Vito
Curt	Mick	Wolf

The authors label the following names "wimpy." They warn that these names can get one's son "picked last for every team, shunned in every game of spin the bottle, turned down for every blind date" (p. 169):

Arnold	Courtney	Marvin
Bernard	Eugene	Percy
Bruce	Herbert	Sylvester
Cecil	Ira	Wilbert

For girls, we begin with "feminine" names, which the authors describe as "clearly female without being too fussy, sweet without being syrupy, soft without being limp" (p. 143). In this largest grouping of girls' names, we find:

Abigail	Gillian	Pamela
Alexandra	Holly	Rebecca
Amy	Jennifer	Sandra
Caroline	Katherine	Shannon
Christine	Lauren	Stephanie
Deborah	Lisa	Tina
Elizabeth	Megan	Wendy
Emily	Nicole	

(text continues on p. 376)

SELF-ASSESSMENT

ARE YOU A "CHESTY" MALE OR A "FLUFFY" FEMALE? THE ANDRO SCALE

What about you? Do you adhere to strict, traditional gender roles? Are you, in the words of psychologist Sandra Bem, a "chesty" male or a "fluffy" female? Or is psychological androgyny—the expression of both "masculine" and "feminine" traits—more your style? ■

Directions: To find out, indicate whether the following items are mostly true or mostly false for you by checking the box under the T or the F. Use the tables in the Appendix to compare your score to those of a national sample of respondents. Then have some other people in your life take the test. How many chesty males and fluffy females do you know?

T	F		
☐	☐	1.	I like to be with people who assume a protective attitude toward me.
☐	☐	2.	I try to control others rather than permit them to control me.
☐	☐	3.	Surfboard riding would be dangerous for me.
☐	☐	4.	If I have a problem I like to work it out alone.
☐	☐	5.	I seldom go out of my way to do something just to make others happy.
☐	☐	6.	Adventures where I am on my own are a little frightening to me.
☐	☐	7.	I feel confident when directing the activities of others.
☐	☐	8.	I will keep working on a problem after others have given up.
☐	☐	9.	I would not like to be married to a protective person.
☐	☐	10.	I usually try to share my problems with someone who can help me.
☐	☐	11.	I don't care if my clothes are unstylish, as long as I like them.
☐	☐	12.	When I see a new invention, I attempt to find out how it works.
☐	☐	13.	People like to tell me their troubles because they know I will do everything I can to help them.
☐	☐	14.	Sometimes I let people push me around so they can feel important.
☐	☐	15.	I am only very rarely in a position where I feel a need to actively argue for a point of view I hold.
☐	☐	16.	I dislike people who are always asking me for advice.
☐	☐	17.	I seek out positions of authority.
☐	☐	18.	I believe in giving friends lots of help and advice.
☐	☐	19.	I get little satisfaction from serving others.
☐	☐	20.	I make certain that I speak softly when I am in a public place.
☐	☐	21.	I am usually the first to offer a helping hand when it is needed.
☐	☐	22.	When I see someone I know from a distance, I don't go out of my way to say "Hello."
☐	☐	23.	I would prefer to care for a sick child myself rather than hire someone to nurse him or her.
☐	☐	24.	I prefer not being dependent on anyone for assistance.
☐	☐	25.	When I am with someone else, I do most of the decision making.

T	F		
☐	☐	26.	I don't mind being conspicuous.
☐	☐	27.	I would never pass up something that sounded like fun just because it was a little hazardous.
☐	☐	28.	I get a kick out of seeing someone I dislike appear foolish in front of others.
☐	☐	29.	When someone opposes me on an issue, I usually find myself taking an even stronger stand than I did at first.
☐	☐	30.	When two persons are arguing, I often settle the argument for them.
☐	☐	31.	I will not go out of my way to behave in an approved way.
☐	☐	32.	I am quite independent of the people I know.
☐	☐	33.	If I were in politics, I would probably be seen as one of the forceful leaders of my party.
☐	☐	34.	I prefer a quiet, secure life to an adventurous one.
☐	☐	35.	I prefer to face my problems by myself.
☐	☐	36.	I try to get others to notice the way I dress.
☐	☐	37.	When I see someone who looks confused, I usually ask if I can be of any assistance.
☐	☐	38.	It is unrealistic for me to expect to do my best all of the time.
☐	☐	39.	The good opinion of one's friends is one of the chief rewards for living a good life.
☐	☐	40.	If I get tired while playing a game, I generally stop playing.
☐	☐	41.	When I see a baby, I often ask to hold him or her.
☐	☐	42.	I am quite good at keeping others in line.
☐	☐	43.	I like to be with people who are less dependent than I.
☐	☐	44.	I don't want to be away from my family too much.
☐	☐	45.	Once in a while I enjoy acting as if I were tipsy.
☐	☐	46.	I feel incapable of handling many situations.
☐	☐	47.	I delight in feeling unattached.
☐	☐	48.	I would make a poor judge because I dislike telling others what to do.
☐	☐	49.	Seeing an old or helpless person makes me feel that I would like to take care of him or her.
☐	☐	50.	I usually make decisions without consulting others.
☐	☐	51.	It doesn't affect me one way or another to see a child being spanked.
☐	☐	52.	My goal is to do at least a little bit more than anyone else has done before.
☐	☐	53.	To love and to be loved is of greatest importance to me.
☐	☐	54.	I avoid some hobbies and sports because of their dangerous nature.
☐	☐	55.	One of the things which spurs me on to do my best is the realization that I will be praised for my work.
☐	☐	56.	People's tears tend to irritate me more than to arouse my sympathy.

Source: Reprinted from Berzins, Welling, & Wetter, 1977.

Beyond feminine is "feminissima"—a group of names that, were they dresses, "would be pale pink, with ruffles and lace and big bows and sprigs of flowers. . . . They are the sweetest of the sweet, the most feminine of the feminine" (p. 140). Examples:

Adriana	Felicia	Priscilla
Ariel	Giselle	Sabrina
Babette	Heather	Samantha
Cecilia	Lisabeth	Taffy
Crystal	Marcella	Tiffany
Dawn	Melissa	Vanessa
Desirée	Melody	
Evangeline	Monique	

Finally, we arrive at our list of androgynous names. Note that many of them are surnames:

Arden	Jody	Morgan
Avery	Jordan	Page
Blaine	Kelly	Parker
Cameron	Kelsey	Reed
Carter	Kendall	Robin
Casey	Kyle	Schuyler
Chris	Lane	Sloan
Dana	Leslie	Taylor
Drew	Mackenzie	Walker
Glenn	Meredith	Whitney
Harper		

Whatever you choose, let us hope that your child does not upbraid you over the years by saying, "How could you name me *that?*"

adjustment and modern life

COSTS OF GENDER-ROLE STEREOTYPING

The guidelines for traditional gender roles remain clearly drawn in our society (Bem, 1993). These stereotypes are learned early, and they influence the child's efforts to become a competent person. Although biology appears to play a role in gender-typing, it is unclear where biological influences leave off and psychological influences begin.

As mentioned at the beginning of this chapter, Sandra Lipsitz Bem (1993) writes that three beliefs about women and men have prevailed throughout the history of Western culture: (1) that women and men have basically different psychological and sexual natures, (2) that men are the superior, dominant gender, and (3) that gender differences and male superiority are "natural." What does "natural" mean? Throughout most of history, people viewed naturalness in terms of religion, or God's scheme of things (Bem, 1993). For the past century or so, naturalness has been seen in biological, evolutionary terms—at least by most scientists. In any event, it is also ingrained, at least in traditionalists, that when we "buck" our "natural" gender roles, we endanger male-female relationships and the fabric of society.

These deeply ingrained ideas have their costs. Put succinctly, they have left millions of individuals confused and frustrated. In many, many cases our self-concepts do not fit the gender schema of our society. It is asking a lot for people who are unacquainted with psychological theory and research to realize that the gender schema may be largely arbitrary. Many people who are uncomfortable with the gender-related social demands made of them are likely to doubt themselves rather than society. This is one of the many costs of gender-role stereotyping. The costs of gender-role stereotyping largely have to do with sexism. Let us consider what is meant by sexism. Then we turn our attention to the costs of stereotyping in terms of educational channeling, limitations on activities and career choices, and the interpersonal arena.

Sexism

Sexism is the prejudgment that a person, because of gender, will possess negative traits. These traits are assumed to prevent adequate performance in certain jobs or social situations. Until recently, sexism excluded women from many occupations, with medicine and law serving as visible examples.

Sexism may lead us to interpret the same behavior in different ways when shown by women or by men. We may see the male as "self-assertive," but the female as "pushy." We may view him as "flexible," but her as "fickle" and "indecisive." He may be "rational," when she is "cold." He is "tough" when necessary, but she is "bitchy." When the businesswoman dons stereotypical masculine behaviors, the sexist reacts negatively by branding her abnormal or unhealthy.

Sexism can also make it difficult for men to show stereotypical feminine behaviors. A "sensitive" woman is simply sensitive, but a sensitive man may be

SEXISM • The prejudgment that a person, on the basis of gender, will possess negative traits or perform inadequately.

seen as a "sissy." A woman may seem "polite," when a man showing the same behavior is labeled "passive" or "weak." Only recently have men begun to enter occupational domains restricted largely to women in this century, such as nursing, secretarial work, and teaching elementary school.

Truth or Fiction Revisited

Of course it isn't true that an essay written by a woman is poorer in quality than an essay written by a man (even when the same essay is being rated). However, research into sexism has found that the same essay was rated as poorer in quality when authorship was attributed to a woman.

In research on sexism, Sandra and Daryl Bem (1973) had college students rate the quality of professional articles in several fields. When the same article was attributed to a woman, its quality received lower ratings than when it was attributed to a man. Women raters were as guilty as men at assuming male superiority. The prejudiced rating pattern applied to works of art as well.

Rachel Hare-Mustin (1983) argues that women are misunderstood by mental health professionals. Women, for example, are more likely to be depressed than men (Russo, 1990), which has been interpreted as meaning that women are more likely to have psychological problems. But Hare-Mustin points out that women are more often forced to live with low social status, discrimination, and helplessness. Their depression is an appropriate response to their more stressful situations (see Chapter 9). The proper "treatment" of women whose depression stems from these problems is social and economic change—not psychotherapy.

Adjustment in a World of DIVERSITY

School Days, School Days—Dear Old Sexist School Days?

Now that we are aware of the existence of sexism, you might expect that it would have diminished, especially among schoolteachers. Schoolteachers, after all, are generally well educated and fair-minded. They have also been trained to be sensitive to the needs of their young charges in today's changing society.

Truth or Fiction Revisited

It is true that teachers are more likely to accept calling out in class from boys than girls. Teachers seem to have the attitude that "boys will be boys" but that girls should be shaped into "ladylike" behavior.

Studies by Myra and David Sadker (1994) and others (AAUW, 1992) suggest that we have not seen the last of sexism, however. The researchers have found that boys generally dominate classroom communication, whether the subject is math (a traditionally "masculine" area) or language arts (a traditionally "feminine" area). Boys are many times more likely to call out the answers to questions without raising their hands. Teachers—female and male alike—are more likely to tolerate calling out from boys. Girls are more likely to—as the song goes—receive "teachers' dirty looks," or to be reminded that they should raise their hands and wait their turn. Boys, it seems, are expected to be "boys"—that is, impetuous. Girls, however, are reprimanded for "unladylike" behavior.

These researchers also report the following instances of sexism in the classroom:

- At the preschool level, teachers praise boys more often than girls and are more likely to give them detailed instructions.
- Teachers often show higher expectations for boys in math courses. (The expectancies of others tend to translate into our own self-efficacy expectancies.)
- Teachers of math courses spend more time instructing and interacting with boys than girls.

- Girls begin school with greater skills in basic computation and reading, but have lower SAT scores in quantitative and verbal subtests by the time they have graduated from high school. It seems unlikely that girls carry genetic instructions that cause academic potential to self-destruct as the years progress. Instead, it would seem that the educational system, and society at large, does less to encourage girls to develop academic prowess.

The irony is that the educational system of the United States has lifted generation upon generation of the impoverished and the children of immigrants into the mainstream of U.S. life. Sad to say, the system appears to be doing more for males than for females—even in our "enlightened" times.

Costs in Terms of Education

The educational costs of stereotyping and sexism have been enormous. Stereotyping has historically worked to the disadvantage of women. In past centuries, girls were considered unsuited to education. The great Swiss-French philosopher Jean-Jacques Rousseau was in the forefront of an open approach to education. Still, he believed that girls were basically irrational and naturally disposed to childrearing and homemaking—not commerce, science, and industry. Although the daughters of royal or sophisticated families have always managed to receive some tutoring, only in the twentieth century have girls been fully integrated into the public schools. But even within these systems, boys seem to receive more encouragement and more direct instruction. Certain courses still seem to be considered part of the "male domain."

In the United States today, boys and girls are looked upon as about equal in **aptitude** for learning. Yet there remain some differences in expectations, and these stereotypes limit the horizons of both genders.

Truth or Fiction Revisited

It is true that girls were considered unsuited for education throughout most of human history. Not until the twentieth century did girls attend schools in large numbers, and the current advances are limited mainly to industrialized nations.

Reading Consider reading. Reading is a most basic educational skill. Reading opens doorways to other academic subjects. Problems in reading generalize to nearly every area of academic life. It turns out that far more American boys than girls have had reading problems, either reading below grade level or the much more severe problem of **dyslexia.**

Psychologists have many hypotheses as to why girls, as a group, read better than boys. Many of these hypotheses involve biological factors, such as different patterns of specialization of the hemispheres of the brain in boys and girls. But it may also be that cultural factors play a role in gender differences in reading. Evidence for this view is found in the fact that gender differences in reading tend to disappear or be reversed in other cultures (Matlin, 1996). Reading is stereotyped as a feminine activity in the United States and Canada, and girls surpass boys in reading skills in these countries. But boys score higher than girls on most tests of reading in Nigeria and England, where boys have traditionally been expected to outperform girls in academic pursuits, including reading.

Spatial Relations The gender difference that is found in spatial ability may similarly be related to stereotyping, because spatial ability is linked to the number of math courses taken. Children are likely to practice spatial skills in geometry and related courses, and boys take more math courses in high school than girls. One study found no gender differences in spatial ability when the number of math courses taken was considered (Hyde and others, 1990).

Aptitude • A specific ability or talent, such as aptitude for music or for writing.

Dyslexia • Severe impairment of reading ability, characterized, for example, by inability to recall vowel sounds and reversals of letters such as small *b* and small *d*.

Mathematics Boys, as noted, are more likely to take math courses in high school than girls. Math courses open doorways for boys to occupations in the natural sciences, engineering, and economics, among many others. There are several reasons why American boys are more likely than American girls to feel "at home" with math (AAUW, 1992; Sadker & Sadker, 1994), including these:

1. Fathers are more likely than mothers to help children with math homework.
2. Advanced math courses are more likely to be taught by men.

Given these experiences with math, and those described in the "School Days" feature on page 378, we should not be surprised that:

1. By junior high, boys view themselves as more competent in math than girls do, even when they receive identical grades. High self-efficacy expectancies foster motivation and perseverance, so even talented girls may be less likely than boys to work hard at math.
2. By high school, students perceive math as part of the male domain.
3. By junior high, boys are more likely than girls to perceive math as useful.
4. Boys are more likely to have positive feelings about math. Girls are more likely to have math anxiety.
5. It becomes increasingly difficult to convince high school and college women to take math courses, even when they show facility in math.

Some high school girls have been dissuaded from taking math because it has been connected with stereotypical masculine traits such as ambition, independence, self-confidence, and spatial ability. Girls who do take math are less likely to view it as a male domain, however, and have usually had positive early experiences with math.

Now let us consider the limitations that stereotyping tends to impose upon our choices of activities and careers.

Costs in Terms of Activities and Careers

Children show preferences for gender-stereotyped activities and toys by the ages of 2 or 3. Their peers make good enforcers. Three-year-olds, for example, often refuse to play with boys who play with dolls or tea sets, or with girls who play with toy guns, fire trucks, and hammers. Most 5-year-olds are openly critical of children who choose "inappropriate" toys and guide them toward stereotypical toys (Lamb and others, 1980). How many little girls are dissuaded from engineering and architecture because they are given dolls, not fire trucks and blocks? How many little boys are dissuaded from child care and nursing because others look askance at them when they reach for dolls?

Inequities in the Workplace In the workplace, we also find inequities. Here too, it is women who suffer most. We explore the workplace for women in Chapter 17, but here let us note a number of costs to women—and the rest of us:

1. *Pay.* Women earn less than men for comparable work.
2. *Promotions.* Women are less likely than men to be promoted into responsible managerial positions. Many women are prevented from reaching the

top echelons of management by "glass ceilings" (Morrison & Von Glinow, 1990). Women who have (or openly discuss plans to have) children are also often placed in "Mommy Tracks" in their organizations. They are not prevented from working, but they are channeled into less demanding (and less rewarding!) career paths. The organization makes less of an investment in them because of the assumption that mothers cannot make as much of an investment in the organization as child-free women can.

3. *"Toughness."* Once in managerial positions, women often feel pressured to be "tougher" than men in order to seem as tough.
4. *Being "businesslike."* Women managers who are strict and businesslike with employees are often accused of being cold or "unwomanly" by their employees—male and female—whereas men showing the same behavior might be considered "matter-of-fact," or not even be noticed.
5. *Dress.* Once in managerial positions, women feel pressured to pay more attention to their appearance than men do, because co-workers pay more attention to what they wear, how they crop their hair, and so forth. If they don't look crisp and tailored every day, others will think that they are unable to exert the force to remain in command. Yet if they dress up "too much," they are accused of being fashion plates rather than serious workers!
6. *Perils of friendliness.* Women are pressured to pay more attention to their interpersonal behavior than men are, because women who act friendly are often misinterpreted as seductive (Abbey, 1987). The friendly female manager may also be perceived as a potential doormat.
7. *Decision making.* Once in managerial positions, women who do not reach rapid decisions (even if they are poor decisions) may stand accused of being "wishy-washy."
8. *Flexibility.* If women managers change their minds, they run the risk of being labeled fickle and indecisive, rather than flexible and willing to consider new information.
9. *Sexual harassment.* Women are more often subject to sexual harassment on the job. Many male superiors expect sexual favors in return for advancement on the job.
10. *"Feminine" tasks.* Women are expected to engage in traditional feminine tasks, such as making the coffee or cleaning up after the conference lunch, as well as the jobs they were hired to do.
11. *Role overload.* Women usually have the dual responsibility of being the major caretaker for the children.

This has been a partial, not an exhaustive list. Yet it highlights some of the costs of stereotyping in terms of careers. It all adds up to a big headache for women. In many cases, stereotyping discourages women from making their highest possible contributions to the workforce and to the nation.

In case it is not self-evident, let us note that men also have a stake in reversing these pressures on women. Mistreatment of women by men hurts women that are loved and cared about by other men. Also, misery in the workplace does not stop at 5:00 P.M. It carries over into home life. Men are married to women, and men have women as mothers and daughters. So mistreatment on the job impairs the quality of home life. There is also the larger picture. If we as

WHAT DO YOU SAY NOW?

HANDLING A SEXIST REMARK

You have "arrived." You are out of college for only a dozen years, and you have become a vice president for sales at your computer firm. Your letterheads use your initials, "J. T. Hernandez," rather than your first name, so correspondents are surprised to learn that you're a woman.

One of them has called on you at your office. He walks in and raises his eyebrows as you rise to meet him. You hold out your hand, and he takes it in both of his. He gives you a great big grin, winks, and says, "What's a nice girl like you doing in a job like this?"

He is being friendly, but you are fuming. This is a business call and not a blind date.

What do you say now? Write down some possible responses and then check the discussion below.

1. ______________________________
   ____
2. ______________________________
   ____
3. ______________________________
   ____

Let us note first that male readers have probably learned at least one thing *not* to say to businesswomen, unless they purposefully want to sabotage their business relationships with them. Women may wish to consider responses such as the following.

1. "My hand's not cold, Mr. Harbinger. Perhaps we can talk about why you're here." (This is a very negative response to his holding your hand within his own, and may be linked to another response as well.)
2. "We've found out that men just aren't tough enough for this job." (This comment can be made in a pleasant, humorous voice if the goal is to "proceed as normal," or in a biting voice, if the expression of displeasure is the sole goal.)
3. "This is a busy day, Mr. Harbinger. Perhaps you'd care to discuss your reasons for coming here." (This lets your visitor know that he is taking your time and that he is on your "territory." It can be said matter-of-factly, in which case there is the possibility for exploring a business relationship further, or it can be said in a way to let your visitor know that the meeting is perilously close to an end. Either way, it puts you in the driver's seat.)
4. "This is the twentieth century, Mr. Harbinger. We refer to adult females as women, not girls." (This points up the fact that "girl" is a demeaning way of addressing an adult, and it can be linked with responses such as 2 or 3.)
5. A suggestion about what *not* to say: It's probably wise not to take your visitor up on the adjective *nice*—that is, avoid saying anything to suggest that you are not, or are, "nice." The word *nice* has an old-fashioned degrading connotation that you need not deal with.

Some of the suggested responses may at first seem like an overreaction. After all, one could argue that Mr. Harbinger was nonplussed and did not know exactly what to say. Perhaps his remark was innocent, and not an effort at "one-ups-person-ship." If you suspect that he meant no harm, you could make a remark such as one suggested in a more friendly voice, but it might be an error to just let his sexist remark go. It gives him an advantage on your territory, and it might be that no profitable business can be transacted with him while he retains this advantage. In other words, by saying nothing you lose in terms of business as well as self-esteem. By saying something, there is a chance of coming out ahead in business, and you'll certainly feel better about yourself. ■

a society utilize the best talents of all of our people, we produce more, we invent more, and we increase our standard of living.

Men too have sought the freedom to break away from gender-role stereotypes. Men, for example, are now taking positions that were previously restricted to women, such as teaching in elementary school and secretarial work. In recent years, men have even been popping up in positions as nannies, although they are usually hired to work with boys (Willens, 1993).

Costs in Terms of Psychological Well-Being and Interpersonal Relationships

Educational frustrations and problems on the job are stressors that can make us anxious and depressed and interfere with our relationships with others. We have noted the ways in which gender-role stereotyping affects our educations and our careers. Here let us note ways in which stereotyping interferes with our psychological well-being and our interpersonal relationships:

1. Women who accept the traditional feminine gender role appear to have lower self-esteem than women who also show some masculine-typed traits (Flaherty & Dusek, 1980; Spence and others, 1975).
2. Women who accept the traditional feminine gender role find stressful events more aversive than women who also show some masculine-typed traits (Shaw, 1982).
3. Women who accept the traditional feminine gender role are less capable of bouncing back from failure experiences than women who also show some masculine-typed traits (Baucom & Danker-Brown, 1979).
4. Women who accept the traditional feminine gender role are likely to believe that women are to be seen and not heard. Therefore, they are unlikely to assert themselves by making their needs and wants known. As a consequence, they are likely to encounter frustration.
5. Women who accept the traditional feminine gender role are more likely to conform to group pressure (Bem, 1975).
6. Men who accept the traditional masculine gender role are more likely to be upset if their wives earn more money than they do!
7. Men who accept the traditional masculine gender role are less likely to feel comfortable performing the activities involved in caring for children, such as bathing them, dressing them, and feeding them (Bem, 1975; Bem and others, 1976; Helmreich and others, 1979).
8. Men who accept the traditional masculine gender role are less likely to ask for help— including medical help—when they need it (Rosenstock & Kirscht, 1979).
9. Men who accept the traditional masculine gender role are less likely to be sympathetic and tender and to express feelings of love in their marital relationships (Coleman & Ganong, 1985).
10. Men who accept the traditional masculine gender role are less likely to be tolerant of their wives' or lovers' faults (Coleman & Ganong, 1985). ■

SUMMARY

1. **What is a gender-role stereotype?** A stereotype is a fixed, conventional idea about a group, and a gender role is a cluster of stereotypes attributed to one of the genders.

2. **What are the stereotypical masculine and feminine roles in our society?** The masculine gender-role stereotype includes aggressiveness, independence, logic, and competence in the business world or the realm of objects. The feminine gender-role stereotype includes nurturance, passivity, and dependence.

3. **What is sexism?** Sexism is the prejudgment that a person, because of gender, will possess negative traits. Sexism is usually directed against women.

4. **What cognitive gender differences are there?** Girls generally excel in verbal abilities, while boys excel in math and spatial-relations abilities. Girls excel in computational ability in elementary school, but boys excel in mathematical problem solving in high school and college.

5. **What gender differences are there in sexuality?** Men are more likely than women to masturbate and to hold permissive attitudes toward casual sex.

6. **Are there gender differences in aggression?** Boys are more aggressive than girls under most circumstances. Aggressiveness in girls may be inhibited by social anxiety (caused by aggression's inconsistency with the feminine gender-role stereotype) and by empathy with the victim.

7. **Are there other gender differences in personality or behavior?** Men talk and interrupt more often than women do. Males are more likely to make demands and curse. Females require less personal space and they prefer to sit next to companions, while males prefer to sit across from them.

8. **What biological influences contribute to gender differences in personality and behavior?** Greater brain lateralization in boys might be associated with differences in cognitive abilities. Prenatal influences of male sex hormones may increase activity level and masculine gender-typed preferences.

9. **What is the psychodynamic view of gender typing?** According to psychodynamic theory, gender typing stems from resolution of the conflicts of the phallic stage. However, children assume gender roles at much earlier ages than the theory would suggest.

10. **What is the cognitive social view of gender typing?** Cognitive social theory explains gender-typing in terms of observational learning, identification, and socialization. Observational learning may largely account for children's knowledge of "gender-appropriate" preferences and behavior patterns. Children generally identify with adults of the same gender and attempt to broadly imitate their behavior, but only when they perceive it as gender-appropriate. Children are also guided into stereotypical gender-role behaviors by early socialization messages and reinforcement.

11. **What is the gender-schema view of gender typing?** Gender-schema theory proposes that children use the gender schema of their society to organize their perceptions, and that children attempt to blend their self-concepts with the gender schema. Evidence in support of gender-schema theory shows that children process information according to the gender schema.

12. **Does psychological androgyny foster adjustment and personal development?** Apparently so. Psychologically androgynous people show high "identity" and "intimacy"—using the concepts of Erik Erikson. They show both independence and nurturance, depending on the situation. They have higher self-esteem and greater ability to bounce back from failure. Wives of psychologically androgynous husbands are happier than wives of husbands who adhere to a strict stereotypical masculine gender role.

CHAPTER 13

Interpersonal Attraction: Of Friendship, Love, and Loneliness

TRUTH OR FICTION?

✔ T F

- ☐ ☐ Tallness is generally found to be an attractive feature in men, but not in women.
- ☐ ☐ College men prefer college women to be thinner than women imagine.
- ☐ ☐ Beauty is in the eye of the beholder.
- ☐ ☐ People are perceived as being more attractive when they are smiling.
- ☐ ☐ Physical attractiveness is the most important trait we seek in our partners for long-term, meaningful relationships.
- ☐ ☐ Juries are less likely to find attractive individuals guilty of burglary or of cheating on an exam.
- ☐ ☐ "Opposites attract": We are more likely to be attracted to people who disagree with our attitudes than to people who share them.
- ☐ ☐ The most sought-after quality in a friend is warmth.
- ☐ ☐ College students consider selflessness one of the attributes of love.
- ☐ ☐ There is such a thing as love at first sight.
- ☐ ☐ It is possible to be in love with someone who is not also a friend.
- ☐ ☐ Many lonely people report that they have as many friends as people who are not lonely do.
- ☐ ☐ Many people are lonely because of fear of rejection.

OUTLINE

ATTRACTION

- Physical Attractiveness: How Important Is Looking Good?
- Adjustment in a World of Diversity: "Your Daddy's Rich and Your Ma Is Good Lookin'": Gender Differences in the Importance of Physical Attractiveness
- Adjustment in the New Millennium: Who Are the Ideal Men for the New Millennium?
- Adjustment in a World of Diversity: "Let's Make a Deal": On Gender and Lonely Hearts Ads
- Attraction and Similarity: Birds of a Feather Flock Together
- Reciprocity: If You Like Me, You Must Have Excellent Judgment
- Sexual Orientation
- Adjustment in the New Millennium: http://www.planetout.com

FRIENDSHIP

- Qualities of Good Friends
- On Friendship and Love
- Fraternities and Sororities: Are They for You?

LOVE

- Styles of Love
- Romantic Love in Contemporary Western Culture
- The Love Triangle—That Is, the Triangular Model of Love
- Romantic Versus Companionate Love: Is Romantic Love Any Basis for a Marriage?
- Self-Assessment: Has Cupid Shot His Arrow Into Your Heart? Sternberg's Triangular Love Scale

ADJUSTMENT AND MODERN LIFE

COPING WITH LONELINESS

CANDY AND STRETCH. A NEW TECHNIQUE FOR controlling weight gains? No, these are the names Bach and Deutsch (1970) give two people who have just met at a camera club that doubles as a meeting place for singles.

Candy and Stretch stand above the crowd—literally. Candy, an attractive woman in her early thirties, is almost 6 feet tall. Stretch is more plain looking, though wholesome, is in his late thirties, and is 6 feet, 5 inches tall.

Stretch has been in the group for some time. Candy is a new member. Let's listen in on them as they make conversation during a coffee break. As you will see, there are some differences between what they say and what they are thinking:

	THEY SAY	THEY THINK
STRETCH:	Well you're certainly a welcome addition to our group.	(Can't I ever say something clever?)
CANDY:	Thank you. It certainly is friendly and interesting.	(He's cute.)
STRETCH:	My friends call me Stretch. It's left over from my basketball days. Silly, but I'm used to it.	(It's safer than saying my name is David Stein.)
CANDY:	My name is Candy.	(At least my nickname is. He doesn't have to hear Hortense O'Brien.)
STRETCH:	What kind of camera is that?	(Why couldn't a girl named Candy be Jewish? It's only a nickname, isn't it?)
CANDY:	Just this old German one of my uncle's. I borrowed it from the office.	(He could be Irish. And that camera looks expensive.)
STRETCH:	May I? (He takes her camera, brushing her hand and then tingling with the touch.) Fine lens. You work for your uncle?	(Now I've done it. Brought up work.)
CANDY:	Ever since college. It's more than being just a secretary. I get into sales, too.	(So okay, what if I only went for a year. If he asks what I sell, I'll tell him anything except underwear.)

STRETCH:	Sales? That's funny. I'm in sales, too, but mainly as an executive. I run our department. I started using cameras on trips. Last time I was in the Bahamas. I took—	(Is there a nice way to say used cars? I'd better change the subject.) (Great legs! And the way her hips move—)
CANDY:	Oh! Do you go to the Bahamas, too? I love those islands.	(So I went just once, and it was for the brassiere manufacturers' convention. At least we're off the subject of jobs.)
STRETCH:	I did a little underwater work there last summer. Fantastic colors. So rich in life.	(She's probably been around. Well, at least we're off the subject of jobs.) (And lonelier than hell.)
CANDY:	I wish I'd had time when I was there. I love the water.	(Look at that build. He must swim like a fish. I should learn.) (Well, I do. At the beach, anyway, where I can wade in and not go too deep.)

So begins a relationship. Candy and Stretch have a drink and talk. They share their likes and their dislikes. Amazingly, they seem to agree on everything—from cars to clothing to politics. The attraction is very strong, and neither is willing to risk turning the other off by seeming disagreeable.

They spend the weekend together and feel that they have fallen in love. They still agree on everything, but they scrupulously avoid one topic: religion. Their religious differences became apparent when they exchanged last names. But that doesn't mean they have to talk about it.

They also put off introducing each other to their parents. The O'Briens and the Steins are narrow-minded about religion. If the truth be known, so are Candy and Stretch. Candy errs when she tells Stretch, "You're not like the other Jews I know." Stretch also allows his feelings to be voiced now and then. After Candy nurses him through a cold, he remarks, "You know, you're very Jewish." But Candy and Stretch manage to continue playing the games that are required to maintain the relationship. They tell themselves that the other's remarks were mistakes, and after all, anyone can make mistakes.

Both avoid bringing in old friends. Friends and acquaintances might say embarrassing things about religion or provide other sources of disruption. Their relationships thus become narrowed. So does their conversation. In order to avoid fights, they do not discuss certain topics. They are beginning to feel isolated from other people and alienated from their genuine feelings.

One of the topics they avoid discussing is birth control. Because of her religious beliefs, Candy does not use contraception, and she becomes pregnant. Stretch claims that he had assumed that Candy was on the pill, but he does not evade responsibility. Candy and Stretch weigh the alternatives and decide to get married. Although physical intimacy came to them quickly, only gradually do they learn to disclose their genuine feelings to one another—and they need professional counseling to help them do so. And on many occasions their union comes close to dissolving. How do we explain this tangled web of deception? Candy and Stretch pretended to agree on most subjects. They kept each other removed from their families in order to maintain feelings of attraction. In this chapter we explore the meaning of *attraction* and the factors that contribute to feelings of attraction. We shall examine how many of us adjust to fear of rejection by potential dating partners as well as to other difficulties.

Two of the outcomes of interpersonal attraction are friendship and love. Candy and Stretch "fell in love." What is *love?* When the first author was a teenager, the answer was, "Five feet of heaven in a ponytail." But this answer may be deficient in scientific merit. In this chapter, we also attempt to define the enigmatic concept of love.

Attraction and love also have a way of leading to the formation of intimate relationships, a subject we explore in Chapter 14. But not everyone develops friendships or love relationships. Some of us remain alone and lonely. Loneliness is the final topic of this chapter, and we shall have a number of suggestions for overcoming loneliness.

ATTRACTION

Feelings of attraction can lead to liking, perhaps to love, and to a more lasting relationship. In this section we see that **attraction** to another person is influenced by factors such as physical appearance and attitudes. We will see that most people are heterosexual; that is, they are sexually attracted to people of the other sex. However, some people have a gay male or lesbian sexual orientation; that is, they are erotically attracted to people of their own sex.

Physical Attractiveness: How Important Is Looking Good?

You might like to think that we are all so intelligent and sophisticated that we rank physical appearance low on the roster of qualities we seek in a date—below sensitivity and warmth, for example. But physical appearance has been found to be a key factor in attraction and consideration of partners for dates and marriage. Physical attractiveness also influences prospective employers during job interviews (Mack & Rainey, 1990).

ATTRACTION • A force that draws people together.

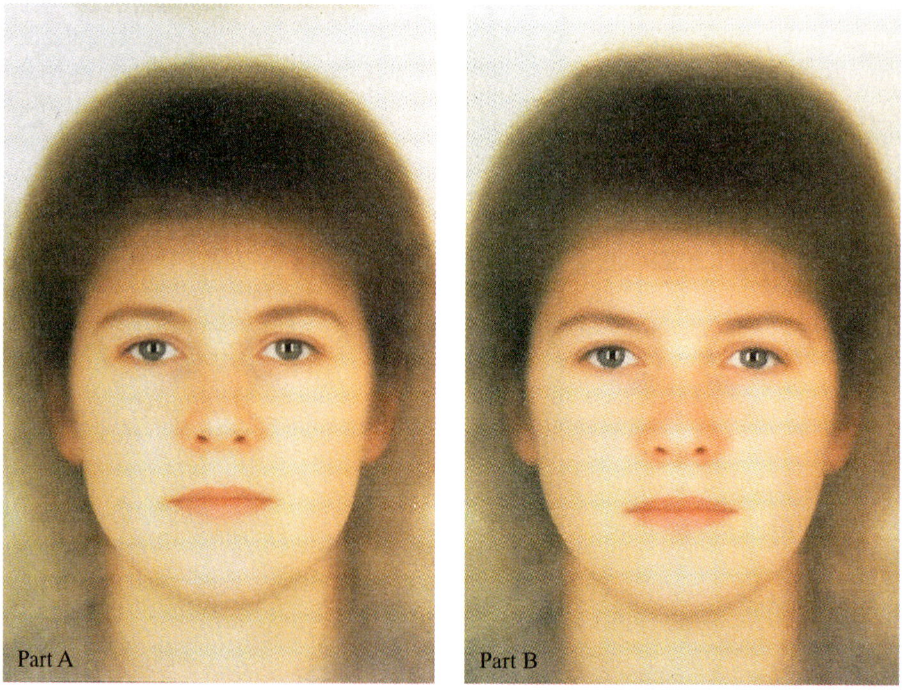

FIGURE 13.1
WHAT FEATURES CONTRIBUTE TO FACIAL ATTRACTIVENESS?
In both England and Japan, features such as large eyes, high cheekbones, and narrow jaws contribute to perceptions of the attractiveness of women. Part A shows a composite of the faces of 15 women rated as the most attractive of a group of 60. Part B is a composite in which the features of these 15 women are exaggerated—that is, developed further in the direction that separates them from the average of the entire 60.

"LOOKING GOOD."
Naomi Campbell, Claudia Schiffer, and Christie Turlington are among those who set the standards for beauty in contemporary American culture. How important is physical attractiveness?

What determines physical attractiveness? Are our standards subjective, or is there some agreement?

Some aspects of beauty appear to be cross-cultural. For example, a study of people in England and Japan found that both British and Japanese men consider women with large eyes, high cheekbones, and narrow jaws to be most attractive (Perret, 1994). In his research, Perret created computer composites of the faces of 60 women and, as shown in Part A of Figure 13.1, of the 15 women who were rated the most attractive. He then used computer enhancement to exaggerate the differences between the composite of the 60 and the composite of the 15 most attractive women. He arrived at the image shown in Part B of Figure 13.1. Part B, which shows higher cheekbones and a narrower jaw than Part A, was rated as the most attractive image. Similar results were found for the image of a Japanese woman. Works of art suggest that the ancient Greeks and Egyptians favored similar facial features.

In our society, tallness is an asset for men, although college women prefer dates who are medium in height. Tall women tend to be viewed less positively (Sheppard & Strathman, 1989). Undergraduate women prefer their dates to be about 6 inches taller than they are, whereas undergraduate men, on the average, prefer women who are about 4½ inches shorter (Gillis & Avis, 1980).

Stretch and Candy were quite tall. Since we tend to associate tallness with social dominance, many women of Candy's height are concerned that their stature will compromise their femininity. Some fear that shorter men are discouraged from asking them out. A few walk with a hunch to minimize their height.

Plumpness is valued in many cultures. Grandmothers who worry that their granddaughters are starving themselves may come from cultures in which plumpness is considered an acceptable or positive feature.[1] In Western society

Truth or Fiction Revisited

It is true that tallness is generally found to be an attractive feature in men, but not in women. Tallness is associated with social dominance, and many males are uncomfortable when they must literally "look up" to women.

[1] But as noted in the discussion of anorexia nervosa in Chapter 7, some granddaughters are literally starving themselves today.

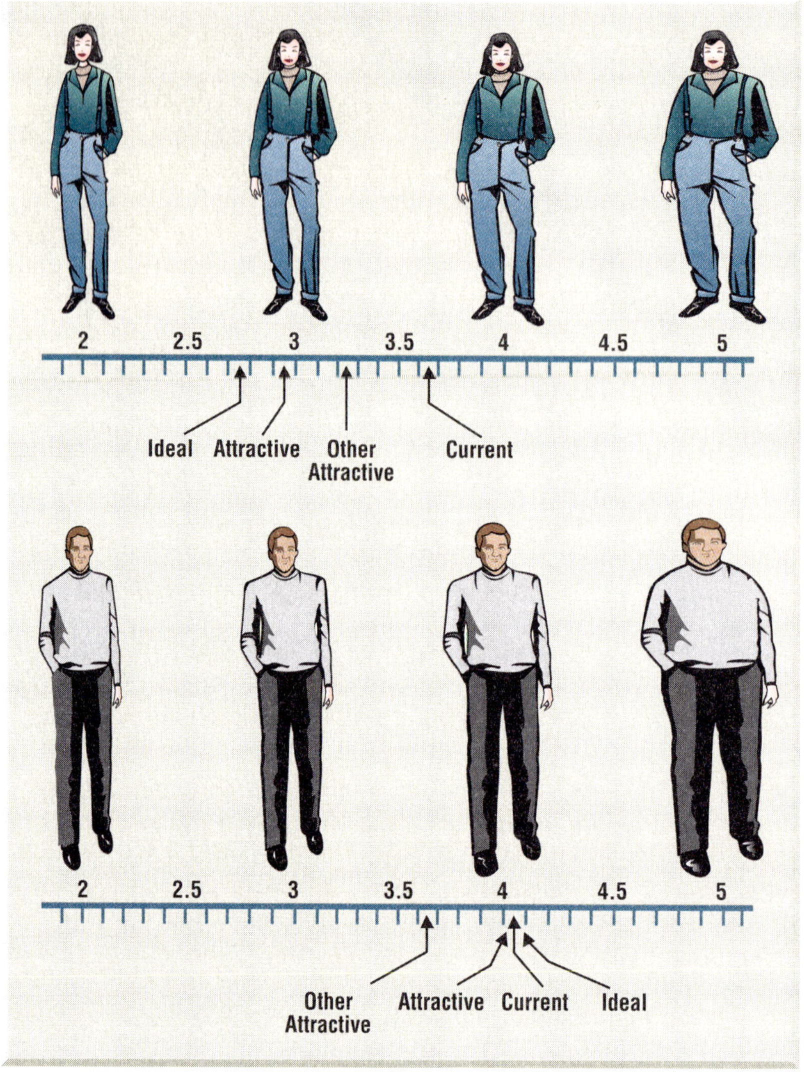

FIGURE 13.2
CAN YOU EVER BE TOO THIN?
The answer to this question is a resounding yes. Research suggests that most college women believe that they are heavier than they ought to be. However, men actually prefer women to be somewhat heavier than women imagine. Physical attractiveness aside, excessive thinness can be deadly, as explained in Chapter 7.

today, both sexes find slenderness engaging (Franzoi & Herzog, 1987). Women generally favor men with a V-shaped body (Horvath, 1981).

Although both genders perceive obese people as unattractive, there are fascinating gender differences in perceptions of the most desirable body shape. College men generally find that their current physique is similar to the ideal male build and to the one that women find most appealing (Fallon & Rozin, 1985). College women, in contrast, generally see themselves as significantly heavier than the figure that is most attractive to males, and heavier still than the ideal female figure (see Figure 13.2). But both genders err in their estimates of the preferences of the opposite gender. Men actually prefer women to be heavier than women expect—about halfway between the girth of the average woman and what the woman thinks is most attractive. And women prefer their men to be somewhat thinner than the men assume.

A flat-chested look was a hallmark of the enchanting profile of the 1920s "flapper" era, but in more recent years, men seem to desire women with medium-size breasts (Kleinke & Staneski, 1980). Interestingly, we tend to perceive large-busted women as less intelligent, competent, moral, and modest than women with smaller breasts (Kleinke & Staneski, 1980). This is clearly a case in which people overattribute a physical feature to dispositional factors!

Truth or Fiction Revisited

It is not true that college men prefer college women to be thinner than the women imagine. College men actually prefer college women to be a bit heavier than the women expect.

Truth or Fiction Revisited

It is not true that beauty is in the eye of the beholder. Although there are individual differences, most of us have adopted cultural standards for beauty, such as preferring slenderness to obesity.

How Behavior Influences Perceptions of Physical Attractiveness Both men and women are perceived as more attractive when they are smiling (Reis and others, 1990). Thus there is good reason to, as the song goes, "put on a happy face" when you are meeting people or looking for a date.

Other aspects of behavior also play a role in attraction. Women viewing videotapes of prospective dates preferred men who acted outgoing and self-expressive. Men viewing videotapes responded negatively to women who role-played the same behavior patterns (Riggio & Wolf, 1984). College men who showed "dominance" (defined in this experiment as control over a social interaction with a professor) in a videotape were rated as more attractive by female viewers. But women showing dominance were not rated as more attractive by men (Sadalla and others, 1987). Despite the liberating forces in recent years, the cultural stereotype of the ideal woman still finds a place for demureness. We are *not* suggesting that self-assertive, expressive women mend their ways to make themselves more appealing to traditional men; assertive women might find nothing but conflict with traditional men anyhow.

Truth or Fiction Revisited

It is true that people are perceived as being more attractive when they are smiling.

What Do You Look for in a Long-Term, Meaningful Relationship? Your second author surveyed college students and found that psychological characteristics such as warmth, fidelity, honesty, and sensitivity were rated higher in importance than physical attractiveness as desirable qualities in a prospective partner for a meaningful, long-term relationship, as can be seen in Table 13.1 (Nevid, 1984). Physical attractiveness won out when subjects were asked to consider the qualities that are most important in a partner for a sexual relationship. Overall, however, men placed greater emphasis on the physical characteristics of their partners for both types of relationships than did women. Women placed more value on qualities such as warmth, assertiveness, wit, and an achievement orientation. The single most highly desired quality students wanted in long-term partners was honesty. Honestly.

Although personal qualities may assume more prominent roles in determining partner preferences in long-term relationships, Nevid argues—most perceptively, to be sure—that physical appeal probably plays a "filtering" role. Unless a prospective date meets minimal physical standards, we might not look beneath the surface for "more meaningful" traits.

Truth or Fiction Revisited

It is not true that physical attractiveness is the most important trait we seek in our partners for long-term, meaningful relationships. Students in one research sample said that honesty was more important in partners for long-term relationships.

Adjustment in a World of DIVERSITY

"Your Daddy's Rich and Your Ma Is Good Lookin'": Gender Differences in the Importance of Physical Attractiveness

Your Daddy's rich
And your Ma is good lookin',
So hush, little baby,
Don't you cry.

From the song "Summertime" (from the opera *Porgy & Bess*)

How important to you is your partner's physical appearance?

In their choice of partners for either short- or long-term relationships, men are apparently swayed more so than women by their partners' physical characteristics (Nevid, 1984). Women place relatively greater emphasis on personal qualities such as warmth, assertiveness, need for achievement, and wit.

TABLE 13.1 RATINGS OF CHARACTERISTICS OF PROSPECTIVE PARTNERS FOR SEXUAL AND MEANINGFUL RELATIONSHIPS

RATINGS BY MEN			
HIGHEST RATED		***LOWEST RATED***	
SEXUAL RELATIONSHIP	**MEAN**	**SEXUAL RELATIONSHIP**	**MEAN**
Build/figure	4.53	Virtue	2.60
Sexuality	4.36	Achievement striving	2.52
Attractiveness	4.31	Strength	2.40
Facial features	4.25	Ethnic background	2.33
Buttocks	4.09	Ears	2.08
Weight	4.07	Ankles	1.89
Legs	4.02	Religion	1.74
Breath	3.94	Money	1.70
Skin	3.92	Knees	1.60
Chest/breasts	3.79	Political views	1.49
MEANINGFUL RELATIONSHIP		**MEANINGFUL RELATIONSHIP**	
Honesty	4.68	Religion	2.74
Personality	4.65	Height	2.71
Fidelity	4.60	Strength	2.65
Sensitivity	4.51	Nose	2.63
Warmth	4.49	Neck	2.56
Kindness	4.47	Hands	2.35
Character	4.41	Money	2.04
Tenderness	4.36	Ears	2.00
Patience	4.34	Political views	1.97
Gentleness	4.31	Knees	1.75

Nevid's findings are replicated in studies on mate selection. Women tend to place greater emphasis than men on traits such as professional status, consideration, dependability, kindness, and fondness for children. Men place relatively greater emphasis on physical allure, cooking ability (can't they turn on the microwave oven themselves?), even thrift (Buss, 1994; Feingold, 1992).

Gender differences in the traits that affect perceptions of attractiveness seem to be rather sexist. Some sociobiologists believe that evolutionary forces favor the survival of men and women with these preferences because they provide reproductive advantages, however (Fisher, 1992). As reviewed in Rathus, Nevid, and Fichner-Rathus (1997), some physical features such as cleanliness, good complexion, clear eyes, good teeth, good hair, firm muscle tone, and a steady gait are found universally appealing to both genders. Perhaps such traits have

TABLE 13.1 (continued)

RATINGS BY WOMEN			
HIGHEST RATED		*LOWEST RATED*	
SEXUAL RELATIONSHIP	**MEAN**	**SEXUAL RELATIONSHIP**	**MEAN**
Attractiveness	4.51	Hands	2.70
Sexuality	4.46	Ethnic background	2.55
Warmth	4.42	Money	2.41
Personality	4.41	Nose	2.40
Tenderness	4.39	Neck	2.30
Gentleness	4.36	Religion	2.00
Sensitivity	4.24	Ears	1.84
Kindness	4.23	Political views	1.78
Build/figure	4.22	Knees	1.31
Character	4.20	Ankles	1.28
MEANINGFUL RELATIONSHIP		**MEANINGFUL RELATIONSHIP**	
Honesty	4.89	Waistline	2.62
Fidelity	4.83	Chest/breasts	2.48
Personality	4.82	Legs	2.46
Warmth	4.80	Hands	2.35
Kindness	4.79	Political views	2.33
Tenderness	4.77	Nose	2.09
Sensitivity	4.75	Neck	1.97
Gentleness	4.73	Ears	1.73
Character	4.70	Knees	1.28
Patience	4.56	Ankles	1.25

Note: Ratings are based on a 5-point scale of judged importance.
Source: Nevid, 1984.

value as markers of better reproductive potential in prospective mates. According to the "parental investment model," a woman's appeal is more strongly connected with her age and health, both of which are markers of reproductive capacity. The value of men as reproducers, however, is more intertwined with factors that contribute to a stable environment for childrearing—such as social standing and reliability (Feingold, 1992). For such reasons, sociobiologists speculate that these qualities may have grown relatively more alluring to women over the millennia (e.g., Buss, 1994; Symons, 1995).

Sociobiological theory is largely speculative, however, and not fully consistent with all the evidence (Kakutani, 1992). Women are attracted to physically appealing men, and women tend to marry men similar to them in physical attractiveness and socioeconomic standing. Aging men are more likely than younger men to die from natural causes. The wealth they accrue may not always be transmitted to their spouses and children, either. Many women may be more able to find reproductive success by mating with a fit, younger male than with an older, higher-status male. Even sociobiologists allow that despite any innate predispositions, many men desire and maintain a sexual interest in older women. Human behavior is certainly flexible.

STEREOTYPES OF ATTRACTIVE PEOPLE: DO GOOD THINGS COME IN PRETTY PACKAGES? By and large, we rate what is beautiful as good. We expect physically attractive people to be poised, sociable, popular, mentally healthy, and fulfilled (Eagly and others, 1991; Feingold, 1992). We expect them to be persuasive and hold prestigious jobs. We even expect them to be good parents and have stable marriages. Physically unattractive individuals are more likely to be rated as outside of the mainstream—for example, politically radical, gay, or psychologically disordered (Brigham, 1980; O'Grady, 1982; Unger and others, 1982). Unattractive college students are even more likely to rate themselves as prone toward developing problems and psychological disorders.

These stereotypes seem to have some basis in reality. It seems that more attractive individuals are less likely to develop psychological disorders, and that the disorders of unattractive individuals are more severe (e.g., Archer & Cash, 1985; Burns & Farina, 1987; Farina and others, 1986). Also, attractiveness correlates positively with popularity, social skills, and sexual experience (Feingold, 1992). The correlations between physical attractiveness and most measures of mental ability and personality are trivial, however (Feingold, 1992).

One way to interpret the data on the correlates of physical attractiveness is to assume that these links are all innate—in other words, we can believe that beauty and competence genetically go hand in hand. We can believe that biology is destiny and throw up our hands in despair. But a more useful way to interpret the data is to assume that we can do things to make ourselves more attractive and also more successful and fulfilled. Recall that having a decent physique or figure (which is something we can work on), grooming ourselves well, and attending to the ways in which we dress are linked to attractiveness. So don't give up the ship.

Truth or Fiction Revisited

It is true that mock juries are less likely to find attractive individuals guilty of burglary or of cheating on an exam. "Good things" are apparently expected to "come in pretty packages."

Attractive people are also more likely to be found innocent of burglary and cheating in mock jury experiments (Mazzella & Feingold, 1994). When found guilty, they are handed down less severe sentences. Perhaps we assume that more attractive people are less likely to need to resort to deviant behavior to achieve their goals. Even when they have erred, perhaps they will have more opportunity for personal growth and be more likely to change their evil ways.

Attractive children learn early of the high expectations of others. Even during the first year of life, adults tend to rate physically attractive babies as good, smart, likable, and unlikely to cause their parents problems (Stephan & Langlois, 1984). Parents, teachers, and other children expect attractive children to do well in school and be popular, well behaved, and talented. Since our self-esteem reflects the admiration of others, it is not surprising that physically attractive people have higher self-esteem (Maruyama & Miller, 1975).

Speaking of esteem (like that transition?), the nearby "Adjustment in the New Millennium" feature considers the traits that contemporary women esteem in men.

THE MATCHING HYPOTHESIS: WHO IS "RIGHT" FOR YOU? Have you ever refrained from asking out an extremely attractive person for fear of rejection? Do you feel more comfortable when you approach someone who is a bit

ADJUSTMENT *in the* NEW MILLENNIUM

Who Are the Ideal Men for the New Millennium?

We thank readers for suggesting that this feature is about your authors. However, we discuss the results of a *Psychology Today* poll in this feature (Keen & Zur, 1989). *Psychology Today* readers are more affluent (two of five had an annual household income of at least twice the national average) and better educated (two of three held at least a bachelor's degree) than the general public, but they are probably very similar to the readers of this textbook.

The finding of most interest to your authors is that the "John Wayne" macho men and the workaholic/hard-driving business types definitely seem to be "out" for the new millennium, whereas the sensitive, communicative man is "in."

Table 13.2 reports the percentage of respondents who endorsed various traits of the ideal man. Social responsiveness, a strong presence, and take-charge qualities were important, but suaveness, Type A behavior, and toughness clearly made the undesirable list. So we have another vote, apparently, for the importance of communication and psychological androgyny in producing satisfying relationships! Oh yes, being trim is also in—the fitness craze persists.

The *Psychology Today* survey also reported that many men are already living up to these ideals. Thirty-seven percent of the female respondents judged the man they were closest to—whether he was a husband, lover, father, friend, or brother—to be ideal. Another 52 percent considered the man they were closest to to be good. That adds up to an encouraging 89 percent.

Advice to male readers: stop being tough and cool and start listening. This means *you*. ■

TABLE 13.2 PSYCHOLOGY TODAY READERS' PERCEPTIONS OF THE IDEAL MAN

TRAIT	*PERCENT WHO ENDORSE TRAIT*
Receptive, responsive to the initiatives of others	89%
Strong intellectual, moral, or physical presence	87
Pays attention to diet, exercise, health	87
Expresses feelings of sadness	86
Stops often to wonder, appreciate, dream	82
Follows inner authority	77
Even-tempered, moderate	77
Easy to be with	75
Nonjudgmental	74
Willingly accepts help	70
A doer, takes charge	68
. . .	
Suave, urbane	22
Type A personality	20
Always where the action is	20
Introverted	16
Critical	14
Has mood swings	10
Never shows pain	6
Basically ignores his body	2

less attractive? According to the **matching hypothesis,** we actually ask out people who are similar to ourselves in physical attractiveness rather than the local Will Smith or Sandra Bullock lookalike.

The major motive for asking out "matches" seems to be fear of rejection by more attractive people. Shanteau and Nagy (1979) asked female undergraduates to choose between two possible male dates on the basis of physical attractiveness (as suggested by a photograph) and probability that the man would accept the date request (as suggested by statements attached to the photographs, varying from "Sure thing" to "No chance"). Women preferred not to pursue men who were either very unattractive or very unlikely to accept the date. Moderately attractive men who were "highly likely" to accept the date were chosen most often. In a second phase of the experiment, women were asked to choose a date on the basis of the photo alone. Again, most women chose moderately attractive men. Perhaps they assumed that the most attractive men would be less likely to accept the date.

The quest for similarity extends beyond physical attractiveness. Our marital and sex partners tend to be similar to us in race/ethnicity, age, level of education, and religion. Consider some findings of the National Health and Social Life Survey (Michael and others, 1994, pp. 45–47):

- Nearly 94 percent of single White men have White women as their sex partners; 2 percent are partnered with Hispanic American women, 2 percent with Asian American women, and less than 1 percent with African American women.
- About 82 percent of African American men have African American women as their sex partners; nearly 8 percent are partnered with White women and almost 5 percent with Hispanic American women.
- About 83 percent of the women and men in the study chose partners within five years of their own age and of the same or a similar religion.
- Of nearly 2,000 women in the study, not one with a graduate college degree had a partner who had not finished high school.

Why do most people have partners from the same background as their own? One reason is that marriages are made in the neighborhood and not in heaven (Michael and others, 1994). We tend to live among people who are similar to us in background, and we therefore come into contact with them more often than with people from other backgrounds. Another reason is that we are drawn to people whose attitudes are similar to ours. People from a similar background are more likely to have similar attitudes. As we see in the following diversity feature, there are some other ways of making a "match."

MATCHING HYPOTHESIS • The view that people generally seek to develop relationships with people who are similar to themselves in attractiveness and other attributes, such as attitudes.

Adjustment in a World of DIVERSITY

"Let's Make a Deal": On Gender and Lonely Hearts Ads

All the lonely people—where will they all be found? Some of them are found in personal ads in newspapers and magazines. Some samples follow:

> Born-again Christian woman, 33, 4′9″, queen-size, loves children, quiet home life, sunsets. Seeks marriage-minded man, 33 or over. Children, handicap, any height or weight welcome.

> Horseman, handsome, wealthy, 48, 5′10″, 180 lbs, likes dancing, traveling. Seeking beautiful, slender girl, under 35, sweet, honest, neat, without dependents. Send full-length photo, details.
>
> Single, 28, 5′7″, 128 lbs with strawberry-blond hair, blue eyes. Wants to meet secure, sincere gentleman, 32–48, who loves the outdoors and dancing. Preferably Taurus. No heavy drinker need reply. Send photo and letter first.
>
> Tall male, 40, slim, divorced, nice-looking, hardworking nondrinker, owns home and business. Seeks attractive, plump gal, 25–35, not extremely heavy, but plump, kind, sweet, for a lasting relationship. Photo, phone.

Koestner and Wheeler (1988) examined 400 lonely hearts ads from two geographically separate newspapers in the United States. They examined each for the stated attractiveness of the advertiser and the requested attractiveness of the respondent. Consistent with the matching hypothesis, more attractive advertisers generally sought more attractive respondents. But women were more likely to advertise themselves as physically attractive. Men were more likely to tout financial security as a come-on. Physically attractive women were more likely to demand financial security. Wealthy men wanted greater physical appeal in potential mates. At first glance, this finding may seem to counter the matching hypothesis, but wealth and physical beauty are both highly desirable. The overall desirability of advertiser and respondent thus tended to remain constant. Good looks were up for sale. A "deal" could be made.

Now let us turn our attention to other factors, including attitudinal similarity, that affect feelings of attraction.

Attraction and Similarity: Birds of a Feather Flock Together

This is the land of free speech. So do we respect the rights of others to reveal their ignorance by disagreeing with us? Perhaps. But it has been observed since ancient times that we tend to like people who agree with us. Similarity in attitudes and tastes is a key contributor to initial attraction, friendships, and love relationships (Cappella & Palmer, 1990; Griffin & Sparks, 1990).

Truth or Fiction Revisited

Actually, it is not usually true that "opposites attract": We are actually more likely to be attracted to people who share our attitudes than to people who disagree with them.

There is also evidence that we may tend to *assume* that physically attractive people share our attitudes (Marks and others, 1981). Can this be a sort of wish fulfillment? When attraction is strong, as it was with Candy and Stretch, perhaps we like to think that all the kinks in a relationship will be small and can be ironed out.

Not all attitudes are necessarily equal. Men on computer dates at the University of Nevada were more influenced by sexual than religious attitudes (Touhey, 1972). But women were more attracted to men whose religious views coincided with their own. The women may have been relatively less interested in a physical relationship and more concerned about creating a family with cohesive values. Attitudes toward religion and children are generally more important in mate selection than characteristics like kindness and professional status (Howard and others, 1987).

Similarity in tastes is also important. May and Hamilton (1980) found that college women rate photos of male strangers as more attractive when they are listening to music that they like (in most cases, rock) as compared to music that they don't like (in this experiment, "avant-garde classical"). If a dating couple's taste in music does not overlap, one member may look more appealing at the same time the second is losing appeal in the other's eyes—and all because of what is on the stereo. Are we suggesting that you pretend to like the music that turns on your date? Certainly not if you're interested in a long-term relationship! Do you want repulsive music blaring from your stereo for the next 50 years?

The sexual attraction experienced by Candy and Stretch motivated them to pretend that their preferences, tastes, and opinions coincided. They entered an unspoken agreement not to discuss their religious differences. Candy and Stretch used common but maladaptive methods to avoid having to face their attitudinal dissimilarity. They first allowed themselves to misperceive each other's religion. When they realized that they were wrong, they tried to sweep the issue under the rug. When ignoring differences failed, they misrepresented or hid their genuine feelings.

There are other ways of trying to cope with dissimilar attitudes. We can try to convince others to change their attitudes or, perhaps, to convert to our own religions. We can reevaluate our attitudes and explore the possibilities of changing them. We can also choose to end the relationship. But Candy and Stretch were unwilling to do any of these things, because they took their religions seriously and were also strongly attracted to one another. Ah, conflict.

Reciprocity: If You Like Me, You Must Have Excellent Judgment

Has anyone told you how good-looking, brilliant, and mature you are? That your taste is refined? That all in all, you are really something special? If so, have you been impressed by his or her fine judgment?

Reciprocity is a powerful determinant of attraction (Condon & Crano, 1988). We tend to return feelings of admiration. We tend to be more open, warm, and helpful when we are interacting with strangers who seem to like us (Curtis & Miller, 1986).

Sexual Orientation

Sexual orientation refers to the organization or direction of one's erotic interests. **Heterosexual** people are sexually attracted to people of the other gender and are interested in forming romantic relationships with them. **Homosexual** people are sexually attracted to people of their own gender and want to form romantic relationships with them. Homosexual males are also referred to as **gay males** and homosexual females as **lesbians. Bisexual** people are sexually attracted to, and are interested in forming romantic relationships with, both women and men.

RECIPROCITY • The tendency to return feelings and attitudes that are expressed about us.

SEXUAL ORIENTATION • The directionality of one's erotic interests—that is, whether one is sexually attracted to people of the other or the same gender and is interested in forming romantic relationships with people of that gender.

HETEROSEXUAL • Referring to people who are sexually aroused by people of the other gender and are interested in forming romantic relationships with them.

HOMOSEXUAL • Referring to people who are sexually aroused by people of the same gender and are interested in forming romantic relationships with them. (Derived from the Greek *homos,* meaning "same," not from the Latin *homo,* meaning "man.")

GAY MALE • A male homosexual.

LESBIAN • A female homosexual.

BISEXUAL • A person who is sexually aroused by people of either gender and who is interested in forming romantic relationships with them.

Sexual activity with members of one's own gender does not in itself define one's sexual orientation. It may reflect limited sexual opportunities or even ritualistic cultural practices, as in the case of the New Guinean Sambian people. American adolescent boys may masturbate one another while fantasizing about girls. Men in prisons may turn to each other as sexual outlets. Sambian male youths engage exclusively in sexual practices with older males, since it is believed that they must drink "men's milk" to achieve the fierce manhood of the head hunter (Money, 1987). But their behavior turns exclusively heterosexual once they reach marrying age.

The concept of *sexual orientation* is not to be confused with the notion of a sexual preference. Research does not support the view that gay males and lesbians *choose* their sexual orientation any more than heterosexuals choose their orientation (American Psychological Association, 1991). However, a *New York Times*/CBS News Poll found that a nationwide sample of 1,154 adults was evenly split on whether or not sexual orientation is a choice: 44 percent of the respondents saw sexual orientation as a choice, whereas 43 percent saw sexual

TABLE 13.3 ATTITUDES TOWARD GAY MALES AND LESBIANS AMONG PEOPLE WHO SEE SEXUAL ORIENTATION AS A CHOICE AND AMONG PEOPLE WHO SEE SEXUAL ORIENTATION AS SOMETHING THAT CANNOT BE CHANGED (IN PERCENTAGES)

	TOTAL SAMPLE	PEOPLE WHO SEE SEXUAL ORIENTATION AS A CHOICE	PEOPLE WHO BELIEVE THAT SEXUAL ORIENTATION CANNOT BE CHANGED
Say gay males and lesbians should have equal rights in terms of job opportunities	78%	69%	90%
Say it is necessary to pass laws to make sure gay males and lesbians have equal rights	42	30	58
Object to having an airline pilot who is gay	11	18	4
Object to having a doctor who is gay	49	64	34
Object to having a gay male or lesbian as a child's elementary school teacher	55	71	39
Say male-male and female-female relations between consenting adults should be legal	46	32	62
Say gay males and lesbians should be allowed to serve in the military	43	32	54
Would permit their child to play at the home of a friend who has a gay male or lesbian parent	34	21	50
Have a close friend or family member who is a gay male or lesbian	22	16	29

Source: Adapted from *The New York Times,* March 5, 1993, p. A14.

orientation as something that cannot be changed (Schmalz, 1993). As shown in Table 13.3, people who view sexual orientation as a choice are significantly more intolerant of gay males and lesbians than people who see sexual orientation as fixed or invariable. People's theoretical explanations of sexual orientation thus have a profound impact on their attitudes. A survey respondent who sees homosexuality as a choice says, "I just don't think that people are born that way, so I wouldn't want that taught to my child" (Wolfe, 1998, p. 47). But a respondent who sees homosexuality as inborn says, "I think it is something we have to accept because it's part of their nature. What are we going to do, get into gene alteration?" (Wolfe, 1998, p. 47).

Surveys in the United States, Britain, France, and Denmark find that about 3 percent of men identify themselves as gay (Hamer and others, 1993; Janus & Janus, 1993; Laumann and others, 1994). About 2 percent of the U.S. women surveyed say that they have a lesbian sexual orientation (Janus & Janus, 1993; Laumann and others, 1994).

ORIGINS OF SEXUAL ORIENTATION There are psychological and biological theories of sexual orientation, as well as theories that combine elements of both.

L'Abandon (Les Deux Amies). This painting by Henri de Toulouse-Lautrec is of lesbian lovers.

Psychodynamic theory ties sexual orientation to identification with male or female figures. Identification, in turn, is related to resolution of the Oedipus and Electra complexes. In men, faulty resolution of the Oedipus complex would stem from a "classic pattern" of childrearing in which there is a "close, binding" mother and a "detached, hostile" father. Boys reared in such a home environment would identify with their mother and not with their father. Psychodynamic theory has been criticized, however, because many gay males have had excellent relationships with both parents (Isay, 1990). Also, the childhoods of many heterosexuals fit the "classic pattern."

From a learning theory point of view, early reinforcement of sexual behavior (for example, by orgasm achieved through interaction with people of one's own gender) can influence one's sexual orientation. But most people are aware of their sexual orientation before they have sexual contacts (Bell and others, 1981).

Biopsychologists note that there is evidence of familial patterns in sexual orientation (Pillard, 1990; Pillard & Weinrich, 1986). In one study, 22 percent of the brothers of 51 primarily gay men were either gay or bisexual themselves. This is about four times the percentage found in the general population (Pillard & Weinrich, 1986). A study published in *Science* reported that genes connected with sexual orientation may be found on the X sex chromosome and be transmitted from mother to child (Hamer and others, 1993). Moreover, according to research by Bailey and Pillard (1991), identical (MZ) twins have a higher agreement rate for a gay male sexual orientation than do fraternal (DZ) twins: 52 percent for MZ twins versus 22 percent for DZ twins. Although genetic factors may partly determine sexual orientation, psychologist John Money, who has specialized in research on sexual behavior, concludes that sexual orientation is "not under the direct governance of chromosomes and genes" (1987, p. 384).

Sex hormones may play a role in sexual orientation. These hormones promote biological sexual differentiation and regulate the menstrual cycle. They also have organizing and activating effects on sexual behavior. They predispose lower animals toward masculine or feminine mating patterns—a directional or

organizing effect (Crews, 1994). They also affect the sex drive and promote sexual response; these are **activating effects.**

Sexual behavior among many lower animals is almost completely governed by hormones (Crews, 1994). In many species, if the sex organs and brains of fetuses are exposed to large doses of **testosterone** in the uterus (which occurs naturally when they share the uterus with many brothers, or artificially as a result of hormone injections), they become masculine in structure (Crews, 1994). Prenatal testosterone organizes the brains of females in the masculine direction, predisposing them toward masculine behaviors in adulthood. Testosterone in adulthood then apparently activates the masculine behavior patterns.

Because sex hormones predispose lower animals toward masculine or feminine mating patterns, some have asked whether gay males and lesbians might differ from heterosexuals in levels of sex hormones. However, a gay male or lesbian sexual orientation has not been reliably linked to current (adult) levels of male or female sex hormones (Friedman & Downey, 1994). What about the effects of sex hormones on the developing fetus? As just noted, we know that prenatal sex hormones can masculinize or feminize the brains of laboratory animals.

Lee Ellis (1990; Ellis & Ames, 1987) theorizes that sexual orientation is hormonally determined prior to birth and is affected by genetic factors, synthetic male sex hormones (which have sometimes been used to help maintain pregnancy), and maternal stress. Why maternal stress? Stress causes the release of hormones such as adrenaline and steroids, which can affect the prenatal development of the brain. Perhaps the brains of some gay males have been feminized and the brains of some lesbians masculinized prior to birth (Collaer & Hines, 1995; Friedman & Downey, 1994).

In sum, the determinants of sexual orientation are mysterious and complex. Research suggests that they may involve prenatal hormone levels—which can be affected by factors such as heredity, drugs, and maternal stress—and postnatal socialization. However, the precise interaction among these influences is not yet understood.

ADJUSTMENT OF GAY MALES AND LESBIANS Despite the slings and arrows of an often outraged society, it has not been shown that gay males and lesbians are more emotionally unstable or prone to psychological disorders such as anxiety and depression than heterosexuals (B. F. Reiss, 1980). Gay males and lesbians occupy all socioeconomic and vocational levels and follow a variety of lifestyles. The Sixth Army's 1992 Soldier of the Year, José Zuniga (1993), was a gay male.

Bell and Weinberg (1978) found variations in adjustment in the gay community that seem to mirror variations in the heterosexual community. Gay males who lived with partners in stable, intimate relationships—so-called *close couples*—were as well adjusted as married heterosexuals. Older gay men who lived alone and had few sexual contacts were less well adjusted. So, too, are many heterosexuals who lead similar lifestyles. All in all, differences in adjustment seem more likely to reflect the person's lifestyle rather than his or her sexual orientation.

Most gay males and lesbians who share close relationships are satisfied with their quality (Kurdek & Schmitt, 1986a; Peplau & Cochran, 1990). Gay males and lesbians who are in enduring relationships generally report high levels of love, attachment, closeness, caring, and intimacy (Peplau & Cochran, 1990). Like heterosexuals, gay men and lesbians are happier in relationships in which they share power and make joint decisions (Kurdek & Schmitt, 1986b).

ORGANIZING EFFECT • The directional effect of sex hormones—for example, along stereotypically masculine or feminine lines.

ACTIVATING EFFECT • The arousal-producing effects of sex hormones that increase the likelihood of sexual behavior.

TESTOSTERONE • A male sex hormone that promotes development of male sexual characteristics and that has activating effects on sexual arousal.

ADJUSTMENT *in the* NEW MILLENNIUM

http://www.planetout.com

The gay community has been active online for quite some time. An *Out* magazine survey shows that gay men and lesbians are more likely than the general population to use personal computers, modems, and online services. In an average month in the 1990s, 40,000 gay people spent more than 100,000 hours online with America Online's Gay and Lesbian Community Forum.

PlanetOut (http://www.planetout.com), the electronic media company, has become a sort of a "gay global village" in cyberspace. It has received the endorsement of virtually all the leading gay organizations. The Human Rights Campaign Fund, the National Gay and Lesbian Task Force, Parents and Friends of Lesbians and Gays, the Gay and Lesbian Victory Fund, Digital Queers, and the Gay and Lesbian Alliance Against Defamation all provide information on the service.

PlanetOut is also a meeting place for millions of gay men, lesbians, bisexuals, and others who may be reluctant to associate with one another in public. A creative director of Netscape and the former head of design at Apple Computer said that chatting electronically with gay men and lesbians on America Online had given him the courage to discuss his gay sexual orientation openly. "It's something that would have been unthinkable for me even a year or two ago," he said. "If I had relied on more traditional ways of meeting people, like going to bars, or going to meetings of various organizations, or picking up gay publications, it never would have happened" (Lewis, 1995). ■

PLANETOUT'S HOME PAGE.
PlanetOut, the electronic media company, has become a sort of "gay global village" of cyberspace. It is also a meeting place for millions of gay people.

FRIENDSHIP

Friendship, friendship,
What a perfect blendship . . .

Friends play a major role in our lives from the time we are children through late adulthood. For primary schoolers, friendships are based largely on who lives next door or who sits next to whom (Berndt & Perry, 1986; Etaugh & Rathus, 1995). "Friends" are classmates and those with whom kids do things and have fun. With middle schoolers, similarity in interests enters the picture: Friendships become more like "perfect blendships."

By puberty, people want someone with whom they can also share intimate feelings (Damon, 1977). In the teens, it becomes important that friends keep confidences. We want to be able to tell friends "everything" without worrying that they will spread stories (Berndt & Perry, 1986). Girls find intimacy somewhat more important than boys do and form more intimate friendships (Berndt, 1982).

In high school and college, we tend to belong to cliques and crowds. A **clique** (pronounced "click") is a small number of close friends who share confidences. A **crowd** is a larger, loosely knit group of friends who share activities. The crowd may go to the football game together or to a party. But we tend to share our innermost feelings about people at the party within the clique.

Friends also play an important role in late adulthood. The quality of friendliness is associated with psychological well-being among the elderly (Costa & McCrae, 1984; Lowenthal & Haven 1981). People with confidants are generally less depressed and lonely. Having a confidant also heightens morale in the face of tragic events such as illness or the death of a spouse.

Qualities of Good Friends

Psychology Today magazine reported the results of a survey of 40,000 readers on friendship. To readers, loyalty and keeping confidences were the most sought-after qualities in a friend (Parlee, 1979). Overall, qualities deemed important in friends were the following:

Truth or Fiction Revisited

It is not true that the most sought-after quality in a friend is warmth. According to a *Psychology Today* survey, loyalty ranks higher.

1. Ability to keep confidences (endorsed by 89 percent of respondents)
2. Loyalty (88 percent)
3. Warmth and affection (82 percent)
4. Supportiveness (75 percent)
5. Honesty and frankness (73 percent)
6. Humor (72 percent)
7. Willingness to set aside time for me (62 percent)
8. Independence (61 percent)
9. Conversational skills (59 percent)
10. Intelligence (58 percent)
11. Social conscience (49 percent)

Among sophisticated young adults, then, loyalty (keeping confidences is one aspect of loyalty) appears to be the prime requisite for friendship. Also important are the social-supportive aspects of the relationship (including warmth, humor, and willingness to set aside time for the relationship). General positive traits also figure in—honesty, independence, intelligence, and so on.

CLIQUE • A small group of close friends who share confidences.

CROWD • A large number of loosely knit friends who share activities.

On Friendship and Love

Return to Stretch and Candy. Their relationship lacked a quality associated with the most frequently endorsed qualities of friendship—trust and the sharing of confidences. Their relationship was so superficial (despite the physical intimacy) that they hadn't even exchanged information about their religious beliefs and attitudes.

The trials of Candy and Stretch highlight the fact that it is possible to be "in love" when we are not friends. Friendship and love, in other words, do not always mix. We shall see, however, that abiding love relationships tend to combine the two.

Speaking of friends and friendships, let us consider a topic of importance to many students entering college—the possible roles of fraternities and sororities in their lives.

Fraternities and Sororities: Are They for You?

Are fraternities and sororities big on your campus? Are you a brother, a sister, or a pledge? If not, have you felt tempted to join?

On some campuses, belonging to a fraternity or a sorority is the ticket of admission to friendship and social acceptance. There is so much pressure to join fraternities and sororities that people who choose not to join—or who are not invited to join—are looked upon with scorn or suspicion. The assumption seems to be that everyone who can become a brother or a sister does so. Students who do not are seen as rejects.

Fraternities and sororities have a lower profile on other campuses, and some colleges do not allow them at all. These societies often take on more prominence at residential colleges. At residential colleges, fraternities and sororities may provide housing and surrogate parents as well as social diversion.

Let us consider some of the advantages and disadvantages of Greek-letter societies. With this knowledge, you may be able to make a more informed decision about whether they are right for you.

Advantages and Disadvantages of Fraternities and Sororities

Fraternities and sororities confer advantages such as the following:

1. They offer handy sources of social support.
2. They offer a crowd of people with whom to do and share things.
3. They confer prestige upon their members. On many campuses, members of Greek organizations feel superior to nonmembers.
4. They offer the beginnings of a lifelong network that may be of use in obtaining jobs and climbing the corporate ladder.
5. They channel social life into house and college occasions. Rather than wondering what you're going to be doing on a weekend—especially a "big" weekend—you're welcome at the house's parties and functions. If you don't have a date, a brother or sister may fix you up with someone from a brother fraternity or sister sorority, where the members tend to share interests and values. Houses also arrange mixers with brother fraternities or sister sororities. In other words, they do much social screening for members.
6. Joiners become part of a tradition. Fraternities and sororities have histories and aims that affect members in the same way the nation, one's religious group, and the college at large affect the individual.

7. Fraternities and sororities frequently provide high-quality living arrangements. They are often housed in splendid buildings, sometimes in converted mansions.
8. They provide social inducement to play on university and intramural athletic teams. Athletics are valued by many houses, and as a member of a fraternity or sorority, you may also be on the society's intramural teams.
9. They encourage participation in the planning of social occasions and the management of house business. These chores develop administrative and interpersonal skills that can be of help later on.
10. Many houses encourage studying. Some value academics more than others do, but most recognize that the primary goal of college is to receive an education; members are inspired to do so.
11. Upperclass members often provide valuable information about the strengths and weaknesses of various courses and professors.
12. Many fraternities and sororities have superb (legitimately compiled) test files. Members who have taken courses place copies of their exams in the file, and old exams often contain recycled questions. Some professors reuse examinations in their entirety.

Fraternities and sororities thus confer many benefits. But there are drawbacks, and what is of value to one person may be a hindrance to another. It depends on who you are and who you want to be.

Fraternities and sororities have these drawbacks or disadvantages:

1. Fraternities and sororities have expectations for behavior, called norms, that pressure members to conform. Students may try to join societies that reflect their own values, but there is never a perfect fit. When "rushing"—that is, visiting fraternities and sororities so that the houses and students can decide who and where to pledge—*be yourself.* Express your own ideas and values—not what you think the brothers or sisters of the house want to hear. It is a mistake to join a house whose members are very different from you. A moment of glory—being invited to pledge for a prestigious society—may yield to years of mutual discomfort.
2. Members who seek friends among nonmembers may face disapproval. This is the flip side of the advantage of finding an instant cadre of "friends." As we grow, we often reappraise our values and seek different qualities in friends. The society that boosted our self-esteem as first-year students may weigh us down as juniors or seniors.
3. There may be pressure to date the "right kind" of people. This is the flip side of the advantage that fraternities and sororities often provide "built-in" pools of potential dates. A member of a Christian fraternity, Carlos, was dating a Jewish girl, Fran, and he heard a number of comments about it.
4. Exclusivity is also reflected in pressure to socialize with members of your own house and a number of similar "acceptable" houses. Peer pressure may thus prevent you from socializing with groups of people you will find in the "real world" once you graduate—people from diverse racial, ethnic, and socioeconomic groups. You may enter college with an open mind and pledge a house with blinders on.
5. For some, the living arrangements offered by the fraternity or sorority are not satisfactory. Some students prefer an apartment with one or two roommates to the hustle and bustle of the fraternity or sorority house. In many cases, however, members are required to live in the fraternity or sorority house for at least a year.

6. The "opportunity" to play on intramural teams may provide pressure that you don't want. *Are* you athletic? If not, do you want to join a group that prizes athletics? If you are only somewhat athletic, do you prefer to compete against others, which is the "Greek" way, or do you prefer self-developing solitary jogs, bike rides, and swims?
7. The "opportunity" to plan and manage house functions can translate into pressure to assume administrative burdens. Many would prefer to spend their spare time in other ways.
8. Although fraternities and sororities may promote academics on certain levels, there may also be subtle—and, in some cases, explicit—pressures not to study. At athletically oriented houses, being overly cerebral may be seen as nerdish. Then, of course, the profusion of social activities, house responsibilities, and demands of pledging may eat into valuable study time. We have seen many students flunk out of college because they could not limit their involvements with their societies. It does little good to pledge a prestigious house if the demands of pledging cause you to flunk out of college. As a pledge, it is one thing to wear silly clothes to class; it is another to be so busy memorizing the names and addresses of the grandparents of house members that there's no time to study!
9. Then there are the perils of hazing. Over the years, hazing practices have ranged from the silly and annoying to the painful and dangerous. There have been times and places when pledges have been required to eat live goldfish. This may seem yucky (to use a sophisticated term), but goldfish are usually nutritious. However, hazing can also involve running naked in winter or overdosing on alcohol. Now and then, a pledge dies from an alcohol overdose. Now and then, fraternity members go to jail because of it. Hazing practices are usually not so noxious, but they are intended to be demanding hurdles—both to test pledges' sincerity and to build their loyalty to the house. (The thinking goes like this: If pledges tell themselves they went through hell to join, they'll believe that their fraternities and sororities must be very, very special.) You have to decide for yourself just what you'll go through—just where you'll draw the line.

Should *you* pledge a fraternity or a sorority? We wish we could answer this for you, but we can't. We hope that we have given you a number of factors to weigh in making your decision. We will say this: If you're into athletics and a social whirl and don't particularly value solitary, contemplative hours, a fraternity or sorority may be right for you. If you would rather socialize with one or two intimate friends and are not "into" belonging to prestigious groups, a fraternity or sorority could be an unnecessary diversion for you.

LOVE

What makes the world go round? **Love,** of course. Love is one of the most deeply stirring emotions, the ideal for which we will make great sacrifice, the emotion that launched a thousand ships in the Greek epic *The Iliad.*

For thousands of years, poets have sought to capture love in words. Robert Burns, an eighteenth-century poet, wrote that his love was like "a red, red rose." In Sinclair Lewis's novel *Elmer Gantry,* love is "the morning and the evening star." Love is beautiful and elusive. It shines brilliantly and heavenly. Passionate love is also earthy and sexy, involving a solid ration of sexual desire.

LOVE • An intense, positive emotion that involves feelings of affection and the desires to be with and to help another person.

Styles of Love

Psychologists today find that love is a complex concept involving many areas of experience—emotional, cognitive, and motivational (Sternberg, 1988). Psychologists also speak of different kinds of love and different *styles* of love. For example, Clyde and Susan Hendrick (1986) developed a love-attitude scale that suggests the existence of six styles of love among college students. Here are the styles and items, similar to those on the test, that identify them:

1. **Eros** (pronounced "ER-oss"), or romantic love. "My lover fits my ideal"; "My lover and I were attracted to one another immediately."
2. **Ludus** (pronounced "LOO-duss"), or game-playing love. "I keep my lover up in the air about my commitment"; "I get over love affairs pretty easily."
3. **Storge** (pronounced "store-gay"), or friendship love. "The best love grows out of an enduring friendship."
4. **Pragma,** or pragmatic, logical love. "I consider a lover's potential in life before committing myself"; "I consider whether my lover will be a good parent."
5. **Mania,** or possessive, excited love. "I get so excited about my love that I cannot sleep"; "When my lover ignores me I get sick all over."
6. **Agape** (pronounced "ah-gah-pay"), or selfless love. "I would do anything I can to help my lover"; "My lover's needs and wishes are more important than my own."

Most people who are "in love" combine a number of these styles. Using these six styles of love, the Hendricks (1986) found some interesting gender differences. Male college students are significantly more "ludic" (i.e., game-playing) than females. Female college students are significantly more "storgic" (friendly), pragmatic (long-term oriented), and manic[2] (possessive) than males. There were no gender differences in eros (passion) or agape (selflessness).

Romantic Love in Contemporary Western Culture

When people in Western culture speak of falling in love, they are referring to romantic love—not to the sort of attachment that binds parents to children. Nor are they referring to sexual arousal, which people may experience while they are reading an erotic story or looking at photographs in an erotic magazine. To experience **romantic love,** in contrast to attachment or sexual arousal, it may be that one must be exposed to a culture that idealizes the concept. In Western culture, romantic love blossoms with the fairy tales of Sleeping Beauty, Cinderella, Snow White, and their princes charming. It matures with romantic novels, television tales and films, and the colorful narratives of friends and relatives.

The Love Triangle—That Is, the Triangular Model of Love

According to Robert Sternberg (1988), love consists of three primary components: intimacy, passion, and commitment.

Intimacy is the emotional component. It is apparently based on the sharing of intimate (deeply personal) information and feelings of mutual acceptance.

EROS • Romantic love.
LUDUS • The style of love characterized by game playing.
STORGE • A type of love similar to attachment and affection.
PRAGMA • The style of love guided by pragmatic, or practical, considerations, as, for example, whether one's partner is a stable individual.
MANIA • As a type of love, it is a possessive, excited love.
AGAPE • A type of love similar to generosity; selfless love.
ROMANTIC LOVE • A type of love that is characterized by passion and intimacy.

[2] Not to be confused with manic depression (bipolar disorder), the problem discussed in Chapter 9.

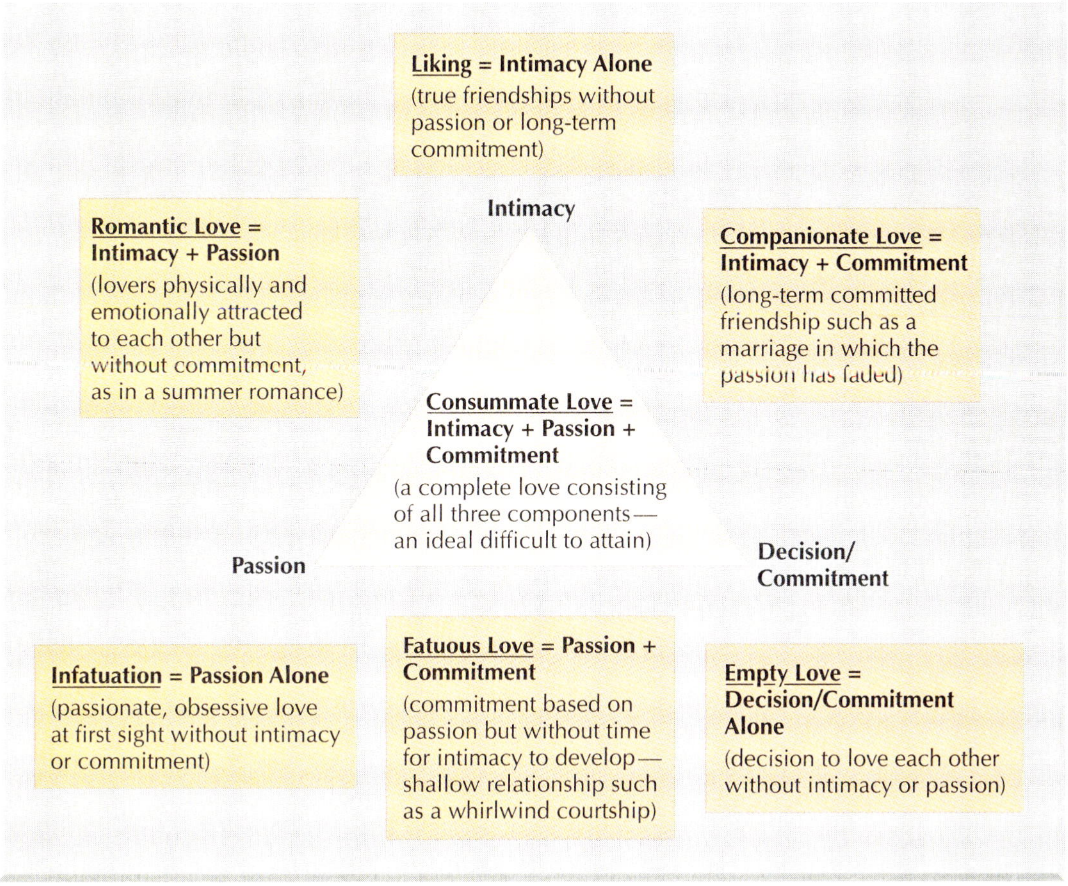

FIGURE 13.3
THE TRIANGULAR MODEL OF LOVE.
According to psychologist Robert Sternberg, love consists of three components, as shown by the vertices of this triangle. Various kinds of love consist of different combinations of these components. Romantic love, for example, consists of passion and intimacy. Consummate love — a state idealized in Western society — consists of all three.

Passion is the motivational force behind love. It involves sexual attraction and the desire for sexual intimacy. Passion gives rise to fascination and preoccupation with the loved one. Passion is rapidly aroused but also quick to fade— especially among adolescents.

Decision making and commitment comprise the cognitive component of love. Initially one decides that he or she is "in love." As time elapses, however, the initial decision becomes a lasting sense of commitment to the other person and the relationship.

Different combinations of the components of love yield different kinds of love (see Figure 13.3 and Table 13.4). *Romantic love* involves passion and intimacy, but not necessarily commitment. Romantic love encourages lovers to champion the interests of the loved one even if it means sacrificing their own interests. In fact, college undergraduates see the desire to help or care for the loved one as central to the concept of romantic love (Steck and others, 1982).

Romantic lovers also idealize one another. They magnify each other's positive features and overlook their flaws.

Romantic love may burn brightly and then flicker out. If commitment develops, romantic love may evolve into *consummate love*, in which all three

Truth or Fiction Revisited

It is true that college students consider selflessness one of the attributes of love. It is assumed that we would place the needs of loved ones before our own.

TABLE 13.4 TYPES OF LOVE ACCORDING TO STERNBERG'S TRIANGULAR MODEL

1. Nonlove	A relationship in which all three components of love are absent. Most of our personal relationships are of this type—casual interactions or acquaintances that do not involve any elements of love.
2. Liking	A loving experience with another person or a friendship in which intimacy is present but passion and commitment are lacking.
3. Infatuation	A kind of "love at first sight" in which one experiences passionate desires for another person in the absence of both intimacy and decision/commitment components of love.
4. Empty love	A kind of love characterized by the decision (to love) and the commitment (to maintain the relationship) in the absence of either passion or intimacy. Stagnant relationships that no longer involve the emotional intimacy or physical attraction that once characterized them are of this type.
5. Romantic love	A loving experience characterized by the combination of passion and intimacy, but without decision/commitment components of love.
6. Companionate love	A kind of love that derives from the combination of intimacy and decision/commitment components of love. This kind of love often occurs in marriages in which passionate attraction between the partners has died down and has been replaced by a kind of committed friendship.
7. Fatuous love	The type of love associated with whirlwind romances and "quicky marriages" in which the passion and decision/commitment components of love are present, but intimacy is not.
8. Consummate love	The full or complete measure of love involving the combination of passion, intimacy, and decision/commitment. Many of us strive to attain this type of complete love in our romantic relationships. Maintaining it is often harder than achieving it.

Source: Adapted from Sternberg, 1988.

FIGURE 13.4
COMPATIBILITY AND INCOMPATIBILITY, ACCORDING TO THE TRIANGULAR MODEL OF LOVE

Within Sternberg's model of love, compatibility can be conceptualized in terms of "love triangles." In Part A there is a perfect match; the triangles are congruent. In Part B there is a good match; the partners are similar according to the three dimensions. Part C reveals a mismatch, with the partners grossly different in all three components of love.

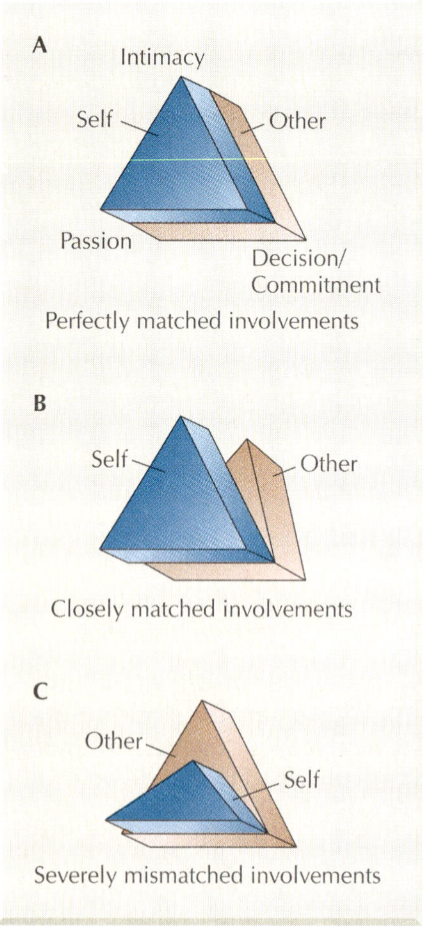

components flower. Consummate love is an ideal toward which many Westerners strive. *Empty love* is characterized by commitment alone. There is neither the warm emotional embrace of intimacy nor the flame of passion. In the case of empty love, one usually tolerates one's partner out of a sense of duty.

Is there such a thing as love at first sight? Yes. But within Sternberg's model, love at first sight is a *fatuous* or foolish love. People may be overwhelmed by feelings of passion and make a rapid commitment to one another before true intimacy develops. Fatuous love may propel whirlwind courtships and rapid marriages that often come to an end when one or both partners wakes up one morning and realizes that the partners are poorly matched and the infatuation is over.

According to Sternberg's model, couples are matched if they possess corresponding levels of passion, intimacy, and commitment. A couple's compatibility can be represented in terms of the fit of the love triangles. Part A of Figure 13.4 shows a perfect match, in which the triangles are congruent. Part B depicts a good match, one in which partners are similar in the three dimensions. Part C shows a mismatch. There are large differences between the partners in all three components. Relationships suffer when partners are grossly mismatched. A relationship may fizzle, rather than sizzle, when one partner has a great deal more passion, or when one wants a permanent commitment and the other's idea of commitment is to stay the night.

Truth or Fiction Revisited

There is such a thing as love at first sight, but it is likely to be fatuous or foolish love. It is not romantic love, and certainly not consummate love.

Romantic Versus Companionate Love: Is Romantic Love Any Basis for a Marriage?

According to the American ideal, when people come of age they will find their perfect match, fall in love, get married, and live happily ever after. In the next chapter we shall see that the high divorce rate sheds some doubt on this fantasy. But for the moment, let us confine ourselves to asking whether romantic love provides a sound basis for marriage.

There is cause for skepticism. Romantic love frequently assails us in a flash. Then it may dissipate as our involvement with the loved one grows. Some philosophers and social critics have argued that romantic love is but a "passing fancy." Marriage, therefore, must be a firm legal institution for the rearing of children and the transmission of wealth from one generation to another. So it is unwise to base marriage on romantic love. From this perspective, marriage is a sober instrument of social stability whereas love, after all, is *l'amour!* In many instances throughout Western history, it was assumed that husbands would take mistresses or visit prostitutes. In a few cases, wives have also been expected to take lovers, especially among the aristocratic upper classes.

A study by Hill and colleagues (1976) appears to support some of the skepticism concerning the durability of romantic love. The researchers followed 200 college couples over a 2-year period, during which more than half broke up. Figure 13.5 suggests the reasons for the breaks. They can be summarized as a combination of boredom and recognition of dissimilarities, two factors also found important in breakups by Byrne and Murnen (1987). Byrne and Murnen

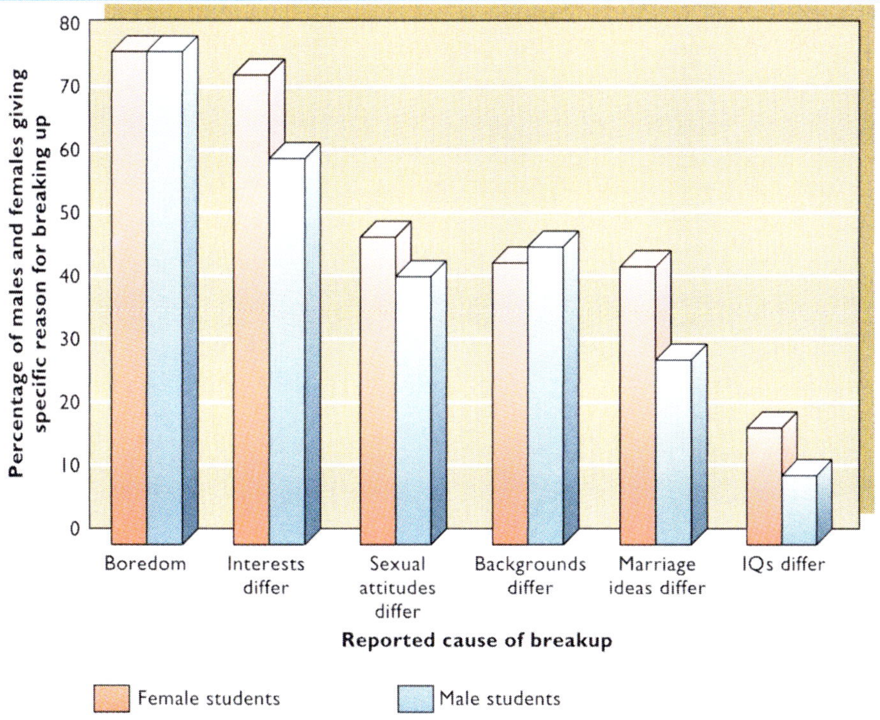

FIGURE 13.5

WHAT HAPPENS WHEN REALITY SETS IN.

Researchers followed some 200 dating couples for a 2-year period, during which more than half of them broke up. Boredom was a major reason given — feelings of passion apparently cooled as time went on. But the couples who broke up also reported the gradual discovery of many differences in opinion, interests, and abilities. If a relationship is to last, perhaps companionate love — which is based on mutual respect and accurate knowledge of one's partner — must wax as the fires of passion wane.

Source: Based on data from Hill, Rubin, & Peplau, 1976.

HAS CUPID SHOT HIS ARROW INTO YOUR HEART? STERNBERG'S TRIANGULAR LOVE SCALE

Which are the strongest components of your love relationship? Intimacy? Passion? Decision/commitment? All three components? Two of them?

To complete the following scale, fill in the blank spaces with the name of one person you love or care about deeply. Then rate your agreement with each of the items by using a 9-point scale in which 1 = "not at all," 5 = "moderately," and 9 = "extremely." Use points in between to indicate intermediate levels of agreement between these values. Then consult the scoring key in the Appendix. ■

Intimacy Component

____ 1. I am actively supportive of ______'s well-being.

____ 2. I have a warm relationship with ______.

____ 3. I am able to count on ______ in times of need.

____ 4. ______ is able to count on me in times of need.

____ 5. I am willing to share myself and my possessions with ______.

____ 6. I receive considerable emotional support from ______.

____ 7. I give considerable emotional support to ______.

____ 8. I communicate well with ______.

____ 9. I value ______ greatly in my life.

____ 10. I feel close to ______.

____ 11. I have a comfortable relationship with ______.

____ 12. I feel that I really understand ______.

____ 13. I feel that ______ really understands me.

____ 14. I feel that I can really trust ______.

____ 15. I share deeply personal information about myself with ______.

Passion Component

____ 16. Just seeing ______ excites me.

____ 17. I find myself thinking about ______ frequently during the day.

(1987) also note that these two factors give rise to a third factor—change in reciprocal evaluations. All in all, early idealized romantic passions give way to objective recognition of differences in attitudes and interests.

People are more likely to maintain their relationship once the romance begins to fade if they have developed **companionate love.** Companionate love

COMPANIONATE LOVE • A type of love that lacks the passion of romantic love. It is based on sharing, mutual respect, and willingness to sacrifice.

____ 18. My relationship with ______ is very romantic.
____ 19. I find ______ to be very personally attractive.
____ 20. I idealize ______.
____ 21. I cannot imagine another person making me as happy as ______ does.
____ 22. I would rather be with ______ than anyone else.
____ 23. There is nothing more important to me than my relationship with ______.
____ 24. I especially like physical contact with ______.
____ 25. There is something almost "magical" about my relationship with ______.
____ 26. I adore ______.
____ 27. I cannot imagine life without ______.
____ 28. My relationship with ______ is passionate.
____ 29. When I see romantic movies and read romantic books, I think of ______.
____ 30. I fantasize about ______.

Decision/Commitment Component

____ 31. I know that I care about ______.
____ 32. I am committed to maintaining my relationship with ______.
____ 33. Because of my commitment to ______, I would not let other people come between us.
____ 34. I have confidence in the stability of my relationship with ______.
____ 35. I could not let anything get in the way of my commitment to ______.
____ 36. I expect my love for ______ to last for the rest of my life.
____ 37. I will always feel a strong responsibility for ______.
____ 38. I view my commitment to ______ as a solid one.
____ 39. I cannot imagine ending my relationship with ______.
____ 40. I am certain of my love for ______.
____ 41. I view my relationship with ______ as permanent.
____ 42. I view my relationship with ______ as a good decision.
____ 43. I feel a sense of responsibility toward ______.
____ 44. I plan to continue my relationship with ______.
____ 45. Even when ______ is hard to deal with, I remain committed to our relationship.

Source: Sternberg, 1988. Reprinted by permission of Basic Books, Inc., Publishers, New York.

requires trust, loyalty, sharing of feelings, mutual respect and appreciation, lack of hypercriticality, and willingness to sacrifice. Companionate love is based on genuine knowledge of the other person, not idealization.

If companionate love blooms, a relationship can survive the fading of extremes of passion. At this point a couple can work together to meet each other's sexual as well as companionate needs. Skills can substitute for the excitement of novelty.

All in all, it sounds a bit like friendship.

In this chapter we have discussed interpersonal attraction—the force that initiates social contact. In the next chapter we follow the development of these social contacts into intimate relationships, particularly as they concern marriage and alternate styles of life.

Truth or Fiction Revisited

It is true that it is possible to be in love with someone who is not also a friend. However, when passion fades, the relationship might suffer.

adjustment and
modern life

COPING WITH LONELINESS

All the lonely people,
Where do they all come from?

FROM "ELEANOR RIGBY," A BEATLES SONG

Sexual attraction was only one reason that Candy and Stretch entered into their troubled relationship. Another was **loneliness.** Being lonely is not the same thing as being alone. Loneliness is a feeling state in which we sense ourselves as painfully isolated or cut off from other people. Being alone is a physical fact, and people with many close friends choose to be alone from time to time so that they can study, work, or just reflect on their feelings about being in the world.

People who are lonely, as compared to people who are not, show behavior patterns such as the following: They spend more time by themselves, are more likely to eat dinner alone and spend weekends alone, engage in fewer social activities, and are unlikely to be dating (Russell, 1982; Russell and others, 1980). Lonely people may report having as many friends as people who are not lonely, but upon closer examination, their friendships are relatively superficial. For example, they are not very likely to share confidences with their friends, and sometimes their "friends" are surprised to learn that lonely people consider them as friends (Williams & Solano, 1983).

Truth or Fiction Revisited

It is true that many lonely people report that they have as many friends as people who are not lonely do. But on closer examination, these "friendships" seem to be relatively superficial.

Loneliness tends to peak during adolescence, when most of us begin to replace close links to our parents with peer relationships. It is no secret that loneliness is linked to feelings of depression. But studies by Kiecolt-Glaser and Glaser of men in their first year following separation or divorce suggest that loneliness is also associated with suppressed immune-system functioning (Lear, 1987). Lonely people, it seems, are actually more likely to get sick!

Causes of Loneliness

The causes of loneliness are many and complex. Lonely people tend to have several of the following characteristics:

1. Lack of social skills, as shown through insensitivity to the feelings of others, not knowing how to make friends, or inability to cope with disagreements (Rubin, 1982)
2. Lack of interest in other people (Cutrona, 1982)
3. Lack of empathy (Lear, 1987)
4. High self-criticism concerning social behavior and expectation of failure in dealing with other people (Check & Melchior, 1990; Lear, 1987)

LONELINESS • A negative feeling state characterized by a sense of painful isolation from other people.

LONELINESS. "All the lonely people — where do they all come from?" Why are so many people lonely? Do they lack social skills? Do they fear rejection? Do they expect the worst from relationships? All of the above, and more. Psychologists have devised many cognitive-behavioral methods for overcoming loneliness, which are outlined in the text.

5. Failure to disclose information about themselves to potential friends (Berg & Peplau, 1982; Solano and others, 1982)
6. Cynicism about human nature
7. Demanding too much too soon, as characterized by misperception of other people as cold and unfriendly in the early stages of developing a relationship (Lear, 1987)
8. Pessimism about life in general
9. External locus of control (Anderson & Riger, 1991)

What To Do

Truth or Fiction Revisited

It is true that many people are lonely because of fear of rejection. Lowering the odds of rejection by enhancing social skills is one way of coping with loneliness.

Psychologists have found that cognitive and behavioral methods are helpful with lonely people. Cognitive therapy for loneliness combats feelings of pessimism, cynicism about human nature (Yes, many people are selfish and not worth knowing, but if we assume that everyone is like that, how can we develop fulfilling relationships?), and fear of social failure.

Social-skills training helps lonely people develop ways of initiating conversations, talking on the telephone, giving and receiving compliments, and handling disagreements without being submissive or aggressive (Rathus, 1978; Rook & Peplau, 1982). You can refresh yourself on assertiveness training by reviewing Chapter 4. In the next chapter we'll have some suggestions for enhancing date-seeking skills.

Also consider the following measures for making friends and combating loneliness:

1. *Make frequent social contacts.* Join committees for student-body activities. Engage in intramural sports. Join social-action groups such as Greenpeace. Join a club such as the psychology club, ski club, or photography club. Get on the school newspaper staff.
2. *Be assertive.* Express opinions. Smile and say "Hi" to interesting-looking people. Sit down next to people at the cafeteria, not in a corner by yourself.

3. *Become a good listener.* Ask people how they're "doing" and what they think about classes or events of the day. Then *listen* to them. Be reasonably tolerant of divergent opinions; no two people are exactly alike. Maintain eye contact and a friendly face.
4. *Let people get to know you.* Try exchanging opinions and talking about your interests. Sure, you'll "turn off" some people—we all do—but how else can you learn whether you have something in common?
5. *Fight fair.* Now and then a friend will disappoint you and you'll want to tell him or her about it, but do so fairly. Begin by asking your friend if it's okay to be honest about something. Then say, "I feel upset because you . . ." Ask if your friend realized that his or her behavior got you upset. Work together to figure out a way to avoid repetition. End by thanking your friend for solving the problem with you.
6. *Tell yourself that you're worthy of friends.* None of us is perfect. Each of us has a unique pattern of traits and insights, and you'll connect with more people than you might expect. Give them a chance.
7. *Go to the counseling center.* Thousands of students are lonely and don't know exactly what to do. Some know what to do but haven't quite got the courage. College counseling centers are familiar with the problem and are a valuable resource. ■

SUMMARY

1. **What is attraction?** Attraction is an attitude of liking or disliking. Attraction involves good or bad affective responses, approach or avoidance behavior, and positive or negative evaluations.

2. **What traits contribute to physical attractiveness in our culture?** In our society, slenderness is found attractive in both genders. Tallness is found attractive in men, but not in women. When we meet new people of the opposite gender, our first impressions focus on their clothing, figures, and faces, although men give the figure more priority than women do. Smiling enhances attractiveness.

3. **What are the stereotypes concerning attractive people?** There is an assumption that good things come in pretty packages. Physically attractive people are assumed to be more successful and well adjusted, but they are also perceived as more vain, self-centered, and given to extramarital affairs. Attractive people are less likely to be judged guilty of crimes. Attractive people have greater social skills. Research suggests that we expect attractive people to show greater social skills and that we elicit skillful behavior from them.

4. **How do attractive people interact socially?** Attractive men have more social interactions with women, but fewer with men than their less attractive peers. Attractive men and women are more likely to date and attend parties than less attractive peers and are more likely to find these activities satisfying.

5. **What is the role of attitudinal similarity in interpersonal attraction?** Experiments reveal that we are most attracted to people who are physically attractive and who share our attitudes.

6. **What is the matching hypothesis?** In keeping with the matching hypothesis, we are more likely to ask out and marry people who are similar to ourselves in attractiveness—largely because of fear of rejection. Examination of lonely hearts ads suggests that people are frequently willing to swap good looks for financial security. Traditional men and nontraditional women are most likely to be attracted to dates who hold similar attitudes.

7. **What are gay male and lesbian sexual orientations?** These are sexual orientations in which people are erotically interested in people of their own gender and are desirous of forming romantic relationships with them. Psychodynamic theory connects sexual orientation with resolution of the Oedipus complex. Learning theorists explain sexual orientation in terms of reinforcement of early sexual experiences. Evidence of a genetic contribution to sexual orientation is accumulating, and prenatal sex hormones may play a role in determining sexual orientation.

8. **What roles do friends play in our lives?** We share activities, interests, and confidences with friends.

9. **What qualities are sought in friends?** We seek loyalty, social support, and generally positive traits, such as frankness and intelligence.

10. **What styles of love are there?** There are several styles of love, including passionate (eros), storgic (affectionate), ludic (game-playing), pragmatic (practical), manic (possessive), and agapic (selfless) styles.

11. **What is passionate, or romantic, love?** Romantic love is a positive, intense emotion that develops in a culture that idealizes the concept. It involves arousal, presence of a person who is attractive to us, and some reason to label the arousal as love.

12. **What is the role of arousal in perceptions of love?** We think of ourselves as being in love when we experience physical arousal in the presence (actual or fantasized) of another person and have some reason to label that arousal love. Experiments support the view that feelings of attraction are enhanced when we experience higher levels of physiological arousal

and can attribute them to the presence of an attractive person.

13. **What factors contribute to loneliness?** Factors such as lack of social skills, fear of social rejection, cynicism about human nature, and general pessimism contribute to loneliness.

14. **What can we do to cope with loneliness?** In order to combat loneliness we can challenge our pessimism and our beliefs about other people. We can also develop social skills. In addition, we can join groups, express our ideas, become good listeners, and, when necessary, fight fair.

CHAPTER 14

Relationships and Communication: Getting From Here to There

TRUTH OR FICTION?

T F

- ☐ ☐ Small talk is a clumsy way to begin a new relationship.
- ☐ ☐ Rapid self-disclosure of intimate information is the best way to deepen a new relationship.
- ☐ ☐ We are less likely to try to iron out the wrinkles in our relationships when new partners are available to us.
- ☐ ☐ Marriage is losing its popularity as a style of life.
- ☐ ☐ Sexual problems are the single most powerful predictor of general marital dissatisfaction.
- ☐ ☐ Sophisticated young adults see nothing wrong with an extramarital fling.
- ☐ ☐ Being single has become a more common American lifestyle over the past few decades.
- ☐ ☐ Single people are "swingers."
- ☐ ☐ Cohabitation is most common among college students.
- ☐ ☐ Couples who were engaged for at least 3 years before getting married have happier marriages than couples who were engaged for only a year.
- ☐ ☐ Disagreement is destructive to a marriage.
- ☐ ☐ The most effective way of handling criticism from a marital partner is to be critical yourself.

OUTLINE

What do you say when you meet someone who is attractive? Do you fumble for words? Do opening lines come easily to you? Do you wait for the other person to take the lead?

Striking up a relationship requires some social skills. Those first few conversational steps can be big ones. In this chapter we first explore stages in the development of **intimate relationships.** Then we discuss the institution of marriage, which remains the goal for most Americans. We examine some alternatives to marriage, including the popular lifestyles of remaining single and cohabitation. Finally, we consider ways of enhancing intimate relationships, including improving communication skills.

STAGES IN RELATIONSHIPS

Relationships, like people, can be thought of as undergoing stages of development. According to Levinger's (1980) **ABCDE model,** relationships can develop through five stages: attraction, building, continuation, deterioration, and ending. During each stage, positive factors incline us to build or maintain the relationship. Negative factors motivate us to dissolve the relationship.

Attraction

Attraction occurs when people become aware of one another. Positive factors at this time include repeated meetings (often brought about by propinquity, or proximity), positive emotions, and personality factors such as a **need for affiliation.** Negative factors include lack of propinquity, negative emotions, and low need for affiliation.

Our impressions of another person are mostly visual during the stage of initial attraction, although we may overhear the other person in conversation or hear others talking about the person. We go from zero contact to initial attraction when we spot a new person across a crowded lunchroom, when we enter a class with new students, or when someone takes a job in a nearby office. We may purposefully go from zero contact to initial attraction through computer matchups or blind dates, but most often we meet other people by accident. And the greatest promoter of such accidents is propinquity.

Intimate relationships • Relationships characterized by sharing of inmost feelings. The term *physical intimacy* implies a sexual relationship.

ABCDE model • Levinger's theory of stages of development in a relationship: attraction, building, continuation, deterioration, and ending.

Building

After initial attraction comes the stage of building. Positive factors in building a relationship include matching physical attractiveness (see discussion of the **matching hypothesis** in Chapter 13), attitudinal similarity, and reciprocal positive evaluations. Negative factors—factors that might encourage us to dissolve the relationship—include nonequivalent physical attractiveness, attitudinal dissimilarity, and reciprocal negative evaluations.

How Do You Get Things Started? Many relationships get off the ground with opening lines and small talk. What do you say when you meet an attractive person and want to get to know him or her better?

Not-So-Small Talk: Auditioning for Love

Early in the stage of building a relationship, we experiment with **surface contact:** We seek common ground (e.g., attitudinal similarity, overlap of interests). We test our feelings of attraction. The decision as to whether or not to pursue the relationship may be made on the basis of **small talk.** At a cocktail party, people may flit about from person to person exchanging small talk, but now and then common ground is found and people begin to pair off.

The "Opening Line": How Do You Get Things Started?

One type of small talk is the greeting, or opening line. Greetings are usually preceded by eye contact. Reciprocation of eye contact may mean that the other person is willing to be approached. Avoidance of eye contact may mean that he or she is not willing, but it can also be a sign of shyness. In any event, if you would like to venture from initial attraction to surface contact, try a smile and some eye contact. When the eye contact is reciprocated, choose an opening line.

Knapp (1984, pp. 162–163) lists a variety of greetings, or opening lines. Here are some of them:

- Verbal "salutes," such as "Good morning"
- Personal inquiries, such as "How are you doing?" (more often pronounced, "How yuh doin'?")
- Compliments, such as "You're extremely attractive"
- References to your mutual surroundings, such as "What do you think of that painting?" or "This is a nice apartment house, isn't it?"
- Reference to people or events outside the immediate setting, such as "How do you like this weather we've been having?"
- References to the other person's behavior, such as "I couldn't help noticing you were sitting alone" or "I see you out on this track every Sunday morning"
- References to your own behavior, or to yourself, such as "Hi, my name is John Smith" (Use your own name, if you like.)

A simple hi or hello is very useful. A friendly glance followed by a cheerful hello ought to give you some idea as to whether your feelings of attraction are reciprocated. If the hello is returned with a friendly smile and inviting eye contact, follow it up with another greeting, such as a reference to your surroundings, the other person's behavior, or your name.

Truth or Fiction Revisited

It is not true that small talk is a clumsy way to begin a new relationship. Small talk can represent a useful search for common ground.

Exchanging "Name, Rank, and Serial Number"

Early exchanges are likely to include name, occupation, marital status, and hometown (Berger & Calabrese, 1975). This has been referred to as exchanging "name, rank, and serial number." Each person is seeking a sociological profile of the other in hope that common ground will provide the footing for pursuing a conversation. An unspoken rule seems to be at work: "If I provide you with some information about myself, you will reciprocate by giving me an equal amount of information about yourself," or "I'll tell you my hometown if you tell me yours" (Knapp, 1984, p. 170). If the person does not follow this rule, it may mean that he or she is not interested. But it could also be that he or she doesn't "know the rules" or that you are turning the other person off.

Need for affiliation • The need to have friends and belong to groups.

Matching hypothesis • The view that we tend to select dates and marriage partners at about our own level of physical attractiveness.

Surface contact • According to Levinger, a phase of a relationship in which we seek common ground and test mutual attraction.

Small talk • A superficial form of conversation that allows people to seek common ground to determine whether they wish to pursue a relationship. Small talk stresses breadth of topic coverage rather than in-depth discussion.

Small talk may sound "phony," but premature self-disclosure of personal information may repel the other person (Rubin, 1975).

SELF-DISCLOSURE: YOU TELL ME AND I'LL TELL YOU . . . CAREFULLY Opening up, or self-disclosure, is central to building intimate relationships. But when you meet someone for the first time, how much is it safe to disclose? If you hold back completely, you may seem disinterested or as if you're hiding something. But if you tell a new acquaintance that your hemorrhoids have been acting up, you are being too intimate too soon.

Truth or Fiction Revisited

It is not true that rapid self-disclosure of intimate information is the best way to deepen a new relationship. People who rapidly disclose intimate information are seen as maladjusted and phony. Timely disclosure is the key.

Research warns us against disclosing certain types of information too rapidly. In one study, **confederates** of the experimenters (Wortman and others, 1976) engaged in 10-minute conversations with subjects. Some confederates were "early disclosers." They shared intimate information early in the conversations. "Late disclosers" revealed the same information but toward the end of the conversation. Subjects rated early disclosers as less mature, less secure, less well adjusted, and more phony than the late disclosers. Subjects wished to pursue relationships with late disclosers but not early disclosers. In general, people who are considered well adjusted or mentally healthy disclose much about themselves but manage to keep a lid on information that could be self-damaging or prematurely revealing.

If the surface contact provided by small talk and initial self-disclosure has been mutually rewarding, partners in a relationship tend to develop deeper feelings of liking for each other (Collins & Miller, 1994). Self-disclosure may continue to build gradually through the course of a relationship as partners come to trust each other enough to share confidences and more intimate feelings.

Women commonly declare that men are reluctant to disclose their feelings (Tannen, 1990). Researchers find that men tend to be less willing to disclose their feelings, perhaps in adherence to the traditional "strong and silent" male stereotype. Yet gender differences in self-disclosure tend to be small. Overall, researchers find that women are only slightly more revealing about themselves than men (Dindia & Allen, 1992). We should thus be careful not to rush to the conclusion that men are always more "tight-lipped."

MUTUALITY: WHEN THE "WE," NOT THE "I'S," HAVE IT If small talk and self-disclosure are mutually rewarding, a couple may develop feelings of liking or love. If attraction and the establishment of common ground cause the couple to think of themselves as "we"—no longer as two "I's" touching at the surface only—they have reached what Levinger refers to as a condition of **mutuality.**

Before we explore advanced stages in relationships, read the box on page 427 for some advice on how readers can hone their date-seeking skills to begin relationships.

Continuation

Once a relationship has been built, it enters the stage of continuation. Factors that contribute to the continuation of a relationship (i.e., positive factors) include looking for ways to enhance variety and maintain interest (e.g., willingness to experiment with social activities and sexual practices), showing evidence of continuing positive evaluation (e.g., Valentine's Day cards), absence of jealousy, perceived equity (e.g., a fair distribution of homemaking, childrearing, and breadwinning chores), and mutual overall satisfaction. Negative factors at this stage include boredom (e.g., falling into a rut), showing evidence of negative evaluation (e.g., arguing, ignoring or forgetting anniversaries and other

CONFEDERATE • A person in league with the researcher who pretends to be a subject in an experiment.

MUTUALITY • According to Levinger, a phase of a relationship in which two people think of themselves as "we."

GET THAT DATE!

All right, now you're aware that your Mr. or Ms. Right exists. What do you do about it? How do you get him or her to go out with you?

Psychologists have found that we may enhance social skills, such as date-seeking skills, through *successive approximations.* That is, we engage in a series of tasks of graded difficulty. We fine-tune our skills and gain confidence at each level. As suggested in the context of assertiveness training (see Chapter 4), we may try out some skills through "behavior rehearsal" with friends. Friends can role-play the person we would like to ask out and provide candid "feedback" about our effectiveness.

Here are a series of graded tasks that can be practiced by readers who want to sharpen their date-seeking skills:

Easy Practice Level Select a person of the opposite gender with whom you are friendly, but one whom you have no desire to date. Practice making small talk. Tapes might include the weather, new films that have come into town, television shows, concerts, museum shows, political events, and personal hobbies.

Select a person you might have some interest in dating. Smile when you pass this person at work, school, or elsewhere, and say "Hi." Engage in this activity with other people of both genders to increase your skills at greeting others.

Speak into your mirror, using behavior rehearsal and role-playing. Pretend you are in the process of sitting next to the person you would like to date, say, at lunch or in the laundry room. Say "Hello" with a broad smile and introduce yourself. Work on the smile until it looks inviting and genuine. Make some comment about the food or the setting—the cafeteria, the office, whatever. Use a family member or confidant to obtain feedback about the effectiveness of your smile, tone of voice, posture, and choice of words.

Medium Practice Level Sit down next to the person you want to date and engage him or her in small talk. If you are in a classroom, talk about a homework assignment, the seating arrangement, or the instructor (be kind). If you are at work, talk about the building or some recent interesting event in the neighborhood. Ask your intended date how he or she feels about the situation. If you are at some group such as Parents Without Partners, tell the other person that you are there for the first time and ask for advice on how to relate to the group.

Engage in small talk about the weather and local events. Channel the conversation into an exchange of personal information. Give your "name, rank, and serial number"—who you are, your major field or your occupation, where you're from, why or how you came to the school or company. The other person is likely to reciprocate and provide equivalent information. Ask how he or she feels about the class, place of business, city, hometown, and so on.

Practice asking the person out before your mirror, a family member, or a confidant. You may wish to ask the person out for "a cup of coffee" or to a film. It is somewhat less threatening to ask someone out to a gathering at which "some of us will be getting together." Or you may rehearse asking the person to accompany you to a cultural event, such as an exhibition at a museum or a concert—it's "sort of" a date, but also less anxiety inducing.

Target Behavior Level Ask the person out on a date. If the person says he or she has a previous engagement or can't make it, you may wish to say something like, "That's too bad," or "I'm sorry you can't make it," and add something like, "Perhaps another time." You should be able to get a feeling for whether the person you asked out was just seeking an excuse or has a genuine interest in you and, as claimed, could not in fact accept the specific invitation.

Before asking the date out again, pay attention to his or her apparent comfort level when you return to small talk on a couple of occasions. If there is still a chance, the person should smile and return your eye contact. The other person may also offer you an invitation. In any event, if you are turned down twice, do not ask a third time. And don't catastrophize the refusal. Look up. Note that the roof hasn't fallen in. The birds are still chirping in the trees. You are still paying taxes. Then give someone else a chance to appreciate your fine qualities. ■

important dates), jealousy, perceived inequity (e.g., one partner desires a traditional distribution of chores, whereas the other partner prefers a nontraditional distribution), and mutual dissatisfaction.

JEALOUSY About 54 percent of adults describe themselves as jealous (Pines & Aronson, 1983). Possessiveness is a related concept that can also make a relationship stressful (Pinto & Hollandsworth, 1984). Highly jealous people are frequently dependent. They may also harbor feelings of inadequacy and report concerns about lack of sexual exclusiveness. (With the advent of AIDS, of course, sexual exclusivity reflects more than concern about how well one will measure up to one's partner's past lovers!) Feelings of jealousy make a relationship less rewarding and lower the individual's self-esteem (Mathes and others, 1985).

Unfortunately, many lovers—including many college students—play jealousy games. They tell their partners about their attractions to other people, they flirt openly, and they even make up stories to spur their partners to pay them more attention or to test the relationship. Another motive for game playing is revenge for a partner's infidelity.

EQUITY Equity basically involves feelings that one is getting as much from the relationship as one is giving to the relationship. We will make great sacrifices for people whom we love, but as a relationship continues over the years, the "accumulation of too much debt" makes the relationship lopsided and unwieldy. Even if the relationship is maintained, there are likely to be resentments that may be expressed openly or indirectly, as in loss of interest in sexual relations. Dating relationships and marriages are more stable when each partner feels that the relationship is equitable (Utne and others, 1984).

Deterioration

Deterioration is the fourth stage in the development of relationships—certainly not a stage that is desirable or inevitable. Positive factors that can prevent deterioration from occurring include investing time and effort in the relationship, working at improving the relationship, and being patient—that is, giving the relationship time for improvement. Negative factors that can advance deterioration include lack of investment of time and effort in the relationship, deciding to end the relationship, or simply allowing deterioration to continue unchecked. According to Levinger (1980), deterioration begins when either or both partners perceive the relationship as less desirable or worthwhile that it had once been.

ACTIVE AND PASSIVE RESPONSES TO A DETERIORATING RELATIONSHIP When partners perceive a relationship to be deteriorating, they respond in active or passive ways (Rusbult and others, 1986; Rusbult & Zembrodt, 1983). Active ways of responding include taking action that might improve the relationship (e.g., enhancing communication skills, negotiating differences, getting professional help) or deciding to end the relationship. Passive responses are essentially characterized by doing nothing—that is, by sitting back and waiting for the problems in the relationship to resolve themselves or to worsen to the point where the relationship ends.

As in coping with other sources of stress, we encourage readers to take an active approach to coping with deteriorating relationships. That is, don't just allow things to happen to you. Make a decision to work to improve things, and if improvement appears to be impossible, consider the possibility of dissolving the relationship. Later in the chapter we shall see that it is irrational (and harmful to a relationship) to believe that ideal relationships need not be worked on. No two of us are matched perfectly. Unless one member of the pair is a doormat, conflicts are bound to emerge. When they do, it is helpful to work to resolve them rather than to let them continue indefinitely or to pretend that they do not exist.

Ending

The ending of a relationship is the fifth and final of Levinger's stages. As with deterioration, it is not inevitable that relationships end. There are a number of factors that can help prevent a deteriorating relationship from ending: presence of some sources of rewards and satisfaction in the relationship, commitment to continue the relationship, and expectation that the relationship will ultimately work out well. Recall that our **self-efficacy expectations** affect how hard we will work to attain our goals: When we believe that our efforts to save a relationship are likely to meet with success, we will work harder at the relationship. A couple of other positive factors also increase the likelihood that a relationship will be saved: Each partner has already made a heavy investment in the relationship, and alternative partners are not readily available (Rusbult, 1983; Rusbult and others, 1982).

On the other hand, relationships are likely to come to an end when negative forces such as the following are in sway: There is little satisfaction in the relationship; alternative partners are available; the partners are not committed to maintaining the relationship, and they expect it to fail. We have a way of living up to our negative expectations as well as to our positive expectations.

The end of a relationship need not be a bad thing. When the partners are incompatible (dissimilar) in basic ways, and when sincere efforts to save the relationship have failed, ending the relationship may provide both partners with the opportunity to build satisfying relationships with other people. One of the reasons that we suggest taking an active approach to coping with deteriorating relationships is that they are then more likely to be dissolved—or fixed—before marriage takes place or while the partners are still young and have not yet established a family. As a consequence, fewer people are likely to "get hurt," and each person is more likely to attract a new, more compatible partner.

Truth or Fiction Revisited

It is true that we are less likely to try to iron out the wrinkles in our relationships when new partners are available to us. When new partners are available, we are not likely to be so strongly motivated to work out our problems with our current partners.

MARRIAGE

Poets and philosophers have been in less-than-perfect agreement about the institution of marriage:

> *It is a truth universally acknowledged, that a single man in possession of a good fortune must be in want of a wife.*
>
> JANE AUSTEN

> *Marriage is like life in this—that it is a field of battle, and not a bed of roses.*
>
> ROBERT LOUIS STEVENSON

> *It is so far from being natural for a man and woman to live in a state of marriage that we find all the motives which they have for remaining in that connection, and the restraints which civilized society imposes to prevent separation, are hardly sufficient to keep them together.*
>
> SAMUEL JOHNSON

SELF-EFFICACY EXPECTATIONS • Our beliefs that we can bring about desired ends through our own efforts.

MARRIAGE — BATTLEFIELD OR A BED OF ROSES?

For most married couples, neither of these extremes apply. Marriage may be flawed, but for most couples in the United States, it remains the preferred style of life.

When two people are under the influence of the most violent, most insane, most delusive, and most transient of passions, they are required to swear that they will remain in that excited, abnormal and exhausting condition until death do them part.

GEORGE BERNARD SHAW

One should always be in love. That is the reason one should never marry.

OSCAR WILDE

All tragedies are finished by death; all comedies are ended by a marriage.

LORD BYRON

Marriage is a great institution, but I'm not ready for an institution, yet.

MAE WEST

Truth or Fiction Revisited

It is not true that marriage is losing its popularity as a style of life. The great majority of us still get married.

Marriage is our most common lifestyle. In some cultures, such as among the Hindus of India, marriage is nearly universal. More than 99 percent of the women in that culture eventually get married. In the United States, the incidence of living together without getting married is on the rise. Nevertheless, 75 to 80 percent of the people in the United States do get married at least once (Saluter, 1995). Today, however, one in three people aged 25 to 34 has never been married (Saluter, 1995).

Throughout Western history, marriage has helped people to adjust to personal and social needs. Marriage regulates and legitimizes sexual relations. Marriage creates a home life and provides an institution for the financial support and socialization of children. Marriage provides a means of determining the father of a woman's children. So marriage also permits the orderly transmission of wealth from one generation to another, and from one family to another.

Notions such as romantic love, equality, and the radical concept that men, like women, should aspire to the ideal of faithfulness are recent additions to the structure of marriage. Today, with the high number of people who believe that sex is acceptable within the bounds of an affectionate relationship, the desire to engage in sexual intercourse is less likely to motivate marriage. But marriage still offers a sense of emotional and psychological security—a partner with whom to share feelings, experiences, and goals. Love is a major motive: In one study, 86 percent of the men and 80 percent of the women reported that they would not get married without love (Campbell & Berscheid, 1976). Among the highly educated, intimacy and companionship are central motives.

To Whom Do We Get Married? Are Marriages Made in Heaven or in the Neighborhood?

I *married beneath me—all women do.*

NANCY ASTOR

Our parents usually no longer arrange our marriages, even if they still encourage us to date the charming son or daughter of that solid couple at church. We tend to marry people to whom we are attracted. They are usually similar to us in physical attractiveness and hold similar attitudes on major issues. They also seem likely to meet our material, sexual, and psychological needs.

The concept of like marrying like is termed **homogamy.** In the United States, we only rarely marry people of different races or socioeconomic classes. According to the National Center for Health Statistics, only 2 percent of U.S. marriages are interracial (Dawson, 1992). According to Reiss (1980), 94 percent of married couples are of the same religion. We are even similar to our mates in height, eye color, intelligence, and personality traits (Buss, 1984; Caspi & Herbener, 1990; Lesnik-Oberstein & Cohen, 1984).

We also follow age homogamy. Husbands are 2 to 3 years older than their wives, on the average. Age homogamy may reflect the tendencies to get married soon after achieving adulthood and to select partners, such as classmates, with whom we have been in proximity. People who are getting remarried, or marrying for the first time at later ages, are less likely to marry partners so close in age.

By and large, however, we seem to be attracted to and to get married to the boy or girl (almost) next door in a quite predictable manner. Marriages seem to be made in the neighborhood—not in heaven. But as we see in the nearby Adjustment in the New Millennium feature, some marriages are made online.

The Marriage Contract: A Way of Clarifying Your Expectations

A*ny intelligent woman who reads her marriage contract, and then goes into it, deserves all the consequences.*

ISADORA DUNCAN

This feature is not about those "prenuptial agreements" that hit the front pages when wealthy couples obtain divorces. It is about informal marriage contracts that help couples clarify and communicate their expectations about their forthcoming unions. Such marriage contracts are *not* legally binding. They are intended to help prevent couples from entering nuptials with "blinders on."

Marriage contracts encourage couples to spell out their marital values and goals. If they desire a traditional marriage in which the husband acts as breadwinner while the wife cooks, cleans, and raises the kids, they can so specify. If they desire a marriage in which each partner has equal right to personal fulfillment through careers, or through extramarital relationships, this, too, can be specified. By discussing who will do what before they get

HOMOGAMY • The principle of like marrying like.

ADJUSTMENT *in the* NEW MILLENNIUM

Modem Matchmaking

Maybe they're not matches made in heaven—but close.

Love seekers are swarming into cyberspace.

Online has become the hot new place for finding sweethearts.

"The Net is what singles bars and mixers used to be," says Stanford University psychologist Al Cooper. "It's turning into the place for smart, eligible people to meet."

Bill Stanfield, 47, says he can't imagine marrying a woman after dating for only a few months. But he and his wife Jacqueline wed "and I've never regretted it. There were no surprises."

Of course, they didn't really date. They met online. "We spent hundreds and hundreds of hours communicating. There were no distractions. . . . I knew my first wife for three years before we got married, but I didn't know her as well as I knew Jackie."

The Stanfields' courtship, peculiar as it sounds, is hardly unique. Love at AOL, an area on America Online designed for searching singles, began in February 1996 with 50 "personal photo ads" posted; now there are 30,000, with more than 700,000 visits to the area monthly. It's the service's most heavily used content area, says Anne Bentley of AOL.

Match.Com, the largest independent dating service on the Web, offers 85,000 member "profiles," adding about 6,000 new faces weekly, corporate vice president Fran Maier reports.

Why such a crowd?

Surveys show Net traffic is dominated by affluent, educated 20- to 40-somethings, often overworked professionals for whom "dating isn't so great," Cooper says. Many are "solid people, good long-term prospects but not good 'daters.' The guys may be a little shy, they're not adept at small talk and don't have great pickup lines."

Finding someone online with similar interests and values can feel a lot easier than hitting bars or "meat market" clubs, Cooper says.

Net liaisons can be "female-friendly too, he adds: Communication is queen; sex stays off the front burner (at least for a while); and guys don't snub women if they're not 10-pluses.

A feeling of intimacy often develops quickly. Online talk lacks nonverbal cues that can put the brakes on romantic encounters, says Santa Clara, California, psychologist Coralie Scherer. Disapproving glances, tone-of-voice changes, hesitance, and breaks in eye contact aren't there. "All you know is what they tell you," says Scherer, so honesty can't make or break the deal.

The Stanfields, who married three months after meeting online, quickly realized they shared a passionate interest in hiking, camping and outdoor beauty. "We were really honest with each other about our personal likes and dislikes, what we want out of life," he says.

But honesty can also be elusive online. "Gender bending" is so common that experts estimate that two out of three "women" in many chat rooms, particularly the sex-oriented ones, are men.

Changing or omitting other truths is common. San Diego psychologist Marlene Maheu tells about one client, "an intelligent, sophisticated professional woman," who recently flew hundreds of miles to meet a Net boyfriend and found "not only was he obese, but he looked considerably older than he claimed to be."

Women play that game, too. New York psychologist Judy Kuriansky, host of a nationally syndicated radio call-in show, [took one] frantic call from a lady about to meet her longtime online sweetheart. She'd neglected to mention she weighed 350 pounds and wondered what to do next.

"Omissions" can be more diabolical—even dangerous. Kuriansky recently heard a self-satisfied Michigan woman describe her "hobby": She'd traveled coast to coast visiting cities she'd always wanted to see, at male expense, after feigning online interest in a throng of men.

Maheu tells of one client recently stalked after giving her phone number to an e-mail friend who used it to find her address. "I've heard of similar situations quite often," Maheu reports.

Several new "Netiquette" books advise how to bring cyberspace romantic encounters safely down to earth. *Looking for Love Online* by Richard Rogers suggests ways to sniff out phonies and crazies, and how to surround in-person meetings with safety nets and escape hatches.

Denise Beaupre, an Attleboro, Massachusetts, single mother, was pretty sure after three months of constant contact that her online friend, Scott Arena, was a wonderful guy. Still, she brought two friends to her first meeting (and one friend brought a taser gun).

"He was a sweetheart from the beginning though. . . . Look, I've been followed home from bars. Online is much safer, if you're careful about it."

Net romance may be most threatening to addicts, those online for many hours a week. And addicts may also behave most deceptively to would-be partners.

University of Pittsburgh psychologist Kimberly Young [reports a link] between Net addiction and clinical depression. Addicts may be "very vulnerable. They're quick to jump into relationships but sensitive to rejection."

Net addicts are also prone to donning online "personas" different from their everyday selves, her research shows.

"The chat rooms now are crowded with people who change their name daily. Who knows who they really are?" grumbles Joan Bounacos. She and husband George met online in 1990, "the good old days," married two years later and know a number of happily married couples matched years ago in cyberspace.

"Too many strange people are online now," Bounacos says, "and they want things to happen quick. . . . We were just good friends for a long time. What you bring to it is what you're going to get out of it."

That's exactly the point, argues psychologist Sherry Turkle, an MIT professor and author of *Life on the Screen*. She's studied several hundred adults who pursued relationships online.

"It's like a living Rorschach test," Turkle says. The absent nonverbal cues and isolation make Net encounters akin to [traditional] psychoanalysis in which patients "projected their greatest desires and fears" onto remote analysts. "They'll tell me, 'I was deceived,' and there is some deception. But when I look at their e-mail transcripts, I see less deception and more projection. These transcripts are often thin; people fill in the gaps as they wish."

How the gaps are filled in is the real tale. It's often a positive one. She's seen people use online encounters "as an occasion for self-reflection. They can learn a lot about themselves."

New York writer Sally Banks says she did just that. And Banks, alumna of several online liaisons, author of *Love Online*, is a bit embarrassed to admit she met her sweetheart, "the best relationship I've ever had," walking their dogs in Central Park. Her romantic forays on the Net harvested the self-revealing fodder for a real-world love.

"All those online relationships made me realize what I needed, what I was really looking for. I'll tell you what happened—I met myself online." ■

Reprinted with permission from Marilyn Elias, "Modem matchmaking," *USA Today*, August 14, 1997, pp. 1D, 2D.

married, couples gain insight into potential sources of conflict and have an opportunity to resolve them—or to reevaluate the wisdom of maintaining their marital plans. Couples include items like the following in the marriage contract:

1. Whether the wife will take her husband's surname or retain her maiden name, or whether one or both will use a hyphenated last name
2. How household tasks will be allocated and who will be responsible for particular everyday activities such as cleaning, washing, cooking, minor home repairs, and so forth
3. Whether or not the couple will have children, and if so, how many and at what time in the marital life cycle
4. What type(s) of contraception to use and who will take the responsibility for birth control measures
5. How child care responsibilities will be divided between the husband and wife, as well as the techniques they will employ in rearing their children
6. Whether they will rent or buy a place to live, and whether residential decisions will accommodate the husband's or wife's career plans (whether the husband, for example, would be willing to move to another city so that the wife could take advantage of a better job offer)
7. How the breadwinning functions will be divided, who will control the family finances, and how economic decisions will be made
8. How in-law relations will be handled, and whether vacations will be spent visiting relatives
9. What proportion of leisure activities will be spent apart from the spouse and what leisure activities will be spent together
10. How their sexual relations will be arranged and whether fidelity will be preserved
11. How they will go about changing specific parts of their marital contract as the marriage progresses

Sound like a tall job? It is. Some critics note that couples entering marriage at an early age are not in a position to foresee the consequences of their current ideas. Rigid adherence to contractual specifications may hamper rather than promote marital adjustment in such cases. Couples, they assert, must be free to change their minds on certain issues and to outgrow the declarations of youth.

True. But a marriage contract is a record of who was thinking what, and when—not a straitjacket. Such a contract can be used to explain *why* one partner now has certain expectations of the other. We need not demand absolute compliance. None of us need feel bound forever by ill-conceived or impractical declarations of youth. But it may be useful to have a record of early expectations, especially when they affect another person.

Marital Satisfaction: Is Everybody Happy?

After ecstasy, the laundry.

ANONYMOUS

How well do we adjust to marriage? Are married people happier than singles? How well do we adjust to children? Are parents happier than couples without children? First let us see what factors contribute to a happy, well-adjusted marriage.

Factors That Contribute to Marital Satisfaction Studies show that communicative ability is a prime component of satisfying relationships (Banmen & Vogel, 1985; Cleek & Pearson, 1985; Floyd & Markman, 1984). Patterns of communication among couples planning marriage predict marital adjustment 5½ years after vows are taken (Markman, 1981). Later in the chapter we shall describe ways of improving communication skills.

Other factors that contribute to marital happiness include spending focused time together (as during courtship), sharing of values, and flexibility (Klagsbrun, 1985). Physical intimacy, emotional closeness, and empathy also help (Tolstedt & Stokes, 1983; Zimmer, 1983).

Snyder (1979) constructed a questionnaire concerning areas of marital distress (see Table 14.1) and found that four areas strongly predicted overall satisfaction: *affective communication,* or expression of affection and understanding; *problem-solving communication,* or ability to resolve disputes; *sexual satisfaction;* and *agreement about finances,* or fighting over money management. The expression of affection and the capacity to resolve problems were consistently more important than problems in childrearing, a history of distress in one partner's immediate family, and sex.

Truth or Fiction Revisited

It is not true that sexual problems are the single most powerful predictor of general marital dissatisfaction. Poor communication, inability to resolve problems, and financial woes seem to be more prominent sources of dissatisfaction.

Some Polls on Marriage Marriage remains a satisfying style of life. In a 1987 Harris poll of 3,000 randomly selected Americans, 89 percent of the respondents, male and female, reported that their relationship with their partner was generally satisfying (Harris, 1988).

The Reverend Andrew M. Greeley (1990) reported the findings of a yet more recent Gallup telephone poll of 657 married couples. Four of five people in the sample stated that knowing what they know now, they would still marry the same person again. Other findings from the survey are noted in Table 14.2.

Table 14.1 Factors Contributing to Marital Satisfaction and Sample Questionnaire Items Used in Their Measurement

1. *Global Distress.* "My marriage has been disappointing in several ways."
2. *Affective Communication.* "I'm not sure my spouse has ever really loved me."
3. *Problem-Solving Communication.* "My spouse and I seem to be able to go for days sometimes without settling our differences."
4. *Time Together.* "My spouse and I don't have much in common to talk about."
5. *Disagreement About Finances.* "My spouse buys too many things without consulting me first."
6. *Sexual Dissatisfaction.* "My spouse sometimes shows too little enthusiasm for sex."
7. *Role Orientation.* "A wife should not have to give up her job when it interferes with her husband's career."
8. *Family History of Distress.* "I was very anxious as a young person to get away from my family."
9. *Dissatisfaction With Children.* "My children rarely seem to care how I feel about things."
10. *Conflict Over Childrearing.* "My spouse doesn't assume his (or her) fair share of taking care of the children."

Source: Snyder, 1979, p. 816.

Do You Endorse a Traditional or a Liberal Marital Role?

What do you believe? Should the woman cook and clean, or should housework be shared? Should the man be the breadwinner, or should each couple define their own roles? Are you traditional or nontraditional in your views on marital roles for men and women? ■

Directions: The following items permit you to indicate the degree to which you endorse traditional roles for men and women in marriage. Answer each one by circling the letters (AS, AM, DM, or DS), according to the code given below. Then turn to the key in the Appendix to find out whether you tend to be traditional or nontraditional in your views. (Ignore the numbers beneath the codes for the time being.) You may also be interested in seeing whether the answers of your date or your spouse show some agreement with your own.

AS = Agree Strongly
AM = Agree Mildly
DM = Disagree Mildly
DS = Disagree Strongly

1. A wife should respond to her husband's sexual overtures even when she is not interested.
   AS AM DM DS
   1 2 3 4
2. In general, the father should have greater authority than the mother in the bringing up of children.
   AS AM DM DS
   1 2 3 4
3. Only when the wife works should the husband help with housework.
   AS AM DM DS
   1 2 3 4
4. Husbands and wives should be equal partners in planning the family budget.
   AS AM DM DS
   1 2 3 4
5. In marriage, the husband should make the major decisions.
   AS AM DM DS
   1 2 3 4
6. If both husband and wife agree that sexual fidelity isn't important, there's no reason why both shouldn't have extramarital affairs if they want to.
   AS AM DM DS
   1 2 3 4
7. If a child gets sick and his wife works, the husband should be just as willing as she to stay home from work and take care of that child.
   AS AM DM DS
   1 2 3 4
8. In general, men should leave the housework to women.
   AS AM DM DS
   1 2 3 4
9. Married women should keep their money and spend it as they please.
   AS AM DM DS
   1 2 3 4
10. In the family, both of the spouses ought to have as much say on important matters.
   AS AM DM DS
   1 2 3 4

Source: Karen Oppenheim Mason, with the assistance of Daniel R. Denison and Anita J. Schacht, *Sex-Role Attitude Items and Scales From U.S. Sample Surveys,* Rockville, MD: National Institute of Mental Health, 1975, pp. 16–19.

TABLE 14.2 PERCENT OF MARRIED PEOPLE WHO REPORT THAT THEY ENGAGE IN THE FOLLOWING ACTIVITIES TOGETHER—AT LEAST "SOMETIMES"

ACTIVITY	*PERCENT*
Talking privately and intimately	91%
Giving back rubs or massages	68
Praying	61
Working out or participating in sports	43
Watching X-rated videotapes	21
Wearing erotic undergarments	20
Swimming in the nude	19

Source: Based on data from Greeley, 1990.

Affairs: Who, What, and Truth and Consequences

> *Women seek soul mates; men seek playmates. Women believe that their affair is justified when it is for love; men, when it's* not *for love.*
>
> —JANIS ABRAHMS SPRING (1997)

There are times when it seems that nearly every married person is having an affair (Alterman, (1997). When French President François Mitterand died a couple of years ago, his wife, his mistress, and his illegitimate daughter were numbered among the mourners. Journalist Eric Alterman (1997) mentions the examples of Kelly Flinn (who was forced to resign from the armed services), Frank Gifford (who retired from *Monday Night Football* in 1998), Bill Cosby (who admitted to an affair but denied that the woman's daughter was his child), and actor Eddie Murphy. And then there was the brouhaha about Bill Clinton and Gennifer Flowers (with whom he admitted to having an affair while he was governor of Arkansas) and, more recently, Monica Lewinsky.

How many people in the United States actually have affairs? Why do people have affairs? Are they for sex only? What are the effects of an affair on a marriage or other primary relationship?

WHO HAS AFFAIRS? How many people "cheat" on their spouses? Viewers of TV talk shows may get the impression that everyone cheats, but surveys paint a different picture. In surveys conducted between 1988 and 1996 by the National Opinion Research Center, about one husband in four or five, and one wife in eight, admit to marital infidelity (Alterman, 1997; "Cheating," 1993). Similarly, more than 90 pecent of the married women and 75 percent of the married men in the NHSLS study reported *remaining loyal* to their mates (Laumann and others, 1994). The vast majority of people who were cohabiting also reported that they were loyal to their partners (Laumann and others, 1994). What can we conclude? Perhaps two things: One is that men are about twice as likely as women to admit to affairs. Yet only a minority of married people admit to affairs.

Those are the conclusions, but note that we said "*admit* to affairs." Having presented the percentages of reported affairs, the fact is that these reports

FIGURE 14.1
WHY DO PEOPLE HAVE AFFAIRS?
Women are more likely than men to justify affairs for reasons of love. Men are more likely than women to cite sexual excitement as the reason.
Sources: Glass & Wright, 1992; Townsend, 1995.

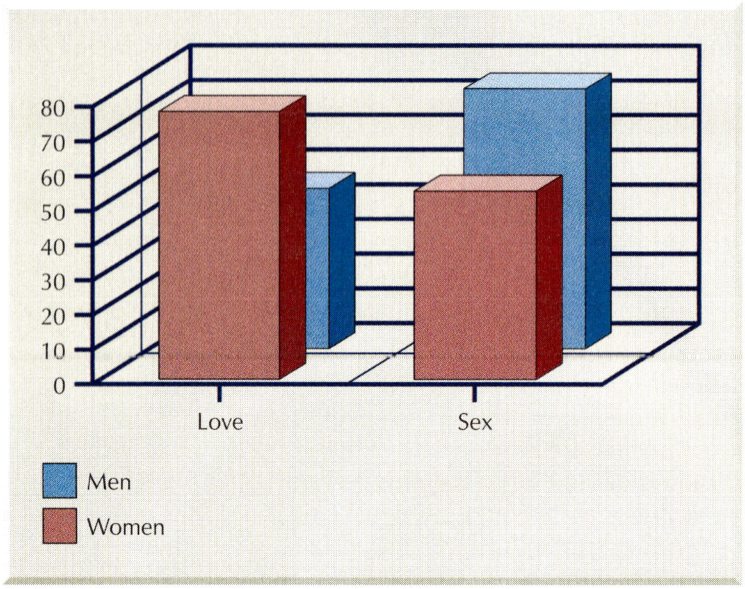

cannot be verified. People may be reluctant to reveal they have "cheated" on their spouses even when they are assured of anonymity. There is likely to be an overall tendency to underreport the incidence of extramarital sex.

WHY DO PEOPLE HAVE AFFAIRS? Some people have affairs for the sake of variety (Lamanna & Riedmann, 1997). Some seek to break the routine of a confining marriage. Others have affairs for reasons akin to the nonsexual reasons sometimes given by adolescents—for example, as a way of expressing hostility (in this case, toward a spouse and not a parent) or as a way of retaliating for injustice. People who have affairs often report that they are not happy with their marital relationships, but curiosity and the desire for personal growth are cited as more common reasons than marital dissatisfaction. Some middle-aged people have affairs to boost their self-esteem or to prove that they are still attractive.

Sexual motives are frequently less pressing than the desire for emotional closeness. Some women say they are seeking someone to whom they can talk or with whom they can communicate (Lamanna & Riedmann, 1997). There is a notable gender difference here. According to Janis Abrahms Spring, author of *After the Affair* (a self-help book designed to help people save their marriages after an affair), men may be seeking sex in affairs ("playmates"). Women, however, are usually seeking "soul mates." Spring (1997) notes that "women believe that their affair is justified when it is for love; men, when it's *not* for love." As you can see in Figure 14.1, 77 percent of the women who have had affairs cite love as their justification, versus 43 percent of the men (Townsend, 1995). Men who have had affairs are more likely to cite a need for sexual excitement as a justification than women are—75 percent versus 55 percent (Glass & Wright, 1992).

These data support the view that women are less accepting of sex without emotional involvement than men are (Townsend, 1995). Men are more likely than women to "separate sex and love; women appear to believe that love and sex go together and that falling in love justifies sexual involvement" (Glass & Wright, 1992, p. 361). Men (whether single, married, or cohabiting) are also generally more approving of extramarital affairs than are women (Glass &

Wright, 1992). But note that these are all *group* differences. Many individual men are primarily interested in the extramarital relationship rather than the sex per se. Similarly, many women are out for the sex and not the relationship.

What Are the Attitudes of Americans Toward Affairs? The sexual revolution does not seem to have changed attitudes toward extramarital affairs. About nine out of ten Americans say that affairs are "always wrong" or "almost always wrong" (Alterman, 1997). Three out of four Americans say that extramarital sex is "always wrong" (Berke, 1997). Another one in seven says that it is "almost always wrong." Only about 1 percent say that extramarital affairs are "not at all wrong." Most married couples embrace the value of monogamy as the cornerstone of their marital relationship (Blumstein & Schwartz, 1990).

Truth or Fiction Revisited

It is not true that today's sophisticated young people see nothing wrong with an occasional fling. The sexual revolution never extended itself to affairs—at least among the majority of people who have primary relationships. The sexual revolution may have liberalized attitudes toward premarital sex, but the message here seems to be that once people make commitments, they are expected to keep them.

How Do Affairs Affect a Primary Relationship? The discovery of infidelity can evoke strong emotional responses. The spouse (or cohabitant) may be filled with anger, jealousy, even shame. Feelings of inadequacy and doubts about one's attractiveness and desirability may surface. Infidelity may be seen by the betrayed individual as a serious breach of trust and intimacy. Primary relationships that are not terminated in the wake of the disclosure may survive only in damaged form (Charny & Parnass, 1995).

The harm an affair does to a primary relationship may reflect the meaning of the affair to the individual and his or her partner. Deborah Lamberti, director of a counseling and psychotherapy center in New York City, points again to women's traditional intertwining of sex with relationships; she argues that "men don't view sex with another person as a reason to leave a primary relationship" (1997, pp. 131–132). Betrayed women may recognize this and be able to tell themselves that their partners are sleeping with someone else just for physical reasons. But women are more concerned about remaining monogamous. Therefore, if a woman is sleeping with another man, she may already have a foot out the door, so to speak. Alterman (1997) also notes that a woman's affair may be an unforgivable blow to a man's ego or pride. A woman may be more likely to see her partner's transgression as a threat to the structure of her life.

If a person has an affair because the relationship is deeply troubled, the affair may be one more factor that speeds its dissolution. The effects on the relationship may depend on the nature of the affair. It may be easier to understand that one's partner has fallen prey to an isolated, unplanned encounter than to accept an extended affair (Charny & Parnass, 1995). In some cases the discovery of infidelity stimulates the couple to work to improve their relationship. If the extramarital activity continues, of course, it may undermine the couple's efforts to restore their relationship. Affairs frequently lead to divorce, and we discuss that topic next.

DIVORCE

Whenever I date a guy, I think, is this the man I want my children to spend their weekends with?

Comedian Rita Rudner

In 1920, about one marriage in seven ended in divorce. By 1960 this figure had risen to one in four. Today nearly half of the marriages in the United States end in divorce (Kirn, 1997; Laumann and others, 1994). More than one quarter (27 percent) of children below the age of 18 live in single-parent households

(Saluter, 1995). Divorced women outnumber divorced men, in part because men are more likely to remarry (Saluter, 1995).

The relaxation of legal restrictions on divorce, especially the introduction of the so-called no-fault divorce, has made divorces easier to obtain. Until the mid-1960s, adultery was the only legal grounds for divorce in New York State. Other states were equally strict. But now no-fault divorce laws have been enacted in nearly every state, allowing a divorce to be granted without a finding of marital misconduct. The increased economic independence of women has also contributed to the rising divorce rate. More women today have the economic means of breaking away from a troubled marriage. Today, more people consider marriage an alterable condition than in prior generations.

People today hold higher expectations of marriage than did their parents or grandparents. They expect marriage to be personally fulfilling as well as expecting it to be an institution for rearing children. Many demand the right to be happy in marriage. The most common reasons given for a divorce today are problems in communication and a lack of understanding. Years ago it was more likely to be lack of financial support.

Why do Americans believe that the divorce rate has risen so high? A *Time*/CNN Poll asked a national sample, "Which is the main reason for the increase in the number of divorces?" Answers are shown in Table 14.3. Respondents were almost equally split in their answer to the question, "Do you believe it should be harder than it is for married couples to get a divorce?" Half (50 percent) said yes, and 46 percent said no.

The Cost of Divorce

Divorce usually has financial and emotional repercussions. When a household splits, the resources may not maintain the former standard of living for both partners. The divorced woman who has not pursued a career may find herself competing for work with younger, more experienced people. The divorced man may not be able to manage alimony and child support and also establish a new home of his own.

Adjustment to divorce can be more difficult than adjustment to death of a spouse. When a spouse dies, legalities are minimal. But divorce may require legal conflict, reams of documents, and seemingly endless waiting periods. (The use of **divorce mediation,** in which the couple are guided through the decisions

TABLE 14.3 THE MAIN REASON FOR THE INCREASE IN THE NUMBER OF DIVORCES IN THE UNITED STATES, ACCORDING TO A *TIME*/CNN POLL

REASON	*PERCENT OF RESPONDENTS CITING REASON AS MAIN REASON*
Marriage is not taken seriously by the couples	45%
Society has become more accepting of divorced people	15
It is easier to get divorced than it used to be	10
People who get divorced are selfish	9
Changes in the earning power of women and men	7
All of the above	9

Source of data: Walter Kirn, The ties that bind, *Time,* August 18, 1997, pp. 48–50.

DIVORCE MEDIATION • A process in which a couple getting a divorce are guided rationally and as amicably as possible through the decisions that must be made.

required by divorce in a cooperative spirit rather than as adversaries, may help reduce some of the stresses of the process [Schwebel and others, 1982].) When someone dies, the rest of the family remains intact. After a divorce, children and others may choose up sides and assign blame. After a death, people receive "compassionate leave" from work and are expected to be less productive for a while. After a divorce, they are commonly criticized. Death is final, but divorced people may nourish "What ifs?" and vacillate in their emotions.

People who are separated and divorced have the highest rates of mental and physical illness in the population (Bloom and others, 1978; Vernbrugge, 1979). Divorced people are subject to greater stress and feel that they exert less control over their lives (Doherty, 1983). Feelings of failure as a spouse and parent, loneliness, and uncertainty prompt feelings of depression. The incidence of divorce is linked closely to the suicide rate (Stack, 1980).

The hardest aspect of divorce may be separating psychologically from one's "ex." Severing links to the past and becoming a whole, autonomous person once more—or in the case of women who had held traditional attitudes, for the first time—can be the greatest challenge but also the most constructive aspect of adjustment to divorce.

ALTERNATE STYLES OF LIFE

Although marriage remains the ideal for most Americans, some choose not to get married. In this section we explore two alternatives to marriage: remaining single and cohabitating. But first note the following "Adjustment in a World of Diversity" feature. It points out that Japan has added a new wrinkle to the single life, as well as to automobiles and VCRs. Single Japanese, that is, may not be caroling "Silent Night, Holy Night" on Christmas Eve.

Adjustment in a World of DIVERSITY

Snug in Their Beds for Christmas Eve—In Japan, December 24th Has Become the Hottest Night of the Year[1]

For young people all over the Christian world, Christmas Eve is a night of magic and wonder. In Japan as well, Christmas Eve has become immensely important—but for rather different reasons.

It has become the sexiest night of the year.

Japanese popular culture has made Christmas Eve a night when every unmarried person must have a date, and it is now expected that the date include an overnight stay. For weeks prior to this night, TV shows, magazines, and manga (adult comic books) are full of reports and advice on which hotels are best for young couples to stay in on Christmas Eve, what each partner should wear, and where the pair should have breakfast the following morning.

Virtually every major hotel in Tokyo is sold out months in advance of December 24th. At the popular Sheraton Grande Hotel, which installed a larger-than-life plastic Nativity scene in its lobby to add to the ambiance, all rooms are reserved—and paid for in advance—by April.

---

[1] Adapted from Reid, T. R. (1990, December 24). Snug in their beds for Christmas Eve: in Japan, Dec. 24 has become the hottest night of the year, *The Washington Post.*

ADJUSTMENT *in the* NEW MILLENNIUM

Modern Bride and *Parenting*, or *Divorce?* Which Will Help You Cope With Relationships in the New Millennium?

Dan Couvrette was married for 10 years. Then in 1994 he was divorced. So he left Canada's largest bridal magazine, *Wedding Bells*, and founded another magazine, *Divorce*, 2 years later. Although half the marriages in the United States end in divorce, *Divorce* is what you call a niche magazine. Its circulation is small, only 80,000 to 90,000 copies a year, and many of these are given away by divorce support groups, churches, lawyers, and divorce mediators.

Divorce is one of many glossy self-help magazines serving a specialized clientele. Others include *POZ*, a magazine for people infected with HIV; *MAMM*, for women with cancer; *Mainstream* and *We*, meeting the needs of physically disabled people; and *Interrace*, intended for interracial couples and their families.

But why *Divorce?* "In my experience," says Couvrette (cited in Stoltz, 1998), "I wanted to know: How am I going to get through it? Is there any hope at the end of it? What steps should I take to make my life better?" These are the kinds of questions *Divorce* is intended to help answer. The magazine is filled with helpful stories on matters such as financial aspects of divorce, questions to ask when negotiating, what to do and what not to do, advice on buying a new home, and how to find a good real estate agent. Recent stories were titled "Divorce Without Devastation," "Stress Busters," "Mediation: It Works!" "Safe at Home!" "Don't Divorce Your Retirement Plans!" and "Jump Start: Back to School."

Many copies of *Divorce* are distributed free, so *Divorce*, like many other magazines, must be supported by its advertisers to be successful. Who advertises in *Divorce?* Advertisers who focus on helping people through divorce and its aftermath include divorce lawyers, therapists, real estate agents, moving services, dating services, private investigators, "forensic accountants" (who claim that they can shed light on a spouse's hidden assets or unexplained hotel expenses), financial planners, book publishers, adult educators, hair and makeover stylists, spas, and resorts. *Divorce* also reaches out to advertisers in areas like automobiles, insurance and banking, and fitness and nutrition. Yet Couvrette admits that he would probably not expect Coca-Cola to advertise in *Divorce*. "It's not like people suddenly start to drink Coke after a divorce," he says, "but they might start taking Prozac." ■

"Christmas Eve is now important as a night for making love," complains poet and social critic Hazuki Kajiwara. This is such a widely accepted aspect of the day here known as *eebu*, the Japanese pronunciation of "eve," that December 24th is frequently referred to as "H-day." The letter *H*, taken from the English word "hormone," is a common symbol here for sex.

The *eebu* phenomenon is carried out in an intensely materialistic, free-spending atmosphere, reflecting the commercial nature of the Christmas season in Japan. In a country less than 1 percent Christian, December 25th is just another working day, yet stores and restaurants here have more Christmas trees, wreaths, and reindeer on display than most places in the United States.

For a couple's Christmas Eve fling, the man is expected to bear all costs. Many "salary men" save all year for this one date. The news magazine *Asahi Journal* printed a breakdown of a fairly standard "Eve course": When the man arrives to pick up his date, he should present her with a $215 silver heart pendant from Tiffany's and then take her out for an evening at Tokyo Disneyland, where admission and extras will cost $100 or so. Then it's on to dinner for two at a French or American restaurant ($385) and a room for the night overlooking Tokyo Bay at the Hilton or the Sheraton Grande ($300, or $650 for a suite). Breakfast in the hotel coffee shop should cost only $35, but a rental limousine to take the couple to their homes so they can quickly change and go to work will cost another $150.

Things would be cheaper if the couple could just go to one of the thousands of "love hotels" here, where a room costs about $30 for two hours. But the popular magazines have decreed that this is too tacky for such a special night.

But *eebu* is hardly a free ride for Japanese women. They must pay the emotional cost.

Women between college age and their mid-thirties have more money and more independence today than ever before in Japanese history. But they are losing their connection to family and peer groups and are struggling to survive on their own.

"Behind the traditional Japanese groupism is a fear of being alone," says Hikaru Hayashi, senior research director at the Hakuhodo Institute, a sociological think tank. For single women, "Christmas Eve enhances the fear that they are not rooted in society."

With everybody making elaborate plans for *eebu*, it is a social necessity for single women to have a date that night. The tribulations of those who don't have become the subject of enormous media attention.

A travel agency has been advertising excursion trips for singles under the headline "Find a Boyfriend by Christmas!" The Tokyo broadcasting system ran a 12-part miniseries called "Christmas Eve." The story concerned a young "office lady" who listened to her friends chattering about the fancy restaurants and hotels they were going to for *eebu* but was ashamed to admit she had no date. In the final episode, a young man called her at the last minute. The two walked off happily into the night, presumably in search of a hotel with a vacant room.

The idea that it might be shameful for a single woman to spend the night with her date is less commonly expressed, but it does occur. Sampei Sato, the editorial cartoonist for the newspaper *Asahi Shimbun*, devoted his space one day to an appeal to young unmarried women to sleep at home rather than in a hotel on Christmas Eve.

The new view of *eebu* has increased the Japanese people's belief that they are unique. "In all the world," said the lead-in to a TV talk show, "only Japan has turned the day before Christmas into a day for sex."

The Singles Scene: Swinging, Lonely, or Both?

Recent years have seen a dramatic increase in the numbers of young adults who are single. Being single, not marriage, is the nation's most common lifestyle among people in their early twenties. Between 1970 and 1988 the percentage of single men in their early twenties rose to nearly 80 percent from about 55 (U.S. Bureau of the Census, 1990). The percentage of single women in their early twenties rose to 61 percent from 36 percent. By their late twenties, some 43 percent of the men and 30 percent of the women in the United States remain unmarried (U.S. Bureau of the Census, 1990).

Several factors contribute to these figures. For example, people are getting married at later ages, more people are going for advanced education, and many

Truth or Fiction Revisited

It is true that being single has become a more common American lifestyle over the past few decades. However, much of the increase stems from the fact that people are delaying marriage. Although more couples are living together without getting married, marriage has not gone out of fashion.

women are placing career objectives ahead of marriage (Lamott, 1993; Lawson, 1993).

Today, however, many young people no longer view being single as a stage of life that precedes marriage. Career women, for example, are no longer financially dependent on men, so a number of them have chosen to remain single (Lamott, 1993; Lawson, 1993). Many young adults are single by choice, and they view being single as an alternative, open-ended lifestyle (Lamott, 1993; Lawson, 1993). Although most single mothers in the United States are young and poorly educated, larger numbers of single, older, well educated professional women have chosen to become mothers in the 1990s (Lamott, 1993; Lawson, 1993). Lamott (1993) points out that there remains a stigma to single mothers; they are frequently referred to as "unwed mothers." However, she notes that unmarried fathers are more likely to be referred to as "single parents," "heroes," even "saints."

There is no single "singles scene." Being single is varied in intent and style of life. For some, it means singles bars and a string of one-night affairs. Some "swinging singles" do not want to be "trapped" with a single partner. They opt for many partners for the sake of novel sexual stimulation, the personal growth that can be attained through meeting many people, and the maintenance of independence. Yet many singles have become disillusioned with frequent yet casual sexual involvements. Singles bars provoke anxieties about physical and sexual abuse, fear of sexually transmitted diseases, and feelings of alienation that diminish the excitement of opportunities for sexual experience.

Truth or Fiction Revisited

It is not true that single people are swingers. The statement is too general to be accurate. Single people follow a number of different kinds of styles of life.

Other single people limit sex to affectionate relationships only. Many singles are delaying marriage until they find Mr. or Ms. Right. Some singles achieve emotional security through a network of friends.

Many single people find that being single is not always as free as it seems. Some complain that employers and co-workers view them with skepticism and are reluctant to assign them responsibility. Their families may see them as selfish, as failures, or as sexually loose. Many single women complain that once they have entered their mid-twenties, men are less willing to accept a "No" at the end of a date. Men assume that the women are no longer virgins and that their motives for saying no are to play games or to snare them into marriage.

The goals and values that seem rock solid in people's twenties may be shaken in their thirties. The singles scene, too, can pall. In their late twenties and thirties, many singles decide that they would prefer to get married and have children. For women, of course, the "biological clock" may seem to be running out during the thirties. Yet some people, men and women alike, choose to remain single for a lifetime.

Remaining single is considered one kind of nontraditional lifestyle. During the "Swinging Sixties" and the 1970s, many Americans experimented with other nontraditional lifestyles, such as **open marriage, group marriage,** and **communes.** Today, open and group marriage and communes, while still found here and there, have something of a nostalgic ring to them. But another nontraditional lifestyle, **cohabitation,** remains widespread.

OPEN MARRIAGE • A marriage in which partners allow each other to develop intimate, sexual relationships with outsiders.

GROUP MARRIAGE • An arrangement in which three or more people share an intimate sexual relationship.

COMMUNE • A communal living arrangement that is usually based on perpetuating a certain philosophical approach to social and economic relationships.

COHABITATION • An intimate relationship in which POSSLQs (pronounced "POSS-'l-cues") live as though they are married, but without legal sanction.

Cohabitation: *There's Nothing That I Wouldn't Do If You Would Be My POSSLQ*

There's Nothing That I Wouldn't Do If You Would Be My POSSLQ is the name of a book by CBS newsperson Charles Osgood. *POSSLQ?* That's the unromantic abbreviation for "Person of Opposite Sex Sharing Living Quarters"—the official term used for cohabiters by the U.S. Bureau of the Census.

Some social scientists believe that cohabitation has become accepted within the social mainstream (Bumpass, 1995). Whether or not this is so, society in general has become more tolerant of it. We seldom hear cohabitation referred to as "living in sin" or "shacking up" anymore. People today are more likely to refer to cohabitation with value-free expressions such as "living together."

Perhaps the current tolerance reflects societal adjustment to the increase in the numbers of cohabiting couples. Or perhaps the numbers of cohabiting couples have increased as a consequence of tolerance. The numbers of households consisting of unmarried adults of the other sex living together in the United States doubled between 1980 and the early 1990s (Steinhauer, 1995). They grew from 1.6 million couples in 1980 to 2.9 million couples in 1990 and 3.3 million in 1992.

WHO COHABITS? Much of the attention on cohabitation has been focused on college students living together, but cohabitation is more prevalent among the less well educated and less affluent classes (Willis & Michael, 1994). The cohabitation rate is about twice as high among African American couples as among White couples. Fifty-five percent of male cohabitors and 41 percent of female cohabitors have never been married (U.S. Bureau of the Census, 1990). Children live with about one cohabiting couple in three (Saluter, 1995).

Truth or Fiction Revisited

It is not true that cohabitation is most common among college students. Cohabitation is actually more prevalent among the less well educated and less affluent.

About one cohabitor in three is divorced. Divorced people are more likely than people who never married to enter cohabiting relationships. Apparently, the experience of divorce makes some people more willing to share their lives than their bank accounts (Steinhauer, 1995).

Willingness to cohabit is related to more liberal attitudes toward sexual behavior, less traditional views of marriage, and less traditional views of gender roles (Huffman and others, 1994). Cohabitors are less likely than married people to attend church regularly (Laumann and others, 1994). Six out of 10 male cohabitors and nearly seven out of 10 female cohabitors are under 35 years of age (Saluter, 1995). Yet the greatest increase since 1980 in the numbers of people cohabiting has not been among young romantics, but among people age 35 and above (Bumpass, 1995).

WHY DO PEOPLE COHABIT? Cohabitation, like marriage, is an alternative to the loneliness that can accompany living alone. Cohabitation, like marriage, creates a home life. Romantic partners may have deep feelings for each other but not be ready to get married. Some couples prefer cohabitation because it provides a consistent relationship without the legal entanglements of marriage (Steinhauer, 1995).

Many cohabitors feel less commitment toward their relationships than married people do (Nock, 1995). Ruth, an 84-year-old woman, has been living with her partner, age 85, for 4 years. "I'm a free spirit," she says. "I need my space. Sometimes we think of marriage, but then I think that I don't want to be tied down" (cited in Steinhauer, 1995, p. C7).

Ruth's comments are of interest because they counter stereotypes of women and older people. However, it is more often the man who is unwilling to make a marital commitment (Yorburg, 1995), as in the case of Mark. Mark, a 44-year-old computer consultant, lives with Nancy and their 7-year-old daughter, Janet. Mark says, "We feel we are not primarily a couple but rather primarily individuals who happen to be in a couple. It allows me to be a little more at arm's length. Men don't like committing, so maybe this is just some sort of excuse" (cited in Steinhauer, 1995, p. C7).

Economic factors come into play as well. Emotionally committed couples may decide to cohabit because of the economic advantages of sharing household expenses. Cohabiting individuals who receive public assistance (Social Security or welfare checks) risk losing support if they get married (Steinhauer, 1995). Some older people live together rather than marry because of resistance from adult children (Yorburg, 1995). Some children fear that a parent will be victimized by a needy senior citizen. Others may not want their inheritances to come into question or may not want to decide where to bury the remaining parent. Younger couples may cohabit secretly to maintain parental support that they might lose if they were to get married or to openly reveal their living arrangements.

STYLES OF COHABITATION People come to cohabit in various ways, leading to different "styles of cohabitation" (Kammeyer and others, 1990):

1. *Part-Time/Limited Cohabitation.* In this style, people start dating and one person starts spending more time at the other's residence. As the relationship deepens, she or he stays overnight more frequently. The visitor gradually brings in more clothes and other belongings. The couple thus drift into cohabitation whether or not they arrive at a decision to do so. Since they did not make a formal arrangement, they may not have resolved issues such as whether to share expenses or date others. This style of cohabitation often ends because of an outside event, such as the end of the school year. Part-time/limited cohabitation can also lead to premarital cohabitation, however.
2. *Premarital Cohabitation.* In premarital cohabitation, people who expect to get married, or who may have made the decision to get married, live together beforehand. Premarital cohabitation sometimes takes the form of a *trial marriage,* in which the couple decide to test their relationship before making a more permanent commitment.
3. *Substitute Marriage.* In this style, the couple decides to make a long-term commitment to live together without getting married. Some people enter into substitute marriages because of fear of a legal commitment. For example, a divorced person may be reluctant to enter another marriage. Some people may believe that a marriage certificate (a "piece of paper") is not necessary to certify their relationship. Many poor people and widows and widowers cohabit rather than get married because marriage would compromise their eligibility for welfare or Social Security payments.

About 40 percent of cohabiting couples eventually marry (Laumann and others, 1994). The majority of cohabiting couples break up within 3 years. Termination of the relationship, not marriage, is the more likely outcome of cohabitation (Willis & Michael, 1994).

Despite experiments such as cohabitation, most Americans remain committed to the ideal of marriage. Many evaluate marriage in much the same way that Winston Churchill evaluated democracy. It's flawed, frustrating, and just plain awful, but when compared to the alternatives, most people still prefer it. The fate of marriage in the new millennium has not yet been written.

adjustment and modern life

MAKING IT WORK: WAYS OF COPING WITH CONLICT IN A RELATIONSHIP

Whether you are married or cohabiting, conflict is inevitable. Conflicts occur over things like money, communication, personal interests, sex, in-laws, friends, and children. If couples have not spelled out their expectations of one another in advance, they are also faced with the chore of deciding who does what. In traditional marriages, responsibilities are delegated according to gender-role stereotypes. The wife cooks, cleans, and diapers. The husband earns the bread and adjusts the carburetor. In nontraditional marriages, chores are usually shared or negotiated, especially when the wife also works (Atkinson & Huston, 1984). However, there is friction when a nontraditional woman gets married to a traditional man (Booth & Edwards, 1985).

The following list is a sampling of the risks that create conflict and endanger the stability of marriages (Booth & Edwards, 1985; Kornblum, 1997):

- Meeting "on the rebound"
- Living too close to, or too distant from, the families of origin
- Differences in race, religion, education, or social class
- Dependence on one or both families of origin for money, shelter, or emotional support
- Marriage before the couple know each other for 6 months, or after an engagement of many years
- Marital instability in either family of origin
- Pregnancy prior to, or during the first year of, marriage
- Insensitivity to the partner's sexual needs
- Discomfort with the role of husband or wife
- Disputes over the division of labor

> ***Truth or Fiction Revisited***
>
> It is not true that couples who were engaged for many years before getting married have happier marriages than couples who were engaged for only a year. It appears that couples who put off marriage for many years have misgivings or conflicts that continue to harm the relationship.

When problems such as these lead to conflict, the following suggestions may be of help.

Challenge Irrational Expectations

People whose marriages are distressed are more likely than people with functional marriages to harbor a number of irrational beliefs (Eidelson & Epstein, 1982). Despite the fact that nearly all couples disagree now and then, they may believe that any disagreement is destructive. They assume that disagreement about in-laws, children, or sexual activities means that they do not love each other or that their marriage is on the rocks. They may believe that their partners should be able to read their minds (and know what they want), that their partners cannot change, that they must be perfect sex partners, and that men and

> ***Truth or Fiction Revisited***
>
> It is not true that disagreement is destructive to a marriage. Disagreement is found in every marriage. The issue is how well the partners manage disagreement. Belief that disagreement is destructive in itself is an irrational belief that can imperil marital adjustment.

women differ dramatically in personality and needs. It is rational, and adjustive to a marriage, for partners to recognize that no two people can agree all the time, to express their wishes rather than depend on "mind reading" (and a sullen face) to get the message across, to believe that we all can change (although change may come slowly), to tolerate some sexual blunders and frustrations, and to treat each other as equals.

Gottman and Krokoff (1989) found that disagreement and the expression of anger could help marital satisfaction in the long run, as long as they were handled properly. Gottman and Krokoff followed marriages for 3 years and found that the following maneuvers had long-term destructive effects:

- Being defensive or making excuses instead of accepting responsibility for problems
- Making countercharges for every charge without indicating that your partner's views may have some validity
- Telling your partner only what you want him or her to stop doing and not what you would like to have done more often
- Erroneously accusing your partner of bad feelings, ideas, or motives that he or she doesn't really have—and then blaming the partner for these feelings, ideas, or motives
- Being stubborn: refusing to accept compromises or tolerate differences
- Making contemptuous remarks or insults
- Whining

On the other hand, Gottman and Krokoff found that the following kinds of interactions led to increased marital satisfaction as time went on:

- At least partly acknowledging partners' points of view
- Carefully listening to accusations
- Understanding how your partner feels, even in the heat of the argument
- Compromising
- Changing one's views

ATTRIBUTION THEORY AND IRRATIONAL BELIEFS Belief that one's partner cannot change for the better is a stable attribution for marital problems (Baucom and others, 1989; Fincham and others, 1987; Fincham & O'Leary, 1983). Stable attributions for problems make efforts to bring about change seem hopeless and are also linked to feelings of depression. Similarly, global attributions ("That's the way my partner *is*," as compared to the specific "That's what my partner's doing that's annoying me") exaggerate the magnitude of problems.

Here is a sampling of other irrational beliefs that increase marital distress:

- "My spouse doesn't love me if he/she doesn't support me at all times."
- "People who love one another don't raise their voices."
- "It's awful if a disagreement isn't resolved immediately."
- "If my spouse really cared about my anxiety/depression/ulcer/exam, he/she wouldn't be acting this way."
- "My spouse has that annoying habit just to bug me."
- "If she/he truly loved me, she/he would know what I want."

These irrational beliefs magnify differences and heighten marital stress instead of helping to relieve it. The last belief is extremely harmful. We may assume that people who really care for us will know what pleases or displeases us even when we don't tell them, but other people cannot read our minds. We should be open and direct about our feelings and preferences (Jacobson, 1984).

Negotiate Differences

In order to effectively negotiate differences about household responsibilities, leisure time preferences, and so on, each spouse must be willing to share the power in the relationship (Rathus & O'Leary, 1990). If a marriage "gets off on the wrong foot," with one spouse dominating the other, the discrepancy in bargaining power may hamper all future negotiations. The disadvantaged spouse may not be heard, resentments may build, and the relationship may eventually dissolve.

One strategy for averting a discrepancy in bargaining power is to list day-to-day responsibilities. Then each spouse can scale them according to their desirability. Chris and Dana ranked the chores shown in Table 14.4 by using this code:

5 = most desirable
4 = desirable
3 = not sure, mixed feelings
2 = undesirable
1 = Are you kidding? Get lost!

Chris wound up washing the dishes and paying the bills. Dana did the cooking and toyed with the car. They agreed to alternate vacuuming and cleaning the bathroom—specifying a schedule for them so that they wouldn't procrastinate and eventually explode with "It's your turn!" Both had careers, so the bread-winning responsibility was divided evenly.

Make a Contract for Exchanging New Behaviors

In **exchange contracting,** you and your partner identify specific behaviors that you would like to see changed, and you offer to modify some of your own disturbing behavior patterns in exchange. Chris and Dana's contract follows on the next page.

EXCHANGE CONTRACTING • A conflict-resolution method in which each member of a couple agrees to change his or her behavior in exchange for the partner's making an equivalent change in behavior.

TABLE 14.4 CHRIS AND DANA'S RANKINGS OF MARITAL CHORES

CHORE	CHRIS'S RANKING	DANA'S RANKING
Washing dishes	3	1
Cooking	1	4
Vacuuming	2	3
Cleaning the bathroom	1	3
Maintaining the automobile	3	5
Paying the bills	5	3

CHRIS: I agree to talk to you at the dinner table rather than watch the news on TV if you, in turn, help me type my business reports one evening a week.

DANA: I agree never to insult your mother if you, in return, absolutely refuse to discuss our sexual behavior with her.

Increase Pleasurable Marital Interactions

Satisfied couples tend to display higher rates of pleasurable behavior toward one another. One spouse also tends to reciprocate the pleasurable behavior shown by the other (Robinson & Price, 1980). So, consider the behaviors listed in Table 14.5 and try to be sure that you are using them, or similar behaviors, at home.

Unfortunately, couples experiencing problems tend to underestimate the pleasurable behaviors shown by their spouses. It may be because poorly

TABLE 14.5 TYPES OF PLEASURABLE BEHAVIORS SHOWN IN MARRIAGE

Paying attention, listening
Agreeing with your spouse (that is, when you do agree)
Showing approval when pleased by your spouse
Positive physical interactions such as touching and hugging
Showing concern
Showing humor; laughing and smiling
Compromising on disagreements
Complying with reasonable requests

adjusted couples may have come to expect the worst from one another, and they either ignore or do not believe efforts to change. If your partner has been trying to bring more pleasure into your life, it might help to show some appreciation. And if you have been trying to bring pleasure to your partner and it has gone unnoticed, it might not hurt to say something like, "Hey! Look at me! I'm agreeing with you, I think you're pretty smart, and I'm smiling!"

Now let us turn our attention to one of the best ways of resolving conflicts in relationships: improving communication skills.

Communicate: How to Enhance Communication Skills

How do you learn about your partner's needs? How do you let your partner know about your own needs? How do you criticize someone you love? How do you accept criticism and maintain your self-esteem? How do you say no? How do you get by impasses?

All these questions focus on the need for communication. Snyder (1979) found that poor affective and problem-solving communication are two of the important factors that interfere with marital satisfaction (see Table 14.1, p. 435). Moreover, people who are dissatisfied with their partners usually list difficulties in communication as one of the major rubs.

Some of us are better communicators than others, perhaps because we are more sensitive to others' needs or perhaps we had the advantage of observing good communicators in our own homes. However, communication is a skill, one that can be learned. Learning takes time and work, but if you are willing, the guidelines we offer here may be of help (Rathus and others, 1997).

HOW TO GET STARTED One of the trickiest aspects of communicating is getting started.

Talk About Talking One possibility is to begin by talking about talking. That is, explain to your partner that it is hard to talk about your conflicts. Perhaps you can refer to some of the things that have happened in the past when you tried to resolve conflicts.

WHAT DO YOU SAY NOW?

DELIVERING CRITICISM

You can't believe it! You've been waiting for an important business call, and it came. There's only one hitch: Your partner was home at the time—you were out—and your partner's not sure *who* called. If only your partner would be more responsible and write down messages!

You can't let it go this time. You're bound and determined to say something. But what?

What do you say now? Note some possible responses in the spaces provided, and then see the following material for some suggestions.

1. ______________________________
2. ______________________________
3. ______________________________

Delivering criticism is tricky. Your goal should be to modify your partner's behavior without arousing extremes of anger or guilt. Consider these guidelines:

1. Specifically communicate what *behavior* disturbs you. Don't insult your partner's personality. Say something like, "Please write down messages for me," not, "You're totally irresponsible."
2. Express dissatisfaction in terms of your own feelings. Say, "You know, it *upsets me* when something that's important to me gets lost, or misplaced," not, "*You* never think about anybody but yourself."
3. Keep complaints to the present. Say, "This was a very important phone call." It may not be helpful to say, "Last summer you didn't write that message from the computer company, and as a result I didn't get the job."
4. Phrase the criticism positively, and combine it with a concrete request. Say something like, "You know, you're usually very considerate. When I need help, I always feel free to ask for it. Now I'm asking for help when I get a phone call. Will you please write down the message for me?" ■

Request Permission to Raise a Topic You can also ask permission to bring up a topic. You can say something like, "Something's been on my mind. Is this a good time to bring it up?" Or try, "I need to get something off my chest, but I really don't know how to start. Will you help me?"

HOW TO LISTEN Listening to your partner is an essential part of communicating. Moreover, by being a good listener, you suggest ways that your partner can behave in listening to you.

Engage in Active Listening First, engage in **active listening.** Don't stare off into space when your partner is talking or offer an occasional, begrudging "mm-hmm" while you're watching TV. In active listening, you maintain eye contact with your partner. You change your facial expression in a demonstration of empathy for his or her feelings. Nod your head as appropriate, and ask helpful questions such as, "Could you give me an example of what you mean?" or, "How did you feel about that?"

ACTIVE LISTENING • Ways of listening that help the speaker to open up and clearly express his or her views.

LISTENING.
Listening to your partner is an essential part of communication. Listening skills include "active listening," paraphrasing, use of reinforcement, and — like client-centered therapists — use of unconditional positive regard.

Use Paraphrasing In paraphrasing you recast what your partner is saying to show that you understand. For instance, if your partner says, "Last night it really bugged me when I wanted to talk about the movie but you were on the phone," you might say something like, "It seemed that I should have known that you wanted to talk about the movie?" or, "It seems that I'm talking more to other people than to you?"

Reinforce Your Partner for Communicating Even if you don't agree with what your partner said, you can genuinely say something like, "I'm glad you told me how you really feel about that," or, "Look, even if I don't always agree with you, I care about you; I always want you to tell me what you're thinking."

Use Unconditional Positive Regard Keep in mind the concept of unconditional positive regard, which is used by person-centered therapists. When you disagree with your partner, do so in a way that shows that you still value your partner as a person. In other words, say something like, "I love you very much, but it bugs me when you . . . " rather than, "You're rotten for . . . "

HOW TO LEARN ABOUT YOUR PARTNER'S NEEDS Listening is essential to learning about your partner's needs, but sometimes you need to do more than listen.

Ask Questions Designed to Draw Your Partner Out Questions can either suggest a limited range of answers or be open-ended. The following yes-or-no questions require a specific response:

- "Do you think I spend too much time on the phone with my sister?"
- "Does it bother you that I wait until we're ready to go to bed before loading the dishwasher?"
- "Do you think I don't value your opinions about cars?"

Yes-or-no questions can provide a concrete piece of information. Open-ended questions, however, encourage exploration of broader issues. For example:

- "What do you like best about the way we make love?" or, "What bothers you about the way we make love?"

- "What are your feelings about where we live?"
- "How would you like to change things with us?"
- "What do you think of me as a father/mother?"

If your partner finds such questions too general, you can offer an example, or you can say something like, "Do you think we're living in an ideal situation? If you had your preferences, how would you change things?"

Use Self-Disclosure Try self-disclosure, not only because you communicate your own ideas and feelings in this way, but also because you invite reciprocation. For example, if you want to know whether your partner is concerned about your relationship with his or her parents, you can say something like, "You know, I have to admit that I get concerned when you call your folks from work. I get the feeling that there are things that you want to talk about with them but not have me know about."

Give Your Partner Permission to Say Something That Might Be Upsetting to You Tell your partner to level with you about a troublesome issue. Say that you realize that it might be clumsy to talk about it, but you promise to try to listen carefully without getting too upset. Consider limiting communication to, say, one difficult issue per conversation. When the entire emotional dam bursts, the chore of "mopping up" can be overwhelming.

How to Make Requests

Take Responsibility for What Happens to You The first step in making requests is internal—that is, taking responsibility for the things that happen to you. If you want your partner to change behavior, you have to be willing to request the change. Then, if your partner refuses to change, you have to take responsibility for how you will cope with the impasse.

Be Specific It might be useless to say, "Be nicer to me," because your partner might not recognize the abrasive nature of his or her behavior and not know what you mean. It can be more useful to say something like, "Please don't cut me off in the middle of a sentence," or, "Hey, you! Give me a smile!"

Use "I" Talk Also, make use of the word *I* where appropriate. "I would appreciate it if you would take out the garbage tonight" might get better results than "Do you think the garbage needs to be taken out?" Similarly, "I like you to kiss me more when we're making love" might be more effective than "Jamie told me about an article that said that kissing makes sex more enjoyable."

Deliver Criticism Correctly There is skill involved in effectively delivering criticism. Your goal should be to modify your partner's behavior without reducing him or her to a quivering mass of fear or guilt.

Evaluate Your Motives First of all, evaluate your motives honestly. Do you want to change behavior or just punish your partner? If you want to punish your partner, you might as well be crude and insulting, but if you want to resolve conflicts, try a more diplomatic approach.

Pick a Good Time and Place Express complaints privately—not in front of the neighbors, in-laws, or children. Your spouse has a right to be angry when you express intimate thoughts and feelings in public places. When you make private thoughts public, you cause resentment and cut off communication. If you're not sure that this is a good time and place, try asking permission. Say something like, "Something is on my mind. Is this a good time to bring it up?"

Be Specific As in making requests, be specific when making complaints. By being specific, you will communicate what *behavior* disturbs you. Avoid insulting your partner's personality. Say, "Please throw your underwear in the hamper," not, "You're a disgusting slob." It is easier (and less threatening) to change problem behavior than to try to overhaul personality traits.

Express Dissatisfaction in Terms of Your Own Feelings This is more effective than attacking the other person (Rogers, 1972). Say, "You know, it *upsets me* that you don't seem to be paying attention to what I'm saying," not, "*You're* always off in your own damn world. You never cared about anybody else and never will."

Keep Complaints to the Present Forget who did what to whom last summer. It may also be counterproductive to say, "Every time I call my mother, there's a fight afterwards!" Bringing up the past muddles the current issue and heightens feelings of anger.

Try to Phrase the Criticism Positively Try to phrase criticism positively, and combine it with a specific request. For example, say, "I love it when you kiss me. Please kiss me more often while we're making love," rather than, "You never kiss me when we're in bed and I'm sick of it." Or say, "You really make my life much easier when you help me with the dishes. How about a hand tonight?" rather than, "Would it really compromise your self-image as Mr. Macho if you gave me a hand with the dishes tonight?"

HOW TO RECEIVE CRITICISM Taking criticism on the job, at home, anywhere, isn't easy. It's helpful to recognize that you might not be perfect and to be prepared for occasional criticism. Your objectives in receiving criticism should be to learn about your partner's concerns, keep lines of communication open, and find or negotiate ways of changing the troublesome behavior. On the other hand, you should not feel that you must take verbal abuse, and you should speak up if the criticism exceeds acceptable boundaries. For example, if your partner says, "You know, you're pretty damned obnoxious," you might say something like, "Say, how about telling me what I did that's troubling you and forgetting the character assassination?" In this way, you are also making a request that your partner be specific.

Ask Clarifying Questions Another way to help your partner be specific is to ask clarifying questions. If your partner criticizes you for spending so much time with your parents, you might ask something like, "Is it that I'm spending too much time with them, or do you feel they're having too much influence with me?"

Paraphrase the Criticism As with being a good listener in general, paraphrase the criticism to show that you understand it.

Acknowledge the Criticism Acknowledge the criticism even if you do not agree with it by saying something like, "I hear you," or, "I can understand that you're upset that I've been investing so much time in the job lately."

Acknowledge your mistake, if you have made a mistake. If you do not believe that you have, express your genuine feelings, using "I" statements and being as specific as possible.

Negotiate Differences Unless you feel that your partner is completely in the wrong, perhaps you can seek ways to negotiate your differences. Say something like, "Would it help if I . . . ?"

How to Cope With Impasses When we are learning to improve our communication skills, we may arrive at the erroneous idea that all of the world's problems, including our own, could be resolved if people would only make the effort of communicating with each other. Communication helps, but it is not the whole story. Sometimes people have deep, meaningful differences. Although they may have good communication skills, they now and then arrive at an impasse. When you and your partner do arrive at an impasse, the following suggestions may be of some use.

Try to See the Situation From Your Partner's Perspective Maybe you can honestly say something like, "I don't agree with you, but I can see where you're coming from." In this way you validate your partner's feelings and, often, decrease the tension between you.

Seek Validating Information Say something like, "I'm trying, but I honestly can't understand why you feel this way. Can you help me understand?"

Take a Break When we arrive at an impasse in solving a problem, allowing the problem to incubate frequently helps (Rathus, 1999). Allow each other's points of view to incubate, and perhaps a solution will dawn on one of you a bit later. You can also schedule a concrete time for a follow-up discussion so that the problem is not swept under the rug.

Tolerate Differentness Recognize that each of you is a unique individual and that you cannot agree on everything. Families function better when members tolerate each other's differentness. By and large, when we have a solid sense of ego identity (of who we are and what we stand for), we are more likely to be able to tolerate differentness in others.

Agree to Disagree Recognize that we can survive as individuals and as partners even when some conflicts remain unresolved. You can "agree to disagree" and maintain self-respect and respect for one another. ■

RECEIVING CRITICISM

Honest criticism is hard to take, particularly from a relative, a friend, an acquaintance, or a stranger.

FRANKLIN P. JONES

You're having dinner one evening when your partner surprises you with, "You've got to do something about your hair." You're threatened and peeved, but you stop and think before answering.

What do you say now? Note some possible responses in the spaces provided, and then see the following for some suggestions.

1. ______________________________

2. ______________________________

3. ______________________________

Although delivering criticism is tricky, taking criticism can be even more difficult. Your objectives should be to learn about your partner's concerns, to keep your lines of communication open, and to find ways of changing the troublesome behavior. Here are some ideas for responding to "You've got to do something about your hair."

1. When we deliver criticism, it helps to be aware of our motives. In receiving criticism, it helps to be aware of the motives of others. Is your partner's concern limited to your hair, or is this criticism only the opening salvo of a war that's about to erupt? When you're not sure, you can help your partner be specific by asking clarifying questions. For example, "Could you tell me exactly what you mean?" or, "My hair?"
2. As with being a good listener in general, you can acknowledge the criticism even if you do not agree with it by saying something like, "I hear you," or "I know you're not thrilled with this style, but it's impossible to control when it gets longer."
3. If you have been letting your hair go because you've been busy, you can accept the criticism by saying something like, "I know. It was my day/week to tidy up, and I blew it."
4. You can follow acceptance of criticism (as in response #3) with a request for help. For example, "Do you suppose you'd be willing to look over the styles with me so that we can settle on something we both can live with?"
5. If none of these responses work, it is possible that your partner has a hidden agenda and is using the remark about your hair as an opening. You can then try something like, "I'm trying to find ways to help the situation, but they don't seem to be working. Is there something else on your mind?"
6. Notice that we have *not* seized the opportunity to retaliate with something like, "You're worried about my hair? What about your teeth and that beach ball you're trying to hide under your shirt?" Although it can be tempting to retaliate, we're assuming that it might be better for the relationship—and for you in the long run—to try to resolve conflict, not heighten it. ■

Truth or Fiction Revisited

It is not true that the most effective way of handling criticism from a marital partner is to be critical yourself. Retaliation heightens tensions and conflicts.

SUMMARY

1. **What is an intimate relationship?** In an intimate relationship, people share their inmost thoughts and feelings.
2. **What are Levinger's stages in the development of a relationship?** According to Levinger, relationships undergo a five-stage developmental sequence: attraction, building, continuation, deterioration, and ending. Relationships need not advance beyond any one of these stages.
3. **What is small talk, and how does it affect the development of relationships?** Small talk is a broad exploration for common ground that permits us to decide whether we wish to advance the relationship beyond surface contact.
4. **What is self-disclosure, and how does it affect the development of relationships?** Self-disclosure is the revelation of personal information. Self-disclosure invites reciprocity and can foster intimacy. However, premature self-disclosure suggests maladjustment and tends to repel people.
5. **Why do people get married?** Today's marriages are usually based on attraction and love and the desires for emotional and psychological intimacy and security.
6. **To whom do we get married?** We tend to marry people similar in race, religion, social class, intelligence, and even eye color.
7. **What factors affect marital satisfaction?** Four factors predict marital satisfaction: affective communication, problem-solving communication, sexual satisfaction, and agreement about finances.
8. **How many marriages end in divorce?** About half of marriages end in divorce. Divorced people usually encounter a great deal of stress and show some decline in health.

9. **Why do people remain single?** Many people remain single because they have not found the right marital partner. Others prefer sexual variety and wish to avoid making a commitment.

10. **What is cohabitation?** Cohabitation is living together without being married. Most cohabiting college students come from stable families and expect to get married someday, but not necessarily to their current partners. Most cohabiting students do not see their behavior as immoral. They tend to encounter adjustment problems similar to those of young married couples.

The Challenges of Life

Chapter 15

Sexual Behavior

Truth or Fiction?

✔ T F

- ☐ ☐ Women, but not men, have a sex organ whose only known function is the sensing of sexual pleasure.
- ☐ ☐ The clitoris becomes engorged with blood and expands during sexual arousal just as the penis does.
- ☐ ☐ A word for the female genital organs derives from the Latin for "something to be ashamed of."
- ☐ ☐ The earlobes swell when people are sexually aroused.
- ☐ ☐ Most Americans believe that some women like to be talked into sex.
- ☐ ☐ Most sexual dysfunctions stem from physical problems.
- ☐ ☐ Only gay males and substance abusers are at serious risk for contracting AIDS.

OUTLINE

OFFSHORE FROM THE MISTY COASTS OF IRELAND lies the small island of Inis Beag. From the air it is a green jewel, warm and inviting. At ground level, things are somewhat different.

For example, the residents of Inis Beag do not believe that women experience orgasm. The woman who chances to find pleasure in sex is considered deviant. Premarital sex is all but unknown. Women engage in sexual relations in order to conceive children and to appease their husbands' carnal cravings. They need not worry about being called on for frequent performances, however, since the men of Inis Beag believe, erroneously, that sex saps their strength. Sex on Inis Beag is carried out in the dark—literally and figuratively—and with the nightclothes on. The man lies on top in the so-called missionary position. In accord with local concepts of masculinity, he ejaculates as fast as he can. Then he rolls over and falls asleep.

If Inis Beag does not sound like your cup of tea, you may find the atmosphere of Mangaia more congenial. Mangaia is a Polynesian pearl of an island, lifting languidly from the blue waters of the Pacific. It is on the other side of the world from Inis Beag—in more ways than one.

From an early age, Mangaian children are encouraged to get in touch with their sexuality through masturbation. Mangaian adolescents are expected to engage in sexual intercourse. They may be found on secluded beaches or beneath the listing fronds of palms, diligently practicing techniques learned from village elders.

Mangaian women are expected to reach orgasm several times before their partners do. Young men want their partners to reach orgasm and compete to see who is more effective at bringing young women to multiple orgasms.

On the island of Inis Beag, a woman who has an orgasm is considered deviant, whereas on Mangaia multiple orgasms are the norm (Rathus and others, 1997). If we take a quick tour of the world of sexual diversity, we also find the following:

- Nearly every society has an incest taboo, but some societies believe that a brother and sister who eat at the same table are engaging in a mildly sexual type of act. The practice is therefore forbidden (Kammeyer and others, 1990).
- What is sexually arousing varies enormously among different cultures. Women's breasts have become eroticized in Western culture and must usually be covered from public view. In some preliterate societies, however, the breasts are considered of interest to nursing children only, and women usually go bare breasted. Among the Abkhasians in the southern part of what used to be the Soviet Union, men regard the female armpit as highly arousing. A woman's armpits are, therefore, a sight for her husband alone (Kammeyer and others, 1990).

- Kissing is practiced nearly universally as a form of petting in the United States but is unknown among many cultures such as the Thonga of Africa and the Siriono of Bolivia. Upon first seeing European visitors kissing, a Thonga tribesman remarked, "Look at them—they eat each others' saliva and dirt."
- Sexual exclusiveness in marriage is valued highly in most parts of the United States, but among the Native American Aleut people of Alaska's Aleutian Islands, it is considered good manners for a man to offer his wife to a houseguest.
- Although U.S. public officials may voice condemnation of premarital sexual relations, couples who engage in them need not fear government reprisal. In China, however, a male college student was expelled from a Beijing university as recently as 1990 when it became known that he had engaged in premarital sexual relations (Southerland, 1990). Other students reported that the punishment was typical.

The residents of Inis Beag and Mangaia have similar anatomic features but vastly different attitudes toward sex. Their attitudes influence their patterns of sexual behavior and the pleasure they find—or do not find—in sex. Like eating, sexual activity is a natural function. As we saw in our quick tour around the world, however, perhaps no other natural function has been influenced so strongly by religious and moral beliefs, cultural tradition, folklore, and superstition (Rathus and others, 1997).

In this chapter, we examine sexual anatomy and sexual response and see that women and men may be more alike in their sexual response than you may have thought. We consider the social problem of rape and what can be done about it. We consider sexual dysfunctions and their treatment. We then provide information in the areas of sexually transmitted diseases and contraception to help students make responsible sexual choices.

THE BIOLOGICAL BASIS OF SEX

Although we may consider ourselves sophisticated about sex, it's surprising how little we know about sexual biology. How many male readers know that women have different orifices for urination and sexual intercourse? How many readers, male and female, know that the penis—sometimes referred to by the slang term *boner*—contains no bones?

In this section we survey some of the details of female and male sexual anatomy. Then we consider the sexual response cycle and the roles of sex hormones in sexual behavior.

Female Sexual Anatomy

The external female genital organs are called the **vulva,** from the Latin for "covering." The vulva is also known as the **pudendum** (pronounced "poo-DEN-dum"), from "something to be ashamed of"—a clear reflection of some ancient Mediterranean sexism. The vulva has several parts (see the bottom part of Figure 15.1): the mons veneris, clitoris, major and minor lips, and vaginal opening. Females urinate through the **urethral** (pronounced "you-WREATH-rull") opening.

The **mons veneris** (pronounced "monz veh-NAIR-iss"; Latin for "hill of love") is a fatty cushion that lies above the pubic bone and is covered with short, curly pubic hair. The mons and pubic hair cushion the woman during intercourse. The woman's most sensitive sex organ, the **clitoris** (pronounced

VULVA • The female external genital organs.
PUDENDUM • Another term for the *vulva.*
URETHRA • A tube that conducts urine—and, in males, the ejaculate—from the body.
MONS VENERIS • The mound of fatty tissue that covers the joint of the pubic bones and cushions the female during intercourse.
CLITORIS • The female sex organ whose only known function is the reception and transmission of sensations of sexual pleasure.

Truth or Fiction Revisited

It is true that women, but not men, have a sex organ whose only known function is the sensing of sexual pleasure. It is the clitoris.

Truth or Fiction Revisited

It is true that the clitoris becomes engorged with blood and expands during sexual arousal just as the penis does.

GLANS • Tip or head.

MAJOR LIPS • Large folds of skin that run along the sides of the vulva. (In Latin, *labia majora.*)

MINOR LIPS • Folds of skin that lie within the major lips and enclose the urethral and vaginal openings. (In Latin, *labia minora.*)

"CLIT-or-iss"; from the Greek for "hill"), lies below the mons and above the urethral opening. The only known function of the clitoris is to receive and transmit pleasurable sensations.

During sexual arousal, the clitoris becomes engorged with blood and expands. The clitoris has a shaft and a tip, or **glans** (pronounced "glanz"). The glans is the more sensitive of the two and may become irritated by prolonged stimulation or by being approached too early during foreplay.

Two layers of fatty tissue, the outer or **major lips** and the inner or **minor lips,** line the entrance to the vagina. The outer lips are covered with hair and are less sensitive to touch than the smooth, pinkish inner lips.

The woman's internal sexual and reproductive organs consist of the vagina, cervix, fallopian tubes, and ovaries (see the top part of Figure 15.1). The vagina contains the penis during intercourse. At rest the vagina is a flattened tube 3 to 5 inches in length. When aroused, it can lengthen by several inches and dilate (open) to a diameter of about 2 inches. A large penis is not required to "fill" the vagina in order for a woman to experience sexual pleasure. The vagina expands as needed. The pelvic muscles that surround the vagina may also be contracted during intercourse to heighten sensation. The outer third of the vagina is highly sensitive to touch.

When a woman is sexually aroused, the vaginal walls produce moisture that serves as lubrication. Sexual relations can be painful for unaroused, unlubricated women. Adequate arousal usually stems from sexual attraction, positive

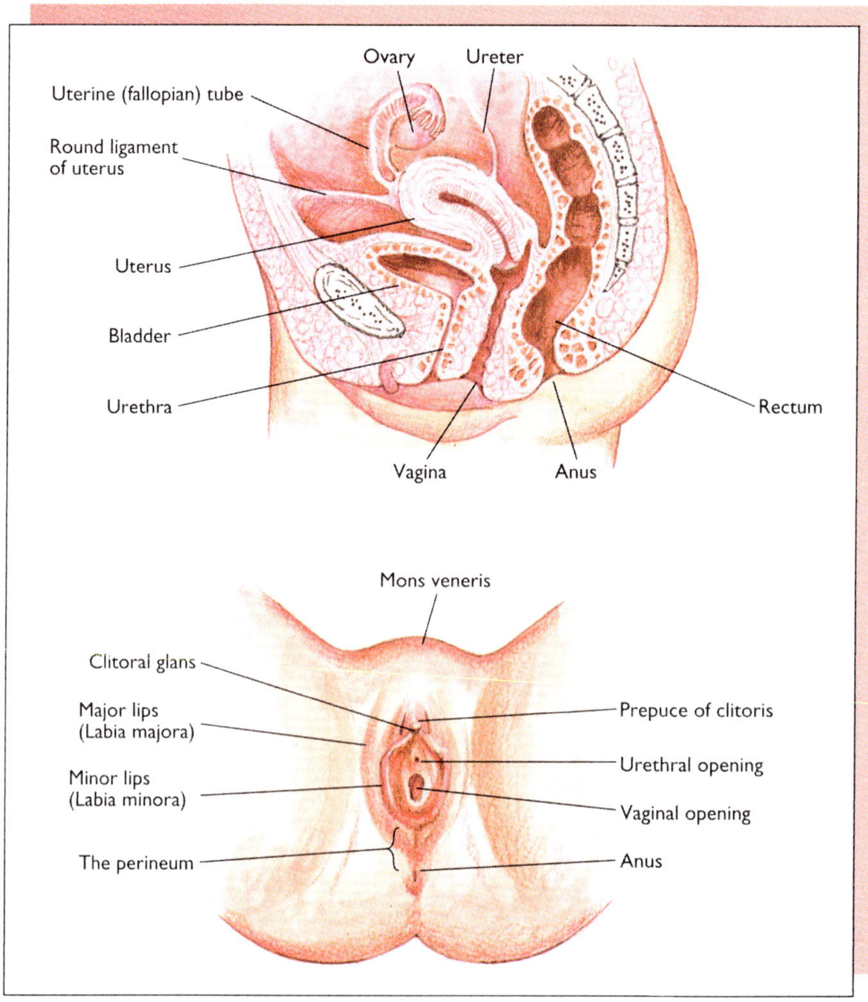

FIGURE 15.1

FEMALE SEXUAL ANATOMY.

The top drawing is a cross section of the internal reproductive organs of the female. The drawing below is an external view of the vulva.

feelings like liking and loving, fantasies, and foreplay. Anxieties concerning sex or a partner may inhibit sexual arousal—for both men and women.

High in the vagina is a small opening called the **cervix** (pronounced "SIR-vicks"; Latin for "neck") that connects that vagina to the uterus. Strawlike fallopian tubes lead from the uterus to the abdominal cavity. Ovaries, which produce ova and the hormones estrogen and progesterone, lie near the uterus and the fallopian tubes. When an ovum is released from an ovary, it normally finds its way into the nearby fallopian tube (although we do not know *how* it does so) and makes its way to the uterus. Conception normally takes place in the tube, but the embryo becomes implanted and grows in the uterus. During labor the cervix dilates, and the baby passes through the cervix and distended vagina.

CERVIX • The lower part of the uterus that opens into the vagina.

Adjustment in a World of DIVERSITY

The Ritual Destruction of Female Sexuality

Despite hundreds of years of tradition, Hajia Zuwera Kassindja would not let it happen to her 17-year-old daughter, Fauziya. Hajia's own sister had died from it. So Hajia gave her daughter her inheritance from her deceased husband. (It amounted to only $3,500, but the gift left Hajia a pauper.) Fauziya used the money to buy a phony passport and flee from the African country of Togo to the United States (Dugger, 1996a).

Upon arrival in the United States, Fauziya requested asylum from persecution. However, she was put into prison for more than a year. But then, in 1996, the Board of Immigration Appeals finally agreed that Fauziya was fleeing persecution, and she was allowed to remain in the United States. She now lives and studies near Washington, D.C.

From what had Hajia's sister died? From what was Fauziya escaping? *Clitoridectomy.*

CLITORIDECTOMY Some predominantly Islamic cultures in Africa and the Middle East ritually mutilate or remove the clitoris as a rite of initiation into womanhood. Clitoridectomy is often performed as a puberty ritual in late childhood or early adolescence (not at birth, like male circumcision).

The clitoris gives rise to feelings of sexual pleasure in women. Its removal or mutilation represents an attempt to ensure the girl's chastity since it is assumed that uncircumcised girls are consumed with sexual desires. Cairo physician Said M. Thabit says, "With circumcision we remove the external parts, so when a girl wears tight nylon underclothes she will not have any stimulation" (cited in MacFarquhar, 1996, p. A3). Some groups in rural Egypt and in the northern Sudan, however, perform clitoridectomies primarily because it is a social custom that has been passed down from ancient times (Toubia, 1994). Some perceive it as part of their faith in Islam. However, nothing in the Koran—the Islamic Bible—authorizes it (Crossette, 1997; MacFarquhar, 1996). Ironically, many young women do not grasp that they are victims. They assume that clitoridectomy is part of being female.

Clitoridectomies are performed under unsanitary conditions without benefit of anesthesia. Medical complications are common, including infections, bleeding, tissue scarring, painful menstruation, and obstructed labor (Toubia, 1994). The procedure is psychologically traumatizing (Toubia, 1994). More radical forms of clitoridectomy have even more serious consequences for health. Some African countries, including Egypt, have outlawed clitoridectomies, but the prohibitions are not always enforced.

More than 100 million women in Africa and the Middle East have undergone removal of the clitoris and the labia minora. Clitoridectomies remain common or even universal in nearly 30 countries in Africa, in many countries in the Middle East, and in parts of Malaysia, Yemen, Oman, Indonesia, and the India-Pakistan subcontinent (Rosenthal, 1995). Thousands of African immigrant girls living in European countries and the United States have also been mutilated (Dugger, 1996b).

Do not confuse male circumcision with the maiming inflicted on girls in the name of circumcision. Former Representative Patricia Schroeder of Colorado depicts the male equivalent of female genital mutilation as cutting off the penis (Dugger, 1996b). The *New York Times* columnist A. M. Rosenthal (1995) calls female genital mutilation the most widespread existing violation of human rights in the world. The Pulitzer Prize–winning African American novelist Alice Walker drew attention to the practice in her best-selling novel *Possessing the Secret of Joy* (1992). She called for its abolition in her book and movie *Warrior Marks.*

OUTLAWED In 1996, the United States outlawed clitoridectomy. The government also directed U.S. representatives to world financial institutions to deny aid to countries that have not established educational programs designed to end the practice (Dugger, 1996b). Yet calls from Westerners to ban the practice in parts of Africa and the Middle East have sparked controversy on grounds of "cultural condescension"—that people in one culture cannot dictate the cultural traditions of another. Yet for Alice Walker, "torture is not culture." As the debate continues, some 2 million African girls are mutilated each year.

Male Sexual Anatomy

Truth or Fiction Revisited

It is true that a word for the female genital organs *(pudendum)* is derived from the Latin for "something to be ashamed of." Ingrained cultural attitudes cause many women to feel embarrassed about their genital organs.

The major male sex organs consist of the penis, testes (or testicles), scrotum, and the series of ducts, canals, and glands that store and transport sperm and produce **semen** (pronounced "SEE-men"). Whereas the female vulva has been viewed historically as "something to be ashamed of," the male sex organs were prized in ancient Greece and Rome. Citizens wore phallic-shaped trinkets, and the Greeks held their testes when offering testimony, in the same way that we swear on a Bible. *Testimony* and *testicle* both derive from the Greek *testis*, meaning "witness." Given this tradition of masculine pride, it is not surprising that Sigmund Freud believed that girls were riddled with penis envy.

The **testes** (pronounced "TESS-tease") produce sperm and the male sex hormone testosterone. The **scrotum** allows the testes to hang away from the body. (Sperm require a lower-than-body temperature.) Sperm travel through ducts up over the bladder and back down to the ejaculatory duct (see Figure 15.2), which empties into the urethra. In females, the urethral opening and the orifice for transporting the ejaculate are different; in males they are one and the same. Although the male urethra transports urine as well as sperm, a valve shuts off the bladder during ejaculation. Thus, sperm and urine do not mix. Several glands, including the prostate, produce semen. Semen transports, activates, and nourishes sperm, enhancing their ability to swim and fertilize the ovum.

The penis consists mainly of loose erectile tissue. Like the clitoris, the penis has a shaft and a tip, or glans, that is highly sensitive to sexual stimulation, especially on the underside. Within seconds following sexual stimulation, blood rushes reflexively into caverns within the penis, just as blood engorges the clitoris. Engorgement with blood—rather than the action of muscle on bone—produces erection.

SEMEN • The whitish fluid that carries sperm. Also called "the ejaculate."

TESTES • Male reproductive organs that produce sperm cells and male sex hormones. Also called *testicles.*

SCROTUM • A pouch of loose skin that houses the testes.

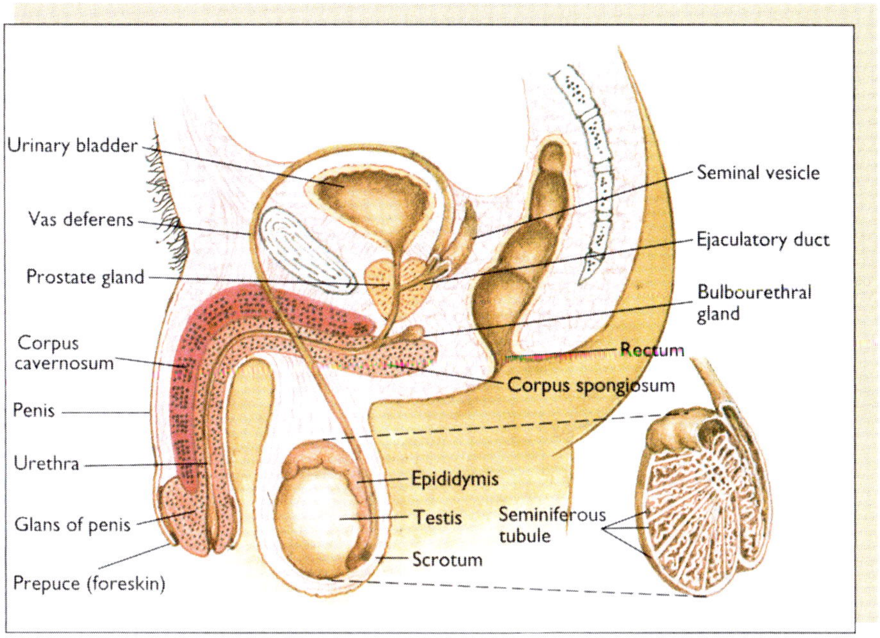

FIGURE 15.2
MALE SEXUAL ANATOMY
A cross section of the internal and external reproductive organs of the male.

The Sexual Response Cycle

Although we may be culturally attuned to focus on gender differences rather than similarities, William Masters and Virginia Johnson (1966) found that the biological responses of males and females to sexual stimulation are quite similar. They use the term *sexual response cycle* to describe the changes that occur in the body as men and women become sexually aroused. Masters and Johnson divide the **sexual response cycle** into four phases: *excitement, plateau, orgasm,* and *resolution.* Figure 15.3 suggests the levels of sexual arousal associated with each phase.

The sexual response cycle is characterized by vasocongestion and myotonia. **Vasocongestion** is the swelling of the genital tissues with blood. It causes erection of the penis and swelling of the area surrounding the vaginal opening. The testes, the nipples, and even the earlobes swell as blood vessels dilate in these areas.

Myotonia is muscle tension. It causes facial grimaces, spasms in the hands and feet, and then the spasms of orgasm. We will now explore these and other bodily changes that make up the sexual response cycle.

Truth or Fiction Revisited

It is true that the earlobes swell when people are sexually aroused.

EXCITEMENT PHASE Vasocongestion during the *excitement phase* can cause erection in young men within seconds. The scrotal skin thickens, becoming less baggy. The testes increase in size and become elevated.

In the female, excitement is characterized by vaginal lubrication, which may start 10 to 30 seconds after sexual stimulation begins. Vasocongestion swells the clitoris and flattens and spreads the vaginal lips. The inner part of the vagina expands. The breasts enlarge, and blood vessels near the surface become more prominent. The nipples may become erect in both men and women. Heart rate and blood pressure also increase.

SEXUAL RESPONSE CYCLE • Masters and Johnson's model of sexual response, which consists of four stages or phases.
VASOCONGESTION • Engorgement of blood vessels with blood, which swells the genitals and breasts during sexual arousal.
MYOTONIA • Muscle tension.

PLATEAU PHASE The level of sexual arousal remains somewhat stable during the *plateau phase* of the cycle. Because of vasocongestion, men show some

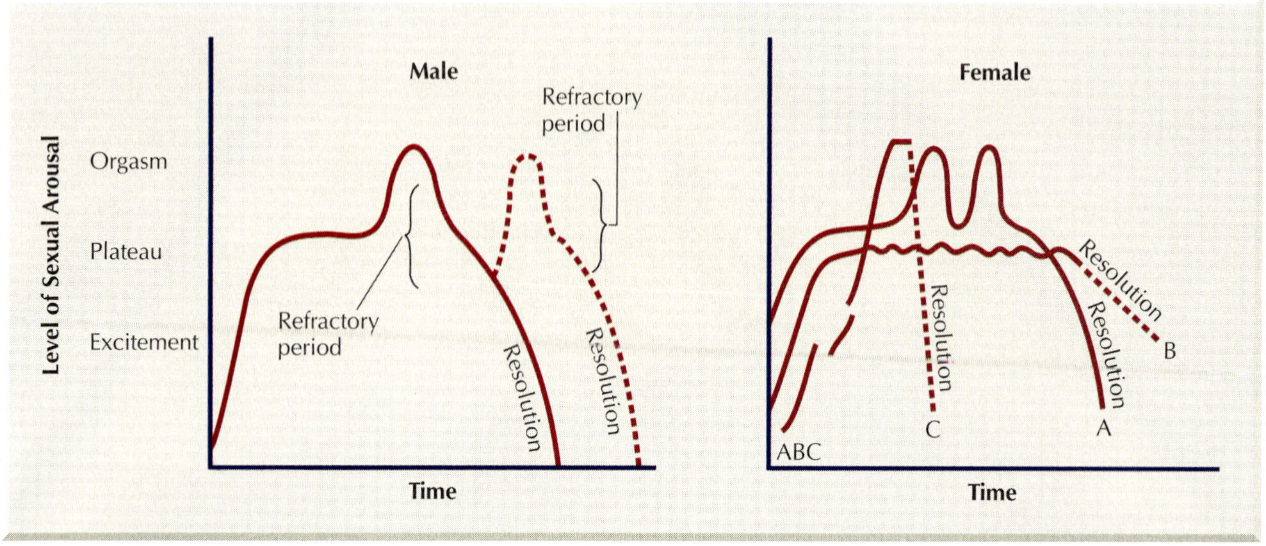

FIGURE 15.3

LEVELS OF AROUSAL DURING THE PHASES OF THE SEXUAL RESPONSE CYCLE

Masters and Johnson divide the sexual response cycle into four phases: excitement, plateau, orgasm, and resolution. During the resolution phase, the level of sexual arousal returns to the prearoused state. For men there is a refractory period following orgasm. As shown by the broken line, however, men can become rearoused to orgasm once the refractory period is past and their levels of sexual arousal have returned to pre-plateau levels. Pattern A for women shows a typical response cycle, with the two peaks suggesting multiple orgasms. Pattern B shows the cycle of a woman who reaches the plateau phase but for whom arousal is "resolved" without reaching the orgasmic phase. Pattern C shows the possibility of orgasm in a highly aroused woman who passes quickly through the plateau phase.

increase in the circumference of the head of the penis, which also takes on a purplish hue. The testes are elevated into position for ejaculation and may reach one and a half times their unaroused size.

In women, vasocongestion swells the outer part of the vagina, contracting the vaginal opening in preparation for grasping the penis. The inner part of the vagina expands farther. The clitoris withdraws beneath the clitoral hood and shortens.

Breathing becomes rapid, like panting. Heart rate may increase to 100 to 160 beats per minute. Blood pressure continues to rise.

ORGASMIC PHASE The *orgasmic phase* in the male consists of two stages of muscular contractions. In the first stage, semen collects at the base of the penis. The internal sphincter of the urinary bladder prevents urine from mixing with semen. In the second stage, muscle contractions propel the ejaculate out of the body. Sensations of pleasure tend to be related to the strength of the contractions and the amount of seminal fluid present. The first 3 to 4 contractions are generally most intense and occur at 0.8-second intervals (5 contractions every 4 seconds). Another 2 to 4 contractions occur at a somewhat slower pace. Rates and patterns can vary from one man to another.

Orgasm in the female is manifested by 3 to 15 contractions of the pelvic muscles that surround the vaginal barrel. The contractions first occur at 0.8-second intervals. As in the male, they produce release of sexual tension. Weaker and slower contractions follow.

Blood pressure and heart rate reach a peak, with the heart beating up to 180 times per minute. Respiration may increase to 40 breaths per minute.

RESOLUTION PHASE After orgasm the body returns to its unaroused state. This is called the *resolution phase.* After ejaculation, blood is released from engorged areas so that the erection disappears. The testes return to their normal size.

In women orgasm also triggers the release of blood from engorged areas. The nipples return to their normal size. The clitoris and vaginal barrel gradually shrink to their unaroused sizes. Blood pressure, heart rate, and breathing also return to their levels before arousal. Both partners may feel relaxed and satisfied.

Unlike women, men enter a *refractory period* during which they cannot experience another orgasm or ejaculate. The refractory period of adolescent males may last only minutes, whereas that of men age 50 and above may last from several minutes to a day. Women do not undergo a refractory period and therefore can become quickly rearoused to the point of repeated (multiple) orgasms with continued sexual stimulation.

Effects of Sex Hormones

Sex hormones promote the differentiation of male and female sex organs in the embryo, regulate the menstrual cycle, and have organizing and activating effects on sexual behavior.

HORMONAL REGULATION OF THE MENSTRUAL CYCLE The ovaries produce **estrogen** and **progesterone** (pronounced "pro-JESS-t'-rone"). Estrogen spurs development of female reproductive capacity and secondary sex characteristics, such as accumulation of fat in the breasts and the hips. Progesterone also has multiple functions. It stimulates growth of the female reproductive organs and maintains pregnancy. Levels of estrogen and progesterone vary markedly and regulate the menstrual cycle. Following **menstruation**—the monthly sloughing off of the inner lining of the uterus—estrogen levels increase, leading to the ripening of an ovum (egg cell) and the growth of the **endometrium** (pronounced "end-oh-MEET-ree-um"), or inner lining of the uterus. **Ovulation** occurs—that is, the ovum is released by the ovary— halfway through the menstrual cycle, when estrogens reach peak blood levels. Then, in response to secretion of progesterone, the inner lining of the uterus thickens, gaining the capacity to support an embryo if fertilization should occur. If the ovum is not fertilized, estrogen and progesterone levels drop suddenly, triggering menstruation once more.

ORGANIZING AND ACTIVATING EFFECTS OF SEX HORMONES Sexual behavior among many lower animals is almost completely governed by hormones (Crews, 1994). Sex hormones have organizing and activating effects (Buchanan and others, 1992). They predispose lower animals toward masculine or feminine mating patterns (a directional or **organizing effect**). Hormones also influence the sex drive and facilitate sexual response **(activating effects**).

Sexual behavior among many lower animals is almost completely governed by hormones (Crews, 1994). In many species, if the sex organs and brains of fetuses are exposed to large doses of **testosterone** in the uterus (which occurs naturally when they share the uterus with many brothers, or artificially as a result of hormone injections), they become masculine in structure (Crews,

ESTROGEN • A generic term for several female sex hormones that foster growth of female sex characteristics and regulate the menstrual cycle.

PROGESTERONE • A female sex hormone that promotes growth of the sex organs, helps maintain pregnancy, and is also involved in regulation of the menstrual cycle.

MENSTRUATION • The monthly shedding of the inner lining of the uterus by women who are not pregnant.

ENDOMETRIUM • The tissue forming the inner lining of the uterus.

OVULATION • The release of an ovum from an ovary.

ORGANIZING EFFECT • The directional effects of sex hormones—for example, along stereotypical masculine or feminine lines.

ACTIVATING EFFECT • The arousal-producing effects of sex hormones.

TESTOSTERONE • A male hormone that promotes development of male sexual characteristics and has activating effects on sexual arousal.

Sex Becomes "Interactive"

There's nothing new about pulling down the curtains so that sex remains a private matter. But a new wrinkle has been added by the black curtains at the computer expositions at the turn of the new millennium. The curtains shield high-tech peep shows that feature nude models on CD-ROMs produced by *Penthouse* and other purveyors of multimedia erotica. Sex has always followed hard on the heels of the technological innovations of the day. Four thousand years ago, the Sumerians celebrated the pleasures of sex in their early cuneiform writing on clay tablets. Shortly after Gutenberg invented the printing press, a volume of erotic engravings appeared. (The year was A.D. 1524, and the work was soon suppressed by the pope.)

Today, we have multimedia interactivity. One could argue, of course, that sex has always been about as interactive a sphere of activity as one could have. But only now has a *Penthouse* model saying "Let's get interactive" become available for your computer.

In one program produced by the CD-ROM company Interotica, entitled *Interactive Adventures,* a narrator introduces himself to a young woman in Los Angeles. The action soon comes to a halt with her face frozen on the monitor. The screen presents the computer operator with a menu of choices: retreating, asking the woman out to dinner, and inviting her to enjoy a sojourn in a hot tub. Retreating and the hot tub proposition offer no rewards. (The hot tub invitation is judged premature by this socially sophisticated program.) But the dinner invitation, followed up by additional "correct" choices, leads to a CD-ROM-mediated "sexual encounter."

Social critics point out that the advanced technology that makes such interactive adventures possible serves to maintain men's low-tech sexist illusions about women. As in pornographic books, films, and videocassettes, women are portrayed as objects whose function is to serve the cruder wishes of men. In such works, "love" is reduced to anonymous encounters in which women seek to fulfill men's sexual desires, not to develop relationships.

Businesspeople are already contemplating new ways of raking in the dollars from interactive erotica. Pay-

1994). Prenatal testosterone organizes the brains of females in the masculine direction, predisposing them toward masculine behaviors in adulthood. Testosterone in adulthood then apparently activates the masculine behavior patterns.

Testosterone is also important in the behavior of human males. Men who are castrated or given antiandrogen drugs, which decrease the amount of androgens in the bloodstream, usually show gradual loss of sexual desire and of the capacities for erection and orgasm. Still, many castrated men remain sexually active for years, suggesting that for many people fantasies, memories, and other cognitive stimuli are as important as hormones in sexual motivation. Beyond minimal levels, there is no clear link between testosterone level and sexual arousal.

ESTRUS • The periodic sexual excitement of many female mammals, during which they can conceive and are receptive to the sexual advances of males.

Female mice, rats, cats, and dogs are receptive to males only during **estrus,** when female sex hormones are plentiful. But women are sexually responsive per-view video sex over modems is likely to replace telephone sex, especially as modems become able to carry greater torrents of information. Today, so-called "hot chats" are popular with computer online services. The services allow people with unusual sexual interests to conduct conversations with people who share their interests anyplace in the country by typing their comments onto their screens. Video versions of the hot chat are also becoming common as we enter the new millennium. If one wishes to remain anonymous during an "interactive" session, one can assume the identity of a make-believe character known as an "avatar." No doubt we will soon be donning the computer-generated screen images of, say, Brad Pitt or Uma Thurman.

Or consider what some futurists refer to as *cybersex* or *virtual sex*. You don headphones, 3-D glasses, and a light bodysuit that has miniature detectors that follow your movements and tiny stimulators for your skin. The detectors and stimulators are connected to computers that record your responses and create the impression of being touched by textures such as virtual satin, virtual wool, or virtual skin. The information superhighway allows you either to interact with another online person who is outfitted with similar gear or to be connected with a canned program.

What are some of the psychological implications of such new forms of interactive sex? If we could electronically dress up as movie stars, would our sense of self and our dignity as individuals suffer?

If we could at a moment's notice access a satisfying virtual sexual encounter with an appealing person (or program) who was only concerned about meeting our needs, would we become less sensitive to the needs of our real-life romantic partners? Would virtual sex provide additional outlets for people whose needs were not being fully met by others? Or would they become the preferred sexual outlets? If they did become preferred outlets, what would be the implications for the family? For children?

Would a virtual sex interaction be grounds for divorce?

Let us note that traditional family life remains a popular ideal despite provocative cuneiform writings on clay tablets, despite arousing engravings (and photographs) in printed media, despite adult films and videotapes, even despite telephone sex and the Internet. On the other hand, we have not yet witnessed the most titillating interactions of the new millennium. ■

during all phases of the menstrual cycle, even during menstruation and after **menopause,** when hormone levels are low. Androgens influence female as well as male sexual response. Women whose adrenal glands and ovaries have been removed (so that they no longer produce androgens) may gradually lose sexual interest and the capacity for sexual response. An active and enjoyable sexual history seems to ward off loss of sexual capacity, suggestive of the importance of cognitive and experiential factors in human sexual motivation.

The message is that sex hormones play a role in human sexual behavior but that our sexual behavior is far from mechanical. Sex hormones initially promote the development of our sex organs. As adults, we may need certain minimal levels of sex hormones to become sexually aroused. However, psychological factors also influence our sexual behavior. In human sexuality, biology is not destiny.

MENOPAUSE • The cessation of menstruation.

ADJUSTMENT *in the* NEW MILLENNIUM

Will We Finally Have "Love Potions" in the New Millennium?

For centuries people have searched for a love potion—a magical formula that could make other people fall in love with you or be strongly attracted to you. Some scientists suggest that such potions may already exist in the form of chemical secretions known as *pheromones.*

Pheromones are odorless chemicals detected through a "sixth sense"—the *vomeronasal organ.* This organ, located in the nose, detects the chemicals and communicates information about them to the hypothalamus, where they might affect sexual response (Azar, 1998). People may use pheromones in many ways. Infants may use them to recognize their mothers, and adults might respond to them in seeking a mate. Lower animals use pheromones to stimulate sexual response, organize food gathering, maintain pecking orders, sound alarms, and mark territories (Azar, 1998). Pheromones induce mating behavior in insects. Male rodents show less sexual arousal when their sense of smell is blocked, but the role of pheromones in sexual behavior becomes less vital as one moves upward through the ranks of the animal kingdom.

Only a few years ago, most researchers did not believe that pheromones played a role in human behavior. Today, however, it appears that people do possess vomeronasal organs (Bartoshuk & Beauchamp, 1994), and this field of research has attracted new interest. Some entrepreneurs have already formed companies that plan to commercialize the use of human pheromones—or shall we say love potions?—in the new millennium. ■

■ RAPE

Parents regularly encourage their daughters to be wary of strangers and strange places—places where they are prey to men. Certainly the threat of rape from strangers is real enough, but only one rape in five is perpetrated by a stranger (Laumann and others, 1994). The great majority are committed by acquaintances. In fact, up to 2 million instances of forced sex may occur within marriage each year, although about one third of women and men are not likely to define forced sex by a husband as rape (see Table 15.1).

Date rape is a pressing concern on college campuses, where thousands of women have been victimized and there is much controversy as to what exactly constitutes rape (Gibbs, 1991). Nine percent of one recent sample of 6,159 college women reported that they had given in to sexual intercourse as a result of threats or physical force (Koss and others, 1987). Consider the case of Ann (Trenton State College, 1991):

> I first met him at a party. He was really good looking and he had a great smile. I wanted to meet him but I wasn't sure how. I didn't want to appear too forward. Then he came over and introduced himself. We talked and found we had a lot in common. I really liked him. When he asked me

TABLE 15.1 WOULD YOU CLASSIFY THE FOLLOWING AS RAPE OR NOT?

		RAPE	NOT RAPE
A man has sex with a woman who has passed out after drinking too much	Female	88%	9%
	Male	77	17
A married man has sex with his wife even though she does not want him to	Female	61	30
	Male	56	38
A man argues with a woman who does not want to have sex until she agrees to have sex	Female	42	53
	Male	33	59
A man uses emotional pressure, but no physical force, to get a woman to have sex	Female	39	55
	Male	33	59
		YES	**NO**
(Do you believe that some women like to be talked into having sex?)	Female	54%	33%
	Male	69	20

Source: From a telephone poll of 500 American adults taken for *Time*/CNN on May 8, 1991, by Yankelovich Clancy Shulman. Sampling error is plus or minus 4.5%. "Not sures" omitted. Reprinted from *Time Magazine,* June 3, 1991, p. 50.

over to his place for a drink, I thought it would be OK. He was such a good listener, and I wanted him to ask me out again.

When we got to his room, the only place to sit was on the bed. I didn't want him to get the wrong idea, but what else could I do? We talked for awhile and then he made his move. I was so startled. He started by kissing. I really liked him so the kissing was nice. But then he pushed me down on the bed. I tried to get up and I told him to stop. He was so much bigger and stronger. I got scared, and I started to cry. I froze, and he raped me.

It took only a couple of minutes and it was terrible, he was so rough. When it was over he kept asking me what was wrong, like he didn't know. He had just forced himself on me and he thought that was OK. He drove me home and said he wanted to see me again. I'm so afraid to see him. I never thought it would happen to me.

If we add to these figures instances in which women are subjected to forced kissing and petting, the numbers grow more alarming. For example, at a major university, 40 percent of 201 male students surveyed admitted to using force to unfasten a woman's clothing, and 13 percent reported that they had forced a woman to engage in sexual intercourse (Rapaport & Burkhart, 1984). Forty-four percent of the college women in the Koss study (Koss and others, 1987) reported that they had "given in to sex play" because of a "man's continual arguments and pressure." (Note from Table 15.1 that most women and men do not believe that men who "argue" women into consenting to sex are committing rape.) Overall, it appears that between one in four and one in seven women in the United States have been raped (Koss, 1993).

KRISTINE, AMY, AND KAREN. These college women are among the many thousands who claim to have been raped by dates. The great majority of rapes are committed by dates or acquaintances, not by strangers. People differ in their perceptions of where encouragement leaves off and rape begins. For this reason, many colleges require students to attend seminars on date rape. Male students are taught that "no" means *stop—now.*

Why Do Men Rape Women?

> Boys . . . *have sex earlier now, with more impunity, with a more casual commitment, in a cultural environment saturated with soft porn and cinematic violence.*
>
> ANNA QUINDLEN (1993)

Why do men force women into sexual activity? Sex is not the only reason. Many social scientists argue that rape is often a man's way of expressing social dominance over, or anger toward, women (Hall & Barongan, 1997). With some rapists, violence appears to enhance sexual arousal. They therefore seek to combine sex and aggression (Barbaree & Marshall, 1991).

Many social critics contend that American culture socializes men—including the nice young man next door—into becoming rapists (Powell, 1996). This occurs because males are often reinforced for aggressive and competitive behavior (Hall & Barongan, 1997). The date rapist could be said to be asserting culturally expected dominance over women.

College men frequently perceive a date's protests as part of an adversarial sex game. One male undergraduate said "Hell, no" when asked whether a date had consented to sex. He added, " . . . but she didn't say no, so she must have wanted it, too. . . . It's the way it works" (Celis, 1991). Consider the comments of Jim, the man who victimized Ann (Trenton State College, 1991):

> I first met her at a party. She looked really hot, wearing a sexy dress that showed off her great body. We started talking right away. I knew that she liked me by the way she kept smiling and touching my arm while she was speaking. She seemed pretty relaxed so I asked her back to my place for a drink. . . . When she said yes, I knew that I was going to be lucky!
>
> When we got to my place, we sat on the bed kissing. At first, everything was great. Then, when I started to lay her down on the bed, she started twisting and saying she didn't want to. Most women don't like to

appear too easy, so I knew that she was just going through the motions. When she stopped struggling, I knew that she would have to throw in some tears before we did it.

She was still very upset afterwards, and I just don't understand it! If she didn't want to have sex, why did she come back to the room with me? You could tell by the way she dressed and acted that she was no virgin, so why she had to put up such a big struggle I don't know.

Rape Myths: Do You Harbor Beliefs That Encourage Rape?

In the United States there are numerous myths about rape—myths that tend to blame the victim, not the aggressor. For example, a majority of Americans aged 50 and above believe that the woman is partly responsible for being raped if she dresses provocatively (see Table 15.2). As a result, they are unlikely to be sympathetic if such a woman complains of being raped. A majority of Americans believe that some women like to be talked into sex.

Other myths include the notions that "women say no when they mean yes," "all women like a man who is pushy and forceful," and "rapists are crazed by sexual desire" (Powell, 1996, p. 139). Still another myth is that deep down inside, women *want* to be raped. All these myths deny the impact of the assault and transfer blame onto the victim. They contribute to a social climate that is too often lenient toward rapists and unsympathetic toward victims.

You may complete the nearby "Self-Assessment" on cultural myths and rape if you want to learn whether you harbor some of the more common myths. We discuss ways of preventing rape in this chapter's "Adjustment and Modern Life" feature.

Truth or Fiction Revisited

It is true that most Americans believe that some women like to be talked into sex. A majority of Americans—including a majority of American *women*—share this belief. Does this encourage men to pressure their dates into sex?

Truth or Fiction Revisited

It is not true that women say no when they mean yes. Myths such as this foster a social climate that encourages rape.

TABLE 15.2 DO YOU BELIEVE A WOMAN WHO IS RAPED IS PARTLY TO BLAME IF:

	AGE	*YES*	*NO*
She is under the influence of drugs or alcohol	18–34	31%	66%
	35–49	35	58
	50+	57	36
She initially says yes to having sex and then changes her mind	18–34	34	60
	35–49	43	53
	50+	43	46
She dresses provocatively	18–34	28	70
	35–49	31	67
	50+	53	42
She agrees to go to the man's room or home	18–34	20	76
	35–49	29	70
	50+	53	41
		YES	*NO*
(Have you ever been in a situation with a man in which you said no but ended up having sex anyway?)	Asked of Females	18%	80%

Source: From a telephone poll of 500 American adults taken for *Time*/CNN on May 8, 1991, by Yankelovich Clancy Shulman. Sampling error is plus or minus 4.5%. "Not sures" omitted. Reprinted from *Time Magazine,* June 3, 1991, p. 51.

SELF-ASSESSMENT

Do You Subscribe to Cultural Myths That Create a Climate That Supports Rape?

Martha Burt (1980) developed a scale to measure cultural myths that support rape. The following statements have been adapted from that scale. ■

Directions: Read each of the following statements. Indicate whether you believe it to be true or false by circling the T or F. Then turn to the key in the Appendix to learn the implications of your answers.

T F 1. A woman who goes to a date's room or apartment on their first date implies that she is willing to engage in sexual activity.

T F 2. Only women who are looking for it get raped.

T F 3. Women often claim that they've been raped just to call attention to themselves.

T F 4. Any woman can successfully defy a rapist if she really wants to.

T F 5. When women go around campus without bras or with short skirts and tight tops, they are asking for trouble.

T F 6. Most rape victims are "easy" or have bad reputations.

T F 7. If a woman necks or pets, she can't expect her partner then to stop just because she says to.

T F 8. Women who hitchhike can't blame men who pick them up if they try to have sex with them.

T F 9. Women who think that they're too good for men need to be taught a lesson.

T F 10. Many women have unconscious wishes to be raped, and so they may unconsciously set up a situation in which they are vulnerable to attack.

T F 11. If a woman gets drunk at a party and has intercourse with a man she's just met there, she should be considered "fair game" to other men at the party who want her, whether she wants to or not.

T F 12. Many women claim that they've been raped as a way of punishing a man for something.

T F 13. Many rapes are fabricated by pregnant women who are trying to protect their reputation.

■ SEXUAL DYSFUNCTIONS

Sexual dysfunctions • Problems in becoming sexually aroused or reaching orgasm.

Many millions of Americans are troubled by **sexual dysfunctions.** It may be that most readers—or their partners—will be troubled by a sexual dysfunction at one time or another. Yet because many people are reluctant to admit to sexual problems, we do not have precise figures on their frequencies. Perhaps our best source of information is the National Health and Social Life Survey (Laumann

TABLE 15.3 CURRENT SEXUAL DYSFUNCTIONS ACCORDING TO THE NHSLS STUDY (PERCENT OF RESPONDENTS REPORTING THE PROBLEM WITHIN THE PAST YEAR)

	MEN	*WOMEN*
Pain during sex	3.0%	14.4%
Sex not pleasurable	8.1	21.2
Unable to reach orgasm	8.3	24.1
Lack of interest in sex	15.8	33.4
Anxiety about performance*	17.0	11.5
Reaching climax too early	28.5	10.3
Unable to keep an erection	10.4	—
Having trouble lubricating	—	18.8

*Anxiety about performance is not itself a sexual dysfunction. However, it figures prominently into sexual dysfunctions.

Source: Adapted from tables 10.8A and 10.8B, pages 370 and 371, in Laumann, E. O., Gagnon, J. H., Michael, R. T., & Michaels, S. (1994). *The social organization of sexuality: Sexual practices in the United States*. Chicago: University of Chicago Press.

and others, 1994). Some of the material from that study appears in Table 15.3. The NHSLS group asked respondents for a *yes* or *no* answer to questions such as "During the last 12 months has there ever been a period of several months or more when you lacked interest in having sex?" Higher percentages of women reported problems in the areas of painful sex, lack of pleasure, inability to reach orgasm, and lack of interest in sex. Higher percentages of men reported reaching orgasm too early and being anxious about their performance. Difficulty keeping an erection (erectile disorder) increases with age from about 6 percent in the group of 18- to 24-year-olds to about 20 percent in the group of 55- to 59-year-olds. The NHSLS figures represent "persistent current problems." The incidences of occasional problems would be higher.

We discuss the following sexual dysfunctions, as defined by the American Psychiatric Association (1994): *hypoactive sexual desire disorder, female sexual arousal disorder, male erectile disorder, orgasmic disorder, premature ejaculation, dyspareunia,* and *vaginismus.*

In **hypoactive sexual desire disorder,** the person shows lack of interest in sexual activity and frequently reports an absence of sexual fantasies. The diagnosis exists because of the assumption that sexual fantasies and interests are normal response patterns that may be blocked by anxiety or other factors.

In the female, sexual arousal is characterized by a lubricating of the vaginal walls that makes entry by the penis possible. Sexual arousal in the male is characterized by erection of the penis. Almost all women now and then have difficulty becoming or remaining lubricated. Almost all men have occasional difficulty attaining erection or maintaining an erection through intercourse. The diagnoses of **female sexual arousal disorder** and **male erectile disorder** are used when these problems are persistent or recurrent.

In **orgasmic disorder,** the man or woman, although sexually excited, is persistently delayed in reaching orgasm or does not reach orgasm at all. Orgasmic disorder is more common among women than men. In some cases, an

HYPOACTIVE SEXUAL DESIRE DISORDER • A sexual dysfunction characterized by lack of interest in sexual activity.

FEMALE SEXUAL AROUSAL DISORDER • A sexual dysfunction characterized by difficulty in becoming sexually aroused, as defined by vaginal lubrication, or by difficulty in sustaining arousal long enough to engage in satisfying sexual relations.

MALE ERECTILE DISORDER • A sexual dysfunction characterized by difficulty in becoming sexually aroused, as defined by achieving erection, or in sustaining arousal long enough to engage in satisfying sexual relations.

ORGASMIC DISORDER • A sexual dysfunction in which one has difficulty reaching orgasm, although one has become sexually aroused.

ADJUSTMENT *in the* NEW MILLENNIUM

Enter the "Brave New World" of Viagra?

Viagra? This is the magic pill for men with erectile dysfunction that was first marketed in 1998. As many as half the men aged 40 and above have at least intermittent problems with erectile dysfunction. Erection is made possible by the flow of blood into the caverns within the penis (a process called vasocongestion), which then stiffens as does a balloon when air or water is pumped in. Viagra achieves its effect by relaxing the muscles that surround the caverns, enabling blood vessels in the region to dilate.

VIAGRA FOR WOMEN? And what about women? Erectile disorder may be seen as a vascular problem or disease. As women get older, they too experience a reduced flow of blood to the genital region, which means that the clitoris becomes less engorged during sexual arousal and may be connected with feelings of lessened sexual arousal overall. About 50 percent of adult women say that they have lost interest in sex or have difficulty becoming aroused (Kolata, 1998c). Some researchers (and some women) have asked whether Viagra or similar drugs may also enhance the sexual experiences of women—when taken by the women, that is (Kolata, 1998b, 1998c). Some women report experiencing greater vaginal lubrication and stronger orgasms as a result of using Viagra. It remains to be seen whether Viagra or a similar drug will reliably increase measures of sexual arousal in women, such as vaginal lubrication, and affect overall sexual desire.

SIDE EFFECTS AND . . . SIDE EFFECTS What are the side effects of Viagra? It can cause headaches (headaches can be caused by changes in the blood supply to the head, and Viagra—taken in pill form—does not affect only the genitals), diarrhea, and distorted color vision (Goldstein and others, 1998). Some users find that things have a blue tinge for a few hours. Given one slang meaning of the word *blue*, this side effect may be rather fitting.

But there is another possible side effect. Consider the case of a 67-year-old retired auto dealer living in Florida. For a number of years, he had been more concerned about his golf game than his sex life: "To tell the truth, I was more concerned about my putting than playing around," he said (cited in Nordheimer, 1998). But his wife asked him if he could see a doctor and have his sexual functioning restored. He did, and treatment was effective. In fact, it was so effective that he began seeing other women and is now living with a woman half his age (Nordheimer, 1998). Then, too, when other problems damage a relationship, no little blue pill (Viagra is blue) can make them just disappear.

Viagra was developed to treat erectile dysfunction, but will people without sexual dysfunctions pop Viagra, and other pills, in an effort to heighten normal sexual experience (Kolata, 1998b)? In the new millennium people may be popping pills left and right to increase their sexual arousal and response. At that time, we will have many issues to consider. One is whether people will become dependent on pills for sexual arousal and response. If a pill makes what is good better, will people lose the ability to settle for what is just good?

Some people of course will argue that people do not have the "right" to toy with what is "normal." Others will say, "Why not?" They might argue that one could extend the argument to outlaw perfume, R-rated movies, sips of wine, and coffee—all of which can enhance sexual arousal and response in one way or another.

Enter the brave new world of Viagra—and its many chemical cousins. ■

individual can reach orgasm without difficulty while engaging in sexual relations with one partner, but not with another.

In **premature ejaculation,** the male persistently ejaculates with minimal sexual stimulation, too soon to permit his partner or himself to enjoy sexual relations fully. In **dyspareunia,** sexual intercourse is associated with recurrent pain

PREMATURE EJACULATION • Ejaculation that occurs prior to the couple's desires.

DYSPAREUNIA • Painful intercourse.

in the genital region. **Vaginismus** is involuntary spasm of the muscles surrounding the vagina, making sexual intercourse painful or impossible.

Causes of Sexual Dysfunctions

Some cases of sexual dysfunctions stem from physical factors such as disease, fatigue, and use of drugs. Hypoactive sexual desire, for example, can reflect diabetes and diseases of the heart and lungs. Fatigue can dampen sexual desire and inhibit orgasm. Depressants such as alcohol, narcotics, and tranquilizers can also impair sexual response. But incidents of such sexual dysfunction will be isolated unless we attach too much meaning to them. Physical factors can also interact with psychological factors. For instance, dyspareunia can heighten anxiety, and extremes of anxiety can, in turn, dampen sexual arousal.

It seems that a larger number of cases stem from psychological factors. For example, the old-fashioned stereotype suggests that although men may find sex pleasurable, sex is a duty for women. Women who share these negative attitudes toward sex may not be fully aware of their sexual potentials. Too, they may be so anxious about sex that the attitudes become a self-fulfilling prophecy. Men, too, may be handicapped by misinformation and sexual taboos.

Physically or psychologically painful sexual experiences can cause future sexual response to be blocked by anxiety. Rape victims may encounter sexual adjustment problems such as vaginismus or orgasmic disorder.

A sexual relationship is usually no better than other aspects of the relationship or marriage. Communication problems are linked to general marital dissatisfaction. Individuals who have problems expressing their sexual desires are at a disadvantage in teaching their partners how to provide pleasure.

Sexual competencies, like other competencies, are based on knowledge and skill, and competencies are based largely on learning. We learn what makes us and others feel good through trial and error, talking and reading about sex, and perhaps, by watching sex films. Many people do not acquire sexual competencies because of lack of knowledge and experimentation—even within marriage.

Irrational beliefs and attitudes contribute to sexual dysfunctions. If we believe that we need others' approval at all times, we may catastrophize the importance of one disappointing sexual episode. If we demand that each sexual encounter be perfect, we make failure inevitable.

In most cases of sexual dysfunction, the physical and psychological factors we have outlined lead to another psychological factor—**performance anxiety**, or fear of whether we shall be able to perform sexually. People with performance anxiety may focus on past failures and current fears rather than lose themselves in erotic sensations and fantasies (Barlow, 1986a). Performance anxiety can make it difficult for a man to attain erection, yet spur him to ejaculate early. Performance anxiety can also prevent a woman from becoming adequately lubricated or can contribute to vaginismus.

Sex therapy programs foster sexual competencies by enhancing sexual knowledge and encouraging sexual experimentation under circumstances in which performance anxiety is unlikely to be aroused.

Truth or Fiction Revisited

It is not true that most sexual dysfunctions stem from physical problems. Most sexual dysfunctions actually appear to stem from psychological factors such as negative attitudes toward sex, lack of sexual skills, and performance anxiety.

Sex Therapy

Sex therapy refers to a number of treatments based on the cognitive social model developed during the past three decades. Sex therapists assume that sexual dysfunctions can be treated by directly modifying the problem behavior that occurs in the bedroom. Fortunately, the great majority of cases of sexual dysfunctions can be successfully treated today. Readers may contact their states'

Vaginismus • Involuntary contraction of the muscles surrounding the vagina, making entry difficult or impossible.

Performance anxiety • Fear concerning whether one will be able to perform adequately.

Sex therapy • Actually, a number of cognitive and behavioral methods that seek to reverse sexual dysfunctions by reducing performance anxiety, reversing defeatist expectations, and fostering sexual competencies.

psychological associations to learn which professionals are competent to help them with problems in this area.

AIDS AND OTHER SEXUALLY TRANSMITTED DISEASES

Sexual relationships can be sources of pleasure and personal fulfillment. They also carry some risks. One of the risks is that of contracting **AIDS** or other sexually transmitted diseases (STDs). According to Theresa Crenshaw, president of the American Association of Sex Educators, Counselors, and Therapists, "You're not just sleeping with one person, you're sleeping with everyone *they* ever slept with."

Although media attention usually focuses on AIDS, a survey of more than 16,000 students at 19 universities found that only 30 were infected with **HIV**, the virus that causes AIDS. That's two (0.2 percent) of every thousand blood samples tested (Gayle and others, 1990). Since AIDS is fatal, this finding is cause for concern. Other sexually transmitted diseases (STDs) are more widespread, however. *Chlamydia trachomatous* (the bacterium that causes chlamydia) was found in 1 sample in 10, or 10 percent of the college population. *Human papilloma virus* (HPV), the organism that causes genital warts, is estimated to be present in one third of college women and 8 percent of men aged 15 to 49 (Cannistra & Niloff, 1996).

AIDS • Abbreviation for *acquired immunodeficiency syndrome*—a fatal sexually transmitted disease caused by the human immunodeficiency virus (HIV), which destroys cells of the immune system, leaving the body vulnerable to opportunistic diseases.

HIV • Abbreviation of *human immunodeficiency virus*—the virus that gives rise to acquired immunodeficiency syndrome (AIDS) by destroying cells of the immune system and leaving the body prey to opportunistic diseases. Sometimes referred to as "the AIDS virus."

Most college students appear to be reasonably well informed about HIV transmission and AIDS (Wulfert & Wan, 1993). Yet many are unaware that chlamydia can go undetected for years. Moreover, if it is not treated it can cause pelvic inflammation and infertility. Many, perhaps most, students are also ignorant of HPV, which is linked to cervical cancer (Cannistra & Niloff, 1996). Yet as many as 1 million new cases of HPV infection occur each year in the United States—more than syphilis, genital herpes, and AIDS combined. Fewer than 2 million Americans are thought to be infected with HIV. However, about

"DYING IN AMERICA AT THE END OF THE MILLENNIUM."
This is a lyric from the Broadway musical *Rent*, which portrays young people with AIDS. They become infected with HIV by means of needle sharing (when injecting heroin), male-female sex, and male-male sex.

SELF-ASSESSMENT

THE AIDS AWARENESS INVENTORY

Some readers are more knowledgeable than others about HIV and AIDS. To find out how much you know about them, place a *T* in the blank space for each item that you believe is true or mostly true. Place an *F* in the blank space for each item that you believe is false or mostly false. Then check your answers against the explanations offered at the end of the chapter.

Before you get started, let us issue a "warning." Some of the items in this Self-Assessment are rated "R." If we were talking about a film, we would say that it contains some sex and nudity. There is no violence, however. The purpose of the questionnaire, like the purpose of this book, is to help you prevent doing violence to yourself. ■

___ 1. AIDS is synonymous with HIV. They are different names for the same thing.

___ 2. You can be infected with HIV only by people who have AIDS.

___ 3. AIDS is a kind of pneumonia.

___ 4. AIDS is a form of cancer.

___ 5. You can't get infected with HIV the first time you engage in sexual intercourse.

___ 6. You can't be infected by HIV unless you engage in male-male sexual activity or share needles to inject ("shoot up") drugs.

___ 7. AIDS is more of a threat to men than to women.

___ 8. You can be infected by HIV and not have any signs or symptoms of illness for many years.

___ 9. You can't be infected with HIV by hugging someone, even if that person is infected with HIV.

___ 10. You can't be infected with HIV by having regular sexual intercourse (intercourse with the penis in the vagina), even if your partner is infected with HIV.

___ 11. You can't be infected with HIV through sexual activity if you're using contraception, even if your partner is infected with HIV.

___ 12. You can't be infected with HIV by oral sex (that is, from kissing, licking, or sucking a penis or a vagina), even if your partner is infected with HIV.

___ 13. Using condoms ("rubbers," "safes") guarantees protection against being infected with HIV, even if your partner is infected with HIV.

___ 14. More than a million people in the United States have AIDS.

___ 15. You can be infected with HIV by donating blood.

___ 16. If you already have a sexually transmitted disease, like chlamydia or genital warts, you can't be infected with HIV.

___ 17. You can't be infected with HIV if you and your sex partner are faithful to one another (don't have sex with anyone else).

___ 18. There are no medical treatments for HIV infection or AIDS.

___ 19. Knowledge of how HIV is transmitted is sufficient to get people to abstain from risky behavior.

___ 20. People are likely to be infected with HIV if they are bitten by insects such as mosquitoes that are carrying it.

TABLE 15.4 CAUSES, METHODS OF TRANSMISSION, SYMPTOMS, DIAGNOSIS, AND TREATMENT OF SEXUALLY TRANSMITTED DISEASES (STDS)

STD AND CAUSE	*METHODS OF TRANSMISSION*	*SYMPTOMS*	*DIAGNOSIS*	*TREATMENT*
Acquired immuno-deficiency syndrome (AIDS): Human immunodeficiency virus (HIV)	HIV is transmitted by sexual intercourse, direct infusion of contaminated blood, or from mother to child during childbirth or breast-feeding.	Infected people may not have any symptoms; they may develop mild flulike symptoms which disappear for many years prior to the development of "full-blown" AIDS. Full-blown AIDS is symptomized by fever, weight loss, fatigue, diarrhea, and opportunistic infections such as Kaposi's sarcoma, pneumonia (PCP), and invasive cancer of the cervix.	Blood, saliva, and urine tests can detect HIV antibodies in the bloodstream. The Western blot blood test may be used to confirm positive results.	There is no safe, effective vaccine for HIV. Combinations of antiviral drugs, including AZT and protease inhibitors, may significantly reduce the amount of HIV in the bloodstream.
Bacterial vaginosis: *Gardnerella vaginalis* bacterium and others	Vaginosis can arise by overgrowth of organisms in vagina, allergic reactions, etc.; it is transmitted by sexual contact.	Women develop a thin, foul-smelling vaginal discharge, irritation of genitals, and mild pain during urination. In men, the penile foreskin and glans become inflamed, urethritis and cystitis develop. Vaginosis may be asymptomatic in both sexes.	Bacterium is cultured and examined.	Treatment is accomplished orally with metronidazole (brand name: Flagyl).
Candidiasis moniliasis, thrush, "yeast infection": *Candida albicans*—a yeastlike fungus	Yeast infections can arise by overgrowth of fungus in vagina or can be transmitted by sexual contact or by sharing a washcloth with an infected person.	Women develop vulval itching; white, cheesy, foul-smelling discharge; soreness or swelling of vaginal and vulval tissues. Men develop itching and burning on urination, or a reddening or "chapping" of the penis.	Diagnosis is usually made on basis of symptoms.	Treatment is accomplished with vaginal suppositories, creams, or tablets containing miconazole, clotrimazole, or teraconazole; modification of use of other medicines and chemical agents; keeping infected area dry.
Chlamydia and **nongonococcal urethritis (NGU):** *Chlamydia trachomatous* bacterium; NGU in men may also be caused by *Ureaplasma urealycticum* bacterium and other pathogens	These diseases are transmitted by vaginal, oral, or anal sexual activity; to the eye by touching one's eyes after touching the genitals of an infected partner; or by passing through the birth canal of an infected mother.	In women, symptoms are frequent and painful urination, lower abdominal pain and inflammation, and vaginal discharge (but most women are symptom-free). In men, symptoms are similar to but milder than those of gonorrhea—burning or painful urination, slight penile discharge (some men are also asymptomatic). A sore throat may indicate infection from oral-genital contact.	For women, cervical smears are analyzed with the Abbott Testpack.	Treatment is accomplished with antibiotics.
Genital herpes: Herpes simplex virus–type 2 (HSV-2)	Herpes is almost always transmitted by means of vaginal, oral, or anal sexual activity; it is most contagious during active outbreaks of the disease.	Painful, reddish bumps appear around the genitals, thigh, or buttocks; in women, they may also be in the vagina or on the cervix. Bumps become blisters or sores that fill with pus and break, shedding viral particles. Other possible symptoms include burning urination, fever, aches and pains, swollen glands and—in women—vaginal discharge.	Sores are clinically inspected; fluid is drawn from the base of a genital sore and is then cultured and examined.	The antiviral drug acyclovir (brand name: Zovirax) may provide relief and prompt healing over, but it is not a cure.

TABLE 15.4 (CONTINUED)

STD AND CAUSE	*METHODS OF TRANSMISSION*	*SYMPTOMS*	*DIAGNOSIS*	*TREATMENT*
Genital warts (venereal warts): Human papilloma virus (HPV)	Transmission is by sexual and other forms of contact, as with infected towels or clothing. Women are especially vulnerable, particularly women who have multiple sex partners.	Painless warts often resembling cauliflowers appear on the penis, foreskin, scrotum, or internal urethra in men, and on the vulva, labia, wall of the vagina, or cervix in women. They may occur around the anus and in the rectum.	Warts are clinically inspected (Because HPV is connected with cervical cancer, regular Pap tests are also advised.)	Methods of removal include cryotherapy (freezing), podophyllin, burning, and surgical removal (by a physician!). Warts may return, however.
Gonorrhea ("clap," "drip"): Gonococcus bacterium (*Neisseria gonorrhoeae)*	Gonorrhea is transmitted by vaginal, oral, or anal sexual activity, or from mother to newborn during delivery.	In men, symptoms are yellowish, thick penile discharge, burning urination. In women, symptoms are increased vaginal discharge, burning urination, and irregular menstrual bleeding (most women show no early symptoms).	Sample discharge is cultured and clinically inspected.	Treatment is accomplished with antibiotics.
Pubic lice ("crabs"): *Pthirus pubis* (an insect)	Transmission is by sexual contact or by contact with an infested towel, sheet, or toilet seat.	Lice cause intense itching in the pubic area and other hairy regions to which lice can attach.	Clinical examination will reveal lice.	Treatment is accomplished with lindane (brand name: Kwell), which is a prescription drug, or with over-the-counter medications containing pyrethrins or piperonal butoxide (brand names: NIX, A200, RID, Triple X).
Syphilis: *Treponema pallidum*	Transmission is by vaginal, oral, or anal sexual activity, or by touching an infectious chancre.	In primary stage, a hard, round painless chancre or sore appears at site of infection within 2 to 4 weeks. Syphilis may progress through secondary, latent, and tertiary stages if left untreated.	Primary-stage syphilis is diagnosed by clinical examination, or fluid from a chancre is examined in a test. Secondary-stage syphilis is diagnosed by blood test (the VDRL).	Treatment is accomplished wih antibiotics.
Trichomoniasis ("trich"): *Trichomonas vaginalis*—a protozoan (one-celled animal)	Trichomoniasis is almost always transmitted sexually.	Women may develop a foamy, yellowish, odorous, vaginal discharge and an itching or burning sensation in vulva; many women are asymptomatic. Men are usually asymptomatic, but mild urethritis is possible.	Microscopic examination of a smear of vaginal secretions or of a culture of the sample (latter method preferred) reveals the disease.	Treatment is accomplished with metronidazole (Flagyl).

56 million are infected with other STD-causing viruses, such as those causing genital warts, herpes, and hepatitis (Barringer, 1993a).

Women experience the effects of STDs disproportionately. They are more likely to develop infertility if an STD spreads through the reproductive system. Each year an estimated 100,000 to 150,000 U.S. women become infertile (unable to get pregnant) because of STDs (Barringer, 1993a). Overall, STDs are believed to account for 15 to 30 percent of cases of infertility among U.S. women. In addition to their biological effects, STDs take an emotional toll and can strain relationships to the breaking point.

In the rest of this section we focus on AIDS, but there are many other STDs that you should be aware of. Information about these STDs is presented in Table 15.4. Readers who want more information are advised to talk to their professor or doctor, consult human sexuality or health textbooks, or visit their college counseling and health center.

AIDS

AIDS is a life-threatening condition in which the person's immune system is so weakened that he or she falls prey to so-called *opportunistic diseases* (diseases that would not have much of a chance of taking hold in people with normal immune systems). It is caused by the human immunodeficiency virus (HIV).

HIV is transmitted by infected blood, semen, vaginal and cervical secretions, and breast milk (Meier, 1997; Royce and others, 1997). The first three fluids may enter the body through vaginal, anal, or oral sex with an infected partner. Other means of infection include sharing a hypodermic needle with an infected person (as is common among people who inject illicit drugs) and transfusion with contaminated blood. There need be no concern about closed-mouth kissing. Note, too, that saliva does not transmit HIV (AIDS Hotline, 1998). *However,* transmission through deep kissing is theoretically possible if blood in an infected person's mouth (e.g., from toothbrushing or gum disease) enters cuts (again, as from toothbrushing or gum disease) in the other person's mouth ("Man transmits HIV," 1997). HIV may also be transmitted from mother to fetus during pregnancy or from mother to child through childbirth or breast-feeding. There is no evidence that public toilets, insect bites, holding or hugging an infected person, or living or attending school with one can transmit the virus.

HIV kills white blood cells called *CD4 lymphocytes* (or, more simply, *CD4 cells*) that are found in the immune system. CD4 cells recognize viruses and "instruct" other white blood cells called *B lymphocytes* to make antibodies, which combat disease. Eventually, however, CD4 cells are depleted and the body is left vulnerable to opportunistic diseases.

AIDS is characterized by fatigue, fever, unexplained weight loss, swollen lymph nodes, diarrhea, and, in many cases, impairment of learning and memory. Among the opportunistic infections that may take hold are Kaposi's sarcoma, a cancer of the blood cells that occurs in many gay males who contract AIDS; PCP (pneumocystis carinii pneumonia), a kind of pneumonia that is characterized by coughing and shortness of breath; and, in women, invasive cancer of the cervix.

People in the United States have been most likely to become infected with HIV by engaging in male-male sexual activity or injecting ("shooting up") illicit drugs (Centers for Disease Control and Prevention, 1997). Other people at particular risk include sex partners of people who inject drugs, babies born to women who inject drugs or whose sex partners inject drugs, prostitutes and men who visit them, and sex partners of men who visit infected prostitutes. People today are unlikely to be infected by means of blood transfusions because blood supplies are routinely screened for HIV (Schreiber and others, 1996).

> ***Truth or Fiction Revisited***
>
> **It is not true that only gay males and substance abusers are at serious risk for contracting AIDS. We all need to be aware of the risk factors and take appropriate precautions.**

One *psychological* risk factor for HIV infection is that people tend to underestimate their risk of infection (Seppa, 1997). This finding is as true for college students (Goldman & Harlow, 1993) as it is for inner-city residents (Hobfoll and others, 1993). Because AIDS has often been characterized as transmitted by anal intercourse (a practice that is fairly common among gay males) and the sharing of contaminated needles, many heterosexual Americans who do not abuse drugs dismiss the threat of AIDS. Yet male-female sexual intercourse accounts for the majority of cases in the world today (Royce and others, 1997). Thus, although gays and drug abusers have been hit hardest by the epidemic, HIV cuts across all boundaries of gender, sexual orientation, ethnicity, and socioeconomic status.

DIAGNOSIS AND TREATMENT OF HIV INFECTION AND AIDS Infection by HIV is generally diagnosed by means of blood, saliva, or urine tests. For many years researchers were frustrated in their efforts to develop effective vaccines and treatments for HIV infection and AIDS. There is still no safe, effective vaccine, but recent developments in drug therapy have raised hopes about treatment.

AZT and similar antiviral drugs—ddI, ddC—inhibit reproduction of HIV by targeting the enzyme called *reverse transcriptase.* A newer generation of drugs, *protease inhibitors,* targets the *protease* enzyme. A "cocktail" of antiviral drugs such as AZT, 3TC, and protease inhibitors—called "triple therapy"—has become the more or less standard treatment and has reduced HIV to below detectable levels in many infected people (Altman, 1997). Many doctors treat people who fear that they have been exposed to HIV with antiviral drugs to reduce the likelihood of infection (Katz & Gerberding, 1997). *If you fear that you have been exposed to HIV, talk to your doctor about it immediately.*

Triple therapy has worked many wonders to date. It cut the U.S. death rate from AIDS-related causes by 26 percent from 1995 to 1996, and by 44 percent from 1996 to 1997 (Altman, 1998; Irvine, 1998). It cut the California and New York death rates from AIDS-related causes by 60 percent and 48 percent, respectively, from 1996 to 1997 (Altman, 1998; Irvine, 1998). But not everyone can tolerate triple therapy. HIV levels also rebound in many who use triple therapy. Even when HIV has been reduced to "undetectable levels" by ordinary means, scientists have been able to find it in "resting" (nonreplicating) CD4 cells by looking harder ("U.S. scientists admit," 1997). Therefore, triple therapy is not a cure. There is also concern that strains of HIV will arise that are not affected by triple therapy (Irvine, 1998). Moreover, there is the danger that the public may assume that AIDS is no longer a threat and decrease funds for AIDS research. Until we do have a cure or a safe, effective vaccine, the most effective way of dealing with AIDS is *prevention* (Fowler, 1998).

For the latest information on AIDS, call the National AIDS Hotline at 1-800-342-AIDS. If you want to receive information in Spanish, call 1-800-344-SIDA.

CONTRACEPTION

Familiarity breeds contempt—and children.

MARK TWAIN

Sexually active college students need to face the question of contraception. Assuming that you'll be okay most of the time is like playing Russian roulette—but you're playing with the well-being of your partner and also, potentially, with the welfare of a child who may be unwanted or be reared by parents who are not ready. Let us consider a number of methods.

TABLE 15.5 METHODS OF CONTRACEPTION: RELIABILITY, REVERSIBILITY, AND PROTECTION AGAINST SEXUALLY TRANSMITTED DISEASES

CONTRACEPTIVE METHOD	*RELIABILITY (POOR–EXCELLENT*)*	*REVERSIBILITY (CAN WOMEN READILY BECOME PREGNANT ONCE METHOD IS DISCONTINUED?)*	*DOES METHOD PROVIDE PROTECTION AGAINST SEXUALLY TRANSMITTED DISEASES?*
Birth control pills containing estrogen and progestin	Excellent	Yes	No
Minipills (contain progestin only)	Excellent	Yes	No
Norplant	Excellent	Yes	No
Depo-Provera	Excellent	Yes	No
Intrauterine device (IUD)	Excellent	Yes (unless fertility is impaired by infection)	No
Diaphragm with spermicide	Fair to Good	Yes	Some protection
Cervical cap	Fair to Good	Yes	Some protection
Male condom	Fair to Good†	Yes	Yes
Male condom with spermicide	Excellent	Yes	Yes
Female condom	Poor to Fair	Yes	Yes
Coitus interruptus (withdrawal)	Poor to Fair	Yes	No
Rhythm methods	Poor to Fair	Yes	No
Douching	Poor	Yes	No
Vasectomy (male sterilization)	Excellent	Not usually	No
Tubal ligation (female sterilization)	Excellent	Not usually	No

* Excellent: Fewer than 5% of women who use method become pregnant within a year.
† About 10% of women whose partners wear a condom become pregnant within a year.
Source: Much of the data is derived from Hatcher and others (1998), *Contraceptive Technology,* 17th edition, New York: Ardent Media.

Table 15.5 summarizes the reliability, reversibility, and degree of protection against STDs provided by various contraceptive methods. Reliability is generally higher for people who use the methods carefully. For example, some women forget to take the pill regularly, and male condoms can tear or slip.

CONTRACEPTIVE PILLS ("THE PILL") "The pill" is the most widely used contraceptive method by unmarried women between the ages of 15 and 44. There are various kinds of pills, but they all contain hormones called estrogens and progestins, singly or in combination. Women cannot conceive children when they are already pregnant, and combination pills (that contain estrogens and progestins) fool the brain into acting as though women are pregnant. So-called minipills contain progestins only. Minipills act in two ways. They thicken the cervical mucus and prevent many sperm from passing into the uterus and fallopian tubes where they normally fertilize egg cells (ova). Minipills also make the inner lining of the uterus unreceptive to the egg. Thus, if the woman does conceive, the fertilized egg is passed from the body. For these reasons, many users look upon the combination pill as a contraceptive—that is, an agent that prevents conception—but they see the minipill as an early way of aborting an embryo. Birth control pills are available only by a doctor's prescription.

The great majority of pregnancies that occur while on the pill reflect failure to follow directions (mostly skipping pills). Pills are taken from 20 to 28 days each month. Users are advised to take them at the same time each day and in sequence to prompt memory.

The great advantage of the pill is that it makes sex spontaneous and usually doesn't interfere with sexual sensations. But the pill does not prevent STDs, so its proper use, in terms of overall health, is within a monogamous sexual relationship with a partner who is known to be free of STDs.

The main drawbacks of pills concern side effects. Minor side effects from estrogen include nausea and vomiting (usually during the first day or two of usage), fluid retention (feeling "bloated"), weight gain, headaches, tenderness in the breasts, and dizziness. More serious—but uncommon—problems include benign tumors, jaundice, gall bladder problems, migraine headaches, and elevated blood pressure. Blood clots, strokes, and hemorrhages are also reported. *There is no clear evidence that oral contraceptives cause cancer.* Breast cancer has been a particular focus of researchers, since breast tissue is sensitive to hormonal changes. Some studies show increased risk of breast cancer among pill users, others show no relationship, and still others show *less* risk of breast cancer among pill users (Reinisch, 1990). Similarly, evidence linking the pill with increased risk of cervical cancer is mixed (Hatcher and others, 1998). The majority of college students may find comfort in the fact that users are not considered at high risk for most disorders until they turn 35. Yet most gynecologists today continue to prescribe the pill for women who are older than 35.

Although there is a tendency to focus on potential problems caused by the pill, it may actually have some *healthful* side effects. For example, the pill appears to reduce the risk of rheumatoid arthritis, ovarian cysts, pelvic inflammatory disease (PID), and fibrocystic (benign) breast growths. The pill regularizes menstrual cycles and reduces premenstrual discomfort and menstrual cramping. It may be helpful in treatment of facial acne and iron-deficiency anemia. The combination pill apparently reduces the risks of ovarian and endometrial cancer (Hatcher and others, 1998).

Progestins foster male characteristics, so women who take the minipill are likely to encounter side effects such as acne, increase in facial hair, thinning of scalp hair, reduction in breast size, vaginal dryness, and missed or shorter periods. When on either kind of pill, women are advised to discuss any physical changes with their physicians.

NORPLANT Norplant, like the pill, works through sex hormones. But the hormones are delivered differently.

Norplant consists of six matchstick-sized silicone tubes that contain progestin. They are surgically embedded under the skin of a woman's upper arm. Surgery takes about 10 minutes and is conducted under local anesthesia. The tubes release a small, steady dose of progestin into the woman's bloodstream, providing protection for as long as 5 years after implantation. The progestin in the Norplant system suppresses ovulation and thickens the cervical mucus so that sperm cannot pass. The contraceptive effect occurs within 24 hours of insertion. After 5 years the spent tubes are replaced.

A major advantage of Norplant is the convenience of having a supply of contraception that is automatically dispensed and literally less than an arm's length away at all times. The woman need not remember to take a pill a day, insert a contraceptive before sex, or check to see that an IUD is in place. Moreover, Norplant is reported to have an extremely low failure rate of less than 1 percent per year across 5 years. The failure rate approximates that of surgical sterilization. Unlike sterilization, however, Norplant is fully reversible. Removal of the implants restores a normal likelihood of pregnancy. The most commonly reported side effect is irregular menstrual bleeding.

DEPO-PROVERA Depo-Provera is the brand name of a long-acting, synthetic form of progesterone that inhibits ovulation. Depo-Provera is injected once every 3 months. Depo-Provera may produce side effects such as weight gain, menstrual irregularity, and spotting between periods. The great advantage is that the woman receives an injection and can forget about contraception for 3 months.

THE "MORNING-AFTER PILL" Morning-after pills also consist of estrogens or progestins. Women ovulate (release an egg cell from an ovary) during the middle of their menstrual cycle, and morning-after pills can prevent implantation of the egg after it has been fertilized. Morning-after pills are higher in hormone content than most birth control pills and are sometimes taken two or more times per day. Because of the high doses, morning-after pills cause nausea in a majority of users.

Morning-after pills are early abortion methods rather than contraceptive devices. For this reason, they have met with opposition by antiabortion groups (Hitt, 1998).

INTRAUTERINE DEVICES (IUDS) The IUD is fixed in the uterus by a physician and can be left in place for a year or more. No one knows exactly how IUDs work. The main theory is that they produce uterine inflammation that (1) can destroy sperm as they travel through to meet eggs in the fallopian tubes and (2) prevent fertilized eggs from becoming implanted after they enter the uterus from a fallopian tube.

The IUD, like the pill, allows for spontaneous sex, and it does not diminish sexual sensations. Also like the pill, it offers no protection against STDs.

Why, then, are IUDs relatively unpopular? For one thing, they can be painful to insert. For another, many users incur infections in the fallopian tubes and may contract pelvic inflammatory disease (PID). These infections can cause infertility. Devices are sometimes expelled by the user. Finally, the uterine wall is sometimes perforated (torn) by the IUD. This potentially lethal problem afflicts hundreds of American users each year.

DIAPHRAGMS Diaphragms are shallow cups with flexible rims that are made of thin rubber. A physician fits them to the contours of the vagina. A cream or jelly that kills sperm (i.e., a spermicide) is spread on the inside of the cup; the cup is then placed against the cervix. The diaphragm is normally inserted within 6 hours before intercourse. When placed properly, the diaphragm fits snugly over the cervix, denying sperm passage into the uterus. As a barrier device, the diaphragm is not reliable. Its main function is to hold the spermicide in place.

A great advantage of the diaphragm is the nearly complete lack of side effects. The occasional woman who is allergic to rubber can switch to a plastic model. About one man or woman in 20 encounters irritation from the spermicide, a problem that is often alleviated by switching brands. On the plus side, the spermicides offer some protection against STDs.

Now, the negatives. The diaphragm is relatively unpopular because it is inconvenient to have to insert it prior to intercourse. It kills the spontaneity. And if it is inserted an hour or so before the date, the woman may wind up watching the clock.

Spermicides, by the way, can be used without diaphragms, but diaphragms hold them in place.

Cervical Caps Cervical caps are made of rubber or plastic and fitted over the cervix. Unlike the diaphragm, they can be kept in place by suction for up to several weeks at a time. They function as a barrier that prevents sperm from reaching the uterus and fallopian tubes, where fertilization normally occurs. An important advantage to the cap is the apparent lack of side effects, although some women find it uncomfortable. Use of the cervical cap can be combined with spermicide, and the combination is apparently about as reliable as that of the diaphragm and spermicide.

Disadvantages are that women must be fitted for the cap and that many women are contoured so that the caps do not remain in place. Also, caps sometimes become dislodged during intercourse. For these reasons, and because caps can be hard to get, they are not used by many American women.

Male Condoms All condoms can be used to prevent pregnancy. Latex condoms ("rubbers") also provide protection from STDs, including HIV infection and AIDS. This is why they are also referred to as *prophylactics* (meaning "agents that protect against disease"). Male condoms made of animal membrane ("skins") offer little or no protection from STDs.

Male condoms are available in pharmacies without prescription, from family planning clinics, and in many locales—including some college dormitories—from vending machines. They are the only device that is worn by the man rather than the woman. They serve as barriers that prevent sperm (and microscopic disease organisms) from entering the woman. Conversely, they protect the man from infected vaginal fluids.

Male condoms are highly reliable when they are put on (and removed!) carefully. Use of a spermicide with a condom is even more reliable.

Use of male condoms changes the psychology of sexual relations. First, it shifts much of the responsibility for contraception to the man. Other methods, with the exception of vasectomy, focus on the woman. In each case, the woman suffers the side effects and the inconvenience and is perceived as responsible for avoiding pregnancy. Avoiding unwanted pregnancy is a shared obligation, of course.

Second, use of condoms makes sex less spontaneous. Third, condoms decrease sexual sensations somewhat, predominantly for the man. For these reasons, many men object to using them. Yet condoms are free of side effects.

Female Condoms The female condom is a polyurethane (plastic) sheath about $6\frac{1}{2}$ inches in length and $1\frac{1}{2}$ to 2 inches in diameter that is shaped like a condom. It is put in the vagina and held in place by flexible plastic rings that are fitted over the vaginal opening and against the cervix. The female condom provides a secure but flexible shield that barricades against sperm but allows the penis to move freely within the vagina during intercourse. The female condom, like the male condom, offers some protection against STDs, but it is not as effective ("Condom for women," 1993). Mary E. Guinan (1992) of the Centers for Disease Control notes that a "hidden epidemic" of HIV infection in women is emerging, and points out that women can use the female condom if their partners refuse to wear a male condom. Cynthia Pearson (1992) of the National Women's Health Network notes that the female condom "for the first time [gives] women control over exposure to sexually transmitted disease, including AIDS." Food and Drug Administration Commissioner David Kessler (1993) remarks, "The female condom is not all we would wish for, but it is better than no protection at all."

The effectiveness of the female condom as a contraceptive device is questionable, however. Early research shows that its use is connected with a 26 percent pregnancy rate during a year of usage ("Condom for women," 1993). Many women also complain that the female condom is bulky and difficult to insert (Stewart, 1992).

COITUS INTERRUPTUS (THE "WITHDRAWAL METHOD") Coitus (pronounced "co-EET-us") interruptus, or the "withdrawal method," is removal of the penis from the vagina prior to ejaculation. Let us tell you a joke: "What do you call couples who use coitus interruptus?" Answer: "Parents."

We include coitus interruptus as a birth control method because you may hear about it from other sources. As implied in the joke, it is unreliable. Even if the man does manage to withdraw before ejaculating, sperm is present in fluids that are typically discharged prior to ejaculation. Enough said?

RHYTHM METHODS There are several rhythm methods—also referred to as natural birth control. Each is based on awareness of the phase of the woman's menstrual cycle. Women can conceive only for about 48 hours after they ovulate. After that, an egg cell (ovum) can no longer be fertilized. Sperm can live for about 72 hours in the female reproductive tract. If the woman knows exactly when she is ovulating, she can avert pregnancy by avoiding intercourse for 3 days prior to ovulation and 2 days afterward.

Most women who have regular 28-day cycles can use the calendar method reliably. Women ovulate 14 days before their periods begin. Regular women can thus track their cycles on calendars and place sex off-limits for a few days before and after ovulation—perhaps 4 days before and 3 days after, just to be safe.

For women with irregular cycles, the math becomes complicated, and the period of abstention becomes protracted. Other rhythm methods involve tracking the woman's basal body temperature or the viscosity (stickiness) of her cervical mucus. These methods are explained in detail in human sexuality textbooks and pamphlets available from gynecologists and family planning clinics. You may also find helpful advice at your college health or counseling center. Ovulation-predicting kits are available without prescription from pharmacies, but they're expensive and can be complicated to use. (They are normally used by people with fertility problems who want to optimize their chances of becoming pregnant.)

There are a number of advantages to rhythm methods. Since they do not use artificial devices, they are acceptable to the Catholic church. (Premarital sex, of course, is not.) Second, there are no side effects. Third, sexual spontaneity and sexual sensations are kept intact—at least on "safe" days. Combining the rhythm method with a condom renders conception highly unlikely. On the other hand, the rhythm method provides no protection from STDs.

DOUCHING Douching is flushing the vagina with a stream of water or another liquid following intercourse. The function of the water is to wash sperm out, although some commercial douches also kill sperm. Douching is usually ineffective because many sperm exceed the range of the douche seconds after ejaculation.

STERILIZATION Sterilization is almost perfectly reliable, and is the most common method used by married people. Sterilization involves surgery, and the major methods in use today are the tubal ligation in women and the vasectomy in men. The tubal ligation cuts and ties back the fallopian tubes, which carry egg cells (ova) from the ovary to the uterus. The vasectomy severs the *vas deferens*, which transport semen from the testes to the penis in men. Although these operations are sometimes reversible—especially when doctors strive to carry them out in a way that enhances the chances of reversibility—they are still considered "permanent." If you want to have children someday, sterilization is not for you. By the way, many college-age people who believe that they will never want to have children change their minds in their late twenties and their thirties.

adjustment and modern life

Rape and AIDS are buzzwords. They are high in the consciousness of most college students, and both of them are best dealt with by *prevention.* This chapter's "Adjustment and Modern Life" section thus describes strategies for preventing these devastating problems.

PREVENTING RAPE (SHOUT "FIRE!" NOT "RAPE!")

Let us begin this section with a disclaimer. We are going to talk about measures that women can take to reduce their vulnerability to rapists. However, we are *not* implying that the prevention of rape is the responsibility of the victim. Society at large harbors many attitudes that have the effect of supporting rape. For example, as noted earlier in the chapter, large numbers of people believe that a woman loses the right to say no if she has "led on" a man or even if she goes with him to his apartment. Also, men are reinforced for aggressive behavior in our society. Many people even expect men to exert social dominance over women. These social attitudes and expectations have catastrophic consequences for women and even for men who are uncomfortable with the stereotypes. It is thus the responsibility of any people who can communicate, such as your authors, to lay the blame at the proper door and to insist on social change. We are doing precisely that—*now.*

Social change is a tedious process, however, and it may never come to pass. Women, unfortunately, can thus profit from being armed with strategies for preventing rape in this less-than-ideal society.

In *The New Our Bodies, Ourselves,* the Boston Women's Health Book Collective (1993) lists a number of such strategies that women can use to lower the likelihood of rape at the hands of strangers. For example:

- Establish signals and arrangements with other women in an apartment building or neighborhood.
- List only first initials in the telephone directory or on the mailbox.
- Use dead-bolt locks.
- Keep windows locked and obtain iron grids for first-floor windows.
- Keep entrances and doorways brightly lit.
- Have keys ready for the front door or the car.
- Do not walk alone in the dark.

- Avoid deserted areas.
- Never allow a strange man into your apartment or home without checking his credentials.
- Drive with the car windows up and the door locked.
- Check the rear seat of the car before entering.
- Avoid living in an unsafe building.
- Do not pick up hitchhikers (including women).
- Do not talk to strange men in the street.
- Shout "Fire!" not "Rape!" People crowd around fires but avoid scenes of violence.

The following tactics may help prevent *date rape* (Rathus & Fichner-Rathus, 1997):

- Avoid getting into secluded situations until you know your date very well. (As noted in the questionnaire on page 476, some men interpret a date's willingness to accompany them to their room as an agreement to engage in sexual activity.) But be aware that victims of date rapes have sometimes gotten to know their assailants.
- Be wary when a date attempts to control you in any way, such as frightening you by driving rapidly or taking you some place you would rather not go.
- Be very assertive and clear concerning your sexual intentions. Some rapists, particularly date rapists, tend to misinterpret women's wishes. If their dates begin to implore them to stop during kissing or petting, they construe pleading as "female game playing." So if kissing or petting is leading where you don't want it to go, speak up.
- When dating a person for the first time, try to date in a group.
- Encourage your college or university to offer educational programs about date rape. The University of Washington, for example, offers students lectures and seminars on date rape and provides women with escorts to get home. Brown University requires all first-year students to attend orientation sessions on rape (Celis, 1991). The point here is for men to learn that "No" means "No," despite the widespread belief that some women like to be "talked into" sex.
- Talk to your date about his attitudes toward women. If you get the feeling that he believes that men are in a war with women, or that women try to "play games" with men, you may be better off dating someone else.
- You can find out about attitudes by discussing items from our "Self-Assessment" questionnaire with a man you are considering dating. You can say something like, "You know, my friend's date said that . . . What do you think about it?" It's a good way to find out if he has attitudes that can lead to trouble.

RESISTING VERBAL SEXUAL PRESSURE

Verbal sexual pressure involves insistence or the use of seduction "lines" that aim to manipulate someone into sex. Forty-two percent of the respondents in a survey of college men at a southeastern university admitted to verbally coercing a woman into sex (Craig and others, 1989). About one in five of the men surveyed at a northwestern university reported having said things to women they did not mean in order to have sexual intercourse (Lane & Gwartney-Gibbs, 1985). College women in the survey were more likely than men to have been pressured, threatened, or forced into sexual relations. One in four of the women said that they had given in to sexual intercourse against their better judgment because they had felt pressured by a man's persistent arguments.

College men are also verbally pressured into sex, however. About 1 in 15 of the men at the northwestern university admitted having engaged in sexual intercourse against their preferences as a result of sexual pressure. In another study, nearly two out of three college men reported they had been pressured into sex at one time or another (Muehlenhard & Falcon, 1990).

Following are sexual pressure lines noted by Powell (1991) that men usually use with women. What would you say in response to each of them? Responses as suggested by Powell (1991) are shown in parentheses.

KIND OF PRESSURE LINE	THE LINE	YOUR RESPONSE
Lines that reassure you about the negative consequences	"Don't worry, I'm sterile."	______________________ ______________________ ______________________ (I know you want to make me feel safer, but . . . well, I'm just not comfortable about sex without a condom. I've known a few people who were more fertile than they thought.)
	"You can't get pregnant the first time."	______________________ ______________________ ______________________ (Hey, where did you get your sex education? People can get pregnant any time they have intercourse, even if it's just for one second.)
	"Don't worry—I'll pull out."	______________________ ______________________ ______________________ (I know you want to reassure me, but people can get pregnant that way, even without ejaculating.)

Kind of Pressure Line	The Line	Your Response
Lines that threaten you with rejection	"If you don't have sex, I'll find someone who will."	______ ______ ______ (I can't believe you are making a threat like this. I'm furious that you you would treat lovemaking like some kind of job, as if anyone will do.)
Lines that attempt to put down the refuser	"You're such a bitch."	______ ______ ______ (I can't believe you want to make love to me and think calling me names will put me in the mood. Good-bye.)
	"Are you frigid?"	______ ______ ______ (I resent being called names just because I tell you what I want to do with my body.)
Lines that stress the beautiful experience being missed	"Our relationship will grow stronger."	______ ______ ______ (I know you really would like to get more involved right now. But I need to wait. And lots of people have had their relationship grow stronger without intercourse.)
Lines that might settle for less	"I don't want to do anything. I just want to lie next to you."	______ ______ ______ (The way we're attracted to each other, I don't think that would be a good idea. As much as I care about you, I'd better not spend the night.)

(continued)

(continued)

Kind of Pressure Line	The Line	Your Response
Lines to make you prove yourself	"If you loved me, you would."	________________ (You know I care a lot about you. But I feel very pressured when you try to get me to do something I'm not ready for. It's not fair to me. Please consider my feelings.)
Lines that attempt to be logical, but aren't	"You're my girlfriend—it's your obligation."	________________ (If you think sex is an obligation, we need to think about this relationship right now.) [*Watch out* for any such talk—it is very common in abusers and rapists. At best, it's an irrational comment by an immature person.]
Lines that are totally transparent	"I'll say I love you after we do it."	________________ (Bye.) [There is no way to deal with a person who would say such a thing.]

Although these sample responses can help you resist specific pressure lines, do not think that saying no to sexual pressure is a privilege that you earn by winning an argument. You have the basic right to control your own body. ■

PREVENTING STDs IN THE AGE OF AIDS

> *You're not just sleeping with one person, you're sleeping with everyone* they *ever slept with.*
>
> DR. THERESA CRENSHAW, PRESIDENT OF THE AMERICAN ASSOCIATION OF SEX EDUCATORS, COUNSELORS, AND THERAPISTS

As shown by the remarks of one young woman, it can be clumsy to try to protect oneself from STDs such as AIDS:

> *It's one thing to talk about "being responsible about STDs" and a much harder thing to do it at the very moment. It's just plain hard to say to someone I am feeling very erotic with, "Oh, yes, before we go any further, can we have a conversation about STDs?" It's hard to imagine murmuring into someone's ear at a time of passion, "Would you mind slipping on this condom or using this cream just in case one of us has STDs?" Yet it seems awkward to bring it up beforehand, if it's not yet clear between us that we want to make love with one another.*
>
> *THE NEW OUR BODIES, OURSELVES*, 1993

Because of the difficulties in discussing STDs with sex partners, some people admit that they wing it. That is, they assume that a partner does not have an STD, or they hope for the best—even in the age of AIDS. Fifty-two percent of the single people aged 18 to 44 responding to a 1991 *New York Times*/CBS News survey reported that they had become more cautious about sex because of concern about AIDS, however (Kagay, 1991). The most common methods of behavior modification were use of condoms and limiting of the numbers of sex partners. Survey respondents overwhelmingly supported education about AIDS in the schools. Forty-two percent thought that children received "too little" information about AIDS in school, whereas only 2 percent believed that children were told "too much." (The remaining 54 percent thought that children received "about the right amount of information" or had no opinion on the matter.)

What can we do to prevent the transmission of HIV and other pathogens? A number of things:

1. *Refuse to deny the prevalence and harmful nature of AIDS.* Many people try to put AIDS and other STDs out of their minds and "wing it" when it comes to sex (Freiberg, 1998). The first and perhaps most important step in protecting oneself against AIDS is thus psychological: keeping it in mind—refusing to play the dangerous game that involves pretending (at least for the moment) that it does not exist. The other measures involve modifying our behavior.
2. *Remain abstinent.* One way of curtailing the sexual transmission of HIV and other pathogens is sexual abstinence. Most people who remain abstinent do so while they are looking for Mr. or Ms. Right, of course. They thus eventually face the risk of engaging in sexual intercourse. Moreover, students want to know just what "abstinence" means. Does it mean avoiding sexual intercourse? Yes. Does abstinence involve avoiding any form of sexual activity with another person? Not necessarily. Kissing,

WHAT DO *You* SAY NOW?

MAKING SEX SAFE(R) IN THE AGE OF AIDS

You've gone out with Chris a few times, and you're keenly attracted. Chris is attractive, bright, witty, shares some of your attitudes, and, all in all, is a powerful turn-on. Now the evening is winding down. You've been cuddling, and you think you know where things are heading.

Something clicks in your mind! You realize that as wonderful as Chris is, you don't know every place Chris has "been." As healthy as Chris looks and acts, you don't know what's swimming around in Chris's bloodstream either.

What do you say now? How do you protect yourself without turning Chris off? Write some possible responses in the spaces provided, and then check below for some ideas.

1. ______________________________

2. ______________________________

3. ______________________________

Ah, the clumsiness! If you ask about STDs, it is sort of making a verbal commitment to have sexual relations, and perhaps you're not exactly sure that's what your partner intends. And even if it's clear that's where you're heading, will you seem too straightforward? Will you kill the romance or the spontaneity of the moment? Sure you might—life has its risks. But which is riskier: an awkward moment or being infected with a fatal illness? Let's put it another way: Are you *really* willing to die for sex? Given that few verbal responses are perfect, here are some things you can try:

1. Ask good-naturedly, "Do you have anything to tell me?" This question is open-ended, and if Chris is as bright as you think, Chris might very well take the hint and tell you what you need to know.
2. If Chris answers "I love you," be happy about it. You could respond with something like, "I'm crazy about you, too." A minute later, add "Do you have anything *else* to tell me?"
3. If Chris says, "Like what?" you can beat around the bush one more time and say something like, "Well, I'm sure you weren't waiting for me all your life locked in a closet. I don't know everywhere you've been."
4. If you're uncomfortable with that, or if you want to be more straightforward, you can say something like, "As far as I know I'm perfectly healthy. Have there been any problems with you I should know about?" Saying that you are healthy invites reciprocity in self-disclosure.
5. Once Chris has expressed unawareness of being infected by any STDs, you might pursue it by mentioning your ideas about prevention. You can say something like, "I've brought something and I'd like to use it" (referring to a condom).
6. Or you can say something like, "I know this is a bit clumsy . . . " (you are assertively expressing a feeling and asking permission to pursue a clumsy topic; Chris is likely to respond with something like, "That's okay" or, "Don't worry—what is it?") ". . . but the world isn't as safe as it used to be, and I think we should talk about what we're going to do."

This is the point: Your partner hasn't been living in a remote cave. Your partner is also aware of the dangers of STDs, especially of AIDS, and ought to be working with you to make things safe and unpressured. If your partner is pressing for unsafe sex and is inconsiderate of your feelings and concerns, you need to reassess whether you really want to be with this person. Someone who wants to have unsafe sex in one relationship may be practicing it in other relationships, too. We think you can do better. ■

hugging, and petting to orgasm (without coming into contact with semen or vaginal secretions) are generally considered safe, although readers may argue about which of these behaviors is consistent with the definition of abstinence.

3. *Engage in a monogamous relationship with someone who is not infected.* Sexual activity within a monogamous relationship with an uninfected person is safe. The questions here are how certain one can be that one's partner is indeed uninfected and monogamous.

For those who are unwilling to abstain from sexual relationships or to limit themselves to a monogamous relationship, some things can be done that make sex safer—if not perfectly safe:

4. *Be selective.* Engage in sexual activity only with people you know well and who do not belong to the high-risk groups for AIDS.
5. *Inspect one's partner's genitals.* People who have been infected by HIV often have other STDs. Visually examining one's partner's genitals for blisters, discharges, chancres, rashes, warts, and lice while engaged in foreplay may yield warning signs of such diseases. An unpleasant odor is also a warning sign.
6. *Wash one's own genitals before and after contact.* Washing beforehand helps protect one's partner, and washing promptly afterward with soap and water helps remove some pathogens. Urinating afterward might be of some help, particularly to men, since the acidity of urine can kill some pathogens in the urethra.
7. *Use spermicides.* Spermicides are marketed as birth control devices, but many creams, foams, and jellies kill HIV and other pathogens as well as sperm. Check with a pharmacist.
8. *Use condoms.* Latex condoms (but not condoms made from animal membrane) protect the man from vaginal (or other) body fluids and protect the woman from having infected semen enter the vagina. A European study followed male-female couples with one partner who was known to be infected with HIV over an average period of 20 months (de Vincenzi, 1994). Among 124 couples who used condoms reliably, not one of the uninfected partners became infected with HIV. Condoms are particularly effective in preventing gonorrhea, syphilis, and AIDS. Combining condoms with spermicides is even more effective.
9. *Consult a physician about medication.* It can be helpful to use antibiotics after unprotected sex to guard against bacterial infections, but routine use of antibiotics may do nothing more than make them less effective when they are really needed. Medication will not shield one from herpes or AIDS, but it may decrease their symptoms or slow their progress.
10. *Have regular medical checkups.* These include blood tests. In this way one can learn about and treat disorders whose symptoms have gone unnoticed. But again, this method is of little avail against herpes and AIDS.
11. *When in doubt, stop.* If one is not sure that sex is safe, one can stop and mull things over or seek expert advice.

If you think about it, this last piece is some rather good general advice. When in doubt, why not stop and think—regardless of whether the doubt is about one's sex partner, one's college major, or a financial investment? When playing cards, it is said that people who hesitate is making discards or making bets are "lost"; that is, they reveal their holdings to their adversaries. In sex and in most other areas of life, however, hesitating when in doubt pays off in many, many ways. ■

SUMMARY

1. **Do sexual practices vary from culture to culture?** Sexual practices vary a great deal! For example, sexual behavior is greatly restricted on Inis Beag, whereas the natives of Mangaia enjoy varied sexual practices from a relatively young age. Societies differ in sexual permissiveness and, to some degree, in the behaviors and stimuli that are deemed sexually arousing.
2. **What biological features are connected with sexual arousal and sexual behavior?** The male and female sex organs respond to sexual stimulation and make reproduction possible. Although the male sex organs are more visible than the female organs, females' organs are complex and, like men's, are oriented toward sexual pleasure.
3. **What are the phases of the sexual response cycle?** The sexual response cycle includes the excitement, plateau, orgasm, and resolution phases.
4. **What are the effects of sex hormones?** Sex hormones promote biological sexual differentiation, regulate the menstrual cycle, and have organizing and activating effects on sexual behavior. In lower animals, sex is controlled largely by hormones and pheromones.
5. **Why do men commit rape?** Rape appears to be motivated more by anger and the desire to exercise power over women than by sexual needs.
6. **What are sexual dysfunctions?** Sexual dysfunctions are problems in becoming sexually aroused or reaching orgasm.
7. **What are the causes of sexual dysfunctions?** Sexual dysfunctions now and then reflect physical factors such as disease, alcohol, or fatigue, but most reflect psychosocial factors such as negative attitudes toward sex, psychosexual trauma, troubled relationships, lack of sexual skills, and irrational beliefs. Any of these may lead to performance anxiety, which compounds sexual problems.
8. **What are sexually transmitted diseases (STDs)?** STDs are diseases that can be transmitted by sexual contact.
9. **What causes STDs?** A variety of pathogens cause STDs. For example, gonorrhea and syphilis are caused by bacteria, and herpes and AIDS are caused by viruses.
10. **Can STDs be cured?** Most STDs can be cured. Gonorrhea and syphilis are cured by antibiotics. Unfortunately, there are no cures for herpes or AIDS.
11. **What's the story on AIDS?** AIDS (acquired immunodeficiency syndrome) is caused by a virus that kills white blood cells in the immune system, leaving the body prey to opportunistic diseases. AIDS is transmitted by sexual intercourse, by sharing contaminated hypodermic needles, and by transfusions and childbirth. Although recently developed methods of treatment have prolonged the lives of people with HIV infection and AIDS, they are not considered a cure.
12. **What is contraception?** Contraception is the prevention of pregnancy.
13. **What are some safe and effective methods of contraception?** There are many safe, effective methods of contraception, as described in the chapter. Male condoms, for example, are highly reliable when used carefully and have virtually no side effects. "The pill" is effective and safe for most women. Sterilization is inappropriate for people who may decide to have children later on.

The Challenges of Life

Chapter 16

Adult Development: Going Through Changes

Truth or Fiction?

T F

- ☐ ☐ Young adulthood is characterized by trying to "make it" in the career world.
- ☐ ☐ There is a dramatic decline in physical strength and ability during middle adulthood.
- ☐ ☐ Women at menopause encounter debilitating hot flashes.
- ☐ ☐ Women tend to lose their sexual desire at menopause.
- ☐ ☐ Menopause brings an end to a woman's child-bearing years.
- ☐ ☐ Most parents suffer from the "empty-nest syndrome" when the youngest child leaves home.
- ☐ ☐ Women in their fifties tend to be more assertive than they are at earlier ages.
- ☐ ☐ Older people who blame health problems on aging are more likely to die in the near future.
- ☐ ☐ Most older people live with children, in institutions, or in retirement communities.
- ☐ ☐ Retired people frequently become disenchanted with their newfound freedom.
- ☐ ☐ The terminally ill undergo a predictable sequence of emotional and cognitive responses.

OUTLINE

There is no cure for birth or death save to enjoy the interval.

George Santayana

What now? You've been through the early childhood years of utter dependency on adults. You've come through elementary school and high school. You're developing plans about a career, and you may be thinking about marriage and a family. Maybe you already have your early career laid out. Some of you are already involved in an enduring relationship or a marriage. Some of you have children. A few of you may even have grandchildren.

What's going to happen as you journey through the remaining years of your adult life? Is everything going to come up roses, right on course? What are some of the typical life experiences of 40-, 50-, and 60-year-olds? Do you ever think about middle and late adulthood? Are you so young that it is almost impossible to imagine that these periods of life will arrive? Given the alternative, let us hope that they do. If you hold negative stereotypes of what it will be like to be a 45-year-old or a 55-year-old, let us also hope that this chapter will replace some of your prejudices with accurate information and positive expectations.

Your authors admit that they cannot foresee what your world, or your life, will be in 20 years or in 40 years. Gail Sheehy (1995) suggests that there may no longer be a "standard" life cycle with predictable stages or phases. Age now has an "elastic quality" (Butler, 1998). People are living longer than ever before and are freer than ever to choose their own destiny. Changes are overleaping themselves at an accelerating pace. Perhaps our homes and our work will bear little resemblance to what they are today. Still, psychologists have made enormous strides in cataloguing and accounting for many of the psychological changes that we undergo as we travel through young, middle, and late adulthood. Although we are unique as individuals, we also have a number of common experiences. Common experiences are beneficial in that they allow us to have some predictive power concerning our own futures. And, so to speak, "forewarned is forearmed." Predictability helps us exert control over our destinies. We can brace ourselves for inevitable negative life changes. We can prepare ourselves to take advantage of our opportunities.

We think that the weight of theory and research concerning adult development is uplifting. There is much future to look forward to. Yes, there are alligators in the streams, and some of the strands of our rope bridges get frayed. Yes, accidents, illnesses, and failures can foreclose opportunities at any time. But for most of us the outlook is reasonably bright—in terms of our physical, cognitive, and personality development.

Get ready for the rest of your life. You may fall short of your wildest dreams. Still, if you remain willing to adjust your horizons in terms of what is possible, you may just find yourself about as happy and productive as you would like to be.

HOW LONG WILL YOU LIVE? THE LIFE-EXPECTANCY SCALE

The life-expectancy scale is one of several used by physicians and insurance companies to estimate how long people will live. Scales such as these are far from precise—which is a very good thing, if you think about it. They make reasonable ballpark predictions based on our heredity, medical histories, and lifestyles, however. ■

Directions: To complete the scale, begin with the age of 72. Then add or subtract years according to the following directions:

Running Total

PERSONAL FACTS

____ 1. If you are male, **subtract 3.**
____ 2. If female, **add 4.**
____ 3. If you live in an urban area with a population over 2 million, **subtract 2.**
____ 4. If you live in a town with under 10,000 people or on a farm, **add 2.**
____ 5. If any grandparent lived to 85, **add 2.**
____ 6. If all four grandparents lived to 80, **add 6.**
____ 7. If either parent died of a stroke or heart attack before the age of 50, **subtract 4.**
____ 8. If any parent, brother, or sister under 50 has (or had) cancer or a heart condition, or has had diabetes since childhood, **subtract 3.**
____ 9. Do you earn over $75,000 a year?* If so, **subtract 2.**
____ 10. If you finished college, **add 1.** If you have a graduate or professional degree, **add 2 more.**
____ 11. If you are 65 or over and still working, **add 3.**
____ 12. If you live with a spouse or friend, **add 5.** If not, **subtract 1** for every 10 years alone since age 25.

LIFESTYLE STATUS

____ 13. If you work behind a desk, **subtract 3.**
____ 14. If your work requires regular, heavy physical labor, **add 3.**
____ 15. If you exercise strenuously (tennis, running, swimming, etc.) five times a week for at least a half hour, **add 4.** If two or three times a week, **add 2.**
____ 16. Do you sleep more than 10 hours each night? **Subtract 4.**
____ 17. Are you intense, aggressive, easily angered? **Subtract 3.**
____ 18. Are you easygoing and relaxed? **Add 3.**
____ 19. Are you happy? **Add 1.** Unhappy? **Subtract 2.**
____ 20. Have you had a speeding ticket in the last year? **Subtract 1.**
____ 21. Do you smoke more than two packs a day? **Subtract 8.** One or two packs? **Subtract 6.** One half to one? **Subtract 3.**
____ 22. Do you drink the equivalent of $1\frac{1}{2}$ oz. of liquor a day? **Subtract 1.**
____ 23. Are you overweight by 50 lbs. or more? **Subtract 8.** By 30 to 50 lbs.? **Subtract 4.** By 10 to 30 lbs.? **Subtract 2.**
____ 24. If you are a man over 40 and have annual checkups, **add 2.**
____ 25. If you are a woman and see a gynecologist once a year, **add 2.**

AGE ADJUSTMENT

____ 26. If you are between 30 and 40, **add 2.**
____ 27. If you are between 40 and 50, **add 3.**
____ 28. If you are between 50 and 70, **add 4.**
____ 29. If you are over 70, **add 5.**
____ Your Life Expectancy

*This figure is an inflation-adjusted estimate.

Source: Robert F. Allen with Shirley Linde (1986), *Lifegain.* Human Resources Institute Press, Tempe Wick Road, Morristown, NJ.

YOUNG ADULTHOOD

Young or early adulthood covers the two decades from the ages of 20 to 40.

Physical Development

Olympic gymnasts are frequently in their early teens, but most of us reach our physical peaks during our twenties. Everything else being equal, during our twenties and the early thirties we are faster, stronger, better coordinated, and have more endurance than we ever had or will have again. Experience interacts with physical development. Many professional athletes come into their own after they have been in the league or on the circuit for a few years.

Cognitive Development

We are also at the height of our cognitive powers during early adulthood. Many professionals show the broadest knowledge of their fields at about the time they are graduating from college or graduate school. At this time their coursework is freshest. They may have just recently studied for comprehensive examinations. Once they enter their fields, they often specialize. As a result, knowledge deepens in certain areas, but understanding of related areas may grow relatively superficial.

Personality Development and Adjustment

Personality development concerns the ways in which we adapt to the challenges of life at various ages. We shall primarily rely on the views of Erik Erikson, Robert Havighurst, Daniel Levinson, and the journalist Gail Sheehy. But there are other noted views, such as Carol Gilligan's insights into factors that affect women.

ERIKSON'S STAGES OF PSYCHOSOCIAL DEVELOPMENT According to Erik Erikson (1963), young adulthood is the stage of **intimacy versus isolation.** Erikson saw the establishment of intimate relationships as a central task of young adulthood. Young adults who have evolved a firm sense of identity during adolescence are now ready to "fuse" their identities with those of other people through marriage and abiding friendships.

Erikson warns that we may not be capable of committing ourselves to others until we have achieved **ego identity.** Achieving ego identity in Erikson's theory is the central task of adolescence. Lack of personal stability may be one reason that teenage marriages suffer a higher divorce rate than adult marriages.

One study found suggestions of Erikson's predicted relationships between ego identity and the achievement of intimacy (Kahn and others, 1985). Men who develop a strong sense of ego identity by young adulthood get married earlier than men who do not. Women with well developed senses of identity, on the other hand, *maintain* more stable marriages. The discrepancy may be explained by the fact that women in our society encounter greater pressure than men to get married—ready or not, so to speak (Gilligan, 1982). For women, then, the test of stability is more likely to be whether they endure in relationships, not whether they enter them (Kahn and others, 1985).

In any event, Erikson argues that people who do not reach out to develop intimate relationships may risk retreating into isolation and loneliness.

INTIMACY VERSUS ISOLATION • Erikson's life crisis of young adulthood, which is characterized by the task of developing abiding intimate relationships.

EGO IDENTITY • According to Erikson, a firm sense of who one is and what one stands for.

Establishing Intimate Relationships. According to Erik Erikson, establishing intimate relationships is a central task of young adulthood.

Havighurst's Developmental Tasks Developmental psychologist Robert Havighurst (1972) lists a number of tasks for each stage of development, beginning in childhood. As we develop, our tasks broaden our social worlds and increase in complexity. Successful achievement of a task at one stage brings fulfillment and eases achievements during subsequent stages.

Havighurst's developmental tasks for young adulthood include the following:

1. Selecting and courting a mate
2. Learning to live contentedly with one's partner
3. Starting a family and becoming a parent
4. Rearing children
5. Assuming the responsibilities of managing a home
6. Beginning a career or job
7. Assuming some civic responsibilities
8. Establishing a social network

Havighurst's tasks exclude many of us, of course—those who remain single, those who postpone (or forgo) childbearing, those who prefer to be and live by themselves, and those who are not civic-minded, to name a few. Havighurst admitted that his list was culture specific and sort of "all American"—that is, the types of behaviors that are championed by Miss America contestants during the interview segment of the pageant.

Havighurst's tasks do not universally apply. Belief that they do gives us too many "oughts" and "shoulds" to live up to. Havighurst's lists serve as useful reminders of stereotypical expectations for each stage of development, however. They inform us of what many people expect. With this rationale, we shall list Havighurst's tasks for each stage of adult development.

Levinson's Seasons According to Daniel Levinson's study of 40 men, which was published in 1978 as *The Seasons of a Man's Life*, we enter the adult

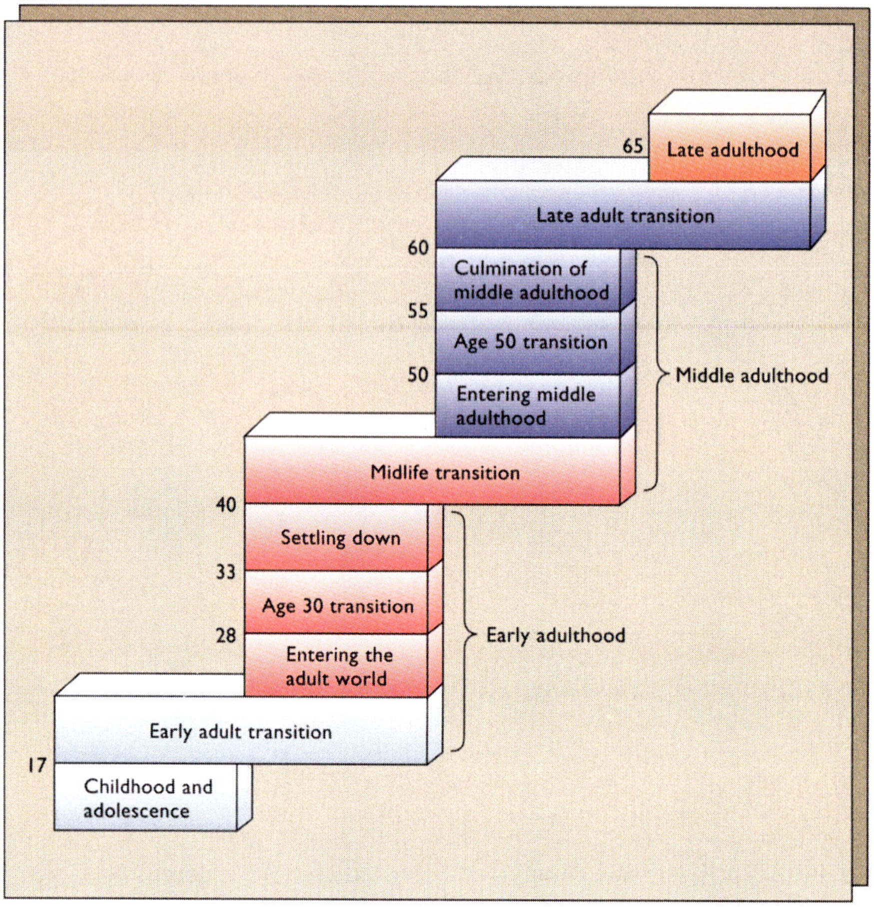

FIGURE 16.1
THE SEASONS OF LIFE.
Daniel Levinson and his colleagues (1978) broke young, middle, and late adulthood down into several periods, including transitions. Our major tasks as we enter the adult world are to explore, and to establish some stability in, our adult roles. During the age 30 transition we reevaluate earlier choices. How does women's adult development differ from men's?

world in our early twenties (see Figure 16.1). Upon entry, we are faced with the tasks of exploring adult roles (in terms of careers and intimate relationships, for example) and of establishing some stability in these roles. At this time, we also often adopt a **dream,** which serves as a kind of blueprint for life.

Truth or Fiction Revisited

It is true that young adulthood is characterized by trying to "make it" in the career world, according to Sheehy, Gould, and other investigators.

SHEEHY'S PASSAGES American surveys show that people in their twenties tend to be fueled with ambition as they strive to establish pathways in life (Sheehy, 1976). Gail Sheehy (1976) labeled the twenties the **Trying 20s.**

In one phase of her work, Sheehy (1976) interviewed 115 people drawn largely from the middle and upper classes, including many managers, executives, and other professionals. In another phase, Sheehy (1981) examined 60,000 questionnaires filled out by readers of *Redbook* and *Esquire* magazines. The young adults in her samples wanted to establish or find their places in the world. They were generally responsible for their own support and made their own choices.

During the twenties, Sheehy noted, we often feel "buoyed by powerful illusions and belief in the power of the will [so that] we commonly insist . . . that what we have chosen to do is the one true course in life" (1976, p. 33). This "one true course" can have many swerves and bends. As we develop, what seemed important one year can lose some of its allure in the next. That which we hardly noted can gain prominence.

DREAM • In this usage, Levinson's term for the overriding drive of youth to become someone important, to leave one's mark on history.

TRYING 20S • Sheehy's term for the third decade of life, when people are frequently occupied with advancement in the career world.

INDIVIDUATION • The process by which one separates from others and gathers control over his or her own behavior.

GENDER DIFFERENCES Most Western men consider separation and **individuation** to be key goals of personality development during young adulthood

(Guisinger & Blatt, 1994). For women, however, the establishment and maintenance of social relationships are also of primary importance (Gilligan and others, 1990, 1991; Jordan and others, 1991). Women, as Carol Gilligan (1982) has pointed out, are likely to undergo a transition from being cared for by others to caring for others. In becoming adults, men are more likely to undergo a transition from being restricted by others to autonomy and perhaps control of other people.

Although there are differences between the development of women and men, college women also develop in terms of individuation and autonomy in young adulthood (Helson & Moane, 1987). Women, like men, assert increasing control over their own lives. They come to accept the differences between romanticized visions of the way the world ought to be and the way it really is. They broaden their psychological understanding of the people who matter to them. On the other hand, they also become more introspective and vulnerable. College women, of course, are relatively liberated and career oriented compared with their less well educated peers.

SEPARATION FROM PARENTS Gould (1975) theorizes about "transformations" in people's ideas about, and relationships with, their parents. He notes common "false assumptions" we tend to share at certain ages. Between the ages of 16 to 22, many of us believe, "My parents will always be my parents. I'll always believe in them." Gould considers the major developmental tasks of these years as moving away from home and abandoning the idea that one's parents are always right.

Between the ages of 22 to 28, Gould notes additional false assumptions about parents. One is that we must do things the ways our parents do if we want to be successful. Another is that our parents will be there to rescue us if things don't work out. It is our task to become increasingly independent of parents during these years. Optimal development requires exploring adult roles, abandoning the notion that we should imitate our parents, and learning to pick ourselves up when we fall down.

THE AGE 30 TRANSITION Levinson labeled the period of 28 to 33 the **age 30 transition.** This is for many a time of reassessment of earlier choices. A number of researchers have noted that women frequently encounter a crisis between the ages of 27 and 30 (Reinke and others, 1985). During the early thirties, many of the women studied by Helson and Moane (1987) felt exploited by others, alone, weak, limited, and as if they would "never get [themselves] together." Concerns about nearing the end of the fertile years, opportunities closing down, and heightened responsibilities at home and work all contribute to these feelings of inadequacy.

For men and women, the late twenties and early thirties are commonly characterized by self-questioning: "Where is my life going?" "Why am I doing this?" Sheehy (1976) labeled the thirties the **Catch 30s** because of such reassessment. During the thirties we often find that the lifestyles we adopted during the twenties do not fit as comfortably as we had imagined.

One response to the disillusionments of the thirties, according to Sheehy,

> is the tearing up of the life we have spent most of our 20s putting together. It may mean striking out on a secondary road toward a new vision or converting a dream of "running for president" into a more realistic goal. The single person feels a push to find a partner. The woman who was previously content at home with children chafes to venture into the world. The childless couple reconsiders children. And almost everybody who is married . . . feels a discontent. (1976, p. 34)

AGE 30 TRANSITION • Levinson's term for the ages from 28 to 33, which are characterized by reassessment of the goals and values of the twenties.

CATCH 30S • Sheehy's term for the fourth decade of life, when many people undergo major reassessments of their accomplishments and goals.

Many people make major life changes in their thirties, forties, even later in life (Sheehy, 1981). Making successful life changes requires risk taking, but risk taking in itself is no guarantee of success. Successful "life-changers" also show foresight, psychological androgyny, and strong belief in their purpose.

SETTLING DOWN According to Levinson, the ages of about 33 to 40 are characterized by settling down. Men during this period still strive to forge ahead in their careers, their interpersonal relationships, and their communities. During the latter half of their thirties, men are also concerned about becoming their own men. They desire independence and autonomy in their careers and adult relationships. Promotions and pay increases are important signs of success.

Sheehy found that young adults who successfully ride out the storm of reassessments of the Catch 30s begin "rooting" at this time. They need to plant roots, to make a financial and emotional investment in their homes. Their concerns become more focused on promotion or tenure, career advancement, and (sigh) long-term mortgages.

MIDDLE ADULTHOOD

Middle adulthood spans the years from 40 to 60 or 65. Levinson and his colleagues (1978) consider the years from 60 to 65 separately as a transition to late adulthood. Let us consider some of the developments of middle adulthood.

Physical Development

At age 40 we do not possess quite the strength, coordination, and stamina that we had during our twenties and thirties. This decline is most obvious in the ranks of professional sports where peak performance is at a premium. Gordie Howe still played hockey at 50 and George Blanda was still kicking field goals at that age, but most professional athletes at those ages can no longer keep up with the "kids."

Truth or Fiction Revisited

It is not true that there is a dramatic decline in physical strength and ability during middle adulthood. The decline is actually quite gradual.

But the years between 40 and 60 are reasonably stable. There is gradual physical decline, but it is minor and only likely to be of concern if we insist on competing with young adults—or with idealized memories of ourselves. On the other hand, many of us first make time to develop our physical potentials during middle adulthood. The 20-year-old couch potato occasionally becomes the 50-year-old marathoner. By any reasonable standard, we can maintain excellent cardiorespiratory condition throughout middle adulthood.

MENOPAUSE **Menopause,** or cessation of menstruation, usually occurs during the late forties or early fifties, although there are wide variations in the age at which it occurs. Menopause is the final stage of a broader female experience, the **climacteric,** which is caused by a falling off in the secretion of the hormones estrogen and progesterone. The climacteric begins with irregular periods and ends with menopause.[1] At this time ovulation also draws to an end. There is some loss of breast tissue and of elasticity in the skin. There can also be a loss of bone density that leads to **osteoporosis** (a condition in which the bones break easily) in late adulthood.

MENOPAUSE • The cessation of menstruation.
CLIMACTERIC • The multiyear process triggered by falloff in production of sex hormones in which menstrual periods become irregular and finally cease.
OSTEOPOROSIS • A condition characterized by porosity, and hence brittleness, of the bones, more common among women.

[1] There are many other reasons for irregular periods, and women who experience them are advised to discuss them with their doctor.

During the climacteric, many women encounter symptoms such as hot flashes (uncomfortable sensations characterized by heat and perspiration) and loss of sleep. However, women are more likely to suffer from depression prior to menopause, when they may feel overwhelmed by the combined demands of the workplace, child rearing, and homemaking (Brody, 1993b). In most cases, the mood changes accompanying menopause are relatively mild. According to psychologist Karen Matthews, who has been following a sample of hundreds of women through menopause, some women do encounter problems, but they are in the minority. "The vast majority have no problem at all getting through the menopausal transition" (Matthews, 1994, p. 25).

Menopause does not signal the end of a woman's sexual interests (Brody, 1993b). Many women find the separation of sex from reproduction to be sexually liberating. Some of the physical problems that may stem from the falloff in hormone production may be alleviated by hormone replacement therapy (Grodstein and others, 1997). A more important issue may be what menopause means to the individual. Women who equate menopause with loss of femininity are likely to encounter more distress than those who do not (Rathus and others, 1997).

Myths About Menopause We are better able to adjust to life's changes when we have accurate information about them. Menopause is a major life change for most women, and many of us harbor misleading and maladaptive ideas about it. Consider the following myths and realities about menopause:

Myth 1. *Menopause is abnormal.* The reality is that menopause is a normal development in women's lives.

Myth 2. *The medical establishment defines menopause as a disease.* No longer. Today menopause is conceptualized as a "deficiency syndrome," in recognition of the dropoff in secretion of estrogen and progesterone. Sad to say, the term *deficiency* also has negative connotations.

Myth 3. *After menopause, women need complete replacement of estrogen.* Not necessarily. Some estrogen is still produced by the adrenal glands, fatty tissue, and the brain. The pros and cons of estrogen replacement therapy are still being debated.

Myth 4. *Menopause is accompanied by depression and anxiety.* Not necessarily. Much of the emotional response to menopause reflects its meaning to the individual rather than physiological changes.

Myth 5. *At menopause, women suffer debilitating hot flashes.* Many women do not have them at all. Those who do usually find them mild.

Myth 6. *A woman who has had a hysterectomy will not undergo menopause afterward.* It depends on whether the ovaries, which are the major producers of estrogen, were removed along with the uterus. If they were left in, menopause should proceed as usual.

Myth 7. *Menopause signals an end to women's sexual interests.* Not at all. In fact, many women feel freed by the severing of the links between sexual expression and reproduction.

Myth 8. *Menopause brings an end to a woman's childbearing years.* Not necessarily! After menopause, women no longer produce ova. However, ova from donors have been fertilized in laboratory dishes, and the developing embryos have been successfully implanted in the uteruses of postmenopausal women (Sauer and others, 1990).

Truth or Fiction Revisited

It is not true that women at menopause encounter debilitating hot flashes. The statement is too general to be true. Many women do not have hot flashes at all, and for most of those who do, they are mild.

Truth or Fiction Revisited

It is not true that women tend to lose their sexual desire at menopause. Some women, in fact, feel sexually liberated because of the separation of sexual expression and reproduction.

Truth or Fiction Revisited

It is not necessarily true that menopause brings an end to a woman's childbearing years. Recent developments in reproductive technology permit the implantation of embryos in the uteruses of postmenopausal women.

Myth 9. *A woman's general level of activity is lower after menopause.* Research shows that many postmenopausal women become peppier and more assertive.

Myth 10. *Men are not affected by their wives' menopause.* Many of them are, of course. But men could become more supportive if they knew more about menopause and if their wives felt freer to communicate about it with them.

Adjustment in a World of DIVERSITY

Is There a Manopause?

Gail Sheehy (1993) relates a joke often told by men who have entered their fifties and sixties. It goes like this:

> An older man is walking down the street when he hears a frog talking. The frog says, "If you pick me up and kiss me, I'll turn into a beautiful woman." The man picks up the frog and puts it in his pocket. The frog complains, "Aren't you going to kiss me? I'll turn into a ravishing woman and you can have me all you want." The man replies, "I'd rather have a talking frog in my pocket."

The joke is supposed to represent male menopause. It suggests that once male menopause occurs, a novel event, such as a talking frog, may hold more allure than sex.

Men cannot experience menopause, of course. Yet now and then we hear the term *male menopause,* or "manopause." Middle-aged or older men may be loosely alluded to as menopausal. This epithet is doubly offensive: It reinforces the negative, harmful stereotypes of aging people, especially aging women, as crotchety and irritable. Nor is the label consistent with the biology or psychology of aging. Alternate terms are *andropause* (referring to a dropoff in androgens, or male sex hormones) and *viropause* (referring to the end of virility) (Cowley, 1996).

For women, menopause is a time of relatively acute age-related declines in sex hormones and fertility. In men, however, the decline in the production of male sex hormones and fertility is more gradual. Moreover, some viable sperm are produced even in late adulthood. It therefore is not surprising to find a man in his seventies or older fathering a child. On the other hand, many men in their fifties and sixties experience intermittent problems in achieving and maintaining erections (Laumann and others, 1994), which may or may not have to do with hormone production.

Sexual performance is only one part of the story, however. Between the ages of 40 and 70, the typical American male loses 12 to 20 pounds of muscle, about 2 inches in height, and 15 percent of his bone mass. Men as well as women are at risk for osteoporosis (Brody, 1996b). (People can fend off osteoporosis in late adulthood by using calcium supplements in earlier years. Postmenopausal women can also help prevent osteoporosis by means of estrogen replacement therapy [Delmas and others, 1997; Nieves and others, 1998].) The amount of fat in the body nearly doubles. The eardrums thicken, as do the lenses of the eyes, resulting in some loss of hearing and vision. There is also loss of endurance as the cardiovascular system and lungs become less capable of responding effectively to exertion.

Some of these changes can be slowed or even reversed. Exercise helps maintain muscle tone and keep the growth of fatty tissue in check. A diet rich in calcium and vitamin D can help ward off bone loss in men as well as in women. Hormone replacement may also help, but is controversial. Although testosterone replacement appears to boost strength, energy, and the sex drive, it is connected with increased risks of prostate cancer and cardiovascular disease (Cowley, 1996).

Even though sexual interest and performance decline, men can remain sexually active and father children at advanced ages. For both genders, attitudes toward the biological changes of aging—along with general happiness—may affect sexual behavior as much as biological changes do.

Cognitive Development

Cognitive development in adulthood has many aspects: creativity, memory functioning, and intelligence. People can be creative for a lifetime. Picasso was painting in his nineties. Grandma Moses did not even begin painting until she was 78 years old. The architect Frank Lloyd Wright designed New York's spiral-shaped Guggenheim Museum when he was 89 years old.

People are probably at their height in terms of learning and memory in young adulthood. Memory functioning declines with age. It is common enough for older people to have trouble recalling the names of common objects or people they know. Memory lapses can be embarrassing, and older people sometimes lose confidence in their memories, which then lowers their motivation to remember things (Cavanaugh & Green, 1990). But declines in memory are not usually as large as people assume (Abeles, 1997b). Memory tests usually measure ability to recall meaningless information. Older people show better memory functioning in areas in which they can apply their experience, especially in their areas of specialization, to new challenges (Graf, 1990). For example, who would do a better job of learning and remembering how to solve problems in chemistry—a college history major or a retired professor of chemistry?

People also obtain the highest intelligence test scores in young adulthood (Baltes, 1997, Kaufman and others, 1989). Yet people tend to retain their verbal skills, as demonstrated by their vocabularies and general knowledge, into advanced old age. It is their performance on tasks that require speed and visual-spatial skills, such as putting puzzles together, that tends to fall off (Lindenberger and others, 1993; Schaie, 1994; Schaie & Willis, 1991).

CRYSTALLIZED VERSUS FLUID INTELLIGENCE Consider the difference between *crystallized intelligence* and *fluid intelligence.* **Crystallized intelligence** represents one's lifetime of intellectual attainments, as shown by vocabulary and accumulated facts about world affairs. Therefore, crystallized intelligence generally increases over the decades. **Fluid intelligence** is defined as mental flexibility and is demonstrated by the ability to process information rapidly, as in learning and solving problems in new areas of endeavor (Horn, 1982).

In terms of people's worth to their employers, familiarity in solving the kinds of problems found on the job (their crystallized intelligence) may be more important than their fluid intelligence. Experience on the job enhances people's specialized vocabularies and their knowledge of the area. People draw upon fluid intelligence when the usual solutions no longer work, but experience is often more valuable than fluid intelligence.

CRYSTALLIZED INTELLIGENCE • Knowledge and ability to solve specific problems, as evidenced by vocabulary, accumulated information, and acquired skills.

FLUID INTELLIGENCE • Mental flexibility and general learning ability.

THE SEATTLE LONGITUDINAL STUDY Psychologist Walter Schaie and his colleagues (Schaie, 1993, 1994) have been studying the cognitive development of adults for four decades and discovered factors that contribute to intellectual functioning across the life span:

1. *General health.* People in good health tend to retain higher levels of intellectual functioning into late adulthood. Therefore, paying attention to one's diet, exercising, and having regular medical checkups contribute to intellectual functioning as well as physical health.
2. *Socioeconomic status (SES).* People with high SES tend to maintain intellectual functioning more adequately than people with low SES. High SES is also connected with above-average income and levels of education, a history of stimulating occupational pursuits, and the maintenance of intact families.
3. *Stimulating activities.* People who maintain their level of intellectual functioning also tend to attend cultural events, travel, participate in professional organizations, and read extensively.
4. *Marriage to a spouse with a high level of intellectual functioning.* The spouse whose level of intellectual functioning is lower at the beginning of a marriage tends to narrow the gap as time goes by. Perhaps that partner is continually challenged by the other.
5. *Openness to new experience.* Being open to new challenges of life apparently helps keep us young—at any age.

Personality Development and Adjustment

ERIKSON'S STAGES OF PSYCHOSOCIAL DEVELOPMENT Erikson (1963) labels the life crisis of the middle years as that of **generativity versus stagnation.** In other words, are we still striving to produce or to rear our children well, or are we marking time, treading water? Generativity by and large requires doing things that we believe are worthwhile. In so doing, we enhance and maintain our self-esteem. Generativity also involves the Eriksonian ideal of helping shape the new generation. This shaping may involve rearing our own children or working to make the world a better place. Many of us find great satisfaction in these tasks.

HAVIGHURST'S DEVELOPMENTAL TASKS Havighurst's tasks for middle adulthood include the following:

1. Facilitating our children's transition from home life to "making it" in the outside world
2. Developing engrossing leisure activities
3. Relating to one's spouse as a person
4. Assuming important social and civic responsibilities
5. Maintaining satisfactory performance in one's career
6. Adjusting to the physical changes that attend middle age
7. Adjusting to aging parents

We remind you of the disclaimer made in the section on young adulthood. Havighurst's tasks in many cases reflect ideals more than realities. We urge readers not to consider them standards by which they should judge themselves.

GENERATIVITY VERSUS STAGNATION • Erikson's term for the crisis of middle adulthood, characterized by the task of being productive and contributing to younger generations.

Levinson's Seasons According to Levinson, there is a **midlife transition** at about 40 to 45 that is characterized by a dramatic shift in psychological perspective. Previously we had thought of our ages largely in terms of the number of years that have elapsed since birth. Once the midlife transition takes place, we tend to think of our ages in terms of the number of years we have left. During this transition, it strikes men that life may be more than halfway over. There may be more to look back upon than forward to. Men recognize that they'll never be president or chairperson of the board. They'll never play shortstop for the Dodgers. They mourn their own youth and begin to adjust to the specter of old age and the finality of death.

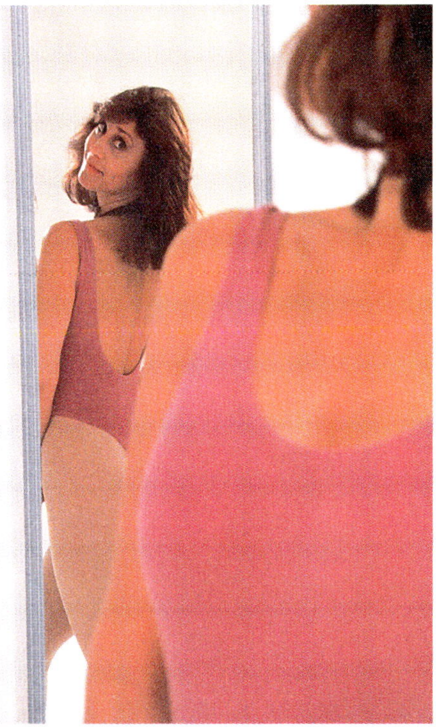

Midlife Crisis or "Middlescence"? According to Gail Sheehy, many middle-aged people undergo a second quest for identity (the first occurs during adolescence). They are trying to decide what they will do with their "second adulthoods" — the three to four healthy decades they may have left.

The Midlife Crisis The midlife transition may trigger a crisis referred to as the **midlife crisis.** The middle-level, middle-aged businessperson looking ahead to another 10 to 20 years of grinding out accounts in a Wall Street cubbyhole may encounter severe depression. The housewife with two teenagers, an empty house from 8:00 A.M. to 4:00 P.M., and a 40th birthday on the way may feel that she is coming apart at the seams. Both feel entrapment and loss of purpose. Some people are propelled into extramarital affairs by the desire to prove to themselves that they remain attractive.

Levinson's views were based on interviews with 40 men. However, surveys with thousands of adults suggest that there may not really be a midlife crisis. The midlife crisis, as conceived by Levinson, involves feelings of personal mortality, emotional instability, loss of meaning, and dissatisfaction with life at home and on the job. Researchers Robert McCrae and Paul Costa surveyed more than 10,000 men and women whose ages ranged from 30 to 60 and did not find any "spike" in measures of instability and dissatisfaction around the age of 40. Nor was the decade of the forties notably more troubled than the previous or succeeding decades (McCrae & Costa, 1990).

Mastery Sheehy (1995) is much more optimistic than Levinson. She terms the years from 45 to 65 "the Age of Mastery" because people are frequently at the height of their productive powers during this period. Sheehy believes that the key task for people aged 45 to 55 is to decide what they will do with their "second adulthoods"—the 30 to 40 healthy years that may be left for them once they reach 50. She believes that both men and women can experience great success and joy if they identify meaningful goals and pursue them wholeheartedly.

"Middlescence" Yet people need to define themselves and their goals. Sheehy coined the term **middlescence** to describe a period of searching that is in some ways similar to adolescence. Both are times of transition. Middlescence involves a search for a new identity: "Turning backward, going around in circles, feeling lost in a buzz of confusion and unable to make decisions—all this is predictable and, for many people, a necessary precursor to making the passage into midlife" (Sheehy, 1995).

The Dream: Inspiration or Tyrant? Until midlife, the men studied by the Levinson group were largely under the influence of their dreams. At midlife, we must deal with the discrepancies between our dreams and our achievements. Middle-aged people who free themselves from their dreams find it easier to enjoy the passing pleasures of the day.

Midlife transition • Levinson's term for the ages from 40 to 45, which are characterized by a shift in psychological perspective from viewing ourselves in terms of years lived to viewing ourselves in terms of the years we have left.

Midlife crisis • A crisis experienced by many people during the midlife transition when they realize that life may be more than halfway over and reassess their achievements in terms of their dreams.

Middlescence • Sheehy's term for a period of searching for identity that occurs during middle adulthood.

ADJUSTMENT in the NEW MILLENNIUM

Two Views of Parenting in the New Millennium

Childfree by Choice

As we approached the new millennium, the first wave of the baby boomers reached the age of menopause. For many of them, the biological clock that so many had anxiously watched wound down forever. Perhaps one woman in six had been infertile. But another 15 percent of them had chosen not to bear children. They were childfree by choice.

To many, the decision not to have children still violates norms of feminine conduct. Little girls are still given dolls and baby carriages as toys. Religious traditionalists still view motherhood as a woman's obligation and primary source of fulfillment. Traditional psychologists and psychiatrists have also believed in the psychological value of motherhood. Erik Erikson wrote, "A woman who does not fulfill her innate need to fill her uterus with embryonic tissue is likely to be frustrated or neurotic."

According to psychoanalyst Jeanne Safer (1996), the conventional wisdom and traditional teachings are all wrong. Women who choose to remain childfree feel fully womanly in their menopausal years. Many believe that they have pioneered new psychological territory for women to come. They have shown that women can make psychologically healthy informed choices about reproduction. Women are free to see motherhood as a way of life that may or may not suit them. Women can find fulfillment regardless of whether they choose motherhood.

Safer bases her conclusions on her own experience and on interviews with 50 women who, like her, had made conscious decisions to remain childfree. She found that most of the women had few regrets. Most of them were excited about the future. Most had never been happier. Consider some vignettes:

Jane was a dancer who at the age of 35 married a man who did not want children. At 40, she went to medical school. She now has a child psychiatry practice and has repaid her loans. "I make a difference in children's lives and still go out at night," she explained.

Then there's Anna, an acupuncturist. "My life is really beginning at 50," Anna said, as she and her bridegroom prepared for a trip around the world.

One woman, unnamed, spent 10 years as a war correspondent in the Middle and Far East. "I've had such an eventful time," she told Safer, "I wouldn't mind dying now. Would I have been able to go into Afghanistan with the rebels if I'd had a child waiting at home?"

Robin is a secretary in a Long Island suburb. She is surrounded by other people's children. Yet she says, "There's no gene for motherhood. I'm happy with my life. I feel no need to undo what I didn't do—and I will leave lots of love behind me."

Lauren is a housewife and community activist. She admits that she has not experienced the "kind of self-knowledge you only get from having kids." On the other hand, she has gained "time to reflect that most people don't have."

Leslie, a gallery owner, is also approaching 50. Yet only recently has she been able to tell acquaintances

SHEEHY'S PASSAGES Levinson's study was carried out with men. Women, as suggested by Sheehy and other writers (e.g., Reinke and others, 1985), may undergo a midlife transition years earlier. Sheehy (1976) writes that women enter midlife about 5 years earlier than men, at about 35 rather than 40. Entering midlife triggers a sense of urgency, of a "last chance" to do certain things. Once they turn 35, women are usually advised to have their fetuses routinely tested for Down's syndrome and other chromosomal disorders. At age 35, women also enter higher risk categories for side effects from birth control pills. They are that she chose to remain childfree. "I felt a stigma in my earlier years," she explained. "I was afraid people would judge me or feel sorry for me, because I mistrusted my decision to be different. Now I know that I made that choice out of strength."

Many of the women attributed their happiness to the opportunities for self-expression and community service that remaining childfree has provided. They are the centers of their own attention. Yet they are not selfish or cold. Rather, they have made the decision that it is all right for them to focus on their own lives.

All of the 50 women said that they felt proud that they actively grappled with their motherhood dilemma. They hadn't just fallen into motherhood as had so many of their peers. They did not regret remaining childfree, even though many wondered what motherhood would have been like. Still others saw themselves permanent outsiders to the core concern of most other women. Yet they enjoyed their unconventional lives, the intimacy of their marriages, and their freedom and privacy.

And then there were those who decided to have children later on . . .

What Biological Clock?

At the beginning of the new millennium, we also find more and more parents with gray hair at Little League games and PTA meetings—even while most of the other parents are still trying to cope with their acne (Matus, 1996). The trend is clear. Bearing children is no longer defined as an event of young adulthood. Although fertility declines with age (Rathus and others, 1997), fathers have traditionally had children in middle and late adulthood. But today increasing numbers of women in the United States are bearing children in middle age. The birthrate for women aged 40 to 44 doubled between 1974 and 1994 (Clay, 1996a). In 1997, a 63-year-old woman gave birth. The trend to bear children at later ages continues.

Mothers in Their Forties What kinds of mothers do middle-aged women make? According to Los Angeles psychologist Renee Cohen (1996), they make good ones. These mothers are usually settled in their work and marriage. Their decisions to bear children are well thought out. Because they have usually completed their education, established their career, and traveled, they are less likely to resent children for interfering with their lives.

"By the time older people decide to become parents," notes Cohen (1996, p. 37), "nothing is haphazard. Everything is planned. By having a baby, they're opening a new chapter in their lives."

Older Fathers Older men also tend to be more involved as fathers, whether they are having their first child or parenting a second family (Clay, 1996b). Younger fathers tend to get embroiled in power struggles and physical discipline with their children, but "all of the studies on parenting show that the older the parent, the more nurturing, laid back, flexible, and supportive they are" (Pollack, 1996, p. 37).

Unlike younger men, men who choose fatherhood in their forties are less likely to view themselves as distant breadwinners whose major role in the home is to provide discipline. More mature fathers are more likely to see themselves as team players who share parenting with their wives. Moreover, they are likely to have more time and patience for fatherhood because they have already established themselves in their careers. ■

often given baseline mammograms and considered at greater risk for various cancers.

Yet women frequently experience a renewed sense of self in their forties and fifties as they emerge from middlescence (Apter, 1995; Sheehy, 1995). Many women in their early forties are already emerging from some of the fears and uncertainties that are first confronting men. For example, Helson and Moane (1987) found that women at age 43 are more likely than women in their early thirties to feel confident; to exert an influence on their community; to feel

SELF-ASSESSMENT

WHAT ARE YOUR ATTITUDES TOWARD AGING?

What are your assumptions about late adulthood? Do you see older people as basically different from the young in their behavior patterns and their outlooks, or just as a few years more mature?

To evaluate the accuracy of your attitudes toward aging, mark each of the following items true (T) or false (F). Then turn to the answer key in the Appendix. ■

T	F	1.	By age 60 most couples have lost their capacity for satisfying sexual relations.
T	F	2.	The elderly cannot wait to retire.
T	F	3.	With advancing age people become more externally oriented, less concerned with the self.
T	F	4.	As individuals age, they become less able to adapt satisfactorily to a changing environment.
T	F	5.	General satisfaction with life tends to decrease as people become older.
T	F	6.	As people age they tend to become more homogeneous—that is, all old people tend to be alike in many ways.
T	F	7.	For the older person, having a stable intimate relationship is no longer highly important.
T	F	8.	The aged are susceptible to a wider variety of psychological disorders than young and middle-aged adults.
T	F	9.	Most older people are depressed much of the time.
T	F	10.	Church attendance increases with age.
T	F	11.	The occupational performance of the older worker is typically less effective than that of the younger adult.
T	F	12.	Most older people are just not able to learn new skills.
T	F	13.	When forced to make a decision, elderly persons are more cautious and take fewer risks than younger persons.
T	F	14.	Compared to younger persons, aged people tend to think more about the past than the present or the future.
T	F	15.	Most elderly people are unable to live independently and reside in nursing homes and other institutions.

secure and committed; to feel productive, effective, and powerful; and to extend their interests beyond their family.

EMPTY-NEST SYNDROME • A sense of depression and loss of purpose experienced by some parents when the youngest child leaves home.

THE EMPTY-NEST SYNDROME In earlier decades psychologists placed great emphasis on the so-called **empty-nest syndrome.** It applied to women in particular. It was assumed that women experienced a profound sense of loss when the youngest child went off to college, got married, or moved into an apartment. Because of overcommitment to rearing a family and lack of planning for a productive life once the "nest" is empty, women were thought to lose their sense of meaningfulness and to become depressed.

Perhaps the empty-nest syndrome was a serious problem in the past. Research findings have shown a more optimistic picture, however. Sure, there can be problems, and these apply to both parents. Perhaps the largest of these is letting go of one's children after years of mutual interdependence. The stresses of letting go can be compounded when the children are ambivalent about becoming independent.

Yet many women report increased marital satisfaction and personal changes like greater mellowness, self-confidence, and stability after the children have left home (Reinke and others, 1985). Middle-aged women show increased dominance and assertiveness, an orientation toward achievement, and greater influence in the worlds of politics and work (Sheehy, 1995). It is as if they are cut free from traditional shackles by the knowledge that their childbearing years are behind them. In fact, this is a time of increased freedom for both parents. They have frequently grown free of financial worries as well and are free to travel. They have the opportunity to experiment with new activities, which is one of the reasons that the fifties can be characterized as "freestyle." Let us also remember that the day of the traditional family, with the mother in the home and the father in the workforce, is fast becoming a nostalgic memory. The great majority of today's mothers—even mothers with young children—work. Therefore, they are likely to simply continue in their careers when the children leave the home. And more than half of the women who had stayed at home enter the workforce when the children leave home. Some return to college—or enter college for the first time.

Family role reversals are not uncommon once the children have left home (Wink & Helson, 1993). Given traditional sociocultural expectations of men and women, men are frequently more competent than their wives in the world outside the family during the early stages of marriage, and their wives are more emotionally dependent. But in the postparental period these differences may decrease or reverse direction, both because of women's enhanced status in the workplace and because of the decreased influence of the mother role.

Truth or Fiction Revisited

It is not true that most parents suffer from the "empty-nest syndrome" when the youngest child leaves home. There can be some conflicts concerning letting go, but for most parents, the final child's leaving home ushers in a period of newfound freedom.

Truth or Fiction Revisited

It is true that women in their fifties tend to be more assertive than they are at earlier ages. Perhaps menopause helps free them from traditional feminine, passive social roles.

LATE ADULTHOOD

It's never too late to be what you might have been.

George Eliot

Did you know that an *agequake* is coming? With improved health care and knowledge of the importance of diet and exercise, more Americans than ever before have entered **late adulthood**, that is they are 65 or older (Abeles, 1997a). In 1900, only 1 American in 30 was over 65, as compared with 1 in 9 in 1970. By 2030, 1 American in 5 will be 65 or older ("Longer, healthier, better," 1997; see Figure 16.2).

The agequake will shake America. It has already influenced the themes of TV shows and movies. Many consumer products are designed to appeal to older consumers. Leisure communities dot the Sun Belt. Older people today differ from their counterparts of a generation or two ago in that age is becoming less likely to determine their behavior and mental processes (Butler, 1998). However, the prospects are not the same for men and women, or for people from different ethnic backgrounds.

Late adulthood • The last stage of life, beginning at age 65.

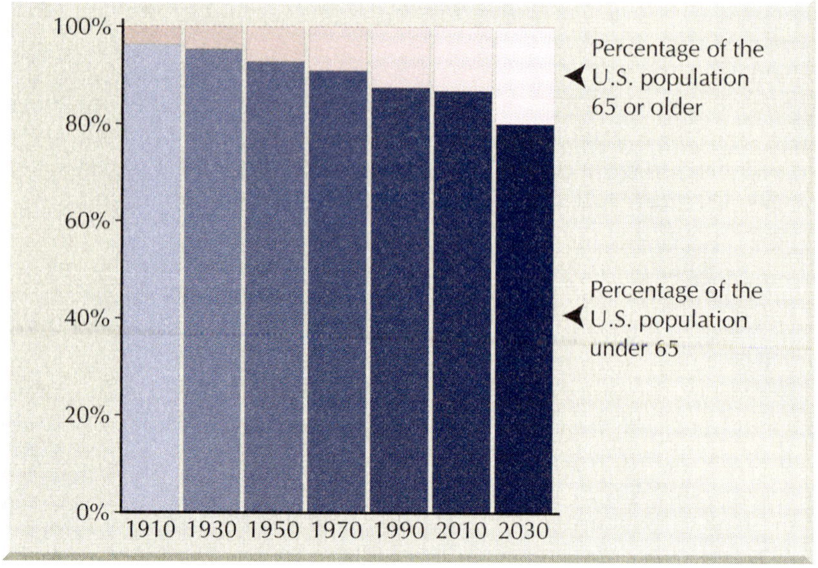

FIGURE 16.2
LIVING LONGER.
As we enter the new millennium, more people in the United States are living to be age 65 or above.

Adjustment in a World of DIVERSITY

Gender, Ethnicity, and Aging

Although Americans in general are living longer, there are gender and ethnic differences in life expectancy. For example, women in our society tend to live longer, but older men tend to live *better* ("Longer, healthier, better," 1997). White Americans from European backgrounds live longer on the average than do Hispanic Americans, African Americans, and Native Americans. Life expectancy for Hispanic Americans falls somewhere between the figures for African Americans and White Americans. The longevity of Asian Americans falls closer to that of White Americans than to that of African Americans. Native Americans have the lowest average longevity of the major racial/ethnic groups in our society (Nevid and others, 1998).

GENDER DIFFERENCES Women in the United States outlive men by 6 to 7 years. Why? For one thing, heart disease, the nation's leading killer, typically develops later in women than in men. Men are also more likely to die because of accidents, cirrhosis of the liver, strokes, suicide, homicide, AIDS, and cancer (excepting cancers of the female sex organs) (Nevid and others, 1998). Many deaths from these causes are the end result of unhealthy habits that are more typical of men, such as excessive drinking and reckless behavior.

Many men are also reluctant to have regular physical exams or to talk to their doctors about their health problems. "In their 20's, [men are] too strong to need a doctor; in their 30's, they're too busy, and in their 40's, too scared" ("Doctors tie male mentality," 1995). Women are much more likely to examine themselves for signs of breast cancer than men are even to recognize the early signs of prostate cancer.

Although women tend to outlive men, their prospects for a happy and healthy old age are dimmer. Men who beat the statistical odds by living beyond their seventies are far less likely than their female counterparts to live alone, suffer from chronic disabling conditions, or be poor.

Older women are more likely than men to live alone largely because they are five times more likely than men to be widowed (Nevid and others, 1998). Older women are also twice as likely as older men to be poor. Several factors account for this difference. Women now age 65 or older were less likely to hold jobs. If they had jobs, they were paid far less than men and received smaller pensions and other retirement benefits. Because more women than men live alone, they more often must shoulder the burdens of supporting a household without being able to draw on the income of a spouse or other family member.

ETHNICITY Why are there ethnic differences in life expectancy? Socioeconomic differences play a role. Members of ethnic minority groups in our society are more likely to be poor, and poor people tend to eat less nutritious diets, encounter more stress, and have less access to health care. There is a 7-year difference in life expectancy between people in the highest income brackets and those in the lowest. Yet other factors, such as cultural differences in diet and lifestyle, the stress of coping with discrimination, and genetic differences, may also partly account for ethnic group differences in life expectancy.

Physical Development

A number of changes—some of them problematic—do occur during the later years (Wade, 1998b; Figure 16.3). Changes in calcium metabolism lead to increased brittleness in the bones and heightened risk of breaks from accidents like falls. The skin becomes less elastic, subject to wrinkles and folds. As we grow older, our immune systems also function less effectively, leaving us more vulnerable to disease.

The senses become less acute. Older people see and hear less acutely. Because of a decline in the sense of smell, they may use more spice to flavor their food. Older people require more **reaction time** to respond to stimuli. Older drivers need more time to respond to traffic lights, other vehicles, and road conditions.

On the other hand, older people can do a great deal to retain vigor, preserve a reasonably youthful profile, and fend off disease. Exercise helps them maintain flexibility and cardiovascular condition. Because of their increased brittleness of bones and rigidity of joints, fast or prolonged walking are excellent aerobic choices for older people (Pena & Bricklin, 1990). Older people can continue to fight heart disease and cancer by eating diets low in cholesterol and saturated fats (Wolk and others, 1998). It was once thought that high cholesterol levels were less important in older people than in younger people. Research shows, however, that men aged 65 and older with high blood levels of cholesterol (250 milligrams or more per 100 milliliters of blood serum) are more than twice as likely to suffer heart attacks as are peers whose blood cholesterol levels were 200 milligrams or lower (Brody, 1990a). So diet and exercise can make inroads against some physical changes that were once considered inevitable.

Cognitive Development

Older people show some decline in general intellectual ability as measured by scores on intelligence tests. The dropoff is most acute on timed items, such as those on many of the "performance" scales of the Wechsler Adult Intelligence Scale. Performance items contain tasks such as putting puzzles together, copying designs with blocks, and learning to associate meaningless symbols with numbers—all of them to be completed within time limits.

REACTION TIME • The amount of time required to respond to a stimulus.

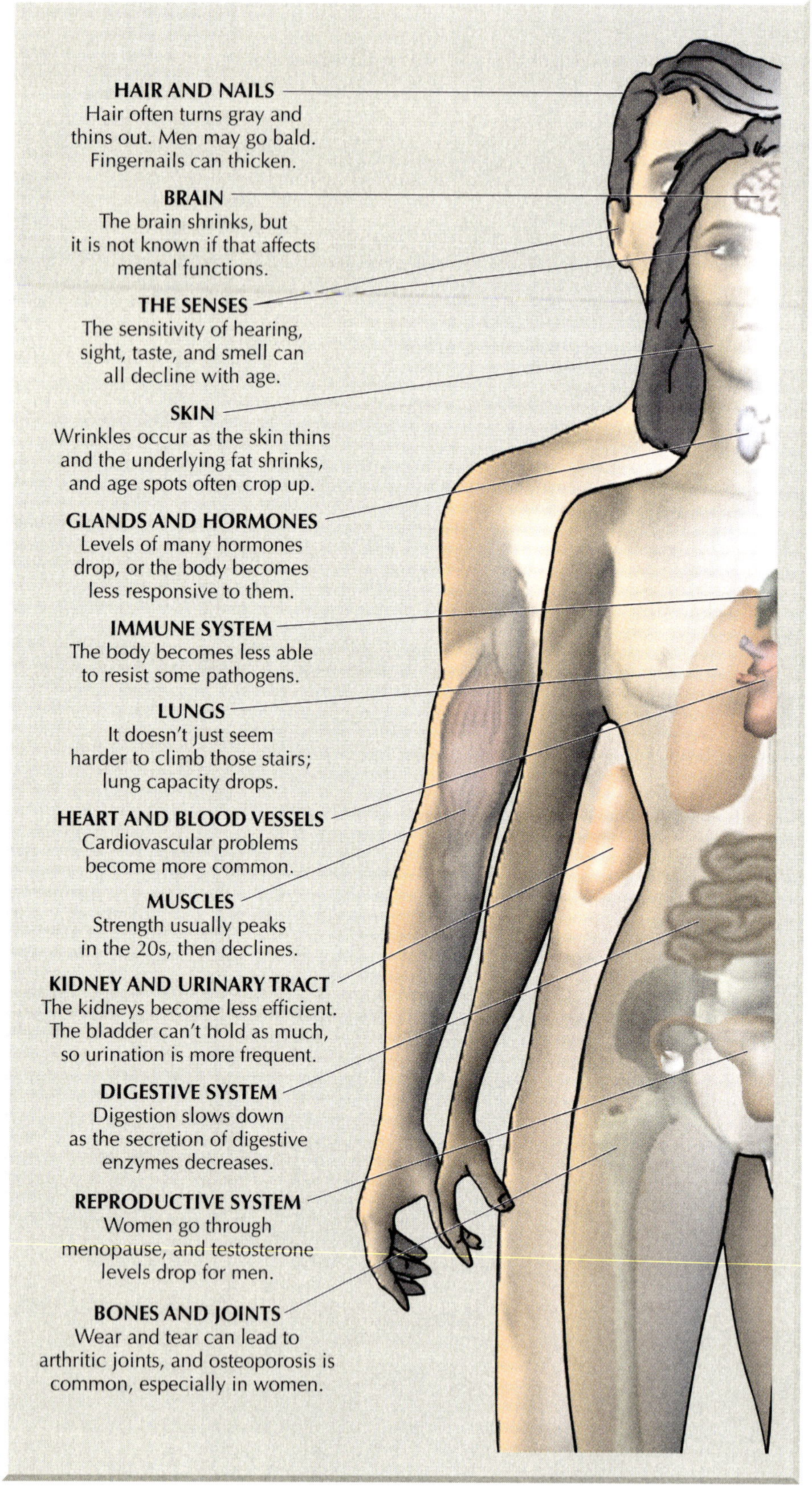

FIGURE 16.3

THE RELENTLESS MARCH OF TIME.

A number of physical changes occur during the later years.

Although there are some changes in reaction time, intellectual functioning, and memory among older people, they are not as large as many people tend to assume they are (Benson, 1995). Moreover, we understand very little about *why* they occur. Loss of sensory acuity and of motivation to do well may contribute to lower scores. In his later years, psychologist B. F. Skinner (1983) argued that much of the falloff is due to an "aging environment" rather than an aging person. That is, in many instances the behavior of older people goes unreinforced. Note that nursing home residents who are rewarded for remembering recent events show improved scores on tests of memory (Langer and others, 1979; Wolinsky, 1982). Skinner (1983) suggested many strategies that older people can adopt to enhance their sensory and motor functioning, memory, and even to cope with mental fatigue.

In some cases, supposedly irreversible cognitive changes may also reflect psychological problems such as depression. Such changes are neither primarily cognitive nor irreversible. If the depression is treated effectively, intellectual performance may also improve.

However, older people often combine years of experience with high levels of motivation on the job. In these cases, forced retirement can be an arbitrary and painful penalty for no sin other than turning 65 or 70.

THEORIES OF AGING Although it may be hard to believe that it will happen to us, everyone who has so far walked the Earth has aged—not a bad fate, considering the alternative. Why do we age? Various factors, some of which are theoretical, apparently contribute to aging.

Heredity plays a role. **Longevity** runs in families. People whose parents and grandparents lived into their eighties and nineties have a better chance of reaching these years themselves.

Environmental factors influence aging. People who exercise regularly appear to live longer. Disease, stress, obesity, and cigarette smoking can contribute to an early death. Fortunately, we can exert control over some of these factors.

Older people apparently show better health and psychological well-being when they retain control over their lives (Rodin & Langer, 1977; Wolinsky, 1982). Unfortunately, some older people are placed in nursing homes and surrender independence because of a decline in health and finances. Today this problem is widely recognized, and many communities make efforts to support older people in their own homes—particularly in the areas of bathing, dressing, and homemaking (Lewin, 1990, Stock, 1995). Even in the nursing home, older people fare better when they are kept informed and allowed to make decisions concerning their activities and care.

The theory of **programmed senescence** sees aging as determined by a biological clock that ticks at a rate governed by instructions in the genes. Just as genes program children to grow and reach sexual maturation, they program people to deteriorate and die. The fact that longevity runs in families may support the role of genes in aging.

The **wear-and-tear theory** does not suggest that people are programmed to self-destruct. Instead, environmental factors such as pollution, disease, and ultraviolet light are assumed to contribute to wear and tear of the body over time. The body is like a machine whose parts wear out through use. Cells lose the ability to regenerate themselves, and vital organs are worn down by the ravages of time.

ALZHEIMER'S DISEASE **Alzheimer's disease** is a progressive form of mental deterioration that may affect as many as 4 million Americans (Teri & Wagner,

LONGEVITY • A long span of life.

PROGRAMMED SENESCENCE • The view that aging is determined by a biological clock that ticks at a rate governed by genes.

WEAR-AND-TEAR THEORY • The view that factors such as pollution, disease, and ultraviolet light contribute to wear and tear on the body, so that the body loses the ability to repair itself.

ALZHEIMER'S DISEASE • A disorder caused by falloff in production of acetylcholine and degeneration of brain cells and characterized by memory loss and disorientation.

ADJUSTMENT in the NEW MILLENNIUM

Will We Discover a Real Fountain of Youth?

We are living longer than ever and, in many ways, better than ever. A hundred years ago, the average American could expect to live to be 48. Today that figure has been pushed back to the late seventies, and in Japan, it is 80. A major reason for the increase is the lowered mortality rate among infants and children. Other reasons include cleaner drinking water, use of sewer systems, antibiotics, vaccines, and refrigeration. Even scrubbing up before surgery and washing hands before preparing food and eating help. Then, of course, there is the eradication of some diseases, such as smallpox, and a medical arsenal of heavy weaponry against chronic diseases, such as cancer and cardiovascular disorders.

Today, if everything were to go right, it is conceivable that one could live to the maximum human life span of 110 to 120. In 1980 the U.S. Census Bureau counted 15,000 Americans over the age of 100. Today there may be 50,000 or more centenarians. By the year 2050, there may be 1.5 million! Moreover, the early detection and treatment of age-related diseases, hormone replacement, and nutritional advances are helping to make late adulthood an ever more vigorous and fulfilling time of life (Hall, 1998).

Even so, the life expectancy in the United States will probably only increase by 10 to 15 years by 2050, to an age of 85 or 90 (Haney, 1998). What, if anything, can we look forward to in the way of pushing back the life span? Let's consider possibilities under exploration today.

CALORIE RESTRICTION "Slim is in" in fashion as we approach the new millennium. The question is whether slimness also increases the life span. Food restriction—in the form of cutting back calories by at least one third of the normal intake—has been shown to significantly increase the life span in many species of animals, including rats, mice, and fruit flies (Roth, 1998). The animals live nearly 50 percent longer than their free-feeding peers. Calorie restriction appears to reset the metabolism from "growth mode" to "maintenance mode." The body operates more efficiently, and even susceptibility to chronic diseases seems to decrease. However, there is no experimental research on the effectiveness of such calorie restriction with humans, and one wonders whether people would put up with it. The goal of George Roth and other researchers at the National Institute on Aging is to see whether they can develop some sort of pill that achieves the same effects and extends the human life span by half a century!

VITAMINS Vitamins? Yes, vitamins. Our cells continually produce chemicals called free radicals, which are connected with cancer and other kinds of health problems. Most free radicals are naturally disarmed by chemicals called antioxidants. Some antioxidants are made by the body. Others, like beta carotene and vitamins C and E, are found in food. Today it appears that beta carotene is best obtained through yellow vegetables such as carrots, sweet potatoes, and squash. (Beta carotene supplements may actually be harmful.) Vitamin C and E supplements are probably helpful for many people—in moderation. Although nobody expects that vitamins will allow people to live forever, they may help us better withstand some of the effects of aging. But check with your doctor first. Don't start popping megadoses on your own.

1992). Alzheimer's affects about 10 percent of people over the age of 65. The risk increases dramatically with advanced age (Selkoe, 1992). Although Alzheimer's is connected with aging, it is a disease and not part of a normal aging process (Kolata, 1991). The disease is associated with the degeneration of cells in an area of the brain (the hippocampus) that normally produces large

Hormones Researchers are also investigating the effects of replacing naturally occurring hormones whose levels decline as we age: melatonin, DHEA, and human growth hormone.

Melatonin is something of a biological clock that is secreted by the pineal gland. It helps regulate the sleep-wake cycle. The question is whether it also affects aging. There is some evidence that melatonin supplements may extend life in mice, but we are waiting to hear whether it has a healthful effect on people.

DHEA (dehydroepiandrosterone) is an adrenal hormone that the body converts into other hormones, including sex hormones. DHEA appears to help bolster the immune system, but DHEA production begins to decline at the ages of 25 to 30, possibly increasing our susceptibility to disease. Research with animals suggests that DHEA replacement might enhance the functioning of the immune system and thus reduce the risk of some forms of cancer, slow the effects of aging, give the libido a boost, and perhaps extend life (Brody, 1998a). But research with people has so far yielded inconclusive results and there are potential hazards, such as increased risks of breast and prostate cancer, liver problems, and heart problems (the latter, in women) (Brody, 1998a).

Human growth hormone is crucial in childhood and adolescence. The question is whether decreasing levels of growth hormone account for effects of aging such as loss of bone density and muscle mass. Researchers found that injections of growth hormone reverse a number of the effects of aging in a sample of older men. The hormone decreased their body fat, increased their muscle mass, improved their bone density, and thickened their skin (Nevid and others, 1998). However, it has not been shown that the men lived longer than they would have otherwise.

Telomerase Telomerase is an enzyme that has the effect of helping cells continue to divide. "Who cares?" you ask? Cells reproduce by dividing, and most cells in the human body renew themselves 50 times or more by the time we reach the end of our life spans. One theory of aging holds that we age and die because cells can no longer divide.

What stops them from dividing? Many factors may be involved, but one is telomeres. Our chromosomes consist of twisting ladders of DNA, which holds our genetic codes. Yet at the ends of the ladders—top and bottom—are segments of "junk DNA" called *telomeres.* They carry no genetic messages themselves but may protect the DNA that does. Each time cells divide, the telomeres shorten, placing one apparent limit on cell division. But the enzyme telomerase prevents telomeres from shortening and may eventually be used to extend life by enabling cells to divide a greater number of times (Shay and others, 1998).

Playing With Genes While telomerase may extend life by lengthening the ends of strips of genetic material, another approach involves changing the genetic code itself—genetic engineering. Researchers have multiplied the life spans of fruit flies through genetic engineering. Thomas Johnson (1998) of the University of Colorado has shown that one can increase the life spans of simple worms fourfold by adding and subtracting genes. Johnson suggests that people may have some genetic equivalent to the worms, and that learning to regulate these genes or to mimic their effects with medicines could greatly extend the human life span. Skeptics argue that human aging is probably caused by several genes acting in complex harmony. But Johnson counters, "I personally am convinced that sometime we are going to be able to engineer new drugs and practices that dramatically extend human life span, perhaps another doubling."

We will see whether the new millennium brings a true fountain of youth. ■

amounts of the chemical messenger **acetylcholine** (ACh). Brain cells collect plaques (dark areas of cellular "garbage") and die off in large numbers. The affected area of the brain and ACh are involved in the formation of new memories. For this reason, one of the cardinal symptoms of Alzheimer's disease is progressive memory loss and disorientation. But memories for remote (distant)

Acetylcholine • A neurotransmitter involved in memory formation and other functions.

events may remain reasonably intact. The older the individual, the greater the risk of Alzheimer's disease. The causes of Alzheimer's are unclear, but they may involve some combination of genetic factors, early viral infections, and accumulations of metals such as zinc and aluminum in the brain.

Alzheimer's usually comes on gradually among older people, over a period of 8 to 20 years. At first victims note memory loss and frequently get lost—even in their own homes. Eventually they may become highly disoriented; fail to recognize other people, including family members; show childish emotions; and lose the ability to take care of their own hygiene and dress.

Researchers are investigating ways of controlling Alzheimer's disease (Tanzi, 1995). They range from diets low in metals to the transplanting of ACh-producing cells into the brain. Older people with Alzheimer's or with less dramatic memory problems can make behavioral adjustments as well. All of us, not only older people, profit from keeping pads and pencils near the phone so that we can readily record messages. We can keep calendars and mark down scheduled events, even routine daily events. Persons with memory loss can mark off each day as it passes. Medicine containers with compartments for each day of the week are available at pharmacies. The establishment of daily routines and environmental prompts is of great value to older people (Skinner, 1983).

Personality Development and Adjustment

Personality theorists offer various views of late adulthood. According to Erikson, late adulthood is the stage of **ego integrity versus despair.** The basic conflict is to maintain the belief that life is meaningful and worthwhile in the face of the inevitability of death. Ego integrity derives from wisdom, from acceptance of one's life span as finite and occurring at a certain point in the sweep of history. We spend most of our lives accumulating things and relationships. Erikson argues that adjustment in the later years requires the wisdom to be able to let go.

Erikson was optimistic. He believed that we can maintain a sense of trust through life and avoid feelings of despair. And research does suggest that most older people are reasonably well satisfied with their lives.

According to Robert Peck (1968), who has extended Erikson's views, a number of psychological shifts aid us in adjusting to late adulthood:

1. Coming to value wisdom more than physical strength and power
2. Coming to value friendship and social relationships more than sexual prowess[2]
3. Retaining emotional flexibility so that we can adjust to changing family relationships and the ending of a career
4. Retaining mental flexibility so that we can form new social relationships and undertake new leisure activities
5. Keeping involved and active and concerned about others so that we do not become preoccupied with physical changes or the approach of death
6. Shifting interest from the world of work to retirement activities

Havighurst also denotes a number of developmental tasks of late adulthood:

1. Adjusting to physical changes
2. Adjusting to retirement and to changes in financial status

EGO INTEGRITY VERSUS DESPAIR • Erikson's term for the crisis of late adulthood, characterized by the task of maintaining one's sense of identity despite physical deterioration.

---

[2] However, most of us continue, or can continue, to enjoy sexual expression for a lifetime, and we should not fall prey to the stereotype of the elderly as asexual (Rathus and others, 1997).

"SUCCESSFUL AGING"?
The later years were once seen mainly as a prelude to dying. As we approach the new millennium, however, many older people — termed "successful agers" — are seeking new challenges.

3. Establishing satisfying living arrangements
4. Learning to live with one's spouse in retirement (e.g., coping with being home much of the time)
5. Adjusting to the death of one's spouse
6. Forming new relationships with aging peers
7. Adopting flexible social roles

ADJUSTMENT AMONG OLDER PEOPLE Sheehy's characterizations of the sixties, seventies, and eighties are filled with cause for optimism. Research appears to bear out her point of view. Despite the changes that occur with aging, the majority of people in their seventies report being generally satisfied with their lives (Margoshes, 1995). A study of people retired for 18 to 120 months found that 75 percent rated retirement as mostly good (Hendrick and others, 1982). Over 90 percent were generally satisfied with life, and more than 75 percent reported their health as good or excellent.

Adjustment among older people, as among younger people, is related to financial security and health. The sicker we are, the less likely we are to be well adjusted. Also, there is a link between financial status and physical health. Poor older people are more likely to report ill health than the financially secure (Birren, 1983). This finding would seem to call for better health care for the aged, and it does. But it may also be that people who have been healthier over the years are also better able to provide for their own financial security.

Among older people, as among younger people, there remains a relationship between social support and adjustment. Older couples are less lonely and more happy than the single or the widowed (Barrow & Smith, 1983). Widows with children are also better adjusted than other widows, a prospect that contributes to some people's desire for children. Once retired, couples tend to spend more time together and their relationship tends to improve and take on greater importance (Atchley, 1985).

SUCCESSFUL AGING The concept of "successful aging" has sprung into the lexicons of developmental psychologists (Margoshes, 1995). The idea is not simply to put a positive spin on the inevitable. Psychologists have found that "successful agers" have a number of characteristics that can inspire all of us to lead more enjoyable and productive lives.

One component of successful aging is reshaping one's life to concentrate on what people find to be important and meaningful. Laura Carstensen's (1995) research on people aged 70 and older reveals that successful agers form emotional goals that bring them satisfaction. For example, rather than cast about in multiple directions, they may focus on their families and friends. Successful agers may have less time left than those of us in earlier stages of adulthood, but they tend to spend it more wisely (Garfinkel, 1995).

Paul and Margret Baltes (1995) use the term "selective optimization and compensation" to describe the manner in which successful agers lead their lives. That is, successful agers no longer seek to compete in arenas best left to younger people—such as certain kinds of athletic or business activities. Rather, they focus on matters that allow them to maintain a sense of personal control. Moreover, they use available resources to make up for losses. If their memories are not quite what they once were, they make notes or other reminders. If their senses are no longer as acute, they use devices such as hearing aids or allow themselves more time to take in information. There are also ingenious individual strategies. The great pianist Arthur Rubinstein performed into his eighties, when he had lost much of his speed. In his later years, however, he would slow down before playing faster passages to enhance the impression of speed during faster passages (Margoshes, 1995).

Truth or Fiction Revisited

It is true, according to research by Rakowski, that older people who blame health problems on aging rather than on specific factors such as a virus are more likely to die in the near future.

A second component of successful aging is a positive outlook. For example, some older people attribute occasional health problems—such as aches and pains—to specific and unstable factors, such as a cold or jogging too long. Others attribute aches and pains to global and stable factors such as aging itself. Not surprisingly, those who attribute these problems to specific, unstable factors are more optimistic that they will surmount them. They thus have a more positive outlook or attitude. Of particular interest here is research conducted by William Rakowski (1995). Rakowski followed 1,400 people aged 70 and older with nonlethal health problems such as aches and pains. He found that those who blamed the problems on aging itself were significantly more likely to die in the near future than those who blamed the problems on specific, unstable factors.

A third component of successful aging is challenging oneself. Many individuals look forward to late adulthood as a time when they can rest from life's challenges. However, sitting back and allowing the world to pass by is a prescription for vegetating, not living life to its fullest. Consider an experiment conducted by Curt Sandman and Francis Crinella (1995) with 175 people of an average age of 72. They randomly assigned participants either to a foster grandparent program with neurologically impaired children or to a control group and followed them for 10 years. As compared to people in the control group, the foster grandparents carried out various physical challenges, such as walking a few miles each day, and also had new social interactions. At assessment, the foster grandparent program had improved participants' overall cognitive functioning, including memory functioning, and their sleep patterns. Moreover, the foster grandparents showed superior functioning in these areas as compared to people assigned to the control group.

Doing less is no prescription for health and adjustment among older people. Focusing in on what is important, maintaining a positive attitude, and accepting new challenges is as important for older people as for any of us.

LIVING ARRANGEMENTS There are some stereotypes concerning living arrangements for older people. One has them living with children; another, in institutions (Stock, 1995). Still another has them buying recreational vehicles and taking off for condominiums or retirement communities in the Sun Belt.

Truth or Fiction Revisited

It is not true that most older people live with children, in institutions, or in retirement communities. Most older people own their own homes and remain in the communities where they had previously lived and worked.

First let us put to rest the stereotype that older people are generally dependent on others. According to the U. S. Bureau of the Census (1995), the majority of heads of households who are 65 years of age or older own their own homes. However, perhaps one third of older adults will spend at least some time in a nursing home (Kemper & Murtaugh, 1991). The populations of nursing homes are disproportionately old, with most residents aged 80 or older.

Despite the stereotype of taking off for the Sun Belt, the majority of older people remain in their hometowns and cities. Moving is stressful at any age. Most older people prefer to remain in familiar locales. When older people do decide to move, however, careful plans and adequate finances decrease the stress of moving (Hendrick and others, 1982).

ECONOMICS Here, too, there are some stereotypes. Older people are often portrayed as living in poverty or at the mercy of their children and external forces, such as government support. Unfortunately, some of these stereotypes are based on reality. People who no longer work are usually dependent on savings and fixed incomes such as pensions and Social Security payments. The flip side of the coin is that nationwide, only about 13 percent of those aged 65 and above live below the poverty level (Schultz, 1982; U.S. Bureau of the Census, 1985). But the financial status of older African Americans is worse. Two out of three live below the poverty level.

KINSHIP AND GRANDPARENTHOOD There is a saying that grandparents have more relaxed relationships with their grandchildren than they did with their own children. Perhaps. Certainly their perspectives have grown broader over the years. Whereas parents may fret and worry, grandparents may have learned that children will turn out to be all right most of the time. Also, they can reap the enjoyment of grandchildren without bearing the brunt of the responsibility for caring for them.

More than 80 percent of older people have children and interact with them regularly (Lee, 1980). They frequently pass power to the family's middle generation and sometimes allow their children to manage their finances. They frequently attempt to balance their own needs for maintaining independence with their needs for continuing involvement with their children and grandchildren. How often they see the children and grandchildren, and whether they have the right to make "suggestions," become key issues. Although many older people worry that their families might no longer want them around, they are not usually rejected by their children (Francis, 1984).

Grandparents are frequently valued by their children for the roles they play with their grandchildren. On a practical level, retired grandparents can help babysit and pick the children up from school. Many adults regret that moving to new locales to climb the corporate ladder has separated their children from their grandparents. Grandparents also often serve as special sources of wisdom, love, and understanding. They are frequently more relaxed and less demanding with their grandchildren than with their own children.

RETIREMENT Although life changes can be stressful, retirement can be a positive step. According to an analysis of U.S. Department of Labor data on 1,200 older men, "most people are perfectly happy not to have to get up each morning to go to work" (Crowley, 1985, p. 80). Many retirees enjoy their leisure. Some continue in part-time labor, paid or voluntary. Most people who deteriorate rapidly after retirement were unhealthy prior to retirement (Crowley, 1985).

Atchley (1985) has theorized that many older people undergo a six-phase developmental sequence of retirement:

1. *The preretirement phase.* This phase involves fantasies about retirement—positive and negative. Company preretirement programs and retired friends can foster adjustment by providing accurate information about financial realities and postretirement lifestyles.

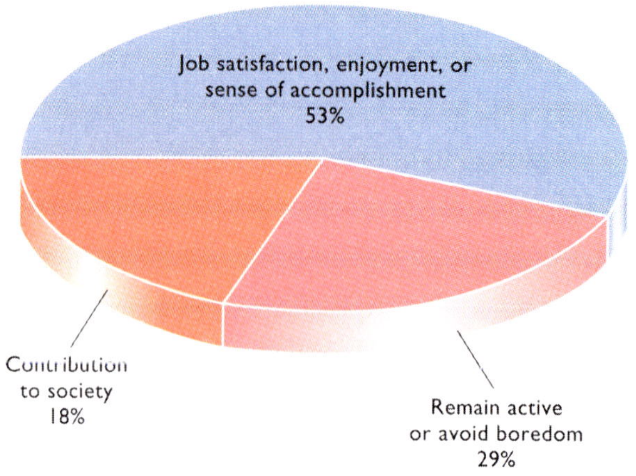

FIGURE 16.4
WHY RETIRED PEOPLE RETURN TO WORK.
As reported in *The Wall Street Journal,* one third of a surveyed group of retired senior executives returned to full-time work within 18 months of retirement. Their reasons are shown in the chart.

2. *The honeymoon phase.* This phase often involves the euphoria that accompanies newfound freedom. It is a busy period during which people do the things they had fantasized doing once they had the time—as financial resources permit.
3. *The disenchantment phase.* As one's schedule slows down and one discovers that fantasized activities are less stimulating than anticipated, disenchantment can set in.
4. *The reorientation phase.* Now a more realistic view of the possibilities of retirement develops. Now retirees frequently join volunteer groups and increase civic involvements.
5. *The stability phase.* Now the retirement role has been mastered. Routine and stability set in; there is more accurate self-awareness of one's needs and strengths and weaknesses.
6. *The termination phase.* Retirement can come to an end in different ways. One is death; another is the assumption of the sick role because of disability. Still another is return to work.

Truth or Fiction Revisited

It is true that retired people frequently become disenchanted with their newfound freedom. Many of them return to work.

As noted in Figure 16.4, some people return to some form of work after retiring. For them, the benefits of employment outweigh the lure of leisure.

ON DEATH AND DYING

Death is the last great taboo. Psychiatrist Elisabeth Kübler-Ross comments on our denial of death in her landmark book *On Death and Dying:*

> We use euphemisms, we make the dead look as if they were asleep, we ship the children off to protect them from the anxiety and turmoil around the house if the [person] is fortunate enough to die at home, [and] we don't allow children to visit their dying parents in the hospitals. (1969, p. 8)

In this section we explore aspects of death and dying. We consider the pioneering theoretical work of Kübler-Ross and the writings of more recent theorists. In the "Adjustment and Modern Life" feature, we examine issues concerning dying with dignity, the funeral, and bereavement.

Theoretical Perspectives

KÜBLER-ROSS'S THEORY From her work with terminally ill patients, Kübler-Ross found some common responses to news of impending death. She identified five stages of dying through which many patients pass. She suggests that older people who suspect that approach of death may undergo similar responses. The stages are as follows:

1. *Denial.* In this stage, people feel, "It can't be me. The diagnosis must be wrong." Denial can be flat and absolute. It can fluctuate so that one minute the patient accepts the medical verdict; the next, the patient starts chatting animatedly about distant plans.
2. *Anger.* Denial usually gives way to anger and resentment toward the young and healthy and, sometimes, toward the medical establishment— "It's unfair. Why me?"
3. *Bargaining.* Next, people may bargain with God to postpone death, promising, for example, to do good deeds if they are given another 6 months, another year.
4. *Depression.* With depression come feelings of loss and hopelessness— grief at the specter of leaving loved ones and life itself.
5. *Final acceptance.* Ultimately, inner peace may come, quiet acceptance of the inevitable. This "peace" is not contentment; it is nearly devoid of feeling.

SHNEIDMAN'S THEORY Psychologist Edwin Shneidman (1984) acknowledges the presence of feelings such as those described by Kübler-Ross. He does not see them linked in sequence, however. Shneidman suggests, instead, that people show a variety of emotional and cognitive responses. They can be fleeting or relatively stable, ebb and flow, and reflect pain and bewilderment. People's responses reflect their personalities and their philosophies of life.

Research is more supportive of Shneidman's views than Kübler-Ross's. Reactions to nearing death turn out to be varied. Some people are reasonably accepting of the inevitable; others are despondent; still others are terrorized. Some people show a rapid shifting of emotions, ranging from rage to surrender, from envy of the young and healthy to yearning for the end (Shneidman, 1984).

Truth or Fiction Revisited

It is not true that terminally ill people undergo a predictable sequence of emotional and cognitive responses. Kübler-Ross's theory has not been borne out by research.

SELF-ASSESSMENT

How Concerned Are You About Death?

Contemplation of death evokes a variety of thoughts and feelings. To some degree, our philosophies about the place of death in human existence and about what—if anything—follows death affects our responses. The Death Concern Scale consists of 30 statements that measure the anxiety or apprehension we feel when we think about death. The key to the questionnaire is in the Appendix. ■

Directions: The questionnaire contains two parts. Respond to questions 1 through 11 by using the code below:

1 = Never
2 = Rarely
3 = Sometimes
4 = Often

____ 1. I think about my own death.
____ 2. I think about the death of loved ones.
____ 3. I think about dying young.
____ 4. I think about the possibility of my being killed on a city street.
____ 5. I have fantasies of my own death.
____ 6. I think about death just before I go to sleep.
____ 7. I think of how I would act if I knew I were to die within a given period of time.
____ 8. I think of how my relatives would act and feel upon my death.
____ 9. When I am sick I think about death.
____ 10. When I am outside during a lightning storm I think about the possibility of being struck by lightning.
____ 11. When I am in an automobile I think about the high incidence of traffic fatalities.

Respond to questions 12 through 30 by circling one of the answers according to the code given below and then writing the corresponding number in the blank space:

SA = I strongly agree
A = I somewhat agree
D = I somewhat disagree
SD = I strongly disagree

____ 12. I think people should first become concerned about death when they are old.

SA	A	D	SD
1	2	3	4

____ 13. I am much more concerned about death than those around me.

SA	A	D	SD
4	3	2	1

____ 14. Death hardly concerns me.

SA	A	D	SD
1	2	3	4

____ 15. My general outlook just doesn't allow for morbid thoughts.

SA	A	D	SD
1	2	3	4

____ 16. The prospect of my own death arouses anxiety in me.
SA A D SD
4 3 2 1

____ 17. The prospect of my own death depresses me.
SA A D SD
4 3 2 1

____ 18. The prospect of the death of my loved ones arouses anxiety in me.
SA A D SD
4 3 2 1

____ 19. The knowledge that I will surely die does not in any way affect the conduct of my life.
SA A D SD
1 2 3 4

____ 20. I envision my own death as a painful, nightmarish experience.
SA A D SD
4 3 2 1

____ 21. I am afraid of dying.
SA A D SD
4 3 2 1

____ 22. I am afraid of being dead.
SA A D SD
4 3 2 1

____ 23. Many people become disturbed at the sight of a new grave but it does not bother me.
SA A D SD
1 2 3 4

____ 24. I am disturbed when I think about the shortness of life.
SA A D SD
4 3 2 1

____ 25. Thinking about death is a waste of time.
SA A D SD
1 2 3 4

____ 26. Death should not be regarded as a tragedy if it occurs after a productive life.
SA A D SD
1 2 3 4

____ 27. The inevitable death of a person poses a serious challenge to the meaningfulness of human existence.
SA A D SD
4 3 2 1

____ 28. The death of the individual is ultimately beneficial because it facilitates change in society.
SA A D SD
1 2 3 4

____ 29. I have a desire to live on after death.
SA A D SD
4 3 2 1

____ 30. The question of whether or not there is a future life worries me considerably.
SA A D SD
4 3 2 1

Source: Reprinted with permission from Louis S. Dickstein (1972), Death concern: Measurement and correlates, *Psychological Reports, 30,* p. 565.

adjustment and modern life

DYING WITH DIGNITY

Dying people, like other people, need self-confidence, security, and dignity. They may also need relief from pain, and a medical controversy is raging concerning giving them addictive pain-killing drugs (e.g., narcotics) that are unavailable to the general public. We believe that the dignity and pain of dying people should take precedence over broader political issues. It is desirable for medical staff to anticipate and prevent extremes of pain rather than only respond to patients' requests. Moreover, the dying patient should decide how much medicine is enough.

The dying often need to share their feelings. It may be helpful to encourage them to talk about what they are feeling. It can also be helpful just to be there—not to withdraw from them when they fear themselves withdrawing from what they hold dear.

Pattison (1977) suggests a number of guidelines for helping dying people, such as the following:

- Providing social support
- Providing accurate information as to what might be experienced in terms of pain and loss of body functions and control
- Acknowledging the reality of the impending loss of family and other people
- Helping the person make final financial and legal arrangements
- Allowing the person to experience grief
- Assuming maintenance of necessary body functions in a way that allows the person to maintain dignity
- Pointing out that people should not blame themselves for loss of control over body functions

The Hospice Movement

The term *hospice* derives from the same root that has given rise to the words *hospital* and *hospitality.* It has come to refer to homelike environments in which terminally ill people can face death with physical and emotional supports that provide them with dignity (Cunningham, 1996; Wilkes, 1996).

In contrast to hospitals, hospices do not restrict visiting hours. Family and friends work with specially trained staff to provide support. In contrast to hospital procedures, patients are given as much control over their lives as they can handle. So long as their physical conditions permit, patients are encouraged to make decisions as to their diets, activities, and medication—including a "cocktail" that consists of sugar, narcotics, alcohol, and a tranquilizer. The cocktail is intended to reduce pain and anxiety without clouding cognitive functioning—although this goal cannot be perfectly met. Relatives and friends may maintain contact with staff to work through their grief once the patient has died.

EUTHANASIA The term *euthanasia* derives from the Greek roots *eu,* meaning "well," and *thanatos,* meaning "death." *Thanatos* was adopted by Sigmund Freud as the name of his theoretical death instinct. "Thanatopsis" is the name of William Cullen Bryant's poem about death, to which we refer again later. If the hospice cocktail is controversial, euthanasia—also referred to as "mercy killing"—is more so.

Euthanasia is sometimes considered when there is no hope for a patient's recovery, when the patient is unconscious (as in a coma), or when the patient is in relentless pain and requests death (Glick, 1992; Quill, 1993). It can be brought about in two ways. In positive or active euthanasia, the patient is given high doses of drugs, such as barbiturates or morphine, that induce death painlessly. As of this writing, positive euthanasia has different legal standings in various states, though it is illegal in most states. A physician dubbed "Dr. Death" in the press, Jack Kevorkian, has been put on trial for aiding terminally ill people who are in pain to commit suicide. Yet many physicians admit to using does of depressants that are larger than necessary to control patients' pain (Quill, 1993). Negative or passive euthanasia, by contrast, refers to *not* preventing death. Negative euthanasia can involve denying comatose patients medicine, food, or life-support systems such as respirators. The legal status of negative euthanasia varies.

The Living Will

The **living will** is a legal document through which people request that they not be kept "alive" by artificial support systems, such as respirators, when there is no hope for recovery. The will is intended to spare people the indignity of being kept alive by tubes and intricate equipment and to spare their families the misery of visiting them in the hospital setting and coping with their states. The living will is intended to bring the inevitable to a conclusion so that the family can deal with it and get on with their lives.

The Funeral

The funeral is an organized, ritualistic way of responding to death in which a community acknowledges that one of its members has died. When as individuals, we might not know how to cope with the passing of a family member, the funeral provides customary things to do. The funeral may reflect religious beliefs and cultural formalities. For religious people, the funeral cognitively ties in a family member's death to the ongoing progress of time and the universe. But it also enlists professionals to "do the right thing" when our grief might impair our own decision-making skills. In a sense, we also prepare for the loss of our own family members when we attend the funerals of people who are further removed.

Funerals involve the following:

1. *Separation of the dead from the living.* The dead person is physically removed and prepared for disposition.
2. *Visitation.* Many religions provide for defined periods of time during which people come to the funeral home (or comparable setting) to see the body and socially support the family of the deceased. If the deceased person is a public figure, he or she may "lie in state" for a defined period, allowing the public to come by and adjust.

LIVING WILL • A document that expresses the wish not to be kept alive by extraordinary support systems in the event of terminal illness and inability to express this decision at the time.

3. *Ritual.* This is the ceremony that recounts the life of the deceased person, testifying as to its meaning. In the United States, most funeral rites are defined by religious customs.
4. *The procession.* The people who attend the funeral follow the body to the place of disposition, such as the cemetery. Moving *to* the cemetery is thought to help family and friends accept the loss. Later, moving *away from* the cemetery is symbolic of family and friends beginning to get on with their lives.
5. *Committing the body to its final resting place.* In this act the finality of death is again underscored. Again, the need for the survivors to go on is suggested.

Bereavement

Those who are left behind, as those who learn of impending death, undergo a complex range of powerful emotions. The term **bereavement** refers to the state of the survivors. It implies feelings of sadness and loneliness, and a process of mourning.

There are many aspects to bereavement: sorrow, emptiness and numbness, anger ("Why did he or she have to die?" "How could they let this happen?" "What do I do now?"), loneliness—even relief, as when the deceased person has suffered over a prolonged period and we feel that we have reached the limits of our abilities to help sustain him or her. Death also makes us mindful of our own mortality.

Investigators have also derived stages or phases of grief and mourning. First there is often numbness and shock, accompanied by the need to maintain as many routines as possible (Boksay, 1998). Then there is preoccupation with and intense yearning for the loved one. Next, as the loss of the loved one sinks in more and more, there is depression, despair, and disorganization. Loss of appetite, insomnia, and forgetfulness are all normal reactions at this time. It may take 2 years or more for the mourner to accept the loss.

Many mourners find it helpful to "rework" the events leading up to the loss, such as the details of what happened in the hospital. You may listen to the spouse of the deceased describe these events for an hour and then be surprised to hear him or her go through it again, with equal intensity, when another person drops by.

Usually, the most intense grief is encountered after the funeral, when the relatives and friends have gone home and the bereaved person is finally alone. Then he or she may have to finally come to grips with the reality of an empty house, of being truly alone. For this reason, it is helpful to space one's social support over a period of time, not to do everything at once. Mourning takes time. Support is helpful throughout the process.

The bereaved do usually "come back" from their losses. They may never forget the deceased person, but they become less preoccupied. They resume routines at work or in the home. They may never be as happy or satisfied with life, but most of the time they resume functioning. Sometimes they grow in compassion because of their loss. They gain a deeper appreciation of the value of life.

Bereavement • The saddened, lonely state of those who have experienced the death of a loved one.

"Lying Down to Pleasant Dreams . . . "

The American poet William Cullen Bryant is best known for his poem "Thanatopsis," which he composed at the age of 18. "Thanatopsis" expresses Erik Erikson's goal of ego integrity, Erikson's optimism that we can maintain a sense of trust through life. By meeting squarely the challenges of our adult lives, perhaps we can take our leave with dignity. When our time comes to "join the innumerable caravan"—the billions who have died before us—perhaps we can depart life with integrity.

Live, wrote the poet, so that

> . . . when thy summons comes to join
> The innumerable caravan that moves
> To the pale realms of shade, where each shall take
> His chamber in the silent halls of death,
> Thou go not, like the quarry-slave at night,
> Scourged to his dungeon, but, sustained and soothed
> By an unfaltering trust, approach thy grave
> Like one who wraps the drapery of his couch
> About him, and lies down to pleasant dreams.

Bryant, of course, wrote "Thanatopsis" at 18, not 85, the age at which he died. At that advanced age his feelings, his pen, might have differed. But literature and poetry, unlike science, need not reflect reality. They can serve to inspire and warm us.

SUMMARY

1. **How are the stages of adulthood divided?** Most researchers divide adulthood into young adulthood (ages 20 to 40), middle adulthood (ages 40 to 60 or 65), and late adulthood (age 65 and older).
2. **Who are the major theorists of adult personality development?** They include Erik Erikson, who theorized stages of psychosocial development; Robert Havighurst, who catalogued developmental tasks; Daniel Levinson, who described the "seasons" of men's lives; and journalist Gail Sheehy, who proposed various "passages" we go through. Psychologists such as Judith Bardwick and Carol Gilligan have focused on the development of women.
3. **How do these theorists describe the major events of young adulthood?** Erikson sees the establishment of intimate relationships as the central task. Other theorists focus on striving to advance in the career world. Many suggest some sort of reassessment at about age 30, and Levinson proposes that we settle into our roles at about 35.
4. **What gender differences are there in the development of personality during young adulthood?** Men's development seems to be characterized by a transition from restriction to control, and women's development, according to Gilligan, is characterized by a transition from being cared for to caring for others. Many women are conflicted about success in the career world because of a career's impact on family life.
5. **What cognitive and physical changes take place during middle adulthood?** There is a slight and gradual decline in overall cognitive abilities and in physical functioning. Because of falloff in estrogen production, women usually encounter the climacteric in the forties and menopause in the late forties or early fifties.
6. **What is menopause, and how does it affect women?** Menopause is a normal process whose symptoms are mild for most women. Menopause is cessation of menstruation, and it can have complex and powerful meanings for women. Despite stereotypes of middle-aged women as irritable and depressed, women are frequently peppier and more assertive following menopause.
7. **What is the midlife transition?** The midlife transition is a psychological shift from how many years we have lived to how many years we have left. In men it usually arrives at about age 40 and is triggered by a marker event, such as death of a parent or peer. According to Sheehy, women undergo a midlife transition about 5 years earlier than men do, and it is triggered by awareness of the approach of the end of the childbearing years.
8. **What is the midlife crisis?** The midlife crisis is a period of major reassessment during which we evaluate the discrepancies between our achievements and our youthful dreams. We recognize our limits, including our mortality.
9. **What is the empty-nest syndrome?** It refers to feelings of depression and loss of purpose that are theorized to affect parents, especially mothers, when the last child leaves home. Although an "empty nest" requires adjustment and the ability to let go, many parents enjoy their newfound freedoms.
10. **What physical and cognitive changes take place during late adulthood?** Older people show less sensory acuity, and reaction time increases. Some presumed cognitive deficits may actually reflect declining motivation or psychological problems such as depression. There is continued decline in strength, stamina, and the immune system, increasing vulnerability to disease.
11. **Why do people age?** Heredity plays a role in longevity. We do not know exactly why people age, although one possibility is that cells lose the abilities to maintain themselves and reproduce adequately. But environmental factors such as exercise, proper diet, and the maintenance of responsibility can apparently delay aging.
12. **What are the major challenges and changes of late adulthood?** Tasks of late adulthood include adjusting to retirement and maintaining one's ego identity in the face of physical decline.
13. **How well adjusted are older people?** Most older people rate their life satisfaction and their health as generally good. Retirement can be a positive step, so long as it is voluntary. Having adequate financial resources is a major contributor to satisfaction among older people.
14. **Are there stages to death and dying?** Kübler-Ross identifies five stages of dying among the terminally ill: denial, anger, bargaining, depression, and final acceptance. However, research by other investigators

shows that psychological reactions to approaching death are varied and related to the person's personality and philosophy of life.

15. **How does the funeral affect the adjustment of survivors?** The funeral provides rituals that relieve the bereaved of the need to plan and take charge during the crisis of death. The rituals help the bereaved accept the finality of death and point to a return to communal life.

The Challenges of Life

CHAPTER 17

The Challenge of the Workplace

TRUTH OR FICTION?

✓ T	F	
☐	☐	Many million-dollar lottery winners feel aimless and dissatisfied if they quit their jobs after striking it rich.
☐	☐	Women who wear perfume to interviews are more likely to get the job.
☐	☐	It's a good idea to ask for the lowest salary you can get by with at a job interview.
☐	☐	Evaluators tend to appraise workers' performance objectively—on the basis of how well they do, not how much they like them.
☐	☐	Efficient, skillful employees are evaluated more highly than hard-working employees who must struggle to get the job done.
☐	☐	Allowing employees to piece together their own work schedules is demoralizing to workers and interferes with productivity.
☐	☐	Apathetic workers are most likely to experience job burnout.
☐	☐	Stressed workers have more accidents on the job.
☐	☐	Women earn only about two thirds the income of men in the United States.
☐	☐	Sexual harassment, like beauty, is in the eye of the beholder. What one person considers sexual harassment may be seen as a compliment or normal sexual invitation by someone else.
☐	☐	Anybody who has the ability to get ahead would be satisfied with prestigious vocations such as college professor, psychologist, physician, or lawyer.

OUTLINE

Work is the refuge of people who have nothing better to do.

OSCAR WILDE

A CENTURY AGO, THE BRITISH PLAYWRIGHT George Bernard Shaw pronounced, "Drink is the greatest evil of the working class." Upon sober reflection, he added, "Work is the greatest evil of the drinking class."

Humor aside, work in Shaw's day for most people involved back-breaking labor or mind-numbing factory work, sunrise to sunset, 6 days a week. In this chapter, we shall see that most of today's workers, living in a more affluent, technologically advanced society, are less likely to abide being cogs—even well-paid cogs—in the industrial machine.

We first examine motives for working. Then we follow the stages of vocational development and see how knowledge of our coping styles can enhance career decision making. We see how industrial/organizational psychologists have contributed to our knowledge of factors that enhance job satisfaction. Then we look at women on the job. We see that women are populating the professions and to some degree closing the earnings gap with men.

SEEKING SELF-FULFILLMENT IN THE WORKPLACE

In this section we explore motives for working and values concerning the workplace, and we see that some time-honored motives and values may be headed toward obsolescence.

Extrinsic Versus Intrinsic Motives for Working

One of the major reasons for working, if not *the* major reason, is economic. Work provides us with the means to pay our bills. The paycheck, fringe benefits, security in old age—all these are external or **extrinsic** motives for working. But work also satisfies many internal or **intrinsic** motives, including the opportunity to engage in stimulating and satisfying activities (Katzell & Thompson, 1990). Professional women, who must often balance the demands of jobs and families, are more likely to quit their jobs because of intrinsic factors such as boredom and lack of challenge than because of extrinsic factors such as flexible hours and the availability of on-site day care (Deutsch, 1990). Moreover, many million-dollar lottery winners who quit their jobs encounter feelings of aimlessness and dissatisfaction (Kaplan, 1978).

EXTRINSIC • External, coming from outside.
INTRINSIC • Internal, coming from within.

THE SOCIAL VALUE OF WORK. Work does more than merely provide an income. For example the workplace also extends our social contacts. It introduces us to friends, lovers, challenging adversaries. At work, we may meet others who share our interests. We may form social networks that in our highly mobile society sometimes substitute for family.

Other intrinsic reasons for working include the work ethic, self-identity, self-fulfillment, self-worth, the social values of work, and social roles:

1. *The work ethic.*

   In works of labor, or of skill,
   I would be busy too;
   For Satan finds some mischief still
   For idle hands to do.

   ISAAC WATTS

   The work ethic holds that we are morally obligated to engage in productive labor, to avoid idleness. Adherents to the work ethic view life without work as unethical, even for the wealthy.

2. *Self-identity.* Occupational identity becomes intertwined with self-identity. We are likely to think, "I *am* a nurse" or "I *am* a lawyer" rather than "I work as a nurse" or "I work as an attorney." We may think of ourselves as *having careers* or occupations, not as simply *holding jobs.*
3. *Self-fulfillment.* We often express our personal needs, interests, and values through our work. We may choose a profession that allows us to express these interests. The self-fulfilling values of the work of the astronaut, scientist, and athlete may seem obvious. But factory workers, plumbers, police officers, and firefighters can also find self-enrichment as well as cash rewards for their work.
4. *Self-worth.* Recognition and respect for a job well done contribute to self-esteem. For some, self-worth may ride on accumulating money. For a writer, self-worth may hinge on acceptance of a poem or article by a magazine. When we fail at work, our self-esteem plummets as sharply as the bank account.
5. *Social values of work.* The workplace extends our social contacts. It introduces us to friends, lovers, challenging adversaries. At work, we may meet others who share our interests. We may form social networks that in our highly mobile society sometimes substitute for family.

Truth or Fiction Revisited

It is true that many million-dollar lottery winners feel aimless and dissatisfied if they quit their jobs after striking it rich. We work not only for extrinsic rewards such as the paycheck and financial security, but also for intrinsic rewards, such as the opportunity to engage in challenging activities and broaden social contacts.

6. *Social roles.* Work roles help define our functions in the community. Communities have their public identities: druggist, shoemaker, teacher, doctor.

VOCATIONAL DEVELOPMENT

If one advances confidently in the direction of his dreams, and endeavors to live the life which he has imagined, he will meet with a success unexpected in common hours.

HENRY DAVID THOREAU, *WALDEN*

"Any child can grow up to be president." "My child—the doctor." "You can do anything, if you set your mind to it." America—land of opportunity. America—land of decision anxiety.

In societies with caste systems, such as old England or India, children grew up to do what their parents did. They assumed that they would follow in their parents' footsteps. The caste system saved people the need to decide what they would "do" with themselves. Unfortunately, it also squandered special talents and made a mockery of personal freedom.

What we "do" is most important. "*What* do you do?" is a more important question at social gatherings than "*How* do you do?" It is usually the first question raised in small talk. Occupational prestige is central to social standing.

There is a bewildering array of career possibilities. *The Dictionary of Occupational Titles*, published by the U.S. Department of Labor, lists more than 20,000 occupations. Most of us do not select careers by leafing through the dictionary, of course. Most of us make our choices from a relatively narrow group of occupations, based on our experiences and our personalities. Some of us postpone career decisions so that when we have graduated from college we are no closer to settling on a career than when we began college. Many of us "fall into" careers not because of particular skills and interests, but because of what is available at the time, family pressures, or the lure of high income or a certain lifestyle. Sometimes we take the first job that comes along after graduation. Sometimes we are lucky and things work out. Sometimes we are not lucky and we hop from job to job. And it may be that the fifth job suits us better than the first.

We need not rely on luck to find a career. There are a number of stages in vocational development to be aware of. There are ways of finding out what occupations are likely to fit us.

Stages of Vocational Development

A number of theories of vocational development have been presented. We will orient our discussion around the classic stage theory of Donald Super, but we will expand it to include contemporary realities.

1. *Fantasy.* The first stage involves the child's unrealistic conception of self-potential and of the world of work. This stage of fantasy dominates from early childhood until about age 11. Young children focus on glamour professions, such as acting, medicine, sports, and law enforcement. They show little regard for practical considerations, such as the fit between these occupations and their abilities, or the likelihood of "getting anywhere" in them. For example, the first author's daughter Allyn, at age 6, was thoroughly committed to becoming a rock star. Her sister Jordan, 4 at the time, intended with equal intensity to become a ballerina. But they also

intended to become teachers, authors, psychologists, art historians (like their mother), and physicians.

2. *Tentative choice.* During the second stage, children narrow their choices and begin to show some realistic self-assessment and knowledge of occupations. From about 11 through high school, children base their tentative choices on their interests, abilities, and limitations, as well as glamour. At the age of 16 Allyn no longer expects to be a rock star; now she plans to trip the life fantastic in musical theater.
3. *Realistic choice.* The following stage is characterized by realistic choice. Beyond age 17 or so, choices become narrowed and more realistic. Students weigh job requirements, rewards, even the futures of occupations. They appraise themselves more accurately. Ideally, they try to mesh their interests, abilities, and values with a job. They may also direct their educations toward supplying the knowledge and skills that they will need to enter the occupation. Keep in mind, however, that many of us never make realistic choices and thus "fall into" occupations.
4. *Maintenance.* Maintenance involves settling into the vocational role, which often happens in the second half of the thirties. Although the individual may change positions within a company or within a career (such as "publishing" or "education"), there is often a sense of development and forward movement. But people can also get trapped in dead-end jobs during this stage. Their employers may come to view them as cogs in the wheel and attend to them only when and if something goes wrong.
5. *Career change.* Here is where we diverge from standard views. Because of corporate downsizing and mergers, today's workers no longer feel the loyalty to their employers that they once did. Thus they are more likely to job hop when the opportunity arises. People are also living longer, healthier lives in rapidly changing times. They are staying in school longer and returning to school later for education, training, and retraining. Fewer are putting in their time till the age of 65 in the hope of retiring. Rather they are seeking fulfillment in the workplace and remain ambitious well into their middle years, and often in late adulthood (Levinson, 1996; Sheehy, 1995). Today it is the norm, rather than the exception, for people to switch careers more than once. Message to readers: Keep your eyes open and maintain a sense of flexibility. The opportunities you find in your thirties, forties, fifties, and even sixties and beyond may be things that are literally undreamed of today. If you are restless, it may be a sign of psychological health rather than instability. Take the time to explore your feelings and options. Have the courage to try new things.
6. *Retirement.* The fifth stage in Super's scheme is the retirement stage, during which the individual severs bonds with the workplace.

No, we have haven't already retired you. In the chapter's "Adjustment and Modern Life" feature, we offer advice on finding a career that fits. Now we talk about *getting* you a job.

Writing a Résumé

When you apply for a job, you usually send a résumé with a cover letter. A résumé is intended to convince a hiring manager that you are well qualified for the position and that interviewing you will be a worthwhile investment. But until you are called in for an interview, your résumé *is* you. So give it the same attention you would give your grooming.

In a moment, we get into the mechanics of the résumé. First, it helps to know who will be looking at it and deciding whether to toss it into the "circular file"—that is, the wastepaper basket. Résumés are usually first screened by a secretary or administrative assistant. That person may chuck it if it's sloppy, illegible, incomplete, or incompatible with the job requirements. Then it is usually seen by an employment or personnel manager. This individual may screen it out if it is incompatible with job requirements or does not show the required specifications. Employment managers also discard résumés that show inadequate experience or education, incompatible salary requirements, and lack of U.S. citizenship or permanent resident status. They also eliminate résumés that are too long. A résumé is a *summary* of your qualifications. It's not a diary or a book. Keep your résumé to one page unless it is truly impossible to do so.

The hiring officer—this may be the person who would be supervising you in the job—may screen out your résumé if it shows that you lack the right qualifications. You may also be eliminated if you're *over*qualified. Why? If you're too highly skilled or too well educated for the job, you probably won't be happy in it. If you're not happy, you won't give it your best. You may even quit early.

In sum, be neat. Show that you are right for the job. Don't use the same résumé for all positions. Instead, keep a general résumé on file. Then fine-tune it for the specific position.

And be honest. Use the job description to decide which of your qualifications to highlight—not as a basis for lying. If you lie about your qualifications, two bad things can happen. First, you can be eliminated if your dishonesty is found out from references or through the interview. Second, you may get the job! If you're not qualified, you'll probably be miserable in it.

PARTS OF THE RÉSUMÉ Résumés consist of the following:

1. A heading
2. A statement of your job objective
3. A summary of your educational background
4. A summary of your work experience
5. Personal information
6. A list of references

The Heading The heading contains your name, address, and telephone number. If you are living at home, the heading should be as follows:

LARRY J. SIEGEL
12 Hazleton Road
Newton Centre, Massachusetts 02159
Telephone: (617) 735-2495

If you are living at school, you might want to provide both a temporary and a permanent address:

AZALEA HAINES

Temporary Address:	*Permanent Address (after 5/26/99):*
Brubacher Hall, Room 135	156 Franklin Avenue
1435 Washington Avenue	Cedarhurst, New York 11735
Albany, New York 12115	*Telephone:* (516) 429-1945
Telephone: (518) 573-1295	

The Job Objective Tailor the job objective to the opening. Don't be too general or too blatantly specific. Is the advertised job for a computer sales trainee in Phoenix, Arizona? A job objective of "Marketing or sales" might be too general. It might suggest that you do not know what you're after. A job objective of "Computer sales trainee in the southwestern United States" is too obvious and just plain silly. Also avoid saying things that will screen you out, like "Sales trainee with rapid advancement opportunities to management." You're being considered for the sales trainee position, not president of the company!

A reasonable objective would be "Sales, computer equipment," or "Sales of technical merchandise."

Educational Background For each school attended, include the following:

1. The degree awarded (or expected)
2. Name of school (and address, if school is not well known)
3. Year graduated (or expected to graduate)
4. Major field or specialties
5. Grade point average (when 3.0 or better)
6. Honors and awards
7. Professional certificates (e.g., teaching, interior design)
8. Extracurricular activities

List schools attended in reverse chronological order. That is, put the most recent school first. For example:

Education	BA:	Arizona State University, Tempe, 1998
	Major:	Psychology
	GPA:	3.8/4.0
	Honors:	Magna Cum Laude
	Activities:	President, Psychology Club, 1997–1998
	AA:	Mesa Community College, Phoenix, 1996
	Major:	Psychology
	Diploma:	Scottsdale High School, Scottsdale, Arizona, 1994

In the preceding example, the solid GPA, the honors earned at Arizona State, and the presidency of the psychology club are all listed. The less impressive performances in high school and at Mesa are not detailed. List the most important extracurricular activities. Be sure to indicate when and where you played a leadership role. Most students approaching graduation do not have extensive work experience. Having been editor of the yearbook, president of a club, or captain of a team is thus a notable achievement.

Work Experience Don't list childhood jobs of baby-sitting and lawn mowing, unless you organized and ran baby-sitting or lawn mowing businesses in your hometown. Pay particular attention to the jobs that are related to the position you are seeking. If you can show that you have been pursuing the same field for a number of years, you will look more organized and motivated. These are desirable job qualities. Of particular importance are internships and full-time positions. Also of interest are responsible summer and part-time positions. Don't pad your résumé with irrelevant, unimportant positions. Remember that you're applying for a job as a fresh graduate. You need not look like a mature professional on the move from one executive position to another.

For each position, include the following:

1. Title of position
2. Dates of employment
3. Whether job was full- or part-time; number of hours per week
4. Name of employer

5. Division of employer or location of employment
6. Brief statement of job responsibilities, using action verbs (see sample below)
7. Brief statement of chief achievements

Don't list the names of your supervisors, unless you are willing to have all of them called by your prospective employer. List positions in reverse chronological order—most recent position first. Consider this example:

Work Experience:	February 1997–May 1998 San Diego State University *Assistant to the Director, University Art Gallery*
	Responsibilities: Catalogued art works in permanent collection; arranged shipping of works for exhibitions; assisted in the hanging of exhibitions; arranged printing of exhibition catalogues and mailers
	Major Achievements: Curated Christo exhibition; co-authored exhibition catalogue *Conceptual Art*
	June 1987–September 1996 (And so forth.)

Personal Information This is a section in which you may indicate your age, marital status, number of children, citizenship, health, and so on. You may want to omit this section. There are pitfalls. Some employers hold the prejudice that women with children are only interested in a second income and would be absent whenever a minor crisis or an illness hit the household. Other employers are prejudiced against married women when a job calls for travel. Discrimination based on gender is illegal, of course. Nevertheless, a hiring manager can screen you out without an explanation. Also, lack of U.S. citizenship or of permanent resident status can knock you out of contention.

When you are graduating from college, employers expect you to be youthful. Why tell them that you went back to school once your kids entered their teens and that you're 40 years old? We know you're great, but prospective employers may be prejudiced against people starting their professional lives at later ages. If that's you, consider omitting your high school education (why give away the graduation date?). Or you may omit your years of preprofessional work—unless, of course, you had notable achievements.

They'll see that you're older than 21 in the job interview. But then you will overwhelm the interviewer with your mature judgment, strong motivation, and clear sense of direction. First, you've got to get to the interview.

References References would be placed last on the résumé. It's probably best not to use them unless they are specifically requested. The prospective employer may check them out before inviting you to an interview. The slightest bit of negative information may knock you out of contention. It's better to say "References will be furnished upon request" in your cover letter.

THE COVER LETTER The cover letter accompanies your résumé. It contains the following information:

1. Explanation of the purpose of the letter
2. Explanation of how you learned about the opening
3. Comparison of your qualifications and the job requirements
4. Statements of desired salary and geographic limitations (optional)

TABLE 17.1 A COVER LETTER TO ACCOMPANY A RÉSUMÉ

SECTION OF LETTER	*REMARKS*
I enclose my résumé in application for the position of computer sales trainee, as described in the job notice sent to my college's placement office.	1. Refers to enclosed résumé (okay) 2. States writer is applying for position (okay) 3. Says how writer learned of position (okay)
My education and work experience appear to fit well indeed with your job requirements. My major field is business, with a specialty in marketing. I have four courses in computer science. I hold a part-time position in the college computer center, where I advise students how to use our mainframe and microcomputers. Moreover, I have held part-time and summer sales positions, as outlined in the résumé.	Good! The writer shows extensive experience (for a fresh college graduate) both in sales and in computers.
Salary is relatively unimportant to me. However, my wife is employed in town here, so I would not be able to relocate.	Mistakes! Visualize someone tossing your application into the circular file (wastepaper basket). Salary is always important—to the employer if not to you. Say nothing about salary unless a statement of "salary requirements" is specifically required in the job listing. Also, don't go into marital status and possible relocation problems. You can deal with them after you get to the interview. Here you've knocked yourself out of contention by admitting that family commitments may prevent you from doing your job.
I look forward to the prospect of an interview. I can get off from work or miss a class or two if I have to.	Yes, no. Yes to desiring an interview; ditch the preoccupation with the mechanics of breaking free for the interview (nobody cares about stuff like this except you).
References will be furnished upon request.	Fine—keep it short. Don't include references unless you are asked for them.
Thanks for your consideration.	Spell out "Thank you"; otherwise, fine.

5. Request for an interview or other response to the letter
6. Statement that references will be sent upon request
7. Thanks for the prospective employer's consideration

Consider the cover letter and remarks shown in Table 17.1.

Congratulations! Your résumé and cover letter were very good. In fact, you've been invited to an interview. Now what?

How to Make a Positive Impression at a Job Interview

A job interview is both a social occasion and a test. First impressions and neatness count, so dress well and look your best. Everything else being equal, people who look their best usually get the job (Mack & Rainey, 1990). You're probably best advised not to wear perfume or cologne. Baron (1983) found that women interviewers rate applicants who wear perfume or cologne more positively, but that male interviewers rate fragrant applicants—male and female alike—more negatively. Male interviewers may be more rigid than females and think that serious things do not come in fragrant packages.

Truth or Fiction Revisited

It is not true that women who wear perfume to interviews are more likely to get the job. The statement is too broad to be true, because it only applies when their interviewers are women. Male interviewers are more likely to frown on female applicants who wear perfume—and also on male applicants who wear cologne.

WHAT DO *You* SAY NOW?

HOW TO WOW THE JOB INTERVIEWER

Okay. Your résumé and cover letter have gotten your foot in the door. This exercise will help you prepare for that all-important job interview. In this exercise, we ask a question and then provide room for an answer. Next we offer our thoughts on the subject and try to alert you as to what your interviewer is looking for. We don't always supply a specific answer. The specific words will have to be consistent with the nature of your field, the organization to which you have applied, your geographical setting, and so on.

All right, the person ahead of you leaves and it's your turn for an interview. Here are the questions. What do you say now?

1. *How are you today?*

Our recommendation: Don't get cute or fancy. Say something like, "Fine, thank you. How're you?"

2. *How did you learn about the opening?*

Don't say, "I indicated that in my application." Yes, you probably did specify this on your application or in the cover letter for your résumé, but your interviewer may not be familiar with the letter or may want to follow a standard procedure. So answer concisely.

3. *What do you know about our organization?*

Your interviewer wants to learn whether you know something about his or her organization or applied everywhere with equal disinterest. Do your homework and show that you know quite a bit. Suggest how the organization is an ideal setting for you to reach your vocational goals.

4. *What are you looking for in this job?*

WHAT DO YOU SAY NOW?
What do you say in a job interview? Your interviewer wants to hear that you have concrete goals, are a motivated worker, and are knowledgeable about the organization. You should also prepare some solid questions of your own.

This is another opportunity to show that you have concrete goals. That's what interviewers are looking for. Mention things like the opportunity to work with noted professionals in your field, the organizational personality (organizations, like people, have personalities), the organization's leadership in its field, and so on. *Don't* say "It's close to home." You can say that you know that salaries are good, but also refer to opportunities for personal growth and self-fulfillment.

5. *What do you plan to be doing 10 years from now?*

Your interviewer wants to hear that you have a clear cognitive map of the corporate ladder, and that your career goals are consistent with company needs. Preplan a coherent answer, but also show flexibility—perhaps that you're interested in exploring a couple of branches of the career ladder. You want your interviewer to think that you're not rigid and that you recognize that the organization will affect your concept of your future.

6. *Are you willing to relocate after a year or two if we need you in another office/plant?*

Your interviewer wants to hear that you are willing—that your ties to the company would be more important than your geographical ties. *Don't* say that your fiancé or spouse is flexible. It implies that he or she really is not, and you just don't want to get into this.

7. *What are your salary needs?*

Entry-level salaries are often fixed, especially in large organizations. But if you are asked this question, don't fall into the trap of thinking you're more likely to get the job if you ask for less. Mention a reasonably high—not absurdly high—figure. You can mention the figure with an explanation that reemphasizes your experience and training. Good things don't come cheap, and organizations know this. And why should they think more of you than you think of yourself?

Truth or Fiction Revisited

It is not true that it is a good idea to ask for the lowest salary you can get by on at a job interview. Quote a relatively high but reasonable figure. Show that your work is valuable.

8. *What is the first thing you would do if you were to take the job?*

Your interviewer probably wants to know (1) if you're an active, take-charge type of person and (2) whether you do have an understanding of what is required. *Don't* say you'd be shocked or surprised. Say something like, "I'd get to know my supervisors and co-workers to learn the details of the organization's goals and expectations for the position." Or it might be appropriate to talk about organizing your workspace, or evaluating and ordering equipment, depending on the nature of the occupation.

9. *Do you realize that this is a very difficult (or time-consuming) job?*

It is or it isn't, but the interviewer doesn't want to hear that you think the job's a snap. The interviewer wants to hear that you will dedicate yourself to your work and that you have boundless energy. One legitimate response is to ask your interviewer to amplify a bit on the remark so that you can fine-tune your eventual answer.

10. *What do you see as your weaknesses?*

Trap time! *Don't* make a joke and say that you can't get along with anyone or know nothing about the job! Your interviewer is giving you a chance to show that you are arrogant by denying weaknesses or to drop some kind of bombshell—that is, admit to a self-disqualifying problem. Don't do either. Turn the question into an opportunity for emphasizing strengths. Say something like, "I think my weakness is that I have not already done this job (or worked for your organization), and so we cannot predict with certainty what will happen. But I'm a fast learner and pretty flexible, so I'm confident that I'll do a good job."

11. *Do you have any questions?*

Have some! Intelligent questions are signs that you are interested and can handle the job. Prepare a few good questions before the interview. In the unlikely event that the interviewer manages to cover them all during his or her presentation, you can say something like, "I was going to ask such and such, but then you said that such and such. Could you amplify on that a bit?"

12. Finally, what do you say when the interview is over?

Say something like, "Thank you for the interview. I look forward to hearing from you." ■

Maintain direct eye contact with your interviewer, but look alert, cooperative, and friendly—don't stare. (A hard stare is perceived as an aversive challenge.)

One good way to prepare for an academic test is to try to anticipate your instructor's questions. Anticipating reporters' questions helps prepare the president for press conferences. Similarly, anticipating the interviewer's questions will help prepare you for the interview. Once you have written down a list of likely questions, rehearse answers to them. Practice them aloud. You can recruit a friend to role-play the interviewer.

A good student doesn't have to say something in every class. Similarly, a good job candidate doesn't have to do most of the talking at an interview. Be patient: Allow the interviewer to tell you about the job and the organization without feeling that you must jump in. Look interested. Nod now and then. Don't champ at the bit.

We consider the kinds of questions you will be asked in the "What Do You Say Now?" feature on the preceeding pages. Some of the interviewer's questions will be specific to your field, and we cannot help you anticipate those. But those that are likely to be found in any interview are found in the feature.

Developmental Tasks in Taking a Job

You've got it! The job you've been dreaming about! Your academic work has paid off, and you did brilliantly at the interview. Good salary, solid opportunities for advancement, and the promise of self-development in a field that you enjoy—all of these are yours. From here on in, it's smooth sailing, right? Not necessarily.

If the job you have landed fits your education, experience, and coping styles, the chances are that you will do well indeed. But we undertake a number of developmental tasks when we take a new job:

1. *Making the transition from school to the workplace.* You have already mastered the school world, and change can be threatening as well as exciting. You are also going from the top of the school world (graduation) to a relatively low position in the organizational hierarchy. Moreover, you are moving from a system in which there is measurable progress, including courses completed each term and movement up the educational ladder each year. In a job one can go for years without a promotion.
2. *Learning how to carry out the job tasks.* Job tasks include executing occupational skills and also meshing your own attitudes and values with those of the organization. Learning the organization's explicit (written) and implicit (unwritten) rules is a job in itself.
3. *Accepting responsibility for your job tasks and functions.*
4. *Accepting your subordinate status within the organization or profession.* Perhaps you were extremely popular on campus. Perhaps you were leader of an athletic team. Perhaps you were an honors student. Despite all these accomplishments and your sterling qualities, you are a newcomer on the job. Act accordingly. (You needn't grovel, of course, but accept the facts that you are new and sort of wet behind the ears.)
5. *Learning how to get along with your co-workers and supervisor.* Sure, you have some social skills. But you are in a new setting with new people. They have new expectations with you. Expect a few bumps in the social road.

6. *Showing that you can maintain the job, make improvements, and show progress.* Yes, this is not fourth grade and you are not likely to be graded on your potential. You will have to show that you are worth what you are being paid.
7. *Finding a sponsor or mentor to "show you the ropes."*
8. *Defining the boundaries between the job and other areas of life.* Where do work and concerns about work end? Where do your personal interests and social relationships begin? Try not to bring home your troubles on the job. (And try not to bring your troubles at home into your job.)
9. *Evaluating your occupational choice in the light of supervisor appraisal and measurable outcomes of your work.* Is the job really for you? If you have given it a solid amount of time and evaluated it carefully, and it does not seem to fit you, investigate why and consider a change.
10. *Learning to cope with daily hassles on the job, frustrations, and successes and failure.* Jobs have their stresses, and some stress management may be in order. Check out the suggestions in this chapter and in Chapter 11.

■ ADJUSTMENT IN THE WORKPLACE

Work provides a major opportunity for personal growth and may also demand major adjustments. In this section we have a look at factors that contribute to satisfaction on the job.

Satisfaction on the Job

It is one thing to land a job. It is another to be satisfied with it. A recent Gallup poll (1991) found that most workers are not completely satisfied with most aspects of their jobs (Figure 17.1).

Talk is rife about dissatisfaction on the assembly line. Some refer to feelings of alienation and dissatisfaction among factory workers as "blue-collar blues." Some factory workers find their work boring or dehumanizing. They complain that supervisors treat them with disrespect and fail to use them as resources for learning how to improve working conditions and productivity.

As pointed out in *Theory Z* (Ouchi, 1981), Japanese managers frequently involve workers with their companies by requesting and acting on their opinions. Managers also eat in the same cafeterias as line workers. Everyone feels "in it together." In the United States, there is usually an adversary relationship between labor and management. Each side feels the other is "out for all they can get" and willing to exploit the opposition in any way they can. Japanese workers are also often given lifetime jobs—a "gift" that can create great loyalty to the company, but one that frequently prevents upward mobility.

How to Enhance Job Satisfaction *and Productivity:* Improving the Quality of Work Life Is Also Good Business

For some of us, the responsibility for our job satisfaction is in our own hands. Many professionals open their own practices and charge competitive fees for their services. We can form partnerships and corporations or open shops or industrial plants. Our lots, in essence, are what we make of them.

WHAT FACTORS CONTRIBUTE TO SATISFACTION IN THE WORKPLACE?
Job satisfaction depends on intrinsic factors as well as the paycheck. Workers tend to be more satisfied when their jobs fit their personalities, they receive adequate training and instruction, they are evaluated fairly, and stress is kept under control.

FIGURE 17.1
SATISFACTION OF U.S. WORKERS WITH VARIOUS ASPECTS OF THEIR JOBS.
According to a Gallup poll, the majority of U.S. workers are not completely satisfied with the important aspects of their jobs

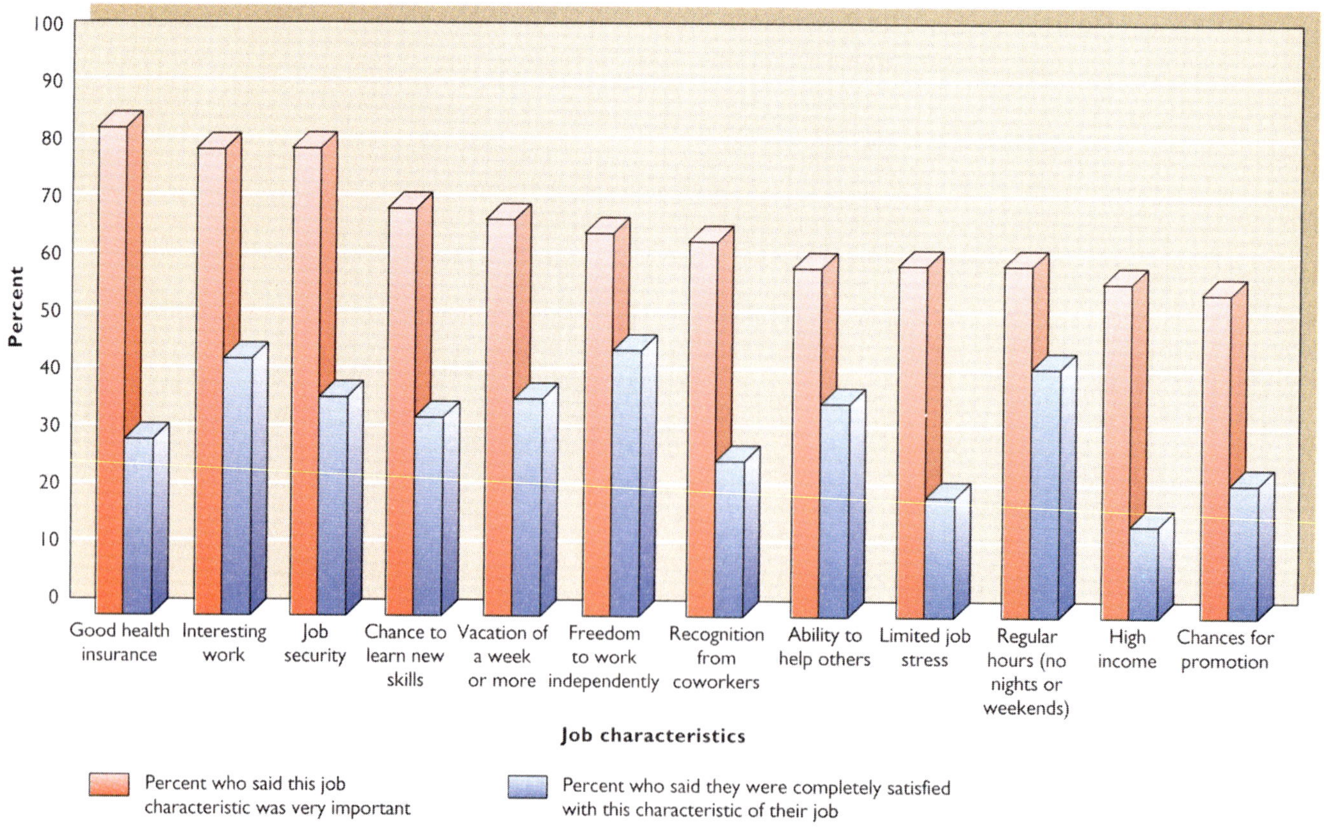

ADJUSTMENT in the NEW MILLENNIUM

Careers—What's Hot, What's Not

What career are you planning for? Will you be writing software for video games and super-efficient voice-recognition technology? Will you be teaching youngsters in primary schools? Will you be hashing out the . . . hash in a restaurant? Will you start up your own business? Will you be *Dr.* ______ (fill in your name)? What career dreams do you entertain?

According to the U.S. Department of Labor's Bureau of Labor Statistics, some 15 million new jobs will be created in the United States by the year 2005. You may choose to take one of them. Where will the jobs be in the new millennium?

Services, Services, Services The government expects that service-producing industries will account for most of the new jobs. More than a million jobs will be lost among machine operators, fabricators, laborers, crafts people, and repair people. Advances in technology, including new generations of robots, will continue to replace people on the assembly line. Jobs in agriculture, forestry, fishing, and related occupations are also expected to decline. Job openings in these fields will stem from replacement needs. There was a song that went, "How're you going to keep them down on the farm after they've seen Paris?" (pronounced "PAR-EE"). Perhaps the song today should go, "How're you going to keep them down on the farm after they've seen MTV?" But the matter is two-sided. If people are less desirous of farm jobs, technology has steadily decreased the number of human hands that are required to do the job.

Within the burgeoning area of services, the lion's share of the new opportunities will be found in health, education, and business ("America's job growth," 1998). Why health? Well, the population is aging, and older people require more health care. But many of these jobs will not require college graduates. To contain costs, hospitals are discharging patients sooner, which will increase the need for personal and home care aides, and home health aides. But there will also be an increase in the use of innovative medical technology for diagnosis and treatment, and these jobs will require technical training at the very least. Nurses will also be in strong demand. Why education? Because there will be many young children, and because older people are retooling. Why business? The business of the United States, as they say, is business, and within business we find the fabulous high-tech sector.

High-Tech Rules There will be very rapid growth in jobs for computer specialists—especially software writers and systems analysts (Harmon, 1998). The country is relying more heavily on computer software than ever before, and the demand for people who can develop and use software has vastly outstripped the supply. The shortage is expected to worsen because a *million* new programming jobs are expected to open up within the next decade. In fact, the industry estimates that 200,000 to 400,000 jobs requiring computer software skills are going begging *right now.* Systems analysts figure out how to piece it all together—that is, how to make computer hardware and software work for *your* business or organization. If you're going to need them, perhaps you want to join them.

Good News There is especially good news for today's college students. Openings in occupations that require a bachelor's degree or more will grow at almost twice the rate projected for jobs that require less education and training. Moreover, these jobs will pay much better than average wages.

Want more specifics? Visit your college or university's placement office. (Tell them who sent you.) ■

For others, such as factory workers, the responsibility for the quality of their work life often appears to be in the hands of supervisors and managers. In a sense, this is illusionary; except in situations of extreme deprivation, workers usually choose to work in a certain plant in a certain location. When there is

(text continues on p. 559)

SELF-ASSESSMENT

HOW DO YOU FEEL ABOUT YOUR WORK? THE JOB SATISFACTION INDEX

How satisfied are you with your work? Part-time students may be holding full-time jobs, and full-time students may be holding part-time jobs. In any event, you can assume that the rest of us—both men and the great majority of women—will be holding jobs at some time in the future. The Job Satisfaction Index provides a number of questions that concern your job-related attitudes, feelings, and behavior patterns. ■

Directions: Consider your present job as you read each item, and decide which choice describes you best. For each item, mark your answer in the spaces provided on page 558. Then turn to the scoring key in the Appendix.

1. Do you watch the clock when you are working?
   a. Constantly
   b. At slack times
   c. Never
2. When Monday morning comes, do you
   a. Feel ready to go back to work?
   b. Think longingly of being able to lie in the hospital with a broken leg?
   c. Feel reluctant to start with, but fit into the work routine quite happily after an hour or so?
3. How do you feel at the end of a working day?
   a. Dead tired and fit for nothing
   b. Glad that you can start living
   c. Sometimes tired, but usually pretty satisfied
4. Do you worry about your work?
   a. Occasionally
   b. Never
   c. Often
5. Would you say that your job
   a. Underuses your ability?
   b. Overstrains your abilities?
   c. Makes you do things you never thought you could do before?
6. Which statement is true for you?
   a. I am rarely bored with my work.
   b. I am usually interested in my work, but there are patches of boredom.
   c. I am bored most of the time I am working.
7. How much of your work time is spent making personal telephone calls or with other matters not connected with the job?
   a. Very little
   b. Some, especially at crisis times in my personal life
   c. Quite a lot
8. Do you daydream about having a different job?
   a. Very little
   b. Not a different job, but a better position in the same kind of job
   c. Yes
9. Would you say that you feel
   a. Pretty capable most of the time?
   b. Sometimes capable?
   c. Panicky and incapable most of the time?
10. Do you find that
    a. You like and respect your colleagues?
    b. You dislike your colleagues?
    c. You are indifferent to your colleagues?

11. Which statement is most true for you?
   a. I do not want to learn more about my work.
   b. I quite enjoyed learning my work when I first started.
   c. I like to go on learning as much as possible about my work.
12. Mark the qualities you think are your best points:

____ a. Sympathy	____ f. Physical stamina
____ b. Clear-thinking	____ g. Inventiveness
____ c. Calmness	____ h. Expertise
____ d. Good memory	____ i. Charm
____ e. Concentration	____ j. Humor

13. Now mark the qualities that are demanded by your job:

____ a. Sympathy	____ f. Physical stamina
____ b. Clear-thinking	____ g. Inventiveness
____ c. Calmness	____ h. Expertise
____ d. Good memory	____ i. Charm
____ e. Concentration	____ j. Humor

14. Which statement do you most agree with?
   a. A job is only a way to make enough money to keep yourself alive.
   b. A job is mainly a way of making money, but should be satisfying if possible.
   c. A job is a whole way of life.
15. Do you work overtime?
   a. Only when it is paid
   b. Never
   c. Often, even without pay
16. Have you been absent from work (other than for normal vacations or illness) in the last year?
   a. Not at all
   b. For a few days only
   c. Often, even without pay
17. Would you rate yourself as
   a. Very ambitious?
   b. Unambitious?
   c. Mildly ambitious?
18. Do you think that your colleagues
   a. Like you, enjoy your company, and get on well with you in general?
   b. Dislike you?
   c. Do not dislike you, but are not particularly friendly?
19. Do you talk about work
   a. Only with your colleagues?
   b. With friends and family?
   c. Not if you can avoid it?
20. Do you suffer from minor unexplained illnesses and vague pains?
   a. Seldom
   b. Not too often
   c. Frequently
21. How did you choose your present job?
   a. Your parents or teachers decided for you.
   b. It was all you could find.
   c. It seemed the right thing for you.
22. In a conflict between job and home, such as an illness of a member of the family, which would win?
   a. The family every time
   b. The job every time
   c. The family in a real emergency, but otherwise probably the job
23. Would you be happy to do the same job if it paid one-third less?
   a. Yes
   b. You would like to, but could not afford to.
   c. No

(continued)

(continued)

24. If you were made redundant (unnecessary), which of these would you miss most?
    a. The money
    b. The work itself
    c. The company of your colleagues
25. Would you take a day off to have fun?
    a. Yes
    b. No
    c. Possibly, if there was nothing too urgent for you to do at work
26. Do you feel unappreciated at work?
    a. Occasionally
    b. Often
    c. Rarely
27. What do you most dislike about your job?
    a. That your time is not your own
    b. The boredom
    c. That you cannot always do things the way you want to
28. Do you keep your personal life separate from work? (Check with your partner on this one.)
    a. Pretty strictly
    b. Most of the time, but there is some overlap
    c. Not at all
29. Would you advise a child of yours to take up the same kind of work as you do?
    a. Yes, if he or she had the ability and temperament.
    b. No, you would warn him or her off.
    c. You would not press it, but you would not discourage him or her either.
30. If you won or suddenly inherited a large sum of money, would you
    a. Stop work for the rest of your life?
    b. Take up some kind of work that you have always wanted to do?
    c. Decide to continue, in some way, the same work you do now?

Answers

1.	a. ___	b. ___	c. ___	14.	a. ___	b. ___	c. ___
2.	a. ___	b. ___	c. ___	15.	a. ___	b. ___	c. ___
3.	a. ___	b. ___	c. ___	16.	a. ___	b. ___	c. ___
4.	a. ___	b. ___	c. ___	17.	a. ___	b. ___	c. ___
5.	a. ___	b. ___	c. ___	18.	a. ___	b. ___	c. ___
6.	a. ___	b. ___	c. ___	19.	a. ___	b. ___	c. ___
7.	a. ___	b. ___	c. ___	20.	a. ___	b. ___	c. ___
8.	a. ___	b. ___	c. ___	21.	a. ___	b. ___	c. ___
9.	a. ___	b. ___	c. ___	22.	a. ___	b. ___	c. ___
10.	a. ___	b. ___	c. ___	23.	a. ___	b. ___	c. ___
11.	a. ___	b. ___	c. ___	24.	a. ___	b. ___	c. ___
12.	a. ___	b. ___	c. ___	25.	a. ___	b. ___	c. ___
	d. ___	e. ___	f. ___	26.	a. ___	b. ___	c. ___
	g. ___	h. ___	i. ___	27.	a. ___	b. ___	c. ___
	j. ___			28.	a. ___	b. ___	c. ___
13.	a. ___	b. ___	c. ___	29.	a. ___	b. ___	c. ___
	d. ___	e. ___	f. ___	30.	a. ___	b. ___	c. ___
	g. ___	h. ___	i. ___				
	j. ___						

choice, plants that offer more in the way of extrinsic and intrinsic rewards will attract and keep better workers.

Increasing the quality of work life turns out to be good business for everyone. First, increased job satisfaction decreases employee turnover and absenteeism—two expensive measures of job dissatisfaction. Second, there is a link between enhanced productivity and the quality of work life. Many of the methods for increasing productivity also contribute to the satisfaction of the worker (Katzell & Thompson, 1990). We discuss many of these methods now.

Improved Recruitment and Placement Worker motivation is enhanced right at the beginning when the right person for the job is hired. When the company's needs mesh with the worker's, both profit. Unfortunately, people sometimes get hired for reasons that are irrelevant to their potential to perform well in the job. Sometimes people are hired because they are physically attractive (Mack & Rainey, 1990). On other occasions relatives or friends of friends are chosen. By and large, however, businesses seek employees who can do the job and are likely to be reasonably satisfied with it. Employees who are satisfied with their jobs are less likely to be absent or quit. Industrial/organizational psychologists facilitate recruitment procedures by analyzing jobs, specifying the skills and personal attributes that are needed, and constructing tests and interviews to determine whether candidates have those skills and attributes. These procedures can enhance job satisfaction and productivity.

Psychologists help improve methods of selecting, training, and evaluating managers for sensitive positions (Hogan and others, 1994). As we reach the new millennium, only 15 percent of new workers will be White males, as compared with more than 40 percent during the 1980s. As the workforce becomes more diverse—including more minority and female employees—we should be increasing the numbers of minority group members and women in management (Hogan and others, 1994). This can be accomplished with the assistance of psychologists who develop appropriate testing and selection procedures.

As we reach the year 2000 and many jobs grow more cognitively complex, research will be needed to help us refine our abilities to match abilities and job requirements (Goldstein & Gilliam, 1990).

Training and Instruction Training and instruction are the most commonly reported methods for enhancing productivity (Katzell & Thompson, 1990). Adequate training socializes workers to the corporate culture and provides them with appropriate skills. It also reduces the stresses on workers by equipping them to solve the problems they will face. Capacity to solve challenging problems enhances worker feelings of self-worth.

There are many dimensions according to which training can take place (Schein, 1990). For example, training can be carried out individually or in groups and formally or informally. The training process can aim to destroy individuality and replace it with a socialized "corporate" personality, or it can enhance individuality. If training procedures are incompatible with workers' personalities, they will be a major source of stress.

Use of Constructive Criticism Criticism is necessary if workers are to improve. However, at work as in personal life, it is important that criticisms be delivered constructively, not destructively (Weisinger, 1990). In Table 17.2 constructive criticisms ("the good") in appraisal of workers' performances are contrasted with destructive criticisms ("the bad"). Poor use of criticism is a great cause of conflict. It saps workers' motivation and self-efficacy expectancies. Proper criticism leads workers to feel that they are being helped to perform better (Baron, 1990).

TABLE 17.2 CRITICISM: THE GOOD, THE BAD, AND THE UGLY

CONSTRUCTIVE CRITICISM (GOOD)	*DESTRUCTIVE CRITICISM (BAD AND UGLY)*
Specific: The supervisor is specific about what the employee is doing wrong. For example, she or he says, "This is what you did that caused the problem, and this is why it caused the problem."	**Vague:** The supervisor makes a blanket condemnation, such as "That was an awful thing to do" or "That was a lousy job." No specifics are given.
Supportive: The supervisor gives the employee the feeling that the criticism is meant to help him or her perform better on the job.	**Condemnatory of the employee:** The supervisor attributes the problem to an unchangeable cause, such as the employee's personality.
Helpful in problem solving: The supervisor helps employees improve things or solve their problems on the job.	**Threatening:** The supervisor attacks the employee, as by saying, "If you do this again, you'll be docked" or "Next time, you're fired."
Timely: The supervisor offers the criticism as soon as possible after the problem occurs.	**Pessimistic:** The supervisor seems doubtful that the employee will be able to improve.

UNBIASED APPRAISAL OF WORKERS' PERFORMANCE Workers fare better and productivity is enhanced when they receive guidance and reinforcers that are based on accurate appraisal of their performance. In an ideal world, appraisal of workers' performances would be based solely on how well they do their jobs. Research shows that cognitive biases are at work, however.

First, supervisors tend to focus on the *worker* rather than the worker's performance. Raters form general impressions of liking or disliking workers. They may then evaluate them according to liking and not on task performance (Williams, 1986). The tendency to rate workers according to general impressions can be mitigated by instructing raters to focus on how well the worker carries out specific tasks.

Truth or Fiction Revisited

Sad to say, it is not true that evaluators tend to appraise worker performance objectively. How well they like the workers turns out to be an important factor as well. Rating workers on the basis of how well they are liked is a common bias in the appraisal process.

Learning theorists have suggested that the criteria for appraisal be totally objective—based on publicly observable behaviors and outlined to workers and supervisors prior to performance. Ideally, workers are rated according to whether or not they engage in targeted behavior patterns. Workers are not penalized for intangibles such as "poor attitude."

Truth or Fiction Revisited

It is not necessarily true that efficient, skillful employees are evaluated more highly than hard-working employees who must struggle to get the job done. The hard-working strugglers usually get rated more positively. Even on the job, in other words, individuals are often given an A for effort.

Another bias is the tendency to evaluate workers according to how much effort they put into their work (Dugan, 1989; Tsui & O'Reilly, 1989). Hard work is not necessarily good work. (Do you think that students who work harder than you should be given higher grades on tests, even when you get all the answers right and they make errors?) It is fairer to focus on how well workers perform targeted behaviors and to evaluate them on this basis.

GOAL SETTING Workers should know precisely what is wanted of them. Too often, goals are vague. Workers are told that they should "work hard" or "be serious" about their jobs, but hard work and seriousness are ill defined. Lack of knowledge creates anxiety and contributes to poor performance (Frayne & Latham, 1987). When workers know exactly what is wanted, they can better conform to these expectations. Setting concrete goals at high but attainable levels makes work challenging but keeps stress at acceptable levels.

FINANCIAL COMPENSATION When possible, performance should be linked to financial reward. It can be demoralizing when productive workers receive no more pay than nonproductive workers. If financial incentives for productivity are to be used, the assessment of productivity must be made fairly and objectively.

A number of psychologists suggest that supervisors handle problem performances in a manner consistent with principles of behavior modification. For example, punishment of unacceptable behavior does not in itself teach acceptable behavior. It can also create hostility. It is preferable, through careful assessment and training, to provide workers with the skills to perform adequately and then to reinforce the targeted behaviors.

WORK REDESIGN Psychologists understand the importance of creating settings in which workers can feel pride and accomplishment. An assembly-line worker may repeat one task hundreds of times a day and never see the finished product. To make factory work more meaningful, workers at one Volvo assembly plant in Sweden have been organized into small groups that elect leaders and distribute tasks among themselves. In another work-redesign program, workers move along the assembly line with "their" truck chassis, which gives them the satisfaction of seeing their product take shape. In an experiment at Motorola, one worker builds an entire pocket radio pager and signs the product when finished. The janitorial staff at a Texas Instruments work site meets in small groups to set goals and distribute cleaning tasks among themselves. Texas Instruments reports a cleaner plant, lowered costs, and decreased turnover.

The **quality circle**, practiced widely in Japan, has also been catching on in the United States. Ironically, this method, in which workers meet regularly to discuss problems and suggest solutions, was brought to Japan after World War II by H. Edwards Deming, an American. Quality circles give workers a greater sense of control over their jobs and increase their commitment to the company. Control and commitment also enhance psychological hardiness. Moreover, workers are in the best position to understand problems that prevent them from performing optimally.

WORK SCHEDULES When there is no company reason for maintaining a strict 9-to-5 schedule, workers frequently profit from **flextime**, or being able to modify their own schedules to meet their personal needs. In one approach to flextime, workers put in four 10-hour workdays, rather than five 8-hour days. One study found that flextime lowered absenteeism (Narayanan & Nath, 1982).

At Honeywell, a "mothers' shift" allows women to coordinate their work schedules with school hours. Mothers may also have college students fill in for them during their children's summer vacations. Are we ready for a "fathers' shift"?

Truth or Fiction Revisited

It is not true that allowing employees to piece together their own work schedules is demoralizing to workers and interferes with productivity. Flextime can help workers cope with parenthood, for example, and as a result boost their morale on the job.

INTEGRATION OF NEW WORKPLACE TECHNOLOGY As we head toward the year 2000, robots and other devices are replacing some workers and enabling others to enhance their productivity. The standard office workstation now includes a computer. Fax machines and computerized payments are replacing the mails. Innovations in workplace technology pose at least two challenges for psychologists: One is to ascertain that they do, in fact, make organizations more productive. The other is to determine whether or not they continue to "fit" workers rather than deprive them of job satisfaction (Turnage, 1990).

Work and Stress

Work for most of us involves more than 40 hours a week. When we figure in commuting, preparation, lunchtime, continuing education, and just thinking about the job, many of us put at least half our waking hours into our work.

QUALITY CIRCLE • A regularly scheduled meeting in which a group of workers discuss problems and suggest solutions in order to enhance the quality of products.

FLEXTIME • A modification of one's work schedule from the standard 9:00 A.M. to 5:00 P.M. to meet personal needs.

Stress at work also spills over into stress at home. Frustrations and resentments about the workplace can make us tired and short-tempered. They can contribute to family arguments. In a vicious cycle, family conflict may then compound problems at work.

CAUSES OF STRESS IN THE WORKPLACE The left-hand part of Figure 17.2 shows how various features of the workplace can contribute to stress. Among the aspects of the physical environment that can produce stress are poor lighting, air pollution (including cigarette or cigar smoke produced by co-workers and clients), crowding, noise, and extremes of temperature. Individual stressors include work overload, boredom, conflict about one's work (e.g., a lawyer's being asked by superiors to defend a person who seems guilty or politicians' having to seek the support of groups whose values are inconsistent with their own in order to get elected), excessive responsibility, and lack of forward movement. Group stressors include bothersome relationships with supervisors, subordinates, and peers.

Organizational stressors include lack of opportunity to participate in decision making, ambiguous or conflicting company policies, too much or too little organizational structure, low pay, racism, and sexism.

FIGURE 17.2
A MODEL FOR THE EFFECTS OF STRESS IN THE WORKPLACE
As shown in this model, various factors such as the physical environment and organizational stressors affect the worker. Workplace stressors can also interact with stresses from home and factors in the personality to produce a number of negative outcomes.

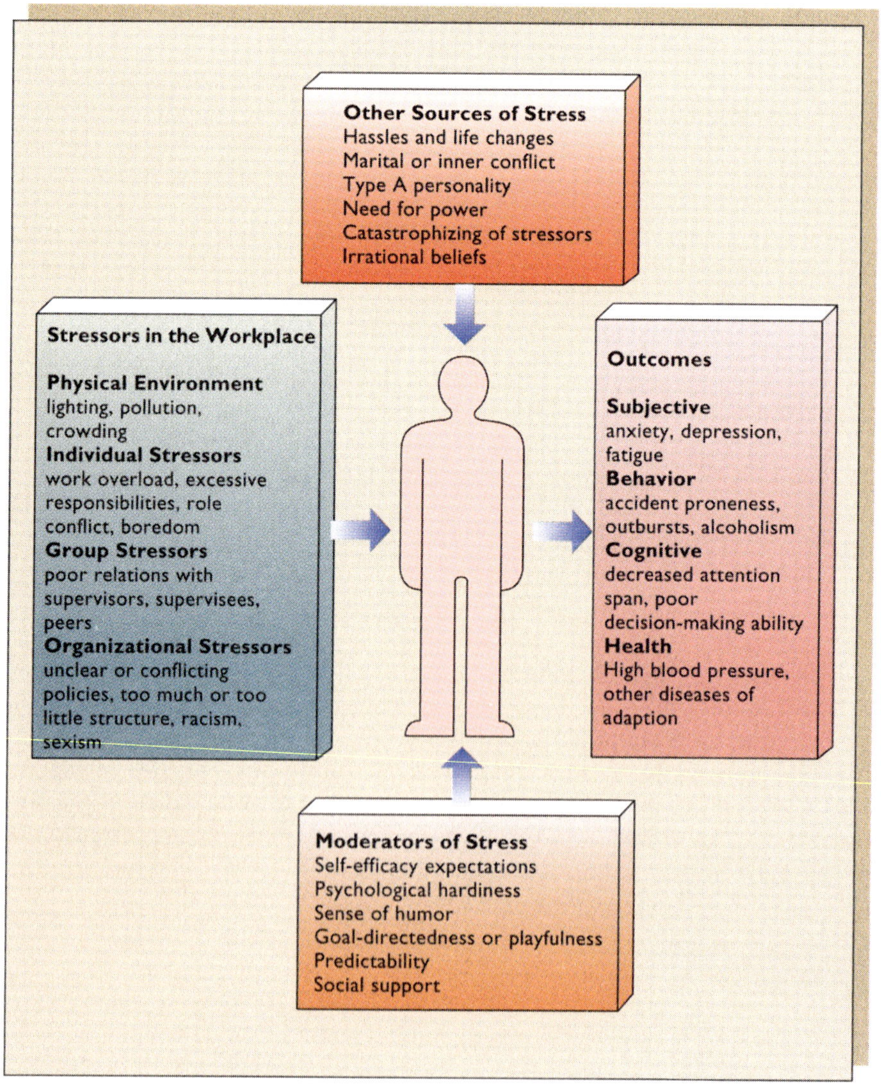

The Role of the Worker The central part of Figure 17.2 shows the worker and the sources of stress that may be acting on him or her. For example, marital or inner conflict may compound any conflicts encountered in the workplace. A Type A personality may turn the easiest, most routine task into a race to beat the clock. Irrational needs for excessive approval may sap the effect of rewards.

Effects of Stress in the Workplace The right-hand side of the figure suggests a number of subjective, behavioral, cognitive, physiological, and organizational outcomes from the interaction of these sources of stress. On a subjective level, stressed workers can experience anxiety, depression, frustration, fatigue, boredom, loss of self-esteem, and *burnout.*

Burnout **Burnout** is a state of physical and psychological exhaustion that is brought on by overcommitment to one's work or similar causes. Workaholics tend to overextend themselves. They become so consumed by their work that they neglect other areas of life, such as social relationships and leisure activities.

Burnout is common among people with daunting workloads. People are most likely to experience burnout when they enter their fields with idealistic fervor and then find that they are "banging their heads against brick walls." Typically, burnout victims are competent, efficient people who become overwhelmed by the demands of their jobs and recognition that they are unlikely to have the impact they had anticipated (Freudenberger, 1989). Teachers, nurses, mental health workers, police officers, social workers, and criminal and divorce lawyers seem particularly prone to job burnout.

Burnout is also common among people who have high levels of *role conflict, role overload,* or *role ambiguity.* People in role conflict face competing demands for their time. They feel pulled in several directions at once. Their efforts to meet competing demands eventually lead to burnout. People with role overload find it hard to say no. They take on more and more responsibilities until they burn out. People with *role ambiguity* are uncertain as to what other people expect of them. Thus, they work hard at trying to be all things to all people.

Behaviorally, stressed workers may become accident-prone, engage in excessive eating or smoking, turn to alcohol or other drugs, and show temperamental outbursts.

The cognitive effects of excessive stress on the job include poor concentration and loss of ability to make sound decisions. Physiological effects include high blood pressure and the "diseases of adaptation" discussed earlier. The organizational effects of excessive stress include absenteeism, alienation from coworkers, decreased productivity, high turnover rate, and loss of commitment and loyalty to the organization.

Burnout develops gradually. The warning signs may not appear for years, but here are some of them:

- Loss of energy and feelings of exhaustion, both physical and psychological
- Irritability and shortness of temper
- Stress-related problems, such as depression, headaches, backaches, or apathy
- Difficulty concentrating or feeling distanced from one's work
- Loss of motivation
- Lack of satisfaction or feelings of achievement at work
- Loss of concern about work in someone who was previously committed
- Feeling that one has nothing left to give

Truth or Fiction Revisited

It is not true that apathetic workers are most likely to experience job burnout. Burnout actually afflicts the most dedicated workers.

Truth or Fiction Revisited

It is true that stressed workers have more accidents on the job. Perhaps stress decreases workers' attention to potentially harmful details. Or perhaps some of the same conditions that are stressful are physically harmful.

Burnout • A response to job stress encountered by competent, idealistic workers and characterized by exhaustion, cynicism, and, when possible, a change of jobs.

PREVENTING BURNOUT[1] People may become burned out when they are overextended. Yet burnout is not inevitable. Here are some suggestions for preventing burnout:

1. *Establish your priorities.* Make a list of the things that are truly important to you. If your list starts and ends with work, rethink your values. Ask yourself some key questions: Am I making time for the relationships and activities that bring a sense of meaning, fulfillment, and satisfaction to life? Getting in touch with what's truly important to you may help you reorder your values and priorities.
2. *Set reasonable goals.* People at risk of burnout drive themselves to extremes. Set realistic long-term and short-term goals for yourself and don't push yourself beyond your limits.
3. *Take things one day at a time.* Work gradually toward your goals. Burning the candles at both ends is likely to leave you burned (out).
4. *Set limits.* People who risk burnout often have difficulty saying no. They are known as the ones who get things done. Yet the more responsibilities they assume, the greater their risk of burnout. Learn your limits and respect them. Share responsibilities with others. Delegate tasks. Cut back on your responsibilities before things pile up to where you have difficulty coping.
5. *Share your feelings.* Don't keep feelings bottled up, especially negative feelings like anger, frustration, and sadness. Share your feelings with people you trust. It is stressful to keep feelings under wraps.
6. *Build supportive relationships.* Developing and maintaining relationships helps buffer us against the effects of stress. People headed toward burnout may become so invested in their work that they let supportive relationships fall to the wayside.
7. *Do things you enjoy.* Balance work and recreation. Do something you enjoy every day. Breaks clear your mind and recharge your batteries. All work and no play make Jack (or Jill) burn out.
8. *Take time for yourself.* Set aside time for yourself. Say no or later. With all the demands that others place on your shoulders, you need some time for yourself. Make it part of your weekly schedule.
9. *Don't skip vacations.* People who are headed for burnout often find reasons to skip vacations. Big mistake. Vacations give you time off from the usual stresses.
10. *Be attuned to your health.* Be aware of stress-related symptoms. These include physical symptoms such as fatigue, headache or backache, and reduced resistance to colds and the flu. They include psychological symptoms such as anxiety, depression, irritability, or shortness of temper. Changes in health may represent the first signs of burnout. Take them as signals to examine the sources of stress in your life and do something about them. Consult health professionals about any symptoms that concern you. Get regular checkups to help identify developing health problems.

HOW TO COPE WITH STRESS ON THE JOB Psychologists have found that many measures can be taken to decrease stress in the workplace. One can begin with an objective analysis of the workplace to determine whether physical

---

[1]Reprinted with permission from Nevid and others (1998), pp. 57–58.

conditions are hampering rather than enhancing the quality of life. Much job stress arises from a mismatch between job demands and the abilities and needs of the employee (Chemers and others, 1985). To prevent mismatches, companies can use more careful screening measures (e.g., interviewing and psychological testing) to recruit employees whose personalities are compatible with job requirements and then provide the training and education needed to impart the specific skills that will enable workers to perform effectively. Job requirements should be as specific and clear as possible.

Workers need to feel they will find social support from their supervisors if they have complaints or suggestions. Companies can also help workers manage stress by offering counseling and supportive therapy, education about health, and gyms. Kimberly-Clark, Xerox, Pepsi-Cola, Weyerhauser, and Rockwell International, for example, have all made significant investments in gyms that include jogging tracks, exercise cycles, and other equipment. Johnson & Johnson's Live-for-Life program not only addresses stress management per se, but also focuses on weight control, exercise, smoking reduction, nutrition, and alcohol abuse. Workers whose companies provide such programs are generally more fit, take fewer sick days, and report greater job satisfaction than workers at companies that provide medical screenings only (Glasgow & Terborg, 1988).

Workers whose companies do not help them manage stress can tackle this task on their own by using methods such as relaxing, examining whether perfectionism or excessive needs for approval are heightening the tension they encounter at work, or attempting to enhance their psychological hardiness, along the lines suggested in Chapter 11. Of course, they can always consult psychologists for additional ideas. If these measures are not sufficient, they may wish to carefully weigh the pluses and minuses and decide whether to change their jobs or shift careers.

Stress Management in the Workplace. Many organizations help workers manage stress by offering counseling, supportive therapy, health education, even fitness programs.

WOMEN IN THE WORKPLACE

When we speak about role overload, we should keep in mind that were are talking about the situation of the typical American woman who has children who have not yet left the home. Let us momentarily climb atop our soapbox to note that the United States is somewhat unusual in that it still lacks coherent policies for helping dual-wage-earning families. Most industrialized nations provide families with allowances for children and paid leave when babies are born (Rauch, 1989; Zedick & Mosier, 1990). Only a minority of U.S. companies do so.

So working women usually work two shifts, one in the workplace and one at home. For example, about 90 percent of working women—including married and single mothers—continue to bear the major responsibility for child care (Lewin, 1995a). (But a sizable minority of fathers—about 13 percent—are the primary care providers for their children [Casper, 1997].) Women miss work twice as often as men do when the kids are sick (Wasserman, 1993). Women, moreover, still carry out the great majority of the household chores—including cleaning, cooking, and shopping (see Figure 17.3). Between work, commuting, child care, and housework, American working women are putting in nearly 15 hours a day!

So *why* do women work? As you can see in the following "Adjustment in a World of Diversity" feature, the answer is that women work for the same reasons as men do: to earn money, to structure their time, meet people, and find challenge and self-fulfillment. Nevertheless, it is sometimes heard that women are less committed than men to their jobs. Employers who deny women equal access to training and promotions sometimes justify discrimination by citing higher quit rates for women. However, women and men in the same job cate-

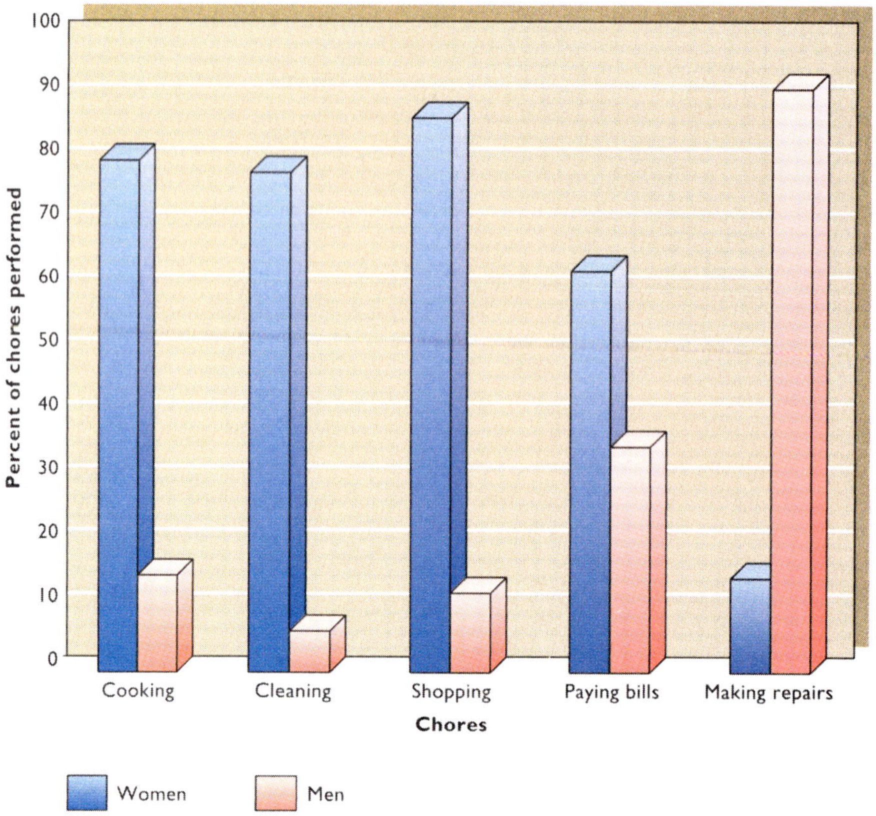

FIGURE 17.3

WHEN MOMMY'S GOT A JOB, WHO DOES THE CLEANING, COOKING, AND SHOPPING? YOU GUESSED IT.

Most American women put in a second shift when they get home from the workplace. With the exception of making repairs, most child care and homemaking chores are left to women.

gories show comparable quit rates (Deutsch, 1990). Women are overrepresented in lower-echelon and dead-end jobs; and workers of both genders in dead-end jobs have higher quit rates than workers in higher-paying, challenging positions. The job role, not the gender of the worker, seems to be the predictor of commitment.

Adjustment in a World of DIVERSITY

Why Does Mommy Work?

Why do women work? So that the family can afford a second car? So that the family can go on vacation? To send the kids off to camp in the summer? Not according to a poll by Louis Harris and Associates (cited in Lewin, 1995a). These stereotypes are long outdated. Women no longer work to provide the family with a supplemental income. Women, like men, work to support the family.

Perhaps we are more familiar with the high-powered mothers like Jane Pauley, Michelle Pfeiffer, even Hillary Rodham Clinton. These women either outearn their husbands or support their children on their own. But out of the spotlight, the earning power of the ordinary woman has been growing by leaps and bounds. According to the Harris poll, wives share about equally with their husbands in supporting their families. Nearly half of them—48 percent—reported that they provided at least half of their family's income. We're not talking vacation money here. We mean half of the mortgage, half of the clothing, half of the medical bills, even half of the new pairs of Nikes and the mountain bikes (Lewin, 1995a).

So why do most of us still think of women as primarily mothers? Why haven't we paid more attention to their new roles as providers? Perhaps it is because working mothers continue to do what mothers were doing before they became such a, well, force in the workforce. That is, 9 of 10 working mothers still bear the primary responsibility for the children, the cooking, and the cleaning (Lewin, 1995a).

Are these mothers overburdened? Perhaps. The Harris poll survey found that working mothers are pressed for time. They are worried about not having enough time with their families and about balancing the demands of work and a home life. Nevertheless, when they were asked whether they would like to surrender some of their responsibilities, 53 percent of working women said no. Even more ironic, full-time working mothers reported that they felt more likely to feel valued for their contributions at home than full-time homemakers were.

Despite their new earning power, working mothers are still primarily concerned about their children. When they were asked what made them feel successful at home, about one man and woman in four mentioned good relationships and spending time together. The next-largest group of women (22 percent) reported good, well adjusted, healthy children. But 20 percent of men mentioned money or being able to afford things. Only 8 percent of the men mentioned well adjusted kids. Just 5 percent of the women mentioned money.

So mom is still "traditional"—if by traditional we mean doing what mom has been expected to do. She is still looking after the house and kids. But now she also pays half the bills.

The Workplace for Women

Despite some recent breaking down of traditional gender-segregation, many occupations largely remain "men's work" or "women's work." Women still account for the great majority of secretaries and schoolteachers, but only a small percentage of police officers and mechanics. On the other hand, the percentage of women in medical and law schools has recently risen to nearly equal the numbers of men entering these professions. But in other professional fields, the gap has not narrowed as much, particularly in fields such as math, science, and engineering.

THE EARNINGS GAP Women overall earn about two thirds of the income of men (U.S. Bureau of the Census, 1995). Note these sad but fascinating examples of the earnings gap:

- Male physicians earn about $7 more an hour than female physicians ("Study finds smaller pay gap," 1996).
- Male college professors earn about 30 percent more than female college professors (Honan, 1996).
- The median salary of female scientists with bachelor's degrees and up to 2 years of experience was 73 percent that of their male colleagues in 1990, $21,000 versus $29,500. Those with doctorates made 88 percent of the median male salary, $35,500 versus $40,400 ("Women lagging," 1994).
- The average female high school graduate earns less than the average male grade school *dropout.*
- Men with only an eighth-grade education earn more than the average female *college graduate.*

Why this gap in earnings? Some of it can be explained by the fact that most women still work in traditionally low-paying occupations such as waitress, housekeeper, clerk, sales, and light factory work. Even in the same job area, such as sales, men are usually given higher-paying, more responsible positions.

Truth or Fiction Revisited

It is true that women average only about two thirds of the earnings of men. Women are usually found in lower-paying positions, but even women in comparable work generally earn less than their male counterparts.

SEXUAL HARASSMENT.
Is this behavior acceptable in the workplace? Many women have switched jobs or colleges because of sexual harassment.

Men in sales are more likely to vend high-ticket items such as automobiles, microcomputers, and appliances.

Even though nearly as many women as men now graduate from medical schools, men tend to gravitate toward higher paying specialties, such as surgery ("Study finds smaller pay gap," 1996). Female physicians are more likely to enter lower paying medical specialties, such as pediatrics and psychiatry. Men are also more likely than women to be in positions of power on medical school faculties.

Male college professors earn more than women for several reasons. Since women are relative newcomers to academia, they are more likely to be found in lower-paying entry positions, such as assistant professorships (Honan, 1996). When men and women reach full professorships, the gap in pay narrows to under 10 percent. Another reason is that women are more likely than men to choose lower-paying academic fields, such as education and English (Honan, 1996). Men are more likely to be found on faculties in business, engineering, and the hard sciences, where the pay is higher.

REDUCING THE EARNINGS GAP The Equal Pay Act of 1963 requires equal pay for equal work. The Civil Rights Act of 1964 prohibits discrimination in hiring, firing, or promotion on the basis of race, ethnic origin, or gender. Measures such as the following can improve the quality of work life and reduce the earnings gap for women:

1. *More realistic career planning.* The average woman today spends about 28 years in the workforce, but plans for a much shorter tenure. Young women should assume that they will be working for several decades so that they will avail themselves of opportunities for education and training.
2. *Providing employers with accurate information about women in the workforce.* If more employers recognized that women spend so many years in the workforce, and that commitment to a job reflects the type of work rather than the gender of the worker, they might be more motivated to open the doors to women.
3. *Heightening awareness of the importance of the woman's career in dual-career marriages.* Husbands may also hold stereotypes that damage their wives' chances for career advancement and fulfillment. A couple should not blindly assume that the man's career always comes first. The man can share child rearing and housekeeping chores so that each may reap the benefits of employment.
4. *Maintaining employment continuity and stability.* Promotions and entry into training programs are usually earned by showing a stable commitment to a career and, often, one's employer. Many couples permit both partners to achieve these benefits by postponing childbearing or sharing child rearing tasks.
5. *Increasing job flexibility and providing child care facilities.* Employers can also assist women workers through flextime, providing on-site child care facilities, and granting extended maternity and *paternity* leaves.
6. *Recruiting qualified women into training programs and jobs.* Educational institutions, unions, and employers can actively recruit qualified women for positions that have been traditionally held by men.

Sexual Harassment

Sexual harassment is one of the common and vicious obstacles women—and sometimes men—face in the workplace. If it is sometimes difficult to draw the line between legitimate persuasion and attempted date rape, it can be even more difficult to distinguish between a legitimate (if unwanted) sexual invitation and sexual harassment (Adler, 1993b). Sexual harassers often claim that charges of harassment are exaggerated. They say that the victim "overreacted" to normal male-female interactions or "took me too seriously" (Powell, 1996; Rathus and others, 1998).

Where does "normal male-female interaction" end and sexual harassment begin? (See Figure 17.4.) One commonly accepted definition of sexual

FIGURE 17.4

WHAT IS SEXUAL HARASSMENT?

Despite all the publicity that has attended sexual harassment in recent years, many people claim not to know where legitimate expressions of sexual interest end and sexual harassment begins. Where exactly do you draw the line?

The U.S. Navy ("What is sexual harassment?" 1993) has drawn up some guidelines that may be of help:

> Sexual harassment includes a wide range of behaviors. Some of these are obvious and easy to recognize, while others fall into gray areas and may be perceived as sexual harassment even if the action was not intended that way.
>
> Adding to the confusion is the fact that a person's intention is not the only deciding factor in these cases. The way the action or "joke" is perceived by the recipient and others in the workplace, and its impact, also determines if it is sexual harassment.
>
> To make it easier to understand, think of behavior in terms of a traffic light with green, yellow, and red zones.

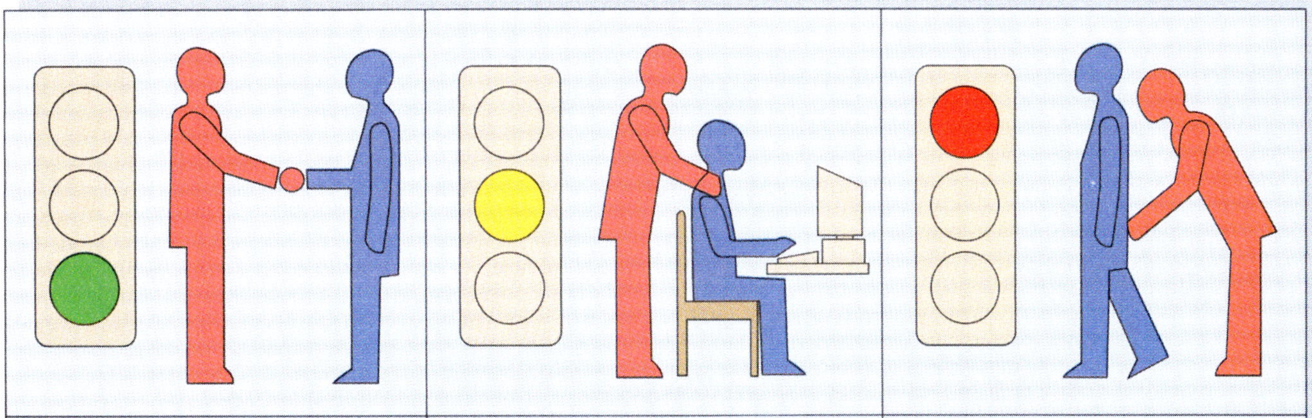

These actions do not constitute sexual harassment. They are typical interactions and common courtesies that happen regularly in an office environment. Some examples: • Performance counseling • Touching which could not be perceived in a sexual way, such as placing a hand on a person's elbow • Counseling on (professional) appearance • Everyday social interaction such as saying, "Hello, how are you?" or "Did you have a good weekend?" • Expressing concern or encouragement • A polite compliment or friendly conversation	Many of these behaviors fall into the gray areas but some are obvious examples of sexual harassment. Examples: • Violating "personal" space (getting too close) • Whistling • Questions about personal life • Lewd or off-color jokes • Leering or staring • Repeated requests for a date after being told no •(Hanging) suggestive posters or calendars (where they may offend others) • Foul language • Unwanted letters or poems • Sexually suggestive touching • Sitting or gesturing sexually	These behaviors are always considered to be sexual harassment. Examples are: • Sexual favors in return for employment rewards and threats if sexual favors are not provided • (Hanging or using) sexually explicit pictures, including calendars or posters (where they may offend others) • Sexually explicit remarks • Using office (or other) status to request a date • Obscene letters or comments • Grabbing, forced kissing, fondling • Sexual assault and rape

WHAT DO *You* SAY NOW?

RESISTING SEXUAL HARASSMENT

What do you do if you are sexually harassed by another student, a professor, or an employer? Do you try to ignore it and hope for the best—that it will be mild or that the harasser will come to his or her senses and cut it out? Do you take action? If so, what do you do? Write down some of your thoughts on the matter in the spaces provided. Then compare them with the suggestions offered by Powell (1996), which are noted below.

1. ______________________________

2. ______________________________

3. ______________________________

Did your own ideas overlap with any of the following suggestions?

1. Impart a professional attitude. Harassment is often stopped cold if you respond to the harasser in a curt, businesslike manner.
2. Discourage harassment and promote the kind of social behavior you want. Speak up. If your professor asks you to come to the office after dinner to review your paper to avoid being disturbed, say that you would rather talk over the paper during office hours. Stick to business. If the harasser does not take this suggestion, be more direct: "Mr. Smith, I'd like to keep our relationship purely student-professor, okay?" Harassed professors may tell persistent students, "Let's keep our interactions public and professional, okay?"
3. Don't get into a situation in which you are alone with the harasser. Have a friend wait outside while you consult the professor in his office. Or see the harasser right before or after class, when other people are milling about.
4. Keep a record of incidents of harassment to document the problem in case you decide to lodge an official complaint.
5. Put the harasser on direct notice that you recognize the harassment for what it is and that you want it to stop. It may help to describe the offensive behavior so that there are no misunderstandings: "When we were in the office, you brushed up against me several times."
6. Confide about harassment to reliable friends, school counselors or advisers, or parents or relatives. Harassment is stressful, and social support helps us cope with stress. Other people may also have helpful advice.
7. Many campuses have offices where complaints about sexual harassment are filed and acted on. Check with the dean of students or the president's office.
8. See a lawyer. Sexual harassment is illegal, and the organization—or school—that lets it take place is responsible for it. ■

harassment consists of *deliberate or repeated unsolicited verbal comments, gestures, or physical contact of a sexual nature that is not wanted by the recipient.* Sexual harassment includes the following (Powell, 1996):

- Verbal abuse or harassment
- Unwelcome sexual overtures or advances
- Pressure to engage in sexual activity
- Remarks about a person's body, clothing, or sexual activities
- Leering at, or ogling, someone's body
- Telling unwanted dirty jokes in mixed company

Truth or Fiction Revisited

It is not true that sexual harassment, like beauty, is in the eye of the beholder. In some cases, it may be unclear as to whether sexual advances were welcome or unwelcome. In most cases, however, government guidelines are clear enough to identify sexual harassment.

- Unnecessarily touching, patting, or pinching someone
- Whistles and catcalls
- Brushing up against someone's body
- Demands to engage in sexual activity that are accompanied by suggested or concrete threats concerning someone's status as a worker or a student, as in a professor's pressuring students for sexual favors through threats of low grades or negative letters of recommendation

adjustment and modern life

FINDING A CAREER THAT FITS

Our work is very important to us. Therefore, it is vital that we seek to have a career that fits us. A proper fit, in terms of our aptitudes, interests, and personal traits, enhances our satisfaction from day to day.

Put it another way: It may matter little that we are bringing home the bacon if we hate getting up in the morning to face our jobs. If we do not fit our jobs, we find them more stressful. We are unlikely to try to do our best (Chemers and others, 1985). When our performance is poor or mediocre, we are unlikely to get ahead. Our income might not keep pace with that of peers who better fit the job environment. Our self-esteem may plummet as peers are promoted ahead of us. We may become alienated from the job. We may even get fired.

Many occupations call for combinations of these **coping styles.** A copywriter in an advertising agency might be both artistic and enterprising. Clinical and counseling psychologists tend to be investigative, artistic, and socially oriented. Military people and beauticians tend to be realistic and conventional. (But military leaders who plan major operations and form governments are also enterprising; and individuals who create new hairstyles and fashions are also artistic.)

Holland has created the Vocational Preference Inventory in order to assess these coping styles. These styles are also measured by vocational tests.

Now that we have seen the value of finding a good person-environment fit in our occupations, let us consider ways in which psychology can help us make effective choices. Two of them involve using the balance sheet and psychological tests.

How to Use the Balance Sheet and Psychological Tests to Make Career Decisions

We first discussed the balance sheet in the context of making personal decisions. In Chapter 11, we saw how Meg used it to decide whether to get a divorce. Balance sheets can also be applied to career decisions. The balance sheet can also help you weigh your goals, pinpoint potential sources of frustration, and plan how to get more information or to surmount obstacles.

Samantha, a first-year liberal arts major, wondered whether she should strive to become a physician. There were no physicians in her family with whom to explore the idea. A psychologist in her college counseling center advised her to fill out the balance sheet shown in Table 17.3 to help weigh the pluses and minuses of medicine.

Samantha's balance sheet helped her see that she needed dozens of pieces of information to decide. For example, how would she react to intense, prolonged studying? What were her chances of being accepted by a medical school? How did the day-to-day nitty-gritty of medical work fit her coping style and her psychological needs?

COPING STYLE • Holland's term for the way in which one approaches occupational demands: realistic, investigative, artistic, social, enterprising, conventional, or a combination of these.

TABLE 17.3 SAMANTHA'S BALANCE SHEET FOR THE ALTERNATIVE OF TAKING PREMEDICAL STUDIES

AREAS OF CONSIDERATION	*POSITIVE ANTICIPATIONS*	*NEGATIVE ANTICIPATIONS*
Tangible gains and losses for Samantha	1. Solid income	1. Long hours studying 2. Worry about acceptance by medical school 3. High financial debt upon graduation
Tangible gains and losses for others	1. Solid income for benefit	1. Little time for family life of family
Self-approval or disapproval	1. Pride in being a physician	
Social approval or disapproval	1. Other people admire doctors	1. Some women (still!) frown on women doctors

Samantha's balance sheet for the alternative showed that although she knew that other people admired physicians, she had not considered how she would feel about herself as a physician. It encouraged her to seek further information about her personal psychological needs.

The need for information is not limited to those contemplating a career in medicine. The types of questions that we must consider about any career are shown in Table 17.4.

To gather more information, Samantha's counselor used a number of psychological tests. Most career counselors test to some degree. They combine test results with interview information and knowledge of their clients' personal histories to attain a rounded picture of their clients' interests, abilities, and personalities.

One of the tests Samantha took was a Wechsler Adult Intelligence Scale (WAIS). The WAIS and the Stanford-Binet Intelligence Scales are the most widely used intelligence tests. Samantha's WAIS score—her **intelligence quotient**—was in the 130s, which means that her general level of intellectual functioning was on a par with that of people who performed well in medicine. Her verbal, mathematical, and spatial relations skills showed no deficiencies. Thus, any academic problems were likely to reflect lack of motivation or of specific prerequisites, not lack of ability. But her counselor also told Samantha that "The best predictor of future behavior is past behavior." Since premedical programs are dominated by chemistry, Samantha's solid performance in high school chemistry was promising.

The balance sheet suggested that Samantha had only superficially asked herself about how she would enjoy being a physician. She had recognized that physicians are generally admired, and she assumed that she would have feelings of pride. But would the work of a physician be consistent with her coping style? Would her psychological needs be met? The counselor provided helpful personality information through the an interest inventory and the Edwards Personal Preference Schedule (EPPS).

Interest inventories are widely used tests in college counseling and testing centers. Most items require that test-takers indicate whether they like, are indifferent to, or dislike various occupations (e.g., actor/actress, architect), school subjects (algebra, art), activities (adjusting a carburetor, making a

INTELLIGENCE QUOTIENT • A score on an intelligence test. Abbreviated *IQ*.

SELF-ASSESSMENT

What's Your Vocational Type? Attend the Job Fair and Find Out!

There are a number of different approaches to predicting whether or not we are likely to adjust to various job environments, or occupations. By and large, they involve matching our traits to the job. Psychologist John Holland has developed a theory of matching coping styles to occupations. To obtain insight into your own coping styles, let's attend a job fair. ■

Directions: Figure 17.5 shows an aerial view of a job fair in a college gymnasium. What happened is this. When the fair got under way, students and prospective employers began to chat. As time elapsed, they found mutual interests and collected into parts of the gym according to those interests.

All right, now *you* enter the room. Groups have already formed, but you decide not to stick to yourself. You catch snatches of conversation in an effort to decide which group to join.

Now consider the types of people in the six groups by reading the descriptions in Figure 17.5.

Which group would you most like to join? Write the letter that signifies the group (R, I, A, S, E, or C) here: ____

What is your second choice? After you had met and chatted with the folks in the first group, with whom else might you like to chat? Write the letter here: ____

Now, which group looks most *boring* to you? With which group do you have nothing in common? Which group would you most like to avoid? Write the letter signifying the group that should have stayed at home here: ____

Where, then, did you fit in at the fair? What might it mean for your vocational adjustment? Predicting our adjustment involves matching our traits to the job. The job fair helps people decide where they do and do not fit in.

Holland has predicted how well people will enjoy a certain kind of work by matching six coping styles—realistic, investigative, artistic, social, enterprising, and conventional—to the job. Each of the groups in Figure 17.5 represents a coping style:

1. *Realistic.* Persons with a realistic coping style tend to be concrete in their thinking, mechanically oriented, and interested in jobs that involve motor activity. Examples include farming; unskilled labor, such as attending gas stations; and skilled trades, such as construction and electrical work.
2. *Investigative.* Investigative people tend to be abstract in their thinking, creative, and introverted. They are frequently well adjusted in research and college and university teaching.
3. *Artistic.* Artistic individuals tend to be creative, emotional, interested in subjective feelings, and intuitive. They tend to gravitate toward the visual arts and the performing arts.
4. *Social.* Socially oriented people tend to be extroverted and socially concerned. They frequently show high verbal ability and strong needs for affiliating with others. Jobs such as social work, counseling, and teaching children often fit them well.
5. *Enterprising.* Enterprising individuals tend to be adventurous and impulsive, domineering, and extroverted. They gravitate toward leadership and planning roles in industry, government, and social organizations. The successful real estate developer or tycoon is usually enterprising.

speech), amusements (golf, chess, jazz or rock concerts), and types of people (babies, nonconformists). The preferences of test-takers are compared with those of people in various occupations. Areas of general interest (e.g., sales, science, teaching, agriculture) and specific interest (e.g., mathematician, guidance counselor, beautician) are derived from these comparisons. Test-takers may also gather information about their coping styles, according to Holland's model.

Interest inventories are one kind of personality test. Some personality tests help psychologists learn about personal problems. Others are used with well adjusted individuals to heighten the chances of finding the right person-

6. *Conventional.* Conventional people tend to enjoy routines. They show high self-control, need for order, and the desire for social approval; they are not particularly imaginative. Jobs that suit them include banking, accounting, and clerical work.

FIGURE 17.5
COPING STYLES AND CAREERS.
Imagine yourself at a job fair like that pictured here. In such fairs, students and prospective employers begin to chat. As time elapses, they find mutual interests and collect into groups accordingly. Consider the types of people in the six groups by reading the descriptions for each. Which group would you most like to join? What does your choice suggest about your coping style? If you wanted to learn more about your coping style, what resources would be available to you?

environment fit in the workplace. Commonly used tests for measuring personality traits are the California Psychological Inventory and Edwards Personal Preference Schedule (EPPS).

The EPPS pairs a number of statements expressive of psychological needs, and test-takers indicate which of each pair of statements is more descriptive of them. In this way it can be determined, for example, whether test-takers have a stronger need for dominance than for deference (taking direction from others), or a strong need for order or a need to be helped by others. All in all, the relative strength of 15 psychological needs is examined.

TABLE 17.4 TYPES OF INFORMATION NEEDED TO MAKE SATISFYING CAREER DECISIONS

1. *Intellectual and educational appropriateness: Is your intended career compatible with your own intellectual and educational abilities and background?*
Have you taken any (preprofessional) courses that lead to the career? Have you done well in them? What level of intellectual functioning is shown by people already in the career? Is your own level of intellectual functioning comparable? What kinds of special talents and intellectual skills are required for this career? Are there any psychological or educational tests that can identify where you stand in your possession of these talents or in the development of these skills? If you do not have these skills, can they be developed? How are they developed? Is there any way of predicting how well you can do at developing them? Would you find this field intellectually demanding and challenging? Would you find the field intellectually sterile and boring?
Information Resources: College or university counseling or testing center, college placement center, private psychologist or vocational counselor, people working in the field, professors in or allied to the field.
2. *Intrinsic factors: Is your intended career compatible with your coping style, your psychological needs, and your interests?*
Does the job require elements of the realistic coping style? Of the investigative, artistic, social, enterprising, or conventional coping style? What is your coping style? Is there a good person-job-environment fit? Is the work repetitious, or is it varied? Do you have a marked need for change (perpetual novel stimulation), or do you have a greater need for order and consistency? Would you be working primarily with machinery, with papers, or with other people? Do you prefer manipulating objects, doing paperwork, or interacting with other people? Is the work indoors or outdoors? Are you an indoors or an outdoors person? Do you have strong needs for autonomy and dominance, or do you prefer to defer to others? Does the field allow you to make your own decisions, permit you to direct others, or require that you closely take direction from others? Do you have strong aesthetic needs? Is the work artistic? Are you Type A, Type B, or somewhere in between? Is this field strongly competitive or more relaxed?
Information resources: Successful people in the field (Do you feel similar to people in the field? Do you have common interests? Do you like them and enjoy their company?), written job descriptions, psychological tests of personality (e.g., coping style and psychological needs), and interests.
3. *Extrinsic Factors: What is the balance between the investment you would have to make in the career and the probable payoff?*
How much time, work, and money would you have to invest in your educational and professional development in order to enter this career? Do you have the financial resources? If not, can you get them? (Do the sacrifices you would have to make to get them—such as long-term debt—seem worthwhile?) Do you have the endurance? The patience? What will the market for your skills be like when you are ready to enter the career? In 20 years? Will the financial rewards adequately compensate you for your investment?
Information resources: College financial aid office, college placement office, college counseling center, family, people in the field.

The interest inventory suggested that Samantha would enjoy investigative work, science—including medical science—and mathematics. However, she was not particularly socially oriented. Well adjusted physicians usually show a combination of investigative and social coping styles.

Truth or Fiction Revisited

It is not true that anyone who has the ability to get ahead would be satisfied with prestigious vocations such as college professor, psychologist, physician, or lawyer. We may be miserable in occupations that are inconsistent with our coping styles and other psychological attributes.

The EPPS showed relatively strong needs for achievement, order, dominance, and endurance. All these factors meshed well with premedical studies—the long hours, the willingness to delay gratification, and the desire to learn about things—to make them fit together and work properly. The EPPS report dovetailed with the interest inventory's report to the effect that Samantha was not particularly socially oriented in her coping style: The EPPS suggested that Samantha had a low need for **nurturance,** for caring for others and promoting their well-being.

With this information in hand, Samantha recognized that she really did not sense a strong desire to help others through medicine. Her medical interests were mainly academic. But after some reflection, she chose to pursue premedical studies and to expand her college work in chemistry and other sciences to lay the groundwork for alternative careers in medically related sciences. The courses promised to be of interest even if she did not develop a strong desire to help others or was not accepted by medical school. Contingency plans like these are useful for all of us. If we can consider alternatives, even as we head down the path toward a concrete goal, we are better equipped to deal with unanticipated roadblocks.

NURTURANCE • A psychological trait or need characterized by caring for people (or other living organisms) or rearing them.

SUMMARY

1. **Why do we work?** Workers are motivated both by extrinsic rewards (money, status, security) and intrinsic rewards (the work ethic, self-identity, self-fulfillment, self-worth, and the social values of work).

2. **What are the stages of vocational development?** Super identifies five stages of development: fantasy, tentative, realistic choice, maintenance, and retirement stages.

3. **What are the developmental tasks in taking a new job?** These include making the transition from school to the workplace, learning the job tasks, accepting responsibility and subordinate status, and learning how to cope with co-workers, supervisors, successes, and failures.

4. **What measures can be taken to enhance job satisfaction?** Measures that contribute to job satisfaction include careful recruitment and selection, training and instruction, unbiased appraisal and feedback, goal setting, linking financial compensation to productivity, work redesign, allowing workers to make appropriate decisions, and flexible schedules.

5. **What sources of stress do we find in the workplace, and what can we do about them?** There are physical, individual, group, and organizational stressors. We can cope with them by evaluating our appraisal of them, enhancing our person-environment fit, and managing stress.

6. **What can be done to improve the workplace for women?** Women profit from more realistic career planning, maintaining employment continuity, child care facilities, and training programs.

7. **What is sexual harassment?** One commonly accepted definition of sexual harassment consists of *deliberate or repeated unsolicited verbal comments, gestures, or physical contact of a sexual nature that is unwelcome.*

8. **What is the relationship between a person's coping style and adjustment in an occupation?** Holland identified six coping styles: realistic, investigative, artistic, social, enterprising, and conventional. Persons with certain coping styles better fit, or are better adjusted in, certain occupations. For example, scientists are investigative and beauticians are realistic and conventional.

9. **How can we use the balance sheet to help make career decisions?** Use of the balance sheet helps us weigh the pluses and minuses of following a particular career path, and also helps us identify gaps in the information we need to make a decision.

10. **How can we use psychological tests to help us make career decisions?** Psychological tests measure our intelligence, aptitudes (as in music), interests, and personality traits. We can then compare our scores on these measures to those of people who are well adjusted in various occupations.

CHAPTER 18

Having and Rearing Children

TRUTH OR FICTION?

✓ T F

- ☐ ☐ Fertilization takes place in the uterus.
- ☐ ☐ "Yuppies" are more likely than nonprofessionals to develop fertility problems.
- ☐ ☐ Developing embryos have been successfully transferred from the womb of one woman to the womb of another.
- ☐ ☐ Pregnant women who smoke risk having children who are low in birth weight.
- ☐ ☐ Soon after birth, babies are slapped on the buttocks to clear passageways for air and stimulate independent breathing.
- ☐ ☐ The way the umbilical cord is cut determines whether a child will have an "inny" or an "outy" for a "belly button."
- ☐ ☐ Women who give birth by the Lamaze method do not have pain.
- ☐ ☐ Children with strict parents are more likely to become competent.
- ☐ ☐ Breast-feeding and bottle-feeding are equally healthful for the child.
- ☐ ☐ Divorce is more stressful for young children than for adolescents.
- ☐ ☐ Children who are placed in day care are more aggressive than children who are cared for in the home.
- ☐ ☐ Parents who have been victims of child abuse are more likely to abuse their own children.

OUTLINE

Truth or Fiction Revisited

It is not true that fertilization takes place in the uterus. Fertilization normally takes place in the fallopian tubes, not the uterus.

ON A SUMMERLIKE DAY IN OCTOBER, SUSAN AND her husband Dan rush out to their jobs as usual. While Susan, a buyer for a New York department store, is arranging for dresses from the Chicago manufacturer to arrive in time for the spring line, a very different drama is unfolding in her body. Hormones are causing a follicle (egg container) in one of her ovaries to rupture and release an egg cell, or ovum. Susan, like other women, possessed from birth all the egg cells she would ever have. How this ovum was selected for development and release this month is unknown. But for a day or so following **ovulation,** Susan will be capable of becoming pregnant.

When it is released, the ovum begins a slow journey down a 4-inch-long fallopian tube to the uterus. It is within this tube that one of Dan's sperm cells will unite with it.

Like many other couples, Susan and Dan engaged in sexual intercourse the previous night. But unlike most other couples, their timing and methodology were preplanned. Susan had used a nonprescription kit bought in a drugstore to predict when she would ovulate. She had been chemically analyzing her urine for the presence of **luteinizing hormone.** Luteinizing hormone surges about 1 to 2 days prior to ovulation, and the results placed this day at the center of the period of time when Susan was likely to conceive.

When Susan and Dan made love, he ejaculated hundreds of millions of sperm, with about equal numbers of Y and X sex chromosomes. By the time of conception only a few thousand had survived the journey to the fallopian tubes. Several bombarded the ovum, attempting to penetrate. Only one succeeded. It carried a Y sex chromosome. When a Y-bearing sperm unites with an ovum, all of which contain X sex chromosomes, the couple will conceive a boy. When an X-bearing sperm fertilizes the ovum, a girl is conceived. The fertilized ovum, or **zygote,** is 1/175th of an inch across—a tiny stage for the drama yet to unfold.

The genetic material from Dan's sperm cell combines with that in Susan's egg cell. Susan is 37 years old, and in 4 months she will have an amniocentesis to check for Down's syndrome in the fetus, a chromosomal disorder that occurs more frequently among the children of couples in their thirties and forties. Amniocentesis also provides information about other problems and the gender of the unborn child. So months before their son is born, Susan and Dan will start thinking about boys' names and prepare their nursery for a boy.

In this chapter, we focus on a number of issues concerning having and rearing children. First is the central question of whether or not to have children. Educated people today are choosing whether to have children, not just having them as a matter of course. Then we consider the not-so-simple matter of conception, and we see how contemporary couples cope with infertility problems. We follow prenatal development and see how parents can make that crucial period as healthful as possible for the embryo and fetus. We explore the psychological, biological, and political issues concerning childbirth and focus on ways in which women can exercise control over their own bodies throughout the process. We report research concerning the patterns of childrearing that are associated with competence in children. Finally, we examine a selection of issues in childrearing that will be of use to readers: breast-feeding versus bottle-feeding, effects of divorce on children, child abuse, and day care.

CHILDREN: TO HAVE OR NOT TO HAVE

Once upon a time, marriage was equated with children. According to the "motherhood mandate," it was traditional for women to bear at least two children. Married women who could bear children usually did. Today the motherhood mandate, like other traditions, has come under reconsideration. More than ever, people see themselves as having the right to *choose* whether or not they will have children. For example, in 1970, 40 percent of households were made up of married couples with children. In 1995, only 25 percent of households consisted of married couples with children (Bryson, 1995).

The decision to have or not to have children is a personal one—one of the most important decisions we make. Let us now follow what happens during the earliest days of development.

CONCEPTION

Conception is the culmination of a fantastic voyage in which one of several hundred thousand ova produced by the woman unites with one of several hundred *billion* sperm produced by the man. Each month one egg (occasionally more than one) is released from its ovarian follicle about midway during the menstrual cycle. It enters a nearby fallopian tube.

The sperm cells that approach the egg secrete an enzyme that briefly thins the gelatinous layer that surrounds the egg, allowing one sperm to enter. The chromosomes from the sperm cell line up across from the corresponding chromosomes in the egg cell to form 23 new pairs with a unique set of genetic instructions.

Infertility

For couples who want children, few problems are more disconcerting than inability to conceive. Physicians are usually not concerned until couples who are trying to conceive have not done so for 6 months. The term *infertility* is usually not applied until the couple has not conceived for a year.

About 15 percent of couples in the United States have fertility problems (Howards, 1995). In about 4 of 10 cases, the problem lies with the man. In the other 6, it lies with the woman. When both members of the couple are infertile and no medical intervention can be of help, the couple can adopt. However, a number of methods have been developed to enhance couples' fertility.

Fertility problems in the male are low sperm count, low sperm **motility,** and damaged sperm. The causes include genetic and hormonal factors, environmental toxins, disease, excess heat, advanced age, and use of drugs—prescription and illicit (Jones & Toner, 1993).

Women may encounter infertility because of (1) lack of ovulation, (2) endometriosis, or (3) obstructions or malfunctions of the reproductive tract (Jones & Toner, 1993).

The most frequent problem, failure to ovulate, may stem from causes such as hormonal irregularities, malnutrition, and stress. *Fertility drugs* such as

OVULATION • The releasing of an ovum from an ovary.
LUTEINIZING HORMONE • A hormone produced by the pituitary gland that causes ovulation.
ZYGOTE • A fertilized ovum.
CONCEPTION • The combining of the genetic material of a sperm cell and an ovum, creating a zygote.
MOTILITY • Self-propulsion.

SELF-ASSESSMENT

SHOULD YOU HAVE A CHILD?

Whether or not to have a child is a heady decision. Children have a way of needing a generation (or a lifetime) of love and support. So we have no simplistic answers to this question, no standardized questionnaire that yields a score for a "go."

Instead, we review some of the considerations involved in choosing to have, or not to have, children. Researchers have found several for each choice. The lists may offer you some insight into your own motives. Sure, you can check the blank spaces of the pros and cons to see how many pros you come up with and how many cons. But we're not pretending that each item in the list is equal in weight or that the totals should influence you. You be the judge. It's your life (and, perhaps, your children's lives) and your choice. ■

REASONS TO HAVE CHILDREN Following are a number of reasons for having children. Check those that seem to apply to you.

____ 1. *Personal experience.* Having children is a unique experience. To many people, no other experience compares with having the opportunity to love them, to experience their love, to help shape their lives, and to watch them develop.

____ 2. *Personal pleasure.* There is fun and pleasure in playing with children, taking them to the zoo and the circus, and viewing the world through their fresh, innocent eyes.

____ 3. *Personal extension.* Children carry on our genetic heritage, and some of our own wishes and dreams, beyond the confines of our own mortality. We name them after ourselves or our families, and see them as extensions of ourselves. We identify with their successes.

____ 4. *Relationship.* Parents have the opportunity to establish extremely close bonds with their children.

____ 5. *Personal status.* Within our culture, parents are afforded respect just because they are parents. Consider the commandment: "Honor thy Father and thy Mother."

____ 6. *Personal competence.* Parenthood is a challenge. Competence in the social roles of mother and father is a potential source of gratification to people who cannot match this competence in their vocational or other social roles.

____ 7. *Personal responsibility.* Parents have the opportunity to be responsible for the welfare and education of their children.

____ 8. *Personal power.* The power that parents hold over their children is gratifying to some people.

____ 9. *Moral worth.* Some people feel that having children provides the opportunity for a moral, selfless act in which they place the needs of others—their children—ahead of their own.

REASONS NOT TO HAVE CHILDREN Following are reasons cited by many couples for deciding not to have children. Check those that apply.

____ 1. *Strain on resources.* The world is overpopulated and it is wrong to place additional strain on limited resources.

____ 2. *Increase in overpopulation.* More children will only geometrically increase the problem of overpopulation.

____ 3. *Choice, not mandate.* Motherhood should be a choice, not a mandate.

____ 4. *Time together.* Childfree couples can spend more time together and develop a more intimate relationship.

____ 5. *Freedom.* Children can interfere with plans for leisure time, education, and vocational advancement. Childfree couples are more able to live spontaneously, to go where they please and do as they please.

____ 6. *Other children.* People can enjoy other than their own children. Adoption is a possibility.

____ 7. *Dual careers.* Members of childfree couples may both pursue meaningful careers without distraction.

____ 8. *Financial security.* Children are a financial burden, especially considering the cost of a college education.

____ 9. *Community welfare.* Childfree couples have a greater opportunity to become involved in civic concerns and community organizations.

____ 10. *Difficulty.* Parenthood is demanding. It requires sacrifice of time, money, and energy, and not everyone makes a good parent.

____ 11. *Irrevocable decision.* Once you have children, the decision cannot be changed.

____ 12. *Failure.* Some people fear that they will not be good parents.

____ 13. *Danger.* The world is a dangerous place, with the threats, for example, of crime and nuclear war. It is better not to bring children into such a world.

clomiphene and pergonal contain hormones that help regulate ovulation. They have also been linked to multiple births. Local infections such as **pelvic inflammatory disease** (PID) may impede passage of sperm or ova through the fallopian tubes and elsewhere. Antibiotics are sometimes helpful.

Endometriosis can block the fallopian tubes and also worsens the "climate" for conception for reasons that are not well understood. Endometriosis has been labeled the "Yuppies' disease" because its effects are cumulative and experienced most strongly by women who have postponed bearing children. Hormone treatments and surgery are sometimes successful in reducing endometriosis to the point where women can conceive.

A number of recent methods have been developed to help women with blocked fallopian tubes and related problems bear children.

Truth or Fiction Revisited

It is true that "yuppies" are more likely than nonprofessionals to develop fertility problems. This is because young urban professionals tend to postpone childbearing, and the likelihood of infertility increases with the years.

ARTIFICIAL INSEMINATION Low (or zero) sperm count is the most common problem with men. In some cases, multiple ejaculations of men with low sperm counts have been collected and quick-frozen. The sperm are then injected into the woman's uterus during ovulation. This is one **artificial insemination** procedure. In another, sperm from a donor are injected into the woman's uterus.

IN VITRO FERTILIZATION Louise Brown, the world's first "test-tube baby," was born in England in 1978 after having been conceived by means of **in vitro fertilization** (IVF). In this method, ova are surgically removed from the mother's ovary and allowed to ripen in a laboratory dish. Then they are fertilized by the father's sperm. If the man's sperm have low motility, their penetration of the egg can be facilitated by making a slit in the wall of the egg or by direct injection (Kolata, 1993c). The fertilized egg is then injected into the mother's uterus and becomes implanted in the uterine wall.

DONOR IVF "I tell her Mommy was having trouble with, I call them ovums, not eggs," one mother explains to her 5-year-old daughter (cited in Stolberg, 1998, p. 1). "I say that I needed these to have a baby, and there was this wonderful woman and she was willing to give me some, and that was how she helped us. I want to be honest that we got pregnant in a special way."

The "special way" referred to by this 50-year-old Los Angeles therapist is *donor* IVF. It is used when the mother-to-be does not produce ova. In donor IVF, an ovum from another woman is fertilized and injected into her uterus, where it becomes implanted and develops to term. The numbers of babies born in this manner has mushroomed over the past decade (Stolberg, 1998).

Truth or Fiction Revisited

It is true that developing embryos have been successfully transferred from the womb of one woman to the womb of another. Embryonic transfer is one method for coping with infertility.

EMBRYONIC TRANSFER A related method under study for women who do not produce ova is termed **embryonic transfer.** A volunteer is artificially inseminated by the infertile woman's partner. After several days, the embryo is removed from the volunteer and placed within the uterus of the mother-to-be, where it becomes implanted in the uterine wall and is carried to term.

SURROGATE MOTHERS Surrogate mothers have been used increasingly in recent years for women who are infertile or cannot carry embryos. The surrogate mother may be artificially inseminated by the husband of an infertile woman and carry the baby to term, or she may carry to term an embryo that is transferred to her uterus. In the first case, the baby carries the genes of only one parent. The surrogate mother in either case is usually paid a fee and signs a contract to surrender the child at birth.

PELVIC INFLAMMATORY DISEASE • Any of a number of diseases that infect the abdominal region, impairing fertility. Abbreviated *PID*.

ENDOMETRIOSIS • Inflammation of endometrial tissue (that forms the inner lining of the uterus) sloughed off into the abdominal cavity rather than out of the body during menstruation. A disease characterized by abdominal pain and impairment of fertility.

ARTIFICIAL INSEMINATION • Injection of sperm into the uterus in order to fertilize an ovum.

IN VITRO FERTILIZATION • Fertilization of an ovum in a laboratory dish.

EMBRYONIC TRANSFER • The transfer of an embryo from the uterus of one woman to that of another.

ADJUSTMENT *in the* NEW MILLENNIUM

Sperm and Egg "Donations" for Overnight Delivery?

Ellen is a 34-year-old Australian whose ovaries were ravaged by cancer treatments. She tried without luck to find an Australian woman who would donate eggs to her for 2 years. Then she learned about the Los Angeles Egg Donor Program, which advertised that it had access to "extremely bright, attractive and kindhearted" women who would donate eggs. Oh, yes, their intelligence test scores were on file.

So Ellen selected a donor from a file that included photos and data on her personality, education, family history—even her special talents. Then Ellen and her husband flew to Los Angeles. The eggs were fertilized in a laboratory dish by her husband's sperm and implanted in Ellen's uterus. The first attempt did not work, but a later attempt with a frozen embryo from the program did, and Ellen's daughter was born 9 months later.

NOT UNUSUAL Ellen's case is not unusual. The United States has become a center for infertile foreigners who are seeking sperm or egg donors. Some would-be parents want babies with an "American look," but nearly all prefer to have children of their own race. In the case of sperm donors, the American look translates into a tall man with brown or blond hair, blue or green eyes, and—of course—dimples. Of course, there are no guarantees that donors come as advertised. There have even been cases of consumer fraud.

Many foreigners turn to the United States because other countries, including England and Australia, do not permit payments to egg donors. Most countries also place limits on donation of sperm. But in the United States there are few restrictions on the buying and selling of sperm and eggs.

Donation is easy for a man: He just ejaculates into a container. Then his sperm are frozen and medically tested for health problems. Egg donors take powerful hormones to stimulate their ovaries to produce upwards of 10 eggs, and then the eggs are surgically removed. Many women who seek egg donors are women whose ovaries are not producing viable eggs. An egg from a donor is fertilized in a laboratory, and then the embryo is implanted in the recipient's uterus or frozen for future use.

In the United States commercial sperm banks advertise that they have sperm that are free of HIV and other sexually transmitted diseases. They offer to ship frozen semen around the world overnight. Donated eggs are available from centers that advertise hundreds of donors, with no waiting lists. Enthusiastic customers typically fork over between $100 and $200 for sperm and about $5,000 for eggs. Catalogues of American donors, complete with color photos, are posted on the Internet for prospective customers.

"There was no delay," Ellen said (Kolata, 1998). "We ordered it. It was like ordering a hamburger. [In Australia] it's like getting blood from a stone."

WEB SITES Prospective customers can go to Web sites, such as those of Cryobank and of the Beverly Hills Center for Surrogate Parenting and Egg Donation, and click on traits they want in donors, in categories such as religion, ethnic background, height, weight, color of eyes or hair, hair texture, blood type, education, and occupation. Some centers even allow customers to check out donors' favorite books and movies, and their philosophies of life. Donors who meet the criteria pop up. How many of us will be surfing the Web for parents in the new millennium? ■

The first kind of surrogate motherhood may seem to be the mirror image of artificial insemination of a woman with the sperm of a donor. But sperm donors usually do not know the identity of the women who have received their sperm. Nor do they observe their children developing within the mothers-to-be. However, surrogate mothers are involved in the entire process of prenatal development. They can become attached to their unborn children. Turning them over to another woman once they are born can instill a devastating sense of loss. For this reason, some surrogate mothers have refused to part with their babies. Court cases have resulted, as with the famous *"Baby M"* and *Johnson* v. *Calvert* cases (Angell, 1990; Behrens, 1990). Many of the legal issues surrounding surrogate motherhood are unresolved.

PRENATAL DEVELOPMENT

During the months following conception, the single cell formed by the union of sperm and egg will multiply—becoming two, then four, then eight, and so on. Tissues, organs, and structures will form that gradually take the unmistakable shape of a human being. By the time a fetus is ready to be born, it will contain hundreds of billions of cells—more cells than there are stars in the Milky Way galaxy.

Prenatal development is divided into three periods: the germinal stage (approximately the first 2 weeks), the embryonic stage (the first 2 months), and the fetal stage. It is also common to speak of prenatal development as lasting for three trimesters of 3 months each.

The period from conception to implantation is called the **germinal stage** or the **period of the ovum.** Prior to implantation, the baby is nourished solely by the yolk of the original egg cell, and it does not gain in mass. It can gain in mass only from outside nourishment, which it obtains once implanted in the uterine wall.

The **embryonic stage** lasts from implantation until about the eighth week of development. During this stage, the major body organ systems differentiate. The circulatory systems of mother and unborn child do not mix. A membrane in the **placenta** permits only certain substances to pass through. Oxygen and nutrients are passed from the mother to the embryo. Carbon dioxide and other wastes are passed from the child to the mother, where they are removed by the mother's lungs and kidneys. Unfortunately, a number of other substances can pass through the placenta. They include some microscopic disease organisms—such as those that cause syphilis and German measles—and some drugs, including aspirin, narcotics, alcohol, and tranquilizers.

The fetus begins to turn and respond to external stimulation at about the ninth or tenth week. By the end of the first trimester, the major organ systems have been formed. The second trimester is characterized by further maturation of fetal organ systems and dramatic gains in size. During the third trimester, the heart and lungs become capable of sustaining independent life. The fetus gains about 5½ pounds and doubles in length. Newborn boys average about 7½ pounds; newborn girls, about 7 pounds.

Environmental Influences

Scientific advances have helped us chronicle the details of prenatal development and have made us keenly aware of the types of things that can go wrong. Fortunately, they have also alerted us to ways of preventing many of these problems. Here, we consider some of the environmental factors that have an impact on our prenatal development: maternal disorders, Rh incompatibility, drugs, smoking, and parental age.

MATERNAL DISORDERS Environmental agents that harm the developing embryo or fetus are referred to as **teratogens,** from the Greek *teras,* meaning "monster." They include drugs like thalidomide and alcohol, Rh-positive antibodies, metals like lead and mercury, radiation, excessive hormones, and

GERMINAL STAGE • The period of development between conception and the implantation of the embryo in the uterine wall.
PERIOD OF THE OVUM • Another term for *germinal stage.*
EMBRYONIC STAGE • The stage of prenatal development that lasts from implantation through the eighth week, characterized by the development of the major organ systems.
PLACENTA • An organ connected to the fetus by the umbilical cord. The placenta serves as a relay station between mother and fetus for exchange of nutrients and wastes.
TERATOGEN • An agent that gives rise to abnormalities in the embryo or fetus.

AN EXERCISE CLASS FOR PREGNANT WOMEN.
Years ago the rule of thumb was that pregnant women should not exert themselves. Today it is recognized that exercise during pregnancy is healthful. Exercise promotes strength and cardiovascular fitness, which are assets during childbirth — and, of course, at other times.

pathogens. Many pathogens cannot pass through the placenta and infect the embryo, but extremely small organisms, such as those responsible for syphilis, mumps, chicken pox, and measles, can. Pregnant women may also incur disorders such as toxemia that are not passed on to the child but affect the child by altering the uterine environment.

Let us now consider the effects of alcohol and cigarettes. Effects of other teratogens are summarized in Table 18.1.

Alcohol Heavy maternal use of alcohol is linked to death of the fetus and neonate, malformations, and growth deficiencies. Many children of severe alcoholics have **fetal alcohol syndrome**, or *FAS* (USDHHS, 1992). FAS infants are often undersized, with smaller-than-average brains. They have distinct facial features, including widely spaced eyes, a flattened nose, and an underdeveloped upper jaw. There may be mental retardation, lack of coordination, limb deformities, and heart problems. FAS babies are short for their weight and tend not to catch up.

Although research suggests that light drinking is unlikely to harm the fetus in most cases (Jacobson & Jacobson, 1994), FAS has been found even among the children of mothers who drank only 2 ounces of alcohol a day during the first trimester (Astley and others, 1992). Moreover, individual sensitivities to alcohol may vary widely (Jacobson & Jacobson, 1994). The critical period for the development of the facial features associated with FAS seems to be the third and fourth week of pregnancy (Coles, 1994). At this time, women may not yet realize that they are pregnant. They may think that they are "late." Many women have light bleeding at implantation, and it is possible to confuse this "spotting" with menstruation. The message is this: Women who drink until pregnancy is confirmed may be waiting too long.

Cigarettes Nicotine and carbon monoxide, two of the ingredients of cigarette smoke, are transmitted to the fetus. The effects of nicotine are uncertain, but carbon monoxide decreases the amount of oxygen. Insufficient oxygen, or **anoxia,** has been linked to mental retardation, learning disorders, and a host of behavioral problems.

Women who smoke during pregnancy are likely to deliver babies who weigh less than those of women who do not smoke (USDHHS, 1992). Women who smoke during pregnancy are also more likely to have stillbirths, or babies who

FETAL ALCOHOL SYNDROME • A cluster of symptoms shown by children of women who drink during the embryonic stage, including characteristic facial features and developmental delays. Abbreviated *FAS.*

ANOXIA • Deprivation of oxygen.

TABLE 18.1 POSSIBLE EFFECTS ON THE FETUS OF CERTAIN AGENTS DURING PREGNANCY

AGENT	*POSSIBLE EFFECT*
Accutane (an acne drug)	Malformation, stillbirth
Alcohol	Mental retardation, addiction, hyperactivity, undersize
Aspirin (large doses)	Respiratory problems, bleeding
Bendectin	Possibility of cleft palate or heart deformities still uncertain
Caffeine (coffee, many soft drinks, chocolate, etc.)	Stimulates fetus; other effects uncertain
Carbamazepine (and other anticonvulsant drugs)	Possibility of spina bifida still uncertain
Cigarettes	Undersize, premature delivery, fetal death
Cocaine	Spontaneous abortion, neurological problems
Diethylstilbestrol (DES)	Cancer of the cervix or testes
Heavy metals (lead, mercury)	Hyperactivity, mental retardation, stillbirth
Heavy sedation during labor	Brain damage, asphyxiation
Heroin, morphine, other narcotics	Addiction, undersize
Marijuana	Possibility of early delivery, neurological problems, or birth defects still uncertain
Paint fumes (substantial exposure)	Mental retardation
PCB, dioxin, other insecticides and herbicides	Under study (possible stillbirth)
Progestin	Masculinization of female embryos; possibility of heightened aggressiveness still uncertain
Rubella (German measles)	Mental retardation, nerve damage impairing vision and hearing
Streptomycin	Deafness
Tetracycline	Yellow teeth, deformed bones
Thalidomide	Deformed or missing limbs
Vitamin A (large doses)	Cleft palate, eye damage
Vitamin D (large doses)	Mental retardation
X rays	Malformation of organs

Note: Many chemical and other agents have been found harmful to the fetus, or are strongly implicated in fetal damage. Pregnant women should consult their physicians about their diets, vitamin supplements, and use of any drugs—including over-the-counter drugs.

die soon after birth. Smoking may also have long-term effects on academic performance.

Truth or Fiction Revisited

It is true that pregnant women who smoke risk having children who are low in birth weight. Smoking deprives the fetus of oxygen.

PARENTAL AGE The twenties are an ideal time for women to bear children. Women in their middle teens and younger, and women in their late thirties and beyond show greater incidences of miscarriage, birth defects, prematurity, and infant mortality.

These negatives dismay many career women who delay marriage and childbearing. Psychologically, many women, like many men, feel that they are

TABLE 18.2 CHROMOSOMAL AND GENETIC ABNORMALITIES

Cystic fibrosis	A genetic disease in which the pancreas and lungs become clogged with mucus, impairing the processes of respiration and digestion.
Down's syndrome	A condition characterized by a third chromosome on the 21st pair in which the child shows a characteristic fold of skin over the eye and mental retardation. Risk increases with the age of the parents.
Hemophilia	A sex-linked disorder in which the blood fails to clot properly.
Huntington's chorea	A fatal neurological disorder with onset in middle adulthood.
Neural-tube defects	Disorders of the brain or spine, such as *anencephaly,* in which part of the brain is missing, and *spina bifida,* in which part of the spine is exposed or missing. Anencephaly is fatal shortly after birth, but some spina bifida victims survive for a number of years, albeit with severe handicaps.
Phenylketonuria	A disorder in which children cannot metabolize phenylalanine, which builds up in the form of phenylpyruvic acid and causes mental retardation. Diagnosed at birth and controlled by diet.
Retinoblastoma	A form of blindness caused by a dominant gene.
Sickle-cell anemia	A blood disorder that mostly afflicts African Americans and obstructs small blood vessels, decreasing their capacity to carry oxygen and heightening the risk of occasionally fatal infections
Tay-Sachs disease	A fatal neurological disorder that afflicts Jews of East European origin.

coming into their own as people in their thirties, after they have had a chance to swim in the world of business. On the positive side, well educated women over the age of 35 who receive adequate prenatal care have only a slightly higher risk of stillbirths, premature babies, or low-birth-weight babies than younger women do (Berkowitz and others, 1990). As noted by an obstetrician at the University of California at San Diego, "Given sound genetic diagnosis and counseling, together with appropriate prenatal care and the judicious management of labor and delivery, the increasing number of women postponing first pregnancies can look forward to excellent outcomes" (Resnik, 1990).

Chromosomal and Genetic Abnormalities

A number of diseases reflect chromosomal or genetic abnormalities. Some genetic abnormalities, like phenylketonuria, are caused by a single pair of genes. Others are caused by combinations of genes. Multifactorial problems reflect the interaction of nature (a genetic predisposition) and nurture (environmental factors). Diabetes mellitus, epilepsy, and peptic ulcers are multifactorial problems. A number of chromosomal and genetic abnormalities are summarized in Table 18.2.

CHROMOSOMAL ABNORMALITIES Occasionally people do not have the normal complement of 46 chromosomes, leading to behavioral and physical abnormalities. The risk of chromosomal abnormalities rises with the age of the parents (Hamamy and others, 1990).

In **Down's syndrome** the 21st pair of chromosomes has an extra, or third, chromosome. This abnormality becomes increasingly likely among older parents. With young mothers, Down's syndrome occurs in about one birth in 1,500. By age 35 the figure rises to one birth in 365, and by age 45 to one birth in every 32 (Samuels & Samuels, 1986).

DOWN'S SYNDROME • A chromosomal abnormality characterized by mental retardation and caused by an extra chromosome in the 21st pair.

Children with Down's syndrome show a downward-sloping fold of skin at the inner corners of the eyes, a round face, protruding tongue, and a broad, flat nose. Their motor development lags behind that of normal children, and they are moderately to severely mentally retarded.

Genetic Abnormalities A number of disorders are caused by defective genes. These include the enzyme disorder **phenylketonuria** (PKU), sickle-cell anemia and Tay-Sachs disease (see Table 18.2). All three are transmitted by recessive genes. Thus, children will not contract them unless both parents carry the gene. If both parents are carriers, they will be transmitted to one child in four. One child in four will *not* carry the recessive gene. The other two children in four will, like their parents, be carriers.

Children with PKU cannot metabolize the protein *phenylalanine*, which builds up as phenylpyruvic acid and damages the central nervous system. The results are mental retardation and emotional disturbance. PKU can be detected in newborn children through blood or urine tests and controlled by diet.

Sickle-cell anemia is found in many groups, but is carried by about 3 million African Americans (nearly 1 African American in 10). One Hispanic American in 20 is also a carrier. In sickle-cell anemia, red blood cells take on a sickle shape and clump together, obstructing small blood vessels and decreasing the oxygen supply. The result is increased likelihood of pneumonia, heart and kidney failure, painful and swollen joints, and jaundice.

Tay-Sachs disease is a fatal degenerative disease of the central nervous system that is most prevalent among Jews of East European origin. About 1 in 25 American Jews carries the recessive gene for the defect, so the chance that a Jewish couple will both carry the gene is about 1 in 625. Victims of Tay-Sachs disease gradually lose muscle control, become blind and deaf, retarded and paralyzed, and die by the age of 5.

Some genetic defects, such as **hemophilia,** are carried on only the X sex chromosome. They are referred to as sex-linked and are more likely to be contracted by boys than girls. Other sex-linked abnormalities include Duchenne's muscular dystrophy, diabetes, color blindness, and some types of night blindness.

Genetic Counseling and Testing

Genetic counseling aims to help parents avert predictable tragedies. In this procedure, information about a couple's genetic backgrounds is compiled to determine the possibility that their union may result in genetically defective children. Some couples whose natural children would be at high risk for genetic diseases elect to adopt.

Pregnant women may also confirm the presence of certain chromosomal and genetic abnormalities through amniocentesis or chorionic villus sampling (CVS). Amniocentesis is usually carried out about 14 to 17 weeks after conception. CVS can be done at 9 to 12 weeks. In **amniocentesis,** fluid is withdrawn from the amniotic sac (also called the bag of waters) containing the fetus. Sloughed-off fetal cells are grown in a culture, and examined microscopically. In **chorionic villus sampling,** a small tube is inserted through the vagina and into the uterus, and pieces of material are snipped off from the outer membrane that envelops the amniotic sac and fetus. Most health care professionals prefer amniocentesis to CVS because the procedure carries somewhat lower risks. But parents often want to know whether their babies are normal before the results of amniocentesis are in. Therefore, many health care providers now carry out amniocentesis at 12 to 13 weeks into pregnancy (Gilbert, 1993).

Phenylketonuria • A genetic abnormality in which phenylpyruvic acid builds up and causes mental retardation.

Sickle-cell anemia • A genetic disorder that decreases the blood's capacity to carry oxygen.

Tay-Sachs disease • A fatal genetic neurological disorder.

Hemophilia • A genetic disorder in which blood does not clot properly.

Genetic counseling • Advice concerning the probabilities that a couple's children will show genetic abnormalities.

Amniocentesis • A procedure for drawing and examining fetal cells sloughed off into amniotic fluid in order to determine the presence of various disorders.

Chorionic villus sampling • A method for detecting genetic abnormalities that samples the membrane enveloping the amniotic sac and fetus.

These tests are commonly carried out with women who become pregnant past the age of 35 because of increased chances of Down's syndrome. The tests also detect sickle-cell anemia, Tay-Sachs disease, spina bifida, muscular dystrophy, and Rh incompatibility in the fetus. The tests also permit parents to learn the gender of their unborn child. The tests carry some risks, however, and it would be unwise to have them done solely for this purpose.

Another method is the formation of a picture of the fetus through **ultrasound.** The picture is called a *sonogram.* Ultrasound is so high in pitch that it cannot be detected by the human ear. However, it can be bounced off the unborn child in the same way that radar is bounced off airborne objects. Ultrasound is used with amniocentesis to determine the position of the fetus. Ultrasound is also used to locate fetal structures when intrauterine transfusions are necessary for the survival of the unborn child in Rh disease.

A variety of disorders can be detected by testing parents' blood. The genes causing sickle-cell anemia and Tay-Sachs disease can be detected in this way. If both parents carry the genes, their presence in the fetus can be confirmed by amniocentesis or CVS. Another blood test, the **alphafetoprotein assay,** detects neural-tube defects.

ULTRASOUND • Sound waves too high in pitch to be sensed by the human ear.

ALPHAFETOPROTEIN ASSAY • A blood test that assesses the mother's blood level of alphafetoprotein, a substance that is linked with fetal neural-tube defects.

FETOSCOPY • Surgical insertion of a narrow tube into the uterus in order to examine the fetus.

In **fetoscopy** a narrow tube is surgically inserted through the abdomen into the uterus to allow examination of the fetus. A small lens can be attached to the scope, permitting visual examination. A small needle may also be attached, which enables the direct withdrawal of a blood sample from the fetus. Fetoscopy, like CVS, is riskier than amniocentesis. Use is thus limited.

Adjustment in a World of DIVERSITY

Some Notes on Prenatal Care: A Tale of Three Neighborhoods

The United States is many nations, not one. The United States may have the world's most sophisticated medical technology, yet the care that is received by poor people—and, often, middle-class people—places many of us in the "Third World."

TABLE 18.3 INFANT HEALTH STATISTICS FOR THREE NEW YORK CITY NEIGHBORHOODS

INFANT HEALTH STATISTICS	*EAST HARLEM*	*ASTORIA–LONG ISLAND CITY*	*KIPS BAY–YORKVILLE*
Infant deaths per 1,000 live births	23.4	14.9	7.3
Low-birth-weight babies per 100 live births (less than 5.5 pounds)	18.5	6.1	6.0
Very low-birth-weight babies per 100 live births (less than 3.3 pounds)	3.8	0.98	0.87
Live births per 100 in which mothers received late or no prenatal care	35.8	10.4	6.1

Note: This table shows infant health statistics for three New York City neighborhoods. East Harlem is a heavily studied inner-city area that is characterized by poverty and a high proportion of minority residents. The Astoria–Long Island City area is populated by middle-income residents. Kips Bay–Yorkville is a high-income area.
Source: Department of Health, City of New York, 1990.

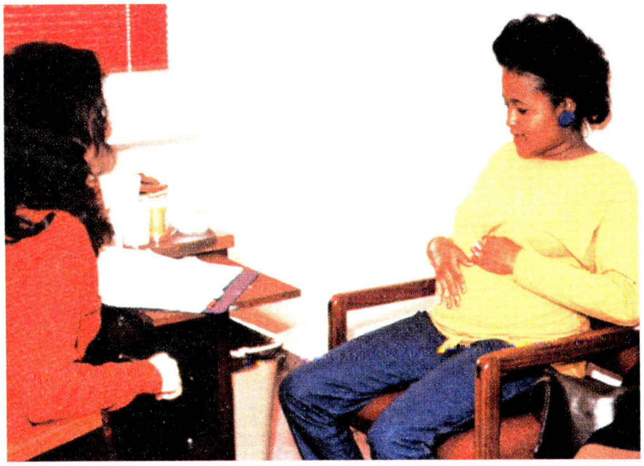

PRENATAL CARE — NATIONS WITHIN NATIONS.
Although the United States has the world's most advanced medical technology, this technology is not equally available to all people who live in the United States. Affluent people are highly likely to receive a comprehensive prenatal care program. Less affluent people receive more sporadic care, if they receive care at all.

Consider Table 18.3, which shows infant health statistics obtained from public records in New York City in 1990. Note that the predominantly White residents of the relatively wealthy Kips Bay–Yorkville area have healthier newborns than residents of East Harlem (a low-income neighborhood made up mostly of African Americans and Hispanic Americans) or of the mainly White, middle-income residents of Astoria–Long Island City. East Harlem mothers, like other low-income mothers (McLaughlin and others, 1992), were more likely than their middle- and upper-income counterparts to have babies with low birth weights and babies who died during infancy. Maternal malnutrition and use of chemical substances such as alcohol and tobacco during pregnancy have all been linked to low birth weights and increased mortality during the first year of life (McLaughlin and others, 1992; Wardlaw & Insel, 1990).

The differences in infant health shown in the table are also connected with the incidence of prenatal care received by the mothers in the three neighborhoods. According to 1990 New York City Department of Health records, nearly 36 percent of East Harlem mothers receive either late prenatal care or none, as compared with about 6 percent in Kips Bay–Yorkville and about 10 percent in Astoria–Long Island City. Research has shown, however, that comprehensive prenatal care is connected with higher birth weights (McLaughlin and others, 1992).

There is some possibility that genetic factors are involved in the tendency for African American children to be born underweight, but use of health care appears to play a more important role. For example, a study of newborn babies in Illinois shows that African American women who were born in sub-Saharan Africa have fewer underweight babies than African American women who were born in the United States (Kilborn, 1998).

CHILDBIRTH

During the last days of her pregnancy, Susan continued to, as she put it, "drag myself into work. I wasn't just going to sit home all day watching *As the World Turns* like a dunce." Your first author has (secretly) watched *As the World Turns* since the character Dr. Bob Hughes was a little boy, so he ignored the remark. (Your second author does not watch soap operas.) She added,

> But since I was so exhausted by the time I got to the office, I sat behind my desk like—well—half a dunce. I also couldn't get my mind off the pregnancy—what it was going to be like when I finally delivered Jason,

or, I should say, when he finally delivered me. I'd had the amniocentesis, but I was still hoping and praying everything would be normal with him. And it was just so darned[1] hard to get around.

During the last weeks of pregnancy it is normal, especially for first-time mothers, to worry about the mechanics of delivery and whether the child will be normal. As they near full **term,** women become increasingly heavy and literally bent out of shape. It may require a feat of balance and ingenuity to get up from a chair or out of bed. Sitting behind a steering wheel—and reaching the wheel—becomes a challenge of life. Muscle tension from supporting the fetus and intrauterine material may cause backaches. At this time, many women have the feeling that their pregnancies will never come to an end.

They do, of course. Or else this book would not have been written.

The mechanisms that initiate and maintain labor are not fully understood, but the fetus may chemically signal the mother when it is mature enough to sustain independent life. Fetal hormones may stimulate the placenta and uterus to secrete prostaglandins. Prostaglandins, in turn, cause labor contractions by exciting the muscles of the uterus. Later during labor the pituitary gland releases **oxytocin,** a hormone that stimulates contractions strong enough to expel the baby.

Now let us consider the stages of childbirth, methods of childbirth, and some of the problems that can attend childbirth. In our discussion we shall refer to the many things that women can do to moderate the impact of stress, such as enhancing predictability, exercising control, and receiving social support.

The Stages of Childbirth

Childbirth begins with the onset of regular uterine contractions and is described in three stages.

THE FIRST STAGE In the first stage of childbirth, uterine contractions cause the cervix to become **effaced** and **dilated** so that the baby may pass. Most of the pain of childbirth is caused by the stretching of the cervix. When the cervix dilates easily and quickly, there may be little or no pain.

The first stage may last from a few minutes to a couple of days. Twelve to 24 hours is about average for a first pregnancy. Later pregnancies require about half the time. Initial contractions are not usually very painful. They may be spaced 15 to 20 minutes apart and last from 45 seconds to a minute.

As time elapses, contractions become frequent, regular, and strong. A woman is usually informed to go the hospital when they are 4 to 5 minutes apart.

THE SECOND STAGE The second stage begins when the baby first appears at the opening of the birth canal. The second stage is shorter than the first, lasting from a few minutes to a few hours, and ending with the birth of the baby.

With each contraction, the skin surrounding the birth canal stretches farther, and the baby is pushed farther along. When the baby's head starts to emerge from the birth canal, it is said to have *crowned.* Typically, the baby then fully emerges within a few minutes.

TERM • A set period of time.
OXYTOCIN • A pituitary hormone that stimulates labor contractions.
EFFACE • To rub out or wipe out; to become thin.
DILATE • To make wider or larger.

[1]This word has been modified in order to maintain the decorum required of a college textbook.

When the baby's head has crowned, the obstetrician, nurse, or midwife may perform an **episiotomy.** Most women do not feel the incision because pressure from the baby's emerging head tends to numb the area. The incision may cause itching and, in some cases, stabbing pain as it heals. Discomfort from an episiotomy may interfere with sexual relations for months following delivery. Still, most physicians argue that an episiotomy is preferable to random tearing when they see that the tissue of the **perineum** is becoming severely effaced.

In the New World The baby's passageway to the outside world is at best a tight fit. For this reason, the baby's head and facial features may be distended. The head may be elongated, the nose flattened, the ears bent. It can look as though our new arrival had been in a prizefight. Parents are frequently concerned about whether things will return to their proper shapes, but usually they do.

Once the baby's head emerges from the mother's body, mucus is usually aspirated from its mouth by suction, so that the passageway for breathing will not be obstructed. Aspiration is frequently repeated when the baby is fully delivered. Because of the use of suction, the baby is no longer routinely held upside down to help expel mucus. There is also no need for the baby to be slapped on the buttocks to stimulate independent breathing, as we see in old films.

Once the baby is breathing on its own, the **umbilical cord,** through which it had received oxygen from the mother, is clamped and severed. The stump will dry and fall off. Whether the child will have an "inny" or an "outy" has nothing to do with the expertise or cosmetic preferences of the obstetrician.

The baby may then be taken by a nurse, so that various procedures can be performed while the mother is in the third stage of labor. The baby is usually given an identification bracelet and footprinted. Drops of silver nitrate or an antibiotic ointment (erythromycin) are put into the baby's eyes to prevent infection. The newborn may also receive an injection of vitamin K to ensure that its blood will clot in case of bleeding.

Truth or Fiction Revisited

It is not true that babies are slapped on the buttocks soon after birth to clear passageways for air and to stimulate independent breathing. The contemporary method for clearing passageways and stimulating breathing is aspiration.

Truth or Fiction Revisited

It is not true that whether a child will have an "inny" or an "outy" for a belly button depends on the way that the umbilical cord is cut. The stump dries and falls off on its own.

THE THIRD STAGE During the third or *placental* stage of childbirth, which may last from a few minutes to an hour or more, the placenta separates from the uterine wall and is expelled along with fetal membranes. There may be some bleeding, and the uterus begins the process of contracting to a smaller size. The attending physician sews the episiotomy and any tears in the perineum.

Methods of Childbirth

Until the twentieth century, childbirth typically was an intimate home procedure involving the mother, a **midwife,** family, and friends. Today in the United States it is most often a hospital procedure performed by a physician. He or she may use surgical instruments, antibiotics, and anesthetics to help protect mother and child from infection, complications, and pain. While the use of modern medicine has saved lives, it has also made childbearing more impersonal. Social critics argue that it has, to a large degree, wrested control over their own bodies from women and, through drugs, denied them the experience of giving birth.

Next, we consider a number of contemporary methods for facilitating childbirth.

MEDICATED CHILDBIRTH

In sorrow thou shalt bring forth children.

GENESIS 3:16

EPISIOTOMY • A surgical incision in the perineum that widens the vaginal opening, preventing random tearing during childbirth.

PERINEUM • The area between the female's genital region and the anus.

UMBILICAL CORD • A tube that connects that fetus to the placenta.

MIDWIFE • A woman who helps other women in childbirth.

The Bible suggests that the ancients saw suffering during childbirth as a woman's lot. But today, some anesthesia is used in more than 90 percent of American deliveries.

General anesthesia puts the woman to sleep. Sodium pentothal, a barbiturate, is frequently used and injected into the vein of the arm. Tranquilizers such as Valium and Librium and orally taken barbiturates are not anesthetics. They reduce anxiety, which can compound the stress of pain. Narcotics such as Demerol also blunt perception of pain.

General anesthetics, tranquilizers, and narcotics decrease the strength of uterine contractions during delivery and, by crossing the placenta, lower the responsiveness of the baby. There is little suggestion of serious long-term effects, however.

Regional anesthetics, or **local anesthetics**—also termed *blocks*—attempt to dull the pain of childbirth without depressing the mother's nervous system or putting her to sleep. But local anesthesia does diminish the strength and activity levels of babies, at least shortly following birth. Again, we are not aware of serious long-term effects.

Women who have general anesthesia show more negative feelings about childbirth and the baby than women using other methods. Women who receive blocks have relatively more positive feelings about childbirth and their babies but feel detached from the birth process.

Truth or Fiction Revisited

It is not true that women who give birth by the Lamaze method do not have pain. However, they may have less pain than other women and cope better overall.

PREPARED CHILDBIRTH: THE LAMAZE METHOD The French obstetrician Fernand Lamaze (1981) visited the Soviet Union in 1951 and found that many Russian women appeared to bear babies without anesthetics or pain. Lamaze took back to Western Europe with him the techniques of the Russian women, and during the 1950s they were brought to the United States as the **Lamaze method,** or *prepared childbirth.* Lamaze argues that women can learn to *dissociate* uterine contractions from pain and fear by associating *other* responses with contractions. Women can be taught to think of pleasant images such as beach scenes during delivery. They can also lessen pain through breathing and relaxation exercises.

A woman attends Lamaze classes accompanied by a "coach." The coach—usually the father—will aid her during delivery by timing contractions, offering moral support, and directing her patterns of breathing and relaxation. During each contraction, the woman breathes in a specific, rehearsed manner. She is taught how to relax muscle groups throughout the body, then to contract a single muscle while others remain at ease. The rationale is that during labor she will be able, on cue, to keep other muscles relaxed while the uterus contracts. In this way she will conserve energy, minimize tension and pain, and feel less anxiety. Too, muscles that will be used during delivery, such as leg muscles, are strengthened through exercise.

The woman is also educated about childbirth and given an agenda of things to do during delivery. The father is integrated into the process. The marital relationship is apparently strengthened and the woman feels less alone during delivery as a result (Dooker, 1980; Wideman & Singer, 1984). The father as well as the mother take pride in "their" accomplishment. Women apparently also report less pain and ask for less medication when their husbands are present (Henneborn & Cogan, 1975). (If she can put up with one pain, she can put up with another?)

The Lamaze method appears to decrease the stress of childbirth. Women using the method have generally positive feelings about childbirth and about their babies. Still, they usually report some pain and often request anesthetics. How, then, does the Lamaze method help? Perhaps in part, it is because women enhance their self-efficacy expectancies by taking charge

GENERAL ANESTHESIA • The process of eliminating pain by putting the person to sleep.

LOCAL ANESTHETIC • A method that reduces pain in an area of the body.

LAMAZE METHOD • A childbirth method in which women are educated about childbirth, learn to relax and breathe in patterns that conserve energy and lessen pain, and have a coach (usually the father) present during childbirth. Also termed *prepared childbirth.*

of their own delivery (Dooker, 1980). They become knowledgeable and see themselves as the actors in the process, not as victims who need the guidance of the doctor. The breathing and relaxation exercises do not fully eradicate pain, but they give the woman coping strategies and something else to focus on.

CESAREAN SECTION In a **cesarean section,** the baby is delivered by surgery rather than through the vagina. Incisions are made in the abdomen and the uterus, and the baby is removed. The incisions are sewn. In most cases the mother is capable of walking about on the same day, although there is discomfort. In previous years, the incisions left visible scars, but today C-sections tend to be performed near the top line of the pubic hair. This "bikini cut" is all but invisible.

C-sections are most likely to be advised when normal delivery is difficult or threatening to the mother or child. Vaginal deliveries can become difficult if the baby is large or in distress, or if the mother's pelvis is small or she is tired or weak. Herpes and HIV infections in the birth canal can be bypassed by C-section. Babies are normally born head first, and C-sections are also likely to be performed if the baby is going to be born feet first or sideways.

Use of the C-section has mushroomed. Today nearly 1 of every 4 births is by C-section (DiMatteo and others, 1996; Paul, 1996). Compare this figure to about 1 in 10 births in 1975. The increased rate of C-sections reflects advances in medical technology, such as use of fetal monitors that allow doctors to detect fetal distress, fear of malpractice suits, financial incentives for hospitals and physicians, and, simply, current medical practice (DiMatteo and others, 1996). The Centers for Disease Control and Prevention (CDC) believes that 15 cesareans per 100 births can be medically justified (Paul, 1996).

Some negative emotional consequences are connected with C-sections. For example, women who have C-sections report being less satisfied with the birth process, are less likely to breast-feed, and interact somewhat less with their infants in the hospital and upon arrival back home (DiMatteo and others, 1996).

Medical opinion once held that once a woman had a C-section, subsequent deliveries also had to be by C-section. Otherwise, uterine scars might rupture during labor. Research has shown that rupture is rare, however (McMahon and others, 1996). Today, many women with previous C-sections are delivering vaginally.

The Postpartum Period

The weeks following delivery are called the **postpartum period.** The first few days of postpartum are often happy enough. The long wait is over. The fear and pain of labor are done with. In the great majority of cases the baby is normal, and the mother may be pleased that she is getting her "figure back." However, women are more likely to feel depressed within a few weeks after bearing children than they are otherwise (Pitman and others, 1990; Troutman & Cutrona, 1990).

MATERNAL DEPRESSION Women may encounter various emotional problems during the postpartum period. Among these are maternity blues, postpartum depression, and postpartum psychosis (DeAngelis, 1997c).

Maternity blues—also called "baby blues"—affects as many as three quarters of women during the first few weeks after delivery (DeAngelis, 1997c). Baby blues are characterized by sadness, crying, and irritability. The hormonal changes that accompany and follow delivery may help trigger the baby blues.

CESAREAN SECTION • A method of childbirth in which the baby is delivered through abdominal surgery.

POSTPARTUM PERIOD • The period that immediately follows childbirth.

MATERNITY BLUES • Crying and feelings of sadness, anxiety and tension, irritability, and anger that many women experience for a few days after childbirth.

SELECTING AN OBSTETRICIAN

WHAT DO *You* SAY NOW?

Congratulations! You're pregnant. You are about to have one of the most stimulating experiences of your life. But pregnancy is stressful physically and carries a number of life changes. One of the things that you need to do very soon is to select an obstetrician. Doing so will make things more healthful and less stressful for you and your baby. Many women learn about obstetricians from friends and relatives. Others, especially women in a new locale, rely on the phonebook.

In either case, there are things you will want to know about the obstetrician, questions that you will need to ask. Many of them concern the degree to which the obstetrician will allow you to be in control of your own childbirth. Write down some of the things you would be interested in asking in the spaces below, and then see the following material for some suggestions.

1. ______________________________
____
2. ______________________________
____
3. ______________________________
____
4. ______________________________
____

1. As in consulting any helping professional, you might be interested in inquiring about the obstetrician's academic credentials and experience. Degrees, licenses, and certificates about residencies should be displayed. If they are not, you might want to ask why. Now get going on your other questions. Ask a lot of them; you're going to be bursting with questions over the next several months, and if your obstetrician does not handle them well now, you would be in for a long, uncomfortable haul with him or her.
2. You might want to ask what kinds of problems the obstetrician runs into most often and how he or she handles them. This is an indirect way of inquiring about frequency of cesareans, for example, and you never know what bombshells will be dropped when you ask an open-ended question.
3. Of course, you can follow up by asking directly, "What percentage of your deliveries are cesareans?" Remember that 25 percent seems to be the norm these days. If you lean in the direction of not wanting a C-section unless absolutely necessary, you can also ask something like, "I've been reading that too many cesareans are done these days. What do you think?"
4. Ask something like, "What are your attitudes toward medication?" You'll quickly get a sense of whether the obstetrician is open minded about medication and willing to follow your lead.
5. Ask something like, "What do you see as the role of the father during childbirth?" You'll quickly learn whether the obstetrician's attitudes coincide with your own.
6. You may also want to ask questions about the obstetrician's beliefs concerning routine testing, weight gains, vitamin supplements, use of amniocentesis or ultrasound, and a whole range of issues. Each will give you an opportunity to determine how the obstetrician is relating to you as a person as well as to obtain specific information.
7. Finally, we have something not to say, but to observe. See how the obstetrician handles you during the initial examination. You should have the feeling that you are being handled gently, respectfully, and competently. If you're not sure, try some comparison shopping. It's your body and your child, and you have the right to gather enough information so that you are confident you are making the right choice. ■

POSTPARTUM DEPRESSION • More severe, prolonged depression that afflicts some women after childbirth, and is characterized by sadness, apathy, feelings of worthlessness, difficulty concentrating, and physical symptoms.

Baby blues are more common following a first pregnancy, and they may reflect, in part, the mother's adjustment to the changes that are about to take place in her daily life. New fathers too may feel overwhelmed or unable to cope. Perhaps more fathers might experience "paternity blues" but for the fact that mothers generally perform most of the childrearing chores.

As many as 1 woman in 5 to 10 experiences a more serious problem called **postpartum depression** (PPD). PPD can last for several weeks or months following delivery (DeAngelis, 1997c; O'Hara and others, 1991). PPD is characterized by extreme sadness, apathy, despair, feelings of worthlessness, difficulty concentrating, and changes in sleep and appetite patterns. Although the disorder is labeled as depression, some women show more anxiety or obsessive-compulsiveness (as in ruminating endlessly over details) than sadness.

PPD may reflect a combination of physiological and psychological factors, including a dropoff in estrogen (Gilbert, 1996a). Women with PPD are also more likely than those with baby blues to have had feelings of depression prior to and during pregnancy (O'Hara and others, 1991). PPD, like the baby blues, may be heightened by concerns about maternal adequacy and the life changes that the new baby will entail (Ruble and others, 1990). Stresses such as marital problems and the challenges of adjusting to a sick or unwanted baby also increase susceptibility to PPD (Terry and others, 1996; Zelkowitz & Milet, 1996).

Infants with so-called difficult temperaments may also contribute to PPD. Their intense emotional reactions, crying, and irregular sleeping and eating habits are stressful in themselves. They also place a severe strain on the mother's sense of competence (Cutrona & Troutman, 1986; Whiffen & Gotlib, 1989).

Psychosocial factors such as high self-esteem and social support are helpful to the mother at this time (Campbell and others, 1992; Leadbeatter & Linares, 1992; Terry and others, 1996). So is psychotherapy (O'Hara, 1996). Antidepressant medications and increasing estrogen levels are also helpful in many cases (Gilbert, 1996a). Some women whose main symptoms are anxiety and tension profit from relaxation training (Feingold, 1997). But even without social support, psychotherapy, or medication, the moods of most depressed mothers improve within a few months (Fleming and others, 1992).

Perhaps 1 new mother in 1,000 experiences **postpartum psychosis.** This is a break in reality that may have rapid upswings in mood as well as downs, even hallucinations and delusions. Some mothers with postpartum psychosis physically abuse their infants—but reaction occurs in only a minority of the women diagnosed with this condition (Feingold, 1997).

HOW TO BE AN AUTHORITATIVE PARENT: REARING COMPETENT CHILDREN

This book has aimed to enhance readers' competence to cope with the challenges of their lives. Research by psychologist Diana Baumrind suggests that we, as parents, may also be able to foster what Baumrind calls **instrumental competence** in our children. Instrumentally competent children can manipulate their environments to achieve desired effects. They are also energetic and friendly. Compared to other children, they show self-reliance and independence, maturity in the formation of goals, achievement motivation, cooperation, self-assertion, and exploratory behavior.

How does competence develop? Diana Baumrind (1973; Lamb & Baumrind, 1978) studied the relationship between parenting styles and the development of competence. She focused on four aspects of parental behavior: strictness; demands for the child to achieve intellectual, emotional, and social maturity; communication ability; and warmth and involvement. The three most important parenting styles she found are the *authoritative, authoritarian,* and *permissive* styles.

1. *Authoritative parents.* The parents of the most competent children rate high in all four areas of behavior (see Table 18.4). They are strict (restrictive) and demand mature behavior. However, they temper their strictness

POSTPARTUM PSYCHOSIS • Depression following childbirth in which there is relatively further impairment in ability to meet the demands of daily life than found in postpartum depression.

INSTRUMENTAL COMPETENCE • Ability to manipulate the environment to achieve desired effects.

TABLE 18.4 PARENTING STYLES

	PARENTAL BEHAVIOR			
STYLE OF PARENTING	**RESTRICTIVENESS**	**DEMANDS FOR MATURE BEHAVIOR**	**COMMUNICATION ABILITY**	**WARMTH AND SUPPORT**
AUTHORITARIAN	High (use of force)	Moderate	Low	Low
AUTHORITATIVE	High (use of reasoning)	High	High	High
PERMISSIVE	Low (easygoing)	Low	Low	Low

Note: According to Baumrind, the children of authoritative parents are most competent. The children of permissive parents are the least mature.

and demands with willingness to reason with their children, and they do so with love and support. They expect a lot, but they explain why and offer help. Baumrind labeled these parents **authoritative** parents to suggest that they know what they want but are also loving and respectful of their children.

2. *Authoritarian parents.* **Authoritarian** parents view obedience as a virtue to be pursued for its own sake. They have strict guidelines about what is right and wrong, and they demand that their children adhere to those guidelines. Both authoritative and authoritarian parents are strict. However, authoritative parents explain their demands and are supportive, whereas authoritarian parents rely on force and communicate poorly with their children. They do not respect their children's points of view, and they may be cold and rejecting. When their children ask them why they should behave in a certain way, authoritarian parents often answer, "Because I say so!"
3. *Permissive parents.* **Permissive** parents are generally easygoing with their children. As a result, the children do pretty much whatever they wish. Permissive parents are warm and supportive, but poor at communicating.

Research evidence shows that warmth is superior to coldness in rearing children. Children of warm parents are more likely to be socially and emotionally well adjusted and to internalize moral standards—that is, to develop a conscience (MacDonald, 1992; Miller and others, 1993).

Strictness also appears to pay off, provided that it is tempered by reason and warmth. Children of authoritative parents have greater self-reliance, self-esteem, social competence, and achievement motivation than other children do (Baumrind, 1991; Dumas & LaFreniere, 1993; Putallaz & Hefflin, 1990). Children of authoritarian parents are often withdrawn or aggressive, and they usually do not do as well in school as children of authoritative parents (Olson and others, 1992; Westerman, 1990). Children of permissive parents seem to be the least mature. They are frequently impulsive, moody, and aggressive. In adolescence, lack of parental monitoring is often linked to delinquency and poor academic performance.

So it seems that we can offer a tentative prescription for promoting competence in children:

1. Be reasonably restrictive. Don't allow your children to "run wild." But exert control by using reasoning rather than force.
2. Do not hesitate to demand mature behavior. However, temper these demands by knowledge of what your child *can* do at a given stage of development.

Truth or Fiction Revisited

It is true that children with strict parents are most likely to become competent. This is especially so when the parents also reason with their children and are loving and supportive.

AUTHORITATIVE • Descriptive of parents who demand mature behavior, reason with their children, and provide love and encouragement.

AUTHORITARIAN • Descriptive of parents who demand obedience for its own sake.

PERMISSIVE • Descriptive of parents who do not make demands of, or attempt to control, their children.

3. Explain why you make certain demands to your children. At an early age, the explanation can be simple: "That hurts!" or "You're breaking things that are important to Mommy and Daddy!" The point is to help your child develop a sense of values that he or she can use to form judgments and self-regulate behavior.
4. Frequently express love and caring—use lots of hugs and kisses. Show strong approval of your child's achievements (playing independently for a few minutes at the age of 2 is an achievement).

The choices are yours. But Baumrind's research may be of more than descriptive value.

ISSUES IN CHILDREARING

There are too many issues to elaborate on in any single book, much less part of one chapter. In this section we focus on two issues that are of concern to today's parents. First, since most of the women reading this book will be career women, they are likely to be interested in the research on breast-feeding versus bottle-feeding. Half of today's marriages end in divorce, so the second topic concerns the effects of divorce on children. Later, the chapter's "Adjustment and Modern Life" feature addresses two other important topics: day care and child abuse.

Breast-Feeding Versus Bottle-Feeding: Does It Make a Difference?

The decision as to whether or not to breast-feed is not taken lightly by most parents. There are a number of concerns about their relative physical and psychological merits. There are also political issues in that breast-feeding is associated with the stereotypical feminine role. Many mothers therefore ask themselves what breast- or bottle-feeding will mean for them as women.

Why do parents bottle-feed their children? Personal preferences concerning lifestyles and financial pressures prompt many new mothers to remain in the workforce. Some parents prefer to share child-feeding responsibilities, and the father is equipped to hold a bottle. Other women simply find bottle-feeding more convenient.

MOTHER'S MILK: THE ULTIMATE FAST FOOD? Mother's milk has been referred to as the ultimate fast food and as the perfect health food. The American Academy of Pediatrics summarizes the benefits of breast-feeding as follows ("Breast-Feeding Revision," 1997):

- Breast milk is tailored specifically to human digestion.
- Breast milk contains all essential nutrients in their most usable form.
- Breast milk varies in nutritional content according to the changing needs of the infant.
- Breast milk contains antibodies that can prevent problems such as ear infections and bacterial meningitis.
- Breast milk helps protect against infant diarrhea and childhood lymphoma (a form of cancer).
- Breast milk is less likely than formula to give rise to allergic responses and constipation.
- Breast milk even reduces the likelihood of obesity in later life.

Truth or Fiction Revisited

It is not true that breast-feeding and bottle-feeding are equally healthful for the child. Breast milk contains the mother's antibodies and is less likely than formula to give rise to allergic responses.

- Breast-feeding is even healthful for the mother, reducing the risk of early breast cancer, ovarian cancer, and the hip fractures that result from osteoporosis following menopause.

Perhaps because of knowledge of these benefits, the majority (about 60 percent) of American women breast-feed their babies. However, the Academy recommends breast-feeding for at least a year, and only about 20 percent of women continue past 6 months ("Breast-Feeding Revision," 1997).

The Children of Divorce

Divorce requires many adjustments for children as well as for parents. In addition to the miseries of the divorce itself, divorce carries a multitude of life changes.

Divorce turns the children's world topsy-turvy. The simple things that had been taken for granted are no longer simple: Activities such as eating meals and going on trips with both parents, curling up with both parents to read a book or watch television, and kissing both parents at bedtime come to an end. Divorced parents must support two households, not one. Children of divorce thus most often suffer downward movement in socioeconomic status. If the downward movement is not severe, it may require minor adjustments. But many children who live in father-absent homes scrape by below the poverty level. In severe cases, the downward trend can mean moving from a house into a cramped apartment, or from a more desirable to a less desirable neighborhood. The mother may suddenly be required to join or rejoin the workforce and place her children in day care. Such women typically suffer the stresses of task overload, as well as the other problems of divorce.

Truth or Fiction Revisited

It is true that divorce is more stressful for young children than for adolescents. Younger children do not understand what is happening as well and haven't developed methods for coping as well as adolescents have.

One of the major conflicts between parents is differences in childrearing practices. Children of parents who get a divorce have frequently heard them arguing about how they should be reared, so young children may erroneously blame themselves. Younger children also tend to be fearful of the unknown. Adolescents have had more of an opportunity to learn that they can exert some control over what happens to them (Kurdek and others, 1981).

The great majority of the children of divorce live with their mothers. Fathers usually see their children frequently during the first months after the divorce, but visitation often drops precipitously (Clingempeel & Repucci, 1982). Also, about two thirds of fathers do not keep up child support, exacerbating the family's downward trend in socioeconomic status.

Research results are mixed concerning the effects of divorce. Children's problems tend to increase during the first year after divorce, but they regain much of their equilibrium after 2 years. There are some gender differences. Boys have greater problems adjusting to conflict or divorce, manifested by conduct problems at school and increased anxiety and dependence (Grych & Fincham, 1993; Holden & Ritchie, 1991). After a couple of years go by, girls by and large cannot be distinguished in terms of general adjustment from girls from intact families.

Wallerstein and Blakeslee (1989) suggest more lasting problems. Even 10 years after divorce, about 40 percent of the children in their case studies show problems like anxiety, academic underachievement, self-depreciation, and anger. The authors also report a "sleeper effect." Children who are apparently adjusting have problems later on, such as when they are about to enter their own intimate relationships. They may find, for example, that they do not trust their partners to make lasting commitments.

Researchers attribute children's problems not only to divorce itself, but also to a decline in the quality of parenting that may follow (Wallerstein &

"Good evening. I am Martha's son by a previous marriage."

Blakeslee, 1989). The organization of family life tends to deteriorate. The family is more likely to eat their meals "pick-up style." Children are less likely to get to school on time or to bed at a regular hour. It is more difficult for a single mother to set limits on her son's behavior. A research group headed by E. Mavis Hetherington (1977) found that divorced parents, on the whole, are significantly less likely to show the authoritative behaviors that foster instrumental competence (see Table 18.4). They make fewer demands for mature behavior, decline in communication ability, and show less nurturance and warmth. Disciplinary methods become inconsistent. Not only do children believe that they can get away with more, they also come to see their worlds as unstructured places. As a consequence, their anxiety levels increase.

Children's adjustment to divorce is facilitated when parents maintain their commitment to the children and set aside their own disputes long enough to agree on childrearing practices (Hetherington, 1979; Wallerstein & Blakeslee, 1989). It is helpful for divorced parents to encourage each other to continue to play roles in their children's lives and to avoid saying negative things about each other in front of the children.

STEPPARENT FAMILIES Today 70 percent to 75 percent of divorced people get remarried, usually within 5 years. Of the children born today, 35 percent can expect to spend some part of their lives in a stepfamily. So the effects of stepparenting are also a key issue in American family life.

Most investigators find that living in stepfamilies as opposed to nuclear families has little psychological impact (Ganong & Coleman, 1984). Stepfathers can have positive effects on stepsons, and stepmothers on stepdaughters. In a study of the effects of stepparenting on middle schoolers, positive stepmother-stepchild relationships were associated with lower aggression in boys and girls and with higher self-esteem in girls (Clingempeel & Segal, 1986). Frequent visits with the nonresident natural mother appeared to impair stepmother-stepdaughter relations. Perhaps they encouraged resistance by stepdaughters to forming a relationship with the stepmother. On the other hand, stepmother-stepdaughter relationships generally improved over time.

However, there are some risks to living in stepfamilies. For example, the incidence of infanticide (killing infants) is 60 times as great in stepfamilies as in genetically related families (Daly & Wilson, 1998). The incidence of sexual abuse by a stepparent is about eight times as high as by a parent. There are traditional psychosocial explanations for the incidences of such problems in stepfamilies—referring, for example, to the greater emotional instability and economic stress that is often found in stepfamilies. But sociobiologists speculate that genes might have something to do with it. Perhaps, the theory goes, stepparents are less invested in rearing the children of other people and may even see other people's children as standing in the way of their chances of passing on their own genes through their own biological children (Brody, 1998b).

SHOULD CONFLICTED PARENTS STAY TOGETHER FOR THE SAKE OF THE CHILDREN? It is good for divorced parents to cooperate in rearing their children. Is it also better for the children for parents to remain together despite their differences? It depends on how they behave in front of the children. Marital conflict or fighting is connected with the same kinds of problems as divorce (Amato & Keith, 1991; Davies & Cummings, 1994). It causes psychological distress in both children and adolescents (Erel & Burman, 1995; Harold and others, 1997). Developmental psychologist E. Mavis Hetherington actually argues that "Divorce is often a positive solution to destructive family functioning" (1979, p. 857). Many questions about the long-term effects of divorce on children remain unanswered.

adjustment and modern life

One of the facts of modern life is that most American mothers are in the workforce. As we cross into the new millennium, fewer than 10 percent of U.S. families fit the once traditional model of the breadwinner husband and the full-time homemaker wife (Saluter, 1995). Today about two mothers in three work outside the home. This figure includes more than half of mothers of children who are younger than 1 year of age (U.S. Bureau of the Census, 1995). When both parents spend the day on the job, the children must be cared for by others. Millions of American preschoolers are placed in day care, although some older "latchkey" children come home from school and care for themselves until their parents arrive. Parents, of course, are very concerned about what happens to children placed in day care. Our first topic thus concerns the effects of day care. We also offer pointers on selecting a day care center.

Another fact of modern life is that nearly 3 million children in the United States are reported to be neglected or abused by parents each year (Fein, 1998). Our second topic in this section is thus child abuse—why parents abuse their children and what can be done about it.

DEALING WITH DAY CARE

Today only a small minority of American families fit the traditional model in which the husband is the breadwinner and the wife is a full-time homemaker (U.S. Bureau of the Census, 1998). Most mothers, including more than half of mothers of children younger than 1 year of age, work outside the home (U.S. Bureau of the Census, 1998). As a consequence, millions of American preschoolers are placed in day care. Parents and psychologists are concerned about what happens to children in day care. What, for example, are the effects of day care on cognitive development and social development?

In part, the answer depends on the quality of the day care center. A large-scale study funded by the National Institute on Child Health and Human Development found that children in high-quality day care did as well on cognitive and language tests as children who remained in the home with their mother (Azar, 1997c). Children whose day care providers spent time talking to them and asking them questions achieved the highest scores on tests of cognitive and language ability. A Swedish study found that children in high-quality day care outperformed children who remained in the home on tests of math and language skills (Broberg and others, 1997).

Studies of the effects of day care on parent-child attachment are somewhat mixed. On the one hand, children in full-time day care show less distress when their mothers leave them and are less likely to seek out their mothers when they return. Some psychologists suggest that this distancing from the mother could signify insecure attachment (Belsky, 1990). Others suggest, however, that the children are simply adapting to repeated separations from, and reunions with, their mother (Field, 1991; Lamb and others, 1992; Thompson 1991).

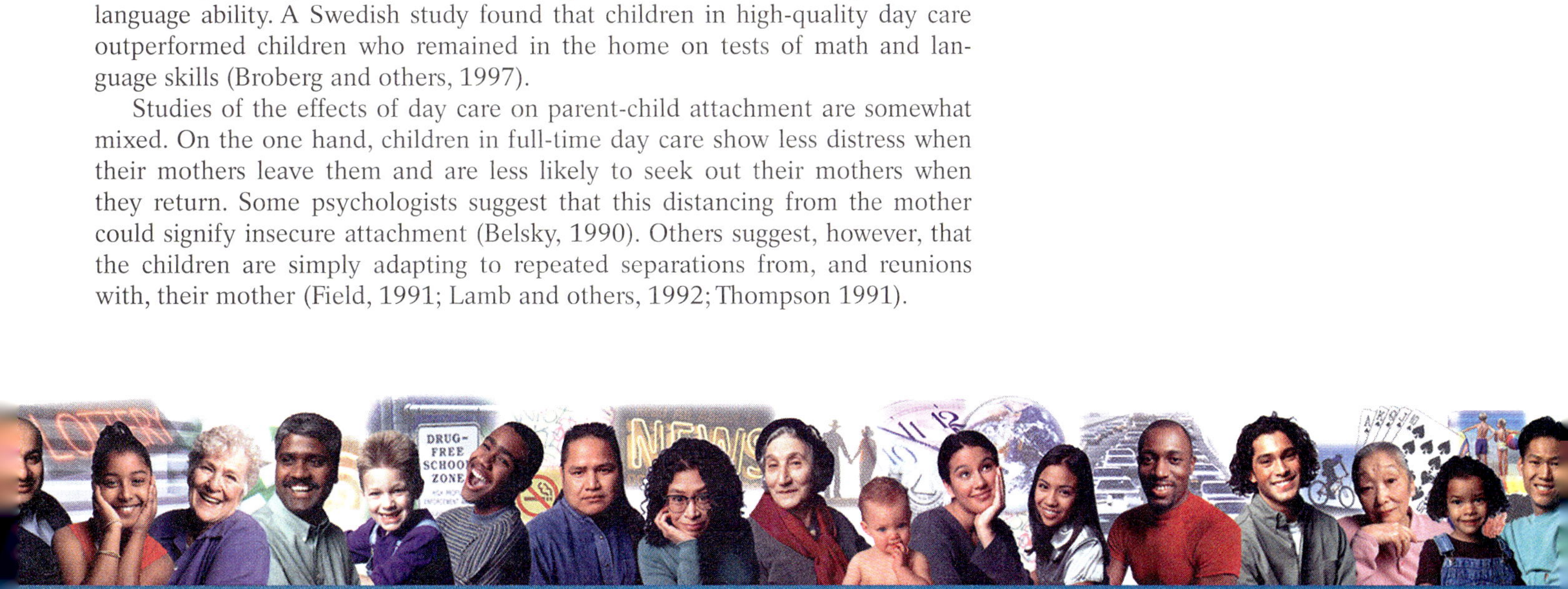

What Are the Effects of Day Care? Because most mothers in the United States are in the workforce, day care is a major factor in the lives of millions of children. Parents are understandably concerned that their children will be provided with positive and stimulating experiences.

Truth or Fiction Revisited

It is true that children placed in day care are more aggressive than children cared for in the home. Perhaps they are so because they have become more independent.

Day care seems to have both positive and negative influences on children's social development. First, the positive: Children in day care are more likely to share their toys and to be independent, self-confident, and outgoing (Clarke-Stewart, 1991; Field, 1991). However, some studies have found that children in day care are less compliant and more aggressive than are other children (Vandell & Corasaniti, 1990). Perhaps some children in day care do not receive the individual attention or resources they need. When placed in a competitive situation, they become more aggressive in an attempt to meet their needs. On the other hand, Clarke-Stewart (1990) interprets the greater noncompliance and aggressiveness of children placed in day care as signs of greater independence rather than social maladjustment.

Selecting a Day Care Center

Because it is economically, vocationally, and socially unrealistic for most parents to spend the day at home, most parents strive to secure day care that will foster the social and emotional development of their children. Because parents share the responsibility for their children, this is a task for fathers as well as mothers.

Selecting a day care center can be an overwhelming task. Standards for day care centers vary from locale to locale, so licensing is no guarantee of adequate care. To help make a successful choice, parents can weigh factors such as the following:

1. Is the center licensed? By what agency? What standards must be met to acquire a license?
2. What is the ratio of children to caregivers? Everything else being equal, caregivers can do a better job when there are fewer children in their charge.
3. What are the qualifications of the center's caregivers? How well aware are they of children's needs and patterns of development? Have they been screened for criminal backgrounds? Children fare better when their caregivers have specific training in child development. Years of day care experience and formal degrees are less important. If the adminis-

trators of a day care center are reluctant to discuss the training and experience of their caregivers, consider another center.

4. How safe is the environment? Do toys and swings seem to be in good condition? Are dangerous objects out of reach? Would strangers have a difficult time breaking in? Ask something like, "Have children been injured in this center?" Administrators should report previous injuries without hesitation.
5. What is served at mealtime? Is it nutritious and appetizing? Will *your child* eat it? Some babies are placed in day care at age 6 months or younger, and parents will need to know what formulas are used.
6. Which caregivers will be responsible for your child? What are their backgrounds? How do they seem to relate to children? To *your* child?
7. What toys, games, books, and other educational materials are provided?
8. What facilities are provided to promote the motor development of your child? How well supervised are children when they use things like swings and tricycles?
9. Are the hours offered by the center convenient for your schedule?
10. Is the location of the center convenient?
11. Do you like the overall environment and "feel" of the center?

As you can see, the considerations can be overwhelming. Perhaps no day care center within reach will score perfectly on every factor. Some factors are more important than others, however. Perhaps this list of considerations will help you focus your primary concerns.

COPING WITH CHILD ABUSE

Dr. Linda Cahill is the medical director of the Child Protection Center at Montefiore Medical Center in the Bronx. She reviewed the cases of six children who were scheduled to be seen one morning:

- A preschool girl whose mother feared that her interest in her genital organs was a sign that she had been molested
- A disabled boy who reported that he had been sexually assaulted by a school aide ("I can't believe people," Dr. Cahill said. "The idea that people who are supposed to watch children—disabled children—could do this" [cited in Fein, 1998].)
- A 6-year-old girl who was being neglected by her mother
- A 9-year-old boy and his 6-year-old sister who were found involved in sexual playacting in their foster home (such playacting can be a sign of sexual abuse)
- A teenager who had been sexually molested by her stepfather
- A boy with neurological problems who had been abandoned by his mother

Nearly 3 million children in the United States are neglected or abused by their parents or other caregivers each year (Fein, 1998). More than half a million of these suffered serious injuries. Nearly 1,000 died (Fein, 1998). In a national poll

of 1,000 parents, 5 percent admitted to having physically abused their children (Lewin, 1995b). One in five (21 percent) admitted to hitting their children "on the bottom" with a hard object such as a belt, stick, or hairbrush. Most parents (85 percent) reported that they often shouted, yelled, or screamed at their children. Nearly half (47 percent) reported spanking or hitting their children on the bottom with their bare hands. And 17 percent admitted to calling their children "dumb" or "lazy" or a similar name.

Even if these percentages seem high, the fact is that abuse—spousal as well as child abuse—tends to be underreported. Why? Some family members are afraid that reporting abuse will destroy the family unit. Others are reluctant to disclose abuse because they are financially dependent on the abuser or do not trust the authorities (Seppa, 1996).

Why do parents abuse their children? Factors that contribute to child abuse include situational stress, a history of child abuse in at least one parent's family of origin, acceptance of violence as a way of coping with stress, failure to become attached to the children, substance abuse, and rigid attitudes toward child rearing (Belsky, 1993; Kaplan, 1991). Unemployment and low socioeconomic status are especially important sources of stress leading to abuse (Lewin, 1995b; Trickett and others, 1991).

Children who are abused are quite likely to develop personal and social problems and psychological disorders. They are less likely than other children to venture out to explore the world (Aber & Allen, 1987). They are more likely to have psychological problems such as anxiety, depression, and low self-esteem (Wagner, 1997). They are less likely to be intimate with their peers and more likely to be aggressive (DeAngelis, 1997b; Parker & Herrera, 1996; Rothbart & Ahadi, 1994). As adults, they are more likely to be violent toward their dates and spouses (Malinosky-Rummell & Hansen, 1993).

Truth or Fiction Revisited

It is true that child abusers have frequently been abused as children. However, the majority of them do not abuse their own children.

Child abuse runs in families to some degree (Simons and others, 1991). However, *the majority of children who are abused do not abuse their own children as adults* (Kaufman & Zigler, 1989). Why does abuse run in families? Several hypotheses have been offered (Belsky, 1993):

- Parents serve as role models. According to Strauss (1995), "Spanking teaches kids that when someone is doing something you don't like and they won't stop doing it, you hit them."
- Children adopt parents' strict philosophies about discipline. Exposure to violence in their own home leads some children to view abuse as normal. Certainly, people can find justifications for violence—if they are seeking them. ("Spare the rod, spoil the child.")
- Abused children develop hostile personalities. When they have their own children, they are thus liable to continue the pattern of abuse and neglect.

What to Do

Dealing with child abuse is frustrating in itself. Social agencies and courts can find it difficult to distinguish between "normal" hitting or spanking and abuse. Because of the American belief that parents have the right to rear their children as they wish, police and courts usually try to avoid involvement in domestic quarrels and family disputes.

However, the alarming incidence of child abuse has spawned new efforts at detection and prevention. Many states require helping professionals such as psychologists and physicians to report any suspicion of child abuse. Many states legally require *anyone* who suspects child abuse to report it to authorities.

Many locales also have child abuse hot lines. Their phone numbers are available from the telephone information service. Private citizens who suspect child abuse may call for advice. Parents who are having difficulty controlling aggressive impulses toward their children are encouraged to use the hot lines. Some hot lines are serviced by groups such as Parents Anonymous, which involve parents who have had similar difficulties and which may help callers diffuse feelings of anger in less harmful ways.

SUMMARY

1. **How does conception take place?** An ovum is released by an ovary and fertilized by a sperm cell in a fallopian tube.
2. **What kinds of fertility problems do people have?** The most common problem among men is insufficient sperm production, and common problems among women are endometriosis and blocked fallopian tubes.
3. **What are some ways of coping with fertility problems?** They include adoption, artificial insemination, in vitro fertilization, embryonic transfer, and surrogate motherhood.
4. **What are the stages of prenatal development?** They are the germinal stage, the embryonic stage, and the fetal stage.
5. **How do maternal diet and disorders, drugs, and parental age affect prenatal development?** Inadequate diets lead to lags in development, particularly motor development. Some maternal pathogens can be passed through the placenta so that the child is given congenital disease. Maternal drinking is linked to fetal alcohol syndrome, and maternal smoking is connected with undersized babies and problems in learning. Parents of advanced ages put the child at risk for chromosomal disorders.
6. **What are some chromosomal and genetic abnormalities?** Chromosomal abnormalities include Down's syndrome. Genetic abnormalities include PKU, sickle-cell anemia, and Tay-Sachs disease.
7. **How can we learn whether something is wrong with the baby before it is born?** A number of methods are used, including parental blood tests, amniocentesis, and ultrasound.
8. **Does anesthesia during childbirth harm the baby?** It seems to make the baby relatively sluggish for a number of hours after birth, but no severe long-term effects have been clearly identified.
9. **What is the Lamaze method?** The Lamaze method prepares the mother and a coach for childbirth by education, relaxation exercises, and muscle-strengthening exercises.
10. **What is postpartum depression?** Actually, there are three kinds of postpartum depression: maternity blues, which is a transient and mild condition that affects about half of new mothers, and postpartum depression and postpartum psychosis, which are more severe disorders. Each problem may reflect the interaction of hormonal influences and concern about the mother role.
11. **How can parents rear competent children?** Baumrind found that parents of the most competent children make demands for mature behavior, clearly communicate their values and beliefs, give their children a great deal of love, and applaud their children's accomplishments.
12. **Does it matter whether a child is breast-fed or bottle-fed?** Breast-feeding is connected with fewer allergies and gives the child some of the mother's antibodies, helping fend off certain diseases. Most children thrive with either method, however.
13. **What happens to the children when the parents get a divorce?** There is usually emotional turmoil and, often, downward movement in socioeconomic status. Adolescents usually adjust better than younger children, and girls adjust better than boys.
14. **Should parents stay together for the sake of the children?** Not if they're going to fight in front of the

children. But if they can agree on childrearing practices and express their other disagreements in private, the children might be better off with both of them.

15. **Why do parents abuse their children?** Child abuse frequently reflects current stresses and attitudes, or personal experiences suggestive that it is "normal" to hit one's children.

16. **What are the effects of day care?** Day care apparently doesn't interfere with parent-child bonds of attachment. Day care appears to foster social skills, but day care children are also somewhat more aggressive than children cared for in the home—possibly because they become used to competing for limited resources.

Scoring Keys for Self-Assessments

SCORING KEY FOR THE SOCIAL DESIRABILITY SCALE (CHAPTER 1, PP. 22–23)

Place a checkmark on the appropriate line below each time your answer agrees with the one listed in the scoring key. Record the total number of checkmarks below.

1. T ____	10. F ____	18. T ____	26. T ____
2. T ____	11. F ____	19. F ____	27. T ____
3. F ____	12. F ____	20. T ____	28. F ____
4. T ____	13. T ____	21. T ____	29. T ____
5. F ____	14. F ____	22. F ____	30. F ____
6. F ____	15. F ____	23. F ____	31. T ____
7. T ____	16. T ____	24. T ____	32. F ____
8. T ____	17. T ____	25. T ____	33. T ____
9. F ____			

INTERPRETATION

LOW SCORERS (0–8)+
About one respondent in six earns a score between 0 and 8. Such respondents answered in a socially *undesirable* direction much of the time. It may be that they are more willing than most people to respond to tests truthfully, even when their answers might meet with social disapproval.

AVERAGE SCORERS (9–19)
About two respondents in three earn a score from 9 through 19. They tend to show an average degree of concern for the social desirability of their responses, and it may be that their general behavior represents an average degree of conformity to social rules and conventions.

HIGH SCORERS (20–33)
About one respondent in six earns a score between 20 and 33. These respondents may be highly concerned about social approval and respond to test items in such a way as to avoid the disapproval of people who may read their responses. Their general behavior may show high conformity to social rules and conventions.

SCORING KEY FOR THE EXPECTANCY-FOR-SUCCESS SCALE (CHAPTER 2, P. 52)

To calculate your total score for the expectancy-for-success scale, first reverse the scores for the following items: 1, 2, 4, 6, 7, 8, 14, 15, 17, 18, 24, 27, and 28. That is, change a 1 to a 5, a 2 to a 4, leave a 3 alone, change a 4 to a 2, and a 5 to a 1. Then add the scores.

The range of total scores can vary from 30 to 150. The higher your score, the greater your expectancy for success in the future—and, according to social learning theory, the more motivated you will be to apply yourself in facing difficult challenges.

Fibel and Hale administered their test to undergraduates taking psychology courses and found that women's scores ranged from 65 to 143 and men's from 81 to 138. The average score for each gender was 112 (112.32 for women and 112.15 for men).

RESULTS OF THE *PSYCHOLOGY TODAY* POLL ON SATISFACTION WITH BODY PARTS (CHAPTER 3, P. 80)

Table A.1 suggests that most respondents to the *Psychology Today* poll had a positive image of their physical selves. Women were generally less satisfied with their bodies than men, perhaps because society tends to focus more on women's bodies than on men's. Both women and men reported general approval of their sexual features (*not* shown in Table A.1), with only one woman in four expressing dissatisfaction with her breasts and an even smaller percentage of men (15 percent) expressing dissatisfaction with the size of their sex organs.

When the investigators compared responses from people of various age groups, they found no major declines in body satisfaction with advancing age. Older men, in fact, were more satisfied with their mid-torsos than younger men. Older respondents of both sexes were more satisfied with their complexions—presumably because adolescent-type acne problems were no longer a source of concern. However, older respondents were less satisfied with their teeth, and older women voiced dissatisfaction with the objects of so many detergent commercials: their hands.

With the generally positive thrust of responses to the poll, would you conclude that a twenty-first century clinic specializing in ready-to-go body reshaping might suffer for business? Not necessarily. Keep in mind that *Psychology Today* readers are better educated, more affluent, and somewhat more liberal than the general public, and readers who filled out the questionnaire might not even fully represent readers of the magazine. People with very negative body images may find such questionnaires punishing and avoid them, and so there could be a positive bias in the results. On the other hand, the description of the

TABLE A.1 RESULTS OF THE *PSYCHOLOGY TODAY* POLL ON SATISFACTION WITH BODY PARTS (IN PERCENTS)

BODY PART	*QUITE OR EXTREMELY DISSATISFIED*		*SOMEWHAT DISSATISFED*		*SOMEWHAT SATISFIED*		*QUITE OR EXTREMELY SATISFIED*	
BODY PART/AREA	**WOMEN**	**MEN**	**WOMEN**	**MEN**	**WOMEN**	**MEN**	**WOMEN**	**MEN**
Overall body appearance	7	4	16	11	32	30	45	55
FACE								
Overall facial attractiveness	3	2	8	6	28	31	61	61
Hair	6	6	13	14	28	22	53	58
Eyes	1	1	5	6	14	12	80	81
Ears	2	1	5	4	10	13	83	82
Nose	5	2	18	14	22	20	55	64
Mouth	2	1	5	5	20	19	73	75
Teeth	11	10	19	18	20	26	50	46
Voice	3	3	15	12	27	27	55	58
Chin	4	3	9	8	20	20	67	69
Complexion	8	7	20	15	24	20	48	58
EXTREMITIES								
Shoulders	2	3	11	8	19	22	68	67
Arms	5	2	11	11	22	25	62	62
Hands	5	1	14	7	21	17	60	75
Feet	6	3	14	8	23	19	57	70
MID-TORSO								
Size of abdomen	19	11	31	25	21	22	29	42
Buttocks (seat)	17	6	26	14	20	24	37	56
Hips (upper thighs)	22	3	27	9	19	24	32	64
Legs and ankles	8	4	17	7	23	20	52	69
HEIGHT, WEIGHT, AND TONE								
Height	3	3	10	10	15	20	72	67
Weight	21	10	27	25	21	22	31	43
General muscle tone or development	9	7	21	18	32	30	38	45

Source: Berscheid, Walster, and Bohrnstedt, 1973.

typical *Psychology Today* reader is similar to that of the typical college student. So perhaps these results reflect those of your peers.

RESPONSES OF A NATIONAL SAMPLE TO THE SURVEY OF VALUES (CHAPTER 3, PP. 86–87)

Table A.2 shows the average rankings of values as determined by a recently drawn national sample of adults. The sample ranked security, peace, and freedom at the top of the list. Beauty, pleasure, and social recognition were ranked near the bottom of the list. Accomplishment and physical comfort were placed about halfway down the list. Apparently, we're an idealistic bunch who place hard work ahead of physical pleasure—or so it seems from the survey of values. There are a number of interesting response patterns. In one, peace and freedom were ranked second and third on the list, but it appears that peace and freedom were not perceived as being linked to national security, which was ranked eleventh. Friendship was also apparently considered more valuable than love.

TABLE A.2 RANKINGS OF VALUES, ACCORDING TO A NATIONAL SAMPLE

Family security	1	True friendship	10
A world at peace	2	National security	11
Freedom	3	Equality	12
Self-respect	4	Inner harmony	13
Happiness	5	Mature love	14
Wisdom	6	An exciting life	15
A sense of accomplishment	7	A world of beauty	16
A comfortable life	8	Pleasure	17
Salvation	9	Social recognition	18

Source: Rokeach and Ball-Rokeach and others, 1989.

SCORING KEY TO SELF-ACCEPTANCE SCALE (CHAPTER 3, PP. 90–91)

To score this key, first *reverse* the numbers you wrote in for the following items: 2, 7, 15, 19, 21, 25, 27, and 32. For each of these items, change a 1 to a 5, change a 2 to a 4, do not change a 3, change a 4 to a 2, and change a 5 to a 1. Then add the numbers assigned to each item and write your total score here: _____.

INTERPRETATION

Your total score can vary from 36 to 180.

LOW SCORERS (36–110)
Scorers in this range are expressing little self-acceptance. The lower your score, the less your self-acceptance. Your low self-acceptance is apparently related to feelings that there is something wrong with you, to general lack of confidence, and to shyness or withdrawal when social opportunities arise. Although many factors are related to low self-acceptance, one of them may be poor social skills. If your lack of self-acceptance and your social interactions are sources of distress to you, you may profit from trying some personal problem solving or seeking professional counseling.

AVERAGE SCORERS (111–150)
Most of us score in this range. Most of us tend to be more self-accepting in some areas than in others, to have more self-confidence in some areas than in others, to feel more comfortable with some people than with others. Our self-acceptance can be enhanced in some cases by challenging irrational goals and self-expectations. In other cases, we may profit from enhancing our vocational, personal, or interpersonal skills.

TABLE A.3 PERCENTILES FOR SCORES ON THE RAS

WOMEN'S SCORES	*PERCENTILE*	*MEN'S SCORES*
55	99	65
48	97	54
45	95	48
37	90	40
31	85	33
26	80	30
23	75	26
19	70	24
17	65	19
14	60	17
11	55	15
8	50	11
6	45	8
2	40	6
−1	35	3
−4	30	1
−8	25	−3
−13	20	−7
−17	15	−11
−24	10	−15
−34	5	−24
−39	3	−30
−48	1	−41

Source: Nevid and Rathus, 1978.

HIGH SCORERS (151–180)
Scorers in this range are highly self-accepting and self-confident. Your consistent sense of worth tends to provide you with support as you meet new people and confront new challenges.

SCORING KEY FOR THE RATHUS ASSERTIVENESS SCHEDULE (CHAPTER 4, P. 108)

Tabulate your score as follows: For those items followed by an asterisk (*), change the signs (plus to minus, minus to plus). For example, if the response to an asterisked item was 2, place a minus sign (−) before the two. If the response to an asterisked item was −3, change the minus sign to a plus sign (+) by adding a vertical stroke. Then total the scores for the 30 items.

Scores on the assertiveness schedule can vary from +90 to −90. Table A.3 will show you how your score compares to those of 764 college women and 637 men from 35 campuses across the United States. For example, if you are a woman and your score was 26, it exceeded that of 80 percent of the women in the sample. A score of 15 for a male exceeds that of 55 to 60 percent of the men in the sample.

ANSWER KEY FOR SOCIAL READJUSTMENT RATING SCALE (CHAPTER 5, PP. 134–135)

Add all the scores in the Total column to arrive at your final score.

INTERPRETATION

Your final score is indicative of the amount of stress you have experienced during the past 12 months:

From 0 to 1500 = Minor stress
1,501–3,500 = Mild stress
3,501–5,500 = Moderate stress
5,501 and above = Major stress

Research has shown that the probability of encountering physical illness within the *following* year is related to the amount of stress experienced during the *past* year. That is, college students who experienced minor stress have a 28 percent chance of becoming ill; mild stress, a 45 percent chance; moderate stress, a 70 percent chance; and major stress, an 82 percent chance. Moreover, the seriousness of the illness also increases with the amount of stress.

It should be recognized that these percentages reflect previous research with college students. Do not assume that a great deal of stress dooms you to illness. Also keep in mind that a number of psychological factors moderate the impact of stress, as described in this chapter. For example, psychologically hardy college students would theoretically withstand the same amount of stress that could enhance the risk of illness for nonhardy individuals.

ANSWER KEY FOR "ARE YOU TYPE A OR TYPE B?" SELF-ASSESSMENT (CHAPTER 5, P. 142)

Yes answers suggest the Type A behavior pattern, which is marked by a sense of time urgency and constant struggle. In appraising your type, you need not be overly concerned with the precise number of yes answers; we have no normative data for you. But as Friedman and Rosenman (1974, p. 85) note, you should have little trouble spotting yourself as "hard core" or "moderately afflicted"—that is, if you are honest with yourself.

ANSWER KEY FOR THE LOCUS OF CONTROL SCALE (CHAPTER 5, PP. 152–153)

Place a checkmark in the blank space each time your answer agrees with the answer in the key. The number of checkmarks is your total score.

1. Yes ____	11. Yes ____	21. Yes ____	31. Yes ____
2. No ____	12. Yes ____	22. No ____	32. No ____
3. Yes ____	13. No ____	23. Yes ____	33. Yes ____
4. No ____	14. Yes ____	24. Yes ____	34. No ____
5. Yes ____	15. No ____	25. No ____	35. Yes ____
6. No ____	16. Yes ____	26. No ____	36. Yes ____
7. Yes ____	17. Yes ____	27. Yes ____	37. Yes ____
8. Yes ____	18. Yes ____	28. No ____	38. No ____
9. No ____	19. Yes ____	29. Yes ____	39. Yes ____
10. Yes ____	20. No ____	30. No ____	40. No ____

INTERPRETATION

LOW SCORERS (0–8)
About one respondent in three earns a score of from 0 to 8. Such respondents tend to have an internal locus of control. They see themselves as responsible for the reinforcements they attain (and fail to attain) in life.

AVERAGE SCORERS (9–16)
Most respondents earn from 9 to 16 points. Average scorers may see themselves as partially in control of their lives. Perhaps they see themselves as in control at work, but not in their social lives—or vice versa.

HIGH SCORERS (17–40)
About 15 percent of respondents attain scores of 17 or above. High scorers tend largely to see life as a game of chance and success as a matter of luck or the generosity of others.

SCORING KEY FOR LIFE ORIENTATION TEST (CHAPTER 6, P. 163)

In order to arrive at your total score for the test, first *reverse* your score on items 3, 8, 9, and 12. That is, 4 is changed to 0; 3 is changed to 1, 2 remains the same, 1 is changed to 3, and 0 is changed to 4. Now add the numbers for items 1, 3, 4, 5, 8, 9, 11, and 12. (Items 2, 6, 7, and 10 are "fillers"; that is, your responses are not scored as part of the test.) Your total score can vary from 0 to 32.

Scheier and Carver (1985) provide the following norms for the test, based on administration to 357 undergraduate men and 267 undergraduate women. The average (mean) score for men was 21.03 (standard deviation = 4.56), and the mean score for women was 21.41 (standard deviation = 5.22). All in all, approximately two undergraduates (men and women combined) obtained scores between 16 and 26. Scores above 26 may be considered quite optimistic, and scores below 16 may be considered quite pessimistic. Scores between 16 and 26 are within a broad average range, and higher scores within this range are relatively more optimistic.

KEY FOR EATING SMART QUIZ (CHAPTER 6, PP. 186–187)

How do you rate?

0–12: *A warning signal.* Your diet is too high in fat and too low in fiber-rich foods. It would be wise to assess your eating habits to see where you could make improvements.

13–17: *Not bad! You're partway there.* You still have a way to go. Review the American Cancer Society dietary guidelines (p. 186) and compare them to your answers. This will help you determine where you can make a few improvements.

18–36: *Good for you! You're eating smart.* You should feel very good about yourself. You have been careful to limit your fats and eat a varied diet. Keep up the good habits and continue to look for ways to improve.

Note that a poor score on the quiz does not guarantee that you will get cancer, and a high score does not guarantee that you will not. However, your score will help you assess the risks of your current dietary habits, and the guidelines will suggest ways in which you can reduce your risk of cancer.

The American Cancer Society notes that "This eating quiz is really for self-information and does not evaluate your intake of essential vitamins, minerals, protein or calories. If your diet is restricted in some ways (i.e., you are a vegetarian or have allergies), you may want to get professional advice" (1987).

SCORING KEY TO THE "CHECK YOUR PHYSICAL ACTIVITY AND HEART DISEASE IQ" SELF-ASSESSMENT (CHAPTER 7, P. 209)

1. True. Heart disease is almost twice as likely to develop in inactive people. Being physically inactive is a risk factor for heart disease along with cigarette smoking, high blood pressure, high blood cholesterol, and being overweight. The more risk factors you have, the greater your chance for heart disease. Regular physical activity (even mild to moderate exercise) can reduce this risk.
2. False. Most Americans are very busy but not very active. Every American adult should make a habit of getting 30 minutes of low to moderate levels of physical activity daily. This includes walking, gardening, and walking up stairs. If you are inactive now, begin by doing a few minutes of activity each day. If you only do some activity every once in a while, try to work something into your routine every day.
3. True. Low- to moderate-intensity activities, such as pleasure walking, stair climbing, yardwork, moderate to heavy housework, dancing, and home exercises can have both short- and long-term benefits. If you are inactive, the key is to get started. One great way is to take a walk for 10 to 15 minutes during your lunch break, or take your dog for a walk every day. At least 30 minutes of physical activity every day can help improve the health of your heart and lower your risk of heart disease.
4. True. It takes only a few minutes a day to become more physically active. If you don't have 30 minutes in your schedule for an exercise break, try to find two 15-minute periods or even three 10-minute periods. Once you discover how much you enjoy these exercise breaks, they'll become a habit you can't live without.
5. False. People who engage in regular activity experience many positive benefits. Regular physical activity gives you more energy, reduces stress, helps you to relax, and helps you to sleep better. It helps to lower high blood pressure and improves blood cholesterol levels. Physical activity helps to tone your muscles, burns off calories to help you lose extra pounds or stay at your desirable weight, and helps control your appetite. It can also increase muscle strength, help your heart and lungs work more efficiently, and let you enjoy your life more fully.
6. False. Low-intensity activities—if performed daily—can have some long-term health benefits and can lower your risk of heart disease. Regular, brisk, and sustained exercise for at least 30 minutes, three to four times a week, such as brisk walking, jogging, or swimming, is necessary to improve the efficiency of your heart and lungs and to burn off extra calories. These kinds of activities are called aerobic—meaning the body uses oxygen to produce the energy needed for the activity. Other activities may give you other benefits such as increased flexibility or muscle strength, depending on the type of activity.
7. False. Although we tend to become less active with age, physical activity is still important. In fact, regular physical activity in older persons increases their capacity to do everyday activities. In general, middle-aged and older people benefit from regular physical activity just as young people do. What is important, no matter what your age, is tailoring the activity program to your own fitness level.
8. True. Many activities require little or no equipment. For example, brisk walking only requires a comfortable pair

of walking shoes. Also, many communities offer free or inexpensive recreation facilities and physical activity classes. Check your shopping malls, as many of them are open early and late for people who do not wish to walk alone, in the dark, or in bad weather.

9. False. The most common risk in exercising is injury to the muscles and joints. Such injuries are usually caused by exercising too hard for too long, particularly if a person has been inactive for some time. To avoid injuries, try to build up your level of activity gradually, listen to your body for early warning pains, be aware of possible signs of heart problems (such as pain or pressure in the left or mid-chest area, left neck, shoulder, or arm during or just after exercising, or sudden light-headedness, cold sweat, pallor, or fainting), and be prepared for special weather conditions.
10. True. You should ask your doctor before you start (or greatly increase) your physical activity if you have a medical condition such as high blood pressure, have pains or pressure in the chest and shoulder area, tend to feel dizzy or faint, get very breathless after mild exertion, are middle-aged or older and have not been physically active, or plan a fairly vigorous activity program. If none of these apply, start slow and get moving.
11. False. Regular physical activity can help reduce your risk of having another heart attack. People who include regular physical activity in their lives after a heart attack improve their chances of survival and can improve how they feel and look. If you have had a heart attack, consult your doctor to be sure you are following a safe and effective exercise program that will help prevent heart pain and further damage from overexertion.
12. True. Pick several different activities that you like doing because you will be more likely to stay with it. Plan short-term as well as long-term goals. Keep a record of your progress, and check it regularly to see the progress you have made. Get your family and friends to join in. They can help keep you going.

SCORING KEY FOR THE "WHY DO YOU DRINK?" SELF-ASSESSMENT (CHAPTER 8, PP. 234–235)

Why do you drink? Score your questionnaire by seeing how many items you answered in accord with the reasons for drinking listed in the table below. The key is suggestive

ADDICTION (ITEMS ANSWERED AS FOLLOWS SUGGEST PHYSIOLOGICAL DEPENDENCE)	*PLEASURE/TASTE*	*SOCIAL REWARD*	*SCAPEGOATING (ITEMS ANSWERED AS FOLLOWS SUGGEST THAT YOU MAY USE ALCOHOL AS AN EXCUSE FOR FAILURE OR SOCIAL MISCONDUCT)*
1. T	2. T	3. T	14. T
6. F	5. T	8. T	15. T
32. T	16. T	23. T	20. T
38. T	27. T	41. T	21. T
40. T	28. T		39. T
45. T	35. T		
	37. T		

ANXIETY/TENSION REDUCTION	*TRANSFORMING AGENTS (ITEMS ANSWERED AS FOLLOWS USE ALCOHOL TO TRY TO CHANGE YOUR EXPERIENCES FOR THE BETTER)*	*RELIGION*	*HABIT*	*SOCIAL POWER*	*CELEBRATION*
7. T	2. T	11. T	17. T	2. T	10. T
9. T	4. T		29. T	13. T	24. T
12. T	19. T		44. T	19. T	25. T
15. T	22. T			30. T	43. T
18. T	28. T				
26. T	30. T				
31. T	34. T				
33. T	36. T				
42. T					

only. If you scored several items on the *addiction* factor, it may be wise to seriously examine what your drinking means to you. However, a few test items are not binding evidence of addiction.

SCORING KEY FOR "WHY DO YOU SMOKE?" SELF-ASSESSMENT (CHAPTER 8, P. 238)

1. Enter the number you have circled for each question in the spaces below, putting the number you have circled to question A over line A, to question B over line B, and so on.
2. Add the three scores on each line to get your totals. For example, the sum of your scores over lines A, G, and M gives you your scores on Stimulation; lines B, H, and N give the score on Handling, and so on.

							Totals
___	+	___	+	___	=		______________
A		G		M			**Stimulation**
___	+	___	+	___	=		______________
B		H		N			**Handling**
___	+	___	+	___	=		______________
C		I		O			**Pleasurable Relaxation**
___	+	___	+	___	=		______________
D		J		P			**Crutch: Tension Reduction**
___	+	___	+	___	=		______________
E		K		Q			**Craving: Psychological Addiction**
___	+	___	+	___	=		______________
F		L		R			**Habit**

Scores can vary from 3 to 15. Any score of 11 and above is high; any score of 7 and below is low.

INTERPRETATION

What kind of smoker are you? What do you get out smoking? What does it do for you? This test is designed to provide you with a score on each of six factors relating to smoking. Your smoking may be characterized by only one of these factors or by a combination of two or more factors. In any event, this test will help you identify what you use smoking for and what kind of satisfaction you think you get from smoking.

The six factors measured by this test describe different ways of experiencing or managing certain kinds of feelings. Three of these feeling states represent the positive feelings people get from smoking: a sense of increased energy or stimulation, the satisfaction of handling or manipulating things, and the enhancing of pleasurable feelings accompanying a state of well-being. The fourth relates to a decrease of negative feelings states such as anxiety, anger, shame, and so forth. The fifth is a complex pattern of the increasing and decreasing craving for a cigarette, representing the psychological addiction to smoking. The sixth is habit smoking, which takes place in an absence of feeling—purely automatic smoking.

A score of 11 or above on any factor indicates that this factor is an important source of satisfaction for you. The higher your score (15 is the highest), the more important a particular factor is in your smoking behavior and the more useful the discussion of that factor can be in your efforts to quit.

SCORING KEY FOR THE SUINN TEST ANXIETY BEHAVIOR SCALE (CHAPTER 11, PP. 346–347)

To attain your total STABS score, first assign points to your checkmarks according to the following code:

Not at all = 1
A little = 2
A fair amount = 3
Much = 4
Very much = 5

Add the numbers to find your total score. (You may want to include items on which you scored a 4 or a 5 in your cognitive restructuring program.)

The following norms for the 20-item STABS were attained with Northeastern University students. There were no gender differences.

STABS SCORE	*PERCENTILE*
68	95
61	80
57	75
52	60
49	50
45	35
41	25
38	20
32	10

SCORING KEY FOR SELF-RATING DEPRESSION SCALE (CHAPTER 11, P. 350)

The first step in scoring the depression scale is to circle the points you earned according to the space you checked on page 350 (see next page).

ITEM NUMBER	NONE OR A LITTLE OF THE TIME	SOME OF THE TIME	GOOD PART OF THE TIME	MOST OR ALL OF THE TIME
1.	1	2	3	4
2.	4	3	2	1
3.	1	2	3	4
4.	1	2	3	4
5.	4	3	2	1
6.	4	3	2	1
7.	1	2	3	4
8.	1	2	3	4
9.	1	2	3	4
10.	1	2	3	4
11.	4	3	2	1
12.	4	3	2	1
13.	1	2	3	4
14.	4	3	2	1
15.	1	2	3	4
16.	4	3	2	1
17.	4	3	2	1
18.	4	3	2	1
19.	1	2	3	4
20.	4	3	2	1

Now add up the points you have earned and write the total here: _________.

INTERPRETATION

Scores can vary between 20 and 80.

LOW SCORERS (20–32)
There is little evidence of feelings of depression. People who score in this range generally feel hopeful about the future and are full of energy. It is normal to feel depressed from time to time, and they may do so, but now things are probably looking up.

MEDUM SCORERS (33–50)
People who score in this range may be experiencing mild to moderate feelings of depression. They probably feel somewhat low in energy, are not enjoying life very much right now, and are uncertain of their abilities to take charge of the future. Sometimes the source of these feelings is apparent enough—social, academic, or vocational problems. In such cases, it is usually worthwhile to take a little time out and try to solve these problems. However, if they have tried to solve their problems and failed, or if these feelings have persisted without apparent cause, it is probably worthwhile to consider professional help.

HIGH SCORERS (51–80)
People who score in this range are reporting serious levels of depression that are likely to impair their abilities to function from day to day. Life may look hopeless right now, and thoughts of suicide may occur from time to time. Seeking an evaluation by a mental health professional such as a psychologist or psychiatrist is strongly recommended.

SCORING KEY FOR THE ANDRO SCALE (CHAPTER 12, PP. 374–375)

People who score high on masculinity alone on this scale endorse traditionally masculine attitudes and behaviors, whereas people who score high on femininity alone hold traditionally feminine ways of relating to the world. Many psychologists now believe that you will experience life more fully and be better adjusted if you score relatively high on both masculinity and femininity. Scoring high on both suggests that you are psychologically androgynous and can summon up characteristics attributed to both genders, as needed. That is, you can be assertive but caring, logical but emotionally responsive, strong but gentle.

You can determine your own masculinity and femininity scores by seeing how many of your answers agree with those on the key in Table A.4.

Use Table A.5 to compare your masculinity and femininity scores to those of 386 male and 723 female University of Kentucky students. Your percentile score (%) means that your own score equaled or excelled that of the percentage of students shown.

TABLE A.4 KEY FOR DETERMINING TOTAL MASCULINITY AND FEMININITY SCORES

MASCULINITY			*FEMININITY*		
ITEM NO.	KEY	SCORE: 1 IF SAME AS KEY, 0 IF NOT	ITEM NO.	KEY	SCORE: 1 IF SAME AS KEY, 0 IF NOT
2.	T	____	1.	T	____
3.	F	____	5.	F	____
4.	T	____	9.	F	____
6.	F	____	13.	T	____
7.	T	____	14.	T	____
8.	T	____	16.	F	____
10.	F	____	18.	T	____
11.	T	____	19.	F	____
12.	T	____	20.	T	____
15.	F	____	21.	T	____
17.	T	____	22.	F	____
25.	T	____	23.	T	____
26.	T	____	24.	F	____
27.	T	____	28.	F	____
29.	T	____	32.	F	____
30.	T	____	36.	T	____
31.	T	____	37.	T	____
33.	T	____	39.	T	____
34.	F	____	41.	T	____
35.	T	____	43.	T	____
38.	F	____	44.	T	____
40.	F	____	45.	T	____
42.	T	____	49.	T	____
46.	F	____	51.	F	____
47.	T	____	53.	T	____
48.	F	____	55.	T	____
50.	T	____	56.	F	____
52.	T	____			
54.	F	____			
Total Masculinity Score: (maximum score = 29)		____	Total Femininity Score: (maximum score = 27)		____

Note: To determine your masculinity and femininity scores on the ANDRO Scale, place a 1 in the appropriate blank space each time your answer agrees with the answer (T or F) shown on the key. Place a 0 in the space each time your answer disagrees with the answer shown on the key. Then add up the totals for each.

Source: Berzins and others, 1977.

KEY FOR STERNBERG'S TRIANGULAR LOVE SCALE (CHAPTER 13, PP. 414–415)

First add your scores for the items on each of the three components—Intimacy, Passion, and Decision/Commitment—and divide each total by 15. This procedure will yield an average rating for each subscale. An average rating of 5 on a particular subscale indicates a moderate level of the component represented by the subscale. A higher rating indicates a greater level. A lower rating indicates a lower level. Examining your ratings on these components will give you an idea of the degree to which you perceive your love relationship to be characterized by these three components of love. For example, you might find that passion is stronger than decision/commitment, a pattern that is common in the early stages of an intense romantic relationship. You might find it interesting to complete the questionnaire a few months or perhaps a year or so from now to see how your feelings about your relationship change over time. You might also ask your partner to complete the scale so that the two of you can compare your respective scores. Comparing your ratings for each component with those of your partner will give you an idea of the degree to which you and your partner see your relationship in a similar way.

TABLE A.5 PERCENTILE RANKINGS OF MASCULINITY AND FEMININITY SCORES OF COLLEGE STUDENT SAMPLE

MASCULINITY SCORES				*FEMININITY SCORES*			
RAW SCORE	MALES (%)	FEMALES (%)	COMBINED (%)	RAW SCORE	MALES (%)	FEMALES (%)	COMBINED (%)
29	99	99	99	27	99	99	99
28	99	99	99	26	99	99	99
27	99	99	99	25	99	99	99
26	99	99	99	24	99	99	99
25	98	99	99	23	99	98	99
24	96	98	97	22	99	94	96
23	92	96	94	21	98	87	92
22	88	96	92	20	95	78	86
21	80	94	87	19	91	65	78
20	73	93	83	18	85	53	69
19	63	88	75	17	76	42	59
18	54	83	68	16	65	32	48
17	47	78	60	15	56	24	40
16	39	72	56	14	47	17	32
15	30	65	48	13	37	12	25
14	23	58	40	12	28	6	17
13	17	50	33	11	20	4	12
12	13	41	27	10	14	3	8
11	10	34	22	9	7	2	4
10	6	28	17	8	4	1	3
9	4	21	13	7	3	0	2
8	2	16	9	6	2	0	1
7	2	11	6	5	2	0	1
6	1	9	5	4	1	0	0
5	1	5	3	3	0	0	0
4	0	2	1	2	0	0	0
3	0	1	0	1	0	0	0
2	0	0	0	0	0	0	0
1	0	0	0				
0	0	0	0				

Source: Berzins and others, 1977.

SCORING KEY FOR QUESTIONNAIRE ON ENDORSEMENT OF TRADITIONAL OR LIBERAL MARITAL ROLES (CHAPTER 14, P. 436)

Below each of the scoring codes (AS, AM, DM, and DS) there is a number. Underline the numbers beneath each of your answers. Then add the underlined numbers to obtain your total score.

The total score can vary from 10 to 40. A score of 10 to 20 shows moderate to high traditionalism concerning marital roles, whereas a score of 30 to 40 shows moderate to high liberalism. A score between 20 and 30 suggests that you are a middle-of-the-roader.

Your endorsement of a traditional or a liberal marital role is not a matter of right or wrong. However, if you and your potential or actual spouse endorse significantly different marital roles, there may be role conflict ahead. It may be worthwhile to have a frank talk with your partner about your goals and values to determine whether the two of you have major disagreements and are willing to work to resolve them.

SCORING KEY FOR THE MYTHS-THAT-SUPPORT-RAPE QUESTIONNAIRE (CHAPTER 15, P. 476)

Each item is false. But our concerns over your responses do not simply address their accuracy. The issue is whether you endorse cultural beliefs that tend to contribute to rape. For example, if you believe that women harbor unconscious desires to be raped, you may also tend to believe that rape victims "get what they have coming to them" and your sympathies may actually lie with the assailant.

ANSWERS TO THE AIDS AWARENESS INVENTORY

1. False. AIDS is the name of a disease syndrome. AIDS stands for *acquired immunodeficiency syndrome.* (A syndrome is a group of signs or symptoms of a disease.) HIV stands for *human immunodeficiency virus,* which is the microscopic disease organism that causes AIDS. When the immune system is weakened beyond a certain point, people are prey to illnesses that normally would not gain a foothold in the body. At this time, they are said to have AIDS.
2. False. HIV is transmitted by people who are infected with it, whether or not they have yet developed AIDS.
3. False. AIDS is a syndrome that is characterized by a weakened immune system. People with AIDS are apt to develop illnesses that otherwise wouldn't stand much of a chance of taking hold. These illnesses are called "opportunistic infections." The confusion of AIDS with pneumonia may come about because one opportunistic illness is a form of pneumonia. *Pneumocystis carinii pneumonia*—PCP for short. Before the emergence of AIDS, PCP was found mainly in people with cancer whose immune systems had been weakened, usually as a side effect of chemotherapy (therapy with chemicals or drugs).
4. False. The confusion about AIDS and cancer may stem from the fact that men with weakened immune systems are prone to developing a rare form of blood cancer, *Kaposi's sarcoma,* which leaves purplish spots all over the body.
5. False. Sure you can. There is also a myth that you cannot become pregnant the first time you engage in sexual intercourse, but you most certainly can.
6. False. Men who engage in sexual activity with other men and people who inject drugs have been at relatively higher risk for being infected by HIV, especially in the United States and Canada. However, *anyone* can be infected by HIV if the virus enters her or his bloodstream.
7. False. As of today, more men than women have developed AIDS, at least in the United States. This is largely because until now, HIV was transmitted predominantly by male-male sexual activity and sharing needles for injecting drugs. The first group consists solely of males, and the second group is mostly male. The incidences of HIV infection and AIDS are now growing more rapidly among women than men, however—in the United States and elsewhere. Women, moreover, are more vulnerable than men are to being infected with HIV through male-female sexual intercourse.
8. True. An average of about 10 years passes between the time adolescents or adults are infected by HIV and the time they develop AIDS.
9. True. In order to be infected with HIV, the virus must get into your bloodstream. This will not happen through hugging someone, even if that person is infected. This is why people who care for HIV-infected children can lavish affection on them without fear of being infected themselves.
10. False. This erroneous belief may reflect the connection between sexual orientation and AIDS in many people's minds. You most assuredly can be infected by HIV in this manner, whether you are a woman or a man.
11. False. You most certainly can. Some forms of contraception such as the birth control pill and rhythm methods afford no protection against infection by HIV. Other methods such as spermicides provide some protection, but cannot be considered safe.
12. False. It appears that you can be infected by HIV through oral sex, even though this avenue of transmission is unlikely (digestive juices such as saliva and the normal acids that are found in the digestive tract kill HIV). Some people appear to have been infected in this manner, however.
13. False. Using condoms substantially reduces the risk of HIV infection, but does not guarantee safety.
14. False. It is estimated that more than a million people in the United States are infected with HIV, but only a fraction of them have developed AIDS to date.
15. False. It is not true that you can be infected by HIV by donating blood. The needles are sterile (free of infection) and are used only once.
16. False. Some people believe, erroneously, that they cannot be placed in "double jeopardy" by sexually transmitted diseases. People who have another sexually transmitted disease are actually *more* likely, not less likely, to be infected by HIV. There are at least two reasons for this. One is that they may have sores in the genital region that provide convenient ports of entry for HIV into the bloodstream. The second is that the risky sexual behavior that led to one kind of infection can easily lead to others.
17. False. You cut your risks through a monogamous relationship, but you must consider two questions: First, what was your faithful partner doing before the two of you became a couple? Second, do you or your partner engage in *nonsexual* forms of behavior that could result in HIV infection, such as shooting up drugs?
18. False. There are several medical treatments for HIV infection and AIDS, as well as for many of the opportunistic illnesses that attack people who have developed AIDS. Moreover, combinations of drugs, including protease inhibitors, seem to be quite promising. The question is whether any of these treatments will permanently clear the bloodstream of HIV or prolong life indefinitely.

19. False. Would that it were so! Knowledge of possible consequences alone is often not enough to encourage people to modify risky behavior.

20. False. You do not have to be concerned about the insects that mill about in next summer's heated air. There is no documented case of HIV having been transmitted in this manner.

ANSWER KEY TO ATTITUDES TOWARD AGING (CHAPTER 16, P. 518)

1. False. Most healthy couples continue to engage in satisfying sexual activities into their seventies and eighties.
2. False. This is too general a statement. Those who find their work satisfying are less desirous of retiring.
3. False. In late adulthood we tend to become more concerned with internal matters—our physical functioning and our emotions.
4. False. Adaptability remains reasonably stable throughout adulthood.
5. False. Age itself is not linked to noticeable declines in life satisfaction. Of course, we may respond negatively to disease and losses, such as death of a spouse.
6. False. Although we can predict some general trends for the elderly, we can also do so for the young. The elderly remain heterogeneous in personality and behavior patterns.
7. False. Elderly people with stable intimate relationships are more satisfied.
8. False. We are susceptible to a wide variety of psychological disorders at all ages.
9. False. Only a minority are depressed.
10. False. Actually church attendance declines, although there is no difference in verbally expressed religious beliefs.
11. False. Although reaction time may increase and general learning ability may undergo a slight decline, the elderly usually have little or no difficulty at familiar work tasks. In most jobs, experience and motivation are more important than age.
12. False. Learning may just take a bit longer.
13. False.
14. False. Elderly people do not direct a higher proportion of thoughts toward the past than younger people do; but we may spend more time daydreaming at any age if we have more time on our hands.
15. False. Only about 10 percent of the elderly require some form of institutional care.

KEY TO THE DEATH CONCERN SCALE (CHAPTER 16, PP. 532–533)

Scores on the Death Concern Scale can vary from 30 to 120. Add the points for each of the 30 items and write your total score here: _________.

INTERPRETATION

LOW SCORERS (30–67)
Low scorers admit to little if any concern about death. A low score may reflect a personal philosophy in which death is viewed as meaningful and acceptable within the scheme of things. A low score can also suggest that you are really reluctant to consider and accept the reality of death. A third possibility is that you tend not to think about things that do not immediately affect you, and death, perhaps, may seem a long way off. Upon reflection, you should have little difficulty deciding which possibility applies to you.

AVERAGE SCORERS (68–80)
Average scorers show some concern about death, but they are not excessively anxious about it.

HIGH SCORERS (81–120)
High scorers probably experienced a great deal of anxiety when they first saw the title of the questionnaire. They are likely to be highly apprehensive about death and to show anxiety whenever the topic is raised. Perhaps they have had more than their share of illnesses or have become sensitized by the deaths of loved ones. High scorers are sometimes generally anxious people for whom apprehension about death is not an isolated concern. People who find themselves preoccupied with death sometimes profit from discussing their concerns with counselors.

SCORING KEY FOR JOB SATISFACTION INDEX (CHAPTER 17, PP. 556–558)

To find your score, compare your answers to those shown in the scoring key. Allot yourself the number of points indicated by each answer. Add your points and write your total in here: _________

1.	a. 1	b. 3	c. 5
2.	a. 5	b. 1	c. 3
3.	a. 3	b. 1	c. 5
4.	a. 5	b. 3	c. 1
5.	a. 1	b. 3	c. 5
6.	a. 5	b. 3	c. 1
7.	a. 5	b. 3	c. 1
8.	a. 5	b. 3	c. 1
9.	a. 5	b. 3	c. 1
10.	a. 5	b. 3	c. 1
11.	a. 1	b. 3	c. 5

12 and 13: Give yourself 5 points each time the qualities you marked are a match:

a. ____
b. ____
c. ____
d. ____
e. ____
f. ____
g. ____
h. ____
I. ____
j. ____

14.	a. 1	b. 3	c. 5	23.	a. 5	b. 3	c. 1
15.	a. 3	b. 1	c. 5	24.	a. 1	b. 5	c. 3
16.	a. 5	b. 3	c. 1	25.	a. 1	b. 5	c. 3
17.	a. 5	b. 1	c. 3	26.	a. 3	b. 1	c. 5
18.	a. 5	b. 1	c. 3	27.	a. 3	b. 1	c. 5
19.	a. 3	b. 5	c. 1	28.	a. 1	b. 3	c. 5
20.	a. 5	b. 3	c. 1	29.	a. 5	b. 1	c. 3
21.	a. 3	b. 1	c. 5	30.	a. 1	b. 3	c. 5
22.	a. 1	b. 5	c. 3				

INTERPRETATION

LOW SCORERS (28–80)
Your score suggests that you are dissatisfied with your current job, but it does not suggest why. Examine your situation and ask yourself whether your dissatisfaction is related to factors such as a mismatch of your personal characteristics and the behaviors required by the job or personal conflicts with a supervisor. If you suspect a mismatch between your traits and the job requirements, vocational testing and counseling may be of help. If interpersonal problems or other factors are preventing you from finding satisfaction with your work, you may be interested in pursuing methods of conflict resolution discussed in Chapter 14 or other solutions. Why not share your concerns with a counselor, a trusted co-worker, or a family member?

AVERAGE SCORER (81–150)
Your level of job satisfaction is about average. Perhaps you would like better pay, a bit less job-related stress, and some more appreciation, but by and large your job seems to provide you with some social or personal benefits in addition to the paycheck.

HIGH SCORERS (151 AND ABOVE)
Your job seems to be a source of great satisfaction to you. You apparently enjoy the daily ins and outs of your work, get along with most of your colleagues, and feel that what you are doing is right for you. If something is lacking in your life, it probably is not to be found in the job. On the other hand, is it possible that your commitment to your work is interfering with your development of a fully satisfying family and leisure life?

References

AAUW. (1992). See American Association of University Women.
Abbey, A. (1987). Misperceptions of friendly behavior as sexual interest: A survey of naturally occurring incidents. *Psychology of Women Quarterly, 11,* 173–194.
Abeles, N. (1997a). Psychology and the aging revolution. *APA Monitor, 28*(4), 2.
Abeles, N. (1997b). Memory problems in later life. *APA Monitor, 28*(6), 2.
Aber, J. L., & Allen, J. P. (1987). Effects of maltreatment of young children on young children's socioemotional development: An attachment theory perspective: *Developmental Psychology, 23,* 406–414.
Abramowitz, J. S. (1997). Effectiveness of psychological and pharmacological treatments for obsessive-compulsive disorder. *Journal of Consulting and Clinical Psychology, 65,* 44–52.
Adams, A., Carnine, D., & Gersten K. (1982). Instructional strategies for studying content area texts in the intermediate grades. *Reading Research Quarterly, 18,* 27–53.
Adelson, A. (1990, November 19). Study attacks women's roles in TV. *The New York Times,* p. C18.
Ader, D. N., & Johnson, S. B. (1994). Sample description, reporting, and analysis of sex in psychological research. *American Psychologist, 49,* 216–218.
Ader, R. (1993). Conditioned responses. In B. Moyers (Ed.), *Healing and the mind.* New York: Doubleday.
Adler, N. E., Boyce, T., Chesney, M. A., Cohen, S., Folkman, S., Kahn, R. L., & Syme, S. L. (1994). Socioeconomic status and health: The challenge of the gradient. *American Psychologist, 49,* 15–24.
Adler, T. (1990). Distraction, relaxation can help "shut off" pain. *APA Monitor, 21*(9), 11.
Adler, T. (1993a). Sex harassment at work hurts victim, organization. *APA Monitor, 24*(8), 25–26.
Adler, T. (1993b). Sleep loss impairs attention—and more. *APA Monitor, 24*(9), 22–23.
Agras, W. S., & Kirkley, B. G. (1986). Bulimia: Theories of etiology. In K. D. Brownell & J. P. Foreyt (Eds.), *Handbook of eating disorders.* New York: Basic Books.
Agras, W. S., Southam, M. A., & Taylor, C. B. (1983). Long-term persistence of relaxation-induced blood pressure lowering during the working day. *Journal of Consulting and Clinical Psychology, 51,* 792–794.
AIDS hotline. (1998). Personal communications.
Aiello, J. R., Baum, A., & Gormley, F. (1981). Social determinants of residential crowding stress. *Personality and Social Psychology Bulletin, 7,* 643–644.
Aiello, J. R., & Thompson, D. E. (1980). Personal space, crowding, and spatial behavior in a cultural context. In I. Altman, J. F. Wohlwill, & A. Rapoport (Eds.), *Human behavior and environment, Vol. 4.* New York: Plenum Publishing.
Alexander, R. A., & Barrett, G. U. (1982). Equitable salary increase judgments based upon merit and nonmerit considerations: A cross-national comparison. *International Review of Applied Psychology, 31,* 443–454.
Allison, K. W., Crawford, I., Echemendia, R., Robinson, L. V., & Knepp, D. (1994). Human diversity and professional competence. *American Psychologist, 49,* 792–796.
Allport, G. W., & Oddbert, H. S. (1936). Trait names: A psycholexical study. *Psychological Monographs, 47,* 2–11.
Alterman, E. (1997, November). Sex in the '90s. *Elle,* pp. 128–134.
Altman, L. K. (1989, May 18). Exercise seen as help regardless of weight. *The New York Times,* p. B9.
Altman, L. K. (1997, January 19). With AIDS advance, more disappointment. *The New York Times,* pp. A1, A14.
Altman, L. K. (1998, February 3). Big drop in AIDS deaths attributed to drug therapies. *The New York Times;* America Online.
Amato, P. R. (1983). Helping behavior in urban and rural environments: Field studies based on taxonomic organization of helping episodes. *Journal of Personality and Social Psychology, 45,* 571–586.
Amato, P. R., & Keith, B. (1991). Parental divorce and the well-being of children: A meta-analysis. *Psychological Bulletin, 110,* 26–46.
American Association of University Women. (1992). *How schools shortchange women: The A.A.U.W. report.* Washington, DC: A.A.U.W. Educational Foundation.
American Psychiatric Association. (1990). *The practice of electroconvulsive therapy.* Washington, DC: American Psychiatric Press.
American Psychiatric Association. (1994). *Diagnostic and statistical manual of the mental disorders* (4th ed.). Washington, DC: American Psychiatric Association.
American Psychological Association. (1992). Ethical principles of psychologists and code of conduct. *American Psychologist, 47,* 1597–1611.
American Psychological Association. (1993). Guidelines for providers of psychological services to ethnic, linguistic, and culturally diverse populations. *American Psychologist, 48,* 45–48.
America's job growth: The decade ahead. (1998, January 26). *Business Week;* America Online.
Andersen, B. L. (1992). Psychological interventions for cancer patients to enhance the quality of life. *Journal of Consulting and Clinical Psychology, 60,* 552–568.
Andersen, B. L. (1996). Psychological and behavioral studies in cancer prevention and control. *Health Psychology, 15,* 411–412.
Andersen, B. L., and others. (1998, January 7). *Journal of the National Cancer Institute.* Cited in Stress may decrease cancer defenses. (1998, January 6). Associated Press; America Online.
Anderson, C. A. (1989). Temperature and aggression: The ubiquitous effects of heat on the occurrence of human violence. *Psychological Bulletin, 106,* 74–96.
Anderson, C. A., & Bushman, B. (1998). Will global warming inflame our tempers? *APA Monitor, 29*(2), 8.
Anderson, C. A., & DeNeve, K. M. (1992). Temperature, aggression, and the negative affect escape model. *Psychological Bulletin, 111,* 347–351.
Anderson, C. A., & Riger, A. L. (1991). A controllability attributional model of problems in living: Dimensional and situational interactions in the prediction of depression and loneliness. *Social Cognition, 9,* 149–181.
Anderson, J R. (1985). *Cognitive psychology and its implications* (2d ed.). San Francisco: W. H. Freeman.
Anderson, L. P. (1991). Acculturative stress: A theory of relevance to Black Americans. *Clinical Psychology Review, 11,* 685–702.
Andrews, B., & Brown, G. W. (1993). Self-esteem and vulnerability to depression. *Journal of Abnormal Psychology, 102,* 565–572.
Angell, M. (1990). New ways to get pregnant. *New England Journal of Medicine, 323,* 1200–1202.
Angell, M. (1993). Privilege and health—What is the connection? *New England Journal of Medicine, 329,* 126–127.
Angier, N. (1994, December 1). Researchers link obesity in humans to flaw in a gene. *The New York Times,* pp. A1, B15.
Annunziata, J., & Jacobson-Kram, P. (1995). *Solving your problems together: Family therapy for the whole family.* Washington, DC: American Psychological Association.
APA Task Force on Diversity Issues at the Precollege and Undergraduate Levels of Education in Psychology. (1998). *APA Monitor, 29*(2), 41.
Appel, L. J., and others. (1997). A clinical trial of the effects of dietary patterns on blood pressure. *New England Journal of Medicine, 336,* 1117–1124.
Apter, T. (1995). *Secret paths.* New York: W. W. Norton.
Archer, J. (1996). Sex differences in social behavior. *American Psychologist, 51,* 909–917.
Archer, R. P., & Cash, T. F. (1985). Physical attractiveness and maladjustment among psychiatric patients. *Journal of Social and Clinical Psychology, 3,* 170–180.
Arkin, R. M., Detchon, C. S., & Maruyama, G. M. (1982). Roles of attribution, affect, and

cognitive interference in test anxiety. *Journal of Personality and Social Psychology, 43,* 1111–1124.

Asarnow, J. R., Carlson, G. A., & Guthrie, D. (1987). Coping strategies, self-perceptions, hopelessness, and perceived family environments in depressed and suicidal children. *Journal of Consulting and Clinical Psychology, 55,* 361–366.

Astley, S. J., and others. (1992). Analysis of facial shape in children gestationally exposed to marijuana, alcohol, and/or cocaine. *Pediatrics, 89,* 67–77.

Atchley, R. C. (1985). *Social forces and aging: An introduction to social gerontology.* Belmont, CA: Wadsworth.

Atkinson, J., & Huston, T. L. (1984). Sex role orientation and division of labor early in marriage. *Journal of Personality and Social Psychology, 46,* 330–345.

Audrain, J. E., Klesges, R. C., & Klesges, L. M. (1995). Relationship between obesity status and the metabolic effects of smoking in women. *Health Psychology, 14,* 116–123.

Ayanian, J. Z. (1993). Heart disease in black and white. *New England Journal of Medicine, 329,* 656–658.

Ayllon, T., & Haughton, E. (1962). Control of the behavior of schizophrenic patients by food. *Journal of the Experimental Analysis of Behavior, 5,* 343–352.

Azar, B. (1995). Several genetic traits linked to alcoholism. *APA Monitor, 26*(5), 21–22.

Azar, B. (1996b). Scientists examine cancer patients' fears. *APA Monitor, 27*(8), 32.

Azar, B. (1996c). Studies investigate the link between stress and immunity. *APA Monitor, 27*(8), 32.

Azar, B. (1997a). Nature, nurture: Not mutually exclusive. *APA Monitor, 28*(5), 1, 28.

Azar, B. (1997b). Environment is key to serotonin levels. *APA Monitor, 28*(4), 26, 29.

Azar, B. (1997c). It may cause anxiety, but day care can benefit kids. *APA Monitor, 28*(6), 13.

Azar, B. (1998). Communicating through pheromones. *APA Monitor, 29*(1), 1, 12.

Bach, G. R., & Deutsch, R. M. (1970). *Pairing.* New York: Peter H. Wyden.

Bachrach, L. L. (1992). What we know about homelessness among mentally ill persons. In H. R. Lamb, L. L. Bachrach, & F. I. Kass (Eds.), *Treating the homeless mentally ill.* Washington, DC: American Psychiatric Press.

Baenninger, M. A., & Elenteny, K. (1997). Cited in Azar, B. Environment can mitigate differences in spatial ability. *APA Monitor, 28*(6), 28.

Bailey, J. M., & Pillard, R. C. (1991). A genetic study of male sexual orientation. *Archives of General Psychiatry, 48,* 1089–1096.

Bal, D. G. (1992). Cancer in African Americans. *Ca—A Cancer Journal for Clinicians, 42,* 5–6.

Baltes, P. B. (1997). On the incomplete architecture of human ontogeny: Selection, optimization, and compensation as foundation of developmental theory. *American Psychologist, 52,* 366–380.

Baltes, P. B., & Baltes, M. (1995). Cited in Margoshes, P. (1995). For many, old age is the prime of life. *APA Monitor, 26*(5), 36–37.

Bandura, A. (1977). *Social learning theory.* Englewood Cliffs, NJ: Prentice-Hall.

Bandura, A. (1986). *Social foundations of thought and action: A social-cognitive theory.* Englewood Cliffs, NJ: Prentice-Hall.

Bandura, A. (1989). Human agency in social cognitive theory. *American Psychologist, 44,* 1175–1184.

Bandura, A. (1991). Human agency: The rhetoric and the reality. *American Psychologist, 46,* 157–162.

Bandura, A., Blanchard, E. B., & Ritter, B. (1969). The relative efficacy of desensitization and modeling approaches for inducing behavioral, affective, and cognitive changes. *Journal of Personality and Social Psychology, 13,* 173–199.

Bandura, A., & Rosenthal, T. L. (1966). Vicarious classical conditioning as a function of fear arousal. *Journal of Personality and Social Psychology, 3,* 54–62.

Bandura, A., Ross, S. A., & Ross, D. (1963). Imitation of film-mediated aggressive models. *Journal of Abnormal and Social Psychology, 66,* 3–11.

Bandura, A., Taylor, C. B., Williams, S. L., Medford, I. N., & Barchas, J. D. (1985). Catecholamine secretion as a function of perceived coping self-efficacy. *Journal of Consulting and Clinical Psychology, 53,* 406–414.

Banks, S. M., and others. (1995). The effects of message framing on mammography utilization. *Health Psychology, 14,* 178–184.

Baquet, C. R., Horm, J. W., Gibbs, T., & Greenwald, P. (1991). Socioeconomic factors and cancer incidence among Blacks and Whites. *Journal of the National Cancer Institute, 83,* 551–557.

Barbaree, H. E., & Marshall, W. L. (1991). The role of male sexual arousal in rape: Six models: *Journal of Consulting and Clinical Psychology, 59,* 621–631.

Barboza, D. (1998, January 19). Video world is smitten by a gun-toting, tomb-raiding sex symbol. *The New York Times,* p. D3.

Barlow, D. H. (1986a). Causes of sexual dysfunction: The role of anxiety and cognitive interference. *Journal of Consulting and Clinical Psychology, 54,* 140–148.

Barlow, D. H. (1986b). Behavioral conception and treatment of panic. *Psychopharmacology Bulletin, 22,* 802–806.

Barlow, D. H. (1991). Introduction to the special issue on diagnoses, definitions, and *DSM-IV:* The science of classification. *Journal of Abnormal Psychology, 100,* 243–244.

Barlow, D. H. (1995, June 21). Cited in Goleman, D. "Virtual reality" conquers fear of heights. *The New York Times,* p. C11.

Barlow, D. H. (1996). Health care policy, psychotherapy research, and the future of psychotherapy. *American Psychologist, 51,* 1050–1058.

Barnes, M. L., & Buss, D. M. (1985). Sex differences in the interpersonal behavior of married couples. *Journal of Personality and Social Psychology, 48,* 654–661.

Baron, R. A. (1983). *Behavior in organizations.* Boston: Allyn and Bacon.

Baron, R. A. (1990). Countering the effects of destructive criticism. *Journal of Applied Psychology, 75,* 235–245.

Baron, R. A., & Byrne, D. (1997). *Social psychology: Understanding human interaction* (8th ed.). Boston: Allyn and Bacon.

Baron, R. A., Mandel, D. R., Adams, C. A., & Griffen, L. M. (1976). Effects of social density in university residential requirements. *Journal of Personality and Social Psychology, 34,* 434–446.

Barr, C. E., Mednick, S. A., & Munk-Jorgensen, P. (1990). Exposure to influenza epidemics during gestation and adult schizophrenia. *Archives of General Psychiatry, 47,* 869–874.

Barringer, F. (1989, June 9). Divorce data stir doubt on trial marriage. *The New York Times,* pp. A1, A28.

Barringer, F. (1992b, July 19). More Americans are saying, "I don't." *The New York Times,* p. E2.

Barringer, F. (1993a, April 1). Viral sexual diseases are found in 1 of 5 in U.S. *The New York Times,* pp. A1, B9.

Barringer, F. (1993b, April 15). Sex survey of American men finds 1% are gay. *The New York Times,* pp. A1, A18.

Barrow, G. M., & Smith, P. A. (1983). *Aging, the individual, and society* (2d ed.). St. Paul: West.

Bartoshuk, L. M., & Beauchamp, G. K. (1994). Chemical senses. *Annual Review of Psychology, 45,* 419–449.

Basic Behavioral Science Task Force of the National Advisory Mental Health Council. (1996a). Basic behavioral science research for mental health: Vulnerability and resilience. *American Psychologist, 51,* 22–28.

Basic Behavioral Science Task Force of the National Advisory Mental Health Council (1996b). Basic behavioral science research for mental health: Sociocultural and environmental practices. *American Psychologist, 51,* 722–731.

Baucom, D. H., & Aiken, P. A. (1984). Sex role identity, marital satisfaction, and response to behavioral marital therapy. *Journal of Consulting and Clinical Psychology, 52,* 438–444.

Baucom, D. H., & Danker-Brown, P. (1979). Influence of sex roles on the development of learned helplessness. *Journal of Consulting and Clinical Psychology, 47,* 928–936.

Baucom, D. H., & Danker-Brown, P. (1983). Peer ratings of males and females possessing different sex role identities. *Journal of Personality Assessment, 44,* 334–343.

Baucom, D. H., & Danker-Brown, P. (1984). Sex

role identity and sex stereotyped tasks in the development of learned helplessness in women. *Journal of Personality and Social Psychology, 46,* 422–430.

Baucom, D. H., Epstein, N., Sayers, S., & Goldman Sher, T. (1989). The role of cognitions in marital relationships: Definitional, methodological, and conceptual issues. *Journal of Consulting and Clinical Psychology, 57,* 31–38.

Baum, A. (1988). Disasters, natural and otherwise. *Psychology Today, 22*(4), 57–60.

Baum, A., Fisher, J. D., & Solomon, S. (1981). Type of information, familiarity, and the reduction of crowding stress. *Journal of Personality and Social Psychology, 40,* 11–23.

Baum, A., & Fleming, I. (1993). Implications of psychological research on stress and technological accidents. *American Psychologist, 48,* 665–672.

Baum, A., Friedman, A. L., & Zakowski, S. G. (1997). Stress and genetic testing for disease risk. *Health Psychology, 16,* 8–19.

Baum, A., Gatchel, R. J., & Schaeffer, M. A. (1983). Emotional, behavioral, and physiological effects of chronic stress at Three Mile Island. *Journal of Consulting and Clinical Psychology, 51,* 565–572.

Baum, A., & Valins, S. (1977). *Architecture and social behavior.* Hillsdale, NJ: Erlbaum.

Baum, M. J., and others. (1977). Hormonal basis of proceptivity and receptivity in female primates. *Archives of Sexual Behavior, 6,* 173–192.

Baumeister, R. F. (1984). Choking under pressure: Self-consciousness and paradoxical effects of incentives on skillful performance. *Journal of Personality and Social Psychology, 46,* 610–620.

Baumeister, R. F., & Covington, M. V. (1985). Self-esteem, persuasion, and retrospective distortion of initial attitudes. *Electronic Social Psychology, 1,* 1–22.

Baumgardner, A. H., Heppner, P. P., & Arkin, R. M. (1986). Role of causal attribution in personal problem solving. *Journal of Personality and Social Psychology, 50,* 636–643.

Baumrind, D. (1973). The development of instrumental competence through socialization. In A. D. Pick (Ed.), *Minnesota Symposia on Child Development, Vol. 7.* Minneapolis: University of Minnesota Press.

Baumrind, D. (1986). Sex differences in moral reasoning: Response to Walker's (1984) conclusion that there are none. *Child Development, 57,* 511–521.

Baumrind, D. (1991). The influence of parenting style on adolescent competence and substance abuse. *Journal of Early Adolescence, 11,* 56–95.

Beardslee, W. R., Bemporad, J., Keller, M. B., & Klerman, G. L. (1983). Children of parents with major affective disorder: A review. *American Journal of Psychiatry, 140,* 825–832.

Beatty, W. W. (1979). Gonadal hormones and sex differences in nonreproductive behaviors in rodents: Organizational and activational influences. *Hormones and Behavior, 12,* 112–163.

Beck, A. T. (1991). Cognitive therapy: A 30-year retrospective. *American Psychologist, 46,* 368–375.

Beck, A. T. (1993). Cognitive therapy: Past, present, and future. *Journal of Consulting and Clinical Psychology, 61,* 194–198.

Beck, A. T., Brown, G., Berchick, R. J., Stewart, B. L., & Steer, R. A. (1990). Relationship between hopelessness and ultimate suicide. *American Journal of Psychiatry, 147,* 190–195.

Beck, A. T., & Freeman, A. (1990). *Cognitive therapy of personality disorders.* New York: Guilford Press.

Beck, A. T., Rush, A. J., Show, B. F., & Emery, G. (1979). *Cognitive therapy of depression.* New York: Guilford Press.

Beck, J., Elsner, A., & Silverstein, C. (1977). Position uncertainty and the perception of apparent movement. *Perception and psychophysics, 21,* 33–38.

Becker, L. B., and others. (1993). Radical differences in the incidence of cardiac arrest and subsequent survival. *New England Journal of Medicine, 329,* 600–606.

Becker, M. H., & Maiman, L. A. (1980). Strategies for enhancing patient compliance. *Journal of Community Health, 6,* 113–135.

Beers, T. M., & Karoly, P. (1979). Cognitive strategies, expectancy, and coping style in the control of pain. *Journal of Consulting and Clinical Psychology, 47,* 179–180.

Behrens, D. (1990, September 21). Test-tube baby in tug-of-war. *New York Newsday,* pp. 3, 23.

Behrman, R. E., & Vaughn, V. C. III. (1983). *Pediatrics.* Philadelphia: W. B. Saunders.

Bell, A. P., & Weinberg, M. S. (1978). *Homosexualities: A study of diversity among men and women.* New York: Simon and Schuster.

Bell, A. P., Weinberg, M. S., & Hammersmith, S. K. (1981). *Sexual preference: Its development in men and women.* Bloomington: University of Indiana Press.

Bell, P. A. (1981). Physiological comfort, performance, and social effects of heat stress. *Journal of Social Issues, 37,* 71–94.

Bell, P. A., & Baron, R. A. (1981). Ambient temperature and human violence. In P. F. Brain & D. Benton (Eds.), *A multidisciplinary approach to aggression research.* Amsterdam: Elsevier.

Belle, D. (1990). Poverty and women's mental health. *American Psychologist, 45,* 385–389.

Belsky, J. (1990). Developmental risks associated with infant day care: Attachment insecurity, noncompliance and aggression? In I. S. Cherazi (Ed.), *Psychosocial issues in day care* (pp. 37–68). New York: American Psychiatric Press.

Belsky, J. (1993). Etiology of child maltreatment. *Psychological Bulletin, 114,* 413–434.

Bem, D. J. (1972). Self-perception theory. In L. Berkowitz (Ed.), *Advances in experimental social psychology, Vol. 6.* New York: Academic Press.

Bem, D. J. (1993). Social influence. In R. L. Atkinson, R. C. Atkinson, E. E. Smith, & D. J. Bem, *Introduction to psychology* (11th ed., pp. 596–627). Fort Worth: Harcourt Brace Jovanovich.

Bem, S. L. (1974). The measurement of psychological androgyny. *Journal of Consulting and Clinical Psychology, 42,* 151–162.

Bem, S. L. (1975). Sex role adaptability: One consequence of psychological androgyny. *Journal of Personality and Social Psychology, 31,* 634–643.

Bem, S. L. (1981). Gender schema theory: A cognitive account of sex typing. *Psychological Review, 88,* 354–364.

Bem, S. L. (1983). Gender schema theory and its implications for child development: Raising gender-aschematic children in a gender-schematic society. *Signs: Journal of Women in Culture and Society, 8,* 598–616.

Bem, S. L. (1985). Androgyny and gender schema theory: A conceptual and empirical integration. In T. B. Sonderegger (Ed.), *Nebraska symposium on motivation.* Lincoln: University of Nebraska Press.

Bem, S. L. (1993). *The lenses of gender.* New Haven: Yale University Press.

Bem, S. L., & Bem, D. J. (1973). Training the woman to know her place: The power of a nonconscious ideology. In L. S. Wrightsman & J. C. Brigham (Eds.), *Contemporary issues in social psychology* (2d ed.). Monterey, CA: Brooks/Cole.

Bem, S. L., & Lenney, E. (1976). Sex typing and the avoidance of cross-sexed behaviors. *Journal of Personality and Social Psychology, 33,* 48–54.

Bem, S. L., Martyna, W., & Watson, C. (1976). Sex typing and androgyny: Further explorations of the expressive domain. *Journal of Personality and Social Psychology, 34,* 1016–1023.

Benecke, W. M., & Harris, M. B. (1972). Teaching self-control of study behavior. *Behaviour Research and Therapy, 10,* 35–41.

Benson, F. (1995). Cited in Margoshes, P. For many, old age is the prime of life. *APA Monitor, 26*(5), 36–37.

Benson, H. (1975). *The relaxation response.* New York: Morrow.

Benson, H., Manzetta, B. R., & Rosner, B. (1973). Decreased systolic blood pressure in hypertensive subjects who practiced meditation. *Journal of Clinical Investigation, 52,* 8.

Berenbaum, H., & Connelly, J. (1993). The effect of stress on hedonic capacity. *Journal of Abnormal Psychology, 102,* 474–481.

Berezin, N. (1980). *The gentle birth book: A practical guide to Leboyer family-centered delivery.* New York: Pocket Books.

Berg, J. H., & Peplau, L. A. (1982). Loneliness: The relationship of self-disclosure and androgyny. *Personality and Social Psychology Bulletin, 8,* 624–630.

Berger, B. G. (1993). Exercise and the quality of life. In R. N. Singer, M. Murphey, & L. K. Tennant (Eds.), *Handbook of research on sport psychology* (pp. 729–760). New York: Macmillan.

Berger, K. S. (1994). *The developing person through the life span* (3d ed.). New York: Worth.

Berke, R. L. (1990, February 14). Survey shows use of drugs by students fell last year. *The New York Times,* p. A16.

Berke, R. L. (1997, June 15). Suddenly, the new politics of morality. *The New York Times,* p. E3.

Berkman, L. F., & Syme, S. L. (1979). Social networks, host resistance, and mortality: A nine-year follow-up study of Alameda County residents. *American Journal of Epidemiology, 109,* 186–204.

Berkowitz, G. S., and others. (1990, March 8). *New England Journal of Medicine.*

Berkowitz, L. (1990). On the formation and regulation of anger and aggression: A cognitive-neoassociationistic analysis. *American Psychologist, 45,* 494–503.

Berman, J. S., Miller, R. C., & Massman, P. J. (1985). Cognitive therapy versus systematic desensitization: Is one therapy superior? *Psychological Bulletin, 97,* 451–461.

Bernal, M. E., & Castro, F. G. (1994). Are clinical psychologists prepared for service and research with ethnic minorities? *American Psychologist, 49,* 797–805.

Berndt, T. J. (1982). The features and effects of friendships in early adolescence. *Child Development, 53,* 1447–1460.

Berndt, T. J., & Perry, T. B. (1986). Children's perceptions of friendships as supportive relationships. *Developmental Psychology, 22,* 640–648.

Bernstein, B. E. (1977). Effect of menstruation on academic performance among college women. *Archives of Sexual Behavior, 6,* 289–296.

Bernstein, W. M., Stephenson, B. O., Snyder, M. L., & Wicklund, R. A. (1983). Causal ambiguity and heterosexual affiliation. *Journal of Experimental Social Psychology, 19,* 78–92.

Berntzen, D., & Götestam, K. G. (1987). Effects of on-demand versus fixed-interval schedules in the treatment of chronic pain with analgesic compounds. *Journal of Consulting and Clinical Psychology, 55,* 213–217.

Berscheid, E., Walster, E., & Borhnstedt, G. (1973). Body image, the happy American body: A survey report. *Psychology Today,* 7(6), 119–123, 126–131.

Berzins, J. I., Welling, M. A., & Wetter, R. E. (1977). The PRF ANDRO Scale: User's manual. Unpublished manuscript: University of Kentucky.

Betancourt, H., & López, S. R. (1993). The study of culture, ethnicity, and race in American psychology. *American Psychologist, 48,* 629–637.

Betz, N. E., & Hackett, G. (1981). The relationships of career-related self-efficacy expectations to perceived career options in college women and men. *Journal of Counseling Psychology, 28,* 399–410.

Bianchi, S. M., & Spain, D. (1997). *Women, work and family in America.* Population Reference Bureau.

Biran, M., & Wilson, G. T. (1981). Treatment of phobic disorders using cognitive and exposure methods: A self-efficacy analysis. *Journal of Consulting and Clinical Psychology, 49,* 886–899.

Birch, K. (1981). Is empathic emotion a source of altruistic motivation? *Journal of Personality and Social Psychology, 40,* 290–302.

Birren, J. E. (1983). Aging in America: Roles for psychology. *American Psychologist, 38,* 298–299.

Bixler, R. H. (1989). Diversity: A historical/comparative perspective. *Behavioral and Brain Sciences, 12,* 15–16.

Bjorklund, D. F., & Kipp, K. (1996). Parental investment theory and gender differences in the evolution of inhibition mechanisms. *Psychological Bulletin, 120,* 163–188.

Black, S. T. (1993). Comparing genuine and simulated suicide notes: A new perspective. *Journal of Consulting and Clinical Psychology, 61,* 699–702.

Blackburn, I. M., and others. (1981). The efficacy of cognitive therapy in depression: A treatment trial using cognitive therapy and pharmacotherapy, each alone and in combination. *British Journal of Psychiatry, 139,* 181–189.

Blake, R. (1985). Neurohormones and sexual preference. *Psychology Today, 19*(1), 12–13.

Blakeslee, S. (1992, January 7). Scientists unraveling chemistry of dreams. *The New York Times,* pp. C1, C10.

Blakeslee, S. (1993, September 7). Human nose may hold an additional organ for a real sixth sense. *The New York Times,* p. C3.

Blakeslee, S. (1994, April 13). Black smokers' higher risk of cancer may be genetic. *The New York Times,* p. C14.

Blakeslee, S. (1995, May 16). The mystery of music. *The New York Times,* pp. C1, C10.

Blanchard, E. B. (1992). Psychological treatment of benign headache disorders. *Journal of Consulting and Clinical Psychology, 60,* 537–551.

Blanchard, E. B., and others. (1990a). Placebo-controlled evaluation of abbreviated progressive muscle relaxation and of relaxation combined with cognitive therapy in the treatment of tension headache. *Journal of Consulting and Clinical Psychology, 58,* 210–215.

Blanchard, E. B., and others. (1990b). A controlled evaluation of thermal biofeedback and thermal feedback combined with cognitive therapy in the treatment of vascular headache. *Journal of Consulting and Clinical Psychology, 58,* 216–224.

Blanchard, E. B., and others. (1991). The role of regular home practice in the relaxation treatment of tension headache. *Journal of Consulting and Clinical Psychology, 59,* 467–470.

Blanchard, R., Steiner, B. W., & Clemmensen, L. H. (1985). Gender dysphoria, gender reorientation, and the clinical management of transsexualism. *Journal of Consulting and Clinical Psychology, 53,* 295–304.

Blass, T. (1991). Understanding behavior in the Milgram obedience experiment: The roles of personality, situations, and their interactions. *Journal of Personality and Social Psychology, 60,* 398–413.

Blatt, S. J., Quinlan, D. M., Pilkonis, P. A., & Shea, M. T. (1995). Impact of perfectionism and need for approval on the brief treatment of depression: The National Institute of Mental Health Treatment of Depression Collaborative Research Program revisited. *Journal of Consulting and Clinical Psychology, 63,* 125–132.

Blatt, S. J., Zuroff, D. C., Quinlan, D. M., & Pilkonis, P. A. (1996). Interpersonal factors in brief treatment of depression. *Journal of Consulting and Clinical Psychology, 64,* 162–171.

Block, J. (1983). Differential premises arising from differential socialization of the sexes: Some conjectures. *Child Development, 54,* 1335–1354.

Block, J. (1995). A contrarian view of the five-factor approach to personality description. *Psychological Bulletin, 117,* 187–215.

Bloom, B. J., Asher, S. J., & White, S. W. (1978). Marital disruption as a stressor: A review and analysis. *Psychological Bulletin, 85,* 867–894.

Bloom, B. L. (1992). Computer assisted psychological intervention. *Clinical Psychology Review, 12,* 169–197.

Blumstein, P., & Schwartz, P. (1990). Intimate relationships and the creation of sexuality. In D. P. McWhirter, S. A. Sanders, & J. M. Reinisch (Eds.), *Homosexuality/heterosexuality: Concepts of sexual orientation* (pp. 307–320). New York: Oxford University Press.

Bodenhausen, G. V., & Wyer, R. S. (1985). Effects of stereotypes on decision making and information-processing strategies. *Journal of Personality and Social Psychology, 48,* 267–282.

Boksay, I. (1998, February 11). Mourning spouse's death: Two years. Associated Press; America Online.

Bond, C. R., & McMahon, R. J. (1984). Relationships between marital distress and child behavior problems, maternal personal adjustment, maternal personality, and maternal parenting behavior. *Journal of Abnormal Psychology, 93,* 348–351.

Booth, A., & Edwards, J. N. (1985). Age at marriage and marital instability. *Journal of Marriage and the Family, 47,* 67–75.

Booth-Kewley, S., & Friedman, H. S. (1987). Psychological predictors of heart disease: A quantitative review. *Psychological Bulletin, 101,* 343–362.

Borkovec, T. D., & Costello, E. (1993). Efficacy

of applied relaxation and cognitive-behavioral therapy in the treatment of generalized anxiety disorder. *Journal of Consulting and Clinical Psychology, 61,* 611–619.

Boskind-White, M., & White, W. C. (1983). *Bulimarexia: The binge/purge cycle.* New York: W.W. Norton.

Boskind-White, M., & White, W. C. (1986). Bulimarexia: A historical-sociocultural perspective. In K. D. Brownell & J. P. Foreyt (Eds.), *Handbook of eating disorders.* New York: Basic Books.

Boston Women's Health Book Collective. (1993). *The new our bodies, ourselves.* New York: Simon and Schuster.

Boyd-Franklin, N. (1995). *A multisystems model for treatment interventions with innercity African American families.* Master lecture delivered to the meeting of the American Psychological Association, New York, August 12.

Braun, A. R., & Balkin, T. J. (1998, January 6). Cited in Wade, N. Was Freud wrong? Are dreams the brain's start-up test? *The New York Times.*

Breast-feeding revision. (1997, December 9). *The New York Times,* p. F9.

Brenner, J. (1992, February 6). Cited in Williams, L. Woman's image in a mirror. Who defines what she sees? *The New York Times,* pp. A1, B7.

Bride, A. B. (1990). Mental health effects of women's multiple roles. *American Psychologist, 45,* 381–384.

Bridgwater, C. A. (1982). What candor can do. *Psychology Today, 16*(5), 16.

Brigham, J. C. (1980). Limiting conditions of the "physical attractiveness stereotype": Attributions about divorce: *Journal of Research in Personality, 14,* 365–375.

Broberg, A., Hwang, P., Wessels, H., & Lamb, M. (1997). Cited in Azar, B. It may cause anxiety, but day care can benefit kids. *APA Monitor, 28*(6), 13.

Brody, J. E. (1989, May 18). Flurry of new findings about caffeine stirs hopes and fears—as well as general confusion. *The New York Times,* p. B8.

Brody, J. E. (1990a, January 19). High cholesterol poses heart risk in older men. *The New York Times,* p. A19.

Brody, J. E. (1990b, January 23). Scientists trace aberrant sexuality. *The New York Times,* pp. C1, C12.

Brody, J. E. (1990c, January 25). Exercise can improve many aspects of a disabled person's life. *The New York Times,* p. B11.

Brody, J. E. (1992, January 8). Migraines and the estrogen connection. *The New York Times,* p. C12.

Brody, J. E. (1993a, August 4). A new look at an old quest for sexual stimulants. *The New York Times,* p. C12.

Brody, J. E. (1993b, December 1). Liberated at last from the myths about menopause. *The New York Times,* p. C15.

Brody, J. E. (1996a, August 28). PMS need not be the worry it was just decades ago. *The New York Times,* p. C9.

Brody, J. E. (1996b, September 4). Osteoporosis can threaten men as well as women. *The New York Times,* p. C9.

Brody, J. E. (1997, March 26). Race and weight. *The New York Times,* p. C8.

Brody, J. E. (1998a, February 3). Personal health: Hormone hoopla, hormone truth. *The New York Times;* America Online.

Brody, J. E. (1998b, February 10). Genetic ties may be factor in violence in stepfamilies. *The New York Times,* pp. F1, F4.

Brooks-Gunn, J., & Ruble, D. N. (1980). The menstrual attitude questionnaire. *Psychosomatic Medicine, 42,* 503–511.

Brown, L. S. (1992). A feminist critique of the personality disorders. In L. Brown & M. Balou (Eds.), *Personality and psychopathology: Feminist reappraisals.* New York: Guilford Press.

Brown, M., & Massaro, S. (1996). New brain studies yield insights into cocaine binging and addiction. *Journal of Addictive Diseases, 15*(4).

Brown, P. L. (1987, September 14). Studying seasons of a woman's life. *The New York Times,* p. B17.

Browne, A. (1993). Violence against women by male partners: Prevalence, outcomes, and policy implications. *American Psychologist, 48,* 1077–1087.

Brownell, K. D. (1997). We must be more militant about food. *APA Monitor, 28*(3), 48.C5.

Brownell, K. D., & Wadden, T. A. (1992). Obesity: Understanding a serious, prevalent, and refractory disorder. *Journal of Consulting and Clinical Psychology, 60,* 505–517.

Buchanan, C. M., Eccles, J. S., & Becker, J. B. (1992). Are adolescents the victims of raging hormones? Evidence for activational effects of hormones on moods and behavior at adolescence. *Psychological Bulletin, 111,* 62–107.

Buchsbaum, M. S., & Haier, R. J. (1987). Functional and anatomical brain imaging: Impact on schizophrenia research. *Schizophrenia Bulletin, 13,* 115–132.

Buffone, G. W. (1980). Exercise as therapy: A closer look. *Journal of Counseling and Psychotherapy, 3,* 101–115.

Buffone, G. W. (1984). Running and depression. In M. L. Sachs & G. W. Buffone (Eds.), *Running as therapy: An integrated approach.* Lincoln: University of Nebraska Press.

Bulman, R. J., & Wortman, C. B. (1977). Attribution of blame and coping in the "real world": Severe accident victims react to their lot. *Journal of Personality and Social Psychology, 35,* 351–363.

Bumpass, L. (1995, July 6). Cited in Steinhauer, J. No marriage, no apologies. *The New York Times,* pp. C1, C7.

Burish, T. G., Snyder, S. L., & Jenkins, R. A. (1991). Preparing patients for cancer chemotherapy: Effect of coping preparation and relaxation interventions. *Journal of Consulting and Clinical Psychology, 59,* 518–525.

Burns, D. D., & Nolen-Hoeksema, S. (1992). Therapeutic empathy and recovery from depression in cognitive-behavioral therapy. *Journal of Consulting and Clinical Psychology, 60,* 441–449.

Burns, G. L., & Farina, A. (1987). Physical attractiveness and self-perception of mental disorder. *Journal of Abnormal Psychology, 96,* 161–163.

Burros, M. (1988, January 6). What Americans really eat: Nutrition can wait. *The New York Times,* pp. C1, C6.

Burt, M. R. (1980). Cultural myths and supports for rape. *Journal of Personality and Social Psychology, 38,* 217–230.

Buss, A. H. (1983). Social rewards and personality. *Journal of Personality and Social Psychology, 44,* 553–563.

Buss, A. H. (1986). *Social behavior and personality.* Hillsdale, NJ: Erlbaum.

Buss, D. M. (1984). Toward a psychology of person-environment (PE) correlation: The role of spouse selection. *Journal of Personality and Social Psychology, 47,* 361–377.

Buss, D. M. (1994). *The evolution of desire: Strategies of human mating.* New York: Basic Books.

Buss, D. M., Gomes, M., Higgins, D. S., & Lauterbach, K. (1987). Tactics of manipulation. *Journal of Personality and Social Psychology, 52,* 1219–1229.

Butler, R. (1998). Cited in CD-ROM that accompanies Nevid, J. S., Rathus, S. A., & Rubenstein, H. *Health in the new millennium.* New York: Worth.

Byrne, D., & Murnen, S. (1987). Maintaining love relationships. In R. J. Sternberg & M. L. Barnes (Eds.), *The anatomy of love.* New Haven: Yale University Press.

Byrnes, J., & Takahira, S. (1993). Explaining gender differences on SAT-math items. *Developmental Psychology, 29,* 805–810.

Calhoun, J. B. (1962). Population density and social pathology. *Scientific American, 206,* 139–148.

Califano, J. A. (1995). The wrong way to stay slim. *New England Journal of Medicine, 333,* 1214–1216.

Campbell, S. B., Cohn, J. F., Flanagan, C., Popper, S., & Meyers, T. (1992). Course and correlates of postpartum depression during the transition to parenthood. *Development and Psychopathology, 4,* 29–47.

Cannistra, S. A., & Niloff, J. M. (1996). Cancer of the uterine cervix. *New England Journal of Medicine, 334,* 1030–1038.

Cannon, W. B. (1929). *Bodily changes in pain, hunger, fear, and rage.* New York: Appleton.

Cappella, J. N., & Palmer, M. T. (1990). Attitude similarity, relational history, and attraction. The mediating effects of kinesic and vocal behaviors. *Communication Monographs, 5,* 161–183.

Carey, G. (1992). Twin imitation for antisocial behavior: Implications for genetic and family environment research. *Journal of Abnormal Psychology, 101,* 18–25.

Carey, G., & DiLalla, D. L. (1994). Personality and psychopathology: Genetic perspectives. *Journal of Abnormal Psychology, 103,* 32–43.

Carmody, D. (1990, March 7). College drinking: Changes in attitude and habit. *The New York Times,* p. B5.

Carpenter, W. T., Jr., & Buchanan, R. W. (1994). Schizophrenia. *New England Journal of Medicine, 330,* 681–690.

Carstensen, L. (1995). Cited in Margoshes, P. For many, old age is the prime of life. *APA Monitor, 26*(5), 36–37.

Carstensen, L. (1997, August 17). *The evolution of social goals across the life span.* Paper presented to the American Psychological Association, Chicago.

Carver, C. S., & Gaines, J. G. (1987). Optimism, pessimism, and postpartum depression. *Cognitive Therapy and Research, 11,* 449–462.

Casper, L. (1997). My daddy takes care of me! Fathers as care providers. U.S. Bureau of the Census: *Current Population Reports,* P70-59.

Caspi, A., & Herbener, E. S. (1990). Continuity and change: Assortative marriage and the consistency of personality in adulthood. *Journal of Personality and Social Psychology, 58,* 250–258.

Cassileth, B. R., and others. (1985). Psychosocial correlates of survival in advanced malignant diseases? *New England Journal of Medicine, 312,* 1551–1555.

Castelli, W. (1994, February 8). Cited in Brody, J. E. Scientist at work—William Castelli. *The New York Times,* pp. C1, C10.

Caulfield, M., and others. (1994). Linkage of the angiotensinogen gene to essential hypertension. *New England Journal of Medicine, 330,* 1629–1633.

Cavanaugh, J. C., & Green, E. E. (1990). I believe, therefore I can: Self-efficacy beliefs in memory aging. In E. A. Lovelace (Ed.), *Aging and cognition: Mental processes, self-awareness, and interventions.* North-Holland, Elsevier.

CDC (Centers for Disease Control and Prevention). (1995, April 21). Children aged 10 to 14; America Online.

Celis, W. (1991, January 2). Students trying to draw line between sex and an assault. *The New York Times,* pp. 1, B8.

Centers for Disease Control and Prevention. (1997). *HIV/AIDS surveillance report: U.S. HIV and AIDS cases reported through December 1996, 8*(2).

Cepeda-Benito, A. (1993). Meta-analytical review of the efficacy of nicotine chewing gum in smoking treatment programs. *Journal of Consulting and Clinical Psychology, 61,* 822–830.

Chadwick, P. D. J., & Lowe, C. F. (1990). Measurement and modification of delusional beliefs. *Journal of Consulting and Clinical Psychology, 58,* 225–232.

Chaiken, S., & Eagly, A. H. (1983). Communication modality as a determinant of persuasion: The role of communicator salience. *Journal of Personality and Social Psychology, 45,* 241–256.

Charny, I. W., & Parnass, S. (1995). The impact of extramarital relationships on the continuation of marriages. *Journal of Sex and Marital Therapy, 21,* 100–115.

Chassin, L., Curran, P. J., Hussong, A. M., & Colder, C. R. (1996). The relation of parent alcoholism to adolescent substance use. *Journal of Abnormal Psychology, 105,* 70–80.

Cheating going out of style but sex is popular as ever. (1993, October 19). *Newsday,* p. 2.

Check, J. M., & Melchior, L. A. (1990). Shyness, self-esteem, and self-consciousness. In H. Leitenberg (Ed.), *Handbook of social and evaluation anxiety.* New York: Plenum.

Chemers, M. M., Hays, R. B., Rhodewalt, F., & Wysocki, J. (1985). A person-environment analysis of job stress: A contingency model explanation. *Journal of Personality and Social Psychology, 49,* 628–635.

Chesney, M. A. (1993). Health psychology in the 21st century: Acquired immunodeficiency syndrome as a harbinger of things to come. *Health Psychology, 12,* 259–268.

Chesno, F. A., & Kilmann, P. R. (1975). Effects of stimulation intensity on sociopathic avoidance learning. *Journal of Abnormal Psychology, 84,* 144–151.

Chitayat, D. (1993, February). Presentation to the Fifth International Interdisciplinary Congress on Women, University of Costa Rica, San Jose, Costa Rica.

Chronicle of Higher Education. (1992, March 18), A35–A44.

Cialdini, R. B., & Fultz, J. (1990). Interpreting the negative mood-helping literature via "mega"-analysis: A contrary view. *Psychological Bulletin, 107,* 210–214.

Cinciripini, P. M., Cinciripini, L. G., Wallfisch, A., Haque, W., & Van Vunakis, H. (1996). Behavior therapy and the transdermal nicotine patch. *Journal of Consulting and Clinical Psychology, 64,* 314–323.

Cinciripini, P. M., Lapitsky, L., Seay, S., Wallfisch, A., Kitchens, K., Van Vunakis, H. (1995). The effects of smoking schedules on cessation outcome: Can we improve on common methods of gradual and abrupt nicotine withdrawal? *Journal of Consulting and Clinical Psychology, 63,* 314–323.

Clark, L. A., Watson, D., & Mineka, S. M. (1994). Temperament, personality, and the mood and anxiety disorders. *Journal of Abnormal Psychology, 103,* 103–116.

Clarke-Stewart, K. A. (1990). "The 'effects' of infant day care reconsidered": Risks for parents, children, and researchers. In N. Fox & G. G. Fein (Eds.), *Infant day care: The current debate* (pp. 61–86). Norwood, NJ: Ablex.

Clarke-Stewart, K. A. (1991). A home is not a school: The effects of child care on children's development. *Journal of Social Issues, 47* 105–123.

Clay, R. A. (1996a). Beating the "biological clock" with zest. *APA Monitor, 27*(2), 37.

Clay, R. A. (1996b). Older men are more involved fathers, studies show. *APA Monitor, 27*(2), 37.

Clay, R. A. (1997). Meditation is becoming more mainstream. *APA Monitor, 28*(9), 12.

Cleckley, H. (1964). *The mask of sanity.* St. Louis, Mosby.

Cleek, M., & Pearson, T. (1985). Perceived causes of divorce: An analysis of interrelationships. *Journal of Marriage and the Family, 47,* 179–183.

Clingempell, W. G., & Repucci, N. D. (1982). Joint custody after divorce: Major issues and goals for research. *Psychological Bulletin, 91,* 102–127.

Clingempeel, W. G., & Segal, S. (1986). Stepparent-stepchild relationships and the psychological adjustment of children in stepmother and stepfather families. *Child Development, 57,* 474–484.

Cloninger, C. R., & Gottesman, I. I. (1987). Genetic and environmental factors in antisocial behavior disorders. In S. A. Mednick and others (Eds.), *The causes of crime: New biological approaches.* New York: Cambridge University Press.

Clore, G. L., & Byrne, D. (1977). The process of personality interaction. In R. B. Cattell & R. M. Dreger (Eds.), *Handbook of modern personality theory.* Washington, DC: Hemisphere.

Coates, T. J. (1990). Strategies for modifying sexual behavior for primary and secondary prevention of HIV disease. *Journal of Consulting and Clinical Psychology, 58,* 57–69.

Coe, C. (1993). Cited in Adler, T. Men and women affected by stress, but differently. *APA Monitor, 24*(7), 8–9.

Cohen, L. A. (1987, November). Diet and cancer. *Scientific American,* pp. 42–48, 533–534.

Cohen, R. (1996). Cited in Clay, R. A. Beating the "biological clock" with zest. *APA Monitor, 27*(2), 37.

Cohen, S., Evans, G. W., Stokols, D., & Krantz, D. S. (1986). *Behavior, health, and environmental stress.* New York: Plenum Publishing.

Cohen, S., Tyrrell, D. A. J., & Smith, A. P. (1991). Psychological stress and susceptibility to the common cold. *New England Journal of Medicine, 325,* 606–612.

Cohen, S., Tyrrell, D. A. J., & Smith, A. P. (1993). Negative life events, perceived stress, negative affect, and susceptibility to the common cold. *Journal of Personality and Social Psychology, 64,* 131–140.

Cohen, S., & Wills, T. A. (1985). Stress, social supports and the buffering hypothesis. *Psychological Bulletin, 98,* 310–357.

Cohn, E. G. (1990). Weather and violent crime. *Environment and Behavior, 22,* 280–294.

Coleman, L. (1990, August 2). Cited in Goleman, G. The quiet comeback of electroshock therapy. *The New York Times,* p. B5.

Coleman, M., & Ganong, L. H. (1985). Love and sex role stereotypes: Do macho men and feminine women make better lovers? *Journal of Personality and Social Psychology, 49,* 170–176.

Coles, C. (1994). Critical periods for prenatal alcohol exposure: Evidence from animal and human studies. *Alcohol Health and Research World, 18*(1), 22–29.

Collins, D. L., Baum, A., & Singer, J. E. (1983). Coping with chronic stress at Three Mile Island: Psychological and biochemical evidence. *Health Psychology, 2,* 149–166.

Collins, N. L., & Miller, L. C. (1994). Self-disclosure and liking: A meta-analytic review. *Psychological Bulletin, 116,* 457–475.

Comas-Diaz, L. (1994, February). Race and gender in psychotherapy with women of color. *Winter roundtable on cross-cultural counseling and psychotherapy: Race and gender.* New York: Teachers College, Columbia University.

Condiotte, M. M., & Lichtenstein, E. (1981). Self-efficacy and relapse in smoking cessation programs. *Journal of Consulting and Clinical Psychology, 49,* 648–658.

Condom for women nearing an approval for U.S. market. (1993, April 28). *The New York Times,* p. A13.

Condon, J. W., & Crano, W. D. (1988). Inferred evaluation and the relation between attitude similarity and interpersonal attraction. *Journal of Personality and Social Psychology, 54,* 789–797.

Cooney, J. L., & Zeichner, A. (1985). Selective attention to negative feedback in Type A and Type B individuals. *Journal of Abnormal Psychology, 94,* 110–112.

Cooney, N. L., Litt, M. D., Morse, P. A., Bauer, L. O., & Gaupp, L. (1997). Alcohol cue reactivity, negative-mood reactivity, and relapse in treated alcoholic men. *Journal of Abnormal Psychology, 106,* 243–250.

Cooper, J. R., Bloom, F. E., & Roth, R. H. (1991). *The biochemical basis of neuropharmacology.* New York: Oxford University Press.

Coopersmith, S. (1967). *The antecedents of self-esteem.* San Francisco: W. H. Freeman.

Costa, P. T., Jr., & McCrae, R. R. (1984). Personality as a lifelong determinant of wellbeing. In C. Z. Malatesta & C. E. Izard (Eds.), *Emotion in adult development.* Beverly Hills, CA: Sage.

Cousins, N. (1979). *Anatomy of an illness as perceived by the patient: Reflections on healing and regeneration.* New York: Norton.

Cowley, G. (1988, April 11). Science and the cigarette. *Newsweek,* pp. 66–67.

Cowley, G. (1996, September 16). Attention: Aging men. *Newsweek,* pp. 68–77.

Craig, M. E., Kalichman, S. C., & Follingstad, D. R. (1989). Verbal coercive sexual behavior among college students. *Archives of Sexual Behavior, 18,* 421–434.

Cramer, R. E., McMaster, M. R., Bartell, P. A., & Dragna, M. (1988). Subject competence and minimization of the bystander effect. *Journal of Applied Social Psychology, 18,* 1133–1148.

Creamer, M., Burgess, P., & Pattison, P. (1992). Reaction to trauma: A cognitive processing model. *Journal of Abnormal Psychology, 101,* 452–459.

Crews, D. (1994). Animal sexuality. *Scientific American, 270*(1), 108–114.

Crick, F., & Mitchison, G. (1983). The function of dream sleep. *Nature, 304,* 111–114.

Crossette, B. (1997, December 29). Court backs Egypt's ban on mutilation. *The New York Times,* p. A3.

Crowley, J. (1985). Cited in Zuckerman, D. Retirement: R & R or risky? *Psychology Today, 19*(2), 80.

Croyle, R. T., Smith, K. R., Botkin, J. R., Baty, B., & Nash, J. (1997). Psychological responses to BRCA1 mutation testing. *Health Psychology, 16,* 63–72.

Crusco, A. H., & Wetzel, C. G. (1984). The Midas touch: The effects of interpersonal touch on restaurant tipping. *Personality and Social Psychology Bulletin, 10,* 512–517.

Culbertson, F. M. (1997). Depression and gender. *American Psychologist, 52,* 25–31.51.

Cunningham, M. R., Shaffer, D. R., Barbee, A. P., Wolff, P. L., & Kelley, D. J. (1990). Separate processes in the relation of elation and depression to helping. *Journal of Experimental Social Psychology, 26,* 13–33.

Cunningham, R. (1996). *Hospice: A special kind of caring.* Hospice Federation of Massachusetts.

Curfman, G. D. (1993a). The health benefits of exercise. *New England Journal of Medicine, 328,* 574–576.

Curfman, G. D. (1993b). Is exercise beneficial—or hazardous—to your heart? *New England Journal of Medicine, 329,* 1730–1731.

Curran, P. J., Stice, E., & Chassin, L. (1997). The relation between adolescent use and peer alcohol use. *Journal of Consulting and Clinical Psychology, 65,* 130–140.

Curtis, R. C., & Miller, K. (1986). Believing another likes or dislikes you: Behavior making the beliefs come true. *Journal of Personality and Social Psychology, 51,* 284–290.

Cutrona, C. E. (1982). Transition to college: Loneliness and the process of social adjustment. In L. A. Peplau & D. Perlman (Eds.), *Loneliness: A sourcebook of current theory, research, and therapy.*

Cutrona, C. E., & Troutman, B. R. (1986). Social support, infant temperament, and parenting self-efficacy: A mediational model of postpartum depression. *Child Development, 57,* 1507–1518.

Daly, M., & Wilson, M. (1998, February 10). Cited in Brody, J. E. Genetic ties may be factor in violence in stepfamililes. *The New York Times,* pp. F1, F4.

Damaged gene is linked to lung cancer. (1996, April 6). *The New York Times,* p. A24.

Damon, W. (1977). *The social world of the child.* San Francisco: Jossey-Bass.

Danforth, J. S., and others. (1990). Exercise as a treatment for hypertension in low-socioeconomic-status Black children. *Journal of Consulting and Clinical Psychology, 58,* 237–239.

Daniel, W. F., & Crovitz, H. F. (1983a). Acute memory impairment following electroconvulsive therapy: 1. Effects of electrical stimulus and number of treatments. *Acta Psychiatrica Scandinavica, 67,* 1–7.

Daniel, W. F., & Crovitz, H. F. (1983b). Acute memory impairment following electroconvulsive therapy: 2. Effects of electrode placement. *Acta Psychiatrica Scandinavica, 67,* 57–68.

Darley, J. M. (1993). Research on morality. *Psychological Science, 4,* 353–357.

Darley, J. M., & Gross, P. H. (1983). A hypothesis-confirming bias in labeling effects. *Journal of Personality and Social Psychology, 44,* 20–33.

Darley, J. M., & Latané, B. (1968). Bystander intervention in emergencies: Diffusion of responsibility. *Journal of Personality and Social Psychology, 8,* 377–383.

Darrow, W. W. (1983, November). *Social and psychological aspects of acquired immune deficiency syndrome.* Paper presented at the annual meeting of the Society for the Scientific Study of Sex, Chicago.

Darwin, C. A. (1872). *The expression of the emotions in man and animals.* London: J. Murray.

D'Atri, D. (1975). Psychophysiological responses to crowding. *Environment and Behavior, 1,* 237–252.

Dauber, R. B. (1984). Subliminal psychodynamic activation in depression: On the role of autonomy issues in depressed college women. *Journal of Abnormal Psychology, 93,* 9–18.

Davidson, J. R., & Foa, E. G. (1991). Diagnostic issues in posttraumatic stress disorder. *Journal of Abnormal Psychology, 100,* 346–355.

Davidson, L. M., Baum, A., & Collins, D. L. (1982). Stress and control-related problems at Three Mile Island. *Journal of Applied Social Psychology, 12,* 349–359.

Davidson, N. E. (1995). Hormone-replacement therapy—Breast versus heart versus bone. *New England Journal of Medicine, 332,* 1638–1639.

Davies, P. T., & Cummings, E. M. (1994). Marital conflict and child adjustment. *Psychological Bulletin, 116,* 387–411.

Davis, K. L., Kahn, R. S., Ko, G., & Davidson, M. (1991). Dopamine in schizophrenia. *American Journal of Psychiatry, 148,* 1474–1486.

Dawson, M. L. (1992, December 3). The genetic blending of Afro-Amerasians. *The New York Times,* p. A24.

DeAngelis, T. (1991). Hearing pinpoints gaps in research on women. *APA Monitor, 22*(6), 8.

DeAngelis, T. (1995a). Firefighters' PTSD at dangerous levels. *APA Monitor, 26*(2), 36–37.

DeAngelis, T. (1995b). Mental health care is elusive for Hispanics. *APA Monitor, 26*(7), 49.

DeAngelis, T. (1997a). Body-image problems affect all groups. *APA Monitor, 28*(3), 44–45.

DeAngelis, T. (1997b). Abused children have more conflicts with friends. *APA Monitor, 28*(6), 32.

DeAngelis, T. (1997c). There's new hope for women with postpartum blues. *APA Monitor, 28*(9), 22–23.

Decline in smoking levels off and officials urge a tax rise. (1993, April 2). *The New York Times,* p. A10.

Deffenbacher, J. L., & Suinn, R. M. (1988). Systematic desensitization and the reduction of anxiety. *The Counseling Psychologist, 16*(1), 9–30.

De La Cancela, V., & Guzman, L. P. (1991). Latino mental health service needs: Implications for training psychologists. In H. F. Myers and others (Eds.), *Ethnic minority perspectives on clinical training and services in psychology* (pp. 59–64). Washington, DC: American Psychological Association.

Delanoy, R. L., Merrin, J. S., & Gold, P. E. (1982). Moderation of long-term potentiation (LTP) by adrenergic agonists. *Neuroscience Abstracts, 8,* 316.

Delmas, P. D., and others. (1997). Effects of raloxifene on bone mineral density, serum cholesterol concentrations, and uterine endometrium in postmenopausal women. *New England Journal of Medicine, 337,* 1641–1648.

DeLongis, A., Coyne, J. C., Dakof, G., Folkman, S., & Lazarus, R. S. (1982). Relationship of daily hassles, uplifts, and major life events to health status. *Health Psychology, 1,* 119–136.

Department of Health and Human Services. (1986). The health consequences of involuntary smoking: A report of the surgeon general. (Publication no. DHHS [CDC] 87-8398). Washington, DC: U.S. Government Printing Office.

DePaulo, B. M., Rosenthal, R., Eisenstat, R. A., Rogers, P. L., & Finkelstein, S. (1978). Decoding discrepant nonverbal cues. *Journal of Personality and Social Psychology, 38,* 313–323.

DeRubeis, R. J. (1983, December). *The cognitive-pharmacotherapy project: Study design, outcome, and clinical follow-up.* Paper presented to the Association for the Advancement of Behavior Therapy, Washington, DC.

Deutsch, C. H. (1990, April 29). Why women walk out on jobs. *The New York Times,* p. F27.

Devine, P. G. (1989). Stereotypes and prejudice: Their automatic and controlled components. *Journal of Personality and Social Psychology, 56,* 5–18.

Diener, E. (1980). Deindividuation: The absence of self-awareness and self-regulation in group members. In P. Paulus (Ed.), *The psychology of group influence.* Hillsdale, NJ: Erlbaum.

Diethrich, E. (1982). *The Arizona Heart Institute's heart test.* New York: Cornerstone Library.

DiLalla, D. L., Carey, G., Gottesman, I. I., & Bouchard, T. J., Jr. (1996). Heritability of MMPI personality indicators of psychopathology in twins reared apart. *Journal of Abnormal Psychology, 105,* 491–499.

DiLalla, L. F., & Gottesman, I. I. (1991). Biological and genetic contributors to violence—Widom's untold tale. *Psychological Bulletin, 109,* 125–129.

DiMatteo, M. R., & DiNicola, D. D. (1982). *Achieving patient compliance: The psychology of the medical practitioner's role.* New York: Pergamon Press.

DiMatteo, M. R., and others. (1996). Cesarean childbirth and psychosocial outcomes: A meta-analysis. *Health Psychology, 15,* 303–314.

Dindia, K., & Allen, M. (1992). Sex differences in self-disclosure. A meta-analysis. *Psychological Bulletin, 112,* 106–124.

Docherty, N. M., and others. (1996). Working memory, attention, and communication disturbances in schizophrenia. *Journal of Abnormal Psychology, 105,* 212–219.

Dockery, D. W., and others. (1993). An association between air pollution and mortality in six U.S. cities. *New England Journal of Medicine, 329,* 1753–1759.

Doctors tie male mentality to shorter life span. (1995, June 14). *The New York Times,* p. C14.

Doherty, W. J. (1983). Impact of divorce on locus of control orientation in adult women: A longitudinal study. *Journal of Personality and Social Psychology, 44,* 834–840.

Donnerstein, E. I., & Wilson, D. W. (1976). Effects of noise and perceived control on ongoing and subsequent aggressive behavior. *Journal of Personality and Social Psychology, 34,* 774–781.

Dooker, M. (1980, July/August). Lamaze method of childbirth. *Nursing Research,* 220–224.

Dooley, D., & Catalano, R. (1980). Economic change as a cause of behavioral disorder. *Psychological Bulletin, 87,* 450–468.

Dowd, M. (1984, March 12). Twenty years after the murder of Kitty Genovese, the question remains: Why? *The New York Times,* pp. B1, B4.

Doyne, E. J., and others. (1987). Running versus weight lifting in the treatment of depression. *Journal of Consulting and Clinical Psychology, 55,* 748–754.

Drobes, D. J., & Tiffany, S. T. (1997). Induction of smoking urge through imaginal and in vivo procedures. *Journal of Abnormal Psychology, 106,* 15–25.

Dubbert, P. M. (1992). Exercise in behavioral medicine. *Journal of Consulting and Clinical Psychology, 60,* 613–618.

Duckitt, J. (1992). Psychology and prejudice: A historical analysis and integrative framework. *American Psychologist, 47,* 1182–1193.

Dugan, K. W. (1989). Ability and effort attributions. *Academy of Management Journal, 32,* 87–114.

Dugger, C. W. (1996a, September 11). A refugee's body is intact but her family is torn. *The New York Times,* pp. A1, B6.

Dugger, C. W. (1996b, October 12). New law bans genital cutting in United States. *The New York Times,* pp. A1, A28.

Duke, M. P., & Nowicki, S. (1972). A new measure and social learning model for interpersonal distance. *Journal of Experimental Research in Personality, 6,* 119–132.

Dumas, J. E., & LaFreniere, P. J. (1993). Mother-child relationships as sources of support or stress. *Child Development, 64.*

Dunning, J. (1997, July 16). Pursuing perfection: Dancing with death. *The New York Times,* p. C11.

Eagly, A. H. (1978). Sex differences in influenceability. *Psychological Bulletin, 85,* 85–116.

Eagly, A. H. (1995). The science and politics of comparing women and men. *American Psychologist, 50,* 145–158.

Eagly, A. H., Ashmore, R. D., Makhijani, M. G., & Longo, L. C. (1991). What is beautiful is good, but . . . : A meta-analytic review of research on the physical attractiveness stereotype. *Psychological Bulletin, 110,* 109–128.

Eagly, A. H., & Chaiken, S. (1992). *The psychology of attitudes.* Fort Worth, TX: Harcourt Brace Jovanovich.

Eagly, A. H., & Steffen, V. J. (1984). Gender stereotypes stem from the distribution of men and women into social roles. *Journal of Personality and Social Psychology, 46,* 735–754.

Eagly, A. H., Wood, W., & Chaiken, S. (1978). Causal inferences about communicators and their effect on opinion change. *Journal of Personality and Social Psychology, 36,* 424–435.

Eccles, J. S., & Hoffman, L. W. (1984). Sex roles, socialization, and occupational behavior. In H. W. Stevenson & A. E. Siegel (Eds.), *Research in child development and social policy, Vol. 1.* Chicago: University of Chicago Press.

Eden, C., & Sims, D. (1981). Computerized vicarious experience: The future for management induction? *Personnel Review, 10,* 22–25.

Edwards, D. J. A. (1972). Approaching the unfamiliar: A study of human interaction differences. *Journal of Behavioral Sciences, 1,* 249–250.

Edwards, R. (1995). American Indians rely on ancient healing techniques. *APA Monitor, 26*(8), 36.

Eidelson, R. J., & Epstein, N. (1982). Cognition and relationship maladjustment: Development of a measure of dysfunctional relationship beliefs. *Journal of Consulting and Clinical Psychology, 50,* 715–720.

Elias, S., & Annas, G. (1986). Social policy considerations in noncoital reproduction. *Journal of the American Medical Society, 255,* 62–68.

Elkin, I., Parloff, M. B., Hadley, S. W., & Autrey, J. H. (1985). NIMH treatment of depression collaborative research program. *Archives of General Psychiatry, 42,* 305–316.

Ellickson, P. L., Hays, R. D., & Bell, R. M.

(1992). Stepping through the drug use sequence: Longitudinal scalogram analysis of initiation and regular use. *Journal of Abnormal Psychology, 101,* 441–451.

Ellington, J. E., Marsh, L. A., & Critelli, J. E. (1980). Personality characteristics of women with masculine names. *Journal of Social Psychology, 111,* 211–218.

Ellis, A. (1977). The basic clinical theory of rational-emotive therapy. In A. Ellis & R. Grieger (Eds.), *Handbook of rational-emotive therapy.* New York: Springer.

Ellis, A. (1993). Reflections on rational-emotive therapy. *Journal of Consulting and Clinical Psychology, 61,* 190–201.

Ellis, L., & Ames, M. A. (1987). Neurohormonal functioning and sexual orientation: A theory of homosexuality-heterosexuality. *Psychological Bulletin, 101,* 233–258.

Ellsworth, P. C., Carlsmith, J. M., & Henson, A. (1972). The stare as a stimulus to flight in human subjects. *Journal of Personality and Social Psychology, 21,* 302–311.

Emery, R. E. (1989). Family violence. *American Psychologist, 44,* 321–328.

Engels, G. I., Garnefski, N., & Diekstra, R. F. W. (1993). Efficacy of rational-emotive therapy. *Journal of Consulting and Clinical Psychology, 61,* 1083–1090.

Erel, O., & Burman, B. (1995). Interrelatedness of marital relations and parent-child relations: A meta-analytic review. *Psychological Bulletin, 118,* 108–132.

Erikson, E. H. (1963). *Childhood and society.* New York: W. W. Norton.

Erikson, E. H. (1983). Cited in Hall, E. A conversation with Erik Erikson. *Psychology Today, 17*(6), 22–30.

Eron, L. D. (1982). Parent-child interaction, television violence, and aggression of children. *American Psychologist, 37,* 197–211.

Eron, L. D. (1987). The development of aggressive behavior from the perspective of a developing behaviorism. *American Psychologist, 42,* 435–442.

Evans, G. W., Jacobs, S. V., & Frager, N. B. (1982). Behavioral responses to air pollution. In A. Baum & J. E. Singer (Eds.), *Advances in environmental psychology* (Vol. 4). Hillsdale, NJ: Erlbaum.

Evans, R. I., and others. (1970). Fear arousal, persuasion, and actual versus implied behavioral change: New perspective utilizing a real-life dental hygiene program. *Journal of Personality and Social Psychology, 16,* 220–227.

Exline, R. V. (1972). Visual interaction: The glances of power and preference. In J. K. Cole (Ed.), *Nebraska symposium on motivation, Vol. 19.* Lincoln: University of Nebraska Press.

Eysenck, H. J., & Eysenck, M. W. (1985). *Personality and individual differences.* New York: Plenum.

Fabian, W. D., Jr., & Fishkin, S. M. (1981). A replicated study of self-reported changes in psychological absorption with marijuana intoxication. *Journal of Abnormal Psychology, 90,* 546–553.

Fairbanks, L. A., McGuire, M. T., & Harris, C. J. (1982). Nonverbal interaction of patients and therapists during psychiatric interviews. *Journal of Abnormal Psychology, 91,* 109–119.

Fallon, A. E., & Rozin, P. (1985). Sex differences in perceptions of desirable body shape. *Journal of Abnormal Psychology, 94,* 102–105.

Farber, E. & Egeland, B. (1987). *The invulnerable child.* New York: Guilford Press.

Farina, A., Burns, G. L., Austad, C., Bugglin, C. S., & Fischer, E. H. (1986). The role of physical attractiveness in the readjustment of discharged psychiatric patients. *Journal of Abnormal Psychology, 95,* 139–143.

Farley, F. (1993). Wisconsin on the Potomac. *APA Monitor, 24*(4), 3.

Farrell, A. D., Camplair, P. S., & McCullough, L. (1987). Identification of target complaints by computer interview. *Journal of Consulting and Clinical Psychology, 55,* 691–700.

Fazio, R. H. (1986). How do attitudes guide behavior? In R. M. Sorrentino & E. T. Higgins (Eds.), *The handbook of motivation and cognition: Foundations of social behavior.* New York: Guilford Press.

Fazio, R. H., Chen, J., McDonel, E. C., & Sherman, S. J. (1982). Attitude accessibility, attitude-behavior consistency, and the strength of the object-evaluation association. *Journal of Experimental Social Psychology, 18,* 339–357.

Fazio, R. H., Sanbonmatsu, D. M., Powell, M. C., & Kardes, F. R. (1986). On the automatic activation of attitudes. *Journal of Personality and Social Psychology, 50,* 229–238.

Fazio, R. H., Sherman, S. J., & Herr, P. M. (1982). The feature-positive effect in the self-perception process: Does not doing matter as much as doing? *Journal of Personality and Social Psychology, 42,* 404–411.

Feder, B. J. (1997, April 20). Surge in the teenage smoking rate left the tobacco industry vulnerable. *The New York Times,* pp. A1, A28.

Feder, H. H. (1984). Hormones and sexual behavior. *Annual Review of Psychology, 35,* 165–200.

Fein, E. (1998, January 5). A doctor puts herself in the world of abused children. *The New York Times.*

Fein, G. G., Schwartz, P. M., Jacobson, S. W., & Jacobson, J. L. (1983). Environmental toxins and behavioral development: A new role for psychological research. *American Psychologist, 38,* 1188–1197.

Feingold, A. (1992). Good-looking people are not what we think. *Psychological Bulletin, 111,* 304–341.

Feingold, A. (1994). Gender differences in personality: A meta-analysis. *Psychological Bulletin, 116,* 429–456.

Feingold, S. (1997). Cited in DeAngelis, T. There's new hope for women with postpartum blues. *APA Monitor, 28*(9), 22–23.

Feltz, D. L. (1982). Path analysis of the causal elements in Bandura's theory of self-efficacy and an anxiety-based model of avoidance behavior. *Journal of Personality and Social Psychology, 42,* 764–781.

Fenigstein, A. (1979). Does aggression cause a preference for viewing media violence? *Journal of Personality and Social Psychology, 37,* 2307–2317.

Fibel, B., & Hale, W. D. (1978). The generalized expectancy for success scale—A new measure. *Journal of Consulting and Clinical Psychology, 46,* 924–931.

Field, T. M. (1991). Young children's adaptations to repeated separations from their mothers. *Child Development, 62,* 539–547.

Fincham, F. D., Beach, S., & Baucom, D. H. (1987). Attribution processing in distressed and nondistressed couples: 4. Self-partner attribution differences. *Journal of Personality and Social Psychology, 52,* 739–748.

Fincham, F. D., & O'Leary, K. D. (1983). Causal inferences for spouse behavior in maritally distressed and nondistressed couples. *Journal of Social and Clinical Psychology, 1,* 42–57.

Findley, M. J., & Cooper, H. M. (1983). Locus of control and academic achievement: A literature review. *Journal of Personality and Social Psychology, 44,* 419–427.

Finn, P. R., and others. (1997). Heterogeneity in the families of sons of alcoholics. *Journal of Abnormal Psychology, 106,* 26–36.

Fischman, J. (1987). Getting tough. *Psychology Today, 21*(12), 26–28.

Fisher, H. E. (1992). *Anatomy of love: The natural history of monogamy, adultery and divorce.* New York: W. W. Norton.

Fisher, J. D., Bell, P. A., & Baum, A. (1984). *Environmental psychology* (2d ed.). New York: Holt, Rinehart and Winston.

Fiske, S. T. (1989). *Interdependence and stereotyping: From the laboratory to the Supreme Court (and back).* Paper presented to the annual meeting of the American Psychological Association, New Orleans.

Fiske, S. T. (1993). Controlling other people: The impact of power on stereotyping. *American Psychologist, 48,* 621–628.

Fiske, S. T., & Taylor, S. E. (1984). *Social cognition.* Reading, MA: Addison-Wesley.

Fitch, G. (1970). Effects of self-esteem, perceived performance, and choice of causal attribution. *Journal of Personality and Social Psychology, 16,* 311–315.

Flack, J. M., and others. (1995). Panel I: Epidemiology of minority health. *Health Psychology, 14,* 592–600.

Flaherty, J. F., & Dusek, J. B. (1980). An investigation of the relationship between psychological androgyny and components of self-concept. *Journal of Personality and Social Psychology, 38,* 984–992.

Fleming, A. S., Klein, E., & Corter, C. (1992). The effects of a social support group on depression, maternal attitudes and behavior in new mothers. *Journal of Child Psychology & Psychiatry, 33,* 685–698.

Fleming, M. Z., MacGowan, B. R., Robinson, L., Spitz, J., & Salt, P. (1982). The body image of the postoperative female-to-male transsexual. *Journal of Consulting and Clinical Psychology, 50,* 461–462.

Fleming, R., Baum, A., Gisriel, M. M., & Gatchel, R. J. (1982). Mediation of stress at Three Mile Island by social support. *Journal of Human Stress, 8*(3), 14–22.

Flippo, J. R., & Lewinsohn, P. M. (1971). Effects of failure on the self-esteem of depressed and nondepressed subjects. *Journal of Consulting and Clinical Psychology, 36,* 151.

Floderus-Myrhed, B., Pederson, N., & Rasmuson, I. (1980). Assessment of heritability for personality based on a short form of the Eysenck Personality Inventory: A study of 12,898 twin pairs. *Behavior Genetics, 10,* 153–162.

Flor, H., & Birbaumer, N. (1993). Comparison of the efficacy of electromyographic biofeedback, cognitive-behavioral therapy, and conservative medical intervention in the treatment of chronic musculoskeletal pain. *Journal of Consulting and Clinical Psychology, 61,* 653–658.

Floyd, F. J., & Markman, H. J. (1984). An economical observational measure of couples' communication skill. *Journal of Consulting and Clinical Psychology, 52,* 97–103.

Fogelman, K. (1980). Smoking in pregnancy and subsequent development of the child. *Child Care, Health, and Development, 6,* 233–251.

Folkman, S., & Lazarus, R. S. (1985). If it changes it must be a process: Study of emotion and coping during three stages of a college examination. *Journal of Personality and Social Psychology, 48,* 150–170.

Ford, E. S., and others. (1991). Physical activity behaviors in lower and higher socioeconomic status populations. *American Journal of Epidemiology, 133,* 1246–1256.

Foreyt, J. P. (1986). Treating the diseases of the 1980s: Eating disorders. *Contemporary Psychology, 31,* 658–660.

Foster, G. D., Wadden, T. A., Vogt, R. A., & Brewer, G. (1997). What is a reasonable weight loss? Patients' expectations and evaluations of obesity treatment outcomes. *Journal of Consulting and Clinical Psychology, 65,* 79–85.

Fowler, R. D. (1998). Join the fight against AIDS. *APA Monitor, 29*(2), 3.

Fox, M. (1998, February 13). U.S. experts see obesity as epidemic. Reuters; America Online.

Francis, D. (1984). *Will you still need me, will you still feed me, when I'm 84?* Bloomington: Indiana University Press.

Franck, K. D. (1979). Friends and strangers: The social experience of living in urban and nonurban settings. *Journal of Social Issues, 36,* 52–71.

Franck, K. D., Unseld, C. T., & Wentworth, W. E. (1974). *Adaptation of the newcomer: A process of construction.* Unpublished manuscript, City University of New York.

Franzoi, S. L., & Herzog, M. E. (1987). Judging physical attractiveness: What body aspects do we use? *Personality and Social Psychology Bulletin, 13,* 19–33.

Frayne, C. A., & Latham, G. P. (1987). Application of social learning theory to employee self-management of attendance. *Journal of Applied Psychology, 72,* 387–392.

Freedman, D. X. (1993, August 8). On "Beyond wellness." *The New York Times Book Review,* p. 6.

Freedman, J. L., & Fraser, S. C. (1966). Compliance without pressure: The foot-in-the-door technique. *Journal of Personality and Social Psychology, 4,* 195–202.

Freedman, J. L., Wallington, S. A., & Bless, E. (1967). Compliance without pressure: The effect of guilt. *Journal of Personality and Social Psychology, 7,* 117–124.

Freiberg, P. (1998). Prevention studies take a variety of tacks. *APA Monitor, 29*(2), 33.

Freud, S. (1909). Analysis of a phobia in a 5-year-old-boy. In *Collected Papers, Vol. 3,* trans. A. & James Strachey. New York: Basic Books, 1959.

Freud, S. (1933). New introductory lectures. In *Standard edition of the complete psychological works of Sigmund Freud, Vol. 22.* London: Hogarth Press, 1964.

Freudenberger, H. J. (1989). Burnout: Past, present, and future concerns. In *Professional Burnout in Medicine and the Helping Professions.* New York: Haworth Press.

Friedman, M., & Ulmer, D. (1984). *Treating Type A behavior and your heart.* New York: Fawcett Crest.

Friman, P. C., & Christopherson, E. R. (1983). Behavior therapy and hyperactivity: A brief review of therapy for a big problem. *The Behavior Therapist, 6,* 175–176.

Frodi, A. M., Macauley, J., & Thome, P. R. (1977). Are women always less aggressive than men? A review of the experimental literature. *Psychological Bulletin, 84,* 634–660.

Fromm, E. (1956). *The art of loving.* New York: Harper & Row.

Galassi, J. P. (1988). Four cognitive-behavioral approaches: Additional considerations. *The Counseling Psychologist, 16*(1), 102–105.

Galassi, J. P., Frierson, H. T., & Sharer, R. (1981). Behavior of high, moderate, and low test anxious students during an actual test situation. *Journal of Consulting and Clinical Psychology, 49,* 51–62.

Galassi, J. P., Frierson, H. T., Jr., & Siegel, R. G. (1984). Cognitions, test anxiety, and test performance: A closer look. *Journal of Consulting and Clinical Psychology, 52,* 319–320.

Gallagher, R. (1996). Cited in Murray, B. College youth haunted by increased pressures. *APA Monitor, 26*(4), 47.

Ganellen, R. J., & Blaney, P. H. (1984). Hardiness and social support as moderators of the effects of life stress. *Journal of Personality and Social Psychology, 47,* 156–163.

Gardner, H. (1983). *Frames of mind: The theory of multiple intelligences.* New York: Basic Books.

Garfinkel, R. (1995). Cited in Margoshes, P. For many, old age is the prime of life. *APA Monitor, 26*(5), 36–37.

Garnets, L., & Kimmel, D. (1991). In Goodchilds, J. D. (Ed.), *Psychological perspectives on human diversity in America.* Washington, DC: American Psychological Association.

Gavin, J. (1988). *Body moves: The psychology of exercise.* Stackpole Books.

Gayle, H. D., and others. (1990). Prevalence of human immunodeficiency virus among university students. *New England Journal of Medicine, 323,* 1538–1541.

Gebhardt, D. L., & Crump, C. E. (1990). Employee fitness and wellness programs in the workplace. *American Psychologist, 45,* 262–272.

Geen, R. G. (1981). Behavioral and physiological reactions to observed violence: Effects of prior exposure to aggressive stimuli. *Journal of Personality and Social Psychology, 40,* 868–875.

Geer, J. T., O'Donohue, W. T., & Schorman, R. H. (1986). Sexuality. In M. G. H. Coles and others (Eds.), *Psychophysiology: Systems, processes, and applications.* New York: Guilford Press.

Geiger, H. J. (1996). Race and health care. *New England Journal of Medicine, 335,* 815–816.

Gelman, D., and others. (1985, August 12). The social fallout from an epidemic. *Newsweek,* pp. 28–29.

George, J. M. (1991). State or trait: Effects of positive mood on prosocial behaviors at work. *Journal of Applied Psychology, 76,* 299–307.

Gerard, H. B., Wilhelmy, R. A., & Conolley, E. S. (1968). Conformity and group size. *Journal of Personality and Social Psychology, 8,* 79–82.

Gerson, M. (1980). The lure of motherhood. *Psychology of Women Quarterly, 5,* 207–218.

Gerson, M. (1984). Feminism and the wish for a child. *Sex Roles, 11,* 389–399.

Gibbs, N. (1991, June 3). When is it rape? *Time,* pp. 48–54.

Gil, K. M., and others. (1996). Effects of cognitive coping skills training on coping strategies and experimental pain sensitivity in African American adults with sickle cell disease. *Health Psychology, 15,* 3–10.

Gilbert, S. (1993, April 25). Waiting game. *The New York Times Magazine,* pp. 70–72, 92.

Gilbert, S. (1996a, May 1). Estrogen patch appears to lift severe depression in new mothers. *The New York Times,* p. C12.

Gilbert, S. (1996b, August 28). More men may seek eating disorder help. *The New York Times,* p. C9.

Gilbert, S. J. (1981). Another look at the Milgram obedience studies: The role of the gradated series of shocks. *Personality and Social Psychology Bulletin, 7,* 690–695.

Gillen, B. (1981). Physical attractiveness: A determinant of two types of goodness. *Personality and Social Psychology Bulletin, 7,* 277–281.

Gilligan, C. (1982). *In a different voice.* Cambridge, MA: Harvard University Press.

Gilligan, C., Lyons, P., & Hanmer, T. J. (Eds.). (1990). *Making connections.* Cambridge, MA: Harvard University Press.

Gilligan, C., Rogers, A. G., & Tolman, D. L. (Eds.). (1991). *Women, girls, and psychotherapy.* New York: Haworth.

Gillin, J. C. (1991). The long and the short of sleeping pills. *New England Journal of Medicine, 324,* 1735–1736.

Gillis, J. S., & Avis, W. E. (1980). The male-taller norm in mate selection. *Personality and Social Psychology Bulletin, 6,* 396–401.

Gladue, B. A., Green, R., & Hellman, R. E. (1984). Neuroendocrine response to estrogen and sexual orientation. *Science, 225,* 1496–1499.

Glaser, R., and others. (1991). Stress-related activation of Epstein-Barr virus. *Brain, Behavior, and Immunity, 5,* 219–232.

Glass, D. C. (1977). *Stress and coronary-prone behavior.* Hillsdale, NJ: Erlbaum.

Glass, D. C., & Singer, J. E. (1972). *Urban stress.* New York: Academic Press.

Glass, S. P., & Wright, T. L. (1992). Justifications of extramarital relationships: The association between attitudes, behaviors, and gender. *Journal of Sex Research, 29,* 361–387.

Glick, H. R. (1992). The right to die: Policy innovation and its consequences. New York: Columbia University Press.

Gold, D. R., and others. (1996). Effects of cigarette smoking on lung function in adolescent boys and girls. *New England Journal of Medicine, 335,* 931–937.

Goldberg, L. W. (1978). Differential attribution of trait-descriptive terms to oneself as compared to well-liked, neutral, and disliked others. *Journal of Personality and Social Psychology, 36,* 1012–1028.

Goldfried, M. R. (1988). Application of rational restructuring to anxiety disorders. *The Counseling Psychologist, 16*(1), 50–68.

Goldfried, M. R., Linehan, M. M., & Smith, J. L. (1978). Reduction of test anxiety through cognitive restructuring. *Journal of Consulting and Clinical Psychology, 46,* 32–39.

Goldman, J. A., & Harlow, L. L. (1993). Self-perception variables that mediate AIDS-preventive behavior in college students. *Health Psychology, 12,* 489–498.

Goldman, K. (1993, June 1). Jordan & Co. play ball on Madison Avenue. *The Wall Street Journal,* p. B9.

Goldman, W., & Lewis, P. (1977). Beautiful is good: Evidence that the physically attractive are more socially skillful. *Journal of Experimental Social Psychology, 13,* 125–130.

Goldstein, I. L., & Buxton, V. M. (1982). Training and human performance. In M. D. Dunnette & E. A. Fleishman (Eds.), *Human Performance and Productivity, 1,* 135–177.

Goldstein, I. L., & Gilliam, P. (1990). Training system issues in the year 2000. *American Psychologist, 45,* 134–143.

Goleman, D. J. (1996a, May 28). Evidence mounting for role of fetal damage in schizophrenia. *The New York Times,* pp. C1, C3.

Goleman, D. J. (1996b, November 19). Research on brain leads to pursuit of designer drugs. *The New York Times,* pp. C1, C3.

Golub, S. (1976). The effect of premenstrual anxiety and depression on cognitive function. *Journal of Personality and Social Psychology, 34,* 99–104.

Goodgame, R. W. (1990). AIDS in Uganda —Clinical and social features. *New England Journal of Medicine, 323,* 383–389.

Goodheart, D. E. (1985). Some psychological effects associated with positive and negative thinking about stressful event outcomes. *Journal of Personality and Social Psychology, 48,* 216–232.

Goodman, L. A., Koss, M. P., Fitzgerald, L. F., Russo, N. F., & Keita, G. W. (1993). Male violence against women: Current research and future directions. *American Psychologist, 48,* 1054–1058.

Goodwin, F. K., & Jamison, K. R. (1990). *Manic-depressive illness.* New York: Oxford University Press.

Gortmaker, S. L., and others. (1993). Social and economic consequences of over-weight in adolescence and young adulthood. *New England Journal of Medicine, 329,* 1008–1012.

Gotlib, I. H. (1984). Depression and general psychopathology in university students. *Journal of Abnormal Psychology, 93,* 19–30.

Gottesman, I. I. (1991). *Schizophrenia genesis: The origins of madness.* New York: Freeman.

Gottman, J. M., & Krokoff, L. J. (1989). Marital interaction and satisfaction: A longitudinal view. *Journal of Consulting and Clinical Psychology, 57,* 47–52.

Gould, R. (1975). Adult life stages: Growth toward self-tolerance. *Psychology Today, 8,* 74–81.

Goy, R. W., & Goldfoot, D. A. (1976). Neuroendocrinology: Animal models and problems of human sexuality. In E. A. Rubenstein and others (Eds.), *New directions in sex research.* New York: Plenum Publishing.

Goy, R. W., & McEwen, B. S. (1982). *Sexual differentiation of the brain.* Cambridge, MA: MIT Press.

Grady, D. (1997, January 21). Brain-tied gene defect may explain why schizophrenics hear voices. *The New York Times,* p. C3.

Graf, P. (1990). Life-span changes in implicit and explicit memory. *Bulletin of the Psychonomic Society, 28,* 353–358.

Greeley, A. M. (1990). Faithful attraction. *Psychology Today, 23,*(3).

Green, B. L., Grace, M. C., Lindy, J. D., Titchener, J. L., & Lindy, J. G. (1983). Levels of functional impairment following a civilian disaster. The Beverly Hills Supper Club fire. *Journal of Consulting and Clinical Psychology, 51,* 573–580.

Green, R. (1987). *The "sissy boy syndrome" and the development of homosexuality.* New Haven: Yale University Press.

Greenbaum, P., & Rosenfeld, H. M. (1978). Patterns of avoidance in response to interpersonal staring and proximity: Effects of bystanders on drivers at a traffic intersection. *Journal of Personality and Social Psychology, 36,* 575–587.

Greene, B. A. (1992). Still here: A perspective on psychotherapy with African American women. In J. Chrisler & D. Howard (Eds.), *New directions in feminist psychology.* New York: Springer.

Greene, B. A. (1993). African American women. In L. Comas-Diaz & B. Greene (Eds.), *Women of color and mental health.* New York: Guilford Press.

Greene, B. (1994). Ethnic-minority lesbians and gay men. *Journal of Consulting and Clinical Psychology, 62,* 243–251.

Greene, J. (1982). The gambling trap. *Psychology Today, 16*(9), 50–55.

Greist, J. H. (1984). Exercise in the treatment of depression. *Coping with mental stress: The potential and limits of exercise intervention.* Washington, DC: National Institute of Mental Health.

Griffin, E., & Sparks, G. G. (1990). Friends forever: A longitudinal exploration of intimacy in same-sex friends and platonic pairs. *Journal of Social and Personal Relationships, 7,* 29–46.

Grodstein, F., and others. (1997). Postmenopausal hormonal therapy and mortality. *New England Journal of Medicine, 336,* 1769–1775.

Grossman, S. (1991, December 22). Cited in Undergraduates drink heavily, survey disclosed. *The New York Times,* p. 46.

Grove, W. M., and others. (1991). Familial prevalence and coaggregation of schizotypy indicators: A multitrait family study. *Journal of Abnormal Psychology, 100,* 115–121.

Gruber, V. A., & Wildman, B. G. (1987). The impact of dysmenorrhea on daily activities. *Behavior Research and Therapy, 25,* 123–128.

Grunberg, N. (1993). Cited in Adler, T. Gum, patches aren't enough; to quit, counseling is advised. *APA Monitor, 24*(5), 16–17.

Grych, J. H., & Fincham, F. D. (1993). Children's appraisals of marital conflict. *Child Development, 64,* 215–230.

Guinan, M. E. (1992, February 1). Cited in Leary, W. E. U.S. panel backs approval of first condom for women. *The New York Times,* p. 7.

Guisinger, S., & Blatt, S. J. (1994). Individuality and relatedness. *American Psychologist, 49,* 104–111.

Gunther, V., Gritsch, S., & Meise, U. (1992). Smoking cessation—Gradual or sudden stopping? *Drug and Alcohol Dependence, 29,* 231–236.

Guyll, M., & Contrada, R. J. (1998). Trait

hostility and ambulatory cardiovascular activity: Responses to social interaction. *Health Psychology, 17,* 30–39.

Haaga, D. A. F., & Davison, G. C. (1993). An appraisal of rational-emotive therapy. *Journal of Consulting and Clinical Psychology, 61,* 215–220.

Hafner, K. (1993, August 29). Woman computer nerd—and proud. *The New York Times,* pp. F1, F4.

Hakim, A. A., and others. (1998). Effects of walking on mortality among nonsmoking retired men. *New England Journal of Medicine, 338,* 94–99.

Hall, C. S. (1984). "A ubiquitous sex difference in dreams" revisited. *Journal of Personality and Social Psychology, 46,* 1109–1117.

Hall, E. T. (1968). Proxemics. *Current Anthropology, 9,* 83–107.

Hall, G. C. I. (1997). Cultural malpractice: The growing obsolescence of psychology with the changing U.S. population. *American Psychologist, 52,* 642–651.

Hall, G. C. I., & Barongan, C. (1997). Prevention of sexual aggression. *American Psychologist, 52,* 5–14.

Hall, J. A., & Braunwald, K. G. (1981). Gender cues in conversation. *Journal of Personality and Social Psychology, 40,* 99–100.

Hall, J. A., & Taylor, M. C. (1985). Psychological androgyny and the masculinity-femininity interaction. *Journal of Personality and Social Psychology, 49,* 429–435.

Hall, J. A., and others. (1990). Performance quality, gender, and professional role: A study of physicians and nonphysicians in 16 ambulatory-care practices. *Medical Care, 28,* 489–501.

Hall, L. L. (1998, February). Next stop, immortality. *Penthouse;* Web site.

Hall, R. G., Sachs, D. P. L., Hall, S. M., & Benowitz, N. L. (1984). Two-year efficacy and safety of rapid smoking therapy in patients with cardiac and pulmonary disease. *Journal of Consulting and Clinical Psychology, 52,* 574–581.

Hall, S. M., Havassy, B. E., & Wasserman, D. A. (1990). Commitment to abstinence and acute stress in relapse to alcohol, opiates, and nicotine. *Journal of Consulting and Clinical Psychology, 58,* 175–181.

Hall, S. M., Tunstall, C., Rugg, D., Jones, R. T., & Benowitz, N. (1985). Nicotine gum and behavioral treatment in smoking cessation. *Journal of Consulting and Clinical Psychology, 53,* 256–258.

Halldin, M. (1985). Alcohol consumption and alcoholism in an urban population in central Sweden. *Acta Psychiatrica Scandinavica, 71,* 128–140.

Halmi, K. A., Eckert, E., LaDu, T. J., & Cohen, J. (1986). Treatment efficacy of cyproheptadine and amitriptyline. *Archives of General Psychiatry, 43,* 177–181.

Halpern, D. F. (1997). Sex differences in intelligence: Implications for education. *American Psychologist, 52,* 1091–1102.

Hamamy, H., and others. (1990). Consanguinity and the genetic control of Down syndrome. *Clinical Genetics, 37,* 24–29.

Hamer, D., and others. (1993, July 26). Cited in Henry, W. A. Born gay? *Time,* pp. 36–39.

Hamilton, M., and others. (1990). *The Duke University Medical Center book of diet and fitness.* New York: Fawcett Columbine.

Haney, D. (1997, September 30). AIDS virus resisting new drugs. *Daily Record,* pp. A1, A10.

Haney, D. (1998, January 31). Science targets old age. The Associated Press; America Online.

Haney, M., and others. (1994). Cocaine sensitivity in Roman high and low avoidance rats is modulated by sex and gonadal hormone status. *Brain Research, 645*(1–2), 179–185.

Hansen, G. O. (1975). Meeting house challenges: Involvement—the elderly. In *Housing issues.* Lincoln: University of Nebraska Press.

Harder, D. W., Gift, T. E., Strauss, J. S., Ritzler, B. A., & Kokes, R. F. (1981). Life events and two-year outcome in schizophrenia. *Journal of Consulting and Clinical Psychology, 49,* 619–626.

Hare-Mustin, R. (1983). An appraisal of the relationship between women and psychotherapy: 80 years after the case of Dora. *American Psychologist, 38,* 593–601.

Harlap, S., & Shiono, P. H. (1980). Alcohol, smoking, and incidence of spontaneous abortions in the first and second trimester. *Lancet, 2,* 173–176.

Harmon, A. (1998, January 13). With boom in high technology, software jobs go begging. *The New York Times;* America Online.

Harold, G. T., Fincham, F. D., Osborne, L. N., & Conger, R. D. (1997). Mom and Dad are at it again: Adolescent perceptions of marital conflict and adolescent psychological distress. *Developmental Psychology, 33,* 333–350.

Harris, G. T., Rice, M. E., & Quinsey, V. L. (1994). Psychopathy as a taxon. *Journal of Consulting and Clinical Psychology, 62,* 387–397.

Harris, L. (1988). *Inside America.* New York: Vintage.

Hass, R. G., & Linder, D. E. (1972). Counterargument availability and the effects of message structure on persuasion. *Journal of Personality and Social Psychology, 23,* 219–233.

Hatcher, R. A., and others. (1998). *Contraceptive technology* (17th ed.). New York: Irvington.

Hatfield, E. (1983). What do women and men want from love and sex? In E. R. Allgeier & N. B. McCormick (Eds.), *Changing boundaries: Gender roles and sexual behavior.* Palo Alto, CA: Mayfield.

Havighurst, R. J. (1972). *Developmental tasks and education* (3d ed.). New York: McKay.

Hays, K. F. (1995). Putting sport psychology into (your) practice. *Professional Psychology: Research and Practice, 26,* 33–40.

Hays, R. B. (1984). The development and maintenance of friendship. *Journal of Social and Personal Relationships, 1,* 75–98.

Helmreich, R. L., Spence, J. T., & Holahan, C. J. (1979). Psychological androgyny and sex-role flexibility: A test of two hypotheses. *Journal of Personality and Social Psychology, 37,* 1631–1644.

Helson, R., & Moane, G. (1987). Personality change in women from college to midlife. *Journal of Personality and Social Psychology, 53,* 176–186.

Hendrick, C., & Hendrick S. (1986). A theory and method of love. *Journal of Personality and Social Psychology, 50,* 392–402.

Hendrick, C. D., Wells, K. S., & Faletti, M. V. (1982). Social and emotional effects of geographical relocation on elderly retirees. *Journal of Personality and Social Psychology, 42,* 951–962.

Hendrick, J., & Hendrick, C. D. (1977). *Aging in mass society: Myths and realities.* Cambridge, MA: Winthrop.

Hendrick, S., Hendrick, C., Slapion-Foote, M. J., & Foote, F. H. (1985). Gender differences in sexual attitudes. *Journal of Personality and Social Psychology, 48,* 1630–1642.

Hennigan, K. M., Cook, T. D., & Gruder, C. L. (1982a). Cognitive tuning set, source credibility, and the temporal persistence of attitude change. *Journal of Personality and Social Psychology, 42,* 412–425.

Hennigan, K. M., and others. (1982b). Impact of the introduction of television on crime in the United States. *Journal of Personality and Social Psychology, 42,* 461–477.

Hepworth, J. T., & West, S. G. (1988). Lynchings and the economy: A time-series reanalysis of Hovland and Sears (1940). *Journal of Personality and Social Psychology, 55,* 239–247.

Hersen, M., Bellack, A. S., Himmelhoch, J. M., & Thase, M. E. (1984). Effect of social skill training, amitriptyline, and psychotherapy in unipolar depressed women. *Behavior Therapy, 15,* 21–40.

Hetherington, E. M. (1979). Divorce: A child's perspective. *American Psychologist, 34,* 851–858.

Hetherington, E. M., Cox, M., & Cox, R. (1977). The aftermath of divorce. In J. H. Stevens, Jr., & M. Matthews (Eds.), *Mother-child, father-child relations.* Washington, DC: National Association for the Education of Young Children.

Hewitt, P. L., Flett, G. L., & Ediger, E. (1996). Perfectionism and depression. *Journal of Abnormal Psychology, 105,* 276–280.

Hilgard, E. R. (1977). *Divided consciousness: Multiple controls in human thought and action.* New York: Wiley-Interscience.

Hill, C. (1987). Affiliation motivation: People who need people . . . but in different ways. *Journal of Personality and Social Psychology, 52,* 1008–1018.

Hill, C., Rubin, Z., & Peplau, L. A. (1976). Breakups before marriage: The end of 103 affairs. *Journal of Social Issues, 32,* 147–168.

Hinds, M. W., Kolonel, L. N., Hankin, J. H., &

Lee, J. (1984). Dietary vitamin A, carotene, vitamin C and risk of lung cancer in Hawaii. *American Journal of Epidemiology, 119,* 227–237.

Hitt, J. (1998, January 18). Who will do abortions here? *The New York Times Magazine*, pp. 20–27, 42, 45–46, 54–55.

Hittleman, J. N., O'Donohue, N., Zilkha, S., & Parekh, A. (1980). *Mother-infant assessment of the LeBoyer "nonviolent" method of childbirth.* Paper presented to the meeting of the American Psychological Association, Montreal.

Hobfoll, S. E., Jackson, A. P., Lavin, J., Britton, P. J., & Shepherd, J. B. (1993). Safe sex knowledge, behavior, and attitudes of inner-city women. *Health Psychology, 12,* 481–488.

Hobfoll, S. E., Ritter, C., Lavin, J., Hulsizer, M. R., & Cameron, R. P. (1995). Depression prevalence and incidence among inner-city pregnant and postpartum women. *Journal of Consulting and Clinical Psychology, 63,* 445–453.

Hobson, J. A. (1992, January 7). Cited in Blakeslee, S. Scientists unraveling chemistry of dreams. *The New York Times,* pp. C1, C10.

Hobson, J. A. (1998, January 6). Cited in Wade, N. Was Freud Wrong? Are Dreams the Brain's Start-Up Test? *The New York Times.*

Hoffman, C., & Hurst, N. (1990). Gender stereotypes: Perception or rationalization? *Journal of Personality and Social Psychology, 58,* 197–208.

Hoffman, M. L. (1981). Is altruism part of human nature? *Journal of Personality and Social Psychology, 40,* 121–137.

Hogan, R., Curphy, G. J., & Hogan, J. (1994). What we know about leadership. *American Psychologist, 49,* 493–504.

Holahan, C. J. (1986). Environmental psychology. In M. R. Rosenweig & L. W. Porter (Eds.), *Annual Review of Psychology, 37,* 381–407.

Holden, G. W., & Ritchie, K. L. (1991). Linking extreme marital discord, child rearing, and child behavior problems. *Child Development, 62,* 311–327.

Holland, J. (1993, July 20). Cited in Rosenthal, E. Listening to the emotional needs of cancer patients. *The New York Times,* pp. C1, C7.

Hollenbeck, A. R., and others. (1984). Labor and delivery medication influences parent-infant interaction in the first postpartum month. *Infant Behavior and Development, 7,* 201–209.

Hollon, S., & Beck, A. T. (1986). Research on cognitive therapies. In S. L. Garfield & A. E. Bergin (Eds.), *Handbook of psychotherapy and behavior change* (3d ed.). New York: Wiley.

Holmes, D. S. (1984). Meditation and somatic arousal reduction: A review of the experimental evidence. *American Psychologist, 39,* 1–10.

Holmes, T. H., & Rahe, R. H. (1967). The social readjustment rating scale. *Journal of Psychosomatic Research, 11,* 213–218.

Honan, W. H. (1996, April 11). Male professors keep 30% lead in pay over women, study says. *The New York Times,* p. B9.

Hong, W. K., and others. (1990). Prevention of second primary tumors with isoretinoin in squamous-cell carcinoma of the head and neck. *New England Journal of Medicine, 323,* 795–800.

Honts, C., Hodes, R., & Raskin, D. (1985). *Journal of Applied Psychology, 70*(1).

Hopper, J. L., & Seeman, E. (1994). The bone density of female twins discordant for tobacco use. *New England Journal of Medicine, 330,* 387–392.

Horn, J. L. (1982). The aging of human abilities. In J. Wolman (Ed.), *Handbook of developmental psychology.* Englewood Cliffs, NJ: Prentice-Hall.

Horney, K. (1967). *Feminine psychology.* New York: W. W. Norton.

Horvath, T. (1981). Physical attractiveness: The influence of selected torso parameters. *Archives of Sexual Behavior, 10,* 21–24.

House, J. S., Robbins, C., & Metzner, H. L. (1982). The association of social relationships and activities with mortality: Prospective evidence from the Tecumseh Community Health Study. *American Journal of Epidemiology, 116,* 123–140.

Howard, J. A., Blumstein, P., & Schwartz, P. (1987). Social or evolutionary theories: Some observations on preferences in mate selection. *Journal of Personality and Social Psychology, 53,* 194–200.

Howard, K. I., Kopta, S. M., Krause, M. S., & Orlinsky, D. E. (1986). The dose-effect relationship in psychotherapy. *American Psychologist, 41,* 159–164.

Howard-Pitney, B., LaFramboise, T. D., Basil, M., September, B., & Johnson, M. (1992). Psychological and social indicators of suicide ideation and suicide attempts in Zuni adolescents. *Journal of Consulting and Clinical Psychology, 60,* 473–476.

Howards, S. S. (1995). Current concepts: Treatment of male infertility. *New England Journal of Medicine, 332,* 312–317.

Howes, M. J., Hokanson, J. E., & Loewenstein, D. A. (1985). Induction to depressive affect after prolonged exposure to a mildly depressed individual. *Journal of Personality and Social Psychology, 49,* 1110–1113.

Huesmann, L. R., Eron, L. D., Klein, R., Brice, P., & Fischer, P. (1983). Mitigating the imitation of aggressive behaviors by changing children's attitudes about media violence. *Journal of Personality and Social Psychology, 44,* 899–910.

Huffman, T., Chang, K., Rausch, P., & Schaffer, N. (1994). Gender differences and factors related to the disposition toward cohabitation. *Family Therapy, 21*(3), 171–184.

Hughes, P. L., Wells, L. A., Cunningham, C. J., & Ilstrup, D. M. (1986). Treating bulimia with desipramine. *Archives of General Psychiatry, 43,* 182–186.

Hull, J. G., Van Treuren, R. R., & Virnelli, S. (1987). Hardiness and health: A critique and alternative approach. *Journal of Personality and Social Psychology, 53,* 518–530.

Hultquist, C. M., and others. (1995). The effect of smoking and light activity on metabolism in men. *Health Psychology, 14,* 124–131.

Hunter, J. E., & Schmidt, F. L., (1983). Quantifying the effects of psychological interventions on employee job performance and work-force productivity. *American Psychologist, 38,* 473–478.

Hyde, J. S., Fennema, E., & Lamon, S. J. (1990). Gender differences in mathematics performance: A meta-analysis. *Psychological Bulletin, 107,* 139–155.

Hyde, J. S., & Plant, E. A. (1995). Magnitude of psychological gender differences. *American Psychologist, 50,* 159–161.

Ilgen, D. R. (1990). Health issues at work: Opportunities for industrial/organizational psychology. *American Psychologist, 45,* 273–283.

Infant deaths drop but Black babies lag. (1993, March 12). *The New York Times,* p. A17.

Insko, C. A. (1985). Balance theory, the Jordan paradigm, and the Wiest tetrahedron. In L. Berkowitz (Ed.), *Advances in experimental social psychology.* New York: Academic Press.

Ironson, G. (1993). Cited in Adler, T. Men and women affected by stress, but differently. *APA Monitor, 24*(7), 8–9.

Irvine, M. (1998, January 10). California AIDS deaths drop sixty percent. Associated Press; American Online.

Jacklin, C. N., & Maccoby, E. E. (1983). Issues of gender differentiation. In M. D. Levine and others (Eds.), *Developmental-behavioral pediatrics.* Philadelphia: W. B. Saunders.

Jacobs, T. J., & Charles, E. (1980). Life events and the occurrence of cancer in children. *Psychosomatic Medicine, 42,* 11–24.

Jacobson, E. (1938). *Progressive relaxation.* Chicago: University of Chicago Press.

Jacobson, J. L., & Jacobson, S. W. (1994). Prenatal alcohol exposure and neurobehavioral development: Where is the threshold? *Alcohol Health and Research World, 18*(1) 30–36.

Jacobson, N. S. (1984). A component analysis of behavioral marital therapy: The relative effectiveness of behavior exchange and communication/problem-solving training. *Journal of Consulting and Clinical Psychology, 52,* 295–305.

Jacobson, N. S., & Hollon, S. D. (1996). Cognitive-behavior therapy versus pharmacotherapy. *Journal of Consulting and Clinical Psychology, 64,* 74–80.

Jacox, A., Carr, D. B., & Payne, R. (1994). New clinical-practice guidelines for the management of pain in patients with cancer. *New England Journal of Medicine, 330,* 651–655.

Janerich, D. T., and others. (1990). Lung cancer and exposure to tobacco smoke in the household. *New England Journal of Medicine, 323,* 632–636.

Janicak, P. G., and others. (1985). Efficacy of ECT: A meta-analysis. *American Journal of Psychiatry, 142,* 297–302.

Janis, I. L., & Mann, L. (1977). *Decision-making.* New York: Free Press.

Janus, S. S., & Janus, C. L. (1993). *The Janus report on sexual behavior.* New York: Wiley.

Jeffery, R. W. (1991). Population perspectives on the prevention and treatment of obesity in minority populations. *American Journal of Clinical Nutrition, 53,* 1621S–1624S.

Jemmott, J. B., and others. (1983). Academic stress, power motivation, and decrease in secretion rate of salivary secretory immunoglobin A. *Lancet, 1,* 1400–1402.

Jennings, J., Geis, F. L., & Brown, J. (1980). Influence of television commercials on women's self-confidence and independent judgment. *Journal of Personality and Social Psychology, 38,* 203–210.

Jensen, M. P., & Karoly, P. (1991). Control beliefs, coping efforts, and adjustment to chronic pain. *Journal of Consulting and Clinical Psychology, 59,* 431–438.

Johnson, K. W., and others. (1995). Panel II: Macrosocial and environmental influences on minority health. *Health Psychology, 14,* 601–612.

Johnson, T. (1998, January 31). Cited in Haney, D. Science targets old age. Associated Press; America Online.

Johnston, L. D., O'Malley, P. M., & Bachman, J. G. (1996). National survey results on drug use from the Monitoring the Future study, 1975–1994. Volume II. College Students and Young Adults. U.S. Department of Health and Human Services, Public Health Service, National Institutes of Health: National Institute on Drug Abuse.

Jones, H. W., & Toner, J. P. (1993). The infertile couple. *New England Journal of Medicine, 329,* 1710–1715.

Jones, J. (1991). In J. D. Goodchilds (Ed.), *Psychological perspectives on human diversity in America.* Washington, DC: American Psychological Association.

Jones, J. L., & Leary, M. R. (1994). Effects of appearance-based admonitions against sun exposure on tanning intentions in young adults. *Health Psychology, 13,* 86–90.

Jones, M. C. (1924). Elimination of children's fears. *Journal of Experimental Psychology, 7,* 381–390.

Jordan, J. V., Kaplan, A. G., Miller, J. B. Stiver, L. P., & Stiver, J. L. (Eds.). (1991). *Women's growth in connection.* New York: Guilford Press.

Jorgensen, R. S., Johnson, B. T., Kolodziej, M. E., & Schreer, G. E. (1996). Elevated blood pressure and personality. *Psychological Bulletin, 120,* 293–320.

Judd, C. M., & Park, B. (1988). Out-group homogeneity: Judgments of variability at the individual and group levels. *Journal of Personality and Social Psychology, 54,* 778–788.

Julien, R. M. (1986). *A primer of drug action* (2d ed.). San Francisco: Freeman.

Just, N., & Alloy, L. B. (1997). The response styles theory of depression: Tests and an extension of the theory. *Journal of Abnormal Psychology, 106,* 221–229.

Kagay, M. R. (1991, June 18). Poll funds AIDS causes single people to alter behavior. *The New York Times,* p. C3.

Kahn, S., Zimmerman, G., Csikszentmihalyi, M., & Getzels, J. W. (1985). Relations between identity in young adulthood and intimacy at midlife. *Journal of Personality and Social Psychology, 49,* 1316–1322.

Kakutani, M. (1992). Is it love, or just the imperatives of reproduction? *The New York Times,* p. C16.

Kamarck, T. W., and others. (1997). Mental stress is linked to blocked blood vessels. *Circulation, 96,* 3842–3848.

Kamarck, T. W., and others. (1998). Effects of task strain, social conflict, and emotional activation on ambulatory cardiovascular activity: Daily life consequences of recurring stress in a multiethnic adult sample. *Health Psychology, 17,* 17–29.

Kammeyer, K. C. W., Ritzer, G., Yetman, N. R. (1990). *Sociology: Experiencing changing societies.* Boston: Allyn & Bacon.

Kane, J. M. (1996). Schizophrenia. *New England Journal of Medicine, 334,* 34–41.

Kanner, A. D., Coyne, J. C., Schaefer, C., & Lazarus R. S. (1981). Comparison of two modes of stress measurement: Daily hassles and uplifts versus major life events. *Journal of Behavioral Medicine, 4,* 1–39.

Kaplan, H. R. (1978). *Lottery winners.* New York: Harper & Row.

Kaplan, S. J. (1991). Physical abuse and neglect. In M. Lewis (Ed.), *Child and adolescent psychiatry: A comprehensive textbook* (pp. 1010–1019). Baltimore: Williams & Wilkins.

Karabenick, S. A., & Meisels, M. (1972). Effects of performance evaluation on interpersonal distance. *Journal of Personality, 40,* 275–286.

Karlin, R. A., McFarland, D., Aiello, J. R., & Epstein, Y. M. (1976). Normative mediation of reactions to crowding. *Environmental Psychology and Non-Verbal Behavior, 1,* 30–40.

Kassirer, J. P., & Angell, M. (1998). Losing weight—An ill-fated New Year's resolution. *New England Journal of Medicine, 338,* 52–54.

Katz, M. H., & Gerberding, J. L. (1997). Postexposure treatment of people exposed to the human immunodeficiency virus through sexual contact or injection-drug use. *New England Journal of Medicine, 336,* 1097–1100.

Katzell, R. A., & Thompson, D. E. (1990). Work motivation: Theory and practice. *American Psychologist, 45,* 144–153.

Kaufman, A. S., Reynolds, C. R., & McLean, J. E. (1989). Age and WAIS-R intelligence in a national sample of adults in the 20- to 74-year age range: A cross-sectional analysis with educational level controlled. *Intelligence, 13,* 235–253.

Kaufman, J., & Zigler, E. (1989). The intergenerational transmission of child abuse. In D. Cicchetti & V. Carlson (Eds.), *Child maltreatment: Theory and research on the causes and consequences of child abuse and neglect* (pp. 129–150). Cambridge, England: Cambridge University Press.

Kaufman, M., and others. (1998, February 3). *Journal of American Medical Association.* Cited in Cocaine found to constrict arteries in brain. Reuters; America Online.

Kazdin, A. E., & Wilcoxin, L. A. (1976). Systematic desensitization and nonspecific treatment effects: A methodological evaluation. *Psychological Bulletin, 83,* 729–758.

Keating, C. F., and others. (1985). Psychosocial enhancement of immunocompetence in a geriatric population. *Health Psychology, 4,* 25–41.

Keefe, F. J., Dunsmore, J., & Burnett, R. (1992). Behavioral and cognitive-behavioral approaches to chronic pain. *Journal of Consulting and Clinical Psychology, 60,* 528–536.

Keen, S., & Zur, O. (1989). Who is the new ideal man? *Psychology Today, 1989, 23*(11), 54–60.

Keesey, R. E. (1986). A set-point theory of obesity. In K. D. Brownell & J. P. Foreyt (Eds.), *Handbook of eating disorders: Physiology, psychology, and treatment of obesity, anorexia, and bulimia.* New York: Basic Books.

Keil, J. E., and others. (1993). Mortality rates and risk factors for coronary disease in Black as compared with White men and women. *New England Journal of Medicine, 329,* 73–78.

Keita, G. P. (1993, February). Presentation to the Fifth International Interdisciplinary Congress on Women, University of Costa Rica, San Jose, Costa Rica.

Keller, M. B., First, M., & Koscis, J. H. (1990, August/September). Major depression and dysthymia. In American Psychiatric Association, *DSM-IV Update.* Washington, DC: American Psychiatric Association.

Kellerman, J., Lewis, J., & Laird, J. D. (1989). Looking and loving: The effects of mutual gaze on feelings of romantic love. *Journal of Research in Personality, 23,* 145–161.

Kelly, J. A., & Murphy, D. A. (1992). Psychological interventions with AIDS and HIV: Prevention and treatment. *Journal of Consulting and Clinical Psychology, 60,* 576–585.

Kelman, H. C. (1997). Group processes in the resolution of international conflicts. *American Psychologist, 52,* 212–220.

Kemper, P., & Murtaugh, C. M. (1991). Lifetime use of nursing home care. *New England Journal of Medicine, 324,* 595–600.

Kendall, P. C., & Norton-Ford, J. D. (1982). Therapy outcome research methods. In P. C. Kendall & J. N. Butcher (Eds.), *Handbook of research methods in clinical psychology.* New York: Wiley.

Kennedy, D. T., & Stephan, W. G. (1977). The

effects of cooperation and competition on ingroup-outgroup bias. *Journal of Applied Social Psychology, 7,* 115–130.

Kennedy, P. (1993). *Preparing for the twenty-first century.* New York: Random House.

Kenrick, D. T., & Gutierres, S. F. (1980). Contrast effects and judgments of physical attractiveness. *Journal of Personality and Social Psychology, 38,* 131–140.

Kenrick, D. T., & MacFarlane, S. W. (1986). Ambient temperature and horn honking: A field study of the heat/aggression relationship. *Environment and Behavior, 18,* 179–191.

Kerpelman, J. P., & Himmelfarb, S. (1971). Partial reinforcement effects in attitude acquisition and counterconditiong. *Journal of Personality and Social Psychology, 19,* 301–305.

Kessler, D. A. (1993, April 28). Cited in Condom for women nearing an approval for U.S. market. *The New York Times,* p. A13.

Kessler, D. A. (1995). Nicotine addiction in young people. *New England Journal of Medicine, 333,* 186–189.

Keye, W. R. (1983). Update: Premenstrual syndrome: *Endocrine and Fertility Forum, 6*(4), 1–3.

Kiecolt-Glaser, J. K. (1993). Cited in Adler, T. Men and women affected by stress, but differently. *APA Monitor, 24*(7), 8–9.

Kiecolt-Glaser, J. K., & Glaser, R. (1988). Psychological influences on immunity: Implications for AIDS. *American Psychologist, 43,* 892–898.

Kiecolt-Glaser, J. K., & Glaser, R. (1992). Psychoneuroimmunology: Can psychological interventions modulate immunity? *Journal of Consulting and Clinical Psychology, 60,* 569–575.

Kiecolt-Glaser, J. K., and others. (1985). Psychosocial enhancement of immunocompetence in a geriatric population. *Health Psychology, 4,* 25–41.

Kilborn, P. T. (1998, January 26). Black Americans trailing Whites in health, studies say. *The New York Times,* p. A16.

Kilbride, J. E., Komin, S., Leahy, P., Thurman, B., & Wirsing, R. (1981). Culture and the perception of social dominance from facial expression. *Journal of Personality and Social Psychology, 40,* 615–626.

Killen, J. D., Fortmann, S. P., Newman, B., & Varady, A. (1990). Evaluation of a treatment approach combining nicotine gum with self-guided behavioral treatments for smoking relapse prevention. *Journal of Consulting and Clinical Psychology, 58,* 85–92.

Kinderman, P., & Bentall, R. P. (1997). Causal attributions in paranoia and depression. *Journal of Abnormal Psychology, 106,* 341–345.

Kinnunen, T., Doherty, K., Militello, F. S., & Garvey, A. J. (1996). Depression and smoking cessation. *Journal of Consulting and Clinical Psychology, 64,* 791–798.

Kirn, W. (1997, August 18). The ties that bind. *Time,* pp. 48–50.

Klagsbrun, G. (1985). *Married people: Staying together in the age of divorce.* New York: Bantam Books.

Klein, D. F., & Rabkin, J. G. (1984). Specificity and strategy in psychotherapy research and practice. In R. L. Spitzer & J. R. W. Williams (Eds.), *Psychotherapy research: Where are we and where should we go?* New York: Guilford Press.

Kleinke, C. L. (1977). Compliance to requests made by gazing and touching experimenters in field settings. *Journal of Experimental Social Psychology, 13,* 218–223.

Kleinke, C. L. (1986). Gaze and eye contact. *Psychological Review, 100,* 78–100.

Kleinke, C. L., & Staneski, R. A. (1980). First impressions of female bust size. *Journal of Social Psychology, 110,* 123–134.

Kleinke, C. L., & Walton, J. H. (1982). Influence of reinforced smiling on affective responses in an interview. *Journal of Personality and Social Psychology, 42,* 557–565.

Klepinger, D. H., and others. (1993). Perceptions of AIDS risk and severity and their association with risk-related behavior among U.S. men. *Family Planning Perspectives, 25,* 74–82.

Klesges, R. C., and others. (1997). How much weight gain occurs following smoking cessation? *Journal of Consulting and Clinical Psychology, 65,* 286–291.

Klosko, J. S., Barlow, D. H., Tassinari, R., & Cerny, J. A. (1990). A comparison of alprazolam and behavior therapy in treatment of panic disorder. *Journal of Consulting and Clinical Psychology, 58,* 77–84.

Knapp, M. L. (1984). *Interpersonal communication and human relationships.* Needham Heights, MA: Allyn & Bacon.

Kobasa, S. C. (1979). Stressful life events, personality, and health: An inquiry into hardiness. *Journal of Personality and Social Psychology, 37,* 1–11.

Kobasa, S. C. (1985). Personality and health: Specifying and strengthening the conceptual links. In P. Shaver (Ed.), *Self, situations, and social behavior.* Beverly Hills, CA: Sage Press.

Kobasa, S. C., Maddi, S. R., & Kahn, S. (1982). Hardiness and health: A prospective study. *Journal of Personality and Social Psychology, 42,* 168–177.

Kobasa, S. C., Maddi, S. R., & Zola, M. A. (1983). Type A and hardiness. *Journal of Behavioral Medicine, 6,* 41–51.

Kobasa, S. C., & Puccetti, M. C. (1983). Personality and social resources in stress resistance. *Journal of Personality and Social Psychology, 45,* 839–850.

Kobasa, S. C. O. (1990). Stress-resistant personality. In R. E. Ornstein & C. Swencionis (Eds.), *The healing brain* (pp. 219–230). New York: Guilford Press.

Kobasa, S. C. O., Maddi, S. R., Puccetti, M. C., & Zola, M. A. (1994). Effectiveness of hardiness, exercise, and social support as resources against illness. In A. Steptoe & J. Wardle (Eds.), *Psychosocial processes and health* (pp. 247–260). Cambridge, England: Cambridge University Press.

Koestner, R., & Wheeler, L. (1988). Self-presentation in personal advertisements: The influence of implicit notions of attraction and role expectations. *Journal of Social and Personal Relationships, 5,* 149–160.

Kohlberg, L. (1969). *Stages in the development of moral thought and action.* New York: Holt, Rinehart and Winston.

Kohlberg, L. (1981). *The philosophy of moral development: Moral stages and the idea of justice.* San Francisco: Harper & Row.

Kolata, G. (1991, February 26). Alzheimer's researchers close in on causes. *The New York Times,* pp. C1, C7.

Kolata, G. (1993a, May 6). Cancer-causing gene found with a clue to how it works. *The New York Times,* pp. 1, B15.

Kolata, G. (1993b, August 11). New pregnancy hope: A single sperm. *The New York Times,* p. C11.

Kolata, G. (1993c, August 11). New pregnancy hope: A single sperm. *The New York Times,* p. C11.

Kolata, G. (1996, August 27). Gene therapy shows first signs of bypassing arterial blockage. *The New York Times,* p. C3.

Kolata, G. (1997, February 24). With cloning of a sheep, the ethical ground shifts. *The New York Times,* pp. A1, B8.

Kolata, G. (1998, January 5). Infertile foreigners see opportunity in the U.S. *The New York Times.*

Kolbert, E. (1994, January 21). Demons replace dolls and bicycles in world of children of the quake. *The New York Times,* p. A19.

Kolko, D. J., & Rickard-Figueroa, J. L. (1985). Effects of video games on the adverse corollaries of chemotherapy in pediatric oncology patients: A single-case analysis. *Journal of Consulting and Clinical Psychology, 53,* 223–228.

Koocher, G. P. (1971). Swimming, competence, and personality change. *Journal of Personality and Social Psychology, 18,* 275–278.

Koop, C. E. (1988, May 17). Excerpts from Koop report on smoking. *The New York Times,* p. C4.

Koss, M. P. (1990). The women's mental health research agenda: Violence against women. *American Psychologist, 45,* 374–380.

Koss, M. P. (1993). Rape: Scope, impact, interventions, and public policy responses. *American Psychologist, 48,* 1062–1069.

Koss, M. P., Gidycz, C. A., & Wisniewski, N. (1987). The scope of rape: Incidence and prevalence of sexual aggression and victimization in a national sample of higher education students. *Journal of Consulting and Clinical Psychology, 55,* 162–170.

Kramer, P. D. (1993). *Listening to Prozac.* New York: Viking.

Krug, E. G., and others. (1998, February 5). *New England Journal of Medicine, 338,* Cited in Haney, D. Q. (1998, February 4), Suicide increases after floods. Associated Press; America Online.

Kübler-Ross, E. (1969). *On death and dying.* New York: Macmillan.

Kuczmarski, R. J. (1992). Prevalence of overweight and weight gain in the United States. *American Journal of Clinical Nutrition, 55*(Suppl.), 495S–502S.

Kupfer, D. J., & Reynolds, C. F. (1997). Management of insomnia. *New England Journal of Medicine, 336,* 341–346.

Kurdek, A., Blisk, D., & Siesky, A. E. (1981). Correlates of children's long-term adjustment to their parents' divorce. *Developmental Psychology, 17,* 565–579.

Kurdek, L. A., & Schmitt, J. P. (1986a). Relationship quality of gay men in closed or open relationships. *Journal of Homosexuality, 12*(2), 85–99.

Kurdek, L. A., & Schmitt, J. P. (1986b). Relationship quality of partners in heterosexual married, heterosexual cohabiting, gay, and lesbian relationships. *Journal of Personality and Social Psychology, 51,* 711–720.

Lacks, P., & Morin, C. M. (1992). Recent advances in the assessment and treatment of insomnia. *Journal of Consulting and Clinical Psychology, 60,* 586–594.

LaFramboise, T. (1994). Cited in DeAngelis, T. History, culture affect treatment for Indians. *APA Monitor, 27*(10), 36.

Lakka, T. A., and others. (1994). Relation of leisure-time physical activity and cardiorespiratory fitness to the risk of acute myocardial infarction in men. *New England Journal of Medicine, 330,* 1549–1554.

Lamanna, M. A., & Riedmann, A. (1997). *Marriages and families* (6th ed.). Belmont, CA: Wadsworth.

Lamaze, F. (1981). *Painless childbirth.* New York: Simon & Schuster.

Lamb, M. E. (1981). The development of father-infant relationships. In M. E. Lamb (Ed.), *The role of the father in child development.* New York: Wiley.

Lamb, M. E., & Baumrind, D. (1978). Socialization and personality development in the preschool years. In M. E. Lamb (Ed.), *Social and personality development.* New York: Holt, Rinehart and Winston.

Lamb, M. E. Easterbrooks, M. A., & Holden, G. W. (1980). Reinforcement and punishment among preschoolers: Characteristics, effects, and correlates. *Child Development, 51,* 1230–1236.

Lamb, M. E., Sternberg, K. J., & Prodromidis, M. (1992). Nonmaternal care and the security of infant-mother attachment: A reanalysis of the data. *Infant Behavior and Development, 15,* 71–83.

Lamberti, D. (1997, November). Cited in Alterman, E. Sex in the '90s. *Elle,* pp. 128–134.

Lamott, A. (1993, August 5). When going it alone turns out to be not so alone at all. *The New York Times,* pp. C1, C9.

Landy, F. J., & Farr, J. L. (1983). *The measurement of work performance: Methods, theory, and applications.* New York: Academic Press.

Lane, K. E., & Gwartney-Gibbs, P. A. (1985). Violence in the context of dating and sex. *Journal of Family Issues, 6,* 45–59.

Lang, A. R., Goeckner, D. J., Adesso, V. J., & Marlatt, G. A. (1975). Effects of alcohol on aggression in male social drinkers. *Journal of Abnormal Psychology, 84,* 508–518.

Lang, S. S., & Patt, R. B. (1994). *You don't have to suffer.* New York: Oxford University Press.

Langer, E. J., Rodin, J., Beck, P., Weinan, C., & Spitzer, L. (1979). Environmental determinants of memory improvement in late adulthood. *Journal of Personality and Social Psychology, 37,* 2003–2013.

Laudenslager, M. L., Ryan, S. M., Drugan, R. C., Hyson, R. L., & Maier, S. F. (1983). Coping and immunosuppression: Inescapable but not escapable shock suppresses lymphocyte proliferation. *Science, 221,* 568–570.

Laumann, E. O., Gagnon, J. H., Michael, R. T., & Michaels, S. (1994). *The social organization of sexuality.* Chicago: University of Chicago Press.

Lawson, C. (1993, August 5). "Who is my daddy?" can be answered in different ways. *The New York Times,* pp. C1, C9.

Lawton, C., & Morrin, K. (1997). Cited in Azar, B. Environment can mitigate differences in spatial ability. *APA Monitor, 28*(6), 28.

Lazarus, A. A. (1990). If this be research . . . *American Psychologist, 45,* 670–671.

Lazarus, R. S. (1984a). Puzzles in the study of daily hassles. *Journal of Behavioral Medicine, 7,* 375–389.

Lazarus, R. S. (1984b). The trivialization of distress. In B. L. Hammonds & C. J. Scheirer (Eds.), *Psychology and health: The master lecture series.* Washington, DC: American Psychological Association.

Lazarus, R. S. (1991a). Cognition and motivation in emotion. *American Psychologist, 46,* 352–367.

Lazarus, R. S. (1991b). *Emotion and adaptation.* New York: Oxford University Press.

Lazarus, R. S., DeLongis, A., Folkman, S., & Gruen, R. (1985). Stress and adaptational outcomes: The problem of confounded measures. *American Psychologist, 40,* 770–779.

Lazarus, R. S., & Folkman, S. (1984). *Stress, appraisal, and coping.* New York: Springer.

Leadbeater, B. J., & Linares, D. (1992). Depressive symptoms in Black and Puerto Rican adolescent mothers in the first 3 years postpartum. *Development and Psychopathology, 4,* 451–468.

Lear, M. (1987, December 20). The pain of loneliness. *The New York Times Magazine,* pp. 47–48.

Leary, W. E. (1991, October 22). Black hypertension may reflect other ills. *The New York Times,* p. C3.

Leary, W. E. (1995, May 2). Millions suffering needlessly, study says. *The New York Times,* p. C5.

Leary, W. E. (1997, January 14). Researchers investigate (horrors!) nicotine's potential benefits. *The New York Times,* p. C3.

LeBon, G. (1895). *The crowd.* New York: Viking, 1960.

Lefcourt, H. M., & Martin, R. A. (1986). *Humor and life stress: Antidote to adversity.* New York: Springer-Verlag.

Lefcourt, H. M., Miller, R. S., Ware, E. E., & Sherk, D. (1981). Locus of control as a modifier of the relationship between stressors and moods. *Journal of Personality and Social Psychology, 41,* 357–369.

Lefley, H. P. (1990). Culture and chronic mental illness. *Hospital and Community Psychiatry, 41,* 277–286.

Leibel, R. L., Rosenbaum, M., & Hirsch, J. (1995). Changes in energy expenditure resulting from altered body weight. *New England Journal of Medicine, 332,* 621–628.

Leibowitz, S. F. (1986). Brain monoamines and peptides: Role in the control of eating behavior. *Federation Proceedings, 45,* 599–615.

Leitenberg, H., & Henning, K. (1995). Sexual fantasy. *Psychological Bulletin, 117,* 469–496.

Leor, J., Poole, K., & Kloner, R. A. (1996). Sudden cardiac death triggered by an earthquake. *New England Journal of Medicine, 334,* 413–419.

Lerman, C. (1997). Psychological aspects of genetic testing. *Health Psychology, 16,* 3–7.

Lerman, C., and others. (1998). Depression and self-medication with nicotine: The modifying influence of the dopamine D4 receptor gene. *Health Psychology, 17,* 56–62.

Lesnik-Oberstein, M., & Cohen, L. (1984). Cognitive style, sensation seeking, and assortive mating. *Journal of Personality and Social Psychology, 46,* 112–117.

Leutwyler, K. (1997). Depression's double standard. *Scientific American mysteries of the mind, Special Issue* Vol. 7, No. 1, 53–54.

Levinger, G. (1983). Development and change. In H. H. Kelley and others (Eds.), *Close relationships.* New York: W. H. Freeman.

Levinson, D. J., and others. (1978). *The seasons of a man's life.* New York: Knopf.

Levy, S. M., Herberman, R. B., Maluish, A. M., Schlien, B., & Lippman, M. (1985). Prognostic risk assessment in the primary breast cancer by behavioral and immunological parameters. *Health Psychology, 4,* 99–113.

Lewin, T. (1990, March 28). Strategies to let elderly keep some control. *The New York Times,* pp. A1, A22.

Lewin, T. (1995a). Women are becoming equal providers. *The New York Times,* p. A27.

Lewin, T. (1995b, December 7). Parents poll shows higher incidence of child abuse. *The New York Times,* p. B16.

Lewinsohn, P. M., & Graf, M. (1973). Pleasant activities and depression. *Journal of Con sulting and Clinical Psychology, 41,* 261–268.

Lewinsohn, P. M., Rohde, P., & Seeley, J. R. (1994a). Psychosocial risk factors for future suicide attempts. *Journal of Consulting and Clinical Psychology, 62,* 297–305.

Lewinsohn, P. M., and others. (1994b). Adolescent psychopathology: II. Psychosocial risk factors for depression. *Journal of Abnormal Psychology, 103,* 302–315.

Lewis, P. H. (1995, August 21). PlanetOut: "Gay global village" of cyberspace, *The New York Times,* p. D3.

Lex, B. W. (1987). Review of alcohol problems in ethnic minority groups. *Journal of Consulting and Clinical Psychology, 55,* 293–300.

Lichtenstein, E., & Glasgow, R. E. (1992). Smoking cessation: What have we learned in the past decade? *Journal of Consulting and Clinical Psychology, 60,* 518–527.

Lieber, C. S. (1990, January 14). Cited in Barroom biology: How alcohol goes to a woman's head, *The New York Times,* p. E24.

Lindenberer, U., Mayr, U., & Kliegl, R. (1993). Speed and intelligence in old age. *Psychology and Aging, 8,* 207–220.

Lindpaintner, K. (1995). Finding an obesity gene—a tale of mice and men. *New England Journal of Medicine, 332,* 679–680.

Linville, P. W., Fischer, G. W., & Salovey, P. (1989). Perceived distribution of the characteristics of in-group and out-group members. *Journal of Personality and Social Psychology, 57,* 165–188.

Lipton, D. N., McDonel, E. C., & McFall, R. M. (1987). Heterosocial perception in rapists. *Journal of Consulting and Clinical Psychology, 55,* 17–21.

Long, B. C. (1984). Aerobic conditioning and stress inoculation: A comparison of stress-management interventions. *Cognitive Therapy and Research, 8,* 517–542.

Longer, healthier, better. (1997, March 9). *The New York Times Magazine,* pp. 44–45.

Louie, V. (1993, August 8). For Asian-Americans, a way to fight a maddening stereotype. *The New York Times,* p. F9.

Lowenthal, M. F., & Haven, C. (1981). Interaction and adaptation: Intimacy as a critical variable. In L. D. Steinberg (Ed.), *The life cycle.* New York: Columbia University Press.

Luborsky, L., Barber, J. P., & Beutler, L. (1993). Introduction to special section: A briefing on curative factors in dynamic psychotherapy. *Journal of Consulting and Clinical Psychology, 61,* 539–541.

Luborsky, L., & DeRubeis, R. J. (1984). The use of psychotherapy treatment manuals: A small revolution in psychotherapy research style. *Clinical Psychology Review, 4,* 5–15.

Luchins, A. S. (1957). Primacy-recency in impression formation. In C. I. Hovland (Ed.), *The order of presentation in persuasion.* New Haven, CT: Yale University Press.

Ludwick-Rosenthal, R., & Neufeld, R. W. J. (1993). Preparation for undergoing an invasive medical procedure. *Journal of Consulting and Clinical Psychology, 61,* 156–164.

Lurie, N., and others. (1993). Preventive care for women: Does the sex of the physician matter? *New England Journal of Medicine, 329,* 478–482.

Lydiard, R. B., Brawman, A., Mintzer, O., & Ballenger, J. C. (1996). Recent developments in the psychopharmacology of anxiety disorders. *Journal of Consulting and Clinical Psychology, 64,* 660–668.

Lykken, D. T. (1982). Fearlessness: Its carefree charm and deadly risks. *Psychology Today, 16*(9), 20–28.

Lykken, D. T. (1996, July 21). Cited in Goleman, D. A set point for happiness. *The New York Times,* p. E2.

Lykken, D. T., McGue, M., Tellegen, A., & Bouchard, T. J., Jr. (1992). Emergenesis: Genetic traits that may not run in families. *American Psychologist, 47,* 1565–1577.

Maas, J. W., and others. (1939). Studies of catecholamine metabolism in schizophrenia/psychosis—I. *Neuropsychopharmacology, 8,* 97–109.

Maccoby, E. E. (1990). Gender and relationships: A developmental account. *American Psychologist, 45,* 513–520.

Maccoby, E. E., & Jacklin, C. N. (1980). Sex differences in aggression: A rejoinder and reprise. *Child Development, 51,* 964–980.

MacDonald, K. (1992). Warmth as a developmental construct. *Child Development, 63,* 753–773.

MacFarquhar, N. (1996, August 8). Mutilation of Egyptian girls: Despite ban, it goes on. *The New York Times,* p. A3.

Mack, D., & Rainey, D. (1990). Female applicants' grooming and personnel selection. *Journal of Social Behavior and Personality, 5,* 399–407.

MacKenzie, T. D., Bartecchi, C. E., & Schrier, R. W. (1994). The human costs of tobacco use. *New England Journal of Medicine, 330,* 975–980.

Mackie, D. M., Worth, L. T., & Asuncion, A. G. (1990). Processing of persuasive in-group messages. *Journal of Personality and Social Psychology, 58,* 812–822.

Macklin, E. D. (1980). Nonmarital heterosexual cohabitation. In A. Skolnick & J. H. Skolnick (Eds.), *Family in transition* (3d ed.). Boston: Little, Brown.

MacPhillamy, D. J., & Lewinsohn, P. M. (1971). *Pleasant Events Schedule, Form III-S.* University of Oregon, Mimeograph.

Maddi, S. R. (1980). *Personality theories: A comparative analysis.* Homewood, IL: Dorsey Press.

Maddi, S. R., & Kobasa S. C. (1984). *The hardy executive: Health under stress.* Homewood, IL: Dow Jones–Irwin.

Maher, B. A., & Maher, W. B. (1994). Personality and psychopathology. *Journal of Abnormal Psychology, 103,* 72–77.

Maier, S. F., Watkins, L. R., & Fleshner, M. (1994). Psychoneuroimmunology: The interface between behavior, brain, and immunity. *American Psychologist, 49* 1004–1017.

Malgady, R. G., Rogler, L. H., & Costantino, G. (1990). Culturally sensitive psychotherapy for Puerto Rican children and adolescents: A program of treatment outcome research. *Journal of Consulting and Clinical Psychology, 58,* 704–712.

Malinosky-Rummell, R., & Hansen, D. H. (1993). Long-term consequences of childhood physical abuse. *Psychological Bulletin, 114,* 68–79.

Man transmits HIV with kiss. (1997, July 11). *USA Today,* p. 3D.

Mandler, G. (1984). *Mind and body: The psychology of emotion and stress.* New York: W. W. Norton.

Marcus, M. G. (1976). The power of a name. *Psychology Today, 10*(5), 75–76, 108.

Marecek, J. (1995). Gender, politics, and psychology's ways of knowing. *American Psychologist, 50,* 162–163.

Marenberg, M. E., and others. (1994). Genetic susceptibility to death from coronary heart disease in a study of twins. *New England Journal of Medicine, 330,* 1041–1046.

Margoshes, P. (1995). For many, old age is the prime of life. *APA Monitor, 26*(5), 36–37.

Markman, H. J. (1981). Prediction of marital distress: A five-year follow-up. *Journal of Consulting and Clinical Psychology, 49,* 760–762.

Marks, G., Miller, N., & Maruyama, G. (1981). Effect of targets' physical attractiveness on assumption of similarity. *Journal of Personality and Social Psychology, 41,* 198–206.

Markus, H., & Kitayama, S. (1991). Culture and the self. *Psychological Review, 98*(2), 224–253.

Marlatt, G. A., & Gordon, J. R. (1980). Determinants of relapse: Implications for the maintenance of behavior change. In P. O. Davidson & S. M. Davidson (Eds.), *Behavioral medicine: Changing health lifestyles.* New York: Brunner/Mazel.

Marriott, M. (1991, June 5). Beyond "yuck" for girls in science. *The New York Times,* p. A26.

Marshall, D. D. (1971). Sexual behavior on Mangaia. In D. S. Marshall & R. C. Suggs (Eds.), *Human sexual behavior: Variations in the ethnographic spectrum.* New York: Basic Books.

Marteau, T. M., Dundas, R., & Axworthy, D. (1997). Long-term cognitive and emotional impact of genetic testing for carriers of cystic fibrosis. *Health Psychology, 16,* 51–62.

Martin, C. L. (1987). A ratio measure of sex stereotyping. *Journal of Personality and Social Psychology, 52,* 489–499.

Martin, J. E., and others. (1997). Prospective evaluation of three smoking interventions in 205 recovering alcoholics. *Journal of Consulting and Clinical Psychology, 65,* 190–194.

Martin, R. A., & Lefcourt, H. M. (1983). Sense of humor as a moderator of the relation between stressors and moods. *Journal of Personality and Social Psychology, 45,* 1313–1324.

Martínez, R. (1994, January 20). One quake, two worlds. *The New York Times,* p. A21.

Maruyama, G., & Miller, N. (1975). *Physical attractiveness and classroom acceptance.* Social Science Research Institute Report No. 75-2, University of Southern California.

Marx, E. M., Williams, J. M. G., & Claridge, G. C. (1992). Depression and social problem solving. *Journal of Abnormal Psychology, 101,* 78–86.

Masters, W. H., & Johnson, V. E. (1966). *Human sexual response.* Boston: Little, Brown.

Masters, W. H., & Johnson, V. E. (1979). *Homosexuality in perspective.* Boston: Little, Brown.

Mathes, E. W., Adams, H. E., & Davies, R. M. (1985). Jealousy: Loss of relationship rewards, loss of self-esteem, depression, anxiety, and anger. *Journal of Personality and Social Psychology, 48,* 1552–1561.

Matlin, M. W. (1996). *The psychology of women* (3d ed.). Fort Worth, TX: Harcourt Brace College Publishers.

Matthews, K. (1994). Cited in Azar, B. Women are barraged by media on "the change." *APA Monitor, 25*(5), 24–25.

Matthews, K., and others. (1997). Women's Health Initiative. *American Psychologist, 52,* 101–116.

Matus, I. (1996). Cited in Clay, R. A. Beating the "biological clock" with zest. *APA Monitor, 27*(2), 37.

Mazzella, R., & Feingold, A. (1994). The effects of physical attractiveness, race, socioeconomic status, and gender of defendants and victims on judgments of mock jurors. *Journal of Applied Psychology, 24*(15), 1315–1344.

McCann, I. L., & Holmes, D. S. (1984). Influence of aerobic exercise on depression. *Journal of Personality and Social Psychology, 46,* 1142–1147.

McCrae, R. R. (1996). Social consequences of experiential openness. *Psychological Bulletin, 120,* 323–337.

McCrae, R. R., & Costa, P. T., Jr. (1990). *Personality in adulthood.* New York: Guilford Press.

McCrae, R. R., & Costa, P. T., Jr. (1997). Personality trait structure as a human universal. *American Psychologist, 52,* 509–516.

McCutchan, J. A. (1990). Virology, immunology, and clinical course of HIV infection. *Journal of Consulting and Clinical Psychology, 58,* 5–12.

McGrath, E., Keita, G. P., Strickland, B. R., & Russo, N. F. (1990). *Women and depression: Risk factors and treatment issues.* Washington, DC: American Psychological Association.

McIntosh, J. L., Hubbard, R. W., Santos, J. F., & Overholser, J. C. (1995). *Elder suicide.* Washington, DC: American Psychological Association.

McLaughlin, F. J., and others. (1992). Randomized trial of comprehensive prenatal care for low-income women: Effect on infant birth weight. *Pediatrics, 89,* 128–132.

McMahon, M. J., and others. (1996). Comparison of a trial of labor with an elective second cesarean section. *New England Journal of Medicine, 335,* 689–695.

McMinn, M. R., & Wade, N. G. (1995). Beliefs about the prevalence of dissociative identity disorder, sexual abuse, and ritual abuse among religious and nonreligious therapists. *Professional Psychology: Research and Practice, 26,* 257–261.

McNally, R. J. (1990). Psychological approaches to panic disorder. *Psychological Bulletin, 108,* 403–419.

McNamara, M. L. L., & Bahr, H. M. (1980). The dimensionality of marital role satisfaction. *Journal of Marriage and the Family, 42,* 45–54.

Meade, V. (1994). Psychologists forecast future of the profession. *APA Monitor, 25*(5), 14–15.

Meichenbaum, D. (1993). Changing conceptions of cognitive behavior modification. *Journal of Consulting and Clinical Psychology, 61,* 202–204.

Meichenbaum, D. H., & Butler, L. (1980). Toward a conceptual model for the treatment of test anxiety: Implications for research and treatment. In I. G. Sarason (Ed.), *Test anxiety: Theory, research, and application.* Hillsdale, NJ: Erlbaum.

Meier, B. (1997, June 8). In war against AIDS, battle over baby formula reignites. *The New York Times,* pp. A1, A16.

Messenger, J. C. (1971). Sex and repression in an Irish folk community. In D. S. Marshall & R. C. Suggs (Eds.), *Human sexual behavior: Variations in the ethnographic spectrum.* New York: Basic Books.

Meyer, T. (1997). Americans are getting fatter. Associated Press; America Online.

Meyerowitz, B. E., Richardson, J., Hudson, S., & Leedham, B. (1998). Ethnicity and cancer outcomes: Behavioral and psychosocial considerations. *Psychological Bulletin, 123,* 47–70.

Meyers, A. W., and others. (1997). Are weight concerns predictive of smoking cessation? *Journal of Consulting and Clinical Psychology, 65,* 448–452.

Michels, R., & Marzuk, P. M. (1993a). Progress in psychiatry. (Part I). *New England Journal of Medicine, 329,* 552–560.

Michels, R., & Marzuk, P. M. (1993b). Progress in psychiatry. (Part 2). *New England Journal of Medicine, 329,* 628–638.

Mikesell, R. H., Lusterman, D., & McDaniel, S. (Eds.). (1995). *Family psychology and systems therapy.* Washington, DC: American Psychological Association.

Milgram, S. (1963). Behavioral study of obedience. *Journal of Abnormal and Social Psychology, 67,* 371–378.

Milgram, S. (1974). *Obedience to authority.* New York: Harper & Row.

Miller, N. B., Cowan, P. A., Cowan, C. P., Hetherington, E. M., & Clingempeel, W. G. (1993). Externalizing in preschoolers and early adolescents. *Developmental Psychology, 29,* 3–18.

Miller, N. E. (1969). Learning of visceral and glandular responses. *Science, 163,* 434–445.

Miller, N. E. (1985). Rx: Biofeedback. *Psychology Today, 19*(2), 54–59.

Miller, N. E., & Dollard, J. (1941). *Social learning and imitation.* New Haven, CT: Yale University Press.

Miller, S. M. (1980). Why having control reduces stress: If I can stop the roller coaster I don't want to get off. In J. Garber & M. E. P. Seligman (Eds.), *Human helplessness: Theory and research.* New York: Academic Press.

Miller, S. M., Shoda, Y., & Hurley, K. (1996). Applying cognitive-social theory to health-protective behavior: Breast self-examination in cancer screening. *Psychological Bulletin, 199,* 70–94.

Mills, J., & Harvey, J. (1972). Opinion change as a function of when information about the communicator is received and whether he is attractive or expert. *Journal of Personality and Social Psychology, 21,* 52–55.

Mineka, S. (1991, August). Paper presented to the annual meeting of the American Psychological Association, San Francisco. Cited in Turkington, C. Evolutionary memories may have phobia role. *APA Monitor, 22*(11), 14.

Mintz, L. B., Bartels, K. M., & Rideout, C. A. (1995). Training in counseling ethnic minorities and race-based availability of graduate school resources. *Professional Psychology: Research and Practice, 26,* 316–321.

Mischel, W., & Shoda, Y. (1995). A cognitive-affective system theory of personality. *Psychological Review, 102,* 246–268.

Mjoseth, J. (1998). New diagnostic system could benefit psychologists. *APA Monitor, 29*(2), 29.

Mokuau, N. (1990). The impoverishment of native Hawaiians and the social work challenge. *Health and Social Work, 15,* 235–242.

Moncher, M. S., Holden, G. W., & Trimble, J. E. (1990). Substance abuse among Native-American youth. *Journal of Consulting and Clinical Psychology, 58,* 408–415.

Money, J. (1987). Sin, sickness, or status? Homosexual gender identity and psychoneuroendocrinology. *American Psychologist, 42,* 384–399.

Money, J., & Lamacz, M. (1989). *Vandalized lovemaps.* Buffalo, NY: Prometheus Books.

Morris, W. N., Miller, R. S., & Spangenberg, S. (1977). The effects of dissenter position and task difficulty on conformity and response conflict. *Journal of Personality, 45,* 251–256.

Morrison, A. M., & Von Glinow, M. A. (1990). Women and minorities in management. *American Psychologist, 45,* 200–209.

Mortola, J. F. (1998). Premenstrual syndrome—Pathophysiologic considerations. *New England Journal of Medicine, 338,* 256–257.

Moser, C. G., & Dyck, D. G. (1989). Type A behavior, uncontrollability, and the activation of hostile self-schema responding. *Journal of Research in Personality, 23,* 248–267.

Motowidlo, S. T. (1982). Sex role orientation and behavior in a work setting. *Journal of Personality and Social Psychology, 42,* 935–945.

Moyers, B. (1993). *Healing and the mind.* New York: Doubleday.

Mullen, B., and others. (1987). Newscasters' facial expressions and voting behavior of viewers: Can a smile elect a president? *Journal of Personality and Social Psychology, 53.*

Murray, B. (1995). Black psychology relies on traditional ideology. *APA Monitor, 26*(6), 33–34.

Murstein, B. I., & Fontaine, P. A. (1993). The public's knowledge about psychologists and other mental health professionals. *American Psychologist, 48,* 839–845.

Murtagh, D. R. R., & Greenwood, K. M. (1995). Identifying effective psychological treatments for insomnia.: A meta-analysis. *Journal of Consulting and Clinical Psychology, 63,* 79–89.

Narayanan, V. K., & Nath, R. (1982). A field test of some attitudinal and behavioral consequences of flexitime. *Journal of Applied Psychology, 67,* 214–218.

National Center for Health Statistics. (1996, March). News Releases and Fact Sheets. *Monitoring Health Care in America: Quarterly Fact Sheet.*

National Institute of Mental Health. (1985). *Electroconvulsive therapy: Consensus Development Conference statement.* Bethesda, MD: U.S. Department of Health and Human Services.

National Institutes of Health. (1985). *National cancer program: 1983–1984 director's report and annual plan, FY 1986–1990.* (NIH Publication No. 85-2765). Washington, DC: U.S. Government Printing Office.

Neisser, U., Boodoo, G., Bouchard, T. J., Jr., Boykin, A. W., Brody, N., Ceci, S. J., Halpern, D. F., Loehlin, J. C., Perloff, R., Sternberg, R. J., & Urbina, S. (1996). Intelligence: Knowns and unknowns. *American Psychologist, 51,* 77–101.

Nevid, J. S. (1984). Sex differences in factors of romantic attraction. *Sex Roles, 11*(5/6), 410–411.

Nevid, J. S., & Javier, R. A. (1993). Unpublished manuscript, St. John's University.

Nevid, J. S., & Rathus, S. A. (1978). Multivariate and normative data pertaining to the RAS with the college population. *Behavior Therapy, 9,* 675.

Nevid, J. S., Rathus, S. A., & Greene, B. A. (1994). *Abnormal psychology in a changing world* (2d ed.). Englewood Cliffs, NJ: Prentice-Hall.

Nevid, J. S., Rathus, S. A., & Greene, B. A. (1997). *Abnormal psychology in a changing world* (2d ed.). Englewood Cliffs, NJ: Prentice-Hall.

Nevid, J. S., Rathus, S. A., & Rubenstein, H. R. (1998). *Health in the new millennium.* New York: Worth Publishers.

Newcomb, T. M. (1971). Dyadic balance as a source of clues about interpersonal attraction. In B. I. Murstein (Ed.), *Theories of attraction and love.* New York: Springer.

Newcomb, T. M. (1981). Heiderian balance as a group phenomenon. *Journal of Consulting and Clinical Psychology, 40,* 862–867.

Newcombe, N., & Arnkoff, D. B. (1979). Effects of speech style and sex of speaker on person perception. *Journal of Personality and Social Psychology, 37,* 1293–1303.

Newcombe, N., Bandura, M. M., & Taylor, D. G. (1983). Sex differences in spatial ability and spatial activity. *Sex Roles, 9,* 377–386.

Newlin, D. B., & Thomson, J. B. (1990). Alcohol challenge with sons of alcoholics: A critical review and analysis. *Psychological Bulletin, 108,* 383–402.

Newman, J., & McCauley, C. (1977). Eye contact with strangers in city, suburb, and small town. *Environment and Behavior, 9,* 547–558.

Newman, R. (1994). Prozac: Panacea? Psychological steroid? *APA Monitor, 25*(4), 34.

Nieves, J., and others. (1998, January 16). *Journal of Clinical Nutrition.* Cited in Calcium plus hormones found to strengthen bones. Reuters; America Online.

Nisbett, R. E., & Ross, L. (1980). *Human inference: Strategies and shortcomings of social judgment.* Englewood Cliffs, NJ: Prentice-Hall.

Nock, S. L. (1995). A comparison of marriages and cohabiting relationships. *Journal of Family Issues, 16*(1), 53–76.

Nolen-Hoeksema, S. (1991). Responses to depression and their effects on the duration of depressive episodes. *Journal of Abnormal Psychology, 100,* 569–582.

Nolen-Hoeksema, S., & Girgus, J. S. (1994). The emergence of gender differences in depression during adolescence. *Psychological Bulletin, 115,* 424–443.

Nolen-Hoeksema, S., Morrow, J., & Fredrickson, B. L. (1993). Response styles and the duration of depressed mood. *Journal of Abnormal Psychology, 102,* 20–28.

Norvell, N., & Belles, D. (1993). Psychological and physical benefits of circuit weight training in law enforcement personnel. *Journal of Consulting and Clinical Psychology, 61,* 520–527.

Novaco, R. (1977). A stress inoculation approach to anger management in the training of law enforcement officers. *American Journal of Community Psychology, 5,* 327–346.

O'Brien, C. P. (1996). Recent developments in the pharmacotherapy of substance abuse. *Journal of Consulting and Clinical Psychology, 64,* 677–686.

O'Grady, K. E. (1982). Sex, physical attractiveness, and perceived risk for mental illness. *Journal of Personality and Social Psychology, 43,* 1064–1071.

O'Hara, M. W. (1996, May 1). Cited in Gilbert, S. Estrogen patch appears to lift severe depression in new mothers. *The New York Times,* p. C12.

O'Hara, M. W., Schlecte, J. A., Lewis, D. A., & Varner, M. W. (1991). Controlled prospective study of postpartum mood disorders: Psychological, environmental and hormonal variables. *Journal of Abnormal Psychology, 99,* 3–15.

Oliver, M. B., & Hyde, J. S. (1993). Gender differences in sexuality: A meta-analysis. *Psychological Bulletin, 114,* 29–51.

Olson, S. L., Bates, J. E., & Kaskie, B. (1929). Caregiver-infant interaction antecedents of children's school-age cognitive ability. *Merrill-Palmer Quarterly, 38,* 309–330.

O'Malley, M. N., & Becker, L. A. (1984). Removing the egocentric bias: The relevance of distress cues to evaluation of fairness. *Personality and Social Psychology Bulletin, 10,* 235–242.

Ortega, D. F., & Pipal, J. E. (1984). Challenge seeking and the Type A coronary-prone behavior pattern. *Journal of Personality and Social Psychology, 46,* 1328–1334.

Ouimette, P. C., Finney, J. W., & Moos, R. H. (1997). Twelve-step and cognitive-behavioral treatment for substance abuse. *Journal of Consulting and Clinical Psychology, 65,* 230–240.

Paffenbarger, R. S., Jr., and others. (1986). Physical activity, all-cause mortality, and longevity of college alumni. *New England Journal of Medicine, 314,* 605–613.

Paffenbarger, R. S., Jr., and others. (1993). The association of changes in physical-activity level and other lifestyle characteristics with mortality among men. *New England Journal of Medicine, 328,* 538–545.

Page, R. A. (1977). Noise and helping behavior. *Environment and Behavior, 9,* 311–334.

Pagel, M., & Becker, J. (1987). Depressive thinking and depression: Relations with personality and social resources. *Journal of Personality and Social Psychology, 52,* 1043–1052.

Pajares, F., & Miller, M. D. (1994). Role of self-efficacy and self-concept beliefs in mathematical problem solving. *Journal of Educational Psychology, 86,* 193–203.

Palinkas, L. A., and others. (1992). Ethnic differences in stress, coping, and depressive symptoms after the Exxon *Valdez* oil spill. *Journal of Nervous & Mental Disease, 180,* 287–295.

Pappas, G., Queen, S., Hadden, W., & Fisher, G. (1993). The increasing disparity of mortality between socioeconomic groups in the United States, 1960 and 1986. *New England Journal of Medicine, 329,* 103–109.

Pardine, P., & Napoli, A. (1983). Physiological reactivity and recent life-stress experience. *Journal of Consulting and Clinical Psychology, 51,* 467–469.

Parker, J. G., & Herrera, C. (1996). Interpersonal processes in friendship: A comparison of abused and nonabused children's experience. *Developmental Psychology, 32,* 1025–1038.

Parlee, M. B. (1979). The friendship bond: *Psychology Today's* survey report on friendship in America. *Psychology Today, 13*(4), 43–54, 113.

Parron, D. L., Solomon, F., & Jenkins, C. D. (Eds.). (1982). *Behavior, health risks, and social disadvantage.* Washington, DC: National Academy Press.

Patsiokas, A. T., Clum, G. A., & Luscomb, R. C. (1980). Cognitive characteristics of suicide attempters. *Journal of Consulting and Clinical Psychology, 47,* 478–484.

Patterson, D. R., & Ptacek, J. T. (1997). Baseline pain as a moderator of hypnotic analgesia for burn injury treatment. *Journal of Consulting and Clinical Psychology, 65,* 60–67.

Pattison, E. M. (1977). *The experience of dying.* Englewood Cliffs, NJ: Prentice-Hill.

Paul, R. H. (1996). Toward fewer cesarean sections—The role of a trial of labor. *New England Journal of Medicine, 335,* 735–736.

Paulus, P. B. (1979). Crowding. In P. B. Paulus (Ed.), *Psychology of group influence.* Hillsdale, NJ: Erlbaum.

Paulus, P. B., Cox, V., McCain, G., & Chandler, J. (1975). Some effects of crowding in a prison environment. *Journal of Applied Social Psychology, 5,* 86–91.

Pavlov, I. (1927). *Conditioned reflexes.* London: Oxford University Press.

Pearlman, C. A., & Greenberg, R. (1973). Posttrial REM sleep: A critical period for consolidation of shuttlebox avoidance. *Animal Learning and Behavior, 1,* 49–51.

Pearlman, K., Schmidt, F. L., & Hunter, J. E. (1980). Test of a new model of validity generalization: Results for job proficiency and training criteria in clerical occupations. *Journal of Applied Psychology, 65,* 373–406.

Pearson, C. A. (1992, February 1). Cited in Leary, W. E. U.S. panel backs approval of first condom for women. *The New York Times,* p. 7.

Peck, R. C. (1968). Psychological developments in the second half of life. In B. L. Neugarten (Ed.), *Middle age and aging.* Chicago: University of Chicago Press.

Pedersen, N. L., Plomin, R., McClearn, G. E., & Friberg, L. (1988). Neuroticism, extraversion, and related traits in adult twins reared apart and reared together. *Journal of Personality and Social Psychology, 55,* 950–957.

Pelham, W. E., and others. (1993). Separate and combined effects of methylphenidate and behavior modification on boys with attention deficit-hyperactivity disorder in the classroom. *Journal of Consulting and Clinical Psychology, 61,* 506–515.

Pempus, E., Sawaya, C., & Cooper, R. E. (1975). *"Don't fence me in": Personal space depends on architectural enclosure.* Paper presented to the American Psychological Association, Chicago.

Pena, N., & Bricklin, M. (1990). The future of fitness. *Prevention, 42*(1), 41–43.

Penn, D. L., Corrigan, P. W., Bentall, R. P., Racenstein, J. M., & Newman, L. (1997). Social cognition in schizophrenia. *Psychological Bulletin, 121,* 114–132.

Penn, N. E., Kar, S., Kramer, J., Skinner, J., & Zambrana, R. E. (1995). Panel VI. Ethnic minorities, health care systems, and behavior. *Health Psychology, 14,* 641–648.

Peplau, L. A., & Cochran, S. D. (1990). A relationship perspective on homosexuality. In D. P. McWhirter, S. A. Sanders, & J. M. Reinisch (Eds.), *Homosexuality/Heterosexuality: Concepts of sexual orientation* (pp. 321–349). New York: Oxford University Press.

Peplau, L. A., & Perlman, D. (1982). Perspectives on loneliness. In L. A. Peplau & D. Perlman (Eds.), *Loneliness: A sourcebook of current theory, research, and therapy.* New York: Wiley.

Perls, F. S. (1971). *Gestalt therapy verbatim.* New York: Bantam Books.

Perry, D. G., & Bussey, K. (1979). The social learning theory of sex differences: Imitation is alive and well. *Journal of Personality and Social Psychology, 37,* 1699–1712.

Peterson, E. D., and others. (1997). Racial variation in the use of coronary-revascularization procedures. *New England Journal of Medicine, 336,* 480–486.

Petraitis, J., Flay, B. R., & Miller, T. Q. (1995). Reviewing theories of adolescent substance use. *Psychological Bulletin, 1995,* 67–86.

Pettingale, K. W., and others. (1985). Mental attitudes to cancer: An additional prognostic factor. *Lancet, 1,* 750.

Petty, R. E., Cacioppo, J. T., Strathman, A. J., & Priester, J. R. (1994). To think or not to think: Exploring two routes to persuasion. In S. Shavitt & T. C. Brock (Eds.), *Persuasion* (pp. 113–147). Boston: Allyn & Bacon.

Petty, R. E., Gleicher, F., & Baker, S. M. (1991). Multiple roles for affect in persuasion. In J. Forgas (Ed.), *Emotion and social judgments.* London: Pergamon Press.

Phinney, J. S. (1996). When we talk about American ethnic groups, what do we mean? *American Psychologist, 51,* 918–927.

Phinney, J. S., Chavira, V., & Williamson, L. (1992). Acculturation attitudes and self-esteem among high school and college students. *Youth and Society, 23*(3), 299–312.

Pihl, R. O., Peterson, J., & Finn, P. (1990). Inherited predisposition to alcoholism: Characteristics of sons of male alcoholics. *Journal of Abnormal Psychology, 99,* 291–301.

Pillard, R. C. (1990). The Kinsey Scale: Is it familial? In D. P. McWhirter, S. A. Sanders, & J. M. Reinisch (Eds.), *Homosexuality/Heterosexuality: Concepts of sexual orientation* (pp. 88–100). New York: Oxford University Press.

Pillard, R. C., & Weinrich, J. D. (1986). Evidence of familial nature of male homosexuality. *Archives of Sexual Behavior, 43,* 808–812.

Pines, A., & Aronson, E. (1983). Antecedents, correlates, and consequences of sexual jealousy. *Journal of Personality, 51,* 108–136.

Pinto, R. P., & Hollandsworth, J. G., Jr. (1984). A measure of possessiveness in intimate relationships. *Journal of Social and Clinical Psychology, 2,* 273–279.

Pitman, R. K., and others (1990). Psychophysiologic responses to combat imagery of Vietnam veterans with posttraumatic stress disorder versus other anxiety disorders. *Journal of Abnormal Psychology, 99,* 49–54.

Pollack, A. (1992, January 14). It's Asians' turn in Silicon Valley. *The New York Times,* pp. D1, D5.

Pollack, W. S. (1996). Cited in Clay, R. A. Older men are more involved fathers, studies show. *APA Monitor, 27*(2), 37.

Pomerleau, O. F., Collins, A. C., Shiffman, S., & Pomerleau, C. S. (1993). Why some people smoke and others do not: New perspectives. *Journal of Consulting and Clinical Psychology, 61,* 723–731.

Pope-Davis, D. B., Reynolds, A. L., Dings, J. G., & Nielson, D. (1995). Examining multicultural counseling competencies of graduate students in psychology. *Professional Psychology: Research and Practice, 26,* 322–329.

Porter, N., Geis, F. L., Cooper, E., & Newman, E. (1985). Androgyny and leadership in mixed-sex groups. *Journal of Personality and Social Psychology, 49,* 808–823.

Powch, I. G., & Houston, B. K. (1996). Hostility, anger-in, and cardiovascular reactivity in White women. *Health Psychology, 15,* 200–208.

Powell, E. (1991). *Talking back to sexual pressure.* Minneapolis: CompCare Publishers.

Powell, E. (1996). *Sex on your terms.* Boston: Allyn & Bacon.

Powley, T. L. (1977). The ventromedial hypothalamic syndrome, satiety, and a cephalic phase hypothesis. *Psychological Review, 84,* 89–126.

Prewett, M. J., van Allen, P. K., & Milner, J. S. (1978). Multiple electroconvulsive shocks and feeding and drinking behavior in the rat. *Bulletin of the Psychonomic Society, 12,* 137–139.

Price, D. D., and others. (1984). A psychophysical analysis of acupuncture analgesia. *Pain, 19,* 27–42.

Price, L. H., & Heninger, G. R. (1994). Lithium in the treatment of mood disorders. *New England Journal of Medicine, 331,* 591–598.

Putallaz, M., & Heflin, A. H. (1990). Parent-child interaction. In S. R. Asher & J. D. Coie (Eds.), *Peer rejection in childhood.* New York: Cambridge University Press.

Qualls, P. J., & Sheehan, P. W. (1981). Imagery encouragement, absorption, capacity, and relaxation during electromyographic feedback. *Journal of Personality and Social Psychology, 41,* 370–379.

Quattrone, G. A. (1982). Overattribution and unit formation: When behavior engulfs the person. *Journal of Personality and Social Psychology, 42,* 593–607.

Quill, T. E. (1993). *Death and dignity: Making choices and taking charge.* New York: W. W. Norton.

Quindlen, A. (1993, April 11). The good guys. *The New York Times,* p. E13.

Rakowski, W. (1995). Cited in Margoshes, P. For many, old age is the prime of life. *APA Monitor, 26*(5), 36–37.

Rapaport, K., & Burkhart, B. R. (1984). Personality and attitudinal characteristics of sexually coercive college males. *Journal of Abnormal Psychology, 93,* 216–221.

Rappaport, N. B., McAnulty, D. P., & Brantley, P. J. (1988). Exploration of the Type A behavior pattern in chronic headache sufferers. *Journal of Consulting and Clinical Psychology, 56,* 621–623.

Rathus, J. H., & O'Leary, K. D. (1990, April). *Clients' perceptions of what helped in cognitive and marital therapy.* Paper presented to the Eastern Psychological Association, Philadelphia.

Rathus, S. A. (1973). A 30-item schedule for assessing assertive behavior. *Behavior Therapy, 4,* 398–406.

Rathus, S. A. (1978). Assertiveness training: Rationales, procedures, and controversies. In J. M. Whiteley & J. V. Flowers (Eds.), *Approaches to assertion training.* Monterey, CA: Brooks/Cole.

Rathus, S. A. (1988). *Understanding child development.* New York: Holt, Rinehart and Winston.

Rathus, S. A. (1996). *Psychology in the new millennium* (6th ed.). Forth Worth, TX: Harcourt Brace College Publishers.

Rathus, S. A., & Fichner-Rathus, L. (1994). *Making the most of college* (2d ed.). Englewood Cliffs, NJ: Prentice-Hall.

Rathus, S. A., & Fichner-Rathus, L. (1997). *The right stand.* New York: Addison Wesley Longman.

Rathus, S. A., & Nevid, J. S. (1977). *Behavior therapy.* Garden City, NY: Doubleday.

Rathus, S. A., Nevid, J. S., & Fichner-Rathus, L. (1997). *Human sexuality in a world of diversity* (3d ed.). Boston: Allyn & Bacon.

Redd, W. H., and others. (1987). Cognitive/attentional distraction in the control of conditioned nausea in pediatric cancer patients receiving chemotherapy. *Journal of Consulting and Clinical Psychology, 55,* 391–395.

Reddy, D. M., Baum, A., Fleming, R., & Aiello, J. R. (1981). Mediation of social density by coalition formation. *Journal of Applied Social Psychology, 11,* 529–537.

Rehm, L. P. (1978). Mood, pleasant events, and unpleasant events. *Journal of Consulting and Clinical Psychology, 46,* 854–859.

Reid, T. R. (1990, December 24). Snug in their beds for Christmas Eve: In Japan, December 24th has become the hottest night of the year. *Washington Post.*

Reinisch, J. M. (1990). *The Kinsey Institute new report on sex: What you must know to be sexually literate* (pp. 348–349). New York: St. Martin's Press.

Reinke, B. J., Holmes, D. S., & Harris, R. L. (1985). The timing of psychosocial changes in women's lives. *Journal of Personality and Social Psychology, 48,* 1353–1364.

Reis, H. T., Senchak, M., & Solomon, B. (1985). Sex differences in the intimacy of social interaction. *Journal of Personality and Social Psychology, 48,* 1205–1217.

Reis, H. T., and others. (1990). What is smiling is beautiful and good. *European Journal of Social Psychology, 20,* 259–267.

Reiser, M. (1992). *Memory and mind and brain.* New York: Basic Books.

Reiss, B. F. (1980). Psychological tests in homosexuality. In J. Marmor (Ed.), *Homosexual behavior* (pp. 299–311). New York: Basic Books.

Reiss, I. L. (1980). *Family systems in America* (3d ed.). New York: Holt, Rinehart and Winston.

Repetti, R. L. (1993). Short-term effects of occupational stressors on daily mood and health complaints. *Health Psychology, 12,* 125–131.

Resnick, M., and others. (1992, March 24). *Journal of the American Medical Association.* Cited in Young Indians prone to suicide, study finds. *The New York Times,* March 25, 1992, p. D24.

Rhodes, J. E., & Jason, L. A. (1990). A social stress model of substance abuse. *Journal of Consulting and Clinical Psychology, 58,* 395–401.

Rich, C. L., Ricketts, J. E., Thaler, R. C., & Young, D. (1988). Some differences between men and women who commit suicide. *American Journal of Psychiatry, 145,* 718–722.

Richardson, D. C., Bernstein, S., & Taylor, S. P. (1979). The effect of situational contingencies on female retaliative behavior. *Journal of Personality and Social Psychology, 37,* 2044–2048.

Richman, J. (1993). *Preventing elderly suicide.* New York: Springer.

Richter, C. P. (1957). On the phenomenon of sudden death in animals and man. *Psychosomatic Medicine, 19,* 191–198.

Ridon, J., & Langer, E. J. (1977). Long-term effects of control-relevant intervention with the institutionalized aged. *Journal of Personality and Social Psychology, 35,* 897–902.

Riggio, R. E., & Woll, S. B. (1984). The role of nonverbal cues and physical attractiveness in the selection of dating partners. *Journal of Personality and Social Psychology, 1,* 347–357.

Riley, V. (1981). Psychoneuroendocrine influences on immunocompetence and neoplasia. *Science, 212,* 1100–1109.

Rizley, R. (1978). Depression and distortion in the attribution of causality. *Journal of Abnormal Psychology, 87,* 32–48.

Roberts, A. H. (1969). Self-control procedures in the modification of smoking behavior: A replication. *Psychological Reports, 24,* 675–676.

Robins, C. J., & Hayes, A. M. (1993). An appraisal of cognitive therapy. *Journal of Consulting and Clinical Psychology, 61,* 205–214.

Robinson, E. A., & Price, M. G. (1980). Pleasurable behavior in marital interaction: An observational study. *Journal of Consulting and Clinical Psychology, 48,* 117–118.

Robinson, F. P. (1970). *Effective study* (4th ed.). New York: Harper & Row.

Rodin, J., & Langer, E. J. (1977). Long-term effects of a control-relevant intervention with the institutionalized aged. *Journal of Personality and Social Psychology, 35,* 897–902.

Rodriguez, N., Ryan, S. W., Kemp, H. V., & Foy, D. W. (1997). Posttraumatic stress disorder in adult female survivors of childhood sexual abuse: A comparison study. *Journal of Consulting and Clinical Psychology, 65,* 53–59.

Rogers, C. R. (1951). *Client-centered therapy.* Boston: Houghton Mifflin.

Rogers, C. R. (1974). In retrospect: 46 years. *American Psychologist, 29,* 115–123.

Rogers, C. R., & Dymond, R. F. (Eds.). (1954). *Psychotherapy and personality change.* Chicago: University of Chicago Press.

Rogers, R. W., & Deckner, C. W. (1975). Effects of fear appeals and physiological arousal upon emotions, attitudes, and cigarette smoking. *Journal of Personality and Social Psychology, 32,* 222–230.

Rogers, R. W., & Prentice-Dunn, S. (1981). Deindividuation and anger-mediated interracial aggression: Unmasking regressive racism. *Journal of Personality and Social Psychology, 41,* 63–73.

Rokeach, M., & Ball-Rokeach, S. J. (1989). Stability and change in American value priorities, 1968–1981. *American Psychologist, 44,* 775–784.

Rook, K. S., & Dooley, D. (1985). Applying social support research: Theoretical problems and future directions. *Journal of Social Issues, 41,* 5–28.

Rook, K. S., & Peplau, L. A. (1982). Perspectives on helping the lonely. In L. A. Peplau & D. Perlman (Eds.), *Loneliness: A sourcebook of current theory, research, and therapy.* New York: Wiley.

Rose, J. S., Chassin, L., Presson, C. C., & Sherman, S. J. (1996). Prospective predictors of quit attempts and smoking cessation in young adults. *Health Psychology, 15,* 261–268.

Rose, R. J. (1995). Genes and human behavior. *Annual Review of Psychology, 46,* 625–654.

Rosenbaum, M., & Hadari, D. (1985). Personal efficacy, external locus of control, and perceived contingency of parental reinforcement among depressed, paranoid, and normal subjects. *Journal of Personality and Social Psychology, 49,* 539–547.

Rosenbaum, M., Leibel, R. L., & Hirsch, J. (1997). Obesity. *New England Journal of Medicine, 337,* 396–407.

Rosenberg, L., and others. (1990, January 25). *New England Journal of Medicine, 322.*

Rosenberg, M. S., & Repucci, N. D. (1985). Primary prevention of child abuse. *Journal of Consulting and Clinical Psychology, 53,* 576–585.

Rosenblatt, R. (1994, March 20). How do tobacco executives live with themselves? *The New York Times Magazine,* pp. 34–41, 55, 73–76.

Rosenkrantz, L., & Satran, P. R. (1988). *Beyond Jennifer & Jason: An enlightened guide to naming your baby.* New York: St. Martin's Press.

Rosenthal, A. M. (1995, June 13). The possible dream. *The New York Times,* p. A25.

Rosenthal, E. (1993a, March 28). Patients in pain find relief, not addiction, in narcotics. *The New York Times,* pp. 1, 24.

Rosenthal, E. (1993b, July 20). Listening to the emotional needs of cancer patients. *The New York Times,* pp. C1, C7.

Ross, L., & Nisbett, R. E. (1991). *The person and the situation.* New York: McGraw-Hill.

Ross, M. J., & Berger, R. S. (1996). Effects of stress inoculation training on athletes' postsurgical pain and rehabilitation after orthopedic injury. *Journal of Consulting and Clinical Psychology, 64,* 406–410.

Rossouw, J. E., and others. (1990). The value of lowering cholesterol after myocardial infarction. *New England Journal of Medicine, 323,* 1112–1119.

Roth, G. (1998, January 31). Cited in Haney, D. Science targets old age. Associated Press; America Online.

Rothbart, M. K., & Ahadi, S. A. (1994). Temperament and the development of personality. *Journal of Abnormal Psychology, 103,* 55–66.

Rothbaum, B. O. (1995). *American Journal of Psychiatry.*

Rothbaum, B. O., Foa, E. B., Riggs, D. S., Murdock, T., & Welsh, W. (1992). A prospective examination of post-traumatic stress disorder in rape victims. *Journal of Traumatic Stress, 5,* 455–475.

Rotheram-Borus, M. J., Koopman, C., & Haignere, C. (1991). Reducing HIV sexual risk behaviors among runaway adolescents. *Journal of the American Medical Association, 266,* 1237–1241.

Rotheram-Borus, M. J., Trautman, P. D., Dopkins, S. C., & Shrout, P. E. (1990). Cognitive style and pleasant activities among female adolescent suicide attempters. *Journal of Consulting and Clinical Psychology, 58,* 554–561.

Rotter, J. B. (1990). Internal versus external control of reinforcement. *American Psychologist, 45,* 489–493.

Rotton, J., & Frey, J. (1985). Air pollution, weather, and violent crimes: Concomitant time-series analysis of archival data. *Journal of Personality and Social Psychology, 49,* 1207–1220.

Royce, R. A., Seña, A., Cates, W., Jr., & Cohen, M. S. (1997). Sexual transmission of HIV. *New England Journal of Medicine, 336,* 1072–1078.

Rubin, Z. (1975). Disclosing oneself to a stranger. Reciprocity and its limits. *Journal of Experimental Social Psychology, 11,* 233–260.

Rubin, Z. (1982). Children without friends. In L. A. Peplau & D. Perlman (Eds.), *Loneliness: A sourcebook of current theory, research, and therapy.* New York: Wiley.

Rubinow, D. R., & Schmidt, P. J. (1995). The treatment of premenstrual syndrome—forward into the past. *New England Journal of Medicine, 332,* 1574–1575.

Rudman, D., and others. (1990). Effects of human growth hormone in men over 60 years old. *New England Journal of Medicine, 323*(1), 1–6.

Ruiz, P., & Ruiz, P. P. (1983). Treatment compliance among Hispanics. *Journal of Occupational Psychiatry, 14,* 112–114.

Rusbult, C. E. (1983). A longitudinal test of the investment model. *Journal of Personality and Social Psychology, 45,* 101–117.

Rusbult, C. E., Johnson, D. J., & Morrow, G. D. (1986). Impact of couple patterns of problem solving on distress and nondistress in dating relationships. *Journal of Personality and Social Psychology, 50,* 744–753.

Rusbult, C. E., Musante, L., & Soloman, M. (1982). The effects of clarity of decision rule and favorability of verdict on satisfaction with resolution of conflicts. *Journal of Applied Social Psychology, 12,* 304–317.

Rusbult, C. E., & Zembrodt, I. M. (1983). Responses to dissatisfaction in romantic involvements: A multi-dimensional scaling analysis. *Journal of Experimental Social Psychology, 19,* 274–293.

Rush, A. J., Beck, A. T., Kovacs, M., Weissenberger, J., & Hollon, S. D. (1982). Comparison of the effects of cognitive therapy and pharmacotherapy on hopelessness and self-concept. *American Journal of Psychiatry, 139,* 862–866.

Rush, A. J., Khatami, M., & Beck, A. T. (1975). Cognitive and behavior therapy in chronic depression. *Behavior Therapy, 6,* 398–404.

Russell, D. (1982). The measurement of loneliness. In L. A. Peplau & D. Perlman (Eds.), *Loneliness: A sourcebook of current theory, research, and therapy.* New York: Wiley.

Russo, A. (1996). Cited in Azar, B. Training is enhanced by virtual reality. *APA Monitor, 26*(3), 24.

Russo, N. F. (1990). Overview: Forging research priorities for women's mental health. *American Psychologist, 45,* 368–373.

Rüstemli, A. (1986). Male and female personal space needs and escape reactions under intrusion: A Turkish sample. *International Journal of Psychology.*

Rutkowski, G. K., Gruder, C. L., & Romer, D. (1983). Group cohesiveness, social norms, and bystander intervention. *Journal of Personality and Social Psychology, 44,* 545–552.

Sadalla, E. K., Kenrick, D. T., & Vershure, B. (1987). Dominance and heterosexual attraction. *Journal of Personality and Social Psychology, 52,* 730–738.

Sadker, M., & Sadker, D. (1994). *How America's schools cheat girls.* New York: Scribners.

Saegert, S. C., & Hart, R. (1976). The development of sex differences in the environmental competence of children. In P. Burnett (Ed.), *Women in society.* Chicago: Maaroufa Press.

Safer, J. (1996, January 17). Childless by choice. *The New York Times,* p. A19.

Salgado de Snyder, V. N., Cervantes, R. C., & Padilla, A. M. (1990). Gender and ethnic differences in psychosocial stress and generalized distress among Hispanics. *Sex Roles, 22,* 441–453.

Saluter, A. F. (1992). Marital status and living arrangements: March 1992. *Current Population Reports,* Series P20-468.

Saluter, A. F. (1995). Marital status and living arrangements: March 1995. *Current Population reports,* Series P20-491.

Samuels, M., & Samuels, N. (1986). *The well pregnancy book.* New York: Simon & Schuster.

Sandman, C., & Crinella, F. (1995). Cited in Margoshes, P. For many, old age is the prime of life. *APA Monitor, 26*(5), 36–37.

Santee, R. T., & Maslach, C. (1982). To agree or not to agree: Personal dissent amid social pressure to conform. *Journal of Personality and Social Psychology, 42,* 690–700.

Sarason, I. G. (1984). Stress, anxiety, and cognitive interference: Reactions to tests. *Journal of Personality and Social Psychology, 46,* 929–938.

Sauer, M. V., Paulson, R. J., & Lobo, R. A. (1990). A preliminary report on oocyte donation extending reproductive potential to women over 40. *New England Journal of Medicine, 323,* 1157–1160.

Scanzoni, J., & Polonko, K. (1980). A conceptual approach to explicit marital negotiation. *Journal of Marriage and the Family, 42,* 31–44.

Scarr, S., & Kidd, K. K. (1983). Developmental behavior genetics. In M. Haith & J. J. Campos (Eds.), *Handbook of child psychology.* New York: Wiley.

Scarr, S., & Weinberg, R. A. (1983). The Minnesota adoption studies: Genetic differences and malleability. *Child Development, 54,* 260–267.

Schachter, S., & Latané, B. (1964). Crime, cognition, and the autonomic nervous system. In D. Levine (Ed.), *Nebraska symposium on motivation.* Lincoln: University of Nebraska Press.

Schaeffer, M., & Baum, A. (1982, August). *Consistency of stress response at Three Mile Island.* Paper presented to the American Psychological Association.

Schafer, J., & Brown, S. A. (1991). Marijuana and cocaine effect expectancies and drug use patterns. *Journal of Personality and Social Psychology, 59,* 558–565.

Schaie, K. W. (1939). The Seattle Longitudinal

Studies of adult intelligence. *Current Directions, 2,* 171–175.

Schaie, K. W. (1994). The course of adult intellectual development. *American Psychologist, 49,* 304–313.

Schaie, K. W., & Willis, S. L. (1991). Adult personality and psychomotor performance. *Journal of Gerontology: Psychological Sciences, 46,* 275–284.

Schaller, M., & Maas, A. (1989). Illusory correlation and social categorization: Toward an integration of motivational and cognitive factors in stereotype formation. *Journal of Personality and Social Psychology, 56,* 709–721.

Scheier, M. F., & Carver, C. S. (1985). Optimism, coping, and health: Assessment and implications of generalized outcome expectancies. *Health Psychology, 4,* 219–247.

Scheier, M. F., and others. (1989). Dispositional optimism and recovery from coronary artery bypass surgery: The beneficial effects on physical and psychological well-being. *Journal of Personality and Social Psychology, 57,* 1024–1040.

Schenker, M. (1993). Air pollution and mortality. *New England Journal of Medicine, 329,* 1807–1808.

Schiedel, D. G., & Marcia, J. E. (1985). Ego identity, intimacy, sex-role orientation, and gender. *Developmental Psychology, 21,* 149–160.

Schifter, D. E., & Ajzen, I. (1985). Intention, perceived control, and weight loss: An application of the theory of planned behavior. *Journal of Personality and Social Psychology, 49,* 843–851.

Schmauk, F. J. (1970). Punishment, arousal, and avoidance learning in sociopaths. *Journal of Abnormal Psychology, 76,* 443–453.

Schmidt, F. L., Hunter, J. E., & Pearlman, K. (1981). Task differences as moderators of aptitude test validity in selection: A red herring. *Journal of Applied Psychology, 66,* 161–185.

Schmidt, P. J., and others. (1998). Differential behavioral effects of gonadal steroids in women with and in those without premenstrual syndrome. *New England Journal of Medicine, 338,* 209–216.

Schotte, D. E., Cools, J., & Payvar, S. (1990). Problem-solving deficits in suicidal patients: Trait vulnerability or state phenomenon? *Journal of Consulting and Clinical Psychology, 58,* 562–564.

Schreiber, G. B., and others. (1996). The risk of transfusion-transmitted viral infections. *New England Journal of Medicine, 334,* 1685–1690.

Schuckit, M. A. (1996). Recent developments in the pharmacotherapy of alcohol dependence: *Journal of Consulting and Clinical Psychology, 64,* 669–676.

Schultz, J. H. (1982). Inflation's challenge to aged income security. *Gerontologist, 22*(2), 115–116.

Schulz, R., & Heckhausen, J. (1996). A life span model of successful aging. *American Psychologist, 51,* 702–714.

Schwartz, B., and others. (1998, February 4). *Journal of the American Medical Association.* Cited in Fallik, D. Women, educated get more headaches. Associated Press; America Online.

Schwartz, M. W., & Seeley, R. J. (1997). Neuroendocrine responses to starvation and weight loss. *New England Journal of Medicine, 336,* 1802–1811.

Schwartz, R. M., & Gottman, J. M. (1976). Toward a task analysis of assertive behavior. *Journal of Consulting and Clinical Psychology, 44,* 910–920.

Schwarz, N., Bless, H., & Bohner, G. (1991). Mood and persuasion: Affective states influence the processing of persuasive communications. In M. Zanna (Ed.), *Advances in experimental social psychology, vol. 24.* New York: Academic Press.

Schwebel, A. I., and others. (1982). Research-based intervention with divorced families. *Personnel and Guidance Journal 60,* 523–528.

Schweinhart, L. J., & Weikart, D. P. (Eds.). (1993). *Significant benefits: The High/Scope Perry Preschool Study through age 27.* Ypsilanti, MI: High/Scope Press.

Scott, J. (1994, May 9). Multiple personality cases perplex legal system. *The New York Times,* pp. A1, B10, B11.

Seligman, M. E. P. (1996, August). Predicting and preventing depression. Master lecture presented to the meeting of the American Psychological Association, Toronto.

Selkoe, D. J. (1992). Aging brain, aging mind. *Scientific American, 267*(3), 134–142.

Selye, H. (1976). *The stress of life* (rev. ed.). New York: McGraw-Hill.

Selye, H. (1980). The stress concept today. In I. L. Kutash, L. B. Schlesinger, and others (Eds.), *Handbook on stress and anxiety.* San Francisco: Jossey-Bass.

Senneker, P., & Hendrick, C. (1983). Androgyny and helping behavior. *Journal of Personality and Social Psychology, 45,* 916–925.

Seppa, N. (1996). APA releases study on family violence. *APA Monitor, 27*(4), 12.

Seppa, N. (1997). Young adults and AIDS: "It can't happen to me." *APA Monitor, 28*(1) 38–39.

Shadish, W. R., Hickman, D., & Arrick, M. C. (1981). Psychological problems of spinal injury patients: Emotional distress as a function of time and locus of control. *Journal of Consulting and Clinical Psychology, 49,* 297.

Shadish, W. R., & Ragsdale, K. (1996). Random versus nonrandom assignment in controlled experiments. *Journal of Consulting and Clinical Psychology, 64,* 1290–1305.

Shadish, W. R., and others. (1997). Evidence that therapy works in clinically representative conditions. *Journal of Consulting and Clinical Psychology, 65,* 355–365.

Shanteau, J., & Nagy, G. (1979). Probability of acceptance in dating choice. *Journal of Personality and Social Psychology, 37,* 522–533.

Shaw, J. S. (1982). Psychological androgyny and stressful life events. *Journal of Personality and Social Psychology, 43,* 145–153.

Shay, J., and others. (1998, January 16). *Science.* Cited in Researchers Claim Fountain of Youth. Associated Press; America Online.

Shaywitz, S., Cohen, D., & Shaywitz, B. (1980). Behavior and learning difficulties in children of normal intelligence born to alcoholic mothers. *The Journal of Pediatrics, 96,* 978–982.

Sheehy, G. (1976). *Passages: Predictable crises of adult life.* New York: Dutton.

Sheehy, G. (1981). *Pathfinders.* New York: Morrow.

Sheehy, G. (1993, April). The unspeakable passage—Is there a male menopause? *Vanity Fair,* pp. 164–167, 218–227.

Sheehy, G. (1995). *New passages: Mapping your life across time.* New York: Random House.

Shepherd, J., and others. (1995). Prevention of coronary heart disease with pravastatin in men with hypercholesterolemia. *New England Journal of Medicine, 333,* 1301–1307.

Sheppard, J. A., & Strathman, A. J. (1989). Attractiveness and height: The role of stature in dating preference, frequency of dating, and perceptions of attractiveness. *Personality and Social Psychology Bulletin, 15,* 617–627.

Sher, K. J., Wood, M. D., Wood, P. K., & Raskin, G. (1996). Alcohol outcome expectancies and alcohol use. *Journal of Abnormal Psychology, 105,* 561–574.

Sherwin, R., & Sherry, C. (1985). Campus sexual norms and dating relationships: A trend analysis. *Journal of Sex Research, 21,* 258–274.

Shettles, L. B. (1972, June). Predetermining children's sex. *Medical Aspects of Human Sexuality,* p. 172.

Shiffman, S. (1982). Relapse following smoking cessation: A situation analysis. *Journal of Consulting and Clinical Psychology, 50,* 71–86.

Shiffman, S. (1984). Coping with temptations to smoke. *Journal of Consulting and Clinical Psychology, 52,* 261–267.

Shiffman, S. (1993a). Smoking cessation treatment: Any progress? *Journal of Consulting and Clinical Psychology, 61,* 718–722.

Shiffman, S. (1993b). Assessing smoking patterns and motives. *Journal of Consulting and Clinical Psychology, 61,* 732–742.

Shiffman, S., and others. (1997). A day at a time: Predicting smoking lapse from daily urge. *Journal of Abnormal Psychology, 106,* 104–116.

Shipley, R. H. (1981). Maintenance of smoking cessation: Effect of follow-up letters, smoking motivation, muscle tension, and health locus of control. *Journal of Consulting and Clinical Psychology, 49,* 982–984.

Shipley, R. H., Butt, J. H., Horwitz, B., & Farbry, J. E. (1978). Preparation for a stressful medical procedure: Effect of amount of stimulus preexposure and coping style. *Journal of Consulting and Clinical Psychology, 46,* 499–507.

Shneidman, E. S. (Ed.). (1984). *Death: Current perspectives* (3d. ed.). Palo Alto, CA: Mayfield.

Shotland, R. L., & Heinold, W. D. (1985). Bystander response to arterial bleeding: Helping skills, the decision-making process, and differentiating the helping response. *Journal of Personality and Social Psychology, 49,* 347–356.

Silverman, L. H. (1984). Beyond insight: An additional necessary step in redressing intrapsychic conflict. *Psychoanalytic Psychology, 1,* 215–234.

Simons, A. D., Angell, K. L., Monroe, S. M., & Thase, M. E. (1993). Cognition and life stress in depression: Cognitive factors and the definition, rating, and generation of negative life events. *Journal of Abnormal Psychology, 102,* 584–591.

Simons, A. D., Gordon, J. S., Monroe, S. M., & Thase, M. (1995). Toward an integration of psychologic, social, and biologic factors in depression. *Journal of Consulting and Clinical Psychology, 63,* 369–377.

Simons, A. D., McGowan, C. R., Epstein, L. H., Kupfer, D. J., & Robertson, R. J. (1985). Exercise as a treatment for depression: An update. *Clinical Psychology Review, 5,* 553–568.

Simons, R. L., Whitbeck, L. B., Conger, R. D., & Chyi-In, W. (1991). Intergenerational transmission of harsh parenting. *Developmental Psychology, 27,* 159–171.

Simpson, M., & Perry, J. D. (1990). Crime and climate: A reconsideration. *Environment and Behavior, 22,* 295–300.

Singer, D. G. (1983). A time to reexamine the role of television in our lives. *American Psychologist, 38,* 815–816.

Sistrunk, F., & McDavid, J. W. (1971). Sex variable in conforming behavior. *Journal of Personality and Social Psychology, 17,* 200–207.

Skinner, B. F. (1938). *The behavior of organisms: An experimental analysis.* New York: Appleton.

Skinner, B. F. (1948). *Walden two.* New York: Macmillan.

Skinner, B. F. (1972). *Beyond freedom and dignity.* New York: Knopf.

Skinner, B. F. (1979). *The shaping of a behaviorist.* New York: Knopf.

Skinner, B. F. (1983). Intellectual self-management in old age. *American Psychologist, 38,* 239–244.

Skinner, B. F. (1987). Whatever happened to psychology as the science of behavior? *American Psychologist, 42,* 780–786.

Slater, E., & Haber, J. D. (1984). Adolescent adjustment following divorce as a function of familial conflict. *Journal of Consulting and Clinical Psychology, 52,* 920–921.

Slater, E., & Shields, J. (1969). Genetic aspects of anxiety. In M. H. Luder (Ed.), *Studies of anxiety.* Ashford, England: Headley Brothers.

Sleek, S. (1996). Side effects undermine drug compliance. *APA Monitor, 26*(3), 32.

Sleek, S. (1997). Resolution raises concerns about conversion therapy. *APA Monitor, 27*(10), 15.

Smith, A., & Stansfield, S. (1986). Aircraft noise exposure, noise sensitivity, and everyday errors. *Environment and Behavior, 18,* 214–226.

Smith, M. L., & Glass, G. V. (1977). Meta-analysis of psychotherapy outcome studies. *American Psychologist, 32,* 752–760.

Smith, M. L., Glass, G. V., & Miller, T. I. (1980). *The benefits of psychotherapy.* Baltimore: The Johns Hopkins University Press.

Smith, R. E., Smoll, F. L., & Ptacek, J. T. (1990). Conjunctive moderator variables in vulnerability and resiliency research: Life stress, social support and coping skills, and adolescent sport injuries. *Journal of Personality and Social Psychology, 58,* 360–370.

Smith, T. W. (1983). Change in irrational beliefs and the outcome of rational-emotive psychotherapy. *Journal of Consulting and Clinical Psychology, 51,* 156–157.

Smoke rises. (1993, December 27). *The New York Times,* p. A16.

Smolowe, J. (1993, July 26). Choose your poison. *Time,* pp. 56–57.

Snyder, D. (1979). Multidimensional assessment of marital satisfaction. *Journal of Marriage and the Family, 41,* 813–823.

Snyder, M., & Cunningham, M. R. (1975). To comply or not to comply: Testing the self-perception explanation of the foot-in-the-door phenomenon. *Journal of Personality and Social Psychology, 31,* 64–67.

Snyder, M., Tanke, E. D., & Berscheid, E. (1977). Social perception and interpersonal behavior: On the self-fulfilling nature of social stereotypes. *Journal of Personality and Social Psychology, 35,* 656–666.

Solano, C. H., Batten, P. G., & Parish, E. A. (1982). Loneliness and patterns of self-disclosure. *Journal of Personality and Social Psychology, 43,* 524–531.

Sommers-Flanagan, J., & Sommers-Flanagan, R. (1995). Intake interviewing with suicidal patients: A systematic approach. *Professional Psychology: Research and Practice, 26,* 41–47.

Sonstroem, R. J. (1984). Exercise and self-esteem. *Exercise and Sport Sciences Reviews, 12,* 123–155.

Southerland, D. (1990, May 27). Limited "sexual revolution" seen in China: Nationwide survey shows more liberal attitudes developing in conservative society. *Washington Post.*

Spanos, N. P., Weekes, J. R., & Bertrand, L. D. (1985). Multiple personality: A social psychological perspective. *Journal of Abnormal Psychology, 94,* 362–376.

Spence, J. T., Helmreich, R., & Stapp, J. (1975). Ratings of self and peers on sex-role attributes and their relation to self-esteem and concepts of masculinity and femininity. *Journal of Personality and Social Psychology, 32,* 29–39.

Spinhoven, P., Labbe, M. R., & Rombouts, R. (1993). Feasibility of computerized psychological testing with psychiatric outpatients. *Journal of Clinical Psychology, 49,* 440–447.

Spreat, S., & Behar, D. (1994). Trends in the residential (inpatient) treatment of individuals with a dual diagnosis. *Journal of Personality and Social Psychology, 61,* 43–48.

Sprecher, S. (1989). The importance to males and females of physical attractiveness, earning potential, and expressiveness in initial attraction. *Sex Roles, 21,* 591–607.

Spring, J. A. (1997, November). Cited in Alterman, E. Sex in the '90s. *Elle.*

Squire, L. R. (1977). ECT and memory loss. *American Journal of Psychiatry, 134,* 997–1001.

Squire, L. R., & Slater, P. C. (1978). Bilateral and unilateral ECT: Effects on verbal and nonverbal memory. *American Journal of Psychiatry, 135,* 1316–1320.

Stack, S. (1980). The effects of marital dissolution on suicide. *Journal of Marriage and the Family, 42,* 83–92.

Stacy, A. W., Newcomb, M. D., & Bentler, P. M. (1991). Cognitive motivation and drug use: A 9-year longitudinal study. *Journal of Abnormal Psychology, 100,* 502–515.

Stampfer, M. J., and others. (1991). A prospective study of cholesterol, apolipoproteins, and the risk of myocardial infarction. *New England Journal of Medicine, 325,* 373–381.

Staples, S. I. (1996). Human responses to environmental noise. *American Psychologist, 51,* 143–150.

Staub, E., Tursky, B., & Schwartz, G. (1971). Self-control and predictability: Their effects on reactions to aversive stimulation. *Journal of Personality and Social Psychology, 18,* 157–162.

Steck, L., Levitan, D., McLane, D., & Kelley, H. H. (1982). Care, need, and conceptions of love. *Journal of Personality and Social Psychology, 43,* 481–491.

Stehr, P. A., and others. (1985). Dietary vitamin A deficiencies and stomach cancer. *American Journal of Epidemiology, 121,* 65–70.

Steinem, G. (1992). *Revolution from within.* Boston: Little, Brown.

Steiner, M., and others. (1995). Fluoxetine in the treatment of premenstrual dysphoria. *New England Journal of Medicine, 332,* 1529–1534.

Steinhauer, J. (1995, July 6). No marriage, no apologies. *The New York Times,* pp. C1, C7.

Steinmetz, J. L., Lewinsohn, P. M., & Antonuccio, D. O. (1983). Prediction of individual outcome in a group intervention for depression. *Journal of Consulting and Clinical Psychology, 51,* 331–337.

Stephan, C. W., & Langlois, J. H. (1984). Baby beautiful: Adult attributions of infant competence as a function of infant attractiveness. *Child Development, 55,* 576–585.

Sternberg, R. J. (1988). *The triangle of love: Intimacy, passion, commitment.* New York: Basic Books.

Stewart, F. H. (1992, February 1). Cited in Leary, W. E. U.S. panel backs approval of first condom for women. *The New York Times,* p. 7.

Stier, D. S., & Hall, J. A. (1984). Gender differences in touch: An empirical and theoretical review. *Journal of Personality and Social Psychology, 47,* 440–459.

Stillman, M. J. (1977). Women's health beliefs about cancer and breast self-examination. *Nursing Research, 26,* 121–127.

Stock, R. (1995, June 1). Wrongheaded views persist about the old. *The New York Times,* p. C8.

Stokols, D., & Novaco, R. (1981). Transportation and well-being: An ecological perspective. In J. F. Wohlwill & P. B. Everett (Eds.), *Transportation and behavior.* New York: Plenum Publishing.

Stolberg, S. G. (1998, January 18). Quandary on donor eggs: What to tell the children. *The New York Times,* pp. 1, 20.

Stolz, M. (1998, January 19). Success in failures: Life style magazine finds its niche in the marriages that don't work. *The New York Times,* p. D7.

Storms, M. D. (1980). Theories of sexual orientation. *Journal of Personality and Social Psychology, 38,* 783–792.

Stout, D. (1996, October 18). Direct link found between smoking and lung cancer. *The New York Times,* pp. A1, A19.

Straube, E. R., & Oades, R. D. (1992). *Schizophrenia.* San Diego: Academic Press.

Strauss, M. (1995, May 11). Cited in Collins, C. Spanking is becoming the new don't. *The New York Times,* p. C8.

Strickland, B. (1991). Cited in DeAngelis, T. Hearing pinpoints gaps in research on women. *APA Monitor, 22*(6), 8.

Strom, S. (1993, April 18). Human pheromones. *The New York Times,* p. V12.

Struckman-Johnson, C., Struckman-Johnson, D., Gilliland, R. C., & Ausman, A. (1994). Effect of persuasive appeals in AIDS PSAs and condom commercials on intentions to use condoms. *Journal of Applied Social Psychology, 24*(24), 2223–2244.

Strupp, H. H. (1996). The tripartite model and the *Consumer Reports* study: *American Psychologist, 51,* 1017–1024.

Stuckey, M. F., McGhee, P. E., & Bell, N. J. (1982). Parent-child interaction: The influence of maternal employment. *Developmental Psychology, 18,* 635–644.

Study finds smaller pay gap for male and female doctors. (1996, April 11). *The New York Times,* p. B9.

Stunkard, A. J., Harris, J. R., Pedersen, N. L., & McLearn, G. E. (1990). A separated twin study of the body mass index. *New England Journal of Medicine, 322,* 1483–1487.

Sue, S. (1988). Psychotherapeutic services for ethnic minorities: Two decades of research findings. *American Psychologist, 43,* 301–308.

Sue, S. (1991). In J. D. Goodchilds (Ed.), *Psychological perspectives on human diversity in America.* Washington, DC: American Psychological Association.

Suinn, R. M. (1982). Intervention with Type A behaviors. *Journal of Consulting and Clinical Psychology, 50,* 933–949.

Suinn, R. A. (1995). Anxiety management training. In K. Craig (Ed.), *Anxiety and depression in children and adults* (pp. 159–179). New York: Sage.

Suls, J., Wan, C. K., & Costa, P. T., Jr. (1995). Relationship of trait anger to resting blood pressure. *Health Psychology, 14,* 444–456.

Susser, E. S., & Lin, S. P. (1992). Schizophrenia after prenatal exposure to the Dutch Hunger Winter of 1944–1945. *Archives of General Psychiatry, 49,* 983–988.

Sweeney, P. D., & Gruber, K. L. (1984). Selective exposure: Voter information preferences and the Watergate affair. *Journal of Personality and Social Psychology, 46,* 1208–1221.

Symons, D. (1995, June 14). Cited in Goleman, D. Sex fantasy research said to neglect women. *The New York Times,* p. C14.

Tailoring treatments for alcoholics is not the answer. (1997). *APA Monitor, 28*(2), 6–7.

Talbott, E., and others. (1985). Occupational noise exposure, noise-induced hearing loss, and the epidemiology of high blood pressure. *American Journal of Epidemiology, 121,* 501–514.

Tanaki, R. (1993). *A different mirror: A history of multicultural America.* Boston: Little, Brown.

Tanzi, R. E. (1995). A promising animal model of Alzheimer's disease. *New England Journal of Medicine, 332,* 1512–1513.

Taub, A. (1993, April 8). Narcotics have long been known safe and effective for pain. *The New York Times,* p. A20.

Tavris, C., & Sadd, S. (1977). *The Redbook report on female sexuality.* New York: Delacorte.

Taylor, C. B., Farquhar, J. W., Nelson, E., & Agras, D. (1977). Relaxation therapy and high blood pressure. *Archives of General Psychiatry, 34,* 339–343.

Taylor, C. B., Killen, J. D., and the Editors of Consumer Reports Books. (1991). *The facts about smoking.* Yonkers, NY: Consumer Reports Books.

Taylor, S. E. (1983). Adjustment to threatening events: A theory of cognitive adaptation. *American Psychologist, 38,* 1161–1173.

Taylor, S. E. (1990). Health psychology: The science and the field. *American Psychologist, 45,* 40–50.

Taylor, S. P., & Epstein, S. (1967). Aggression as a function of the interaction of the sex of the aggressor and the sex of the victim. *Journal of Personality, 35,* 474–486.

Teri, L., & Wagner, A. (1992). Alzheimer's disease and depression. *Journal of Consulting and Clinical Psychology, 60,* 379–391.

Terry, D. J., Mayocchi, L., & Hynes, G. J. (1996). Depressive symptomology in new mothers: A stress and coping perspective. *Journal of Abnormal Psychology, 105,* 220–231.

Tetlock, P. E. (1983). Accountability and complexity of thought. *Journal of Personality and Social Psychology, 45,* 74–83.

Thase, M. E., & Kupfer, D. J. (1996). Recent developments in the pharmacotherapy of mood disorders. *Journal of Consulting and Clinical Psychology, 64,* 646–659.

Thigpen, C. H., & Cleckley, H. M. (1984). On the incidence of multiple personality disorder. *International Journal of Clinical and Experimental Hypnosis, 32,* 63–66.

Thomas, G. C., Batson, C. D., & Coke, J. S. (1981). Do good samaritans discourage helpfulness? *Journal of Personality and Social Psychology, 40,* 194–200.

Thompson, R. A. (1991). Infant daycare: Concerns, controversies, choices. In J. V. Lerner & N. L. Galambos (Eds.), *Employed mothers and their children* (pp. 9–36). New York: Garland.

Thoresen, C., & Powell, L. H. (1992). Type A behavior pattern: New perspectives on theory, assessment, and intervention. *Journal of Consulting and Clinical Psychology, 60,* 595–604.

Timpson, J., and others. (1988). Depression in a Native Canadian in northwestern Ontario: Sadness, grief or spiritual illness? *Canada's Mental Health, 36*(2–3), 5–8.

Tolstedt, B., & Stokes, J. (1983). Relation of verbal, affective, and physical intimacy to marital satisfaction. *Journal of Counseling Psychology, 30,* 573–580.

Torgersen, S. (1983). Genetic factors in anxiety disorders. *Archives of General Psychiatry, 40,* 1085–1089.

Toubia, N. (1994). Female circumcision as a public health issue. *New England Journal of Medicine, 331,* 712–716.

Touhey, J. C. (1972). Comparison of two dimensions of attitude similarity on heterosexual attraction. *Journal of Personality and Social Psychology, 23,* 8–10.

Townsend, J. M. (1995). Sex without emotional involvement: An evolutionary interpretation of sex differences. *Archives of Sexual Behavior, 24,* 173–206.

Trickett, P. K., Aber, J. L., Carlson, V., & Cicchetti, D. (1991). Relationship of socioeconomic status to the etiology and developmental sequelae of physical child abuse. *Developmental Psychology, 27,* 148–158.

Trobst, K. K., Collins. R. L., & Embree, J. M. (1994). The role of emotion in social support provision. *Journal of Social and Personal Relationships, 11,* 45–62.

Troutman, B. R., & Cutrona, C. E. (1990). Nonpsychotic postpartum depression among adolescent mothers. *Journal of Abnormal Psychology, 99,* 69–78.

Tsui, A. S., & O'Reilly, C. A. III. (1989). Beyond simple demographic effects. *Academy of Management Journal, 32,* 402–423.

Tucker, J. S., Friedman, H. S., Wingard, D. L., &

Schwartz, J. E. (1996). Marital history at midlife as a predictor of longevity. *Health Psychology, 15,* 94–101.
Turnage, J. J. (1990). The challenge of new workplace technology for psychology. *American Psychologist, 45,* 171–178.
Tzuriel, D. (1984). Sex role typing and ego identity in Israeli, Oriental, and Western adolescents. *Journal of Personality and Social Psychology, 46,* 440–457.

Ugwuegbu, D. C. E. (1979). Racial and evidential factors in juror attribution of legal responsibility. *Journal of Experimental Social Psychology, 15,* 133–146.
Ukestad, L. K., & Wittrock, D. A. (1996). Pain perception and coping in female tension headache sufferers and headache-free controls. *Health Psychology, 15,* 65–68.
Ullman, C. (1982). Cognitive and emotional antecedents of religious conversion. *Journal of Personality and Social Psychology, 43,* 183–192.
Unger, R. K., Hilderbrand, M., & Madar, T. (1982). Physical attractiveness and assumptions about social deviance: Some sex-by-sex comparisons. *Personality and Social Psychology Bulletin, 8,* 293–301.
USBC (U.S. Bureau of the Census). (1990). *Statistical abstract of the United States* (110th ed.). Washington, DC: U.S. Government Printing Office.
USBC (U.S. Bureau of the Census). (1993). *Statistical abstract of the United states* (113th ed.). Washington, DC: U.S. Government Printing Office.
USBC (U.S. Bureau of the Census). (1995). *Statistical abstract of the United States* (115th ed.). Washington, DC: U.S. Government Printing Office.
USBC (U.S. Bureau of the Census). (1998). *Statistical abstract of the United States* (118th ed.). Washington, DC: U.S. Government Printing Office.
USDHHS (U.S. Department of Health and Human Services). (1990, February). *Smoking and health, a national status report.* Washington, DC: U.S. Government Printing Office.
USDHHS (U.S. Department of Health and Human Services). (1991, March). *Health United States, 1990.* DHHS Pub. No. (PHS) 91-1232. Hyattsville, MD: Centers for Disease Control, National Center for Health Statistics.
USDHHS (U.S. Department of Health and Human Services). (1992). *For a strong and healthy baby.* DHHS Publication No. (ADM) 92-1915. Washington, DC: U.S. Government Printing Office.
USDHHS (U.S. Department of Health and Human Services). (1993, Winter). *Mothers target of passive smoking intervention effort. Heart Memo.* Public Health Service, National Institutes of Health, National Heart, Lung and Blood Institute, Office of Prevention, Education, and Control.
U.S. Riot Commission (1968). *Report of the National Advisory Commission on Civil Disorders.* New York: Bantam Books.
U.S. scientists admit cocktail might not cure AIDS. (1997, November 13). Reuters; America Online.
Utne, M. K., Hatfield, E., Traupmann, J., & Greenberger, D. (1984). Equity, marital satisfaction, and stability. *Journal of Social and Personal Relationships, 1,* 323–332.

Vaillant, G. E. (1994). Ego mechanisms of defense and personality psychopathology. *Journal of Abnormal Psychology, 103,* 44–50.
Van Brunt, L. (1994, March 27). About men: Whites without money. *The New York Times Magazine,* p. 38.
Vance, M. L. (1990, July 5). Cited in Angier, N. Human growth hormone reverses effects of aging. *The New York Times,* pp. A1, B6.
Vandell, D. L., & Corasaniti, M. A. (1990). Child care and the family: Complex contributors to child development. In K. McCartney (Ed.), *New Directions for Child Development, 49,* 23–37. San Francisco: Jossey-Bass.
Vandenberg, S. G., Singer, S. M., & Pauls, D. L. (1986). *The heredity of behavior disorders in adults and children.* New York: Plenum Press.
VandenBos, G. R. (1996). Outcome assessment of psychotherapy. *American Psychologist, 51,* 1005–1006.
Venables, P. H. (1996). Schizotypy and maternal exposure to influenza and to cold temperature. *Journal of Abnormal Psychology, 105,* 53–60.
Vernbrugge, L. M. (1979). Marital status and health. *Journal of Marriage and the Family, 41,* 267–285.
Vernbrugge, L. M. (1983). Multiple roles and physical health of women and men. *Journal of Health and Social Behavior, 24,* 16–30.
Vernon, S. W., and others. (1997). Correlates of psychologic distress in colorectal cancer patients undergoing genetic testing for hereditary colon cancer. *Health Psychology, 16,* 73–86.
Verplanken, B. (1991). Persuasive communication of risk communication: A test of cue versus message processing effects in a field experiment. *Personality and Social Psychology Bulletin, 17,* 188–193.
Visintainer, M. A., Volpicelli, J. R., & Seligman, M. E. P. (1982). Tumor rejection in rats after inescapable or escapable shock. *Science, 216*(23), 437–439.
Vitousek, K., & Manke, F. (1994). Personality variables and disorders in anorexia nervosa and bulimia nervosa. *Journal of Abnormal Psychology, 103,* 137–147.
Von Krafft-Ebing, R. (1886). *Psychopathia sexualis.* (Reprinted by Putnam, New York, 1965).
Voyer, D., Voyer, S., & Bryden, M. P. (1995). Magnitude of sex differences in spatial abilities. *Psychological Bulletin, 117,* 250–270.
Wachtel, P. L. (1994). Cyclical processes in personality and psychopathology. *Journal of Abnormal Psychology, 103,* 51–54.
Wadden, T. A., and others. (1997). Exercise in the treatment of obesity. *Journal of Consulting and Clinical Psychology, 65,* 269–277.
Wade, N. (1998a, January 6). Was Freud wrong? Are dreams the brain's start-up test? *The New York Times.*
Wade, N. (1998b, January 13). Can life span be extended? Biologists offer some hope. *The New York Times,* pp. F1, F7.
Wade, N. (1998c, January 18). Longevity's new lease on life. *The New York Times,* pp. WK1, WK4.
Wagner, R. K. (1997). Intelligence, training, and employment. (1997). *American Psychologist, 52,* 1059–1069.
Walker, W. B., & Franzini, L. R. (1985). Low-risk aversive group treatments, physiological feedback, and booster treatments for smoking cessation. *Behavior Therapy, 16,* 263–274.
Wallerstein, J. S., & Blakeslee, S. (1989). *Second chances: Women and children a decade after divorce.* New York: Ticknor & Fields.
Wallston, B. S., & Wallston, K. A. (1984). Social psychological models of health behavior: An examination and integration. In A. Baum, S. E. Taylor, & J. E. Singer (Eds.), *Handbook of psychology and health: Vol. 4. Social psychological aspects of health.* Hillsdale, NJ: Erlbaum.
Walsh, B. T., and others. (1984). Treatment of bulimia with phenelzine: A double-blind, placebo-controlled study. *Archives of General Psychiatry, 41,* 1105–1109.
Walsh, M. R. (1993, August). Teaching the psychology of women and gender for undergraduate and graduate faculty. Workshop of the Psychology of Women Institute presented at the meeting of the American Psychological Association, Toronto, Canada.
Wang, P., Springen, K., Schmitz, T., & Bruno, M. (1987, October 12). A cure for stress? *Newsweek,* pp. 64–65.
Wardlaw, G. M., & Insel, P. M. (1990). *Perspectives in nutrition.* St. Louis: Times Mirror/Mosby College Publishing.
Wasserman, J. (1993, September 3). It's still women's work. *Daily News,* p. 7.
Watson, C. M. (1993). *Love potions: A guide to aphrodisiacs and sexual pleasures.* Jeremy P. Tarcher/Perigree.
Watson, J. B. (1924). *Behaviorism.* New York: Norton.
Watson, J. B., & Rayner, R. (1920). Conditioned emotional reactions. *Journal of Experimental Psychology, 3,* 1–14.
Webb, W. (1993). Cited in Adler, T. Sleep loss impairs attention—and more. *APA Monitor, 24*(9), 22–23.
Weber, R., & Crocker, J. (1983). Cognitive processes in the revision of stereotypic beliefs. *Journal of Personality and Social Psychology, 45,* 961–977.

Weidner, G., Boughal, T., Connor, S. L., Pieper, C., & Mendell, N. R. (1997). Relationship of job strain to standard coronary risk factors and psychological characteristics in women and men of the Family Heart Study. *Health Psychology, 16,* 239–247.

Weinberg, R. S., Yukelson, S., & Jackson, A. (1980). Effect of public and private efficacy expectations on competitive performance. *Journal of Sport Psychology, 2,* 340–349.

Weinberg, S. L., & Richardson, M. S. (1981). Dimensions of stress in early parenting. *Journal of Consulting and Clinical Psychology, 49,* 688–693.

Weiner, K. (1992, January 8). Cited in Goleman, D. J. Heart seizure or panic attack? Disorder is a terrifying mimic. *The New York Times,* p. C12.

Weinstein, M. S. (1980). *Health in the city: Environmental and behavioral influences.* New York: Pergamon Press.

Weinstein, N. D. (1993). Testing four competing theories of health-protective behavior. *Health Psychology, 12,* 324–333.

Weisinger, H. (1990). *The critical edge: How to criticize up and down your organization and make it pay off.* New York: Harper & Row.

Weiss, R. D., & Mirin, S. M. (1987). *Cocaine.* Washington, DC: American Psychiatric Press.

Weisz, J. R., Sweeney, L., Proffitt, V., & Carr, T. (1993). Control-related beliefs and self-reported depressive symptoms in late childhood. *Journal of Abnormal Psychology, 102,* 411–418.

Wells, C. (1991). *Women, sport, & performance: A physiological perspective* (2d ed.). Champaign, IL: Human Kinetics Publishers.

Weniger, B. G., & Brown, T. (1996). The march of AIDS through Asia. *New England Journal of Medicine, 335,* 343–345.

Westerman, M. A. (1990). Coordination of maternal directives with preschoolers' behavior in compliance-problem and healthy dyads. *Developmental Psychology, 26,* 621–630.

Whalen, C. K., & Henler, B. (1991). Therapies for hyperactive children: Comparisons, combinations, and compromises. *Journal of Consulting and Clinical Psychology, 59,* 126–137.

What is sexual harassment? (1993, June 19). *The New York Times,* p. L9.

Whiffen, V. E., & Gotlib, I. H. (1989). Infants of postpartum depressed mothers: Temperament and cognitive status. *Journal of Abnormal Psychology, 98,* 274–279.

Whipp, B., & Ward, S. (1992). Will women soon outrun men? *Nature, 355*(2), 25.

Whisman, M. A., Miller, I. W., Norman, W. H., & Keitner, G. I. (1991). Cognitive therapy with depressed inpatients. *Journal of Consulting and Clinical Psychology, 59,* 282–288.

Whitcher, S. J., & Fisher, J. D. (1979). Multidimensional reaction to therapeutic touch in a hospital setting. *Journal of Personality and Social Psychology, 37,* 87–96.

White, G. L. (1981). Some correlates of romantic jealousy. *Journal of Personality, 49,* 129–146.

White, J. L., & Nicassio, P. M. (1990, November). *The relationship between daily stress, pre-sleep arousal and sleep disturbance in good and poor sleepers.* Paper presented at the annual meeting of the Association for the Advancement of Behavior Therapy, San Francisco.

White, J. L., and others. (1994). Measuring impulsivity and examining its relationship to delinquency. *Journal of Abnormal Psychology, 103,* 192–205.

White, M. (1975). Interpersonal distance as affected by room size, status, and sex. *Journal of Social Psychology, 95,* 241–249.

Whitehead, W. E. (1994). Assessing the effects of stress on physical symptoms. *Health Psychology, 13,* 99–102.

Whitley, B. E., Jr. (1983). Sex role orientation and self-esteem: A critical meta-analysis. *Journal of Personality and Social Psychology, 44,* 765–788.

Wideman, M. V., & Singer, J. E. (1984). The role of psychological mechanisms in preparation for childbirth. *American Psychologist, 34,* 1357–1371.

Widiger, T. A., and others. (1996). DSM-IV antisocial personality disorder field trial. *Journal of Abnormal Psychology, 105,* 3–16.

Wiens, A. N., & Menustik, C. E. (1983). Treatment outcome and patient characteristics in an aversion therapy program for alcoholism. *American Psychologist, 38,* 1089–1096.

Wilcox, B. L. (1981). Social support, life stress, and psychological adjustment. *American Journal of Community Psychology, 9*(4), 371–386.

Wilder, D. A. (1977). Perception of groups, size of opposition, and social influence. *Journal of Experimental Social Psychology, 13,* 253–268.

Wilder, D. A. (1986). Social categorization: Implications for creation and reduction of intergroup bias. In L. Berkowitz (Ed.), *Advances in experimental social psychology.* Orlando, FL: Academic Press.

Wilder, D. A. (1990). Some determinants of the persuasive power of in-groups and out-groups: Organization of information and attribution of independence: *Journal of Personality and Social Psychology, 59,* 1202–1213.

Wilder, D. A., & Thompson, J. E. (1980). Intergroup contact with independent manipulations on in-group and out-group interaction. *Journal of Personality and Social Psychology, 38,* 589–603.

Wildman, B. G., & White, P. A. (1986). Assessment of dysmenorrhea using the Menstrual Symptom Questionnaire: Factor structure and validity. *Behavior Research and Therapy, 24,* 547–551.

Wilkerson, I. (1992, September 4). Hurricane haunts children long after winds have died. *The New York Times,* pp. A1, A10.

Wilkes, P. (1996, July 21). The next pro-lifers. *The New York Times Magazine,* pp. 22–27, 42, 45, 50.

Willens, M. (1993, May 13). Breaking a stereotype: More men are being hired as nannies. *The New York Times,* p. C6.

Williams, C. J. (1990, February 12). Cited in Schmidt, W. E. Valentine in a survey: Marital fidelity. *The New York Times,* p. A18.

Williams, D. E., & D'Alessandro, J. D. (1994). A comparison of three measures of androgyny and their relationship to psychological adjustment. *Journal of Social Behavior and Personality, 9*(3) 469–480.

Williams, J. E., & Best, D. L. (1994). Cross-cultural views of women and men. In W. J. Lonner & R. Malpass (Eds.), *Psychology and culture.* Boston: Allyn & Bacon.

Williams, J. G., & Solano, C. H. (1983). The social reality of feeling lonely: Friendship and reciprocation. *Personality and Social Psychology Bulletin, 9,* 237–242.

Williams, J. H. (1980). Sexuality in marriage. In B. B. Wolman & J. Money (Eds.), *Handbook of human sexuality.* Englewood Cliffs, NJ: Prentice-Hall.

Williams, K. (1986, February 7). *The role of appraisal salience in the performance evaluation process.* Paper presented at a colloquium, State University of New York at Albany.

Williams, L. (1992, February 6). Woman's image in a mirror: Who defines what she sees? *The New York Times,* pp. A1, B7.

Williams, R. M., Goldman, M. S., & Williams, D. L. (1981). Expectancy and pharmacological effects of alcohol on human cognitive and motor performance: The compensation for alcohol effect. *Journal of Abnormal Psychology, 90,* 267–270.

Willis, R. J., & Michael, R. T. (1994). Innovation in family formation: Evidence on cohabitation in the United States. In J. Eruisch & K. Ogawa (Eds.), *The family, the market and the state in aging societies.* London: Oxford University Press.

Wilmore, J. (1991). Importance of differences between men and women for exercise testing and exercise prescription. In J. Skinner (Ed.), *Exercise testing and exercise prescription* (pp. 41–56). Malverne, PA: Lea & Febbiger.

Wilson, T. D., & Linville, P. W. (1982). Improving the performance of college freshmen: Attribution therapy revisited. *Journal of Personality and Social Psychology, 42,* 367–376.

Winerip, M. (1998, January 4). Binge nights. *The New York Times,* Education Life, Section 4A, pp. 28–31, 42.

Wingard, D. L., Berkman, L. F., & Brand, R. J. (1982). A multivariate analysis of health-related practices: A nine-year mortality follow-up of the Alameda County Study. *American Journal of Epidemiology, 116,* 765–775.

Wink, P., & Helson, R. (1993). Personality change in women and their partners. *Journal of Personality and Social Psychology, 65,* 597–606.

Winkleby, M., Fortmann, S., & Barrett, D.

(1991). Social class disparities in risk factors for disease: Eight-year prevalence patterns by level of education. *Preventive Medicine, 19,* 1–12.

Wissow, L. S. (1995). Child abuse and neglect. *New England Journal of Medicine, 332,* 1425–1431.

Wolfe, A. (1998, February 8). The homosexual exception. *The New York Times Magazine,* pp. 46–47.

Wolfe, L. (1981). *The Cosmo report.* New York: Arbor House.

Wolinsky, J. (1982). Responsibility can delay aging. *APA Monitor, 13*(3), 14, 41.

Wolk, A., and others. (1998, January 12). *Archives of Internal Medicine.* Cited in Study: Some fats reduce cancer risk. (1998, January 11). Associated Press; America Online.

Wolpe, J. (1990). *The practice of behavior therapy* (4th ed.). New York: Pergamon Press.

Wolpe, J., & Lazarus, A. A. (1966). *Behavior therapy techniques.* New York: Pergamon Press.

Wolpe, J., & Plaud, J. J. (1997). Pavlov's contributions to behavior therapy: The obvious and the not so obvious. *American Psychologist, 52,* 966–972.

Wolraich, M. L., and others. (1990). Stimulant medication use by primary care physicians in the treatment of attention-deficit hyperactivity disorder. *Pediatrics, 86,* 95–101.

Women scientists lagging in industry jobs (1994, January 18). *The New York Times,* p. C5.

Wood, J. M., & Bootzin, R. R. (1990). The prevalence of nightmares and their independence from anxiety. *Journal of Abnormal Psychology, 99,* 64–68.

Wood, W. (1982). Retrieval of attitude-relevant information from memory: Effects on susceptibility to persuasion and on intrinsic motivation. *Journal of Personality and Social Psychology, 42,* 798–810.

Wood, W., & Eagly, A. H. (1981). Steps in the positive analysis of causal attributions and message comprehension. *Journal of Personality and Social Psychology, 40,* 246–259.

Wortman, C. B., Adesman, P., Herman, E., & Greenberg, P. (1976). Self-disclosure: An attributional perspective. *Journal of Personality and Social Psychology, 33,* 184–191.

Wu, C., & Shaffer, C. R. (1987). Susceptibility to persuasive appeals as a function of source credibility and prior experience with the attitude object. *Journal of Personality and Social Psychology, 52,* 677–688.

Wulfert, E., & Wan, C. K. (1993). Condom use: A self-efficacy model. *Health Psychology, 12,* 346–353.

Yoder, J. D., & Kahn, A. S. (1993). Working toward an inclusive psychology of women. *American Psychologist, 48,* 846–850.

Yorburg, B. (1995, July 9). Why couples choose to live together. *The New York Times,* p. 14.

Zagorski, M. G. (1997, January 14). Cited in Leary, W. E. Researchers investigate (horrors!) nicotine's potential benefits. *The New York Times,* p. C3.

Zamansky, H. S., & Bartis, S. P. (1985). The dissociation of an experience. *Journal of Abnormal Psychology, 94,* 243–248.

Zane, N., & Sue, S. (1991). Culturally responsive mental health services for Asian Americans: Treatment and training issues. In H. F. Myers and others (Eds.), *Ethnic minority perspectives on clinical training and services in psychology* (pp. 49–58). Washington, DC: American Psychological Association.

Zatz, S., & Chassin, L. (1985). Cognitions of test-anxious children under naturalistic test-taking conditions. *Journal of Consulting and Clinical Psychology, 53,* 393–401.

Zedick, S., & Mosier, K. L. (1990). Work in the family and employing organization. *American Psychologist, 45,* 240–251.

Zelkowitz, P., & Milet, T. H. (1996). Postpartum psychiatric disorders: Their relationship to psychological adjustment and marital satisfaction in the spouses. *Journal of Abnormal Psychology, 105,* 281–285.

Zigler, E., Taussig, C., & Black, K. (1992). Early childhood intervention: A promising preventative for juvenile delinquency. *American Psychologist, 47,* 997–1006.

Zimmer, D. (1983). Interaction patterns and communication skills in sexually distressed, maritally distressed, and normal couples: Two experimental studies. *Journal of Sex and Marital Therapy, 9,* 251–265.

Zinbarg, R. E., & Barlow, D. H. (1996). Structure of anxiety disorders. *Journal of Abnormal Psychology, 105,* 181–193.

Ziv, T. A., & Lo, B. (1995). Denial of care to illegal immigrants—Proposition 187 in California. *New England Journal of Medicine, 332,* 1095–1098.

Zuckerman, M., Miserandino, M., & Bernieri, F. (1983). Civil inattention exists—in elevators. *Personality and Social Psychology Bulletin, 9,* 578–586.

Zuniga, J. (1993, July 11). My life in the military closet. *The New York Times Magazine,* 40–45, 58, 64.

Zweigenhaft, R. L. (1975). Name styles in America and name styles in New Zealand. *Journal of Social Psychology, 97,* 289–290.

Zweigenhaft, R. L. (1977). The other side of unusual names. *Journal of Social Psychology, 103,* 291–302.

Zweigenhaft, R. L., Hayes, K. N., & Haagen, C. H. (1980). The psychological impact of names. *Journal of Social Psychology, 110,* 203–210.

Name Index

Subject Index

Credits and Acknowledgments

PHOTO CREDITS

CHAPTER 1 p. 0: © 1998 Scott Spiker / Alaska Stock. p. 5: Richard Pasley / Stock, Boston. p. 9: Courtesy University of the Arts, Philadelphia. Photography Tom Crane © 1993. p. 18: Robert McElroy / Woodfin Camp & Associates. p. 24: Leverett Bradley / Tony Stone Images. **CHAPTER 2** p. 34: Jeff Isaac Greenberg / Photo Researchers. p. 39: Bob Daemmrich Photos / The Image Works. p. 53: Jerry Wachter / Photo Researchers. p. 57: Jeff Isaac Greenberg / Photo Researchers. p. 60: Jim Pickerell / Stock, Boston. **CHAPTER 3** p. 70: The artist with her work, 1994. © Hung Liu, *Burial at Little Golden Village*, 1994. Oil on canvas, 74×96". Collection of Bernice and Harold Steinbaum. Courtesy of Steinbaum Krauss Gallery, NYC. p. 74: Harriet Gans / The Image Works. p. 77: Jeffrey Greenberg / The Picture Cube. p. 79: Dorothy Littel Greco / The Image Works. p. 98: © The Stock Market / George Disario 1999. **CHAPTER 4** p. 102: © The Stock Market / Alon Reninger / Contact Press Images 1999. p. 107: NIKE. p. 112: From the film OBEDIENCE © 1965 by Stanley Milgram. Distributed by Penn State Media Sales. p. 113: From the film OBEDIENCE © 1965 by Stanley Milgram. Distributed by Penn State Media Sales. p. 116: Jeff Albertson / Stock, Boston. p. 120: David Young-Wolff / PhotoEdit. **CHAPTER 5** p. 128: © Kerrick James / The PhotoFile. p. 132 (left): David Ball / The Picture Cube. p. 132 (right): John Coletti / Stock, Boston. p. 143: Dana White / PhotoEdit. **CHAPTER 6** p. 160: Jim Cummins / Tony Stone Images. p. 166: David Young-Wolff / PhotoEdit. p. 171: Biology Media / Photo Researchers. p. 174: Bob Daemmrich Photos / The Image Works. p. 180: Bruce Ayres / Tony Stone Images. **CHAPTER 7** p. 192: Sam Sargent / ImageQuest. p. 195: Charles Gupton / Tony Stone Images. p. 199: David Dempster / Offshoot. p. 201: David Young-Wolff / PhotoEdit. p. 207: Courtesy of Eidos Interactive. p. 217: Topham / The Image Works. p. 220: P. Didier / Superstock. **CHAPTER 8** p. 228: Anne Marie Rousseau / The Image Works. p. 232: Jeff Greenberg / PhotoEdit. p. 237: Reprinted by permission of the American Cancer Society, Inc. p. 240: © The Stock Market / Roy Morsch 1999. **CHAPTER 9** p. 252: Sandy Skoglund / Superstock. p. 261: Joe Carini / The Image Works. p. 264: Robert Ellison / Black Star. p. 272: Superstock. p. 276: Richard Frieman / Photo Researchers. **CHAPTER 10** p. 286: Erich Hartmann / Magnum. p. 290: Rhoda Sidney / PhotoEdit. p. 294: Rick Friedman / Black Star. p. 307: Bob Daemmrich / Stock, Boston. p. 311: P. Petersen / Custom Medical Stock. **CHAPTER 11** p. 320: Richard Hamilton Smith / Tony Stone Images. p. 323: Jeff Isaac Greenberg / Photo Researchers. p. 327: Hank Morgan / Rainbow. p. 330: David Lissy / The Picture Cube. p. 339: © Joel Gordon 1999. **CHAPTER 12** p. 358: John Chiasson / Gamma Liaison. p. 361: Paul Conklin / PhotoEdit. p. 364: Seth Resnick / Stock, Boston. p. 368: From the film OBEDIENCE © 1965 by Stanley Milgram. Distributed by Penn State Media Sales. p. 369 (left): Diana Ong / Superstock. p. 369 (right): Michael Greenlar / The Image Works. **CHAPTER 13** p. 386: Leslie Sponseller / Tony Stone Images. p. 390: D. Perrett, K. May, S. Yoshikawa, University of St. Andrews / SPL / Photo Researchers, Inc. p. 391: Reuters / Ian Waldie / Archive Photos. p. 402: Private Collection / Hayward Gallery, London. p. 405: http://www.planetout.com. p. 418: Mark Antman / The Image Works. **CHAPTER 14** p. 422: Ron Chapple / FPG. p. 425: Joseph Nettis / Photo Researchers. p. 430: John Feingersh / Stock, Boston. p. 453: Richard Lord Enterprises / The Image Works. **CHAPTER 15** p. 460: Joan Marcus. p. 474: Per Breiehagen / Time Magazine. p. 480: Joan Marcus. p. 502: © The Stock Market / Roy Morsch 1999. p. 507: © The Stock Market / Roy Morsch 1999. p. 515: Tom & Dee Ann McCarthy / PhotoEdit. p. 527: Bob Daemmrich Photos / The Image Works. p. 540: © The Stock Market / William Taufic 1999. p. 543: Ron Chapple / FPG. p. 550: © Joel Gordon 1999. p. 554: Alan Carey / The Image Works. p. 565: Michael Heron / Monkmeyer. p. 568: Bob Daemmrich / Stock, Boston. p. 578: © The Stock Market / Ronnie Kaufman 1999. p. 586: Robert McElroy / Woodfin Camp and Associates. p. 591: © Suzanne Arms / Jeroboam. p. 604: Joseph Schuyler / Stock, Boston.

LITERARY ACKNOWLEDGMENTS

CHAPTER 1 p. 12: Beckham, E. F. (1993). Campus diversity: Facing new realities. *The Ford Foundation Report, 23*(4). Reprinted by permission. p. 13: *Chronicle of Higher Education* (1992, March 18), A35. Copyright 1992, The Chronicle of Higher Education. Reprinted by permission. p. 14: Pion, G. M. (1996). The shifting gender composition of psychology: Trends and implications for the discipline. *American Psychologist 51,* 509–528. Copyright © 1996 by the American Psychological Association. Reprinted by permission. p. 21: Adapted from Laumann E. O., Gagnon, J. H., Michael, R. T., & Michaels, S. (1994). *The social organization of sexuality: Sexual practices in the United States.* p. 179. Copyright 1994. Reprinted by permission of The University of Chicago Press. **CHAPTER 2** p. 42: Erikson, E. H. (1950). *Childhood and society,* 2nd ed. Copyright 1950, © 1963 by W. W. Norton & Company, Inc., renewed © 1978, 1991 by Erik H. Erikson. Reprinted with permission of W. W. Norton & Company, Inc. p. 52: Hale & Fibel (1978). Expectancy for success scale. *Journal of Clinical Psychology,* 931. Copyright © 1978 by The American Psychological Association. Reprinted by permission. p. 61: Based on Markus, H., & Kitayama, S. (1991). Culture and the self. *Psychological Review, 98*(2), 224–253. Copyright © 1991 by the American Psychological Association. Reprinted by permission. p. 63: Ostling, R. N. (1993). One nation under gods: Not without conflict: An unprecedented variety of faiths blooms across the land. *Time, 24*(21), 62–63. **CHAPTER 3** p. 77: Takaki, R. (1993). *A different mirror.* Copyright © 1993 by Ronald Takaki. Reprinted by permission of Little, Brown & Co. p. 80: Berscheid, E., Walster, E., & Bohrnstedt, G. (1973, November). Body image. *Psychology Today Magazine.* Copyright © 1973 (Sussex Publishing Co. Inc.). Reprinted by permission. p. 87: Copyright 1967 by Milton Rokeach. Permission to reproduce granted by Holgren Test, 873 Persimmon Avenue, Sunnyvale, CA 94087. p. 90: Self-Acceptance Scale. Copyright © Emanuel E. Berger. Reprinted by permission of Mrs. Emanuel E. Berger. p. 98: Jackson, M. (1990). "The Man in the Mirror." International copyright secured. All rights of Mijac Music administered by WB Music Corp. All rights reserved. Used by permission of Warner Bros. Publications U.S. Inc. Miami, FL 33014. **CHAPTER 4** p. 108: Rathus, S. (1973). A 30-item schedule for assessing assertive behavior. *Behavior Therapy, 4,* 398–406. Reprinted by permission. **CHAPTER 5** p. 131: Murray, B. (1996). College youth haunted by increased pressures. *APA Monitor 26*(4), 47. Copyright © 1996 by the American Psychological Association. Reprinted by permission. p. 135: Blake, P., Fry, R., & Pesjack, M. (1984). *Self assessment and behavioral change manual,* 43–47. New York: Random House. Reprinted with permission of The McGraw-Hill Companies. p. 144: Ruben Martinez (1994, January 29). One quake, two worlds. *The New York Times,* A21. Copyright © 1994 by The New York Times Company. Reprinted by permission. **CHAPTER 6** p. 163: Scheier, M. F., & Carver, C. S. (1985). Optimism, coping and health: Assessment and implications of generalized outcome expectancies. *Health Psychology 4,* 219–247. Reprinted by permission of Lawrence Erlbaum & Associates, Mahwah, NJ. p. 179: Brody, J. E. (1996, August 28). PMS need not be the worry it was just decades ago. *The New York Times,* C9. © 1996 by The New York Times Company. Reprinted by permission. p. 187: Permission granted by the American Cancer Society, Inc. **CHAPTER 7** p. 195: New York Times poll (1988, January 6), C6. © 1988 by The New York Times Company. Reprinted by permission. p. 208 (top): Hakim, A. A., Petrovitch, H., Burchfiel, C. M., Ross, G. W., Rodriguez, B. L., White, L. R., Yano, K., Curb, J. D., & Abbott, R. D. (1998). Effects of walking on mortality among nonsmoking retired men. *The New England Journal of Medicine, 338*(2), 96. Copyright © 1998 Massachusetts Medical Society. All rights reserved. Used with permission. p. 208 (bottom): Hakim, A. A., Petrovitch, H., Burchfiel, C. M., Ross, G. W., Rodriguez, B. L., White, L. R., Yano, K., Curb, J. D., & Abbott, R. D. (1998). Effects of walking on mortality among nonsmoking retired men. *The New England Journal of Medicine, 338*(2), 96. Copyright © 1998 Massachusetts Medical Society. All rights reserved. Used with permission. **CHAPTER 9** p. 256: American Psychiatric Association (1994). *Diagnostic and statistical manual of the mental disorders,* 4th ed. Washington, DC: The American Psychiatric Association. p. 257: American Psychiatric Association (1994). *Diagnostic and statistical manual of the mental disorders,* 4th ed. Washington, DC: The American Psychiatric Association. p. 260: Nevid, J. S., Rathus, S. A., & Greene, B. (1997). *Abnormal psychology in a changing world,* 3rd ed. Copyright © 1997. Reprinted by permission of Prentice-Hall, Upper Saddle River, NJ. p. 265: Resnick, H. S., Kilpatrick, D. G., Dansky, B. S., Saunders, B. E., & Best, C. L. (1993). Prevalence of civilian trauma and posttraumatic stress disorder in a representative national sample of women. *Journal of Consulting and Clinical Psychology, 61,* 984–991. Copyright © 1993 by The American Psychological Association. Reprinted by permission. p. 263: Nevid, J. S., Rathus, S. A., & Greene, B. (1997). *Abnormal psychology in a changing world,* 3rd ed. Copyright © 1997. Reprinted by permission of Prentice-Hall, Upper Saddle River, NJ. p. 264: Nevid, J. S., Rathus, S. A., & Greene, B. (1997). *Abnormal psychology in a changing world,* 3rd ed. Copyright © 1997. Reprinted by permission of Prentice-Hall, Upper Saddle River, NJ. p. 271: Nevid, J. S., Rathus, S. A., & Greene, B. (1997). *Abnormal psychology in a changing world,* 3rd ed. Copyright © 1997. Reprinted by permission of Prentice-Hall, Upper Saddle River, NJ. p. 273: Williams, J. M. G. (1984). *The psychological treatment of depression: A guide to the theory and practice of cognitive behaviour therapy.* Copyright © 1984 by J. Mark G. Williams. Adapted by permission of the Free Press, a division of Simon & Schuster. **CHAPTER 10** p. 295: Rathus, S. A., & Nevid, J. S. (1977). *Behavior therapy,* 52–54. Reprinted by permission of Bantam Doubleday Dell Publishing Group, Inc. p. 301: Rush, A. J., Khatami, M., & Beck, A. T. (1975). Cognitive and behavior therapy in chronic depression. *Behavior Therapy, 6,* 398–404. Reprinted by permission of the Association for Advancement of Behavior Therapy. **CHAPTER 11** p. 341: Wolpe, J., & Lazarus, A. A. (1966). *Bevavior therapy techniques,* 177–180. Reprinted by permission of Pergamon Press, a Division of Simon & Schuster. p. 345: Galassi, J. P., Frierson, H. T., & Sharer, R. (1981). Behavior of high, moderate, and low test anxious students during an actual test situation. *Journal of Consulting and Clinical Psychology, 49,* 56, 58. Copyright © 1981 by The American Psychological Association. Reprinted by permission. p. 346: The full 98-item STABS is copyright by R. M. Suinn and not to be duplicated in any way. Orders may be obtained from: Dr. Richard M. Suinn, 808 Cheyenne Dr., Fort Collins, CO 80525. p. 352: Lewinsohn, P. M., & Graf, M. (1973). Pleasant activities and depression. *Journal of Consulting & Clinical Psychology, 41,* 261–268. Copyright © 1973 by The American Psychological Association. Reprinted by permission. p. 354: MacPhillamy, D. J., & Lewinsohn, P. M. (1971). The pleasant events schedule: Studies on reliability, validity and scale intercorrelation. *Journal of Consulting & Clinical Psychology, 50,* 363–380. University of Oregon, mimeograph. Reprinted by permission of The

American Psychological Association. **CHAPTER 12** p. 361: This guest feature was written by Rafael Art Javier, Ph.D. Dr. Javier is Clinical Professor of Psychology and Director of the Center for Psychological Services and Clinical Studies at St. John's University, Jamaica, NY. Dr. Javier was born in the Dominican Republic and educated in philosphy in the Dominican Republic, Puerto Rico, and Venezuela, and in psychology and psychoanalysis at New York University. Dr. Javier is a practicing psychoanalyst and maintains a research interest in psychotherapy with ethnic minorities. p. 363: Williams, J. E., & Best, D. L. (1994). Cross-cultural views of women and men. In W. J. Lonner & R. S. Malpass (Eds.), *Psychology and culture.* Copyright © 1994 by Allyn & Bacon. Reprinted by permission. p. 369: Richardson, D. C., Bernstein, S., & Taylor, S. P. (1979). The effect of situational contingencies on female retaliative behavior. *Journal of Personality & Social Psychology, 37,* 2044–2048. Copyright © 1979 by The American Psychological Association. Reprinted by permission. p. 373: Rosenkrantz, L., & Satran, P. (1988). *Beyond Jennifer and Jason,* 160. Reprinted by permission of St. Martin's Press. p. 374. Berzins, J. I., Welling, M. A., & Wetter, R. E. (1977). *The PRF ANDRO Scale: User's manual.* Unpublished manuscript: University of Kentucky. Reprinted by permission of the author. **CHAPTER 13** p. 392: Fallon, A. E., & Rozin, P. (1985). Sex differences in perceptions of desirable body shape. *Journal of Abnormal Psychology, 94,* 102–105. Copyright © 1985 by The American Psychological Association. Reprinted by permission. p. 390: Pockriss, L., & Vance, P. (1959). "What Is Love?" Copyright © 1959 (renewed) by Music Sales Corporation (ASCAP) and Emily Music Corporation. International copyright secured. All rights reserved. Reprinted by permission. p. 393: Gershwin, G., Heyward, D., Heyward, D., & Gershwin, I. (1935). "Summertime." © 1935 (Renewed 1962) George Gershwin Music, Ira Gershwin Music, and DuBose and Dorothy Heyward Memorial Fund. All rights administered by WB Music Corp. All rights reserved. Used by permission of Warner Bros. Publications U.S. Inc., Miami, FL 33014. p. 394: Nevid, J. S. (1984). Sex differences in factors of romantic attraction. *Sex Roles, 11*(5/6), 401–411. Reprinted by permission of Plenum Publishing. p. 397: Based on data in Keen, S., & Zur, O. (1989). Who is the new ideal man? *Psychology Today, 23*(11), 54–60. Copyright © 1989 (Sussex Publishers, Inc.). Reprinted by permission. p. 401: *New York Times* (1993, March 5), A41. Copyright © 1993 by The New York Times Company. Reprinted by permission. p. 406: Porter, C. (1939). "Friendship," introduced in *DuBarry Was a Lady.* Copyright 1939. All Rights of Chappell & Co. Administered by WB Music Corp. All rights reserved. Used by permission of Warner Bros. Publications U.S. Inc., Miami, FL 33014. p. 412: Adapted from Sternberg, R. J. (1988). *The triangle of love: Intimacy, passion, commitment.* New York: Basic Books. Reprinted by permission of the author. p. 417: Lennon, J., & McCartney, P. (1965). "Eleanor Rigby." © 1965, 1966 Northern Songs Ltd. Copyright renewed. All rights controlled & administered by EMI Blackwood Music Inc. under license from ATV Music Corp. (Maclen Music). All rights reserved. International copyright secured. Used by permission. **CHAPTER 14** p. 432: Elias, M. (1997, August 14). Modem match-making. *USA Today,* 1D, 2D. Reprinted by permission. p. 435: Snyder, D. K. (1994). Multidimensional assessment of marital satisfaction. *Journal of Marriage and the Family, 41,* 4, 813–823. Copyright (1994) by the National Council on Family Relations, 3989 Central Ave. N.E., Ste. 550, Minneapolis, MN 55421. Reprinted by permission. p. 440: Data from Kirn, W. (1997, August 18). The ties that bind. *Time* magazine, 48–50. Copyright 1997. Reprinted by permission. p. 441: *The Washington Post* (1990, December 24). Snug in their beds for Christmas Eve: In Japan, December 24th has become the hottest night of the year. © 1990, Washington Post Writers Group. Reprinted with permission. p. 450: © The New Yorker Collection 1983 Ed Koren from cartoonbank.com. All rights reserved. **CHAPTER 15** p. 473: From a telephone poll of 500 American adults taken for TIME/CNN on May 8, 1991 by Yankelovich, Clancy, and Schulman. Sampling error is plus or minus 4.5%. "Not sures" omitted. Reprinted from *Time* magazine, June 3, 1991, p. 50. Copyright 1991, Time, Inc. Reprinted by permission. p. 475: From a telephone poll of 500 American adults taken for TIME/CNN on May 8, 1991 by Yankelovich, Clancy, and Schulman. Sampling error is plus or minus 4.5%. "Not sures" omitted. Reprinted from *Time* magazine, June 3, 1991, p. 50. Copyright 1991, Time, Inc. Reprinted by permission. p. 477: Adapted from Laumann, E. O., Gagnon, J. H., Michael, R. T., & Michaels, S. (1994). *The social organization of sexuality: Sexual practices in the United States,* 370–371. Copyright 1994. Reprinted by permission of The University of Chicago Press. p. 492: Boston Women's Health Book Collective (1993). *The new our bodies, ourselves.* Copyright © 1984, 1992 by The Boston Women's Health Book Collective. Published by Simon & Schuster, New York. Reprinted by permission. p. 493: Rathus, S. A., & Fichner-Rathus, L. (1997). *The right start.* © 1997. Reprinted by permission of Addison Wesley Educational Publishers Inc. p. 494: E. Powell (1991). *Talking back to sexual pressure.* Comp Care Publishers, a Division of Comprehensive Care, Minneapolis. Reprinted by permission. p. 497: Boston Women's Health Book Collective (1993). *The new our bodies, ourselves.* Copyright © 1984, 1992 by The Boston Women's Health Book Collective. Published by Simon & Schuster, New York. Reprinted by permission. p. 505: Allen, R. F., with Linde, S. (1986). *Lifegain.* Human Resources Institute, 115 Dunder Rd., Burlington, VT. Reprinted by permission. p. 508: Levinson, D. (1978). *The seasons of a man's life.* Reprinted by permission of Alfred A. Knopf, Inc. p. 522: *New York Times* (1998, January 13). *Illustration* by Juan Velasco in The relentless march of time, F1. © 1998 by The New York Times Company. Reprinted by permission. p. 532: Dickstein, L. S. (1972). Death concern: Measurement and correlates. *Psychological Reports, 30,* 563–571. © Psychological Reports, 1972. Reprinted by permission. p. 554: *New York Times* (1992, August 31). Pulse: On the job, B1. © 1992 by The New York Times Company. Reprinted by permission. p. 564: Nevid, J. S., Rathus, S. A., & Rubenstein, H. R. (1998). *Health in the new millennium,* 57–58. Reprinted by permission of Worth Publishers. p. 566: Data from Families and Work Institute (1997). *National study of the changing workforce.* Used by permission of Families and Work Institute, New York, NY. p. 601: © The New Yorker Collection 1983 Robert Weber from cartoonbank.com. All rights reserved.